CW01183124

THE
CODEBREAKERS

The Story of Secret Writing

DAVID KAHN

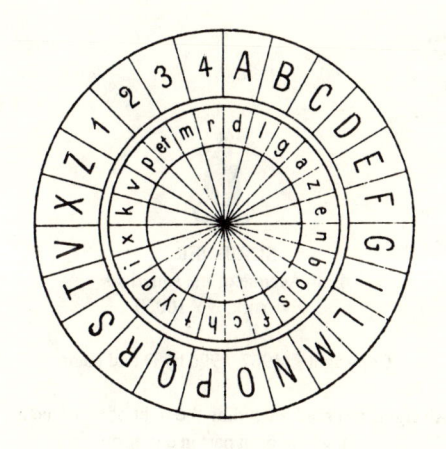

SCRIBNER

SCRIBNER
1230 Avenue of the Americas
New York, NY 10020

Copyright © 1967, 1996 by David Kahn

All rights reserved, including the right of reproduction
in whole or in part in any form.

SCRIBNER and design are trademarks of
Macmillan Library Reference USA, Inc. under license by
Simon & Schuster, the publisher of this work.

Manufactured in the United States of America

7 9 10 8

Library of Congress Cataloging-in-Publication Data is available.

ISBN 0-684-83130-9

*To
my Parents
and
my Grandmother*

CONTENTS

Preface to the Revised Edition ... ix
Preface ... xi
A Few Words ... xv

1. One Day of Magic ... 1

THE PAGENT OF CRYPTOLOGY

2. The First 3,000 Years ... 71
3. The Rise of the West ... 106
4. On the Origin of a Species ... 125
5. The Era of the Black Chambers ... 157
6. The Contribution of the Dilettantes ... 189
7. Crises of the Union ... 214
8. The Professor, the Soldier, and the Man on Devil's Island ... 230
9. Room 40 ... 266
10. A War of Intercepts: I ... 298
11. A War of Intercepts: II ... 321
12. Two Americans ... 351
13. Secrecy for Sale ... 394
14. Duel in the Ether: The Axis ... 435
15. Duel in the Ether: Neutrals and Allies ... 478
16. Censors, Scramblers, and Spies ... 513
17. The Scrutable Orientals ... 561
18. Русская Криптология ... 614
19. N.S.A. ... 672

SIDESHOWS

20. The Anatomy of Cryptology	737
21. Heterogeneous Impulses	763
22. Rumrunners, Businessmen, and Makers of Non-secret Codes	802
23. Ciphers in the Past Tense	854
24. The Pathology of Cryptology	873

PARACRYPTOLOGY

25. Ancestral Voices	895
26. Messages from Outer Space	938

THE NEW CRYPTOLOGY

27. Cryptology Goes Public	969
Bibliography	985
Notes to Text	989
Acknowledgments	1145
Notes to Illustrations	1146
Index	1153

PREFACE TO THE REVISED EDITION

The need to revise this book existed even before it was published on September 27, 1967. I had written what I hoped would be the definitive history of the subject. I did not know at the time of such great matters as the Polish-British-American mastery of the German Enigma cipher machine, which had such great effects on World War II, or of such lesser ones as the tactical value of German front-line telephone taps. Nor did I—or anyone—know of things that had not yet been invented, such as public-key cryptography. The first glimmering that the world of cryptology would not stand still for me came four months after publication, when North Korea seized the U.S. electronic reconnaissance ship *Pueblo* in January 1968. It marked the first of a series of events that showed the need for revision. I had, indeed, made some minor corrections in printings three through seven, but then I concentrated on other projects.

There followed, however, the Ultra disclosures. the creation of public-key cryptography, and the enormous growth in computer communications, including particularly the appearance of the Internet, where cryptography affords the best means for privacy. At about the same time, the absorption of Macmillan, the original publisher, by Simon & Schuster brought a young, energetic editor named Scott Moyers to handle *The Codebreakers*. He saw that I could fulfill my obligation to cryptology and at the same time help the book sell better by incorporating the new material as a single chapter. This made sense, and that is what I've done.

I have sought to cover the major events, both external and internal, that have affected cryptology in the past quarter century. It is amazing how much these have changed the field. Fortunately for me, while they have added information, they do not change the past, so the first edition remains valid. I hope that this new edition will prove as useful—and perhaps as pleasurable—to readers as the previous one.

DAVID KAHN

Great Neck, New York
May 1996

PREFACE

CODEBREAKING is the most important form of secret intelligence in the world today. It produces much more and much more trustworthy information than spies, and this intelligence exerts great influence upon the policies of governments. Yet it has never had a chronicler.

It badly needs one. It has been estimated that cryptanalysis saved a year of war in the Pacific, yet the histories give it but passing mention. Churchill's great history of World War II has been cleaned of every single reference to Allied communications intelligence except one (and that based on the American Pearl Harbor investigation), although Britain thought it vital enough to assign 30,000 people to the work. The intelligence history of World War II has never been written. All this gives a distorted view of why things happened. Furthermore, cryptology itself can benefit, like other spheres of human endeavor, from knowing its major trends, its great men, its errors made and lessons learned.

I have tried in this book to write a serious history of cryptology. It is primarily a report to the public on the important role that cryptology has played, but it may also orient cryptology with regard to its past and alert historians to the sub rosa influence of cryptanalysis. The book seeks to cover the entire history of cryptology. My goal has been twofold: to narrate the development of the various methods of making and breaking codes and ciphers, and to tell how these methods have affected men.

When I began this book, I, like other well-informed amateurs, knew about all that had been published on the history of cryptology in books on the subject. How little we really knew! Neither we nor any professionals realized that many valuable articles lurked in scholarly journals, or had induced any cryptanalysts to tell their stories for publication, or had tapped the vast treasuries of documentary material, or had tried to take a long view and ask some questions that now appear basic. I believe it to be true that, from the point of view of the material previously published in books on cryptology, what is new in this book is 85 to 90 per cent.

Yet it is not exhaustive. A foolish secrecy still clothes much of World War II cryptology—though I believe the outlines of the achievements are known—and to tell just that story in full would require a book the size of this.

Even in, say, the 18th century, the unexplored manuscript material is very great.

Nor is this a textbook. I have explained at length only two basic methods of solution, though I have sketched many others. For some readers even this will be too much; them I advise to skip this material. They will not have a full understanding of what is going on, but that will not cripple their comprehension of the stories. For readers who want more detail on these methods, I recommend Helen F. Gaines's *Elementary Cryptanalysis*, partly because it is a competent work, partly because it is the only work of its kind in English now easily available (in a paperback reprint, entitled *Cryptanalysis*). In French, there is Luigi Sacco's outstanding *Manuel de cryptographie* (the Italian original is out of print). Nearly all the other books in print are juveniles. Readers interested in cryptanalysis may also join the American Cryptogram Association, which publishes a magazine with articles on how to solve ciphers and with cryptograms for solution.

In my writing, I have tried to adhere to two principles. One was to use primary sources as much as possible. Often it could not be done any other way, since nothing had been published on a particular matter. The other principle was to try to make certain that I did not give cryptology sole and total credit for winning a battle or making possible a diplomatic coup or whatever happened if, as was usual, other factors played a role. Narratives which make it appear as if every event in history turned upon the subject under discussion are not history but journalism. They are especially prevalent in spy stories, and cryptology is not immune. The only other book-length attempt to survey the history of cryptology, the late Fletcher Pratt's *Secret and Urgent*, published in 1939, suffers from a severe case of this special pleading. Pratt writes thrillingly—perhaps for that very reason—but his failure to consider the other factors, together with his errors and omissions, his false generalizations based on no evidence, and his unfortunate predilection for inventing facts vitiate his work as any kind of a history. (Finding this out was disillusioning, for it was this book, borrowed from the Great Neck Library, that interested me in cryptology.) I think that although trying to balance the story with the other factors may detract a little from the immediate thrill, it charges it with authenticity and hence makes for long-lasting interest: for this is how things really happened.

In the same vein, I have not made up any conversations, and my speculations about things not a matter of record have been marked as such in the notes. I have documented all important facts, except that in a few cases I have had to respect the wishes of my sources for anonymity.

The manuscript was submitted to the Department of Defense on March 4, 1966.

It is impossible to adequately thank all those who have helped me with this book, giving generously of their time and talents. But perhaps I can at

Preface

least indicate the size of my debts and publicly express my gratitude to those who have helped.

Foremost is Bradford Hardie, M.D., of El Paso, Texas, who translated a veritable stream of documents in German and read the galleys. His constant warm encouragement was like manna. My good friend Edward S. (Buddy) Miller of Malverne, New York, read many of the early chapters in manuscript and made extremely penetrating and valuable observations on them. Howard T. Oakley of Scotch Plains, New Jersey, and Kaljo Käärik, Ph.D., of Enskede, Sweden, read chapters, provided information, and exchanged views.

Many cryptologists or relatives of cryptologists took the time to talk with me or reply to my queries. I have acknowledged these debts in my notes, but I must pay special tribute to former Ambassador J. Rives Childs, who replied in detail to numerous questions and lent me his entire set of papers from his work in World War I; to Admiral Sir William James, who read the chapter on Room 40 and ransacked his voluminous memory for answers to many queries; to the late Yves Gyldén, who spent four days with me in Sweden; to Naotsune Watanabe and to Shiro Takagi, who wrote detailed reports of their World War II cryptanalytic experiences; to Dr. Hans Rohrbach, who set up some important appointments for me by long-distance telephone; to Harold R. Shaw, who wrote a 27-page reminiscence of his wartime work; to the Boris Hagelins, senior and junior, for hospitality and information; to Mrs. Malcolm Hay of Seaton, for information and photographs; to Parker Hitt, for an important memorandum and for the gift of his invaluable cipher papers; and to Mr. and Mrs. William F. Friedman for numerous kindnesses, though they steadfastly refused to discuss his government work, and for a gift made in 1947, upon my graduation from high school, that was a major step in my cryptologic education.

Many scholars very kindly replied to my queries about cryptology in their fields, and I have also acknowledged these in my notes. But especially generous were T. C. H. Raper of the India Office Library, London, who did a great deal of research on my behalf; C. E. Bosworth of St. Andrews University, Scotland, who furnished important background material in addition to a critical article; and Robert Wolfe, Philip Brower, and W. Neil Franklin of the National Archives, Washington, who replied with courtesy and dispatch to volleys of requests. Without the incredible resources of the New York Public Library and the courteous help of its staff in making them available, this book in its present form would not exist. A great deal of credit is due Mrs. Suzanne Oppenheimer, who typed the bulk of the book from execrable copy, and to Mrs. Harriet Simons, who typed the other chapters. Jenny Hauck made the photographic layouts. Geoffrey C. Jones of Lee-on-the-Solent, England, compiled the index, with some technical assistance by me.

The design department of The Macmillan Company and the Alden Press of Oxford, England, have overcome the many production problems to produce a very handsome book.

In a larger sense, I owe a great deal to former colleagues on *Newsday*, especially to Al Marlens, my former city editor, who taught me most of what I know about reporting and writing, and also to Bernie Bookbinder, who demonstrated that concern for the human must always be paramount; to Stan Isaacs, who showed how a subject can transcend itself; and to Stan Brooks, whose "Keep it light and bright!" galled me at the time but has since delivered me—I hope—from solemnity.

The errors are, of course, mine. If any reader cares to tell me of any corrections or additions, including personal reminiscences, I shall be very grateful to him.

DAVID KAHN

Windsor Gate
Great Neck, New York
Paris

A FEW WORDS

EVERY TRADE has its vocabulary. That of cryptology is simple, but even so a familiarity with its terms facilitates understanding. A glossary may also serve as a handy reference. The definitions in this one are informal and ostensive. Exceptions are ignored and the host of minor terms are not defined—the text covers these when they come up.

The **plaintext** is the message that will be put into secret form. Usually the plaintext is in the native tongue of the communicators. The message may be hidden in two basic ways. The methods of **steganography** conceal the very existence of the message. Among them are invisible inks and microdots and arrangements in which, for example, the first letter of each word in an apparently innocuous text spells out the real message. (When steganography is applied to electrical communications, such as a method that transmits a long radio message in a single short spurt, it is called **transmission security**.) The methods of **cryptography**, on the other hand, do not conceal the presence of a secret message but render it unintelligible to outsiders by various transformations of the plaintext.

Two basic transformations exist. In **transposition**, the letters of the plaintext are jumbled; their normal order is disarranged. To shuffle *secret* into ETCRSE is a transposition. In **substitution**, the letters of the plaintext are replaced by other letters, or by numbers or symbols. Thus *secret* might become 19 5 3 18 5 20, or XIWOXV in a more complicated system. In transposition, the letters retain their identities—the two *e*'s of *secret* are still present in ETCRSE—but they lose their positions, while in substitution the letters retain their positions but lose their identities. Transposition and substitution may be combined.

Substitution systems are much more diverse and important than transposition systems. They rest on the concept of the **cipher alphabet**. This is the list of equivalents used to transform the plaintext into the secret form. A sample cipher alphabet might be:

plaintext letters   a b c d e f g h i j k l m n o p q r s t u v w x y z
cipher letters   L B Q A C S R D T O F V M H W I J X G K Y U N Z E P

This graphically indicates that the letters of the plaintext are to be replaced by the cipher letters beneath them, and vice versa. Thus, *enemy* would become CHCME, and SWC would reduce to *foe*. A set of such correspondences is still called a "cipher alphabet" if the plaintext letters are in mixed order, or even if they are missing, because cipher letters always imply plaintext letters.

Sometimes such an alphabet will provide multiple substitutes for a letter. Thus plaintext *e*, for example, instead of always being replaced by, say, 16, will be replaced by any one of the figures 16, 74, 35, 21. These alternates are called **homophones.** Sometimes a cipher alphabet will include symbols that mean nothing and are intended to confuse interceptors; these are called **nulls.**

As long as only one cipher alphabet is in use, as above, the system is called **monalphabetic.** When, however, two or more cipher alphabets are employed in some kind of prearranged pattern, the system becomes **polyalphabetic.** A simple form of polyalphabetic substitution would be to add another cipher alphabet under the one given above and then to use the two in rotation, the first alphabet for the first plaintext letter, the second for the second, the first again for the third plaintext letter, the second for the fourth, and so on. Modern cipher machines produce polyalphabetic ciphers that employ millions of cipher alphabets.

Among the systems of substitution, **code** is distinguished from **cipher.** A code consists of thousands of words, phrases, letters, and syllables with the **codewords** or **codenumbers** (or, more generally, the **codegroups**) that replace these plaintext elements. A portion of a code might look like this:

codenumber	plaintext
3964	emplacing
1563	employ
7260	en-
8808	enable
3043	enabled
0012	enabled to

This means, of course, that 0012 replaces *enabled to*. In a sense, a code comprises a gigantic cipher alphabet, in which the basic plaintext unit is the word or the phrase; syllables and letters are supplied mainly to spell out words not present in the code. In ciphers, on the other hand, the basic unit is the letter, sometimes the letter-pair (**digraph** or **bigram**), very rarely larger groups of letters (**polygrams**). The substitution and transposition systems illustrated above are ciphers. There is no sharp theoretical dividing line between codes and ciphers; the latter shade into the former as they grow larger. But in modern practice the differences are usually quite marked. Sometimes the two are distinguished by saying that ciphers operate on plaintext units of regular length (all single letters or all groups of, say, three letters), whereas codes operate on plaintext groups of variable length (words, phrases, individual letters, etc.). A more penetrating and useful distinction is that code operates

A Few Words

on linguistic entities, dividing its raw material into meaningful elements like words and syllables, whereas cipher does not—cipher will split the *t* from the *h* in *the*, for example.

For 450 years, from about 1400 to about 1850, a system that was half a code and half a cipher dominated cryptography. It usually had a separate cipher alphabet with homophones and a codelike list of names, words, and syllables. This list, originally just of names, gave the system its name: **nomenclator**. Even though late in its life some nomenclators grew larger than some modern codes, such systems are still called "nomenclators" if they fall within this historical period. An odd characteristic is that nomenclators were always written on large folded sheets of paper, whereas modern codes are almost invariably in book or booklet form. The **commercial code** is a code used in business primarily to save on cable tolls; though some are compiled for private firms, many others are sold to the public and therefore provide no real secrecy.

Most ciphers employ a **key**, which specifies such things as the arrangement of letters within a cipher alphabet, or the pattern of shuffling in a transposition, or the settings on a cipher machine. If a word or phrase or number serves as the key, it is naturally called the **keyword** or **keyphrase** or **keynumber**. Keys exist within a general system and control that system's variable elements. For example, if a polyalphabetic cipher provides 26 cipher alphabets, a keyword might define the half dozen or so that are to be used in a particular message.

Codewords or codenumbers can be subjected to transposition or substitution just like any other group of letters or numbers—the transforming processes do not ask that the texts given to them be intelligible. Code that has not yet undergone such a process—called **superencipherment**—or which has been deciphered from it is called **placode**, a shortening of "plain code." Code that has been transformed is called **encicode**, from "enciphered code."

To pass a plaintext through these transformations is to **encipher** or **encode** it, as the case may be. What comes out of the transformation is the **ciphertext** or the **codetext**. The final secret message, wrapped up and sent, is the **cryptogram**. (The term "ciphertext" emphasizes the result of encipherment more, while "cryptogram" emphasizes the fact of transmission more; it is analogous to "telegram.") To **decipher** or **decode** is for the persons legitimately possessing the key and system to reverse the transformations and bare the original message. It contrasts with **cryptanalyze**, in which persons who do not possess the key or system—a third party, the "enemy"—break down or solve the cryptogram. The difference is, of course, crucial. Before about 1920, when the word **cryptanalysis** was coined to mean the methods of breaking codes and ciphers, "decipher" and "decode" served in both senses (and occasionally still do), and in quotations where they are used in the sense of solve, they are retained if they will not confuse. Sometimes cryptanalysis is called **codebreaking**; this includes solving ciphers. The original intelligible text that emerges from either decipherment or cryptanalysis is again called **plaintext**. Messages sent without encipherment are **cleartext** or **in clear**, though they are sometimes called **in plain language**.

Cryptology is the science that embraces cryptography and cryptanalysis, but the term "cryptology" sometimes loosely designates the entire dual field of both rendering signals secure and extracting information from them. This broader field has grown to include many new areas; it encompasses, for example, means to deprive the enemy of information obtainable by studying the traffic patterns of radio messages, and means of obtaining information from radar emissions. An outline of this larger field, with its opposing parts placed opposite one another, and with a few of the methods of each part given in parentheses, would be:

SIGNAL SECURITY	SIGNAL INTELLIGENCE
Communication Security	Communication Intelligence
Steganography (invisible inks, open codes, messages in hollow heels) and Transmission Security (spurt radio systems)	Interception and Direction-Finding
Traffic Security (call-sign changes, dummy messages, radio silence)	Traffic Analysis (direction-finding fixes, message-flow studies, radio fingerprinting)
Cryptography (codes and ciphers, ciphony, cifax)	Cryptanalysis
Electronic Security	Electronic Intelligence
Emission Security (shifting of radar frequencies)	Electronic Reconnaissance (eavesdropping on radar emissions)
Counter-Countermeasures ("looking-through" jammed radar)	Countermeasures (jamming, false radar echoes)

This book employs certain typographic conventions for simplicity and economy. Plaintext is always set lower case; when it occurs in the running text (as opposed to its occurrence in the diagrams), it is also in *italics*. Ciphertext or codetext is set in SMALL CAPS in the text, keys in LARGE CAPS. They are distinguished in the diagrams by labels. Cleartext and translations of foreign-language plaintext are in roman within quotation marks. The sound of a letter or syllable or word, as distinguished from its written form, is placed within diagonals, according to the convention widely followed in linguistics; thus /t/ refers to the unvoiced stop normally represented by that letter and not to the graphic symbol *t*.

D. K.

1

ONE DAY OF MAGIC

AT 1:28 on the morning of December 7, 1941, the big ear of the Navy's radio station on Bainbridge Island near Seattle trembled to vibrations in the ether. A message was coming through on the Tokyo–Washington circuit. It was addressed to the Japanese embassy, and Bainbridge reached up and snared it as it flashed overhead. The message was short, and its radiotelegraph transmission took only nine minutes. Bainbridge had it all by 1:37.

The station's personnel punched the intercepted message on a teletype tape, dialed a number on the teletypewriter exchange, and, when the connection had been made, fed the tape into a mechanical transmitter that gobbled it up at 60 words per minute.

The intercept reappeared on a page-printer in Room 1649 of the Navy Department building on Constitution Avenue in Washington, D.C. What went on in this room, tucked for security's sake at the end of the first deck's sixth wing, was one of the most closely guarded secrets of the American government. For it was in here—and in a similar War Department room in the Munitions Building next door—that the United States peered into the most confidential thoughts and plans of its possible enemies by shredding the coded wrappings of their dispatches.

Room 1649 housed OP-20-GY, the cryptanalytic section of the Navy's cryptologic organization, OP-20-G. The page-printer stood beside the desk of the GY watch officer. It rapped out the intercept in an original and a carbon copy on yellow and pink teletype paper just like news on a city room wire-service ticker. The watch officer, Lieutenant (j.g.) Francis M. Brotherhood, U.S.N.R., a curly-haired, brown-eyed six-footer, saw immediately from indicators that the message bore for the guidance of Japanese code clerks that it was in the top Japanese cryptographic system.

This was an extremely complicated machine cipher which American cryptanalysts called PURPLE. Led by William F. Friedman, Chief Cryptanalyst of the Army Signal Corps, a team of codebreakers had solved Japan's enciphered dispatches, deduced the nature of the mechanism that would effect those letter transformations, and painstakingly built up an apparatus that cryptographically duplicated the Japanese machine. The Signal Corps had then constructed several additional PURPLE machines, using a hodgepodge of

1

manufactured parts, and had given one to the Navy. Its three components rested now on a table in Room 1649: an electric typewriter for input; the cryptographic assembly proper, consisting of a plugboard, four electric coding rings, and associated wires and switches, set on a wooden frame; and a printing unit for output. To this precious contraption, worth quite literally more than its weight in gold, Brotherhood carried the intercept.

He flicked the switches to the key of December 7. This was a rearrangement, according to a pattern ascertained months ago, of the key of December 1, which OP-20-GY had recovered. Brotherhood typed out the coded message. Electric impulses raced through the maze of wires, reversing the intricate enciphering process. In a few minutes, he had the plaintext before him.

It was in Japanese. Brotherhood had taken some of the orientation courses in that difficult language that the Navy gave to assist its cryptanalysts. He was in no sense a translator, however, and none was on duty next door in OP-20-GZ, the translating section. He put a red priority sticker on the decode and hand-carried it to the Signal Intelligence Service, the Army counterpart of OP-20-G, where he knew that a translator was on overnight duty. Leaving it there, he returned to OP-20-G. By now it was after 5 a.m. in Washington—the message having lost three hours as it passed through three time zones in crossing the continent.

The S.I.S. translator rendered the Japanese as: "Will the Ambassador please submit to the United States Government (if possible to the Secretary of State) our reply to the United States at 1:00 p.m. on the 7th, your time." The—"reply" referred to had been transmitted by Tokyo in 14 parts over the past 18½ hours, and Brotherhood had only recently decrypted the 14th part on the PURPLE machine. It had come out in the English in which Tokyo had framed it, and its ominous final sentence read: "The Japanese Government regrets to have to notify hereby the American Government that in view of the attitude of the American Government it cannot but consider that it is impossible to reach an agreement through further negotiations." Brotherhood had set it by for distribution early in the morning.

The translation of the message directing delivery at one o'clock had not yet come back from S.I.S. when Brotherhood was relieved at 7 a.m., and he told his relief, Lieutenant (j.g.) Alfred V. Pering, about it. Half an hour later, Lieutenant Commander Alwin D. Kramer, the Japanese-language expert who headed GZ and delivered the intercepts, arrived. He saw at once that the all-important conclusion of the long Japanese diplomatic note had come in since he had distributed the 13 previous parts the night before. He prepared a smooth copy from the rough decode and had his clerical assistant, Chief Yeoman H. L. Bryant, type up the usual 14 copies. Twelve of these were distributed by Kramer and his opposite number in S.I.S. to the President, the secretaries of State, War, and Navy, and a handful of top-ranking Army and Navy officers. The two others were file copies. This decode was part of a whole series of Japanese intercepts, which had long ago been given a

One Day of Magic

collective codename, partly for security, partly for ease of reference, by a previous director of naval intelligence, Rear Admiral Walter S. Anderson. Inspired, no doubt, by the mysterious daily production of the information and by the aura of sorcery and the occult that has always enveloped cryptology, he called it MAGIC.

When Bryant had finished, Kramer sent S.I.S. its seven copies, and at 8 o'clock took a copy to his superior, Captain Arthur H. McCollum, head of the Far Eastern Section of the Office of Naval Intelligence.

```
From:  Tokyo
To:    Washington
December 7, 1941
Purple (Urgent - Very Important)

#907.          To be handled in government code.

               Re my #902ª.

               Will the Ambassador please submit to the United

States Government (if possible to the Secretary of State)

our reply to the United States at 1:00 p.m. on the 7th, your

time.


a - JD-1:7143 - text of Japanese reply.
```

MAGIC's *solution of the Japanese one o'clock delivery message*

He then busied himself in his office, working on intercepted traffic, until 9:30, when he left to deliver the 14th part of Tokyo's reply to Admiral Harold F. Stark, the Chief of Naval Operations, to the White House, and to Frank Knox, the Secretary of the Navy. Knox was meeting at 10 a.m. that Sunday morning in the State Department with Secretary of War Henry L. Stimson and Secretary of State Cordell Hull to discuss the critical nature of the American negotiations with Japan, which, they knew from the previous 13 parts, had virtually reached an impasse. Kramer returned to his office about 10:20, where the translation of the message referring to the one o'clock delivery had arrived from S.I.S. while he was on his rounds.

Its import crashed in upon him at once. It called for the rupture of Japan's negotiations with the United States by a certain deadline. The hour set for the Japanese ambassadors to deliver the notification—1 p.m. on a Sunday—was highly unusual. And, as Kramer had quickly ascertained by drawing a navigator's time circle, 1 p.m. in Washington meant 7:30 a.m. in Hawaii and a couple of hours before dawn in the tense Far East around Malaya, which Japan had been threatening with ships and troops.

Kramer immediately directed Bryant to insert the one o'clock message into the reddish-brown looseleaf cardboard folders in which the MAGIC intercepts were bound. He included several other intercepts, adding one at the last minute, then slipped the folders into the leather briefcases, zipped these shut, and snapped their padlocks. Within ten minutes he was on his way.

He went first to Admiral Stark's office, where a conference was in session, and indicated to McCollum, who took the intercept from him, the nature of the message and the significance of its timing. McCollum grasped it at once and disappeared into Stark's office. Kramer wheeled and hurried down the passageway. He emerged from the Navy Department building and turned right on Constitution Avenue, heading for the meeting in the State Department eight blocks away. The urgency of the situation washed over him again, and he began to move on the double.

This moment, with Kramer running through the empty streets of Washington bearing his crucial intercept, an hour before sleepy code clerks at the Japanese embassy had even deciphered it and an hour before the Japanese planes roared off the carrier flight decks on their treacherous mission, is perhaps the finest hour in the history of cryptology. Kramer ran while an unconcerned nation slept late, ignored aggression in the hope that it would go away, begged the hollow gods of isolationism for peace, and refused to entertain—except humorously—the possibility that the little yellow men of Japan would dare attack the mighty United States. The American cryptanalytic organization swept through this miasma of apathy to reach a peak of alertness and accomplishment unmatched on that day of infamy by any other agency in the United States. That is its great achievement, and its glory. Kramer's sprint symbolizes it.

Why, then, did it not prevent Pearl Harbor? Because Japan never sent any message saying anything like "We will attack Pearl Harbor." It was therefore impossible for the cryptanalysts to solve one. Messages had been intercepted and read in plenty dealing with Japanese interest in warship movements into and out of Pearl Harbor, but these were evaluated by responsible intelligence officers as on a par with the many messages dealing with American warships in other ports and the Panama Canal. The causes of the Pearl Harbor disaster are many and complex, but no one has ever laid any of whatever blame there may be at the doors of OP-20-G or S.I.S. On the contrary, the Congressional committee that investigated the attack praised them for fulfilling their duty in a manner that "merits the highest commendation."

As the climax of war rushed near, the two agencies—together the most efficient and successful codebreaking organization that had ever existed—

scaled heights of accomplishment greater than any they had ever achieved. The Congressional committee, seeking the responsibility for the disaster, exposed their activity on almost a minute-by-minute basis. For the first time in history, it photographed in fine-grained detail the operation of a modern codebreaking organization at a moment of crisis. This is that film. It depicts OP-20-G and S.I.S. in the 24 hours preceding the Pearl Harbor attack, with the events of the past as prologue. It is the story of one day of MAGIC.

The two American cryptanalytic agencies had not sprung full-blown into being like Athena from the brow of Zeus. The Navy had been solving at least the simpler Japanese diplomatic and naval codes in Rooms 1649 and 2646 on the "deck" above since the 1920s. Among the personnel assigned to cryptanalytical duties were some of the Navy's approximately 50 language officers who had served in Japan for three years studying that exceedingly difficult tongue. One of them was Lieutenant Ellis M. Zacharias, later to become famous as an expert in psychological warfare against Japan. After seven months of training in Washington in 1926, he took charge of the naval listening station on the fourth floor of the American consulate in Shanghai, where he intercepted and cryptanalyzed Japanese naval traffic. This post remained in operation until it was evacuated to Corregidor in December, 1940. Long before then, radio intelligence units had been set up in Hawaii and in the Philippines, with headquarters in Washington exercising general supervision.

The Army's cryptanalytical work during the 1920s was centered in the so-called American Black Chamber under Herbert O. Yardley, who had organized it as a cryptologic section of military intelligence in World War I. It was maintained in secrecy in New York jointly by the War and State departments, and perhaps its greatest achievement was its 1920 solution of Japanese diplomatic codes. At the same time, the Army's cryptologic research and code-compiling functions were handled by William Friedman, then as later a civilian employee of the Signal Corps. In 1929, Henry L. Stimson, then Secretary of State, withdrew State Department support from the Black Chamber on ethical grounds, dissolving it. The Army decided to consolidate and enlarge its codemaking and codebreaking activities. Accordingly, it created the Signal Intelligence Service, with Friedman as chief, and, in 1930, hired three junior cryptanalysts and two clerks.

The following year, a Japanese general suddenly occupied Manchuria and set up a puppet Manchu emperor, and the government of the island empire of Nippon fell into the hands of the militarists. Their avarice for power, their desire to enrich their have-not nation, their hatred for white Occidental civilization, started them on a decade-long march of conquest. They withdrew from the League of Nations. They began beefing up the Army. They denounced the naval disarmament treaties and began an almost frantic ship-building race. Nor did they neglect, as part of their war-making capital, their cryptographic assets. In 1934, their Navy purchased a commercial German cipher machine called the Enigma; that same year, the Foreign Office adopted it, and it evolved into the most secret Japanese system of cryptography. A variety of other cryptosystems supplemented it. The War, Navy, and Foreign ministries shared the superenciphered numerical HATO code for intercommunication. Each ministry also had its own hierarchy of codes. The Foreign Office, for example, employed four main systems, each for a specific level of security, as well as some additional miscellaneous ones.

Meanwhile, the modern-style shoguns speared into defenseless China, sank the American gunboat *Panay*, raped Nanking, molested American hospitals and missions in China, and raged at American embargoes on oil and steel scrap. It became increasingly evident that Nippon's march of aggression would eventually collide with American rectitude. The mounting curve of tension was matched by the rising output of the American cryptanalytic agencies. A trickle of MAGIC in 1936 had become a stream in 1940. Credit for this belongs largely to Major General Joseph O. Mauborgne, who became Chief Signal Officer in October, 1937.

Mauborgne had long been interested in cryptology. In 1914, as a young first lieutenant, he achieved the first recorded solution of a cipher known as the Playfair, then used by the British as their field cipher. He described his technique in a 19-page pamphlet that was the first publication on cryptology issued by the United States government. In World War I, he put together several cryptographic elements to create the only theoretically unbreakable cipher, and promoted the first automatic cipher machine, with which the unbreakable cipher was associated. He was among the first to send and receive radio messages in airplanes. As Chief Signal Officer, he retained enough of his flair for cryptanalysis to solve a short and difficult challenge cipher. He was also talented in other directions: he played the violin well and was an accomplished artist, exhibiting at, among others, the Chicago Art Institute.

When he became head of the Signal Corps, he immediately set about augmenting the important cryptanalytic activities. He established the S.I.S. as an independent division reporting directly to him, enlarged its functions, set up branches, started correspondence courses, added intercept facilities, increased its budget, and put on more men. In 1939, when war broke out in Europe, S.I.S. was the first agency in the War Department to receive more funds, personnel, and space. Perhaps most important of all, Mauborgne's intense interest inspired his men to outstanding accomplishments. More and more codes were broken, and as the international situation stimulated an increasing flow of intercepts, the MAGIC intelligence approached flood stage.

Mauborgne retired in September, 1941, leaving an expanded organization running with smooth efficiency. By then the Japanese had completed the basic outline for a dawn attack on Pearl Harbor. The plan had been conceived in the fertile brain of Admiral Isoroku Yamamoto, Commander-in-Chief Combined Fleet, Imperial Japanese Navy. Early in the year, he had ordered a study of the operation, contending that "If we have war with the United States, we will have no hope of winning unless the United States fleet in Hawaiian waters can be destroyed." By May, 1941, studies had shown the feasibility of a surprise air attack, statistics had been gathered, and operational planning was under way.

In the middle of that month, the U.S. Navy took an important step in the radio intelligence field. It detached a 43-year-old lieutenant commander from his intelligence berth aboard U.S.S. *Indianapolis* and assigned him to reorganize and strengthen the radio intelligence unit at Pearl Harbor. The officer was Joseph John Rochefort, the only man in the Navy with expertise in three closely related and urgently needed fields: cryptanalysis, radio, and the Japanese language. Rochefort, who had begun his career as an enlisted man, had headed the Navy's cryptographic section from 1925 to 1927. Two years later, a married man with a child, he was sent, because of his outstanding abilities, as a language student to Japan, a hard post to which ordinarily only bachelor officers were sent. This three-year tour was followed by half a year in naval intelligence; most of the next eight years were spent at sea.

Finally, in June of 1941, Rochefort took over the command of what was then known as the Radio Unit of the 14th Naval District in Hawaii. To disguise its functions he renamed it the Combat Intelligence Unit. His mission was to find out, through communications intelligence, as much as possible about the dispositions and operations of the Japanese Navy. To this end he was to cryptanalyze all minor and one of the two major Japanese naval cryptosystems.

His chief target was the flag officers' system, the Japanese Navy's most difficult and the one in which it encased its most secret information. From about 1926 to the end of November, 1940, previous editions had provided the U.S. Navy with much of its information on the Japanese Navy. But the new version—a four-character code with a transposition superencipherment—was stoutly resisting the best efforts of the Navy's most skilled cryptanalysts, and Rochefort was urged to concentrate on it. The other major system, the main fleet cryptographic system, the most widely used, comprised a code with five-digit codenumbers to which were added a key of other numbers to complicate the system. The Navy called it the "five numeral system," or, more formally, JN25b—the JN for "Japanese Navy," the 25 an identifying number, the b for the second (and current) edition. Navy cryptanalytic units in Washington and the Philippines were working on this code. Rochefort's unit did not attack this but did attack the eight or ten lesser codes dealing with personnel, engineering, administration, weather, fleet exercises.

But cryptanalysis was only part of the unit's task. The great majority of its 100 officers and men worked on two other aspects of radio intelligence—direction-finding and traffic analysis.

Direction-finding locates radio transmitters. Since radio signals are heard best when the receiver points at the transmitter, sensitive antennas can find the direction from which a signal is coming by swinging until they hear it at its loudest. If two direction-finders take bearings like that on a signal and a control center draws the lines of direction on a map, the point at which they cross marks the position of the transmitter. Such a fix can tell quite precisely where, for example, a ship is operating. Successive fixes can plot its course and speed.

To exploit this source of information, the Navy in 1937 established the Mid-Pacific Strategic Direction-Finder Net. By 1941, high-frequency direction-finders curved in a gigantic arc from Cavite in the Philippines through Guam, Samoa, Midway, and Hawaii to Dutch Harbor, Alaska. The 60 or 70 officers and men who staffed these outposts reported their bearings to Hawaii, where Rochefort's unit translated them into fixes. For example, on October 16, the ship with call-sign KUNA 1 was located at 10.7 degrees north latitude, 166.7 degrees east longitude—or within Japan's mandated islands.

These findings did not serve merely to keep an eye on the day-to-day locations of Japanese warships. They also formed the basis of the even more fruitful technique of traffic analysis. Traffic analysis deduces the lines of command of military or naval forces by ascertaining which radios talk to which. And since military operations are usually accompanied by an increase in communications, traffic analysis can infer the imminence of such operations by watching the volume of traffic. When combined with direction-finding, it can often approximate the where and when of a planned movement.

Radio intelligence thus maintains a long-range, invisible, and continuous surveillance of fleet movements and organization, providing a wealth of information at a low cost. Of course it has its limitations. A change of the call-signs of radio transmitters can hinder it. The sending of fictitious messages can befuddle it. Radio silences can deafen it. But it cannot be wholly prevented except by unacceptable restrictions on communications. Hence the Navy relied increasingly on it for its information on Japanese naval activities as security tightened in Japan during 1941, and almost exclusively after July, when the President's trade-freezing order deprived the Navy of all visual observations of Japanese ships not on the China coast.

It was in July that a Japanese tactic set up a radio pattern that was later to deceive the Combat Intelligence Unit. The Nipponese militarists had decided to take advantage of France's defeat and occupy French Indochina. The naval preparations for the successful grab were clearly indicated in the radio traffic, which went through the usual three stages that preceded major Japanese operations. First appeared a heavy flurry of messages. The Commander-in-Chief Combined Fleet busily originated traffic, talking with many commands to the south, thereby indicating the probable direction of his advance. Then came a realignment of forces. In the lingo of the tranalysis people, certain chickens (fleet units) no longer had their old mothers (fleet commanders). Call-sign NOTA 4, which usually communicated with OYO 8, now talked mostly with ORU 6. Accompanying this was a considerable confusion

One Day of Magic

in the routing of messages, with frequent retransmissions caused by the regrouping: Admiral z not here; try Second Fleet. Then followed the third phase: radio silence. The task force was now under way. Messages would be addressed to it, but none would emanate from it.

During all this, however, not only were no messages heard from the aircraft carriers, none were sent to them, either. This blank condition exceeded radio silence, which suppresses traffic in only one direction—from the mobile force—not in both. American intelligence reasoned that the carriers were standing by in home waters as a covering force in case of counterattack, and that communications both to and from them were not heard because they were being sent out by short-range, low-powered transmissions that died away before reaching American receivers. Such a blank condition had obtained in a similar tactical situation in February. American intelligence had drawn the same conclusions then and had been proven right. Events soon confirmed the July assessment as well. Twice, then, a complete blank of carrier communications combined with indications of a strong southward thrust had meant the presence of the carriers in Empire waters. But what happened in February and July was not necessarily what would happen in December.

During the summer and fall of 1941, the pressure of events molded America's two cryptanalytic agencies closer and closer to the form they were to have on December 7. The Signal Intelligence Service, which had 181 officers, enlisted men, and civilians in Washington and 150 at intercept stations in the field on Pearl Harbor Day, had been headed since March by Lieutenant Colonel Rex W. Minckler, a career Signal Corps officer. Friedman served as his chief technical assistant. S.I.S. comprised the Signal Intelligence School, which trained Regular Army and Reserve officers in cryptology, the 2nd Signal Service Company, which staffed the intercept posts, and four Washington sections of the S.I.S. proper: the A, or administrative, which also operated the tabulating machinery; the B, or cryptanalytic; the C, or cryptographic, which prepared new U.S. Army systems, studied the current systems for security, and monitored Army traffic for security violations; and the D, or laboratory, which concocted secret inks and tested suspected documents.

The B section, under Major Harold S. Doud, a West Point graduate, had as its mission the solution of the military and diplomatic systems not only of Japan but of other countries. In this it apparently achieved at least a fair success, though no Japanese military systems—the chief of which was a code employing four-digit codenumbers—were readable by December 7 because of a paucity of material. Doud's technical assistant was a civilian, Frank B. Rowlett, one of the three original junior cryptanalysts hired in 1930. The military man in charge of Japanese diplomatic solutions was Major Eric Svensson.

The Navy's official designation of OP-20-G indicated that the agency was the G section of the 20th division of OPNAV, the Office of the Chief of Naval

Operations, the Navy's headquarters establishment. The 20th division was the Office of Naval Communications, and the G section was the Communication Security Section. This carefully chosen name masked its cryptanalytic activities, though its duties did include U.S. Navy cryptography.

Its chief was Commander Laurence F. Safford, 48, a tall, blond Annapolis graduate who was the Navy's chief expert in cryptology. In January, 1924, he had become the officer in charge of the newly created research desk in the Navy's Code and Signal Section. Here he founded the Navy's communication-intelligence organization. After sea duty from 1926 to 1929, he returned to cryptologic activities for three more years, when sea duty was again made necessary by the "Manchu" laws, which required officers of the Army and Navy to serve in the field or at sea to win promotion. He took command of OP-20-G in 1936. One of his principal accomplishments before the outbreak of war was the establishment of the Mid-Pacific Strategic Direction-Finder Net and of a similar net for the Atlantic, where it was to play a role of immense importance in the Battle of the Atlantic against the U-boats.

Safford's organization enjoyed broad cryptologic functions. It printed new editions of codes and ciphers and distributed them, and contracted with manufacturers for cipher machines. It developed new systems for the Navy. It comprehended such subsections as GI, which wrote reports based on radio intelligence from the field units, and GL, a record-keeping and historical-research group. But its main interest centered on cryptanalysis.

This activity was distributed among units in Washington, Hawaii, and the Philippines. Only Washington attacked foreign diplomatic systems and naval codes used in the Atlantic theater (primarily German). Rochefort had primary responsibility for the Japanese naval systems. The Philippines chipped away at JN25 and did some diplomatic deciphering, with keys provided by Washington. That unit, which like Rochefort's was attached for administrative purposes to the local naval district (the 16th), was installed in a tunnel of the island fortress of Corregidor. It was equipped with 26 radio receivers, apparatus for intercepting both high- and low-speed transmissions, a direction-finder, and tabulating machinery. Lieutenant Rudolph J. Fabian, 33, an Annapolis graduate who had had three years of communication intelligence in Washington and the Philippines, commanded. The 7 officers and 19 men in his cryptanalytic group exchanged possible recoveries of JN25b codegroups with Washington and with a British group in Singapore; each group also had a liaison man with the other.

Of the Navy's total radio-intelligence establishment of about 700 officers and men, two thirds were engaged in intercept or direction-finding activities and one third—including most of the 80 officers—in cryptanalysis and translation. Safford sized up the personnel of his three units this way: Pearl Harbor had some of the best officers, most of whom had four or five years of radio intelligence experience; the crew at Corregidor, which in general had only two or three years' experience, was "young, enthusiastic, and capable";

One Day of Magic

Washington—responsible for both overall supervision and training—had some of the most experienced personnel, with more than ten years' experience, and many of the least: 90 per cent of the unit had less than a year's experience.

Under Safford in the three subsections most closely involved with cryptanalysis were Lieutenant Commanders George W. Welker of GX, the intercept and direction-finding subsection, Lee W. Parke of GY, the cryptanalytical subsection, and Kramer of GZ, the translation and dissemination subsection. GY attacked new systems and recovered new keys for solved systems, such as PURPLE. But while it made the initial breaks in code solutions, the detailed recovery of codegroups (which was primarily a linguistic problem as compared to the more mathematical cipher solutions) was left to GZ. Four officers in GY, assisted by chief petty officers, stood round-the-clock watches. Senior watch officer was Lieutenant (j.g.) George W. Lynn; the others were Lieutenants (j.g.) Brotherhood, Pering, and Allan A. Murray. GY had others on its staff, such as girl typists who also did the simple deciphering of some diplomatic messages after the watch officers and other cryptanalysts had found the keys.

Kramer was in an odd position. Though he worked in OP-20-GZ, he was formally attached to OP-16-F2—the Far Eastern Section of the Office of Naval Intelligence. This arrangement was intended in part to throw off the Japanese, who might have inferred some measure of success in codebreaking if a Japanese-language officer like Kramer were assigned to communications, in part to have an officer with a broad intelligence background distribute MAGIC so that he could answer the recipients' questions. Kramer, 38, who had studied in Japan from 1931 to 1934, had had two tours in O.N.I. proper before being assigned full time to GZ in June, 1940. An Annapolis graduate, chess fan, and rifle marksman, he lived in a world in which everything had one right way to be done. He chose his words with almost finicky exactness (one of his favorites was "precise"); he kept his pencil mustache trimmed to a hair; he filed his papers tidily; he often studied his MAGIC intercepts several times over before delivering them. Included in this philosophy was his duty. He performed it with great responsibility, intelligence, and dedication.

The first task of OP-20-G and of S.I.S. was to obtain raw material for the cryptanalysts. And in peacetime America that was not easy.

Section 605 of the Federal Communications Act of 1934, which prohibits wiretaps, also prohibits the interception of messages between foreign countries and the United States and territories. General Malin Craig, Chief of Staff from 1937 to 1939, was acutely aware of this, and his attitude dampened efforts to intercept the Japanese diplomatic messages coming into America. But after General George C. Marshall succeeded to Craig's post, the exigencies of national defense relegated that problem in his mind to the status of a legalistic quibble. The cryptanalytic agencies pressed ahead in their intercept programs. The extreme secrecy in which they were cloaked helped them avoid detection. They concentrated on radio messages, since the cable companies, fully cognizant of the legal restrictions, in general refused to turn over any foreign communications to them. Consequently, 95 per cent of the intercepts were radio messages. The remainder was split between cable intercepts and photographs of messages on file at a few cooperative cable offices.

To pluck the messages from the airwaves, the Navy relied mainly on its listening posts at Bainbridge Island in Puget Sound; Winter Harbor, Maine; Cheltenham, Maryland; Heeia, Oahu; and Corregidor and to a lesser degree on stations at Guam; Imperial Beach, California; Amagansett, Long Island and Jupiter, Florida. Each station was assigned certain frequencies to cover. Bainbridge Island, which was called Station S, copied solid the schedule of Japanese government messages between Tokyo and San Francisco. Its two sound recorders guarded the radiotelephone band of that circuit; presumably it was equipped to unscramble the relatively simple sound inversion that then provided privacy from casual eavesdropping. Diplomatic messages were transmitted almost exclusively by commercial radio using roman letters. The naval radiograms, however, employed the special Morse code devised for kata kana, a syllabic script of Japanese. The Navy picked these up with operators trained in Japanese Morse and recorded them on a special typewriter that it had developed for the roman-letter equivalents of the kana characters. The Army's stations, called Monitor Posts, were: No. 1, Fort Hancock, New Jersey; No. 2, San Francisco; No. 3, Fort Sam Houston, San Antonio; No. 4, Panama; No. 5, Fort Shafter, Honolulu; No. 6, Fort Mills, Manila; No. 7, Fort Hunt, Virginia; No. 9, Rio de Janeiro.

At first both services airmailed messages from their intercept posts to Washington. But this proved too slow. The Pan-American Clipper, which carried Army intercepts from Hawaii to the mainland, departed only once a week on the average, and weather sometimes caused cancellations, forcing messages to be sent by ship. As late as the week before Pearl Harbor, two Army intercepts from Rio did not reach Washington for eleven days. Such delays compelled the Navy to install teletypewriter service in 1941 between Washington and its intercept stations in the continental U.S. The station would perforate a batch of intercepts onto a teletype tape, connect with Washington through a teletypewriter exchange, and run the tape through mechanically at 60 words per minute, cutting toll charges to one third the cost of manually sending each message individually. Outlying stations of both the Army and Navy picked out Japanese messages bearing certain indicators, enciphered the Japanese cryptograms in an American system, and radioed them to Washington. The reencipherment was to keep the Japanese from knowing of the extensive American cryptanalytic effort. Only the three top Japanese systems were involved in this expensive radio retransmission: PURPLE, RED (a machine system that antedated PURPLE, which had supplanted it at major embassies, but that was still in use for legations such as Vladivostok), and the J series of enciphered codes. The Army did not install a teletype for intercepts from its continental posts until the afternoon of December 6, 1941; the first messages (from San Francisco) were received in the early morning hours of December 7.

The intercept services missed little. Of the 227 messages pertaining to Japanese-American negotiations sent between Tokyo and Washington from March to December, 1941, all but four were picked up.

In Honolulu, where a large Japanese population produced nightmares of antlike espionage and potential sabotage, the 14th Naval District's intelligence officer, Captain Irving S. Mayfield, had long sought to obtain copies of the cablegrams of Consul General Nagao Kita. If Rochefort's unit could solve these, Mayfield figured, he might know better which Japanese to shadow and what information they sought.

His intuitions were sound. On March 27, 1941, not two weeks after Mayfield himself took up his duties, a young ensign of the Imperial Japanese Navy, 25-year-old Takeo Yoshikawa, who had steeped himself in information about the American Navy, arrived in Honolulu to serve as Japan's only military espionage agent covering Pearl Harbor. Under the cover-name "Tadasi Morimura," he was assigned to the consulate as a secretary. He promptly made himself obnoxious—and drew suspicion upon himself within the consulate staff—by coming to work late or not at all, getting drunk frequently, having women in his quarters overnight, and even insulting the consul himself on occasion. But he managed to tour the islands, and within a month was sending such messages as: "Warships observed at anchor on the 11th [of May, 1941] in Pearl Harbor were as follows: Battleships, 11: *Colorado*, *West Virginia*, *California*, *Tennessee*...." These were sent in the consulate's diplomatic systems, not in naval code.

But Mayfield's hopes of peering into these secret activities through the window of a broken code were stymied by the refusal of the cable offices to violate the statute against interception. His desires grew more intense as another source failed to yield any information of counterespionage activity. For months one of his enlisted men, Theodore Emanuel, had tapped half a dozen of the consulate's telephone lines, recorded the 50 or 60 calls made on them each day, and turned the recordings over to Lieutenant Denzel Carr for translation and summarization. But this eavesdropping produced at best some juicy items about bachelor Kita's sex life (such as his chasing a maid around a bedpost one night after a sake-soaked Japanese wedding); there was little to help Mayfield.

So when David Sarnoff, president of the Radio Corporation of America, vacationed in Hawaii, Mayfield spoke to him. It was subsequently arranged that thenceforth R.C.A.'s Japanese consulate messages would be quietly given to the naval authorities. But the consulate rotated its business among the several cable companies in Honolulu, and R.C.A.'s turn was not due until December 1.

In Washington, however, intercepts overwhelmed GY and S.I.S. The tiny staff of cryptanalysts simply could not cope with all of them expeditiously. This difficulty was resolved in two ways.

One was to cut out duplication of effort. At first, both services solved all their Japanese diplomatic intercepts. But beginning more than a year before Pearl Harbor, messages originating in Tokyo on odd-numbered days of the month were handled by the Navy, those on even days, by the Army. Each began breaking the messages sent in from its own intercept stations until it reached the Tokyo date of origin; it would then retain them or send them over as the dates indicated. The cryptanalysts utilized the extra time to attack as-yet-unbroken systems and to clean up backlogs.

The other method was to concentrate on the important intercepts and let the others slide, at least until the important ones were completed. But how can a cryptanalyst tell which messages are important until he has solved them? He cannot, but he can assume that messages sent in the more secret systems are the more important. All dispatches cannot be transmitted in a single system because the huge volume of traffic would enable cryptanalysts to break it too quickly. Hence most nations set up a hierarchy of systems, reserving the top ones for their vital needs.

Japan was no exception. Though her Foreign Office employed an almost bewildering variety of different codes, resorting, from time to time, to the Yokohama Specie Bank's private code, a Chinese ideographic code list, and codes bearing kata kana names, such as TA, JI, or HEN, it relied in the main on four systems. American cryptanalysts ranked these on four levels according to the inherent difficulty of their solution and the messages that they generally carried. Intercepts were then solved in the order of this priority schedule.

Simplest of all, and hence the lowest in rank and last to be read (excluding plain language), was the LA code, so called from the indicator group LA that preceded its codetexts. LA did little more than put kata kana into roman letters for telegraphic transmission and to secure some abbreviation for cable economy. Thus the kana for *ki* was replaced by the code form CI, the kana for *to* by IF, the two-kana combination of *ka + n* by CE. Its two-letter codewords, all of either vowel-consonant or consonant-vowel form and including such as ZO for 4, were supplemented by a list of four-letter codewords, such as TUVE for *dollars*, SISA for *ryoji* ("consul"), and XYGY for *Yokohama*. A very typical LA message is serial 01250 from the Foreign Minister to Kita, dated December 4, which begins in translation: "The following has been authorized as the year-end bonus for employee typists of your office." This sort of code is generally called a "passport code" because it usually serves for messages covering the administrative routine of a mission, such as issuance of passports and visas. LA was a particularly simple one to solve, partly because it had been in

One Day of Magic

effect since 1925, partly because of the regularities in its construction. For example, all kana that ended in *e* had as code equivalents groups beginning with A (*ke* = AC, *se* = AD), and all that began with *k* had code equivalents beginning or ending with C. Identification of one kana would thus suggest the identification of others.

One rung up the cryptographic ladder was the system known to the Japanese as *Oite* and to American codebreakers as PA-K2. The PA part was a two- and four-letter code similar to the LA, though much more extensive and with codegroups disarranged. The K2 part was a transposition based on a keynumber. The letters from the PA encoding were written under this keynumber from right to left and then copied out in mixed order, taking first the letter under number 1, then the letter under number 2, until the row was completed. The process was repeated for successive rows.

For example, on December 4 Yoshikawa wired the Foreign Minister that "At 1 o'clock on the 4th a light cruiser of the *Honolulu* class hastily departed—Morimura." In romaji (the roman-letter version of the kata kana) this became *4th gogo 1 kei jun (honoruru) kata hyaku shutsu ko—morimura*. In PA, with the parentheses getting their own codegroups (OQ and UQ), it assumed this form: BYDH DOST JE YO IA OQ GU RA HY HY UQ VI LA YJ AY EC TY FI BANL, with FI indicating *use four-letter code*. (The code clerk made two errors. After encoding *kata* by VI, he encoded an extra *ta* into LA and an unnecessary *re* into TY.) This was then written under the keynumber from right to left, with an extra letter I as a null to complete the final five-letter group:

10	15	11	16	2	8	1	5	17	3	7	13	19	4	18	6	12	9	14
B	Y	D	H	D	O	S	T	J	E	Y	O	I	A	O	Q	G	U	R
A	H	Y	H	Y	U	Q	V	I	L	A	Y	J	A	Y	E	C	T	Y
			F		I	B			A	N			L			I		

Transcribed line by line according to the numbers (s under 1 first, D under 2 second, etc.), prefixed with system indicator GIGIG and key indicator AUDOB, the message number, and the telegraphic abbreviation of *Sikuyu* ("urgent"), the message (with three more errors: the Y under 13 became the J in CJYHH, the F under 2 became the E in IYJIE, and the T under 9 became the I in AUIAY) became the one actually sent over Kita's name:

GAIMUDAIJIN TOKIO
SIKYU 02500 GIGIG AUDOB SDEAT QYOUB DGORY HJOIQ YLAVE AUIAY CJYHH IYJIE ALBIN

                                                                                   KITA

PA-K2 did not pose much of a problem to experienced American cryptanalysts. Rochefort estimated that his unit could crack a PA-K2 message in from six hours to six days, with three days a good average. The transposition was vulnerable because each line was shuffled identically; the cryptanalyst could slice a cryptogram into groups of 15 or 17 or 19 and anagram these simultaneously until the predominant vowel-consonant alternation appeared on all lines; the underlying code could then be solved by assuming that the most frequent codegroups represented the most frequent kana (*i*, followed by *ma*, *shi*, *o*, etc.) and filling out the skeleton words that resulted. Since the system had remained in use for several years, this reconstruction had long been accomplished by the Washington agencies. Hence solution involved only unraveling any new transposition and, with luck, might take only a few hours. It could also take a few days. Primarily because of PA-K2's deferred position in the priority list, an average of two to four days elapsed between interception and translation.

The code clerk in Honolulu enveloped Yoshikawa's final messages in PA-K2 only because higher-level codes had been destroyed December 2 on orders from Tokyo. Normally, espionage reports of shipping movements and military activities, sent routinely by Japanese consuls from their posts all over the world, were framed on that next level of secrecy. Here prevailed a succession of codes called TSU by the Japanese and the J series by Americans. These were even more extensive and more thoroughly disarranged than PA, and they were transposed by a system of far greater complexity than the rather simple and vulnerable K2. Furthermore, the code and the transposition were changed at frequent intervals. Thus J17-K6 was replaced on March 1 by J18-K8, and that in turn by J19-K9 on August 1.

The transposition was the real stumbling block. Like the K2, it used a keynumber, but it differed in being copied off vertically instead of horizontally, and in having a pattern of holes in the transposition blocks. These holes were left blank when the code groups are inscribed into the block. For example, letting the alphabet from A to Y serve as the code message:

5	1	3	4	6	2
A	B	■	C	D	E
F	■	■	G	■	H
I	J	■	■	■	K
L	M	N	O	P	■
Q	■	■	R	S	T
U	V	W	X	Y	

The letters were transcribed in columns in the order of the keynumbers, skipping over the blanks: BJMV EHKT NW CGORX AFILQU DPSY. This would be sent in the usual five-letter groups.

The first step in solving a columnar transposition like this, but without blanks, is to cut the cryptogram into the approximately equal segments that

One Day of Magic

the cryptanalyst believes represent the columns of the original block. The blanks vastly increase the difficulty of this essential first step because they vary the length of the column segments. The second step is to reconstruct the

ak ew /類	'ew	fo	ge	gu	hy	if	in
ak	相成	内話	的確	ツイデ	チェッコ スロヴァキア	ゼン	二十日
av	立場	相成タ(シ)	内紛	轉電	積リ	本年	獨逸
ba	ワガ	立至(ル)	相成致 シタ(ル)	内密	本月	ツウ	ゼンケン
ce	在...大使	我方	直ニ	明カ	乍ラ	テツ	通知
di	二月	在...代理大使	本日	タダシ	アン	十九日	會談
eg	來訪	本國政府	在...公使	メレ	對案	豫メ	ナイ
em	本國	ラン	然ルベ(ク)在...代理公使		會議	態度	アラザ(ル)
ew	ベク	豫テ	レイ	會計	在...總事	ヤク	タキ
fo	ガン	ベン	考(フ)	レン	十八日	在...總領事 代理 (事務代理)	ハツ
ge	承認	難(ク)	四月	カレ	聯合	ヘイ	在...領事
gu	會見	三月	ガワ	ベンポウ	發表	聯盟	然ルニ
hy	メン	極(メ)	主張	ゲキ	ベシ	カタ	八月
if	希臘	面談	ヘン	十七日	ゲン	ベツ	電信
in	移民	平和	面會	心得	クン	傳達	別電(第...號)
ix	返電	イン	佛國	訓電	電送	主義	原因
mu	總理大臣	ノ如(ク)	否ヤ	ドク	見計(ヒ)	七月	シュク
no	列ヘバ	訓示	十六日	一方	ジツ	見込	試(ミ)
pi	訓令	同盟	總領事	情報	一般	英國	ミン
od	エイ	不取敢	條件	總督	ノミ	一般的	假令
oy	申添(フ)	條項	取扱(ヒ)	五月	ツツ	述ベ	委細
re	, comma	十五日	專ラ	取計(ヒ)	波蘭	國民	ニ依ル
sa	故	一 横線	波斯	モシ	國際	西比利亞	ステート メント
uc	從來	行懸	...點線	コン	六月	取極(メ)	露國
uz	何分	ゾン	コンミット	/斜線	太平洋	若ハ	取消(シ)
wu	十四日	困難	ゼンゴ	行惱(ミ)	% パーセント	增	求(メ)
xy	根本	前段	ナン	ゾウ	ユウ	?疑問點	歐米

A page of a Japanese codebook (about 1931)

block by trying one segment next to the other until a codeword-like pattern appears. Here again the blanks, by introducing gaps in unknown places between the letters of the segments, greatly hinder the cryptanalyst.

The problems of solving such a system are illustrated by the fact that J18-K8 was not broken until more than a month after its introduction. The cryptanalysts had to make a fresh analysis for each pattern of blanks and each transposition key. The key changed daily, the blank-pattern three times a month. Hence J19-K9 solutions were frequently delayed. The key and pattern for November 18 were not recovered until December 3; those for November 28, not until December 7. On the other hand, solution was sometimes effected within a day or two. Success usually depended on the quantity of intercepts in a given key. About 10 or 15 per cent of J19-K9 keys were never solved.

This situation contrasts with that of PURPLE, the most secret Japanese system, in which all but 2 or 3 per cent of keys were recovered and in which most messages were solved within hours. Did the Japanese err in assessing the security of their systems? Yes and no. PURPLE was easier to keep up with once it was solved, but it was a much more difficult system to break in the first place than J19-K9. The solution of the PURPLE machine was, in fact, the greatest feat of cryptanalysis the world had yet known.

The cipher machine that Americans knew as PURPLE bore the resounding official Japanese title of 97-shiki O-bun In-ji-ki. This meant Alphabetical Typewriter '97, the '97 an abbreviation for the year 2597 of the Japanese calendar, which corresponds to 1937. The Japanese usually referred to it simply as "the machine" or as "J,"[*] the name given it by the Imperial Japanese Navy, which had adapted it from the German Enigma cipher machine and then had lent it to the Foreign Ministry, which, in turn, had further modified it. Its operating parts were housed in a drawer-sized box between two big black electrically operated Underwood typewriters, which were connected to it by 26 wires plugged into a row of sockets called a plugboard. To encipher a message, the cipher clerk would consult the thick YU GO book of machine keys, plug in the wire connections according to the key for the day, turn the four disks in the box so the numbers on their edges were those directed by the YU GO, and type out the plaintext. His machine would record that plaintext while the other, getting the electric impulses after the coding box had twisted them through devious paths, would print out the ciphertext. Deciphering was the same, though the machine irritatingly printed the plaintext in the five-letter groups of the ciphertext input.

The Alphabetical Typewriter worked on roman letters, not kata kana. Hence it could encipher English as well as romaji—and also roman-letter codetexts, like those of the J codes. Since themachin e could not encipher numerals or punctuation, the code clerk first transformed them into three-letter codewords, given in a small code list, and enciphered these. The receiving clerk would restore the punctuation, paragraphing, and so on, when typing up a finished copy of the decode.

* Not the same thing as the American name J for the J series of Japanese codes.

The guts and heart of the machine were the plugboards and the coding wheels. They diverted the current flowing along the connections from the input typewriter to the output one so that when the *a* key was depressed on the input keyboard an *a* would not be typed on the output machine. The diversion began with the plugboard connections. If the coding box were not present, a plugboard wire would take the electric impulse from the *a* key of the plaintext typewriter and bring it directly to, say, the R typebar of the ciphertext machine. Other wires would similarly connect the plaintext keys to noncorresponding ciphertext typebars. This would automatically produce a cipher, though a very elementary one. Each time plaintext *a* was depressed ciphertext R would appear. So simple a system affords no security. The plugboard connections can be changed from message to message, or even within a message, but this does not noticeably augment the system's strength.

Here is where the four coding wheels came in. Interposed between the plugboard of the plaintext typewriter and that of the ciphertext machine, they were shifted constantly with respect to one another by their supporting assembly. The enciphering current had to traverse their winding wire paths to get from one typewriter to the other, and the constant shifting continually set up different paths. Thus impulses from a given plaintext letter were switched through the box along ever varying detours to emerge at ever differing ciphertext letters. Plaintext *a* might be represented in a long message by all 26 letters. Conversely, any given ciphertext letter might stand for any one of 26 plaintext letters. Switches on the coding wheels could be flicked one way or the other; this constituted part of the key and was done by the code clerk before enciphering. Usually the plugboard connections were changed each day.

These factors united to produce a cipher of exceptional difficulty. The more a cipher deviates from the simple form in which one ciphertext letter invariably replaces the same plaintext letter, the harder it is to break. A cipher might replace a given plaintext letter by five different ciphertext letters in rotation, for example. But the Alphabetical Typewriter produced a substitution series hundreds of thousands of letters long. Its coding wheels, stepping a space—or two, or three, or four—after every letter or so, did not return to their original positions to re-create the same series of paths, and hence the same sequence of substitutes, until hundreds of thousands of letters had been enciphered. The task of the cryptanalysts consisted primarily of reconstructing the wiring and switches of the coding wheels—a task made more burdensome by the daily change of plugboard connections. Once this was done, the cryptanalyst still had to determine the starting position of the coding wheels for each day's messages. But this was a comparatively simple secondary job.

American cryptanalysts knew none of these details when the Japanese Foreign Office installed the Alphabetical Typewriter in its major embassies in the late 1930s. How, then, did they solve it? Where did they begin? How did they even know that a new machine was in service, since the Japanese government did not announce it?

The PURPLE machine supplanted the RED machine,* which American cryptanalysts had solved, and so probably their first clue to the new machine was the disconcerting discovery that they could no longer read the important Japanese messages. At the same time, they observed new indicators for the PURPLE system. Clues to the system's nature came from such characteristics of its ciphertext as the frequency of letters, the percentage of blanks (letters that did not appear in a given message), and the nature and number of repetitions. Perhaps the codebreakers also assumed that the new machine comprised essentially a more complicated and improved version of the one it replaced. In this they were right.

Their first essays at breaking into the cipher both accompanied and supplemented their attempts to determine the type of cipher. Their previous success with the RED machine and with the lesser systems had given them insight into the Japanese diplomatic forms of address, favorite phrases, and style (paragraphs were often numbered, for example). These provided the cryptanalysts with probable words—words likely to be in the plaintext—that would help in breaking the cipher. Opening and closing formulas, such as "I have the honor to inform Your Excellency" and "Re your telegram," constituted virtual cribs. Newspaper stories suggested the subject matter of intercepts. The State Department sometimes made public the full texts of diplomatic notes from Japan to the American government, in effect handing the cryptanalysts the plaintext (or its translation) of an entire dispatch. (State reportedly did not pass the texts of confidential notes to the cryptanalysts, though this would have helped them considerably and was done by other foreign ministries.) Japan's Foreign Office often had to circulate the same text to several embassies, not all of which had a PURPLE machine, and a code clerk might have inadvertently encoded some cables in PURPLE, some in other systems—which the cryptanalysts could read. A comparison of times of dispatch and length, and *voilà!*—another crib to a cryptogram. Errors were, as always, a fruitful source of clues. As late as November, 1941, the Manila legation repeated a telegram "because of a mistake on the plugboard." How much more common must errors have been when the code clerks were just learning to handle the machine! The sending of the identical text in two different keys produces "isomorphic" cryptograms that yield exceedingly valuable information on the composition of the cipher.

The cryptanalysts of S.I.S. and OP-20-G, then, matched these assumed plaintexts to their ciphertexts and looked for regularities from which they

---

* Whence, apparently, its codename. In American prewar military and naval parlance, the codeword ORANGE meant *Japan* in official papers such as war plans, and even in personal letters between high-ranking officers. In the 1930s, Lieutenant Jack S. Holtwick, Jr., a Navy cryptanalyst, built a machine to solve a Japanese diplomatic cipher that was abandoned in 1938. American cryptanalysts could very naturally have called it the ORANGE machine. As the successors of this system appeared, each increasingly enigmatic, their American codenames might well have progressively deepened in hue.

One Day of Magic

could derive a pattern of encipherment. This kind of work, particularly in the early stages of a difficult cryptanalysis, is perhaps the most excruciating, exasperating, agonizing mental process known to man. Hour after hour, day after day, sometimes month after month, the cryptanalyst tortures his brain to find some relationship between the letters that hangs together, does not dead-end in self-contradiction, and leads to additional valid results. "Most of the time he is groping in the darkest night," one solver has written. "Now and again a little flicker of light gleams across the darkness, tantalizing him with a glimpse of a path. Hopefully he dashes to it only to find himself in another labyrinth. His knowledge that night is inevitably followed by day keeps his waning courage up, and he steers his course towards where the morning sun is soon to appear. Except that sometimes he is engulfed in an interminable polar night."

It must have seemed like that interminable night to the cryptanalysts who began attacking the new Japanese machine. The codebreakers went just so far—and for months could not push on further. As William Friedman recalled, "When the PURPLE system was first introduced it presented an extremely difficult problem on which the Chief Signal Officer [Mauborgne] asked us to direct our best efforts. After work by my associates when we were making very slow progress, the Chief Signal Officer asked me personally to take a hand. I had been engaged largely in administrative duties up to that time, so at his request I dropped everything else that I could and began to work with the group."

Friedman was (and is) the world's greatest cryptologist. Then in his late forties, he was a quiet, studious man, well liked by his associates, of average height and build, and a natty dresser given to bow ties. Trained as a geneticist, he had become interested in cryptology in 1915 at a research institution in Illinois called the Riverbank Laboratories. He served as a cryptanalyst with the American Expeditionary Forces in World War I, and returned to Riverbank to write an 87-page tract that revolutionized cryptanalysis by introducing statistical methods for the first time. Hired by the Signal Corps in 1921, he applied these methods to a cipher-machine solution that placed America in the forefront of world cryptology. During these years, his wife, the former Elizabeth Smith, whom he had met and married at Riverbank, was solving rumrunners' codes for the Coast Guard. He wrote textbooks in cryptanalysis that are models of clarity. He became head of S.I.S. when it was founded and continued to exercise his extraordinary cryptanalytic abilities. His genius soon manifested itself in the attack on PURPLE.

Lighting his way with some of the methods that he himself had developed, he led the cryptanalysts through the murky PURPLE shadowland. He assigned teams to test various hypotheses. Some prospected fruitlessly, their only result a demonstration that success lay in another direction. Others found bits and pieces that seemed to make sense. (OP-20-G cooperated in this work, with Harry L. Clark making especially valuable contributions, but S.I.S. did most of it.) Friedman and the other codebreakers began to segregate the ciphertext letters into cycles representing the rotation of the coding wheels—gingerly at first, then faster and faster as the evidence accumulated. The polyalphabetic class of ciphers, to which PURPLE belonged, is based ultimately upon an alphabet table, usually 26 letters by 26. To reconstruct the PURPLE tables, the cryptanalysts employed both direct and indirect symmetry of position— names only slightly less forbidding than the methods they denote. Errors, caused perhaps by garbled interceptions or simple mistakes in the cryptanalysis, jarred these delicate analyses and delayed the work. But slowly it progressed. A cryptanalyst, brooding sphinxlike over the cross-ruled paper on his desk, would glimpse the skeleton of a pattern in a few scattered letters; he tried fitting a fragment from another recovery into it; he tested the new values that resulted and found that they produced acceptable plaintext; he incorporated his essay into the over-all solution and pressed on. Experts in Japanese filled in missing letters; mathematicians tied in one cycle with another and both to the tables. Every weapon of cryptanalytic science—which in the stratospheric realm of this solution drew heavily upon mathematics, using group theory, congruences, Poisson distributions—was thrown into the fray.

Eventually the solution reached the point where the cryptanalysts had a pretty good pencil-and-paper analog of the PURPLE machine. S.I.S. then constructed a mechanism that would do automatically what the cryptanalysts could do manually with their tables and cycles. They assembled it out of ordinary hardware and easily available pieces of communication equipment, such as the selector switches used for telephones. It was hardly a beautiful piece of machinery, and when not running just right it spewed sparks and made loud whirring noises. Though the Americans never saw the 97-shiki O-bun In-ji-ki, their contraption bore a surprising physical resemblance to it, and of course exactly duplicated it cryptographically.

S.I.S. handed in its first complete PURPLE solution in August of 1940, after 18 or 20 months of the most intensive analysis. In looking back on the effort that culminated in this, the outstanding cryptanalytic success in the whole history of secret writing up to its time, Friedman would say generously:

> Naturally this was a collaborative, cooperative effort on the part of all the people concerned. No one person is responsible for the solution, nor is there any single person to whom the major share of credit should go. As I say, it was a team, and it was only by very closely coordinated teamwork that we were able to solve it, which we did. It represents an achievement of the Army cryptanalytic bureau that, so far as I know, has not been duplicated elsewhere, because we definitely know that the British cryptanalytic service and the German cryptanalytic service were baffled in their attempts and they never did solve it.

Friedman, was, despite his partial disclaimer, the captain of that team. The solution had taken a terrific toll. The restless turning of the mind tormented

One Day of Magic

by a puzzle, the preoccupation at meals, the insomnia, the sudden wakening at midnight, the pressure to succeed because failure could have national consequences, the despair of the long weeks when the problem seemed insoluble, the repeated dashings of uplifted hopes, the mental shocks, the tension and the frustration and the urgency and the secrecy all converged and hammered furiously upon his skull. He collapsed in December. After three and a half months in Walter Reed General Hospital recovering from the nervous breakdown, he returned to S.I.S. on shortened hours, working at first in the more relaxed area of cryptosecurity. By the time of Pearl Harbor he was again able to do some cryptanalysis, this time of German systems.

Meanwhile, S.I.S. constructed a second PURPLE machine and gave it to the Navy. A third was sent to England in January of 1941 on *King George V*, Britain's newest and largest battleship, which had just brought over her new ambassador to the United States, Lord Halifax. Two Army and two Navy cryptanalysts accompanied the machine. In return the United States received British cryptanalytic information, presumably about German codes and ciphers. This machine eventually reached the British codebreaking group at Singapore, and was evacuated with it to Delhi after the Japanese swarmed down Malaya. A fourth machine was sent to the Philippines, while a fifth was built as an extra for S.I.S. A machine for Hawaii was under construction at the time of Pearl Harbor; this became instead a second machine sent to England for use there by Great Britain.

OP-20-G contributed importantly to the ease and speed of daily PURPLE solutions when 27-year-old Lieutenant (j.g.) Francis A. Raven discovered the key to the keys. After a number of PURPLE messages had been solved, Raven observed that the daily keys within each of the three ten-day periods of a month appeared to be related. He soon found that the Japanese simply shuffled the first day's key to form the keys for the next nine days, and that the nine shuffling patterns were the same in all the ten-day periods. Raven's discovery enabled the cryptanalysts to predict the keys for nine out of ten days. The cryptanalysts still had to solve for the first day's key by straightforward analysis, but this task and its delays were eliminated for the rest of the period. Furthermore, knowledge of the shuffles enabled the codebreakers to read all the traffic of a period even though they could solve only one of the daily keys.

This fine piece of work, on the shoulders of the tremendous initial Friedman–S.I.S. effort, resulted in the paradoxical situation of Americans reading the most difficult Japanese diplomatic system more quickly and easily than some lower-grade systems. They also became very facile in reading two-step systems in which PURPLE superenciphered an already coded message. The Japanese did this from time to time to provide extra security, usually with the CA code, the personal code of an ambassador or head of mission. A year after S.I.S. handed in its first PURPLE solution, the cryptanalysts solved a message enciphered in "the highest type of secret classification used by the Japanese Foreign Office." The message was first enciphered in CA; this was then juggled according to the K9 transposition (normally used with the J19 code), and the transposed codetext was then enciphered on the PURPLE machine. The solution, which on the basis of the number of combinations involved might have been expected to take geologic eons, was completed in just four days.

The question of who should receive this hard-won, easily-lost information was the knottiest, most nagging, most intractable problem in the whole operation of MAGIC. It involved a delicate balancing of security against utility. On the one hand was the need to turn the results to as much good effect as possible, and the more persons who saw it the greater its value would be. "I see no use in breaking a cipher," one admiral remarked dryly, "unless you use its contents." On the other hand was the danger that too wide a distribution would jeopardize this invaluable intelligence by increasing the possibility of a leak. In general, policy leaned heavily toward security, toward minimizing the risk as much as practicable by narrowly restricting the number of recipients.

In an agreement dated January 23, 1941, the intelligence chiefs of the Army and the Navy listed those eligible to see MAGIC. The ten named comprised perhaps the most elite group in the American power structure of the day: the President, the secretaries of State, War, and Navy, the Chief of Staff, the Chief of Naval Operations, the heads of the Army and Navy War Plans divisions, and the heads of the Army and Navy intelligence divisions. In practice, of course, many others saw the intercepts, such as McCollum, the heads of the Army and Navy communications divisions (which controlled the cryptanalytic bureaus), and the cryptanalysts and translators themselves. In time so did others not on the original list nor involved in the processing. By December the Navy's Assistant Chief of Naval Operations was regularly reading MAGIC. On the White House staff, President Roosevelt's right-hand man, Harry Hopkins, and the President's military and naval aides saw MAGIC; in fact, when Hopkins was confined to the Navy Hospital in November of 1941, Kramer brought it over to him specially. While Marshall interpreted the rules strictly and did not even entrust one of his closest assistants, Colonel Walter Bedell Smith, secretary to the general staff, with a key to the MAGIC briefcase, other officials, like Hull, Knox, and Stark, let their aides handle the details and so see the intercepts. In addition, at least four subordinate State Department officers saw MAGIC with fair regularity: Sumner Welles, the Under Secretary; Dr. Stanley K. Hornbeck, advisor on political relations; Maxwell M. Hamilton, chief of the Far Eastern desk, and Joseph W. Ballantine, a Far Eastern expert.

Excluded from this tiny group were the field commanders of major military and naval forces. Security mainly controlled, but the feeling that this high-level, mainly political information should be analyzed in Washington contributed to this decision. But while the actual intercepts—indeed, the very existence of MAGIC—were kept from them, such intelligence extracted from it as Washington thought would help them was sent to them, usually attributed to "highly reliable sources." For example, on July 8, Lieutenant General Walter C. Short, commanding in Hawaii, was told that "Movement of Jap shipping from Japan has been suspended and additional merchant vessels are being requisitioned." This information came from MAGIC.

The Philippines constituted a special case. Cavite was the Navy's most favorably situated intercept post for Tokyo radio traffic, particularly Tokyo–Berlin, of which Hawaii, the East and West coasts, and England combined could not get more than 50 per cent. To cut the number of retransmissions of intercepts from Cavite to Washington, and thus reduce the danger of Japanese discovery of the MAGIC operation, the Navy in March sent out a PURPLE machine to the Philippines. OP-20-GY radioed the daily PURPLE and J19 keys to Fabian's unit; he applied these to the messages intercepted by his and the Army's intercept stations. He was then to forward the important solutions by radio. This procedure was practically abandoned later in the year, when almost every PURPLE message was important and all intercepts bearing its indicator were retransmitted to Washington. The Philippines were also regarded as the most threatened American outpost, and since diplomatic MAGIC was available right there because of a geographical accident, it went to General Douglas MacArthur and to Admiral Thomas C. Hart.

In sending the MAGIC keys to Fabian, OP-20-GY employed a restricted cipher. Had the messages been sent using the general Navy keys, any of the many ships and shore installations holding those keys could have read them. Worse, had the Japanese worked an Oriental MAGIC of their own on these general keys, they would have learned of America's most precious secret. The most secure naval cryptosystem was the E.C.M., or Electric Coding Machine, a device similar to but much stronger than PURPLE, which used a kind of codewheel called a rotor. The MAGIC cipher used the E.C.M. with a special set of rotors, resulting, in effect, in a new cipher. Traffic in this cryptochannel, called COPEK, was kept down, and extra precautions were taken to guard against occurrences that might aid cryptanalysis. Only officers of the radio intelligence organizations in Washington, Cavite, and Honolulu held the rotors. They also used COPEK to exchange information on Japanese naval codes that they were solving.

Rochefort in Hawaii could read the COPEK messages sending diplomatic-code keys to Fabian, and it may have been from him that Lieutenant Commander Edwin T. Layton, intelligence officer for the Pacific Fleet, learned that the Asiatic Fleet had the diplomatic MAGIC. On March 11, 1941, he asked McCollum to send it out to him. The head of the Far Eastern branch of naval intelligence declined, expounding what might be called the official line. On April 22 he wrote:

> I thoroughly appreciate that you would probably be much helped in your daily estimates if you had at your disposal the DIP. This, however, brings up

matters of security, et cetera, which would be very difficult to solve.... It seems reasonable to suppose that the Department should be the origin for evaluated political situations, as its availability of information is greater than that of any command afloat, however large, its staff is larger and it should be in a position to evaluate the political consequences.... I should think that the forces afloat should, in general, confine themselves to the estimate of the strategic and tactical situations with which they will be confronted when the time of action arrives. The material you mentioned can necessarily have but passing and transient interest as action in the political sphere is determined by the Government as a whole and not by the forces afloat.... In other words, while you and the Fleet may be highly interested in politics, there is nothing that you can do about it.

The inconsistency of this position reflects Washington's more basic inconsistency of, on the one hand, trying to keep MAGIC from the field commanders for security reasons and, on the other, constructing PURPLE machines for them.

Nevertheless, despite Washington's determination not to send MAGIC to the field, not to use the ordinary Navy cipher for it, and never to identify it as such in dispatches, the Navy in July wired Admiral Husband E. Kimmel, commanding the Pacific Fleet, a whole series of messages that gave the very serial numbers of the Japanese diplomatic messages in summarizing their contents! And on July 19, Washington began a message "PURPLE 14 July Canton to Tokyo" and continued with a quote from it. This practice ceased in August, suggesting tightened security, but again on December 3 the Navy clearly indicated Japanese intercepts as the source of its information.

The tightening may have resulted from several scares that Washington had just had. In March, State lost MAGIC memorandum No. 9. A horrified Army intelligence officer once found another MAGIC memorandum casually discarded in the wastebasket of Brigadier General Edwin M. (Pa) Watson, the President's military aide. In Boston the F.B.I. picked up a man connected with the cryptanalytic work who was attempting to sell information on it. The worst frights of all came in the spring of 1941.

On the afternoon of April 28, Hans Thomsen, counselor of the German embassy in Washington, cabled his Foreign Ministry, in a message not read by the U.S.: "As communicated to me by an absolutely reliable source, the State Department is in possession of the key to the Japanese coding system and is therefore also able to decipher telegrams from Tokyo to Ambassador Nomura here regarding Ambassador Oshima's reports from Berlin." After thinking about it for a few days, Berlin gave this information to its Axis ally through Baron Hiroshi Oshima, the Japanese ambassador to Germany. He passed it to Tokyo on May 3 in a cable saying he believed it, and Tokyo, on May 5, asked Washington "whether you have any suspicion" of the matter. The American codebreakers, who had been following the Japanese messages from Berlin to Tokyo to Washington, held their breath. They remembered how Japan had canceled her J12 code in 1940 on her first inkling that the British and Dutch were reading it. But Nomura's reply—"The most stringent precautions are taken by all custodians of codes and ciphers"—evidently soothed the Foreign Office, for it contented itself with issuing stricter regulations for coding.

Then, on May 20, Nomura told Tokyo: "Though I do not know which ones, I have discovered the United States is reading some of our codes." The cryptanalysts shuddered. Would they have to start all over again? Nothing happened at once, but a few days later an incident made it appear that only the shipment of new systems from Japan was delaying the change of codes. On May 30, Japan prohibited her merchant vessels all over the world from further use of Code s. More to the point, she did so less than 24 hours after she learned that U.S. narcotics agents had removed codes from the tanker *Nichi Shin Maru* near San Francisco during a search.

The dreaded change of code, which would have cost the United States her best source of information just as it was needed more and more, now seemed inevitable. But morning after morning, the messages bore the same aspect and continued to break down under the same treatment. After days of anxious waiting, Navy cryptanalysts read a cable from Tokyo to Mexico on June 23, warning the legation: "There are also some suspicions that they [the Americans] read some of our codes. Therefore, we wish to exercise the utmost caution in accomplishing this mission."

Was this to be the extent of the Japanese security precautions? It seemed incredible, yet it appeared so. The cryptosystems continued unchanged. The Foreign Office capped its ludicrous cryptosecurity program of pointless warnings and regulation changes with a step that was almost as effective as the others: on November 25, it directed its embassies to print "Kokka Kimitsu" ("State Secret") in red enamel on the right of the number plate of their cipher machines. Perhaps they thought that this incantation would prevent cryptanalysis as an amulet was supposed to ward off sickness!

But if the Foreign Office discredited the rumors of solution (because, in its natural pride, it could not imagine its codes being anything but impregnable), the American recipients of MAGIC knew that they were all too true. In 1939, the director of naval intelligence had personally brought MAGIC in a looseleaf folder to a recipient, waited there while he read it, then took the folder on to the next recipient. The increasing volume of MAGIC had slowly eaten away at this original iron security. Colonel Rufus S. Bratton, chief of the Far Eastern section of Army intelligence, found himself wasting so much time chaperoning his single copy that he began to have duplicates and triplicates made. The number of copies grew from 4 in early 1941 to 14 by December. Subordinates assumed the time-consuming messenger function. Kramer took over for the Navy. Bratton, who had a higher rank and more responsibilities than Kramer (his opposite number was Kramer's superior, McCollum), had to delegate some of this work still further. Three assistants in the Japan subsection of his Far Eastern section, Lieutenant Colonel Carlisle C. Dusenbury, Major Wallace H. Moore, and Second Lieutenant J. Bayard Schindel, made some of his rounds for him. Instead of carrying around a single folder, copies were left with the recipient.

Marshall saw danger in all this: "I intervened very directly and required that it [MAGIC] be locked in a pouch and delivered by pouch, the pouch unlocked and it be read by the recipient and put back in the pouch." The "pouches" were actually zippered briefcases made by the Washington leather shop of Becker & Co. Each had a padlock to which there were only two keys, one held by the disseminator, one by the recipient, either personally or by his aide. This crackdown—about September—compelled the executive officer of the military intelligence division, who had been seeing MAGIC while his chief was on leave, to surrender his key and to stop reading the intercepts. The Navy soon adopted the Marshall precautions. Kramer, for example, often sat next to the recipient and explained references, furnished background, answered questions, and so forth—which is why so valuable an officer was given the apparently menial messenger task. Nevertheless, departures from this ideal occurred. The messenger could not very well stand over the Secretary of War or the Chief of Naval Operations while the messages were being read. In the State Department, the pouch was actually left overnight and exchanged the next day for a new one.

Still, the documents circulated in a cloud of mystery and continuous precaution. When Kramer telephoned in advance to recipients to find out where they were before delivering the intercepts, he would say only guarded words like, "I have something important that you should see." Bratton's immediate superior frequently saw him "leave his office with several parcels under his arm and be gone for several hours," and, because he knew that *his* superior wanted it that way, never asked about it. He also received packages from S.I.S. chief Minckler when Bratton was out; these he locked up in his safe and turned over to Bratton on his return without having looked into them. Before MAGIC was given to State, Army and Navy officers met with Hull to explain how a loose word could suddenly extinguish the light shed by these intercepts. When Knox received the documents at his apartment, he did not explain them to his wife. At high-level conferences, recipients took care not to mention MAGIC when men not privy to the secret attended. All copies had to be returned. No recipient could retain them for reference, though back copies were sometimes included in new folders when later messages referred to them. The cryptanalytic agencies each filed two copies, one by date, one by subject, and the Far Eastern sections of Army and Navy intelligence each kept one. All other copies were burned.

Before an intercept could even begin the rounds that would end in this fiery immolation, it ordinarily had to be translated, and translation was the bottleneck of the MAGIC production line. Interpreters of Japanese were even scarcer than expert cryptanalysts. Security precluded employing Nisei or any but the most trustworthy Americans. The Navy scoured the country for acceptable translators, and through prodigious efforts in 1941 it doubled its GZ translation staff—to six. These included three whom Kramer called "the most highly skilled Occidentals in the Japanese language in the world."

But ability in standard Japanese alone did not suffice. Each translator had to have at least a year's experience in telegraphic Japanese as well before he could be trusted to come through with the correct interpretation of a dispatch. This is because telegraphic Japanese is virtually a language within a language, and, as McCollum, himself a Japanese-language officer, explained, "the so-called translator in this type of stuff almost has to be a cryptographer himself. You understand that these things come out in the form of syllables, and it is how you group your syllables that you make your words. There is no punctuation.

"Now, without the Chinese ideograph to read from, it is most difficult to group these things together. That is, any two sounds grouped together to make a word may mean a variety of things. For instance, 'ba' may mean horses or fields, old women, or my hand, all depending on the ideographs with which it is written. On the so-called translator is forced the job of taking unrelated syllables and grouping them into what looks to him to be intelligible words, substituting then such of the Chinese ideographs necessary to pin it down, and then going ahead with the translation, which is a much more difficult job than simple translation."

Hence the situation of Mrs. Dorothy Edgers. She had lived for thirty years in Japan and had a diploma from a Japanese school to teach Japanese to Japanese students up to high-school level. Yet, because she had only two weeks' experience in GZ at the time of Pearl Harbor, Kramer considered her "not a reliable translator" in this field. And on the important messages, only reliable translators could be used. To unclog this bottleneck, messages in the minor systems were given only a partial translation. If a translator saw that they dealt with administrative trivia, they were frequently not formally translated at all.

With manifold streamlinings like that, with enlarged staffs, with the fluidity gained by experience, OP-20-G and S.I.S. gradually increased the speed and quantity of their output. In 1939, the agencies had often required three weeks to funnel a message from interceptor to recipient. In the latter part of 1941 the process sometimes took as little as four hours. Occasionally an agency broke down a late intercept that bore on a point of Japanese-American negotiations and rushed it to the Secretary of State an hour before he was to meet with the Japanese ambassadors. Volume attained overwhelming proportions. By the fall of 1941, 50 to 75 messages a day sluiced out of the two agencies, and at least once the quantity swelled to 130. Some of these messages ran to 15 typewritten pages.

The top-echelon recipients of MAGIC clearly could not afford the time to read all this traffic. Much of it was of secondary importance anyway. Kramer and Bratton winnowed the wheat from this chaff. Reading the entire output, they chose an average of 25 messages a day for distribution. At first Kramer supplemented his translations with gists for recipients too busy to read every word of the actual intercepts, starring the important ones, but he abandoned these in mid-November under the pressure of getting out the basic material. Bratton, who had been delivering summaries of MAGIC in the form of Intelligence Bulletins, began on August 5 to distribute MAGIC verbatim at Marshall's orders. This, however, had the effect of increasing the volume. Marshall complained that to absorb every word of it he would have had to "retire as Chief of Staff and read every day." To save the recipients' time, Bratton checked the important messages on a list in the folder with a red pencil; Kramer slid paper clips onto them. The recipients always read the flagged messages; the others they did not always read thoroughly, but they did leaf through the folder and skim them.

Distribution was usually made twice a day. Intercepts that had come in overnight went out in the morning, those processed during the day went out at the end of the afternoon. Especially important messages were delivered at once, often to the recipients' homes if late in the evening. Each agency sent its MAGIC copies on to the other with exemplary promptitude, despite a natural competition between them. As Bratton put it: "I was further urged on by the fact that if the Chief of Naval Operations ever got one of these things before General Marshall did and called him up to discuss it on the telephone with him, and the General hadn't gotten his copy, we all caught hell." (Marshall demurred: "I don't think I gave anybody hell much.")

Delivery to the White House and the State Department incurred difficulties. Under the January 23 agreement, the Army and Navy at first alternated in servicing the two. The Army, however, discontinued its deliveries to the White House after its turn in May, partly because of Watson's wastebasket security bungle, partly because it felt that these diplomatic matters should go to the President through the State Department. The Navy continued its deliveries through the President's naval aide, Captain John R. Beardall, though once in the summer Kramer himself carried a particularly "hot" message—probably dealing with negotiations the next day—to Roosevelt. Near the end of September, a month originally scheduled for Army delivery, during which nothing was delivered to the White House, the President said he wanted to see the intercept information. In October naval intelligence sent him memoranda based on MAGIC, but on Friday, November 7, Roosevelt said he wanted to see MAGIC itself. Beardall told him that it was an Army month. The President replied that he knew that and that he was either seeing MAGIC or getting information on it from Hull, but that he still wanted to see the original intercepts. He feared that condensing them would distort their meaning. On Monday, a conference agreed that the Navy would furnish the White House

One Day of Magic

with MAGIC and the Army the State Department. At 4:15 p.m., Wednesday, November 12, Kramer made the first distribution to the White House under this system.

Thus, by the fall of 1941, MAGIC was being demanded at the topmost level of government. It had become a regular and vital factor in the formation of American policy. Hull, who looked upon MAGIC "as I would a witness who is giving evidence against his own side of the case," was "at all times intensely interested in the contents of the intercepts." The chief of Army intelligence regarded MAGIC as the most reliable and authentic information that the War Department was receiving on Japanese intentions and activities. The Navy war plans chief thought that MAGIC, which was largely diplomatic at this time, affected his estimates by about 15 per cent. The high officials not only read MAGIC avidly and discussed it at their conferences, they acted upon it. Thus the decision to set up the command of United States Army Forces, Far East, which was headed by General MacArthur, stemmed directly from intercepts early in 1941 showing that Germany was pressuring Japan to attack Britain in Asia in the hope of involving the United States in the war; on the basis of this information, the command was created in July to deter Japan by enhancing American prestige in the Western Pacific—and it is a fact that Japan did not then comply with Germany's wishes.

The intricate mechanism of the American cryptanalytic effort pumped MAGIC to its eager recipients smoothly, speedily, and lavishly. Messages flew back and forth along the COPEK channel as if along nerve cells. Intercepts poured into Washington with less and less of a time lag. S.I.S. and GY grew increasingly adept at solution; the translators picked out the important messages ever more surely. Bratton and Kramer hustled from place to place with their locked briefcases. MAGIC gushed forth in profusion. So effectively did the cryptanalytic agencies perform that Marshall could say of this "priceless asset," this most complete and up-to-the-minute intelligence that any nation had ever had concerning a probable enemy, this necromantic gift of the gods of which one could apparently never have enough, that "There was too much of it."

In October the cabinet of Prince Konoye fell, and the Emperor summoned General Hideki Tojo to form a new government. One of the first acts of the new Foreign Minister, Shigenori Togo, was to call in the chief of the cable section. Togo, remembering a book that Herbert O. Yardley had written disclosing his 1920 solution of Japanese diplomatic codes, asked the cable chief, Kazuji Kameyama, whether their current diplomatic communications were secure. Kameyama reassured him. "This time," he said, "it's all right."

With the assumption of total power by the militarists under Tojo, the last real hopes for peace died. Almost at once, events began to slide toward war. On November 4, Tokyo sent to her ambassadors at Washington the text of her proposal B, which Togo described as "absolutely final." The ambassadors held it while they pursued other avenues, even though Tokyo, on November 5, told them that "Because of various circumstances, it is absolutely necessary that all arrangements for the signing of this agreement be completed by the 25th of this month."

That same day, Yamamoto promulgated Combined Fleet Top Secret Order Number 1, the plan for the Pearl Harbor attack. Two days later, he set December 8 (Tokyo time) as Y-day and named Vice Admiral Chuichi Nagumo as Commander, First Air Fleet—the Pearl Harbor strike force. In the days that followed, the 32 ships that were to compose the force slipped, one by one, out to sea and vanished. Far from any observation, they headed north to rendezvous in a bay of barren Etoforu Island, one of the chill, desolate Kuriles north of the four main islands of Japan. Behind them the ships left their regular wireless operators to carry on an apparently routine radio traffic in their own "fists," or sending touch, which is as distinctive as handwriting.

As the force was gathering, the Foreign Office, which knew only that the situation was tense and was never told in advance of the time, place, or nature of the planned attack, prepared an open-code arrangement as an emergency means of notification. Tokyo sent Circular 2353 to Washington on November 19:

> Regarding the broadcast of a special message in an emergency.
> In case of emergency (danger of cutting off our diplomatic relations), and the cutting off of international communications, the following warning will be added in the middle of the daily Japanese language short-wave news broadcast:
> 1) In case of Japan–U.S. relations in danger: HIGASHI NO KAZE AME ("east wind rain")
> 2) Japan–U.S.S.R. relations: KITA NO KAZE KUMORI ("north wind cloudy")
> 3) Japan–British relations: NISHI NO KAZE HARE ("west wind clear")
>
> This signal will be given in the middle and at the end as a weather forecast and each sentence will be repeated twice. When this is heard please destroy all code papers, etc. This is as yet to be a completely secret arrangement.
> Forward as urgent intelligence.

This open code related the winds to the compass points in which the named countries stood in regard to Japan: the U.S. to the east, Russia to the north, England to the west. Tokyo also set up an almost similar code for use in the general intelligence (not news) broadcasts.

As the secret messages establishing these open codes whistled through the air, Navy intercept Station S at Bainbridge Island heard and nabbed them. The station teletyped them to GY, which identified them as J19 and began cryptanalysis.

Many of the ships of the Pearl Harbor strike force had by then gathered in bleak Tankan Bay, where the only signs of human presence were a small concrete pier, a wireless shack, and three fishermen's huts. Snow covered the surrounding hills. In the gray twilight of November 21, the great carrier

One Day of Magic

Zuikaku glided into the remote harbor to complete the roster. The force swung at anchor, awaiting the order to sortie.

A few hours later, on November 20 (Washington time), the Japanese ambassador to the United States, Admiral Kichisaburo Nomura, and his newly arrived associate, Saburo Kurusu, presented Japan's ultimatum to Hull. It would have required the United States to reverse its foreign policy, acquiesce in further Japanese conquests, supply Japan with as much oil as she required for them, abandon China, and in effect surrender to international immorality. While Hull began drafting a reply, Tokyo cabled its ambassadors in message 812 that "There are reasons beyond your ability to guess why we wanted to settle Japanese-American relations by the 25th, but if within the next three or four days you can finish your conversations with the Americans; if the signing can be completed by the 29th (let me write it out for you—twenty-ninth); if the pertinent notes can be exchanged; if we can get an understanding with Great Britain and the Netherlands; and in short if everything can be finished, we have decided to wait until that date. This time we mean it, the deadline absolutely cannot be changed. After that things are automatically going to happen." Two days later, Togo wirelessed: "The time limit set in my message No. 812 is in Tokyo time."

The calendar had become a clock, and the clock had begun to tick.

On November 25, Yamamoto ordered the Pearl Harbor strike force to sortie next day. At 6 a.m. on November 26, the 32 ships of the force—six carriers, two battleships, and a flock of destroyers and support vessels—weighed anchor and sliced across the wrinkled surface of Tankan Bay. They steamed slightly south of east, heading into the "vacant sea"—the wintry North Pacific, whose wastes were undefiled by merchant tracks and whose empty vastness would swallow up the force. They had been ordered to return if detected before December 6 (Tokyo time); if discovered on December 7, Nagumo would decide whether or not to attack. Strict radio silence was enjoined. Aboard the battleship *Hiei*, Commander Kazuyoshi Kochi, a communications officer for the force, removed an essential part of his transmitter and put it in a wooden box, which he used as a pillow. The force drove eastward through fog, gale winds, and high seas. No one saw them.

Meanwhile, Hull, after a frantic week of drafting, consultations, and redraftings, had completed the American reply to Japan's proposal. It called upon Japan to withdraw all forces from China and Indochina and in return promised to unfreeze Japanese funds and resume trade. Nothing was said about oil. On November 26, the day that he handed it to Nomura and Kurusu, a message came from Tokyo setting up an open code for them for telephone use to speed up their reports. In it, *the President* was MISS KIMIKO, *Hull* was MISS FUMEKO, *Japanese–American negotiations* were to be referred to as a MARRIAGE PROPOSAL, the criticality of the situation as the imminence of the birth of a child, *the China question* as SAN FRANCISCO, and so on. They had occasion to use it the very next night to report on an interview with Hull. Kurusu talked for seven minutes, starting at 11:27 p.m. Washington time, with Kumaicho Yamamoto, the chief of the American bureau of the Japanese Foreign Office.* American interceptors had their recording machine running even before the Japanese started theirs, and succeeded in capturing even this rare form of communication. Kramer translated the conversation, interpreted the rather amateurish application of the open code (even detecting an attempt to bolster it with some extraneous comments), added the colorful description of vocal nuances and pauses, and distributed it with the routine MAGIC intercepts the following day.

[Secret]

From: Washington
To: Tokyo
27 November 1941 (2327–2334 EST)
(Telephone Code)—(See JD–1: 6841) (S. I. S. #25344)
Trans-Pacific
Telephone
(Conversation between Ambassador Kurusu and Japanese Foreign Office American Division Chief, Yamamoto.)

Literal translation	Decode of Voice Code
(After connection was completed:)	
KURUSU: "Hello, hello. This is Kurusu."	
YAMAMOTO: "This is Yamamoto."	
KURUSU: "Yes, Hello, hello."	
(Unable to get Yamamoto for about six or eight seconds, he said aside, to himself, or to someone near him:)	
KURUSU: "Oh, I see, they're making a record of this, huh?"	
(It is believed he meant that the six-second interruption was made so that a record could be started in Tokyo. Interceptor's machine had been started several minutes earlier.)	
KURUSU: "Hello. Sorry to trouble you so often."	
YAMAMOTO: "How did the matrimonial question get along today?"	"How did the negotiations go today?"
KURUSU: "Oh, haven't you got our telegram† yet? It was sent—let me see—at about six—no, seven o'clock. Seven o'clock. About three hours ago.	
"There wasn't much that was different from what Miss Fumeko said yesterday."	"There wasn't much that was different from Hull's talks of yesterday."

* Not to be confused with Admiral Isoroku Yamamoto.

One Day of Magic

Literal translation	*Decode of Voice Code*

YAMAMOTO: "Oh, there wasn't much difference?"

KURUSU: "No, there wasn't. As before, that southward matter—that south, SOUTH—southward matter, is having considerable effect. You know, southward matter."

YAMAMOTO (Obviously trying to indicate the serious effect that Japanese concentrations, etc. in French Indo-China were having on the conversations in Washington. He tries to do this without getting away from the "Miss Fumeko childbirth, marriage" character of the voice code.):

YAMAMOTO: "Oh, the south matter? It's effective?"

KURUSU: "Yes, and at one time, the matrimonial question seemed as if it would be settled."

"Yes, and at one time it looked as though we could reach an agreement."

KURUSU: "But—well, of course, there are other matters involved too, but—that was it—that was the monkey wrench. Details are included in the telegram† which should arrive very shortly. It is not very long and you'll be able to read it quickly."

YAMAMOTO: "Oh, you've dispatched it?"

KURUSU: "Oh, yes, quite a while ago. At about 7 o'clock."

(Pause.)

KURUSU: "How do things look there? Does it seem as if a child might be born?"

"Does it seem as if a crisis is at hand?"

YAMAMOTO (In a very definite tone): "Yes, the birth of the child seems imminent."

"Yes, a crisis *does* appear imminent."

KURUSU: (In a somewhat surprised tone, repeating Yamamoto's statement:)

"It *does* seem as if the birth is going to take place?"
(Pause.)

"A crisis *does* appear imminent?"

KURUSU: "In which direction . . ."

(Stopped himself very abruptly at this slip which went outside the character of the voice code. After a slight pause he quickly recovered, then to cover up the slip, continued:)

KURUSU: "Is it to be a boy or a girl?"

YAMAMOTO (Hesitated, then laughing at his hesitation took up Kurusu's cue to reestablish the voice code character of the talk. The "boy, girl, healthy" byplay has no other significance.):

YAMAMOTO: "It seems as if it will be a strong healthy boy."

KURUSU: "Oh, it's to be a strong healthy boy?"
(Rather long pause.)

Literal translation	Decode of Voice Code
YAMAMOTO: "Yes." "Did you make any statement (to the newspapers) regarding your talk with Miss Kimiko today?"	"Did you make any statement regarding your talks with the President today?"
KURUSU: "No, nothing. Nothing except the mere fact that we met." YAMAMOTO: "Regarding the matter contained in the telegram‡ of the other day, although no definite decision has been made yet, please be advised that effecting it will be difficult." KURUSU: "Oh, it is difficult, huh?" YAMAMOTO: "Yes, it is." KURUSU: "Well, I guess there's nothing more that can be done then." YAMAMOTO: "Well, yes." (Pause.) YAMAMOTO: "Then, today . . ." KURUSU: "Today?"	
YAMAMOTO: "The matrimonial question, that is, the matter pertaining to arranging a marriage—don't break them off." KURUSU: "Not break them? You mean talks." (Helplessly:) KURUSU: "Oh, my." (Pause, and then with a resigned laugh:) KURUSU: "Well, I'll do what I can." (Continuing after a pause:) KURUSU: "Please read carefully what Miss Kimiko had to say as contained in today's telegram."†	"Regarding negotiations, don't break them off." "Please read carefully what the President had to say as contained in today's telegram."†
YAMAMOTO: "From what time to what time were your talks today?" KURUSU: "Oh, today's was from 2:30." (Much repeating of the numeral 2.) KURUSU: "Oh, you mean the duration? Oh, that was for about an hour." YAMAMOTO: "Regarding the matrimonial question." "I shall send you another message. However, please bear in mind that the matter of the other day is a very difficult one." KURUSU: "But without anything,—they want to keep carrying on the matrimonial question. They do. In the meantime we're faced with the excitement of having a child born. On top of that Tokugawa is	"Regarding the negotiations." "But without anything,—they want to keep on negotiating. In the meantime we

One Day of Magic

Literal translation	Decode of Voice Code
really champing at the bit, isn't he? Tokugawa is, isn't he?" (Laughter and pause.)	have a crisis on hand and the army is champing at the bit. You know the army."
KURUSU: "That's why I doubt if anything can be done." YAMAMOTO: "I don't think it's as bad as that." YAMAMOTO: "Well,—we can't sell a mountain."	"Well,—we can't yield."
KURUSU: "Oh, sure, I know that. That isn't even a debatable question any more." YAMAMOTO: "Well, then, although we can't yield, we'll give you some kind of a reply to that telegram." KURUSU: "In any event, Miss Kimiko is leaving town tomorrow, and will remain in the country until Wednesday."	"In any event, the President is leaving town tomorrow, and will remain in the country until Wednesday."
YAMAMOTO: "Will you please continue to do your best." KURUSU: "Oh, yes. I'll do my best. And Nomura's doing everything too." YAMAMOTO: "Oh, all right. In today's talks, there wasn't anything of special interest then?" KURUSU: "No, nothing of particular interest, except that it is quite clear now that that southward—ah—the south, the south matter is having considerable effect." YAMAMOTO: "I see. Well, then, good-bye." KURUSU: "Good-bye."	

25443
JD–1: 6890   (M) Navy Trans. 11–28–41 ( )

† JD–1: 6915 (S. I. S. #25495). Outline of interview on November 27 with Roosevelt-Hull-Kurusu-Nomura.
‡ Probably #1189 (S. I. S. #25441–42). (JD–1: 6896). Washington reports the two proposals presented by the U.S. on November 26.

The same day that this conversation was held, Tokyo circularized its major embassies with still another open code. While the winds code envisioned abolition of all communication with the embassies, this new code—called the INGO DENPO ("hidden word") code—was intended for a less critical situation. It seems to have been arranged at the request of the consul in Singapore in case code but not plain language telegrams were prohibited. It set up such equivalences as ARIMURA = *code communications prohibited*; HATTORI = *relations between Japan and (name of country) are not in accordance with* *expectation*;* KODAMA = *Japan*; KUBOTA = *U.S.S.R.*; MINAMI = *U.S.A.*; and so on. "In order to distinguish these cables from others," Tokyo said, "the English word STOP will be added at the end as an indicator. (The Japanese word OWARI [end] will not be used.)"

The next day, November 28, the Navy cracked the transposition for the J19 message of nine days earlier and learned of the winds code arrangement. The cryptanalytic agencies saw at once that this arrangement, which dispensed with the entire routine of coding, cabling, delivery, and decoding, could give several hours' advance warning of Japan's intentions. They erupted into activity to try to intercept it. This wrenched facilities away from the commercial (for Japanese diplomatic), naval, and radiotelephone circuits with which the agencies were familiar and put them on voice newscasts.

The Army asked the Federal Communications Commission to listen for the winds code execute. Army stations at Hawaii and San Francisco tuned to the newscasts, as did Navy stations at Corregidor, Hawaii, and Bainbridge Island, and four or five along the Atlantic seaboard. Rochefort placed his four best language officers—Lieutenants Forrest R. Biard, J. R. Bromley, Allyn Cole, Jr., and G. M. Slonim—on a 24-hour watch on frequencies suggested by Washington and on others that his unit had found. The Dutch in Java and the British in Singapore listened. In Washington, Kramer made up some 3 × 5 cards for distribution to MAGIC recipients. They bore only the portentous phrases, "East Wind Rain: United States. North Wind Cloudy: Russia. West Wind Clear: England."

Soon plain-language intercepts were swamping GZ. Bainbridge ran up bills of $60 a day to send them in. Kramer and the other translators, already burdened, now had also to scan 100 feet of teletype paper a day for the execute; previously only three to five feet per week of plain-language material had come in. The long strips were thrown into the wastebasket and burned after checking. Several times the GY watch officers telephoned Kramer at his home at night to ask him to come to the office and check a possible execute. It always proved false.

Meanwhile, other signs of increasing tension were not lacking. On the 29th, Baron Oshima in Berlin reported that the German Foreign Minister, Joachim von Ribbentrop, had told him, "Should Japan become engaged in a war against the United States, Germany, of course, would join the war immediately." Next day, Tokyo replied, "Say very secretly to them that there is extreme danger that war may suddenly break out between the Anglo-Saxon

---

* This is the literal translation made by Mr. Cory of GZ and given in MAGIC. But Friedman and others have contended that it does not take into account the Japanese tendency to speak in circumlocution and by indirection. The spirit of it might better be rendered into English, Friedman suggested, as "on the brink of catastrophe" or "on the verge of disaster." Kramer conceded that the words should not be interpreted as mildly as the English seems to indicate, but could imply "relations are reaching a crisis." The British translated this phrase as "Relations between Japan and (name of country) are extremely critical."

One Day of Magic

nations and Japan through some clash of arms and add that the time of the breaking out of this war may come quicker than anyone dreams." Both these messages were translated on December 1, and Roosevelt considered the latter so important that he asked for a copy of it to keep. Kramer, after paraphrasing it for security's sake, gave him one.

At Pearl Harbor, Rochefort had just been presented with an unpleasant confirmation of that tautening situation. The Japanese fleet reassigned its 20,000 radio call-signs at midnight, December 1—only 30 days after the previous change. It was the first time in Rochefort's experience that a switch had occurred so soon after a previous one.

The one on November 1 had been expected; it had followed by the usual six months the regular spring call-sign shift. With the facility born of long experience, Rochefort's Combat Intelligence Unit identified in fairly rapid order the senders and receivers of a large percentage of the traffic. The unit observed the rising volume and southward routing of messages on the 200 radio circuits of the Japanese Navy. This fitted in almost perfectly with the widely known Japanese buildup for what the world thought was a strike at Siam or Singapore. By the third week in November, the unit had sensed the formation of a Third Fleet task force and its imminent departure in the direction of those areas. Aircraft carriers were not addressed during this buildup, nor did they transmit. To Rochefort, the situation shaped up like those of February and July, when Japanese fleet units moved south to support the takeover in French Indochina while the carriers remained in home waters as a reserve. They were there, he felt, to protect the exposed flank of the Japanese forces from the American fleet, which, from its bases at Cavite and Pearl, could sever the supply lines of the aggressor.

Rochefort's view was shared by fleet intelligence officer Layton. He knew that the two main carrier divisions had not appeared in the traffic for at least two weeks, and maybe three. He suspected their presence in home waters, but since he lacked positive indications of it, he omitted his presumptions from a report on the Japanese fleet that he submitted to Kimmel on December 1. Whereupon, Layton recalled:

> Admiral Kimmel said, "What! You don't know where Carrier Division 1 and Carrier Division 2 are!"
> I replied, "No, sir, I do not. I think they are in home waters, but I do not know where they are. The rest of these units, I feel pretty confident of their location." Then Admiral Kimmel looked at me, as sometimes he would, with somewhat a stern countenance and yet partially with a twinkle in his eye, and said:
> "Do you mean to say that they could be rounding Diamond Head and you wouldn't know it?" or words to that effect. My reply was that "I hope they would be sighted before now," or words to that effect.

On the same day that Layton gave his report to Kimmel, the Office of Naval Intelligence produced a memorandum of "Japanese Fleet Locations" that Layton, when he saw it, considered as "dotting the i's and crossing the t's" of his own estimates. It placed *Akagi* and *Kaga* (Carrier Division 1), and *Koryu* and *Kasuga* in southern Kyushu waters, and *Soryu* and *Hiryu* (Carrier Division 2) and *Zuikaku, Shokaku, Hosho*, and *Ryujo* at the great naval base of Kure. All this was just a more precise way of saying "home waters."

These estimates were based on the November observations. The call-sign change of December 1 obliterated the intricate communication networks that the radio intelligence units had so painstakingly built up and forced them to begin anew. The Japanese bedeviled them with new communication-security measures. Dispatches were sent "on the umbrella"—broadcast to the fleet at large and copied by all ships. This sort of blanket coverage made identification difficult. Multiple addresses were used. They sent dummy traffic, which, however, did not confuse the listeners. Just before the change, the communicators passed many old messages. Rochefort's unit spotted them, and guessed that they were attempts either to pad the volume or to get through to the addressee before the change caused routing difficulties.

On December 2, after only two days of analyzing the new calls, Rochefort's unit stated in its Communications Intelligence Summary: "Carriers—Almost a complete blank of information of the Carriers today. Lack of identifications has somewhat promoted this lack of information. However, since over two hundred service calls have been partially identified since the change on the first of December and not one carrier call has been recovered, it is evident that carrier traffic is at a low ebb." In the next day's summary appeared the last mention of carriers before December 7, and it was rather negative: "No information on submarines or carriers."

Other messages, however, clearly indicated the drive to the south, which Japan made no attempt to conceal. Twice before, Rochefort, Fabian, Layton, and O.N.I. had seen exactly the same conditions, and twice before their reasoning that the carriers were being held in empire waters had been proved right. Now, they thought, they were seeing it happen again. Temporarily oblivious to the possibility of a surprise attack on Pearl Harbor, they watched the forces moving against Malaya as hypnotically as a conjuror's audience stares at the empty right hand while the left is pulling the ace out of a sleeve.

American preconceptions were reinforced by two PURPLE messages of December 1, which the Navy read that same day. In the first, Tokyo directed Washington: "When you are faced with the necessity of destroying codes, get in touch with the naval attaché's office there and make use of chemicals they have on hand for this purpose. The attaché should have been advised by the Navy Ministry regarding this." Five days earlier, the cryptanalysts had read Tokyo's detailed instructions on how to destroy the PURPLE machine in an emergency. These two code-destruction messages appeared to be just precautionary measures in a tense situation, and this impression was strengthened by the second message of December 1. It seemed to virtually announce a Japanese invasion of British and Dutch possessions and to relegate conflict with the United States to a subsequent date: "The four offices in London, Hongkong, Singapore and Manila have been instructed to abandon the use of the code machines and to dispose of them. The machine in Batavia has been returned to Japan. Regardless of the contents of my circular message #2447 [which MAGIC did not have], the U.S. (office) retains the machines and the machine codes." American officials breathed easier. The messages appeared to give the United States a bit more of what it needed most—time, time to build up its pitifully weak Army and Navy.

While the world gazed with tunnel vision toward Southeast Asia, and American radio intelligence envisioned the Japanese carriers in home waters, six of them—*Akagi, Kaga, Hiryu, Soryu, Shokaku,* and *Zuikaku*—were in fact butting eastward through the high winds and waves of the vacant sea. Late in the afternoon of December 2, Tokyo time, the force picked up, apparently on a blanket broadcast, an electrifying open-code message intended for it: NIITAKA-YAMA NOBORE ("Climb Mount Niitaka"). It informed the strike force that the decision for war had been made and directed it to *Proceed with attack.* Niitaka-yama, also known as Mount Morrison, is a peak on Formosa whose 12,956-foot elevation made it the highest point of what was then the Japanese empire. The symbolism could not have been lost on the officers. The force refueled from its tankers.

There was trouble in Honolulu. The F.B.I. had, early in November, begun to tap the telephone of the manager of an important Japanese firm in the hope of obtaining some clues to possible espionage activity. The tap was in addition to those placed on the Japanese consulate by Mayfield, who was helped by an employee of the telephone company whom the 14th Naval District Intelligence Office had cultivated as its contact. Unexpectedly, however, a telephone repairman came across the jumper wire that the F.B.I. had put across the connections in the junction box. The Navy's contact man immediately tipped off Mayfield's office, which warned the F.B.I.—who promptly complained to the telephone company that their confidence had been breached. Mayfield, fearful that the commotion would disclose his own telephone surveillances and that such disclosure would give the Japanese an excuse for almost any action, pulled his taps. His recording operator jotted a wistful farewell under his final notes. "At 4 p.m. Honolulu time in the 1941st year of Our Lord, December 2 inst., I bade my adieu to you my friend of 22 months standing. Darn if I won't miss you!! Requiescat in Peace." The F.B.I., however, maintained its other taps.

Earlier that day, the consulate had received Circular #2445 in J19, relayed by Washington from Tokyo:

Take great pains that this does not leak out.

You are to take the following measures immediately:

1. With the exception of one copy each of the O [PA-K2] and the L [LA] codes, you are to burn all telegraph codes (this includes the codebooks for communication between the three departments [HATO] and those for use by the Navy).

2. As soon as you have completed this operation, wire the one word HARUNA.

3. Burn all secret records of incoming and outgoing telegrams.

4. Taking care not to arouse outside suspicion, dispose of all secret documents in the same way.

Since these measures are in preparation for an emergency, keep this within your consulate and carry out your duties with calmness and care.

The codes were duly burned, including the TSU, or J19, in which the circular was transmitted. That evening Kita sent HARUNA. Henceforth the consulate code secretary, Samon Tsukikawa, would have to transmit the spy messages of Yoshikawa, alias Morimura, in the simpler PA-K2.

The first such message arranged four signaling systems by which a spy might report on the condition of the ships in Pearl Harbor. The arrangement had been submitted to Yoshikawa by an Axis spy in Hawaii, Bernhard Julius Otto Kühn. Nazi Propaganda Minister Josef Goebbels had transferred him to the islands in 1935 after a contretemps with Kühn's daughter Ruth, who had become Goebbels' mistress when she was 16. In his signaling system, Kühn stipulated that numbers from 1 to 8 would mean such things as *A number of carriers preparing to sortie* (which was 2) and *Several carriers departed between 4th and 6th* (which was 7). Then he arranged that bonfires, house lights shown at certain times and places, or want ads broadcast over radio station KGMG would mean certain numbers. For example, 7 would be represented by two lights shown in the window of a house on Lanikai Beach between 2 and 3 a.m., or by two sheets between 10 and 11 a.m., by lights in the attic window of a house in Kalama between 11 and 12 p.m., or by a want ad offering a complete chicken farm for sale and listing P.O. Box 1476. If all these failed, a bonfire on a certain peak of Maui Island between 8 and 9 p.m. would indicate 7. The purpose of the system was to eliminate dangerous personal contacts between Kühn and the Japanese. Kühn tested it on December 2, found that it worked, and passed it to Yoshikawa. He had it encoded (in PA-K2) and sent to Tokyo in two long parts on December 3.

It was now the third day of the month in which the Japanese consulate gave its cable business to R.C.A. Following Sarnoff's instructions, George Street, district manager of the firm, had had the Japanese consulate messages copied on a blank sheet of paper with no identification of the sender or addressee. About 10 or 11 a.m., December 3, Mayfield called at the branch office and Street slipped him a blank envelope containing the messages. As soon as Mayfield returned to the District Intelligence Office, he had a messenger bring them down to Rochefort.

In Washington that Wednesday, the Signal Intelligence Service solved a

One Day of Magic

PURPLE message from Tokyo—and the readers of MAGIC, who only two days earlier had been lulled by the supposition that Japan might temporarily spare the United States, were stunned by the realization that the arrow of war might be loosed momentarily. For the message ordered the Washington embassy to "burn all [codes] but those now used with the machine and one copy each of O code [PA-K2] and abbreviating code [LA].... Stop at once using one code machine unit and destroy it completely... wire... HARUNA." Under Secretary of State Welles saw it and felt that "the chances had diminished from one

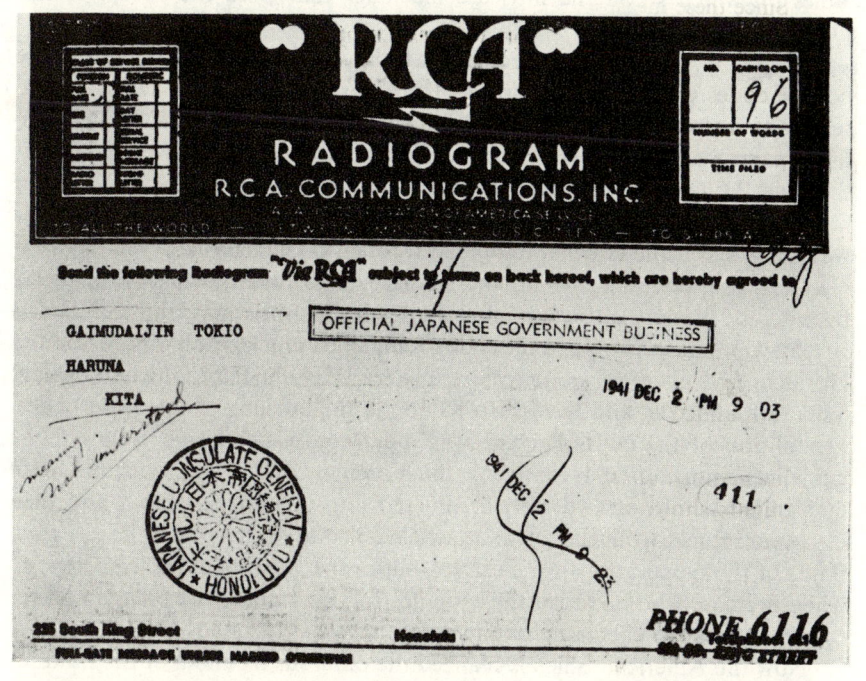

Consul Nagao Kita sends the codeword HARUNA *to report his codes destroyed*

in a thousand to one in a million that war could then be avoided." When the President's naval aide, Beardall, brought the message to Roosevelt, he said in substance, "Mr. President, this is a very significant dispatch." After the Chief Executive had read it carefully, he asked Beardall, "When do you think it will happen?"—referring to the outbreak of war. "Most any time," replied the naval aide, who thought that the moment was getting very close.

At the Japanese embassy at 2514 Massachusetts Avenue, the code clerks were executing these destruction orders. The code room stood at the southeast corner of the embassy, with windows overlooking the embassy parking lot and another legation next door. Half a dozen desks clustered in the middle of the room. Two cipher machines waited on desks against the west wall and a third, broken, rested in the walk-in safe. In utter disregard of the regulations promulgated for the security of communications, the embassy had hired an elderly Negro janitor named Robert to dust and clean the code room and its supersecret furnishings each day. The code clerks did make some obeisance to the security regulations by not allowing him in the room unless some Japanese were in it. But the situation was, to say the least, ironical. While the Japanese Foreign Office was exercising almost superhuman security precautions and American cryptanalysts were suffering nervous breakdowns to solve the PURPLE machine, an American citizen was running his duster over tables on which stood the intricate machines that were the vortex of this silent struggle.

But just as the Japanese seemed not to have given serious thought to the possibility of Robert's being a spy, so the Americans seemed to have given no serious thought to the possibility that a spy might have been insinuated into the Japanese embassy to ease their cryptanalytic burden. Of course, even if they had thought about it, they might have rejected the idea, for discovery of the spy would have meant an automatic change of codes. The danger of this was much less if the systems were read through cryptanalysis.

The paper codes of the Japanese consisted of folders whose four or six pages could be opened into a single long sheet. Embassy Counselor Sadao Iguchi, who was in charge of the code room, directed telegraph officer Masana Horiuchi and code clerks Takeshi Kajiwara, Hiroshi Hori, Juichi Yoshida, Tsukao Kawabata, and Kenichiro Kondo in the burning of the paper codes. Demolition of the code machine was more complicated, and followed the guidelines transmitted recently by the Foreign Office. The machines were dismantled with a screwdriver, hammered into unrecognizability, and then dissolved in acid from the naval attaché's office to destroy them thoroughly. Some of these operations were carried out in the gardens of the embassy; so when Bratton, who had read the code-destruction intelligence, sent an officer to the embassy to check, he obtained immediate confirmation.

Now the American officials realized the ominous meaning of the HARUNA messages that had been intercepted as they were sent from New York, New Orleans, and Havana and that had been received just that day in S.I.S. The Army and Navy high command universally regarded the destruction of codes as virtual certainty that war would break out within the next few days. As Stark's deputy put it: "If you rupture diplomatic negotiations you do not necessarily have to burn your codes. The diplomats go home, and they can pack up their codes with their dolls and take them home. Also, when you rupture diplomatic negotiations you do not rupture consular relations. The consuls stay on. Now, in this particular set of dispatches they not only told their diplomats in Washington and London to burn their codes, but they told their consuls in Manila, in Hong Kong, Singapore, and Batavia to burn their codes and that did not mean a rupture of diplomatic relations; it meant war."

A few hours after the code-destruction MAGIC reached Stark, he dispatched the electrifying news to Kimmel and Hart:

One Day of Magic

> Highly reliable information has been received that categoric and urgent instructions were sent yesterday to Japanese diplomatic and consular posts at Hongkong X Singapore X Batavia X Manila X Washington and London to destroy most of their codes and ciphers at once and to burn all other important confidential and secret documents X

He followed this five minutes later with another message:

> Circular twenty four forty four from Tokyo one December ordered London X Hongkong X Singapore and Manila to destroy PURPLE machine XX Batavia machine already sent to Tokyo XX December second Washington also directed destroy PURPLE X all but one copy of other systems X and all secret documents XX British Admiralty London today reports embassy London has complied

In Washington urgency drove out all thoughts of security. The strict injunction against ever mentioning MAGIC was completely overlooked. When Kimmel got the message, he asked Layton what "PURPLE" was. So tight had security been that neither of them knew. They checked with Lieutenant Herbert M. Coleman, the fleet security officer, who told them that it was a cipher machine similar to the Navy's.

Marshall authorized his intelligence chief, Brigadier General Sherman Miles, to direct the military attaché in Tokyo to destroy most of his codes and ciphers:

> Memorize emergency key word #2 for use of SIGNUD without repeat without indicators destroy document Stop SIGNNQ SIGPAP and SIGNDT should be retained and used for all communications except as last resort when these documents should be destroyed and memorized SIGNUD used Stop Destroy all other War Department ciphers and codes at once and notify by code word BINAB Stop Early rupture of diplomatic relations with Japan has been indicated State Department informed you may advise ambassador

Next day after lunch the Navy followed suit in advising its Far Eastern attachés:

> Destroy this system at discretion and report by word JABBERWOCK Destroy all registered publications except CSP 1085 and 6 and 1007 and 1008 and this system and report execution by sending in plain language BOOMERANG

At 8:45 p.m. that night, Thursday, December 4, the watch officer of the F.C.C.'s Radio Intelligence Division telephoned the Office of Naval Intelligence to ask if it could accept a certain message. The O.N.I. officer was not sure and said he would call back. At 9:05 GY watch officer Brotherhood called the F.C.C. and was given a Japanese weather report that sounded like something the F.C.C. man had been told to listen for. He read it to Brotherhood: "Tokyo: today—wind slightly stronger, may become cloudy tonight; tomorrow—slightly cloudy and fine weather. Kanagawa prefecture: today—north wind cloudy; from afternoon—more clouds. Chiba prefecture: today—north wind clear, may become slightly cloudy. Ocean surface: calm." Brotherhood was relieved that it included nothing about EAST WIND RAIN, which would have meant the United States, but in any case this message seemed to lack something that would have been required in a true execute. For one thing, the phrase NORTH WIND CLOUDY, which would have meant Russia, was not repeated twice. Nevertheless, Brotherhood telephoned Rear Admiral Leigh Noyes, director of naval communications, who remarked that he thought the wind was blowing from a funny direction. The consensus was that it was not a genuine execute, and the search continued.

In Tokyo, where it was December 5, Foreign Minister Togo received representatives of the Army and Navy general staffs. A general and an admiral wanted to discuss the delicate matter of the precise timing of Japan's final note to the United States. Drafted in English by the director of the Foreign Office's American bureau, the note had been approved by the Liaison Conference, a six-man war cabinet, at its meeting the day before. It rejected Hull's offer of the 26th and concluded: "The Japanese Government regrets to have to notify hereby the American Government that in view of the attitude of the American Government it cannot but consider that it is impossible to reach an agreement through further negotiations."

Article I of the 1907 Hague Convention governing the laws of war provides that "... hostilities ... must not commence without previous and explicit warning, in the form either of a reasoned declaration of war or of an ultimatum with conditional declaration of war." Togo had suggested to the Liaison Conference that the note was far stronger than an ultimatum and that to include a specific declaration of war would be "merely to reiterate the obvious." The conferees had gratefully acceded to this casuistry, since it enabled them to comply with the prior-notification requirement without endangering the surprise of the attack. Since the Hague Convention does not specify how long in advance such notification must be given, Premier Tojo and the other conferees thought to shave the time as much as possible. Dawn in Hawaii was about noon in Washington. The Liaison Conference had tentatively set 12:30 p.m., Sunday, December 7 (Washington time), as the time of delivery of the note.

But when the two military men called upon Togo the next day to fix the exact time, Vice Admiral Seiichi Ito, vice chief of the naval general staff, told the foreign minister [Togo later wrote] "that the high command had found it necessary to postpone presentation of the document thirty minutes beyond the time previously agreed upon, and that they wanted my consent thereto. I asked the reason for the delay, and Ito said that it was because he had miscalculated. ... I inquired further what period of time would be allowed between notification and attack; but Ito declined to answer this, on the plea of operational secrecy. I persisted, demanding assurance that even with the hour of delivery changed from twelve-thirty to one there would remain a sufficient time thereafter before the attack occurred; this assurance Ito gave. With this—being able to learn no more—I assented to his request. In leaving, Ito said: 'We

One Day of Magic

want you not to cable the notification to the Embassy in Washington too early.'" In this demand lay the seeds of Japan's juridical culpability.

Yoshikawa, in Honolulu, had continued sending his ship-disposition reports after the switch to PA-K2. They were an odd mélange of accuracy, error, and outright falsehoods. On December 3, for example, he correctly reported that the liner *Lurline* had arrived from San Francisco but stated that a military transport had departed when no such thing had occurred. The next day he informed Tokyo about the hasty departure of a cruiser of the *Honolulu* class; no such ship either entered or cleared the harbor on the 4th. Then, on the 5th, he cabled that three battleships had arrived in Pearl Harbor, making a total—which he reported with deadly accuracy—of eight anchored in the harbor. His messages, sent over Kita's signature, were decoded in the Foreign Office and routed to the North American section, where Toshikazu Kase passed them immediately to the Navy Ministry. Here they were redrafted, encoded in a naval code, and transmitted on a special frequency not normally used by the Navy and without any direct address to the Pearl Harbor strike force. Commander Koshi decoded it and brought to his chief this latest information.

The communication-security precautions paid off. Whether or not the messages slipped by the American radio monitors in Hawaii mattered little. Mere interception would not have helped much. The messages bore no external indication of their intended recipient, and they could not have been read. Rochefort's attack on Japanese naval codes had achieved some minor successes in late October and November, but he could read only about 10 per cent of the naval traffic, and much of this consisted of weather and other minor systems. The information obtained, Rochefort said, "was not in any sense vital." Cavite was spottily reading JN25 messages—which revealed nothing about Pearl Harbor—until December 4, when the superencipherment was suddenly changed. As a message that moved on the COPEK channel put it: "Five numeral intercepts subsequent to zero six hundred today indicate change of cipher system including complete change differentials and indicator subtractors X All intercepts received since time indicated checked against all differentials three previous systems X No dupes." Corregidor was not to get the initial break into the new superencipherment until December 8. And the only other system in which the Yoshikawa messages might have been forwarded—the flag officers' system—remained unsolved.

A possibility of warning was opened at the source, however, when Yoshikawa's original messages became available to Rochefort's unit. Mayfield had picked up another batch of cables in the surreptitious fashion from Street on Friday morning and immediately sent them down to Rochefort's unit by messenger. Solving them was not part of its duty,* but when a superior

---

* This may be why Rochefort did not simply request the keys from Washington via COPEK.

officer and colleague asks one to do a favor, it is hard to say no. Rochefort assigned the messages to Chief Radioman Farnsley C. Woodward, 39, who had had some experience with Japanese diplomatic codes at the Shanghai station from 1938 to 1940. He had some help from Lieutenant Commanders Thomas H. Dyer, Rochefort's senior cryptanalyst, and Wesley A. Wright, Dyer's assistant. Although the unit was not working on the diplomatic systems, it had information on them in the Navy's R.I.P.s, or Radio Intelligence Publications, with which all radio intelligence units were supplied. The R.I.P. gave, however, only the PA code list, leaving the onerous reconstruction of the current K2 transposition to the cryptanalyst. The half-dozen or so dispatches, plus some in LA, reached Woodward about 1:30 or 2 p.m. Friday, and he immediately began the first of a series of 12- and 14-hour days to read them. He had no difficulty with the LA messages, which were translated into English by Marine Corps Captain Alva Lasswell, but these yielded "nothing but junk." The K2, however, eluded him, and he worked on it far into the night.

At about 5 p.m. that day, a trans-Pacific telephone call came through to Mrs. Motokazu Mori, wife of a dentist prominent in Hawaii's Japanese community. She was the Honolulu correspondent for the militaristic Tokyo newspaper *Yomiuri Shimbun*. Mrs. Mori had received a wire from her editor the previous day asking her to arrange a telephone interview with a prominent Japanese on conditions in Hawaii. She cabled an acknowledgment but, unable to get anyone, she took the call herself.

Yomiuri: Hello, is this Mori?
Mrs. Mori: Hello. This is Mori.
Yomiuri: I am sorry to have troubled you. Thank you very much.
Mrs. Mori: Not at all.
Yomiuri: . . . I would like to have your impression on the conditions you are observing at present. Are airplanes flying daily?
Mrs. Mori: Yes, lots of them fly around.
Yomiuri: Are they large planes?
Mrs. Mori: Yes, they are quite big.
Yomiuri: Are they flying from morning till night?
Mrs. Mori: Well, not to that extent, but last week they were quite active in the air.

There ensued Q-and-A about the number of sailors, relations between Japanese and Americans, factory construction, population growth, whether the airplanes carried searchlights, Hawaii weather, newspaper comment, and comparison of impressions made during stopovers in Hawaii by two ambassadors to the United States, Kurusu of Japan and Maxim Litvinoff of Russia. The interview continued:

Yomiuri: Do you know anything about the United States fleet?
Mrs. Mori: No, I don't know anything about the fleet. Since we try to avoid talking about such matters, we do not know much about the fleet. At any rate,

One Day of Magic

the fleet here seems small. I don't [know if] all of the fleet has done this, but it seems that the fleet has left here.

Yomiuri: Is that so? What kind of flowers are in bloom in Hawaii at present?

Mrs. Mori: Presently, the flowers in bloom are fewest out of the whole year. However, the hibiscus and the poinsettia are in bloom now.

The editor seemed a little confused about the hibiscus, but the interview continued with discussions about liquor and the number of first- and second-generation Japanese. Finally the editor thanked Mrs. Mori. She asked him to hold on for a moment, but he had already hung up.

Unknown to both of them, someone had been listening. And that someone thought that the talk about hibiscus and poinsettias sounded mighty suspicious—especially on an expensive transoceanic telephone connection, and especially at a time of extraordinarily tense relations.

In Tokyo it was a little after 1 p.m. on Saturday, December 6. The Japanese reply to Hull's note of the 26th had recently been sent to the cable room of the Foreign Ministry for transmission to the embassy in Washington. Kazuji Kameyama, the cable chief, broke it into fourteen approximately equal parts to facilitate handling and ordered these enciphered on the 97-shiki O-bun In-ji-ki. He also enciphered a shorter "pilot" message from Togo alerting the embassy that the reply was on the way and instructing it "to put it in nicely drafted form and make every preparation to present it to the Americans just as soon as you receive instructions." At 8:30 p.m., the pilot message was telegraphed from the cable room to Tokyo's Central Telegraph Office, from where, 45 minutes later, it was radioed to the United States. Bainbridge Island intercepted it and relayed it to OP-20-G. By five minutes past noon on Saturday, December 6 (Washington time), OP-20-G had delivered the teletype copy to S.I.S., which promptly ran it through the PURPLE machine. By 2 p.m. Bratton had it, translated and typed. An hour later it was in the hands of the Army distributees. S.I.S. had officially closed at 1 p.m. and was not due to reopen until 6, when it was to go on 24-hour status. But this notification of the imminent receipt of the long-awaited reply to Hull's note of the 26th led to telephoning employees Mary J. Dunning and Ray Cave about 2:30 and asking them to report to work. By 4 both were there.

In Tokyo, Kameyama had released the first 13 parts of the Japanese note to the Central Telegraph Office. Following the instructions of the American bureau, he retained the crucial 14th part, which broke off negotiations. Shortly after 10 p.m., commercial radio began sending the 13 parts to Washington. Most of them took less than ten minutes to transmit, but even though two transmitters were used, it was not until two minutes before 2 a.m. that the tail of the last part had gone. Bainbridge, of course, was listening, and it picked the parts up in this order: 1, 2, 3, 4, 10, 9, 5, 12, 7, 11, 6, 13, 8. One batch arrived by teletype at OP-20-G at eleven minutes before noon, Saturday, December 6, Washington time, and the other at nine minutes of 3 that afternoon. Though it was Saturday, December 6, an even date and hence an Army date of responsibility, the Navy handled the dispatches because it knew that S.I.S. was not expected to work that afternoon, and it considered the intercepts of great importance. Decryptment did not go very smoothly, however. Something seemed to be in error. GY knew the key, but it was producing garbles every few letters. The cryptanalysts tried to correct them.

Meanwhile, a decode into Japanese of the long PA-K2 message that Yoshikawa had sent concerning Kühn's visual-signal system for Hawaii was placed on the desk of Mrs. Edgers in GZ. "At first glance," she said, "this seemed to be more interesting than some of the other messages I had in my basket, and so I selected it and asked one of the other men, who were also translators working on other messages, whether or not this shouldn't be done immediately and was told that I should and then I started to translate it. Well, it so happened that there was some mistake in the message that had to be corrected and so that took some time. That was at 12:30 or perhaps it was a little before or after 12:30; whatever time it was, we were to go home. It being Saturday, we worked until noon. I hadn't completed it, so I worked overtime and finished it, and I would say that between 1:30 and 2 was when I finished my rough draft translation." Mrs. Edgers left it in the hands of Chief Yeoman Bryant. But the message was still not entirely clear, and she had not yet had enough experience for her translations to be sent out without further checking. Kramer, busy with the 13 parts, did not examine it in detail.

To speed processing of the 13 parts, GY, learning that some people were in S.I.S., sent over parts 1 and 2. But when Major Doud of S.I.S. ordered Miss Cave to OP-20-G to help in the smooth typeups, the two parts were returned to GY for solution there, probably because of the garbles. But other messages also coming in were retained by S.I.S.

At 3 o'clock, Kramer, in GZ, had checked with GY to find out whether any more Tokyo traffic had come in before releasing his translators for the day. Since the critical matter of a diplomatic note is often found in the last sentences, GY broke down the last part intercepted for him. The first part of the first line indicated in Japanese that this was part 8 of a 14-part message. After about three lines of Japanese text in the preamble, the message came out in English, just as the Foreign Office had sent it. Kramer could let his translators go home. Interspersed throughout the English text were many of the three-letter codewords indicating punctuation, paragraphing, and numbering, but these posed no problem since they had been recovered long ago.

At 4 o'clock, when Linn took over the GY watch, the garbles still had not been cleared. He decided to start from the very beginning, to check the key, find what was wrong, and redecrypt the messages rather than to try to guess at the garbled letters and possibly make serious errors that would distort the sense. Discarding all the previous work caused a serious jam on the Navy's one PURPLE machine, and about 6 p.m. GY again called on S.I.S. for help.

One Day of Magic 51

Parts 9 and 10 were sent over; an hour later, the decrypts came back in longhand. By 7:30, the last of the 13 parts was being decrypted.

Not all the garbles had been scrubbed out. Part 3 had a 75-letter smudge that could not be read at all, Part 10 a 45-letter blur, and Part 11 one of 50 letters. Part 13 went awry in two patches. One deciphered as *andnd* and the other as *chtualylokmmtt*; GY thought the first should be *and as* and the second *China, can but*.*

In the Japanese embassy, about a mile away, the code clerks had completed deciphering the first seven or eight parts of the message by dinnertime. Then they all repaired to the Mayflower Hotel for a farewell dinner for Hidenari Terasaki, head of Japanese espionage for the western hemisphere, who had been ordered to another post.

While they were enjoying themselves, American code clerks at the Department of State were at work encoding a personal appeal for peace from the President of the United States to the Emperor of Japan. This had been off again, on again since October, Roosevelt apparently wishing to save it for a last resort. Now he decided that the time had come. The message was on its way by 9 o'clock. It traversed the 7,000 miles to Tokyo in an hour. But it took ten hours to get from the Central Telegraph Office to the American embassy.

As the President was addressing a message of peace to the Emperor, the men of the Japanese strike force were listening to a message of war. Shortly before, Admiral Nagumo had topped off the fuel tanks of his combat ships for the final dash. His crews waved farewell to the slow-moving tankers. Now the officers read a stirring message from Yamamoto to all hands: "The moment has arrived. The fate of the empire is at stake. Let every man do his best." Banzais rent the air. Up the mast of *Akagi* fluttered the very flag that had flown at Japan's great naval victory over Russia in 1905. It was a moment of great emotion. Nagumo altered course to due south and bent on 26 knots. Through a mounting sea, the battle force plunged toward its target.

Lovely, peaceful, that target lay "open unto the fields, and to the sky," oblivious to the onrushing armada of destruction. But many people were seeking clues to Japanese intentions, particularly concerning sabotage, which was regarded as a serious threat. Among these was Robert L. Shivers, special agent in charge of the F.B.I.'s Honolulu office and the man who, under authority of the Attorney General, had ordered the tap on the overseas phone that picked up Mrs. Mori's interview. By noon he had received a transcript in English of the call, and soon after 4 p.m. was conferring about it with Mayfield and the Army assistant G-2, Lieutenant Colonel George W. Bicknell, in

* The correct plaintexts were simply *and*, with the extra *nd* probably an inadvertent repetition, and *China, it must*, with the LYL probably a codeword for *comma*.

his office on the sixth floor of the **Alexander Young Hotel** in Honolulu. Mayfield consulted with Lieutenant Carr, who had translated the Navy telephone taps and who happened to be duty officer that afternoon at the District Intelligence Office; both thought that Carr should listen to the original recording to see if any hidden meaning was concealed in the intonations. Shivers said he would have it by 10 the following morning. Bicknell, whose job included heading the Army's counterintelligence in Hawaii, was convinced that the hibiscus and poinsettias smelled of espionage. He telephoned his boss, Colonel Kendall J. Fielder, the G-2, and said he wanted to see him and General Short immediately on a matter of importance.

They were both on their way to dinner at Schofield Barracks, and Fielder asked if it couldn't wait until tomorrow. Bicknell said it was too important; Fielder agreed to see him. Bicknell drove hurriedly out to Fort Shafter, where Fielder and Short had their homes side by side, and at about 6 p.m. the three men discussed the message for a while, but though they considered it "very suspicious, very fishy," Fielder said, "we couldn't solve it, we couldn't make heads nor tails out of it." The flower references seemed totally out of place, as if they were indeed conveying secret military information by open code, but, on the other hand, the Japanese spoke quite openly about airplanes and the fleet. The whole thing was very baffling, and they never did reach a conclusion about it.

They did not know that the *Yomiuri Shimbun* was then being hawked on the streets of Tokyo with an atmosphere feature on Hawaii based on the Mori interview—complete with reference to flowers. Nor, apparently, did they realize that the Japanese did not need so weak and dangerous a system. They could send much more detailed reports by cable in their diplomatic code. And, in one of the most ironical of situations at Pearl Harbor, they were doing precisely that at that very minute. While the three American army officers were standing on Short's porch worrying about the hibiscus, the R.C.A. office was time-stamping "1941 Dec 6 PM 6 01" on a message from the consulate. It was signed "Kita" but it came from Yoshikawa. It was brief (only 44 groups) and cheap ($6.82), but it reported that "(1) On the evening of the 5th, the battleship *Wyoming* and one sweeper entered port. Ships at anchor on the 6th were: 9 battleships, 3 minesweepers, 3 light cruisers, 17 destroyers. Ships in dock were: 4 light cruisers, 2 destroyers. Heavy cruisers and carriers have all left. (2) It appears that no air reconnaissance is being conducted by the fleet air arm." Yoshikawa was, as usual, partly right and partly wrong. He mistook *Utah* for *Wyoming*. His figure on the battleships was correct, but in harbor that afternoon were 6 light and 2 heavy cruisers, 29 destroyers, 4 minesweepers, 8 minelayers, and 3 seaplane tenders. With this message Yoshikawa completed his assignment. It was the last cable sent by the Japanese consulate in Hawaii for many years.

By 8:45 p.m. in Washington, the 13 parts had been typed in smooth copies

One Day of Magic 53

and put up in folders. Kramer began telephoning the recipients to find out where they were so he could bring the MAGIC to them. He also called his wife, Mary, who agreed to chauffeur him during his deliveries. They reached the White House first, at about 9:15. The naval aide, Beardall, had told the President that some MAGIC would be delivered that evening, and at about 4

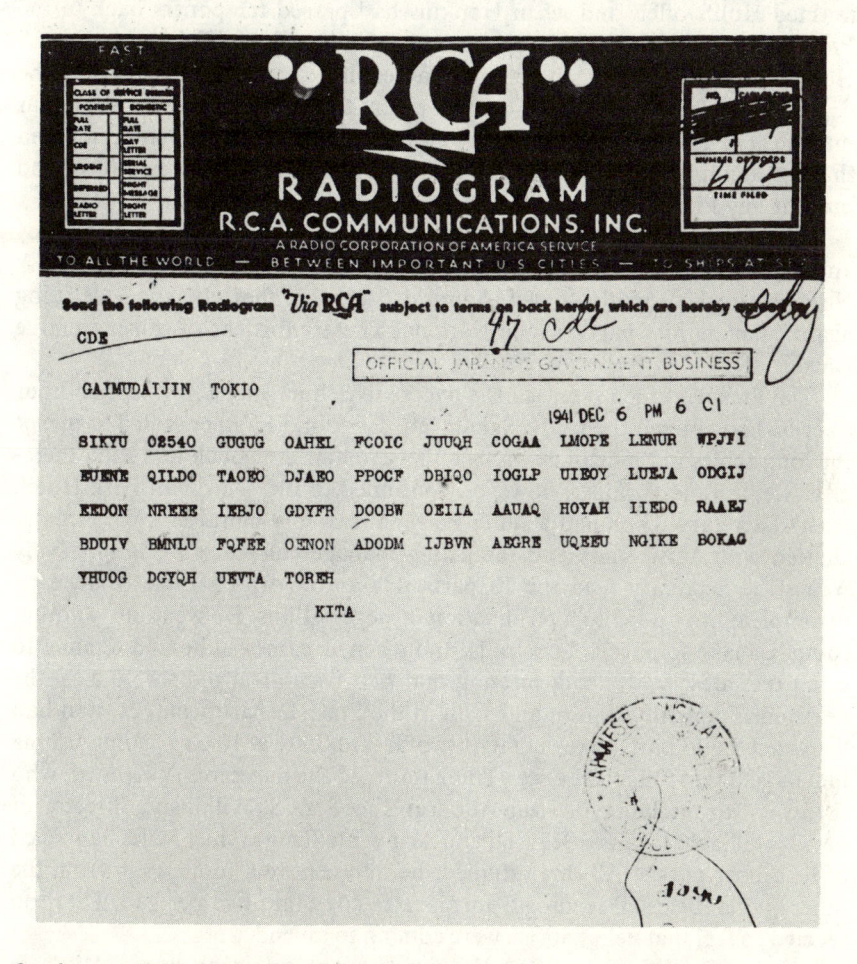

On the eve of Pearl Harbor, Takeo Yoshikawa sends his final message over Consul Kita's signature, using the PA-K2 code, to report that the U.S. fleet is still in port

p.m. he had ordered his communications assistant, Lieutenant Lester R. Schulz, to stand by and bring it to the President. Schulz was waiting in Beardall's small office in the corner of the basement mail room in the White House when Kramer arrived. The Roosevelts had been entertaining at a large dinner party, but the President had excused himself. Schulz obtained permission to bring the MAGIC to the President, and an usher accompanied him to the oval study on the second floor and announced him. Roosevelt was seated at his desk. Only Harry Hopkins was with him. Schulz unlocked the briefcase with the key that Beardall had given him, removed the sheaf of MAGIC, and handed it to the President. He read the 13 parts in about ten minutes while Hopkins paced slowly up and down. Then Hopkins read them. The 13th part rejected Hull's offer, and when Hopkins had passed the papers back to the President, Roosevelt turned to him and said, in effect, "This means war." Hopkins agreed, and for about five minutes they discussed the situation, the deployment of Japanese forces, the movement towards Indochina, and similar matters. The President mentioned his message to Hirohito. Hopkins remarked that it was too bad that the United States could not strike the first blow and prevent any kind of surprise in the inevitable war.

"No," the President said in effect, "we can't do that. We are a democracy and a peaceful people." He raised his voice: "But we have a good record." He tried unsuccessfully to get Admiral Stark on the telephone, deciding against having him paged at the National Theater for fear of causing undue alarm.

The President then returned the papers to Schulz and, about half an hour after he had entered the study, Schulz left. He found Kramer seated at one of the long tables in the mail room. Schulz gave him the pouch and soon thereafter went home. Kramer, however, continued to the Wardman Park Hotel, where Secretary Knox had a suite. For about twenty minutes, while Kramer chatted with Mrs. Knox and the acting manager of Knox's *Chicago Daily News*, the Secretary read the 13 parts. He agreed with Kramer that, even incomplete, it pointed to a termination of negotiations. He went into another room to make some telephone calls, and when he came out he told Kramer to bring the latest MAGIC to a meeting that had been arranged for 10 a.m. the next morning with Stimson and Hull in the State Department. (Bratton had delivered the 13 parts to the night duty officer at State at 10 p.m., admonishing him to get them to Hull at once.) Knox returned the intercepts to Kramer, who then went to the home of Rear Admiral Theodore S. Wilkinson, director of naval intelligence, where Beardall and Army intelligence chief Miles happened to be dinner guests. All three studied the intercept in a room away from the other guests, Beardall reading from an extra copy that Kramer had. They too seemed to feel that negotiations were coming to an end.

It was after midnight when Kramer left the Wilkinson house. His wife drove him back to the Navy Department, where he put the MAGIC back in his safe in GZ and checked to see if the 14th part had yet come in. It had not. Finally he went home himself.

In S.I.S., meanwhile, the new teletype that would expedite the forwarding of intercepts was being set up in the "cage," the barred room where PURPLE traffic was processed. Monitor Post 2 was requested to send in some intercepts as a test. In San Francisco, Harold W. Martin, the noncom in charge, punched onto the teletype tape the intercepts that the post had picked up since airmailing in the bulk of the day's material, as well as the earlier ones. Among the later ones was Yoshikawa's final message, which thus became one of the first to move on the direct wire as a real, nontest item. S.I.S. received it a little after midnight. But PA-K2 was a low-priority system, and the message had originated in a consular office. It was set aside to be worked on later.

Besides, S.I.S. had more important things to worry about. Like OP-20-G, it was going frantic in a search for the 14th part. Captain Robert E. Schukraft, head of the intercept section, and Frank B. Rowlett, the civilian cryptanalyst in charge of the Japanese diplomatic solutions, checked and rechecked to see whether one of the stations had picked it up and had somehow neglected to forward it. The message preambles had said that it existed, but they could find no trace of it. Neither suspected that the Japanese Foreign Office had deliberately held up transmission of this final conclusive part for security's sake.

Neither did the code clerks at the Japanese embassy. They had returned from Terasaki's party about 9:30, and by midnight had completed deciphering of the 13 parts. While they waited for the final section, they busied themselves by disposing of the remnants of the cipher machine they had destroyed the night before. But they did nothing to fulfill the orders of the pilot message to prepare the dispatch for immediate presentation.

Finally, fourteen hours after the last part of the previous 13 parts had been transmitted, the Foreign Office released the crucial 14th part that broke off negotiations. At 4 p.m., Tokyo time, it ordered it transmitted via both R.C.A. and Mackay Radio & Telegraph Company to ensure its correct reception. An hour and a half later, it wired to the Central Telegraph Office the coded message ordering the 1 p.m. delivery of the 14-part note. This too was sent via the two companies.

As usual, the indefatigable ear of Bainbridge Island detected the ethereal pulses of both messages. It picked up the Mackay transmission of the 14th part between 12:05 and 12:10 a.m., December 7, local time, and the even briefer one o'clock message between 1:28 and 1:37 a.m. It teletyped them to GY in a single transmission, the 14th part as serial No. 380 of Station S, the one o'clock as No. 381. Brotherhood, who was GY watch officer, ran them through the PURPLE machine. He evidently had some trouble with the 14th part, for it took an hour to break. But by 4 a.m. he had it in English. The three-letter codegroups were quickly translated into punctuation; the message would need little more than typing. The one o'clock message, however, turned out to be in Japanese. He sent it to S.I.S. for translation, knowing that translators were on duty because S.I.S. was beginning its round-the-clock tours. It was a little past 5 a.m., Washington time.

In the embassy of Nippon, the code clerks who had waited all through the night for the 14th part were, on Counselor Iguchi's advice, being sent home. Just as they were climbing wearily into their beds, the naval attaché arrived and found the mailbox stuffed with cablegrams. The duty officer telephoned the clerks at their homes about 8 a.m. and ordered them back to work.

A few hundred miles north of Oahu, the Japanese task force, bristling with guns, planes, and hate for Americans, bore down on the Pacific Fleet. A few hours earlier, a message had arrived from Tokyo that caused Commander Mitsuo Fuchida, the pilot who was to head the first wave of the air attack, to breathe a sigh of relief. It had been relayed from Yoshikawa, and it reported that no barrage balloons had yet been emplaced to protect the fleet from air attack. The same message also caused Commander Minoru Genda to sigh with relief. It stated that the battleships appeared not to be protected by torpedo nets. Genda had conceived the plan of shallow-water torpedo attack on the anchored American ships.

A little more than an hour after the hands of Honolulu clocks had snipped off December 6 and opened out into the first hours of December 7, the Pearl Harbor strike force received Tokyo's relay of Yoshikawa's final message. The American ships were still in harbor, awaiting the ax stroke with fat complacency. They were apparently not even protected by air search. Was it all a decoy? The strike force's radio officer, Commander Kanjiro Ono, listened intently to Honolulu's radio station KGMB for any inkling that the Americans knew of them. He heard only the soft melodies of the islands. On *Hiryu*, the flight deck officer slipped bits of paper between each plane's radio transmitter key and its contact point to make sure that radio silence, so carefully preserved for almost two weeks, would not be accidentally broken in the last few hours to destroy the element of surprise.

As Yoshikawa's final report was being decoded aboard *Akagi*, Kramer returned to the Navy Department he had left only seven hours before, and began working again. It was 7:30 on the morning of Sunday, December 7.

Brotherhood's decryptment of the 14th part was on his desk when he arrived. It took him about half an hour to ready a smooth version, and at 8 o'clock he delivered the neatly typed copy to McCollum. Other copies went to S.I.S. for its distribution. Kramer then worked on other traffic in his office, interrupting himself only once, at 8:45, to bring a copy of the 14th part to naval intelligence chief Wilkinson on his arrival at the Navy Department. At 9:30 he set out to deliver the full 14 parts to the meeting of the three secretaries. He stopped at the office of the Chief of Naval Operations to make sure that Stark had been given the message, which he had, and then walked and trotted to the White House. He got there at about 9:45 and gave the MAGIC pouch to Beardall, who had assigned himself to duty that morning because he thought the 14th part of the message that he had seen at Wilkinson's house the night before might be coming in.

Beardall brought the folder to the President, who was in his bedroom. Roosevelt said good morning to him, read the intercept, and commented that it looked like the Japanese were going to break off negotiations. Then he returned the MAGIC, and Beardall took it back to the Navy Department.

Kramer, meanwhile, had hurried across the west lawn of the White House to the ugly, ornate State Department building, arriving at about ten minutes of 10. The Army courier appeared at almost the same moment with the MAGIC for Hull and Stimson. Three State Department officials who saw MAGIC—Hornbeck, Ballantine, and Hamilton—were shown the 14th part by Hull's aide, John Stone, and the group discussed the situation in general terms until the secretaries arrived a few minutes later. Kramer gave his pouch to Knox and headed back to the Navy Department.

Meanwhile, the translation of the one o'clock message had come up from S.I.S. It was placed in Bratton's hands about 9 a.m. while he was reading the 14th part. It "immediately stunned me into frenzied activity because of its implications, and from that time on I was busily engaged trying to locate various officers of the general staff and conferring with them on the exclusive subject of this message and its meaning," he said later. He tried first to get in touch with Marshall, calling him at his quarters at Fort Myer, and was told by an orderly that the chief of staff had gone on his customary Sunday morning horseback ride. Bratton directed the orderly:

"Please go out at once, get assistance if necessary, and find General Marshall, ask him to—tell him who I am and tell him to go to the nearest telephone, that it is vitally important that I communicate with him at the earliest practicable moment." The orderly said he would. Bratton called Miles, told him of the message, and urged him to come down to the office at once. Between 10 and 10:30, Marshall called Bratton back. The colonel offered to drive out at once with the one o'clock message, but Marshall told him not to bother, that he was coming down to his office at once. Bratton obeyed.

Kramer arrived back in GZ at about 10:20, and found there the one o'clock message. It struck him as forcibly as it had Bratton. He at once had Yeoman Bryant prepare a new set of folders for immediate delivery of the intercept. Included in the new set were other messages which S.I.S. had decrypted, and on which Kramer had been working earlier in the morning: Tokyo serial No. 904, which directed the ambassadors not to use an ordinary clerk in preparing the 14-part ultimatum for presentation to the Secretary of State, so as to preserve maximum security; serial No. 909, thanking the two ambassadors for all their efforts; and serial No. 910, ordering destruction of the remaining cipher machine and all machine codes.

Kramer was about to dart out again when Pering, the GY watch officer, brought in a message in plain-language Japanese, ending with the telltale STOP that indicated it was an INGO DENPO message: KOYANAGI RIJIYORI SEIRINOTUGOO ARUNITUKI HATTORI MINAMI KINEBUNKO SETURITU KIKINO KYOKAINGAKU SIKYUU DENPOO ARITASI STOP TOGO. Kramer recognized KOYANAGI as the codeword for *England*, and HATTORI as a codeword whose meaning he did not recall. He consulted his code list and saw that it meant *Relations between Japan and (name of country) are not in accordance with expectation.* But in his haste he overlooked that the common Japanese word *minami*, which means "south," had an INGO DENPO meaning of *U.S.A.* He interpreted the message as "Please have director Koyagani send a wire stating the sum which has been decided to be spent on the South Hattori Memorial Library in order that this business may be wound up." Consequently, he dictated a decode that omitted *United States*: *Relations between Japan and England are not in accordance with expectation.* Yeoman Bryant inserted this and three other minor messages that had come over from the Army into the folders. Kramer meanwhile made a navigator's time circle that indicated that one o'clock in Washington was dawn in Hawaii and the very early hours of the morning in the Far East around Singapore and the Philippines, which everybody seemed to be watching. He shoved the folders into the briefcase and dashed out the door.

He went first to Stark's office, where the officers were discussing the 14th part, summoned McCollum, gave him the pouch that included the final code-destruction and one o'clock messages, and mentioned to him the significance of the latter's timing. McCollum grasped it at once and disappeared into Stark's office. Kramer wheeled and hurried down the passageway. He emerged from the Navy Department building and turned right on Constitution Avenue, heading for the meeting in the State Department eight or ten blocks away. The urgency of the situation washed over him again, and he began to move on the double.

He half trotted, half walked to State, getting there at about 10:45. Hull, Knox, and Stimson were still meeting. Kramer saw them grouped around the conference table when the door to Hull's office was opened briefly. He gave the MAGIC messages to Stone, explaining to him how the one o'clock time of delivery of the ultimatum tied in with the movement of a big Japanese convoy down the coast of Indochina, and mentioning in passing that the time in Hawaii would be 7:30 a.m. The final code-destruction message was self-explanatory. Kramer carried a MAGIC pouch to the White House, and then returned, perspiring, to the Navy Department, to busy himself with still more MAGIC. At about 12:30, he spotted the omission of *United States* from the INGO DENPO message. Because the one o'clock meeting was so close, he telephoned the recipients with the correction, a practice he had followed several times in the past, but reached only McCollum and Bratton. He told them that *United States* was to be inserted in file number 7148. The force of it had been considerably lessened by the one o'clock message, but Kramer, conscientious beyond the basic requirements of duty, nevertheless planned to send around a corrected version.

Safford later estimated that OP-20-G handled three times as much material that weekend as on a normal one; the GY log shows at least 28 messages in PURPLE alone handled that Sunday. And these messages were processed

One Day of Magic

much more expeditiously than at any other time in the past, Kramer said. The cryptanalysts had done their duty, and had done it superbly. Events now passed out of their hands.

In Tokyo, the President's message to the Emperor had finally been delivered to Grew after a delay of ten hours. The chief of the censorship office had ordered that all foreign cables be held up for five hours one day and ten hours the next. The order had been issued at the request of a lieutenant colonel on the general staff, who asked that this be done "as a precaution." The President's "triple priority" message arrived on one of the ten-hour days, was stalled for the required time, and was finally delivered at 10:30 p.m., Tokyo time.

Grew immediately arranged for a meeting with Togo and, when the message had been decoded, drove to Togo's official residence at 12:15 a.m. He requested—as is the right of all ambassadors—an audience with the head of state to present the message, then read it aloud to Togo and gave him a copy. Togo promised to present the matter to the Throne and, despite the lateness of the hour, telephoned the Lord Keeper of the Privy Seal for an audience. Ministers of state would be received at any hour, and the audience was arranged for 3 a.m. Togo began having the message translated.

It was then about 5:30 a.m., December 7, in Hawaii. The Japanese task force was only 250 miles north of Pearl Harbor. More than 2,000 Americans with less than three hours to live slept or played in blissful ignorance of that fact. The hands of clocks in the Foreign Office in Tokyo, in the code room at the Japanese embassy in Washington, in the War and Navy departments, in Pearl Harbor, circled around and around, but not so quickly as the spinning propellers of Nagumo's ships. At 5:30, two cruisers catapulted off a pair of scout planes to make sure the Americans were still there.

The clerks at the embassy had straggled back to work between 9:30 and 10. They began decoding the longer cables first, as experience had shown that these were usually the more important. At the same time, the embassy's first secretary, Katzuso Okumura, was typing up the first 13 parts of the ultimatum. He had been chosen because the Foreign Office had forbidden the use of an ordinary typist in the interests of secrecy and he was the only senior official who could operate a typewriter at all decently. At about 11:30, code clerk Juichi Yoshida adjusted the Alphabetical Typewriter to the proper keys and typed out a short code message. To the consternation of the entire staff, it turned out to be an instruction to deliver the 14-part message to Secretary Hull at 1 p.m., Washington time. The 14th part had not even been decoded from the sheaf of incoming cables! And only one code machine was left to decipher all the messages!

A few blocks away, General Marshall had just arrived at the War Department. On his desk was the MAGIC folder with the 14-part message on top and the one o'clock message under it. He began to read the ultimatum carefully, some parts several times. Bratton and Brigadier General Leonard T. Gerow, the war plans chief, tried to get him to look at the one o'clock message, but it is rather difficult for subordinates to interrupt a four-star general, and he finished the ultimatum before finding the time-of-delivery message. It struck him with the same sense of urgency that it had the others, and he picked up the telephone to call Stark to see if he wanted to join him in sending a warning message to American forces in the Pacific.

At approximately the same time, Ambassador Nomura was calling Hull to request an appointment at 1 p.m. And 230 miles north of Hawaii, the first wave of Japanese planes was thundering off the flight decks of the carriers.

Stark was at that moment discussing the significance of the one o'clock message with Captain R. E. Schuirman, Navy's liaison with State. He told Marshall that he felt that enough warnings had been sent and that more would just confuse the commanders. Marshall thereupon wrote out the dispatch he wanted sent:

> Japanese are presenting at one p.m. Eastern Standard Time today what amounts to an ultimatum also they are under orders to destroy their code machine immediately Stop Just what significance the hour set may have we do not know but be on alert accordingly Stop

On his desk Marshall had a scrambler telephone with which he could have called Short in Hawaii. The scrambling apparatus stood in a room next to his office, thus obviating the possibility of tapping the conversation in unscrambled form, as was done with the Mori message. But Marshall knew that scramblers afforded protection merely against casual listeners; they could be penetrated by a determined eavesdropper with proper equipment. He had on several occasions warned the President about security on his transatlantic telephone conversations with Ambassador Bullitt in France and later with Churchill—a wise move, for, though he did not know it, the Nazis had already penetrated that scrambler. The Japanese had evidenced some interest in the San Francisco–Honolulu scrambler, and Marshall was acutely sensitive "that the Japanese would have grasped at most any straw" to suggest to the isolationists that the administration had committed an overt act that had forced the Japanese hand. Japanese interception of a scrambler warning might thus have sent the country to war divided. So Marshall shunned the scrambler telephone and relied on the slightly slower but much more secure method of enciphering a written message.

As he was completing the message, Stark called him back. He had reconsidered and wanted Marshall to add the usual admonition to show the message to the naval opposites. Marshall added: "Inform naval authorities of this communication." Stark offered the Navy communication facilities, but Marshall said that the Army's could get the message out as quickly.

Marshall gave the message to Bratton to take it to the War Department

One Day of Magic

message center for transmission to the commanding generals in the Philippines, Hawaii, the Caribbean, and West Coast, after vetoing a suggestion that it be typed first. As Bratton was leaving, Gerow called out that if there was any question as to priority, to send it to the Philippines first. Bratton, greatly agitated, gave the message to Colonel Edward French in the message center and asked how long it would take to get it out. French told him that it would be encoded in three minutes, on the air in eight, and in the hands of the addressees in twenty. Bratton returned and reported to Marshall, who did not understand the explanation and sent him back for a clarification. He still was not sure and sent Bratton back a third time, after which he was finally satisfied with the answer.

Meanwhile, French had had the message typed anyway and then ordered it encoded on a machine that was operated from a typewriter keyboard. During the few minutes that this took, he checked his Honolulu circuit, and found that since early morning interference had been so bad that the small 10-kilowatt War Department radio could not "bust" through it. He knew that R.C.A. in San Francisco had a 40-kilowatt transmitter which would have no difficulty in getting through, and that Western Union in San Francisco had a tube running across the street from its office to this R.C.A. office. He had also learned on the previous day that R.C.A. was installing a teletype circuit from its office in Honolulu to Short's headquarters at Fort Shafter. French figured that this would therefore be his most expeditious route; after the message had been encoded, he personally carried it over to his bank of six Western Union teletypes and, at 12:01 p.m. December 7, sent it on its way. Western Union forwarded it at 12:17, and 46 minutes later it was received by R.C.A. in Honolulu. Local time was 7:33 a.m. The first wave of Japanese planes was then only 37 miles away—so close that the Army radar operators at Opana Point, who had tracked the flight for several hours and had been told to "Forget it" when they first reported it, were about to lose it in the dead zone of the nearby hills. But though the teletype connection for Fort Shafter had been completed the day before, it was not in operation pending tests on Monday. R.C.A. put Marshall's message in an envelope marked "Commanding General" for hand delivery.

In Tokyo, Togo had been received by the Emperor. He read the text of Roosevelt's message, then a draft of the imperial reply that he and Tojo had prepared. It stated that the 14-part note was to be considered as Japan's response. Hirohito assented, and at 3:15 a.m. Togo withdrew from the Divine Presence. Deeply moved, he recalled, "I passed solemnly, guided by a Court official, down several hundred yards of corridors, stretching serene and tranquil. Emerging at the carriage entrance of the Sakashita Gate, I gazed up at the brightly shining stars, and felt bathed in a sacred spirit. Through the Palace plaza in utter silence, hearing no sound of the sleeping capital but only the crunching of the gravel beneath the wheels of my car, I pondered that in a few short hours would dawn one of the eventful days of the history of the world." Even as he pondered, Japanese planes were circling over Pearl Harbor.

In stark contrast to the calm stillness of Tokyo was the hectic bustle of the Japanese embassy on Massachusetts Avenue.

Soon after the one o'clock message had been decoded, Okumura finished typing the first 13 parts. But he decided that this rough draft did not suit the formality of a document to be delivered to the Secretary of State. He began retyping it from the very beginning, being assisted now by a junior interpreter, Enseki. His task was complicated by two messages sent up from the code room, one ordering the insertion of a sentence that had been accidentally dropped, one changing a word. This required the retyping of several pages, including one just completed with a great deal of trouble. At about 12:30, the code room finally gave him the 14th part of the ultimatum, but Okumura was nowhere near finished with the first 13. Nomura kept poking his head in the door to hurry him on. A few minutes after one, when it was evident that the document would not be finished for some time, the Japanese called Hull to request a postponement to 1:45, saying that the document they wished to present was not yet ready. Hull acquiesced.

At almost exactly the time that the call to Hull was being placed, Commander Fuchida and his flight of 51 dive bombers, 49 high-level bombers, 40 torpedo planes, and 43 fighters arrived over Pearl Harbor. He fired a "black dragon" from his signal pistol to indicate that the squadrons should deploy in the assault pattern for complete surprise. Nine minutes later, he wirelessed the message "To, to, to"—the first syllable of the Japanese word for "Charge!" and the signal to attack. As the planes moved into position for their runs, he felt so certain that he had achieved complete surprise that, at 7:53, two minutes before the first bomb even fell, he jubilantly radioed "TORA! TORA! TORA!" ("Tiger! Tiger! Tiger!")—the prearranged codeword that indicated surprise. On *Akagi*, Nagumo turned to a brother officer and grasped his hand in a long, silent handshake. At 7:55, the first bomb exploded at the foot of the seaplane ramp at the southern end of Ford Island in the middle of Pearl Harbor.

Okumura was still typing. His fingers struggled with the keys as torpedoes capsized *Oklahoma*, as bombs sank *West Virginia*, as 1,000 men died in the searing inferno of *Arizona*. At 1:50 p.m. Washington time, 25 minutes after the attack had started, he reached the end of his typing marathon. The two ambassadors, who were waiting in the vestibule, started for the State Department as soon as it was handed to them.

> The Japanese envoys arrived at the Department at 2:05 and went to the diplomatic waiting room [Hull wrote]. At almost that moment the President telephoned me from the White House. His voice was steady but clipped.
> He said, "There's a report that the Japanese have attacked Pearl Harbor."
> "Has the report been confirmed?" I asked.

One Day of Magic

He said, "No."

While each of us indicated his belief that the report was probably true, I suggested that he have it confirmed, having in mind my appointment with the Japanese Ambassadors....

Nomura and Kurusu came into my office at 2:20. I received them coldly and did not ask them to sit down.

Nomura diffidently said he had been instructed by his Government to deliver a document to me at one o'clock, but that difficulty in decoding the message had delayed him. He then handed me his Government's note.

I asked him why he had specified one o'clock in his first request for an interview.

He replied that he did not know, but that was his instruction.

I made a pretense of glancing through the note. I knew its contents already but naturally could give no indication of this fact.

After reading two or three pages, I asked Nomura whether he had presented the document under instructions from his Government.

He replied that he had.

When I finished skimming the pages, I turned to Nomura and put my eye on him.

"I must say," I said, "that in all my conversations with you during the last nine months I have never uttered one word of untruth. This is borne out absolutely by the record. In all my fifty years of public service I have never seen a document that was more crowded with infamous falsehoods and distortions—infamous falsehoods and distortions on a scale so huge that I never imagined until today that any Government on this planet was capable of uttering them."

Nomura seemed about to say something. His face was impassive, but I felt he was under great emotional strain. I stopped him with a motion of my hand. I nodded toward the door. The Ambassadors turned without a word and walked out, their heads down.

The warlords' hopes of shaving the warning time to the closest possible margin had quite literally gone up in the smoke of attack, and Japan had started hostilities without giving prior notification. Later, this failure to declare war would be made part of the charges on which the Japanese war criminals were tried—and convicted, some of them paying with their lives. Togo would try to exonerate himself by throwing the blame on the embassy personnel for neglecting to decipher the cables promptly and to type the ultimatum at once. Perhaps some lawyer's talking point might have been salvaged if the ambassadors had grabbed Okumura's original copy, no matter how messy, and taken it to Hull at 1 p.m., or if they had taken the first few pages of the fair copy at 1 p.m. and directed the embassy staff to rush the other pages over as completed. But even if the entire document had been delivered on time, the 25 minutes that remained until the attack would not have been sufficient time for all the steps needed to prevent surprise: reading the document, guessing that a military attack was intended, notifying the War and Navy departments, composing, enciphering, transmitting, and deciphering an appropriate warning, and alerting the outpost forces. This was just what the shoguns intended. But just as a multitude of human errors on the part of Americans, cascading one atop the other, helped make tactical surprise perfect, so a series of similar human errors on the part of the Japanese deprived them of their last vestige of legality.

Shortly after the attack commenced, Tadao Fuchikama, a messenger for

```
From:   Tokyo
To:     Washington
7 December 1941
(Purple-Eng)

#902            Part 14 of 14

                (Note: In the forwarding instructions to the
                radio station handling this part, appeared the
                plain English phrase "VERY IMPORTANT")


                7. Obviously it is the intention of the American
Government to conspire with Great Britain and other countries
to obstruct Japan's efforts toward the establishment of
peace through the creation of a New Order in East Asia,
and especially to preserve Anglo-American rights and interests
by keeping Japan and China at war. This intention has
been revealed clearly during the course of the present
negotiations. Thus, the earnest hope of the Japanese
Government to adjust Japanese-American relations and to
preserve and promote the peace of the Pacific through
cooperation with the American Government has finally been
lost.

                The Japanese Government regrets to have to notify
hereby the American Government that in view of the attitude
of the American Government it cannot but consider that it is
impossible to reach an agreement through further negotiations.


JD-1:7143       SECRET      (M) Navy trans. 7 Dec. 1941 (S-TT)
25843
```

The fourteenth part of the Japanese ultimatum, as distributed to MAGIC *recipients*

the Honolulu office of R.C.A., picked up a batch of cables for delivery. He knew that the war had started and that it was the Japanese who were attacking the ships in the harbor, but he felt he had his job to do anyway. He glanced at the addresses on the envelopes, including the one marked "Commanding General," and planned an efficient route. Shafter was well down the list. His motorcycle progressed slowly through the jammed traffic; once he was stopped by National Guardsmen who had almost taken him for a para-

One Day of Magic

trooper. At 11:45, almost two hours after the last attackers had vanished, Marshall's warning message was delivered to the signal officer. It got to the decoding officer at 2:40 that afternoon and to Short himself at 3. He took one look at it and threw it into the wastebasket, saying that it wasn't of the slightest interest.

In Tokyo, Grew was awakened at 7 a.m. by the telephone, summoning him to a meeting at 7:30 with Togo. On Grew's arrival, the Foreign Minister gave him the Emperor's reply to the President. He thanked Grew for his cooperation and saw him off at the door. Four hours had elapsed since the attack had

-11-

and China at war. This intention has been revealed clearly during the course of the present negotiation. Thus, the earnest hope of the Japanese Government to adjust Japanese-American relations and to preserve and promote the peace of the Pacific through cooperation with the American Government has finally been lost.

The Japanese Government regrets to have to notify hereby the American Government that in view of the attitude of the American Government it cannot but consider that it is impossible to reach an agreement through further negotiations.

December 7, 1941.

The last page of the Japanese note as typed by First Secretary Katzuso Okumura and handed to Secretary of State Cordell Hull while Pearl Harbor was being attacked

begun, but Togo never mentioned it. Shortly thereafter, Grew learned of the outbreak of hostilities from an extra of the *Yomiuri Shimbun* hawked outside his window. The Japanese soon closed the embassy gates and prohibited cipher telegrams. Grew ordered execution of the State Department regulation to destroy all codes. The embassy's second and third secretaries, Charles E. Bohlen and James Espy, locked the code room from the inside and destroyed the several score documents. "No Japanese interrupted that process," Grew wrote, "nor could he have, since the heavy door of the code room was securely locked. None of our codes, nor any part of them, nor any of our confidential correspondence fell into the hands of the Japanese."

The Japanese themselves were not so smart. They did all right in Washington, breaking up their last code machine and burning all remaining codes after encoding a final message that they were so doing—the last message sent on the Washington–Tokyo circuit, and read, of course, by the American codebreakers. But in Honolulu, police guarding the consulate after the attack smelled papers burning and saw smoke coming from behind a door. Fearing a conflagration, they broke in and found the consulate staff burning its remaining documents in a washtub on the floor. The police confiscated what proved to be the telegraph file plus five burlap sacks full of torn papers. These reached Rochefort's unit that evening. Woodward was still working long hours in an attempt to break the PA-K2 messages that Mayfield had brought. Since the attack, the fear of sabotage had swelled to enormous proportions. "Nothing coming to light," his notes read, "so it was decided to reverse the process of deciphering, allowing for the encoding party to have either purposely encrypted the messages in this manner or possibly to have made an error in using the system employed due to confusion. This netted results."

At about 2 a.m. on December 9, he cracked one of the messages picked up in the consulate. It was one sent from the Foreign Ministry to Kita on the 6th: "Please wire immediately re the latter part of my #123 any movements of the fleet after the 4th." With this, he was soon able to unlock the other PA-K2 messages—including the long one setting up Kühn's light-signaling system. At about the same time in OP-20-GZ, Kramer, who had been too busy with the 13 parts on Saturday to work on this message, was breaking out charts of Oahu and Maui to help in degarbling the message, which was finally reduced to plaintext by Thursday. Marshall later said that it was the first message that clearly indicated an attack on Pearl to him—but this was, of course, after the fact. The information from it was immediately passed to counterintelligence units in Hawaii, where invasion was thought highly probable. Their agents interrogated residents in the neighborhood of the houses mentioned in the dispatch and listened to recordings of KGMB want ads, but found that the signal system had never been used. They arrested Kühn, who confirmed this. He was convicted on espionage charges and imprisoned at Leavenworth Penitentiary until after the war, when he was paroled to leave the country.

On December 7, while Honolulu was still reeling from the devastation of the attack, F.C.C. monitors there picked up a Japanese-language news broadcast from station JZI in Japan. The announcer boasted of a "death-defying raid" at Pearl, reported other events, and, about halfway through the broadcast, declared: "Allow me to especially make a weather forecast at this time: west wind clear." The O.N.I. translator noted that "as far as I can recollect, no such weather forecast has ever been made before" and that "it may be some sort of code." It was the long-awaited winds code execute, apparently sent indicating war with Britain to make sure that some Japanese

One Day of Magic

outpost that had not reported destroying its codes by the codeword HARUNA would burn them.

Shortly after noon in Washington on the day after the attack, the President of the United States stood before a stormily applauding joint session of Congress and opened a black looseleaf notebook. When the cheers had subsided into a hushed solemnity, he began to speak:

> Yesterday, December 7, 1941—a date which will live in infamy—the United States of America was suddenly and deliberately attacked by naval and air forces of the Empire of Japan.

He alluded to the fatal Japanese delay in delivering the ultimatum:

> The United States was at peace with that nation and, at the solicitation of Japan, was still in conversation with its Government and its Emperor looking toward the maintenance of peace in the Pacific. Indeed, one hour after Japanese air squadrons had commenced bombing in Oahu, the Japanese Ambassador to the United States and his colleague delivered to the Secretary of State a formal reply to a recent American message. While this reply stated that it seemed useless to continue the existing diplomatic negotiations, it contained no threat or hint of war or armed attack.

The war was on. The most treacherous onslaught in history had succeeded. Japan had cloaked the strike force in absolute secrecy. She had dissembled with diplomatic conversations and with jabs toward the south. She had—in a precaution whose wisdom she but dimly realized—swathed her plans in a communications security so all-enveloping that not a whisper of them ever floated onto the airwaves.

But if the cryptanalysts had no chance to warn of the attack and save American lives before the war, they found ample opportunities to exert their subtle and pervasive talents during the struggle. In the 1,350 days of conflict in which an angry America turned Japan's tactical victory at Pearl Harbor into total strategic defeat, the cryptanalysts, in the words of the Joint Congressional Committee, "contributed enormously to the defeat of the enemy, greatly shortened the war, and saved many thousands of lives."

That, however, is another story.

The Pageant of Cryptology

2

THE FIRST 3,000 YEARS

ON A DAY nearly 4,000 years ago, in a town called Menet Khufu bordering the thin ribbon of the Nile, a master scribe sketched out the hieroglyphs that told the story of his lord's life—and in so doing he opened the recorded history of cryptology.

His was not a system of secret writing as the modern world knows it; he used no fully developed code of hieroglyphic symbol substitutions. His inscription, carved about 1900 B.C. into the living rock in the main chamber of the tomb of the nobleman Khnumhotep II, merely uses some unusual hieroglyphic symbols here and there in place of the more ordinary ones. Most occur in the last 20 columns of the inscription's 222, in a section recording the monuments that Khnumhotep had erected in the service of the pharaoh Amenemhet II. The intention was not to make it hard to read the text. It was to impart a dignity and authority to it, perhaps in the same way that a government proclamation will spell out "In the year of Our Lord One thousand eight hundred and sixty three" instead of just writing "1863." The anonymous scribe may also have been demonstrating his knowledge for posterity. Thus the inscription was not secret writing, but it incorporated one of the essential elements of cryptography: a deliberate transformation of the writing. It is the oldest text known to do so.

As Egyptian civilization waxed, as the writing developed and the tombs of the venerated dead multiplied, these transformations grew more complicated, more contrived, and more common. Eventually the scribes were replacing the usual hieroglyphic form of a letter, like the full-face mouth representing /r/, by a different form, like a profiled mouth. Sometimes they used new hieroglyphs whose first sound represented the letter desired, as a picture of a pig, "rer," would mean /r/. Sometimes the sounds of the two hieroglyphs differed but their images resembled one another. The horned asp, representing /f/, was replaced by the serpent, representing /z/. And sometimes the scribes used a hieroglyph on the rebus principle, as in English a picture of a bee might represent b; thus a sailboat, "khentey," stands for another Egyptian word *khentey*, which means "who presides at"—this latter being part of a title of the god Amon, "he who presides at Karnak." These procedures of acrophony and the rebus are essentially those of ordinary Egyptian writing; it was through them that the hieroglyphics originally acquired their sound values. The Egyptian transformations merely carry them further, elaborate them, and make them more artificial.

The transformations occur in funerary formulas, in a hymn to Thoth, in a chapter of the Book of the Dead, on the sarcophagus of the pharaoh Seti I, in royal titles displayed in Luxor, on the architrave of the Temple of Luxor, on stele, in laudatory biographic inscriptions. There is nothing meant to be concealed in all this; indeed, many of the statements are repeated in ordinary form right next to the altered ones. Why, then, the transformations? Sometimes for essentially the same reason as in Khnumhotep's tomb: to impress the reader. Occasionally for a calligraphic or decorative effect; rarely, to indicate a contemporary pronunciation; perhaps even for a deliberate archaism as a reaction against foreign influence.

But many inscriptions are tinctured, for the first time, with the second essential for cryptology—secrecy. In a few cases, the secrecy was intended to increase the mystery and hence the arcane magical powers of certain religious texts. But the secrecy in many more cases resulted from the understandable desire of the Egyptians to have passersby read their epitaphs and so confer upon the departed the blessings written therein. In Egypt, with its concentration upon the afterlife, the number of these inscriptions soon proliferated to such an extent that the attention and the goodwill of visitors flagged. To revive their interest, the scribes deliberately made the inscriptions a bit obscure. They introduced the cryptographic signs to catch the reader's eye, make him wonder, and tempt him into unriddling them—and so into reading the blessings. It was a sort of Madison Avenue technique in the Valley of the Kings. But the technique failed utterly. Instead of interesting the readers, it evidently destroyed even the slightest desire to read the epitaphs, for soon after the funerary cryptography was begun, it was abandoned.

The addition of secrecy to the transformations produced cryptography. True, it was more of a game than anything else—it sought to delay comprehension for only the shortest possible time, not the longest—and the cryptanalysis was, likewise, just a puzzle. Egypt's was thus a quasi cryptology in contrast to the deadly serious science of today. Yet great things have small beginnings, and these hieroglyphs did include, though in an imperfect fashion, the two elements of secrecy and transformation that comprise the essential attributes of the science. And so cryptology was born.

In its first 3,000 years, it did not grow steadily. Cryptology arose independently in many places, and in most of them it died the deaths of its civilizations. In other places, it survived, embedded in a literature, and from this the next generation could climb to higher levels. But progress was slow and jerky. More was lost than retained. Much of the history of cryptology of this time is a patchwork, a crazy quilt of unrelated items, sprouting, flourishing, withering. Only toward the Western Renaissance does the accreting know-

The First 3,000 Years

ledge begin to build up a momentum. The story of cryptology during these years is, in other words, exactly the story of mankind.

China, the only high civilization of antiquity to use ideographic writing, seems never to have developed much real cryptography—perhaps for that reason. Diplomats and military authorities relied mainly on oral statements, memorized and delivered by messenger. For written messages, the Chinese would often write on exceedingly thin silk or paper, which they rolled into a ball and covered with wax. The messenger hid the wax ball, or "la wan," somewhere about his person, or in his rectum, or he sometimes swallowed it. This, of course, was a form of steganography.

Actual cryptography often involved open codes. If a man's name included the ideogram for "chrysanthemum," the correspondents would refer to him as "the yellow flower." But for military purposes, the 11th-century compilation, *Wu-ching tsung-yao* ("Essentials from Military Classics"), recommended a

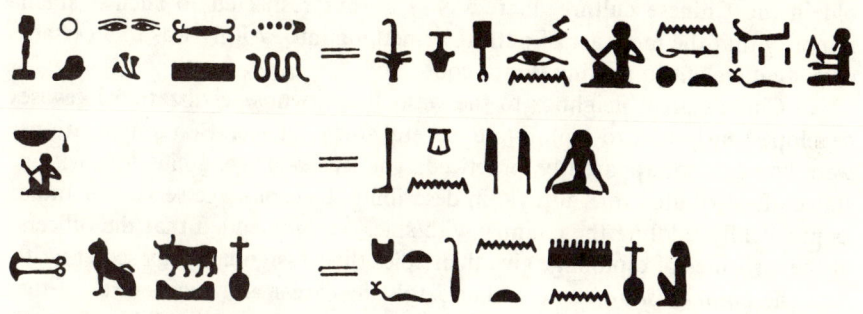

Hieroglyphic encipherments of proper names and titles, with cipher hieroglyphs at left, plain equivalents at right

true if small code. To a list of 40 plaintext items, ranging from requests for bows and arrows to the report of a victory, the correspondents would assign the first 40 ideograms of a poem. Then, when a lieutenant wished, for example, to request more arrows, he was to write the corresponding ideogram at a specified place on an ordinary dispatch and stamp his seal on it. The general could put down the same character with his own seal to indicate approval, or his seal without the character to indicate disapproval. Even if the message were intercepted, the code portion would remain secret.

It is questionable, however, whether such methods were much used. The greatest conqueror of them all, Genghis Khan, seems never to have made use of cryptography. Nor do ciphers seem possible. The ideographic nature of the language precludes them. The cipher-like technique of altering the form of the ideograms by shifting lines or elements from one place to another in the pattern would be, one authority has said, neither practical nor effective. In fact, one of the apparently few cryptologic episodes in the history of China involves a Western alphabet.

In 1722, Yin-t'ang, ninth son of the late Emperor Shêng-tsu, lost out to his elder brother, Yin-chên, in a struggle for the throne. He was banished to Sining. With him went his supporter, a Portuguese missionary named João Mourão, who had taught him the Latin alphabet. Yin-t'ang used it for a code with his son. Early in 1726, a letter from the son in this alphabet was intercepted by agents of Emperor Yin-chên. Ever alert for such an opportunity, the emperor used it as evidence to condemn his brother's activities as treasonable, expel him from the Imperial Clan, and remove him from Sining to Paoting, Chihli. Here Yin-t'ang was confined in a small house surrounded by high walls; he received his food by pulleys. Within a few months he was dead of dysentery. The emperor announced that his brother had been called to justice by the netherworld. Mourão himself died in confinement at about the same time.

Why did China, so far ahead of other civilizations in so many things, not develop cryptography? An astute comment by Professor Owen Lattimore of the University of Leeds may give the reason. "Although writing is extremely old in the Chinese culture, literacy was always restricted to such a small minority that the mere act of putting something into writing was to a certain extent equivalent to putting it into code."

In China's great neighbor to the west, India, whose civilization likewise developed early and to high estate, several forms of secret communications were known and, apparently, practiced. The *Artha-śāstra*, a classic work on statecraft attributed to Kauṭilya, in describing the espionage service of India as practically riddling the country with spies, recommended that the officers of the institutes of espionage give their spies their assignments by secret writing. The *Lalita-Vistara*, a work that extols the career and excellencies of the Buddha, tells how Buddha astounded the tutor who was to teach him writing by enumerating 64 different kinds. Some of these, such as the perpendicular writing, or the disordered writing, or the scattered writing, or the cross writing, are sometimes regarded as cryptographic, though many are fanciful and probably never existed.

Perhaps most interesting to cryptologists, amateur or professional, is that Vātsyāyana's famous textbook of erotics, the *Kāma-sūtra*, lists secret writing as one of the 64 arts, or yogas, that women should know and practice. It is 45th in a list that begins with vocal music and runs through prestidigitation, solution of verbal puzzles, and exercises in enigmatic poetry. The yoga is called "mlecchita-vikalpā." In his commentary on the *Kāma-sūtra*, Yaśodhara describes two kinds of mlecchita-vikalpā. One is called "kauṭiliyam," in which the letter substitutions are based upon phonetic relations—the vowels become consonants, for example. A simplification of this form is called "durbodha." Another kind of secret writing is "mūladevīya." Its cipher alphabet consists merely of the reciprocal one

a	kh	gh	c	t	ñ	n	r	l	y
k	g	ṅ	ṭ	p	ṇ	m	ṣ	s	ś

with all other letters remaining unchanged. Mūladevīya existed in both a spoken form—as such it figures in Indian literature and is used by traders, with geographical variations—and a written form, in which case it is called "gūḍhalekhya."

Beyond these unquestioned types of cryptography, ancient India made use of allusive language, a sort of impromptu open code called "sābhāṣa," and a finger communication, "nirābhāṣa," in which the phalanges stand for the consonants and the joints for the vowels. Deaf and dumb people still use it, as do traders and moneylenders.

Whether India owes this profusion of mentions of cryptography to actual use or to her great interest in grammar and language in general—the world's first grammarian, Pāṇini, was an Indian—remains in question. That cryptology is not mentioned in the classic drama of political intrigue, the *Mudrā-Rākṣasa*, suggests that it was not widely used. On the other hand, the *Artha-śāstra*, which was written sometime between 321 and 300 B.C., recommended that ambassadors use cryptanalysis to obtain intelligence: "If there is no possibility of carrying on any such conversation (conversation with the people regarding their loyalty), he [the envoy] may try to gather such information by observing the talk of beggars, intoxicated and insane persons, or of persons babbling in sleep, or by observing the signs made in places of pilgrimage and temples, or by deciphering paintings or secret writings." (One begins to wonder whether Kauṭilya, by putting cryptanalysis in the company of such sources, meant to praise or damn it.) Nevertheless, though he gives no suggestions on how to solve either paintings or secret writings, the fact that he knows that solution is possible bespeaks some cryptologic sophistication. His is, moreover, the first reference in history to cryptanalysis for political purposes.

The fourth great civilization of antiquity, the Mesopotamian, rather paralleled Egypt early in its cryptographic evolution, but then surpassed it, attaining a surprisingly modern level of cryptography. Its oldest encipherment appears in a tiny cuneiform tablet only about 3 by 2 inches, dating from about 1500 B.C. and found on the site of ancient Seleucia on the banks of the Tigris. It contains the earliest known formula for the making of glazes for pottery. The scribe, jealously guarding his professional secret, used cuneiform signs—which could have several different syllabic values—in their least common values. His method resembles George Bernard Shaw's way of using the /f/ sound of GH in "tough," the /i/ sound of O in "women," and the /sh/ sound of TI in "nation" to write *fish* as GHOTI. The scribe also truncated sounds by ignoring the final consonant of several syllabic signs, and spelled the same word with different signs at different places. Interestingly, as knowledge of glaze-making spread, the need for secrecy evaporated, and later texts were written in straightforward language.

The Babylonian and Assyrian scribes sometimes used rare or unusual cuneiform signs in signing and dating their clay tablets. These ending formulas, called "colophons," were short and stereotyped, and the substitution of the unusual signs for the usual were not intended to conceal but simply to show off the scribe's knowledge of cuneiform to later copyists. Nothing precisely like this exists in the modern world, because literacy is so widespread and spelling so standardized. But comparable might be a businessman's writing "We beg to acknowledge receipt of your communication of the 25th ult." instead of "Thank you for your letter of May 25," or a schoolboy's using long words where short would do—both seeking to impress their readers with their learning.

In the final period of cuneiform writing, in colophons written at Uruk (in present-day Iraq) under the Seleucid kings in the last few score years before the Christian era, occasional scribes converted their names into numbers. The encipherment—if such it be—may have been only for amusement or to show off. Because colophons are so stereotyped, and because several of the enciphered ones have only one or two number signs among many plaintext, Assyriologists have been able to "cryptanalyze" them. For example, a tablet giving lunar eclipses for from 130 to 113 B.C. includes in its colophon "palih 21 50 10 40 1a...." Comparing this with the identical formula in plaintext in another tablet, Otto Neugebauer determined that 21 = *Anu*, 50 = *u*, 10 40 = *An-tu*. The formula reads: "He who worships Anu and Antu shall not remove it [the tablet]." With the help of these equivalencies, Erle Leichty attacked the signature at the foot of a large tablet reciting a myth of the goddess Ishtar that might be an indirect source of the biblical story of Esther, whose name might be another version of "Ishtar." The signature reads "tuppi ¹21 35 35 26 44 apil ¹21 11 20 42," or "tablet of Mr. 21 35 35 26 44, son of Mr. 21 11 20 42." Leichty suggested that the solution was "tablet of Mr. Anu-aba-uttirri, son of Mr. Anu-bel-su-nu," whose father-son relationship is well known.

Other tablets employ the same numbers with the same values. No simple relationship between the equivalencies appears. "A check of the various lexical series shows that the numbers are not based on a counting of signs either forward from the beginning of the series, nor backward from the end," wrote Leichty. "It is of course possible that a tablet of equations between numbers and signs existed." He suggested that two little tablet-fragments from Susa (in present-day Iran) might comprise such a codebook, but added that they were too short to be certain. The broken pieces of clay list cuneiform numbers in order in a vertical column; opposite them stand cuneiform signs. Unfortunately, none of the numbers used in the cryptograms occur on these fragments (except for 35, whose cuneiform sign is blurred to illegibility), and so it is not possible to determine whether these tablets served as the codebook for the colophon cryptography. But if they are indeed codebooks, they are the oldest in the world.

The Holy Scriptures themselves have not escaped a touch of cryptography —or protocryptography, to be precise, for the element of secrecy is lacking.

The First 3,000 Years

As with the hieroglyphics in the tomb of Khnumhotep or the colophons of the Mesopotamian scribes, the transformations are present without any apparent desire to conceal. Probably the main motives in the biblical transformations, as with the others, were the human ones of pride and a longing for immortality, attained here by making a textual alteration which, as later scribes faithfully copied it, would transmit a bit of one's self down through the centuries. If this was in fact the idea, it most certainly succeeded.

Hebrew tradition lists three different transformations in the Old Testament (none are recorded for the New). In Jeremiah 25:26 and 51:41, the form

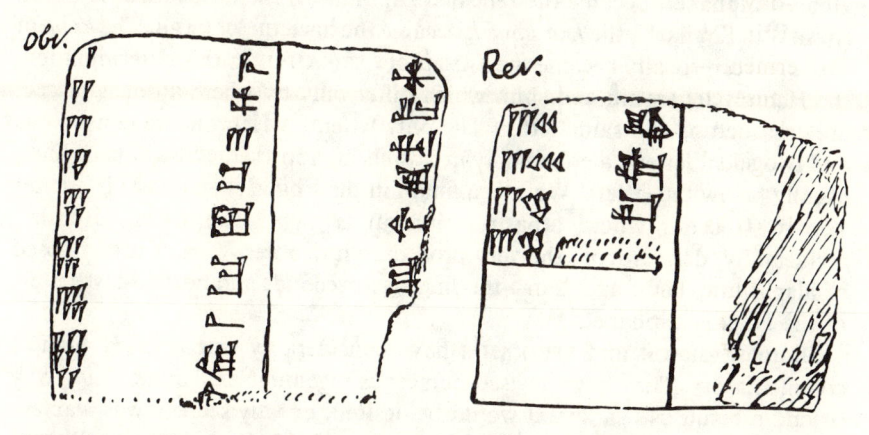

A cuneiform tablet from Susa lists the numbers from 1 to 8 and from 32 to 35 opposite parallel columns of cuneiform signs in what might be the oldest codebook in the world

SHESHACH appears in place of *Babel* ("Babylon"). The second occurrence strikingly demonstrates the lack of a secrecy motive, since the phrase with SHESHACH is immediately followed by one using "Babylon":

> How is Sheshach taken!
> And the praise of the whole earth seized!
> How is Babylon become an astonishment
> Among the nations!

Confirmation that SHESHACH is really a substitute for *Babel* and not a wholly separate place comes from the Septuagint and the Targums, the Aramaic paraphrases of the Bible, which simply use "Babel" where the Old Testament version has SHESHACH. The second transformation, at Jeremiah 51:1, puts LEB KAMAI ("heart of my enemy") for *Kashdim* ("Chaldeans").

Both transformations resulted from the application of a traditional substitution of letters called "atbash," in which the last letter of the Hebrew alphabet replaces the first, and vice versa; the next-to-last replaces the second, and vice versa; and so on. It is the Hebrew equivalent of $a = $ z, $b = $ Y, $c = $ X, ..., $z = $ A.

aleph	beth	gimel	daleth	he	waw	zayin	heth	teth	yod	kaph
א	ב	ג	ד	ה	ו	ז	ח	ט	י	כ

ת	ש	ר	ק	צ	פ	ע	ס	נ	מ	ל
taw	sin shin	resh	qoph	sadhe	pe	ayin	samekh	nun	mem	lamed

Consequently, in *Babel*, the repeated *b*, or *beth*, the second letter of the Hebrew alphabet, became the repeated SH, or SHIN, the next-to-last letter, in SHESHACH. Similarly, the *l*, or *lamed*, became the hard CH, or KAPH. The *kaph* of *Kashdim* reciprocally became the LAMED of LEB KAMAI. In this determination, the Hebrew letters sin and shin, which differ only by where a dot is placed, are regarded as the same letter. The only letters in Hebrew are consonants and two silent letters, aleph and ayin; vowels are represented by dots or lines, usually below the letters. What is a final *i* in the English LEB KAMAI is a letter YOD in Hebrew, whose atbash reciprocal is *mem*. The word "atbash," incidentally, derives from the very procedure it denotes, since it is composed of aleph, taw, beth, and shin—the first, last, second, and next-to-last letters of the Hebrew alphabet.

Both SHESHACH and LEB KAMAI have considerably embarrassed biblical commentators. They have devised numerous ingenious explanations for why so odd a result as LEB KAMAI would be desired, or why secrecy was wanted. Some have even thought Sheshach the name of a Babylonian district. But the idea of simple scribal manipulation, which would mean that such desires never even existed, and which is advanced by modern authorities and bolstered by the similar examples from other cultures and by the predilection of scribes for amusing themselves with word and alphabet games, seems the best explanation.

The two transformations by atbash are straightforward and universally recognized. The third transformation in the Old Testament, which resulted from a different substitution system, is disputed. The system is called "albam." It splits the Hebrew alphabet in half and equates the two halves. Thus, the first letter of the first half, aleph, substitutes for the first letter of the second half, lamed, and vice versa; the second of the first half, beth, for the second of the second half, mem, and vice versa; and so on. The term "albam" derives from the first four letters of this arrangement. According to the *Midrash Rabbah* (Numbers 18:21), the name TABEEL in Isaiah 7:6 is an albam transformation for *Remala*, or "Remaliah," who figures in verses 1 and 4. But while the albam works for the first two letters (the third, lamed, retains its identity because it would otherwise be transformed into a silent aleph), the "solution" does not clarify the text. The *Midrash Rabbah* does not give any reasons for thinking it albam. Most authorities seem to regard "Tabeel" as a corruption or some form of contemptuous epithet, and not as albam. In this connection it might be noted that many authorities also think that the meaningless names Shadrach, Meshach, and Abed-nego represent distortions, deliberate or accidental, of the names of real kings or countries. Shadrach, for example, may stand for Marduk—Hebrew samekh and mem look alike, and the transposition of consonants is not an uncommon linguistic phenomenon.

Hebrew literature records a third traditional form of letter substitution. It is called "atbah," and, like atbash and albam, its name stems from its system. This is based on Hebrew numbers, which, like Roman numbers, were written with the letters of the Hebrew alphabet. Within the first nine letters of the alphabet, the substitutes were chosen so that their numerical value would add up to 10. Thus, aleph, the first letter, would be replaced by teth, the ninth, and vice versa; beth, the second, by heth, the eighth, and vice versa. The remaining letters were paired on a similar system that would total to the Hebrew digital version of 100. In decimal notation, this means that the two letters will add up to 28. Thus mem, the 13th letter, and samekh, the 15th, replace one another. What happens to the 19th letter and those beyond is not clear. The 5th letter, he, and the 14th, nun, which under the system would represent themselves, are made to replace each other. This rather confusing system of atbah is not used in the Bible, though there is at least one use in the Babylonian Talmud (*Seder Mo'ed*, Sukkah, 52b). This example plays on the word "witness" and its atbah substitution "master" to make a moral point.

These three substitutes are used here and there throughout Hebrew writing, particularly atbash, which is the most common. Their importance consists, however, in that the use of atbash in the Bible sensitized the monks and scribes of the Middle Ages to the idea of letter substitution. And from them flowed the modern use of ciphers—as distinct from codes—as a means of secret communication.

While SHESHACH and LEB KAMAI are an imperfect cryptography because, although they are transformations, they lack the element of secrecy, another "cryptogram" in the Bible—perhaps the most famous in the world—is imperfect for the opposite reason. It was shrouded in secrecy, but it apparently involved no transformation!

This is the message of the handwriting on the wall. It appeared ominously at Belshazzar's feast: MENE MENE TEKEL UPHARSIN. The real mystery is not what the words meant but why the king's wise men could not read it. The Bible says nothing about secret or unusual writing, and the words themselves are ordinary roots in Aramaic (the language, related to Hebrew, in which the book of Daniel is written) meaning "numbered," "weighed," and "divided." When Belshazzar summoned Daniel, the latter had no difficulty in reading the handwriting and interpreting the three words: "MENE, God hath numbered thy kingdom, and brought it to an end. TEKEL, thou art weighed in the balances, and art found wanting. PERES, thy kingdom is divided [perisa] and given to the Medes and Persians [paras]," with the extra play on PERES, which, in Aramaic, would be identical with UPHARSIN. The message may also reflect a series of pieces of money whose names stem from the Aramaic roots: a mina, a tekel (the Aramaic equivalent for shekel, which is $\frac{1}{60}$th of a mina), and a peres, which is a half-mina. Though the order is illogical, the series might symbolize the breaking up of the Babylonian empire and its wealth. Dr. Cyrus Gordon has devised an ingenious American equivalent that makes this clear: "You will be quartered, halved, and cent to perdition."

With all these interpretations possible, it seems strange that the Babylonian priests could not read what was essentially a plain-language message. Perhaps they feared to give the bad news to Belshazzar, or perhaps God blinded them and opened the eyes of Daniel. Whatever the reason, Daniel alone penetrated the enigma and became, in consequence, the first known cryptanalyst. And just as there were giants in the earth in those days, so the biblical reward for cryptanalysis far exceeded any that has been given ever since: "They clothed Daniel with purple, and put a chain of gold around his neck, and made proclamation concerning him that he should rule as one of three in the kingdom."

"Queen Anteia, Proetus's wife, had fallen in love with the handsome youth," the "incomparable Bellerophon ... who was endowed with every manly grace, and begged him to satisfy her passion in secret." So Homer begins the story in the *Iliad* that includes the world's first conscious reference to—as distinct from use of—secret writing.

"But Bellerophon was a man of sound principles and refused. So Anteia went to King Proetus with a lying tale. 'Proetus,' she said, 'Bellerophon has tried to ravish me. Kill him—or die yourself.' The king was enraged when he heard this infamous tale. He stopped short of putting Bellerophon to death—it was a thing he dared not do—but he packed him off to Lycia with sinister credentials from himself. He gave him a folded tablet on which he had traced a number of devices with a deadly meaning, and told him to hand this to his father-in-law, the Lycian king, and thus ensure his own death."

The Lycian king feasted Bellerophon for nine days. "But the tenth day came, and then, in the first rosy light of Dawn, he examined him and asked to see what credentials he had brought him from his son-in-law Proetus. When he had deciphered the fatal message from his son-in-law, the king's first step was to order Bellerophon to kill the Chimera," a fire-breathing monster with a lion's head, a goat's body, and a serpent's tail. Bellerophon did. The Lycian king then tried one ruse after another to carry out the surreptitious instructions, but Bellerophon successively battled the Solymi, defeated the Amazons, and slew the best warriors of Lycia, who had ambushed him. In the end the Lycian king relented, realizing that the youth stood under the divine protection of the gods, and gave him his daughter and half his kingdom.

This is the only mention of writing in the *Iliad*. Homer's language is not precise enough to tell exactly what the markings on the tablets were. They were probably nothing more than ordinary letters—actual substitution of symbols for letters seems too sophisticated for the era of the Trojan War. But the mystery that Homer throws around the tablets does suggest that some rudimentary form of concealment was used, perhaps some such allusion as "Treat this man as well as you did Glaucus," naming someone whom the king had had assassinated. The whole tone of the reference makes it fairly certain that here, in the first great literary work of European culture, appear that culture's first faint glimmerings of secrecy in communication.

A few centuries later, those glimmerings had become definite beams of light. Several stories in the *Histories* of Herodotus deal specifically with methods of steganography (not, however, with cryptography). Herodotus tells how a Median noble named Harpagus wanted to avenge himself on his relative, the king of the Medes, who years before had tricked him into eating his own son. So he hid a message to a potential ally in the belly of an unskinned hare, disguised a messenger as a hunter, and sent him off down the road, carrying the hare as if he had just caught it. The road guards suspected nothing, and the messenger reached his destination. At it was Cyrus, king of Persia, whose country was then subject to Medea and who had himself been the target of a babyhood assassination attempt by the Medean king. The message told him that Harpagus would work from within to help him dethrone the Medean king. Cyrus needed no further urging. He led the Persians in revolt; they defeated the Medes and captured the king, and Cyrus was on his way to winning the epithet "the Great."

Herodotus tells how another revolt—this one against the Persians—was set in motion by one of the most bizarre means of secret communication ever recorded. One Histiaeus, wanting to send word from the Persian court to his son-in-law, the tyrant Aristagoras at Miletus, shaved the head of a trusted slave, tattooed the secret message thereon, waited for a new head of hair to grow, then sent him off to his son-in-law with the instruction to shave the slave's head. When Aristagoras had done so, he read on the slave's scalp the message that urged him to revolt against Persia.

One of the most important messages in the history of Western civilization was transmitted secretly. It gave to the Greeks the crucial information that Persia was planning to conquer them. According to Herodotus,

> The way they received the news was very remarkable. Demaratus, the son of Ariston, who was an exile in Persia, was not, I imagine—and as is only natural to suppose—well disposed toward the Spartans; so it is open to question whether what he did was inspired by benevolence or malicious pleasure. Anyway, as soon as news reached him at Susa that Xerxes had decided upon the invasion of Greece, he felt that he must pass on the information to Sparta. As the danger of discovery was great, there was only one way in which he could contrive to get the message through: this was by scraping the wax off a pair of wooden folding

tablets, writing on the wood underneath what Xerxes intended to do, and then covering the message over with wax again. In this way the tablets, being apparently blank, would cause no trouble with the guards along the road. When the message reached its destination, no one was able to guess the secret until, as I understand, Cleomenes' daughter Gorgo, who was the wife of Leonidas, discovered it and told the others that, if they scraped the wax off, they would find something written on the wood underneath. This was done; the message was revealed and read, and afterwards passed on to the other Greeks.

The rest is well-known. Thermopylae, Salamis, and Plataea ended the danger that the flame of Western civilization would be extinguished by an Oriental invasion. The story is not without a certain bitter irony, however, for Gorgo, who may be considered the first woman cryptanalyst, in a way pronounced a death sentence on her own husband: Leonidas died at the head of the heroic band of Spartans who held off the Persians for three crucial days at the narrow pass of Thermopylae.

It was the Spartans, the most warlike of the Greeks, who established the first system of military cryptography. As early as the fifth century B.C., they employed a device called the "skytale," the earliest apparatus used in cryptology and one of the few ever devised in the whole history of the science for transposition ciphers. The skytale consists of a staff of wood around which a strip of papyrus or leather or parchment is wrapped close-packed. The secret message is written on the parchment down the length of the staff; the parchment is then unwound and sent on its way. The disconnected letters make no sense unless the parchment is rewrapped around a baton of the same thickness as the first: then words leap from loop to loop, forming the message.

Thucydides tells how it enciphered a message from the ephors, or rulers, of Sparta, ordering the too-ambitious Spartan prince and general Pausanius to follow the herald back home from where he was trying to ally himself with the Persians, or have war declared against him by the Spartans. He went. That was about 475 B.C. About a century later, according to Plutarch, another skytale message recalled another Spartan general, Lysander, to face charges of insubordination. Xenophon also records the skytale's use in enciphering a list of names in an order sent to another Spartan commander.

The world owes its first instructional text on communications security to the Greeks. It appeared as an entire chapter in one of the earliest works on military science, *On the Defense of Fortified Places*, by Aeneas the Tactician. He retold some of Herodotus' stories, and listed several systems. One replaced the vowels of the plaintext by dots—one dot for alpha, two for epsilon, and so on to seven for omega. Consonants remained unenciphered. In a steganographic system, holes representing the letters of the Greek alphabet were bored through an astragal or a disk. Then the encipherer passed yarn through the holes that successively represented the letters of his message. The decipherer would presumably have to reverse the entire text after unraveling the thread. Another steganographic system was still in use in the 20th century:

The First 3,000 Years

Aeneas suggested pricking holes in a book or other document above or below the letters of the secret message. German spies used this very system in World War I, and used it with a slight modification in World War II—dotting the letters of newspapers with invisible ink.

Another Greek writer, Polybius, devised a system of signaling that has been adopted very widely as a cryptographic method. He arranged the letters in a square and numbered the rows and columns. To use the English alphabet, and merging *i* and *j* in a single cell to fit the alphabet into a 5 × 5 square:

	1	2	3	4	5
1	a	b	c	d	e
2	f	g	h	ij	k
3	l	m	n	o	p
4	q	r	s	t	u
5	v	w	x	y	z

Each letter may now be represented by two numbers—that of its row and that of its column. Thus $e = 15$, $v = 51$. Polybius suggested that these numbers be transmitted by means of torches—one torch in the right hand and five in the left standing for *e*, for example. This method could signal messages over long distances. But modern cryptographers have found several characteristics of the Polybius square, or "checkerboard," as it is now commonly called, exceedingly valuable—namely, the conversion of letters to numbers, the reduction in the number of different characters, and the division of a unit into two separately manipulable parts. Polybius' checkerboard has therefore become very widely used as the basis of a number of systems of encipherment.

These Greek authors never said whether any of the substitution ciphers they described were actually used, and so the first attested use of that genre in military affairs come from the Romans—and from the greatest Roman of them all, in fact. Julius Caesar tells the story himself in his *Gallic Wars*. He had proceeded by forced marches to the borders of the Nervii, and

> There he learned from prisoners what was taking place at Cicero's station, and how dangerous was his case. Then he persuaded one of the Gallic troopers with great rewards to deliver a letter to Cicero. The letter he sent written in Greek characters, lest by intercepting it the enemy might get to know of our designs. The messenger was instructed, if he could not approach, to hurl a spear, with the letter fastened to the thong, inside the entrenchment of the camp. In the dispatch he wrote that he had started with the legions and would speedily be with him, and he exhorted Cicero to maintain his old courage. Fearing danger, the Gaul discharged the spear, as he had been instructed. By chance it stuck fast in the tower, and for two days was not sighted by our troops; on the third day it was sighted by a soldier, taken down, and delivered to Cicero. He read it through and then recited it at a parade of the troops, bringing the greatest rejoicing to all.

The garrison, heartened, held out until Caesar arrived and relieved them.

Later, Caesar improved on this technique and, in doing so, impressed his name permanently into cryptology as he did into so many other fields. Suetonius, the gossip columnist of ancient Rome, says that Caesar wrote to Cicero and other friends in a cipher in which the plaintext letters were replaced by letters standing three places further down the alphabet, D for *a*, E for *b*, etc. Thus, the message *Omnia Gallia est divisa in partes tres* would be enciphered (using the modern 26-letter alphabet) to RPQLD JDOOLD HVW GLYLVD LQ SDUWHV WUHV. To this day, any cipher alphabet that consists of the standard sequence, like Caesar's:

plain a b c d e f g h i j k l m n o p q r s t u v w x y z
cipher D E F G H I J K L M N O P Q R S T U V W X Y Z A B C

is called a Caesar alphabet, even if it begins with a letter other than D. A later writer, Aulus Gellius, seems to imply that Caesar sometimes used more complicated systems. But Caesar's nephew Augustus, first emperor of Rome and less able than his uncle in a number of ways, also employed a weaker cipher. "When Augustus wrote in cipher," said Suetonius, "he simply substituted the next letter of the alphabet for the one required, except that he wrote AA for *x*" (the last letter of the Roman alphabet).

Cryptography seems to have been not at all uncommon in the Roman state. Suetonius's phraseology implies that the two Caesars employed it habitually and not on a single isolated occasion. Cicero used SAMPSICERAMUS and ARABARCHES and HIEROSOLYMARIUS as mocking codenames for *Pompey*; they all allude to persons and places of importance in Pompey's career. Many Latin writers mention rudimentary forms of secret communication. A grammarian named Probus, probably Valerius Probus, even wrote a treatise on the ciphers of Julius Caesar; this has not survived, and is the first of several Lost Books of Cryptology.

It must be that as soon as a culture has reached a certain level, probably measured largely by its literacy, cryptography appears spontaneously—as its parents, language and writing, probably also did. The multiple human needs and desires that demand privacy among two or more people in the midst of social life must inevitably lead to cryptology wherever men thrive and wherever they write. Cultural diffusion seems a less likely explanation for its occurrence in so many areas, many of them distant and isolated.

The Yezidis, an obscure sect of about 25,000 people in northern Iraq, use a cryptic script in their holy books because they fear persecution by their Moslem neighbors. Tibetans use a kind of cipher called "rin-spuns" for official correspondence; it is named for its inventor Rin-c'(hhen-)spuns(-pa), who lived in the 1300s. The Nsibidi secret society of Nigeria keeps its pictographic script from Europeans as much as possible because it is used chiefly to express love in rather direct imagery, and samples appear to be at least as pornographic as they are cryptographic. The cryptography of Thailand developed under Indian influence. An embryonic study of the subject even appears in a grammatical work entitled *Poranavakya* by Hluang Prasot Aksaraniti (Phe). One system, called "the erring Siamese," substitutes one delicate Siamese letter for another. In another system, consonants are divided into seven groups of five letters; a letter is indicated by writing the Siamese number of its group and placing vertical dots under it equal in number to the letter's place in its group. A system called "the hermit metamorphosing letters" writes the text backwards.

"The erring Siamese"—a form of Thai cryptography with plaintext in upper lines, cipher in lower

As isolated an area as the Maldive Islands in the Indian Ocean uses two kinds of secret writing. "Harha tana" involves reciprocal substitution between consecutive letters of their alphabet, the "gabuli tana," so that h = RH and rh = H, and so forth, the first equivalent perhaps giving rise to the name of the system. "De-fa tana" effects substitutions between the halves of the gabuli tana. In Malaya, natives call their cryptographic alphabet the "gangga malayu"; it consists of the slightly altered or inverted characters of the Malayan Arabic alphabet, with some Javanese marks. In Armenia in the 16th century, two scribes employed a Polybius-like checkerboard to inject an air of special hidden knowledge into religious texts; a third composed his ciphertext by writing two letters whose numerical value equaled that of the plaintext letter—z, with value 6, became GG, each G having a value 3.

Persia, in the first half-millennium after Christ, apparently made use of cryptography for political purposes. A chronicler mentioned a "script called 'shāh-dabīrīya,' and the kings of the Persians used to speak it among themselves to the exclusion of commoners and prevent the rest of the people of the kingdom from [learning] it for fear that one who was not a king should discover the secrets of the kings." He also referred to "another script called 'rāz-sahrīya,' in which the kings used to write secrets [in correspondence] with those of other nations that they wished, and the number of its consonants and vowels is forty, and each of the consonants and vowels has a known form, and there is no trace in it of the Nabataean language." Though the historian gave no examples, a 10th-century compiler of a handbook for secretaries, in setting down two monalphabetic substitutions, said that they were of Persian origin. One substituted the names of birds for the letters of the alphabet. The other equated the letters of the alphabet with the names of the 28 astronomical lunar mansions: the two horns of the ram, the ram's belly, the Pleiades, and so on.

At the Coptic monastery of St. Jeremias in Saqqara, Egypt, perhaps just before it was abandoned late in the sixth century A.D., a man enciphered a message in monalphabetic substitution and scratched it on the wall inside the door to a courtyard in a curious bid for immortality. "In the name of God before all things," the inscription calls out beseechingly across the centuries, "I, Victor, the humble poor man—remember me." Victor's encipherment of his plea gave him his wish. At the site of another Coptic monastery, the seventh-century one of Epiphanius at Sheikh-abd-el-Gourna in southern Egypt, there was found an unusual object in the cell of a priest named Elias. It was a dried-out piece of wood about a foot long and four inches high, bearing two lines of writing in black ink. The top line is a slightly garbled verse in Greek, notable not for its beauty but because it includes all the letters of the Coptic Greek alphabet. It spills over for five letters into the bottom line, which contains 21 letters of that alphabet, divided into four unequal sections that are reversed and shuffled. How Priest Elias used it is not known, but it does seem fairly certain that this wooden tablet, now in the Metropolitan Museum of Art in New York, is the oldest surviving cipher key (as distinguished from the codelike cuneiform tablets) in the world.

The hardy plant of cryptography sprouted not only in these sunblasted climes but also in the damp, chill lands to the north. Two non-Latin scripts of Europe, Teutonic runes and Celtic oghams, were occasionally enciphered.

Runes flourished in Scandinavia and in Anglo-Saxon Britain during the seventh, eighth, and ninth centuries. They were nearly always used for religious purposes. A stark, angular script, its alphabet was divided into three groups

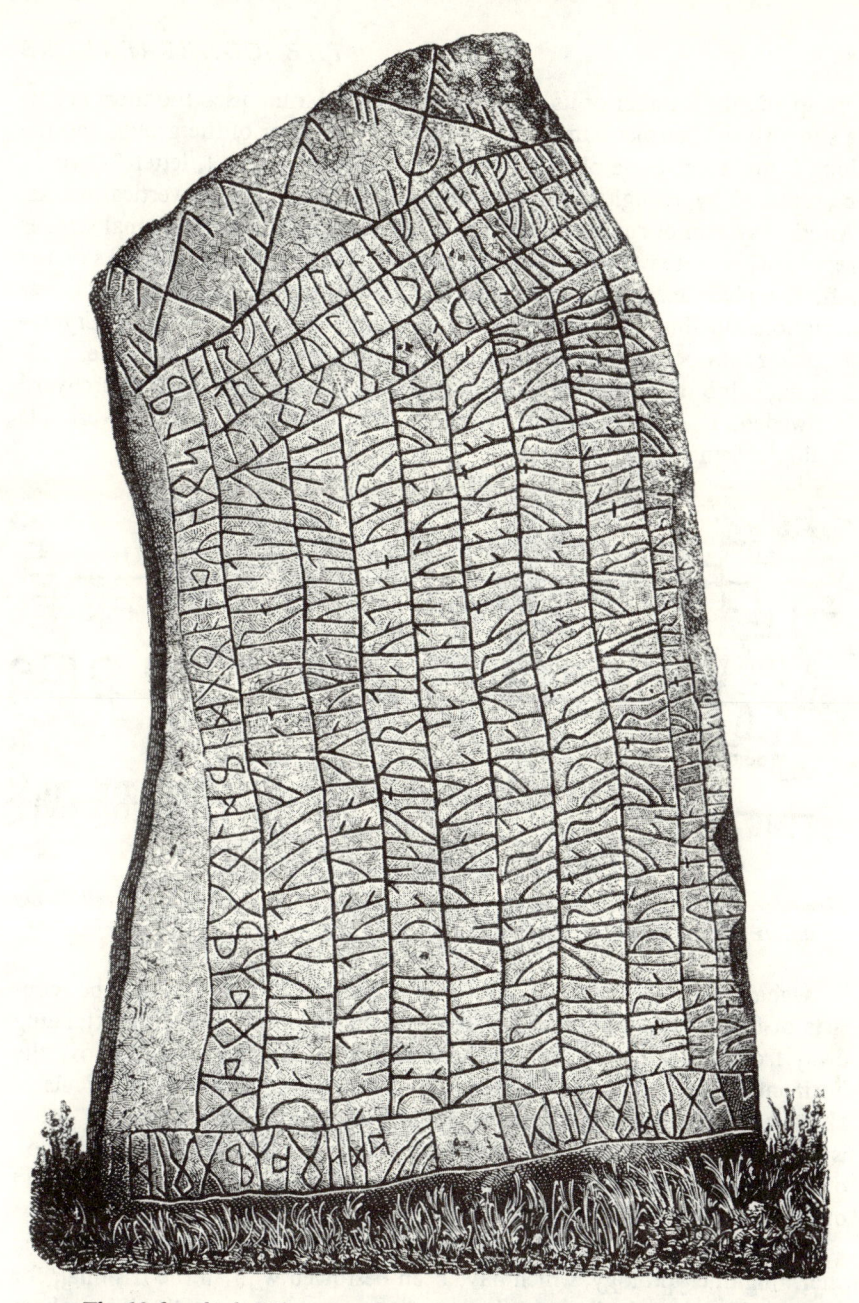

The 13-foot-high Rök stone of Sweden, covered with enciphered runes

of eight runic letters each. The letter thorn, for example, which looked somewhat like a modern *p* and represented the initial sounds of "thin" and "then," was the third letter of the first group. All systems of runic cryptography replaced runic letters by groups of marks indicating the number of a letter's group and the number of its place in that group. Isruna used the short *i* rune, a short vertical stroke named "is," to give the number of the group, and the long *i* rune to give the place number. Thus thorn—group 1, letter 3—would be replaced by a single short vertical mark and three longer vertical marks. Another system of runic cryptography, hahalruna, attached diagonal strokes representing these numbers to a vertical shaft, putting the group marks on the left, the place marks on the right. Sometimes shafts were crossed. Other variations on this theme were lagoruna, stopfruna, and clopfruna. Cryptographic runes occur in many places, most profusely on the Rök stone, a 13-foot-high slab of granite standing at the western end of the Rök churchyard in Sweden. It includes among its more than 770 runic letters a veritable catalog of runic cryptography.

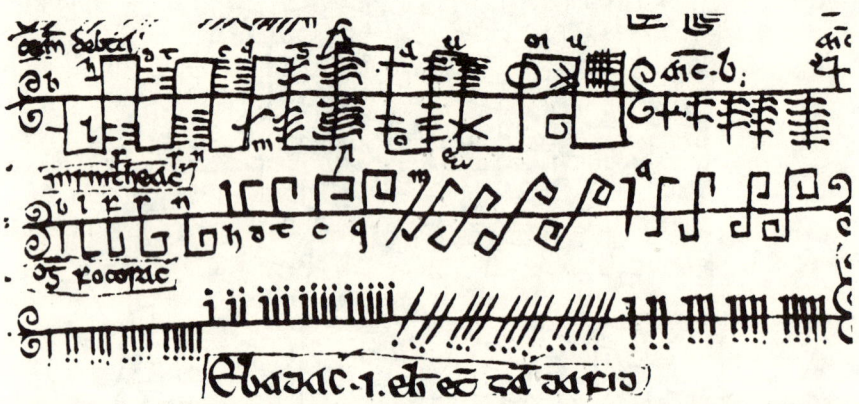

Three forms of enciphered ogham: head of quarreling, interwoven, and well-footed ogham as shown in the "Book of Ballymote"

Ogham survives chiefly in inscriptions on tombstones. Its alphabet consists of five groups of five letters, represented by one to five lines extending away from a horizontal line. In the first group, the lines extend above the horizontal line; in the second group, below it; in the third, perpendicularly above and below; in the fourth, diagonally above and below; the fifth group is heterogeneous. Methods for enciphering them are catalogued in the "Book of Ballymote," a 15th-century compilation of historical, genealogical, and other facts of importance.

The most delightful thing about these systems is their names, the most charming in cryptology, which have been bestowed with all the Irish flair for poetry, blarney, and wit. There is, for an example, a system called "the ogham that bewildered Bres," in which the name of the letter stands for the letter, as if one were to encipher *who* as DOUBLE-YOU AITCH OH. The name comes from a story that a message thus concealed was given to the ancient hero Bres as he was going into battle, and so confused him by its complications that he lost the battle while trying to figure it out. "Sanctuary ogham" puts a stroke between every pair of letters. "Serpent through the heather" runs a wavy line above and below the successive letters. "Great speckle" has a single mark of appropriate slant and length for the letter, followed by as many dots, less one, as there are strokes in the letter. In "twinned ogham" each letter is doubled; in "host ogham," tripled. "Vexation of a poet's heart" reduces the lines to short marks extending beyond an empty rectangle. In "point against eye," the alphabet is reversed. In "fraudulent ogham" the letters are replaced by symbols one step further on. And a system in which the chaotic order of the substitutes seems to have resulted from an infuriated Irishman's knocking them about with a shillelagh is called "outburst of rage ogham." Probably none of these ever actually enciphered ogham. They seem to have been just dreamed up for fun. But the bottom of one of the pages of the "Book of Ballymote" is written in another system called "Bricriu's ogham." With some emendation, it can be interpreted as a fragment of an ancient Druidic liturgy —probably the only one known to the modern world, and, fittingly, the only place in which enciphered oghams were ever used.

In the Europe of the Latin alphabet—from which modern cryptology would spring—cryptography flickered weakly. With the collapse of the Roman empire, Europe had plunged into the obscurity of the Dark Ages. Literacy had all but disappeared. Arts and sciences were forgotten, and cryptography was not excepted. Only during the Middle Ages occasional manuscripts, with an infrequent signature or gloss or "deo gratias" that a bored monk put into cipher to amuse himself, fitfully illuminate the cryptologic darkness, and, like a single candle guttering in a great medieval hall, their feeble flarings only emphasize the gloom.

The systems used were simple in the extreme. Phrases were written vertically or backwards; dots were substituted for vowels; foreign alphabets, as Greek, Hebrew, and Armenian, were used; each letter of the plaintext was replaced by the one that follows it; in the most advanced system, special signs substituted for letters. For almost a thousand years, from before 500 to 1400, the cryptology of Western civilization stagnated. An "advanced" system is as likely to appear in the 600s as in the 1400s—though the really simple systems do fade away by the end of the period.

A few names glimmer through the mists. Tradition attributes to St. Boniface, the Anglo-Saxon missionary who founded monasteries in Germany in the eighth century, the importation to the continent of cryptographic puzzles based on a dots-for-vowels system. The brilliant monk Gerbert, who reigned as Pope Sylvester II from 999 to 1003 and whose learning became legendary, kept notes in a syllabic system called "tyronian notes," a shorthand reputedly developed by Tullius Tyro, a freed slave of Cicero's. He even wrote his name in it on two of his bulls. Hildegard von Bingen, an 11th-century nun who saw apocalyptic visions and was later canonized, had a cipher alphabet which she claimed came to her in a flash of inspiration. In the early 800s, an Irishman named Dubthach concocted a cryptogram while at the castle of the king of Wales as a kind of malicious IQ test for visiting compatriots. He apparently wanted to embarrass them in revenge for some humiliation he had suffered at home, and was confident that "no Irish scholar, much less British," would be able to read it. But four clever sons of Eire—Caunchobrach, Fergus, Domminnach, and Suadbar—turned the tables on him by solving the cryptogram, which consisted of a short Latin plaintext written in Greek letters. Then they prudently sent the answer back to their teacher, urging him to "give this information to such of our simple and unsophisticated Irish brethren as may think of sailing across the British sea, lest perchance otherwise they might be made to blush in the presence of Mermin, the glorious king of the Britons, not being able to understand that inscription."

The only writer of the Middle Ages to describe cryptography instead of

A cryptogram composed and written by Geoffrey Chaucer

just using it was Roger Bacon, the English monk of startlingly modern speculations. In his Epistle on the *Secret Works of Art and the Nullity of Magic*, written about the middle of the 1200s, Bacon stated: "A man is crazy who writes a secret in any other way than one which will conceal it from the vulgar," and then listed seven deliberately vague methods of doing so. Among them are the use of consonants only, figurate expressions, letters from exotic alphabets, invented characters, shorthand, and "magic figures and spells."

Far and away the most famous of all those who had an acquaintance with cryptology in the Middle Ages was an English customs official, amateur astronomer, and literary genius named Geoffrey Chaucer. In a work called *The Equatorie of the Planetis*, which describes the workings of an astronomical instrument and which appears to be a companion piece to his *Treatise on the Astrolabe*, Chaucer included six short passages in cipher. He enciphered them with a symbol alphabet in which, for example, *a* is represented by a sign resembling a capital V and *b* by one looking like a script alpha. One passage reads: "This table servith for to entre in to the table of equacion of the mone on either side." The encipherments give simplified directions for using the equatorie—never mind about the complicated technical explanation, just do this and that and the answer comes out right. The cryptograms are in Chaucer's own hand, making them some of the most illustrious encipherments in history.

During all these years, cryptology was acquiring a taint that lingers even today—the conviction in the minds of many people that cryptology is a black art, a form of occultism whose practitioner must, in William F. Friedman's apt phrase, "perforce commune daily with dark spirits to accomplish his feats of mental jiu-jitsu."

In part it is a kind of guilt by association. From the early days of its existence, cryptology had served to obscure critical portions of writings dealing with the potent subject of magic—divinations, spells, curses, whatever conferred supernatural powers on its sorcerers. The first faint traces of this appeared in Egyptian cryptography. Plutarch reported that "sundry very ancient oracles were kept in secret writings by the priests" at Delphi. And before the fall of the Roman empire, secret writing was serving as a powerful ally of the necromancers in guarding their art from the profane.

One of the most famous magic manuscripts, the so-called Leiden papyrus, discovered at Thebes and written in the third century A.D. in both Greek and a very late form of demotic, a highly simplified version of hieroglyphics, employs cipher to conceal the crucial portions of important recipes. For example, in a section telling how to give a man an incurable skin disease, the papyrus uses secret signs to encipher the words for "skin disease" and the names of the lizards: "You wish to produce a *skin-disease* on a man and that it shall not be healed, a *hantous*-lizard and a *hafleele*-lizard, you cook them with oil, you wash the man with them." The plaintext in most of the cipher sections (including one telling how to make a woman desire a man, which doesn't work) is in Greek, and the cipher alphabet consists basically of Greek letter signs. Cryptology served magical purposes frequently throughout the Middle Ages, and even in the Renaissance was still disguising important parts of alchemical formulas. A manuscript compiled at Naples between 1473 and 1490 by Arnaldus de Bruxella uses five lines of cipher to conceal the crucial part of the operation of making a philosopher's stone.

The association of magic and cryptology was reinforced by other factors. Mysterious symbols were used in such esoteric fields as astrology and alchemy—where each planet and chemical had a special sign, like the circle and arrow for Mars—just as they were in cryptology. Like words in cipher, spells and incantations, such as "abracadabra," looked like nonsense but in reality were potent with hidden meanings.

A very important factor was the confusion of cryptology with the Jewish kabbalah, a mystical philosophy that also interested many Christians of an occultistic turn of mind. One of its basic tenets was that language, which comes from God, reflects the fundamental spiritual nature of the world, and so expresses creation itself. Kabbalists thus produced new revelations about existence by wringing hidden meanings from every word, every letter, even every vowel point and accent mark in the Torah. "Truth," they would say, "stands more firmly than falsehood"—an assertion based on the fact that the letters of the Hebrew word for "falsehood" all balance precariously on one leg, somewhat like an English r, whereas those of the word for "truth" all rest solidly on two feet, like h. Among their devices was gematria, which gave the letters of Hebrew words their numerical values, added them up, and then interpreted the result, often by comparing it with other words having the same total. For example, Genesis 14:14 says that Abraham came to the aid of his nephew Lot with 318 servants. But 318 is the numerical value of the name of Abraham's servant, Eliezer. Hence the 318 were really only one—Eliezer. Less important than gematria were notarikon, which regarded the letters of words as abbreviations for whole sentences, and temurah, an interchange of letters according to various rules, including atbash. These practices work upon the same raw material as cryptology, but unlike cryptology they are flexible and speculative. Some of their laxness seemed to infect cryptology, while their mystical pronouncements seemed to add further magical elements.

Later writers boasted of their ability to solve ciphers in the same breath that they bragged of their prowess in recording human voices, in telepathy, and in communicating with people far underground or miles away. One influential writer, an abbot who believed in magic, then under condemnation by the church, wrote about it under the guise of the more innocuous cryptology—and thus intensified the association between them. Later writers discussed the two together either because they believed they went together or to impress their readers with their own dread powers. Much of this supernatural claptrap besmirched cryptology.

But, important as all these were, the view that cryptology is black magic in itself springs ultimately from a superficial resemblance between cryptology and divination. Extracting an intelligible message from ciphertext seemed to be exactly the same thing as obtaining knowledge by examining the flight of birds, the location of stars and planets, the length and intersections of lines in the hand, the entrails of sheep, the position of dregs in a teacup. In all of these, the wizardlike operator draws sense from grotesque, unfamiliar, and apparently meaningless signs. He makes known the unknown. Of course the analogy errs. Augury, astrology, palmistry, haruspication, and the other divinatory techniques are all ultimately subjective and invalid, while cryptology is objective and perfectly valid. Nevertheless, the appearance often overwhelmed this reality. The simpleminded saw magic even in ordinary deciphering. Others, more sophisticated, saw it in cryptanalysis, whose drawing the veil from something concealed and buried seemed to them both mysterious and miraculous. They equated cryptology and magic.

All this stained cryptology so deeply with the dark hues of esoterism that some of them still persist, noticeably coloring the public image of cryptology. People still think cryptanalysis mysterious. Book dealers still list cryptology under "occult." And in 1940 the United States conferred upon its Japanese diplomatic cryptanalyses the codename MAGIC.

In none of the secret writing thus far explored has there been any sustained cryptanalysis. Occasional isolated instances occurred, as that of the four Irishmen, or Daniel, or any Egyptians who may have puzzled out some of the hieroglyphic tomb inscriptions. But of any science of cryptanalysis, there was nothing. Only cryptography existed. And therefore cryptology, which involves both cryptography and cryptanalysis, had not yet come into being so far as all these cultures—including the Western—were concerned.

Cryptology was born among the Arabs. They were the first to discover and write down the methods of cryptanalysis. The people that exploded out of Arabia in the 600s and flamed over vast areas of the known world swiftly engendered one of the highest civilizations that history had yet seen. Science flowered. Arab medicine and mathematics became the best in the world—from the latter, in fact, comes the word "cipher." Practical arts flourished. Administrative techniques developed. The exuberant creative energies of such a culture, excluded by its religion from painting or sculpture, and inspired by it to an explication of the Holy Koran, poured into literary pursuits. Storytelling, exemplified by Scheherazade's *Thousand and One Nights*, word-riddles, rebuses, puns, anagrams, and similar games abounded; grammar became a major study. And included was secret writing.

Their interest appeared early. In the Arabic year 241, which is 855,* the scholar Abū Bakr Aḥmad ben ʿAlī ben Waḥshiyya an-Nabatī included several traditional cipher alphabets used for magic in his book *Kitāb shauq al-mustahām fī maʿrifat rumūz al-aqlām* ("Book of the Frenzied Devotee's Desire to Learn About the Riddles of Ancient Scripts"). One alphabet, called "dâwoûdî," meaning "Davidian," from the name of the king of Israel, was developed from Hebrew letters by changes in cursive form, by adding tails to letters, or by dropping parts of them. The copyist in 1076 of a treatise on magic operations enciphered such words as "opium" in dâwoûdî. It was considered the magic alphabet par excellence, and was sometimes called "rihani," a form of a word meaning "magic." Another classic substitution alphabet survived as late as 1775, when it was used in a spy letter to the regent of Algiers. This script was known in Turkey as "Miṣirli" ("Egyptian"), in Egypt as "Shāmī" ("Syrian"), and in Syria as "Tadmurī" ("Palmyrene"). In a manuscript on the art of war, probably of 14th-century Egyptian origin, cipher concealed the crucial ingredients of compounds to be hurled into besieged strongholds. Extremist sects in Islam cultivated cryptography to conceal their writings from the orthodox.

In rare cases, the Moslem states used ciphers—not codes, which they seem

---

* Unless otherwise noted, all dates are A.D.

not to have known—for political purposes, perhaps deriving this practice from the Persian empire, upon which they modeled much of their administration. A few documents with ciphertext survive from the Ghaznavid government of conquered Persia, and one chronicler reports that high officials were supplied with a personal cipher before setting out for new posts. But the general lack of continuity of Islamic states and the consequent failure to develop a permanent civil service and to set up permanent embassies in other countries militated against cryptography's more widespread use. Arabic

The Arabic "Davidian" substitution cipher

writers occasionally allude to it. A genealogical tract said of an eighth-century secretary, Mullūl ben Ibrāhīm ben Yaḥzā aṣ-Ṣanhāǧī, that "he was eloquent and quickly understood divers languages; he wrote in Syriac [perhaps meaning the classical Shāmī cipher alphabet] and in secret characters etc., and he excelled in this." The monumental survey of history written in Egypt in the 14th century by 'Abd al-Raḥmān Ibn Khaldūn, *The Muqaddimah*, which Arnold Toynbee has called "undoubtedly the greatest work of its kind that has ever yet been created by any mind in any time or place," noted that officials of the governmental tax and army bureaus "use a very special code among themselves, which is like a puzzle. It makes use of the names of perfumes, fruits, birds, or flowers to indicate the letters, or it makes use of forms different from the accepted forms of the letters. Such a code is agreed upon by the correspondents between themselves, in order to be able to convey their thoughts in writing." The names of the birds recalls the Persian system that also used them, and points to a Persian origin for at least this cipher, and by implication for others.

The special cryptography of the tax officials, called "qirmeh," simplified the forms of the Arabic letters, reduced the size of their bodies and elongated their tails, dropped diacritic points, ran words together and sometimes superimposed or intermingled them, and abbreviated many words. It first appeared in Egypt in the 16th century, and most of the financial records in Istanbul, Syria, and Egypt until the latter part of the 19th century were written in qirmeh. It was used only in documents pertaining to tax affairs, in order to keep revenue information secret.

The Arabic knowledge of cryptography was fully set forth in the section on cryptology in the Ṣubḥ al-a 'sha, an enormous, 14-volume encyclopedia written to afford the secretary class a systematic survey of all the important branches of knowledge. It was completed in 1412 and succeeded in its task. Its author, who lived in Egypt, was Shihāb al-Dīn abu 'l-'Abbās Aḥmad ben 'Ali ben Aḥmad 'Abd Allāh al-Qalqashandi. The cryptologic section, "Concerning the concealment of secret messages within letters," has two parts, one dealing with symbolic actions and allusions, the other with invisible inks and cryptology. The section falls under a larger heading, "On the technical procedures used in correspondence by the secretaries in eastern and western lands and in the Egyptian territories, ranging over the whole period from the appearance of Islam up to our own time," which, in turn, is within a unit headed "On the forms of correspondence."

Qalqashandi attributed most of his information on cryptology to the writings of Tāj ad-Dīn 'Alī ibn ad-Duraihim ben Muḥammad ath-Tha'ālibī al-Mausilī, who lived from 1312 to 1361 and held various teaching and official posts under the Mamelukes in Syria and Egypt. Except for a theological treatise, none of his writings is extant, but he is reported to have authored two works on cryptology. One was a poem, "Urjūza fi 'l-mutarjam," in a loose meter often used for didactic poems and perhaps chosen for mnemonic purposes. The other work consisted of a prose commentary on the poem "Miftāh al-kunūz fi īdah al-marmūz." Though this must be included among the Lost Books of cryptology, most of its information was probably preserved in Qalqashandi.

Qalqashandi began by explaining that necessity sometimes compels concealment "because an enemy places some obstacle or similar thing between the sender and the addressee, e.g., between two rulers or two other persons. [It is used] when circumventory actions are of no avail, either because of interceptory ambushes or because of thorough probes into all letters coming from either of the two parties corresponding"—the latter remark a significant revelation of the need for cryptography and of the probable practice of cryptanalysis.

After explaining that one may write in an unknown language to obtain secrecy, Ibn ad-Duraihim, according to Qalqashandi, gave seven systems of cipher: (1) One letter may replace another. (2) The cryptographer may write a word backward. *Muhammad* (in the consonantal Arabic alphabet) would become DMHM. (3) He may reverse alternate letters of the words of a message. (4) He may give the letters their numerical value in the system in which the Arabic letters are used as numbers, and then write this value in Arabic numerals. *Muhammad* becomes 40+8+40+4, and the cryptogram looks like a list of figures. (5) The cryptographer may replace each plaintext letter with two Arabic letters, whose numerical value adds up to the numerical value of the plaintext letter. After giving some examples, Qalqashandi states that "other letters can be used, so long as they add up to the number of the original letter." (6) "He may substitute for each letter the name of a man or something like that." (7) The cryptographer may employ the lunar mansions as substitutes for the letters, or list the names of countries, fruits, trees, etc., in a certain order, or draw birds or other living creatures, or simply invent special symbols as ciphertext replacements. The similarity of this list to Ibn Khaldūn's suggests that both writers took their information from a 10th-century manual for secretaries by Abū Bakr Muḥammad ben Yaḥyā aṣ-Ṣūlī, who gave both the bird and lunar substitutions, reporting that they are Persian in origin.

This list encompassed, for the first time in cryptography, both transposition and substitution systems, and, moreover, gave, in system 5, the first cipher ever to provide more than one substitute for a plaintext letter. Remarkable and important as this is, however, it is overshadowed by what follows—the first exposition on cryptanalysis in history.

It appeared in full maturity in Qalqashandi's paraphrase of Ibn ad-Duraihim, but its beginnings are probably to be found in the intense and minute scrutiny of the Koran by whole schools of grammarians in Basra, Kufa, and Baghdad to elucidate its meanings. Among other studies, they counted the frequency of words to attempt a chronology for the chapters of the Koran, certain words being considered as having been used only in the later chapters. They examined words phonetically to see whether they were native Arabic or foreign loanwords. This led to generalizations about the composition of Arabic words. For example, one grammarian, referring to the lingual letters ra', lām, and nūn, and the labials fā', bā', and mīm, declared: "Now when the six (labial and lingual) letters were pronounced and emitted by the tongue, they proved easy to form, and became common in speech-patterns. So no true quinquiliteral roots are free from them, or at least from one of them." This very rule reappeared in Ibn ad-Duraihim's work. Also of great importance in the discovery of linguistic phenomena that led to cryptanalysis was the development of lexicography. In making a dictionary, considerations of letter-frequency and of which letters go or do not go together virtually thrust themselves upon the lexicographer. For example, the Arabs recognized early that zā' was the rarest letter in Arabic and, contrariwise, that the omnipresence of

The First 3,000 Years

the definite article "al-" made alif and lām the most common letters in normal style.

It is therefore quite understandable that the Arab world's first great philologist, the first man to conceive the idea of a comprehensive dictionary, a shining light of the Basra school of grammarians, wrote a "Kitāb al-muʿammā" ("Book of Secret Language") relatively early in history. This was Abū ʿAbd al-Raḥmān al-Khalīl ibn Aḥmad ibn ʿAmr ibn Tammām al Farāhīdī al-Zadī al Yaḥmadī, who lived from the Arabic year 100 to between 170 and 175 (or A.D. 718/719 to between 786 and 791). Al-Khalīl was inspired to write the "Kitāb al-muʿammā"—which apparently is yet another Lost Book—by his solution of a cryptogram in Greek sent him by the Byzantine emperor. When he was asked how he managed to solve it, he said, "I said (to myself), the letter must begin 'In the name of God' or something of that sort. So I worked out its first letters on that basis, and it came right for me."

This description, and the fact that it took him a month before he could solve it, suggests that the Arabs had not yet formulated the more analytical techniques of cryptanalysis based upon letter-frequency. This makes sense— 150 years or so after the Hegira they would probably still be in the early stages of their linguistic explorations. But by the time of Ibn ad-Duraihim, 600 years later, these studies would have ramified enough to stimulate some unknown genius to apply their findings to the solution of ciphers. Indeed, Ibn ad-Duraihim's discussion of cryptanalysis, as reflected in Qalqashandi, is so mature that it implies a fairly long preceding period of development. The technique was at least moderately well known, for Ibn Khaldūn wrote in *The Muqaddimah*: "Occasionally, skillful secretaries, though not the first to invent a code [and with no previous knowledge of it], nonetheless find rules [for solving it] through combinations which they evolve for the purpose with the help of their intelligence, and which they call 'solving the puzzle [cryptanalysis].' Well-known writings on the subject are in the possession of the people. God is knowing and wise."

The Ibn ad-Duraihim–Qalqashandi exposition begins at the beginning: the cryptanalyst must know the language in which the cryptogram is written. Because Arabic, "the noblest and most exalted of all languages," is "the one most frequently resorted to" (in that part of the world), there follows an extensive discussion of its linguistic characteristics. Lists are given of letters that are never found together in one word, of letters that rarely come together in a word, of combinations of letters that are not possible ("Thus tha' may not precede shin."), and so on. Finally, the exposition gives a list of letters in order of "frequency of usage in Arabic in the light of what a perusal of the Noble Koran reveals." The writers even note that "In non-Koranic writings, the frequency may be different from this." With these basics completed, Qalqashandi goes on:

> Ibn ad-Duraihim has said: When you want to solve a message which you have received in code, begin first of all by counting the letters, and then count

how many times each symbol is repeated and set down the totals individually. If the person devising the code has been very thorough and has concealed the word-divisions in the body of the messages, then the first thing to be worked out is the symbol which divides up the words. To do this, you take a letter and work on the assumption that the next letter is the word-divider. Then you go all through the message with it, having regard for the possible combinations of letters of which the words may be composed, as has been previously explained. If it fits, [then all right]; if not, you take the next letter after the second one. If that fits, [then all right]; if not, you take the next letter after that, and so on, until you are able to ascertain the division of the words. Next, look which letters occur most frequently in the message, and compare this with the pattern of letter-frequency previously mentioned. When you see that one letter occurs in the message more often than the rest, then assume that it is alif; then assume that the next most frequent is lām. The accuracy of your conjecture should be confirmed by the fact that in a majority of contexts, lām follows alif. . . . Then the first words which you try to work out in the message are the two-lettered ones, through estimating the most feasible combinations of their letters, until you are sure you have discovered something correct in them; then look at their symbols and write down the equivalents by them [whenever they occur in the message]. Apply the same principle to the message's three-lettered words until you are sure you have got something, then write out the equivalents [all through the message]. Apply the same principle to the four- and five-lettered words, according to the previous procedure. Whenever there is any doubt, posit two or three or more conjectures and write each one down until it becomes certain from another word.

Qalqashandi follows this clear explanation with a four-page example of solution taken from Ibn ad-Duraihim. The cryptogram consists of two lines of verse enciphered with symbols of apparently arbitrary invention. At the end, he notes that eight letters were not used and that they are exactly the same eight that stand at the foot of the frequency list. "This, however, is pure chance: a letter may be somewhat misplaced from the position it has been assigned in the above-mentioned list," he observes—an observation that argues a fair amount of experience in cryptanalysis. To nail everything down, Qalqashandi gives a second example from Ibn ad-Duraihim, with a rather longer message. With this three-page illustration, he concludes the cryptologic section of his work.

To what extent the Arabs used the abilities so brilliantly evident here in the solution of military or diplomatic cryptograms, and what effects they had upon Moslem history, is not known. What does seem certain is that, like the Arabic civilization itself, this knowledge fell into desuetude and was soon lost. An episode of 250 years later dramatizes the decline.

In 1600, the Sultan of Morocco, Aḥmad al-Manṣūr, sent an embassy headed by his confidential secretary, 'Abd al-Waḥid ibn Mas'ud ibn Muḥammad Anūn, to Queen Elizabeth of England to ally himself with her against Spain. The ambassador reported back in a monalphabetically enciphered dispatch, which shortly thereafter apparently somehow fell into the hands of

The First 3,000 Years 99

an Arab, evidently intelligent, but as evidently ignorant of his great cryptologic heritage. In a memorandum, he wrote:

> Praise be to Allah! Writing of the secretary 'Abd al-Waḥid ibn Mas 'ud Anūn. I found a note written in his hand in which he had noted in secret characters some information destined for our protector Abū l'Abbas al-Mansūr. This information relates to the Sultana of the Christians (May God destroy them!) who was in the country of London in the year 1009. From the moment when the note fell into my hands, I never stopped studying from time to time the signs which it bore. ... About 15 years more or less passed, until the moment when God (Glory to Him!) did me the favor of permitting me to comprehend these signs, although no one taught them to me. ...

Fifteen years! For what Ibn ad-Duraihim would have solved in a few hours! Yet that has always been the story of civilizations.

Analyzing the frequency and contacts of letters is the most universal, most basic of cryptanalytic procedures. A knowledge of it is requisite to an understanding of all subsequent techniques of substitution cryptanalysis. Hence it seems worthwhile to give in some detail, with an English plaintext, an example of such a solution, much as Qalqashandi did in Arabic.

Cryptanalysis rests upon the fact that the letters of language have "personalities" of their own. To the casual observer, they may look as alike as troops lined up for inspection, but just as the sergeant knows his men as "the goldbrick," "the kid," "the reliable soldier," so the cryptanalyst knows the letters of the alphabet. Though in a cryptogram they wear disguises, the cryptanalyst observes their actions and idiosyncrasies, and infers their identity from these traits. In ordinary monalphabetic substitution, his task is fairly simple because each letter's camouflage differs from every other letter's and the camouflage remains the same throughout the cryptogram.

How would he go about doing this for the following cryptogram?

GJXXN	GGOTZ	NUCOT	WMOHY	JTKTA	MTXOB	YNFGO
GINUG	JFNZV	QHYNG	NEAJF	HYOTW	GOTHY	NAFZN
FTUIN	ZANFG	NLNFU	TXNXU	FNEJC	INHYA	ZGAEU
TUCQG	OGOTH	JOHOA	TCJXK	HYNUV	OCOHQ	UHCNU
GHHAF	NUZHY	NCUTW	JUWNA	EHYNA	FOWOT	UCHNP
HOGLN	FQZNG	OFUVC	NZJHT	AHNGG	NTHOU	CGJXY
OGHTN	ABNTO	TWGNT	HNTXN	AEBUF	KNFYO	HHGIU
TJUCE	AFHYN	GACJH	OATAE	IOCOH	UFOXO	BYNFG

The cryptanalyst would begin by counting each letter's frequency (how often it occurs in a text) and its contacts (which letters it touches, and how many different ones). The frequency count of this cryptogram is this:

```
17  4 13  0  7 17 23 26  5 12  3  2  2
 A  B  C  D  E  F  G  H  I  J  K  L  M

36 25  1  5  0  0 23 20  3  6  9 13  8
 N  O  P  Q  R  S  T  U  V  W  X  Y  Z
```

A widely used frequency table of 200 letters of normal English is this:

	16	3	6	8	21	4	3	12	13	1	1	7	6
	A	B	C	D	E	F	G	H	I	J	K	L	M
percentage:	8	1.5	3	4	13	2	1.5	6	6.5	.5	.5	3.5	3

	14	16	4	½	13	12	18	6	2	3	1	4	½
	N	O	P	Q	R	S	T	U	V	W	X	Y	Z
percentage:	7	8	2	.25	6.5	6	9	3	1	1.5	.5	2	.25

But it is not possible to simply list the letters in the cryptogram in the order of frequency, and then, lining that list up with one giving the letters of normal text in their order of frequency, mechanically replace the cipher with the "plain." In this case, the two lists are:

letters in order of frequency

in normal text   e t a o n i r s h d l u c m p f y w g b v j k q x z
in cryptogram   N H O G T U A F C Y J X Z E W I Q B K V L M P

Brute substitution of letters of the upper row for those of the lower at the beginning of the cryptogram would give this "plaintext": *oluueooanceihanpjatd* ... Obviously, the two frequency counts do not match. Which is not surprising, since they are based on different texts, using different words with different letters in them. But whereas the relative frequencies may shift slightly, making, say, *i* more frequent than *a* in a particular case, the letters generally do not stray very far from their home areas in the frequency table. Thus, *e, t, a, o, n, i, r, s,* and *h* will normally be found in the high-frequency group; *d, l, u, c,* and *m* in the medium-frequency group; *p, f, y, w, g, b,* and *v* in the lows, and *j, k, q, x,* and *z* in the rare group. Furthermore, a sharp break in frequency usually sets off the highs from the mediums; the lowest of the highs, *h,* is normally 6 per cent, while the highest of the mediums, *d,* is only 4 per cent. This step-down is quite visible in the cryptogram's frequency count:

N	H	O	G	T	U	A	F	C	Y	J	X	Z	E	W	I	Q	B	K	V	L	M	P
36	26	25	23	23	20	17	17	13	13	12	9	8	7	6	5	5	4	3	3	2	2	1

It is the drop between F and C. Though one of the usual nine highs has slipped out of its category, the remaining eight letters above the division are almost certainly all high-frequency letters. N probably represents *e,* which is outstandingly the most common letter (about one in every eight of normal text). Frequency alone cannot tell much more than this.

But contact can. Every letter has a cluster of preferred associations that constitute its most distinguishing characteristic. The cryptanalyst can spot these almost by eye if he sets up a contact chart for the high-frequency cipher letters like the one on the following page. In the chart, the letter being counted stands at the left, with the other letters strung out in order of frequency in a line to the right. Each tally above a letter in the line means that the letter in that line has preceded the subject letter in one instance, while each tally below means that it has followed the subject letter.

CONTACT CHART FOR HIGH-FREQUENCY CIPHER LETTERS

```
36  N    N H O G T U A F C Y J X Z E W I Q B K V L M P
26  H    N H O G T U A F C Y J X Z E W I Q B K V L M P
25  O    N H O G T U A F C Y J X Z E W I Q B K V L M P
23  G    N H O G T U A F C Y J X Z E W I Q B K V L M P
23  T    N H O G T U A F C Y J X Z E W I Q B K V L M P
20  U    N H O G T U A F C Y J X Z E W I Q B K V L M P
17  A    N H O G T U A F C Y J X Z E W I Q B K V L M P
17  F    N H O G T U A F C Y J X Z E W I Q B K V L M P
13  C    N H O G T U A F C Y J X Z E W I Q B K V L M P
13  Y    N H O G T U A F C Y J X Z E W I Q B K V L M P
12  J    N H O G T U A F C Y J X Z E W I Q B K V L M P
```

The chart shows that H has preceded N three times—in other words, that the digraph HN has occurred three times—and has followed it, to make NH, just once.

In a chart like this, plaintext *e* is about as hard to recognize under its cipher masquerade as a six-and-a-half-foot-tall man at a costume party. It is president of this republic of letters because it leads all the rest in frequency, yet it is democratic enough to contact more different letters more often than any other letter, including a goodly number in the low-frequency bracket. Indubitably, N here is President *e*.

Next most distinctive are the three high-frequency vowels, *a*, *i*, and *o*. Like rival dowagers at a society ball, they avoid one another as much as possible. A glance at the contact chart shows that ciphertext O, U, and A are the most mutually exclusive. (H, which rarely associates with U and A, is ruled out as a vowel possibility because it contacts O so often.) Thus, these three letters probably represent the three high-frequency plaintext vowels. Which is which can often be ascertained by the fact that the plaintext digraph *io* is fairly frequent while the other five combinations (*oi, ia, ai, oa, ao*) are fairly rare. The contact chart shows these frequencies: OA, 2; OU, 1; and UO, UA, AO, and AU, all zero. If OA = *io*, then U would be *a*, and OU would be *ia*, which happens to be the most common of the other five digraphs. Better still, NU, which appears five times, would stand for *ea*, the most frequent of all the digraphs involving vowels, while UN, which does not exist in this message, would stand for *ae*, the rarest. This is a nice corroboration for the vowel identification. Even if identification of the individual vowels is not possible, it is nearly always wise to begin the analysis by determining which letters are the four high-frequency vowels.

What about consonants? The easiest to spot is plaintext *n* because four fifths of the letters that precede it are vowels. The contact chart shows that ciphertext T is preceded by ciphertext N, O, U, and A 17 times out of 23. It is a good bet for *n*.

The behavior of Y in the chart is striking. It runs before N (= *e*) like a herald and never follows it, while on the other hand it invariably tags along behind H and never precedes it. It behaves, in fact, just like plaintext *h*. The digraph *he* is one of the most common in English, while *eh* is very rare; *th* is the most common of all, and *ht* is also fairly rare. If Y = *h*, then ciphertext H must be *t*—an assumption that fits in well with its frequency. In telegraphic texts where *the* is deleted, plaintext *h* can usually be spotted because—just the opposite of *n*—it precedes vowels about ten times as often as it follows them.

The only two high-frequency letters remaining to be identified are *r* and *s*. The basic difference between them is that *r*, rather like a social climber, associates much more with the vowels—dowagers *a*, *i*, and *o* as well as President *e*—than does *s*, while *s*, a proletarian at heart, mingles with the consonants, the blue-collar laborers of the alphabet. These differences in their contacts hold both absolutely and relatively. In the chart, however, inspection of the contact bars for G and F, the only two high-frequency letters left, yields contradictory evidence: F contacts the identified vowels more often than G—21 times to G's 17—but it also contacts the three high-frequency consonants (*t*, *n*, *h*) more—4 times to G's 3—even though its frequency is lower.

It is not necessary to force the decision, for even without these identifications, 160 out of the 280 letters in the message have been given tentative plaintext equivalents. The acid test as to whether they are right, of course, consists in substituting them into the cryptogram and seeing whether they make sense. In doing so, many cryptanalysts use pencils of different colors for the plain- and the ciphertext to make them easier to distinguish. They also leave a lot of space between the lines of the ciphertext to allow for multiple hypotheses, erasures, underlining of repetitions, and so on.

```
G J X X N G G O T Z N U C O T W M O H Y J T K T A M T X O B
      e     in ea   in     ith  n  no  n   i

Y N F G O G I N U G J F N Z V Q H Y N G N E A J F H Y O T W
h e   i     e a         e       the   e o     t h i n

G O T H Y N A F Z N F T U I N Z A N F G N L N F U T X N X U
i n t h e o     e     n a   e   o e     e   e   a n   e   a

F N E J C I N H Y A Z G A E U T U C Q G O G O T H J O H O A
  e         e t h o     o   a n a       i   i n t   i t i o

T C J X K H Y N U V O C O H Q U H C N U G H H A F N U Z H Y
n         t h e a   i     i t   a t   e a   t t o   e a   t h
```

Just this portion of the message will suffice for its solution. The cryptanalyst uses these tentative identifications to root out the meanings of other cipher letters. He does this by guessing at what the missing letters should be to make up intelligible text. For example, near the beginning the plaintext sequence *-ith-* appears. This could be a portion of the word *with*.

No cryptanalyst, if asked, could at this point give any proof that his assumption is correct. All it is now is a kind of guess, guided only by the porous laws of probability. Successive guesses will either increasingly confirm it or contradict it, causing the cryptanalyst to discard it. But each successive assumption is put forth at first upon the same slim basis as this. Eventually, the internal consistency of the final result piles up such an immense weight of probability that the validity of the solution becomes a virtual certainty. But the cryptanalyst who seeks proof absolute for each assumption as he makes it will never find it—and he will never solve the cipher.

Here, however, *with* seems likely. This assumption means that M = *w*, and this equivalence can be filled in wherever M appears in the cryptogram, to see whether it suggests any more new words. Just ten letters down the line, it forms the sequence *with-n-nown-i-* ..., which suggests the phrase *with unknown*. The long plaintext sequence *-int-ition-* provides a check: the J = *u* identity fits right in to form the word *intuition*. The new plaintext letters are inserted and used to provide clues to still more letters. This process of reconstructing the plaintext—perhaps the easiest and the most fun in cryptanalysis—is called "anagramming."*

It can be greatly speeded by a parallel reconstruction: that of the key alphabet. If the ciphertext letters are written under a normal alphabet that serves as the plaintext alphabet, their mere arrangement will often donate additional equivalences. The ciphertext listings thus far recovered are these:

plaintext   a b c d e f g h i j k l m n o p q r s t u v w x y z
ciphertext U   N   Y O   K   T A   H J   M

Because it is difficult to remember an incoherent string of 26 letters that constitutes the set of cipher equivalents, cipher alphabets are often based on a single word that is easy to memorize. Various derivations are possible, but the simplest is just to write out the keyword, omitting repeated letters, then to follow it with the remaining letters of the alphabet. Thus the cipher alphabet springing from the keyword CHIMPANZEE would be:

plaintext   a b c d e f g h i j k l m n o p q r s t u v w x y z
ciphertext C H I M P A N Z E B D F G J K L O Q R S T U V W X Y

The portion of the ciphertext alphabet following the keyword contains long alphabetical sequences. Often the cryptanalyst can complete segments that have been partially filled in, and thus recover more equivalencies. For example, if he sees QR-TU, he needs no great wit to realize that the missing letter must be s.

One such segment leaps to the eye in the partial alphabet recovered from

---

* This usage of the term seldom conflicts with its traditional sense of rearranging letters of one text to spell another, like *night* to *thing*.

the cryptogram: HJ-M. Only K or L can fit there, but since ciphertext K has already been assigned to plaintext *k* (from *unknown*), L must slide in to represent *v*, thereby giving the cryptanalyst a free identification. The technique can help in another way: to decide between F and G for *r* and *s*. If F = *s* and G = *r*, the sequence in the key alphabet under *r* and *s* would run backwards:

    ...rs...
    ...GF...

This is unlikely, so F = *r* and G = *s*. The cipher alphabet also gives ideas for plaintext equivalencies. For example, U = *a* in the alphabet, so if the cryptanalyst sees a V in the cryptogram, he may try *b* as one possibility for its plaintext to complete the UV segment under *ab*. In this case, it happens to work out right. With these new values inserted in the top two lines, the solution is virtually finished:

```
G J  X X  N G G O T  Z N U C O T  W M O H Y J  T K T  A M T X O B
s u    e s s i n    e a    i n    w i t h u n k n o w n    i

Y N F  G O G I  N U G J  F N Z V Q H Y N G N E  A J  F H Y O T W
h e r  s i s    e a s u r e      b    t h e s e      o u r t h i n
```

The two x's must be two *c*'s to make *success*; then B must be *p* to form *ciphers*; E must be *f*, for *four*; W, *g* for *things* and *-ing*; and so forth. At this point, hypotheses pour in literally faster than they can be written down. The plaintext (with punctuation supplied) reads: "*Success in dealing with unknown ciphers is measured by these four things in the order named: perseverance, careful methods of analysis, intuition, luck. The ability at least to read the language of the original text is very desirable but not essential.*" Such is the opening sentence of Parker Hitt's *Manual for the Solution of Military Ciphers*.

The full key alphabet, including equivalents for plaintext *j*, *q*, and *z*, which did not appear, is based on the keyphrase NEW YORK CITY:

```
plaintext   a b c d e f g h i j k l m n o p q r s t u v w x y z
ciphertext  U V X Z N E W Y O R K C I T A B D F G H J L M P Q S
```

The careful examination of the propensities of the various plaintext letters may seem unnecessary. In the case of monalphabetic substitutions with word divisions, solution may often be obtained by taking a stab at common words (*the*, *and*), guessing at pattern words whose repeated letters form a distinctive configuration (WXYZY might be *there*), or comparing short words (HX, XH, HL, PL, and PX might be *on*, *no*, *of*, *if*, and *in*). But a knowledge of the characteristics of plaintext lies at the heart of the solution of more complex ciphers, where that plaintext is concealed more effectively. Naturally, in shorter cryptograms, solutions do not run quite as smoothly as the longer ones that allow the statistics of language enough play to become reliable. For these more difficult problems, expert solvers offer novices two tips: (1) make contact charts: the drudgery usually pays off in faster and more accurate identifications; (2) when stumped, and no likely plaintext values are visible, try *something* and see where it leads; even if it proves wrong, it has narrowed down the possibilities. No cryptogram was ever solved by staring at it. Finally, it should be noted that monalphabetic substitutions that use numbers or symbols as their ciphertext equivalents are solvable in the same way as those using letters. The difference in the camouflage does not alter the features of the underlying language.

3

THE RISE OF THE WEST

WESTERN CIVILIZATION began the use of political cryptology that it has continued uninterrupted to the present as it emerged from the feudalism of the Middle Ages. The secret writing of that time was as embryonic as other elements of what was to become the world's dominant civilization. Its use was at first infrequent and irregular; the systems were rudimentary, even in the church, still the greatest and most wide-ranging power of its day. But there were no longer any regressions, no thousand-year hiatuses. Cryptology only progressed. And from the earliest days there existed the two basic modern forms: codes and ciphers.

The substitutions of code stemmed in part from abbreviations, in part from obscure epithets and imagery used in oracles and magic half to reveal, half to conceal meanings. The oldest cryptographic document in the Vatican archives includes substitutions of both origins. This is a little list of name-equivalents compiled in 1326 or 1327 for use in the struggle between the pro-pope Guelphs and the pro-Holy Roman Emperor Ghibellines in central Italy. It replaced the title *official*—evidently representing anyone of authority—by the single letter O. The *Ghibellines* became EGYPTIANS and the *Guelphs* the CHILDREN OF ISRAEL. A decade later, another list moved away from the jargon and introduced some secrecy to its abbreviations when it gave LORD A as the equivalent for *our lord*. Finally, on an undated slip of paper, perhaps a little later than the second list, appears the first modern code. It is very small but it manifests undiluted the essential attribute: the paramountcy of secrecy in its substitutions (though they secondarily enjoy the advantages of abbreviation): A = *king*, D = *the Pope*, S = *Marescallus*, and so on.

Ciphers, of course, had been used by monks all through the Middle Ages for scribal amusement, and the Renaissance knew from its study of such classic texts as Suetonius that the ancient world had used ciphers for political purposes. Hence the basic concept was already known. As early as 1226, a faint political cryptography appeared in the archives of Venice, where dots or crosses replaced the vowels in a few scattered words. A century and a half later, in 1363, the Archbishop of Naples, Pietro di Grazie, enciphered vowels fairly regularly in his correspondence with the papal curia and with cardinals. In 1379, the antipope Clement VII, who had fled to Avignon the previous year

The Rise of the West 107

to begin the Great Schism of the Roman Catholic Church, in which two popes claimed to reign, saw the need of new ciphers for his new establishment. One of his secretaries, Gabrieli di Lavinde, a man from Parma who had perhaps worked in one of the chancelleries of the northern Italian city-states, compiled a set of individual keys for 24 correspondents of Clement, among them Niccolò of Naples, the Duke of Montevirdi, and the Bishop of Venice.

Lavinde's collection of keys—the oldest extant in modern Western civilization—includes several that combine elements of both code and cipher. In addition to a monalphabetic substitution alphabet, often with nulls, nearly every key comprised a small repertory of a dozen or more common words or names with two-letter code equivalents. They constitute the earliest examples of a cryptographic system that was to hold sway over all Europe and America for the next 450 years: the nomenclator. The nomenclator united the cipher substitution alphabet of letters and the code list of word, syllable, and name equivalents; it is a cross between the two basic systems. Code and cipher were

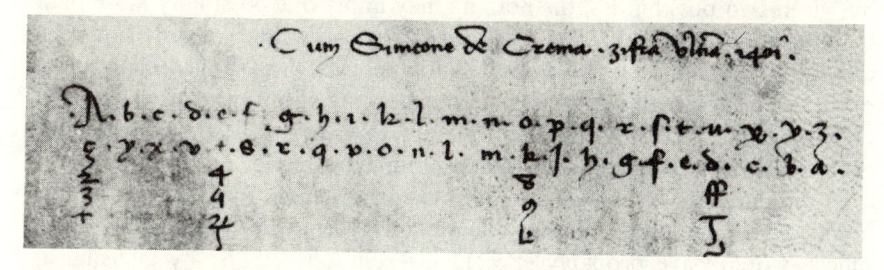

The West's earliest known homophonic substitution cipher, used at Mantua with Simeone de Crema in 1401

separated in the early nomenclators but were merged in the later. The nomenclator eventually expanded its word-substitution lists from the few dozen names of Lavinde to the 2,000 or 3,000 syllables and words of those of Czarist Russia in the 1700s.

The first substitution alphabets provided only a single substitute for each plaintext letter. Later ones supplied multiple substitutes. The first known Western instance of multiple cipher-representations occurs in a cipher that the Duchy of Mantua prepared in 1401 for correspondence with one Simeone de Crema. Each of the plaintext vowels has several possible equivalents. This testifies silently that, by this time, the West knew cryptanalysis. There can be no other explanation for the appearance of these multiple substitutes, or homophones. The cipher secretary of Mantua introduced them to hinder anyone who might try to solve an intercepted dispatch, for each extra cipher symbol means that much more work, that much more that has to be dug out by the cryptanalyst. That the homophones were applied to vowels, and not just indiscriminately, indicates a knowledge of at least the outlines of frequency analysis.

Where did that knowledge come from? It probably developed indigenously. Though it is true that contact with the Moslem and other civilizations during the Crusades triggered the cultural explosion of the Renaissance, and that Arabic works of science, mathematics, and philosophy poured into Europe from Moorish centers of scholarship in Spain, it seems unlikely that cryptanalysis emigrated from there. It was considered more a branch of grammar than of science or mathematics; it was linked too closely in Arabic tradition to the language of the Koran; its importance was much less than that of medicine or algebra or alchemy; in any case, neither Ibn ad-Duraihim's nor Qalqashandi's works, the only ones known to give a full explanation of the technique, were translated. It is possible but improbable that a diplomat to one of the Arabic lands may have brought back a knowledge of cryptanalysis. But cultural diffusion such as this would probably leave some written records, and none exist for any transfer of cryptanalysis from Islam to Christendom. It is dangerous to infer something from nothing, but given two possibilities, the nothing may imply one possibility more than the other: and it would rather be expected that no written records would be created if cryptanalysis developed spontaneously. The bright chancellery official who succeeded in puzzling out the meaning of the enciphered words in a captured dispatch would be hardly likely to give away, either orally or in writing, the knowledge that could bring him extra money and prestige.

Though no known documents attest to such a genesis for Western political cryptanalysis—and none object to it, either—it seems the most probable. The official would have probably effected his solutions at first by guessing at words, much as did the four Irishmen who solved Dubthach's cryptogram. As through repeated cryptanalyses he became more acquainted with the personalities of the letters, he might have eventually stumbled on the principle of frequency analysis. The same development may have taken place separately in several principalities, and it is not inconceivable that one new solver may have reasoned his way to frequency analysis by wondering why a cryptographer in another city used homophones for vowels!

What is certain is that, as the secular principalities of Italy began to use cipher regularly in the 1390s and early 1400s, their cipher alphabets gradually began to include homophones for vowels. So slow was cryptology's development, however, that not until the mid-1500s did consonants begin to get homophones. Likewise, the code lists of the nomenclators did not expand much until well into the 1500s.

The growth of cryptology resulted directly from the flowering of modern diplomacy. In this, for the first time, states maintained permanent relations with one another. The resident ambassadors sent home regular reports—they have been called "honorable spies"—and the jealousy, suspicion, and intrigues among the Italian city-states made it often necessary to encipher these. As the practice implies, the reports were sometimes opened and read, and, if necessary, cryptanalyzed. By the end of the century, cryptology had become important enough for most states to keep full-time cipher secretaries occupied in making up new keys, enciphering and deciphering messages, and solving intercepted dispatches. Sometimes the cryptanalysts were separate from the cipher secretaries and were called in only when needed.

Perhaps the most elaborate organization was Venice's. It fell under the immediate control of the Council of Ten, the powerful and mysterious body that ruled the republic largely through its efficient secret police. Venice owed her preeminence largely to Giovanni Soro, who was perhaps the West's first great cryptanalyst. Soro, appointed cipher secretary in 1506, enjoyed remarkable success in solving the ciphers of numerous principalities. His solution of a dispatch of Mark Anthony Colonna, chief of the army of the Holy Roman Emperor Maximilian I, requesting 20,000 ducats or the presence of the emperor with the army, gave an insight into Colonna's problems. So great was Soro's fame that other courts sharpened their ciphers, and as early as 1510 the papal curia was sending him ciphers that no one in Rome could solve. In 1526, Pope Clement VII (not to be confused with the antipope of the same name) twice sent him intercepts for solution, and Soro twice succeeded —once with three long dispatches from Maximilian I's successor, the Holy Roman Emperor Charles V of Spain, to his emissary at Rome, and once with letters addressed by the Duke of Ferrara to his ambassador in Spain. When one of Clement's messages fell into the hands of the Florentines, Clement, exclaiming "Soro can decipher any cipher!" sent him a copy of the message to see whether it was secure. He was reassured when Soro reported that he could not solve it—but one wonders whether Soro was not simply lulling the pope into a false security.

On May 15, 1542, Soro, who was two years from the grave, was given two assistants, and from then on Venice had three cipher secretaries. Their office was in the Doge's Palace above the Sala di Segret, and here they worked behind barred doors. When cipher dispatches of foreign powers fell into the hands of the Venetians, their translation was ordered at once. No one was allowed to disturb the cryptanalysts and, reportedly, they were not permitted to leave their office until the solution was obtained. It then had to be delivered without delay to the signory. The cryptologists' usual salary was ten (later twelve) ducats a month, paid semiannually. The art was taught in a kind of school, which even held examinations each September. The cryptologists also wrote treatises explaining their techniques. That by Soro, written in the early 1500s on the solution of Latin, Italian, Spanish, and French ciphers, is another Lost Book of cryptology, for though he turned it over to the Council of Ten on March 29, 1539, no trace of it can be found in the archives. Fragmentary notes written by his successor, Giovanni Battista de Ludovicis, survive, and so do careful thorough surveys of the field by other cipher secretaries, Girolamo Franceschi, Giovanni Francesco Marin, and Agostino Amadi, whose manual is especially fine and whose work was so outstanding that Venice rewarded him by giving his two sons pensions of ten ducats a month for life. The Council of Ten held contests in ciphers, and advances in the art were rewarded: a Marco Rafael, later a favorite of Henry VIII of England, received 100 ducats in 1525 for a new method of invisible writing. If the cipher secretaries made valuable suggestions, they would get a raise. On the other hand, if they betrayed any of the state cryptologic secrets, they could be put to death.

The council was as alert to protect its own ciphers as it was to solve those of its rivals. It kept a number of nomenclators ready to replace compromised ones, and it did not hesitate to use them. For example, new ciphers were sent on August 31, 1547, to the Venetian envoys to Rome, England, France, Turkey, Milan, and the Holy Roman Emperor. On June 5, 1595, a returning ambassador reported that Venetian ciphers had been solved and on June 12, the council ordered a wholesale replacement of the ambassadorial nomenclators with new ones prepared by Pietro Partenio, then the most expert of the cipher secretaries. Earlier, Soro had instituted a "general cipher" (a nomenclator) to permit the ambassadors to communicate among themselves; this was in addition to the "special cipher" each ambassador held for messages to and from home.

But Venice was not the only locale of expert cryptanalysts during the Renaissance. In Florence, Pirrho Musefili, Conte della Sasseta, solved literally scores of messages during the decade from 1546 to 1557, reconstructing, among others, nomenclators used between Henry II of France and his envoy in Denmark, another between the same king and his emissary at Siena, a cipher of Cardinal di Mendoze of Naples. His expertise was so renowned that others came to him, as they had to Soro, to solve ciphers for them. A papal cryptologist, discussing contemporaries, said that to Musefili "is due first place and all honor." Among his clients were the Duke of Alba and the King of England, who sent him a cryptogram that had been found in a sole of a pair of golden shoes from France. Musefili's successor, Camillo Giusti, was reputed to be even more expert. They extended a fine tradition, since the ciphers devised by their predecessors for the ruling Medici family, particularly those of Lorenzo the Magnificent, display a lively appreciation of the methods of cryptanalysis. Further attesting to cryptology's importance is its mention in a book, *The Art of War*, by another well-known Florentine—Niccolò Machiavelli.

The cruel, sinister, and resolute dukes of Sforza, oligarchs of Milan, were also well served in their cryptology. One of their secretaries, Cicco Simonetta, wrote the world's first tract devoted entirely to cryptanalysis. In Pavia on July 4, 1474, he set down thirteen rules for solving monalphabetic substitution ciphers in which word divisions are preserved. The manuscript, on two narrow strips of paper, begins: "The first requisite is to see whether the document is in Latin or in the vernacular, and this can be determined in the following manner: See whether the words of the document in question have only five different terminations, or less, or more; if there are only five or less, you are justified in concluding that it is in the vernacular...." Nine years later, Milanese cryptology was boasting the clever trick of using two symbols to mark as nulls all the ciphertext signs between them. The greatest compliment to Milan came in a backhanded fashion from the cryptologists of Modena, who early in the 15th century provided a more elaborate nomenclator for their envoy to Milan than for any other.

Courts outside Italy had cryptanalysts as well. In France, Philibert Babou, sieur de la Bourdaisière, who held the post of first secretary of state, solved intercepted dispatches for Francis I. One observer saw Babou "ofttimes decipher, without the alphabet, it must be understood, many intercepted

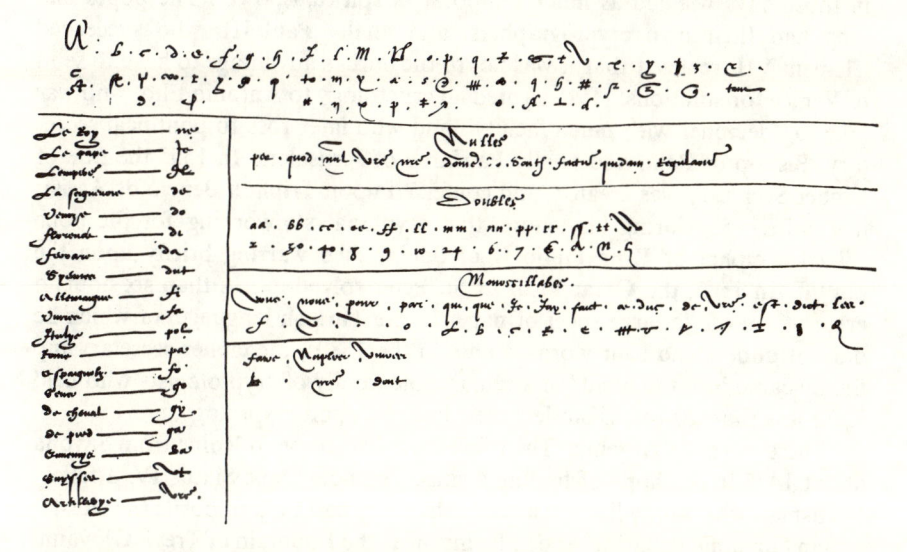

A typical early nomenclator, compiled at Florence, in 1554, during the reign of Cosimo de' Medici

dispatches, in Spanish, Italian, German, although he did not understand any of it, or very little,* with patience to work at it three weeks continually day and night, before getting a single word out of it: that first breach made, all the rest came very soon after, quite like in a demolition of walls." While Babou was thus slaving for the king, it might be noted, the king was enthusiastically taking Babou's pretty wife as his mistress. Babou received many

---

* It is quite possible to solve a cryptogram in a language that one "does not know," provided that "not knowing" means only that one does not understand the sense of the words, which is the case here. For a solution, the cryptanalyst must have only a general idea of the formation and structure of the words of a language. Solutions of this kind are not at all uncommon. Obviously, the more the cryptanalyst knows about a language, the more easily he can solve cryptograms in it. If he has never seen a sentence in the language, then the solution is virtually impossible—"virtually" because the alternations of vowels and consonants common to all languages may yet afford some clues.

favors from the king, but one wonders whether they were for cryptology or cuckoldry.

England opened the letters of the Venetian ambassador to the court of Henry VIII—presumably those of other ambassadors as well—and undoubtedly solved or tried to solve their ciphers. The Venetian ambassador, however, well schooled by the excellent cryptologists of his city, paraphrased the enciphered sections of his instructions before communicating them to the English to prevent their serving as a massive crib to the key.

Among the more expert of the cryptologic experts of the Renaissance were those who labored in the service of His Holiness, the Supreme Pontiff, who in those days wielded as much temporal as spiritual power. The popes had long had their own cryptographers, and finally Paul III, who succeeded Clement VII, realized that it was not to the curia's advantage to have to send to Venice for solutions. He delegated all cryptology to Antonio Elio, who was able to "decipher with much facility" and who later rose to pontifical secretary, Bishop of Pola, and finally Patriarch of Jerusalem. In 1555 the title of Cipher Secretary was created, and conferred upon Triphon Bencio de Assisi; it was in 1557, during his tenure, that cryptanalysts working for the pope solved a cipher of King Philip II of Spain, then warring briefly upon the pontiff. In 1567, the Great Vicar of St. Peter solved in less than six hours a cryptogram on "a large sheet of paper in the Turkish language, of which he did not understand four words." Late in the 1580s, the cipher secretaryship finally came into the hands of a remarkable family of cryptologists who held it for less than 20 years, but left their impress upon cryptology.

These were the Argentis. Their forebears had come to Rome from Savona about 1475 in the hope of finding a sinecure under Pope Sixtus IV, a fellow townsman; the family lived in a house that they had built opposite the cloister of San Giacomo della Muratte in Rome, near the Fountain of Trevi. Giovanni Batista Argenti entered the papal service as a personal clerk to Antonio Elio, who taught him cryptology. Though Giovanni Batista burned to become papal secretary of ciphers, he had to give way before some nepotistic claims, and it was not until he was well into his fifties, after Sixtus V became pope, that Giovanni Batista finally got his wish. By then it was almost too late: when Pope Gregory XIV ascended the throne of St. Peter in 1590, he had to persuade Argenti to retain the office because of the irksome trips to France and Germany that it entailed. Giovanni Batista realized that he was weakening; he hastened to teach cryptology to his nephew, Matteo Argenti, and expired April 24, 1591.

Matteo, 30, succeeded to his uncle's office. Five popes renewed his appointment. He taught cryptology to his younger brother, Marcello, who was cipher secretary to a cardinal, in the evident hope of perpetuating the family in the job. But Matteo was unexpectedly relieved of his office on June 15, 1605—apparently the victim of a power play in the curia, for the pope called him in to tell him that he was not at fault and to give him a pension of

The Rise of the West

100 ducats. Matteo used his new leisure to compile a 135-page, calf-bound manual of cryptology that lists many of the nomenclators devised by his uncle and that, out of his own experience, summarizes the best in Renaissance cryptology.

The Argentis were the first to use a word as a mnemonic key to mix a cipher alphabet, a practice that became widespread. They wrote out the keyword, omitting any repeated letters, then followed it with the remaining letters of the alphabet:

```
p   i   e   t   r   o   a   b   c   d   f   g   h   l   m   n   q   s   u   z
10  11  12  13  14  15  16  17  18  19  20  21  22  23  24  25  26  27  28  29
```

Knowing that the invariable sequence of *u* after *q* in plaintext advertises the identity of both letters, the Argentis merged the two into a single unit for encipherment purposes. Noticing that the frequent doubled letters within (Italian) words were always consonants, they deleted the second of such a pair: *sigillo* would be written *sigilo*. They realized, of course, that the basic method of solving ciphers using homophones, or homophonic substitutions, is to search for partial repetitions, such as:

```
13    24    81    66    41
13    24    49    66    41
```

If these result from the similar but not identical encipherments of the same word, then 49 stands for the same letter as 81. Given sufficient text, whole sets of these equivalencies can be built up, and the cryptogram then solved by the ordinary method of letter-frequency. To impede such comparisons, the Argentis ordered nulls larded throughout the cryptogram at a rate of no less than three to eight per line.

By prohibiting word separations, punctuation and accentuation, and words in clear, they eliminated all clues stemming from these highly fertile sources. They ran all the ciphertext digits together and, to make it difficult even to determine the proper ciphertext numbers, they mixed single digits with pairs, so that a cryptanalyst dividing the text into straight pairs would get a totally false picture. They prevented confusion in deciphering by making sure that digits used as singles were excluded from those composing the pairs. Moreover, they cleverly assigned the single digits to high-frequency plaintext equivalents that would raise the single digits' frequency in the ciphertext high enough that they would not stand out by their rarity. For example, from a cipher by Matteo:

```
a   b   c   d   e   f   g   h   i   l   m   n   o   p   q   r   s   t   u   z   et  con non che  nulls
1   86  02  20  62  22  06  60  3   24  26  84  9   66  68  28  42  80  04  88  08  64  00  44   5, 7
                82                                                                           40
```

Thus *Argenti* might be enciphered 5128068285480377. They sometimes made use of polyphones—cipher symbols that have two or three plaintext meanings. These plaintext equivalents were chosen so as not to mislead the decipherer, but their mutual symbol, simultaneously reflecting two different letter personalities, would behave in a very schizoid manner, quite puzzling to the cryptanalyst.

The Argentis did not stop there, however. They fit the cipher to the occasion. If a cipher were to be used to encipher Italian, it would not waste cipher equivalents on plaintext *k*, *w*, and *y*, which Italian does not use. But ambassadors in Germany and Poland got alphabets with *k* and *w*, and those in Spain had *y* in their ciphers. Matteo remarked in a note that few dangers existed for the papal ciphers in Poland, Sweden, and Switzerland, and that the Germans knew so little of cryptology that they preferred to burn intercepted cryptograms instead of trying to solve them. Consequently he recommended—and used—only simple systems in those countries. But Matteo exercised great prudence in constructing ciphers intended for use in France, England, Venice, and Florence—states for whose cryptology he professed great admiration.

Cryptology was used quite as widely as Matteo Argenti's comments indicate. The carefully guarded sheets of folio-sized paper on which the nomenclators were neatly engrossed were as much an instrument of war as the arquebus and, like any other weapon, they followed their flags to all parts of the world, multiplying in direct proportion to conquests. Nowhere is this more evident than with Spain. Her ascent to power can be traced in the proliferation of her ciphers, and these project an interesting image of the cryptology of the day, as practiced by the richest and mightiest nation in Europe.

Knowledge of cryptology had filtered into Iberia at just about the time that Ferdinand and Isabella expelled the Moors and set their unified country on the road to world supremacy. The first systems, introduced in 1480 by councilor Miguel Perez Alzamán, transformed plaintext into Roman numerals. These proved so clumsy that many decipherments bear such marginal notes as "Nonsense," "Impossible," "Cannot be understood," and "Order the ambassador to send another dispatch." It may have been in one of these systems that Christopher Columbus in the New World in 1498 reportedly wrote to his brother to fight off a governor sent from Spain—a cipher letter that was used as a reason for the governor's sending Columbus back to Spain in chains. After Isabella died in 1504, simpler systems were instituted for the increasing number of Spanish envoys. Nothing much was done thereafter until the shrewd, morose, arrogant, and fanatic Philip II ascended the throne of Spain. On May 24, 1556, four months after he became king and three days after his 29th birthday, Philip, who personally supervised the minutest details of his administration, wrote his uncle, the Holy Roman Emperor Ferdinand I, king of Hungary, that he had decided to change the ciphers used during the reign of his father, Charles V, because they had fallen into disuse or had been compromised. He asked his uncle to use a new cipher that he was sending him together with a list of persons who held the key.

The Rise of the West

Philip's first cipher, the new general cipher of 1556, was one of the best nomenclators of the day. It comprised a table of homophonic letter substitutions (two symbols for consonants, three for vowels), a list of equivalents for common digraphs and trigraphs (each digraph was represented by both a symbol and a two-digit number), a small code in which words and titles were represented by two- and three-letter groups, and a provision that symbols with a single dot above them were nulls and that those with two dots above them represented a doubled letter. It set the pattern for Spanish cryptography well into the 17th century, though the separate sections of the nomenclator tended to coalesce, the symbols to give way to numbers, and the code section to enlarge until repertories of 1,000 elements were not uncommon. Not every

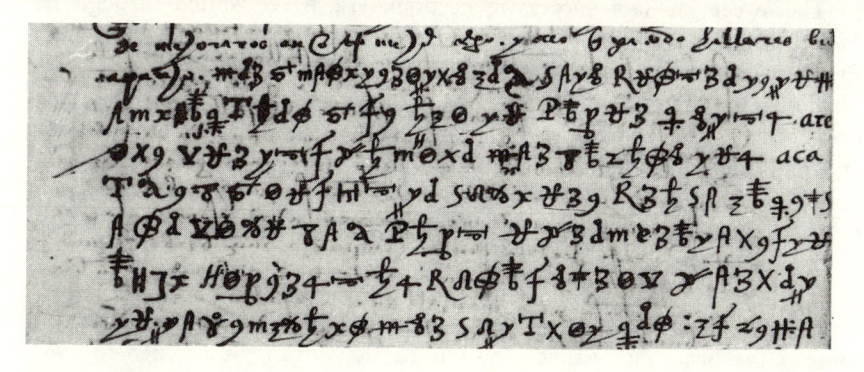

The earliest New World cryptogram extant: a cipher message of Hernán Cortés, June 25, 1532

nomenclator was as complicated, for Philip, like Soro, divided his systems into two classes: the *cifra general*, used for intercommunication among ambassadors in many countries and with the king; and the *cifra particular*, used by Philip with an individual envoy. Ciphers were changed every three or four years: the *cifra general* of 1614 was replaced in 1618, for example, and the *cifra particular* of 1604 with the ministers in Italy indicated on its face that it was to serve only from 1605 to 1609. Numerous separate nomenclators were compiled for correspondence with the viceroys and governors of the new colonies in the Americas. They hid their reports of impending shipments of gold beneath ciphers to foil pirates who might capture a galleon and its dispatches. This practice began as early as the conquistadores. The oldest instance extant of New World cryptography is a letter from Hernán Cortés, dated June 25, 1532, from the Mexico he had recently subdued. Cortés used a small nomenclator, comprising a homophonic monalphabetic substitution in which each letter was represented by two or three symbols, together with a few codewords for proper names.

Spain administered its cryptography in the Despacho Universal, the nerve center of the government, from which couriers departed at all hours of the day and night for all parts of the world. When the capital was moved to Madrid in 1561, the Despacho was installed in the Alcázar with Foreign Secretary Gonzalo Perez in charge.

Decipherment in the intrigue-filled court of Spain did not rest solely on a mere mechanical operation of cryptographic rules. If an ambassador requested the payment of his salary or solicited a bishopric, and the deciphering secretary was not his friend, the passage might remain undeciphered. Philip himself ordered the deciphering secretaries to suppress passages that he did not want his council to know about. On top of these sins of omission were piled those of commission, sometimes so serious that in at least one instance the codeword for *king of England* was confounded with that for *king of France*!

The sweet smell of success in cryptanalysis never wafted through the Moorish chambers of the Alcázar. But Philip's archfoes—Protestant England, France with its Huguenot king, and the rebellious Spanish provinces of the Netherlands—did not blind themselves to this providential source of information. Their cryptanalytic abilities had a pope and most of Europe snickering at Philip, played no small role in foiling his grandiose plans for the conquest and conversion of England, and helped ultimately to execute a sentence of death on that most romantic and captivating of royal ladies, Philip's intended sister-in-law, Mary, Queen of Scots.

In 1589, Henry of Navarre, who was destined to become the most popular king in the history of France (he coined the slogan "A chicken in every peasant's pot every Sunday"), ascended to the throne as Henry IV and found himself embroiled still more fiercely in his bitter contest with the Holy League, a Catholic faction that refused to concede that a Protestant could wear the crown. The League, headed by the Duke of Mayenne, held Paris and all the other large cities of France, and was receiving large transfusions of men and money from Philip of Spain. Henry was tightly hemmed in, and it was at this juncture that some correspondence between Philip and two of his liaison officers, Commander Juan de Moreo and Ambassador Manosse, fell into Henry's hands.

It was in cipher, but he had in his government at the time one François Viète, the seigneur de la Bigotière, a 49-year-old lawyer from Poitou who had risen to become counselor of the parlement, or court of justice, of Tours and a privy counselor to Henry. Viète had for years amused himself with mathematics as a hobby—"Never was a man more born for mathematics," said Tallement des Réaux. As the man who first used letters for quantities in algebra, giving that study its characteristic look, Viète is today remembered as the Father of Algebra. A year before, he had solved a Spanish dispatch addressed to Alessandro Farnese, the Duke of Parma, who headed the Spanish forces of the League. Henry turned the new intercepts over to him to see if Viète could repeat his success.

He could and did. The plaintext of the long letter from Moreo, in particular, was filled with intimate details of the negotiations with Mayenne: "... Your Majesty having 66,000 men in those states [the Netherlands], it would be nothing to allot 6,000 to so pressing a need. Should your refusal become known, all will be lost.... I said nothing about that to the Duke of Parma.... The Duke of Mayenne stated to me that it was his wish to become king; I could not hold back my surprise...." The message was couched in a new nomenclator that Philip had specially given Moreo when he departed for France; it consisted of the usual alphabet with homophonic substitutions, plus a code list of 413 terms represented by groups of two or three letters (LO = *Spain*; PUL = *Navarre*; POM = *King of Spain*) or of two numbers, either underlined (64 = *confederation*) or dotted (9̇4̇ = *Your Majesty*). A line above a two-digit group indicated a null.

Moreo's letter had been dated October 28, 1589, and despite Viète's experience and the quantity of text, it was not until March 15 of the following year that Viète was able to send Henry the completed solution, though he had previously submitted bits and pieces. What Viète did not know was that, 110 miles from Tours, Henry had defeated Mayenne's superior force at Ivry west of Paris the day before, making the solution somewhat academic.

Any chagrin that Viète felt did not deter him from extending his cryptanalytic successes. As he wrote to Henry in the letter forwarding the Moreo solution: "And do not get anxious that this will be an occasion for your enemies to change their ciphers and to remain more covert. They have changed and rechanged them, and nevertheless have been and always will be discovered in their tricks." It was an accurate prediction, for Viète continued to read the enciphered messages of Spain and of other principalities as well. But his pride led him straight into a trap in which a shrewd diplomat drew confidential information from him as deftly as he elicited the secret meaning from elegant and mysterious symbols. Giovanni Mocenigo, the Venetian ambassador to France, said that he was talking one day with Viète at Tours:

> He [Viète] had just told me that a great number of letters in cipher of the king of Spain as well as of the [Holy Roman] Emperor and of other princes had been intercepted, which he had deciphered and interpreted. And as I showed a great deal of astonishment, he said to me:
> "I will give your government effective proofs of it."
> He immediately brought me a thick packet of letters from the said princes which he had deciphered, and added:
> "I want you also to know that I know and translate your cipher."
> "I will not believe it," I said, "unless I see it."
> And as I had three kinds of cipher—an ordinary which I used, a different one which I did not use, and a third, called dalle Caselle—he showed me that he knew the first. Then, to better probe so grave an affair, I said to him,
> "You undoubtedly know our dalle Caselle cipher?"
> "For that, you have to skip a lot," he replied, meaning that he only knew

portions of it. I asked him to let me see some of our deciphered letters, and he promised to let me, but since then he has not spoken further about it to me, and, having left, I have not seen him any more.

Mocenigo was reporting to the Council of Ten, and it was after hearing his remarks that they so promptly replaced their existing keys.

Meanwhile, Philip had learned, from his own interceptions of French letters, that Viète had broken a cipher that the Spanish—who apparently knew little about cryptanalysis—had thought unbreakable. It irritated him, and, thinking that he would cause trouble for the French at no cost to himself, told the pope that Henry could have read his ciphers only by black magic. But the tactic boomeranged. The pope, cognizant of the ability of his own cryptologist, Giovanni Batista Argenti, and perhaps even aware that papal cryptanalysts had themselves solved one of Philip's ciphers 30 years before, did nothing about the Spaniard's complaint; all Philip got for his effort was the ridicule and derision of everyone who heard about it.

One of those who must have been laughing the hardest was probably a 50-year-old Flemish nobleman who had himself just completed solving a cipher of Spain. This was Philip van Marnix, Baron de Sainte-Aldegonde, right-hand man of William of Orange, who led the united Dutch and Flemish revolt against Spain. Marnix, an intimate of John Calvin and composer of what is today the Dutch national anthem, was also a brilliant cryptanalyst. An adversary described him as "noble, wise, gracious, sagacious, eloquent, experienced and with a very acute understanding, knowing the finer points of dealing with people. He is learned in Greek, Hebrew, Latin; he understands and writes the Spanish, Italian, German, French, Flemish, English, Scottish, and other languages very easily—better than any other man of this country. He is about 40 years old, of medium height, of dark complexion, but ugly of face. He is the greatest and most constant anti-Catholic in the world, more than even Calvin himself."

The Spanish cipher message that Marnix solved had been intercepted by Henry IV during his siege of Paris. The writer was, as with Viète's solution, the luckless Juan de Moreo; the addressee was, as before, King Philip. Marnix had joined Henry at the siege; his reputation had apparently preceded him, for the French king himself turned over the three-and-a-half page cryptogram to his Protestant ally. Marnix's solution revealed some of the jealous Moreo's vituperations against the Duke of Parma (who served also as the Spanish governor of the Low Countries), accusing him in venomous terms of subverting Philip's programs there. Henry had Marnix send both the decryptment and the substantiating ciphertext to the duke in August of 1590, in the faint hope of stirring up some discord; the duke, who knew of Moreo's calumnies and considered them beneath his contempt, found Marnix's solution of sufficient interest to preserve it, but took none of the hoped-for actions.

It was not the first time that Marnix had solved Spanish ciphers. Thirteen

The Rise of the West

years before he had done it, and his demonstration of the value of cryptanalysis set in motion a train of events that culminated on a headsman's block.

In 1577, Philip was ruling the Netherlands through his half brother, Don Juan of Austria, its governor. The ambitions of Don Juan, then the first warrior of Christendom by virtue of his crushing defeat of the Turks at Lepanto, were not to be circumscribed by those constricted borders. He dreamed of crossing the Channel into England with a body of troops, dethroning Elizabeth, then marrying the seductive Mary, Queen of Scots, and sharing a Catholic crown of England with her. Philip consented to the invasion and the marriage, both to be begun as soon as Juan had restored peace in the Netherlands.

But England did not sleep. Sir Francis Walsingham, Elizabeth's satanic-looking minister, had built up an efficient organization for secret intelligence that reportedly had 53 agents in its pay on the Continent at one time. Walsingham first got wind that something was afoot when he heard of the marriage proposal. But his suspicions remained unconfirmed until the Huguenot general François de la Noue intercepted some of Don Juan's enciphered letters in Gascony near the end of June, 1577. Since they presumably dealt with affairs in the Low Countries, they were sent to authorities there.

Somehow they reached Marnix. Within a month he had broken the cipher. It was a typical Spanish nomenclator of the period, with a total vocabulary of about 200 words, the usual syllabary, and an alphabet. A peculiarity was that each plaintext vowel was given, in addition to its one literal and two numerical substitutes, a swash symbol as a substitute. Then, if a consonant preceded a vowel, this flourish was joined to the consonant's ciphertext number to form a single combined character representing the two letters.

The solutions seem to have all but disclosed Juan's plan of landing his Spanish veterans in England under the guise of seeking refuge from storms that had blown him off course. William of Orange revealed the contents to Daniel Rogers, one of Walsingham's agents, at a dinner at Alkmaar on July 11, in an attempt to persuade Elizabeth to come to his aid. Wrote Rogers in his report to Walsingham:

> The Prince [William] told me this that her Majesty might perceive how this negotiation of Don John and the Pope's Nuncio agreed with the letters written by Don John and Escovedo [Juan's secretary] in April last, and now intercepted. With that he called for M. de Sainte-"Allagunde," whom he would have to bring the letters with him. ... Sainte-Aldegonde brought nine letters, written all in Spanish, the most part of every one in cipher, excepting one. Three of these were written by Don John, two of them to the King [of Spain], the third to the King's Secretary, Antonio Perez. The rest were all written by Escovedo to the King; it appeared by the seals and signatures they were no forged letters. The Prince also showed me the letter of La Noue, in which were enclosed all the said letters, as he had intercepted them in France. I thought good to pick out of them notes of the chief things contained in them.

120   THE CODEBREAKERS

This report gave England tangible evidence of Philip's aggressive intentions and perhaps provoked an increased watchfulness that served England in good stead when Philip finally did mount his invasion attempt in the Grand

Philip van Marnix's solution of a nomenclator used by Don Juan de Austria, in 1577

Armada eleven years later. Juan's plot came to naught because he failed to negotiate peace with the rebels, which he needed before he could begin with England. But Walsingham, having learned of Marnix's rare talent, induced the nobleman to solve messages for him. On March 20, 1578, he wrote to William Davison, an English agent in Flanders: "It is very important to her Majesty's service to have this letter of the ambassador of Portugal deciphered with speed. Please therefore deal earnestly and speedily with St. Alagondye in that behalf. The cipher is so easy that it requires no great trouble."

For once the sanguine expectations of a superior concerning the lack of difficulty of an assigned task proved correct. On April 5, Davison replied: "Sainte-Aldegonde is this day gone toward Worms. . . . His leisure before going did not suffice to decipher the letters you sent me with your last, but he procured me another to perform it. I send it herewith. . . ." The lengthy letter revealed the ambassador complaining to his king about how Elizabeth feigned illness to avoid an audience he was seeking.

Walsingham must have been dazzled by possibilities he never suspected when he first received Marnix's solutions, for he took steps to assure himself of the rich flow of information provided by cryptanalysis without having to depend on foreign experts. Later that very year he had a bright young man in Paris devouring enciphered messages. This was Thomas Phelippes, England's first great cryptanalyst.

Phelippes was the son of London's collector of customs, a not inconsequential post to which he himself later succeeded. He traveled widely in France, probably as a roving representative for Walsingham. On his return, he became one of the minister's most confidential assistants. He was an indefatigable worker, corresponding tirelessly in his calligraphic hand with Walsingham's numerous agents. His letters show a fair acquaintance with literary allusions and classical quotations, and he appears to have been able to solve ciphers in Latin, French, and Italian and, less proficiently, in Spanish. The only known physical description of him comes from the pen of Mary of Scots herself, who describes Phelippes, whose hair and beard were blond, as "of low stature, slender every way, eated in the face with small pocks, of short sight, thirty years of age by appearance."

Mary's unflattering comments betrayed her suspicions about Phelippes— suspicions that were well founded. For Phelippes and his master, Walsingham, were casting a jaundiced eye on Mary for reasons that, in their turn, were equally well founded. Mary was the heir apparent to the throne of England. She was also nominally queen of Scotland, though she had been ejected in a tangled series of events and had been prevented from returning by the opposition of the strong Protestant party there to her indiscretions. She was a remarkable woman: beautiful, possessed of great personal charm, commanding the loyalty of her subordinates, courageous, unshakably devoted to her religion, but also unwise, stubborn, and capricious. Various Catholic factions had schemed more than once to seat her on the throne of England and so restore the realm to the Church. The chief result had been to confine Mary to various castles in England and to alert Walsingham to seek an opportunity to extirpate once and for all this cancer that threatened to destroy his own queen, Elizabeth.

The opportunity arose in 1586. A former page of Mary's, Anthony Babington, began organizing a plot to have courtiers assassinate Elizabeth, incite a general Catholic uprising in England, and crown Mary. A conspiracy that involved the overthrow of the government naturally had ramifications all over the country, and Babington also gained the support of Philip II, who promised to send an expedition to help, once Elizabeth was safely dead. But the plan depended ultimately on the acquiescence of Mary, and to obtain this Babington had to communicate with her.

This was no easy task. Mary was then being held incommunicado under house arrest at the country estate of Chartley. But a handsome former seminarian named Gilbert Gifford, recruited by Babington as a messenger, discovered a way of smuggling Mary's letters into Chartley in a beer keg. It worked so well that the French ambassador gave Gifford all the correspondence that had been accumulating for Mary for the past two years.

Much of it was enciphered. But this was only part of the care that Mary took to ensure the security of her communications. She insisted that important letters be written within her suite and read to her before they were enciphered. Dispatches had to be sealed in her presence. The actual encipherment was usually performed by Gilbert Curll, her trusted secretary, less often by Jacques Nau, another secretary. Mary not infrequently ordered changes in her nomenclators, which were much smaller and flimsier than the diplomatic ones.

What neither Mary nor Babington knew was that, despite their elaborate precautions, their correspondence was being delivered to Walsingham and Phelippes as quickly as they wrote it. Gilbert Gifford was a double-agent, a ne'er-do-well who had offered his services to Walsingham. Walsingham, seeing an unparalleled opportunity to insinuate his antennae into Mary's circles, employed Gifford to turn over to him all Mary's letters, which he copied and then passed on. It included the two-year backlog entrusted to Gifford by the French ambassador, and the rapidly growing volume of traffic generated by Babington's festering plot. These enciphered missives were being solved by Phelippes almost as quickly as he got his hands on them. As the conspiracy reached a crescendo of preparation in the middle of July, he was sometimes reading two or more in a day: two letters from the queen bear notations "decifred 18 July 1586," two others are marked as deciphered July 21, and there are still other cipher letters in the same packet in the records that bear no notations.

During these three months, Walsingham cannily made no arrests, but simply let the plot develop and the correspondence accumulate in the hope that Mary would incriminate herself. His expectations were fulfilled. Early in July, Babington specified the details of the plan in a letter to Mary, referring to the Spanish invasion, her own deliverance, and "the dispatch of the

The Rise of the West 123

usurping competitor." Mary considered her reply for a week and, after composing it carefully, had Curll encipher it; she sent it off to Babington on July 17. It was to prove fatal, for in it Mary acknowledged "this enterprise" and advised Babington of ways "to bring it to good success." Phelippes, on solving it, immediately endorsed it with the gallows mark.

But Walsingham still lacked the names of the six young courtiers who were to commit the actual assassination. So when the letter reached Babington, it bore a postscript that was not on it when it left Mary's hands; in it Babington was asked for "the names and qualities of the six gentlemen which are to accomplish the designment." Both the forgery and the encipherment in the correct key seem to be the work of Phelippes.

It proved unnecessary. Babington needed to go abroad to organize the invasion; at Walsingham's suggestion, there was a mix-up in the passports. Babington, suspecting nothing, boldly came to the minister for help in cutting

Enciphered postscript to letter of Mary, Queen of Scots, forged by Thomas Phelippes

the red tape. While he was dining at the nearby tavern with one of Walsingham's men, a note came, calling for his arrest. He caught a glimpse of it and, saying he was going to pay the bar bill and leaving his cloak and sword on the back of his chair, he slipped out and escaped. The hue and cry set up by his pursuers panicked the six young men. They fled for their lives, but within a month both they and Babington were caught and condemned to death after a two-day trial. Before they were executed, the authorities prudently extracted from Babington the cipher alphabets he had used with Mary.

These, and Mary's letters, served as thoroughly incriminatory evidence in the Star Chamber proceedings that convicted her of high treason. Mary received the announcement that Elizabeth had signed her death warrant with majestic tranquillity, and at eight on the morning of February 8, 1587, after eloquently reiterating her innocence and praying aloud for her church, for Elizabeth, for her son, and for all her enemies, mounted the platform with solemn dignity, knelt, and received the axeman's three strokes with the courage that had marked every other action of her life. Thus did Mary,

Queen of Scots, exit this transient life and enter the more enduring one of legend, as her motto had prophesied: "In my end is my beginning." There seems little doubt that she would have died before her time, the politics of the day being what they were. But there seems equally little doubt that cryptology hastened her unnatural end.

4
ON THE ORIGIN OF A SPECIES

"DATO and I were strolling in the Supreme Pontiff's gardens at the Vatican and we got to talking about literature as we so often do, and we found ourselves greatly admiring the German inventor who today can take up to three original works of an author and, by means of movable type characters, can within 100 days turn out more than 200 copies. In a single contact of his press he can reproduce a copy of an entire page of a large manuscript. And so we went from topic to topic marveling at the ingenuity that men showed in various enterprises, till Dato gave expression to his warm admiration for those men who can exploit what are called 'ciphers.' "

So wrote Leon Battista Alberti near the beginning of the succinct but suggestive work that earned him the title of Father of Western Cryptology. Alberti was the first of a group of writers who, element by element, developed a type of cipher to which most of today's systems of cryptography belong. The species is polyalphabetic substitution.

As the name implies, it involves two or more cipher alphabets. Because the different alphabets use the same symbols (usually letters) for ciphertext, a given symbol can represent different plaintext letters, depending on which alphabet is being used. This naturally will confuse the cryptanalyst, which of course is the point. But it could also confuse the cryptographer, unless he knew which alphabet was then in use, and this knowledge implies some kind of rotation or rule for bringing the alphabets into play. All this differs from the simple use of homophones or their much rarer opposites, polyphones. A given homophone always represents the same plaintext letter, and a given polyphone always represents the same choice of plaintext letters, usually two or three at the most. Their relation to their plaintext elements remains fixed. In polyalphabetic substitution the relationship is variable. It thus marked a great stride forward in cryptology, though it did not supplant the nomenclator in political cryptography for more than 400 years. In the 20th century, the ways of varying the plain-to-cipher relationship reached such proportions of complexity as to afford cryptographers guarantees of extraordinary security.

It was the amateurs of cryptology who created the species. The professionals, who almost certainly surpassed them in cryptanalytic expertise, concentrated on the down-to-earth problems of the systems that were then in use but are now outdated. The amateurs, unfettered to these realities, soared into the empyrean of theory. There were four whose thought took wings: a famous architect, an intellectual cleric, an ecclesiastical courtier, and a natural scientist.

The architect was Alberti, a man who, perhaps better than anyone except Leonardo da Vinci, epitomizes the Renaissance ideal of the universal man. Born in 1404, the illegitimate but favored son of a family of rich Florentine merchants, Alberti enjoyed extraordinary intellectual and athletic aptitudes. His family cultivated these with lavish care, educating him in the law at the University of Bologna and sending him on a grand tour of Europe in his mid-twenties. A severe illness that caused a partial loss of memory interrupted a career which might have led to a bishopric, and Alberti turned his attention from law to arts and sciences. As an architect, he completed the Pitti Palace, erected the first Fountain of Trevi in Rome (since replaced in a renovation), and constructed, among many other buildings, the church of Sant'Andrea at Mantua, which served as the model for many Renaissance churches, and the temple of Malatesta at Rimini.

His talent was universal. He painted, composed music, and was regarded as one of the best organists of his day. He was given one of the leading roles in an imaginary philosophical dialogue. Writings poured from his pen: poems, fables, comedies, a treatise on the fly, a funeral oration for his dog, a misogynistic essay on cosmetics and coquetry, the first scientific investigation of perspective, books on morality, law, philosophy, family life, sculpture, and painting. His *De Re Aedificatoria*, the first printed book on architecture, written while Gothic churches were still being built, helped shape the thoughts of those who built such utterly non-Gothic structures as St. Peter's Basilica in Rome. It stands as "the theoretical cornerstone of the architecture of the Renaissance." Alberti was a superb athlete, supposedly able to fling a coin so it rang against the high vault of a cathedral and capable of riding the wildest horses. Jacob Burckhardt, author of the classic *The Civilization of the Renaissance in Italy*, singled out Alberti as one of the truly all-sided men who tower above their numerous many-sided contemporaries. And another great Renaissance scholar, John Symonds, declared that "He presents the spirit of the 15th century at its very best."

Among his friends was the pontifical secretary, Leonardo Dato, one of the learned men of his age, who during that memorable stroll in the Vatican gardens brought the conversation around to cryptology. "You've always been interested in these secrets of nature," Dato said. "What do you think of these decipherers? Have you tried your hand at it, as much as you know how to?"

Alberti smiled. He knew that Dato's duties included ciphers (it was before the curia had a separate cipher secretary). "You're the head of the papal secretariat," he teased. "Could it be that you had to use these things a few times in matters of great importance to His Holiness?"

"That's why I brought it up," Dato replied candidly. "And because of the post I have, I want to be able to do it myself without having to use outside interpreters. For when they bring me letters in cipher intercepted by spies, it's no joking matter. So please—if you've thought up any new ideas having to do with this business, tell me about them." So Alberti promised that he would do some work on it so that Dato would see that it was profitable to have asked him, and the result was the essay that he wrote in 1466 or early 1467, when he was 62 or 63.

He implied that he thought up the idea of frequency analysis all by himself, but the conception that he set forth is far too matured for that. Nevertheless, his remarkably lucid Latin essay, totaling about 25 manuscript pages, constitutes the West's oldest extant text on cryptanalysis. "First I shall consider the number of letters and the phenomena which depend on the rules of number," he wrote at the start of his analysis. "Here the vowels claim first place. ... Without a vowel there is no syllable. It follows that if you take a page of some [Latin] poet or dramatist and make separate counts of the vowels and consonants in the lines, you will be sure to find the vowels very numerous.... If all the vowels of a page were put together, to the number of, say, 300, the number of all the consonants together will be about 400. Among the vowels I have noticed that the letter *o*, while not less frequent than the consonants, occurs less often than the other vowels." He continued in this vein through a detailed description of the characteristics of Latin: "When the consonants follow a vowel at the end of the word, this final consonant will never be any except *t*, *s*, and *x*, to which *c* may be added." He touched briefly upon Italian and pointed out that if a cipher message has more than 20 different elements, nulls and homophones may be present because Latin and Italian use only 20 letters.

Only after he had explained how ciphers are solved did he proceed to ways of preventing solution—a wise procedure which is ordinarily neglected by the inventors of cipher systems. Alberti first reviewed different systems of encipherment: substitutions of various kinds, transposition of the letters within a word, placing dots above the letters of a cover text to spell out a secret message, and invisible inks. He capped his work with a cipher of his own invention that he called "worthy of kings" and, like all inventors, claimed was unbreakable. This was the cipher disk that founded polyalphabeticity. With this invention, the West, which up to this point had equaled but had never surpassed the East in cryptology, took the lead that it has never lost.

"I make two circles out of copper plates. One, the larger, is called stationary, the smaller is called movable. The diameter of the stationary plate is one-ninth greater than that of the movable plate. I divide the circumference of each circle into 24 equal parts. These parts are called cells. In the various cells of the larger circle I write the capital letters, one at a time in red, in the usual order of the letters, A first, B second, C third, and then the rest, omitting H and K [and Y] because they are not necessary." This gave him 20 letters, since J, u, and w were not in his alphabet, and in the remaining four spaces he inscribed the numbers 1 to 4 in black. (The red and black seem to signify only that Alberti liked colors.) In each of the 24 cells of the movable circle he inscribed "a small letter in black, and not in regular order like the stationary characters, but scattered at random. Thus we may suppose the first of them to be a, the second g, the third q, and so on with the rest until the 24 cells of the circle are full; for there are 24 characters in the Latin alphabet, the last being et [probably meaning "&"]. After completing these arrangements we place the smaller circle upon the larger so that a needle driven through the centers of both may serve as the axis of both and the movable plate may be revolved around it."

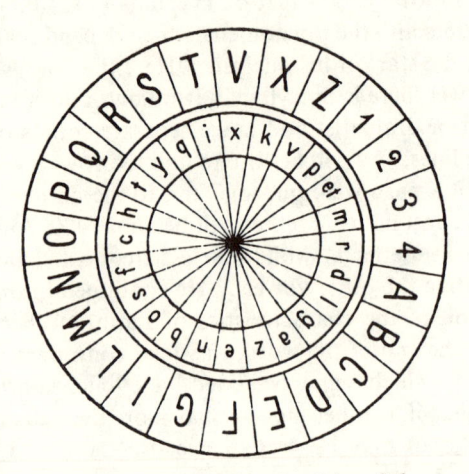

Leon Battista Alberti's cipher disk

The two correspondents—who, Alberti carefully pointed out, must each have identical disks—agree upon an index letter in the movable disk, say k. Then, to encipher, the sender places this prearranged index letter against any letter of the outer disk. He informs his correspondent of this position of the disk by writing, as the first letter of the ciphertext, this letter of the outer ring. Alberti gave the example of k being placed against B. "From this as a starting point all the other characters of the message will acquire the force and sounds of the stationary characters above them."* So far nothing remarkable had happened. But in his next sentence Alberti placed cryptography's feet on the road to its modern complexity. "After writing three or four words, I shall change the position of the index in our formula by turning the circle, so that the index k may be, say, under D. So in my message I shall write a capital D,

* In Alberti's disk, the outer capital letters are the plaintext and the inner lower-case letters are the ciphertext. This contradicts the convention of this book, and is being used in the section on Alberti only to avoid altering his text. The difference is signalized by not using italic for the lower case.

On the Origin of a Species

and from this point on [ciphertext] k will signify no longer B but D, and all the other stationary letters at the top will receive new meanings."

There is the crucial point: "new meanings." Each new position of the inner disk brings different letters opposite one another in the inner and outer rings. Consequently, each shift means that plaintext letters would be replaced with different ciphertext equivalents. For example, the plaintext word NO might be enciphered to fc at one setting and to ze at another. Equally, at each shift a given ciphertext letter would stand for a different plaintext letter than it did at the previous setting. Thus, the fc that formerly represented NO might, at the new setting, stand for plaintext TU. This shift in both plain and cipher equivalents differentiates polyalphabetic from homophonic or polyphonic substitution. In homophonic substitution, plaintext E might be represented by 89, 43, 57, and 64—but those four numbers would always and invariably refer to the same plaintext, whereas in polyalphabetic substitution cipher equivalents have different plaintext meanings. Moreover, while E in homophonic substitution is limited to that group of cipher equivalents, in polyalphabetic substitution it may be replaced by any one of the ciphertext letters. In substitution using polyphones, ciphertext 24 may stand for both plaintext R and plaintext G. But it will invariably stand for just those two letters, whereas a ciphertext symbol in polyalphabetic substitution may stand for any one of all the plaintext letters. To a cryptanalyst, the quicksilver, impermanent nature of cipher symbols in polyalphabetic substitution, which mean one thing here and another there, can be exceedingly baffling; at the same time, the collapse of his expectations of seeing a plaintext A being again represented by the ciphertext symbol that he previously extracted for it can be very frustrating.

Each new setting of Alberti's disk brought into play a new cipher alphabet, in which both the plaintext and the ciphertext equivalents are changed in regard to one another. There are as many of these alphabets as there are positions of his disk, and this multiplicity means that Alberti here devised the first polyalphabetic cipher.

This achievement—critical in the history of cryptology—Alberti then adorned by another remarkable invention: enciphered code. It was for this that he had put numbers in the outer ring. In a table he permuted the numbers 1 to 4 in two-, three-, and four-digit groups, from 11 to 4444, and used these as 336 codegroups for a small code. "In this table, according to agreement, we shall enter in the various lines at the numbers whatever complete phrases we please, for example, corresponding to 12, 'We have made ready the ships which we promised and supplied them with troops and grain.'" These code values did not change, any more than the mixed alphabet of the disk did. But the digits resulting from an encoding were then enciphered with the disk just as if they were plaintext letters. In Alberti's words, "These numbers I then insert in my message according to the formula of the cipher, representing them by the letters that denote these numbers." These numbers thus changed their ciphertext equivalents as the disk turned. Hence 341, perhaps meaning

"Pope," might become mrp at one position and fco at another. This constitutes an excellent form of enciphered code, and just how precocious Alberti was may be seen by the fact that the major powers of the earth did not begin to encipher their code messages until 400 years later, near the end of the 19th century, and even then their systems were much simpler than this.

Alberti's three remarkable firsts—the earliest Western exposition of cryptanalysis, the invention of polyalphabetic substitution, and the invention of enciphered code—make him the Father of Western Cryptology. But although his treatise was published in Italian in a collection of his works in 1568, and although his ideas were absorbed by the Argentis and so influenced the later development of cryptology, they never had the dynamic impact that such prodigious accomplishments ought to have produced. Symonds' evaluation of his work in general may both explain why and summarize the modern view of his cryptological contributions: "This man of many-sided genius came into the world too soon for the perfect exercise of his singular faculties. Whether we regard him from the point of view of art, of science, or of literature, he occupies in each department the position of precursor, pioneer, and indicator. Always original and always fertile, he prophesied of lands he was not privileged to enter, leaving the memory of dim and varied greatness rather than any solid monument behind him."

Polyalphabeticity took another step forward in 1518, with the appearance of the first printed book on cryptology, written by one of the most famous intellectuals of his day. He was born February 2, 1462, in Trittenheim, Germany, where his father, a wealthy winegrower, was known only as Johannes of Heidenberg, his former village. The father died a year later, and the son, also named Johannes, was raised first by his mother and then by a rather stern stepfather, who ridiculed the boy's passion for learning. At 17, Johannes left home and sought entry to the University of Heidelberg, where its chancellor, Johannes of Dalberg, was so impressed by the youth's brilliance that he granted him a pauper's certificate exonerating the tuition fees. Soon thereafter, Johannes of Dalberg, one Rodolphe Huesmann, and the young Johannes formed the Rhenish Literary Society, each taking, according to custom, a Latin and a Greek name. The young man chose "Trithemius," which, while having a certain consonance with the name of his native village of Trittenheim, indicated that he was the third link of the group. He has been known as Johannes Trithemius ever since.

In January, 1482, when the young Trithemius was on his way home from Heidelberg for a New Year's visit, he sought shelter during a heavy snowstorm at the impoverished, 437-year-old Benedictine abbey of Saint Martin at Spanheim, Germany. He was very much attracted by the life of the monks and soon entered the novitiate. A year and a half later, only a little while after taking his final vows, he was elected abbot—either because the monks recognized his brilliance or because they thought that he would be too young to enforce discipline. He maintained his post, however, and at 24 published a book of sermons that gave him an instant fame. He was called upon to preach before princes and religious conventions. His reputation as a savant grew with his prolific writings—several histories, a biographical dictionary of famous Germans, one of famous Benedictines, a chronicle of the dukes of Bavaria and the Counts Palatine, a life of Saint Maximum and one of an archbishop of Mainz. Learned men corresponded with him. He knew the original Dr. Faustus well enough to consider him a charlatan. Powerful rulers like the Margrave of Brandenberg and the Holy Roman Emperor Maximilian I invited him to their castles. And posterity has honored him. His most important work, the *Liber de scriptoribus ecclesiasticis*, a chronological list of about 7,000 theological works by 963 authors that was published in 1494, earned him the title of Father of Bibliography. It was conferred by Theodore Besterman, compiler of the *World Bibliography of Bibliographies*, who said that Trithemius "was not the first to compile bibliographies, but he was certainly the first bibliographically-minded scholar to do so."

These were all solid works. But Trithemius' other writings were darkened by his intense interest, not to say belief, in occult powers. (Like others of his day, he could reconcile this with his pious Christianity because the leading treatises on esoterism, thought to have been written by an Egyptian priest called Hermes Trismesgistus, had actually been compiled by Christians in the second century A.D. and so contained nothing monumentally offensive to the church.) Trithemius wrote on alchemy, classified witches into four carefully defined categories, explained the twelve angelic hierarchies ruled by emperors related to the chief winds and points of the compass. He analyzed history in terms of the 354-year cycles of the seven planetary angels, bearing names like Orifiel and Zachariel, and fixed the creation of the world at 5206 B.C. These writings made him one of the great figures of occult science, and today books on the subject venerate him as a superlative alchemist and as the mentor of two other almost legendary occultists, Paracelsus and Cornelius Agrippa.

In 1499, Trithemius, who after long pondering had finally concluded that some things were unknowable, was said to have been visited in a dream by a spirit who taught him many of these very things. These he wrote down in a volume which he intended to comprise eight books and which he called "Steganographia," from Greek words meaning "covered writing." In the first two books he described some elementary reciprocal vowel-consonant substitutions and several variations on a system in which only certain letters of nonsense words signify the meaning, the other letters being nulls. For example, in the message beginning PARMESIEL OSHURMI DELMUSON THAFLOIN PEANO CHARUSTREA MELANY LYAMUNTO . . . , the decipherer extracts every other letter of every other word, beginning with the second word since the first indicates the specific system. The Latin plaintext begins *Sum tali cautela ut* . . . . But all this may have simply served as a cover for the magical operations described in the third book, which included no cryptography at all.

Here Trithemius slipped again into the shadow world of spirits with names like Vathmiel, Choriel, and Sameron, and discussed methods that sound like telepathy. To convey a message to a desired recipient within 24 hours, for example, one needed simply to say it over an image of a planetary angel at a moment determined by complicated astrological calculations, wrap the image up with an image of the recipient, bury them under a threshold, say the proper incantations ending with "In nomine patris & filii & spiritus sancti, Amen," and the message would arrive, Trithemius assured the reader, without words, writing, or messenger. Trithemius told how to use the network of angels for thought transference and for gaining knowledge of all things happening in the world. Involved is the Kabbalah-like computation of the numerical values of the angels' names; Trithemius, like other hermeticists, regarded Moses as a kind of Jewish Hermes Trismesgistus.

He showed the "Steganographia" in its incompleted state to a visitor, who was so horrified at its barbarous names of seraphim, its obscurantism, its impossible claims, that he denounced it as sorcery. A letter which Trithemius wrote to a friend arrived after the friend had died; the prior of the abbey opened it, was likewise shocked, and passed it around. Trithemius fell under a cloud of working in magic, which the church even then frowned upon. He abandoned the book, but probably did not mind the reputation he was gaining as a wonder-worker, for Trithemius was more than a bit of the braggart and publicity hound. He had concluded his ecclesiastical bibliography with some of his own books—inserted, he said, "at the solicitation of my friends." To a visitor, he boasted that he had taught an illiterate German prince Latin in an hour, and then, before the prince departed, withdrew all his knowledge. He offered to make a thief return everything that he had stolen from the visitor if only the visitor would have faith; of course he did not have enough. Trithemius maintained that he comprehended nothing less than wisdom itself. This sort of thing naturally attracted crowds of the curious and hopeful and started the wild rumors about his magic powers that were circulating even during his life. According to one, the abbot, finding himself at an inn where supplies had run short, tapped on a window and called out in Latin, whereupon a spirit passed in to him a broiled pike and a bottle of wine.

Believing sincerely that his own practices were devoutly Christian, Trithemius did not fight the legend, except to deny that there was anything demonic or un-Christian in his practices. His reputation for esoteric knowledge grew so great, in fact, that the "Steganographia" circulated in manuscript for a hundred years, being copied by many persons eager to suck out the secrets that it was thought to hold. Parts were transcribed for Giordano Bruno, among others. It became famous, and controversy flamed about it. In 1599, for example, the Jesuit Martin Antoine Del Rio called it "full of peril and superstition." Not until 1606 was it printed, and this exacerbated the dispute. The opponents scored a great victory when, on September 7, 1609, the Roman Catholic Church placed it on its Index of Prohibited Books. It stayed there for more than 200 years, throughout numerous reprintings, the last as late as 1721. Many scholars attacked it, and others wrote whole books defending it. But the larger controversy over magic faded as the Age of Reason gained sway, and the book lost its interest.

Even during Trithemius' lifetime, however, it had caused him trouble. In 1506, while he was away on a trip, the monks at Spanheim mutinied, apparently because his reputation as a magician, due in no small measure to the "Steganographia," had brought odium to the monastery. He never returned, but obtained a transfer to the monastery of Saint Jacob in Wurzburg, where, on October 3, 1506, he was elected prior. Early in 1508, he addressed himself to a book carefully restricted to cryptology, as if to prove that that was what he meant all along. He called it the "Polygraphia" because of the multiplicity of ways of writing that it included. He perhaps began it on his 46th birthday, for he finished Book I on February 12, and he wrote each of its six books in an average of ten days. At that rate, he completed it quickly, probably by April 24, the date of its dedication to the Holy Roman Emperor Maximilian I. Like others of his writings, it was not published at once, and Trithemius turned to the composition of other texts. So he lived on quietly at Wurzburg, where he studied, wrote, corresponded, and received visitors, and where, on December 15, 1516, he died.

A year and a half later, the descendants of his old preceptor, Johannes of Dalberg, paid for the publication of the "Polygraphia," which thereby became the first printed book on cryptology. It bore the title *Polygraphiae libri sex, Ioannis Trithemii abbatis Peapolitani, quondam Spanheimensis, ad Maximilianum Caesarem* ("Six Books of Polygraphy, by Johannes Trithemius, Abbot at Wurzburg, formerly at Spanheim, for the Emperor Maximilian"). Johannes Haselberg of Aia completed its printing in July, 1518. It is a handsome small folio of 540 pages in red and black, with a woodcut title page borrowed from an earlier book by Trithemius. It ends with a "Clavis Polygraphiae" which repeats the original woodcut title page and gives a résumé of the preceding six books. It was reprinted in 1550, 1571, 1600, and 1613, and a French translation (heavily edited and modified) by Gabriel de Collanges appeared in 1561 and was reprinted in 1625. This became the subject of one of the world's most notorious plagiarisms when in 1620 a Frisian named Dominique de Hottinga published Collange's work as his own and even complained of how hard it was to do!

By far the bulk of the volume consists of the columns of words printed in large Gothic type that Trithemius used in his systems of cryptography. The first of the six books comprises 384 columns of Latin words, two columns per page, for Trithemius' best-known invention, his Ave Maria. Each word represents the plaintext letter that stands opposite it. Trithemius so selected the words that, as the equivalents for the letters are taken from consecutive tables, they will make connected sense and will appear to be an innocent prayer. Thus *abbot* would be enciphered as DEUS CLEMENTISSIMUS REGENS

POLYGRAPHIAE

LIBRI SEX, IOANNIS TRITHEMII AB
BATIS PEAPOLITANI, QVONDAM
SPANHEIMENSIS, AD MAXI
MILIANVM CAESAREM.

Cum gratia et priuilegio C. M.

·IO. TRITHEMIVS·

The woodcut title page of the first printed book on cryptology. Though taken from an earlier book by the same author, Johannes Trithemius, the illustration was apparently appropriate to this book as well. It shows the author wearing his Benedictine habit and, with his abbot's miter on the floor before him, kneeling to present his book—padlocked, as befits its secret character—to the dedicatee, the Holy Roman Emperor Maximilian I. Seated upon his throne in the imperial castle at Augsburg and wearing the imperial crown and mantle, Maximilian holds his scepter in one hand and blesses Trithemius with the other. Behind Trithemius, another person—either another monk or the publisher—extends towards Maximilian two keys to the book, these symboliz-

On the Origin of a Species

AEVUM INFINIVET. Book II lists 284 similar alphabets. Book III has 1,056 numbered lines of three artificial words per line, arranged in columns. A typical column begins HUBA, HUBE, HUBI, HUBO, and so on down to the 24th word, HUBON. These were to be used like those of the Ave Maria—but just how this was to avoid suspicion is hard to see. Book IV lists 117 columns of artificial words whose second letter varied in each column from *a* to *w* (the last letter of the alphabet Trithemius used, following *z*): BALDACH, ABZACH, ECOZACH, ADONACH, ... These served to construct a cover text in which only

a	Deus	a	clemens
b	Creator	b	clementissimus
c	Conditor	c	pius
d	Opifex	d	pijssimus
e	Dominus	e	magnus
f	Dominator	f	excelsus
g	Consolator	g	maximus
h	Arbiter	h	optimus

The first page of Johannes Trithemius' "Ave Maria" cipher

the second letters of each word would carry the secret message. Taking words from his first three alphabets in order, *bad* would become ABZACH HANASAR ADAMAI. Once again, this does not appear the height of innocence. Perhaps Trithemius just could not stay away from those incantatory words. Book VI gives supposed cipher alphabets of the Franks and Normans, as well as the first printed description of Tironian notes.

It is Book V that contains Trithemius' contributions to polyalphabeticity. Here appears, for the first time in cryptology, the square table, or tableau. This is the elemental form of polyalphabetic substitution, for it exhibits all at once all the cipher alphabets in a particular system. These are usually all the same sequence of letters, but shifted to different positions in relation to the

---

ing Maximilian's spiritual authority and temporal power. In the background Trithemius' chaplain, a young monk, holds his abbot's crozier. At bottom, Trithemius reclines with a fruit-laden branch representing the motto " Ye shall judge the tree by its fruits" and implying that Trithemius' many works make him worthy of acclaim. At upper left, arms of the Holy Roman Empire; at upper right, arms of the engraver; at lower left, arms of Trithemius (the two bass back to back symbolizing his Christianity; the shells, his religious state; the grapes, his father, a winegrower); at lower right, arms of the then Bishop of Würzburg. At sides, philosophers hold an armillary sphere, a sextant, a compass, and a square rule; others hold the banner ends.

plaintext alphabet, as in Alberti's disk the inner alphabet assumed different positions in regard to the outer alphabet. The tableau sets them out in orderly fashion—the alphabets of the successive positions laid out in rows one below the other, each alphabet shifted one place to the left of the one above. Each row thus offers a different set of cipher substitutes to the letters of the plaintext alphabet at the top. Since there can be only as many rows as there are letters in the alphabet, the tableau is square.

The simplest tableau is one that uses the normal alphabet in various positions as the cipher alphabets. Each cipher alphabet produces, in other words, a Caesar substitution. This is precisely Trithemius' tableau, which he called his "tabula recta." Its first and last few lines were:

```
a b c d e f g h i k l m n o p q r s t u x y z w
b c d e f g h i k l m n o p q r s t u x y z w a
c d e f g h i k l m n o p q r s t u x y z w a b
d e f g h i k l m n o p q r s t u x y z w a b c
e f g h i k l m n o p q r s t u x y z w a b c d
. . . . . . . . . . . . . . . . . . . . . . . .
z w a b c d e f g h i k l m n o p q r s t u x y
w a b c d e f g h i k l m n o p q r s t u x y z
```

Trithemius used this tableau for his polyalphabetic encipherment, and in the simplest manner possible. He enciphered the first letter with the first alphabet, the second with the second, and so on. (He gave no separate plaintext alphabet, but the normal alphabet at the top can serve.) Thus a plaintext beginning *Hunc caveto virum*... became HXPF GFBMCZ FUEIB.... In this particular message, he switched to another alphabet after 24 letters, but in another example he followed the more normal procedure of repeating the alphabets over and over again in groups of 24.

The great advantage of this procedure over Alberti's is that a new alphabet is brought into play with each letter. Alberti shifted alphabets only after three or four words. Thus the ciphertext would mirror the obvious pattern of repeated letters of a word like *Papa* ("Pope"), or in English, *attack*, and the cryptanalyst could seize upon this reflection to break into the cryptogram. The letter-by-letter encipherment obliterates this clue.

Trithemius' system is also the first instance of a progressive key, in which all the available cipher alphabets are exhausted before any are repeated. Modern cipher machines very often embody such key progressions. Naturally, they avoid the chief defects of Trithemius' primitive system: its paucity of alphabets and the rigid order of their use.

Trithemius' influence in cryptology was very great, owing in part to his reputation and in part to his having authored the first printed book on the subject. Letter-by-letter encipherment quickly became customary in polyalphabetic theorizing, and the tableau established itself as a standard item in cryptology. It formed the basis of innumerable ciphers, and so important did it become that some German authors attempted to enshrine their compatriot as the Father of Cryptology on this basis alone. But valuable as his contributions were, they do not justify that accolade.

If the first two steps in polyalphabeticity were made by men who were giants in their time, the third was taken by a man who was so unexceptional that he left almost no traces. This is Giovan Batista Belaso; the sum total of knowledge about him consists of the facts that he came from Brescia of a noble family, served in the suite of one Cardinal Carpi, and, in 1553, brought out a little booklet entitled *La cifra del. Sig. Giovan Batista Belaso.* In this he proposed the use of a literal, easily remembered, and easily changed key—he called it a "countersign"—for a polyalphabetic cipher. Wrote Belaso: "This countersign may consist of some words in Italian or Latin or any other language, and the words may be few or many as desired. Then we take the words we wish to write, and put them on paper, writing them not too close together. Then over each of the letters we place a letter of our countersign in this form. Suppose, for example, our countersign is the little versetto VIRTUTI OMNIA PARENT. And suppose we wish to write these words: *Larmata Turchesca partira a cinque di Luglio.* We shall put them on paper in this manner:

VIRTUTI OMNIA PARENT VIRTUTI OMNIA PARENT VI
larmata turch escapa rtiraac inque dilugl io"

The keyletter that is paired with a given plaintext letter indicates the alphabet of the tableau that is to be used to encipher that plaintext letter. Thus, *l* is to be enciphered by the V alphabet, *a* by the I alphabet, and so on. The system permits great flexibility: no longer did all messages have to be enciphered with one of a relatively few standard sequences of alphabets, but different ambassadors could be given individual keys, and, if it were feared that a key had been stolen or solved, a new one could be substituted with the greatest of ease. Keys caught on at once, and the Belaso invention laid the foundation for today's exceedingly complex arrangements, in which not one but several keys are employed and are varied at odd intervals.

Belaso, however, like Trithemius, employed standard alphabets as his cipher alphabets. It remained for a young prodigy, who later organized the first scientific society of modern times, to revive the mixed alphabets of Alberti and to wrap Alberti's notions together with those of Trithemius and Belaso into the modern concept of polyalphabetic substitution.

Giovanni Battista Porta was born in Naples in 1535, was raised by a cultured and intelligent uncle, and was composing essays in Latin and Italian by the time he was ten. After the usual grand tour, he returned to Naples and, at 22, published his first book, a study of oddities and scientific curiosa entitled *Magia naturalis.* Later, he brought together in his home in Naples a group of men similarly interested in natural magic—the study of the mysteries of nature by experimental means, as opposed to spirit magic like Trithemius'. Here they met periodically and performed experiments. This was the Accademia Secretorum Naturae, whose members called themselves the Otiosi (Men of Leisure). It was the first of all associations of scientists, and as such it began the transformation of scientific inquiry from an individual eccentricity to the organized and socially sanctioned pursuit that it now is. The Otiosi were soon suspected of dabbling in the occult, however, and Porta was called to Rome to explain reports of witches' salves and necromantic arts. He cleared himself before Pope Paul V, returning cautioned but unblemished. In fact, his "magic" was only that of a parlor conjuror—tricks cloaked in mystery but easily explained. He also served as vice president of another early scientific society, the Accademia dei Lincei (Academy of Lynxes), one of whose members was Galileo.

Between 1586 and 1609, Porta produced books on the asserted relation of human physiognomy to animal characteristics, which influenced the Italian criminologist Cesare Lombroso in defining "the criminal type," on meteorology, the refraction of light, pneumatics, the design of villas, astronomy, astrology, distillation, and the improvement of memory, as well as 14 prose comedies, two tragedies, and one tragicomedy. An expanded version of the *Magia naturalis*, in 20 books, recorded many of the experiments of the Otiosi and, as popular as the original, was translated and was reprinted no fewer than 27 times. Called the "most delightful and browsable of scientific books," it includes such oddities as ways of making merry by turning women's faces red, green, or pimply, and by using a juggler's prank of burning hare's fat to cause women to cast off all their clothes. (Not all of Porta's tricks worked.) Book XVI gave numerous recipes for secret ink and for such tricks as writing invisibly on an egg and on human skin so that "messengers may be sent, who shall neither know that they carry letters nor can they be found about them," and hiding missives in living creatures (by feeding a letter in meat to a dog, then killing him to retrieve it). Porta sometimes embroidered the truth a little in reporting the facts both of his experiments and of his life. But he was the first to recognize the heating effect of light rays and to expound an ecological grouping of plants. He died in 1615 at 80, leaving the memory of a mild-tempered and pleasant man.

Porta was only 28 when, in 1563, he published the book on which his fame as a cryptologist rests. *De Furtivis Literarum Notis* is an extraordinary book. Even today, four centuries later, it retains its freshness and charm and—remarkably—its ability to instruct. Its great quality is its perspective: Porta saw cryptology in the round. Its four books, dealing respectively with ancient ciphers, modern ciphers, cryptanalysis, and a list of linguistic peculiarities that will help in solution, encompassed the cryptologic knowledge of the time. He rehearsed the standard ciphers of his forefathers, but he did not hesitate to criticize: the venerable pig-pen, or Freemasons', or Rosicrucians' cipher, is used, he sneered, by "rustics, women and children." Among the "modern"

On the Origin of a Species 139

systems—many of which are probably Porta's own—appeared the first digraphic cipher in cryptology, in which two letters were represented by a single symbol.

He classified systems into three kinds: the changing of a letter's order (transposition), of a letter's form (substitution by symbol), and of a letter's value (substitution by a letter of another alphabet). This was one of the earliest, if crude, instances of the now standard division of ciphers into transposition

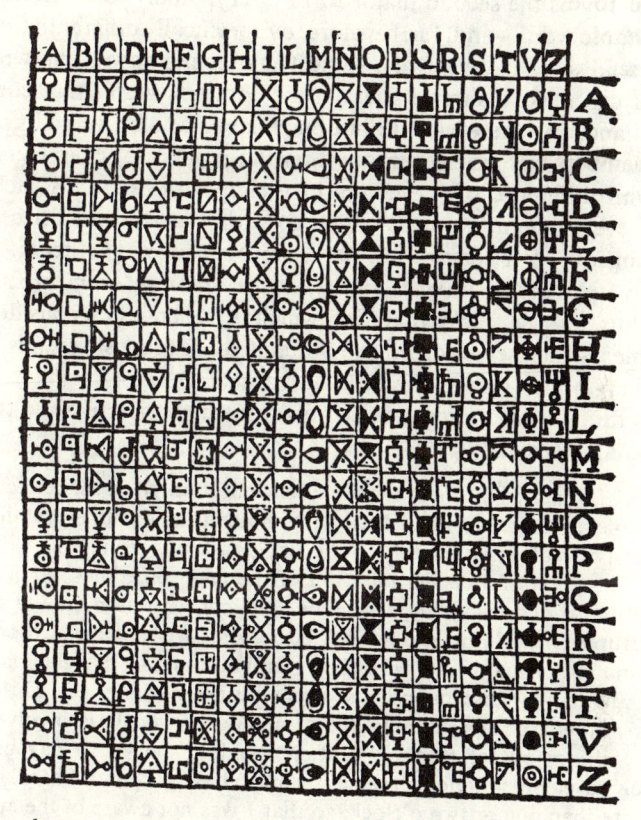

The earliest known digraphic system: Giovanni Battista Porta replaced each pair of letters with the sign at the intersection of their row and columns

and substitution. He urged the use of synonyms in plaintexts, noting that "It will also make for difficulty of interpretation if we avoid the repetition of the same word." Like the Argentis, he suggested deliberate misspellings of plaintext words: "For it is better for a scribe to be thought ignorant than to pay the penalty for the detection of plans," he wrote. The book included a set of movable rococo cipher disks, and at one point Porta explained how they may be converted to a square table. His grasping of this relationship illuminates more clearly than anything else his thorough comprehension of the subject.

He spiced his book with some eyebrow-raising sample plaintexts. Perhaps the most startling is "I deflowered the object of my affections today," used for six encipherments in a row. He gave the first published description in Europe of how to solve a monalphabetic cipher with no word divisions or with false word divisions, at a time when cryptanalysts often depended on the presence of word divisions.

Porta anticipated all other writers on the subject by describing what is regarded today as the second major form of cryptanalytical technique—that of the probable word—and, furthermore, by specifically differentiating it from linguistic analysis: "... when the subject matter is known," he wrote, "the interpreter can make a shrewd guess at the common words that concern the matter in hand, and these can without much labor be discovered by observing for each word in the passages in question the number of characters and the likeness and difference of the letters in their positions.... In each subject there are several common words which go with it as it were of necessity; for example, in love, *love, heart, fire, flame, to be burned, life, death, pity,* and *cruelty* have place, and in war, *soldier, leader, general, camp, arms, to fight,* etc.... Thus, a form of interpretation which is not based on consideration of the documents themselves or on the attempt to distinguish vowels and consonants therein may lighten the task."

He proffered some sapient advice on work techniques, as valid today as it was in Renaissance Italy:

> There is required the most complete concentration, the most perfect diligence, so that the mind, free from all distracting thoughts, and with everything else put aside, may devote itself entirely to the single task of carrying the whole undertaking to a successful conclusion. Still, if the task sometimes requires unusual concentration and expenditure of time, this concentration should not go on uninterrupted; the brain should not be racked over-anxiously. For excessive pains and prolonged mental effort bring on brain-fag, so that the mind is afterwards less fit for these things, and accomplishes nothing.... This has often been my experience at such times as I came upon particularly involved ciphers, in the working-out of these. For after spending the whole day in this task (scarcely seven or eight hours seemed to me to have gone by), I hardly thought it was more than one or two o'clock, so that I was not aware of the approach of evening except through the shadows and the failing of the light.

Finally, Porta unconsciously revealed some practical experience in one sentence: "It will be found of no small importance besides for the message to have been written by the hand of the author, or a skilled scribe, for if, after it has been intercepted, it be copied wrong, or if it have started off from the hands of someone who was ignorant of the art of cipher, it will readily result that, since the writing is confused, every way of interpreting it will be blocked." Knowledge like that comes only from wrestling with the dropped or transposed or altered letters that appear so regularly in the transmission of real cryptograms, since the problems one finds in books are invariably letter-

One of Giovanni Battista Porta's cipher disks

perfect and highly susceptible to solution. It may be that he did some cryptanalysis for the papal curia.

But what of Porta's contribution to polyalphabeticity? It consists essentially of a lamination of existing elements—the letter-by-letter encipherment of Trithemius, the easily changed key of Belaso, and the mixed alphabet of Alberti—into a modern system of polyalphabetic substitution. Unfortunately for Porta, though he specifically stated that "The order [of the letters in the tableau] . . . may be arranged arbitrarily, provided no letter is omitted," he illustrated the system only with standard alphabets, and a lazy posterity, while naming this trivial system for him, cheated him of full recognition of his contribution. He wisely used a long key—CASTUM FODERAT LUCRETIA PECTUS ALGAZEL—and advised the choice of "irrelevant words" for keys, because "The further removed they are from common knowledge, the greater safety do they afford to the writing." No great originality may be claimed for Porta's contribution to polyalphabeticity, but it remains the first time that the modern concept of polyalphabeticity was enunciated.

Perhaps the full measure of Porta's remarkable abilities may best be taken by his brash tackling of the toughest problem of Renaissance cryptology —the solution of polyalphabetic ciphers. Despite the high esteem in which these ciphers were then universally held, Porta refused to admit their invincibility and thought out some methods of attack. These are rather artificial, but their importance lies not in their intrinsic value, which is low, but in the bold attitude that engendered them—the only attitude that leads to any success in cryptanalysis.

In his first solution, Porta mounted an assault on a progressive-alphabet cipher with mixed alphabets. It was produced by a cipher disk with a normal plaintext alphabet clockwise on the fixed portion and a series of fantastic cipher signs on the mobile portion, which turned one space clockwise after the encipherment of each letter. Porta observed that if three letters appear in alphabetical sequence in a plaintext word (as *def* in *deficio* or *stu* in *studium*) the one-space progression of the disk would bring the same cipher sign successively opposite each of them, resulting in a threefold repetition of that sign in the ciphertext. Using this as a basis, Porta solved a contrived cryptogram and reconstructed the symbol alphabet. In his second solution, given in a chapter added in the 1602 edition of *De Furtivis*, Porta modified his first method to solve another trick polyalphabetic cryptogram that had standard alphabets but that used a literal key. Here, a threefold repetition of a ciphertext letter signaled that a key with three letters in normal alphabetical order had enciphered a plaintext that had three letters in reverse alphabetical order. During his discussion, he came within a hair's breadth of achieving the true general solution he sought: "Since there are . . . 51 letters between the first three MMM and the same three letters repeated in the thirteenth word, I conclude that the key has been given three times and decide correctly that it consists of 17 letters." He never capitalized on this observation. Had he done so, he would have kept the polyalphabetic cipher from ever gaining the exaggerated reputation for security that glowed like a protective aura around it for 300 years.

De Furtivis, like Porta's other books, went through several editions and, in 1591, it received the ultimate accolade: it was pirated by an unscrupulous printer of London, John Wolfe, who counterfeited the original 1563 edition almost to perfection. A legitimate 1593 edition, published under the title of *De Occultis Literarum Notis*, included at the rear cryptology's first set of synoptic tables. These showed in graphic form the path the cryptanalyst must follow in his analysis of a given cryptogram, with the forks he must take if the message shows one characteristic as opposed to another. Porta's overall rank in the cryptology of his day was well stated by Dr. Charles J. Mendelsohn, who has delved more deeply into this period than any other scholar: "He was, in my opinion, the outstanding cryptographer of the Renaissance. Some unknown who worked in a hidden room behind closed doors may possibly have surpassed him in general grasp of the subject, but among those whose work can be studied he towers like a giant."

Though Porta had molded together the three basic elements that are essential to a modern concept of polyalphabeticity, refinements were always possible, and two other men of the 16th century devised improvements upon Belaso's key procedure.

It is clear that a key that changes with each message provides more security than one that is used over and over for several messages. The ultimate, of course, is a key that changes with each message. The two men devised an exceedingly clever way to ensure this change: use the message itself as its own key. This is called an "autokey." The first system was flawed and consequently unusable; the inventor is remembered chiefly for a contribution to steganography. The second worked perfectly. But though it afforded guarantees of security far above those of simple keywords, and though the author described it with clarity, and though his book is one of the most famous in cryptology, the system fell into utter oblivion and its inventor owes his fame to a crude and degenerate form of polyalphabetic substitution with which he had nothing to do and which he would have spurned.

The inventor of the first and imperfect autokey system was Girolamo Cardano, a Milanese physician and mathematician who is known today chiefly as one of the first popularizers of science and as author of the world's first text on the theory of probability.

Born in 1501, Cardano had an overwhelming desire simply to be remembered—not even caring whether the memory was of good or of ill. He tried to assure himself a place in posterity by a stupendous volume of writing. In the 131 books that he published during his lifetime and the 111 that he left behind in manuscript, he discussed mathematics, astronomy, astrology, physics, chess, gambling (which included his pioneering investigation of probability), the immortality of the soul, consolation, marvelous cures, dialectics, death, Nero, gems and colors, the zeal of Socrates, poisons, air, water, nourishment, dreams, urine, teeth, music, morals, and wisdom. Somehow he did not give cryptology a book of its own, but inserted his information in his two best-selling popularizations of science. The first was *De Subtilitate*, a collection of illustrations and attempted explanations of scientific phenomena that included such topics as suggestions for teaching the blind to read and write by touch. Published in 1550, *De Subtilitate* embodied both the soundest physical learning of its time and its most advanced spirit of speculation. The public liked Cardano's anecdotal exposition and his bizarre illustrations so much that he followed it six years later with a sort of continuation entitled *De Rerum Varietate*. Both books were translated and pirated by printers throughout Europe.

In his two discussions of cryptology, Cardano described the classic methods of antiquity, attempted a classification which leads to an unfortunate self-contradiction, gave directions for surreptitiously opening letters, laid down some elementary rules for solving messages and for developing secret ink, and offered a few methods of his own, accompanied by the usual laud: "In the case of the methods that we give, [cryptanalysis] would require an Apollo." One of these is his autokey.

He employed the plaintext as a key to encipher itself, starting the key over from the beginning with each new plaintext word:

key	S	I	C	S	I	C	E	S	I	C	E	R	G	O	E	L
plain	s	i	c	e	r	g	o	e	l	e	m	e	n	t	i	s
cipher	N	T	F	Z	C	L	T	Z	V	H	R	Y	V	I	P	E

But while the autokey was a brilliant idea, Cardano formulated it defectively. First, it allows plural decipherments. With Cardano's (standard) alphabets, cipher N could stand for a plaintext *f* keyed with an F as well as for plaintext *s* and key S. Second, and worse, the decipherer is in exactly the same position as the cryptanalyst in trying to figure out the first plaintext word. This, once obtained, unlocks the rest of the message.* Consequently this formulation has been justly neglected, and the immortality that Cardano so desperately sought he achieved in cryptology with a system of steganography, which bears his name.

The Cardano grille consists of a sheet of stiff material, such as cardboard, parchment, or metal, into which rectangular holes, the height of a line of writing and of varying lengths, are cut at irregular intervals. The encipherer lays this mask over a sheet of writing paper and writes the secret message through the perforations, some of which will take a whole word, others a single letter, others a syllable. He then removes the grille and fills in the remaining spaces with an innocuous-sounding cover message. Cardano prescribed copying the message three times to smooth out any irregularities in the writing that might give the secret away. The decipherer simply places his grille on the message he receives and reads the hidden text through the "windows." The method's chief defect, of course, is that awkwardness in phrasing may betray the very

---

* In 1564, Bellaso (now spelling his name with a double *l*) published a third edition of his booklet in which he described a form of autokey without these obstacles. It keys the first letter of the message with the first alphabet and successive letters of the first word with successive alphabets. Then it keys the first letter of the second word with the first letter of the first word, successive letters being keyed with the succeeding alphabets. This procedure —partly autokey, partly progressive—is repeated to the end of the message.

On the Origin of a Species

secret that that phrasing should guard: the existence of a hidden message. Nevertheless, a number of countries made use of the Cardano grille in their diplomatic correspondence in the 1500s and 1600s.

Cardano also achieved the dubious renown of being the first cryptologist to cite the enormous number of variations inherent in a cryptographic system as "proof" of the impossibility of a cryptanalyst's ever reaching a solution during his lifetime. After describing a monalphabetic substitution in which the 27 permutations of three-letter groups (AAA, AAB, AAC, ABA, ... CCC) stand for the 24 letters of the alphabet and three common words, he stated: "The [number of possible] arrangements of alphabets will require 28 digits" and "such a number of arrangements could not be contained in many books." He meant that the number of ways in which the 27 plaintext elements could be mated to possible ciphertext equivalents in trial solutions would require 28 digits to write out. As a matter of fact, it would require 29 digits, since the number of combinations is:

$27 \times 26 \times 25 \times \ldots \times 2 \times 1$, or 10,888,869,450,418,352,160,768,000,000. Cardano heads a long line of cryptographers in erroneously placing cryptographic faith in large numbers—a line that stretches right down to today. His own example refutes his argument. Cryptanalysts do not solve monoalphabetics—or any ciphers for that matter—by testing one key after another. With a 26-letter alphabet, $26 \times 25 \times \ldots \times 1$, or 403,291,461,126,605,635,584,000,000, different cipher alphabets are possible. If the cryptanalyst tried one of these every second, he would need six quintillion years, or longer than the known universe has been in existence, to run through them all. Yet most monoalphabetics are solved in a matter of minutes.

The comedy of errors and neglect that constitutes so much of the historiography of cryptology reached a climax of irony when it came to the inventor of the second and acceptable autokey system. It ignored this important contribution and instead named a regressive and elementary cipher for him though he had nothing to do with it. And so strong is the grip of tradition that, despite modern scholarship, the name of Blaise de Vigenère remains firmly attached to what has become the archetypal system of polyalphabetic substitution and probably the most famous cipher system of all time.

Vigenère was not a nobleman. The "de" in his name simply indicates that his family came from the village of Vigenère or Viginaire. He himself was born in the village of Saint-Pourçain, about halfway between Paris and Marseilles, on April 5, 1523. At 17, he was taken from his studies and sent to court and, five years later, to the Diet of Worms as a very junior secretary. This gave him his initiation into diplomacy, and his subsequent travels through Europe broadened his experience. At 24, he entered the service of the Duke of Nevers, to whose house he remained attached the rest of his life, except for periods at court and as a diplomat. In 1549, at 26, he went to Rome on a two-year diplomatic mission.

It was here that he was first thrown into contact with cryptology, and he seems to have steeped himself in it. He read the books of Trithemius, Belaso, Cardano, and Porta, and the unpublished manuscript of Alberti. He evidently conversed with the experts of the papal curia, for he tells anecdotes that he could have heard only in the shoptalk of these cryptologists. There was, for example, the one about the fellow who was not at all embarrassed to ask the Cardinal du Bellay to give him the enormous sum of 2,000 écus for a cipher he had devised—but was redfaced to learn that his system had been solved in less than three hours. Vigenère left the court at 39 to pursue his interrupted studies, but in 1566 he was sent again to Rome as secretary to King Charles IX. Here he renewed his acquaintance with the cryptologic experts, and this time he appears to have been admitted to their secret chambers, for it is he who reports having seen the Great Vicar of St. Peter solve a Turkish cryptogram in six hours. Finally, in 1570, at 47, Vigenère quit the court for good, turned over his annuity of 1,000 livres a year to the poor of Paris, married the much younger Marie Varé, and devoted himself to his writing.

He turned out some 20-odd books before he died of a throat cancer in 1596. Most of his translations and historical works have fallen into oblivion, though his *Traicté des Comètes* has been credited with helping to destroy the superstition that comets are fireballs flung by an angry God to warn a wicked world. But the book which is constantly cited by workers in its field is his *Traicté des Chiffres*, which was written in 1585 despite the distraction of a year-old baby daughter and which appeared, elegantly rubricated, in 1586, and was reprinted the following year.

It is a curious work. In its more than 600 pages, it distilled not only much of the cryptologic lore of Vigenère's day (with the major exception of cryptanalysis, which he called, in a quaint phrase, "un inestimable rompement de cerveau"—"a worthless cracking of the brain"), but a hodgepodge of other topics. It contained the first European representation of Japanese ideograms. It digressed into the foundations of alchemy, licit and illicit magic, the secrets of the kabbalah, the mysteries of the universe, recipes for making gold, and philosophic speculations. "All the things in the world constitute a cipher," its author declared. "All nature is merely a cipher and a secret writing. The great name and essence of God and his wonders, the very deeds, projects, words, actions, and demeanor of mankind—what are they for the most part but a cipher?" And so on. There may be some allegorical truth to this—Pascal himself was to say that the Old Testament was a cipher—but it hardly advanced the science of cryptology.

Despite these ramblings, the *Traicté* is reliable in its cryptologic information. Vigenère was scrupulous in assigning credit for material from other authors, and he quoted them accurately and with comprehension. He relished a good story, such as the one about the practical joke played on one Paulo Pancatuccio. Pancatuccio, Vigenère said, had been employed by the pope to solve documents in cipher, "in which in truth he was fairly well versed, and performed several minor miracles of the lesser kind." Certain "bons compagnons," wishing to humble his pride, contrived to have a letter in cipher, marked "most important," fall into Pancatuccio's hands. The opening words were in a very simple transposition cipher, and Pancatuccio solved it readily, only to read: "O poor wretched slave that you are to your decipherments, on which you waste all your oil and your pains, what does it profit you to eat out your heart in the quest of these vain curiosities, presuming by your laborious researches to be able to attain to the discovery of the secrets of others, which are reserved to God alone?" More in the same vein followed, ending with a challenge to see if Pancatuccio could get at the meaning of "one little letter" of the succeeding message. It was written in a complicated cipher; Vigenère thoroughly described it, but never said whether the indignant Pancatuccio even bothered to try solving it.

Among the numerous ciphers that Vigenère discussed (such as concealing a message in a picture of a field of stars) were polyalphabetics. Each of his used a Trithemius-like tableau, though Vigenère provided for mixed alphabets at the top and the side. He listed a variety of key methods: words, phrases, lines of poetry, the date of the dispatch, progressive use of all the alphabets. He then put forth his autokey system. Like Cardano's, it used the plaintext as the key. But it perfected Cardano's in two ways. First, it provided a priming key. This consisted of a single letter, known to both encipherer and decipherer, with which the decipherer could decipher the first cryptogram letter and so get a start on his work. With this, he would get the first plaintext letter, then use this as the key to decipher the second cryptogram letter, use that plaintext as the key to decipher the third cryptogram letter, and so on. Secondly, Vigenère, unlike Cardano, did not recommence his key with each plaintext word, which is a weakness, but kept it running continuously.

key	D	A	U	N	O	M	D	E	L	E	T	E	R	N	E
plain	a	u	n	o	m	d	e	l	'	é	t	e	r	n	e	l
cipher	X	I	A	H	G	U	P	T	M	L	S	H	I	X	T

The system works well and affords fair guarantees of security; it has been embodied in a number of modern cipher machines.

Vigenère also described a second autokey in which the cryptogram itself serves as the key after a priming key:

key	D	X	H	E	E	C	O	U	M	X	G	N	A	B	Q
plain	a	u	n	o	m	d	e	l	'	é	t	e	r	n	e	l
cipher	X	H	E	E	C	O	U	M	X	G	N	A	B	Q	O

This has the advantage of being an incoherent key but has the great disadvantage of leaving the key in full view of the cryptanalyst.

In spite of Vigenère's clear exposition of his devices, both were entirely forgotten and only entered the stream of cryptology late in the 19th century after they were reinvented. Writers on cryptology then added insult to injury by degrading Vigenère's system into one much more elementary.

The cipher now universally called the Vigenère employs only standard alphabets and a short repeating keyword—a system far more susceptible to solution than Vigenère's autokey. Its tableau consists of a modern tabula recta: 26 standard horizontal alphabets, each slid one space to the left of the one above. These are the cipher alphabets. A normal alphabet for the plaintext stands at the top. Another normal alphabet, which merely repeats the initial letters of the horizontal ciphertext alphabets, runs down the left side. This is the key alphabet. Both correspondents must know the keyword. The encipherer repeats this above the plaintext letters until each one has a keyletter. He seeks the plaintext letter in the top alphabet and the keyletter in the side. Then he traces down from the top and in from the side. The ciphertext letter stands at the intersection of the column and the row. The encipherer repeats this process with all the letters of the plaintext. To decipher, the clerk begins with the keyletter, runs in along the ciphertext alphabet until he strikes the cipher letter, then follows the column of letters upward until he emerges at the plaintext letter at the top. For example:

key   T Y P E T Y P E T Y P E T Y P E T Y P E T
plain   n o w i s t h e t i m e f o r a l l g o o d m e n
cipher G M L M L R W I M G B I Y M G E E J V S H B B I G

This system is clearly more susceptible to solution than Vigenère's original. Nevertheless, a legend grew up that this degenerate form of Vigenère's work was the indecipherable cipher par excellence, a legend so hardy that as late as 1917, more than half a century after it had been exploded, the Vigenère was being touted as "impossible of translation" in a journal as respected as *Scientific American*!

The cryptanalysts of the time did not create the legend. They knew very well that the cipher was not "impossible of translation"—because they themselves had occasionally translated it. "I may at this point mention," wrote Porta, "a letter of this sort sent me a while ago by a dabbler in ciphers who lived at Rome. To his surprise, I interpreted it within the very hour I received it—because the key of the message was the proverb OMNIA VINCIT AMOR, which is familiar to almost everybody." And Giovanni Batista Argenti noted under a Porta-like cipher in his book of cipher keys:

Qaetepeeeacszmddfictzadqgbpleaqtacui.

(In principio erat) such is the motto or key* with which the Illustrious and Excellent Signor Iacomo Boncampagni [nephew of Pope Gregory XIII], Duke of Sora, my patron, wrote the above line in cipher and gave it to me Sunday 8

---

* The key in full is actually IN PRINCIPIO ERAT VERBUM. The third-to-last letter of the ciphertext, c, should be i.

On the Origin of a Species

October 1581 in the Tusculana villa, telling me that it was not possible to find it out, and I quickly found out the counterciphner which was of 10 alphabets and the motto. The line written above means and is this:

Arma virumque cano troie qui primus ab oris.

Matteo Argenti also boasted of solving a test polyalphabetic, but he may simply have been claiming his uncle's success as his own.

	a	b	c	d	e	f	g	h	i	j	k	l	m	n	o	p	q	r	s	t	u	v	w	x	y	z
A	A	B	C	D	E	F	G	H	I	J	K	L	M	N	O	P	Q	R	S	T	U	V	W	X	Y	Z
B	B	C	D	E	F	G	H	I	J	K	L	M	N	O	P	Q	R	S	T	U	V	W	X	Y	Z	A
C	C	D	E	F	G	H	I	J	K	L	M	N	O	P	Q	R	S	T	U	V	W	X	Y	Z	A	B
D	D	E	F	G	H	I	J	K	L	M	N	O	P	Q	R	S	T	U	V	W	X	Y	Z	A	B	C
E	E	F	G	H	I	J	K	L	M	N	O	P	Q	R	S	T	U	V	W	X	Y	Z	A	B	C	D
F	F	G	H	I	J	K	L	M	N	O	P	Q	R	S	T	U	V	W	X	Y	Z	A	B	C	D	E
G	G	H	I	J	K	L	M	N	O	P	Q	R	S	T	U	V	W	X	Y	Z	A	B	C	D	E	F
H	H	I	J	K	L	M	N	O	P	Q	R	S	T	U	V	W	X	Y	Z	A	B	C	D	E	F	G
I	I	J	K	L	M	N	O	P	Q	R	S	T	U	V	W	X	Y	Z	A	B	C	D	E	F	G	H
J	J	K	L	M	N	O	P	Q	R	S	T	U	V	W	X	Y	Z	A	B	C	D	E	F	G	H	I
K	K	L	M	N	O	P	Q	R	S	T	U	V	W	X	Y	Z	A	B	C	D	E	F	G	H	I	J
L	L	M	N	O	P	Q	R	S	T	U	V	W	X	Y	Z	A	B	C	D	E	F	G	H	I	J	K
M	M	N	O	P	Q	R	S	T	U	V	W	X	Y	Z	A	B	C	D	E	F	G	H	I	J	K	L
N	N	O	P	Q	R	S	T	U	V	W	X	Y	Z	A	B	C	D	E	F	G	H	I	J	K	L	M
O	O	P	Q	R	S	T	U	V	W	X	Y	Z	A	B	C	D	E	F	G	H	I	J	K	L	M	N
P	P	Q	R	S	T	U	V	W	X	Y	Z	A	B	C	D	E	F	G	H	I	J	K	L	M	N	O
Q	Q	R	S	T	U	V	W	X	Y	Z	A	B	C	D	E	F	G	H	I	J	K	L	M	N	O	P
R	R	S	T	U	V	W	X	Y	Z	A	B	C	D	E	F	G	H	I	J	K	L	M	N	O	P	Q
S	S	T	U	V	W	X	Y	Z	A	B	C	D	E	F	G	H	I	J	K	L	M	N	O	P	Q	R
T	T	U	V	W	X	Y	Z	A	B	C	D	E	F	G	H	I	J	K	L	M	N	O	P	Q	R	S
U	U	V	W	X	Y	Z	A	B	C	D	E	F	G	H	I	J	K	L	M	N	O	P	Q	R	S	T
V	V	W	X	Y	Z	A	B	C	D	E	F	G	H	I	J	K	L	M	N	O	P	Q	R	S	T	U
W	W	X	Y	Z	A	B	C	D	E	F	G	H	I	J	K	L	M	N	O	P	Q	R	S	T	U	V
X	X	Y	Z	A	B	C	D	E	F	G	H	I	J	K	L	M	N	O	P	Q	R	S	T	U	V	W
Y	Y	Z	A	B	C	D	E	F	G	H	I	J	K	L	M	N	O	P	Q	R	S	T	U	V	W	X
Z	Z	A	B	C	D	E	F	G	H	I	J	K	L	M	N	O	P	Q	R	S	T	U	V	W	X	Y

The modern Vigenère tableau

Both the Porta and the Argenti solutions owe their success to the easily guessable nature of their keys—a common proverb in one, the first words of the Gospel of St. John in the other. The Argenti solution was further simplified by a plaintext consisting of the first line of Vergil's *Aeneid*. Even without these aids, polyalphabetics might occasionally have been solved if several other conditions obtained: if the cryptograms retained original word divisions, if the cipher alphabets were normal, and if the cryptanalyst recognized that keys repeat. He could then guess at words in the plaintext and recover part of the key that would have been used; if it made sense, he would try to guess the rest of it or, failing that, try to decipher other portions of the cryptogram. Such hit-or-miss solutions were not entirely beyond the reach of the Renaissance. Porta recognized key repetition in his artificial solution: "I conclude that the key has been given three times and decide correctly that it consists of 17 letters." And Vigenère hints at such knowledge when he comments that "the longer the key is, the more difficult it is to solve the cipher."

Yet the mere elimination of word divisions would greatly reduce the possibility of striking the right plaintext, and simply mixing the cipher alphabets would deny the Renaissance cryptanalyst any opportunity whatever for solution. The cryptographers of the time ran words together as standard practice, and they knew of techniques for mixing alphabets. Hence they had the power to make polyalphabetics unbreakable to their contemporaries. This explains Matteo's paean: "The key cipher is the noblest and the greatest in the world, the most secure and faithful that never was there man who could find it out."

Why, then, did the nomenclator reign supreme for 300 years after Porta? Why did cryptographers not use this "noblest" and "most secure" cipher instead?

Apparently because they disliked its slowness and distrusted its accuracy. Encipherment in a polyalphabetic system, with its need to keep track of which alphabet was in use at every point and to make sure that the ciphertext letter was taken from that alphabet, could not compare in speed with a nomenclator encipherment. A former ambassador of Louis XIV, François de Callières, declared in 1716 in his classic manual of diplomacy, *De la Manière de Negocier avec les Souveraens*, that unbreakability could be attained by "an infinite number of different keys" based upon "a general Model." "I do not speak," he added, in an apparent reference to polyalphabetics, "of certain ciphers, invented by professors in a University and upon rules of Algebra or Arithmetick; which are impractical by reason of their too great Length, and of the Difficulties in using them; but of common Cyphers which all Ministers make use of, and with which one may write a Dispatch almost as fast as with ordinary Letters." The well-informed author of an anonymous 17th-century "Traitté de l'art de deschiffrer" in the Royal Archives at Brussels stated that chancelleries do not use polyalphabetics because it takes too long to encipher them and because the dropping of a single ciphertext letter garbles the message from that point on. In 1819, William Blair, in a superb encyclopedia article on cryptology, likewise argued that polyalphabetic substitution "requires too much time" and that "by the least mistake in writing is so confounded, that the confederate with his key shall never set it in order again."

One might think that cipher clerks might have corrected such garbles by trial and error, especially in those more leisurely days. But they were not cryptanalysts and may not have known, or have wanted to know, how to

On the Origin of a Species

make the necessary trials. Serious garbles would thus render the dispatch unreadable until a courier went out and returned with a correction; thus the cipher would have prevented communication instead of safeguarding it. Garbles of just this type, so bad that messages could not be read, compelled two highly intelligent Americans, both Framers of the Constitution, to abandon the use of a polyalphabetic system.

Although a lack of speed and a proneness to error kept polyalphabetics from supplanting the nomenclator, they cropped up now and again. The author of the "Traitté" says that they were used in Holland from time to time. On October 12, 1601, the Jesuits sent a numerical polyalphabetic with keyword CUMBRE to Peru for communications with Rome. And, despite the myth of their unbreakability, polyalphabetics were broken occasionally. The Argentis, who would not use them for regular traffic, sometimes gave them to cardinals for personal use. One such was the "cifra con mons. rev^{mo} Panicarola apresso l'ill^{mo} signor [Enrico] cardinal Caetano legato in Francia, 3 Ottobre 1589." Pope Sixtus V had dispatched Caetano to France to further Holy League efforts against Henry IV. The cipher's first two alphabets, with their key letters at left, were:

AB	a	b	c	d	e	f	g	h	i	l
	m	n	o	p	q	r	s	t	u	z

CD	a	b	c	d	e	f	g	h	i	l
	n	o	p	q	r	s	t	u	z	m

The Argentis made its two keys prudently long (FUNDAMENTA EIUS IN MONTIBIS SANCTIS and GLORIOSA DICENTUR DE TE QUIA POTENTER AGIS), assigned K, X, and Y as nulls, and attached a small nomenclator of letters with dots, macrons, or circumflexes over them. They had considered giving Panicarola a polyalphabetic whose alphabets included the ten digits and so might be considered mixed, but instead settled on this normal-alphabet one—"easier and more secure," they said.

It was the cipher's undoing. The curia used it to tell Caetano in the middle of the following year that Sixtus had died—obviously news of the greatest importance. One of Henry's Huguenot commanders, chronicling the interception of the messages, wrote that "because the letters were in double cipher* and very difficult, it was necessary to put them in the hands of Chorrin, who disentangled all that had stopped the others and in his time has not had his equal in this perfection." Chorrin, who was a contemporary of Viète and who, from this feat alone, would appear to be his equal in ability if not in fame, also solved some other letetrs for Henry's minister of finance, Sully.

At about the same time, the cipherers of Elizabethan England set sail upon

---

* A term meaning polyalphabetics, derived from the two "keys" needed—one the cipher alphabet, the other the keyword or keyphrase. It survives in modern French usage as "double-key cipher."

the uncharted seas of polyalphabeticity with Drake-like daring. They employed a Porta-like tableau to correspond with several envoys, and a Vigenère for a Mr. Asheley. Another system comprises the oldest device of its type in the world. It consists of a vertical strip of stout cardboard on which is written a normal plaintext alphabet. Slits were cut in the cardboard down both sides of the alphabet, and through these slits was inserted a sheet of paper on which ten different cipher alphabets were vertically inscribed. The paper could be moved through the slits so as to bring the desired cipher alphabets against the plaintext one. This facilitated the reading of ciphertext equivalents.

Writers on cryptology in the 1600s occasionally referred to the solution of polyalphabetics. They did so in vague terms, probably reflecting their own indefinite thinking and the loss of knowledge that let the myth of unbreakability take root. Thus Antonio Maria Cospi, secretary to the grand duke of Tuscany, mentioned in his 1639 *La interpretazione delle cifre* "two kinds of ciphers, some simple and some composite ... the latter practically impossible to discover and decipher." And later he wrote that "The present method may not be at all useless for the interpretation of the more difficult simple ciphers ... no more than for that of double and composite ciphers." The author of the Brussels "Traitté," who demonstrated his capability when he solved a French royal cipher for Spain in 1676, floundered when he came to polyalphabeticity. He could only suggest the almost useless technique of trying one probable plaintext letter after another until a coherent combination appeared in the key he derived. Understandably, he did not illustrate his protracted method; the number of combinations is so great that he would be at it yet. His failure contrasts markedly with the technical mastery displayed in the rest of the treatise.

The time and place of the writing of that "Traitté," the author's failure with polyalphabeticity, and his allegiance to Spain make it probable that he was a cryptanalyst named Martin, who figured in an incident that shows how rare and fortuitous was the solution of a polyalphabetic. The Cardinal de Retz, that liberal and popular French prelate-politician, narrated in his *Mémoires* how he escaped from the château of Nantes on August 8, 1654, after two years of political imprisonment. He digressed to discuss ciphers:

> I had one with Madame La Palatine, which we called The Indecipherable, because it always seemed to us that no one could penetrate it without knowing the word that had been agreed upon. We placed such complete confidence in it that we never hesitated to write freely and to send the most important and the most confidential secrets by ordinary courier. It was in this cipher that I wrote to the Premier President [of the Parlement of Paris] that I would escape on August 8 ... The Prince [of Condé], who had one of the best decipherers in the world, named, it seems to me, Martin, held this cipher six weeks with me in Brussels.*
> And he told me that Martin had confessed to him that it was indecipherable....
> It was broken down sometime afterwards by [Guy] Joly [a counselor to the

---

* Retz visited Condé in Brussels in 1658.

Châtelet tribunal in Paris and one of Retz's followers], who, though not a professional decipherer, hit upon its key while reflecting on it and brought it to me at Utrecht, where I was at the time.

Retz was trying to show "how little confidence one can place in ciphers," but the fact that it took a lucky guess by an intimate to effect the only solution in six years seems rather to enhance the cipher's value.

The most interesting polyalphabetic solution of the nomenclator years came a century later. Its interest derives from a cryptanalyst who has become a very prototype in a field utterly removed from cryptanalysis, and whose obsession with that field was such that he even turned cryptanalysis to account in it.

It all happened in 1757, when he was talking about magic, alchemy, and chemistry with his friend, the wealthy Madame d'Urfé. She showed him a cipher manuscript describing the transmutation of baser metals into gold, and told him that she did not need to keep it locked up because she alone held the key. She gave it to him, remarking that she did not believe in cryptanalysis. "Five or six weeks later," he stated in his memoirs, "she asked me if I had deciphered the manuscript which had the transmutation procedure. I told her that I had." But Madame d'Urfé, still skeptical, replied:

> "Without the key, sir, excuse me if I believe the thing impossible."
> "Do you wish me to name your key, madame?"
> "If you please."
> I then told her the word, which belonged to no language, and I saw her surprise. She told me that it was impossible, for she believed herself the only possessor of that word which she kept in her memory and which she had never written down.
> I could have told her the truth—that the same calculation which had served me for deciphering the manuscript had enabled me to learn the word—but on a caprice it struck me to tell her that a genie had revealed it to me. This false disclosure fettered Madame d'Urfé to me. That day I became the master of her soul, and I abused my power. Every time I think of it, I am distressed and ashamed, and I do penance now in the obligation under which I place myself of telling the truth in writing my memoirs.

But this did not stop him at the time from amazing the lady with some hocus-pocus in producing the keyword (NABUCODONOSOR, an Italian spelling of "Nebuchadnezzar"), and then taking his leave "bearing with me her soul, her heart, her wits and all the good sense that she had left."

The cryptanalyst? Casanova.

Less dramatic solutions of polyalphabetics occurred early in the 1800s before a retired German infantry major published the general solution in 1863. It may seem that so many solutions should have dispelled the myth of polyalphabetic unbreakability. But they were isolated instances, scores of years apart, so unusual that standard works on cryptology do not mention them. Polyalphabetics remained freaks of cryptologic usage. The professionals avoided them. Their very unpopularity protected them. Had they been used more, perhaps the coincidences that lit the way to the general solution would have forced themselves upon cryptologists. But the world fixated upon the nomenclator, and so the legend of unbreakability flourished.

It was fed by the lesser writings of the time. These books shed no new light on polyalphabetics and none on the political cryptology of their day. They are divorced from the realities, and generally content themselves with commentaries on earlier works, chiefly Trithemius, and with describing a few trivial inventions. Neglect justly entombs most. A few are of minor interest.

The Florentine Jacopo Silvestri published the second printed book on cryptology at Rome in 1526. His *Opus novum* ... begins with a Dantesque scene of the author fleeing the plague at Rome to a small country estate near the Tiber. There he received a visit from an Etruscan friend, who, discoursing with him on ancient modes of writing, discussed cryptology. Silvestri's friend begged him to write down his knowledge of it for universal advantage. But most of the 88 pages of the *Opus novum* are merely given over to a vocabulary that can serve as the basis for a small code.

In 1624, Augustus II, Duke of Braunschweig-Lüneberg (afterwards Hanover) in Germany, issued his *Cryptomenytices et Cryptographiae libri IX* under the pseudonym Gustavus Selenus. This was a play on his name, GUSTAVUS being an anagram (with the interchangeable *u* and *v* of the time) of *Augustus*, and Selene, the Greek goddess of the moon, which is "luna" in Latin, standing for *Lüneberg*. The duke, who was cousin to the grandfather of George I of England, is probably the highest ranking author of a book on cryptology; both he and the present queen of England descend from Ernest the Confessor, of the house of Guelph. He prefaced the almost 500 small-folio pages of his volume with 17 pages of tributes from his courtiers ("As, what night in dusty cloak conceals, bright Cynthia soon with torch full-flaming shows,/So, too, Gustavus now, Selenus called, uncovers things that time has long in shadow held"). One such, a particularly laudatory one entitled a "Sportive Poem," was contributed to this volume of the supposedly unknown Selenus by none other than the gracious Duke Augustus himself! But the work, while containing some cipher systems, mainly defends the occultism of Trithemius.

The most celebrated scholar of his day, the Jesuit Athanasius Kircher, who had won fame by his "solution" of hieroglyphics and by his having been lowered into the crater of Vesuvius to study underground forces (a feat that, with a book on the subterranean world, won him the title of Father of Vulcanology), published his *Polygraphia nova et universalis* at Rome in 1663. The book contains chiefly processes of encipherment, as well as a multilingual, cross-indexed code which is one of the earliest essays at a universal language. Two years later, his student, Gaspar Schott, a Jesuit physicist, brought out *Schola steganographia* at Nuremberg. Schott's book, like his teacher's, is largely a compilation of cipher systems.

Only two English works of the period merit attention. The first book in English on cryptology appeared anonymously in 1641, but *Mercury, or the Secret and Swift Messenger* was the offspring of John Wilkins, a "lustie, strong growne... broad shouldered" young chaplain who later married Oliver Cromwell's sister and became Bishop of Chester and a founder and first secretary of the Royal Society. A succinct volume, very well grounded in the classics, *Mercury* introduced the words *cryptographia* (defined by Wilkins as "secrecy in writing") and *cryptologia* ("secrecy in speech") into English. The author reserved the term *cryptomeneses*, or "private intimations," for the art of secret communication in general. In addition to summing up the knowledge of the time, Wilkins depicted three kinds of geometrical cipher, a mystifying system in which a message is represented by dots, lines, or triangles. The letters of the alphabet, in normal or mixed order, were written out at known spatial intervals; this served as the key. This line of letters was held at the top of a sheet of paper, and the message was spelled out by marking a dot for each plaintext letter underneath that letter in the key alphabet, each dot lower than its predecessor. The dots could then be connected by twos to form lines, by threes to form triangles, or all together to form what would look like a graph—or they could be left as dots. The receiver, who had an identically proportioned key, noted the positions of the dots, the ends of the lines, or the apexes of the triangles against the alphabetical scale to read the plaintext.

The second English book on the subject excelled. *Cryptomenytices Patefacta* was written by John Falconer, about whom nothing is known except that he was a distant relative of the Scottish philosopher David Hume, was reportedly entrusted with the private cipher of the future King James II, and died in France while following James into temporary exile there. The book came out posthumously in 1685, with its author listed only as "J.F." It proved so popular that it was reissued in 1692 with a new title page that clearly indicates just what its 180 pages comprise: *Rules for Explaining and Decyphering all Manner of Secret Writing....*

Falconer's cryptanalytical bias sharpened his comments on the standard systems, and led him to make a praiseworthy assault on that old bugbear, polyalphabetic substitution. He suggested guessing at the short words in a cryptogram, deducing the keyletters (these were standard alphabets), and seeing whether "they can be joyned to make up part of the Key." Knowing the number of letters in the key is a great help, he says, "since thereby you have the several Returns of each Alphabet." The technique is quite valid for cryptograms with word divisions, and bespeaks an acute mind. Falconer also gave what seems to be the earliest illustration of keyed columnar transposition, a cipher that is today the primary and most widely used transposition cipher, having served (with modifications) for French military ciphers, Japanese diplomatic superencipherments, and Soviet spy ciphers.

These five books, plus the even less important ones that were also published at this period, have—with the possible exception of Falconer's—a certain air of unreality about them. There is good reason for this. The authors borrowed their knowledge from earlier volumes and puffed it out with their own hypothesizing, which seems never to have been deflated by contact with the bruising actuality of solving cryptograms that they themselves had not made up. The literature of cryptology was all theory and no practice. The authors did not know the real cryptology that was being practiced in locked rooms here and there throughout Europe, by uncommunicative men working stealthily to further the grand designs of state.

5
THE ERA OF THE BLACK CHAMBERS

RÉALMONT was under siege. The royal army, under Henry II of Bourbon, Prince of Condé, had invested it at dawn Wednesday, April 19, 1628. But the Huguenots, inside the battlements of the little town in southern France, were putting up a stiff defense. They cannonaded Condé from a tower and contemptuously rejected his demands that they surrender, saying that they would die instead. Condé brought up five big cannon from Albi, a dozen miles away, and on Sunday ranged them in an ominous line facing Réalmont.

That same day his soldiers captured an inhabitant of the town who was trying to carry an enciphered message to Huguenot forces outside. None of Condé's men could unriddle it, but during the week the prince learned that it might be solved by the scion of a leading family of Albi who was known to have an interest in ciphers.

Condé sent him the cryptogram. The young man solved it on the spot. It revealed that the Huguenots desperately needed munitions and that, if they were not supplied, they would have to yield. This was news indeed, for despite the destruction of a number of houses by the Catholic batteries, the town was continuing to resist stoutly with no sign of surrender. Condé returned the cryptogram to the inhabitants, and on Sunday, April 30, 1628, though its fortifications were still unbreached and its defenses still apparently adequate for a long siege, Réalmont suddenly and unexpectedly capitulated. With this dramatic success began the career of the man who was to become France's first full-time cryptologist: the great Antoine Rossignol.

When word of the incident reached Cardinal Richelieu, the astute and able Gray Eminence of France, he at once attached this useful talent to his suite. Rossignol proved his worth almost immediately. The Catholic armies under Richelieu surrounding the chief Huguenot bastion of La Rochelle intercepted some letters in cipher, which the young codebreaker of Albi read with ease. He told His Eminence that the starving citizens were eagerly awaiting help that the English had promised to send by sea. When the fleet arrived, the primed guardships and forts so intimidated it that it stood off the port's entrance and made no serious attempt to force a passage. A month later, the city capitulated in full sight of the English vessels—and the great French tradition of expertise in cryptology had been founded.

Rossignol very quickly established himself in the royal service. By 1630, his solutions had made him rich enough to build a small but elegant chateau at Juvisy, 12 miles south of Paris, later surrounding it with a charming informal garden designed by Le Nôtre, the gardener of Versailles. Here Louis XIII stopped to visit the young cryptanalyst in 1634, 1635 and 1636 on his returns to Paris from Fontainebleau.

In the swashbuckling court of that monarch, and then in the resplendent one of Louis XIV, Rossignol served with an extraordinary facility. The stronghold of Hesdin surrendered a week sooner than it otherwise would have because he solved an enciphered plea for help, and then composed a reply in the same cipher telling the townspeople how futile their hopes were. How many other towns he compelled to surrender, how many diplomatic coups he made possible, how many betrayals he uncovered among the great nobles in those days of shifting allegiances, he never discussed. This reticence caused some at the court to charge that he never actually solved a single cipher, and that the cardinal spread inflated rumors about his abilities to discourage would-be conspirators. But in fact Richelieu was frequently telling his subordinates such things as, "It is necessary to make use, in my opinion, of the letters of the man who has been arrested by the civil authorities at Mézières, that is to say, have them put into Rossignol's hands to see if there is something important in them." Or, eight years later, in 1642, writing to Messieurs de Noyers and de Chavigny: "I saw, in some extracts, that Rossignol sent me, a truce negotiation of the King of England with the Prince of Orange; I do not think that it can have any effect, but . . . it is up to you, gentlemen, to keep your eyes peeled."

Louis XIII, on his deathbed, recommended Rossignol to his queen as one of the men most necessary to the good of the state. Two years later, on February 18, 1645, Richelieu's successor, Cardinal Mazarin, named him a master of the Chamber of Accounts and a counselor of state. Like Richelieu, Mazarin himself sometimes sent him intercepts. In 1656, for example, he forwarded a letter of the Cardinal de Retz instructing Rossignol to solve it. Under Louis XIV, Rossignol often worked in a room next to the king's study at Versailles. From here issued the streams of solutions that helped the Sun King direct the polity of France.

Rossignol had, at 45, improved his social position by marrying 23-year-old Catherine Quentin, the daughter of a nobleman and the niece of a bishop. Their marriage was a happy one, full of playfulness and endearments, and they had two children, Bonaventure and Marie.

One of their best friends was the poet Boisrobert, who originated the idea of the Académie Française. He loved to hold forth at the excellent Rossignol table, which he liked for its fine wines and Madame Rossignol's charm as a hostess. (In a 13-line poem to her, he declared her friendship "sweeter than sugar with cream.") When he found himself out of favor at court, he complained about his unhappiness in a poem to his influential cryptologist-friend.

The Era of the Black Chambers

Rossignol showed it to Mazarin, who singled out Boisrobert at the next audience and praised the poem loudly. Boisrobert, delighted at this sign of favor, addressed a paean of thanks to Rossignol. Perhaps out of gratitude, he later praised him extravagantly in the first poem ever written to a cryptologist. Some of the choicer of the 66 lines of the untitled Épistre 29 in his *Épistres en Vers* read:

Il n'est plus rien dessous les Cieux	31	There's not a thing beneath the skies;
Qu'on puisse cacher à tes yeux;		That can be hidden from thine eyes;
Et crois que ces yeux de Lyncée*		Those Lynceus eyes, which, I believe,
Lisent mesme dans la pensée.		Our most internal thoughts perceive.
Que ton service est éclatant	35	How marvelous thy skill, and bright,
Et que ton Art est important!		And how important thine art's might!
On gagne par luy des Provinces,		For with it provinces are gained,
On sçait tous les secrets des Princes,		All princes' secrets ascertained,
Et par luy, sans beaucoup d'efforts,		And by it, with an effort small,
On prend les villes & les forts.	40	Are towns and forts compelled to fall.
. . . .		. . . .
Certes j'ignore ton adresse,	57	Indeed, thy art's beyond my ken
Je ne comprends point la finesse		And I shall never comprehend
De ton secret; mais je sçay bien		Thy secret; but I now can tell
Qu'il t'a donné beaucoup de bien;	60	That it hath served thee very well.
Tu le mérites, & je gage		Thou dost deserve it. Have no fears—
Qu'il t'en donnera davantage;		Thy skill shall prosper thee for years.
Tousjours fortune te rira,		Too, Fortune will upon thee smile,
Et, tant que guerre durera,		And long as wars the land defile
Bellone† exaltera tes Chiffres	65	Bellona shall, in strife to come,
Parmy les tambours & les fiffres.		Thy cipher praise, 'midst fife and drum.

Rossignol's work gave him access to some of the greatest secrets of the state and the court, and consequently made him a figure of some prominence in the glittering court of Louis XIV. He appears in some of the major memoirs of that period. Tallement des Réaux tells some unflattering stories about him and calls him "a poor species of man" in his *Historiettes*. But the Duke of Saint-Simon, whose *Mémoires* are a monument of French literature, wrote that Rossignol was "the most skillful decipherer of Europe.... No cipher escaped him; there were many which he read right away. This gave him many intimacies with the king, and made him an important man." Rossignol also became the first person to have his biography written solely because of his cryptologic abilities. Charles Perrault, who is better known as the formulator of the Mother Goose tales, included a two-page sketch of Rossignol's life, complete with engraved portrait, in his "Illustrious Men Who Have Appeared in France During This Century," in the company of such as

---

* Lynceus was an Argonaut whose glances were so piercing that they penetrated the bowels of the earth.

† Bellona was the Roman goddess of war.

Richelieu. Mazarin regarded his good will as important enough to write a letter of regret in 1658 for some injury done to Rossignol at Paris—and to follow it up two months later with a note to a court official pressing him to do justice to the cryptanalyst "for the insult and violence that has been done him." A more particular sign of importance appears in the largesse that the king showered upon him: 14,000 écus in 1653, 150,000 livres in 1672, and an annuity, late in his life, of 12,000—to name just some of his payments.*

All the power, wealth, flattery, and royal favor that came to Rossignol at court quite turned his small-town head. To pace the galleries of the Louvre with haughty dukes and princes of France, to wear rich lace-trimmed coats with enormous cuffs, and stockings of whitest silk, to play at that new game, billiards, with the king himself—and to have this publicized in an engraving—to run up bills at the wigmaker's, to learn before the rest of the world did who had become the king's new mistress, best of all, to return home to Albi exuding the aura of the court. "Monseigneur," he gloated one day to Richelieu about his former neighbors, "they do not dare to approach me. They regard me as a favorite—me, who lives with them just as before. They are amazed at my civility." Richelieu could only shrug his shoulders.

Nevertheless, Rossignol's abilities were undeniable. And they served France not only in cryptanalysis but in cryptography, where they wrought the most important technical improvement that nomenclators underwent in their 400-year reign.

When Rossignol began his career, nomenclators listed both their plain and code elements in alphabetical order (or alphabetical and numerical order, if the code was numerical). Plain and code paralleled one another. This relatively simple arrangement had existed since nomenclators emerged during the early Renaissance. The only deviation occurred in occasional small nomenclators when short lists of names were written down haphazardly; the code elements, however, always ascended in alphabetical order. Rossignol must have soon observed in his cryptanalyses that parallelism of plain and code assisted him in recovering plaintext. If, for example, he ascertained in an English dispatch that 137 stood for *for* and 168 for *in*, he would know that 21 could not represent *to* because codenumbers for words beginning with *t* would have to stand higher than those for words beginning with *i*. Moreover, he would know that the codenumber for *from*, which comes alphabetically between *for* and *in*, would have to fall between their codenumbers 137 and 168, and he could search accordingly.

* One story about Rossignol should be deflated, however. This is that his solutions were made "in a fashion so marvelous to his contemporaries that the device with which a lock is opened when the key has been lost is still called in French a *rossignol*." While the fact of the current usage is true, its implied origin is false. Unfortunately for so charming an etymology, this particular use of the term *rossignol* appears as criminal argot in police documents as early as 1406—almost two centuries before the cryptologist was born. Since the word also means "nightingale," it may be possible that the thieves adopted it as slang for a picklock because its nighttime solos of clicks and rasps were music to their ears.

The Era of the Black Chambers

From here, it was a simple step to depriving other cryptanalysts of such clues by destroying the parallel arrangement. This he did, mixing the code elements relative to the plain. Two lists were now required, one in which the plain elements were in alphabetical order and the code elements randomized, and one to facilitate decoding in which the code elements stood in alphabetical or numerical order while their plain equivalents were disarranged. These two lists soon came to be called "tables à chiffrer" and "tables à déchiffrer," and the mixed type of nomenclator became a "two-part" nomenclator to contrast it with the older "one-part" type. The two-part nomenclator has been compared to a bilingual dictionary. In the first half, the native words are listed alphabetically and the foreign appear in mixed order; in the second half, the foreign words progress alphabetically and the native words are jumbled.

This innovation apparently began to go into service about the middle of Rossignol's stewardship. Circumstances probably deserve most of the credit for his getting the idea first. At that time, other countries employed different people for making nomenclators and for breaking them. The cryptanalysts were called in only when needed; clerks compiled the nomenclators. France alone was rich and active enough to need and support a full-time cryptanalyst, who could also apply his knowledge to improving France's secret communications.

The two-part construction spread rapidly to other countries. At the same time, nomenclators continued to grow. The greater the size the greater the security, for it meant just that many more elements that the cryptanalyst had to recover. By the 1700s some nomenclators ran to 2,000 or 3,000 elements. But these were very expensive to compile in two-part form, and so, for reasons of economy and to the detriment of security, some nomenclators regressed to a modified two-part form. The code elements paralleled the plain in segments of a few dozen groups, but the segments themselves were in mixed order. For example, a Spanish nomenclator, a cifra general of 1677, has the syllables from *bal* to *ble* represented by the numbers from 131 to 149, but *bli*, following *ble*, is encoded by 322. This series continues to *Bigueras* at 343, while 150 reappears farther down the list as the codegroup for *c*.

As he grew old, Rossignol retired to his country home at Juvisy though he reportedly continued to perform his special magic to the end of his life. His last days were brightened by an unmistakable demonstration of royal esteem: the Sun King made a detour in a progress back to Fontainebleau to visit him at Juvisy—this in an age when courtiers vied for the privilege of removing the king's pajamas at grand and petit levees each morning! Rossignol died soon after, in December of 1682, only a few days short of his 83rd birthday on January 1.

He had been the cryptologist of France in that incomparable moment when Molière was her dramatist, Pascal her philosopher, La Fontaine her fabulist, and the supreme autocrat of the world her monarch. Rossignol was, like them, a superlative practitioner of his art at the foremost court of Europe in the very splendor of its golden age.

   His work was carried on by his son, whom he had tutored. Bonaventure succeeded to his father's 12,000 livres a year, and in 1688 was raised from counselor to the parlement to president of the Chamber of Accounts. A contemporary describes him as an "intriguer, very ugly, who has gained great well-being from deciphering letters." He numbered among his friends the great letter writer, Madame de Sévigné. When he died, in 1705, the Marquis de Dangeau remarked in his *Mémoires* that he was the finest decipherer in Europe. The *Mercure Galant* likewise praised him, saying that "the King himself admitted being vexed by his death: which alone may suffice for his eulogy." Saint-Simon would only concede that "he became adept at it, but not to the point of his father. They were," he summed up, "honest and unassuming men, who both waxed fat on the king, who even left a pension of 5,000 livres for those members of the family who were not old enough to decipher." Bonaventure's eldest son had been killed in an accident, and his second son, Antoine-Bonaventure, who had been destined for a career in the church, switched to what had become the family trade. He inherited the Rossignol acuity in cryptanalysis, and eventually succeeded his father as president of the Chamber of Accounts.

   One of the most important contributions of the Rossignols was to make crystal clear to the rulers of France the importance of cryptanalyzed dispatches in framing their policy. So effectively did their work demonstrate this that the war minister, Louvois, vigorously encouraged anyone who could provide such intelligence. On July 2, 1673, while Antoine Rossignol was still alive, Louvois ordered 200 écus remitted to one Vimbois "for having found the cipher," and, four days later, 600 livres to one Sieur de La Tixeraudière for his solution. The next year, he thanked the Count of Nancre at the Flanders frontier for sending him an enemy cipher table, saying "that if the man of whom you speak can help you succeed [in solving some enciphered letters], you may assure him that His Majesty will grant him what he asks." Still another of Louvois' cryptanalysts was named Luillier. All these endeavors coalesced into a central black chamber, or Cabinet Noir, which regularly read the ciphered dispatches of foreign diplomats throughout the 1700s.

   These successes quickened the French appreciation of the need to prevent cryptanalysis of their own systems. Their precautionary measures included frequent changes and an ironclad control. In 1676, Louvois sent a dozen two-part nomenclators to the provincial governors, and a few months later followed them up with a detailed order of the king about how they were each to be placed into individual packets and carefully marked. In 1690, when Louis XIV again ordered a change in the chiffre général, Louvois instructed the governors to return the old tables and reminded them to use the homophones in the new nomenclator and not always to repeat the same cipher

The Era of the Black Chambers

character. And in 1711, Louis, though a crabbed and tired old man then only four years from his grave, was ordering still another set of nomenclators sent to these governors. Extant records of the ministry of war for the reign of his successor, Louis XV, comprehend nomenclator after nomenclator, all of several hundred number groups in thoroughly disarranged fashion, for use with various individuals. One of several special "Canada Tables" was for the Marquis de Montcalm; it is dated 1755, just before that general sailed to defend New France against the British and to die a hero's death in battle with Wolfe on the Plains of Abraham. In the repertory of a 1756 nomenclator, destined for France's colonial efforts in Asia, the proper names of the East glow like rubies: *the Mogul, the Nabob, Pondichéry, India* itself. A note on another nomenclator, intended for use among ten persons, demonstrates the care with which they were used: "Suppressed," reads the notation, "M. de Marainville having lost his."

The prudence was not excessive. One day near the end of Louis XV's reign in 1774, a marshal of France brought a package from Vienna into the king's presence. When Louis undid it, he was astonished to see not only dispatches of the king of Prussia to secret agents in Paris and Vienna, but also plaintext copies of his own most secret enciphered correspondence, and messages between the head of his spy organization and his ambassador in Stockholm, who participated in the coup that set up the strongly pro-French Gustavus III as absolute monarch of Sweden. Louis was told that the package had come from the Abbot Georgel, secretary to France's ambassador to Austria. Georgel had met a masked man at midnight in Vienna and had been given the packet in return for 1,000 ducats. When he opened it in his room, he found that he could obtain twice weekly all the discoveries of the black chamber of Vienna, in which the correspondence of all powers was surreptitiously opened, solved, and read. Georgel made the deal, and continued to meet the mysterious agent at midnight, sending the documents to Louis twice a week by special courier.

Black chambers were common during the 1700s, but that of Vienna—the Geheime Kabinets-Kanzlei—was reputed to be the best in all Europe.

It ran with almost unbelievable efficiency. The bags of mail for delivery that morning to the embassies in Vienna were brought to the black chamber each day at 7 a.m. There the letters were opened by melting their seals with a candle. The order of the letters in an envelope was noted and the letters given to a subdirector. He read them and ordered the important parts copied. All the employees could write rapidly, and some knew shorthand. Long letters were dictated to save time, sometimes using four stenographers to a single letter. If a letter was in a language that he did not know, the subdirector gave it to a cabinet employee familiar with it. Two translators were always on hand. All European languages could be read, and when a new one was needed, an official learned it. Armenian, for example, took one cabinet polyglot only a few months to learn, and he was paid the usual 500 florins for his new knowledge. After copying, the letters were replaced in their envelopes in their original order and the envelopes resealed, using forged seals to impress the original wax. The letters were returned to the post office by 9:30 a.m.

At 10 a.m., the mail that was passing through this crossroads of the continent arrived and was handled in the same way, though with less hurry because it was in transit. Usually it would be back in the post by 2 p.m., though sometimes it was kept as late as 7 p.m. At 11 a.m., interceptions made by the police for purposes of political surveillance arrived. And at 4 p.m., the couriers brought the letters that the embassies were sending out that day. These were back in the stream of communications by 6:30 p.m. Copied material was handed to the director of the cabinet, who excerpted information of special interest and routed it to the proper agencies, as police, army, or railway administration, and sent the mass of diplomatic material to the court. All told, the ten-man cabinet handled an average of between 80 and 100 letters a day.

Astonishingly, their nimble fingers hardly ever stuffed letters into the wrong packet, despite the speed with which they worked. In one of the few recorded blunders, an intercepted letter to the Duke of Modena was erroneously resealed with the closely similar signet of Parma. When the duke noticed the substitution, he sent it to Parma with the wry note, "Not just me—you too." Both states protested, but the Viennese greeted them with a blank stare, a shrug, and a bland profession of ignorance. Despite this, the existence of the black chamber was well known to the various delegates to the Austrian court, and was even tacitly acknowledged by the Austrians. When the British ambassador complained humorously that he was getting copies instead of his original correspondence, the chancellor replied coolly, "How clumsy these people are!"

Enciphered correspondence was subjected to the usual cryptanalytic sweating process. The Viennese enjoyed remarkable success in this work. The French ambassador, who was apprised of its successes through Georgel's purchases from the masked man, remarked in astonishment that "our ciphers of 1200 [groups] hold out only a little while against the ability of the Austrian decipherers." He added that though he suggested new ways of ciphering and continual changes of ciphers, "I still find myself without secure means for the secrets I have to transmit to Constantinople, Stockholm, and St. Petersburg."

The Viennese owed at least some of their success to their progressive personnel policies. Except in emergencies, the cryptanalysts worked one week and took off one week—apparently to keep them from cracking under the intense mental strain of the work. Though the pay was not high, substantial bonuses were given for solutions. For example, bonuses totalling 3,730 florins were disbursed between March 1, 1780, and March 31, 1781, for the solution of 15 important keys. Perhaps the most important incentive was the prestige accorded to the cryptanalysts by direct royal recognition of their value. Karl VI personally handed the cryptanalysts their bonuses and thanked them for their work. Empress Maria Theresa conferred frequently with the officials of the black chamber about the cipher service and the cryptanalytic ability of other countries; that remarkable woman demonstrated her grasp of the principles involved by inquiring whether any of her ambassadors had corresponded too much in a single nomenclator and ought to be given a new key. The cryptanalysts sometimes even got paid for not solving a cipher: if a key was stolen from an embassy, the codebreakers would get a kind of unemployment compensation because they had no opportunity to win their bonus. In 1833, for example, the cabinet got three fifths of the solution bonus when the key of the French envoy was stealthily removed, copied, and replaced in a cupboard in the bedroom of the secretary of the French legation within a single night.

The cryptanalysts' training likewise aimed at stimulating extra effort. Young men about 20, of high moral caliber, who spoke French and Italian fluently and knew some algebra and elementary mathematics, were assigned to cryptanalysts as trainees. They were kept ignorant of the real work going on while they learned to construct keys, and then tested as to whether they could break the systems they had constructed. If they failed, they were transferred to another civil service job. If they proved competent, they were introduced to the secrets of the black chamber and sent to other countries for linguistic training. The starting salary was 400 florins a year, and this was doubled when they solved their first cipher. Their instructors were paid extra for the tutelage. Since all directors had to be cryptanalysts, this was the way for a young man to become director of the black chamber—a high-status post which paid salaries varying between the extraordinarily good rates of 4,000 and 8,000 florins, which often brought awards of such medals as the Order of St. Stephan, and which gave direct and frequent access to the monarch, with all that that privilege implied.

A good glimpse into the achievements of the Geheime Kabinets-Kanzlei is afforded by the letters of one of its best directors, Baron Ignaz de Koch, who served from 1749 to 1763 with the cover-title of secretary to Maria Theresa. On September 4, 1751, he sent to the Austrian ambassador in France some cryptanalyzed correspondence which "makes one see more and more the main principles that direct the cabinet in France." Two weeks later, in referring to some other cryptanalyses, he wrote, "This is the eighteenth cipher that we have got through during the course of the year; ... we are regarded, unhappily, as being too able in this art, and this thought makes the courts that fear that we can engross their correspondence change their keys at every instant, so to speak, each time sending ones more difficult and more laborious to decipher." Among letters solved during its existence were those of Napoleon, Talleyrand, and a host of lesser diplomats. These solutions were often made the basis of Austrian strategy.

England, too, had its black chamber. Its origins may be found in the cryptanalyses of a young man who stumbled into cryptology at the same age and at about the same time that Rossignol did, and who may be considered his counterpart. This was John Wallis, better known as the greatest English mathematician before Newton.

He was born on November 23, 1616, in Ashford, Kent, where his father was rector. He studied at Emanuel College, Cambridge, became a fellow of Queen's College there, and was ordained a minister. He was known to divert himself with arithmetical problems, and one evening early in 1643, when he was serving as chaplain to the widowed Lady Vere, a gentleman brought him a letter that had been found after the capture of Chichester by a parliamentary army during the Puritan Revolution. Wallis told him that he could not tell whether he could solve it or not, "Adding withall, that if it were nothing but barely a new Alphabet, as at the first Sight it seemed to bee, I thought it might possibly bee done. The Gentleman," Wallis wrote afterward, "who did not expect such an answer, told mee Hee would leave it with all his Heart, if I had any Thought of reading it: And accordingly did so. After Supper (for it was somewhat late in the Evening when I first saw it) having a while considered what Course to take, I set about it, and within a few Houres (before I slept) I had overcome the Difficulty, and transcribed the Letter in a legible Character. This good Successe upon an easy Cipher (for so it was) made me confident, that I might with the like ease read any other, which was no more intricate than that."

But the next one, a numerical, was so much more difficult than the first, which was a long monalphabetic with word divisions, that Wallis turned it down. His career would have been nipped before it had budded—except that, soon thereafter, Wallis was somehow prevailed upon to try a cryptogram that had lain about for two years because no one could be found to solve it. The cipher numbers in this letter ranged beyond 700, and, wrote Wallis, as the first cryptogram "was one of the easiest, so this second was one of the hardest that I have ever met with." Several times he gave it up as "desperate," but after about three months, "I did at last overcome the Difficulty."

This feat made his fortune. At the behest of Parliament, he solved in 1643 some of the dispatches of Charles I during the civil war, and was rewarded, first, with the living of St. Gabriel's Church in London, and then with the place of secretary to the Westminster Assembly. Additional solutions for Parliament led to his appointment in 1649 as Savilian professor of geometry at Oxford at the age of 32. In 1660, Charles II's negotiations with Presbyterian ministers in London for his Restoration were "made known to mee," said Thomas Scot, director of intelligence for Parliament, "first by one Mr Harvy, since dead and after by Major Adams, who kept them daily Company here, but very much more by letters intercepted which commonly were every word & syllable in Cypher, and decyphered by a learned gentleman incomparably able that way, Do^r Wallis of Oxford (who never concerned himself in the matter, but only in ye art & ingenuity); it is a jewell for a Princes vse and service in that kind." Though Charles knew of Wallis' parliamentary services through Scot's confession, he found him so valuable that soon after he ascended the throne he was employing the man who had recently worked against him. Indeed, so indispensable did Wallis prove that Charles compensated him not only with small sums of bounty but eventually with an appointment as a chaplain to the king.

Wallis seems to have been largely self-taught. He studied the works of Porta and others, but learned little from them because, he says, they chiefly treated of methods of encipherment. "So that I saw, there was little Help to bee expected from others; but that if I should have further occasions of that Kind, I must trust to my owne Industry and such observations as the present Case should afford. And indeed," he continues perceptively, "the Nature of the Thing is scarce capable of any other Directions; every new Cipher allmost being contrived in a new Way, which doth not admit any constant Method for the finding of it out."

The mind that, without aid, could find its way so unerringly through the labyrinth of cryptology could also blaze new trails in the unexplored fields of mathematics. This Wallis did. His *Arithmetica Infinitorum* arrived at results that Newton used as a springboard to develop the calculus and that contained the germ of the binomial theorem. Wallis invented the symbol ∞ for infinity, and he was the first to give the value of π by interpolation—a term, incidentally, that he coined. In later years, he taught himself to calculate mentally to while away sleepless nights, performing such astounding feats as extracting the square root of a number of 53 digits and dictating the answer (which proved correct) to 27 places.

Hale and vigorous of body, of medium height with a small head, he was set down by that vivid chronicler John Aubrey as "a person of reall worth" who "may stand very gloriously upon his owne basis, and need not be beholding to any man for Fame, yet he is so extremely greedy of glorie, that he steales feathers from others to adorne his own cap; e.g., he lies at watch at Sir Christopher Wren's discourses, Mr. Robert Hooke's, Dr. William Holder, &c; putts downe their notions in his Note booke, and then prints it, without owneing the author. This frequently, of which they complain." Wallis helped found the Royal Society, but despite his accomplishments, Samuel Pepys, who met him on December 16, 1665/6, noted in his diary, "Here was also Dr. Wallis, the famous scholar and mathematician; but he promises little."

Wallis' most active period, cryptologically, came late in life, when he was employed as cryptanalyst to William and Mary. In 1689, he reported to William's Secretary for War, the Earl of Nottingham, that in the past two weeks he had forwarded three packets of solutions and now had lying before him five letters in three or four different ciphers, all new to him. He told Nottingham, who was always pressing him for solutions, that he could not yet give the plaintext of some cryptograms, though, he went on, "I have already employed about seven weeks on them, and have studied hard thereupon eight or ten hours in a day, or more than so very often, which, in a business of this nature, is hard service for one of my years [then more than 70] unless I would crack my brains at it." Nottingham, in fact, was once so anxious to have a solution to letters from Louvois to one of his generals that he told Wallis that he had ordered the messenger who brought the cryptograms to wait until Wallis had solved them. Wallis managed to break the nomenclator in four days and, on returning the plaintext, tactfully apprised Nottingham of a few cryptologic realities to explain why he had let the messenger go.

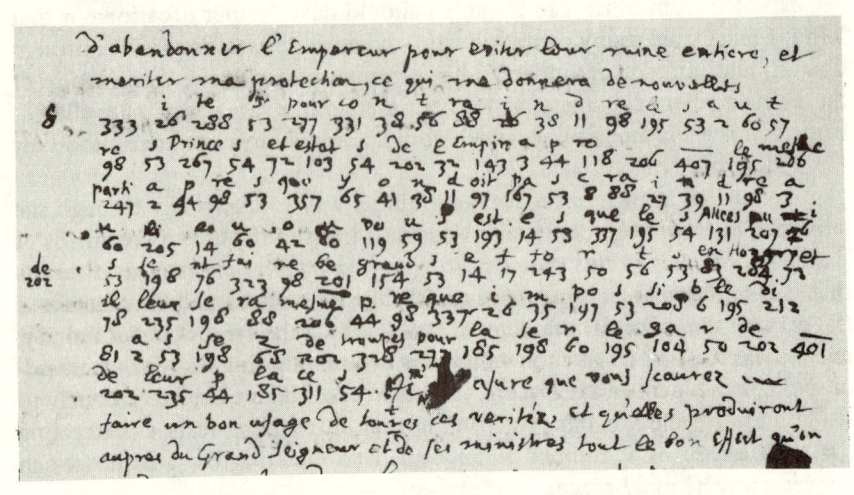

John Wallis' solution of a dispatch of Louis XIV of France of June 9, 1693

His solutions—nearly all nomenclators, a few monalphabetics—had a considerable impact on current events. In the summer of 1689, he solved the correspondence between Louis XIV and his ambassador in Poland. In one dispatch, Louis was caught urging the King of Poland to declare war against Prussia with him; in another, he was discovered promoting a self-serving marriage between the Prince of Poland and the Princess of Hanover. Wallis described the value of this work in a letter asking for a raise: "The deciphering of some of those letters having quite broke all ye French King's measures in Poland for that time; & caused his Ambassadors to be thence thrust out with disgrace. Which one thing," he adds pointedly, "was of much greater advantage to his Matie & his Allies, than all that I am like to receive on that account."

Though Wallis entreated Nottingham not to publicize his solutions for fear France would again change her ciphers, as she had done nine or ten times before (probably under the expert Rossignol tutelage), word of his prowess somehow spread. The King of Prussia gave him a gold chain for solving a cryptogram, and the Elector of Brandenburg a medal for reading 200 or 300 sheets of cipher. The Elector of Hanover, not wanting to depend on a foreign cryptanalyst, got Wallis' fellow intellectual, Baron Gottfried von Leibnitz, to importune him with lucrative offers to instruct several young men in the art. When Wallis put off Leibnitz' query as to how he did these amazing things by saying that there was no fixed method, Leibnitz quickly acknowledged it and, hinting that Wallis and the art might die together, pressed his request that he instruct some younger people in it. Wallis finally had to say bluntly that he would be glad to serve the elector if need be, but he could not send his skill abroad without the king's leave.

The shrewd old cryptanalyst, who was frequently asking for more money for his solutions, then used Leibnitz' arguments to his own advantage in successfully urging the secretaries of state to pay for his tutoring of his grandson in cryptanalysis. They agreed in 1699, but it was not until Wallis wrote to the king in 1701, saying that the young man had made such good progress that he had solved one of the best English ciphers and a very good French one, that they were jointly granted £100 a year, retroactive to 1699.

Wallis' career thus strikingly parallels Rossignol's. The two men were approximately contemporaneous (Rossignol was not quite 17 years older). Both made their first cryptanalyses in their late twenties on ciphers stemming from civil warfare in their countries. Both had a mathematical bent, and both were largely self-taught in cryptology. Both owed their worldly success to this unusual talent. Both lived into their eighties. And both became their countries' Fathers of Cryptology in a literal as well as a figurative sense. There were differences, of course. Rossignol had to assist at the more autocratic French court; Wallis seems to have done most of his work at Oxford and in other country places far from London. Rossignol probably supervised French cryptography, but Wallis apparently prescribed an English cipher only once, and that very informally. It is therefore unlikely that these cryptologic titans of the two most powerful and most contentious countries of Europe ever clashed cryptologically. Thus the problem as to who might have been the better must remain—unlike the cryptograms to which they addressed themselves with such success—forever unsolved.

On Wallis' death on October 28, 1703, the grandson whom he had tutored, William Blencowe, an undergraduate at Magdalen College, assumed the cryptanalytical duties, though he was only 20 years old. His grandfather's tutorial fee of £100 reverted to him as Decypherer, and he thus became the first Englishman both to bear that title officially and to be paid a regular salary for cryptanalysis. Blencowe did so well that six years later this salary was doubled, and he stood high in the royal favor: Queen Anne intervened in his behalf during a dispute with All Souls College at Oxford, where he was a fellow. But he shot himself in a fit of temporary insanity during his recovery from a violent fever in 1712. He was succeeded by Dr. John Keill, 50-year-old professor of astronomy at Oxford, who, though a fellow of the Royal Society, proved totally incompetent. On May 14, 1716, Keill was replaced by Edward Willes, a 22-year-old minister at Oriel College, Oxford.

Willes embarked at once upon a career unique in the annals of cryptology and the church. He not only managed to reconcile his religious calling with an activity once condemned by churchly authorities, but also went on to become the only man in history to use cryptanalytic talents to procure ecclesiastical rewards. Within two years, he had been named rector of Barton, Bedfordshire, for solving more than 300 pages of cipher that exposed Sweden's attempt to foment an uprising in England. He virtually guaranteed his future when he testified before the House of Lords in 1723. Here, Francis Atterbury, Bishop of Rochester, was being tried by his peers for attempting to set a pretender on the English throne.

The pretender's cause exhorted the allegiance of many in England, and the nation's attention focused on Atterbury's trial. Most of the facts about the alleged conspiracy had come from his intercepted correspondence, and the most inculpatory evidence had been extracted from the portions in cipher by Willes and by Anthony Corbiere, a former foreign service official in his mid-thirties who had also been appointed a Decypherer in 1719. The Lords "thought it proper to call the Decypherers before them, in order to their being satisfied of the Truth of the Decyphering." To demonstrate this, Willes and Corbiere deposed,

> That several Letters, written in this Cypher, had been decyphered by them separately, one being many Miles distant in the Country, and the other in Town; and yet their Decyphering agreed;
>
> That Facts, unknown to them and the Government at the Time of their Decyphering, had been verified in every Circumstance by subsequent Discoveries; as, particularly, that of H——'s Ship coming in Ballast to fetch O—— to *England* which had been so decyphered by them Two Months before the Government had the least Notice of *Halstead's* having left *England*;
>
> That a Supplement of this Cypher, having been found among *Dennis Kelly's* Papers the latter End of *July*, agreed with the Key they had formed of that Cypher the *April* before;
>
> That the Decyphering of the Letters signed *Jones Illington* and 1378, being afterwards applied by them to others written in the same Cypher, did immediately make pertinent Sense, and such as had an evident Connexion and Coherence with the Parts of those Letters that were out of Cypher, though the Words in Cypher were repeated in different Paragraphs, and differently combined.

The two Decypherers appeared before the Lords on several occasions to swear to their solutions. Atterbury twice objected and was twice overruled. But on May 7, as Willes was testifying to the cryptanalysis of the three most incriminatory letters of all, and the bishop felt the noose tightening around him, he persisted in questioning Willes on the validity of the reading though the House had supported Willes' refusal to answer. He raised such a commotion that he and his counsel were ordered to withdraw, and the Lords voted upon the proposition, "that it is the Opinion of this House that it is not consistent with the public Safety, to ask the Decypherers any Questions, which may tend to discover the Art or Mystery of Decyphering." It was resolved in the affirmative, the solutions were accepted, and Atterbury, largely on this evidence, was found guilty, deprived of office, and banished from the realm.

Willes, on the other hand, became Canon of Westminster the next year. His salary more than doubled to £500. He succeeded to ever more important posts every four or six years thereafter, and finally, in 1742, when the oldest of his three sons, Edward, Jr., obtained a patent as a Decypherer, he was created Bishop of St. David's, being translated the next year to the more prestigious see of Bath and Wells. The bishop and his son shared the substantial salary of £1,000 a year. In 1752, he brought another son, William, into the business at an eventual £200, and six years later a third son, Francis, who for some reason served without pay.

Bishop Willes died in 1773 and was buried in Westminster Abbey. His sons Edward, Jr., and Francis inherited a large share of his fortune and landed property and, living as wealthy squires at Barton and Hampstead, continued their cryptanalytic work. Their brother William had retired in 1794, but his three sons, Edward, William, and Francis Willes joined the Decyphering Branch in the 1790s.

Though the Willes family dominated the cryptanalytic branch, others worked in it. Corbiere was paid through such sinecures as his appointment as naval officer at Jamaica, though he never stirred from England, and as Commissioner of Wines Licenses, which sounds like the cushiest of posts. He rose to Under Secretary of the Post Office but continued his cryptanalytic work, which ended after 24 years only with his death in 1743, when he was receiving £800. The other cryptanalysts at various times were James Rivers, Frederick Ashfield, John Lampe, George Neubourg, John Bode, Jr., one Scholing, and a Boelstring.

These men received their foreign interceptions from the Secret Office and their domestic ones from the Private Office, both subdivisions of the Post Office. The Secret Office was quartered in three rooms adjoining the Foreign Office and entered privately from Abchurch Lane. Fire and candles burned constantly in one room; the staff lodged in the others. It included men who made their life's work the specialty of unsealing diplomatic packets with such deftness that they could be resealed without evidence of tampering; one such opener was J. E. Bode, father of John Bode, Jr. He regularly spent three hours on the dispatches of the King of Prussia, opening them and then resealing them with special wax and carefully counterfeited seals. Perhaps surprisingly in a bastion of human rights, its interceptions enjoyed full legality. The statute of 1657 that established the postal service declared outright that the mails were the best means of discovering dangerous and wicked designs against the commonwealth. Leases of 1660 and 1663, confirmed by the Post Office Act of 1711, permitted government officials to open mail under warrants that they themselves issued. They sidestepped this bothersome procedure by promulgating all-inclusive general warrants.* The Secret Office sent interceptions en clair to the king and those in cipher to the cryptanalysts.

They were known collectively as the Decyphering Branch. Unlike the Secret Office, the branch had no specific location. Its tiny staff of experts worked largely at home, receiving their material by special messenger. Nor had it any formal organization, the senior Decypherer being merely first among equals. More secret than the Secret Office, the branch's funds came from secret-service money issued to the Secretary of the Post Office from Parliament's surplus revenue. Security was tight—in all of England probably only 30 people knew what diplomatic correspondence was being read at any given moment. Nevertheless, most men of affairs were aware of the practice of opening private letters, and they often enciphered their correspondence or entrusted it to private messengers when secrecy was essential.

After the Elector of Hanover succeeded to the English throne as George I in 1714, retaining the rule of the German state, the Decyphering Branch collaborated with the black chamber maintained at Nienburg by the Hanoverian government. Cryptanalysts Bode, Lampe, and Neubourg had even been imported from there—an ironic development in view of Wallis' refusal to divulge his techniques to Hanover a few years earlier. Mail opening became habitual. George and his successors took a constant personal interest in the work, often encouraging talent with royal bounty. Correspondence was closely watched for cribs that were passed to the Decyphering Branch.

During the 1700s, the branch's output averaged two or three dispatches a week, and sometimes one a day. Its cryptanalysts solved the dispatches of France, Austria, Saxony and other German states, Poland, Spain, Portugal, Holland, Denmark, Sweden, Sardinia, Naples and other Italian states, Greece, Turkey, Russia, and, later, the United States. The record of French interceptions covers two centuries and comprises five volumes of intercepts totaling 2,020 pages plus three volumes of keys. Perhaps more typical is the Spanish dossier—three volumes of intercepts from 1719 to 1839 totaling 872 pages. Not all of the messages were solved at the time of their interception. Many were held either until enough had accumulated for a successful attack or until a need arose for their solution.

The solutions were read by the king and a few of the top ministers. They warned the government of the intrigues of foreign rulers and ambassadors and of impending war. An intercepted message between the Spanish ambassadors

---

* This activity forms the legal precedent for the modern tapping of telephones, at least in Britain. Significantly, however, the source of the power to intercept communications has never been determined. The Crown simply exercised it and, despite occasional debate, has continued to do so, presumably with the tacit approval of the public as necessary for the safety of the state.

The Era of the Black Chambers

in London and Paris clearly suggested that Spain had allied herself with France against England in the Seven Years' War. It was read at the British cabinet meeting of October 2, 1761. The Great Commoner, William Pitt the Elder, cited it as support for his proposal that England take the initiative, declare war before Spain did, and capture the fleet of treasure ships then transporting gold to Spain from her American possessions. His counsel was rejected, and he resigned. The war came anyway—after the immense cargo of bullion had been unloaded at Cadiz.

Solution of a 1716 French dispatch by England's Decyphering Branch

The success of the cryptanalysts of France and England was undoubtedly due in large measure to their skill. But, as always, there was another side to it which François de Callières pointed out in his superb little work on diplomacy. The cryptanalysts, he said, "owe the Esteem they have gain'd solely to the negligence of those who give bad Cyphers, and to that of Ministers and their Secretaries, who make not a right use of them."

He omitted the important factor of economics. In England in the 1700s, the Decyphering Branch at first tested and, after 1745, prepared England's diplomatic nomenclators. These generally had four-figure codegroups and numerous homophones; they were printed on large sheets and pasted on boards for the cipher clerks' use. The cryptanalysts, who should have known, thought that it was "little less than impossible to find them out." But their initial strength, which was due to the extent of the lexicon and the many homophones, eventually proved a weakness: the foreign service was reluctant to change a nomenclator that, in the late 1700s, cost £150, or to order separate nomenclators for separate countries. Thus some remained in use for a dozen years or more, and some simultaneously served several embassies. For example, in 1772 and 1773, Paris, Stockholm, and Turin had Ciphers and Deciphers K, L, M, N, O, and P; Florence had K, L, O, and P; Venice, K and L for use with Florence and M and N for other purposes; Naples, M and N; and Gibraltar, O and P.

But Callières correctly remarked failures to make a "right use" of ciphers. Time and again, diplomats enciphered documents handed to them by the governments to which they were accredited, giving those governments' cryptanalysts ideal cribs. They repeated in clear dispatches sent in cipher. Because of language difficulties, they used foreigners in secret work. And often their chiefs simply did not want to believe in cryptanalysis because it meant more work for them. In 1771, for example, the French ambassador to England complained that he had only two old ciphers and that there was in London "a bishop [Willes] charged with the decipherment of the dispatches of foreign ministers who succeeds in finding the key of all ciphers." His superior replied that not even a bishop could translate French ciphers, "which have no kind of system and of which it is not possible to find the key because one does not exist." Then, after rather heavy-handedly pointing out that ciphers are sometimes compromised through the indiscretions of those who hold them, he added, "I do not believe in decipherers any more than in magicians."

This sentiment found its most pointed expression in Voltaire's remark that "those who boast of deciphering a letter without being instructed in the affairs of which it treats, and without having any preliminary help, are greater charlatans than those who boast of understanding a language which they have not even studied." For once, one of his epigrams rang false.

Across the Atlantic, cryptology reflected the free, individualistic nature of the people from which it sprang. No black chambers, no organized development, no paid cryptanalysts. But this native cryptology, which had much of the informal, shirtsleeve quality of a pioneer barn-raising, nevertheless played its small but helpful role in enabling the American colonies to assume among the powers of the earth their separate and equal station. Indeed, the first incident occurred even before those colonies had declared their independence.

It started in August of 1775. A baker named Godfrey Wenwood was visited in Newport, Rhode Island, by a girl whom he had formerly known intimately. She asked him for help in getting in touch with some British officers so that she could give them a letter. Wenwood, a rebel patriot, grew suspicious. He

The Era of the Black Chambers

persuaded her to give him the letter for delivery and to depart before his fiancée learned of her visit. But he did not forward it.

Instead, he consulted a schoolmaster friend. The friend broke the seal and found inside three pages covered with line after neatly printed line of small Greek characters, odd symbols, numbers, and letters. Unable to penetrate the mystery, he handed the missive back to Wenwood, who tucked it away while he considered the matter further. But soon thereafter he received a letter from the girl, who complained that "you never Sent wot you promest to send." His suspicions now thoroughly aroused, Wenwood went up through channels and at the end of September was standing in the headquarters of Lieutenant General George Washington, showing him the letter.

The commander in chief could not read the cryptogram either, but he could question the girl. She was brought in that evening, and though, Washington said later, "for a long time she was proof against every threat and persuasion to discover the author," intensive interrogation wore her down.

Last lines of the cipher message of the Tory spy, Dr. Benjamin Church

The next day, she finally revealed that the letter had been given to her by her current lover, Dr. Benjamin Church, Jr. Washington was astounded. Church was his own director general of hospitals. A prosperous Boston physician who was a leader in the Massachusetts Congress and a colleague of Samuel Adams and John Hancock in the new House of Representatives, he had just asked to resign as hospitals chief. Washington had turned down his request because of his own "unwillingness to part with a good officer." Could so distinguished a man be engaged in a clandestine and possibly traitorous correspondence? But he was brought in under guard.

The letter was his, he readily admitted, intended for his brother, Fleming Church, who was in Boston—though it was addressed to "Major [Maurice] Cane in Boston on his majisty's service." If deciphered, it would be found to contain nothing criminal. But though he repeatedly protested his loyalty to the Colonial cause, he did not offer to put the contents of his letter into plain language.

Washington cast about for someone who could solve it. He located the Reverend Mr. Samuel West, 45, a rather absentminded pastor who was, ironically, a Harvard classmate of Church's. West, who later served as a delegate to the Constitutional Convention of 1787, was interested in alchemy and became convinced that prophetic portions of the Bible predicted the course of events of the American Revolution.

When Washington's need for a cryptanalyst became known, Elbridge Gerry, 31, chairman of the Massachusetts committee of military supply, volunteered his help. Gerry went on to greater fame as fifth Vice President of the United States and concocter of the political grotesquery known today as the "gerrymander." He also suggested the name of Colonel Elisha Porter of the Massachusetts militia, who had been a year ahead of him at Harvard. Gerry and Porter teamed to attack the message, and West worked by himself through the night.

Washington received the two solutions of what proved to be a monalphabetic substitution on October 3. They were identical. Church was reporting to Thomas Gage, the British commander, on American ammunition supply, on a plan for commissioning privateers, on rations, recruiting, currency, a proposed attack on Canada, artillery that he had counted at Kingsbridge, New York, troop strength in Philadelphia, and the mood of the Continental Congress. It ended: "Make use of every precaution or I perish."

This, to Washington, refuted Church's protestations that he had deliberately transmitted the information to the redcoats to impress them with patriot strength and so deter them from attacking just when American ammunition was low. It also convinced most Colonial leaders of his guilt. " . . . what a complication of madness and wickedness must a soul be filled with to be capable of such perfidy!" ejaculated an angry Rhode Island delegate. And the paymaster general of the Continental forces commented, "I have now no difficulty to account for the knowledge Gage had of all our Congress secrets, and how some later plans have been rendered abortive." It also developed that information furnished by Church caused Gage to send troops to Boston to capture American stores at Concord—a move that resulted in the historic clash at Lexington that began the American Revolution.

Church was imprisoned. The Massachusetts legislature expelled him. When he was paroled briefly, a mob assailed him. Congress rejected a British proposal to exchange him. Finally, in 1780, Massachusetts exiled him to the West Indies under pain of death should he return. But the small schooner in which he sailed was never heard of again, and the first American to have lost his liberty as a result of cryptanalysis evidently lost his life because of it as well.

Cryptology served another traitor much better. No mere monalphabetic substitution for ambitious Benedict Arnold. He played for much higher stakes and his systems excelled in security. The correspondence between Arnold, in charge at West Point, and John André, an engaging young British major whose gallantry caused some to call him the "English Nathan Hale," was conducted in several types of code. Arnold apparently handled his own cryptographic duties, but encoding and decoding at the Tory end devolved largely upon Jonathan Odell, a Loyalist clergyman of New York, and upon Joseph Stansbury, a Philadelphia merchant also partial to the Crown.

At first they employed a book code based on volume I of the fifth Oxford edition of the legal classic, Blackstone's *Commentaries*. "Three Numbers make a Word," André instructed Stansbury, "the 1st is the Page the 2d the Line the third the Word." Words not in the book were to be spelled out, and these codenumbers distinguished from the others by drawing a line through the last number, which then represented the position of a letter in that line instead of a word.

They promptly ran into unsuspected practical difficulties. Only a very few of the encoded words (the messages were encoded only in part) could be found whole, such as *general* (35.12.8) and *men* (7.14.3). Arnold managed to find the word *militia*, but he had to search to page 337 to find it, whereas the other words in his message of June 18, 1779, came from pages 35, 91, and 101. Most of the words and the proper names had to be spelled out in an enormously cumbersome fashion that required tedious counting for each letter and then the writing of four digits as its ciphertext equivalent. *Sullivan*, for instance, became (with a stroke through the final number of each group) 35.3.1 35.3.2 34.2.4 35.2.5 35.3.5 35.7.7 35.2.3 35.5.2. Arnold consequently abandoned the system after sending one message in the Blackstone code, and receiving only one from Stansbury to Odell.

The conspirators switched to the best-selling *Universal Etymological English Dictionary* of Nathan Bailey as a codebook; the words, being listed alphabetically, were considerably easier to locate. Then they turned to a small dictionary, which has not been identified. Through its pages sifted the bulk of the clandestine correspondence relating to Arnold's betrayal of West Point to the British in return for money, security, and honor. Both sides enciphered their codenumbers by adding 7 to each of the three figures—including the middle digit which, representing the column, always appeared as 8 or 9 in what would have been a giveaway to the system. But the security of the system was never put to the test of Colonial cryptanalysis, for the attempted betrayal was blocked by the capture of André before any of the missives were intercepted. He was hanged; Arnold escaped—to a life of ignominy.

British spy cryptography was surpassed by that of the two most important American agents. Samuel Woodhull of Setauket, Long Island, and Robert Townsend of New York City supplied Washington with reams of information about the redcoat occupation of New York during 1779. They wrote their reports in a one-part nomenclator of about 800 elements that had been constructed by one of Washington's spymasters, Major Benjamin Tallmadge of the Second Connecticut Dragoons. Tallmadge extracted the words he thought would be needed from a copy of John Entick's *New Spelling Diction-*

ary, wrote them in columns on a double sheet of foolscap, and assigned numbers to them. Personal and geographic names followed in a special section. Thus, 28 = *appointment*, 356 = *letter*, 660 = *vigilant*, 703 = *waggon*,

Benedict Arnold's dictionary-code message of July 15, 1780, to Major John André, reading, in part, "If I point out a plan of cooperation by which S[ir Henry Clinton] shall possess him self of West Point, the garrison &c &c &c, twenty thousand pounds sterling I think will be a cheap purchase for an object of so much importance...." Arnold's code signature, 172.9.192, stands for his codename, MOORE.

711 = *George Washington*, 723 = *Townsend*, 727 = *New York*, 728 = *Long Island*. In addition, the following semimixed alphabet permitted the encipherment of words not in the code list:

```
a b c d e f g h i j k l m n o p q r s t u v w x y z
E F G H I J A B C D O M N P Q R K L U V W X Y Z S T
```

Tallmadge provided copies of these pocket codes to both spies and to Washington, and kept one himself. A typical letter from Woodhull, dated at Setauket, August 15, 1779, began: "Sir: Dqpeu Beyocpu agreeable to 28 met 723 not far from 727 and received a 356, but on his return was under the necessity to destroy the same, or be detected...." (DQPEU BEYOCPU was Jonas Hawkins, a messenger.) The spies further masked their identity under codenames, Woodhull being CULPER SR. and Townsend CULPER JR.

The CULPERS used invisible ink extensively. Washington supplied them, getting it from Sir James Jay, who had been a physician in London and was the brother of John Jay, the American statesman who became the first Chief Justice. Sir James recounted the story of the ink in a letter he wrote years later to Thomas Jefferson:

> When the affairs of America, previous to the commencement of hostilities, began to wear a serious aspect, and threatened to issue in civil war, it occurred to me that a fluid might possibly be discovered for invisible writing, which would elude the generally known means of detection, and yet could be rendered visible by a suitable counterpart. Sensible of the great advantages, both in a political and military line, which we might derive from such a mode of procuring and transmitting intelligence, I set about the work. After innumerable experiments, I succeeded to my wish. From England I sent to my brother John in New York, considerable quantities of these preparations.... In the course of the war, General Washington was also furnished with them, and I have letters from him acknowledging their great utility, and requesting further supplies.... By means of this mode of conveying intelligence, I transmitted to America the first authentic account which Congress received, of the determination of the British Ministry to reduce the Colonies to unconditional submission; the ministry at the time concealing this design, and holding out conciliatory measures. My method of communication was this: To prevent the suspicion which might arise were I to write to my brother John only, who was a member of Congress, I writ with black ink a short letter to him, and likewise to 1 or 2 other persons of the family, none exceeding 3 or 4 lines in black ink. The residue of the blank paper I filled up, invisibly, with such intelligence and matters as I thought would be useful to the American Cause.... In this invisible writing I sent to [Benjamin] Franklin and [Silas] Deane, by the mail from London to Paris, a plan of the intended Expedition under Burgoyne from Canada.

By July, 1779, Washington was writing CULPER SR.: "All the white Ink I now have (indeed all that there is any prospect of getting soon) is sent in phial No. 1 by Col. Webb. The liquid in No. 2 is the counterpart which renders the other visible by wetting the paper with a fine brush after the first has been used and is dry. You will send these to C——R, JUNR., as soon as possible, and I beg that no mention may ever be made of your having received such liquids from me or anyone else." But though Washington urged the use of a cover-text in black ink, the CULPERS customarily wrote their message on a blank sheet of paper, inserting the sheet at a predetermined point in a whole package of the same letter paper.

Numerous letters in this "stain"—as Washington and the CULPERS generally called the secret ink—successfully eluded British inspection and transported considerable information to the American commander in chief. The reports of the CULPERS were filled with detail on such matters as how many troops were stationed where, what warships were anchored in New York harbor, what provisions were entering the town, and so forth. Washington found their reports "intelligent, clear and satisfactory" and said of CULPER JR. that "I rely upon his intelligence."

The redcoats used invisible ink even earlier than the Americans. Only a few days after the Battle of Lexington, British headquarters in Boston received a secret-ink letter which revealed some of the military plans of the New England patriot forces. ". . . the first movement will be to make a feint attack upon the Town of Boston," the invisible portion read in part, "& at the same time to attempt the castle with the main body of their Army." The handwriting shows the document to be from Benjamin Thompson, a hated Tory, who, after a series of colorful adventures, became Count Rumford of the Holy Roman Empire and a widely known scientist. He used gallotannic acid for his ink, which the British developed by ferrous sulphate—a procedure described by Porta, from whose *Natural Magick* Thompson, who had been avid for science since his teens, had probably borrowed it.

When it came to ciphers, the British provided themselves with a veritable menagerie of systems. Sir Henry Clinton, British commander in New York, had a small one-part nomenclator; he also had a monoalphabetic substitution in which $a = 51$, $b = 52$, $c = 53$, and so on. He had a truncated alphabet tableau of twelve lines. He even had a pigpen cipher. Still other specimens inhabited this cryptographic zoo, but the only one Clinton is known to have used in the early part of the war is a degenerate form of grille called the dumbbell cipher, from the hourglass shape of its one large hole.

In the summer of 1777, Clinton had to inform General John Burgoyne, driving south down the Hudson in an attempt to cut the colonies in two, that he would have trouble pushing north to a meeting because his superior, Sir William Howe, had taken most of his troops to Philadelphia. On August 10, Clinton wrote as part of his secret message a heartfelt *Sir W's move just at this time the worst he could take.* His cover-text for this portion, which necessarily had to include many of these words, stated just the opposite: SIR W'S MOVE JUST AT THIS TIME HAS BEEN CAPITAL; WASHINGTON'S HAVE BEEN THE WORST HE COULD TAKE IN EVERY RESPECT. But it was patently absurd for a commander to assert that the loss of his troops was "capital"; the example throws a sharp light on the weakness of the grille. Whether the message got through or not, and if it did whether it disheartened Burgoyne, is unknown. It is known that, deprived of the help of Clinton's column from the south, he lost the

Battle of Saratoga, which helped determine the ultimate outcome of the Revolution.

While code and cipher systems proliferated throughout the Revolution, cryptanalysis hibernated. The basic reason seems to be that, with the exception of an infrequent episode like that of the Church cipher, no cryptograms were intercepted. It was not until the war neared its end that enough messages were captured to make recurrent cryptanalyses possible. Most of the messages were solved by James Lovell, a member of the Continental Congress who may be called the Father of American Cryptanalysis.

Lovell, born in Boston on October 31, 1737, graduated from Harvard in 1756 and then taught for eighteen years in his father's South Grammar School in Boston. His father was a fervid Loyalist, but James was named as the first orator to commemorate the Boston Massacre, and in 1775 was arrested by the British as an American spy. After his exchange, he was elected a delegate to the Continental Congress. He took his seat in 1777, and promptly distinguished himself for zeal and industry, particularly on the Committee on Foreign Affairs. It is said that he never once in the next five years visited his wife and children. He offered a design for the Great Seal of the United States, which, however, was rejected. He quit Congress in April of 1782 and was appointed receiver of continental taxes in Boston, and, in 1789, naval officer for the district of Boston and Charlestown, the post he held until his death in 1814.

He was regarded as gifted in intrigue and as a lover of mystery. Where he learned cryptology is not known, but as early as 1777, he was endorsing Arthur Lee's proposal that the Committee of Secret Correspondence use a dictionary as a codebook. Two years later, he urged Major General Horatio Gates, whom he preferred over Washington as commander in chief, to "Ask Dr. Joseph Gardner, one of my best earthly friends, to let your clerk copy an alphabet which he had from me." The system was a Vigenère using numbers instead of cipher letters; Lovell keyed a letter in it to Gates with the name JAMES. The same system, with key CR, served him in enciphering letters to John and Abigail Adams in 1781. The following year, after a mail robbery had compromised the nomenclator of 846 elements used by Virginia's delegates to Congress, one of them, the acid-tongued Edmund Randolph, proposed to another, James Madison, that they employ "the cypher which we were taught by Mr. Lovell. Let the keyword be the name of the negro boy who used to wait on our common friend Mr. Jas. Madison." This name was CUPID, the system a numerical Vigenère. It is significant that Lovell was here popularizing a system that was relatively obscure and little used, but that was then the only type that lay beyond the known limits of cryptanalysis. Later, however, errors compelled its abandonment.

Lovell's successes in solution came at the most opportune time. In the fall of 1781, Lord Cornwallis, Britain's second-in-command in America, had moved his troops north from the Carolinas to Virginia. He was convinced that that colony had to be taken before the southern colonies could be held, and he marched down the James River toward the coast in the hope of receiving reinforcements by sea from his chief, General Clinton, in New York. He planned to reduce Virginia, conquer the Carolinas, and quell the revolution for His Britannic Majesty, King George III.

It was at this juncture that the American commander in the South, Nathanael Greene, sent to Congress, as he had done before, some intercepted redcoat cryptograms that no one in his headquarters could read, enclosing them in a general report. The British correspondence was among Cornwallis and several of his subordinates.

Greene's report was read in Congress September 17. Four days later, Lovell had solved the enclosures. A few were in a simple monalphabetic substitution, but most were in a bastard system that combined the poorest features of mon- and polyalphabeticity. A single numerical cipher alphabet enciphered four to ten lines monalphabetically, and then shifted to provide new ciphertext equivalents. For example, the positions were as follows for lines 1, 10, and 14 of the first page of the first letter:

line	a	b	c	d	e	f	g	h	i	k	l	m	n	o	p	q	r	s	t	u	v	w	x	y	z
1	19	9	17	13	16	7	12	8	14	15	26	4	18	21	3	2	11	5	24	29	1	25	23	22	6
10	23	22	6	19	9	17	13	16	7	12	8	14	15	26	4	18	21	3	2	11	5	24	29	1	25
14	5	24	29	1	25	23	22	6	19	9	17	13	16	7	12	8	14	15	26	4	18	21	3	2	11

Any number above 30 was a null, and these were sprinkled freely throughout the message. Changes in alphabets were signaled by both a bracketlike mark and a series of four to seven nulls. No pattern appeared in the shifting; presumably it followed a list prearranged by the correspondents.

Unfortunately, the tactical situation had changed too much for the information in the Carolina intercepts to be of much good. But the keys that Lovell had recovered might possibly prove valuable some time in the future, and so he took the precaution of writing Washington: "It is not improbable that the Enemy have a plan of cyphering their letters which is pretty general among their Chiefs. If so, your Excellency will perhaps reap Benefit from making your Secretary take a Copy of the Keys and observations which I send to General Greene, through your Care."

Lovell could not have been shrewder. The system that he had solved was, as he had guessed, also in service between Cornwallis and Clinton, who was the commander in chief of all British forces in America. Cornwallis had by now retired to Yorktown to await Clinton's reinforcements. But Washington had encircled the town with 16,000 men, while the French admiral, the Count de Grasse, with 24 French ships of the line, barred relief by sea. On October 6, just after the French and American allies had driven a parallel close to the British lines, Washington wrote Lovell, "My Secretary has taken a Copy of the Cyphers, and by the help of one of the Alphabets has been able to decipher

The Era of the Black Chambers 183

one paragraph of a letter lately intercepted going from L'd Cornwallis to Sir H'y Clinton." The letter presumably gave Washington insight into conditions inside the British fortifications.

Clinton, meanwhile, managed to maintain contact with Cornwallis by small boat. But the vessels that he sent out from New York on September 26 and October 3 were captured by the rebels. One of them had been driven ashore near Little Egg Harbor, where the Tory who was carrying one set of dispatches hid them under a large stone before he was captured and brought

James Lovell's solution of a 1781 letter to Lord Cornwallis

to Philadelphia. "By means of a little address and a promise of a pardon," as one American put it, he was persuaded to recover them. The search took at least two days, either because "the beach is so extensive and so many places like each other," as the president of Congress, Thomas McKean, wrote Washington, or because the man was delaying. He still had not returned with them to Philadelphia by 3 p.m. October 13, nor, apparently, by the next morning. At that time, Lovell sent to Washington through a French officer what appears to have been a supplementary British system: "I found, as I had before supposed, that they sometimes use Entick's Dictionary marking the Page Column and Word as 115.1.4. Tis the Edition of 1777 London by Charles Dilley."

The Tory returned with the dispatches some time during October 14. Lovell attacked them at once and with immediate success, since he found to his joy that they were written in the same alphabets as the rest of the Clinton-Cornwallis correspondence. The more important message of the two that were apparently intercepted was the one sent in duplicate by Clinton on September 30 and received by Cornwallis on October 10. "My Lord," it began, "Your Lordship may be assured that I am doing every thing in my power to relieve you by a direct move, and I have reason to hope, from the assurances given me this day by Admiral Graves, that we may pass the bar by the 12th of October, if the winds permit, and no unforeseen accident happens: this, however, is subject to disappointment, wherefore, if I hear from you, your wishes will of course direct me, and I shall persist in my idea of a direct move, even to the middle of November...."

By the evening of October 14, Lovell was writing to Washington: "Since I wrote that Letter [of the morning], I have been happy in decyphering what the President of Congress sends by this Opportunity. The use of the same Cypher by all the British Commanders is now pretty fairly concluded. The Enemy play a grand Stake, May the Glory redound to the Allied Force under your Excellency's Command!"

This went out with a letter of the president of Congress, who told Washington: "My intelligence was true: the inclosed copies of two original letters from Sir Henry Clinton to Lord Cornwallis which I have in cyphers, and which have been faithfully decyphered by Mr. Lovell (whose key I had the honor to forward to you about a fortnight ago) more than prove the fact."

At the same time, McKean also sent the solutions to de Grasse, whose ships were to prevent Graves and Clinton from relieving Cornwallis. "The British General and Admiral seem to be desperate, and willing to risque all on the intended attempt," he wrote de Grasse, adding prophetically, "If they fail it appears here that they are disposed to give up the contest for North America." De Grasse continued to blockade Cornwallis and to watch for the British fleet. Five days after Lovell had completed his cryptanalytic exposure of British plans, Cornwallis surrendered. But victory was not quite complete. Washington recognized this when, on the following day, October 20, he received the copies of the solutions that McKean had sent him and lost "not an instant" in forwarding them to de Grasse. Doubly warned, the French admiral prepared for the British attack. On October 30, he scared off the English fleet and set the seal of final victory on the American War for Independence.

With the coming of victory, the difficulties attendant upon the establishment of a new nation compelled the Founding Fathers not only to continue their secret communications, but to extend and improve them. In the fall of 1781, Robert A. Livingston, Secretary of Foreign Affairs, had forms printed that bore on one side the numbers 1 to 1700 and on the other an alphabetical list of letters, syllables, and words. They served as a convenient basis for correspondents to produce individual nomenclators by assigning the code numbers to the plaintext elements in whatever order they wished.

They were widely used. Madison and Thomas Jefferson constructed a code on one of them in 1785, using it at least until 1793. It was in that year that

The Era of the Black Chambers 185

Madison, vacationing in Fredericksburg, found himself staring at this enlightening passage in a letter from Jefferson because he had left his key in Philadelphia: "We have decided unanimously to 130 . . . interest if they do not 510 . . . to the 636. Its consequences you will readily seize but 145 . . . though the 15. . . ." Another code composed on the Livingston forms, endorsed "Mr. Monroe's cypher," was used by Monroe in 1805 when he was minister to England, by James A. Bayard in 1814 when he helped negotiate the treaty that ended the War of 1812, and as late as 1832 by President Andrew Jackson in letters to a diplomatic agent. It therefore seems to have been one of the first official codes of the United States under the Constitution.

The nomenclator compiled in 1785 by Jefferson for use with Madison and Monroe

Other emissaries used systems of secret communication while the America that they were representing was still little more than thirteen united colonies. Benjamin Franklin, in France in 1781, assigned consecutive numbers to each of the 682 letters and punctuation marks in a long passage in French to concoct a homophonic substitution cipher:

```
v o u l e z - v o u s  s  e  n  t  i  r  l  a  d  i  f  f  e  r  e  n  c  ...
1 2 3 4 5 6 7 8 9 10 11 12 13 14 15 16 17 18 19 20 21 22 23 24 25 26 27 28 ...
```

One message began, I HAVE JUST RECEIVED A 14, 5, 3, 10, 28, 76, 203, 66, 11, 12, 273, 50, 14, . . . the numbers deciphering to *neuucmiissjon*. The double *u* was necessary because the French passage has no *w*. Plaintext *e* was represented by more than 100 different numbers. Another early representative, William Carmichael, minister in Madrid, seems to have made the first recorded suggestion for a standard American diplomatic cryptography. In a letter to Jefferson in Paris on June 27, 1785, he wrote: "It has long been my surprise that Congress hath not instructed those they employ abroad on this head [ciphers]: For this purpose a common cypher should be sent to each of their Ministers and Chargé Des Affaires."

Still other systems were used. Before they settled on the Livingston-form nomenclator, Jefferson and Madison agreed to use a French-English lexicon as a codebook. The Lee brothers, Arthur, Richard Henry, and William, corresponded from 1777 to 1779 in a dictionary code, probably the same Entick's of 1777 that Clinton had used and Lovell discovered.

The most far-reaching cryptogram in domestic American history used not one but three systems of cryptography. It served as evidence in the sensational trial for treason of the man who had lost the Presidency by a single vote in 1800 and who became Vice President instead—Aaron Burr.

After killing Alexander Hamilton in a duel in 1804, Burr headed west, fired with his dream of carving out a colonial empire in the Southwest at the expense of Spain, with whom war then seemed imminent. Whether this empire was to be the United States' or Burr's was never clear. His military accomplice in this grandiose scheme was General James Wilkinson, who, unknown to Burr, was a paid Spanish agent. Though Burr had used a cardboard cipher disk with numbers for polyalphabetic substitution in 1800 and in a letter to his son-in-law in 1804, he and Wilkinson decided to combine into a single system of cryptography for their great work a symbol code in which, for example, a circle stood for "President," a symbol cipher in which a dash represented *a*, and a dictionary code based on the 1800 Wilmington edition of the ubiquitous Entick's. On October 8, 1806, as Wilkinson waited in camp at Natchitoches, Louisiana, a messenger arrived with a cipher letter in this system from Burr dated July 22, in which he outlined his final plans for the great adventure.

Its exact wording will never be known. Wilkinson erased, altered, and redeciphered it time and again to suit his varying conveniences. In its final version, it began: "Your letter post marked 13th May is received. I have at length 263.13ed 176.3. and have 35.3 93.10ed. . . ." It went on to tell how Burr was planning to move westward down the Ohio and the Mississippi with about 500 or 1,000 men to meet Wilkinson and "there to determine whether it will be expedient in the first instance to seize on or pass by Baton Rouge." Wilkinson used it, not to meet Burr, but to double-cross him. He sent one of the decipherments to President Thomas Jefferson, who promptly ordered the breakup of Burr's expedition.

The former Vice President was arrested and tried for treason, with Chief Justice John Marshall presiding. The letter formed one of the chief exhibits. Under cross-examination, Wilkinson brazenly admitted that he had changed the document to save himself from implication. At one point he averred that the decipherment was hasty, inaccurate, and done piecemeal; at another, that it was a careful, tedious, and lengthy bit of work. This sort of vacillation by the chief prosecution witness threw a reasonable doubt on Burr's guilt, and the jury acquitted him. But the court of public opinion, roused by the evidence of the cryptogram, convicted him. For the remainder of his life Burr could never expunge the stain on his name that his enciphered message had helped place there.

During these formative years, the black chambers of Europe did not disdain to read the communications of the fledgling nation just because it was weak and far away. As early as 1777 Britain's black chamber was developing American letters in secret ink: the British chemists marked two of them, apparently sent between Paris and London, with "all written in white ink" and "R,15th." One has Benjamin Franklin's name in the margin.

The following year, a letter from an American businessman in London to Franklin's secretary in Paris was solved. In 1780, Francis Willes, Bishop Willes' son, solved a packet of letters from the Marquis de Lafayette, then in Philadelphia, to France's Minister of Foreign Affairs, the Count de Vergennes. One dispatch, of May 20, in an extensive two-part nomenclator, proved to be a long and informative report summarizing the overall situation as Lafayette saw it—the Continental currency has greatly depreciated, New York can be taken if the French troops arrive in time, Washington is thinking of conquering Canada, and the ability, honesty, and constancy of "mes amis Américains." The packet had been thrown overboard when the vessel carrying it was captured by the British, but some tars jumped in and retrieved it. The solutions were shown to King George III, who may have obtained thereby some valuable clues as to how to conduct his American war.

Later the Decyphering Branch read correspondence between American ministers in London, The Hague, and Berlin—in the latter city a future President named John Quincy Adams—between July, 1798, and February, 1800. The letters, enciphered in a homophonic substitution, seem to have been solved in retrospective solutions. In 1841, Britain lifted the flap of a two-part U.S. nomenclator and peeked at the American minister to Spain reporting on the successful conclusion of financial negotiations with that country.

By then the Decyphering Branch had only two members. Of the three grandsons of Bishop Willes who had joined in the 1790s, just one, Francis Willes, carried on the family tradition. His brother William had assisted only briefly, and his other brother, Edward, had died in 1812, the last to hold the title of Decypherer. Francis became so overworked that he enrolled his nephew, the Reverend Mr. William Willes Lovell (apparently no relation to James Lovell) as assistant.

Nor was France idle. On September 26, 1812, the American minister, writing to President Madison, carefully enciphered the names of two French officials who were backing his claims against Napoleon and made a point of asking the President to keep them confidential. But the cryptologic descendants of the Rossignols had their own way of finding out for the Little Emperor that the two were Cambacérès and Talleyrand.

These were the dying gasps of the black chambers. The winds of change, stirred up in part by the example of the nation whose codes were being solved,

188   THE CODEBREAKERS

in part by the machines of the Industrial Revolution, freshened into the political gales of the 1840s which blew down most of Europe's remaining absolutism and the totalitarian agencies that propped it up. Europe's new birth of freedom tolerated no government opening of mail. In England, a tremendous public and parliamentary outcry over the surreptitious opening of letters forced the government to discontinue the interception of diplomatic

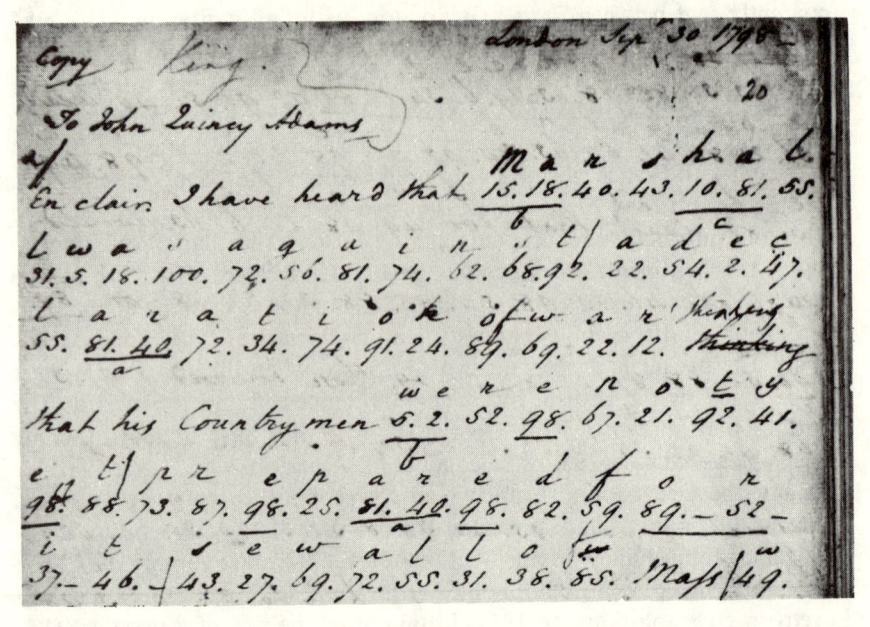

Decyphering Branch solution of a 1798 diplomatic dispatch to John Quincy Adams, American Minister in Berlin

correspondence in June of 1844. That October the government dissolved the Decyphering Branch, pensioning off Willes and Lovell. In Austria, the Geheime Kabinets-Kanzlei closed its doors in 1848. In France, the Cabinet Noir, which had been withering ever since the Revolution, passed away as well in that convulsive year. And in that same decade, the same vast social forces that ended the era of the black chambers simultaneously fostered an invention that transformed cryptography.

6
THE CONTRIBUTION OF THE DILETTANTES

THE TELEGRAPH made cryptography what it is today. Samuel F. B. Morse sent "What hath God wrought!" in 1844. The next year his lawyer and promotional agent, Francis O. J. Smith, published a commercial code entitled *The Secret Corresponding Vocabulary; Adapted for Use to Morse's Electro-Magnetic Telegraph*, in whose preface he declared that "secrecy in correspondence, is far the most important consideration." This was provided by a superencipherment. Nine years later, an article on telegraphy in England's *Quarterly Review* likewise emphasized the primacy of security:

> Means should also be taken to obviate one great objection, at present felt with respect to sending private communications by telegraph—the violation of all secrecy—for in any case half-a-dozen people must be cognizant of every word addressed by one person to another. The clerks of the English Telegraph Company are sworn to secrecy, but we often write things that it would be intolerable to *see* strangers read before our eyes. This is a grievous fault in the telegraph, and it *must* be remedied by some means or other. . . . At all events, some simple yet secure cipher, easily acquired and easily read, should be introduced, by which means messages might to all intents and purposes be "sealed" to any person except the recipient.

As the most exciting invention of the first half of the century, the telegraph stirred as much interest in its day as Sputnik did in its. The great and widely felt need for secrecy awakened the latent interest in ciphers that so many people seem to have, and kindled a new interest in many others. Dozens of persons tried to dream up their own unbreakable ciphers. Nearly all were amateurs, the professionals (except for a few code clerks) having lost their jobs when the black chambers were abolished. A surprising number of these dabblers were intellectual and political leaders of the day who beamed their powerful and original minds on the engrossing field of cryptology. Their contributions enriched it with dozens of new cipher systems.

As businessmen and the public used the telegraph more and more, they found that their fears about lack of privacy were exaggerated. The clerks dealt impersonally with the messages. The telegraph companies respected their confidentiality. And commercial codes like Smith's, which replaced words and phrases by single codewords or codenumbers to cut telegraph tolls, afforded sufficient security for most business transactions by simply precluding an at-sight comprehension of the meaning. The brokers and traders soon realized that the main advantage of these codes was their economy.

Smith's pioneering venture was followed by dozens, then scores, then hundreds of commercial codes. Though a few had as many as 100,000 entries and some specialized ones only a few hundred, considerations of optimum manageability and selling price concentrated most in the neighborhood of Smith's 50,000-entry size. They improved on his in two ways. They provided dictionary words as codewords instead of the letter-and-number groups that he had used. It was easier, cheaper, and more reliable to send ALBACORE to mean *alone* than the A.1645 of Smith's *Vocabulary*. And they greatly increased the number of phrases, thereby raising their toll-saving potential. Smith listed only 67 phrases, collected on a single page, compared to his 50,000 words; later codes had 10 or 20 times as many phrases as individual words.

Government ministries used the telegraph, too. At first they must have encoded with their nomenclators. But although secrecy was paramount for them, they liked the telegraphic economy of a large code—especially as they telegraphed more and more. So when the time arrived to compile a new nomenclator, they abandoned that form, copied the commercial form, and produced a full-fledged code. The nomenclators had had their 1,- or 2,000 codenumbers in mixed order, but the war and foreign ministries balked at the expense of drawing up a 50,000-entry code in two parts, and they had no professional cryptanalysts to warn them of the danger of the one-part format. They relied for security upon small editions, big safes, extensive lexicon (large codes are harder to break than small ones, other things being equal), and superencipherment, retaining codenumbers to facilitate this instead of switching to codewords. This evolution was essentially complete by the 1860s. The large, one-part code had replaced the small, two-part nomenclator in high-level military and diplomatic cryptography.

Meanwhile, the telegraph, author of this development, was creating something new in war—signal communications, or voluminous command and reconnaissance messages. Of course such messages had existed before, with torches, pigeons, and couriers, but in so rarefied a form that they were not even called "signal communications." The telegraph enabled commanders, for the first time in history, to exert instantaneous and continuous control over great masses of men spread over large areas. It filled a need, for universal military conscription had begun to raise such armies to fight the nationalistic warfare of democracies (as contrasted with the small, professional armies that fought the dynastic wars of kings), the new railroad transported these large forces rapidly over great distances, and the industrial society supported them. These developments, together with the breech-loading gun, brought about the era of modern warfare.

The Contribution of the Dilettantes

No longer could a general sit horseback atop a hill and survey the battle, like Napoleon or Hannibal, sending messengers to hand-carry instructions to wheel or to counterattack. The forces engaged were too numerous, the field too vast. He had to work from a command post far in the rear, following the progress of the battle by telegraph on maps that showed more than his naked eye could ever see. He could issue orders by telegraph that would coordinate the movement of one out-of-sight wing with that of another, bring up reserves to block an enemy charge, order up food and ammunition in a hurry. The number of messages grew correspondingly. The command post became virtually a communications center.

These tactical messages required protection: telegraph wires could be tapped. Neither the old nomenclator nor the new code would do. They were too easy to capture in combat, too hard to reissue quickly and frequently to the numerous and widespread telegraph posts. Signal officers turned away from them. They looked instead to that neglected child of cryptography, the cipher. Ciphers could be printed cheaply on a single sheet of paper and distributed with ease. Secrecy was based upon variable keys, so capture of the general system and even of one of the keys would not compromise all an army's secret messages. Solutions would be prevented by rapid key changes. Ciphers were ideal for battle-zone messages, and the first of the modern wars, the American Civil War, used them for just that. Thus was born a new genre in cryptography: the field cipher.

The first one was waiting in the wings. This was polyalphabetic substitution, in the form of the straight-alphabet Vigenère with short repeating keyword. The old objections to its use, which boiled down to the impossibility of correcting a garbled dispatch quickly enough, vanished with the telegraph. It fulfilled the requirements of noncompromisability of the general system and of ease of key changes. Moreover, it had the reputation of being unbreakable —which, if its cryptograms were not divided into words, it largely was. The military adopted it at once.

Then, in 1863, a retired Prussian infantry major discovered the general solution for the periodic polyalphabetic substitution. At one stroke he demolished the only impregnable structure in cryptography. Signal officers, compelled to provide secure communications, hunted frantically for new field ciphers. They found many good ideas in the writings of the dilettante cryptographers who had proposed ciphers for the protection of private messages. Soon some of these systems were serving in the various armies of Europe and the Americas. More ideas came from army officers who had studied cryptography in the courses in signal communication that the national military academies, such as St. Cyr, had added in the mid-1800s. Inevitably, cryptanalysts—who were either amateurs or soldiers with a professional interest, for full professionals there were none—replied with new techniques for breaking the new ciphers. From the slow crawl of nomenclator days, when the introduction of a special group meaning *Disregard the preceding group* would constitute a remarkable technical advance, the race between offense and defense in cryptology accelerated to its modern pace.

The history of cryptology from the decade that saw both the death of the black chambers and the birth of the telegraph to World War I is thus a story of internal development. Without Rossignols or Willeses, and without major wars or diplomatic struggles, cryptology could not influence world events, and, except for one or two unusual cases, it did not. The telegraph launched this evolution of cryptology. It broke the monopoly of the nomenclator. The nomenclator had reigned for 450 years as a general, all-purpose system, but it could not meet the new requirements either of high-level diplomatic or military communications or of low-level signal communications, which the telegraph had engendered. Each called for its own kind of cryptosystem, a specialized one. Signal officers ranked these systems in a hierarchy, rising from the simple and flexible and easily solved to the extensive and hard to solve. The telegraph thus stimulated the invention of many new ciphers and, by reaction, many new methods of cryptanalysis, and compelled their arrangement in a scale of complexity.

Many of these ciphers and techniques have become classic and are in use today. Moreover, cryptography still functions through a hierarchy and employs a multitude of special systems. The telegraph thereby furnished cryptography with the structure and the content that it still has. It made it what it is today.

All these things have antecedents, and just as the telegraph itself did, so were there precursors of the cryptographic systems that it engendered. What may be the earliest printed forerunner of the codes of today appeared at Hartford in 1805. *A Dictionary; to Enable Any Two Persons to Maintain a Correspondence, With a Secrecy, Which Is Impossible for Any Other Person to Discover* was a small book listing words and syllables in alphabetical order; these were to be numbered serially by the correspondents, omitting one number in every ten so that no two sets of correspondents would have the same code equivalents.

One cipher system invented before the telegraph was so far ahead of its time, and so much in the spirit of the later inventions, that it deserves to be classed with them. Indeed, it deserves the front rank among them, for this system was beyond doubt the most remarkable of all. So well conceived was it that today, more than a century and a half of rapid technological progress after its invention, it remains in active use.

But then it was invented by a remarkable man, a well-known writer, agriculturalist, bibliophile, architect, diplomat, gadgeteer, and statesman named Thomas Jefferson. He called it his "wheel cypher," and it seems likely that he invented it either during 1790 to 1793 or during 1797 to 1800. During the first period he was America's first Secretary of State, and the responsibilities of conducting foreign policy, the need to protect communications from

The Contribution of the Dilettantes

England and France, the divided American cabinet, the spirit of invention that he found as administrator of the patent law, all spurred his own natural inventiveness; he was then also in contact with Dr. Robert Patterson, a mathematician of the University of Pennyslvania and vice president of the American Philosophical Society, who was interested in ciphers. During the later period, he was again in close contact with Patterson, who in 1801 sent him a cipher. Jefferson's explanation of the wheel cypher is characteristically clear and economical:

Turn a cylinder of white wood of about 2. Inches diameter & 6. or 8. I. long. bore through its center a hole sufficient to recieve an iron spindle or axis of 1/8 or 1/4 I. diam. divide the periphery into 26. equal parts (for the 26. letters of the alphabet) and, with a sharp point, draw parallel lines through all the points of division from one end to the other of the cylinder, & trace those lines with ink to make them plain. then cut the cylinder crosswise into pieces of about 1/6 of an inch thick. they will resemble back-gammon men with plane sides. number each of them, as they are cut off, on one side, that they may be arrangeable in any order you please. on the periphery of each, and between the black lines, put all the letters of the alphabet, not in their established order, but jumbled & without order, so that no two shall be alike. now string them in their numerical order on an iron axis, one end of which has a head, and the other a nut and screw; the use of which is to hold them firm in any given position when you chuse it. they are now ready for use, your correspondent having a similar cylinder, similarly arranged.

Suppose I have to cypher this phrase. "Your favor of the 22^d is recieved."

I turn the 1st wheel till the letter y. presents itself
I turn the 2^d & place it's . . o. by the side of the y. of the 1st wheel.
I turn the 3^d & place it's . . u. by the side of the o. of the 2^d
4th . . . . . r. by the side of the u. of the 3^d
5th . . . . . f. by the side of the r. of the 4th
6th . . . . . a. by the side of the f. of the 5th

and so on till I have got all the words of the phrase arranged in one line. fix them with the screw. you will observe that the cylinder then presents 25. other lines of letters, not in any regular series, but jumbled, & without order or meaning. copy any one of them in the letter to your correspondent. when he recieves it, he takes his cylinder and arranges the wheels so as to present the same jumbled letters in the same order in one line. he then fixes them with his screw, and examines the other 25. lines and finds one of them presenting him these letters: "your favor of the 22 is recieved." which he writes down. as the others will be jumbled & have no meaning, he cannot mistake the true one intended. so proceed with every other portion of the letter. numbers had better be represented by letters with dots over them; as for instance by the 6. vowels & 4. liquids. because if the periphery were divided into 36. instead of 26. lines for the numerical, as well as alphabetical characters, it would increase the trouble of finding the letters on the wheels.

When the cylinder of wheels is fixed, with the jumbled alphabets on their peripheries, by only changing the order of the wheels in the cylinder, an immense variety of different cyphers may be produced for different correspondents. for whatever be the number of wheels, if you take all the natural numbers from unit to that inclusive, & multiply them successively into one another, their product will be the number of different combinations of which the wheels are susceptible, and consequently of the different cyphers they may form for different correspondents, entirely unintelligible to each other. . . .

Jefferson went on to say that if the cylinder be six inches long ("which probably will be a convenient length, as it may be spanned between the middle finger & thumb of the left hand, while in use") the number of wheels would total 36, and the number of ways in which they can be strung on the spindle to form different ciphers for different correspondents would come to 36 factorial, or $1 \times 2 \times 3 \times \ldots \times 35 \times 36$, which Jefferson calculated almost exactly

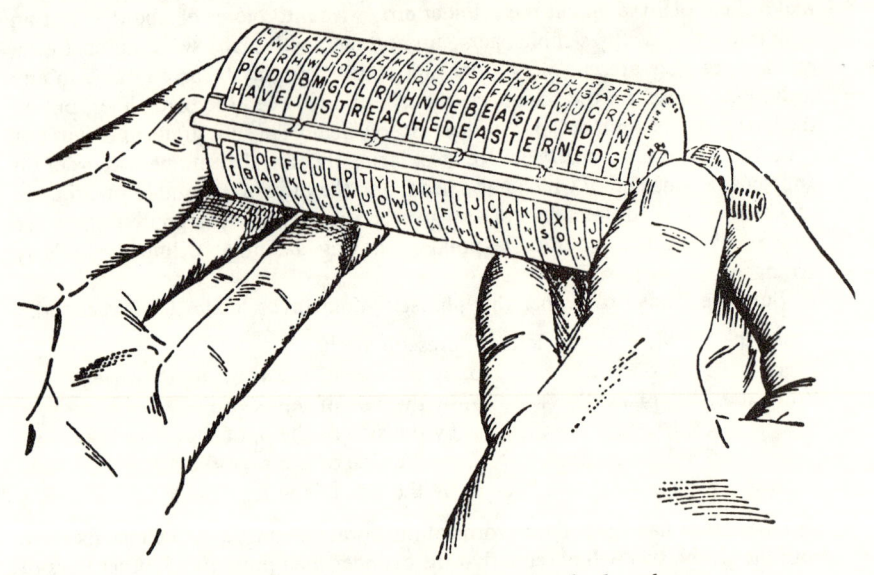

The U.S. Army form of Jefferson's wheel cypher

as "372 with 39 cyphers [zeros] added to it." In fact, 36 factorial is 371,993,326,789,901,217,467,999,448,150,835,200,000,000.

Jefferson's wheel cypher was far and away the most advanced devised in its day. It seems to have come out of the blue rather than as a result of mature reflection upon cryptology. Jefferson continued to use the nomenclator while he was Secretary of State, and the only indication of any cryptographic originality is his selection of a Vigenère as the official cipher for the Lewis and Clark expedition. Moreover, on March 22, 1802, he wrote Dr. Patterson, who had submitted a cipher to Jefferson as president of the American Philosophical Society, that "I have thoroughly considered your cypher, and find it so much more convenient in practice than my wheel cypher, that I am

The Contribution of the Dilettantes

proposing it to the Secretary of state for use in his office," a month later adding that "We are introducing your cypher into our foreign correspondences." Patterson's cipher was a columnar transposition with nulls at the heads of the columns, of a security in no way comparable to Jefferson's. That Jefferson did not see this does not speak too highly of his cryptologic perceptions.

Had the President recommended his own system to Secretary of State James Madison, he would have endowed his country with a method of secret communication that would almost certainly have withstood any cryptanalytic attack of those days. Instead he appears to have filed and forgotten it. It was not rediscovered among his papers in the Library of Congress until 1922, coincidentally the year the U.S. Army adopted an almost identical device that had been independently invented. Later, other branches of the American government used the Jefferson system, generally slightly modified, and it often defeated the best efforts of the 20th-century cryptanalysts who tried to break it down! To this day the Navy uses it. This is a remarkable longevity. So important is his system that it confers upon Jefferson the title of Father of American Cryptography. And so original is it that it sets Jefferson upon a pedestal far more prominent than those accorded to men like Vigenère and Cardano, whose names are usually thought to be household words in the history of secret writing.

In 1817, another American constructed a cryptograph that, like Jefferson's, introduced a new principle into cryptology. Colonel Decius Wadsworth, then 49, was a Yale graduate who twice quit the Army (once to seek his fortune in the fur trade) and twice rejoined when wars with France and Britain threatened; how and why he became interested in secret writing remains unknown. But his attraction to mechanical devices may well have fostered his friendship with Eli Whitney, whose cotton gin he admired and whose muskets with interchangeable parts he inspected and approved for use by the Army. When, in 1812, he became the first chief of ordnance of the U.S. Army, he again backed Whitney strongly. Illness forced him to resign this post and his commission in June of 1821, and Whitney, remembering, brought him to New Haven. Here Whitney could visit him daily and ensure his good care. But on November 8 Wadsworth died.

His innovation was to make the plaintext and ciphertext alphabets different lengths. The device in which he realized this is a brass cipher disk set in a polished wooden case six and a half inches in diameter and almost three inches high. It may have been built for him by Whitney. Its outer alphabet consists of the 26 letters plus the digits from 2 to 8 for a total of 33 elements; the inner alphabet consists of just the 26 letters. A little brass plate marks the one point around the two rings of alphabets at which they are in exact conjunction; two apertures in this plate expose the two letters, one on each ring, that are to be taken as plaintext and cipher equivalents. (No records indicate which alphabet Wadsworth meant to serve as plain and which as cipher; this account assumes the inner to be the plain alphabet.) These two rings of the disk, both of which revolve, are connected to one another inside the case by two gears, one with 33, the other with 26 teeth. The letters and numbers of the outer ring are stamped on brass plugs which may be assembled in any order. Before enciphering, the correspondents agree on a mixed sequence for the ciphertext ring and on a starting juxtaposition for the two sections, such as, say, R in the outer disk opposite V in the inner; the gears may be disengaged to permit this setting.

Suppose, now, that the correspondents are in the Peruvian wool trade and that their message begins with *llama*—a word admirably suited to demonstrate the cryptographic workings of their device. The encipherer will spin the inner disk by means of a little knob on it until the first *l* appears in the inner aperture of the brass plate; he will write down the letter in the outer aperture as the first cipher letter. Then he will turn the inner disk until *l* appears again in the inner aperture. The gears will have transmitted this motion to the outer ring, but because of the difference in the size of the alphabets, the outer disk will have gone through only 26/33rds of a revolution while the inner has completed a full revolution. Consequently, the second ciphertext letter will stand seven places farther forward in the outer alphabet than the first, even though both represent the same plaintext letter. If this process is kept up, the cipher equivalents for *l* would not begin to repeat until all 33 letters and digits of the outer alphabet had been used. This is because 26 and 33 have no factors in common to bring them into conjunction earlier.

The encipherment thus constitutes a progressive system in which all the cipher alphabets are used, like Trithemius' original polyalphabetic encipherment. But the disparity in length between the plain and the cipher alphabets results in two crucial differences. One is that the Wadsworth device employs 33 cipher alphabets instead of the 24 of Trithemius. The other is that these alphabets are brought into play, not one right after another, but in an irregular manner—a manner that depends on the letters of the plaintext. This irregularity defends the cipher much better than Trithemius' regular progression.

Knowledge of Wadsworth's device, which could not have been widely disseminated even while he lived, faded completely soon after he died. Consequently, credit for the discovery of the principle of sliding two alphabets of different lengths against one another has usually been awarded to a widely known British scientist who independently devised a mechanism based on it.

Charles Wheatstone had a remarkably fertile mind. He constructed an electric telegraph before Morse did, invented the concertina, improved the dynamo, studied underwater telegraphy, produced some of the first stereoscopic drawings, published half a dozen papers on acoustics, discussed phonetics and hypothetical speaking machines in print, conducted numerous

The Contribution of the Dilettantes

electrical experiments, and popularized a method for the extremely accurate measurement of electrical resistance now in frequent use and called the "Wheatstone bridge." His work was highly enough regarded for him to be elected a fellow of the Royal Society and to be knighted. He was nominally professor of experimental philosophy at King's College, London, but was so excessively shy that he hardly ever actually lectured. Around 1860, in his late fifties, he solved a long cipher letter of Charles I. It consisted of seven folio pages filled with numerals, each page signed at the top by the king; it proved to be instructions in French for the Sieur de Goffe, enciphered in a small one-part nomenclator (a = 12, 13, 14, 15, 16, 17; b = 18, 19; *France* = 478).

Wheatstone first displayed his Cryptograph at the Exposition Universelle at Paris in 1867. It differed only in detail from Wadsworth's. The Wheatstone apparatus had an outer plaintext alphabet of 27 elements—the 26 letters in

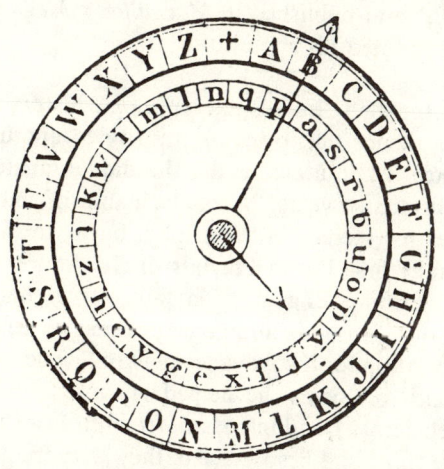

The Wheatstone cipher machine, with plaintext alphabet outside, cipher inside

normal order plus a blank for a word space—and an inner, mixed ciphertext alphabet of the 26 letters. Over these alphabets swung two clocklike hands, which were connected by gears. "At the commencement [of encipherment]," Wheatstone's instructions read, "the long hand must correspond with the blank of the outer circle and the short hand be directly under it. The long hand must be brought successively to the letters of the despatch (outer circle), and the letters indicated on the inner circle by the short hand must be written down. At the termination of each word the long hand must be brought to the blank, and the letter indicated by the short hand also written down. By this arrangement, the cipher is continuous, no intimation being given of the separation of the words. Whenever a double letter occurs, some unused letter (as, for instance, *q*) must always be substituted for the repeated letter; or the latter may be omitted." The variation in the length of the two alphabets means that as the larger hand is completing a revolution, the smaller is already one cell into its second.

The device's simplicity, automaticity, apparent insolubility, and compactness impressed many visitors to the exposition. One of them was Colonel Laussedat of the French commission that looked for military possibilities among the exhibits; he reported favorably on the Wheatstone Cryptograph, even to the point of stating that it "assures the most absolute secrecy."

In fact, a cryptogram produced by this instrument is less secure than a Wadsworth because the Wheatstone difference in alphabet sizes amounts to only one unit. As a result, a doubled ciphertext letter can mean only that their two plaintext letters represent letters in reverse alphabetical order, such as the common digraph *on* or *ts*. These may afford a break into the system. Indeed, this very observation was made, and a solution elucidated by attacking sentences as probably starting with *the*, in an extremely perceptive article signed only "C.P.B." and published in *Macmillan's Magazine* just four years after Wheatstone exhibited his apparatus.

It is another of the many ironies of cryptologic history that Wheatstone's name adheres to a device that owes its priority to another and that never achieved importance, while a cipher that he did originate, and that served with distinction for many years, bears the name of another. Wheatstone invented the cipher for secrecy in telegraphy, but it carries the name of his friend Lyon Playfair, first Baron Playfair of St. Andrews. A scientist and public figure of Victorian England, Playfair was at one time or another deputy speaker of the House of Commons, postmaster general, and president of the British Association for the Advancement of Science. As a commissioner on the public health of towns, he helped lay the foundations of modern sanitation. He lived across London's Hammersmith Bridge from Wheatstone. Because both were short and bespectacled, they were frequently mistaken for one another—once even by Lady Wheatstone. They walked together on Sundays and amused themselves by solving the enciphered personal messages in the London *Times*. They easily read the correspondence of an Oxford student with his young lady in London, and when the student proposed an elopement, Wheatstone inserted an advertisement in the same cipher remonstrating with her. There followed a frantic "Dear Charlie: Write no more. Our cipher is discovered!"—and then silence.

Playfair demonstrated what he called "Wheatstone's newly-discovered symmetrical cipher" at a dinner in January, 1854, given by the president of the governing council, Lord Granville. One of the guests was Queen Victoria's husband, Prince Albert; another was the Home Secretary and future Prime Minister, Lord Palmerston. Playfair explained the system to him, and, while in Dublin a few days later, received two short letters in the cipher from Palmerston and Granville, showing that both had readily mastered it.

The earliest known description of the Playfair cipher, signed by its inventor, Charles Wheatstone, March 26, 1854

The cipher is the first literal one in cryptologic history to be digraphic*—that is, to encipher two letters so that the result depends upon both together. Wheatstone recognized that the cipher would work as well with a rectangle as with a square, but it soon petrified into the latter form. Wheatstone also employed a thoroughly mixed cipher alphabet, which he generated by a keyword transposition—one of the earliest instances of such a method. Beneath a keyword he would write the remaining letters of the alphabet, and then derive the mixed alphabet by reading the columns vertically:

```
M A G N E T I C
B D F H J K L O
P Q R S U V W X
Y Z
```

Which yields: MBPYADQZGFRNHSEJUTKVILWCOX. This important feature soon slipped out of the picture as the cipher fell to the lowest common denominator, just like Vigenère's. The keyword was instead inscribed directly into a 5×5 square with the remaining letters of the alphabet following. (I and J are merged in a single cell.) The practice lessened security but facilitated operation. It may well have been the way Playfair hastily constructed a keysquare based on PALMERSTON to illustrate the cipher at Granville's dinner:

```
P A L M E
R S T O N
B C D F G
H IJ K Q U
V W X Y Z
```

To encipher, the plaintext is divided into pairs. Double letters occurring together in a pair must be separated with an *x*, so that *balloon* would be enciphered as *ba lx lo on*; *i* and *j* are regarded as identical, so that *adjacent* will be enciphered as if it were *adiacent*. Now the letters of each pair may stand in only three relationships to one another with the key square: the two may appear in the same row, in the same column, or in neither. Letters that fall in the same row are each replaced by the letter to its right. Thus, *am* = LE, *hi* = IK, *os* = NT. Each row is considered cyclical, so that the letter to the right of the last letter in a row is the first letter at the left of that row. Thus, *le* = MP, *ui* = HK. Letters that appear in the same column are each replaced by the letter beneath it; the cyclical provision holds. Thus, *ac* = SJ (or SI, as the encipherer wishes); *of* = FQ, *wi* = AW, *br* = HB.

If the plaintext letters appear in neither the same row nor the same column, each is replaced by the letter that lies in its own row and stands in the column occupied by the other plaintext letter. For example, to encipher *sq*, the encipherer first locates them in the square. Then he runs across the row of the

---

* Porta's digraphic table was not literal: it used signs.

The Contribution of the Dilettantes

first plaintext letter (*s*) until he meets the column in which the second plaintext letter (*q*) stands:

```
. . . M .
R S T O N
. . . F .
. . . Q .
. . . Y .
```

The letter at the junction of row and column (o) becomes the first cipher letter. Then the encipherer traces across the row of the second plaintext letter (*q*) until he intersects the column in which the first plaintext letter stands:

```
. A . . .
. S . . .
. C . . .
H IJ K Q U
. W . . .
```

The letter at the intersection (I) becomes the second cipher letter. Thus *sq* = OI. Other encipherments are *af* = MC, *at* = LS, *ed* = LG. The letter in the row of the first plaintext letter is always taken first to preserve the order of the letters, so that *cl* = DA and not AD, which would stand for *lc*, and *we* = ZA.

Decipherment in this is precisely the same as encipherment: if *ow* = SY, then *sy* = OW. In the other two cases, the plaintext letters are found to the left or above the ciphertext letters. Thus, using the same square, a ciphertext reduces as follows:

MT	TD	BN	ES	WH	TI.	MP	TA	LN	NL	NV
lo	rd	gr	an	vi	lx	le	sl	et	te	rz

The *z* at the end is a null to complete the final digraph.

Wheatstone and Playfair explained the cipher to the Under Secretary of the Foreign Office, no doubt pointing out its chief advantage—that two plaintext pairs that have a letter in common may not display the slightest resemblance in ciphertext, as *le* and *te* above were enciphered to MP and NL. Further, once mastered, it rolls along with remarkable ease and rapidity. When the Under Secretary protested that the system was too complicated, Wheatstone volunteered to show that three out of four boys from the nearest elementary school could be taught it in 15 minutes. The Under Secretary put him off. "That is very possible," he said, "but you could never teach it to attachés."

Playfair, reasoning that this reflected more on the diplomats than on the cipher, remained enthusiastic about it. There were good grounds for enthusiasm. In the first place, the cipher's being digraphic obliterates the single-letter characteristics—*e*, for example, is no longer identifiable as an entity. This undercuts the usual monographic methods of frequency analysis.

Secondly, encipherment by digraphs halves the number of elements available for frequency analysis. A 100-letter text will have only 50 cipher digraphs. In the third place, and most important, the number of digraphs is far greater than the number of single letters, and consequently the linguistic characteristics spread over many more elements and so have much less opportunity to individualize themselves. There are 26 letters but 676 digraphs; the two most frequent English letters, *e* and *t*, average frequencies of 12 and 9 per cent; the two most frequent English digraphs, *th* and *he*, reach only 3¼ and 2½ per cent. In other words, not only are there more units to choose among, the units are less sharply differentiated. The difficulties are doubly doubled.

These properties elevated the cipher above most of its contemporaries purely on cryptographic considerations; it was, probably, regarded as unbreakable. Its many practical excellences—no tables or apparatus required, a keyword that could easily be remembered and changed, great simplicity of operation—commended it as a field cipher. Playfair suggested that it be used as just that in the impending Crimean War when he brought it up at the dinner with Prince Albert. No evidence exists that it was used then, but there are reports that it served in the Boer War. Britain's War Office apparently kept it secret because it had adopted the cipher as the British Army's field system. Playfair's unselfish proselytizing for his friend's system unwittingly cheated Wheatstone of his cryptographic heritage; though Playfair never claimed the invention as his own, it came to be known in the War Office as Playfair's Cipher, and his name has stuck to it to this day.

In England in 1857, a 4 × 5-inch card with an alphabet square printed in red and black went on sale for sixpence. It was a new system of secret writing "adapted for telegrams and postcards," the latter an even newer form of communication than the telegraph. Admiral Sir Francis Beaufort, R.N., creator of the Beaufort scale with which meteorologists indicate wind velocities by numbers from 0 (calm) to 12 (hurricane), had originated the cipher, and his brother had published it a few months after the admiral's death. The envelope for the card carried the directions: "Let the key for the foregoing table be a line of poetry or the name of some memorable person or place, which cannot easily be forgotten.... Now look in the side column for the first letter of the text (*t*) and run the eye across the table until it comes to the first letter of the key (*v*), then at the top of the column in which v stands will be found the letter c," which would be the ciphertext.

The alphabet square is essentially the same as the Vigenère, except that it repeats the normal alphabet on all four sides, so that the square extends 27 letters across and 27 down and has A at all four corners. Its encipherment equals that of a Vigenère with reversed alphabets. The system had been originally proposed almost 150 years before Beaufort by one Giovanni Sestri, in a book published in Rome in 1710 that had been widely ignored. But under

The Contribution of the Dilettantes

Beaufort's name the cipher became a standard in the repertory of cryptology, though its theoretical importance is minor.

It has also given rise to a system called the Variant Beaufort. In this, the encipherer starts, not with the plaintext letter but with the keyletter, traces in to the plaintext letter, and then turns upward to emerge at the ciphertext. Actually, the system might better be called the Variant Vigenère, for to decipher it the clerk must perform the operation that constitutes a Vigenère encipherment: find the keyletter on the side and the ciphertext letter at the top, and run into the tableau from both until the plaintext letter is located at the junction. Vigenère and Variant Beaufort thus invert one another—the encipherment of one serves as the decipherment of the other. True Beaufort, on the other hand, is reciprocal within itself, since the same operation of starting with the known letter, tracing in to the keyletter, and rising to find the unknown works for both encipherment and decipherment.

Two years later, an American who at the time was working for a stove and foundry firm gave, like Beaufort, the merest glance to cryptology. Like Beaufort, the result was a single short piece of work. But unlike the admiral's, this work opened important new vistas into untrodden lands, and then sank immediately into a cryptologic obscurity as undeserved as Beaufort's renown.

The inventor was Pliny Earle Chase, then 39, who, after entering Harvard as a prodigy at 15, taught in Philadelphia for seven years until his health forced him into less tiring work in business. In 1861 he resumed teaching, becoming professor of natural science and then professor of philosophy and logic at Haverford College near Philadelphia. He was an absorbing lecturer, particularly in astronomy, and he collaborated on an arithmetic textbook with Horace Mann. But perhaps his most notable accomplishment was his writing more than 250 articles for scholarly magazines. Among them was the one that he penned in 1859 which covered barely three pages in the new *Mathematical Monthly*, but which constitutes the first published description of fractionating, or tomographic, cipher systems.

The basis of these ciphers stretches back across the millennia to Polybius, the Greek historian of the second century B.C. who distributed the alphabet in what is even today sometimes called a "Polybius square," but more often a "checkerboard." Numbers at the side and top indicate the row and the column of a given letter. Similar systems have cropped up throughout cryptography. Some replace the alphabet by three symbols in groups of three ($a = 111$, $b = 112$, $c = 113$, $d = 121$, etc.), some by two in groups of five ($a = 00000$, $b = 00001$, $c = 00010$, etc.). But no one seems to have seen the symbols as manipulable entities instead of just as an unalterable part of the whole.

Until Chase. He severed the coordinates from one another and subjected the resulting fractions to various cryptographic treatments. He began with a checkerboard filled out to ten columns with Greek letters:

	1	2	3	4	5	6	7	8	9	0
1	x	u	a	c	o	n	z	l	p	φ
2	b	y	f	m	&	e	g	j	q	ω
3	d	k	s	v	h	r	w	t	i	λ

Chase wrote his coordinates vertically, so that his sample plaintext, *Philip*, appeared like this:

$$\begin{array}{cccccc} 1 & 3 & 3 & 1 & 3 & 1 \\ 9 & 5 & 9 & 8 & 9 & 9 \end{array}$$

He then multiplied the lower line by 9, obtaining the result:

$$\begin{array}{ccccccc} & 1 & 3 & 3 & 1 & 3 & 1 \\ 8 & 6 & 3 & 9 & 0 & 9 & 1 \end{array}$$

This he restored to literal form by resubstituting back in his checkerboard, 8 (by itself) = L, J, or T, then 16 = N, 33 = S, 39 = I, and so on, with the final ciphertext LNSIΦIX.

Chase proposed other means of transforming the bottom row, such as adding a repeating key or giving the logarithm of the row, and pointed out that even more intricate processes might be used. "But the simpler cypher, provided it is effectual, is the better," he wisely concludes. The Chase systems grant a fairly hermetic security; they are, besides, relatively simple to operate. Yet cryptologic history shows no one ever having used them, even though they are far superior to many systems that have seen service.

Most remarkable of the Victorian congregation of cryptologists was the Lucasian Professor of Mathematics at Cambridge, the pioneer who enunciated the principles on which today's huge electronic computers are based and who himself built their prototypes: Charles Babbage. Most of his cryptologic work was never published and hence never played a role in the science, but it was astonishingly advanced. He was among the first to use mathematical notations and formulas in cryptanalysis; he solved polyalphabetics at a time when the system was still regarded as "le chiffre indéchiffrable;" he appears to have been the first to solve an autokey. The few words that he wrote on the subject are pregnant with observations that bespeak an extraordinary grasp of it.

Born in 1792, he inherited a considerable fortune from his father, a banker. This financed his many interests—studies of railways, archaeology, submarine navigation, occulting lighthouses, tree rings as an indicator of ancient climate, lock picking (for scientific purposes only), what is now known as operational research, and his long, bitter, and totally unavailing campaign against his pet hate—organ-grinders in the streets of London. Babbage was fascinated by statistical phenomena, compiling tables of mortality and logarithms, counting the proportion of letters in various texts, and measuring the pulse and breathing rate of any animals he encountered. Cryptology may have been an offshoot of his statistical interest, which also led to his lifelong attempt to apply machinery to the calculation of mathematical tables. A paper on this at 30 brought him the first gold medal of the Astronomical Society, and Babbage spent the rest of his life trying to realize his vision in his Difference and Analytical Engines. He even resigned his Cambridge professorship after seven years to devote himself more completely to them.

His problem was that he never finished anything. With his two mathematical machines, he was forever getting new ideas and scrapping all that he had done. The government's exasperated withdrawal of financial support (which he had largely matched out of his own pocket) because nothing concrete had been accomplished turned Babbage later in life from a social fellow of interesting conversation and a good sense of humor into a bitter man. Though he took his disappointment to the grave at 78, his ideas ultimately triumphed and, in particular, the logical structure of his Analytical Engine remains fully visible in the big electronic computers of today.

The opening words of the short essay he published on cryptology will ring a familiar bell in the minds of amateurs who have worked until 3 a.m. on a teaser: "Deciphering is, in my opinion, one of the most fascinating of arts, and I fear I have wasted upon it more time than it deserves." Like his acquaintances Wheatstone and Playfair, Babbage delighted in solving the enciphered personal advertisements that abounded in the newspaper "agony columns;" this may account for his further observation that "very few ciphers are worth the trouble of unravelling them."

Babbage is also the only person known to have suffered corporally for his cryptanalyses. It happened at school: "The bigger boys made ciphers, but if I got hold of a few words, I usually found out the key. The consequence of this ingenuity was occasionally painful: the owners of the detected ciphers sometimes thrashed me, though the fault lay in their own stupidity."

His reputation for cryptanalytic ability did not wane in later life, though its rewards became less punishing. In July of 1850, he solved a cipher of Henrietta Maria, queen of Charles I, though he turned down the task of solving the seven-page cryptogram of the king, instead recommending Wheatstone, who succeeded. He solved a note in a kind of shorthand that threw some light on a historical point for the author of a life of John Flamsteed, England's first Astronomer Royal. On April 20, 1854, barrister S. W. Kinglake wrote Babbage from Lincoln's Inn asking for help in solving some cryptic correspondence of importance in a case. Babbage undertook the task himself, solved a sheaf of monalphabetically enciphered letters, and read such intimacies as *Where is it to end* and *You have had warnin*[g] *long ago of what I wished*.

During these years he was also solving polyalphabetics. The messages retained their word divisions, and Babbage seized on these to make his entries. For example, in 1846, he broke an enciphered letter from his nephew, Henry, by guessing that it began *Dear Uncle* and ended with *nephew* and *Henry*. The cryptogram was in Vigenère, the key SOMERSET. He demonstrated a lively appreciation of periodicity—the repetition of the key —and, replying to a public challenge, even managed to extricate the two primary keys TWO and COMBINED from a complicated invented cipher that amounted to a double encipherment in Vigenère, first by one key, then by the other.

"One of the most singular characteristics of the art of deciphering," he declared in his autobiography, *Passages from the Life of a Philosopher*, "is the strong conviction possessed by every person, even moderately acquainted with it, that he is able to construct a cipher which nobody else can decipher. I have also observed that the cleverer the person, the more intimate is his conviction. In my earliest study of the subject, I shared in this belief, and maintained it for many years.

Charles Babbage uses mathematics to solve a cipher

"In a conversation on that subject which I had with the late Mr. Davies Gilbert, President of the Royal Society," he continued, "each maintained that he possessed a cipher which was absolutely inscrutable. On comparison, it appeared that we had both imagined the same law." This proved to be the use of each cipher letter as the key for the following plaintext letter. Both Babbage and Gilbert had independently reinvented, with a mixed alphabet, the autokey of Cardano and Vigenère—though Babbage readily admitted that "I am not sure that it may not be found in the *Steganographia* of Schott, or even of Trithemius." Years later, while explaining the cipher to a friend, "an indistinct glimpse of defeating it presented itself vaguely to my imagination." He went on to solve it, aided, no doubt, by word divisions, but achieving nevertheless the first autokey solution in history. The mixed cipher alphabet raises this to the level of a substantial accomplishment indeed.

Babbage most strikingly demonstrated his originality of thought when he applied algebra to cryptology. His papers are filled with formulas which he used to help him solve ciphers and see their underlying structure more clearly. Unfortunately his notes are too scrappy and incomplete to give any more than a tantalizing glimpse of what he was trying to accomplish. His most imposing formula, which he jotted down on worksheets dealing with a numerical cryptogram sent him by Gilbert, is this:

$$a = \frac{A_1R_1 - A_1R_2 - A_2R_1 + A_2T_2 - A_0R_2 + A_0R_3 - A_1R_2 - A_1R_3}{A_1^2 - 2A_1A_2 + A_2^2 - A_0A_2 + A_0A_3 + A_1A_2 - A_1A_3}$$

It may have been as efficacious as it is formidable, but neither an index to its symbolism nor any clue to its purpose exists.

Babbage's talents in cryptology appear to have been as exceptional as they were in other fields, and they were crippled by the same defect: the inability to leave off improving and to finish a work despite its imperfections. Had he published any specifics of his cryptanalyses, their insights might have upended the science. But his flaw robbed him of this distinction.

Of the man who did explode the bomb that gouged new channels for cryptology, little more is known than the bare outline provided by his service record. This is complete if not detailed, for Friedrich W. Kasiski spent his entire professional career as an officer in East Prussia's 33rd Infantry Regiment. Born November 29, 1805, in what was then Schlochau, West Prussia, and is now Czluchow, Poland, he enlisted in the regiment at 17. He won his commission as a second lieutenant three years later, in 1825—and did not budge out of that rank for 14 years. But he remained a first lieutenant only three years before he was promoted to captain and company commander, a post he held for nine years. He retired in 1852 with the rank of major, and though he served from 1860 to 1868 as the commander of a National Guard-like battalion, he found sufficient leisure to devote some to cryptology, for in 1863 his short but epochal book was published in Berlin by the respected house of Mittler & Sohn.

Three quarters of *Die Geheimschriften und die Dechiffrir-kunst* concentrates on answering the problem that had vexed cryptanalysts for more than 300 years: how to achieve a general solution for polyalphabetic ciphers with repeating keywords. (One chapter zeros in on "The Decipherment of French Writing"—a rather ominous portent in a book dedicated to the Count Albrecht von Roon, the Prussian minister of war who molded the army that humbled France only seven years later.) The polyalphabetic solution opened the doors to the cryptology of today. But the 95-page volume seems to have stirred almost no comment at the time. Kasiski himself lost interest in cryptology. He became an avid amateur anthropologist, joining the Natural Science Society of Danzig, unearthing prehistoric graves, and reporting on his work to learned journals. (One of his scholarly articles was cited in the

Encyclopaedia Britannica.) Kasiski died on May 22, 1881, almost certainly without realizing that he had wrought a revolution in cryptology.

That revolution had begun when Kasiski seized upon a phenomenon that Porta and perhaps others had observed but not recognized. This is that the conjunction of a repeated portion of the key with a repetition in the plaintext produces a repetition in the ciphertext:

```
key       RUNRUNRUNRUNRUNRUNRUNRUNRUNRUN
plaintext tobeornottobethatisthequestion
ciphertext KIOVIEEIGKIOVNURNVJNUVKHVMGZIA
```

Each time that the key RUNR engages the repeated plaintext *to be*, the repeated ciphertext tetragraph KIOV results. Like causes produce like effects. Similarly, when the repeated key-fragment UN operates upon the repeated *th*'s, the ciphertext registers repeated NU's.

Clearly, the keyword must repeat one or more times for a given part of it to encipher two identical bits of plaintext several letters distant from one another. The number of letters between the two resultant ciphertext repetitions will record the number of times that the keyword has repeated. The count of the interval "between" the two repetitions actually includes repeated letters. Thus the interval between the first KIOV and the second is 9, figured like this: 5 letters not repeated and 4 that are. This interval of nine results from the fact that the keyword has three letters and has repeated three times. These repetitions betray the movements of the keyword beneath the surface of the cryptogram just as the ducking of a fishing cork tells of a nibble. Analysis of the intervals between the repetitions can disclose the length of the keyword.

Obviously, not all plaintext repeats will show up as ciphertext repetitions. The two *ti*'s of *that is* and *question* do not because they are enciphered by different key digraphs, nor do the *st*'s of *is the* and *question*. Furthermore, repetitions sometimes appear that are no more than the result of coincidence. For example, *th* keyed by CO will become vv in Vigenère, but so will *ir* keyed by NE. Two appearances of vv thus do not indubitably reflect a repetition of plaintext *th*. These spurious indications are usually called "accidental" repetitions in polyalphabetic cryptanalysis to distinguish them from the "true" repetitions, like KIOV.

Accidental repetitions will naturally give some false clues about the length of the keyword. But since their effect is diffused, whereas that of the true repetitions is concentrated, the real keyword length usually shows up fairly clearly. Knowledge of how many letters are in the keyword tells how many alphabets were used in the polyalphabetic encipherment. This information permits the cryptanalyst to sort the letters of the cryptogram so that all those enciphered with the first keyletter are brought together in one group, all those enciphered with the second keyletter in another group, and so forth. Since all of the, say, *e*'s in the first group were converted under the influence of a single keyletter to the same ciphertext letter, all of the *a*'s to one ciphertext letter,

The Contribution of the Dilettantes

and so on, each of these collections of letters constitutes a monalphabetic substitution cipher and so can be solved like one.

An example using the following cryptogram should make this clear:

ANYVG YSTYN RPLWH RDTKX RNYPV QTGHP HZKFE YUMUS AYWVK

ZYEZM EZUDL JKTUL JLKQB JUQVU ECKBN RCTHP KESXM AZOEN SXGOL

PGNLE EBMMT GCSSV MRSEZ MXHLP KJEJH TUPZU EDWKN NNRWA GEEXS

LKZUD LJKFI XHTKP IAZMX FACWC TQIDU WBRRL TTKVN AJWVB

REAWT NSEZM OECSS VMRSL JMLEE BMMTG AYVIY GHPEM YFARW AOAEL

UPIUA YYMGE EMJQK SFCGU GYBPJ BPZYP JASNN FSTUS STYVG YS

Repetitions of three letters or more have been underlined; bigraphic ones have been ignored here as too frequent, though in shorter cryptograms they are quite valuable. The monoliteral frequency count is:

E S M Y T A K U L N P G J R Z V W B H C X F D I Q O
22 18 16 16 15 14 14 14 13 13 13 12 11 11 11 10 9 8 8 7 7 6 5 5 5 4

It differs strikingly from the count of a monalphabetic substitution. All 26 letters appear several times, while several would be missing from an equally long monalphabetic cryptogram. No one letter stands out remarkably; the two most frequent reach only 7.7 and 6.3 per cent, compared to the 12 per cent in a monalphabetic substitution. The profile shows no plateaus of high-, medium-, low-, and rare-frequency letters. Instead it descends in a gentle, even slope. These characteristics result from the dispersal of individual letter-frequencies among the several alphabets.

With the repetitions located, Kasiski advised the cryptanalyst to "calculate the distance separating the repetitions from one another. . . . and endeavor to break up this number into its factors. . . . The factor most frequently found indicates the number of letters in the key." Cryptanalysts usually perform this operation—now called a "Kasiski examination"—in tabular form.

	positions			
repetition	*first*	*second*	*interval*	*factors*
YVGYS	3	283	280	$2 \times 2 \times 2 \times 5 \times 7$
STY	7	281	274	2×137
GHP	28	226	198	$2 \times 3 \times 3 \times 11$
ZUDLJK	52	148	96	$2 \times 2 \times 2 \times 2 \times 2 \times 3$
LEEBMMTG	99	213	114	$2 \times 3 \times 19$
SEZM	113	197	84	$2 \times 2 \times 3 \times 7$
ZMX	115	163	48	$2 \times 2 \times 2 \times 2 \times 3$
GEE	141	249	108	$2 \times 2 \times 3 \times 3 \times 3$

The most frequent factor is 2, which appears in every instance. But since 2 must be a factor in every even interval, and since keys as short as 2 or 3 letters are extremely unlikely, cryptanalysts usually consider only lengths of 4 and above. In the above list, 4, or 2×2, occurs in five of the eight intervals, 5 in only one, 6 in six, 7 in two, 8 in two, 9 in two, 12 in four, and all others except multiples of these (as 18 and 24) occur but once. At first, 6 seems to be the proper choice on the basis of frequency. On second thought, however, 12 makes an even better showing, considering that a repetition has only half as many chances to show up in a period of 12 as in one of 6. But then the cryptanalyst, checking, sees that the period of 12 would make the $2 \times 3 \times 19$ interval of LEEBMMTG an accidental one, which is exceedingly unlikely, and that a period of 6 would keep it as a key-caused repetition. He therefore returns to the period of 6. The behavior of the YVGYS repetition can only be ignored for the moment.

The cryptanalyst then writes out the cryptogram in lines six letters wide, thus setting beneath one another all the letters presumed enciphered with the same keyletter. He segregates each column and attempts to find the plaintext equivalents of the letters in each one. With the above cryptogram, he finds the following 48 letters in the first column. These represent all the letters homogeneously enciphered by the first keyletter (if the period of 6 is correct) and constitute the 1st, 7th, 13th, 19th, 25th, 31st, and so on, letters in the cryptogram: ASLKVHUWZLJUKHMSGMSZKUWWSLHZWUTJAZSJ MVEWUYJGJJSY.

Meager though its frequency count is, it indubitably reflects a monalphabetic substitution; a polyalphabetic count would be much smoother:

$$\overline{A}\ B\ C\ D\ \overline{E}\ F\ \overline{\overline{G}}\ H\ I\ \overline{\overline{\overline{J}}}\ \overline{\overline{K}}\ \overline{\overline{L}}\ \overline{\overline{M}}\ N\ O\ P\ Q\ R\ \overline{\overline{\overline{S}}}\ \overline{T}\ \overline{\overline{U}}\ \overline{\overline{V}}\ \overline{\overline{W}}\ X\ \overline{Y}\ \overline{\overline{Z}}$$

This is an encouraging sign to the cryptanalyst, for only if his deduction about the period is correct will such a count be monalphabetic.

To the experienced eye, the little hills and dales of that frequency count limn one thing: the normal profile. This is the outline made by the standard frequency count (of English). It does not have to start at *a*; it preserves its shape even in cyclical form, and, when dealing with the Caesar alphabets of the Vigenère family, this is the form in which the cryptanalyst will most often meet it. The single most durable and detectable feature of the normal profile is the long, low peneplane of *uvwxyz*, which extends almost a quarter of the profile and is extremely depressed. This basin is sharply walled off by the *rst* cordillera at one end and the single peak of *a* at the other. The other features of the profile are more easily eroded by decreases in size of sample. The pinnacle of *e* normally soars midway between *a* and the double tower of *hi*, which is followed by the severe drop to *jk*. High-frequency *n* and *o* also rise to twin peaks. In short samples, however, the troughs of the profile are often more reliable indicators than the crests.

This physiognomy appears, in stunted form, in the count above. The low-frequency depression is unmistakable at NOPQR. The *rst* group cannot be

The Contribution of the Dilettantes

matched with KLM, for then high-frequency J would represent q and the high-frequency s would represent z. It must thus coincide with JKL, and though this gives plaintext u a slightly disproportionate frequency, it is one well within the allowable limits. Plaintext c also has too high a frequency, but this is one of the normal abnormalities that the cryptanalyst must expect. In general, then, the match is satisfactory. If both the plain and cipher alphabets are known, as they are here, being both normal alphabets, the identification of a single plaintext letter will align the cipher alphabet with the plain alphabet and thus instantaneously yield the identification of every other cipher letter. In this case, the cryptanalyst fixes the alignment of the plain and the cipher components at the "point" $uvwxyz$ = MNOPQR, with this result:

```
plain  i j k l m n o p q r s t u v w x y z a b c d e f g h
cipher A B C D E F G H I J K L M N O P Q R S T U V W X Y Z
```

This can be cycled to bring the plaintext a to the head, which is the more usual arrangement, but the plain-to-cipher equivalencies will remain the same. These equivalents are, for the 48 letters enciphered by the first keyletter:

```
cipher A S L K V H U W Z L J U K H M S G M S Z K U W W S L H Z W U T J A Z S J M V E W U Y J G J J S Y
plain  i a t s d p c e  h t r c s  p u a o u a h s c e  e  at p h e  c b r i  h a r u d m e c g r o r r a g
```

This is quite an acceptable aggregation of plaintext letters, and the solution picks up momentum.

Perhaps the most important thing that the cryptanalyst learned from the identification of the alphabet as the normal profile was that the cipher belonged to the Vigenère family. This opens the door to a whole variety of special techniques. These are based on the fact that the alphabet, in this family of ciphers, is known. The techniques would work as well for any other polyalphabetic cipher in which the cipher alphabet is known to the cryptanalyst, but such situations arise far more frequently with the Vigenère family because the standard A-to-Z arrangement that it employs is universally known and extensively applied.

One of these special techniques identifies plaintext letters mechanically. It employs cardboard strips with the alphabet printed on them twice, the nine high-frequency letters ($e, t, a, o, n, i, r, s, h$) in red, the others in black. The cryptanalyst aligns the strips under one another to bring the ciphertext letters into a column. The other columns that are automatically formed out to the right represent all the possible solutions for that aggregation of ciphertext letters. The cryptanalyst scans them to see which one is the reddest by virtue of having the most high-frequency letters. Probability theory can predict how likely it is that the reddest column will be the correct one: with nine ciphertext letters, 42 per cent; with twelve, 61 per cent; with fifteen, 74 per cent. If the next-to-reddest column is included, the probabilities that either it or the reddest will prove the correct plaintext rise to 74, 85, and 90 per cent, respectively.

A practical drawback is that since nine letters comprise fully a third of the alphabet, most columns will look fairly red. It is easier to cast out the wrong columns than to choose the right one, and the best criterion for rejection is the presence of too many rare letters. The color principle may be applied to them: blue for the five low-frequency letters. This technique is illustrated in printed form in the accompanying table by using boldface for *j*, *k*, *q*, *x*, and *z*. The ciphertext letters shown are the first ten that have been enciphered by the second keyletter (the 2nd, 8th, 14th, 20th, 26th, and so on, letters of the cryptogram). Now the five low-frequency letters combined have a frequency of about 2 per cent. In a text of 48 letters like this, then, the five should have a total frequency of one letter. The cryptanalyst will be playing it safe if he passes over any full column with three or more boldface letters.

ciphertext	*possible plaintexts*
N	n o p **q** r s t u v w **x** y **z** a b c d e f g h i **j k** l m
T	t u v w **x** y **z** a b c d e f g h i **j k** l m n o p **q** r s
W	w **x** y **z** a b c d e f g h i **j k** l m n o p **q** r s t u v
X	**x** y **z** a b c d e f g h i **j k** l m n o p **q** r s t u v w
Q	**q** r s t u v w **x** y **z** a b c d e f g h i **j k** l m n o p
Z	**z** a b c d e f g h i **j k** l m n o p **q** r s t u v w **x** y
M	m n o p **q** r s t u v w **x** y **z** a b c d e f g h i **j k** l
V	v w **x** y **z** a b c d e f g h i **j k** l m n o p **q** r s t u
M	m n o p **q** r s t u v w **x** y **z** a b c d e f g h i **j k** l
J	**j k** l m n o p **q** r s t u v w **x** y **z** a b c d e f g h i

On this basis, only the column beginning *flop* is acceptable. When these letters are paired with those that would precede them in the plaintext, the correctness of both choices becomes incontrovertible:

1	2	3	4	5	6		1	2	3	4	5	6
A	N	Y	V	G	Y		W	V	K	Z	Y	E
i	f						e	n				
S	T	Y	N	R	P		Z	M	E	Z	U	D
a	l						h	e				
L	W	H	R	D	T		L	J	K	T	U	L
t	o						t	b				
K	X	R	N	Y	P		J	L	K	Q	B	J
s	p						r	d				
V	Q	T	G	H	P		U	Q	V	U	E	C
d	i						c	i				
H	Z	K	F	E	Y		K	B	N	R	C	T
p	r						s	t				
U	M	U	S	A	Y		H	P	K	E	S	X
c	e						p	h				

(and so on)

The Contribution of the Dilettantes

From this point on, the cryptanalyst can complete the solution by guessing at words and seeing what effects they produce. For example, the *he* screams for a *t* to precede it; this would be the E in column 6. A test decipherment with the alphabet in which *t* = E, which, in Vigenère, is the alphabet of keyletter L, proves eminently satisfactory: *e, e, n, t, a, r, m,* . . . .

In the end, the key turns out to be SIGNAL and the plaintext to be as follows: *If signals are to be displayed in the presence of an enemy, they must be guarded by ciphers. The ciphers must be capable of frequent changes. The rules by which these changes are made must be simple. Ciphers are undiscoverable in proportion as their changes are frequent and as the messages in each change are brief. From Albert J. Myer's Manual of Signals.*

The longest repetition, LEEBMMTG, resulted from the coincidence of the repeated *frequent* with the key GNALSIGN, and the next longest, ZUDLJK, from the coincidence of the two *must be*'s with the key NALSIG. On the other hand, the threefold repetition of *ciphers* and the fourfold repetition of *change* did not pole through the fabric of the ciphertext because each encountered different sections of the key. The accidental repetition YVGYS resulted from a freak situation in which the key GNALS enciphered *signa* and then the key SIGNA enciphered *gnals*. Accidental repetitions longer than trigraphs are extremely rare, though they have been known to occur.

What if the alphabets used in the repeating-key system are unknown? The cryptanalyst is faced with the problem of quarrying out plaintext letter after letter, since a single identification will not carry all with it. Usually he conducts a linguistic analysis, and on the basis of contacts, frequency, and so forth, makes a few tentative assumptions. These follow the lines laid down for monalphabetic substitutions. He substitutes these assumptions back into the cryptogram and reconstructs the plaintext bit by bit, often aided by a recovery of the key and reconstruction of the cipher alphabets. The process usually requires 40 to 60 letters per keyletter for success.

7

CRISES OF THE UNION

SHORTLY AFTER the fateful guns spoke at Fort Sumter, a 36-year-old telegrapher was summoned to the Cincinnati house of the commander of the military Department of the Ohio. Anson Stager had risen rapidly to become the first general superintendent of the newly formed Western Union Telegraph Company; on mobilization, he had been given charge of the Department of the Ohio's military telegraphs. He had previously devised a cipher for Ohio's Governor Dennison that had worked just fine in communication with his gubernatorial colleagues in Indiana and Illinois, and Major General George B. McClellan wanted Stager to draw up a military cipher along these lines.

Stager complied. Soon McClellan was relying on the cipher to protect his communications during his successful campaign in West Virginia, and Major General John C. Frémont, commander of the Western Department, transmitted orders for his operations in it. One of its very first users was the detective Allan Pinkerton, founder of the agency that bears his name. The key of the cipher was so short that one colonel carried it on the back of a business card. Its brevity and dependability endeared it to McClellan, who brought it with him later in 1861 when he came east to assume command of the Army of the Potomac. From there it spread rapidly throughout the Union forces, becoming the best as well as the best-known cipher of the Civil War. It was the first military cipher to be used extensively, largely because the Civil War first employed the telegraph on a large scale.

The cipher was a word transposition. Stager's telegraphic experience evidently led him to a system in which the ciphertext consisted—as in the new telegraph codes—of ordinary words, which are far less subject to dangerous garbles than groups of incoherent letters. The system also had an appealing simplicity: the plaintext was written out in lines and transcribed by columns, up some and down others in a specified order. As the war progressed, some simple improvements noticeably strengthened it. Nulls ruffled the transcription. Routes traced mazes of diagonals and interrupted columns through ever larger rectangles. Samuel H. Beckwith, Ulysses S. Grant's cipher operator, suggested that important terms be represented by codewords which he carefully chose to minimize telegraphic error. The cipher expanded from one that could be contained on a single card to one that, at the end of the war, required 12 pages to list routes and 36 for the 1,608 codewords. This was Cipher No. 4, the last of a series of 12 that the North employed at various times.*

A good example of the system is given by the encipherment of this message sent by Abraham Lincoln on June 1, 1863: "For Colonel Ludlow. Richardson and Brown, correspondents of the Tribune, captured at Vicksburg, are detained at Richmond. Please ascertain why they are detained and get them off if you can. The President." Cipher No. 9 was in use, and it provided the following codeword substitutions: VENUS for *colonel*, WAYLAND for *captured*, ODOR for *Vicksburg*, NEPTUNE for *Richmond*, ADAM for *President of U.S.*, and NELLY for *4 : 30 p.m.*, the time of dispatch. The encipherer chose to write out the message in seven lines of five words each with three nulls to complete the rectangle:

For	VENUS	Ludlow	Richardson	and
Brown	correspondents	of	the	Tribune
WAYLAND	at	ODOR	are	detained
at	NEPTUNE	please	ascertain	why
they	are	detained	and	get
them	off	if	you	can
ADAM	NELLY	THIS	FILLS	UP

The route for this configuration ran up the first column, down the second, up the fifth, down the fourth, up the third. Nulls were inserted at the end of each column. With the keyword GUARD heading the message to indicate the size of the rectangle and its route, this ciphertext resulted: GUARD ADAM THEM THEY AT WAYLAND BROWN FOR KISSING VENUS CORRESPONDENTS AT NEPTUNE ARE OFF NELLY TURNING UP CAN GET WHY DETAINED TRIBUNE AND TIMES RICHARDSON THE ARE ASCERTAIN AND YOU FILLS BELLY THIS IF DETAINED PLEASE ODOR OF LUDLOW COMMISSIONER.

This particular telegram was sent from the War Department over the signature of Major Thomas T. Eckert, the general superintendent of military telegraphs, who later became chairman of the board of the Western Union Telegraph Company. Because the flow of orders and reports through Eckert's office gave a more detailed and up-to-the-minute picture of the war than any other source, Lincoln paid it frequent visits. He virtually lived there during battles. The telegraph office and its adjunct, the cipher quarters, were located

---

* These do not include the ciphers—mostly simple word transpositions—that the several military departments employed within their own territory. The Department of the Missouri used these more extensively than any other. A number of other cipher systems were proposed by members of the infant Signal Corps. They generally consisted of various types of polyalphabetic systems, and one of them—a fanlike set of 26 wooden tablets, each with a different ciphertext alphabet on it, designed for use with a keyword by Sergeant Edwin H. Hawley—matured into the first United States patent granted for a cipher device (No. 48,681, July 11, 1865).

in a converted library and its anteroom, respectively, on the second floor of the War Department building, which stood next to the White House. Here Lincoln relaxed and chatted daily with the three young telegrapher-cipher-operators, David Homer Bates, Charles A. Tinker, and Albert B. Chandler. Bates, who was only 18 when the war started, told about it years later:

"Outside the members of his cabinet and his private secretaries, none were brought into closer or more confidential relations with Lincoln than the cipher-operators, . . . for during the Civil War the President spent more of his waking hours in the War Department telegraph office than in any other place, except the White House. . . . His tall, homely form could be seen crossing the well-shaded lawn between the White House and the War Department day after day with unvaried regularity." When Lincoln entered the cipher room he would open a little drawer in one of the desks and read the carbon copies of messages that the operators had made on lettersize tissue paper and placed, unfolded, in that drawer for the President's information.

"It was his habit to read from the top down," Chandler wrote, "and when he came to those which he had already read, with a smile he said, 'Well, I guess I have got down to the raisins.' As I seemed in doubt as to what that might mean, he explained that a little girl, having eaten improperly both in quantity and quality, beginning with a lot of raisins, was made quite ill, and could find relief only in the process which a sick stomach is likely to compel. After an exhausting siege she gave an exclamation of satisfaction that the end of her trouble was near, for she had 'got down to the raisins.' "

Once when Lincoln entered the telegraph office on a day of national fasting, he noticed that all the operators were busy, and he remarked: "Gentlemen, this is fast day, and I am pleased to observe that you are working as *fast* as you can; the proclamation was mine, and that is my interpretation of its bearing on you." When a battle was in progress, the President would look over the shoulders of the young cipher operators as an especially important message was being deciphered. Sometimes he would read the dispatches aloud, and when he reached such codewords as HOSANNA and HUSBAND, both of which meant *Jefferson Davis* in one cipher, or HUNTER and HAPPY, both meaning *Robert E. Lee*, he would invariably translate them as "Jeffy D" or "Bobby Lee."

War is hell, Sherman said, but he didn't know Confederate cryptography. In contrast to the close-knit Union organization, the South apparently extended the states' rights principle into the realm of cryptography and let each commanding officer choose his own codes and ciphers. Thus, just before the Battle of Shiloh, on April 6, 1862, that excellent officer but indifferent cryptographer, General Albert S. Johnston, agreed with his second-in-command, General Pierre Beauregard, upon a Caesar substitution for military use! Two weeks earlier President Jefferson Davis had sent Johnston "a dictionary of which I have the duplicate. . . . the word *junction* would be

Crises of the Union 217

designated by 146. L. 20," meaning, respectively, page number, left-hand column, and word number. Beauregard, in turn, sent Major General Patton Anderson a monalphabetic cipher to assure the secrecy of their communications. The Secretary of the Navy, Stephen B. Mallory, instructed Lieutenant John N. Maffitt, then in Mobile readying the cruiser *Florida* for its spectacularly destructive cruise against Northern shipping, to buy two identical copies of a dictionary for use as a codebook. His colleague, the dashing Commander Raphael Semmes, likewise bought copies of *Reid's English Dictionary* for the same purpose as part of his preparation for his harassment of merchantmen in *Sumter*, the Confederacy's first warship.

A Confederate cipher telegram, in Vigenère

The rebels reposed their major trust, however, in the Vigenère, sometimes using it in the form of a brass cipher disk. In theory, it was an excellent choice, for so far as the South knew the cipher was unbreakable. In practice, it proved a dismal failure. For one thing, transmission errors that added or subtracted a letter (American Morse was peculiarly susceptible to this kind) unmeshed the key from the cipher and caused no end of difficulty. Once Major Cunningham of General Kirby Smith's staff tried for twelve hours to decipher a garbled message; he finally gave up in disgust and galloped around the Union flank to the sender to find out what it said. For another, it could be solved by intuitive techniques. And if the South had difficulty reading Dixie cipher messages, the North did not. "It would sometimes take too long to make translations of intercepted dispatches for us to receive any benefit from them," Ulysses S. Grant wrote. "But sometimes they gave useful information."

During the siege of Vicksburg, Grant's troops captured eight rebels who were trying to slip into the beleaguered city with 200,000 percussion caps. On one of them the Federals found the following cryptogram, which Grant sent to Washington "hoping that someone there may be able to make it out":

Jackson, May 25, 1863

Lieutenant General Pemberton: My XAFV. USLX was VVUFLSJP by the BRCYAJ. 200000 VEGT. SUAJ. NERP. ZIFM. It will be GFOECSZOD as they NTYMNX. Bragg MJTPHINZG a QRCMKBSE. When it DZGJX. I will YOIG. AS. QHY. NITWM do you YTIAM the IIKM. VFVEY. How and where is the JSQMLGUGSFTVE. HBFY is your ROEEL.

J. E. Johnston

Lincoln's three young cipher operators—Tinker, Chandler, and Bates—soon solved it. It proved to be a Vigenère, key MANCHESTER BLUFF, and its clear (after corrections) read as follows (with the two words not solved by the trio in brackets);

Lieutenant General Pemberton: My [*last note*] was *captured* by the *picket*. 200000 *caps have been sent*. It will be *increased* as they *arrive*. Bragg *is sending* a *division*. When it *joins* I will *come to you. Which* do you *think* the *best route*? How and where is the *enemy encamped*? *What* is your *force*?

J. E. Johnston

This was only one of a number of Confederate cryptograms solved by this triumvirate, who, being barely out of their teens, were probably the youngest wartime cryptanalysts in history. The solution did not help Grant take Vicksburg, but it provided the three young men with a Confederate keyword, of which the South apparently used only three during the war. Early in 1865, J. B. Devoe, acting master of the United States Navy, was reporting to the Assistant Secretary of the Navy the two known keywords—MANCHESTER BLUFF and COMPLETE VICTORY (a phrase the Confederates clung to long after that cherished hope had dissipated)—and confessing that "the new key is not known." But the youngsters' most important solution dealt not with military but with political affairs.

In December of 1863, Postmaster Abram Wakeman of New York spotted an envelope addressed to Alexander Keith, Jr., in Halifax, Nova Scotia, who was known to be in frequent communication with rebel agents. Wakeman turned it over to the Secretary of War, who found that the letter inside was written in a complicated mixture of symbol ciphers. After War Department clerks puzzled over the mysterious signs in vain for two days, the cryptogram was given to the "Sacred Three," as Bates, Chandler, and Tinker liked to call themselves. They determined to do what the clerks could not.

They ascertained that the unknown encipherer had intermingled five different kinds of signs plus ordinary letters as substitutes in the letter. But he

Crises of the Union

had imprudently marked off the words with commas and confined himself to a single set of signs within each word. The letter patterns of the plaintext consequently showed through. One 6-letter word repeated its second and sixth letters. It was followed by a 4-letter word that in turn was followed by the cleartext phrase *reaches you*. The three deduced that the sequence should read *before this reaches you*. Bates recognized the ciphertext signs involved as those of the pigpen cipher, which had been used as a price marker in the Pittsburgh

The Confederate agents' message, solved by Tinker, Chandler, and Bates

store in which he had worked as a boy. This permitted prompt reconstruction of the entire pigpen alphabet, driving a substantial wedge into the cryptogram. The identification of signs in the dateline as standing for "N.Y. Dec. 18, 1863" yielded further values, and, working in this way, the three—with the President hovering about anxiously—unlocked the cipher in about four hours. It read:

N Y Dec 18 1863
Hon J P Benjamin   Secretary of State   Richmond Va
   Willis is here   The two steamers will leave here about Christmas Lamar and Bowers left here via Bermuda two weeks ago   12000

rifled muskets came duly to hand and were shipped to Halifax as instructed We will be able to seize the other two steamers as per programme Trowbridge has followed the Presidents orders We will have Briggs under arrest before this reaches you Cost $2000 We want more money How shall we draw   Bills are forwarded to Slidell and rects recd Write as before

J H C

A special cabinet meeting was called, and by 7:30 that evening Assistant Secretary of War Charles A. Dana had started for New York to take charge of an investigation. Two days later, another cryptogram addressed to Keith was intercepted and promptly solved. "Say to Memminger," it read, "that Hilton will have the machines all finished and dies all cut ready for shipping by the first of January   The engraving of the plates is superb." Christopher G. Memminger was the Confederate Secretary of the Treasury; the letter made it clear that plates for printing rebel currency were being made in New York. Hilton, the engraver, was easily located in lower Manhattan, and on the last day of the year the U.S. marshal raided his plant, seizing the plates, machinery, dies, and several million dollars worth of already-printed bonds and money. The plot was broken up, the Confederacy deprived of badly needed plates for printing its paper money. For their central role in all this, the three junior cryptanalysts each received the handsome raise of $25 a month.

The men in gray, who sometimes could not read their own messages, could never solve the Union's. The ravings of the Delphic oracle must have seemed more clear than messages in the federal route transposition. Though many of the North's estimated 6,500,000 telegrams were in cipher, though the Confederates tapped the Union wires, though their cavalry raids must have captured parallel plain and cipher copies of messages, though the system had intrinsic weaknesses—though they had all these clues, the rebels never sorted out the Yankee word-thicket. This would be incredible if they had not vouched for it themselves by publishing a number of messages in their newspapers with a general request for solution. Even the capture of two of the ciphers themselves—No. 12 in July of 1864 and No. 1 in September—failed to help. The Yankees simply got out a new list of routes and jargon words, and the result was always more than the rebels could handle.

Appomattox itself did not still the cryptologic reverberations of the Civil War. In the trunk of John Wilkes Booth, found in his room at the National Hotel after he was shot, officials discovered a Vigenère tableau. This was introduced into evidence at the trial of the eight Southern sympathizers charged with conspiring to assassinate the President in an obvious attempt to link them with the actual killer, though no one testified to their use of the cipher. The prosecution then sought to show that the crime had been instigated by the Confederate government by exhibiting a rebel "cipher reel," which Major Eckert averred to be identical with the Booth cipher. This curiosity, captured on a shelf in the Richmond office of Judah P. Benjamin, Confederate Secretary of State, simply consisted of a Vigenère tableau wrapped around a cylinder; over this, an arm supported two indicators that presumably pointed out the letters. It deciphered no messages at the trial. The burlesque reached a climax when a North Carolina pile-driver named Charles Deuel described how he and a friend solved a cipher that he found floating in the water near where he was working. The plaintext, signed "No. 5," began: "I am happy to inform you that Pet has done his work well. He is safe, and Old Abe is in hell." What connection all these displays had with the accused was never made clear, but they were hanged anyway.

At about the same time that Booth and others were being hunted down and captured, Jefferson Davis was using the third Vigenère key to compose the last official cryptogram of the Confederacy. Sent to his secretary on April 24, almost two weeks after Lee's surrender, it was a message of futile defiance ordering "active operations to be resumed in forty-eight hours." No one knows who chose this final key of the Confederacy, or why, but in view of Davis' own impending fall and the black days of Reconstruction that lay just ahead, it gleams as the most somberly prophetic in the whole history of cryptology: COME RETRIBUTION.

On the morning of Monday, October 7, 1878, the *New York Tribune* trumpeted forth one of the great scoops of American journalism. Under the two-column headline "The Captured Cipher Telegrams," the lead story of the day blared the plaintext of cryptogram after cryptogram that the *Tribune* had solved. The messages, which hearkened back to the most famous electoral dispute in American history, were the first to play a vital role in American politics.

After the popular votes were counted in the presidential election of 1876, the Democratic candidate, Samuel J. Tilden, held a clear lead of 250,000 ballots over his Republican opponent, Rutherford B. Hayes. But which way the deciding electoral college vote went depended on which of the double and conflicting returns from Florida, Louisiana, South Carolina, and Oregon were accepted as valid. Congress created a special electoral commission to settle the matter; by a straight party vote of 8 to 7, it awarded all 22 contested electoral votes to Hayes. This gave him a majority of 1 in the college—and the Presidency.

During the tumultuous legislative session that followed, a Congressional committee was appointed to look into persistent Democratic rumors of Republican purchase of electors' votes. As part of its investigation, the committee subpoenaed 641 political telegrams out of the 29,275 that had clattered back and forth between politicians and their agents in the four states—the vast majority having been burned by Western Union to publicize the privacy of the correspondence entrusted to it. A large bundle of the impounded wires kicked around the committee room during the summer of 1878, and, through a complicated chain beginning with a committee messenger and ending with the Republican National Chairman, 27 of the telegrams in cipher were leaked to the Republican-leaning *Tribune* in the hope that they might embarrass the Democrats.

A few weeks earlier, Manton Marble, one of Tilden's closest political advisors, had written an open letter to the New York *Sun* contrasting dark Republican practices with Tilden's station in "the keen bright sunlight of publicity." Whitelaw Reid, the *Tribune*'s brilliant editor, took a suggestion of the Republican chairman and inserted the cipher telegrams in editorials as subtle commentaries on Marble's letter. The Democrats squirmed as the *Tribune* staff played impishly upon the ciphertexts. Was this cryptic mumbo-jumbo the vaunted Democratic candor? But as more and more dispatches poured in upon Reid from other G.O.P. sympathizers, he conceived a broader scheme. Reckoning that any negotiations that had to be conducted beneath the cloak of cipher would mightily discomfit the Democrats if drawn from under that cover, he set to work to get them read.

Prompted by hints in the editorials, numerous subscribers offered suggestions for their solution. Schuyler Colfax, who had been Vice President during Grant's first term and had been interested in cryptology since his teens, referred Reid to several magazine articles on the subject, but they proved useless. William M. Evarts, the Secretary of State, had a good idea: get a student of mathematics to unearth the law on which the messages were based. But this only promised; it did not produce. Reid even tried the approach direct when he ran into Tilden at fashionable Saratoga that August: "I told him that we had all the cipher dispatches that went between his house and Florida, and asked him, laughingly, for the key. I told him we couldn't make head or tail to them, and wanted him to help us. He smiled and blushed, innocent as a baby, and passed on." Things were getting nowhere.

Meanwhile, the Detroit *Post* had learned from a former business partner of J. N. H. Patrick, one of the Democratic agents, that the Democrats had couched their electoral communications to Oregon in the same dictionary code that Patrick had used in his mining ventures. The encoder had looked up the word in the edition of the *Household English Dictionary* that was published at London in 1876, noted the word's numerical position on the page, and took the corresponding word four pages to the front of the book as the code equivalent. The decoder had reversed the process. For instance, the most damning of the Oregon messages read, in codetext:

BY VIZIER ASSOCIATION INNOCUOUS TO NEGLIGENCE CUNNING MINUTELY PREVIOUSLY READMIT DOLTISH TO PURCHASED AFAR ACT WITH CUNNING AFAR SACRISTY UNWEIGHED AFAR POINTER TIGRESS CUTTLE SUPERANNUATED SYLLABUS DILATORINESS MISAPPREHENSION CONTRABAND KOUNTZE BISCULOUS TOP USHER SPINIFEROUS ANSWER

J. N. H. PATRICK

Crises of the Union 223

The first codeword, BY, is on page 30 as word 29. The decoder counted towards the back to page 34, where the 29th word is *certificate*. The entire plaintext read:

Portland, Nov. 28, [1876]

W. T. Pelton, New York

    Certificate will be issued to one Democrat. Must purchase Republican elector to recognize and act with Democrat and secure vote and prevent trouble. Deposit ten thousand dollars my credit Kountze Brothers, Twelve Wall Street. Answer.

J. N. H. Patrick

On September 4, one of the *Tribune*'s editors, John R. G. Hassard, basing his work on the Detroit *Post*'s revelation, set forth $3\frac{1}{2}$ columns of cryptograms and translations that showed that the Democrats had sought to buy a Republican elector for $10,000 and that the deal had fallen through only through delays in transmission.

But the *Household English Dictionary* was not the key so urgently desired to the messages from the other three states. With no outside help forthcoming for their solution, Reid set his staff to work on the problem in earnest.

Hassard, then 42, had become managing editor in all but name on the death of Horace Greeley in 1872. A tall, lanky man with sandy hair, sidewhiskers, and hazel eyes, always spruce, with a no-nonsense manner, he was gifted with a charm of style and breadth of culture that showed in his graceful editorials. He had converted to Catholicism at 15—a courageous act in the heyday of Know-Nothingism—and, after graduating from St. John's College at the head of his class, abandoned his plans for the priesthood only because of ill health. He served as secretary to the first archbishop of New York, John Hughes, whose biography he later wrote. His dispatches to the *Tribune* from Bayreuth on the premiere of the Nibelungen Ring series in 1876 did more to bring Wagner's music to America than perhaps anything else up to that time. Hassard took on the challenge of the cryptograms himself, and worked on them so uninterruptedly that a cold hung on and developed into tuberculosis. He spent the next ten years in search of health, but succumbed in 1888.

Soon after Hassard started his task, another member of the *Tribune* staff became interested and took up the puzzles independently. This was Colonel William M. Grosvenor, who had become economic editor of the *Tribune* in 1875, three years earlier. A burly, forceful man, then 43, with bristly eyebrows, long hair and beard, and a leonine head, he had demonstrated his statistical skill while editor of the St. Louis *Democrat* by making an elaborate comparison between the whisky production of the St. Louis distillers and the revenue accruing therefrom to the government. It clearly indicated fraud on the part of the liquor interest and led to exposure of the notorious Whisky Ring. A native of Massachusetts, he had commanded a regiment of Negro troops in the Civil War. Grosvenor later became editor of the prestigious

Dun's Review and was frequently consulted by government experts on tariff and currency legislation. His integrity in these matters was so great that on one occasion his advice cost him a fortune in the stock of a printing firm. He was gifted in mathematics and languages, was one of the most expert billiard players in New York, could carry on three games of chess simultaneously, and more than held his own at tennis and whist. He died in 1900.

Grosvenor and Hassard, each in his own home, wrestled with the riddles and obstinacies of an unfamiliar science. They could not have known it, but not only were they mastering a problem that had repulsed many, they were also breaking new ground in that science.

A cipher telegram offering the electoral votes of Florida for $200,000, solved and published by the New York Tribune

"They both did extremely well," Reid said later, "worked independently, compared notes loyally and altogether cooperated in a charming way in a highly important piece of work. Hassard was a little earlier in the field, and to that extent deserves special credit; but Grosvenor was equally keen, and, as well as I can now remember it, about equally successful. Sometimes he and Hassard would attack the same despatch on different lines, and after being foiled again and again, would finally reach the solution the same evening, Hassard in Eighteenth Street and Grosvenor out at Englewood."

Unknown to them, a young mathematician from the U.S. Naval Observatory in Washington had been solving some of the specimen ciphers that Reid had published in the Marble-baiting editorials. This was Edward S. Holden, 31, who had graduated third in the West Point class of 1870 and had gone to

Crises of the Union

the Naval Observatory three years later. In 1879, the year following his work on the cipher telegrams, he was appointed librarian there. In 1885, he became president of the University of California and director of the Lick Observatory, relinquishing the presidency in 1888 on completion of the observatory. He founded the Astronomical Society of the Pacific, organized five eclipse expeditions, and edited the observatory's publications. From 1901 until his death in 1914 he was librarian at West Point, adding 30,000 volumes to the collection, cataloging it, and issuing many bibliographies.

Holden had been attracted by the "novel and ingenious character" of the cryptograms. "By September 7, 1878," he said later, "I was in possession of a rule by which any key to the most difficult and ingenious of these ... could infallibly be found." He approached the *Tribune*, which had liked Evarts' idea of hiring a mathematician, and Hassard sent on a quantity of dispatches. But Hassard and Grosvenor had independently reached the theory of solution that Holden had, and furthermore had solved some messages before he did. None of Holden's solutions reached the *Tribune* before Hassard and Grosvenor had solved those messages, Reid said, and in general his work was regarded as corroborative.

The most important messages, and those to which the new theory of solution applied, were enciphered in a form of word transposition grievously deteriorated from the excellent Civil War system that had evidently inspired it. Only four keys were employed, one each for telegrams of 15, 20, 25, and 30 words, with longer telegrams being enciphered in parts by two or more keys. Sometimes deciphering keys were used to encipher. Code disguised some of the proper names and important words. The enciphering key for 25 words (18, 12, 6, 25, 14, 1, 16, 11, 21, 5, 19, 2, 17, 24, 9, 22, 7, 4, 10, 8, 23, 20, 3, 13, 15) served to encipher this honest offer of corruption from Tallahassee:

    1   2   3   4   5   6   7   8   9 10 11   12
Have just received a proposition to hand over at any hour required
    13   14   15   16   17   18   19   20
Tilden decision of canvassing board and certificate of Governor Stearns
    21 22   23   24   25
for two hundred thousand. Manton Marble.

In the code list, BOLIVIA stood for *proposition*, RUSSIA for *Tilden*, LONDON for *canvassing board*, FRANCE for *Governor Stearns*, MOSELLE for *two*, GLASGOW for *hundred*, EDINBURGH for *thousand*, and MOSES for *Manton Marble*. As transmitted to New York, the message read:

CERTIFICATE REQUIRED TO MOSES DECISION HAVE LONDON HOUR FOR BOLIVIA OF JUST AND EDINBURGH AT MOSELLE HAND A ANY OVER GLASGOW FRANCE RECEIVED RUSSIA OF

The reply to that is extant; it was both clear and in clear: "Telegram here. Proposition too high."

The Hassard-Grosvenor-Holden theory of solution of messages like this fed upon the great quantity of dispatches in each key. It is now considered the general solution for all transposition ciphers, because it works on any transposition whenever two or more cryptograms of the same length in the same key are available for analysis. The method, which they developed empirically for the first time in cryptology, has become known as "multiple anagramming," and though Holden did not use that term, he gave a good description of the technique: "There is one way, and only one way, in which the general problem can be solved, and that is to take two messages, A and B, of the same number of words, and to number the words in each; then to arrange message A with its words in an order which will make sense, and to arrange the words of message B in the same order. There will be one order—and only one—in which the two messages will simultaneously make sense. This is the key."

Holden's description makes explicit one requirement of successful operation of multiple anagramming (that the two messages be the same length) but presupposes the other (that their keys be the same). The technique rests on the fact that, if two messages of the same length are transposed in the same system with identical keys, their individual words will wind up in the same relative positions. To put it differently, if the first word of the plaintext becomes the 15th word of the cryptogram in the first message, the first word of the plaintext of the second message will equally wind up in the 15th position of the second cryptogram. This is transposition's version of like causes producing like effects, and the principle holds for all transposition systems, letter as well as word, irrespective of their mixing process.

The principle may be illustrated with two five-letter cryptograms enciphered with the same key: GHINT and OWLCN. Suppose that the cryptanalyst begins trying to reconstruct the plaintext of the first message by assuming that it begins with *th*. This implies an encipherment key which moved the first plaintext letter (*t*, in this message) to the fifth position (in GHINT) and the second plaintext letter (*h*) to the second position (in GHINT). The cryptanalyst can determine that the same key would require the second message to begin with *nw*—hardly a promising beginning. If the cryptanalyst now tries to anagram the second message instead, he might try *cl* as a starter. The corresponding moves in the first cryptogram would bring *n* and *i* together at the head of the message. This gives good possibilities in both messages, which is, of course, more desirable. The cryptanalyst will continue juggling the two messages, checking one against the other, until he reconstructs them both as *night* and *clown*. The key he recovers will solve any other five-letter cryptograms enciphered by it. The process must be done individually for each key and each cryptogram of different length. Multiple anagramming cannot work with just a single message because without any control the single message could be anagrammed into too many equally likely texts. GHINT alone, for example, could be unscrambled to make *thing* as well as *night*, and there is no cross-check to tell which is right.

The word-transposition system carried the most explosive and the greatest

Crises of the Union

number of messages sent by the Democratic politicians, but it was by no means the only one. Messages from Florida and South Carolina were evidently encoded by a dictionary, but the one used for the Oregon disclosures did not unlock them. The three tyro cryptanalysts had independently noticed that these dispatches included the word *geodesy*, which is a rather unusual term for the pocket dictionary that they reasoned would probably be used. Holden found the right one after an hour and a half's search in the Library of Congress; he telegraphed the news to the *Tribune* just as a bleary-eyed staff member, who had examined 40 or 50 volumes without success, was about to go out and check the one that Hassard and Grosvenor rightly suspected—*Webster's Pocket Dictionary*. It was used in the same way as the Oregon dictionary, though the number of pages turned to the front to select the codeword varied from one to five.

The Democrats also used pairs of numbers in a monalphabetic substitution. Hassard broke this system by guessing that the patterned ciphertext 84 66 33 87 66 27 27 mirrored *canvass*. He cracked a checkerboard substitution when he divined that ITYYITNS in a partially enciphered telegram from Florida stood for the name of the county of *Dade*. The coordinates of the checkerboard (which also served for the two-digit cipher) proved to be ten different letters that spelled a phrase of extraordinary suitability:

	H 1	I 2	S 3	P 4	A 5	Y 6	M 7	E 8	N 9	T 0
H 1										
I 2					k		s			d
S 3	l		n	w					p	
P 4		r		h			t			
A 5		u				o				
Y 6		x				a		f		
M 7					b		g			
E 8		i		c			v		y	
N 9			e			m			j	
T 0										

Of the 400 dispatches that were given to Hassard and Grosvenor, all but three (in a cipher not used elsewhere) were translated. The Democrats, unaware that their own machinations were being bared, raised the cry of fraud in the presidential election as the midterm campaign for Congress grew hot. On October 3, 1878, the *Tribune* reported that solution of the dispatches had been completed and published a few of them as a hint for the Democrats to confess. But they said nothing, and four days later the *Tribune* thundered out the story of Democratic intrigue in Florida and Louisiana. The first story detailed the operations of the ciphers; the second, next day, exposed the texts of the telegrams. On October 16, the South Carolina shenanigans came out. Their

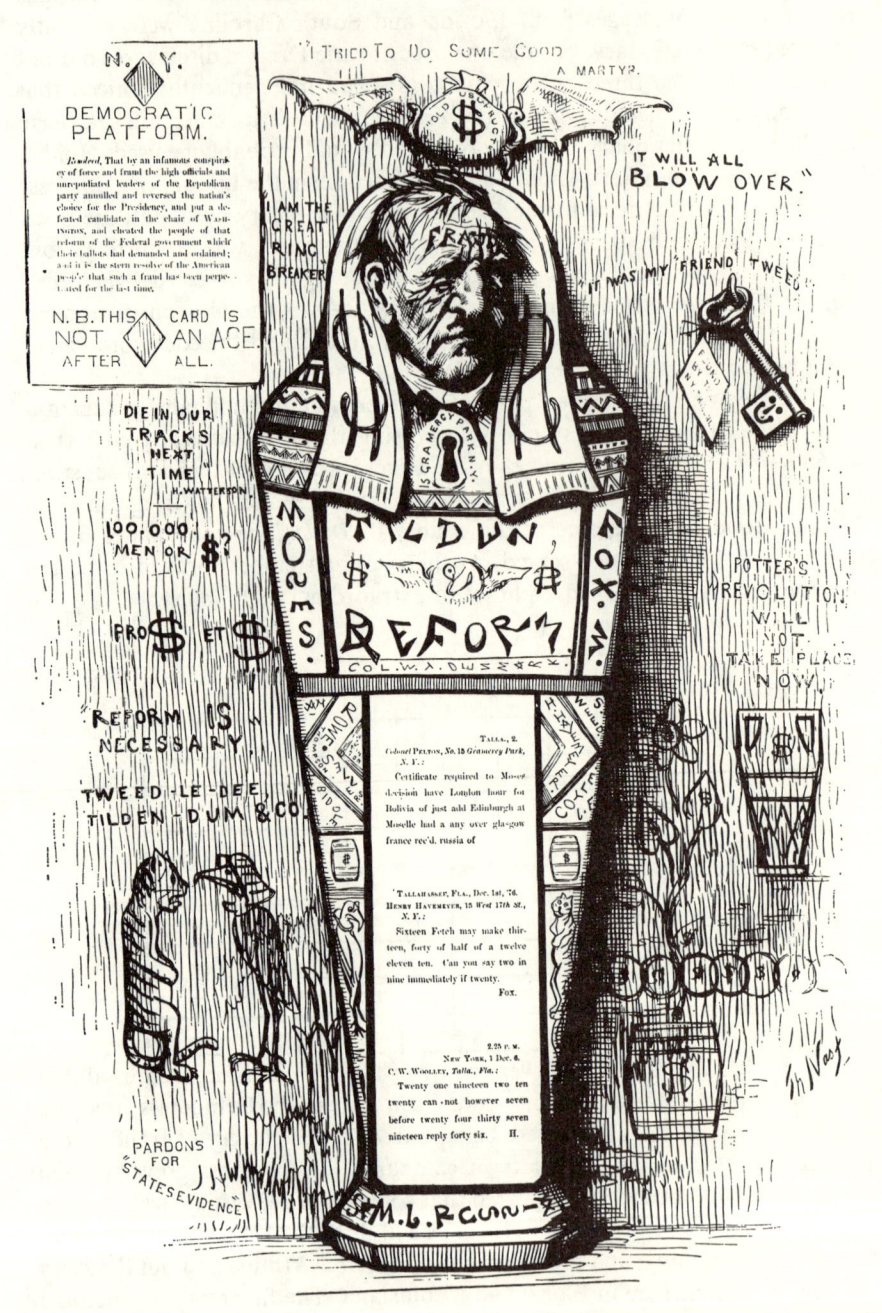

"*Cipher Mumm(er)y. Exhumed by the New York Tribune.*" Cartoon of Samuel Tilden by Thomas Nast in Harper's Weekly

sum was that Colonel William T. Pelton, Tilden's nephew and confidential secretary, had bargained through Marble and others for electoral votes.

The results were sensational. The public marvelled at the ingenuity of the cipher-solvers. Thousands of readers tested the keys and satisfied themselves as to the accuracy of the solutions. The Democrats argued that the telegrams were strictly for Pelton's information, but it seemed clear that only Pelton's hesitation at the price and the subsequent bungling and delay subverted his intentions. The *Tribune* had prepared its exposé thoroughly and presented it skillfully; even its Democratic rival, the *Sun*, was forced to a grudging tribute. The timing, too, was perfect: election was only a few weeks off. In that election, the G.O.P. made emphatic gains in Congress. New York, Pennsylvania, Massachusetts, and Connecticut voted, as the *Tribune* inferred with pardonable pride, to rebuke the cipher fraud.

But the effects did not stop there. The telegrams had been addressed to Pelton at 15 Gramercy Square, New York, Tilden's home, and though Tilden, haggard and with his perpetual cold, swore before the Congressional investigating committee that he had no personal knowledge of what his nephew was doing in his house, and that anything that was done was done without his permission, his reputation was sullied. The disclosures ended his presidential aspirations. As his old supporter, the *Sun*, sadly conceded, "Mr. Tilden will not again be the Presidential candidate of any party."

In fact he was not, and in the election of 1880, James A. Garfield, a personal friend of Reid's, defeated Winfield S. Hancock, the Democratic candidate, by only 7,000 votes out of 9,000,000 in the popular tally but by an unchallengeable 214 to 155 in the electoral ballot. Even a sympathetic biographer of Tilden acknowledged that "As a result of the cipher telegrams the Republicans won an advantage which probably gave them the national election of 1880. Much of the public became convinced that the millionaire candidate for the Presidency had permitted his party directors to dip into his purse to win a decision for the party that was willing to pay the highest price." Cryptanalysis had helped elect a President. The *Tribune*'s triumph stood forth as one of the first great journalistic exposés of governmental corruption, which helped elevate American newspapers to their role of public watchdog. It also carried the *Tribune* into the citadel of Republican power. Reid later banqueted at its tables when he was named ambassador to the Court of St. James's. But perhaps the most lasting value of the Hassard-Grosvenor cryptanalysis and its dramatic disclosure by the *Tribune* was noted by Reid's biographer: "It had pilloried once and for all the single manifestation in our annals of the idea that the Presidency was a purchasable honor."

8

THE PROFESSOR, THE SOLDIER, AND THE MAN ON DEVIL'S ISLAND

ONLY A FEW BOOKS in the history of any science may be called great. Some of these report a technical innovation that radically alters the content of the science. Through the 19th century, Alberti's and Kasiski's were the two great books of this kind in cryptology. Such books look inward.

Other great books look outward. They bring the science up to date—make it consonant with its time—and so renew its utility to men. This they do by assimilating developments in relevant fields (for example, improvements in instrumentation), by summing up the lessons of recent experience and deducing their meaning for the current age, and by reorganizing the concepts of the science according to this new knowledge. This does not mean simple popularization, though such a work usually does have an organic persuasiveness. Rather, it amounts to a reorientation, a new perspective.

For 300 years, the only great book of this kind in cryptology was Porta's. He was the first to delineate a coherent image of cryptology. His ideas remained viable so long because cryptology underwent no essential change; communication was by messenger, and consequently the nomenclator reigned. But his views no longer sufficed after the invention of the telegraph. New conditions demanded new theses, new insights. And in 1883 cryptology got them in the form of its second great book of the outward-looking kind, *La Cryptographie militaire*.

Its author was born Jean-Guillaume-Hubert-Victor-François-Alexandre-Auguste Kerckhoffs von Nieuwenhof on January 19, 1835, at Nuth, Holland, son of a well-to-do landlord and a member of one of the oldest and most honorable families of the Flemish duchy of Limburg. He went to school at a little seminary near Aachen. Afterward, to improve his knowledge of English, he lived in Britain for a year and a half, then returned to the University of Liège, where he received two degrees, one in letters, one in science. After teaching modern languages for four years at two schools in Holland and joining a number of literary societies there, he accompanied a young American, Clarence Prentice, son of the founder of the Louisville *Journal*, through England, Germany, and France as traveling secretary, then went to Meaux, near Paris, where he again taught modern languages.

In 1863, he obtained the chair of modern languages at the high school at Melun, a large town 25 miles southeast of Paris. The next year he married a girl from the area and in 1865, when he was 30, they had their only child, a daughter, Pauline. He stayed at Melun for 10 years, teaching English and German. He supplemented his salary of about 1,600 francs by taking students in to lodge with him—a practice that was officially prohibited but winked at.

During these years he participated in a variety of activities that show the great diversity of his interests. He gave lectures on the formation of languages and on literature, founded a society for the encouragement of education in Melun, gave free courses in English and Italian, served as delegate of the local branch of the French Society of Archaeology to the international congress at Bonn in 1868, and got embroiled in some minor political difficulties after the French defeat of 1870. His learning was broad enough for him to fill in at different times for teachers of Latin, Greek, history, and mathematics.

By this time he had shortened his name to Auguste Kerckhoffs. Bearded, dignified, slow of speech, Kerckhoffs, despite an inability to maintain discipline in his classes and some eccentricities of character, was a "learned, zealous, capable" teacher who awoke his students' interest in their work; his superiors said "his students like him and work with success." Thus when a hostile official wanted to turn down Kerckhoffs' request for a leave for further studies, he discovered that the teacher had "ardent protectors," and the leave was granted.

Kerckhoffs went from 1873 to 1876 to the universities of Bonn and Tübingen, getting his Ph.D. He earned his living by teaching the young Count de São Mamede, who later became secretary to the king of Portugal; Kerckhoffs was made a commander of the Order of Christ for this. He then returned to Paris, where he worked as a private instructor, teaching two younger sons of the São Mamede family. He demonstrated an interest in things military by applying for the chair of German at the Ecole Militaire Superieure in 1878, losing it because a clerk failed to note that he had become naturalized as a French citizen in 1873. In 1881, Kerckhoffs became professor of German at the Ecole des Hautes Etudes Commerciales and at the Ecole Arago, both in Paris. It was during this time that, aged 47, he wrote *La Cryptographie militaire*. It was not his first book: he had already written a Flemish grammar, an English grammar, a German verb manual, a study (in German) on the origins of German drama, and a work examining the relation of art to religion.

His busiest years followed the publication of *La Cryptographie militaire*. A new international language called Volapük ("World-Speak") had been invented by a German priest, Johann Martin Schleyer. About 1885, it caught on in France, and flashed with express-train speed all over the country, not only among intellectuals but among all classes: it was even heard in the streets. From France it radiated throughout the world. The most active propagandist of Volapük was Auguste Kerckhoffs, who, at the second Volapük congress in Munich in 1887, was acclaimed director ("Dilekel," in Volapük) of the International Academy of Volapük. To this body were submitted questions of the grammar, vocabulary, and orthography of the expanding tongue.

As secretary of the French Association for the Propagation of Volapük, Kerckhoffs proselytized the artificial language with ability and vigor. In 1888, 182 textbooks on Volapük appeared—a publication rate of one every other day—and the Macy's of Paris, the Grands Magazins des Printemps, sponsored courses in it. By 1889, 25 periodicals in or about the language were being published and 283 Volapük clubs were meeting all over the globe. When the third Volapük congress was held at Paris in May of 1889, with Kerckhoffs presiding, even the waiters and porters conversed in World-Speak. A new Golden Age of brotherhood, unencumbered by the chains of Babel, seemed to shimmer just ahead.

It was a mirage. For the congresses, which seemed to be the harbingers of that great day, were actually symptoms of critical tensions within the movement. Schleyer's goal of creating the richest and most perfect literary language, in which he was supported by the German Volapükists, clashed with the desire of Kerckhoffs and the other active Volapükists to have the simplest and most practical language for commerce and science. From the beginning, Kerckhoffs had eliminated from his grammatical manuals some of the forms that Schleyer had carried over in Volapük from his native German, such as the endings for the jussive and optative moods of verbs. But the priest insisted that, as the father of Volapük, he should have the final decision on any changes. The tensions mounted, and when the Academy refused to grant Schleyer the full veto he wanted, the movement broke in two.

It splintered into bickering factions entirely unable to agree when Kerckhoffs submitted to the Academy, not individual questions, but a complete grammar, and other members of the Academy retorted with projects of their own. The movement crumpled with unbelievable swiftness: in 1889, it seemed as though it would conquer the world; in 1890, it was moribund. Kerckhoffs resigned as Dilekel in 1891, and, by 1902, of the estimated 210,000 enthusiasts the language had once had, only 159 remained on its List of Correspondents, and only four little clubs clung weakly to life. Kerckhoffs' *Cours complet de Volapük*, his *Dictionnaire Volapük-Français et Français-Volapük*, his *Vollständiger Lehrgang des Volapük* remain only as forgotten monuments to a splendid dream.

Crushed and perhaps embittered by the collapse of what had seemed so needful and so certain, Kerckhoffs one day exploded with some intemperate criticisms of the handling of the state's school examinations so that his contract at the Ecole des Hautes Etudes Commerciales was not renewed in 1891. It was only through the intervention of influential friends that he managed to get a post teaching German at the high school at Mont-de-Marsan, near Bordeaux. Here, his superiors reported on him: "Very diverse and extended knowledge taught with more method, exactness and precision than I would have expected in a spirit that embraces so many things. Highly regarded and highly appreciated." The following year, trying to get closer to Paris, Kerckhoffs moved to the Brittany seaport of Lorient, where he again taught German. In the middle of that school year, his daughter died. He stuck it out for another year, but by 1895, then 60, his health failing, his spirit broken, but living in Paris not far from the Sorbonne, he applied for a year's leave. He renewed it annually until his death in Switzerland, apparently while on vacation, on August 9, 1903.

But if his works on Volapük are defunct, his cryptologic ideas still flourish. *La Cryptographie militaire* first appeared as two installments in the *Journal des Sciences militaires* in January and February of 1883, being reissued later that year as a paperback book by the journal's publisher. It is the most concise book on cryptology ever written. Kerckhoffs had the instinct for the cryptographic jugular, and he compressed into 64 pages virtually the entire known field of cryptology, including polyalphabetics with mixed alphabets, enciphered code, and cipher devices. The book is also one of the most scholarly on cryptology. Its footnotes cite most classical and many modern sources; comments such as "This is not the only historical or bibliographic error for which the Austrian writer must be reproached" show how carefully the author has studied those sources. And the book throbs with life. Kerckhoffs selected an enciphered news-service dispatch as the specimen for a demonstration solution. He discussed current German practice and contrasted it with what was then going on in France. He scrutinized the most recent ciphers, such as the Wheatstone device. He concentrated upon it all his extraordinary range of knowledge, and it is perhaps significant that at least three of the great books of cryptology—Kerckhoffs', Alberti's, and Porta's—were written not by narrow specialists but by well-rounded men who had one foot in each of what C. P. Snow would later call "the two cultures" of science and humanities.

What makes Kerckhoffs' book great, however, is that he sought answers to the problems thrust upon cryptology by new conditions, and that the solutions he proposed were valid, well-grounded, and meritorious. The major problem was to find a system of cryptography that would fulfill the requirements of the new signal communications created by the telegraph—a problem that still commands the interest of cryptologists. While other authors simply discussed various cipher systems rather as if the science of cryptology existed in a vacuum, Kerckhoffs addressed himself directly to the issue of the day. Indeed, it inspired his book: "I have therefore thought that it would be rendering a service to the persons who are interested in the future of military cryptography . . . to indicate to them the principles which must guide them in the contrivance or evaluation of every cipher intended for war service." The principles which he enunciated guide cryptologists even now.

Kerckhoffs took field ciphers as a given; far from realizing that they were creatures of the telegraph, he thought that they had existed in the 1600s. But this historical error did not affect his understanding of current conditions. In considering the problem of finding a good field cipher, he saw that any one that was practical would have to withstand the operational strains of heavy traffic. "It is necessary to distinguish carefully between a system of encipherment envisioned for a momentary exchange of letters between several isolated people and a method of cryptography intended to govern the correspondence between different army chiefs for an unlimited time," he wrote. In that one sentence, Kerckhoffs differentiates pre-telegraphy military communications from post-. The sentence is pregnant with most of the requirements that have come to be demanded of systems of military cryptography, requirements such as simplicity, reliability, rapidity, and so on. This clear recognition of the new order constitutes Kerckhoffs' first great contribution to cryptology.

The second was to reaffirm in a modern context the principle that only cryptanalysts can know the security of a cipher system. Others had, of course, realized this before him: Rossignol invented the two-part nomenclator upon that principle, and the English Decypherers assessed and then compiled England's nomenclators in the 1700s. But it was forgotten after the black chambers were closed, and in any case the simple criteria for appraising the cryptanalytic resistance of a nomenclator no longer applied to the more complex cipher systems then being proposed. The inventors of these systems, instead of submitting their ciphers to the empirical verdict of cryptanalysts, sought instead to evaluate them a priori. They would calculate how many centuries it would take to run through all the combinations necessary to solve their cipher, or would argue how it was logically impossible to break through a certain interlocking feature. Kerckhoffs observed and diagnosed the phenomenon:

> ... I am stupefied to see our scholars and our professors teach and recommend for wartime use systems of which the most inexperienced cryptanalyst would certainly find the key in less than an hour's time.
>
> One can hardly explain this excess of confidence in certain ciphers except by the abandon into which the suppression of black chambers and the security of postal communications have let cryptographic studies fall; it may likewise be believed that the immoderate assertions of certain authors, no less than the complete absence of any serious work on the art of solving secret writing, have largely contributed to give currency to the most erroneous ideas about the value of our systems of cryptography.

Reacting against this, Kerckhoffs demonstrated that cryptanalysis was the only way to enlightenment in cryptography, that only by climbing the steep and thorny path of cryptanalysis could one arrive at the truth about a system of cryptography. Only solution could validly test the security of a cipher. Kerckhoffs never quite stated this in so many words, though he came close. But his whole book cries it out. *La Cryptographie militaire* is essentially a tract on cryptanalysis; its whole bias and emphasis is cryptanalytic. Kerckhoffs established ordeal by cryptanalysis as the only sure trial for military cryptography. It is the form of judgment which is still used.

From these two fundamental principles for selecting usable field ciphers, Kerckhoffs deduced six specific requirements: (1) the system should be, if not theoretically unbreakable, unbreakable in practice; (2) compromise of the system should not inconvenience the correspondents; (3) the key should be rememberable without notes and should be easily changeable; (4) the cryptograms should be transmissible by telegraph; (5) the apparatus or documents should be portable and operable by a single person; (6) the system should be easy, neither requiring knowledge of a long list of rules nor involving mental strain.

These requirements still comprise the ideal which military ciphers aim at. They have been rephrased, and qualities that lie implicit have been made explicit. But any modern cryptographer would be very happy if any cipher fulfilled all six.

Of course, it has never been possible to do that. There appears to be a certain incompatibility among them that makes it impossible to institute all of them at once. The requirement that is usually sacrificed is the first. Kerckhoffs argued strongly against the notion of a field cipher that would simply resist solution long enough for the orders it transmitted to be carried out. This was not enough, he said, declaring that "the secret matter in communications sent over a distance very often retains its importance beyond the day on which it was transmitted." He was on the side of the angels, but a practical field cipher that is unbreakable was not possible in his day, nor is it today, and so military cryptography has settled for field ciphers that delay but do not defeat cryptanalysis.

Perhaps the most startling requirement, at first glance, was the second. Kerckhoffs explained that by "system" he meant "the material part of the system; tableaux, code books, or whatever mechanical apparatus may be necessary," and not "the key proper." Kerckhoffs here makes for the first time the distinction, now basic to cryptology, between the general system and the specific key. Why must the general system "not require secrecy," as, for example, a codebook requires it? Why must it be "a process that ... our neighbors can even copy and adopt"? Because, Kerckhoffs said, "it is not necessary to conjure up imaginary phantoms and to suspect the incorruptibility of employees or subalterns to understand that, if a system requiring secrecy were in the hands of too large a number of individuals, it could be compromised at each engagement in which one or another of them took part." This has proved to be true, and Kerckhoffs' second requirement has become widely accepted under a form that is sometimes called the fundamental assumption of military cryptography: that the enemy knows the general system. But he must still be unable to solve messages in it without knowing the specific key. In its modern formulation, the Kerckhoffs doctrine states that secrecy must reside solely in the keys.

Had Kerckhoffs merely published his perceptions of the problems facing post-telegraph cryptography and his prescriptions for resolving them, he would have assured a place for himself in the pantheon of cryptology. But he did more. He contributed two techniques of cryptanalysis that, while not as wrenching to the science as Kasiski's, play roles of supreme importance in most modern solutions.

The first of these is superimposition. It constitutes the most general solution for polyalphabetic substitution systems. With few exceptions, it lays no restrictions on the type or length of keys, as does the Kasiski method, nor on the alphabets, which may be interrelated or entirely independent. It wants only several messages in the same key. The cryptanalyst must align these one above the other so that letters enciphered with the same keyletter will fall into a single column. In the simplest case, that of a running key that starts over again with each message, he can do this simply by placing all the first letters in the first column, all the second letters in the next column, and so on.

Kerckhoffs demonstrated this procedure with 13 short messages enciphered with a long key. He superimposed his first five cryptograms like this:

	1	2	3	4	5	6	7	8	9	10	11	12	13	14	15	...
Message 1	U	H	Y	B	R	J	I	M	B	C	F	A	M	M	T	...
Message 2	U	H	W	P	R	B	Q	L	K	I	B	L	W	R	E	...
Message 3	I	E	W	H	C	H	Q	K	Q	M	T	M	V	G	J	...
Message 4	U	W	V	R	R	H	I	K	M	C	W	W	E	G	H	...
Message 5	U	H	S	H	A	H	K	S	V	C	J	W	Z	V	X	...

Now, since all these messages were enciphered with the same keytext, all the hidden plaintext letters in the first column were enciphered by the same keyletter, which means that they have been enciphered in the same ciphertext alphabet. Consequently, all the plaintext *a*'s will have the same ciphertext equivalent, all the plaintext *b*'s will likewise have their own unvarying ciphertext equivalent, and so on. Likewise, each ciphertext letter represents only one plaintext letter. This holds true for each column. Each column may thus be attacked as an ordinary monalphabetic substitution, just like the columns in a periodic polyalphabetic.

In cases where the key does not start over again with each message, the cryptanalyst may line up repetitions in several messages to obtain a proper superimposition.

Superimposition does not ask that the alphabet in the first column bear any relation to that in the second. Thus it suits cryptanalysts of such systems as that of C. H. C. Krohn, who published in Berlin in 1873 a dictionary of

3,200 alphabets for secret correspondence; Kerckhoffs remarked scornfully of this number that "it is at once too many and too few." But superimposition does depend for its success on a sufficient depth of column. Kerckhoffs realized this, and used examples to show that if two columns could be found to have been enciphered with the same keyletter, their effective depth was doubled. This is of especially great value with coherent running keys, whose cipher alphabets will be brought into play with the irregular frequency that their keyletters have in plaintext. If all the columns enciphered with the cipher alphabet governed by keyletter E can be recognized, collected, and solved together, about 12 per cent of the plaintext (in an English running key) will be recovered. Identically enciphered columns could be recognized, Kerckhoffs suggested, by finding columns with similar frequency counts.

Kerckhoffs also discerned another way to extort more plaintext from a paucity of ciphertext. Unlike most techniques of cryptanalysis, which ascertain plaintext, this technique determines ciphertext letters—which are, to be sure, immediately converted into plaintext. It may therefore be considered an indirect technique, but it is one of the most powerful in the cryptanalyst's arsenal. Kerckhoffs called it "symmetry of position."

How it works may be seen by looking at part of a tableau with mixed alphabets:

plain	a b c d e f g h i j k l m n o p q r s t u v w x y z
	N E W Y O R K C I T A B D F G H J L M P Q S U V X Z
	E W Y O R K C I T A B D F G H J L M P Q S U V X Z N
cipher	W Y O R K C I T A B D F G H J L M P Q S U V X Z N E
	Y O R K C I T A B D F G H J L M P Q S U V X Z N E W
	. . . .

Now, it is evident that N and E stand next to one another in every cipher alphabet of this tableau (considering the alphabets as cyclical). Similarly, N is separated from Y by an interval of 3 in every cipher alphabet. Again, R stands 6 spaces, or cells, before B in every cipher alphabet. Relations like these may be fixed between any two (or more) ciphertext letters, and they will hold for every cipher alphabet in the tableau. So if the cryptanalyst determines the linear distance between two ciphertext letters in one alphabet, and then determines one of those letters in another alphabet, he can place the second letter in the second alphabet at the known distance. This contributes a ciphertext equivalent which he did not have before and which he can decipher throughout the cryptogram to add a few grains of plaintext to further his solution.

For example, suppose that the cryptanalyst has ascertained, in solving a message based on the above tableau, that K and H represent plaintext *e* and *n*. Consequently, K and H will stand 9 places apart in the ciphertext alphabet:

plain	a b c d e f g h i j k l m n o p q r s t u v w x y z
cipher alphabet I	K H
distance	0 1 2 3 4 5 6 7 8 9

Then suppose that, in another alphabet, he has discovered that ciphertext K represents plaintext *i*. He may immediately count 9 spaces beyond K, thus:

plain	a b c d e f g h i j k l m n o p q r s t u v w x y z
cipher alphabet II	K
distance	0 1 2 3 4 5 6 7 8 9

and insert a ciphertext H at that point. He may now decipher all the ciphertext H's in alphabet II into plaintext *r*'s. If he finds that, say, plaintext *e* is enciphered in this alphabet by W, he will measure the distance between K and W (four spaces forward), and will insert a W four spaces before K in the first ciphertext alphabet, giving him the identity of plaintext *b* in that alphabet. Since the intervals between the letters remain fixed for all the cipher alphabets of this tableau, the proper identification of a few letters in a few alphabets can lead to the determination of many others.

Kerckhoffs went no further than this—a patent symmetry of position. Cryptanalysts see it when they build up skeleton tableaux in solving polyalphabetics with a normal *a*-to-*z* plaintext alphabet. But modern cryptologists have discovered that skeleton tableaux for polyalphabetics with mixed plaintext alphabets will manifest a latent symmetry of position. It enlarges the principle of linear distances to include horizontal and vertical proportions. It is a complicated technique, but an enormously valuable one. Sometimes a chain reaction of placements will reconstitute an entire tableau. More often, it will donate important ciphertext equivalents to the cryptanalyst, or will notify him that a certain assumption contradicts its rules and hence is untenable. Because of today's extensive use of polyalphabetics with both alphabets mixed, latent symmetry of position is an indispensable tool of the modern cryptanalyst.

Finally, Kerckhoffs rounded out his work by popularizing and naming the cryptographic slide, and demonstrating its identity with the polyalphabetic tableau. He called the slide the St.-Cyr system, after the French national military academy where it was taught. A St.-Cyr slide consists of a long piece of paper or cardboard, called the stator, with an evenly spaced alphabet printed on it and with two slits cut below and to the sides of the alphabet. Through these slits runs a long strip of paper—the slide proper—on which an alphabet is printed twice.

If both alphabets are normal, the device comprises a shorthand version of the Vigenère tableau, for any given alphabet of that tableau may be reproduced by finding its keyletter in the slide alphabet and setting this under the A of the stator. The stator alphabet will represent the plaintext alphabet and the slide alphabet the cipher alphabet. The alphabets do not have to be normal;

if they are mixed, the slide (a term that sometimes encompasses the entire device) will represent a tableau with mixed alphabets. Any slide may be expanded into a tableau, and any tableau that is derived from the regular interaction of two alphabets, or components, may be compressed into the more convenient St.-Cyr form. Kerckhoffs also pointed out that a cipher disk was merely a St.-Cyr slide turned round to bite its tail, and he iterated Porta's observation that a cipher disk could be developed into an equivalent tableau. He thus joined the tableau, the cipher disk, and the St.-Cyr slide into a family of related devices that differed only in form.

Such are the many excellences of *La Cryptographie militaire*. It stands perhaps first among the great books of cryptology. Its incisiveness, its clarity, its solid base of scholarly research, its invaluable new techniques, but above all its maturity, its wisdom, and its vision, elevate it to that rank. Perhaps it could only have been done by a man as well-rounded and as sensitive as Kerckhoffs.

It is ironic that the most lasting work of a man whose ideals were as cosmopolitan as Kerckhoffs' should have had nationalistic results. Yet perhaps the most immediate consequence of *La Cryptographie militaire* was its giving France a commanding lead in cryptology, accruing benefits that were cashed during World War I. The Ministry of War bought 300 copies. Signal officers and amateur cryptographers read it, and, in reaction, invented or reinvented systems such as the autokey to circumvent the powerful superimposition technique. A whole literature poured off the presses. France flowered in a cryptologic renaissance.

Yet the French interest in cryptology was not due purely to the intellectual challenge of the subject. Much of the impetus must have come from the smart of France's 1870 defeat by Prussia and her desire for revenge—the same desire that drove her to build up the largest army in Europe. It is significant that while almost two dozen books and pamphlets on cryptology were published in France between 1883 and 1914, to say nothing of scores of articles, only half a dozen appeared in Germany, all third-rate except for a few superb historical studies.

Probably several factors led to this indifference. The 1870 victory may have convinced the Germans that they were doing things right and did not need to change. Germans tend to be regimented and less apt to suggest new ideas to the authorities than the more individualistic French. And Germans seem to have a predilection for working things out in advance according to theory, for erecting elaborate structures based on pure reason. They sought, by the clarity of their logic and the unshakability of their assumptions, to do in cryptography what they did in philosophy—produce the ideal system. Kerckhoffs had shown that this approach is sterile, if not actually dangerous. But the Germans persisted, confident of the superiority of anything Teutonic. Their writers occupied themselves with cryptography to the virtual neglect of cryptanalysis. The French, more pragmatic, submitted their ciphers to the harsh judgment of actual solution.

The course of French prewar cryptology may be traced in its literature. Most of the books were second-rate, unoriginal, deriving their ideas from Kerckhoffs, whom they repeatedly laud. Typical is H. Josse, a captain of artillery who is chiefly noted for condensing Kerckhoffs' six desiderata into a single guiderule that apparently governed the selection of French field ciphers up to World War I: "Military cryptography, properly called, must employ a system requiring only pencil and paper." Josse quoted Kerckhoffs so often that he felt it necessary to insert an apologetic "M. Kerckhoffs, whose name recurs so often in cryptography" after an especially heavy flurry of references. But four fine writers helped make French cryptology the best in the world at the time: de Viaris, Valério, Delastelle, and Bazeries.

The Marquis Gaëtan Henri Léon Viarizio di Lesegno, whose name was gallicized to de Viaris, was born February 13, 1847, at Cherbourg. His father was an artillery captain. At 19, young de Viaris entered the famed École Polytechnique as 48th—and graduated as 102nd (out of 134). He enlisted in the Navy at 21, earning his commission as ensign two years later, but serving for only four years before resigning at 25. He later became an assistant police prefect and an infantry officer.

He apparently became interested in cryptology about the mid-1880s. He devised some of the first cipher machines to integrate a printing mechanism:* after enciphering, the cryptographer pressed a button which imprinted the cipher letter on a paper tape. He published for the first time in cryptology what he called "cryptographic equations." (Babbage had employed such equations in his own work, but had never described them publicly.)

In articles in the scientific journal *Le Génie Civil* for May 12 and 19, 1888 (the first two parts of a series that was later collected into a book), de Viaris proposed that the Greek letter chi (χ) stand for any ciphertext letter, gamma (γ) for any keyletter and the lower-case c for any cleartext letter. He then proved that the algebraic formula $c + \gamma = \chi$ would produce a Vigenère encipherment no different from the standard manipulations of tableau, slide, or disk. If the letters of the alphabet be numbered from zero to 25,

a	b	c	d	e	f	g	h	i	j	k	l	m	n	o	p	q	r	s	t	u	v	w	x	y	z
0	1	2	3	4	5	6	7	8	9	10	11	12	13	14	15	16	17	18	19	20	21	22	23	24	25

the Vigenère may be duplicated mathematically by adding the values for plain and key together and then turning the sum (less 26 if it is 26 or above) back into letter form. For example, a standard tableau encipherment of plaintext *d* with key G yields cipher J. With the formula, these same letters give $3 + 6 = 9$, or J. A different cipher will naturally have a different formula.

---

* The earliest known printing cipher machine appears to be one invented before 1874 by Émile Vinay and Joseph Gaussin, but no description of it is known.

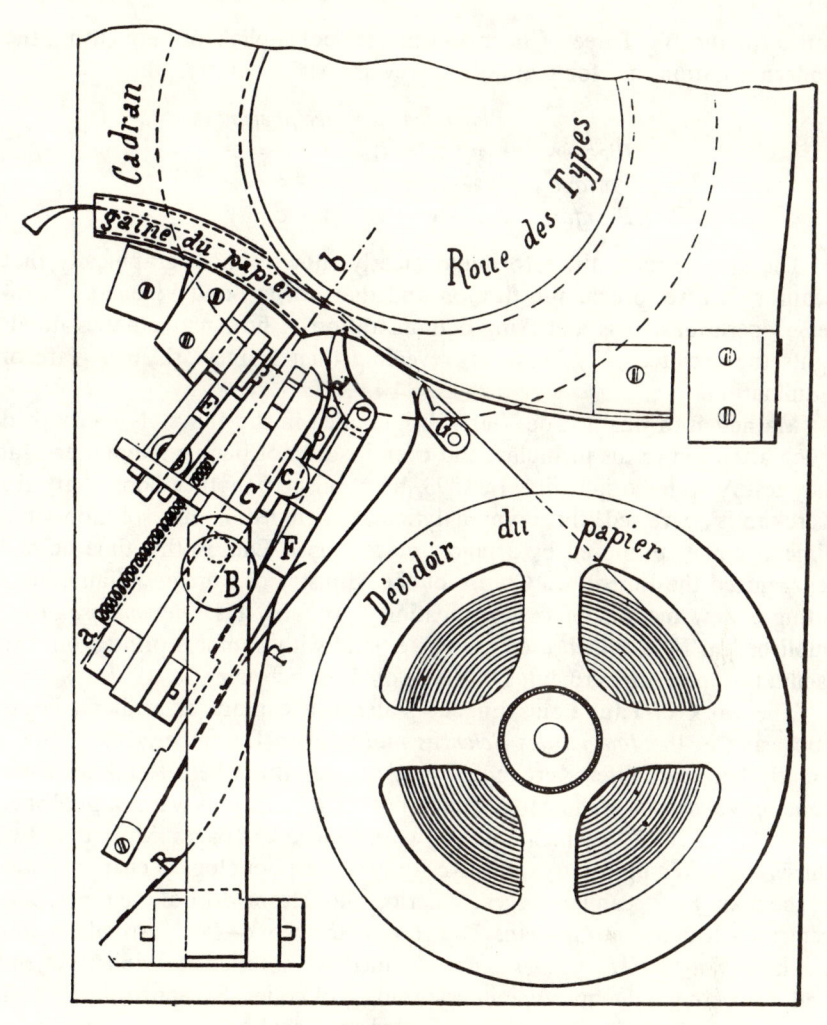

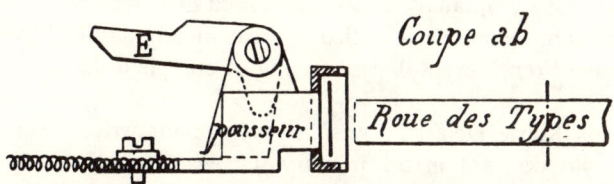

Plan of the Marquis de Viaris' printing cipher device

Those for the Big Three of normal-alphabet polyalphabetics are (using the modern notation of P for plain, K for key and C for cipher):

	enciphering	deciphering
Vigenère	P + K = C	C − K = P
Variant	P − K = C	C + K = P
Beaufort	K − P = C	K − C = P

The symmetry of these formulas clearly shows almost graphically that Beaufort is a reciprocal substitution and that Variant and Vigenère are inverse operations. It is a striking demonstration of how mathematics floodlights the architecture of ciphers, revealing their framework in a glare of illumination.

Mathematics was just de Viaris' bright idea in the 1880s. Nobody paid much attention to his formulas, and even he did not pursue the matter. But they testify to his originality. In 1893, he published another book that, like Kerckhoffs', stressed the cryptanalytic. It included a fine solution of a difficult cipher proposed by a fellow cryptologist. During this time he had reorganized the Bureau du Chiffre of the Ministry of Foreign Affairs, instituting a new method of communication—probably his *Dictionnaire ABC*, published in 1898, which used a flexible band with numbers printed on it to facilitate superencipherment. De Viaris died on February 18, 1901.

The work of Paul Louis Eugène Valério, a captain of artillery, began appearing in the *Journal des Sciences militaires* in December, 1892, almost exactly ten years after Kerckhoffs' first article. But where Kerckhoffs was concise, Valério was exhaustive. The last of ten installments was not published until May of 1895, by which time the work totaled 214 pages. More than two thirds was taken up by an exhaustive study of the phonological characteristics of the main European languages; Valério, who felt the drift of the times, concentrated heavily on German. The rest of the work—later assembled into book form as *De la cryptographie*—detailed the solutions of cipher systems and, for perhaps the first time in cryptology, of codes. Except for his exposition on code cryptanalysis, Valério added little that was new to the science, but his comprehensiveness filled in areas merely outlined by his predecessors and gave French cryptology a feeling of completion and solidity that it had lacked.

Félix Marie Delastelle was the only major writer on cryptology of the time who was not in the military. He was born January 2, 1840, at the Brittany seaport of Saint-Malo to a long line of seafaring ancestors—his father, master of an oceangoing vessel, was apparently lost at sea when Félix was three. After graduating from the College of Saint-Malo, Delastelle got a job as inspector with the government's Tobacco Administration, with duties involving warehousing in cities as large as Marseilles, a post he held for forty years. After his retirement in 1900, the quiet bachelor moved into Ker Kador, an apartment hotel in Paramé, near Saint-Malo, where he devoted full time

The Professor, the Soldier, and the Man on Devil's Island 243

to writing a book on cryptology that would improve on the short one he had written seven years earlier. He signed the foreword at Paramé on May 25, 1901, and the book, *Traité Élémentaire de Cryptographie*, was published the following year by the respected house of Gauthier-Villars. But on April 2, 1902, while he was about to go to the home of his elder brother, Auguste Michel, who had just died, he was stricken with a heart attack, and died the same day.

His book's 156 pages deal mostly with systems of encipherment. Delastelle accused most previous books with considerable justice of being "only catalogues, more or less complete and detailed, of various systems, of which none is studied in depth, even several that differ only in appearance. I therefore believe," he wrote in his foreword, "that I have done something useful in classifying all these systems and in discussing how principles may be deduced from them."

But while the individuality of cipher systems balked this plan, Delastelle's good intentions rewarded him. While searching for a method of bigraphic encipherment that did not require cumbersome 26-by-26 enciphering tables (during which he reasoned his way to an independent invention of the Playfair), Delastelle invented a fractionating system of considerable importance in cryptology. It differed from those of Pliny Earle Chase, who had subjected the letter fractions to substitution before recombining them. Delastelle transposed them. His cipher, the bifid, requires the fundamental bipartite substitution, which he somehow never wrote in checkerboard form:

```
 a  b  c  d  e  f  g  h  i  j  k  l  m
42 22 14 32 34 25 11 53 51 41 15 23 54

 n  o  p  q  r  s  t  u  v  x  y  z
12 55 33 31 52 21 35 13 24 44 43 45
```

The plaintext is written in groups of a specified length, say five letters, and the coordinates are written vertically beneath each letter. Delastelle set up his own plaintext, *Attendez des ordres* ("Wait for orders"), like this:

```
a t t e n   d e z d e   s o r d r   e s
4 3 3 3 1   3 3 4 3 3   2 5 5 3 5   3 2
2 5 5 4 2   2 4 5 2 4   1 5 2 2 2   4 1
```

To form the ciphertext, the coordinates are paired horizontally group by group and reconverted into letters: 43 = Y, 33 = P, 12 = N, 55 = O, and so on. The complete ciphertext: YPNOA PYDZV FHIRB DJ. If a different alphabet serves for the recomposition, the system is called a bifid with conjugated matrices. If tripartite coordinates ($a = 111$, $b = 112$, $c = 113$, etc.) are decomposed, the elements shuffled and then recomposed in different combinations, the system is called a trifid.

Delastelle experimented to nullify Kerckhoffs' symmetry of position by shifting the positions of key, plain, cipher, and index letters in St.-Cyr slides.

The traditional arrangement regards the first letter of the stator alphabet as the index letter; the key is set under this; the plaintext is then located in the stator alphabet and the ciphertext on the slide beneath it. Delastelle burst the bonds and showed that other dispositions would serve as well. For example, the keyletter may be located in the stator alphabet and the plaintext set under it; then the letter designated as the index letter may be located on the slide and the ciphertext found on the stator above it. Because Delastelle did not move the index letter, he found only eight such dispositions. But there are actually twelve, and, despite Delastelle's attempt, all show some kind of symmetry, whether latent or patent, vertical or horizontal, in the plain or in the cipher component.

Étienne Bazeries is the great pragmatist of cryptology. His theoretical contributions are negligible, but he was one of the greatest natural cryptanalysts the science has seen. Ciphers melted under the fierce intensity of his mental processes. Historical cryptograms, new inventions, official systems, the clandestine communications of plotters—all receded, abandoned their ramparts, and finally succumbed to his blazing onslaught. He was also the most opinionated cryptanalyst the science has known. His barbed pronunciamentos, hurled like Jovian thunderbolts, enraged his contemporaries and lashed the usually unruffled waters of cryptology into unwonted tempests.

He was born August 21, 1846, the son of a mounted policeman, in the little Mediterranean fishing village of Port-Vendres, which lies in the shadow of the mighty Pyrenees. Raised there, Étienne learned Catalan at the same time he learned French. Five days after he turned seventeen, he enlisted in the Army's 4th Supply Squadron to avoid the agricultural career his family had planned for him. He fought in the Franco-Prussian War and was taken prisoner of war when Metz fell, but escaped, disguised as a bricklayer. Promotions came slowly but steadily, despite a strong-willed individualism that refused to accept things as they are simply because they are: as a lieutenant, he nervily told a general that the regimental harness injured the squadron's horses. He had been given his lieutenancy in 1874, and the next year was sent to Algeria on the first of three tours of duty there. On his return in 1876, he married Marie-Louise-Elodie Berthon, by whom he had three daughters.

He seems to have become interested in cryptology by solving the cryptograms in the newspapers' personal columns, some of them setting up adulterous assignations, with whose sordid details he regaled his messmates. One day in 1890, while stationed at Nantes, he said aloud to his brother officers at the headquarters of the 11th Corps that the official French military cipher, a complicated form of transposition, could be read without the key. There was a general roar of laughter—but one who did not join the chorus was the corps commander, General Charles Alexandre Fay, one of the best-known officers of the time. He took Bazeries up on the implied challenge and sent him several cryptograms in the system. Bazeries solved them; his comrades and Fay were impressed; even the War Ministry took note, and readied a new system. Then Bazeries topped his own feat by reading the test messages in the new system before it even went into service.

Word of his ability had evidently spread beyond the parade ground, for early the next year a gentleman from Nantes, one Bord, who had invented a printing cryptograph that, Bazeries conceded, was "a jewel of an instrument," submitted eight cryptograms enciphered with it to Bazeries. This was on January 8, 1891; by the 31st, Bord, attempting to salvage the system, was sending him five messages in a more complicated arrangement of the device. Bazeries read two more sets, of increasing complication if not difficulty, until, wanting to halt what had become for him a tedious repetition, he had Bord compose one in his ultimate system. Bazeries easily discovered that it read, "I want to be hanged if you decipher this," hastily implored the inventor not to do anything rash, and observed later that if all those whose ciphers had been solved were to be hanged, the penalty would lose all meaning.

By now his reputation had reached the Quai d'Orsay in Paris, for in August of 1891 the Army placed him temporarily at the disposition of the Bureau du Chiffre of the Ministry of Foreign Affairs. He was promoted in 1892 to the command of his own supply squadron, and served again with the Foreign Ministry in 1894.

These years in and around Paris were his most active, cryptologically. As fast as new ciphers appeared, he smashed them. Among those he solved were the systems of La Feuillade, Hermann, and d'Ocagne, and the devices of Gavrelle and de Viaris—the latter feat one that was soon to boomerang. He became interested in historical ciphers when a commandant on the general staff asked him for help in reading some ciphered dispatches for a study of Louis XIV's military campaigns. Bazeries solved that system, and then rifled the archives for others, succeeding in breaking down nomenclators of Francis I, Francis II, Henry IV, Mirabeau, and Napoleon. He found the campaign ciphers of the great military genius so feeble that he contemptuously put the word "ciphers" in quotation marks in the title of his monograph on them.

He bloodied his knuckles in the arena of real-life cryptanalysis, too. In 1892, French authorities arrested a group of anarchists and brought them to trial. Included in the evidence was a number of cryptograms that had been solved by Bazeries. They used a system called the Gronsfeld, a kind of truncated Vigenère named for the Count of Gronsfeld, who described it to the 17th-century author Gaspar Schott while they went together from Mainz to Frankfort. Its key consists of numbers, each of which indicates the number of letters forward in the normal alphabet that the encipherer is to count from the plaintext letter to the ciphertext letter. For example, with the anarchist key of 456327, the first word of the message of April 30, *Demande*, would be enciphered to HJSDPKI in this manner: counting four letters beyond *d* gives E, F, G, H—and H is the ciphertext letter; five letters beyond *e* stands J, and so on. Bazeries was not up to his usual standard here, however: the mere use of six nulls at the head and the tail of the cryptograms incomprehensibly delayed his solution for an entire fortnight. For some reason, he always considered this solution, which should have been his least distinguished, as his best.

After he retired from the Army in 1899, the Foreign Ministry hired him as a cryptanalyst. He worked partly at home, partly in the office, living much of the time at Versailles. That same year, the ministry recommended him to the police as the man who might solve a series of dispatches captured, with a numerical Beaufort table, in the quarters of one Chevilly, a supporter of the Duke of Orléans, pretender to the throne of France. The messages consisted of groups of four digits, none of which was smaller than 1111 or larger than 3737. This indicated to Bazeries that each pair of numbers stood for a letter, 11 representing A; 12, B; and so on up to 36 for Z and 37 again for A. He was put off for a good while by that rare but extraordinarily bewildering cryptologic mischance: long repetitions in a polyalphabetic cryptogram that result purely from chance and not, as Bazeries long thought, from the interaction of a periodic key with a repeated plaintext. For example, in a telegram of February 17, 1898, the digits 30 24 14 12 repeated at a distance of 21, indicating a period of 3 or of 7; when the cryptogram was solved, the first repetition proved to be the plaintext *lesd* enciphered by ERVE, and the second plaintext *prou* with key IERV. In another telegram, a false trigraphic repetition indicated a period of 8. Bazeries eventually broke the messages down by a series of inspired guesses as to probable words, and found them to fall into two sets, one enciphered with successive lines of the famous poem *Nuit de décembre* by Alfred de Musset, the other with the day and date on which the message was sent. Each message thus had its own key, which would have made it necessary for each to be attacked individually—except that Bazeries, after solving a few, deduced the key to the keys.

Thus he had the satisfaction of solving a message that could not be deciphered by the duke because it was loaded with errors—and of reading the duke's short and pointed reply. The duke's dispatch—3733 3737 1514 1224 2920 2524—was sent at 9:35 a.m. on Tuesday, December 13, 1898, after a long and fruitless night of trying to decipher the incoming message. Bazeries translated it with the key MARDI TREIZE D[ECEMBRE] and discovered one of the most heartfelt expressions of disgust ever vented by a cipherer who has received a garbled wire. Seven null *q*'s gave the message bulk, but the meaningful portion was monosyllabic: *Merde*. "The word," the cryptanalyst remarked with uncharacteristic understatement, "is vigorous." Bazeries later testified to these solutions at the trial of the conspirators in the High Court of Justice.

In 1913, Bazeries bought a house in Céret, a small town not far from his birthplace, in search of health for one of his daughters. Neighbors did not know that the bearded, gray-haired gentleman with the wide forehead and the piercing gaze was known as the Lynx of the Quai d'Orsay, the Napoleon of

Ciphers, the Magician. They seldom saw him, for he came down from Versailles only when he had a major solution to prepare, and then he shut himself up in his house on the Place des Neuf Jets, where he would hire only illiterate servants, and, fortified with his pipes and pots of coffee, assailed the cryptograms that the Foreign Ministry sent down from Paris. Only when exhausted by a long bout would he emerge and head for a day of picnicking in the nearby mountains. His wife and three daughters, Césarine, Fernande, and Paule, dressed in the long, rustling skirts that were then the height of fashion, trailed their cane-swinging father through the village to an upland farm, where he would interrogate the farmers in Catalan and try to convince his daughters to like the local Roussillon wine that his wife could not stand. When World War I came, he assisted in solving German military cryptograms. He did not retire until 1924, when he was 78. He died at Noyon on November 7, 1931, aged 85.

But if he was continually successful in cryptanalysis, he was continually rebuffed in his years-long cryptographic battle to have the military establishment adopt the ciphers he proposed instead of the official ones which, he said, "offer little resistance to solution." He had little trouble in demonstrating their frangibility: in addition to the Nantes solutions, he was given a test cryptogram in the army cipher by a general of artillery during one of his Algerian tours, and he solved it during a 250-mile train ride from Constantine to Philippeville. But, as he himself said, "to prove that a cipher that is being used is worthless is one thing, but it is another to propose something better in its place."

His disdain for the official ciphers stung him into firing off two polyalphabetic systems of his own, both of which the general staff rejected on the ground that they were too complicated. A friendly officer at Nantes—perhaps General Fay—then suggested that he might have greater success if he devised an apparatus that a cipher clerk could use "without knocking his brains out." Bazeries reworked one of his systems, which employed 20 different cipher alphabets, and came up with his "cylindrical cryptograph." It was practically the same as Jefferson's wheel cypher, except that it had 20 disks with 25 letters on their circumferences instead of 36 disks with a full alphabet. He offered it to the Ministry of War on February 12, 1891, backed by a recommendation from Fay, and described it on September 19 of that same year at a convention of the French Association for the Advancement of Sciences in Marseilles. The Army turned it down as too complicated. Bazeries simplified it, and resubmitted it at a meeting of the Military Cryptography Commission on February 9, 1893. Present, Bazeries relates, was the captain who had invented the system then in use, which Bazeries had solved. "We knew," Bazeries wrote later, "that, as a foregone conclusion, he would be hostile to all inventors of cryptologic systems." In fact the Bazeries cylinder—as it is commonly called—was not adopted, but the Marquis de Viaris, perhaps piqued by Bazeries' shattering of his cipher device, exerted himself to solve a series of three messages sent him by Bazeries and thus rationalized the Army's decision.

His method requires possession of the device. This presupposition was quite in line with Kerckhoffs' principle that no military system should require the secrecy of the apparatus. Bazeries accepted the principle and contended that the key alone—the order in which the disks are placed on the spindle—assured the absolute unsolvability of the system. In the de Viaris method, the cryptanalyst begins by turning the disks so that only *a*'s stand on the "plaintext" line. Each successive line—called a "generatrix"—comprises all the ciphertext equivalents for *a* that could possibly exist on that generatrix. Furthermore, the array of equivalents on each generatrix differs

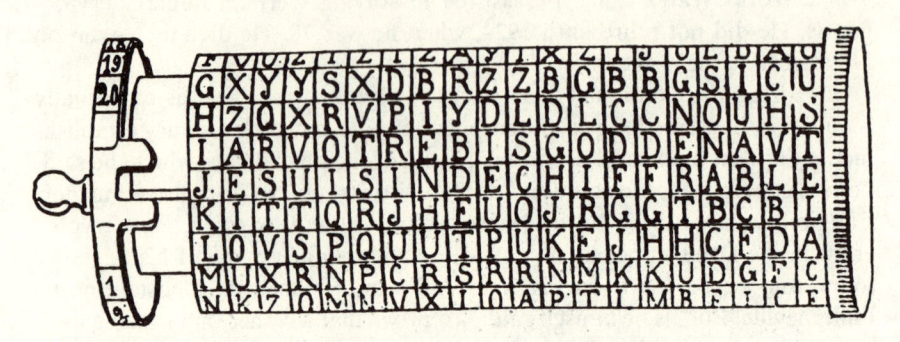

Étienne Bazeries' drawing of his cylinder, with plaintext "I am indecipherable"

from the array on any other generatrix. For example, the first two generatrices under *a* in the orginal Bazeries device were:

disk number	1	2	3	4	5	6	7	8	9	10	11	12	13	14	15	16	17	18	19	20
plaintext	a	a	a	a	a	a	a	a	a	a	a	a	a	a	a	a	a	a	a	a
generatrix 1	B	E	E	Z	Z	Z	L	V	R	F	N	I	U	T	J	I	B	B	C	C
generatrix 2	C	I	B	Y	X	X	O	D	Y	N	D	C	X	I	B	M	C	C	H	F

The patterning results from the peculiar way in which Bazeries constructed his alphabets to make them mnemonic. Some consisted of intercalations of vowels and consonants; others derived from keyphrases tending toward the patriotic ("God protects France," "Honor and country"), the homiletic ("Avoid drafts," "Instruct youth"), and the idiotic ("I like onion fried in oil"). Other alphabets would produce other patterns.

Now, these first two generatrices employ distinctive sets of letters as the substitutes for *a*:

substitutes for a

in generatrix 1	B C	E F	I J	L	N		S T U V		Z
in generatrix 2	B C D	F G	I		M N O			X Y	

The cryptanalyst now assumes that a probable word or word-fragment such as *-ation* has been enciphered wholly on one generatrix in the cryptogram before him. He then lists all the possible first-generatrix substitutes for *a*, for *t*, for *i*, *o*, and *n* in columns next to one another. These five columns he slides along under the cryptogram looking for a five-letter group whose first letter appears among the substitutes for *a*, whose second appears among the substitutes for *t*, and so on. Any such group obviously constitutes a possible first-generatrix substitute for *-ation*.

Suppose the cryptanalyst finds such a group. If the substitute for *a* in that group is v, the disk in use at that point must have been number 8. It is the only disk which substitutes v for *a* on the first generatrix. If the substitute were z, the disk in use must have been either 4, 5, or 6. The choices for the other letters will be similarly limited. The cryptanalyst then assembles a trial grouping of disks based on these choices, and, because the message was enciphered 20 letters at a time, makes trial decipherments at intervals of 20 letters. If little atolls of plaintext break the surface of the ciphertext sea, he obviously has found the right permutation of some of the disks. He can anagram to enlarge the islets into an archipelago, and to eventually merge them into an entire continent of clear. If no solid plaintext emerges, the cryptanalyst must move his list along under the cryptogram until another possibility appears. If none appears with the equivalents from the first generatrix, the cryptanalyst must try with those of the second, and so on. The whole process, de Viaris said, takes longer to explain than to carry out.

Despite this truly fine bit of cryptanalysis, Bazeries would not concede that de Viaris had done what he had in fact done: found a valid solution for the Bazeries cylinder. The inventor pointed out that the cryptogram presented in Marseilles remained unsolved, insisted that it never would be solved, reaffirmed his faith in his brainchild, and, in the words of a later commentator, generally displayed "a woeful lack of that intellectual generosity which a scientist must invariably display towards an antagonist when facing the collapse of his theory, even if a cherished one."

Notwithstanding de Viaris' solution or Bazeries' inordinate faith, the system of simultaneous encipherment with multiple alphabets is a good one, and, with frequent key changes and some modifications, can serve as a quite effective military cipher. Though he probably never knew it, Bazeries was vindicated during his own lifetime when, in 1922, the U.S. Army adopted his system.

The rejection of his cylinder hardly stilled Bazeries' fear that weak military ciphers imperiled his country. His fervent patriotism, his refusal to submit meekly to mere authority, his legitimate conviction that his cryptanalytic accomplishments qualified him to judge the merits of a cipher, all impelled him to put forward one final system. It conformed to the general staff requirement—possibly taken from Josse's dictum—that it need only pencil and paper for its operation.

Basically, it consisted of a monalphabetic substitution that changed with each message combined with a transposition. Each message carried its own key at the head. The key consisted of two letters, which were turned into a number by means of the simple rule A = 1, B = 2, and so on, and this, written out as a phrase, formed the cipher alphabet. Using English, SF becomes 186, or ONE HUNDRED EIGHTY-SIX, giving a key alphabet of ONEHUDRIGTYSXABCFJKLMPQVWZ. After the plaintext was substituted by means of this alphabet, it was divided into groups of three letters and these groups reversed. Vowels could be interpolated as nulls before each such triplet; if such a group began with a ciphertext vowel, a null had necessarily to be inserted before it to prevent confusion. Bazeries felt that the change of key with each message effectively fortified his system, and he offered a sample cryptogram. Though the French cryptanalysts never solved it, the Ministry of War wrote him on April 19, 1899, that "the method does not present sufficient guarantees of security to be adopted."

For once the bureaucrats were right; no monoalphabetic substitution can maintain security in heavy traffic. Bazeries, naturally enough, remained entirely unconvinced, and in 1901 he revenged himself in a bitter, scornful, episodic book called *Les Chiffres Secrets Dévoilés* ("Secret Ciphers Unveiled"). "May this revelation lead the War Department to change its locks," he exclaims in the introduction of a book whose cover is subtly adorned with a photograph of the Bazeries cylinder. He flagellated the general staff for its "willful blindness" in matters cryptologic, rehearsed his tale of injured pride, argued anew for his ciphers, rebutted the official criticism of them. His pages rasp: "The French general staff, in adopting these methods, believed it made progress. It only retreated." He sarcastically praised the Army's "fine spirit of routine" and denounced its ciphers as "a public danger."

The book is not entirely polemic. Bazeries outlined the major systems of cryptology, related some entertaining history, and disclosed how he solved the anarchist and Orléans messages. He surveyed the current literature with Olympian hauteur and convicted authors like Josse and de Viaris of "heresy" when they asserted views contrary to his own. The book exudes his personality. Bazeries invested even an arid technical discussion with his astringent tone: "To abandon the methods of substitution for those of transposition," he pontificated, "is to change a one-eyed horse for a blind one." That Bazeries lost his fight with the administration is cryptology's gain, for the upshot was probably the most readable book in the whole of the science. The author's victory is that in it he lives still.

It will be noted that, despite their differences, both Bazeries and the French general staff agreed almost axiomatically on ciphers for field operations instead of codes. The practice was almost universal during those years, and it testifies to the ascendancy of the field cipher. Spain employed a system in which a mixed plaintext alphabet slid over a list of two-digit ciphertext groups from 10 to 99; the position of the alphabet, and hence the homophonic equivalents for each letter, changed from message to message. The worthlessness of the system was exposed in 1894 by a lieutenant of infantry, Joaquín García Carmona, in his *Tratado de Criptografía*, the finest book on the subject in Spanish and one of the better ones in any language.

In Cuba, José Martí, that island's great apostle of freedom, was using a numerical Vigenère to direct the revolutionary struggle during the early 1890s. For example, on December 8, 1894, he wrote from New York, in his famous plan for the rising in Cuba: "1. Todos los trabajos deberán dirigirse desde ahora con la idea de comenzar, todos unidos, 16, 3, 5, 10, 16, 7 | 17, 16, 7, 22, 19, 6, | 20, 19, 22, 6, 36, 6, | 23, 23, 7, 15, 20, 22." He had applied the key HABANA to a tableau whose alphabets included the Spanish letters *ll* and *ñ*. Deciphered, this portion read, *hbcia* [*hacia*] *fines del presente mes*, making the entire clause: "1. All the work must be directed from now with the idea of beginning, all together, towards the end of the current month." The revolt indeed broke out early in 1895. And even in faraway Ethiopia a polyalphabetic substitution with mixed alphabets played its role during the confused warfare of that ancient land to retain its independence against the colonial powers.

But while armies clung to ciphers, navies and foreign ministries employed codes. These swollen descendants of the nomenclators afforded—when kept secret—greater security than a cipher, and they saved cable tolls for diplomats and signal time for commodores. Most of the codes were one-part, and most listed both codenumbers and codewords as replacements for the plaintext. Each had advantages. The codewords were far less susceptible to transmission error than the codenumbers. The addition or omission of a single Morse dot in a cable could change a codenumber from 7261 to 7262 and alter the reading from *he will* to *he will not*, since the alphabet usually placed such phrases above their negatives in the code. This is less likely to happen with codewords, like MALSANIA and MALSANOS.

On the other hand, codenumbers were easier to handle in superencipherment. Superencipherment consists of enciphering codenumbers or codewords to provide extra security. Straightforward substitution could be used. A sequence of codewords like PALMETO FEODALISER CONTABOR ANGROLLEN could be enciphered in monalphabetic substitution, or Vigenère, or any system, just as if it were ordinary language. (Transposition systems seem not to have been used because they would destroy the codewords. Code language did not regularize into five-letter groups until July 1, 1904, when new cable regulations went into effect.) Likewise, codenumbers could be transformed into letters by a key. Often a 10-letter word with no repeated letters, like REPUBLICAN, served to convert the numbers on the basis of 1 = R, 2 = E, and so on. But such superencipherments were used much less often than two others, based on codenumbers.

One transposed the codenumber digits. For example, 8264 could be shuffled to any of 23 other permutations. This method was proposed by F.-J. Sittler to attain secrecy in his best-selling commercial code, first published in 1868. In the Sittler code, the first two codenumber digits indicated the page, the second the line. The encoder could represent these mnemonically by PA and LI, the codenumber as a whole by PALI, and the encipherment by whatever combination was desired, as IPLA.

The second superencipherment was a form of substitution; the "alphabet" was the ordinary scale of numbers. This method added a keynumber, called an "additive," to the original codenumber, called the "plain code," or "placode." The sum constituted the final cryptogram, called the "enciphered code" or "encicode." In the late 19th century, a single keynumber usually served as the additive for all the codegroups of a message. For example, the placode 2726 7074 8471 might be enciphered with the additive 2898 to yield the encicode 5634 9972 1369—with the extra 1 that would precede 1369 dropped as being understood. A rudimentary form of this additive method had been used a century earlier by Benedict Arnold, who added a 7 to the digits of his dictionary code.

It was possible, however, to obtain the advantages of both easy superencipherment and transmission accuracy by utilizing the code's parallel lists of codenumbers and codewords. The code clerk would note the numerical placode for his phrase, say 3043, mentally add the additive, which would have to be a simple figure like 800, and then take the codeword opposite the intermediate encicode, 3843, as the final encicode. (Somewhat the same thing had been done with dictionary codes in the United States in 1876 by J. N. H. Patrick in his telegrams concerning presidential electors for Oregon.) In this method, the conversion from codenumbers to codewords contributes a security bonus. Cryptanalysts would find it easier to determine the additive for numerical placode-encicode pairs, like 10053 and 12053, than for literal pairs, like CAVARONO and CIANICO, which furnish only the most generalized clue to the number of code elements between them.

This system, probably the most secure and advanced code system of the day, appears to have been used by the United States Navy at the time of the Spanish-American War. It marked the latest stage in Navy secret communications. In 1809, a simple monalphabetic had served for messages from the Navy Department to its future hero, Commander David Porter, at New Orleans. Responsibility for naval cryptography then rested, as it had since the Navy was founded, with the senior member of the Navy Board. In 1842, with the establishment of the bureau system, the cryptographic responsibility was assigned to the Bureau of Construction, Equipment, and Repair. In 1853, it was transferred to the Bureau of Ordnance and Hydrography, and in 1862 to the Bureau of Navigation, which retained it until 1917. In 1877, the Navy was using a Vigenère for at least some of its communications, and in 1887 it printed the Navy Secret Code, which was still in use in 1898, apparently with a superencipherment. Naval cryptography glinted briefly in the tumult surrounding the reception and decoding of one of the most thrilling code messages of the era.

As war approaches: Admiral Dewey gets a coded message from Navy Secretary Long **warning** Keep full of coal, the best that can be had

Ever since rumors had reached the United States of the momentousness of Admiral George Dewey's victory over the Spanish fleet in Manila Bay on May 1, 1898, the country had been in a fever of anxiety to hear the official report. Elaborate preparations had been made to process it. Consul Wildman at Hong Kong, who was expected to get the first word by ship from Manila, was ordered to cable the message without delay. Officials remained on 24-hour duty at the State Department and in the Navy's Bureau of Navigation, which would decode the cable. At 4:40 a.m. on the rainy morning of Saturday, May 7, the message "Hong Kong, McCulloch, Wildman" arrived, indicating that the revenue cutter *McCulloch* had arrived with Dewey's report and that the Admiral's dispatch would follow shortly. Within half an hour, Secretary of the Navy John D. Long was notified. Soon the whole city was wild with excitement.

About 9:30, Mr. Marcan, manager of the Western Union office, appeared at the Navy Department with a sheet containing the mysterious jargon in which Dewey had coded his report. He handed it directly to Long, who looked hard at its 88 codewords, as if he would wrest their meaning from them by sheer force of personality. But all his straining anxiety could not draw an iota of sense from the message, which began:

CRAQUIEREZ REFRENANS VIJFVOETIG IMPAZZAVA PRESABERE INTRUSIVE REGENBUI EDIFIERS RETAPIEZ DECRUSAMES IMPAVIDEZ RIBOTIEZ GOLDKRAUT RIONORAI SANSCRITO . . .

He handed it to Lieutenant (j.g.) Humes S. Whittlesey, one of the cryptographic officers, who disappeared with it into the Bureau of Navigation. Then Long pretended to transact other business at his desk.

Just after 10 o'clock, the Assistant Secretary of the Navy, Theodore Roosevelt, who had been in the Bureau of Navigation, stepped into the midst of the waiting newspapermen and announced, "Dewey has destroyed or captured all six cruisers." Reporters rushed for the telephones; messenger boys pedaled furiously through the rain. Soon thereafter, Long came out and, standing in the corner window where the light was good, read out the plaintext: *Squadron arrived at Manila at daybreak this morning. Immediately engaged the enemy and destroyed the following Spanish vessels: Reina Cristina, Castillia, Don Antonio de Biloa, Don Juan de Austria, Isla de Luzon, Isla de Cuba.* . . . The list of names seemed to run on endlessly. When he finished, cheers rang through the room, and then swept the country. Not until much later did the nation decode the real meaning of the message: that the United States, having conquered possessions around the globe, had started on the road to international commitment.

At 9 a.m. on October 15, 1894, Captain Alfred Dreyfus of the French general staff reported to a meeting of several superior officers at the War Ministry on the Rue Saint-Dominique in Paris. They suspected him of having written a document that offered military information to Germany, the so-called bordereau, or memorandum. After the captain took some dictation to test his handwriting, which resembled that of the bordereau, Major Marquis Mercier du Paty de Clam arose, placed his hand on Dreyfus' shoulder, and intoned, "Captain Dreyfus, in the name of the law I arrest you. You are accused of high treason."

Though the arrest was kept secret at first, the anti-Semitic journal *La Libre Parole* scooped the rest of the Paris press on November 1 with the headline, "High Treason! Arrest of the Jewish Officer, A. Dreyfus!" The newspapers indicated that Dreyfus was in the pay of Germany or Italy, and that very day the Italian military attaché, Colonel Alessandro Panizzardi, wrote to his chief in Rome that neither he nor his German colleague knew anything of the prisoner, though he conceded that Dreyfus may have worked directly for the Italian general staff without Panizzardi's own knowledge. As the clamor mounted in the press, Panizzardi next day felt it necessary to telegraph that, if Dreyfus had not been in contact with Rome, an official denial should be published to quell newspaper comments.

The message of November 2 went out in code and, like all other diplomatic cryptograms passing over the wires of the French Ministry of Posts and Telegraphs, an onionskin copy of Panizzardi's text was sent to the Foreign Ministry for an attempt at solution. This cryptogram, which was to become the most sensational secret message of those gaslight years, read:

Commando stato maggiore Roma
913 44 7836 527 3 88 706 6458 71 18 0288 5715 3716 7567 7943 2107 0018 7606 4891 6165

                                                        Panizzardi

The ministry's Bureau du Chiffre consisted of seven men.* Its chief, Charles-Marie Darmet, who was two weeks short of his 59th birthday when the Panizzardi telegram came in, had joined the ministry as an employee in the archives bureau 40 years previously, and had moved over to the cipher bureau three years later. He had served as a delegate to the Congress of Berlin in 1878, possibly with secret cryptanalytic duties. His rise through the ranks culminated in his appointment on January 22, 1891, as chief of the cipher bureau with a salary somewhere between 7,000 and 10,000 francs. His deputy chief was Albin-Chrysostôme Marnotte, 54, who had served in the cipher bureau for just under 37 years and had become deputy the same day that Darmet became chief. The others were Maurice-Edmé-Ludovic Gaillard, 53, with 23 years in the cipher bureau; Charles Dauchez, 46, also with 23 years' service; Louis-Marie-Léonor Béguin-Billecocq, 29, seven years in the bureau; François Billecocq, 29, four years' service; and Joseph-Gabriel-Claude-

---

* Whether Bazeries, who had been lent to the ministry in September, was serving in the cipher bureau at the time, existing records do not say. His discussion of the Panizzardi telegram in his book is so sketchy that it seems unlikely that he participated in its solution.

Pag.

00	Raziocinio	50	Reggimento Bersaglieri
01	Razionale	51	» Cavalleria
02	Razza	52	» Linea
03	Di buona razza	53	Reggio Calabria
04	Di cattiva razza	54	Reggio d'Emilia
05	(Re) Il Re di	55	Regìa
06	S. M. il Re	56	Regìa cointeressata
07	Reagi-re, Reagente	57	Regime
08	Reagito	58	Passato regime
09	Realista, Reale	59	Sotto il regime
10	Realizza-re, Realizzazione	60	Regina
11	Potete realizzare	61	La Regina di
12	Realizzate	62	S. M. la Regina
13	Realizzato	63	Regio
14	Potuto realizzare	64	Regione, Regionale
15	Realtà, Realmente	65	Registra-re, Registrazione
16	Reazione, Reazionario	66	Registro
17	Prodotta una reazione	67	Regna-re, Regno
18	Recalcitra-re, Recalcitrante	68	Regolamento, Regolamentare
19	Recapito	69	Regola-re, Regolato
20	Reca-re, Recato	70	È in regola
21	Recede-re, Receduto	71	Si ponga in regola
22	Recente, Recentemente	72	Si regoli
23	Recidivo	73	Sono in regola
24	Recinto	74	Regolarità
25	Recipiente	75	Regolarizza-re, Regolarizzato
26	Reciprocità	76	Regresso, Regressivo
27	Reciproco, Reciprocamente	77	Reichsrath
28	Reciso, Recisamente	78	Reichstag
29	Recita-re, Recitazione	79	Reichsmark
30	Reclama-re, Reclamo	80	Reimpo-rre, Reimposizione
31	Reclami	81	Reintegra-re, Reintegrato
32	Recluso, Reclusione	82	Reis
33	Recluta-re, Reclutamento	83	Reiteratamente
34	Recrimina-re, Recriminazione	84	Relativ-o-amente
35	Redattore	85	Relatore
36	Reddito	86	Relatore del Bilancio
37	Redige-re, Redatto	87	» della Commissione
38	Redime-re, Redimibile	88	Relazione
39	Reduce	89	In relazione
40	Referendario	90	Presentata la relazione
41	Refezione	91	Pubblicata la relazione
42	Refrattario	92	Relega-re, Relagazione
43	Refrigerio	93	Religione
44	Regala-re, Regalo	94	Religioso, Religiosamente
45	Reggente	95	Reliquia
46	Regge-re, Reggenza	96	Remissibile
47	Reggia	97	Remissione
48	Reggimento	98	Rende-re, Reso
49	Reggimento Artiglieria	99	Renda

Page 75 of the Baravelli commercial code, used in the Panizzardi telegram

Hippolyte Mézière, 21, two years' service. The three older men had all been made chevaliers of the Légion d'Honneur; the four younger, all with law degrees, seem to have been recruited directly into the cryptanalytic service.

The cryptanalysts recognized Panizzardi's intermixture of one-, two-, three- and four-digit groups in a single message as that of an Italian commercial code published earlier that year in Turin by Paolo Baravelli, an engineer. This code, entitled *Dizionario per corrispondenze in cifra*, was constructed in four sections: table I, in which vowels and punctuation marks were represented by single digits from 0 to 9; table II, in which consonants, grammatical forms, and auxiliary verbs were represented by pairs of digits; table III, consisting of syllables indicated by three-digit groups; and a vocabulary proper, in which words and phrases were represented by four-digit groups. Some four-digit groups were left blank so the user could insert terms he found necessary.

The codebreakers furthermore remembered the Baravelli code from an amusing incident of a few months earlier. In June, a mysterious correspondence had been daily burning up the wires between the Count of Turin, a nephew of the king of Italy, and the Duchess Grazioli, a tall and voluptuous Italian living at the Hotel Windsor in Paris. Colonel Jean Sandherr, the dull and stolid head of French army intelligence, thought it smelled of espionage; Maurice Paléologue, an assistant to the Foreign Minister, whose duties included overseeing the cryptanalytic office, said that it gave off only the perfume of romance. (Paléologue was to become France's World War I ambassador to Russia and a member of the Académie Française.) Soon Sandherr burst into Paléologue's office with a small, flat, highly scented book. It was a Baravelli code. One of Sandherr's agents had stolen it from beneath a packet of the duchess's handkerchiefs while she was at the races. Two days later, Paléologue brought over the translations. They expressed, he said, nothing but "simple, elemental, natural feelings. However, one four-figure sequence which recurred in most of the telegrams remained indecipherable [presumably because it stood for a blank that the couple had filled in themselves]. All that our decoders were able to suggest was that the apocalyptic number stood for something extraordinary, unforgettable and sublime!"

This experience—in its own way extraordinary, unforgettable and sublime—had taught the cryptanalysts that, to achieve secrecy in a volume that was on public sale, the Baravelli employed an artifice common among commercial codes of the day. On each of the 100 pages devoted to the vocabulary, the words, phrases, and blank spaces were distributed in two columns of 50; each was assigned a printed number from 00 to 99. Each page was also numbered at its lower outside corner by two small printed digits that ran from 00 on the first page of the vocabulary to 99 on the last. The user could either superencipher these, or he could fill in his own page number following the large printed "Pag." at the top of each page. He was to combine these two digits with the two digits for the words into the four-digit figure of the vocabulary section.

Similar arrangements were provided in the other sections. Table III (syllables) was set up in precisely the same way, except that the ten pages were given single instead of double digits. Table II (grammatical forms, consonants) was divided into ten groups of ten elements; the first number, indicating the group, was provided with a dotted line on which a substitute could be written; the second number, indicating the element in that group, was printed. The ten numbers of Table I (vowels, punctuation) were each preceded by a dotted line.

The Foreign Ministry cryptanalysts undoubtedly attempted to read Panizzardi's message using all printed numbers—in other words, without any substitutes for the page or group numbers. The attempt yielded:

```
913   44    7836         527   3   88    706     6458      71 ...
us    le    rimprovera,  nar   i   te    ren     pensato   sarà ...
uss               -re    narr  j
                                  ì
```

This gibberish showed that Panizzardi had made use of a superencipherment. It was the task of the French cryptanalysts to determine it—a task made more difficult by the fact that this message was the first sent by Panizzardi in this particular system.

They were abetted, however, by the peculiar construction of the Baravelli code, in which the portion of each placode number representing the line remains invariable because it is printed. With this as a start, and with the agitations of the Dreyfus disclosures, the cryptanalysts had little trouble in determining that the arrested man's name figured in the cryptogram. The plaintext elements available in the Baravelli code permit the word *Dreyfus* to be broken up for encoding in only one way: *dr, e, y, fus*. Both *dr* and *fus* are found in Table III: page 2, line 27 for *dr*; page 3, line 06 for *fus*. The *y* is found in Table II, group 9, line 8; and the *e* in Table I, line 1. In placode form, then, *Dreyfus* would be 227 1 98 306.

Now the Panizzardi telegram includes a similar sequence of codegroups composed of three, one, two, and three digits: 527 3 88 706. Furthermore, the numbers in this sequence that presumably represent the lines—27, 8, and 06 (omitting the single digit from Table I)—are identical with those for *Dreyfus*. Obviously, then, the sequence 527 3 88 706 represented Panizzardi's encicode for *Dreyfus*. From this, the cryptanalysts could see that the digits representing lines were not enciphered. They also had ascertained the encipherment of two of the Table III pages, of one group in Table II, and of a line of Table I.

With this as a start, the Foreign Ministry cryptanalysts produced—perhaps by the very next day—a preliminary decryptment that read: "Arrested [is] Captain Dreyfus who has not had relations with Germany...." This text, highly hypothetical, and in which the only certain word was *Dreyfus*, was shown to Sandherr, who was in intimate and frequent contact with the Foreign Ministry cryptanalysts. He was immediately interested, for the telegram bore on the guilt or innocence of the central figure of a sensational scandal involving his service. By Tuesday, November 6, the cryptanalysts had perceived that the group 913, which they had translated as part of *arrestato* in their first trial, was just Panizzardi's serial number, and they had reached a solution which they considered exact, except for the ending: "If Captain

The Professor, the Soldier, and the Man on Devil's Island

Dreyfus has not had relations with you, it would be wise to have the ambassador deny it officially. Our emissary is warned." These last words seemed to hint darkly at Dreyfus' guilt, and, though that was the very part that was conjectural, Sandherr, who was disposed to think Dreyfus a traitor, borrowed the cryptanalyst's worksheet, with its successive hypotheses stacked up beneath each codegroup and with question marks advertising the conjectural nature of the final four words, *uffiziale rimane prevenuto emissario.* He reported on it to his superiors, remarking to Charles Le Mouton de Boisdeffre, the chief of staff, "Well, General, here's another proof of Dreyfus' guilt." Sandherr had a copy made of the worksheet, which du Paty de Clam studied with interest, and then returned the original to the Ministry of Foreign Affairs.

By the following Saturday, November 10, the cryptanalysts had finally cracked the system of encipherment used by Panizzardi, recovered the placode equivalents, and established the definitive text of the cryptogram. It read, with the placode equivalents:

74	1336	227	1	98	306	5858	31	08	7588
Se	Capitano	Dr	e	y	fus	non	ha	avuto	relazione

2215	2116		4367	0343	8607
costà	sarebbe conveniente		incaricare	ambasciatore	smentire

9518	3306	1791	8865
ufficialmente	evitare	commenti	stampa

Or, in English: "If Captain Dreyfus has not had relations with you, it would be wise to have the ambassador deny it officially, to avoid press comment."

Panizzardi proved to have used a relatively simple system. Line digits were not touched. The two digits of the vocabulary's printed page numbers were transposed and given substitutes according to these alphabets:

first placode digit	0 1 2 3 4 5 6 7 8 9
second encicode digit	9 8 7 6 5 4 3 2 1 0
second placode digit	0 1 2 3 4 5 6 7 8 9
first encicode digit	1 3 5 7 9 0 2 4 6 8

Thus the placode 1336 of *capitano* became 7836, and the 3306 of *evitare* became 7606. The second of the above two alphabets also served to encipher the page, group, and line numbers of Tables III, II, and I, respectively. Thus the placode page 3 of the 306 of *fus* became 7 to give encicode 706; the placode of 98 of *y* became 88; and the placode 1 for *e* became encicode 3.

This version, which in no way implicated Dreyfus, was communicated to Sandherr by Paul-Henri-Phillipe-Horace Delaroche-Vernet, a 28-year-old subordinate of Paléologue's who served as liaison between the cryptanalysts and the Army (and who, in 1908, became chief of the Bureau du Chiffre, holding the post for five years). Sandherr was not pleased with this new version, and he transmitted it to his chiefs with the observation that "with Foreign Affairs, you can't always be certain about these things—they lack a little precision." Then one of his subordinates, Commandant Pierre-Ernest

Matton, a 39-year-old artilleryman who was the army liaison with the Foreign Ministry, had an idea that would lay all skepticism to rest once and for all. He would trick Panizzardi into sending a telegram whose contents were known

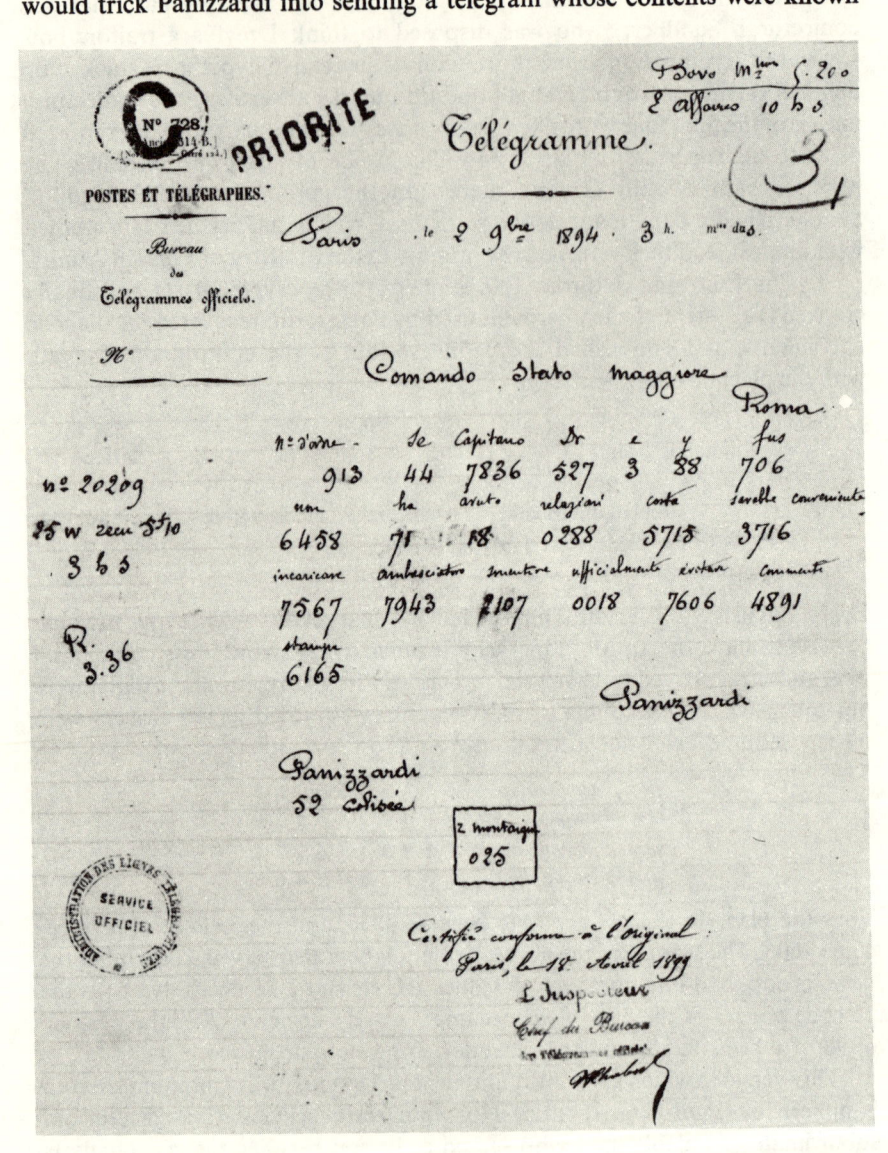

The Panizzardi telegram, with correct solution inserted

to the French; the solution of this would verify or refute the cryptanalysis of the Dreyfus message. Sandherr approved.

Matton framed a message with words chosen from pages in the Baravelli code whose numbers were critical in the encipherment and with proper names that could be divided in only one way. He artfully composed it to be so important that Panizzardi could not ignore it, and so perishable that he would have to telegraph it to Rome. It told how "A certain Y, who is now at X, will leave within a few days for Paris. He is carrying some documents relative to the mobilization of the army, which he obtained in the offices of the general staff. This person lives on Z street." One of the proper names was *Schlissenfurt*, which the Baravelli can handle in only one way. Matton had a double agent slip it to the Italian attaché. Panizzardi fell for the ruse, encoded the message almost verbatim and wired it to Rome at 8:10 a.m. November 13. The usual routine brought the onionskin copy to the cryptanalysts of the Quai d'Orsay. They, not knowing that the Army had the plaintext, solved the message and passed the translation to the Army because of its military import. When Delaroche-Vernet brought it over, Matton says he interrupted the young official and said:

" 'Will you permit me? I am going to get the original.' I went into my office and got out the piece I had written. It was word for word the dispatch they had deciphered. I told him, 'You may be sure now that you have the encipherment.' " The text that exonerated Dreyfus was irrefutably correct.

So conclusive a proof of the solution's validity would seem to have been unchallengeable. But this would be to reckon without the persistence and tenacity of those who felt Dreyfus guilty, or who thought it better to convict Dreyfus wrongfully than to admit the Army had erred and open it to criticism. Boisdeffre and his fellow generals refused to allow the Panizzardi telegram into evidence at Dreyfus' first trial, telling the prosecutor that the variations of the progressively more accurate solutions negated the telegram's value as evidence. Dreyfus was found guilty of treason and interned on Devil's Island.

But knowledge of the telegram could not be suppressed, and the anti-Dreyfus officers finally slipped a false and highly condemnatory version into the subsequent trials and appeals of the case: "Captain Dreyfus arrested; the Minister of War has proofs of his relations with Germany. Parties informed in the greatest secrecy. My emissary is warned." This text appeared as No. 44 in the so-called Secret File; it had been dictated from memory by du Paty de Clam, who seems to have fabricated it from among the various hypotheses he saw on the original worksheet borrowed by Sandherr. This version invalidated itself by the simultaneous presence in it of both *proofs* and *relations*. Both of these stood on line 88 of different pages of the Baravelli code (*provi* on page 71, *relazione* on page 75), and so both obviously could not be the plaintext equivalent for the telegram's encicode 0288.

Faced with such difficulties, Sandherr checked secretly with Commandant Munier, a former secretary of the Military Cryptography Commission, who obliged with some obscurantist professional cant to indicate that the wrong version was cryptologically correct. Finally, on April 27, 1899, Paléologue and two officers deciphered an authenticated copy of the original Panizzardi telegram for the Cour de Cassation. The result was, of course, the same as the final version decrypted by the Foreign Ministry cryptanalysts—the version in which Panizzardi by implication disclaimed any contact with Dreyfus. At last the correct solution entered the record. This alone did not exonerate Dreyfus; it was to take seven more years before he was to receive justice, reinstatement, and the Legion of Honor. (In the interim, the true author of the bordereau was found to be Major Ferdinand Walsin Esterhazy; among his papers, seized on his arrest, were a number of cardboard grilles, presumably for cipher communications with the German military attaché.) But the demonstration of how the false solutions had been used to bolster the trumped-up anti-Dreyfus case helped clear the man on Devil's Island. Du Paty de Clam, the officer who long ago had arrested Dreyfus, himself exclaimed on the importance of the telegram, though he intended his words as a condemnation. "This telegram," he declared, "is, for me, the pivot of the affair."

When the Dreyfus case was finally closed in 1906, holocaust was less than a decade away. During those years, as the tensions increased and the world girded for battle, cryptology received degrees of attention that varied from country to country according to their individual cryptologic traditions. France had the strongest tradition. The published literature from Kerckhoffs on reflected that nation's profound understanding of the subject. Practical applications were amply demonstrated by the Panizzardi telegram, by French solution of the Italian Foreign Office's most secret codes three and five years after the Panizzardi solution, and by France's possession of the German diplomatic code, which enabled her to read critical German messages on the very eve of World War I.

Army cryptology was better than Bazeries' rough tongue gave it credit for. The Military Cryptography Commission, which consisted of approximately ten officers chosen from among all arms who had shown an aptitude for cryptanalysis, tested systems proposed for use by the Army and studied cipher systems used by other nations, particularly Germany. The commission's president was, in 1900, the inspector-general of the military telegraph services, General François Penel, and in that year a 37-year-old engineer, a graduate of the École Polytechnique, was attached to the general staff as adjutant to Penel and secretary to the commission. This was Captain François Cartier, who was to become the chief of the French military cryptologic bureau in World War I. Before that war, Cartier had drafted a memorandum on how to solve German Army cryptograms on the basis of the drill messages, prefixed ÜBCHI, that French radio stations had intercepted during German maneuvers. The commission obtained other information from spies, deserters, and recruits to the Foreign Legion. The members, who did their cryptologic work in their spare time and received extra pay for it, formed a core of cryptologists with valuable experience. All this gave France a preponderant cryptologic superiority in 1914.

The Germans, on the other hand, seem to have disdained studying cryptology. The Junkers felt that their armies could, as in 1870, overrun the French by sheer force of arms. Cryptanalysis played a minor role in intelligence, since it required tapping telegraph wires to intercept texts. The Germans failed to foresee how much radio would be used and how much information would flow in its channels. Hence the general staff obtained what little it knew of other nations' cryptography from its intelligence service and did not waste manpower on such frills as cryptanalysis. As for their own ciphers—were they not German? Which ended the discussion. And so German cryptology goose-stepped toward war with a top-heavy cryptography and no cryptanalysis.

Marching with them in the parade of cryptologic ignorance were most of the other armies of Europe. England had done little more than distribute field ciphers to its tiny Army; Italy was about as interested in cryptology as it was in, say, social reform. There was no organized military cryptanalytic bureau in any country except France—and Austria-Hungary.

Perhaps the Hapsburg background in cryptanalysis, stretching to the Geheime Kabinets-Kanzlei, had conditioned Austria-Hungary to think in those terms. In 1908, she intercepted Italian radiograms, and again in 1911, when they "rained" from the sky at the outbreak of the Italo-Turkish conflict over Tripoli. The alert Colonel Max Ronge, later head of the Nachrichtendienst, or intelligence organization of the general staff, saw the opportunity. In November of 1911, he instituted a cryptanalytic bureau with Captain Andreas Figl as its chief. The staff analyzed Russian cryptograms, which proved very difficult under peacetime conditions, and Ronge purchased some Italian ciphers as a headache-preventative for his cryptanalysts.

He was not the only buyer. In the E. Phillips Oppenheim world of prewar Eastern Europe, codes and ciphers were bid up and up like speculative shares in a stock-market boom. Heading the list were those of Austria-Hungary, which, as the crossroads of Europe, was a virtual ants' nest of espionage.

According to one story, a young and remarkably attractive Italian "countess," who had become friendly with a lieutenant in the Austro-Hungarian headquarters, sneaked a copy of a red-bound code from an open safe there and replaced it with a book that looked remarkably like it—but that had only blank pages! Some time later a code clerk pulled the book out to use it and discovered the substitution. Shock waves of consternation shook the general staff. Frenzied manhunts began. Not until the Russian attaché had laughingly told one of the staff officers that he had been offered the code, but had turned it down because the 400,000 rubles asked was too much, did the Austrians trace who had taken it.

Then there was the time a mysterious gentleman offered the Austrians a handwritten copy of the Serbian code, copied in snatched moments at the risk of life by his nephew, who worked in the Serbian code room. To prove its validity, he said, he would leave it with the Austrians, who would test it on the next two Serb telegrams. They came through the very next day and were duly decoded with the new key; they dealt with some matters of custom duties—the dull routine of embassy affairs. The gentleman got his 10,000 kronen and the Austrians a warm glow of self-satisfaction, especially when they reminded one another how a copied code was less likely to be changed than a stolen one. Soon more Serb messages trickled in. "We took our cipher out of the safe," recalled one former staff member, "arranged our dispatches on the desk, and set to work. And we kept on working—perspiring, groaning, cursing—and could not get an intelligible sentence out of them—not a letter, a syllable, a punctuation point. With the exercise of some imagination we made one of them read, *The male mother of the warship has been built.*

"Then we had a bright idea. We composed a dispatch to the ambassador and put it into cipher with our 10,000-kronen key." They marked it Urgent and sent it off. Soon an angry little Serbian secretary bounced into the Vienna central telegraph office and demanded that three hopelessly garbled telegrams be repeated. They were, of course, the two that the Austrians had first decoded with their new key and the one that they had made up with it. What had happened was that the code was a pure fake, written out by the mysterious gentleman himself, who had an accomplice send two telegrams in them to the Serbian embassy. The Serbs let them lay, undecoded, until the urgent wire shook them into action.

But the Austrians were not always on the losing end. Indeed, they showed no little ingenuity of their own at one time. Through cryptanalysis, they had identified about 150 words of the Italian code used between Rome and Constantinople. Then they bogged down. So they inserted a tidbit of military information into an Italian-language paper published at Constantinople. As they had hoped, the Italian military attaché picked up the item—verbatim, as it turned out—and sent it encoded to Rome. The Austrians began phrasing their paragraphs so as to enlarge their vocabulary, and within just three months they had a fairly workable Italian code of about 2,000 words.

As the tides of history flowed toward war, nations tightened their alliances and intensified their mobilization efforts. At a high-level meeting in London in 1911 to arrange for Anglo-French intercommunications in the event of war, it was decided, among other matters, to prepare an English-French codebook. Cartier, who was at the meeting, later returned for conferences with Britain's Lieutenant Spiers on the code's lexicon and its rules of service; in 1913, he checked the final draft before printing. Soon thereafter, Spiers brought three copies of the codebook to Paris—one for the French G.H.Q., one for the French Army that would have the English on their flank, a third for the French cryptologic section.

The minuteness of these preparations reflected that of War Plan w, which the British and French general staffs had completed by the spring of 1914 and which specified the billet of every battalion in the British Expeditionary Force, down to the places where the troops were to drink their coffee. The Central Powers were no less lax, and finally, in an obscure corner of the Balkans, someone helpfully slew an archduke, and the nations leaped recklessly into the bloody cockpit of war.

9

ROOM 40

BEFORE DAWN on the morning of August 5, 1914, the first day of a world war that was to convulse country after country and to end the lives of millions, an equipment-laden ship slid quietly through the black and heaving waters of the North Sea. Off Emden, where the Dutch coast joins the German, she dropped some grappling gear overboard with a dull splash, and shortly there rose dripping from the sea great snakelike monsters, covered with mud and seaweed. Grunts of men, chopping sounds—and soon they were returned, severed and useless, to the depths. These were Germany's transatlantic cables, her chief communications lifelines to the world, and the vessel was the British cable ship *Telconia*. Though the Committee of Imperial Defence never dreamed of it when it planned the move in 1912, the cutting of these cables, England's first offensive action of the war, forged the first link in a chain that helped to end it.

Germany was now forced to communicate with the world beyond the encircling Entente by radio or over cables controlled by her enemies. She thus delivered into the hands of her foes her most secret and confidential plans, provided only that they could remove the jacket of code and cipher in which Germany had encased them. It was an opportunity for which England was unprepared, but of which she promptly availed herself.

On that first day of the war, the director of naval intelligence, Rear Admiral Henry F. Oliver, walked to lunch with the only man at the Admiralty to take any interest in cryptology, the director of naval education, Sir Alfred Ewing. A few months before, Ewing had devised what he later called a "futile" ciphering mechanism, and he had spoken to Oliver about new methods of constructing ciphers. Oliver mentioned that some naval and commercial radio stations were sending to the Admiralty some messages in code that they had picked up and that these were accumulating on his desk. The Admiralty had no department to deal with enemy cryptograms, he said. Ewing was at once interested, and when he saw the messages that afternoon he recognized that they were probably German naval signals and that their solution could be of great value. He at once undertook the task.

Ewing was then 59, a short, thickset Scot with blue eyes beneath shaggy eyebrows, a quiet voice, and the manner of a benign physician. He had been knighted three years before for his contributions to science, which included pioneering studies of Japanese earthquakes, of magnetism, and of mechanical lagging effects in stressed materials (now known by a word he coined, "hysteresis"), and for his public services, notably his naval education directorship. He was to become president of the British Association for the Advancement of Science and perhaps his country's greatest living expert on mechanical science. And now he was about to found a cryptanalytic bureau that was to become almost legendary and to exert a direct and noticeable effect upon the course of history.

He began by boning up on ciphers in the stacks of the British Museum library and on the construction of codes at Lloyd's of London and at the General Post Office, where commercial codebooks were on file. He called in four teachers at the naval colleges at Dartmouth and Osborne, A. G. Denniston, W. H. Anstie, E. J. C. Green, and G. L. N. Hope, all friends of his with a good knowledge of German, and, sitting together around the table in his office, they inspected the incomprehensible lines of letters and numbers with only the feeblest general idea on how to begin.

Among those first messages was one which, had they been able to solve it, might have affected the entire course of the war. It may have been among the first batch that Oliver showed Ewing, for it had been issued at 1:35 a.m. August 4 by the German naval high command and transmitted by the powerful radio station at Nauen outside Berlin to Admiral Wilhelm Souchon, commander in the Mediterranean. Message 51 read: "Alliance with Turkey concluded August 3. Proceed at once to Constantinople." Souchon started eastward from the central Mediterranean at once in the battle cruiser *Göben* and the light cruiser *Breslau*. The British Mediterranean squadron, convinced that Souchon would try to force the Strait of Gibraltar, patrolled the waters west of Sicily while Souchon coaled at Messina. When a British cruiser finally spotted him heading east out of the Strait of Messina, the squadron made a frantic effort to catch and destroy him, but he eluded them among the isles of Greece. On Sunday, August 10, *Göben* steamed into the Dardanelles, bringing, as Winston Churchill later acknowledged, "more slaughter, more misery and more ruin than has ever before been borne within the compass of a ship." For *Göben's* strength and its bombardments of Russian Black Sea ports brought Turkey into the war and sealed off Russia from her allies, contributing to her eventual capitulation and all that that would mean. Had the Admiralty been able to read Souchon's orders then as they did retrospectively later in the war, England might have won the fateful game of hide-and-seek, with consequences perhaps greater than any other single exploit of the war.

Of all this, nothing was foreseen at Whitehall, where on that very Sunday Ewing was, he wrote to his family, "in the thick of office work, special work quite outside my ordinary lines." The codebooks of several German commercial firms were being rounded up, but they proved of no help. Not much better was a mercantile signal-book used by German outpost vessels that had been taken from a German merchantman in Australia at the outbreak of war. Meanwhile, Russell Clarke, a barrister and a radio ham, set up the first low-frequency intercept station at Hunstanton to bring in the raw material, and soon, with the help of Clarke and another ham, Commander B. Hippisley, intercepts were trickling in by direct land line from 14 coast intercept stations to "Ewing Admiralty."

None of the small band of pioneers had had any real previous knowledge of cryptanalysis, and they made only antlike progress in those first weeks. But Ewing was exhilarated by the job, and it was not until October 25 that he took a Sunday off. By then, England had had a stroke of fortune that gave such an impetus to its cryptanalytic work that it remained far ahead of its enemies through the rest of the war. What happened has best been told in his own style by the minister who then headed the Admiralty, the First Lord, Winston Churchill:

> At the beginning of September, 1914, the German light cruiser *Magdeburg* was wrecked in the Baltic. The body of a drowned German under-officer was picked up by the Russians a few hours later, and clasped in his bosom by arms rigid in death, were the cypher and signal books of the German Navy and the minutely squared maps of the North Sea and Heligoland Bight. On September 6 the Russian Naval Attaché came to see me. He had received a message from Petrograd telling him what had happened, and that the Russian Admiralty with the aid of the cypher and signal books had been able to decode portions at least of the German naval messages. The Russians felt that as the leading naval Power, the British Admiralty ought to have these books and charts. If we would send a vessel to Alexandrov, the Russian officers in charge of the books would bring them to England. We lost no time in sending a ship, and late on an October afternoon Prince Louis [of Battenberg, First Sea Lord] and I received from the hands of our loyal allies these sea-stained priceless documents.

The date was October 13. Russell Clarke, who was as adept with a camera as with a crystal set, copied it by photography at his home. But even the astounding windfall of the *Magdeburg* codebook—perhaps the luckiest in the whole history of cryptology—did not enable Ewing's team to read the German naval messages, for the four-letter codewords in that book did not appear in the dispatches. Finally, Fleet Paymaster Charles J. E. Rotter, a principal German expert, discovered that the code had been superenciphered with a monalphabetic substitution. Solution of such a superencipherment is not too difficult a problem with the codebook in one's possession. As in ordinary plaintext, certain codewords recur more frequently than others and in familiar clusters, letters in one codeword reappear in others in different arrangements, and the codewords themselves possess some structural regularities: in the case of the German naval code, consonants alternated with vowels in the four-letter codewords. When these characteristics are known, the cryptanalyst can spot them almost as well as the more pronounced ones of ordinary language, and can exploit them to solve the superencipherment.

So green were the British cryptanalysts that it took them almost three weeks before they began reading portions of some German naval messages. These, Churchill says, "were mostly of a routine character. 'One of our torpedo boats will be running out into square 7 at 8 p.m.,' etc. But a careful collection of these scraps provided a body of information from which the enemy's arrangements in the Heligoland Bight [bordering the northwest German coast] could be understood with a fair degree of accuracy."

By this time, Ewing's staff had grown to such an extent that they crowded his office, and they were continually irked by having to put their work out of sight when he had visitors on educational subjects. So about the middle of November the entire cryptanalytic group moved to Room 40 in the Old Buildings of the Admiralty. This was a large room with a small room adjoining, with a camp bed for tired staffers. Room 40, O.B., had the advantage of being out of the main stream of Admiralty traffic, yet being relatively handy to the Operations Division, which received its output. Though the cryptanalysts were later designated as I.D. 25 (section 25 of the Intelligence Division), "Room 40" was so convenient and so innocuous a name that it soon became the common identification for the organization. The name stuck even when I.D. 25 moved into larger quarters.

For it expanded rapidly. At the end of December an English trawler brought up a heavy chest containing a number of books and documents that had been jettisoned by one of four German destroyers which had been sunk in an action in the Heligoland Bight October 16. In it was found an important German codebook that was missing from the *Magdeburg* find. The cryptanalysts immediately used it to read signals to German cruisers harassing English shipping, but they did not discover for several months that it also served to encode messages between Berlin and German naval attachés abroad. The increase in traffic required five new men, which brought watches to two-man strength. As additional codes were discovered, more staff was enrolled, frequently in a casual British manner.

Francis Toye, a young war-prison administrator and interpreter who had worked in the British censorship and who later became a widely known music critic, attended a dinner one Thursday evening at the London home of financier Max Bonn. Among the guests was one of Room 40's brighter members, Frank Tiarks, a partner in the banking firm of J. Henry Schroder & Co. and a director of the Bank of England.

"We talked a good deal," Toye recalled, "and after dinner he took me aside and asked me whether I should like to come to the Admiralty. Registering proper—and wholly genuine—surprise, I answered that I could not see what use the Admiralty is likely to have for my services.

" 'Max has just told me that your German is very good,' he replied; 'you are obviously intelligent and presumably, from your record, trustworthy.

There are hundreds of people with one of these qualifications, a number with two, but very few with all three. What about it?'

" 'What about my job, the War Office and all that?' said I.

" 'If you'll come you can leave everything in our hands.'

" 'But of course I'll come if I'm really wanted.'

" 'Very well, I'll check up on you and you'll hear in due course.' . . . About a fortnight later the Commandant sent for me and silently handed me a War Office telegram: 'Lieutenant-Interpreter Toye is to report as soon as possible to the Admiralty for special duty.' So omnipotent and expeditious is the British Admiralty when its mind is once made up; think of the yards of red tape that must have been cut in those two weeks!"

Meanwhile, naval intelligence was building up activities concomitant to cryptanalysis. Major radio direction-finding stations were—largely thanks to Oliver's foresight—set up at Lowestoft, York, Murcar, and Lerwick; they fed their readings into Whitehall, where they proved of immense help in locating the German fleets and the movement of the U-boats. There was no way of avoiding a fix except by maintaining radio silence. This fact was of course known to the Germans, and in view of it England made no attempt to keep its direction-finding activity secret, using it as a smokescreen for its less obvious and more valuable cryptanalytic work. Two other sources of radio intelligence were the identification of ships' radio call-signs and the recognition of a radio operator's "fist," or characteristic way of sending Morse code. If the Admiralty knew that a call-sign heard under way in the North Sea belonged to the 12-gun battleship *Westfalen*, it would pursue tactics different from those if the call-sign was assigned to *U-20*. This radio intelligence, plus cryptanalysis, plus other information streaming into the Admiralty was correlated and interpreted by Admiral Sir Arthur Wilson, a former First Sea Lord and naval elder statesman who was charged by Churchill with advising the top war officials of its substance.

Thus it was that, at about 7 p.m. on December 14, 1914, Wilson came to Churchill to report that intelligence indicated a sortie of German vessels, possibly against British coasts. Less than three hours later the Admiralty ordered units of the British fleet to proceed at once to a "point where they can make sure of intercepting the enemy on his return." So while the German First Cruiser Squadron hurled high-explosive shells into the seacoast towns of Hartlepool and Scarborough early on the morning of the 15th, four British battle cruisers and six of the most powerful battleships in the world were standing 150 miles to the eastward, cutting off their return. As the Germans headed back toward their base in the Jade River at Wilhelmshaven on December 16 after the bombardment, the weather thickened and heavy squalls reduced visibility. But the Admiralty intelligence had placed the light cruiser *Southampton* so precisely in the path of the German vessels that, at 10:30 a.m., Commodore W. E. Goodenough saw their shapes driving through the fog. He could not be sure that they were not British ships on station, however, so

Rembrandt depicts the most famous cryptogram in the world—the handwriting on the wall—in his "Belshazzar's Feast." A celestial hand emerges from smoke to inscribe Mene mene tekel upharsin *vertically in glowing Hebrew letters upon the palace wall as a startled Belshazzar turns and stares.*

The father of Western cryptology, Leo Battista Alberti

Giovanni Battista Porta, the Italian scientist, in 1589

Girolamo Cardano, the Italian writer, aged 49

Blaise de Vigenère, in the last year of his life

Abbot Johannes Trithemius, author of the first printed book on cryptology

François Viète, French cryptanalyst

Philippe van Marnix, solver of Spanish ciphers

Antoine Rossignol, the father of French cryptology

Bishop Edward Willes, head of England's decyphering branch

John Wallis, the father of English cryptology

Elbridge Gerry, who solved a Tory spy cryptogram

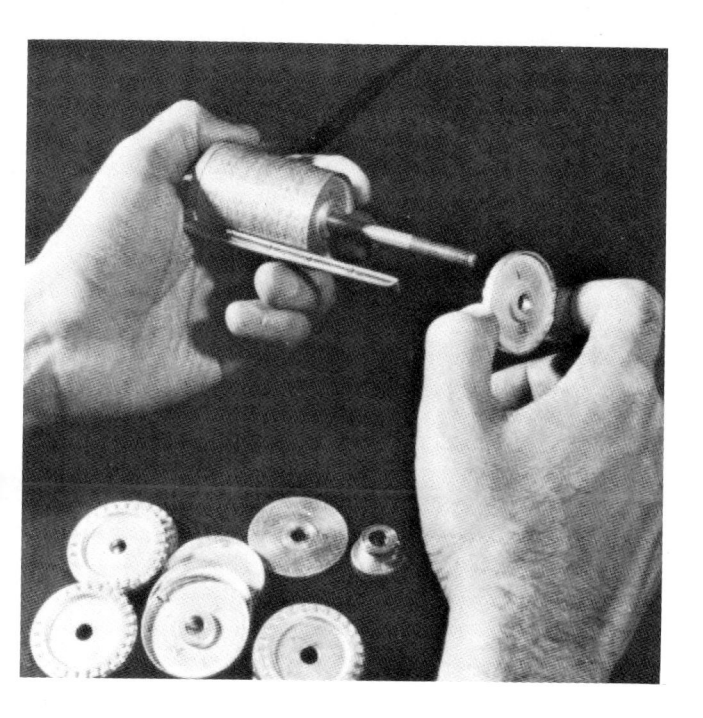

Above, *Thomas Jefferson*, the father of American cryptography; left, *cryptographer assembles Cipher Device* M-94, *U.S. Army version of Jefferson's cypher*

Three Victorian amateur cryptologists: from left, *Sir Charles Wheatstone, inventor of two important cipher systems; Lyon Playfair, First Baron Playfair, who gave his name to one of Wheatstone's ciphers; and Charles Babbage, who solved many difficult ciphers*

Left, *Confederate brass cipher disk;* right, *Edward S. Holden, one of the cryptanalysts of the electoral scandal telegrams of 1876*

Above, *Etienne Bazeries, the great French cryptanalyst, in the 1920s;* left, *Auguste Kerckhoffs, apostle of modern cryptography*

Three World War I British cryptologists: from left, *Nigel de Grey, a solver of the Zimmermann telegram; Malcolm Hay of Seaton, head of the War Office cryptanalytic bureau; O. T. Hitchings, worth "four divisions" to the B.E.F.*

Luigi Sacco, Italian cryptologist, in 1942

Colonel Parker Hitt, mentor of America's World War I cryptology, in France in 1918

Lieutenant Georges Painvin, who was to become the greatest cryptanalyst of World War I, engages in his first attempts at solution in a room at the Chateau de Montgobert, November, 1914

he flashed his recognition signal at them. They failed to reply; he opened fire, but soon lost contact. Two hours later, the heavy British forces sighted the enemy. But when the commander of the German light cruisers saw the giant forms of the British battleships looming up through the drizzle, he, with great presence of mind, blinked the recognition signal that Goodenough had made to him shortly before. Then he turned away and escaped behind the curtains of mist before the deception could be discovered and the 13.5-inch guns could blow him out of the water.

Disappointment was intense in the British Navy, which had been straining to test its mettle against the German High Seas Fleet. But opportunity recurred little more than a month later, when Wilson marched into Churchill's office about noon on January 23, 1915, and announced:

"First Lord, those fellows are coming out again."

"When?"

"Tonight. We have just got time to get Beatty there." Wilson explained that the chief source of his intelligence was Room 40's translation—undoubtedly with the *Magdeburg* codebook—of a message sent at 10:25 a.m. that morning to Rear Admiral Franz von Hipper, reading: "First and Second Scouting Groups, senior officer of destroyers, and two flotillas to be selected by the senior officer scouting forces are to reconnoiter the Dogger Bank. They are to leave harbor this evening after dark and to return tomorrow evening after dark."

England elected the same tactics as before, and units under Vice Admiral Sir David Beatty sailed to block the German homeward trip. This time they were luckier. Contact was made at 7:30 a.m. next morning. When von Hipper saw the numerous English forces, he collected his ships and ran. The British, in their faster super-dreadnought class battleships, gave chase. By 9 a.m., *Lion*, carrying Beatty, could open fire at 20,000 yards. The action soon became general between the four British and the four German capital ships. *Blücher* was sunk, and *Seydlitz* and *Derfflinger* heavily damaged, but confusion in the British squadron after a shell had crippled the flagship allowed the German ships to escape. The Germans staggered into port, flames leaping above their funnels, their decks cumbered with wreckage and crowded with the wounded and the dead, not to stir again for more than a year.

This Battle of the Dogger Bank settled the confidence of the Admiralty in Room 40, and shortly afterwards the terrifying Lord Fisher, the new First Sea Lord, gave Ewing carte blanche to get whatever he needed for the betterment of his work. Ewing augmented his staff, installed improved equipment in his intercept and direction-finding stations, and increased their number to 50.

At about this time, the old German superencipherment failed to yield the correct codegroups. Room 40 was now more familiar with the quirks and characteristics of these codewords, and, after an all-night effort with all available staff, the new key was discovered. It seems to have been this:

placode   a b c d e   f g h i j   k l m n o   p q r s t   u v w x y z
encicode I L D S A M X Z O   B N C V U   G   T W F Y P   R E H

This key was used in a message of February 19, 1915, directing the captain of the interned naval auxiliary *Odenwald* to act according to his judgment and to "avoid expenses for the empire":

placode kytul ocuko ryharoz unu kozapocuko larake nume...
encicode BEFYNUDYBU TEZITUHYVY BUHICUDYBU NITIBAVYCA...

Vowels represented vowels, and consonants, consonants, to retain the pronounceability of the codewords. In the morning Churchill himself called to offer his congratulations.

Solution of the superencipherment—then worthy of a call from the First Lord—soon became routine. The Germans gradually accelerated their key changes from once every three months at the beginning of the war to every midnight in 1916. But by then Room 40 had become so proficient that the new key was sometimes solved as early as 2 or 3 a.m. and nearly always by 9 or 10 a.m.

Consequently, when Vice Admiral Reinhard Scheer, chafing under his enforced inactivity, decided to try to entice the British Grand Fleet to where his submarines could attack it and his High Seas Fleet fall upon a section of it without risking a general engagement, his orders lay at the mercy of British cryptanalysts. But it seems to have been noncryptanalytic intelligence that led the Admiralty to inform its Navy at 5 p.m. May 30, 1916, that the High Seas Fleet was apparently putting out to sea. On this news, virtually the entire Grand Fleet, that mighty armored pride of England, built up steam and sallied forth majestically from Scapa Flow, Invergordon, and Rosyth. It sought the major fleet action that would give England the undisputed control of the seas on which her strategy in the war so heavily depended.

Then there occurred one of those trifling errors on which history so often turns. On sailing, Scheer had transferred the call-sign DK of his flagship *Friedrich der Grosse* to the naval center at Wilhelmshaven in an attempt to conceal his departure. Room 40 was aware of this procedure, but when queried on May 31 as to where call-sign DK was, simply replied, "In the Jade River," without mentioning the transfer. Whitehall radioed Admiral Sir John Jellicoe that directional wireless placed the enemy flagship in harbor at 11:10 a.m. Three hours later, with Jellicoe believing the Germans to be in port, the two fleets made contact in the middle of the North Sea. This rather shook Jellicoe's faith in Admiralty intelligence. It was further jolted when he plotted the position of the German cruiser *Regensburg* as given by an Admiralty report and found that it appeared to be in almost the very same spot as he himself then was! No one then knew that the *Regensburg* navigator had made an error of ten miles in his reckoning and that the fault for the absurd result lay with the German officer and not with the cryptanalysts of Room 40.

After the brief flurries of action, inconclusive and unsatisfactory to both sides, that constituted the Battle of Jutland, Scheer at 9:14 p.m. ordered: "Our own main body is to proceed in. Maintain course S.S.E. 1/4 E; speed 16 knots." At 9:46, he altered it slightly to S.S.E. 3/4 E. Both messages were decrypted with almost unbelievable alacrity by Room 40, and by 10:41 a summary of them had been received aboard the flagship. But Jellicoe had had enough of Admiralty intelligence. Furthermore, the summary had omitted Scheer's 9:06 call for air reconnaissance off the Horn Reefs, which would have confirmed his intentions, and thus there was nothing to contradict a battle report from *Southampton* that suggested a different enemy course. Jellicoe therefore rejected the Admiralty information, which this time was right. As a result, he steered one way, Scheer fled another, and Britain's hope of a decisive naval victory evaporated in a welter of errors, missed chances, and distrust.

After Jutland, the German emphasis on submarine warfare intensified Room 40's concentration on the U-boat messages. These were encoded in the four-letter code of the High Seas Fleet, but were superenciphered by columnar transposition. The Germans called the one for the regular U-boats "gamma epsilon" and that for the larger cruising submarines, whose keyword differed, "gamma u." Keywords changed often but not daily. Three or four staffers specialized in this; they became so adept that they usually managed not only to restore the scrambled codewords to their original form but even to recover the keyword for the transposition tableau. The solutions greatly assisted British operations, and eventually the Germans could no longer chalk off as coincidental the repeated apparitions of substantial British units athwart their course. In August of 1916, they changed their code. But Room 40's direction-finding and call-sign sections were so well oiled that they nevertheless maintained a fair flow of intelligence.

They did not have to bear the burden very long, however, for in September a badly burned but legible copy of the valuable new codebook was recovered from the Zeppelin L-32, which had been downed at Billericay. Nor did the Admiralty rely entirely on fortuitous circumstances. In an attempt to obtain whatever intelligence it could on new apparatus aboard the German submarines, the Admiralty had some months previously sent a diver into a U-boat sunk off the Kentish coast. He was Shipwright E. C. Miller, a thin, pale, but wiry young diving instructor possessed of an unusual courage and capacity to stand pressure at greater depths than most men. On his first descent, he entered through a hole in the U-boat's hull and reconnoitered through a chill blackness with things bumping up against him—which his flashlight showed to be corpses. Pushing through them, he opened a small door aft of the officers' quarters. Inside the compartment was an iron box, which was found to contain the vessels' codes.

Miller brought up so much valuable material that he was sent down again and again. It was not pleasant work. The dogfish, he said, "are always about and will eat anything. In the mating season they naturally resent any intruder, and on lots of occasions when they chased me I offered them my boot, and they never failed to snap at it. ... There were some pretty weird scenes inside the boats. ... I found scores of conger eels, some of them seven to eight feet long and five inches or so thick, all busily feeding. They gave one a bit of a shock." Despite the gruesome aspects of the job, Miller succeeded nearly every time in finding the now familiar iron box, and from one of the 25 U-boats that he explored—no Englishman was more familiar with their interior than he—he recovered the badly needed new German naval code. After the war, he was decorated at Buckingham Palace by the king.

Miller's find helped the cryptanalysts in reading the increasing volume of enemy messages. Room 40 was now approaching the height of its power. Intercepts poured in through the pneumatic tube so fast that at times the discharge of its small containers sounded like a machine gun. (After the war it was estimated that from October, 1914, to February, 1919, Room 40 had intercepted and solved 15,000 German secret communications.) Work went on round the clock on the naval messages, even during the Zeppelin bombings, when the lights were dimmed behind the close-fitting dark blinds. The staff was further increased by wounded officers and by German university scholars, many of whom were commissioned in the Royal Navy Volunteer Reserve so that they could wear uniforms to forestall icy looks from the public. Women were enlisted to free cryptanalysts from clerical tasks. Separate sections were established for naval and political cryptanalysis. Heading the former was A. G. Denniston, one of Ewing's original four musketeers, who proved exceedingly skillful at cryptanalysis, who came back to do similar work in World War II, and who in recognition was made a Companion of St. Michael & St. George and a Commander of the Order of the British Empire. The chief of the political cryptanalysts was George Young, who had a background of diplomacy that included posts in Washington, Athens, Constantinople, Madrid, Belgrade, and Lisbon, whence he quit a sinecure to work in Room 40, and who later succeeded to a baronetcy.

With the increase in traffic, Room 40 ceased simply passing edited intercepts to the Operations Division and began sending daily summaries that integrated the cryptanalytic with the direction-finding and other radio intelligence. Captain H. W. W. Hope was replaced as editor and correlator of the cryptanalyzed naval messages in May of 1917 by Commander William James, who later became administrative head of I.D. 25, or Room 40. Starting in November of 1916, Hugh Cleland Hoy, secretary to the director of naval intelligence, read through the hundreds of intercepts to sift the wheat from the chaff and to send the kernels on to the proper division of government—the Cabinet, the War Office, or Scotland Yard.

The staff included several men who already had or later would achieve a modicum of fame. In addition to Toye, Tiarks, and Ewing himself, there were

Ronald Knox, who later became a Catholic priest and made a highly praised translation of the Bible; Dr. Frank Adcock, dean of Kings College, Cambridge, who was later knighted for his work as one of the three joint editors of the 11-volume *Cambridge Ancient History*, and who also served as a cryptanalyst in World War II; Desmond McCarthy, a widely known author and critic, later knighted, who, like Knox, joined only late in the war; the second Baron Monkbretton, who served as chairman of the London County Council from 1920 to 1930; and W. Lionel Fraser, later chairman of three substantial financial firms—Banque de Paris et des Pays-Bas, Cornhill Insurance Company, and Scandinvest Trust, Ltd.—and president of Babcock and Wilcox, Ltd.; Gerald Lawrence, the actor; and Professor E. Bullough, chiefly known as the son-in-law of the famous actress Eleanora Duse.

Less well known—sometimes unknown—to the public, but outstanding as cryptanalysts, were Ronald Knox's older brother, Dilwyn, who is credited with having solved the three-letter German naval flag code in his bath, and who found cryptanalysis so to his taste that he made a career out of it in the War Office; Dr. John D. Beazley, then a tutor at Oxford and later professor of classical archaeology there, later knighted; Dr. Gilbert Waterhouse, professor of German at the University of Dublin, regarded as a "first-class performer"; Dr. Leonard A. Willoughby, lecturer in German at Oxford and later a Freeman of the City of London; Professor E. C. Quiggin, who enjoyed considerable success with the Austrian messages; and Dr. Douglas Savory, professor of the French language and Romance philology at the University of Belfast, later knighted, who, after Quiggin died, took over the Austrian traffic and produced some important solutions.

Not all in the Room 40 galaxy were cryptanalysts; in fact, in the entire personnel, there were only about 50 of this exalted breed. The others were support troops or worked on the other aspects of radio intelligence. Tiarks and Lawrence, for example, unraveled the directional bearings; the call-sign section, where Toye worked, was directed by W. F. Clarke, son of the attorney who had defended Oscar Wilde. Edward Molyneux, later a famous dress designer, came to work in Room 40 answering a telephone and sorting incoming messages as one of several wounded officers sent over by the War Office. The place was loaded with peers and social types and seemed to be sort of an Eton Alumni Club: McCarthy, Lord Monkbretton, Young, Knox, and others all had attended. The very typists had to be daughters or sisters of naval officers with a knowledge of at least two foreign languages! Their chief was Lady Hambro, who smoked cigars.

The most important personnel change came with the retirement of Ewing and his replacement as immediate overseer of Room 40 by the director of naval intelligence. On May 6, 1916, Ewing had been offered the principalship of the University of Edinburgh. It was an attractive offer, especially to one who had spent the 25 years before becoming director of naval education in 1903 as a professor of engineering or of applied mechanics. In addition,

Ewing was by this time taking little part in actual cryptanalysis, for as his staff had grown, it had come to include persons whose talent for the work far exceeded his own. They would leap or fly to conclusions with an agility incomprehensible, he said, to his own pedestrian wits. He was mainly administrator of the department. He discussed the Edinburgh offer several weeks later with his chief, the new First Lord, Arthur Balfour, who also happened to be chancellor of the University. Balfour told him that he had organized Room 40 so well that he could safely delegate its supervision. Accordingly, Ewing accepted the offer as of October 1, 1916, the date on which he ceased to be director of naval education, a post he had held—not without a certain amusement—during his captaincy of Room 40. He continued to make weekly visits to Whitehall in an advisory capacity, but by the following year the claims of Edinburgh were becoming too insistent for double duty, and on May 31, 1917, he said goodbye to his Admiralty friends once and for all.

The reins of Room 40 had by then been long since in the firm grasp of a most remarkable man, a man who made an unforgettable impression on all those who met him and whose positive brilliance in espionage ably served his country just when it needed it most. He was Captain William Reginald Hall, R.N., director of naval intelligence. He had almost literally been born for intelligence work: his father had been the first director of the Admiralty's intelligence division. Hall had joined the Navy at 14, had been promoted to captain at 35, and, after commanding a cruiser and a battle cruiser, had been appointed to the intelligence directorship in November, 1914. A dapper, alert man with a perfectly domed, prematurely bald head and a large hooked nose, Hall, then in his middle forties, looked like a demonic Mr. Punch in uniform.

But his eyes, with their penetrating, hypnotic quality, were his most remarkable feature. "Such eyes as the man has!" the American ambassador, Walter Hines Page, wrote to President Woodrow Wilson. "For Hall can look through you and see the very muscular movements of your immortal soul while he is talking to you." A nervous tic caused one of his eyes to twitch incessantly, giving him the nickname "Blinker." He burst with energy and confidence. "He was the most stimulating man to work for I have ever known," Toye later wrote. "When ... he spoke to you, you felt that you would do anything, anything at all, to merit his approval." Page summed him up best: "Hall is one genius that the war has developed. Neither in fiction nor in fact can you find any such man to match him. Of the wonderful things that I know he has done, there are several that it would take an exciting volume to tell. The man is a genius—a clear case of genius. All other secret-service men are amateurs by comparison." Hall and Page were soon to swirl together through a grave international gavotte of intrigue and propaganda that was to have the most crucial effects on the war. But neither of them guessed any of that when Hall took over officially from Ewing in the fall of 1916.

Despite its efficiency, England's Room 40 held no monopoly on naval or diplomatic cryptanalysis during the war. In the cryptanalytic section of the French War Ministry, Lieutenant Paul Louis Bassières and the reserve interpreter Paul-Brutus Déjardin reconstructed a German U-boat code as the first triumph of their diplomatic-naval branch. Captain Georges Painvin solved the four-letter German naval code, superencipherment and all, and Commandant Marcel Givierge the three-letter flag code.

Later in the war, the French discovered that each midnight the Nauen station broadcast to U-boats in the Mediterranean the sailing times and itineraries of French ships departing Marseilles—information that had evidently been sent to the Germans by waterfront spies. French radio posts intercepted the coded messages and telegraphed them to the cryptanalytic bureau. Depending on the accuracy of the transmission, the French cryptanalysts took between 30 minutes and an hour to crack the messages. A messenger took the solutions to the Ministry of Marine by bicycle, and by 3 or 4 a.m. the harbormaster at Marseilles had been notified in time for him to alter schedules and foil the waiting submarines. Ships that had already sailed were radioed to change course. In one case, the transport *Alger* could not be contacted at sea because of an electrical storm. It was torpedoed and sunk with a loss of 500 soldiers and considerable matériel. The spies were later captured.

The French sent many of their naval solutions to London, but Room 40 reciprocated as minimally as possible. Hall apparently never sent the *Magdeburg* nor any other in-force naval codebooks to the French. His motives were understandable. England depended for her very existence on control of the seas, and every additional person who knew of the German solutions added to the danger of loss of this supremely valuable intelligence and, consequently, of the nation's maritime mastery. But, in the opinion of Colonel François Cartier, head of the French cryptologic service, Hall exceeded all decent bounds in his jealous hoarding of his cryptanalytic secrets.

Once when Cartier was visiting Hall, he told the director of naval intelligence that his bureau was cryptanalyzing the German naval codes but had only progressed to partial solutions. Hall suggested that Cartier leave the naval traffic to the British, who had an actual copy of the German code, could read the German messages with ease, and would apprise the French of anything of importance to them. Cartier replied by telling Hall how one of the fragmentary French decryptions had enabled them to save one of their auxiliary cruisers from possible torpedoing; the English must have known of the danger from the same intercept, but they had not warned the French. The intelligence chief explained that it was better to lose the ship than to take precautionary measures that risked disclosing the cryptanalysis to the Germans. "Would you feel the same way if the cruiser had been English?" Cartier asked coldly. Hall dodged that one, and a change of code ended the negotiations.

Mutual need sometimes overrode these differences, however, and cryptanalytic collaboration continued among the Allies. England, for example, read the Berlin–Madrid diplomatic messages in both the Spanish and the German codes and offered them to the French; France managed to solve a superencipherment in this traffic the very day that it was put into service, and then sent the solution to Hall. It was in this code that the German naval attaché in Madrid radioed to Germany several times to ask for funds and instructions for agent H-21. The agent, a beautiful dancer better known by her stage name of Mata Hari, was ordered to Paris. But the French had read the messages, which were the first concrete evidence that they had been able to collect that Mata Hari was a German spy. They picked her up, and though she fiercely contended that the money was a payment from her lovers, the messages convicted her. A few months later, courageously refusing a blindfold, she was executed by a twelve-man firing squad.

The French also solved an Austro-Hungarian code, which they later got from Hall, and a naval code of the same country, which was superenciphered in a way that gave rise to such peculiar codewords as PLESDEPOTS, CODYFIGARO, and OGNISEXUAL. The French discovered in May of 1916 that the first four digits of the ten underlying codenumbers were enciphered in two groups of two and the last six digits in two groups of three. The solution proved of great value to the Italians. The Austrians apparently later changed this code, for in the autumn of 1917, Hall learned that the Italians were having little success in obtaining information about the movements of the Austro-Hungarian fleet, despite its extensive use of wireless. He dispatched three of Room 40's staff as a "special secret information service" to study the Austro-Hungarian signals, and the British ambassador to Italy later wrote the foreign secretary that this service "has been of great value to us to obtain rapid and sure information of what was going on on the other side of the Adriatic, and I do not think either we or the Italians would have had much if it had not been for the system which he [Hall] devised and induced the Italians to work."

Just as the reading of secret naval and diplomatic messages was not restricted among the Allies to Room 40, so it was not restricted among the belligerents to the Allies. The Germans had finally set up a cryptanalytic section, with an intercept and transmission post at Neumünster. They succeeded in penetrating the British naval codes (whether by capture or by cryptanalysis is unknown), and during Jutland they read Jellicoe's order massing his destroyers to his rear to shield from a torpedo attack. Neumünster passed this order to Scheer. This, together with other information, confirmed his position well astern of the British battle fleet. He therefore thought it was safe enough for him to cross his enemy's wake—and he did, running safely for home without encountering the superior British dreadnoughts.

Room 40 intercepted and read this message. Whether it specifically motivated them to change or improve their naval systems is unknown, but it is certain that they ended the war with unquestionably the era's finest code.

This is Cypher SA, apparently invented by one J. C. F. Davidson, who received £300 for it. It went into force at noon August 1, 1918, replacing Cypher W.

Despite its name, it was a two-part code, bound in two volumes in the standard lead covers so it would sink when jettisoned in time of danger. The encoding section ran 341 pages and gave five-digit codenumbers for everything from *A* to *Zwyndrecht*, with up to 15 homophones for many plaintext expressions. *Ship*, for example, had that many, but the effective number was even larger because of the 35 phrases containing the word *ship*, as *ship will be*, which itself had three homophones, plus the separate entries for *ships*, *shipping*, *shipped*, and so on. The code included two pages of nulls, tables of digraphs and single letters for spelling words not in the vocabulary, separate sections for numbers, dates, message references, senior officers' names, British navy warships, and names of foreign men-of-war, as well as indicators to shift to a separate "code index" with names of important merchantmen and steamship companies. The 536-page decoding section ran from 00100 (for *Vathy*) to 53698 (for *Nought one four five*), but many numbers were skipped in the codegroup series; at one point, for example, it ran 07401, 07403, 07404, 07406. The instructions called for the use of at least 25 per cent nulls in every message—which had to start with one.

The code's major feature, however, was its extensive use of the polyphone, a codegroup that has multiple meanings. Obviously, if codegroup 07640 can mean either *eight*, or *fifth April*, or *then North-ward*, the task of the cryptanalyst becomes substantially more difficult. This situation prevailed in Cypher SA with a large percentage of the groups. How, then, could the legitimate decoder keep the meanings separate, so that he would not inadvertently select *eight* when *fifth April* is meant? The code distinguished between the three meanings by tagging the three polyphones with an A, a B, or a C both fore and aft of the codenumber. In encoding, the code clerk had to pick the codegroup that had the same letter in front of it as the codegroup preceding had behind it. In other words, a group ending with a B must be followed by one beginning with a B. The code was so constructed that wherever the clerk had to make this selection, a choice of codegroups was provided. All the polyphones, in other words, were homophones (but not vice versa). The code clerk dropped the letters before transmitting the cryptogram. The decoder could pick up the thread with the first group, a null, because all the nulls and many plaintext groups were prefixed with a dash. This meant that they did not have to follow any particular letter, and so could serve as the free end of a chain. The letter at their tail, however, forged the first link in this chain, which the decoder tracked through his codebook.

Polyphones are a powerful weapon for confusing a cryptanalyst, for a codegroup may not always be what it seems. This is not to say that Cypher SA was unbreakable; but it undoubtedly would have demanded considerably more time, more traffic, and more corollary information than others. The connoisseur may also revel in its exquisite ingenuity.

Hall's supersession of Ewing roughly coincided with the end of the great sea battles. This was largely due to Room 40. "Without the cryptographers' department there would have been no Battle of Jutland," Churchill wrote, and Jutland bottled up the German fleet so effectively that it never ventured forth again. The closing of this phase of the war reduced the need for tactical intelligence, and Hall, as aggressive as any man, shifted the emphasis to the strategic. He gained access to the larger and more exciting arena of international affairs through Room 40's diplomatic decryptments. This was usurpation of power, for his province was nominally just naval intelligence, and indeed, while the Foreign Office appreciated his information, it grudged him his powers. But it was helpless to stop him, for his control of Room 40 made him absolute master of the vital information it produced, from disclosures of the far-flung subversions and conspiracies and aggrandizements of

Shershel 268

```
- 51648 C...Shershel           A 10569 B ⎫
- 07510 B...Shetland Islands   B 53472 C ⎬ Ship is
- 18855 B....Shetland Mainland C 03917 A ⎭
- 43026 C...Shetlands
- 53038 A...Shiant Islands    - 35613 A....Ship is not
- 04216 C...Shield—for        - 50968 C....Ship is not to
- 35998 C...Shielday          - 06679 A....Ship is not to be
- 43144 B...Shielded          - 18641 C....Ship is now—at
- 35732 B....Shielded by      - 42583 C....Ship is to
- 10726 B....Shielded from    - 10247 A....Ship is to be
- 53124 C...Shielding         - 53180 C....Ship must
- 06656 B...Shields—for—of    - 07006 A....Ship must be
- 17848 B....Shields, North
- 41802 A....Shields, South    A 51738 B ⎫
- 28814 C...Shift-s            B 41759 C ⎬ Ship of
                               C 10994 C ⎭
```

A page of the encoding section of Admiralty Cypher SA, *showing homophones*

the Central Powers to the coded squeakings of a minor spy. Though Hall did pass this information to other governmental departments (usually in a form that concealed the source), he also stuck his fingers into more than one political pie. Fortunately for Britain, he nearly always came out with plums.

He was doing this even before Ewing left. There was, for example, the German plan for a revolt in Persia, bared by Room 40's cryptanalysis of the plotters' messages. In another case, Trebitsch Lincoln, an embittered former member of Parliament, sent military information to the German consul in neutral Rotterdam in one dictionary code and two jargon codes that were solved by Room 40. In one of the jargon systems, family names meant ships or ports; in the other, various petroleum products stood for them. A message that read CABLE PRICES FIVE CONSIGNMENTS VASELINE, EIGHT PARAFFIN really meant [At] Dover [are] *five first-class cruisers, eight sea-going destroyers.* Lincoln, unfortunately, evaded the British authorities and escaped to New York.

Room 40 also read coded messages involving Sir Roger Casement, the former British consul who, after failing to recruit an anti-English battalion among Irish prisoners-of-war in Germany, sought to raise rebellion in Ireland. Several of these cryptograms were passed between Berlin and German diplomatic posts in the United States. One urged German military support of the rebellion by "troops, arms, and ammunition"; another dealt with the transmission of $500 to Casement by John Devoy, an Irish agitator in America who had arranged for Germany's delivery of 20,000 rifles and ten machine guns for the uprising. Another message read by Room 40 reported to Devoy that Casement's sailing on a submarine was imminent and arranged that the

77

077

```
- 07700 B...Spontaneous-ly        - 07750 A...Dummy group
- 07701 B...Sow-s-ing             - 07751 A...Recurrences—of
- 07703 B...Rodd                  - 07752 B...Report when she
- 07704 C...Vacate-s              - 07754 A...Rush-es-ing
- 07705 B...To what               - 07755 C...Purpose of
- 07707 A...What time—is—are     - 07756 C...Withdrawn from
A 07708 C...Hornet, H.M.S.        - 07758 B...Sheep
B 07708 A...Referring             A 07759 C...12th April
C 07708 B...Wednesday             B 07759 A...Was no-t
- 07709 A...Send-s mails for      C 07759 B...In convoy
- 07710 C...Worth                 - 07760 C...She could
- 07712 B...Riddled by (with)     - 07761 A...That every
A 07713 A...Smoke-s—from—of       - 07763 A...Sulen Isles
B 07713 B...Will be               A 07764 C...Begins
C 07713 C...13th April            B 07764 B...Spell word of 13 letters
- 07714 A...Tsu Sima              C 07764 A...Acknowledge
```

A page of the decoding section of Cypher SA, *showing polyphones*

codeword OATS would be cabled if the U-boat left with Casement aboard as scheduled and the codeword HAY if there was a hitch. On April 12, 1916, among the day's usual batch of intercepts appeared one containing the word OATS. Ten days later, Casement landed near Tralee Bay—and was promptly arrested by waiting authorities. He remained cool, giving a false name and saying he was a writer, but on the way to Adfert Barracks he tried to discard a piece of paper on which was written a small code of phrases he might need, such as *send more explosives.* The police saw it and confiscated it for evidence. He was tried and convicted of high treason. Hall deflated the strong public pressure for a reprieve by surreptitiously circulating through London clubs and the House of Commons specimen pages of Casement's homosexually-inclined "Black Diaries." Casement was hanged on August 3.

Not all Hall's activities were so nefarious. Spy scares were rampant, so much so that when a bird flew up from near where a foreign-looking individual stood, a hysterical bystander called police, convinced that the "alien" was sending messages to the enemy by homing pigeon. One day a self-described "code expert" from the London financial district came to tell Hall that he had solved secret messages relating to the movement of troops that had been concealed as personal advertisements in newspapers. The head of naval intelligence listened attentively and invited him to return when he had further proofs. Then Hall, who was not without a sense of humor, composed a suspicious-sounding message and inserted it in the personal column of *The Times*. Next day the expert arrived, highly agitated, with a "solution" that disclosed that certain battleships were about to sail from the naval ports of Chatham, Portsmouth, and Plymouth. His reaction when Hall told him what had happened is, regrettably, not recorded.

At about half-past ten on the morning of January 17, 1917, the Reverend William Montgomery, a thin, gray-haired scholar of the early church fathers who was serving as a cryptanalyst in the diplomatic section of Room 40, came to tell Hall of what looked like an important message. Montgomery's instincts were right. The cryptogram that he and a youthful colleague, Nigel de Grey, had partially read was to become the single most far-reaching and most important solution in history.

The message was a long one, consisting of about a thousand numerical codegroups. Dated at Berlin January 16, it was addressed to the German ambassador in the United States, Count Johann Heinrich Andreas von Bernstorff, and the two cryptanalysts recognized that it was encoded in a German diplomatic code known as 0075, upon which they had been working for six months. Room 40 knew from its analyses that 0075 was one of a series of two-part codes that the German Foreign Office designated by two zeros and two digits, the two digits always showing an arithmetical difference of 2. Among the others, some of which Room 40 had solved, were 0097, 0086, which was used for German missions in South America, 0064, used between Berlin and Madrid and perhaps elsewhere, 0053, and 0042. Code 0075 was a new code that the German Foreign Office had first distributed in July of 1916 to German missions in Vienna, Sofia, Constantinople, Bucharest, Copenhagen, Stockholm, Bern, Lugano, The Hague, and Oslo. Somehow the British obtained copies of enough of the telegrams in this code to enable Montgomery and de Grey, whose assignment it probably was, to make a start in breaking it. In November, Room 40 began intercepting messages to the German embassy in the United States in the same code, and if Hall guessed that the code and the keys to the superencipherment that it sometimes used had been sent across the Atlantic on the second voyage of the cargo U-boat *Deutschland*, which docked at New London on November 1, 1916, he would have been right.

Montgomery and de Grey could read only parts of the long message. But they could see that it was a double-decker, consisting of Berlin's messages Nos. 157 and 158 to Bernstorff. They could read the signature of the German Foreign Minister, Arthur Zimmermann. As far as they could extricate its sense on the basis of their partial solution of 0075, the second message read:

Most secret for your Excellency's personal information and to be handed on to the Imperial Minister in (? Mexico) with Telegram No. 1 (...) by a safe route.

We propose to begin on the 1st February unrestricted submarine warfare. In doing so, however, we shall endeavor to keep America neutral. (?) If we should not (succeed in doing so) we propose to (? Mexico) an alliance upon the following basis:

[joint] conduct of the war.

[joint] conclusion of peace.

(...)

Your Excellency should for the present inform the President [of Mexico] secretly (? that we expect) war with the U.S.A. (possibly) (...) (Japan) and at the same time to negotiate between us and Japan. (Please tell the President) that (...) or submarines (...) will compel England to peace in a few months. Acknowledge receipt.

Zimmermann.

Montgomery handed this fragmentary solution to Hall, who stared down at the phrases that seemed to jump off the page at him: "unrestricted submarine warfare," "war with the U.S.A.," "propose ... an alliance." He realized at once that here was a weapon of enormous potentiality. He urged Montgomery to hurry the solution, ordered all copies except the original message and a single solution burned, and, without a word to the Foreign Office, sat down by himself to contemplate the situation.

It was as bleak as that winter's day. The war that everyone had expected would last only a few weeks had now dragged into its third year. Nor was there any prospect of an end. France had expended half a million lives at Verdun and only succeeded in restoring the battle line to where it was ten months before. England, which had lost 60,000 men at the Somme in a single day, struggled to gain a few yards of shell-blasted earth, then fell back exhausted. The Hindenburg line remained unbreached. Rumania, a new ally, had been quickly overrun, and Russia, the colossus of the east, was virtually defeated. The stepped-up U-boat campaign increased the economic pressure on the Allies. Worst of all, despite the provocation of the *Lusitania* sinking and despite the tug of ancient common ties, the United States, guided by a President who had just won reelection on the slogan "He kept us out of war," remained obstinately neutral.

Things were no better in Germany. Her initial offensive had stalled at the Marne and her gray-coated troops had been locked in the futile trench slaughter ever since. Civilians were living on potatoes—a result of the stranglehold of the British blockade. Fifteen-year-olds were being conscripted. Greece and Portugal had recently entered the war against her. Like the Allies, she could see no immediate hope for victory.

Except one.

Unleash the submarines, the generals cried, and England would soon be "gasping in the reeds like a fish." The blockaders would become the blockaded. For months the generals had hammered away on this theme, and, as the signs of exhaustion multiplied, they finally prevailed. Foreign Minister Zimmermann, who had long opposed the idea, fell in line. But this big jolly bachelor, the first to break the Junker barrier in the higher regions of the Kaiser's officialdom, perceived that the repeated sinkings of American vessels would sooner or later torpedo American neutrality, and he bethought himself of a scheme to counter this danger. He proposed a military alliance with Mexico, then particularly hostile to the imperialistic Norteamericanos as a result of Pershing's punitive expedition into Mexican territory. He sweetened the proposition with an offer of money and the possibility of support from Japan, standing at America's back, and with still more anti-Yankee inducements.

Unable to deal through the Mexican ambassador, who was in Switzerland, Zimmermann sent his proposal to his minister in Mexico, Heinrich J. F. von Eckardt, by way of Washington. To ensure that it would get there, he routed it two ways, both monitored by Britain. The cruise of *Telconia* was paying off.

One way was called the "Swedish Roundabout" by the British. Sweden, which was neutral in favor of Germany, had since early in the war helped the German Foreign Office get messages past the British cable blockade by sending them as her own. British censorship detected this practice. When Sweden complained in the summer of 1915 that Britain was delaying her messages, Britain informed her that it had positive knowledge of the unneutral practice. The Swedish government admitted this and promised that it would no longer send any German messages to Washington. It did not. Instead, it sent them to Buenos Aires. Here they were transferred from Swedish to German hands and then forwarded to Washington. This was a circuitous route of about 7,000 miles, half of them in flat violation of the prerogatives of a nonbelligerent.

But the cable from Stockholm to South America touched at England. Germany feared that British censorship might recognize the German codegroups in the Swedish messages and would stop the dispatches. So the German Foreign Office disguised the codegroups by enciphering them. This was done with Code 13040 in messages to Latin America and to Washington. Unfortunately for the Germans, the superencipherment did not obliterate all traces of the underlying code, which employed a distinctive mixture of 3-, 4-, and 5-digit codegroups. These traces aroused the suspicions of the ever-alert Room 40; it resolved the superencipherment, and Code 13040 reappeared. Room 40 then looked closely at other official Swedish messages. Many of them proved to be German as well; concealed under one superencipherment, for example, they found Code 0075. But this time England entered no protest. Hall perceived that it was more advantageous to listen to what the Germans were saying than to stop them from talking.

The second route that Zimmermann used was of such simplicity, perfidy, and barefaced gall that it probably remains unequaled in the annals of diplomacy. It had its inception in the pompous mind of Colonel Edward M. House, President Wilson's alter ego and a major exponent of personal diplomacy. On one of his missions to Europe in 1915, House arranged to have coded reports from the embassies cabled directly to him, bypassing the State Department. When, on December 27, 1916, Ambassador Bernstorff discussed a new peace attempt by Wilson with House, he pointed out that the chances would be improved if his government could communicate directly with Wilson through House. House checked with the President. The next day Wilson permitted the German government to send messages in its own code between Washington and Berlin under American diplomatic auspices—an arrangement that was, at best, simpleminded, and that, furthermore, contravened the accepted international practice of requiring the messages to be submitted in clear for transmission in American code.

Germany availed herself of this arrangement to make America seal her own doom by letters she herself bore. Under the aegis of American sovereignty, Zimmermann sent his message striking at that sovereignty. It was delivered to the American embassy in Berlin at 3 p.m. January 16. It could not go direct to Washington, but had to be sent first to Copenhagen—and then to London. Only from there could it go to Washington. Consequently Britain seized this copy as well. Room 40 was "highly entertained" at the sight of the German code in an American cable, but again did not protest.

With two copies of the same text helping to eliminate garbles, Montgomery and de Grey rammed into the cryptogram. De Grey, though at 30 the younger of the two, had been in Room 40 the longer. Slightly built, rather handsome, with dark hair and brown eyes and chiseled, movie-star features, an Eton graduate, he was descended from the peerage as the grandson of the fifth Baron Walsingham (no relation to Sir Francis Walsingham). He had worked for the prestigious publishing house of William Heinemann for seven years before the war, when he joined the Royal Naval Air Service. He came to Room 40 in 1915.

Soon after his work on the cryptogram that became known as the Zimmermann telegram, he left 40 O.B. to serve as head of the naval intelligence mission that Hall had sent to Rome. After the war, he became director of the Medici Society, a publishing house specializing in art prints. In 1939, his government remembered his World War I services, and he joined the cryptanalytic division of the Foreign Office, soon becoming deputy director. A man who listed as his recreations the odd threesome of shooting, gardening, and acting, he also enjoyed carpentry and was useful around the house. He died May 25, 1951, leaving two sons and a daughter.

Montgomery was 45 at the time of his work on the Zimmermann telegram. A Liverpool shipowner's son who studied in private schools or under tutors in England, France, and Germany, he took a bachelor of divinity degree at Presbyterian College, London. But his health prevented an active pastorate and he became a member of St. John's College at Cambridge University. He specialized in early church history, editing the *Confessions* of St. Augustine for the Cambridge Patristic Series and writing a study on the life and thought of the African father. His most memorable work, however, was as a translator. It was said of his translation of Albert Schweitzer's *The Quest of the Historical Jesus* in 1910 that "no German work has ever been rendered into English so idiomatically and yet so faithfully." A modest, reticent man, Montgomery entered the censor's office in 1916, and later that year transferred to Room 40. Cryptanalysis so suited his aptitudes that after the war he continued the work in the Foreign Office, remaining there until his sudden death in October, 1930.

While in Room 40 his familiarity with Scripture unriddled a problem that had baffled most of the other staffers. A Sir Henry Jones had received a blank postcard from Turkey addressed to him at 184 King's Road, Tighnabruaich, Scotland. Sir Henry knew that the card was from his son, who had been captured by the Turks, but Tighnabruaich is a small village, with no King's Road and so few houses that no number would have been needed in any case. The card found its way to Room 40, where nobody seemed able to ascertain what Sir Henry's son was trying to tell him. Finally Montgomery suggested a reference to chapter 18, verse 4, of one of the books of Kings. Second Kings shed no light, but First Kings revealed that "Obadiah took a hundred prophets, and hid them fifty in a cave, and fed them with bread and water." Montgomery interpreted this to mean that Sir Henry's son was safe with other prisoners but in need of food—and this proved to be the case.

But the solution of the Zimmermann telegram required more than a flash of inspiration. It demanded the reconstruction of Code 0075, a two-part code of 10,000 words and phrases numbered from 0000 to 9999 in mixed order. Since a code is, in a sense, a gigantic monalphabetic substitution, the establishment of plaintext equivalents is the "only" task involved. But where the cryptanalyst of cipher deals with only 26 such elements, the cryptanalyst of code must keep his eye on hundreds or thousands, whose characteristics, moreover, because of their reduced frequency, are much scantier and more diffuse than the sharply defined traits of letters.

Solution usually begins with the identification of the groups meaning *stop*. Groups that recur near the end of telegrams are likely candidates. The identification of *stop* or *period* is often aided because often only a few of the many code equivalents are employed. Code clerks, referring frequently to *stop*, come to memorize one or two of its codegroups; they then simply use these groups in encoding instead of hunting up a different one in the codebook. Indeed, cryptanalysts familiar with a given embassy's messages can often tell when a new code clerk has been hired by the sudden efflorescence of new equivalents for *stop*!

The identification of the stops outlines the structure of the message. In English messages, nouns, as the subjects of sentences, will often appear directly after stops. In German, where the predicate often comes at the end of the sentence, the codegroup immediately preceding a stop may be a verb. Other clues come from the stereotyped expressions that diplomats so love in their dispatches: "I have the honor to report to Your Excellency. . . ." Collateral information is of very great value.

The first tentative identifications are usually written in pencil for easy erasing, and such are called "pencil groups." Eventually, further traffic confirms them and they become "ink groups." Solution proceeds much more rapidly if a code is one-part. If codegroup 1234 represents a word beginning with *d*, then 5678 must represent one farther back in the alphabet; this both rules out some guesses and suggests others. Sometimes the meaning of a codegroup can be indicated rather precisely by its location between two ink groups. This is not possible with a two-part code, where the code and plain equivalents are matched in an absolutely arbitrary fashion. Code 0075 was of this type. It required more traffic for its solution than a one-part code, and the identifications came more slowly and with greater difficulty. It had been in service on the Continent for only half a year—not a very long time for a diplomatic code—and portions of many messages remained unreadable.

As more traffic came in (including now the messages to and from Bernstorff), Montgomery and de Grey, working night and day, filled in more and more groups, ever more rapidly. On January 28, de Grey brought Hall part of Bernstorff's protest against Zimmermann's plan of unrestricted submarine warfare, which, to the ambassador's dismay, had been announced to him in message No. 157, the first part of the double-decker. Bernstorff argued vigorously against this plan, for he felt that it negated all his efforts to bring about a détente between the two countries and that it would drive the United States into the war on the side of the Allies.

And in fact, on February 3 Wilson announced to Congress that he was breaking diplomatic relations with Germany, as he had said he would the previous April if Germany continued its course of submarine warfare. Though he added that "only actual overt acts" on Germany's part would make him believe that she really would sink neutral vessels on the high seas, it must have seemed to the war-weary Allies that now, at last, within a few days or a fortnight at most, the United States would enter the war. Day by day, they awaited the final inevitable step.

While waiting, Room 40 continued its work on Code 0075. De Grey had taken to Hall Bernstorff's message giving details of his interview with Wilson severing relations. Recovered codegroups were substituted into the Zimmermann telegram, and on February 5 Hall was able to show a more fully solved version of it to Lord Hardinge at the Foreign Office.

Hall had realized from the first day that Montgomery had brought him the first sketchy solution of the Zimmermann telegram that he had in it a propaganda weapon of titanic proportions. Exposure of this German plot directed against the United States would, in the present circumstances, almost certainly compel that nation to declare war on Germany. This was an immensely strong argument for showing it to the Americans. But for the moment, at least, even stronger considerations militated against it. First, Room

40 and its cryptanalytic capabilities was one of Britain's darkest secrets. How could she disclose the message without Germany's guessing that her codes were being read? Britain might minimize the risk by hinting that the plaintext had been stolen, but the danger would still remain that Germany would suspect the truth, change her codes, and deprive Britain of her most valuable intelligence. In the second place, to reveal the message, Britain would have to admit that it had been supervising the code telegrams of a neutral: Sweden. It would not require much wit for the Americans to surmise that England might also be supervising the code telegrams of another neutral: the United States, which, like Sweden, was working as a messenger boy for the Germans and had, in fact, transmitted this very message. This realization would both embarrass and anger the United States and would not conduce to pro-Allied feelings. In the third place, the solution was still not complete. The missing portions would inevitably raise doubts about the validity of the solution and so weaken its impact. Perhaps the British had failed to solve a word like "not" that would completely alter the sense, the arguments would run. Perhaps the British had not even correctly solved the portion that they were offering as evidence of German duplicity. Moreover, the gaps would shout "codebreaking," preventing any subterfuges about captured codes or a stolen message and exposing the very secret Britain sought to conceal.

But the most powerful argument against disclosure of the German plot, with all the attendant difficulties, was that events might make it unnecessary. Relations had been severed between Germany and the United States. American public opinion seemed to be turning increasingly against Germany. Shipping dared not sail; ports were congested; men were laid off; business languished. Bitterness was growing. It seemed only a matter of a short while until the declaration of war. And so the British continued to wait, and to hope.

Hall, however, while waiting for events to dictate, did not remain idle. His job was only half done if he merely solved the Zimmermann telegram without making it ready for use by his government. Consequently, he conceived a plan that at one stroke might resolve the three difficulties connected with the telegram's exposure, in what still appeared the unlikely event that that might be necessary. He reasoned that the telegram as received in Mexico would differ in small but significant details from the telegram as sent from Berlin. The date would almost certainly be different, and probably the serial number as well. The preamble addressed to Bernstorff ordering him to forward the message would of course be omitted. If Hall could produce the copy from Mexico, perhaps the Germans would spot these slight variations and infer that the plaintext had been betrayed on the American continent and would not change their codes. Other collateral details might confirm a tale of a Mexican theft to the Americans. Moreover, Room 40 perhaps knew, from its numerous solutions of German messages via the Swedish roundabout, that the German mission in Mexico had not used Code 0075 and probably did not hold it. Bernstorff might then have had to re-encode the Zimmermann telegram in another code, which Room 40 might have solved more completely than 0075 and which might therefore enable it to fill in the missing portions in its solution.

On February 5, therefore, Hall began trying to get a copy of the Zimmermann telegram as received in Mexico. An English agent known only as T obtained from the Mexico City telegraph office a copy of the message that Bernstorff had sent to Eckardt by Western Union. Soon Hall had it.

It proved him right in every one of his assumptions. Eckardt did not have Code 0075, and so Bernstorff had had to recode the dispatch in one that Eckardt did have. This was Code 13040, which was an older and simpler code than 0075 and whose superencipherment had led to the discovery of the Swedish roundabout. It had been distributed to German missions in Central and South America between 1907 and 1909 and to Washington, New York, Havana, Port-au-Prince, and La Paz in 1912. Its basic repertory contained about 25,000 plaintext elements with a fair number of homophones—Bernstorff's telegram alone employed six different groups for *zu*—and proper names took up a huge section of 75,000 codenumbers. But Code 13040 was a cross between one-part and two-part codes. In the encoding section, blocks of several hundred codenumbers in numerical order stood opposite the alphabetized plaintext elements, but the blocks themselves were in mixed order. A skeleton code, made up from a few groups from Bernstorff's encoding, will illustrate this:

encoding		*decoding*	
13605	Februar	5144	wenigen
13732	fest	5161	werden
13850	finanzielle	5275	Anregung
13918	folgender	5376	Anwendung
17142	Frieden	5454	ar
17149	Friedenschluss	5569	auf
17166	führung	5905	Krieg
17214	Ganz geheim		
17388	Gebeit		
4377	geheim		
4458	Gemeinsame		

The solution of such a hybrid code stands midway in difficulty between the two pure types: harder than a one-part code but easier than a two-part. The large orderly segments considerably help the cryptanalyst, though his guesses are not as delimited as in a one-part code. For example, the cryptanalyst could not assume, as he could in a one-part solution, that a codegroup for *Krieg* will be higher in number than the codegroup for *Februar*. But if he knows that *Februar* is 13605 and *finanzielle* is 13850, he will know that the codegroup for *fest* must almost certainly fall somewhere between the two. His identifications thus come with greater speed and certainty.

Owing to this weakness, and to the fact that they had had all of the war to work on a great volume of messages, the codebreakers of Room 40 had recovered most of Code 13040's commonly used groups. They could conse-

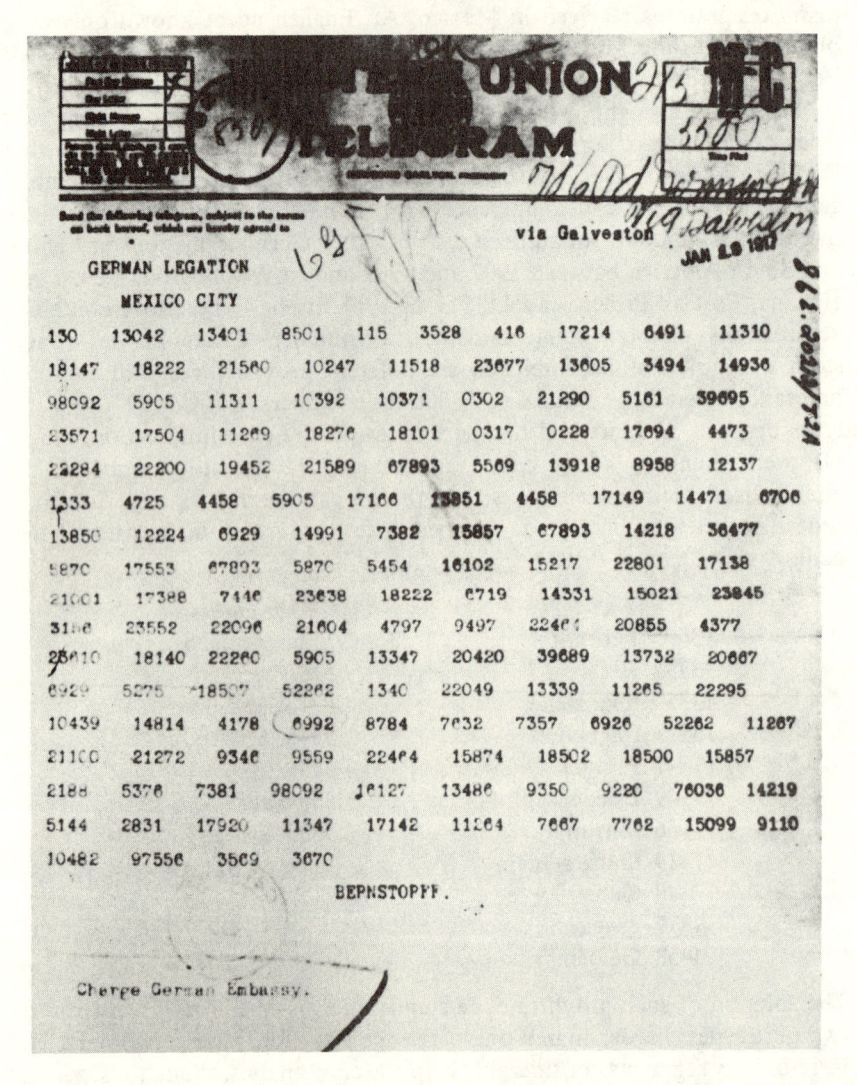

```
                                          via Galveston
GERMAN LEGATION
    MEXICO CITY

130     13042   13401    8501    115    3528     416   17214    6491   11310
18147   18222   21560   10247   11518   23677   13605   3494   14936
98092    5905   11311   10392   10371    0302   21290   5161   39695
23571   17504   11269   18276   18101    0317    0228   17694   4473
22284   22200   19452   21589   67893    5569   13918   8958   12137
 1333    4725    4458    5905   17166   13851    4458   17149   14471   6706
13850   12224    6929   14991    7382   15857   67893   14218   36477
 5870   17553   67893    5870    5454   16102   15217   22801   17138
21001   17388    7446   23638   18222    6719   14331   15021   23845
 3156   23552   22096   21604    4797    9497   22464   20855    4377
 23010  18140   22260    5905   13347   20420   39689   13732   20667
  6929   5275   18507   22262    1340   22049   13339   11265   22295
10439   14814    4178    6992    8784    7632    7357    6926   52262   11267
21100   21272    9346    9559   22464   15874   18502   18500   15857
 2188    5376    7381   98092   16127   13486    9350    9220   76036   14219
 5144    2831   17920   11347   17142   11264    7667    7762   15099    9110
10482    9755    3569    3670

                              BERNSTORFF.
```

Charge German Embassy.

The Zimmermann telegram as re-encoded in Washington into Code 13040 and forwarded to Mexico

quently read all or nearly all of Bernstorff's message to Eckardt, and in those few places where a rare proper name or syllable might have been used for the first time, the partial alphabetical arrangement afforded a strong check on their guesses. This eliminated the problem of having only a partial solution. In addition, it confirmed their almost-complete solution of the original Berlin-to-Washington message and added a few new values to their reconstruction of Code 0075.

The cryptanalysts also found the slight changes in heading that Hall had foreseen. Bernstorff had deleted the Foreign Office preamble and substituted one of his own: "Foreign Office telegraphs January 16: No. 1. Most Secret. Decode yourself." He replaced the Berlin–Washington serial number with a Washington–Mexico City serial number, which was 3. And finally, his message was dated January 19, which, due to the numerous steps in the complicated transmission routes, differed from the January 16 date that the original German text bore.

Fairly early in February, it seems, Hall was ready. With a stroke bordering on genius, he had done his job. His must stand as one of the most subtly dissembling moves in the whole history of espionage. It was now possible to give the message to the Americans, should that prove necessary, with as little risk as possible to Britain's intelligence sources. But though Hall had covered his tracks fairly well, it remained possible that the Germans might guess the truth. Events might yet make it unnecessary to chance this. So Britain held the message and waited.

And waited. The days passed. On the Western Front the lifeblood of the Empire and of the French republic trickled into the earth. The armies shuddered in mortal combat. Still there came no sign that America was going to enter the war. Though it seemed that Germany's announcement of unrestricted torpedoings of American ships had made, as Bernstorff himself had warned in cables read by Room 40, "war unavoidable," the American President seemed unable to do what the British thought that honor, self-respect, and the whole course of recent actions made obligatory. Even Ambassador Page, a long-time friend of the President and a wholehearted sympathizer with the Allied cause, was irked enough to note in his diary, "The danger is that with all the authority he wants (short of a formal declaration of war) the President will again wait, wait, wait—till an American liner be torpedoed! Or till an attack is made on our coast by a German submarine!" Evidently Wilson was waiting for the "overt acts" that he had mentioned in his address to Congress. But perhaps Germany would not actually be so rash as to torpedo American ships and thereby—Britain thought—cut her own throat. More days passed. The Germans did nothing. Tension mounted. The situation was, a British diplomat in America reported, "much that of a soda-water bottle with the wires cut but the cork unexploded."

It exploded on February 22, 1917. Unable to wait any longer, the British gave the cork a push. Hall, with Foreign Office approval if not under its orders, showed the Zimmermann telegram to Edward Bell, a secretary of the American embassy who maintained liaison with the various intelligence offices of the British government. He read an astounding tale of German intrigue against his country:

> We intend to begin on the first of February unrestricted submarine warfare. We shall endeavor in spite of this to keep the United States of America neutral. In the event of this not succeeding, we make Mexico a proposal of alliance on the following basis:
>
> Make war together, make peace together, generous financial support, and an understanding on our part that Mexico is to reconquer the lost territory in Texas, New Mexico and Arizona. The settlement in detail is left to you.
>
> You will inform the President [of Mexico] of the above most secretly, as soon as the outbreak of war with the United States of America is certain and add the suggestion that he should, on his own initiative, invite Japan to immediate adherence and at the same time mediate between Japan and ourselves.
>
> Please call the President's attention to the fact that the ruthless employment of our submarines now offers the prospect of compelling England in a few months to make peace.   Zimmermann.

Bell did not believe it. The notion that anyone in his right mind would consider giving away a chunk of the continental United States was simply too preposterous. But Hall convinced him of its authenticity, and the two went over to Grosvenor Square. When Page saw the message, he realized at once that the entry into war on England's side, which he had so single-mindedly pursued and the President had so obstinately opposed, was at last delivered into his hands. Hall, Bell, Page, and Irwin Laughlin, first secretary of the embassy, spent the day trying to decide how best to instill confidence in the telegram's genuineness, to minimize incredulity, and to maximize its impact. They decided that the British government should officially present the telegram to Page, and in his room at the Foreign Office the next day Arthur Balfour, now secretary of state for foreign affairs, formally communicated it to Page in a moment that Balfour later confessed was "as dramatic a moment as I remember in all my life."

Page worked all night to draft a covering message explaining how the telegram was obtained. At 2 a.m. February 24 he cabled, "In about three hours I shall send a telegram of great importance to the President and Secretary of State," but it was not until 1 p.m. that the Zimmermann telegram, with his explanation, was transmitted. He gave the President the collection of half-truths that Hall had given him—for Hall naturally withheld the deep secret of British cryptanalytic ability, particularly since it might start the Americans wondering whether Britain was reading their code messages as well:

> Early in the war the British government obtained possession of a copy of the German cipher code used in the above message and have made it their business to obtain copies of Bernstorff's cipher telegrams to Mexico, among others, which

are sent back to London and deciphered here. This accounts for their being able to decipher this telegram from the German government to their representative in Mexico, and also for the delay from January 19th until now in their receiving the information. This system has hitherto been a jealously guarded secret and is only divulged to you now by the British government in view of the extraordinary circumstances and their friendly feeling toward the United States. They earnestly request that you will keep the source of your information and the British government's method of obtaining it profoundly secret, but they put no prohibition on the publication of Zimmermann's telegram itself.

Page's pilot telegram rattled the Morse sounders at the State Department at 9 a.m. Saturday, February 24, but the "telegram of great importance" did not arrive until 8:30 that evening. Frank L. Polk, counselor of the department and acting secretary in the absence of Secretary of State Robert L. Lansing, telephoned to ask the President to expect him and carried the four typewritten yellow sheets across the street to the White House. Wilson, Polk reported, showed "much indignation" on reading it, and wanted to make it public at once. But he agreed to Polk's suggestion to await Lansing's return from a long weekend.

On Tuesday, February 27, Lansing came back from White Sulphur Springs. Polk told him about the Zimmermann telegram and showed him an exceptionally long cable of 1,000 codegroups that he had found in the State Department files. It had come for Bernstorff in an American cablegram of January 17 from Berlin and was, Polk felt, almost certainly the coded original. (It was, in fact, the double-decker, which included the Zimmermann telegram.) At 11 that morning, Lansing, armed with this, discussed the whole situation with the President, who exclaimed "Good Lord!" several times at the outrageous German abuse of the cable privileges he had extended them. He consented to Lansing's plan to release the telegram through the press, which Lansing felt "would avoid any charge of using the document improperly and would attract more attention than issuing it openly." Accordingly, at 6 p.m. the next day, E. M. Hood of the Associated Press was called to Lansing's home, given the message and some background details, and pledged to secrecy on the greatest scoop of the war.

The story broke in eight-column streamers in the morning papers of March 1. "Profound sensation," Lansing noted. The nation gasped. In Congress, the House orated patriotically and passed by 403 to 13 a bill to arm merchant ships. But the Senate, more deliberate, wondered whether the whole thing was not just a crude Allied plot. This reaction had been foreseen. Lansing had asked Page to "Please endeavor to obtain copy of German code from Mr. Balfour," but the British had told him that the code was "never used straight, but with a great number of variations which are known to only one or two experts here. They can not be spared to go to America." This was, of course, another half-truth—the 0075 message was probably superenciphered (the "variations") but the 13040 one was not. Polk, meanwhile, exerted tremendous pressure on Newcomb Carlton, the president of Western Union, and finally managed to get a copy of Bernstorff's telegram to Eckardt despite a federal law protecting the privacy of telegrams. Lansing appended this codetext to the wire he sent Page at 8 p.m. the day of the exposé:

> Some members of Congress are attempting to discredit Zimmermann message charging that message was furnished to this government by one of the belligerents. This government has not the slightest doubt as to its authenticity but it would be of the greatest service if the British government would permit you or someone in the Embassy to personally decode the original message which we secured from the telegraph office in Washington, and then cable to Department German text. Assure Mr. Balfour that the Department hesitated to make this request but feels that this course will materially strengthen its position and make it possible for the Department to state that it had secured the Zimmermann note from our own people.

The message, No. 4494, was received the next day, and by 4 p.m. Page cabled back: "Bell took the cipher text of the German messages contained in your 4494 of yesterday to the Admiralty and there, himself, deciphered it from the German code which is in the Admiralty's possession." In fact Bell wrote only a dozen or so plaintext groups before letting de Grey do the rest in his neat handwriting. Page then sent the German text as decoded by Bell and de Grey. But Lansing and the President had already sent up to the Senate a statement that the government possessed evidence establishing the telegram as genuine, and that no further information could be disclosed.

Everyone already had his own pet theory of how the United States had gotten it. Most popular was the spy story. Most farfetched was that four American soldiers had found it on a German agent trying to cross into Mexico. Most plausible was that the telegram had been found among Bernstorff's effects when his baggage was searched at Halifax after his dismissal. Most amusing were the attacks by the British press on the inefficiency of their secret service and its inferiority to the American. (At least one of these was instigated by Hall himself to throw the theorizers off the scent.)

Wilhelmstrasse, too, wondered where the leak had occurred. Though the message as published in the papers did not carry either Bernstorff's heading or his serial number, it did bear the significant date January 19. "Please cable in same cipher," the Foreign Office purred at a quivering Eckardt, who had already tried to blame Bernstorff for the betrayal, "who deciphered cable dispatches 1 [the Zimmermann telegram] and 11 [ordering Eckardt to negotiate at once for the proposed alliance], how the originals and decodes were kept, and, in particular, whether both dispatches were kept in the same place." Six days later, it picked up the clue that Hall had carefully planted: "Various indications suggest that the treachery was committed in Mexico. The greatest caution is indicated. Burn all compromising material."

Eckardt mustered impressive details to exculpate himself: "Both dispatches were deciphered, in accordance with my special instructions, by [Dr.

Nigel de Grey transcribes the Code 13040 version of the Zimmermann telegram into plaintext for the skeptical Americans

Arthur von] Magnus [the legation's corpulent secretary]. Both, as is the case with everything of a politically secret nature, were kept from the knowledge of the chancery officials.... The originals in both cases were burned by Magnus and the ashes scattered. Both dispatches were kept in an absolutely secure steel safe, procured especially for the purpose and installed in the chancery building, in Magnus' bedroom, up to the time when they were burned." Three days later, he sent in his reserves: "Greater caution than is always exercised here would be impossible. The text of telegrams which have arrived is read to me at night in my dwelling house by Magnus, in a low voice. My servant, who does not understand German, sleeps in an annex.... Here there can be no question of carbon copies or waste paper." The shrieks of hilarity that this

"Exploding in his Hands." Cartoon by Rollin Kirby in The [New York] World *just after the Zimmermann telegram was made public*

occasioned Hall, Page, and Room 40 were not heard in Berlin. Its last doubts swept away by the low voice, the steel safe, the scattered ashes, and the non-German-speaking servant, the Foreign Office capitulated. "After your telegram it is hardly conceivable that betrayal took place in Mexico. In face of it the indications which point in that direction lose their force. No blame rests on either you or Magnus."

Meanwhile, the problem of authenticity, which had so troubled the Anglo-American officials and stirred uneasy questioning in the Senate and the press, had been eliminated by Zimmermann himself. Completely unexpectedly, he confessed: "I cannot deny it. It is true." Knowledge of the plot had been blandly disavowed by the Mexicans, the Japanese, and Eckardt, and to this day no one knows why Zimmermann admitted it. His acknowledgment buried the last doubts that the story might have been a hoax.

Suddenly, Americans in the middle of the continent who could not get excited about the distant poppings of a European war jerked awake in the realization that the war was at their border. Texans blinked in astonishment: the Germans meant to give away their state! The Midwest, unmoved because untouched by the submarine issue, imagined a German-officered army crossing the Rio Grande and swung over to the side of the Allies. The Far West blew up like a land mine at the mention of Japan. Within a month, public opinion crystallized. Wilson, who three months before had said that it would be a "crime against civilization" to lead the nation into war, decided that "the right is more precious than peace" and went up to Capitol Hill on April 2 to ask Congress to help make the world safe for democracy. He cited the Zimmermann telegram in his address:

"That it [the German government] means to stir up enemies against us at our very doors, the intercepted note to the German minister at Mexico City is eloquent evidence. We are accepting this challenge of hostile purpose. . . . I advise that the Congress declare the recent course of the Imperial German Government to be in fact nothing less than war against the government and people of the United States, that it formally accept the status of belligerent which has thus been thrust upon it."

The Congress did. Soon the Yanks were coming. The fresh strength of the young nation poured into the trenches of the Western Front to rescue the exhausted Allies. And so it came about that Room 40's solution of an enemy message helped propel the United States into the First World War, enabling the Allies to win, and into world leadership, with all that that has entailed. No other single cryptanalysis has had such enormous consequences. Never before or since has so much turned upon the solution of a secret message. For those few moments in time, the codebreakers held history in the palm of their hand.

10
A WAR OF INTERCEPTS: I

RADIO, envisioned by its inventor as a great humanitarian contribution, was seized upon by the generals soon after its birth in 1895 and impressed as an instrument of war. For it immeasurably magnified the chief military advantage of telegraphy: instantaneous and continuous control of an entire army by a single commander. By eliminating the need for physical linkage by wire, radio speeded communication between headquarters, joined through the ether units that could not connect by wire because of distance, terrain, hostile forces, or rapid movement, opened communications with naval and air forces, and eased the economic burden of producing immense quantities of wire.

But few blessings are unmixed. Just as the telegraph had made military communications much more effective but had also increased the possibility of interception over that of hand-carried dispatches, so radio's vast amplification of military communications was accompanied by an enormously greater probability of interception. The public, omnidirectional nature of radio transmissions, which makes wireless communication so easy to establish, makes it equally easy to intercept. It was no longer necessary to gain physical access to a telegraph line behind the enemy's front to eavesdrop upon his communications. A commander had only to sit in his headquarters and tune his radio to the enemy's wavelength. Radio thereupon introduced two revolutionary factors in the interception of communications: volume and continuity.

Communications are intercepted, of course, so that they may be submitted to cryptanalysis. Now cryptanalysis has a potential that cryptography does not. Cryptanalysis can alter the status quo. Cryptography can at best conserve it. Cryptanalysis can bring countries into war, engender naval battles and win them, compel besieged cities to yield, condemn queens to death and prove innocent the unjustly accused. Cryptanalysis hammers upon the real world. Cryptography does not.

Consequently, the telegraph, which affected only cryptography, had had a wholly internal influence upon cryptology. That a hierarchy of special systems had arisen to displace the nomenclator interested only cryptologists; it did not matter to generals or statesmen. And although the telegraph greatly increased the volume of communications, wiretapping could produce intercepts only at rare and irregular intervals. Cryptanalysis could exercise only transient and haphazard effects. Its potential remained largely unfulfilled. Kerckhoffs accurately regarded it as an auxiliary to cryptography, a means to the end of perfecting military codes and ciphers. Cryptanalysis during the telegraph years was interesting but inconsequential, intriguing but academic —an ideal topic to pass a Victorian tea-time, perhaps, but not much more.

The radio, however, turned over to the commander a copy of every enemy cryptogram it conveyed. It furnished a constant stream of intercepts. And with these, cryptanalysis could bear continually upon operations, could be depended upon for information, could affect events decisively. The generals and the statesmen took notice. This was no longer a polite trifling discussion; this had become a weapon, a pursuit entailing all the savagery of warfare and life against death. Radio made cryptanalysis an end in itself, elevating it to an importance coordinate with that of cryptography, if not superior to it. Radio's impact upon cryptology reverberated in the outside world.

Wire and wireless thus complemented one another. The telegraph created modern cryptography; the radio, modern cryptanalysis. The one developed cryptology internally, the other externally. The telegraph had given cryptology shape and content; now the radio carried it out into the arena of life. One gave it form; the other, meaning. The radio completed the work that the telegraph had begun. And so it was that radio, first widely used in the Great War of 1914 to 1918, brought cryptology to maturity.

On the Western Front, only France was ready. Her prewar activities, more extensive and better conceived than those of any other nation, had prepared her. Posts that had intercepted German radiograms in peace simply continued to do so in war. The cipher system approved by the Commission on Military Cryptography went into effect. The cryptologic section set up by Cartier at the War Ministry was quickly fleshed out with mobilized personnel. His assistant, Major Marcel Givierge, arrived alone at general headquarters to set up a cryptologic section—and a week later had six assistants working round the clock. For the first few days, there was little to do, but when the invading Germans crossed the frontier early in August, passing beyond the wires of their telegraph network, their messages filled the air.

The French hauled them in. At first the only intercept stations were in the great fortresses of Maubeuge, Verdun, Toul, Épinal, and Belfort and at three special posts at Lille, Rheims, and Bésançon. Later in the war France had an elaborate network, with the country divided into three zones centered on Paris, Lyons, and Bordeaux. The capital itself had one intercept station in the Eiffel Tower and another in a Métro station (Trocadéro). A line of six direction-finding stations extended behind the entire front. All these stations were connected by direct wire to the War Ministry at 14 Rue Saint-Dominique in Paris, where Colonel Cartier's office stood next to the telegraph central. The French thus received German radiograms as quickly as the legitimate recipients. During the course of the war, Cartier estimated, they intercepted more than 100,000,000 words, or enough to make a library of a thousand average-sized novels.

At the start, however, the organization was so crude that the French even lacked direction-finders. They had to work instead on an assumption that all German stations emitted at the same strength and that the loudness of the intercepted signal roughly indicated the distance of the transmitter. Operators thus noted whether they heard German signals very loudly, loudly, medium loudly, weakly, or very weakly. By making quantities of such readings and drawing circles on the map with a radius equal to the estimated distance, the French less than two weeks after the outbreak of the war had diagrammed the probable locations of the German stations—a grouping that later proved in large measure correct.

The French also recorded call-signs, volume of traffic, and correspondents for all stations. These soon segregated themselves into four main networks, each of which, the French assumed, belonged to a combat group. The patterns of correspondence defined the headquarters stations, and volume soon differentiated the fast-moving and fast-sending cavalry stations from the infantry. Occasional cleartext signatures disclosed the commanders' names. In this way, the French gradually built up a picture of the German forces facing them.

This was the first radio traffic analysis. It attained a high refinement later in the war. Traffic analysis aided in delineating the enemy order of battle, and frequently forewarned of important enemy activities by detecting an increase in message volume. It also made a preliminary sorting of messages for cryptanalysis. Different enemy armies may use different codes with the same codewords or different keys for a single cipher system, and only the pinpointing of the transmitter by direction-finding and call-sign will enable the cryptanalyst to separate messages in one cryptographic "language" from those in another. It is the modern version of looking at the seal and the signature of an intercepted letter so that cryptograms from Venice will not be mixed with those from Parma. The careful filing of every detail surrounding an intercepted radiogram—its sender, receiver, time, preamble, length—often yielded supplementary benefits.

Early in the war, for example, the French intercepted a German cleartext radiogram, "Was ist Circourt?" The elaborate cross-references permitted an easy identification of the cryptogram that gave rise to the query. Meanwhile, the geographic service furnished the information that the name "Circourt" showed in full on certain German general staff maps while the troop maps had only the initial C. Other characteristics of the cryptogram implied that it dealt with a troop movement, and when it was attacked on this basis and on the now highly probable supposition that it contained the plaintext word

A War of Intercepts: I

Circourt, it succumbed. The French then recovered the key and read all the traffic for the week or so that it remained in force.

The cipher was the ÜBCHI, the famous double columnar transposition that the Germans had used—and the French had known—since even before the war. It employed a keyword or keyphrase prescribed by the high command, which, before actual encipherment, had to be transformed into a numerical sequence. This was done—as is conventional—by numbering the letters of the keyword in their alphabetical order, numbering repeated letters from left to right. For example, with the keyphrase DIE WACHT AM RHEIN, the two A's would be given numbers 1 and 2. There are no B's, so the C would take number 3, the D number 4, the two E's 5 and 6, and so on:

D	I	E	W	A	C	H	T	A	M	R	H	E	I	N
4	9	5	15	1	3	7	14	2	11	13	8	6	10	12

Actual encipherment of a plaintext—say *Tenth division X Attack Montigny sector at daylight X Gas barrage to precede you*—involved six separate steps. The encipherer (1) wrote the plaintext horizontally into a block beneath this numerical sequence:

4	9	5	15	1	3	7	14	2	11	13	8	6	10	12
t	e	n	t	h	d	i	v	i	s	i	o	n	x	a
t	t	a	c	k	m	o	n	t	i	g	n	y	s	e
c	t	o	r	a	t	d	a	y	l	i	g	h	t	x
g	a	s	b	a	r	r	a	g	e	t	o	p	r	e
c	e	d	e	y	o	u								

He (2) transcribed the letters vertically by columns in order of the key-numbers: HKAAY, ITYG, DMTRO, and so on, and (3) inscribed them horizontally into another block under the same numbers. To this he (4) added as many null letters as there were words in the original keyphrase—four, in this case:

4	9	5	15	1	3	7	14	2	11	13	8	6	10	12
h	k	a	y	i	t	y	g	d	m	t	r	o	o	t
t	c	g	c	n	a	o	s	d	n	y	h	p	i	o
d	r	u	o	n	g	o	e	t	t	a	e	x	s	t
r	s	i	l	e	a	e	x	e	i	g	i	t	v	n
a	a	t	c	r	b	e	k	a	i	s				

The encipherer then (5) again took out these letters by columns in key order: YNNER, GDTEA, IAGAB, and so on, and (6) divided them into the standard five-letter groups for transmission: YNNER GDTEA IAGAB HTDRA AGUIT RPXTT OOEET HEIKC RSAOI SVDNT IITOT NMYAG SYSEX KACOL C.

Decipherment was precisely the inverse of this process, except that the decipherer had first to determine the size of the transposition block so that he would know how deep his columns ran. He did this by dividing the number of digits in the key into the number of letters in the message; in this case, 15 into 71. The quotient—here, 4—gave the number of full lines in the block; the remainder—11—the number of letters in the final incomplete line.

Solution of a single message enciphered by double transposition constitutes an exceedingly difficult problem. Why this is so can best be understood from the cryptanalysis of a single columnar transposition. This is a cipher that would pass its plaintext through only one block, taking as its ciphertext the result of step 2 of the double transposition. Obviously, such a ciphertext is composed of segments that were originally the columns of the tableau. A cryptanalyst will cut up that ciphertext into what he thinks might be the columns and then will juxtapose one segment against another until he finds two that look as if they might have stood next to one another in the original block.

With the following 40-letter cryptogram, for example, the cryptanalyst might begin by assuming a keylength of five. The columns would then run eight letters deep, and the cryptanalyst would slice the cryptogram into groups of eight letters and pair the first group with the other four:

EITTI GMI | NH EGRNM T | YTRS GPNN | M RHINU UO | ETI EBIAI.

1 2	1 3	1 4	1 5	2 1	3 1	4 1	5 1
E N	E Y	E M	E E	N E	Y E	M E	E E
I H	I T	I R	I T	H I	T I	R I	T I
T E	T R	T H	T I	E T	R T	H T	I T
T G	T S	T I	T E	G T	S T	I T	E T
I R	I G	I N	I B	R I	G I	N I	B I
G N	G P	G U	G I	N G	P G	U G	I G
M M	M N	M U	M A	M M	N M	U M	A M
I T	I N	I O	I I	T T	N I	O I	I I

He can then either examine these by eye or use various mathematical techniques to see which two segments go together the best. One such technique is to give each assumed digraph its frequency in plaintext and then to add these frequencies; the combination with the highest total is most likely to be right. Thus, in the 1-2 pairing, EN has a normal frequency of 25 (per 2,000 English digraphs), IH of zero, and so on, with the eight digraphs totaling to 69. The other combinations come to 73, 143, 77, 77, 73, 62, and 78, respectively. The cryptanalyst would probably select the 1-4 combination with its

143 total, try to extend its digraphs into trigraphs on both right and left, and continue like that until he has reconstructed the entire block. If nothing looks good, he must modify his original guess as to the keylength and start over.

This process is greatly simplified if all the columns are the same length—a condition that obtains when the block is completely filled. This is called regular columnar transposition. In irregular columnar transposition, where the last line of the block is not full and the columns are consequently of two different lengths, the solution involves some jockeying up and down of the columns to get the proper matches.

This sort of reconstruction is, in exceptional cases, possible on a second-order basis to permit the solution of a single double-transposition cryptogram. In theory the cryptanalyst merely has to build up the columns of the second block by twos and threes so that their digraphs and trigraphs would in turn be joinable into good plaintext fragments. But this is far more easily said than done. Even a gifted cryptanalyst can accomplish it only on occasion; and even with help, such as a probable word like *Circourt*, it is never easy.

Solution becomes relatively simple, however, with several double-transposition cryptograms, all of exactly the same length and enciphered by the same keys. The cryptanalyst can then apply, on a letter-by-letter basis, the multiple-anagramming technique used in 1878 by Hassard, Holden, and Grosvenor on a word-by-word basis. Usually the two messages are written out one underneath the other on strips of paper, the paper is cut vertically so that two letters—one from each message—are on a single slip, and the slips tried one next to the other until plaintext appears on both top and bottom. The method very often succeeds, and French cryptanalysts accordingly sought cryptograms of identical length and key which they could subject to it. The Germans eased their search by keeping a single key in effect for eight or ten days over the entire Western Front. And as summer waned, the intercepts were fluttering onto French desks as thickly as the leaves of the war's first autumn.

But the four or five cryptanalysts that Cartier had under him at the Ministry of War could not concentrate solely on them. They had to lend a hand with the naval traffic, because the Ministry of Marine had no cryptanalysts whatsoever, and with the Berlin–Madrid diplomatic correspondence, because the Foreign Office experts were too overloaded to solve them quickly enough to be useful. Their work was further disrupted when, on September 2, their office was evacuated to Bordeaux with the rest of the government in the face of the German threat to Paris. Despite these difficulties, they began to send daily solutions to general headquarters later that month, when the war had been in progress only a few weeks. Sometimes these consisted of only the gist of messages, for multiple anagramming sometimes restores only patches of plaintext. A complete solution, however, will permit reconstruction of the original transposition key. This reconstruction is a tedious task, but it is worth the effort, for the basic key would unlock all the cryptograms enciphered in it, irrespective of identical-length requirements. On October 1, Cartier and three of his cryptanalysts—Major Adolphe Olivari and Officer-Interpreters Henry Schwab and Gustave Freyss—made this breakthrough for the first time. They communicated the primary ÜBCHI key to the various headquarters for on-the-spot decipherment of local German cryptograms.

It promptly became the hottest topic of conversation in the French army. The news raced through the ranks, and telephone lines were clogged with excited calls about the key recovery. Soldiers chattered about the existence of the key and discussed the contents—real or imagined—of cryptograms. So serious was the breach of security that on October 3 G.H.Q. had to issue an order to try to stop indiscreet talk about it. It didn't help. A few weeks later, after the Germans had changed their key, an officer asked loudly in the vestibule of headquarters whether it had been discovered again. The gossip swelled and expanded until it even reached civilian ears in Bordeaux.

The Germans seemed not to have heard it, however, for they continued to use their double transposition with their infrequent key changes. On October 17, a new key went into effect, but the French, more experienced now, recovered this one four days later. A new change at the beginning of November took only three days to solve; the next key was ascertained the very day it went into service. One of the new solutions enabled the French to bomb Thielt in occupied Belgium at the very moment that Kaiser Wilhelm II was entering it for a review. This story was too good for anyone to keep to himself; soon *Le Matin* published it, specifying the source of information. This time the Germans took notice. On November 18, they instituted an entirely new system.

It was a case of what cryptologists call "illusory complication." For though on its face it appeared more intricate and harder to solve than the double transposition, it proved to be solvable with a single cryptogram instead of the two or more, limited to highly specific conditions, required for multiple anagramming. The cipher consisted of a Vigenère encipherment with key ABC—which could be done in the head—followed by a single columnar transposition. One weakness was that the ciphertext equivalents stood at most two places away from their plaintext in the normal alphabet. The errors of cipher clerks enabled Lieutenant Colonel Anatole Thévenin, a member of the Commission of Military Cryptography who was serving as a part-time cryptanalyst at his post as assistant chief of staff of the 21st Army Corps, to solve it by December 10.

A month later there arrived on Cartier's desk a memorandum suggesting a simplified method of breaking this system, called the ABC by the French. It had been written by Georges Jean Painvin, a 29-year-old reserve lieutenant of artillery on the staff of the 6th Army. Painvin, who had a mind that flashed and cut like a rapier, was destined to become the Perseus of cryptologists in the epic struggle of World War I, slaying one German cryptographic Gorgon after another. Tall and slender, with dark, rather Spanish-looking features and piercing black eyes, Painvin worked with an intense concentration that gave no hint of either the lightning agility of his intelligence or his native charm and generosity. A high-ranking graduate of the famed École Polytechnique, he had taught paleontology at the École Nationale Supérieure des Mines in Paris. He was also an outstanding 'cellist and had once won first prize in this instrument at the Nantes conservatory.

When, after the Battle of the Marne, the fighting settled into the stagnation of trench warfare, Painvin found his afternoons unoccupied. He had become friendly with Captain Victor Paulier, a cryptanalyst who had been sent to the 6th Army from Cartier's bureau, and from him learned about the ÜBCHI. Painvin took up multiple anagramming of the German intercepts much as one might do crossword puzzles, and soon his recreations were crowned with practical success. He recovered several keys which were reported to Cartier, who, after receiving the ABC memorandum, dispatched his congratulations to Painvin.

On several occasions during inspection visits to 6th Army headquarters at the Château de Montgobert near Villers-Cotterets, the Minister of War, Alexandre Millerand, asked the commander, General Michel-Joseph Maunoury, to release Painvin for service at the Bureau du Chiffre. But Painvin had been through too much with the elderly Maunoury to feel able to leave him. Maunoury finally yielded to the pressure, however, and in March of 1915 told Painvin to go for two weeks and see whether he could be of more use with the cryptanalysts than with the 6th Army staff. Painvin went; soon thereafter, Maunoury was grievously wounded. There was now no one to recall the young cryptanalyst, and he remained in Cartier's office for the rest of the war.

That office now headed the first echeloned organization in the history of cryptology. The Bureau du Chiffre, which had returned to the War Ministry building in Paris, employed several dozen people, of whom only about 10 were cryptanalysts. It worked in the cryptologic stratosphere—inter-Allied communications, enemy diplomatic and naval cryptograms, new military systems, and messages from distant fronts. Its chief, Cartier, also directed the intercept service. Under the Bureau du Chiffre was G.H.Q.'s Service du Chiffre, headed by Givierge. Its staff of 15 officers handled the cryptographic correspondence of the French headquarters and solved the strategic cryptograms of the German Army, usually with methods and keys supplied by the Paris bureau.

Beneath it in turn came the cryptologic offices that were attached to the various army and army group headquarters in the same way that those headquarters had their own intelligence, signal, and other specialized organizations for their own needs. Paulier constituted one such office. They had been inaugurated by an order of September 17, 1914, which attached a specialist to each major unit to enforce the cryptographic regulations for their own troops.

France was preparing a general advance and did not want its cipher clerks making the blunders on the radio that they were then making on wire telegraphy. Eventually this one man became three, including cryptanalysts. Their presence near the front enabled them to garner many details helpful in solutions. If, for example, a message was sent to a German artillery unit, and two hours later that unit laid a barrage on a certain sector, the French cryptanalyst would have a number of probable words with which to rip open the message. These army bureaus generally solved low-level tactical communications.

The various branches of the decentralized French organization worked in close cooperation. Results or partial results were flashed from one to another as soon as a break was made: the War Ministry and G.H.Q. later communicated via a teleautograph, which, since it was the only one in existence, they regarded as sufficiently secure to carry some of the most secret messages in France.

By May of 1915 the ABC cipher had vanished. The end of the war of movement greatly reduced the volume of German military radio messages, and for most of 1915 traffic was at a very low level. The lull gave the French a chance to attack other problems. Painvin, Schwab, Givierge, Olivari, and Paulier cudgeled naval dispatches. Officer-Interpreters Bélard and Trannoy struggled with Bulgarian, Greek, and Turkish cryptograms. The several codes used in the busy Berlin–Madrid and Vienna–Madrid diplomatic circuits were under attack, the German-language ones by Painvin, Olivari, and Paul-Brutus Déjardin, the Spanish by Lieutenant Pannier and Officer-Interpreter J. Périère.

The cryptanalysts also engaged in retrospective solution of some of the cryptograms of the first days of the war. These helped explain why the Germans had made the historic turn to the east that led to the crucial Battle of the Marne, where they were stopped, and shed light on the thinking of German commanders during the critical "race to the sea," which established warfare's first continuous front. The picture that emerged of the German way of conducting war was so helpful to the French staff that General Joffre, the commander in chief, wrote to the Minister of War: "I have, like all the army commanders, during the last few days learned to realize the value of the services which have been rendered by the cryptanalytic bureau of your department. Please transmit the thanks of all of us to Major Cartier and his group."

The radio lull ended explosively at the start of 1916. This was the year in which the Germans oscillated wildly over the entire cryptographic spectrum in a frantic hunt for the ideal cipher. But the French kept up with them, and sometimes G.H.Q. received two or three solutions of a new problem within a few hours.

Every possible weakness was exploited in these solutions. Particularly ⁀ful were stereotyped messages. "Night calm; nothing to report" appeared with what Givierge called "terrible regularity" in German transmissions. One command required regular morning reports from its units in line. When the cipher changed, the practice did not, and the French promptly pried open the cipher with the leverage of a known plaintext. The French turned to similar advantage the thoughtless German practice of checking out new systems by enciphering proverbs as test messages. The German version of "The early bird gets the worm" was a particular favorite—but it was the French who profited.

Their familiarity with German habits of phraseology and transmission technique greatly helped. They had gained this insight during the very first days of the war, when the radio operators in General Georg von der Marwitz' cavalry corps on the wheeling German flank became simultaneously intoxicated by their speedy conquests, overwhelmed by the volume of their traffic, and exasperated by the nuisance of ciphering. They began sending messages in clear. Soon, by a kind of cryptologic Gresham's Law, everyone was doing it, while the French took copious notes. They bore down mercilessly on ciphering errors, studied captured notebooks with cryptographic worksheets, compared messages from different sectors that, individually, offered little but, conjointly, suggested much. They fished about wildly for keywords—and, given the German predilection for patriotic terms such as VATERLAND, KAISER, and DEUTSCHLAND, sometimes hooked the prize. They bombarded enemy trenches and feigned preparations for attacks just to get some badly needed probable words into enemy cryptograms. And, above all, they carved away at the ciphers with their keen, surgical minds, dissecting, discarding hypotheses, until at last they cut through to the heart of the system. Painvin in particular shone brilliantly in this pure cryptanalysis.

The first of the new German systems appeared with the outburst of new wireless activity. The French high command believed that these signs presaged a new German attack, and Painvin and Olivari fell upon the intercepts. They quickly decided that half of them were fake—mere meaningless strings of letters. But what messages were the real cryptograms carrying? Within two weeks, they discovered that the system consisted of an interrupted-key Vigenère with key ABCD followed by a single columnar transposition. The key interruptions were controlled by the numbers of the transposition key. The system was an elaboration of the old ABC; they called it the ABCD. The plaintexts proved to be nothing but simple ciphering exercises, portions of communiqués, extracts from newspapers, even trigonometrical formulas. This showed that the entire radio busyness was a German deception, and the cryptanalysts thereby relieved the French staff of some of its worries.

The cumbersome ABCD expired in April. It was replaced for the first time in German cryptography by pure substitution ciphers. These were numerous, but of two general kinds: monalphabetic substitution in which the choice of the 24 available alphabets was left to the encipherer, and polyalphabetic substitution with 12, 24, or 25 mixed alphabets. These grew ever more complicated, but as the development was progressive the French never lost cryptanalytic contact. Painvin solved one that spring thanks to a Bavarian prince's telling his parents, the king and queen, that he had been wounded. The polyalphabetic systems culminated in one used between Berlin and Constantinople. It employed 25 alphabets, required 32 tableaux, and was so excessively complex that only cipher clerks comfortably ensconced in quiet, well-equipped headquarters offices could handle it. In fact, it was *too* elaborate, and the pendulum swung away from substitution to transposition. At the end of 1916, transposition messages again appeared in German military communications.

By January, 1917, the French cryptanalysts recognized these as turning grilles. About all that these grilles have in common with the fixed concealment grille of Cardano is the name and the openings in the mask. The turning grille is usually a square sheet of cardboard divided into cells; one quarter of these are punched out in a pattern such that when the grille is rotated to its four positions, all the cells on the paper beneath will be exposed and none will be exposed more than once. A 6 × 6 grille might look like this:

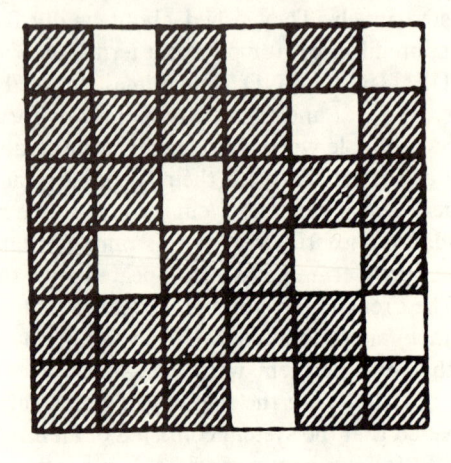

This is laid over a sheet of paper and the first nine letters are written through the apertures. Then it is turned 90 degrees, the next nine letters are written through the openings in their new position, and so on for two more turns. By then each of the 36 cells on the paper will have a letter inscribed in it, and the cryptographer can read it off in any pattern he chooses—usually by rows. Messages longer than 36 letters must repeat the process; in the last section of less than 36 letters, the unwanted cells can simply be blocked out.

The Germans provided their signal troops with a variety of sizes for different length messages. Each grille had a codename: ANNA for 25 letters, BERTA for 36, CLARA, 49, DORA, 64, EMIL, 81, FRANZ, 100. These codenames were changed weekly.

A War of Intercepts: I

Grille systems are particularly susceptible to multiple anagramming—which is the general solution for transposition systems—because their sections are of necessity of equal length. But the system produces intriguing geometrical symmetries, and the French soon devised attacks exploiting this and other weaknesses. The grilles lasted four months.

Britain, too, had her military cryptanalytic bureaus. But she had made no more preparations for them before the war than she had done for Room 40, and her Army cryptanalysts, expert though they became, never achieved the proficiency of the French.

Her setup was essentially the same as France's. The head organization, M.I. 1(b), was attached to the War Office. A field agency was established at British Expeditionary Force headquarters, and individual cryptanalysts were stationed with the several armies.

M.I. 1(b) was still a small, four-man section—1(b)—of the Military Intelligence Division in December of 1915 when Malcolm Vivian Hay of Seaton was placed in charge. Hay, then 34, was the grandson of the second son of the seventh Marquess of Tweeddale and had succeeded to the Seaton Estates near Aberdeen when he was 2. After an education at Beaumont College and abroad, he returned to supervise his farms; he joined the Gordon Highlanders as a captain at the outbreak of war. He was machine-gunned at the Battle of Mons and was captured by the Germans when he was left on the field by the British retreat. Partly paralyzed as a result of his head wound, he was repatriated in February, 1915, as unfit for military duty. After learning to walk with the aid of a cane, he was promoted to major and given command of M.I. 1(b).

He began at once to scour the universities for bright young men, preferably language scholars, to supplement the three original civilians on the staff: J. St. Vincent Pletts, a radio engineer from Marconi's Wireless Telegraph Company; J. D. Crocker, a young Cambridge scholar, and Oliver Strachey of the Indian Civil Service, who liked cryptanalysis so much that he switched after the war from administering the East Indian Railway to codebreaking for the Foreign Office. Hay recruited a remarkable concentration of men who were later to achieve eminence, if listing in *Who's Who* may be taken as an index. Among them were his chief assistant, John Fraser, 32, later professor of Celtic as a fellow of Jesus College, Oxford; Arthur Surridge Hunt, 45, then and later professor of papyrology at Oxford and one of the world's most eminent authorities on ancient writing; David Samuel Margoliouth, 58, professor of Arabic at Oxford, later president of the Royal Asiatic Society and author of many works on Arabic literature and history; Zachary Nugent Brooke, 33, then lecturer in history at Cambridge, later professor of medieval history there and an editor of the *Cambridge Medieval History*; Edward Thurloe Leeds, 39, then assistant keeper of the department of antiquities of the Ashmolean Museum and, after the war, keeper of that first public museum in England; Ellis H. Minns, 42, then and later lecturer in paleography at Cambridge, later knighted; Norman Brooke Jopson of Cambridge, 26, later professor of comparative philology there; George Bailey Sansom of the consular service, 33, later knighted and commercial counselor of the British embassy in Tokyo and author of a *Historical Grammar of Japanese* and of a standard history of Japan; and Henry E. G. Tyndale, 28, later housemaster of Winchester College, one of England's great public schools, an avid mountaineer, and editor of the *Alpine Journal* and of the classic *Whymper's Scrambles Amongst the Alps*. The chief himself, Hay, became well known as a historian, writing half a dozen major historical works (most presenting the Catholic viewpoint on controversial questions) and almost as many on other subjects. His first study, *A Chain of Errors in Scottish History*, concerning early church history, was violently denounced and extravagantly praised. But subsequent works, such as *The Enigma of James II*, were received with more moderate but more extended applause, and his later *The Foot of Pride*, an erudite examination of European anti-Semitism, was universally lauded.

The staff of M.I. 1(b) was to number 84, including 30 women, by the end of the war. To shelter this growing organization, as well as to conceal it from the curious, the War Office requisitioned a largish private house at 5 Cork Street, several blocks from its own building in Whitehall and behind the fashionable Burlington Arcade. Hay immediately instituted a complicated entrance procedure that involved locking visitors in a room temporarily to prevent their wandering about the premises.

Early in the war, the French had provided the English with keys and techniques for the German military ciphers, and with this help, M.I. 1(b) was soon passing valuable information to the army command. Eventually a pool of skilled cryptanalysts was built up, including one who was familiar with Turkish. Perhaps the most brilliant at Cork Street was Captain G. L. Brooke-Hunt of the Royal Engineers, who had served in the Indian Army.

Among his most difficult problems was the "Für GOD" system, which was so-called because all messages in it bore that prefix to show that they were for the German wireless station whose call letters were GOD. These messages were sent irregularly about three times a week from POZ, the powerful German station at Nauen outside of Berlin. They began in 1916 and lasted until the fall of 1918, making the Für GOD the longest-lived German cipher. Because the dispatches bore no signature and no address beyond the call-sign, suspicion grew that the cryptograms concealed instructions to German secret agents.

Brooke-Hunt solved the Für GOD early in 1917. It proved to be a polyalphabetic system using 22 mixed alphabets and 30 incoherent keys of from 11 to 18 letters. The messages were numbered serially from January to December in each year and the keywords repeated in cycles of 30. The dispatches were transmitted by the political section of the German general staff to an expedition sent to North Africa under Captain von Todenwart to foment uprisings by the Arab population. Some of the messages were orders, but many forwarded reports of the slaughter of colonial troops on the Western Front as a result of alleged French placement of them in the most dangerous positions in the line. Von Todenwart was directed to spread these reports as anti-Allied propaganda.

Among the messages were several arranging for a submarine to bring rifles and ammunition to Abd el Malek, a Moroccan nationalist. Hay was in the closest personal touch with Captain Hall at the Admiralty. Information was passed, wheels turned, air commands were notified, and shortly after the U-boat surfaced in the blue Mediterranean she had submerged again—this time involuntarily and for good, taking her cargo with her. Later in the war Brooke-Hunt read with mingled pleasure and regret a Für GOD message declaring that "For security reasons, U-boat arrival notifications will no longer be made."

Hay, who was admired by his subordinates as "a very good chief" (they later gave him a silver loving cup and a book of photographs with cryptographic inscriptions and affectionate remembrances), was given charge of constructing codes and ciphers for British forces early in 1917. He took his responsibilities seriously enough to make a visit to Cartier's office despite his own disability, and later in the war his office sent representatives to the Near East to coordinate cryptologic security there.

But M.I. 1(b) apparently had no hand in the development of perhaps the finest British cryptanalyst of the war. O. T. (for Oswald Thomas) Hitchings had been destined to be a schoolmaster like his father, but he loved music so much that he became an organist instead. Later he taught music in two preparatory schools, and while doing this learned French and German so well by correspondence that he won an honors degree in them from London University. In 1911 he went to Bridlington Grammar School as modern language master. Quiet, conscientious, he volunteered for the Army at the start of the war and went directly to France, where his knowledge of languages was put to use in the Field Censor's Office. One day his colonel asked him if he would like to try solving the German messages that were being intercepted. He said he would, found he had a flair for the work, and by 1918, when he was 42, had risen to the rank of captain and the command of Intelligence E(c), 2d echelon—the Code and Cipher Solution Section of the British Expeditionary Force's general headquarters.

This section was located in Le Touquet, a Channel-side resort town not far from British G.H.Q. at Montreuil, probably for reasons of security. Here the serious, earnest Hitchings was assisted by a debonair, kilted Scot, Duncan Campbell Macgregor. Under them worked the cryptanalysts at the several army headquarters; at one of these an American visitor was astonished to see a German prisoner of war, still wearing his uniform, puzzling over the intercepts of his native land! Hitchings' solutions were so extraordinarily valuable that one colonel exclaimed that he was worth four divisions to the British.

With this superb background in cryptanalysis to instruct them, what systems did the Allies use? The British employed the Playfair with random keysquare. Its use extended even to Lawrence of Arabia. Behind the lines, the French corresponded in a four-digit superenciphered code; they changed it three times between August 1, 1914, and January 15, 1915. Series 65 of this code chiffré was a two-part code of about 2,300 four-digit groups. A tableau de concordance superenciphered number pairs into letter pairs with a straddling gimmick: the first digit was chopped off and enciphered separately, and the subsequent division into pairs straddled the gap between codegroups. This kept a codegroup from being always superenciphered the same way. A sample encoding and encipherment of the plaintext "The relief will take place tomorrow morning" in Series 65 would be:

plaintext	La	relève	au-	ra	lieu	demain	matin
placode	1 65	14 27	50 86	58 75	01 06	57 35	3
encicode	RH BR	AG NU	AU HB	TR BU	GA HI	BI IS	SI

The remarkable French acuity in matters cryptological is nowhere better shown than in the instruction accompanying this code: "Exceptionally, if you do not have the time to encipher entirely, transmit in clear." The French knew that partial encoding, which offered quick and easy entries into a code ("Colonel seriously 6386" could have but one meaning, for example), posed a danger to the compromise of all communications that a single cleartext message, which at best disclosed a single piece of information, did not.

In the field, the French sometimes used a mixed-alphabet polyalphabetic with a running key. But the cipher they relied upon for three years was an interrupted columnar transposition that was, paradoxically, theoretically weaker than the German double transposition. It employed the usual transposition block with a key sequence in which the plaintext was inscribed horizontally. The vertical transcription, however, was preceded by a reading out of letters on certain diagonals. For example, with the message *Enemy has brought up four howitzer batteries and three companies Stop We can hold but we need more fifty calibre machine gun ammunition Third Battalion* (plus three nulls to complete the last five-letter group), and the key (the French used long ones) MADEMOISELLE FROM ARMENTIERES, with the rightward diagonals starting under 3, 5, 7, 8, and 10 to be taken off in that order, followed by the leftward diagonals under 16, 18, 21, and 26:

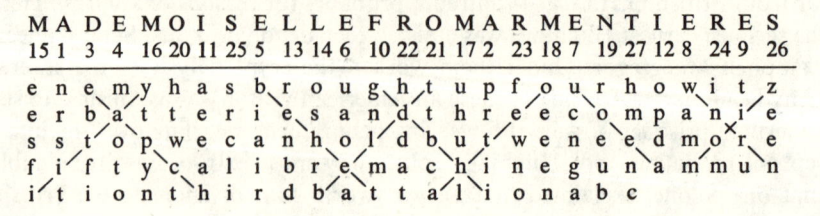

```
M  A D E M O I S E L L E F R O M A R M E N T I E R E S
15 1 3 4 16 20 11 25 5 13 14 6 10 22 21 17 2 23 18 7 19 27 12 8 24 9 26

e n e m y h a s b r o u g h t u p f o u r h o w i t z
e r b a t t e r i e s a n d t h r e e c o m p a n i e
s s t o p w e c a n h o l d b u t w e n e e d m o r e
f i f t y c a l i b r e m a c h i n e g u n a m m u n
i t i o n t h i r d b a t t a l i o n a b c
```

The transcription begins with EAPCH and continues with BEHET. The leftward diagonals skip over any letter previously transcribed; thus, diagonal 21 would read TLB and not TDLEB. Similarly, the vertical transcriptions ignore any letters taken by the diagonals: column 1 would read NRST and not NRSIT. The full transcription, which would naturally be divided into groups of five for transmission, is: EAPCH BEHET UOEA WNRN GDBHI YTII OETA TLB ZIOM NRST PRI BFI MOTO IAIR UAOA CNGA AM TU NM AEEA OPD RNBD OSR EESF TYN UHUL EEEN REUB HTWT TC HDAT FWNO IM SRCLI EE HMNC.

The diagonals break up the columnar segments that the cryptanalyst juxtaposes and adjusts to solve uninterrupted columnar transpositions. But the diagonals constitute segments of their own, and the columns, though fragmented, keep their constituent letters together instead of scattering them, as does the double transposition. The cryptanalyst can seize upon these weaknesses to reconstruct the tableau. The task is admittedly more difficult than with an ordinary columnar transposition, but it can be effected with a single message far more easily than with the German system.

Why, then, did the Germans not solve it for the three years that the French kept it in force?

The reason is absurdly simple: Germany had no cryptanalysts on the Western Front for the first two years of the war.

She had entered the war with no military cryptanalytic service. (An expected side effect appeared in the erratic development of German cryptography. The absence of the stabilizing influence of cryptanalysts resulted in the overcorrective swings from one field cipher to another in 1915 and 1916. The lack of cryptanalytic instruction also forced the Germans to attend the hard-knocks school of cryptography, learning through one painful experience after another the dangers of normal alphabets, patriotic keys, their inherent love of order, and the like.) But even if Germany had had well-trained cryptanalysts available at the start of the war, she would have had little opportunity to use them.

German victories drove the French back into their own territory, where they used their own wire network for communication and thus deprived the enemy of much chance of intercepting radio messages. The same situation freed the French radio for intercept work whereas the Germans had to use their wireless for communication. French cryptanalysis thus owed much of its success to the highly dubious advantage of having the war fought on French territory. One may wonder whether the French would have preferred solving enemy cryptograms or the nondesolation of dozens of villages, orchards, fields, and forests in their northern provinces.

As the war progressed, the French began using radio more and more. By 1916, the Germans awoke to their opportunities and set up the Abhorchdienst ("Intercept Service"). Its main station was at Neumünster, where cryptanalysts, many of them recruited from the ranks of mathematicians, were soon solving Playfairs within a day after a key change. Later, the Germans established a cryptanalytic center at their Western Front G.H.Q. at the Belgian resort of Spa. But they never caught up with the Allies, who had had the inestimable advantage of familiarity with German phraseology and idiosyncrasies, gained in the first chaotic days, and of preventative improvements in their own communications.

Both sides, however, were equally adept at picking up the enemy's frontline telephone messages—an eavesdropping that was facilitated by the fixed nature of trench warfare. Conversations could be heard either by induction through earth pickups, or by actual taps of enemy wires by intrepid soldiers who crawled across no-man's-land. Both sides obtained enormous quantities of intelligence from this source. Officers and men repeatedly violated the strict regulations against transmitting any important information over field telephones.

In 1916, for example, the British sustained casualties in the thousands in a fierce battle to take Ovillers-la-Boiselle on the Somme. Battalions were decimated as they went over the top. When the British finally captured their objective, they found in one enemy dugout a complete transcript of one of their operation orders. A brigade major had read it in full over a field telephone despite the protest of his subordinate that the procedure was dangerous. "Hundreds of brave men perished," the British signal historian related, "hundreds more were maimed for life as the result of this one act of incredible foolishness." The search for protection resulted in the ultimate cryptographic development of the First World War. These were the trench codes.

In February of 1916, General Auguste Dubail, the handsome and energetic commander of the French Army of Lorraine, requested some kind of code for telephone use because indiscretions had drawn so many heavy bombardments onto his reserves. The cryptographic office produced a carnet de chiffre ("cipher notebook"). Important words in telephone messages were to be spelled out in code form by replacing their letters with the two-digit groups of the carnet. Soon a table of 50 common expressions was added, and the carnet authorized for use by wireless telegraphy. This spurred its enlargement into a small code of three-letter groups for use by smaller units. This was called a "carnet réduit" ("condensed notebook") in contrast to the larger headquarters codes.

The carnets were replaced from time to time. Each had a name—OLIVE, URBAIN, and so on—and the initial letter of that name, repeated three times, indicated the carnet that had encoded the message. The carnets were caption codes: the plaintext elements were arranged in categories, such as artillery, infantry, numbers, letters, common words, prepared phrases, place-names, verbs, and so forth. Though the codewords of the early carnets ran in alphabetical order, the topical distribution of the plaintext ruffled the one-part aspect of the code. Later carnets thoroughly mixed the codewords as well.

Germany did not start using codes until a year after France did, but then they evolved in roughly the same way.

The simple Befehlstafel ("command table") came first. A small trench code in which bigrams represented common words or letters, it superseded the grilles in March of 1917. Some Befehlstafeln were in the form of notebooks with variable pagination; others were constructed as cipher disks, in which a change of position would give a change of equivalencies. In June these were supplemented on the regimental level by the Satzbuch ("sentence book"), the German version of the French code chiffré. The 2,000 (later 4,000) plaintext expressions of the Satzbuch were represented by thoroughly mixed three-letter codewords. It provided numerous homophones (*anschluss fehlt*, ["link-up missed"] = KXL, ROQ, UDZ) and many Blinde Signale, or nulls. Unlike the code chiffré, it was not superenciphered; it relied instead on planned obsolescence for security. At first a new codebook was issued about every month, but the interval was gradually cut down to about 15 days. This multiplicity of codes in time was matched by one in space. Where at first the entire front shared a single code, soon army groups and then individual armies had their own Satzbucher.

The French called these codes the "KRU" or "KRUSA" codes, because all their codewords began with one of those five letters. The first one disconcerted the Service du Chiffre, unaccustomed as it was to dealing with two-part German codes. But it recovered quickly and, with Déjardin playing a leading role, reconstituted it sufficiently to read most messages. As the number of codes multiplied, their successful solution depended increasingly on accurate traffic analysis—an accurate separation of the messages of one army from those of another. This was managed, and the French soon were straining to recover the first 100 or 150 groups of each code as quickly as possible, for with this entry the rapid filling out of the repertory was virtually assured. Most of the 30 German codes that France solved during the war must have been Satzbucher. The information obtained during the ten days from December 5 to 15, 1917, a period picked at random, illustrates the value of the cryptanalysis: discovery of four division movements, reconfirmation of the identity of 32 regiments, ascertainment of the presence of a counterattack division north of St. Quentin, and warning of a German surprise attack at the Abia farm, which the alerted French troops repulsed.

In March of 1918, the British predicted that the Germans would soon change their trench codes, probably in the direction of enciphered code. Painvin and Cartier were discussing this possibility with a visitor when Painvin was called to the telephone. French G.H.Q. informed him that what appeared to be that very switch had been made that day over the entire front, replacing the Befehlstafel trench code. The basis of the new system was the Schlüsselheft ("keybook"), a caption code of 1,000 three-digit groups. Only the first two digits of each codegroup were enciphered. This was done with a Geheimklappe ("secret flyleaf"), a 10 × 10 table with placode digits 0 to 9 as coordinates on the top and side and the encicode digits dispersed irregularly inside. Toward the end of the war, the Geheimklappe changed daily.

Though the cruel deadlock of the Western Front riveted the major attentions of the Entente and of Germany, its chief antagonist, battles on the Eastern and the Southern Fronts sacrificed their millions as well to the clash of national ambitions. Russia, isolated by the cruise of the *Göben*, hurled her mighty forces against the German and Austro-Hungarian empires time and again in noble resolution of her treaty obligations; her eventual downfall, in no small degree a matter of cryptology, is a story in itself. In May of 1915, Italy denounced its treaty with the Central Powers and joined the Allies; Rumania followed a year later. Bulgaria lined up with Germany; Greece and Portugal with the Entente. Fighting blasted the Holy Land. All Europe and the Near East flamed.

Thanks to its prewar training, the Austro-Hungarian Army's Dechiffrierdienst handily unwrapped the Russian systems, aided by the innumerable confusions of mobilization. They had gained almost a year of invaluable wartime experience by the time hostilities broke out with Italy. Thus they achieved their first solutions of Italian cryptograms (of no tactical importance) on June 5, 1915, only 13 days after the declaration of war. These first four were followed by 16 others in June, most intercepted by the new station erected at Marburg. On July 5, the Austrians picked up their first dispatch in the cifrario rosso ("red cipher"), the Italian staff cipher, which intelligence chief Ronge had prudently acquired before the war. They had the odd pleasure of reading a reprimand from General Luigi Cadorna, the Italian commander in chief, to Lieutenant General Frugoni for not having pressed an attack vigorously enough.

Five days later, the cifrario rosso key changed. The Italian specialists among the Austrian cryptanalysts, spearheaded by the chief of the entire cryptanalytic section, Major Andreas Figl, cracked it only after considerable work. The number of solutions fell to 13 in July. But as the Austrians accustomed themselves to Italian methods, their successes waxed. By August 12, they had read 63 messages and could send the new key to the several army headquarters, where Figl had just stationed cryptanalysts. Captain Albert de Carlo was assigned to Bozen; Lieutenant Alfred, Baron von Chiari, went to the 11th Army at Adelsburg in the Tyrol and Lieutenant Hugo Scheuble to the 10th Army at Villach in Carinthia. Soon afterwards the Austrians captured the enemy's field radio instructions, and thereupon the number of solutions mounted to 50 and sometimes 70 a day. Though these usually contained only administrative matters, they enabled Colonel Ronge to predict the course of impending offensives.

By now the Austrian cryptanalysts had become so expert that they hardly noticed the changing every six weeks of the key of the field cipher, the cifrario servizio ("service cipher"). In October, the Italians put into front-line service a new system, the cifrario tascabile ("pocket cipher"), and Ronge boasted that "it was another one of my peacetime purchases that was already paying for itself." For once Ronge was wrong: it had been a complete waste of money. The cifrario tascabile was no more or less than a Vigenère with the digits 1 to 0 tacked on to the end of the plaintext alphabet and with cipher alphabets consisting of the digits 10 to 45 in normal order! Passwords usually served as keys. It should have taken the experienced Austrian cryptanalysts perhaps three or four hours at the most to identify and solve the first message or two in the system.

This system was the brainchild of Felice de Chaurand de Saint-Eustache, an Italian colonel who before the war had laboriously solved a correspondence carried on alternately in two enciphered commercial codes, the Sittler and the Mengarini. Subsequently he "enhanced" his cryptologic reputation by devising the cifrario tascabile. It should have rather brutally exposed his ignorance—and it reflects badly on the poverty of prewar Italian cryptology that it did not. Anyone having the slightest acquaintance with the field would have seen the vulnerability of the cifrario tascabile, while anyone who had kept up with the literature would have known that de Chaurand could have solved his code correspondence in a few hours if he had applied Valério's mechanical technique instead of requiring the two months of several hours' work a day that he said, rather pridefully, it took him. Later, for some inexplicable reason, an Italian expeditionary force in Albania corresponded in this very same Mengarini code!

During the big Austrian drive in the spring of 1916, Austrian cryptanalysts preyed not only on the cifrario tascabile, which was an easy killing, but on the other systems as well. One radiogram was intercepted during the evening of May 20; by 3 the next morning Figl's group had read of arrangements for a heavy counterattack with reserves; by 4 countermeasures had been ordered which checked the Italian onslaught. On June 1, the armies' intercept-cryptanalytic posts—which Ronge had codenamed "Penkalas," after a pencil factory's trademark that showed a head with a mechanical pencil behind an oversized ear—detected a change in Italian call-signs and cipher key. Four days later, a new call-sign was heard which later proved to be that of a newly formed Italian 5th Army. On June 8, the Italian 1st Army cipher key changed, and the air force got its own code. The Nachrichtenabteilung put these indications all together and they spelled "attack." Consequently the Austrians were prepared for the Italians' summer offensives on the Isonzo River. The cryptanalysts soon became so expert that the now-daily Italian key changes caused less trouble to them than to the legitimate decipherers. And when a new system was introduced on August 20, they cracked it within 38 hours.

Cryptanalysis had thus become one of the major sources of Austrian intelligence, and by April of 1917, the organization that generated this information had burgeoned into a multisection outfit. Attached to the general staff's Evidenzgruppe were Chiffrengruppe I, under Captain de Carlo, and Chiffrengruppe II, under Captain Richard Imme. Theoretically under the Evidenzgruppe, but, according to Colonel Ronge (who commanded both), the "real" Austrian intelligence service, was the Nachrichtenabteilung of G.H.Q. at Baden. One of its five divisions was the Kriegschiffregruppe ("War Cipher Group"), headed by First Lieutenant Hermann Pokorny, a brilliant cryptanalyst who had solved the first Russian cryptogram of the war, and who later became chief of the Evidenzgruppe. The Kriegschiffregruppe had three sections: an Italian under Major Figl (who later rose to colonel), a Rumanian under Captain Kornelius Savu, and a Russian under Captain Viktor von Marchesetti. Feeding intercepts to them were three major Penkalas: Austro-West, covering the Italian sector; Austro-Sud, the Rumanian; and Austro-Nord, the Russian. The entire complex was referred to by the unofficial title "Dechiffrierdienst."

Savu's group, incidentally, made little progress for a while after Rumania's entry into the war in 1916, but then the ciphers caved in and proved a mine of information, giving the Austrians full warning, for example, of a planned counterattack on September 14. Captain Franz Jansa, in charge of Austro-Sud, and his assistant, Captain Konstantin Marosan, found themselves so overworked that a cryptanalyst had to be attached to 1st Army headquarters. Later the flood slackened, but on occasion the Austrians read messages that the intended recipients could not, showing that they had not lost their touch.

They did not capture all the laurels, however. Italy had made no prewar cryptographic purchases, but she was aided in her efforts to catch up to her enemy by some remarkably inept Austrian cryptography and some remarkably able Italian cryptanalysts.

The first and best of these was Luigi Sacco, an enthusiastic, 32-year-old lieutenant of engineers at the Supreme Command's radio station. He had first become interested in cryptography in 1911, at the time of Italy's war with Turkey. When, during the World War, France rebuffed his attempts to learn about Central Powers cryptography and then failed to send back solutions of the Austrian intercepts that Italy was giving her, Sacco, who had charge of the intercept service, began to attack the messages himself. Though he knew no German, he chipped away so energetically and acutely that he soon managed to hack out fragments of plaintext. These proved valuable enough for him to be placed in charge of a cryptanalytic office attached to the Supreme Command's intelligence service. Called the "Reparto crittografico" ("cryptographic unit"), it was staffed at first with two engineers from Irredentist areas of Austria—Tullio Cristofolini of Trent and Mario Franzotti of Gorizia—and with a distinguished linguist, Professor Remo Fedi. It employed several score of people by the end of the war.

The cryptanalysts achieved their first complete solution of Austro-Hungarian radiograms during the Battle of Gorizia in August of 1917. What systems were then in use are unspecified. But up to that time the Austrians had not displayed any singular excellence in their cryptography. Among the systems in which they had reposed their trust and their lives was a Vigenère with alphabets normal except for the addition of ä, ö, and ü—a circumstance that perhaps explains Ronge's vaunting of his purchase of the closely similar cifrario tascabile. There were also what the Italians called the AK and the SH, in which 50-odd ciphertext digrams represented a plaintext letter, number, or syllable. The AK was sent in its original two-letter groups, whereas the SH was divided into five-letter groups. Not till November, 1917, did the Austrians convert to codes, when they placed into service what the Italians called the CW and the Carnia codes, both of 1,000 groups and for use only within a single army. The Reparto crittografico solved them both.

It also solved a similar code on the basis of a single message in the crucial days just before the Battle of the Piave. As part of the preparations for their summer push, the Austrians had placed a two-part code of 1,000 groups into service on June 15, 1918. At first they used it correctly, but soon repetitions appeared that indicated letter-by-letter encoding, with groups exceeding the frequency of 4 or 5 per cent that would be the normal maximum for word-groups in such a code. On June 20, Italy intercepted two messages with virtually the same unusual ending:

492   073   065   834   729   589   255   073   255   834   729   264

The pattern of repetitions suggested the plaintext *radiostation*, with the two partial repeats 073 ... 834 729 representing the repeated *a-io* and the two 255s standing for the repeated *t*. It checked out, and thus this one lazy Austrian code clerk, who found it easier to encode letter by letter than to hunt up the codegroups for *radio* and *station*, had enabled the Italians to read a goodly portion of his comrades' code communications.

Italy's growing cryptanalytic experience enabled it to solve increasingly difficult problems, such as the superenciphered Austrian diplomatic code (for which Sacco's group had the aid of cleartext messages). The considerably larger naval cryptanalytic staff solved the Austrians' superenciphered naval system. And gradually it dawned on the Italians that if they could read Austrian ciphers, perhaps the Austrians could read theirs. As early as January, 1917, an attempt was made to replace the old systems. It foundered on the complaint that the new methods required too much time for encipherment. Later, improvements were made to the cifrario rosso, but these were quickly nullified when a major army unit transmitted the new key variables in the old system. In June, the cifrario tascabile was replaced by a small codebook, and after the bloody Italian defeat at Caporetto, there was a wholesale change of army systems, to enciphered code. At about the same time, Cartier journeyed to Italy, visiting the intercept posts and talking with Sacco. The Allied military mission that bolstered Italy at the end of 1917 included some cryptologic personnel. All of this noticeably tightened Italian cryptologic practice.

As a result, Austrian cryptanalyses declined sharply in the latter half of the war. Nevertheless, Austria-Hungary had enjoyed the preponderance of cryptanalytic success on the Southern Front. Ronge always cherished as the greatest tribute to his Dechiffrierdienst an unintended one from the foe. A postwar commission of enquiry into the Caporetto disaster reported with anguish that "The enemy had known and deciphered all our codes, even the most difficult and most secret."

11

A WAR OF INTERCEPTS: II

NINETEEN ELEVEN is not a momentous year in American history. The last two territories on the continent, New Mexico and Arizona, were preparing for admission to the Union. The large-girthed William Howard Taft lumbered about the White House, trying to ignore the pyrotechnics of his predecessor, Theodore Roosevelt. C. P. Rodgers made the first airplane flight across the country. Carry Nation died. Perhaps the most impressive event of the twelve-month was Ty Cobb's batting that incredible .420. The year was not outstanding, but it was the year in which the United States took its first faltering steps in official military cryptanalysis.

They were taken at Fort Leavenworth, Kansas. Here America's tiny pre-war Army had its Signal School. In 1911, the school began a series of technical conferences, and on December 20 portions of a paper on "Military Cryptography" by Captain Murray Muirhead of Britain's Royal Field Artillery were read to Conference No. 4. The students responded with some papers of their own. Captain Alvin C. Voris showed how unsuitable the purely administrative War Department Telegraph Code was for troops in the field and proposed a tactical supplement for it. Lieutenant Frederick F. Black praiseworthily made an attempt to mechanize en- and deciphering by putting caps over typewriter keys. Lieutenant Karl Truesdell took a basic first step by compiling 10,000-letter frequency tables for English, German, French, Italian, Spanish, and Portuguese. A few months later, Lieutenant Joseph O. Mauborgne—who was to become Chief Signal Officer—whiled away the long hours of a trans-Pacific crossing by solving an 814-letter Playfair from Muirhead; he described his methods in 1914 in a 19-page pamphlet that is the first published solution of that cipher.

The Muirhead seed ripened best in the fertile mind of a 34-year-old captain of infantry named Parker Hitt. Hitt was the towering figure of American cryptology in those days, both figuratively and literally. Six feet four inches tall, a native of Indianapolis, he had left his studies in civil engineering at Purdue University in 1898 to join the Army. He served in Cuba, won a commission, and saw, if not the world, at least the Philippines, Alaska, and California. After graduating from the Signal School, he stayed on as an instructor. Hitt participated in the technical conferences and, among other things, demonstrated the insecurity of Black's typewriter method by taking only 45 minutes to solve one of the automatic cryptograms.

He discovered that he was "very much interested in cipher work of all kinds" and that he had a real knack for it. When the border command began intercepting Mexican cipher messages as American friction grew with that troubled country, the messages found their way to Hitt. Soon he was solving transposition ciphers, monalphabetics, polyalphabetics (some with mixed alphabets) used by agents of Pancho Villa and others, and a homophonic substitution used by the Constitutionalists. This had four numerical cipher alphabets, all of which remained fixed during the encipherment of a single message, but whose positions were changed from one message to another. The key could be indicated by the letters above the lowest number in each alphabet, or by the four numbers under A. For example, the arrangement used for a message between Saltillo and Juarez, intercepted on November 26, 1916, was:

```
A  B  C  D  E  F  G  H  I  J  K  L  M  N  O  P  Q  R  S  T  U  V  W  X  Y  Z
24 25 26 01 02 03 04 05 06 07 08 09 10 11 12 13 14 15 16 17 18 19 20 21 22 23
41 42 43 44 45 46 47 48 49 50 51 52 27 28 29 30 31 32 33 34 35 36 37 38 39 40
56 57 58 59 60 61 62 63 64 65 66 67 68 69 70 71 72 73 74 75 76 77 78 53 54 55
99             79 80 81 82 83 84 85 86 87 88 89 90 91 92 93 94 95 96 97 98
```

Hitt solved this, and many like it. The system later became more widely known under the name of the Mexican Army Cipher Disk when the four numerical alphabets were placed on revolving disks.

Hitt demonstrated his acuity in cryptanalysis nowhere more strikingly than with a subtle numerical system forwarded him by Lieutenant Colonel Samuel Reber of the Office of the Chief Signal Officer. Reber wrote him on September 21, 1915: "Some time ago while in conversation with the Assistant Chief Engineer of the Western Electric Company, I told him that a good cipher expert could work out almost any cipher, and his letter of August 3rd shows what he thinks in the matter. I am sending you the ciphers. . . ." On the 24th, Hitt, then at the School of Musketry at Fort Sill, Oklahoma, received the cryptograms, which were two strings of unbroken numbers, and the next day, a rainy Saturday, analyzed them. That afternoon he wrote Reber:

"No. 1 consisted of 415 figures and the factors of this are 83 × 5. This led to the conclusion that I had five figure groups to deal with and this was checked affirmatively when I made out a list of these groups and found some duplicates and a few triplicates. The ratio of occurrence of these duplicates and triplicates led me at once to the conclusion that each group represented two let

"The groups ran in value from 00518 to 53339 with large gaps. I then ɪ the small graph of group values and found that I could roughly superimɪ normal frequency table on the graph, but the scale, if I may so call ˙ larger at the A end than at the Z end. This suggested a logarithmic scaˊ reached for a table of logarithms.

A War of Intercepts: II

"00518 showed up as log 1012 and 53339 as log 3415 *exactly*. If A = 10, then 12 = C, 34 = Y and 15 = F. The rest of the solution merely involved the use of the logarithm table on these five figure groups and the reduction of the numerals so found to letters." In a few swift slashes of his mind he thus cracked an ingenious two-step cipher, to Reber's pleasure (though he ungraciously said he could have done it himself if he tried) and to the chagrin of the Western Electric assistant chief engineer.

During 1915 Hitt was working on a project that he had mentioned in a letter to Reber on January 15: "I have a mass of material on cipher work, the accumulation of the last four years, and hope to put it into shape as a pamphlet before I leave here if time permits. Major Wildman has kindly suggested that I do this in order that the pamphlet be used as a basis for the course in cipher work." He enriched his own experience—greater than that of any other person in the country at that time—with theory and new information from European books on cryptology that he borrowed from the Army War College. He finally completed his booklet late in 1915, and the next year the Press of the Army Service Schools at Fort Leavenworth published 4,000 copies of his *Manual for the Solution of Military Ciphers*, selling it at 35 cents the copy.

It was an excellent work. It naturally explained how to solve the standard ciphers, up to periodic polyalphabetics with mixed alphabets and—for perhaps the first time in the literature of cryptology—combined transposition-substitution. But its special merit lay in its practical tone. The book was imbued with a verisimilitude, an air of this-is-how-things-really-are, that stemmed largely from Hitt's grounding in the realities of signal communication. This pragmatic approach cropped up, for example, in the book's discussions of why cryptanalytic offices should be attached to field headquarters and how they should be organized, of the need for accurate intercept and recording procedures and how they may be achieved, and of how to correct errors in enciphering and transmission—a subject of the utmost practical importance and one almost invariably neglected in treatises. Hitt replaced the waxen examples of other books with real cryptograms, several with Spanish plaintexts, whose presence, in view of the Pershing punitive expedition, intensified the feeling of reality. As a military man, Hitt wrote with directness; as one with an extra measure of intelligence, he wrote with clarity; and as one with a touch of the poet, he flavored his 101 pages with a prairie tang all his own. "As to luck," he observed when discussing the fourth of four factors that determine success in cryptanalysis (the others being perseverance, careful analysis and intuition), "there is the old miner's proverb: 'Gold is where you find it.' "

Yet the book was outdated at the moment of its birth. Events in Europe had far outrun its elementary notions. Cryptograms were no longer being solved on the basis of single messages, as in Hitt's examples. Military ciphers had long since attained a complexity never hinted at in the *Manual*. The

French had anticipated his ideas on cryptanalytic organizations. The Spanish-language examples might better have been German. And in view of the trench codes which were then emerging as the dominant form of cryptography, one sentence was singularly inapt: "The necessity for exact expression of ideas practically excludes the use of codes for military work although," he hedged, "it is possible that a special tactical code might be useful for preparation of tactical orders."

All this is true. Yet it remains equally true that the book filled a real need. Many people, struck by the interest in these matters that war always enlarges, wanted to know about cryptology. But the United States was achingly devoid of information: Hitt's was, in surprising fact, the first book on the subject published in America*—and indeed the first devoted to cryptanalysis in English since Philip Thicknesse's 1772 *A Treatise on the Art of Decyphering*! Soldiers and civilians grabbed at it. A second edition became necessary, and this time 16,000 paperbound copies were run off, giving it a greater circulation than any previous book in the history of cryptology. Elementary it may have been, but for those who knew nothing of the subject, a basic work was what was needed. When the United States declared war, Hitt's *Manual* served as the textbook to train future cryptanalysts of the American Expeditionary Forces. Some of this training was done at the Army War College in Washington under the auspices of MI-8, the cryptologic section (number 8) of the Military Intelligence Division, headed by Herbert O. Yardley, and some at the Riverbank Laboratories in Geneva, Illinois, where cryptologic research, mainly aimed at proving that Bacon wrote Shakespeare, had been carried on since before the war. Riverbank also had some texts of its own.

In doing the research for his book, Hitt ran across a military cipher that greatly impressed him as affording more security than any other that he knew. He, and probably all the other young cryptanalysts at the Signal School, stood aghast at what was then the "official" U.S. Army field cipher. This was the Signal Corps cipher disk, a celluloid device with a reversed cipher alphabet revolving inside a standard plaintext alphabet. The Army used it with a repeating keyword to produce a straight periodic Beaufort cipher. It was equivalent to the Confederate cipher disk of 50 years before and inferior to the cipher disk described by Porta three centuries before that—a record of retrogression unmatched, perhaps, by any science in the world. Even though the cipher disk was the "official" system, Hitt's own 2nd Division used a then-popular cipher called the "Larrabee." It was simply an ordinary Vigenère printed so that the plaintext alphabet was repeated for all 26 cipher alphabets. Neither it nor the cipher disk would have delayed an expert cryptanalyst for more than an hour. On May 19, 1914, Hitt had recommended that the Larrabee be replaced by the Playfair as the 2nd Division cipher, but was

* The only previous works on cryptology to appear in the United States were magazine or encyclopedia articles and two pamphlets—Mauborgne's and a totally obscure work of 31 pages by one Harvey Gray, entitled *Cryptography* and published at Boston in 1874.

turned down. Undaunted, he proposed the new cipher that impressed him so much to the director of the Army Signal School on December 19, 1914.

"This device is based, to a certain extent, on the ideas of Commandant Bazeries, of the French Army," he wrote in his memorandum. Hitt in effect peeled the alphabets off the disks of the Bazeries cylinder and stretched them out in strip form. He cut 25 long slips of paper, printed a mixed alphabet on each of them twice, numbered them, and then arranged them in a holder in the order given by a keynumber. To encipher, he slid the slips up or down until they spelled out the first 20 letters of the message in a horizontal line, and then selected any other line, or generatrix, as the ciphertext, repeating this process until the entire message was enciphered. Hitt's first holder was $7 \times 3\frac{1}{4}$ inches. He also made the device in its original Jefferson-Bazeries form by sawing disks off a cylinder of apple wood.

He requested that the device be forwarded to the Chief Signal Officer. About 1917, his old fellow student at the Signal School, Joseph Mauborgne, then in charge of the Signal Corps Engineering and Research Division, fixed the device in the cylindrical form for the Army and mixed the alphabets much more thoroughly than Hitt had, thereby making solution more difficult. In 1922, the Army issued its M-94, which strung 25 aluminum disks the size of a silver dollar on a spindle $4\frac{1}{4}$ inches long. The M-94 remained in Army service until early in World War II. Between the wars, both the Coast Guard and the Radio Intelligence Division of the Federal Communications Commission made use of it. In the 1930s, the Army reverted to Hitt's slide form in its cipher device M-138-A, which improved on the Hitt device by providing 100 slides, 30 of which were used at a time. The State Department adopted the M-138-A in the late 1930s and early 1940s as its most secret method of communication. The Navy likewise used it very widely in World War II. It was commonly called the "strip system." Thus Hitt's few paper slides became one of the most widely used systems in the history of American cryptography.

In 1917, Hitt went to France with Pershing's staff as assistant to the Chief Signal Officer. When the A.E.F's 1st Army was formed, Hitt became its Chief Signal Officer. Though there was no cryptology involved in this job, his book had made him the American expert on the subject, and his advice was often sought. It was even followed, since Hitt was widely respected.

While he was overseas, his wife, Genevieve, who was operating the code room at Fort Sam Houston in San Antonio, struck up a friendship with a young lieutenant and his wife who lived across the way. Their names were Dwight and Mamie Eisenhower, and the friendship of the two families stretched across the years. One morning during World War II the Hitts stumbled across Ike, stretched out asleep in the living room of their home in Front Royal, Virginia, and in the 1950s Parker Hitt attended one of the famous and exclusive stag dinners given by the President at the White House.

When the United States entered the war, its Army had no official codemaking or codebreaking agency. Codes were occasionally compiled, of course, and each unit seemed to prescribe its own field ciphers, as Hitt found out when he tried to replace the Larrabee with the Playfair. Any cryptanalysis was on a strictly informal basis, like the messages that were sent to Hitt, often with a request like that from the acting intelligence officer of the Southern Department on March 7, 1917: "1. The inclosed cipher messages have been received from the Chief of the War College Division, General Staff. 2. It is requested that you decipher them as they are unable to do it in Washington. 3. The results obtained are desired at the earliest practicable date." (Hitt returned these on March 10 saying that they appeared to be in code and that he could not read them.) Usually Hitt had to squeeze this work in among his regular duties. The Riverbank Laboratories also did some informal cryptanalysis for the War Department.

It was obvious, upon the arrival of the first token units of the American Expeditionary Force in France in the spring of 1917, that the A.E.F. would have both cryptographic and cryptanalytic work to do. Consequently, General Orders No. 8 of July 5, 1917, which established the A.E.F. headquarters organization, provided for these functions. It assigned "American codes and ciphers" to the Signal Corps but gave "policy regarding preparation and issue of ciphers and trench codes" to the Intelligence Division, probably because this was also charged with "enemy's wireless and ciphers" and "examining of enemy's ciphers." Having the cryptanalysts supervise the cryptographers was excellent in theory—and it worked out fine in practice. The two organizations that came into being in accordance with this order collaborated closely throughout the war. One was G.2 A.6, the Radio Intelligence Section (the 6) of the Military Information Division (the A) of the Intelligence Section (the 2) of the General Staff (the G). The other was the Code Compilation Section of the Signal Corps. Both were stationed at American G.H.Q. at Chaumont, a town on the Marne about 150 miles east of Paris.

The Code Compilation Section was set up in December of 1917. There had been no real need for it before then because the United States had no troops in the line. In command was Howard R. Barnes, a 40-year-old Ohioan who had been commissioned a captain because of his ten years of experience in the State Department code room. Under him were three lieutenants and a corporal. The unit examined and discarded the three means of secret communications then authorized for the A.E.F.—the War Department Telegraph Code, which, as Voris had pointed out, was unsuited to tactical work, the cipher disk, whose security was nil, and the Playfair, which could not sustain security under regular use, but could and did serve as an emergency system.

Cryptography on the Western Front had evolved through ciphers to codes, and Barnes, bowing to this experience, began the task—never before attempted in the American Army—of compiling a codebook in the field. His section studied an obsolete trench code that the British had reluctantly turned over, made firsthand observations of communication needs at the front, and drew up *The American Trench Code*, of 1,600 elements, and the *Front-Line Code*, of 500. Both were one-part codes to be used with a monoalphabetic superencipherment. The 1,000 copies of the *Trench Code* were distributed only down to regimental headquarters, and the 3,000 copies of the *Front-Line Code* to companies. They served as the American cryptosystems during the first weeks of real A.E.F. participation in the war—the weeks of Château-Thierry and Belleau Wood.

But the system of enciphered code did not last long. Barnes frequently consulted with Hitt—"To him more than to any other officer of the American Army is due whatever success the American Codes may have obtained," he later wrote—and Hitt suggested testing the superencipherment. G.2 A.6 lent Lieutenant J. Rives Childs. On May 17, 1918, Childs was given a copy of the codebook and 44 superenciphered messages. Within five hours—three of them spent just in making frequency counts—he had recovered the encipherment alphabet. At about the same time, Barnes and his men realized that a superencipherment imposed extra delay and extra work upon the encoders at the front, with all the dangers that that entailed. Superenciphered code would have to be junked. But what would the A.E.F. use?

Barnes was in close contact with Major Frank Moorman, chief of G.2 A.6, and it may have been Moorman who proposed that the A.E.F. use unenciphered two-part codes changed either before the Germans could solve them—a period estimated at from two to four weeks—or upon the capture of a book. On May 24, Hitt was writing to Moorman: "I concur in your ideas about the trench code book. I believe that we can republish it every two weeks . . . ." Barnes, who was no cryptanalyst, acquiesced in the views of those who were. Frequent replacement was the principle of the Satzbuch, but the American codes were intended for service closer to the front. Thus the burden of augmenting security was lifted from the front-line soldiers and thrown, in the form of the more complicated two-part arrangement and the rapid replacement of codes, on the relatively undistracted personnel at headquarters.

On June 24, 1918, the Code Compilation Section published the first of the superb series of A.E.F. field codes—the *Potomac*. A 47-page booklet, it contained about 1,800 words and phrases for tactical needs (*during the night* = ANF, *machine gun ammunition* = APU). About 2,000 copies were printed and turned over to G-2 for distribution as far down as battalion headquarters. It went into service on July 15. The *Potomac* set the pattern for subsequent codes, which were printed and held in reserve, one set at army headquarters, a second at General Headquarters. Thus when, as expected, the *Potomac Code* was captured a few weeks after its publication, it took only two days to issue the *Suwanee* to the entire A.E.F. The *Wabash* moved into place as the back-up code and then, 16 days later, into service. It was followed by the *Mohawk*, *Allegheny*, *Hudson*, and *Colorado* codes at intervals of 3, 9, 21, and 22 days.

328   *THE CODEBREAKERS*

The rapid growth of the A.E.F. necessitated an increase in the number of copies printed to 3,200, but this also increased the danger of capture. So with the formation of the 2nd Army, a series of codes named for lakes was instituted on October 7 for the use of that army, while the river series was continued for the 1st Army. The *Champlain, Huron, Osage,* and *Seneca*

Stop...3514		1629...-non
Stopped...3329..4017		1630...6-inch
Storm...4211		1631...'s
Strength...1740..2329		1633...A
Strength of enemy unknown...3961		1636...Was
Strengthen...1679		1638...Does not
Stretcher bearers...3166	Nulls:	1640...Will be
Strike...5056	2809	1644...Bengal flares
Strip...3515	4286	1645...Our wire
Strong...3131	2094	1646...And
Sub...5639	2553	1647...-ied
Succeed...3237	2399	1648...Darkness
Success...1790		1651...Unit
Successful...5746		1652...Indication
Sudden...3136		1654...Yard
Suffer...3058		1655...Enemy machine gun
Suffocate...2770		1658...Prepare
Sun...5890		1659...............
Sunday...2167		1663...Slow
Superior...4160		1665...U
Supplies...1695..2600..5333		1667...Damage
Supply...3005		1669...Together
Supply train...5557		1671...Telegraph
Support...4968..4049..2799		1672...Result
Supported...4162		1673...Troops
Surface...2097		1674...Favorably
Surprise...4414..3141		1675...Make ready
Surrounded...3745		1676...No patrols
Suspect...1871		1679...Strengthen
Sweep...3100		1681...-nt
T...3821..3626..4971..4790		1683... (Null)
Take...3331..2561		1684...49
Take place.. 4904..4403		1685...Question mark
Taken...1972..4083		1691...64
Tank...3287..3408		1693...The

Portions of the encoding and decoding sections of the A.E.F.'s Hudson Code

codes were issued to the 2nd Army at intervals of 8, 13, and 9 days. At the Armistice, the *Niagara Code* was in press and the *Michigan* and *Rio Grande* codes in manuscript. In the five months between June and November, the section turned out nearly three codes a month—a noteworthy achievement, particularly in comparison with what the other belligerents accomplished.

The Code Compilation Section printed its codes under conditions of tightest security at the Adjutant General's printing office at Chaumont. Codes took priority over all other work except general orders and bulletins. Under favorable conditions, a field code would go from manuscript to binder in five or six days. Each code was proofread twice. "During the process of printing," Barnes wrote, "the codes were under the constant supervision of an officer whose duty it was to destroy all spoiled sheets containing impressions even to the mats on the presses. All copies were counted and accounted for and the metal type melted down after the final impression. In many cases, two or three officers were on duty in the printing office keeping the various operations in sight." The size of an edition was determined by G-2. Because the courier service refused to carry the heavy packages of codebooks, G.2 A.6, whose personnel realized the importance of secrecy in communications, took over the actual distribution of copies. Officers at the headquarters where the codes were kept in reserve were ordered to make frequent checks of the number of packages and the seals on them. A British officer was dumfounded when he heard that American codes could be prepared in ten days, saying that it would take his army at least a month.

Their cryptanalytic resistance was, as with the enciphered code, gauged by actual test. This time the results were positive. Members of G.2 A.6 reported that the system, while not insoluble, excelled that of the Germans. Coded messages had been sent to the British for further examination. Hay reported that "We have not been able to solve them or even to get any light. The security appears of a high order." Hitchings wrote: "I am sending you a short survey of our observations on the 41 messages. . . . we have not succeeded in solving them, but you will see in the enclosed survey a few possible lines of attack." And while Parker Hitt had not tried to solve any messages in the code, his general experience led him to say, "We believe that this code system will be better than anything now in use on either side."

These field codes served primarily for communication within each division, though they also encoded messages between divisions and to higher headquarters. Battalions on the flanks of each army exchanged codebooks to permit intercommunication. The A.E.F. supplemented them with a variety of others needed by a modern army and prepared by the Code Compilation Section. Troops in the very first trenches used the *Emergency Code List*, a single sheet with about 50 common expressions represented in two-part arrangement by two-letter groups (CM = *message not understood*; PV =*our artillery is shelling us*). It resembled the carnet de chiffre. New editions were distributed at the same time as new editions of the field codes. For headquarters work Barnes' section produced 1,000 copies of the massive *Staff Code*: 30,400 words and phrases, whose four-letter codewords, in one-part order, were superenciphered digraphically, with different tables for G-1, G-2, G-3, G-4, and G-5. It was probably the largest codebook ever printed in the field. There were also special codes for reporting casualties, for technical

SECRET — EMERGENCY CODE LIST

To be used only with Field Code No. 1.
To be issued down to companies.
To be used only for communications within divisions.
To be completely destroyed, by burning, when in danger of capture or after a new code has been issued.

Precede Every Message in This Code by "C 1"

About to advance...BY	AB...Left
Ammunition exhausted...FB	AF...Enemy machine gun fire serious
Are advancing...PX	AG...Gas is being released
At...SX	AP...Stretcher bearers needed
Attack failed...BM	AV...Recall working party
Attack successful...PF	AW...Casualties heavy
Barrage wanted...XF	AX...Using gas shells
Be ready to attack...ZF	AZ...Relief completed
Being relieved...XA	BD...How is everything
Captured...CB	BF...Right
Casualties heavy...AW	BJ...Situation serious
Casualties light...FZ	BM...Attack failed
Center...PB	BP...Enemy trenches
Enemy...FC	BS...Raiders have left
Enemy barrage commenced...PV	BX...Falling back
Enemy fire has destroyed...SP	BY...About to advance
Enemy machine gun fire serious...AF	CA...Everything O. K.
Enemy trenches...BP	CB...Captured
Everything O. K...CA	CM...Reinforcements needed
Everything quiet...XG	CP...Need water
Falling back...BX	CX...Machine gun ammunition needed
Gas is being released...AG	CZ...Objective reached
Have broken through...SA	FA...Not ready
How is everything...BD	FB...Ammunition exhausted
Increase range...SB	FC...Enemy
Left...AB	FM...Our artillery is shelling us
Look out for signal...SZ	FS...Using high explosive shells
Machine gun ammunition needed...CX	FX...Stopped
Message not understood...PO	FY...Situation improving
Message received...ZX	FZ...Casualties light
Near...SM	PB...Center
Need water...CP	PF...Attack successful
Not ready...FA	PG...Strong attack
Objective reached...CZ	PM...Trenches
Our...XP	PO...Message not understood
Our artillery is shelling us...FM	PV...Enemy barrage commenced
Raiders have left...BS	PX...Are advancing
Recall working party...AV	SA...Have broken through
Reinforcements needed...CM	SB...Increase range
Relief being sent...XY	SC...Troops
Relief completed...AZ	SF...Tank stuck
Rifle ammunition needed...XB	SM...Near
Right...BF	SP...Enemy fire has destroyed
Rush...ZP	SX...At
Situation improving...FY	SZ...Look out for signal
Situation serious...BJ	XA...Being relieved
Stopped...FX	XB...Rifle ammunition needed
Stretcher bearers needed...AP	XF...Barrage wanted
Strong attack...PG	XG...Everything quiet
Tank stuck...SF	XP...Our
Trenches...PM	XY...Relief being sent
Trenches have been occupied...ZJ	ZB...Wire entanglements destroyed

Front-line cryptography: an A.E.F. code list issued for use in the trenches

radio matters, for extra secrecy at six major telegraph posts in reporting troop movements, and for designating the names of organizations and officers over the telephone by using women's names as jargon (*28th Division* = JENNIE; *Chief of Staff* = DOW; *Chief of Staff of 28th Division* = JENNIE DOW). In its ten months of active work, the section printed more than 80,000 codebooks and pamphlets, all numbered, recorded, issued and receipted for.

In addition to these official codes, many A.E.F. units cooked up their own unauthorized ones. In the 82nd Division, for example, officers said GREAT NECK for *Grosreuves* and BUZZARD for *1st Battalion, 326th Infantry*. Some anonymous but avid baseball fan in the 52nd Infantry Brigade produced the gem of these unofficial systems. If *we were under bombardment*, it was WAGNER AT BAT; if the Germans simply lobbed over some *enemy registration fire*, WAGNER BUNTED; if *we were under light bombardment*, WAGNER DOUBLED, and if *we were under heavy bombardment*, WAGNER (whose nickname, it will be remembered, was "Hans") KNOCKED A HOME RUN. Juvenile all this may be, but if codes are to delay enemy comprehension, this one no doubt served its purpose.

But the finest codes in the world, changed at the most rapid intervals, are worthless if wrongly used. Did the American doughboy fulfill his opportunity under these codes to achieve a superior security of communication? He did not. His irritation at the nuisance of encoding and his consequent unconcern for regulations could be matched against any combatant's. Encoding delayed signaling, and combat officers bitterly resented this gumming of communications just when they were most needed. Aversion became so extreme that at one point a general actually gave his division specific orders to use no code before and during an important movement. The order was undoubtedly born of some unhappy experiences, and it was, in any case, less dangerous than any semicoding or other violations of coding regulations, such as sending messages to addressees not having the code, necessitating repeats either in clear or another system. The well-known American disregard for regulations —especially ones as persnickety as these—and the tendency to take the easiest way out caused G.2 A.6 chief Moorman to remark exasperatedly that "there certainly never existed on the western front a force more negligent in the use of their own code than was the American Army."

Violations, in fact, became so numerous that a Security Service was set up to monitor American radio messages (later, telephone conversations as well). Its first station began operating at Toul on July 11, 1918; eventually the A.E.F. had four. The messages were sent to an officer in G.2 A.6 who studied them for practices that would help the Germans in solution. Letters pointed these faults out to commanders. One sent by the adjutant general to the commanding general of the 1st Army relating to a single message of September 17, pointed out that the plaintext *Boche*, spelled out by five code groups, could have been replaced by *German* or *enemy*, each a single code-group, that two groups for *day light* could have been used instead of the 18 for *almost before the crack of dawn*, that *work* could have been written instead of *business* with a saving of seven groups, and so on.

Most of these rather fussy letters were ignored. "Only a few of these were answered," Moorman complained, "and in these cases the action taken was entirely inadequate. In one case an officer was reprimanded by his commander. In others the excuse was made that officers did not know or were too busy or thought they were justified in their action.... in trying to check up and eliminate faults we have found great willingness and ability to refer us to someone else." He proffered a unique solution of his own to end the vexing problem: "My idea would be to hang a few of the offenders. This would not only get rid of some but would discourage the development of others. It would be a saving of lives to do it." Barnes' more moderate idea of assigning a cryptographic control officer to each headquarters was preferred, but it did not go into practice until 20 years later.

Perhaps the most interesting thing about the entire American cryptographic operation was the attitude taken toward it by Barnes and his men. They did not regard their codes as immutable; rather they sought continually to improve them. Further, their efforts encompassed the physical as well as the cryptographic aspects. Paper, for example, was chosen so that it would stand up just long enough for the brief life of the book and would burn easily in case of danger. The typeface—named "Typewriter"—was picked for its legibility in the ill-lit dugouts of the front. The books continually shrank in size from the $7\frac{1}{4} \times 9\frac{3}{4}$ inches of the *Potomac* to the $5\frac{1}{2} \times 7\frac{1}{2}$ of the *Colorado* and subsequent books. In the later books, nulls were prominently bunched next to the encoding columns to encourage their use, and common suffixes, such as *-ing*, were listed conveniently at the bottom of each page. Homophones grew more abundant, and blanks were provided for special terms or names needed within the different divisions. A G-2 circular inviting suggestions brought in many requests to include certain phrases. To use them all would have swollen the book beyond easily manageable proportions, and Barnes winnowed out the many local and transitory ones. But the adaptability of the Code Compiling Section is shown by the fact that almost half of the 1,900 words and phrases in the *Osage Code* were new compared to those in the *Potomac*.

The section never satisfactorily resolved a continuing dispute over the relative merits of letters or numbers as codegroups, though it consulted many telegraphists, radio operators, code clerks, and experienced code officers. Opinion was almost equally divided. Most of the codes used three-letter codegroups, but a few were published with four-digit ones in an apparent experiment to see which actually worked best. The same undogmatic approach was demonstrated in the submission of the books for cryptanalytic tests, and in the testing of 50,000 telegraphic combinations to empirically select those resulting in the fewest errors as codegroups for the *Staff Code*.

In short, the Code Compiling Section was willing to learn, and it did learn a great deal that notably improved American codes. To an astonishing degree, it encapsulated "that practical, inventive turn of mind, quick to find expedients," that historian Frederick Jackson Turner found the frontier had shaped as an American trait. Perhaps this is best epitomized—with the important addition of some American humor—by the codegroup to report that the code had been lost. The early codes did not even have one. The *Hudson Code* displayed in large type on its cover, "Memorize this Group: '2222—Code Lost.'" Then the codegroup for *Code Lost* was changed to DAM.

To the right of the imposing dark stone headquarters building at Chaumont stood an undistinguished, single-story barracks of glass and concrete. Sometimes called the "Glass House," the caserne housed the other half of the American cryptologic effort, the Radio Intelligence Section, G.2 A.6.

Its chief, Moorman, 40, a native of Greenville, Michigan, was a blue-eyed, brown-haired Regular Army man who had worked his way up through the infantry ranks from private. He was a 1915 graduate of the Army Signal School and knew enough about cryptanalysis to devise an ingenious method for almost automatically determining the letters of a Playfair keyword. Hitt thought it valuable enough to include in his *Manual*. In France, however, Moorman did not engage in any actual cryptanalysis, except perhaps to help out, since his work as head of G.2 A.6 was administrative, not operative. As a boss he was well regarded by his men for his fairness and blunt honesty.

His organization began to take rudimentary shape in the fall of 1917 with a mere handful of men, the nucleus of what became a 72-man unit at the period of the A.E.F.'s maximum expansion. They came from the most varied civilian occupations. There were two New York lawyers, both lieutenants—Hugo A. Berthold, who was of Germanic extraction, knew the language well, and became Moorman's chief assistant and head of code cryptanalysis, and Robert Gilmore. Childs, who had solved the superencipherment, had been a reporter on the Baltimore *American* before taking his M.A. at Harvard in 1915. Lieutenant Lee West Sellers was a New York music critic, and Lieutenant John Graham an instructor at Washington and Lee University, later a professor of Romance languages there. There was an architect who had studied Hebrew, Persian, and other Oriental tongues; one man was a chess expert, another an amateur archaeologist. About the only two who had had any experience at all with codes or ciphers were Corporal Joseph P. Nathan, who had worked in the code section of the Grace Line in New York, and one not unknown to later fame, Lieutenant William F. Friedman, who had become interested in the subject several years earlier. In addition to these men, six cryptanalysts were assigned to each army headquarters to decrypt intercepts from their front with keys from G.H.Q.

The work of G.2 A.6 divided into cryptanalysis and four minor areas—traffic analysis, intercepting enemy telephone conversations, following enemy air artillery spotters, and checking monitored American communications for security breaches. These minor functions made more important contributions than it would at first seem. Moorman, for example, originally did not consider the traffic analysis particularly necessary. But he saw its value when his men became skilled enough to draw a map of the German order of battle and to see through German fake messages. They even managed to discover two newly formed armies and thus help give warning of a new German drive. The aircraft teams eavesdropped on the planes as they signaled targets to their batteries and warned Allied troops that they were about to be fired upon; sometimes the G.2 A.6 experts even identified the battery that was about to fire, permitting Allied counterbatteries to shell them first.

The monitoring officer, Lieutenant Woellner, came up with some frightening object lessons. He deduced the entire American order of battle for the assault on the Saint-Mihiel salient from monitored telephone messages, missing the time of attack by 24 hours only because one speaker had misstated it! Most of his information came from a single switchboard operator who complained that certain lines had been broken by tanks and heavy artillery moving into a small woods near him all night. "Whether or not the Germans picked up this message we never learned," Moorman commented disgustedly, "but it is certain that this one operator did all that could be reasonably expected of one man in the matter of telling the Germans when and where the attack would take place and the forces to be engaged."

Like the other sections, the cryptanalysts got off to a slow start. Their training had been all in ciphers, whereas the Germans were using code. In November of 1917, Berthold went to the French cipher bureau, where he picked up some instruction and probably some current KRU solutions as well. With this help, G.2 A.6 discovered that certain nearby German stations radioed regular reports at regular hours—a habit that thenceforth proved fatal to many a Satzbuch. By the end of the first week of a code's month-long life, Moorman said, "we were reading some of the routine messages.... At the end of the second week we were reading many of the messages, and at the end of the third week we practically controlled the code. This really meant that we had for one week a real control of each code."

G.2 A.6's first real victory in the war of the intercepts came with the introduction of the Schlüsselheft. The success was due in large measure to the alertness of the Signal Corps' Radio Section, which operated the network of intercept stations that fed the cryptanalysts their raw material. The first stations were set up in the fall of 1917, and by the end of the war the five posts had snatched 72,688 German messages from the airwaves. Eight direction-finding stations took the astonishing total of 176,913 bearings. The radio operators, frequently working in damp and drafty shacks exposed to enemy fire, won high praise from the cryptanalysts for the accuracy of their interception of long strings of meaningless letters. Often they picked up messages that the other Allies had not heard, and this was what happened on March 11, 1918.

It was at midnight of that date that the Germans placed into service not merely a new code, but one that, from its numerical codegroups, appeared to be of a different breed entirely. The Allies were expecting a major German push, and the appearance of this code was considered another straw in the wind. Its solution would obviously be of importance in giving clues to German activities. Though the British had suggested that a superencipherment might be involved, the precise nature of the system had to be determined, the superencipherment stripped off, and the repertory then built up. This would have imposed much greater difficulties than just solving another Satzbuch edition—except for American alertness.

Forty minutes after midnight, the American intercept post at Souilly picked up one of the first messages in the new system. Station x2 was sending it to Station ÄN:

00:25 CHI-13 845 422 373 792 240 245 068 652 781 245 659 659 504

At 12:52 ÄN replied: CHI-13 OS RGV KZD. Five minutes later x2 sent a second message to ÄN:

00:25 CHI-14 UYC REM KUL RHI KWZ RLF RNQ KRD RVJ UOB KUU UQX UFQ RQK

When these appeared on the desk of Berthold, head of code cryptanalysis, he guessed at once what had happened: x2 sends a 13-group cipher message (CHI-13) in a new system. ÄN responds with OS, a well-known service abbreviation for *Ohne Sinn* ("message unintelligible"), and a reference to CHI-13, followed by two groups from the old KRU code. Whereupon x2 sends a second message, this time in KRU but with the original time group (00:25). The old KRU had been partially solved, and Berthold knew that the RGV of the short ÄN message meant "old." He did not know the meaning of KZD, but it seemed likely in view of what happened that it meant "Send in code," making the whole phrase "Send in old code." Could the Germans have been so stupid as to compromise their new code within an hour after putting it into service by sending the same message in both the old and the new systems?

Berthold's blue eyes fairly snapped and the few pale wisps of hair that lay against his bald pate almost stood up with excitement as he decoded the second x2 message with his reconstructed KRU. It read:

UYC REM KUL RHI KWZ RLF RNQ KRD RVJ UOB KUU UQX UFQ RQK
An [?] Bn. 2   h   i   r   sch   w   i   tt e

The KWZ and UOB appeared to be nulls, used—almost certainly in violation of regulations—as word dividers, and REM probably meant *Kommandant*. When Berthold checked this against the second message, he saw at once that it had the same plaintext. The repetitions of the plaintext *i*'s and *t*'s, which had been masked by the homophones and the lexicon of the KRU code, appeared clearly in the trinumeral message as the repeated 245s and 659s. With these four points as anchors, Berthold could set up the following equivalencies:

845 422 373 792 240 245 068 652 781 245 659 659 504
An   [?]   Bn.   2   h   i   r   sch   w   i   t   t   e

A staff airplane sped his result to the British cryptanalytic bureau, and Berthold telegraphed it in a special codebreakers' code to the French. It was a Rosetta Stone for what turned out to be the new Schlüsselheft. The three bureaus cooperated closely, but it was largely due to Painvin's genius that within two days they had neutralized the Geheimklappe superencipherment and dismembered much of the lexicon. By March 21, when the expected German blow fell, Allied cryptanalysts were reading Schlüsselheft messages better than the German code clerks themselves. Theoretically no important information was supposed to be carried in it, because it was intended only for low-level, front-line communications. But theory succumbed at times of great activity, when the information was most desirable, and the trinumeral messages were laden with valuable nuggets. "The sending of this one message must certainly have cost the lives of thousands of Germans," Moorman said, "and conceivably it changed the result of one of the greatest efforts made by the German armies."

As G.2 A.6 gained experience, it gained speed. Perhaps the most dramatic demonstration came at 9:05 p.m. April 28, when the Germans ordered an attack for 1 a.m. The message was intercepted, telegraphed to headquarters, cryptanalyzed, and employed to warn American troops half an hour before the Hun assault. Despite this rather sensational demonstration, the higher-ups seemed dissatisfied. They felt, Moorman protested, "that we were doing a lot of unnecessary work. What they wanted us to do was pick out the important messages, decode them, and let the rest go. They understood that the greater part of these messages were valueless and so thought what was the use of bothering with them. It was a matter of considerable difficulty to make them see that we had to work them out and that the Germans did not tag their important messages before sending them."

During the summer of 1918 G.2 A.6 received considerable help from a source that was seeking to hamper it. Code discipline had grown lax among the signal troops of the German 5th Army, which faced the American forces, and one Lieutenant Jaeger was detailed to stiffen it. He knew what should be done and issued numerous orders to do it. Unfortunately, he overlooked the circumstance that the German codebooks did not include his name, which therefore had to be spelled out letter by letter every time he affixed it to an order. This was frequently. Its peculiar formation—the repetition of the high-frequency *e*, for example—permitted G.2 A.6 to identify it readily, and this in turn led to important clues concerning the superenciphering Geheimklappe and, in one case, to the identification of 40 groups in a new Schlüsselheft. Perhaps it was Jaeger who, before his assignment to the 5th Army, coined one of the unforgettable slogans of communication security—which was, fittingly enough, read by G.2 A.6: *Weh dem der leugt und Klartext funkt* ("Woe to him who lies and radios in clear"). Jaeger was beloved by his adversaries because he kept them up to date with code changes, and it was with genuine regret that they saw his name disappear from the German traffic.

The older, battle-wise cryptanalytic bureaus of France and England developed increasing respect for their younger protégé as it gradually proved itself, and the tendency was nurtured by the effective liaison work of Childs. A 25-year-old Virginian, he displayed enough diplomatic ability to later become American ambassador to Saudi Arabia, Yemen, and Ethiopia, and sufficient command of French to later write a book in it (on Nicolas Restif de la Bretonne, a bawdy French novelist on whom, along with Casanova, Childs became an international authority). On visits in the spring and summer of 1918, Childs built up friendly relations with Hay, Brooke-Hunt, Hitchings, and Cartier; he enjoyed a particular rapport with Painvin, under whom he studied for a week.

Childs headed the small group that concentrated on German ciphers, a post he had obtained because Moorman mistakenly thought he was an amateur cryptologist from New York with the same name. Moorman made him liaison officer because of his impressive showing with the American trench code superencipherment—though up to that time Childs, despite diligent application of the principles he had been taught, had not solved a single German message. His ignorance was so abysmal that in London Brooke-Hunt lost all interest in him as soon as he discovered it. As a sop he told Childs about the German Für GOD cipher and furnished him with the keys. Childs soon discovered that the apparently incoherent keys were actually monoalphabetically enciphered versions of words like INSTRUMENT-ENMACHER and GOLDARBEITER. It became his personal turning point.

On August 5, an American intercept station picked up a 456-letter message addressed to the German Foreign Office from General Kress von Kressenstein. He had recently been shifted from Syria to Tiflis to prevent the rich oil fields of the Caucasus from falling into Turkish hands. This question of friction between allies acutely interested Britain, for it affected not only her Mesopotamian campaign but also the whole future of Persia and the gateways to India.

The intercept began: PZÄVE PNBJY GJCGB PZAV PFAVG BPFHG YZAN RPBBP GOWIB PCBPR OOBP XBEGH ÄVBRW . . . . Childs took his frequency count, found to his gratification that the immense frequency of ciphertext B could only mean that it represented plaintext e in a monoalphabetic substitution, and within an hour had broken the message. Von Kressenstein was reporting the unconfirmed capture of Baku, heart of the oil basin, by Turkey. The Turkish leader, Enver Pasha, had assured him that he was moving into Baku only to improve his sanitary arrangements, and von Kressenstein was reciprocating this obvious trust. "To make the Turkish advance more difficult," he stated, "I have hampered every shipment of munitions from Batum via Tiflis up to the present time." Childs' solution was important enough to be included verbatim in a printed G-2 survey of the Caucasus and Central Asia. It demonstrated to the Allies that the Turco-German split had gone deep enough for one to deprive the other of the very essentials of combat in a struggle for national existence.

If Childs wondered in his elation why so important a message was being clothed in so flimsy a cipher, he discovered the answer a few days later when

SECRET

GENERAL HEADQUARTERS

GENERAL STAFF, SECOND SECTION (G.2 A.6)

(DISTRIBUTION "E")   June 21, 1918.

SPECIAL CODE REPORT.

The following telegrams were transmitted in the five-letter cipher used by the German High Command. (Argonne Sector or West).

From station DIY to station DVM.
Sent at 08:21   31st May;   intercepted by Neufchatel. (2 parts)
German text: "SIEBEN R D UEBERSCHREITET NEUN KOMMA DREI NULL VORM STRASSE AOUGNY ROMIGNY
ANGRIFF AUF VILLE EN TARDENOIS STATTFINDET NICHT
STAB HOEHE SUEDWESTL. CHERY."

Translation:
"7th Reserve Division will cross road Aougny-Romigny at 9:30 a.m. Attack on Ville en Tardenois will not take place. Staff on heights southwest of Chery."

From station GID to station GWF.
Sent at 08:50   31 May; intercepted by Nancy.
German text: "SCHER PUNKT SCHARF LINKS LEGEN A O K SIEBEN."
Translation:
"Lay cutting-off point sharply to the left. Army Hdqrs. 7"

From station DLK to station DVM.
Sent at 08:50   31st May intercepted By Chalons.
German Text: "SIEBEN FUENF ZEHN VORM. EIGENE INF AM DREI ECKS WALD.
EINS FUENF NULL NULL M SUEDOESTL. ST GEMME SCHLECHTEN.."

Translation:
"7:15 a.m. our infantry at (three corner?) woods, 1500 meters southeast of St Gemme. Bad ...."

From station DLK to station DVM.
Sent at 09:02   31st May; Intercepted by Neufchatel.
German Text: "ANGRIFF IN GUTEM FORTSCHREITEN VORDERE LINIE HAT NORDRAND PASSY ERREICHT."

Translation:
"Attack making good progress. Front line has reached north edge of Passy."

From station DRW to station GIN.
Sent at 12:02   31st May; intercepted by Nancy.
German Text: "HABT IHR F.T. VERBINDUNG ZU GRUPPEN BUND".
Translation: "Have you wireless connection with group liaison center".

G.2 A.6 distributes its solutions of ADFGX cryptograms

he read a message from Berlin in another and far more secure system. "The cipher method prepared by General von Kress was solved here at once. Its further use is forbidden."

Extremely alert, Childs pounced on the freaks of German encipherment and twisted them to American advantage. The Germans, for example, were still using a double transposition that they called the ALACHI as one of their systems of secret communication with their forces in Russian Georgia and the Near East. On July 24, two ALACHI messages were intercepted, one of 226 letters from Berlin to a small post at Tiflis, the other of 152 letters from Tiflis to Constantinople. The Berlin message resisted all attempts at solution, but Childs discovered that the encipherer at Tiflis had omitted the second transposition. He solved it as a simple columnar with a 22-number key. When he applied this key twice to the other message, he read it with ease. It proved to be a message signed by General Erich Ludendorff, the German chief of staff.

In another case, Childs noticed that the second part of a message from Berlin to Constantinople on November 1 was repeated the next day with the addition of only two letters. Using the slight difference as a fulcrum, Childs levered back and forth from one message to another like a bridge player working a ruff and within an hour and a half on the afternoon of November 2 had solved them both. At this time and on this front, German keys remained in effect for three days, and when he used them to read a long message of November 3 in 13 parts, he detonated a small bomb of excitement at G.H.Q.

"By reason of its length," Childs wrote later, "I was persuaded before the message had even been reduced to German plaintext, a long and tedious task, that it was likely to contain information of more than ordinary interest.... Every available German translator of the Section was pressed into service, while I superintended the conversion of the ciphertext to German, of which language I was almost entirely ignorant save for that instinctive feel for the mechanics of it which any cryptographer acquires from such intimate daily contact with it as I had had."

It turned out to be a highly revealing review of the situation in the Balkans as seen by the German commander there, Field Marshal August von Mackensen. The dynamite was in the twelfth part, where Mackensen proposed "that the army of occupation be withdrawn from Rumania at once." The conqueror's jackboots there were enforcing a particularly harsh peace treaty, and it was not beyond conjecture that the Rumanians would rise in fury as soon as the military restraint was removed and fall upon the Germans from behind. This possibility suddenly brightened for the Allies with the information extracted from the Mackensen telegram. Accordingly, as soon as it was deciphered and translated, Berthold grasped Childs by the sleeve and rushed with him and the telegram to the office of the assistant chief of staff. When the colonel there read it, he caught Berthold's excitement, and he dashed out of the office carrying the telegram. He returned to say that its contents had been communicated to the Supreme War Council. A few days later, when Mackensen evacuated Bucharest to the hooting of the crowd, the Rumanian government denounced the peace treaty and declared war anew upon Germany.

The Mackensen message was in the ADFGVX system—probably the most famous field cipher in all cryptology. It was so named because only those six letters appeared in the cryptograms,* though just five were used (no v) when the system sprang into use on March 5, 1918.

The war in the West had by then become a stalemate of exhaustion. The young recruits who the Kaiser had promised in the glorious summer of 1914 would be "home before the leaves fall" had become veterans hardened by almost four years of battle—those few who survived. The flower of England's youth had perished; in France, a generation had climbed out of the trenches and vanished forever.

During the winter, Germany had come to realize that she would have to win in the spring if she were to win at all. The U-boat had failed to starve England into submission, and the United States had entered the war against her. But the collapse of Russia had freed dozens of German divisions for service on the Western Front and, for the first time, Germany held a numerical preponderance there. This, however, was only until America could transport her strong young forces across the Atlantic. It was to be now or never, and the imperial government lashed its weary troops and hungry civilians for the supreme effort that was to bring final victory.

It was no less clear to the Allies that Germany planned to launch a climactic offensive in the spring. There were many signs—the new cipher itself was one. The question was: Where and when would the actual blow fall? The German high command, recognizing the incalculable military value of surprise, shrouded its plans in the tightest secrecy. Artillery was brought up in concealment; feints were flung out here and there along the entire front to keep the Allies off balance; the ADFGVX cipher, which had reportedly been chosen from among many candidates by a conference of German cipher specialists, constituted an element in this overall security, as did the new Schlüsselheft. The Allies bent every effort and tapped every source of information to find out the time and place of the real assault. But one of their most flowing founts—cryptanalysis—appeared to have dried up.

When the first ADFGX messages were brought to Painvin, the best cryptanalyst in the Bureau du Chiffre, he stared at them, ran a hand through his thick black hair with an air of perplexity, and then set to work. The presence of only five letters immediately suggested a checkerboard. Without much hope, he tried the messages as simple monalphabetics; the tests were, as he had expected, negative. He discarded a polyalphabetic checkerboard as too cumbersome, and was left with the hypothesis that the checkerboard substitution had been subjected to a transposition. On this basis he began to work.

Nothing happened. The traffic was too light for him even to determine by frequency counts whether the checkerboard key changed each day, and with-

---

* These six were apparently chosen because their International Morse symbols were sufficiently distinct to minimize garbles: A · —   D — · ·   F · · — ·   G — — ·   V · · · —   X — · · —

out this basic information he did not dare to amalgamate the cryptograms of successive days for a concerted assault. Cartier looked on over his shoulder as he braided and unbraided the letters and mused sadly, "Poor Painvin. This time I don't think you'll get it." Painvin, goaded, worked harder than before. Meanwhile, Berthold achieved his Schlüsselheft entry and Painvin, shifting temporarily to that more fruitful field, completed it. But the enciphered code, used only for trench communications, provided no strategic insights. These would come, if they were to come at all, through solution of the ADFGX, which direction-finding showed was carrying messages between the higher German headquarters, chiefly those of divisions and army corps. Painvin strained even harder.

At 4:30 a.m. March 21, 6,000 guns suddenly fired upon the Allied line at the Somme in the most furious artillery cannonade of the war. Five hours later, 62 German divisions rolled forward on a 40-mile front. The surprise was complete and its success overwhelming. French and British troops reeled back day after day in stunned confusion. The head of intelligence at French G.H.Q. came into the cryptologic bureau three days later and told Major E.-A. Soudart, the replacement for Givierge, who had gone to the front, and his assistant Marcel Guitard: "By virtue of my job I am the best informed man in France, and at this moment I no longer know where the Germans are. If we're captured in an hour, it wouldn't surprise me." Within a week the Germans had punched a hole 38 miles deep in the Allied lines, and it was not until the British and French troops fell back to Amiens that they collected themselves and halted the advance.

The furious advance was reflected in a dramatic upsurge in radio traffic. The first result was disappointment. Painvin's frequency counts showed that the checkerboard key did change daily; presumably the transposition key did also. Solution would therefore require a goodly quantity of text from a single day, but until April 1 the interceptions were too meager. On that day, the French picked up 18 ADFGX messages totaling 512 five-letter groups. Two of them had been sent in three parts, none of the same length: the Germans had had their fingers burned by multiple anagramming early in the war and had learned their lesson.

Studying them, Painvin noticed on April 4 that the first parts of the two messages had identical bits and pieces of text larded in the same order in the cryptograms. This oddity could most likely have resulted from both cryptograms having identical beginnings transposed according to the same key; the identical fragments of text would then represent the identical tops of the columns of the transposition tableau. Sectioning the cryptograms so that each identical fragment started a new segment would yield the columns of the tableau, in the order of their transcription. Painvin did this to CHI-110, the 110-letter first part of a message from VI to B8, and to CHI-104, the 104-letter first part of a message sent 13 minutes later, also from VI but this time to BF:

CHI-110:	(1) ADXDA	(2) XGFXG	(3) DAXXGX	(4) GDADFF	(5) GXDAG
CHI-104:	(1) ADXDD	(2) XGFFD	(3) DAXAGD	(4) GDGXD	(5) GXDFG
CHI-110:	(6) AGFFFD	(7) XGDDGA	(8) DFADG	(9) AAFFGX	(10) DDDXD
CHI-104:	(6) AGAAXG	(7) GXG?D	(8) DFADG	(9) AAFFF	(10) DDDFF
CHI-110:	(11) DGXAXA	(12) DXFFD	(13) DXFAG	(14) XGGAGA	(15) GFGFF
CHI-104:	(11) DGDGF	(12) DXXXA	(13) DXFDAF	(14) XGGAGF	(15) GFGXX
CHI-110:	(16) AGXXDD	(17) AGGFD	(18) AADXFX	(19) ADFGXD	(20) AAXAG
CHI-104:	(16) AGXXA	(17) AGGAA	(18) AADAFF	(19) ADFFG	(20) AAFFA

The problem now was to discover the transposition key, or, to put it another way, to reconstitute the block. A beginning could be made on the principle that the long columns stood at the left. Painvin saw that in both cryptograms columns 3, 6, 14, and 18—meaning the columns headed by these keynumbers—were longer than the other columns. He moved them to the extreme left of the block. Columns 4, 7, 9, 11, 16, and 19 were short in CHI-104 and long in CHI-110; consequently they clustered in a zone to the right of the first four but to the left of the remaining ten columns. The remaining ten were short in both messages and thus pushed to the right. These three zones marked a first approximation to the key.

Unable to wrest any more information from the first parts of the messages, Painvin turned to their third parts in the hope of finding a common ending. Common repetitions showed him that they had indeed a common ending, and this enabled him to properly segmentize them into columns as he had the first parts. He partially divided up each of the three zones within themselves on the same basis of long and short columns. He thus made a second approximation to the transposition key. This showed conclusively that columns 5 and 8 huddled next to one another in the middle of the tableau and that 12 and 20 stood at the extreme right—though in neither case did Painvin yet know whether their order was 5-8 or 8-5, or 12-20 or 20-12.

He went back to the original 18 intercepts of the day, sliced them into 20 segments, and matched segment 5 to segment 8 in all of them. Sixty letter-pairs resulted from this juxtaposition, and Painvin took a frequency count of them—so many AA's, so many AD's. so many AF's, and so on. To his delight the count showed all the characteristics of a monalphabetic substitution. This indicated that the two columns indeed belonged together in the transposition block, for placing two wrong segments side by side would have resulted in a flattish count. It verified his original system assumptions as well as his transposition rough-out.

He made a similar test with the 12-20 combination, and found an equally monoalphabetic count. The most frequent pair was DG, with a frequency of 8, probably representing plaintext *e*. But DG in the 5-8 coupling had a frequency of zero—impossible for German *e*. On the other hand, GD had a frequency of 8. Since Painvin did not know the order of the columns within each pairing, his arbitrary 5-8 order for the frequency count had probably reversed the letter-pairs respective to 12-20. To correlate them, Painvin reversed 5-8 into

A War of Intercepts: II

8-5, turning its GD into DG, which, with its frequency of 8, was a much better candidate for *e*. The former DG became GD, frequency zero. Painvin could now set up a skeleton checkerboard—which he did on the basis that the coordinates would be taken in the order side-top—and could insert his plaintext values in it as he recovered them:

	A	D	F	G	X
A					
D				e	
F					
G					
X					

How could the rest of the transposition block be reconstructed? Since the coordinates were taken repeatedly in the order side-top, side-top, side-top, and since the block had 20 columns, all the side coordinates would have fallen into the 1st, 3rd, 5th, . . . 19th positions during encipherment, and all the top coordinates into the even positions, thus:

position number	1 2 3 4 5 6 7 8 9 10 11 12 13 14 15 16 17 18 19 20
position odd or even	o e o e o e o e o e o e o e o e o e o e
column key number	8 5 12 20
side or top co-ordinates	S T S T S T S T S T S T S T S T S T S T
	S T S T S T S T S T S T S T S T S T S T

If, Painvin thought, the side coordinates could be separated from the top ones, this would separate the odd positions from the evens. The coordinate separation might be effected on the basis of frequency characteristics. The frequency of the side coordinate D should differ from that of the top coordinate D because the total frequency of the five letters in the D row should differ from the total frequency of the five letters in the D column. The same should hold true for the other coordinates. Hence the top coordinates should manifest a different frequency profile than the side coordinates.

Painvin's frequency counts showed that the columns of the cryptograms indeed separated into two groups: one with D as its maximum and G as its minimum, the other group with G as its maximum and F as its minimum. The first group, which included column 12, turned out to stand in the odd positions. Painvin then determined which odd went with which even by matching one with another; only correct pairings showed monalphabetic distributions. Simultaneously he began solving for actual plaintext and building up his checkerboard, and, after 48 hours of incredible labor, Painvin had cracked the first messages in the toughest field cipher the world had yet seen.

His feat shows the cryptanalytic mind at its finest. Painvin spotted opportunities that many would have missed, and when he worked with one, he did not leave it until he had wrung it dry. This technique of extracting every drop of information from each phase of solution before moving on served well, for the cipher prickles with many defenses. Most stem from its fractionating nature—the breaking-up of a plaintext letter's equivalent into pieces, with the consequent dissipation of its ordinary characteristics. The transposition then scatters these characteristics in a particularly effective fashion, while the dissipation, in turn, dulls the clues that normally help reconstruct the transposition.

It is not surprising, therefore, that the Allies never developed a general solution for the ADFGVX. Cryptanalysis nearly always depended on the finding of two messages with identical beginnings or endings or some other quirk. This explains the apparent anomaly that although only ten keys covering as many days were ever recovered on the Western Front, approximately half the ADFGVX messages ever sent were solved: solutions were achieved only on the days of heaviest traffic. From the German point of view, the system was quick and easy, involving only two simple steps. Messages were doubled in length, but this disadvantage was somewhat offset by the presence of only six different letters in the cryptograms, making transmission faster and more accurate.

By the time Painvin had achieved his first solution, the first German offensive had spent its force, and the volume of traffic had diminished. He rummaged through the piles of intercepts to find others with common endings or beginnings and began working on the messages of March 29, which were relatively abundant. On April 26, after three weeks of work, he finally broke through. Meanwhile the Germans again struck with surprise and forced the English back almost to the sea. But Painvin was now getting his feet on the ground, and the subsequent key recoveries came with increasing speed. It took only nine and a half days to discover the key for the April 5 messages. On the morning of May 29, he started to work on the messages of the day before, and two days later had their key. He took up the messages of the 30th at 4 p.m. on May 31 and was reading them at 5 p.m. the next day.

By then the French had been dealt two unpleasant blows—one military, one cryptographic. Ludendorff had again managed to conceal the time and place of a major assault. Fifteen of his divisions fell by surprise on seven. A gray flood of Germans inundated the French positions in the heights of the Chemin-des-Dames and surged forward irresistibly until it lapped the banks of the Marne only 30 miles from Paris, almost submerging the Allied cause. At the same time, Painvin suddenly saw, on June 1, the ADFGX message complicated by the addition of a sixth letter, v. Probably the Germans expanded their checkerboard to 6 × 6. But why? For homophones to further blunt the frequency clues? Or to insert the ten digits? Painvin did not know.

"In short," he said, "I had a moment of discouragement. The last two keys of the 28th and the 30th of May had been discovered under conditions of such rapidity that their exploitation was of the greatest usefulness. The offensive and the German advance still continued. It was of the greatest importance not to lose [cryptanalytic] contact and in my heart I did not want to brusquely

A War of Intercepts: II

shut off this source of information to the interested services of the armies, which had become accustomed to counting on its latest results."

He opened his assault on the cryptograms of June 1 at 5 p.m. Three messages of that date all bore the same time group (00:05) and had all been sent from a transmitter with call-sign GCI. Painvin compared two of them, one to call-sign DAX, the other to DAK, that had almost identical texts of 106 letters each. But aside from indicating a keylength of 21, they led nowhere: they were too similar. He then compared the DAX cryptogram with the third from GCI, a message of 108 letters to DTD that closely resembled the others. These he cut into column segments as he had done with the messages of April 1. He obtained two roughed-out transposition blocks, whose key-order he still did not know.

Painvin assumed, however, that the two plaintexts were the same except for the addition of a single element to the internal address of the DTD message. This would have pushed the identical portion two notches further back in the DTD block than in the DAX one. He had only to seek an arrangement of columns that would produce such a result. Within an hour he had found it:

6 16 7 5 17 2 14 10 15 9 13 1 21 12 4 8 19 3 11 20 18

The solution of the checkerboard followed quickly:

	A	D	F	G	V	X
A	c	o	8	x	f	4
D	m	k	3	a	z	9
F	n	w	l	0	j	d
G	5	s	i	y	h	u
V	p	1	v	b	6	r
X	e	q	7	t	2	g

The DAX plaintext read: *14 ID XX Gen Kdo ersucht vordere Linie sofort drahten XX Gen Kdo 7* ("14th Infantry Division: HQ requests front line [situation] by telegraph. HQ 7th [Corps]"). The DTD text was identical except for its being addressed *216 ID*.

Painvin completed his solution at 7 p.m. on June 2, and sent it at once to G.H.Q. By then the French had managed to halt Ludendorff's push, but they teetered precariously on the brink of defeat. The Germans were shelling Paris from 60 miles away with their long-range guns. The great German successes of March and May had driven two vast salients into Allied territory. They pointed like daggers at Paris. And the great question recurred: Where would Ludendorff strike next? The thin Allied lines could not hold against a massive piledriver blow concentrated on a single point. If Ludendorff could gain the same surprise that he had so successfully achieved in each previous assault, he could puncture the Allied defenses, overrun Paris, and perhaps end the war. The Allies' only hope of stopping him was to absorb his thrust head-on with their reserves. But to do this they had to know where to send them.

The French discussed the possibilities. Would Ludendorff lunge out directly for Paris from the tip of one of his salients despite the danger to their flanks? Or would he first flatten out the large dent between those bulges and then drive forward from a consolidated position? If the latter, where in the huge pocket would he strike? No one knew.

Ludendorff, meanwhile, was having troubles of his own. German military doctrine called for a sudden, intense artillery bombardment to paralyze the defenders before the infantry attacked. This saturation technique required concentrating thousands of field pieces and tons of munitions at the battlefront. At a conference early in June, Ludendorff learned that this concentration was running behind the schedule he had set for his next assault. His successes had strained his lines of transport, and he had been moving his guns and shells only under cover of night to preserve the invaluable advantage of surprise.

And this advantage he had conserved superbly. The hints that drifted out to French G.H.Q. about his intentions were multiple, petty, and contradictory. Nothing would jell. Gloomy intelligence officers could reach no definite conclusions. Another attack was certainly in the offing, but unless they could ascertain its location, France might be lost.

Into this dismal atmosphere on the morning of June 3 burst Guitard of the Service du Chiffre, excitedly waving an intercept. One of the G.H.Q. cryptanalysts, applying the keys that Painvin had sent there, had just read a cryptogram sent at 4:30 a.m., only a few hours earlier:

CHI-126 FGAXA XAXFF FAFFA AVDFA GAXFX FAAAG DXGGX AGXFD XGAGX GAXGX AGXVF VXXAG XFDAX GDAAF DGGAF FXGGX XDFAX GXAXV AGXGG DFAGD GXVAX XFXGV FFGGA XDGAX ADVGG A

Direction-finders reported that it had been transmitted by the German High Command. The addressee, DIC, was known from traffic analysis and direction-finding to be the 18th Army's general staff in Remaugies—a town situated just above the concavity in the German lines. Its plaintext read: *Munitionierung beschleunigen Punkt Soweit nicut* [error for *nicht*] *eingesehen auch bei Tag* ("Rush munitions Stop Even by day if not seen").

Guitard and the intelligence officers recognized at once that the ammunition mentioned in the telegram was that intended for the usual German preassault bombardment, and the location of the addressee of the message told them where that attack would come. Jubilantly they communicated their information to the operations officers: Ludendorff was going to hammer out the dent, and the German sledge would crash down onto the French line between Montdidier and Compiègne, a sector about 50 miles north of Paris.

Aerial reconnaissance confirmed the daylight transport of munitions.

A War of Intercepts: II

Deserters reported that the onslaught would take place June 7. Foch, in supreme command, shifted his reserves into position, thinned out the front lines, upon which the brunt of the cannonade would fall, and braced his secondary defenses. On the 6th, officers were told that "the offensive is imminent." Tension mounted. The 7th passed without enemy action, and the 8th: Ludendorff had postponed the attack for two days to bring up more guns and munitions because, he said, "thorough preparation was essential to success." The French waited tensely but with confidence. At midnight on June 9 the front from Montdidier to Compiègne erupted in a fierce, pelting hurricane of high-explosive, shrapnel, and gas shells. For three hours a German artillery concentration that averaged one gun for no more than ten yards of front poured a continual stream of fire onto the French positions—and Ludendorff's urgent demand for ammunition became clear. But this time, for the first time since Ludendorff began his stupendous series of triumphs, there was no surprise. Painvin's manna had saved the French.

A little before dawn 15 German divisions charged forward. The French were ready. For five days, fighting seesawed back and forth. Initially the Germans took the little villages of Méry and Courcelles, but on June 11, General Charles Mangin counterattacked with five divisions and all the élan the French could muster. He stopped the German advance cold and then swept the gray tide out of the two villages. Again the Germans heaved forward in a great effort. They failed with heavy losses. For the first time that spring, Ludendorff suspended an operation before it had achieved its goal. Mangin, wearing his gold-brocaded képi, laughed beneath the guns of victory. Foch, who realized that other German assaults would come and that he would have to defend against them, knew at last that he would some day take the offensive. He knew then that the war was not lost, and could eventually be won. Within a few weeks, the final German thrusts did come, but they had run out of steam, and the French parried them. Soon the initiative passed to the Allies, bolstered by the Americans, and their powerful counterstrokes drove the German armies back and back until the Kaiser, his militaristic dreams wrecked, abdicated and fled while his generals signed the Armistice at Compiègne. The World War was ended.

For Painvin, who had lost 33 pounds while simply seated at his desk, there was a long leave of convalescence. Afterwards, he engaged in an immensely successful business career, becoming president and director general of Ugine, the chemical giant of France, president of a phosphate company, vice president of a commercial credit firm, administrator of a mortgage society, honorary president of the Union of Chemical Industries and of the central committee of the electrochemical trade, and president of the Chamber of Commerce of Paris. Yet, he said, none of these achievements ever gave him the satisfaction that his ADFGVX solutions did. They left "an indelible mark on my spirit, and remain for me one of the brightest and most outstanding memories of my existence."

The First World War marks the great turning point in the history of cryptology. Before, it was a small field; afterwards, it was big. Before, it was a science in its youth; afterwards, it had matured. The direct cause of this development was the enormous increase in radio communications.

This heavy traffic meant that probably the richest source of intelligence flowed in these easily accessible channels. All that was necessary was to crack the protective sheath. As cryptanalysis repeatedly demonstrated its abilities and worth, it rose from an auxiliary to a primary source of information about the foe; its advocates spoke regularly in the councils of war. Its new status was exemplified in terms clear to every military mind when both Cartier and Givierge became generals. The emergence of cryptanalysis as a permanent major element of intelligence was the most striking characteristic of cryptology's new maturity.

Another was the change in cryptanalysis itself. The science at last outgrew the mode of operation that had dominated it for 400 years. This was chamber analysis, in which a single man wrestles with a single cryptogram alone in his room; John Wallis epitomizes the genre. Chamber analysis began to fail the cryptanalysts in the first days of the war. The German double transposition required at least two messages of the same length for solution, but a great many messages had to be intercepted before the law of averages would hatch those two. As cipher systems grew increasingly complex, cryptanalysis relied more and more on special solutions like this, and so they required many more messages for success than the bewigged practitioners of chamber analysis would have ever thought necessary. They also depended more heavily on such auxiliary aids as traffic analysis and knowledge of surrounding events, because the more that is known about the circumstances in which messages are sent, the easier solutions by special case become. Cryptanalysts thus became much more intimately connected with the real world.

A third characteristic of the new maturity was the evolution of fields of cryptanalytic specialization. Systems of secret communication had ceased to be so few and so homogeneous that a single expert could subdue them all. Their multiplicity and heterogeneity, plus the volume of traffic in each, bred the specialist. Such, for example, was Childs, who worked exclusively on ciphers, while others in G.2 A.6 attacked codes. Perhaps the most interesting specialist of all was the chief of the cryptanalytic office himself. No longer could he seclude himself in a quiet little world of letters and numbers as just the foremost among a group of cryptanalysts, like the English Decypherers. The more active cryptology of the 20th century impinged on so many more areas that the chief had to devote his energies exclusively to learning from other branches of the services what intelligence was most needed, disposing his team of codebreakers to get it, and obtaining information in the form of battle reports, cleartext intercepts, prisoner-of-war interrogations, captured documents, and the like that would help them in their special solutions. The chief had become purely an executive, who himself never picked up a colored pencil or an eraser for an actual solution, though he necessarily needed a thorough knowledge of the technique. His new responsibilities, of course, stemmed in large measure from cryptology's upgraded position. But they also reflected the specialization now required in the burgeoning field, and this division of labor is as much a sign of maturity in cryptology as it is in a society.

Still another sign of that maturity was the emotional apprehension of the role played by the blunders of inexperienced, indolent, and ignorant cryptographic clerks. Cryptologists had had an intellectual awareness of this danger at least since 1605, when Francis Bacon wrote that "in regards of the rawness and unskillfulnesse of the handes, through which they passe, the greatest Matters, are many times carryed in the weakest Cyphars." But it was not until cipher key after cipher key, and code after code, had been betrayed by needless mistakes or stupidities or outright rule violations that the magnitude of the problem was borne in upon them. The problem had swollen to such proportions because so large a volume of messages had to be handled by so many untrained men—against whom were pitted the best brains of the enemy. The experts realized that to eliminate these is to strengthen cryptographic security more effectively than by introducing the most ingenious cipher. The great practical lesson of World War I cryptology was the necessity of infusing an iron discipline in the cryptographic personnel. Errors arising from ignorance can be reduced by explaining how enemy cryptanalysts take advantage of what appears to be the most trivial violation of the rules. Faults arising from laziness can be lessened by a monitoring service that finds and punishes offenders. Givierge enunciated the doctrine that must be impressed upon the cipherers: "Encode well or do not encode at all. In transmitting cleartext, you give only a piece of information to the enemy, and you know what it is; in encoding badly, you permit him to read all your correspondence and that of your friends."

All these developments, however, resulted essentially from the interreaction between cryptology and the outside world; they were externally oriented. World War I originated no developments that were internally oriented, as, for example, was the emergence of the field cipher. On the contrary, two of the most central activities—the actual cryptographic operations, which were performed by hand, and the techniques of solution, which were brute frequency analysis—had exhausted their usefulness.

Manual systems sagged under message loads for which they were never designed. Not a few cryptographic clerks dreamed of machines that would lift the onerous burden from their shoulders. In a sense, the codes that became so popular might be regarded as a rudimentary form of mechanical device that does the work for the encoder: the phrases are prepared and equated with their code equivalents in advance, and the encoder has but to pick out the ones he wants. But the trench codes were to the printing cipher machines of later years as the taxis of the Marne were to the armored troop-carriers of **Panzer** columns.

At the same time, the classic principles of frequency analysis had been stretched to their utmost. They were applied with great subtlety, as in Painvin's matching of frequency distributions to determine the odd and even columns of the ADFGVX transposition block. But no new principles had been evolved, and the old ones had barely coped with such concepts as fractionation.

In these two internal matters, which lie at the core of cryptology, World War I marked not a beginning but an end, had reaped not fulfillment but barrenness. So viable had the science become, however, that this very vacuum, this want, held promise.

12

TWO AMERICANS

THE MOST FAMOUS CRYPTOLOGIST in history owes his fame less to what he did than to what he said—and to the sensational way in which he said it. And this was most perfectly in character, for Herbert Osborne Yardley was perhaps the most engaging, articulate, and technicolored personality in the business.

He was born April 13, 1889, in Worthington, Indiana, and grew up in that little Midwestern town during the tranquil, sunlit years that preceded the First World War. A popular youngster, he was president of his high-school class, editor of the school paper, and captain of the football team, and though only an average student, he had a flair for mathematics. From 16 on he frequented the poker tables of the local saloons, learning the game that was to be a passion of his life. He had wanted to become a criminal lawyer, but instead landed at 23 as a $900-a-year code clerk in the State Department.

It was a case of purest serendipity, for the man and the subject were ideally matched. His romantic mind thrilled to the stream of history that daily poured through his hands in the form of ambassadorial dispatches, and cryptology fired his imagination. He had heard vague tales of cryptanalysts who could pry into secrets of state, and when a 500-word message from Colonel House passed over the wires to President Wilson one night, Yardley, with characteristic audacity, determined to see whether he could solve what must be the most difficult of American codes. He astonished himself by solving it in a few hours.* His success cemented his attachment to cryptanalysis, and he followed this demonstration of the low estate of high-level cryptography with a 100-page memorandum on the solution of American diplomatic codes. While absorbed in possible solutions for a proposed new

---

* The President and his advisor were then using two main systems. One was external—a superencipherment applied to the five-digit numerical groups of what probably was a State Department code. The first digit was enciphered by one of two alternate letters; the two pairs by a vowel-consonant combination. Thus, in one edition of the superencipherment, 40606 became FEDED, 40699, KEDIR, and so on. The other was internal—a jargon code of such less-than-Stygian incognitos as MARS for the Secretary of War, NEPTUNE for the Secretary of the Navy, BLUEFIELDS for William C. Redfield, Secretary of Commerce, ALLEY for Franklin K. Lane, Secretary of the Interior, and MANSION for David F. Houston, Secretary of Agriculture. Yardley does not specify which he solved.

coding method, he diagnosed what has ever since been known among cryptologists as the "Yardley symptom": "It was the first thing I thought of when I awakened, the last when I fell asleep."

Soon after the American declaration of war in April of 1917, he sold the idea of a cryptologic service to the War Department. He succeeded partly because the need was genuine, partly because he himself was an exceedingly convincing young man. Yardley had proven his cryptanalytic ability, and moreover had done well enough in his regular duties to have won raises to $1,400 in 43 months. Major Ralph H. Van Deman, later to be known as the Father of American Intelligence, commissioned the thin, balding 27-year-old as a lieutenant and set him up as the head of the newly created cryptologic section of the Military Intelligence Division, MI-8.

Like Topsy, MI-8 just grew. First to arrive, to take charge of the instruction subsection for training A.E.F. cryptanalysts, was Dr. John M. Manly, a 52-year-old philologist who headed the Department of English at the University of Chicago and was later president of the Modern Language Association; a longtime hobbyist in cryptology, he was to become Yardley's chief assistant and one of his best cryptanalysts. Manly brought with him a bevy of Ph.D.'s clanking with Phi Beta Kappa keys, mostly from the University of Chicago: David H. Stevens, 32, an instructor in English, later director of the division for the humanities of the Rockefeller Foundation; Thomas A. Knott, 37, associate professor of English and later general editor of Webster's Dictionaries, including the colossal 1934 Second New International Unabridged; Charles H. Beeson, 47, associate professor of Latin, later president of the Mediaeval Academy of America, who had gotten his doctorate at Munich and knew German well enough to write scholarly works in it; and Frederick Bliss Luquiens, 41, professor of Spanish at Yale University, general editor of the Macmillan Spanish Series, and author of *An Introduction to Old French Phonology and Morphology*.

The instruction subsection did its teaching at the Army War College. It advanced far enough to offer as Problem 20 "General Principles of attack on enciphered code when the book is known but the system of encipherment unknown." Another subsection popped into being for code and cipher compilation; it produced a military intelligence code, two geographical codes for combat information from France, and a casualty code, which was never used. Soon a communications subsection was handling close to 50,000 words a week. As the organization expanded, it shifted to ever-larger quarters. Beginning in the balcony overhanging the library of the War College, MI-8 moved to the Colonial, an apartment house at 15th and M Streets barely ready for occupancy, and then to a building on the site of what is now the Capitol Theatre on F Street, all in Washington. For security, its offices were always on the top floor.

Growth continued apace. An intercepted letter in a German shorthand instigated a shorthand subsection that soon could read missives in more than

30 systems, most commonly Gabelsberger, Schrey, Stolze-Schrey, Marti, Brockaway, Duploye, Sloan-Duployan, and Orillana. A blank piece of paper discovered in the shoe heel of a woman suspected of working with German espionage in Mexico turned out to bear a message in invisible ink. Fortunately, it proved one of the simpler kinds, which can be developed by heat. But it sparked the establishment of a secret-ink subsection whose expert chemists could detect writing in an invisible ink disguised as a perfume with an actual odor and with only one part in 10,000 of solid matter.

The Germans later replaced inks in so bulky and conspicuous a form as liquids with chemicals that were impregnated into scarves, socks, and other garments. They had only to be dipped in water to create the writing fluid. These miracles of the test tube, called F and P inks by the British chemists who taught the Americans much of what they knew, were so precisely formulated that they would react with only one other chemical to form a visible compound.

Eventually, the Allied chemists discovered a reagent that brought out secret writing in any kind of ink, even clear water. Crystals of iodine, heated gently, sublimated into fumes of a beautiful violet hue that settled more densely in those fibers of paper that had been disturbed by any kind of wetting action, thus tracing the pen's course. The Germans replied by writing in a sympathetic ink and then moistening the entire sheet. The Allies struck back with a chemical streak test that would show whether the paper surface had been dampened. This was almost as incriminating as actual development of a secret-ink letter, for who but a spy would wet a letter? The seesaw battle between the chemists of Germany, traditionally world leaders in that science, and those of the Allies reached a stalemate when both sides discovered the general reagent—one that would develop any secret ink at any time, even on moistened paper. Formulas differ slightly, but all use a mixture of iodine, potassium iodide, glycerine, and water, dabbed on with cotton. The liquid concentrates in the more disturbed fibers and reveals the writing. By the time this general reagent appeared, MI-8's secret-ink subsection was testing 2,000 letters a week for invisible writing and had discovered 50 of major importance. Among them were letters that led to the capture of Maria de Victorica, a beautiful German spy who was planning to import high explosives for sabotage inside the hollow figures of saints and the Virgin Mary!

MI-8 also solved cryptograms. It read diplomatic telegrams of Argentina, Brazil, Chile, Costa Rica, Cuba, Germany, Mexico, Spain, and Panama. The Spanish-language texts constituted the bulk of its cryptanalytic work. The censorship office sent over intercepted cipher letters; most of these turned out to be merely personal notes in very simple systems, though some of the love letters were so torrid that Yardley said, "It rather worried me to see husbands and wives trust their illicit correspondence to such unsafe methods."

Perhaps the most important of the MI-8 solutions was the one that largely resulted in the conviction of the only German spy condemned to death in the

United States during World War I. This was Lothar Witzke, alias Pablo Waberski, who was suspected of setting off the Black Tom explosion. He was captured in January, 1918, by an American agent, who found in his baggage in the Central Hotel in Nogales, Mexico, a cipher letter dated January 15. It did not reach MI-8 until spring, and then it kicked about for a few more months while several men there tried and failed to solve it. Finally Manly took it up.

This quiet scholar, who never married and whose quiet, simple manner contrasted so sharply with his chief's, was to become one of the world's leading authorities on Chaucer. He and his collaborator, Edith Rickert, labored for 14 years to produce their monumental eight-volume work, *The Text of the Canterbury Tales*, in which, by a tedious collation of scribal errors and variant readings in more than 80 manuscripts of the medieval masterpiece, they reconstructed a text that is as close to the poet's own original as the extant evidence allows. The cast of mind that can thus sort out, retain, and then organize innumerable details into a cohesive whole was just what was needed for the Gothic complexity of the 424-letter Witzke cryptogram. In a three-day marathon of cryptanalysis, Manly, aided by Miss Rickert, perceived the pattern of this 12-step official transposition cipher, with its multiple horizontal shiftings of three- and four-letter plaintext groups ripped apart by a final vertical transcription. He drew forth a message from Heinrich von Eckardt, the luckless German minister in Mexico whose very involvement with a cryptogram seemed to mean its cryptanalysis,* to the German consular authorities:

"The bearer of this is a subject of the Empire who travels as a Russian under the name of Pablo Waberski. He is a German secret agent. Please furnish him on request protection and assistance; also advance him on demand up to 1,000 pesos of Mexican gold and send his code telegrams to this embassy as official consular dispatches." When Manly read this to a military commission of colonels and generals who were trying Witzke on spy charges in a hushed courtroom at Fort Sam Houston, San Antonio, the effect was condemnatory. The handsome young spy was sentenced to death. Wilson later commuted it to life imprisonment, however, and Witzke was released in 1923.

In August of 1918, Yardley sailed for Europe to learn as much as he could from America's allies. He obtained entrance to M.I. 1(b) after demonstrating his abilities to Brooke-Hunt and there studied British methods for the solution of different codes and ciphers. The doors of Room 40 remained resolutely locked against him as against everyone else, though Hall did give him a German naval code and a neutral nation's diplomatic codes. In Paris

---

* In addition to this and the Zimmermann telegram, two messages to the diplomat from his home office, encoded in the English-French half of Clifton's *Nouveau Dictionnaire Français*, which had replaced the betrayed Cipher 13040, were solved by MI-8. They disclosed Germany trying to bribe Mexico to remain neutral.

that fall, Yardley met Painvin, who gave him a desk in his office and invited him to his home many evenings. But he never gained access to the French Foreign Ministry cryptanalytic bureau.

He remained in Paris after the Armistice to head the cryptologic bureau of the American delegation to the Peace Conference. At first there was a tremendous rush to get organized, but then the pressure eased, and Yardley, Childs, who was assigned to assist him, and Lieutenant Frederick Livesey, who had been sent over from MI-8, enjoyed the life of playboy cryptologists. A practical soul, Yardley saw no need for the three officers assigned to the bureau to be present at once, and so a rotation of duties was arranged that permitted them to spend most of their time at the international cocktail parties and dancings that were then the rage of Paris.

When it ended, as it had to, Yardley, viewing with distaste a return to the State Department code room, and burning with evangelical fervor over America's need for cryptanalysis, exercised his potent salesmanship on the State and War departments. He won the concurrence of Frank L. Polk, the acting Secretary of State; then, on May 16, 1919, he submitted to the Chief of Staff a plan for a "permanent organization for code and cipher investigation and attack." Three days later the Chief of Staff approved it, and Polk brown-penciled an "O.K." and his initials on it. The plan envisioned joint financial support by the two departments at about $100,000 a year, but actual expenditures never reached that sum. The State Department's contribution of $40,000, which began on July 15, 1919, could not be legally expended within the District of Columbia, and so Yardley soon found himself moving the nucleus of a staff (largely recruited from MI-8) and the necessary paraphernalia—language statistics, maps, newspaper clippings, dictionaries—to New York City.

By October 1 the organization that was to become known as the American Black Chamber was ensconced in the former town house of T. Suffern Tailer, a New York society man and political leader, at 3 East 38th Street. It stayed there little more than a year, however, before moving to new quarters in a four-story brownstone at 141 East 37th Street, just east of Lexington Avenue. It occupied half of the ornate, divided structure, whose high ceilings did little to relieve the claustrophobic construction of its twelve-foot-wide rooms. Yardley's apartment was on the top floor. All external connection with the government was cut. Rent, heat, office supplies, light, Yardley's salary of $7,500 a year, and the salaries of his staff were paid from secret funds. Though the office was a branch of the Military Intelligence Division, War Department payments did not begin until June 30, 1921.

Among the twenty people who started with Yardley or joined him soon thereafter were Dr. Charles J. Mendelsohn from MI-8, a philologist who taught history at City College mornings and worked in the Black Chamber afternoons; Victor Weiskopf, also from MI-8, a former agent of and cryptanalyst for the Justice Department, which allowed him to join Yardley's organization in New York but paid him $200 a month to solve ciphers for it on the side; Livesey, who had been with Yardley in Paris, a Harvard graduate and businessman who later became a State Department economic advisor; Ruth Willson and Edna Ramsaier (who was to become Yardley's second wife), both specialists in Japanese ciphers; and John Meeth, Yardley's chief clerk. Livesey, who became Yardley's prime assistant, was paid $3,000, or about $60 a week.

One of the organization's first assignments was to solve the codes of Japan, with whom friction had been growing. Yardley, in an access of enthusiasm, promised the solution or his resignation within the year. He regretted his impetuousness as soon as he plunged into the task, for he almost foundered in the Oriental intricacies of Japanese plaintext, to say nothing of codetext. After some preliminary study, assisted by Livesey, who had a great aptitude for languages, he ascertained that the Japanese employed a watered-down form of their ideographic writing called "kata kana" for telegraphic and—presumably—cryptologic communication, which was transmitted in Latin letters. Kata kana consists of about 73 syllables, each with a sign of its own which had been given a roman equivalent, and when Yardley had his typists compile frequency tables for the twenty-five plain-language kata kana telegrams he had, he discovered that this script obeyed rules of frequency just like any other. Specifically, the kana *n*, the only nonsyllabic kana, was most common, appearing often at the end of words, followed by *i*, *no*, *o*, *ni*, *shi*, *wa*, *ru*, and *to*, in that order. The list of most common syllables and words began with *ari* and continued with *aritashi*, *daijin*, *denpoo*, *gai*, *gyoo*, and so on. At the end of about four months, the typists had prepared elaborate statistics of frequency and contact for about 10,000 kana.

He then set them to work dividing the ten-letter groups of the Japanese code telegrams into pairs of letters and drawing up similar frequency and contact data for these pairs. He himself went through the approximately 100 code telegrams underlining with colored pencils all repetitions of four letters or more. But despite the most intensive scrutiny and study, no solution was forthcoming. Livesey's linguistic abilities had meanwhile brought him a fair acquaintance with Japanese. He found in a bilingual dictionary that he had bought for 75 cents that the word *owari* meant "conclusion." Could it be the plaintext of certain codegroups found frequently at the end of telegrams? The hypothesis, involving only three kana, proved barren. He examined the plain-language telegrams and pointed out probable words with conspicuous patterns to Yardley. Two of these, which played a vital role in the solution, were "Airurando dokuritsu" ("Ireland independence"), with the repeated *do*, and "Doitsu" ("Germany"), which used three of the same kana in a different order. This was a good clue, but it alone was not the answer. Night after night Yardley would climb the stairs to his apartment, weary, hopeless, discouraged, and fall into bed, only to wake up excitedly a few hours later with a brilliant idea—which invariably turned out to be just another blind alley.

Two Americans

> By now [he wrote] I had worked so long with these code telegrams that every telegram, every line, even every code word was indelibly printed in my brain. I could lie awake in bed and in the darkness make my investigations—trial and error, trial and error, over and over again.
>
> Finally one night I awakened at midnight, for I had retired early, and out of the darkness came the conviction that a certain series of two-letter codewords absolutely *must* equal *Airurando* (Ireland). Then other words danced before me in rapid succession: *dokuritsu* (independence), *Doitsu* (Germany), *owari* (stop). At last the great discovery! My heart stood still, and I dared not move. Was I dreaming? Was I awake? Was I losing my mind? A solution? At last—and after all these months!
>
> I slipped out of bed and in my eagerness, for I knew I was awake now, I almost fell down the stairs. With trembling fingers I spun the dial and opened the safe. I grabbed my file of papers and rapidly began to make notes.

These promptly proved his intuitions correct. The repetitions of RE for *do*, BO for *tsu*, OK for *ri*, and UB for *i* in his equivalences confirmed it:

WI	UB	PO	MO	IL	RE	RE	OS	KO	BO	RE	UB	BO	AS	FY	OK
a	i	ru	ra	n	do	do	ku	ri	tsu	do	i	tsu	o	wa	ri

For an hour Yardley filled in these and other identifications and then, convinced that the opening wedge had been driven, went upstairs, awoke his wife, and went out to get drunk. Actually, considerably more work had to be done before the Black Chamber could read anything approaching sentences. Much of this was done by Livesey, who achieved an important secondary breakthrough when he identified the Japanese plaintext *jooin* ("Senate") and *jooyakuan* ("draft treaty").

Yardley encountered unexpected difficulties in finding a translator for the exotic language, but finally located a kindly, bewhiskered missionary. He looked joltingly incongruous in the Black Chamber, but he enabled Yardley to send the first translations of Japanese telegrams to Washington in February of 1920. He quit after six months when he finally realized the espionage nature of the work, but by then Livesey had accomplished the almost unheard-of feat of learning Japanese in that time.

Yardley called the first code "Ja," the "J" for Japanese, the "a" a serial for the first solution. From 1919 to the spring of 1920 the Japanese introduced eleven different codes, having employed a Polish expert, Captain Kowalefsky, to revise their cryptologic systems. Kowalefsky taught the Japanese how to bi-, tri-, and tetrasect their messages: to divide them into two, three, or four parts, shuffle the parts, and then encipher them in transposed order to bury stereotyped beginnings and endings. Some of the codes contained 25,000 code groups.

During the summer of 1921, the Black Chamber solved telegram 813 of July 5 from the Japanese ambassador in London to Tokyo. It contained the first hints of a conference for naval disarmament—an idea that powerfully gripped the imagination of a war-weary world. Another indication came when Japan suddenly introduced a new code, the YU, for their most secret messages. On solution, it was dubbed "Jp"—the sixteenth solved since Yardley's original break.

A few months before the November opening of the disarmament conference in Washington, daily courier service was set up between the Black Chamber and the State Department. An official grinningly remarked that State's upper echelons were delighted with the cryptanalysts' work and read the solutions every morning with their orange juice and coffee. The conference sought to limit the tonnage of capital ships, and as negotiations were proceeding toward its chief result—the Five-Power Treaty that accorded tonnages in certain ratios to the United States, Britain, France, Italy, and Japan—Yardley's team was reading the secret instructions of the negotiators. "The Black Chamber, bolted, hidden, guarded, sees all, hears all," he wrote later, rather melodramatically. "Though the blinds are drawn and the windows heavily curtained, its far-seeing eyes penetrate the secret conference chambers at Washington, Tokyo, London, Paris, Geneva, Rome. Its sensitive ears catch the faintest whisperings in the foreign capitals of the world."

Each nation naturally tried to obtain the most favorable tonnage ratio for itself; the most aggressive in its efforts was Japan, which even then was dreaming expansionist dreams in Asia but feared to offend the United States. At the height of the conference, when Japan was demanding a ratio of 10 to 7 with the United States and Great Britain, the Black Chamber read what Yardley later called the most important telegram it ever solved.

"It is necessary to avoid any clash with Great Britain and America, particularly America, in regard to the armament limitation question," the Japanese Foreign Office cabled its ambassador in Washington on November 28. "You will to the utmost maintain a middle attitude and redouble your efforts to carry out our policy. In case of inevitable necessity you will work to establish your second proposal of 10 to 6.5. If, in spite of your utmost efforts, it becomes necessary in view of the situation and in the interests of general policy to fall back on your proposal No. 3, you will endeavor to limit the power of concentration and maneuver of the Pacific by a guarantee to reduce or at least to maintain the status quo of Pacific defenses and to make an adequate reservation which will make clear that [this is] our intention in agreeing to a 10 to 6 ratio. No. 4 is to be avoided as far as possible."

Each 0.5 in the ratio meant 50,000 tons of capital ships, or about a battleship and a half. With the information in this message telling the American negotiators that Japan would yield if pressed, all they had to do was press. This Secretary of State Charles Evans Hughes did, and on December 10 Japan capitulated, instructing its negotiator, in a cable read by the Black Chamber, that "there is nothing to do but accept the ratio proposed by the United States." As signed, the Five-Power Treaty allotted capital ships to the

United States, Great Britain, Japan, France, and Italy in the ratio of 10 : 10 : 6 : 3.3 : 3.3. It was considerably less than Japan had hoped for. Hughes sent Yardley a letter of commendation.

During the conference, the Black Chamber had turned out more than 5,000 solutions and translations. Yardley nearly suffered a nervous breakdown, and in February went to Arizona for four months to recover his health. Several of his assistants had already had trouble in this regard. One babbled incoherently; a girl dreamed of chasing around the bedroom a bulldog that, when caught, had "code" written on its side; another could lighten the enormous sack of pebbles that she carried in a recurring nightmare only by finding a stone along a lonely beach that exactly matched one of her pebbles, which she could then cast into the sea. All three resigned.

Security was a constant preoccupation. Mail was sent to a cover address; Yardley's name was not permitted in the telephone book; locks were often changed. Nevertheless, some foreign government must have discovered the organization's activities, for there was at least one attempt to subvert Yardley and, when this failed, the office was broken into and the desks rifled. After this the Black Chamber moved to a large office building at 52 Vanderbilt Avenue, where, by 1925, it had set up the Code Compiling Company as a rather unsubtle cover. The firm, with Yardley as president and Mendelsohn as secretary-treasurer, actually compiled the *Universal Trade Code*, which they sold, together with other commercial codes. Behind this front office, in a locked room, worked the cryptanalysts. Though each piece of paper was scrupulously locked away each night so that nothing was left on the desks, the cryptanalysts were allowed, in those more informal days, to take home problems on which they were working.

Yardley's appropriation had been severely cut in 1924, and half the staff had to be let go, reducing the force to about a dozen. Despite this, Yardley said, the Black Chamber managed to solve, from 1917 to 1929, more than 45,000 telegrams, involving the codes of Argentina, Brazil, Chile, China, Costa Rica, Cuba, England, France, Germany, Japan, Liberia, Mexico, Nicaragua, Panama, Peru, San Salvador, Santo Domingo (later the Dominican Republic), the Soviet Union, and Spain, and made preliminary analyses of many other codes, including those of the Vatican.

Suddenly it all ended. Yardley, who had been obtaining the code telegrams of foreign governments through the cooperation of the presidents of the Western Union Telegraph Company and the Postal Telegraph Company, was encountering increasing resistance from them. Herbert Hoover had just been inaugurated, and Yardley resolved to settle the matter with the new administration once and for all. He decided on the bold stroke of drawing up "a memorandum to be presented directly to the President, outlining the history and activities of the Black Chamber, and the necessary steps that must be taken if the Government had hoped to take full advantage of the skill of its cryptographers." He waited to see which way the wind was blowing before making his move—and found that it was not with him. Yardley went to a speakeasy to listen to Hoover's first speech as President and sensed, in the high ethical strictures that Hoover expressed, the doom of the Black Chamber.

He was right, though its actual closing came from elsewhere. After Henry L. Stimson, Hoover's Secretary of State, had been in office the few months that Yardley thought would be necessary for him to have lost some of his innocence in wrestling with the hardheaded realities of diplomacy, the Black Chamber sent him the solution of an important series of messages. But Stimson was different from previous Secretaries of State, on whom this tactic had always worked. He was shocked to learn of the existence of the Black Chamber, and totally disapproved of it. He regarded it as a low, snooping activity, a sneaking, spying, keyhole-peering kind of dirty business, a violation of the principle of mutual trust upon which he conducted both his personal affairs and his foreign policy. All of this it is, and Stimson rejected the view that such means justified even patriotic ends. He held to the conviction that his country should do what is right, and, as he said later, "Gentlemen do not read each other's mail." In an act of pure moral courage, Stimson, affirming principle over expediency, withdrew all State Department funds from the support of the Black Chamber.* Since these constituted its major income, their loss shuttered the office. Hoover's speech had warned Yardley that an appeal would be fruitless. There was nothing to do but close up shop. An unexpended $6,666.66 and the organization's files reverted to the Signal Corps, where William Friedman had charge of cryptology. The staff quickly dispersed (none went to the Army), and when the books were closed on October 31, 1929, the American Black Chamber had perished. It had cost the State Department $230,404 and the War Department $98,808.49—just under a third of a million dollars for a decade of cryptanalyis.

Yardley, whose job experience had been rather specialized, could not find work, and he went back home to Worthington. The Depression sucked him dry. By August of 1930, he had had to give up an apartment house and a one-eighth interest in a real estate corporation; indeed, he complained that he had to sell nearly everything he owned "for less than nothing." A few months later he was toying with the idea of writing the story of the Black Chamber to make some money to feed his wife and their son, Jack. When his old MI-8 friend, Manly, with whom he had been in contact all during the 1920s, had to turn down his request for a $2,500 loan at the end of January, 1931, Yardley, in desperation, sat down to write what was to be the most famous book on

---

* In 1940, as Secretary of War, he had to reverse himself and accept the cryptanalyses of MAGIC. But the international situation then was totally different. "In 1929," he himself has written, in the third person, "the world was striving with good will for lasting peace, and in this effort all the nations were parties. Stimson, as Secretary of State, was dealing as a gentleman with the gentlemen sent as ambassadors and ministers from friendly nations. . . ." In 1940, Europe was at war, and the United States was on the verge.

cryptology ever published. He described the composition of it in a letter to Manly in the spring of 1931:

> I hadn't done any real work for so long that I told Bye, my agent, and the Sat Eve Post that I would need some one else to write the stuff. I showed a few things to Bye and Costain, the latter editor of POST, and both told me to go to work myself. I sat for days before a typewriter, helpless. Oh, I pecked away a bit, and gradually under the encouragement of Bye I got a bit of confidence. Then Bobbs Merrill advanced me $1000 on outline. Then there was a call to rush the book. I began to work in shifts, working a few hours, sleeping a few hours, going out of my room only to buy some eggs, bread, coffee and cans of tomatoe juice. Jesus, the stuff I turned out. Sometimes only a thousand words, but often as many as 10,000 a day. As the chapters appeared I took them to Bye who read them and offered criticism. Anyway I completed the book and boiled down parts of it for the articles all in 7 weeks.

The Bobbs-Merrill Company, of Indianapolis, published the 375-page book on June 1, but parts of it had already appeared in three articles at two-week intervals in *The Saturday Evening Post*, the leading magazine of the day, which thought so highly of them that it used the first of the series to lead its April 4 issue. Yardley was a superb storyteller, and his narrative skill did not desert him on paper. Largely owing to this and to his vigorous and pungent style, the book itself, *The American Black Chamber*, was an immediate success, and it instantly fixed itself in popular lore as the epitome of books on cryptology. Even today, it is invariably mentioned in any cocktail-party discussion of the subject, and copies remain in demand among secondhand-book dealers. Reviews of it were unanimously good. Critic W. A. Roberts, in a commendatory review, summed up the prevailing opinion: "I think it the most sensational contribution to the secret history of the war, as well as the immediate post-war period, which has yet been written by an American. Its deliberate indiscretions exceed any to be found in the recent memoirs of European secret agents." Reporters hastened to governmental bureaus to inquire whether it was all true. The State Department, with masterfully diplomatic double-talk, was "disposed to discredit" Yardley's statements. At the War Department, officials lied straightforwardly and said that no such organization had been in existence in the past four years.

But beneath this bland surface American cryptologists seethed. Friedman was incensed at what he regarded as an unwarranted slur on the A.E.F. cryptologic effort. Yardley had learned from a report by Moorman about Childs's test-stripping of the superencipherment from the proposed but never used A.E.F. *Trench Code* and about the telephone monitoring of the messages that allowed the G.2 A.6 monitor to deduce the American attack on the St.-Mihiel salient. He inadvertently combined them into a highly dramatic tale in which the Germans knew from cryptanalysis about the American effort to flatten the salient, which consequently "represents only a small part of what might have been a tremendous story in the annals of warfare, had the Germans not been forewarned. The stubborn trust placed in inadequate code and cipher systems had taken its toll at the Front." Yardley was not entirely to blame, for Moorman's report is extremely confusing and does not clearly separate the two episodes, but he ignored the frequent replacement of codebooks, unwarrantedly assumed that the Germans cryptanalyzed the messages, and in general did not check out his facts.

Friedman circularized his A.E.F. colleagues to ask their views. Moorman replied, "I started to read the Yardley articles, but finding that their object seemed to be exaggeration of the importance of the writer with little regard for the truth, I did not finish. I have been surprised at the number of individuals who can write quite plausibly on the subject, 'How I Won the War,' and it was with some regret that I discovered Yardley had joined them." Hitt wrote, "I have never seen in a reputable magazine any series of articles so full of misstatement of fact, uncalled for criticism and innuendo as those by Yardley. A great national weekly has permitted him to pose before its readers as one of the outstanding heroes of the war, poor fellow, and he had to lie to do it."

Manly, who at first had warned Yardley that "you might incur very serious criticism if you disclosed the fact that you had been reading the official messages of the Foreigner," told him after the articles appeared that "I approve the articles and think that they are well done." To Friedman, who had compared Yardley's disclosure of American cryptanalysis to a lawyer's breach of ethics by disclosing confidential material of his client, Manly wrote that he himself would not have revealed any of the cryptanalytic matters dealing with friendly nations, but felt that Yardley's motive was to force the government to set up a cryptanalytic bureau. Friedman replied that "In my opinion the great harm he has done our country will not become fully apparent for many years to come." Some was probably apparent almost immediately, for at least some of the 19 nations named as having their codes broken must have changed them. One Army cryptanalyst recalled that publication of the book caused him and his colleagues considerable extra work at the time.

Yardley himself seems to have been taken a bit aback by the storm he had kicked up. He had at first admitted frankly to Manly that "if I didn't dramatise them [the book and articles] in some manner the reader would go to sleep" and "To write saleable stuff one must dramatise. Things don't happen in dramatic fashion. There is therefore nothing to do but either dramatise or not write at all." But when he saw he had a tiger by the tail he assumed a sanctimonious attitude. "Would it not appear," he rhetorically asked in a letter to the editor of the *New York Evening Post*, "that if such practices [reading other nations' messages] are to be eliminated from the considerations of diplomacy the first step toward such elimination must be an airing, publicly, of the situation? . . . It seems to me that my book may possibly render a real public service in at least pointing out the conditions existing as the first step toward achieving their remedy." He took the offensive against his critics with an article in *Liberty* magazine entitled "Are We Giving Away Our State Secrets?" In this he accused the Department of State of gross negligence in cryptographic matters—"sixteenth-century codes," he had, with some justice, called them in his book—and asserted that his book should have been taken, not "as a story of romance," but "as an exposé of America's defenseless position in the field of cryptography."

It was, however, as a story of romance that *The American Black Chamber* sold 17,931 copies, unprecedented for a book dealing with cryptology, and a highly respectable figure even today. The English edition, entitled *Secret Service in America*, sold 5,480 more. The book was published in French, in Swedish, and in an unauthorized Chinese version, but it was in Japan, as might be expected, that sales skyrocketed. On a per-capita basis, Japanese sales of 33,119 copies were almost four times better than in the United States.

It stirred a tremendous furor there. On July 22, 1931, the Tokyo *Nichi Nichi*, one of the most influential papers in Japan, published a long article giving various views on the book. Everyone tried to save face by throwing the blame on the Foreign Ministry. Typical was the comment of an unnamed member of the House of Peers, who contended that Baron Kujiro Shidehara, then foreign minister and at the time of the conference ambassador to the United States, "must be held responsible." He added, "The disclosure of this breach of faith committed by the United States Government will doubtless serve as a valuable lesson for the future to Japan in participating in international conferences." Baron Nagayasu Ikeda, a bitter critic of Shidehara, declared that "The Japanese authorities are really foolish." The Foreign Ministry had to concede that the American solution "was due to failure of the Japanese Government to effect a change in ciphers occasionally." Then it tried to make the United States lose face by calling the solution "a dishonor," and sought to tar Yardley with the statement that at the time of the conference he had "visited the Japanese embassy in Washington and stated that Japan's cipher telegrams were all deciphered and then proposed to sell the translations. Mr. Yardley is such a man"—unquestionably false. A naval officer expressed amazement that such a book could be published "even in the United States," regret that the United States permitted the solution, and assurance that the Japanese Navy "has taken great trouble to preserve the secrecy of wireless telegrams." The Army, after criticizing the Foreign Ministry's "serious blunder" in not changing ciphers just before the conference, promised to give it advice.

One English-language paper after another in Japan reported the "considerable interest" or "mild sensation" or "serious sensation" that Yardley's revelations were causing in official circles. The respected Osaka *Mainichi* reported that the War and Navy ministries had instructed their attachés in Washington to purchase several copies of the book, and stated that they are "determined to enter the proposed Geneva Conference [on limiting armed forces] with all the precaution in the world." Two of the English-language papers took diametrically opposed editorial views of the solution. The *Japan Chronicle* said, very Britishly, "It is so much like steaming open people's letters—a thing which is distinctly not done," but the *Japan Times* coolly remarked that "trying to decipher the other nation's code is part of the game" and that "about all that one can do is to criticise the Foreign Office rather than rail against the Americans for scoring against our own team."

Interest long remained high. On November 5, 1931, Ambassador W. Cameron Forbes reported to the State Department, which had asked "to be kept fully informed" about the Yardley agitation, that "The 'Black Chamber' evidently made a great impression in Japan. I often hear reference made to it in conversation with various classes of Japanese. According to the publishers of the Japanese edition, more than 40,000 copies have been sold. It remains a best seller at the present time." Contrary to some published reports, however, it did not cause the government to fall (Would that books on cryptology were that powerful!), nor Japan to lodge protests with the United States or repudiate the Five-Power Treaty three years later. It did cause Japan to start treating American naval officers there to study the language with suspicion. It did impress itself so indelibly on the Japanese conscience that, when Shigenori Togo became foreign minister ten years later, he recalled the episode and checked to see whether Japanese communications were then secure. And it contributed to anti-American and antiwhite feeling in Japan.

Consequently, when Stanley K. Hornbeck, a Far Eastern expert in the Department of State, heard that Yardley had written a new book, entitled "Japanese Diplomatic Secrets," revealing many Japanese telegrams sent during the 1922 naval disarmament conference, he wrote in a memorandum of September 12, 1932: "I cannot too strongly urge that, in view of the state of excitement which apparently prevails in Japanese public opinion now, characterized by fear of or enmity toward the United States, every possible effort should be made to prevent the appearance of this book. Its appearance would contribute substantially to the amount of explosive material which seems to be piling up in Japan." Apparently as a result of this, United States marshals seized the manuscript on February 20, 1933, at the offices of The Macmillan Company, to whom Yardley had submitted it after Bobbs-Merrill had declined it, on the grounds that it violated a statute prohibiting agents of the United States government from appropriating secret documents. A Macmillan editor and Yardley's literary agent, George T. Bye, were escorted before the federal grand jury by the Chief Assistant United States Attorney in New York, a man who later achieved fame in other areas, Thomas E. Dewey. No criminal prosecution ensued against either of them or against Yardley.

Instead, the government sought to pass a law in Congress aimed straight at Yardley. "Whoever, by virtue of his employment by the United States," the bill read, "obtains from another or has or has had custody or access to any official diplomatic code or any matter prepared in any such code, or which purports to have been prepared in any such code, and without authorization or competent authority, willfully publishes or furnishes to another any such code or matter, or any matter which was obtained while in the process of transmission between any foreign government and its diplomatic mission in the United States, shall be fined not more than $10,000 or imprisoned not more than 10 years, or both."

As originally introduced in the House of Representatives at the request of the State Department by Hatton W. Sumners, a Texas Democrat, the bill—H.R. 4220, "For the Protection of Government Records"—was longer and more elaborate than the final version, presented above, though with essentially the same substance. In debate, some Representatives charged a State Department cover-up. Others questioned whether the bill would penalize persons who might present plaintext versions of American messages that had been transmitted in encoded form. The persons they were particularly concerned with were members of Congress and newspapermen. As a result of these considerations, the Senate, when it got the House bill, substituted its own version. This was hustled through the chamber while its opponents were out and was actually passed; but when the great California Republican, Hiram W. Johnson, twice governor of California and once a vice presidential candidate, returned to the chamber and found out what had been done in his absence, he asked for and received unanimous consent to have the bill reconsidered.

Two days later, on May 10, 1933, in the midst of the momentous Congressional session that enacted the major reform measures of the New Deal, the Senate held its great debate on the cryptologic bill. Harry F. Byrd of Virginia, in his first term in the Senate, was presiding. Key Pittman of Nevada, a Democrat and the administration's sponsor for the bill in the Senate, declared that "In my opinion it is unconscionable for trusted employees to publish private correspondence between governments which they obtain by virtue of their office. That is all that is covered in the measure, in my opinion." But Homer T. Bone of Washington, also a Democrat, had a question. "I am rather curious to know [how] it is that we have managed to go along from the First Congress to the Seventy-Third without this sort of legislation. What is the purpose of it at this time?" Pittman replied, "Mr. President, I will state that in the past our Government apparently has been very fortunate in having trusted employees in these extremely confidential positions. It has, however, recently found, or believe it has found, that there are grounds for suspecting that that confidence has been violated, and may be violated again." At this juncture a letter from Secretary of State Cordell Hull was, in the jargon of the legislators, spread on the record, stating that restrictions on the press were not even remotely considered in State's proposing the bill. Then Johnson took the floor, and, his indignation tempered by his humor, attacked the bill as a threat to individual liberty:

> On its face the bill is as conventional as a wedding and as respectable as a funeral. . . . But . . . it does not accomplish the result that was set forth when the bill was presented. . . .
>
> It happened that on a certain day young gentlemen from the State Department rushed into the Capitol here, and said that, as a matter of emergency, in order that guns should not rumble at our doors, we should forthwith pass this measure. Indeed, so persuasive were they with the House that the House considered it without ever telling its Members why it was presented and without Members of the House knowing at all the subject matter of the bill or the reason for the emergency. . . . That emergency was a month and a half ago, and the bill has been pending ever since, but nobody has heard of any of the dreadful and terrible things occurring that it was asserted were going to happen unless this bill should forthwith become the law of the land. So the reason for the passage of the bill, so first vehemently asserted, does not exist now and, calmly scrutinizing the past, never did exist.

He then referred, for the first time in the Congressional debate, to Yardley and his book, which he had read and found "more or less interesting." He criticized Yardley for violating "every rule that relates to fiduciary relations," and pointed out that he had written another book containing disarmament conference messages.

> It was then that the great "emergency" arose. His manuscript, as I understand, was confiscated, and after its confiscation, then into the Halls of Congress came these frightened gentlemen to say that it was such a delicate, perilous and immediate emergency that they had to have a new criminal statute. That was the first of April or thereabouts of this year. So this proposed statute was born. Immediately upon the bill being passed by the House—and it was passed in such fashion that no one knew anything about it until it had been passed—the members of the press set up the usual howl of the press about the freedom of the press and how this sort of statute would interfere with them. The result was that, of course, everybody ran to cover and the bill was amended in the twinkling of an eye in order that the press should not be interfered with and the freedom of the press at all hazards should be preserved. . . .
>
> Let us look at the bill as presented. I am speaking more or less academically in respect to this matter. I do not believe in creating unnecessary crimes. If it be essential that a crime should be created in order that punishment shall be meted out, I can recognize, of course, that it is proper for the legislature to undertake it; but unless an absolute necessity exists, I do not like the idea of creating additional crimes. Here is a bill designed to fit a particular case. It is a misfit and never will touch that case. It will rest upon the statute books, a criminal law with harsh penalties, until—far in the future, when its original purpose will have been forgotten—it will be used for another purpose for which it was never intended and may do gross wrong. That has ever been the story of this kind of law made to fit some past particular offense.

Johnson began to read the bill—"Whoever, by virtue of his employment by the United States, obtains from another . . ."—but was interrupted by Senator George W. Norris of Nebraska:

MR. NORRIS: Mr. President, should he not be guilty? If he does such a terrible thing as that, should he not be guilty of a crime?
MR. JOHNSON: Obtaining from another?
MR. NORRIS: Yes.
MR. JOHNSON: Yes, I think so. In these days anybody that obtains anything from another ought to be most condignly punished if he gets it, but the difficulty is with most of us that while we strive we do not succeed. (*Laughter*)

Then Tom Connally of Texas, another Administration manager of the bill, rebutted Johnson's arguments:

What is proposed to be done by this measure? All the bill would do is simply to make it a criminal offense for a scoundrel to betray his confidential relationship with the Government, or for another to conspire with some agent of the Government to get confidential information, and then go out and sell it for money.... My contention is that any citizen ... who is in the employ of the Government and, having access to confidential papers and records, disloyally and improperly uses knowledge so obtained for private gain or private profit ought to be punished.... Mr. President, what is there so wrong about this measure? What is there so terrible about it? Where is the Senator who approves pilfering private records? If there be such, let him rise. Senators who become enraged because of a man's stealing a spotted calf and want to put him in the penitentiary would seem to entertain the idea that a man could sell a public record or a public document and sell it for money to the newspapers and that that would be an act of patriotism and public service. I do not so regard it....

We are interfering with free thieving and free betrayal of trust; that is what we are interfering with. We are interfering with free treachery to their employer and to the Government, that is all.

This view, abetted by the political influence of the Administration, prevailed. By a voice vote the Senate passed the bill. A conference committee of Senators and Representatives decided in favor of the Senate's bill and convinced the House to accept it. On June 10, President Franklin D. Roosevelt signed it, making it Public Law 37, and it lies today on the statute books as Section 952 of Title 18, United States Code.

Four days later, the Bobbs-Merrill Company petitioned the State Department for approval to carry out a 1931 contract with Blue Ribbon Books to reprint 15,000 copies of *The American Black Chamber*. Evidently the firm, not wanting to take any chances under the new law, was seeking a State Department blessing to safeguard it against a Justice Department prosecution. It told the State Department that it would suffer a heavy financial loss if it had to make good its contract with Blue Ribbon without getting any return on sales.

On July 13, William Phillips, the acting Secretary of State (who, ironically, had personally allowed Yardley to resign from the State Department in 1917 to form MI-8), replied: "The granting by this Department of such a permission would imply that the Department felt no objection to the publication and distribution of the book and would in a measure associate the Department with action on the part of the author and the publisher upon which it has not at any time looked with approval." The department, he continued, was therefore unable to grant the permission. But the department did not want to contribute to the company's financial loss, Phillips wrote, and so it would take no action to prevent the sale or distribution of the 4,500 copies already printed by Blue Ribbon. From this refusal of the State Department to grant its "permission" for republication—though some of its officials had wondered privately whether such permissions were part of State's business—grew a legend that *The American Black Chamber* had been suppressed, though no action had been taken in regard to the many copies already in circulation.

Yardley remained unperturbed throughout the whole commotion. Though he had availed himself of the opportunity provided by his senator, Arthur R. Robinson of Indiana, to give his justifications for publishing *The American Black Chamber* ("It would, I hoped, awaken the conscience of the State Department, so that they would revise their own code systems and render American diplomatic secrets invulnerable to attack by foreign cryptographers"), he implied that he was much too busy in his laboratory developing a commercial secret ink to be interested in this piddling legislative trivia. The ink worked, but it did not inundate the nation as a commercial success, and Yardley lost the third finger of his right hand through an infection caused by it.

He tried writing again, but his imagination seemed to need fact to work on, and his adventure novels, *The Red Sun of Nippon* and *The Blonde Countess*, lacked the excitement of his rather fictionalized nonfiction. Metro-Goldwyn-Mayer, however, found the beautiful woman spy, the secret codes, and the infallible cryptologist of *The Blonde Countess* eminently suitable for its purposes. A problem was that no redblooded movie hero would settle for a dull desk job like codebreaking, but the film company fixed that up by destroying the fabric of Yardley's tale and making the hero an unwilling intellectual who wanted only to serve in the trenches overseas. The result was *Rendezvous*, starring William Powell, Rosalind Russell, Binnie Barnes, Cesar Romero, and Lionel Atwill. Yardley was retained by MGM on a generous contract as technical advisor and became friendly with Powell. The film premiered at New York's Capitol Theatre on October 25, 1935. *The New York Times* reviewed it as a "lively and amusing melodrama."

In 1938, after a brief and unsuccessful fling at real-estate speculation in Queens, New York, Yardley was hired by Chiang Kai-shek at about $10,000 a year to solve the messages of the Japanese armies then invading China. In Chungking, he at first passed himself off as an exporter of hides, but no one in the small and tight-knit foreign colony there was fooled for very long. He seems to have enjoyed some success in solving the Japanese ciphers, which appear to have been columnar transposition of the kana symbols.

By then he was changing. He was basically an attractive personality who enjoyed simple masculine pleasures. He would rise at dawn to go duck-hunting, shot a good enough game of golf to have won the Greene County (Indiana) championship in 1932, and played poker with a compulsive intensity wherever and whenever he could. He regaled his companions with a flood of amusing stories, told with the wit and gusto of a natural raconteur. He was the very opposite of stuffy, and did not hesitate to admit that he knew his way around in a Chinese whorehouse. He kept a Chinese and a German mistress* and once organized a virtual Oriental orgy for a young correspondent, later nationally famous, on the ground that it was necessary for him to be blooded as a man. He enjoyed the loyalty and friendship of a great many people, though not everybody liked him. Emily Hahn, in her *China to Me*, said bluntly that she did not, calling him "an American with a loud manner of talking." His original enterprise, which had enabled him to create MI-8 and the Black Chamber, had turned to opportunism with the publication of his book, and then had soured to cynicism under the widespread disgust that followed that violation of confidence, and under the realization that he had traded his soul for a few thousand dollars.

He returned from China in 1940, and, after a brief attempt to be a restaurateur in Washington, went to Canada to set up a cryptanalytic bureau which dealt largely with spy ciphers. He was reportedly forced out under pressure either from Stimson, then Secretary of War, or from the British, though the Canadians did not want to part with him. From 1941 to the end of the war he served as an enforcement officer in the food division of the Office of Price Administration. His popular *The Education of a Poker Player*, in which he offered an informal course of instruction in the game, appeared in 1957. On August 7, 1958, he died of a stroke at his home in Silver Spring, Maryland, and was buried with military honors in Arlington National Cemetery.

The obituaries called him "the father of American cryptography." They were wrong, but they demonstrated the deep impression that Yardley's writing had made on the American consciousness. With all its faults and falsehoods, his book had captured the imagination of the public and inspired untold numbers of amateurs to become interested in cryptology. To the extent that the impact of their fresh ideas enriched American cryptology, the credit must go to him.

While Herbert Yardley may be the best known cryptologist, uncontestably the greatest is William Frederick Friedman. Unlike his contemporary, his eminence is due most emphatically to what he did. Indeed, two more dissimilar men in a single field can scarcely be imagined. Where Yardley was Rabelaisian, outgoing, superficial, free and easy with the details of a good story, and ever ready for the main chance, Friedman tended toward introversion,

---

* At different times.

depth of study, personal security, timidity, dedication, and accuracy, nicety, and validity of work. Despite the relative drabness of these personal traits—or perhaps because of them, Friedman's theoretical contributions and his practical attainments exceed those of any other cryptologist. Yardley's career was like an amazing skyrocket that explodes in fantastic patterns against the heavens. Friedman's was like the sun.

He was born Wolfe Friedman on September 24, 1891, in Kishinev, Russia, the oldest son and second child of Frederick and Rosa Friedman. His father, a Rumanian who spoke eight languages and worked as an interpreter for the Russian Post Office, emigrated to America in 1892, at which time his son's name was changed to William. The family settled in Pittsburgh, where his father managed a sewing machine agency. William graduated in 1909 as one of the ten honor students in a class of 300 at Pittsburgh Central High School; he then went to work as chief clerk in the Erie City Iron Works, a firm that sold steam engines. About that time the back-to-the-farm movement called to city boys, and in the fall of 1910, Friedman and three friends enrolled in Michigan Agricultural College, whose chief attraction was that it was tuition-free.

But Friedman soon discovered that farming held little interest for him. He was an inventive young fellow who liked to fix things and had written some science fiction for his high-school paper; he was rapidly coming to the conclusion that he liked science. At the end of the term he learned that tuition was also free in a scientific field allied to agriculture—genetics—at one of the Ivy League universities, Cornell. He borrowed train fare and arrived in Ithaca, New York, in February, 1911, where he got a job waiting on tables. After commencement in February of 1914, he attended graduate school, managing to fall in love twice, once with a brunette, once with the blonde daughter of a movie-house owner. While he was there, a wealthy textile merchant, George Fabyan, who maintained laboratories in acoustics, chemistry, genetics, and cryptology (to try to prove that Bacon wrote Shakespeare's plays) on his 500-acre estate, Riverbank, at Geneva, Illinois, decided that he needed a geneticist to improve the grains and livestock on his farm. He applied to Cornell for a "would-be-er," not an "as-is-er," and hired Friedman, to begin June 1, 1915.

Fabyan was a man of no formal education but of intelligence and energy. He had a great desire to be "somebody," and that desire motivated his subsidizing the Baconian studies: proof of this revolutionary thesis would cover its patron as well as its actual discoverers with glory. He himself read little, but he absorbed enough from those around him to make his talk on almost any subject sound impressive—at least superficially. He was autocratic, never allowing his staff to disagree with him, but otherwise not unpleasant so long as employees recognized that he was boss. A cardinal article of faith with him was that a well-executed sales campaign could put across almost anything.

Friedman did some genetics work for him, but, because he was handy with a camera, he helped the cryptologists who were looking for Bacon's cipher-signatures in Shakespeare by making photographic enlargements of the Elizabethan printing that figured in the work. The Department of Ciphers of the Riverbank Laboratories consisted of 14 or 15 high-school and college graduates who assigned the individual letters in these Elizabethan texts to one or the other of two fonts of type as part of the Baconian search. Fabyan gave them their living plus a salary of about $50 a month. The staff was fed and housed in Engledew and Hoover Cottages, the cipher laboratories taking up the first floor of Engledew.

The young woman who collated the work of many of the other staff members was Elizebeth Smith. She had been born August 26, 1892, in Huntington, Indiana, the youngest of the nine children of John M. Smith, a dairyman, banker, and county Republican committeeman, and his wife, Sopha, who spelled her daughter's Christian name with an *e* instead of an *a* in the middle because she was not going to have anyone calling her child "Eliza." After completing high school in Huntingdon, Elizebeth attended Wooster College briefly but was graduated from Hillsdale College in Michigan where she had majored in English. While working at the Newberry Library in Chicago, she was recruited by Fabyan and began work there in 1916.

Neither she nor Friedman had given any particular previous thought to cryptology, but they began to get personally interested in the work. It is yet another of the ironies of cryptologic history that the interest of two foremost cryptologists was aroused by a false doctrine—a doctrine, moreover, against which they later were to wage a lifetime battle. For at table at the Riverbank cottages they heard gaudy tales of lusty Elizabethan life, of the not-so-Virgin Queen, of courtiers' intrigues and the secret histories of the great names of English history—all actually invalid decipherments of Shakespeare's plays tending to prove that Bacon had written them, related by the gentle, upright, but self-deluded woman who had "deciphered" them, Mrs. Elizabeth Wells Gallup. These stories stirred Friedman's dormant interest; he began to do some of the cryptology, and inevitably its puissant magic seeped like the fume of poppies into his mind and spirit and intoxicated him. "When it came to the cryptology," he recalled years later, "something in me found an outlet."

An understatement. He soon found himself head of the Department of Ciphers as well as the Department of Genetics at Riverbank. The attraction he felt for cryptology was reinforced by the attraction he felt for a cryptologist: the quick-witted and sprightly Miss Smith. In May of 1917 they were married and started the most famous husband-and-wife team in the history of cryptology.

America had declared war a month before, and Riverbank, which had the only going cryptologic concern in the country, began getting, on an informal basis, cryptograms for solution from various government bureaus. Probably the most important were messages to and from a ring of 125 Hindus who, with German aid, were taking advantage of England's preoccupation in Europe to strike for Indian independence. The intercepts were given to Friedman for solution, and he quickly solved the number cipher used in cablegrams to Berlin. The letters of the plaintext and of the keyword were transformed into digits by means of a 4 × 7 checkerboard with a normal alphabet; the key digits were then added to those of the plaintext to form the ciphertext. One key was LAMP. Each agent had his own key, but Friedman had no trouble in solving them. Nor was he stumped by a system usually regarded by amateurs as the ne plus ultra of cryptographic security: a book cipher.

It came to him in the form of a seven-page typewritten letter. The writer, Heramba Lal Gupta, had enciphered only the important words, leaving large patches of cleartext as valuable clues; he had also repeated the equivalents for many letters instead of seeking new ones and had employed neighboring letters in a single line, thus enabling Friedman to reconstruct the words of the keytext as a check upon and aid to the solution. For example, Friedman guessed from context that 83-1-2 83-1-11 83-1-25 83-1-1 83-1-8 83-1-13 83-1-18 83-1-3 83-1-1 83-1-6   83-1-3 83-1-6 meant *revolution in*, with the 83 the page, the 1 the line on that page, and the third number the letter in that line. (It is interesting to note how the third group sticks out as the equivalent for a low-frequency letter by being so far back in the line.) This gave him ORI . . N . L . . E . U . . as the start of the key line, and this in turn probably let him guess that the line started with *original* or *originally*. He would then have known that 83-1-4 in the very next word was the equivalent for *g* in *Bengal*. By taking full advantage of such clues he built up the entire plaintext without ever knowing what was later discovered—that the key book was Price Collier's *Germany and the Germans*, a scholarly work published in New York in 1913.

The Hindus were prosecuted for trying to purchase the uprising's arms in the United States and to ship them from the West Coast. At the mass trials in Chicago and San Francisco, Friedman gave evidence that in effect convicted the conspirators out of their own mouths. The San Francisco proceeding witnessed one of the most dramatic scenes ever to occur in an American courtroom when one defendant rose, fired two shots from a revolver to assassinate a compatriot who was testifying for the government, and was himself killed by a marshal shooting over the heads of the crowd. In an anticlimax, a jury later found most of the defendants guilty.

A few months after these Hindu solutions, the British submitted five short messages to Riverbank for tests. They had been enciphered by a cipher device invented by J. St. Vincent Pletts of M.I. 1(b), the British War Office cryptanalytic bureau. The machine was a modification of the Wheatstone apparatus, proposed as a field cipher. So highly did the British regard it that one argument advanced against its adoption was that if the Germans captured one and adopted it, the Allies would no longer be able to solve enemy messages! Friedman, however, at once recovered the keyword CIPHER to

(3)
If we
119-1-3
119-2-3
119-1-2
118-2-9
118-2-3
118-3-3

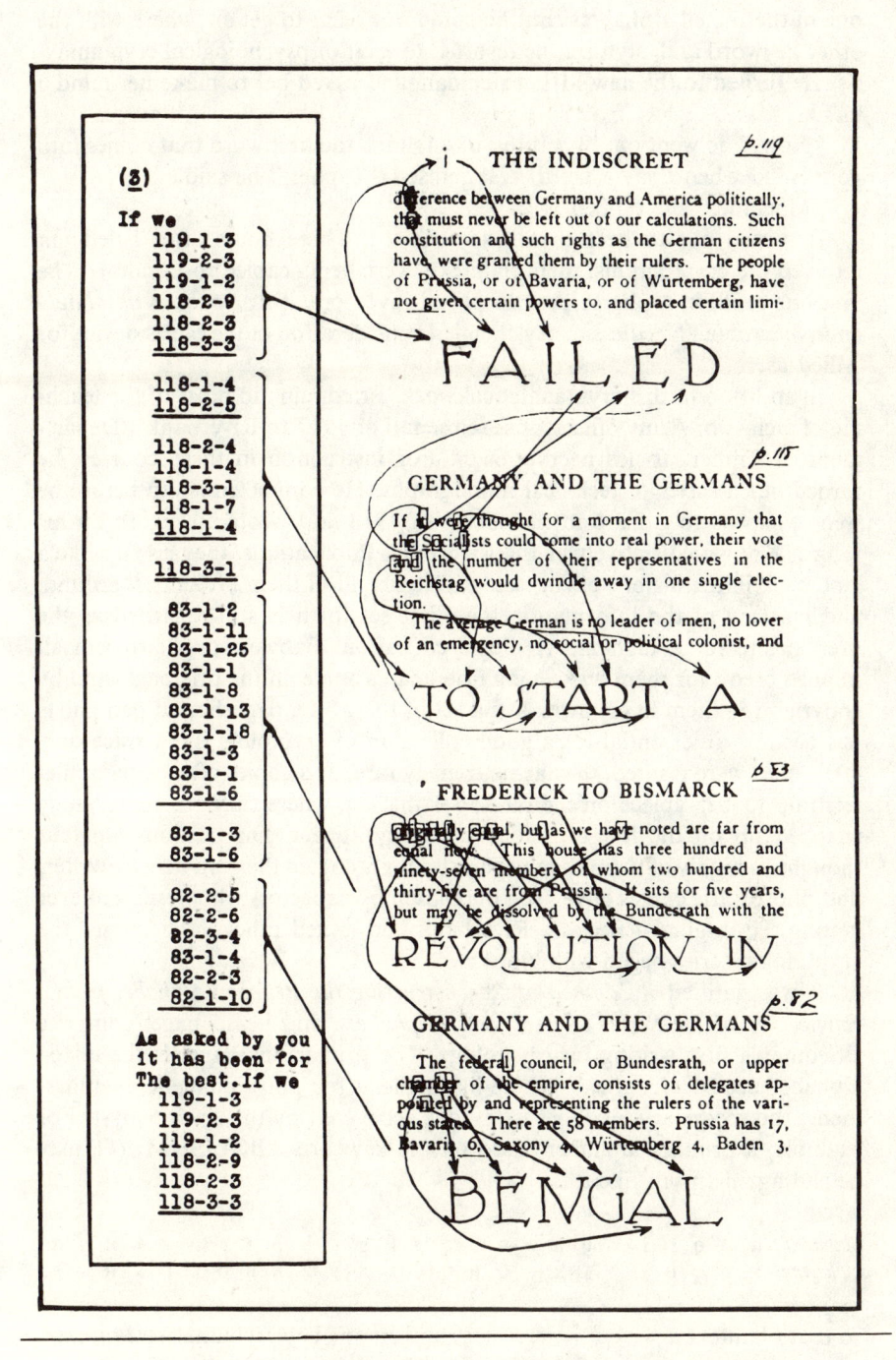

118-1-4
118-2-5

118-2-4
118-1-4
118-3-1
118-1-7
118-1-4

118-3-1

83-1-2
83-1-11
83-1-25
83-1-1
83-1-8
83-1-13
83-1-18
83-1-3
83-1-1
83-1-6

83-1-3
83-1-6

82-2-5
82-2-6
82-3-4
83-1-4
82-2-3
82-1-10

As asked by you
it has been for
The best. If we
119-1-3
119-2-3
119-1-2
118-2-9
118-2-3
118-3-3

THE INDISCREET *p. 119*

difference between Germany and America politically, that must never be left out of our calculations. Such constitution and such rights as the German citizens have, were granted them by their rulers. The people of Prussia, or of Bavaria, or of Würtemberg, have not given certain powers to, and placed certain limi-

FAILED

GERMANY AND THE GERMANS *p. 115*

If it were thought for a moment in Germany that the Socialists could come into real power, their vote and the number of their representatives in the Reichstag would dwindle away in one single election.
The average German is no leader of men, no lover of an emergency, no social or political colonist, and

TO START A

FREDERICK TO BISMARCK *p. 83*

originally equal, but as we have noted are far from equal now. This house has three hundred and ninety-seven members of whom two hundred and thirty-five are from Prussia. It sits for five years, but may be dissolved by the Bundesrath with the

REVOLUTION IN

GERMANY AND THE GERMANS *p. 82*

The federal council, or Bundesrath, or upper chamber of the empire, consists of delegates appointed by and representing the rulers of the various states. There are 58 members. Prussia has 17, Bavaria 6, Saxony 4, Würtemberg 4, Baden 3.

BENGAL

How the Hindus worked the book cipher that William Friedman solved

one of the mixed alphabets. But he could not seem to get anywhere with the other keyword and, stymied, he resorted to a bit of psychological cryptanalysis. He turned to the new Mrs. Friedman, and asked her to make her mind a blank.

"Now," he went on, "I want you to tell me the first word that comes into your mind when I say a word." He paused. "Cipher," he said.

"Machine," she replied.

It turned out to be the very key desired. Three hours after Friedman received the cryptograms, their plaintexts were being cabled to London. (The first one read, in a phrase dear to proud inventors, *This cipher is absolutely undecipherable.*) Needless to say, it ended consideration of the Pletts device for Allied use.

In addition to this cryptanalytical work, Friedman did most of the teaching of a class of Army officers sent in the fall of 1917 to Riverbank's Department of Ciphers to learn cryptology. For instruction in these courses, he turned out a series of technical monographs. He completed seven before he went overseas to G.2 A.6 in the spring of 1918 and wrote an eighth on his return. Known collectively as the Riverbank Publications, they rise up like a landmark in the history of cryptology. Nearly all of them broke new ground, and mastery of the information they first set forth is still regarded as the prerequisite for a higher cryptologic education. Fabyan sought to win an implied credit for them by keeping Friedman's name off the title pages and by copyrighting them in his own. A full set of the white, paperbound pamphlets has become an essential for a good collection of cryptologia, but since only 400 copies were printed, they are extremely rare, and copies of each pamphlet fetch up to $25 apiece on the rare-book market, where they are immediately snapped up on the few occasions that they appear. One zealous amateur thought so highly of them that he painstakingly copied them on his typewriter, and photostatic copies have been purchased by collectors who despair of ever getting the originals. Because Riverbank had issued other publications, the cryptologic series began with No. 15.

It was entitled *A Method of Reconstructing the Primary Alphabet from a Single One of the Series of Secondary Alphabets*, and its 15 pages comprise Friedman's first writing on cryptology. The primary alphabet is the mixed alphabet used to form a Vigenère-like tableau for polyalphabetic encipherment; the secondary alphabet is the one recovered by the cryptanalyst. For example, a primary alphabet based on the keyword ABOLISHMENT may be slid against itself like this

plaintext   a b o l i s h m e n t c d f g j k p q r u v w x y z
ciphertext N T C D F G J K P Q R U V W X Y Z A B O L I S H M E

so that plaintext $a = $ N, $b = $ T, $o = $ C, and so on. The cryptanalyst, however, not knowing the order of the letters in the plaintext alphabet, will arrange them alphabetically in his recovery, thus obscuring the keyword in the lower, or secondary, alphabet. It will look like this (to use Friedman's own example):

plaintext a b c d e f g h i j k l m n o p q r s t u v w x y z
ciphertext N T U V P W X J F Y Z D K Q C A B O G R L I S H M E

Friedman showed that the original alphabet could be recovered by making a chain of letters and then stretching them out at trial intervals of 1, 2, 3, ... 25 letters. To make the chain, the cryptanalyst takes as its first link the letter under *a*, which is N. He then finds this letter in the upper alphabet and takes as the second link the letter beneath it, or Q. He finds *q* in the upper alphabet and takes as the third link the letter beneath it, B. After completing the chain, he writes the letters out in successive trials, leaving ever wider spaces between them until he can see plaintext fragments that might form part of the keyword. Usually he does not have to write out the full chain before feeling that an attempt is useless. In this case, likely sequences appear at an interval of 9—which is the displacement of the two alphabets. Completion of the chain at this interval will produce the original ABOLISHMENT alphabet:

interval	1	2	3	4	5	6	7	8	9	10	11	12	13	14	15	16	17	18	19	20	21	22	23	24	25	26
1	N	Q	B	T	R	O	...																			
2	N		Q		B		T		R	...																
3	N	D		Q	V		B		T		R			O			C			U			E			
.	.	.	.	.	.																					
9	N	T	C	D					Q	R	U	V						B	O	L	I					

Such a determination can be of crucial importance. Knowing the primary alphabet will enable the cryptanalyst to solve much more easily cryptograms based on it but with different periodic keywords. He will also be able to solve much shorter cryptograms. This glimpse of the underlying key system may help him solve messages in other primary alphabets. The technique has many implications, and cryptanalysts must often be grateful to Friedman for devising it.

Riverbank Publication No. 16, *Methods for the Solution of Running-Key Ciphers*, showed in its 42 pages how to crack polyalphabetic ciphers keyed with long texts to defeat Kasiski analyses. Friedman set up an abbreviated tableau in which only the high-frequency keyletters and plaintext letters appeared with their cipher equivalents in the known alphabets. Given a cryptogram, "the first step is to assume that the key-text and plain-text consist solely" of those letters; the possible combinations that could yield the actual letters of the cryptogram are set out, and the cryptanalyst attempts to anagram so that he obtains intelligible text in both key and plain. He then extends the fragments thus obtained by working the one text against the other. No. 17, *An Introduction to Methods for the Solution of Ciphers*, was simply that. No. 18, *Synoptic Tables for the Solution of Ciphers and A Bibliography of Cipher*

Literature, set out cipher systems in a tabular arrangement similar to that devised by Porta.

No. 19 was a highly original attempt to mechanize the solution of transposition ciphers. The basic idea of *Formulae for the Solution of Geometrical Transposition Ciphers* was conceived by Lenox R. Lohr, then a captain taking one of the Riverbank courses and later president of Chicago's Museum of Science and Industry. While the formulas worked perfectly and produced plaintext fragments without the cryptanalyst's having tediously to write out innumerable trial transposition rectangles, the geometrical, or route, transpositions for which they were designed were so rarely used that the work had little practical value. Nevertheless, it was a forerunner of techniques used today with electronic computers. In No. 20, *Several Machine Ciphers and Methods for Their Solution*, Friedman amplified the de Viaris solution of the Bazeries cryptograph, to which he gave the generic name of a "multiplex" system, and devised a solution for the Wheatstone cryptograph, perhaps based on his work with the Pletts device. No. 21, *Methods for the Reconstruction of Primary Alphabets*, written in collaboration with Mrs. Friedman, took up where No. 15 left off. It extended the method of that brochure to secondary alphabets that resulted from the interaction of two different mixed alphabets that had been used as the plain and cipher components.

Riverbank Publication No. 22, written in 1920 when Friedman was 28, must be regarded as the most important single publication in cryptology. It took the science into a new world. Entitled *The Index of Coincidence and Its Applications in Cryptography*, it described the solution of two complicated cipher systems. Friedman, however, was less interested in proving their vulnerability than he was in using them as a vehicle for new methods of cryptanalysis. Fabyan had the pamphlet printed in France in 1922 to save money; General Cartier saw it and thought so highly of it that he had it translated and published forthwith—false-dating it "1921" to make it appear as if the French work had come first!

In it, Friedman devised two new techniques. One was brilliant. It permitted him to reconstruct a primary cipher alphabet without having to guess at a single plaintext letter. But the other was profound. For the first time in cryptology, Friedman treated a frequency distribution as an entity, as a curve whose several points were causally related, not as just a collection of individual letters that happen to stand in a certain order for noncausal (historical) reasons, and to this curve he applied statistical concepts. The results can only be described as Promethean, for Friedman's stroke of genius inspired the numerous, varied, and vital statistical tools that are indispensable to the cryptology of today.

The Index of Coincidence intermingles the two techniques, but they are easier to understand separately. Furthermore, the rudimentary formula used in that publication for the statistical technique has been superseded by one growing out of Friedman's 1925 solution of a cipher machine using cryptographic rotors, or wired codewheels. During this analysis Friedman refined his theory, evolving two parameters of great importance in modern cryptology. Hence, despite the violation of chronology, it seems wiser to begin with the improved theory.

Imagine an urn containing one each of the 26 letters of the alphabet. The chance of drawing any specified letter, say r, is one in 26, or 1/26. Now imagine another, identical urn. The chance of drawing an r is equally one in 26, or 1/26. What are the odds on drawing a pair of r's, one after another, in a two-draw situation? The likelihood of drawing the second r is 1/26 of the chance of drawing the first, which is 1/26. So the chance of drawing two r's in a single event, or "simultaneously," one from each urn, is 1/26 × 1/26. Similarly, the probability of drawing two a's is 1/26 × 1/26, of two b's, 1/26 × 1/26, and so on. Consequently, the chance of drawing a pair of letters—any pair of letters, no matter which pair may come up—is the sum of all these probabilities. It is (1/26 × 1/26) + (1/26 × 1/26) + ... + (1/26 × 1/26), repeated 26 times, or 26 × (1/26 × 1/26), or 1/26. This quantity may be written as the decimal 0.0385.

Assume now an ideal cryptosystem whose ciphertexts yield a perfectly flat frequency count—one with as many a's as b's as c's ... as z's. Polyalphabetics approach this in varying degrees and may, for practical purposes, be regarded as generating such ciphertexts. These texts are called "random" because they are what would be obtained if letters were drawn at random from the urn (each letter being replaced after being noted and the urn shaken to mix the lot, chance alone dictating their identities). If two such random texts are superimposed, the chance that the letter above will be the same as the letter below is the same as the chance of drawing a pair of identical letters from the two urns. This is 0.0385, or, to put it another way, there will be 3.85 such coincidences in every 100 vertical pairs. Experiment will confirm this.

Now imagine an urn filled with 100 letters of English in the proportion in which they are used in normal text—8 a's, 1 b, 3 c's, 13 e's, and so on. The chance of drawing a specified letter is now proportional to its frequency. The probability that an a will emerge is 8/100ths, that an e will is 13/100ths. With two such urns, the chance of drawing two a's is, as before, the product of the individual probabilities, or 8/100 × 8/100; the chance of drawing two e's is consequently 13/100 × 13/100. And the probability of drawing a pair—any pair—of identical letters is the sum of all these pair-probabilities: (8/100 × 8/100) + (1/100 × 1/100) + (3/100 × 3/100) ... , and so on through all 26 letters. This calculation has been made (with a slightly different frequency table). The result is 0.0667.

These two plaintext urns may likewise be replaced by two strings of plaintext. If they are superimposed, there will be as much likelihood that two letters will coincide vertically as there was that two identical letters will be drawn from the two urns. This probability is 0.0667, or 6.67 coincidences per 100 pairs. For example:

```
                                          *           *
text A         wheninthecourseofhumaneventsitbecomesnecessaryforo
text B         fourscoreandsevenyearsagoourfathers broughtforthupo
               *          **                   *        *
text A (cont.) nenationtodissolvethepoliticalbandsthathaveconnect
text B (cont.) nthiscontinentanewnationconceivedinlibertyanddedic
```

There are just seven coincidences in the 100 pairs—precisely what theory predicts.

The quantities 0.0385 and 0.0667 are important enough to be given names. The first is called κ_r, read as "kappa sub r" (for random), the second is κ_p, read "kappa sub p" (for plaintext).* They will naturally differ for other alphabets and other languages. In Russian's 30-letter Cyrillic alphabet, for example, κ_r will be $30 \times 1/30 \times 1/30$, or 0.0333. Changing frequency characteristics alters κ_p. Thus, it is 0.0778 for French, 0.0762 for German, 0.0738 for Italian, 0.0775 for Spanish, and 0.0529 for Russian.

The establishment of the kappa values permits the finding of a quick and easy answer to one of the most important and recurring problems in cryptanalysis: how to superimpose two or more polyalphabetic ciphertexts so that the letters in each column will have the same keyletter. The problem arises in cases in which different messages use the same portion of a very long key, such as that generated by a machine. Discovery of these overlaps opens the door to a Kerckhoffs solution. A test based on the kappa values and called "the kappa test" tells quantitatively whether a given superimposition has brought together identically enciphered texts.

To understand it, one must recognize first that the superimposition of two monalphabetically enciphered texts will result in the κ_p figure of about 6.67 coincidences per 100 vertical pairs, or 6.67 per cent of coincidences. This is because the coincidences will occur whether the letters are clothed in ciphertext disguises or not. The calculation does not ask the letters for their identities. It merely notes their coincidence. By the same token—and this is important—two *polyalphabetic* cryptograms enciphered in the same key and superimposed so that the two occurrences of that key are in synchronization with one another will also show 6.67 per cent of coincidences. The reason is this: In a correct (in-phase) superimposition, the two letters of each vertical pair have the same keyletter. Thus whenever a coincidence occurs in the plaintext, the letters of the pair will be identically enciphered. This results in an identical pair—a coincidence—in the ciphertext. It does not matter that a pair of *e*'s may be enciphered into v's at one point and into Q's at another, or that a coincidence of *a*'s becomes a coincidence of L's here and a coincidence of F's there. The total number of coincidences will remain the same as the number in the plaintext.

On the other hand, if the two cryptograms are improperly superimposed, so that the keys are not in step, any coincidences will result from different

---

* The Greek letter kappa is frequently used in mathematics to designate a constant.

keyletters operating on different plaintext letters to accidentally produce the same ciphertext letter. The coincidences will be caused, in other words, by chance. Chance alone will produce 3.85 coincidences per 100 vertical pairs in random text, and polyalphabetic ciphertext is equivalent to random text. Hence an incorrect superimposition should yield about 3.85 per cent of coincidences. But 3.85 per cent is substantially less than 6.67 per cent, and so a comparison of the percentages of coincidences at various test superimpositions should show which superimposition is correct.

An example should make things clear. A cryptosystem with the Vigenère running key THE BARD OF AVON IS THE AUTHOR OF THESE LINES... starts the key for the first message with the first keyletter, but starts the key for successive messages with the third, fifth, and so on, keyletters. If plaintext 1 is *If music be the food of love, play on*, and plaintext 2 is *Now is the winter of our discontent*, the encipherments will be these:

key   THEBARDOFAVONISTHEAUTHOROFTH
plaintext 1   ifmusicbethefoodofloveplayon
ciphertext 1 BMQVSZFPJTCSSWGWVJLIOLDCODHU

key   (TH)EBARDOFAVONISTHEAUTHOROFTHESE
plaintext 2   nowisthewinterofourdiscontent
ciphertext 2 RPWZVHMERWABWKVJOOKKWJQTGAIFX

A cryptanalyst, receiving these two cryptograms, will superimpose them so that they start at the same point:

ciphertext 1 BMQVSZFPJTCSSWGWVJLIOLDCODHU
ciphertext 2 RPWZVHMERWABWKVJOOKKWJQTGAIFX

Since there are 28 vertical pairs, the cryptanalyst would expect 28 × 0.0667 coincidences or 1.8676, or about 2, for a proper superimposition. But in fact he finds none, so he shifts the second cryptogram one space to the right and tries again. There will now be 27 vertical pairs. The cryptanalyst again calculates the theoretical expected number of coincidences for random and for correctly superimposed texts of this length so that he may compare the values with what he actually observes. Thus, a wrongly superimposed text would yield 27 × 0.0385 = 0.9695, or about 1 coincidence that would be produced by chance alone, while a correct superimposition would yield 27 × 0.0667 = 1.2369. (These fractional differences become more pronounced with longer texts.) One coincidence appears:

ciphertext 1 BMQVSZFPJTCSS WGWVJLIOLDCODHU
ciphertext 2 RPWZVHMERWAB WKVJOOKKWJQTGAIFX

Since the differences between the chance and the caused values are so slight, with so few letters, the cryptanalyst might wonder whether this is not in fact a random result (which in fact it is: the upper W resulting from the encipherment of plaintext *o* with key I, the lower W resulting from the encipherment of plaintext *e* with key S) and try the next superimposition. Here the number of coincidences immediately jumps. This superimposition is obviously correct.

```
                          *                * *
ciphertext 1     B M Q V S Z F P J T C S S W G W V J L I O L D C O D H U
ciphertext 2       R P W Z V H M E R W A B W K V J O O K K W J Q T G A I F X
```

If the cryptanalyst wishes to continue, he will find that at the next superimposition the number of coincidences falls again, to 2, and will return to begin his attack with the third superimposition.

It is like shifting, an inch at a time, two identical picket fences with very wide pales and very narrow slits at irregular locations. From time to time, light will shine through when two slits coincide by chance. But there will be a burst of radiance when the fences are correctly juxtaposed and light can stream through all the slits at once. Similarly with the cryptograms: the right superimposition allows the coincidences that lie in the original plaintext to stand forth, even though the polyalphabetic key produces different ciphertext letters for the same plaintext letter.

The importance of the kappa test in modern cryptology can hardly be overestimated. Computers can automatically make the vertical comparisons necessary to determine coincidences at rates of thousands per second, can check the total against the two theoretical figures, and then can ring a bell to signalize the correct superimposition or can automatically shift the texts one place and try again. Cipher machines employ keys millions of letters long in attempts to preclude superimposition, but in heavy traffic several cryptograms may be enciphered with overlapping portions of these keys. Only the computerized kappa test makes practicable the search for these overlaps through the scores or hundreds of messages that are needed to make finding them likely. If enough are found to permit their alignment in depth, a Kerckhoffs attack—frequency analysis of the columns, plus anagramming of the plaintext along the horizontal, aided by symmetry of position to reconstruct the cipher alphabets—can solve the cryptograms. The kappa test thus opens the door to the solution of the most complex of modern ciphers.

The parameters κ_p and κ_r animate two other Greek-letter tests, the phi and the chi tests. Both derive from the basic principle of coincidence. And just as a frequency count concentrates the spread-out occurrences of individual letters for easier assimilation, so the phi and chi tests coalesce the separate tabulations of a frequency count to make it easier to compare counts. These two tests were devised in 1935 by one of Friedman's assistants, Dr. Solomon Kullback. Since Friedman's original test in *The Index of Coincidence* has been supplanted by the chi test, it seems preferable to give the latter.

The phi test, which is its basis, can determine whether a given frequency count reflects a monalphabetic or a polyalphabetic encipherment. It might be used to see whether a Kasiski determination of a period is correct by testing the letters in the column for monalphabeticity. If the period is correct, the frequency counts of the columns will show as monalphabetic; if not, they will be only random.

To use it, the cryptanalyst first multiplies the total number of letters in the message (N) by that total less one ($N-1$). He then multiplies this product by κ_r to find what is known as the polyalphabetic expected phi (ϕ_r). Then he performs the same operation with κ_p to find what is known as the monalphabetic expected phi (ϕ_p). He sets these two aside and goes through his frequency count of the cryptogram, multiplying each letter's frequency (f) by that frequency less one ($f-1$). He adds up these products. If the sum—the observed phi—is closer to the monalphabetic expected phi than to the polyalphabetic, the frequency count is monalphabetic, and vice versa. For example, with a 26-letter cryptogram the expected phis are:

$$26 \times 25 \times 0.0385 = 25 \text{ for } \phi_r$$
$$26 \times 25 \times 0.0667 = 43 \text{ for } \phi_p$$

The cryptogram's frequency count determines its observed phi:

```
              A   B   C   D   E   F   G   H   I   J   K   L   M
frequency (f) .   2   .   .   1   1   3   4   .   .   .   .   1
f×(f−1)       0 + 2 + 0 + 0 + 0 + 0 + 6 + 12+ 0 + 0 + 0 + 0 + 0 +

              N   O   P   Q   R   S   T   U   V   W   X   Y   Z
frequency (f) .   1   1   2   2   2   2   1   .   1   .   1   .
f×(f−1)       0 + 0 + 0 + 2 + 2 + 2 + 2 + 0 + 0 + 0 + 0 + 0 + 0 = 28
```

The observed phi of 28 is noticeably closer to the polyalphabetic expected phi; the assortment of letters on which the count is based is thus probably polyalphabetic. The test can determine this fairly accurately for small distributions, where the eye cannot discriminate between the two types of count.

The chi test uses this procedure to compare two frequency distributions. It can tell whether the letters they represent have been enciphered with the same key, either mon- or polyalphabetic. For example, it can tell whether two Vigenère cryptograms have the same keyword, or, more importantly, it can pick out the columns in a Kerckhoffs superimposition that have been enciphered by the same keyletter, thus permitting their letter counts—which are usually scanty—to be amalgamated.

Its mechanics remain the same whether a polyalphabetic or a monalphabetic distribution is being tested, the only difference being that κ_r is used in the polyalphabetic calculations and κ_p in the monalphabetic. The chi test compares only two distributions at a time. The procedure is this: Multiply the number of letters in one distribution by the number in the other and by κ_p or κ_r. This is the expected chi. Then multiply the number of a's in one by the number of a's in the other, the number of b's by the number of b's, and so on. Total these products. The sum constitutes the observed chi. If the observed chi is reasonably close to the expected, the distributions represent identically enciphered assortments of letters.

For example, the three following counts have all been found to be monalphabetic. Are they identically enciphered?

```
    A B C D E F G H I J K L M N O P Q R S T U V W X Y Z   total
1   . 1 . 1 . 4 . 1 3 2 1 . 2 4 . . 1 1 . 2 1 1 . . . .    25
2   2 1 2 2 . 2 3 . . 4 . 3 4 . 3 . . . . . 6 . . . 2 1    35
3   . . . 1 . 2 2 1 . 2 . 4 1 1 . . . 1 . . 2 . . 2 . .    19
```

Since they are monalphabetic, κ_p is used for the calculations:

$$\begin{array}{ll} & \text{expected} \\ & \text{chi} \\ \text{1 and 2} & 25 \times 35 \times 0.0667 = 58 \\ \text{1 and 3} & 25 \times 19 \times 0.0667 = 32 \\ \text{2 and 3} & 35 \times 19 \times 0.0667 = 44 \end{array}$$

The individual letter-multiplications produce the following:

```
         A    B    C    D    E    F    G    H    I    J    K    L    M
1×2   0 +  1 +  0 +  2 +  0 +  8 +  0 +  0 +  0 +  8 +  0 +  0 +  8 +
1×3   0 +  0 +  0 +  1 +  0 +  8 +  0 +  1 +  0 +  4 +  0 +  0 +  2 +
2×3   0 +  0 +  0 +  2 +  0 +  4 +  6 +  0 +  0 +  8 +  0 + 12 +  4 +
```

```
                                                            observed
         N    O    P    Q    R    S    T    U    V    W    X    Y    Z      chi
1×2   0 +  0 +  0 +  0 +  0 +  0 +  0 +  6 +  0 +  0 +  0 +  0 +  0 =    33
1×3   4 +  0 +  0 +  0 +  1 +  0 +  0 +  2 +  0 +  0 +  0 +  0 +  0 =    23
2×3   0 +  0 +  0 +  0 +  0 +  0 +  0 + 12 +  0 +  0 +  0 +  0 +  0 =    48
```

The only expected and observed chis that agree to any extent are those for counts 2 and 3; their messages may then be regarded as having identical encipherments and may be combined in all respects, making identification of plaintext letters that much easier. With Kerckhoffs superimpositions in which the columns run only 10 or 15 letters deep, the chi test in effect makes solution practicable.

The same procedure may be used to correctly line up frequency distributions that have been shifted relative to one another—a task almost impossible to do by eye when the counts are small. For example, a cryptanalyst knows that two frequency counts represent the same cipher alphabet but standing at different positions relative to the normal alphabet. He can run the chi test at each of the 26 possible juxtapositions of the two to see at which point they represent identical encipherments. If the cryptanalyst can determine this, he will know the distance that one has to be slid to match the other and so their relative displacement. This knowledge plays an essential role in the other technique that Friedman described in *The Index of Coincidence*.

One of the two ciphers that he was analyzing in that publication was a progressive-alphabet system. For simplicity's sake, this may be imagined as a St.-Cyr slide with a mixed cipher alphabet that shifts forward one space after each plaintext letter is enciphered. The period is 26, and a cryptanalyst would have no trouble in distributing the letters of a cryptogram into 26 columns, each enciphered at a setting of the slide. If the cryptanalyst focuses on one letter of the ciphertext alphabet as it creeps forward with the slide, he will see that this letter adopts at any given position the frequency of the plaintext letter above it. It exists with that frequency in the column representing that setting of the slide, and "deposits" this frequency in a frequency count for that column. At the next setting of the slide, it attires itself in the frequency of the plaintext letter above it at this point, and again sheds the frequency of that plaintext letter in a frequency count for the column representing that setting. The cryptanalyst now looks at his 26 frequency counts, which represent the successive positions of the slide as the key progressed. He singles out this one letter in the successive counts. Its differing frequencies mark the differing plaintext letters it has represented as it has moved along. The point to see is that these successive frequencies reflect the plaintext letters in their order in the plaintext alphabet. If this order happens to be the normal alphabet, things will be simplified, but the order itself is immaterial to what follows.

While this cipher letter is creating this pattern of frequencies, another cipher letter is also creating it. As this other cipher letter moves past the letters of the plaintext alphabet, it too is piling up little mounds of frequencies in the successive column counts. These mounds likewise mirror the order of the letters in the plaintext alphabet. The two patterns will be virtually identical, differing only by the usual and slight variations in plaintext. Now if one letter precedes another on the ciphertext slide by, say, three places, its pattern, as seen cutting through the 26 frequency counts, will obviously be shifted three places forward of the pattern of the other letter. So if the cryptanalyst can determine the displacements of the patterns with respect to one another, he can find the relative positions of those two ciphertext letters in the ciphertext alphabet. By determining the relative displacement of all the ciphertext letters in this fashion, the cryptanalyst can reconstruct the entire ciphertext alphabet! And he can do it without guessing at a single plaintext letter!

Friedman developed the ancestor of the chi test to compare the frequency patterns to determine the displacements. This comparison is a crafty and ingenious idea, with many applications in the cryptanalyses of complex systems, especially machines using cryptographic rotors, which are progressive. But it has had nowhere near the impact of the statistical concept. Friedman presented both ideas in *The Index of Coincidence*, and cryptology has never been the same since.

Before Friedman, cryptology eked out an existence as a study unto itself, as an isolated phenomenon, neither borrowing from nor contributing to other bodies of knowledge. Frequency counts, linguistic characteristics, Kasiski examinations—all were peculiar and particular to cryptology. It dwelt a recluse in the world of science. Friedman led cryptology out of this lonely wilderness and into the broad rich domain of statistics. He connected cryptology to mathematics. The sense of expanding horizons must have resembled that felt by chemists when Friedrich Wöhler synthesized urea, demonstrating that life processes operate under well-known chemical laws and are therefore subject to experimentation and control, and leading to today's vast strides in biochemistry. When Friedman subsumed cryptanalysis under statistics, he likewise flung wide the door to an armamentarium to which cryptology had never before had access. Its weapons—measures of central tendency and dispersion, of fit and skewness, of probability and sampling and significance—were ideally fashioned to deal with the statistical behavior of letters and words. Cryptanalysts, seizing them with alacrity, have wielded them with notable success ever since.

This is why Friedman has said, in looking back over his career, that *The Index of Coincidence* was his greatest single creation. It alone would have won him his reputation. But in fact it was only the beginning.

He and Mrs. Friedman quit Riverbank near the end of 1920. The situation had become intolerable. Fabyan had lured him back after the war with raises and promises of absolute freedom to prove or disprove the existence of ciphers in Shakespeare. But he had squelched every attempt to do so and had embarrassed Friedman into apparently acquiescent silence at lantern-slide lectures on the subject. On January 1, 1921, Friedman began a six-month contract with the Signal Corps to devise cryptosystems. When it expired, he was taken on the civil-service payroll of the War Department at $4,500 a year.

One of his first assignments was to teach a course in military codes and ciphers at the Signal School, then at Camp Alfred Vail, New Jersey. For this he wrote a textbook that, for the first time, imposed order upon the chaos of cipher systems and their terminology. These had sprouted in a bewildering variety, and writers treated them individually, with little comprehension of the close connection between, say, the Vigenère and the Gronsfeld. Friedman sorted them out on the basis of structure instead of aspect, and so logical and useful was this classification that it has become standard. He modeled his nomenclature on his categories, so that the names he minted have the great merit of making the relations between the various genera of ciphers evident on sight. An example is the complementary pair "monalphabet" and "polyalphabet"; Givierge was even then calling polyalphabetic systems by the almost obfuscatory "double substitution," which tells absolutely nothing at all about the system. Friedman's most important coinage was the word "cryptanalysis," which he devised in 1920 to clear up a chronic source of confusion in cryptology—the ambiguity of the verb "decipher," then used to mean both authorized and unauthorized reductions of a cryptogram to plaintext. He titled his book *Elements of Cryptanalysis*, and the term has so prospered that today it circulates in general conversation and print.

While the book's main contribution is its taxonomy, each of its 143 pages of text manifests the author's concern for always making clear to the reader why things happen as they do. As a result, the student understands principles and phenomena, and the lessons stick. Partly because of this pedagogical effectiveness, partly because of its substantive values, Friedman's book, issued by the Chief Signal Officer in May of 1923 as Training Pamphlet No. 3, has guided the development of all American cryptology since then.

At the start of 1922, Friedman became Chief Cryptanalyst of the Signal Corps in charge of the Code and Cipher Compilation Section, Research and Development Division, Office of the Chief Signal Officer. To help him carry on the work of the office he had a single clerk-typist—a cauliflower-eared ex-prizefighter. Because Yardley's Black Chamber was doing the cryptanalysis for the War Department, Friedman's functions were nominally cryptographic. He installed the M-94, or Jefferson-Bazeries cylinder, as the Army's field cipher. Paradoxically, however, his job involved a great deal of cryptanalysis. He was continually testing the new systems of cryptography urged on the Army as "absolutely indecipherable" by zealous amateurs.

Most difficult of these was the machine with five wired codewheels—rotors—invented by Edward H. Hebern, whose principle is today the most widely used in high-level cryptography. Each of the rotors generates a progressive cipher, and in 1925 Friedman devised the kappa test and extended his *Index of Coincidence* analyses to determine the order and starting positions of the rotors. The five progressive ciphers intertwine in a cipher of hideous nightmare complexity, but in a later solution Friedman sorted them out and reconstructed the wiring of the rotors. This work was of the utmost importance, for it laid the foundations for the PURPLE machine solution and for today's many solutions of modern rotor machines. The technique was far in advance of its time. So far as is known, not another cryptanalyst on the globe could duplicate it—and none did, apparently, for more than two decades. With this solution of Friedman's, world leadership in cryptology passed to America.

Friedman's horizons were continually expanding. In 1922, he had filed applications for his first two patents—improvements on a device recently invented by Gilbert S. Vernam. In 1924, he testified before a Congressional committee to his reading of some messages in the Teapot Dome scandal. When Mars made an extremely close approach to Earth a few months later, he joined in the Roaring Twenties wackiness by standing by to translate any revelations the Martians may have condescended to pass along. He had returned to mundane problems by 1927, when he wrote a history and theory of commercial codes for the American delegations to international communications conferences, which were then heatedly discussing the pronounceability of codewords as a basis for cable toll rates. The following year, he served as secretary and technical advisor to the American delegation to the International Telegraph Conference of Brussels. In 1929, he became widely known as one of the world's leading authorities on cryptology when the *Encyclopaedia Britannica* published his article on "Codes and Ciphers."

Meanwhile, the Army had been studying its divided cryptologic operation and, shortly before the State Department withdrew support from Yardley's bureau, had decided to integrate both cryptographic and cryptanalytic functions in the Signal Corps. The closing of the Black Chamber eased the transition, and on May 10, 1929, cryptologic responsibility devolved upon the Chief Signal Officer. To better meet these new responsibilities, the Signal Corps established a Signal Intelligence Service in its War Plans and Training Division, with Friedman as director. Its officially stated mission was to prepare the Army's codes and ciphers, to intercept and solve enemy communications in war, and in peace to do the training and research—a vague enough term—necessary to become immediately operational at the outbreak of war. To carry out these duties, Friedman hired three junior cryptanalysts, all in their early twenties, at $2,000 a year—the first of the second generation of American cryptologists. They were Frank Rowlett, a Virginian, and Solomon Kullback and Abraham Sinkov, close college friends who had taught together in New York City high schools before coming to Washington and who both received their Ph.D.'s in mathematics a few years later. It was the beginning of an expansion that led to the massive cryptologic organization of today.

By this time the Navy, too, had its cryptologic section. Like the Army's, it had evolved gradually.

When the Navy was reorganized during World War I in its present form, with a Chief of Naval Operations, responsibility for cryptography was transferred in October 1917 from the Bureau of Navigation, which had long held it, to the new Office of Naval Communications. The four young assistant communication officers—who were burdened by the unfortunate Navy jargon-abbreviation "ASSCOMS"—coded and decoded messages in their office in the old State-War-Navy departments building, where Yardley also worked. They were doing this work even before the transfer. When an inquiry was held on the loss of a battle signal book, letters flooded in from amateurs all over the country who thought they had the answer to the Navy's code security. It fell to the senior assistant communication officer, Lieutenant (j.g.) W. W. (Poco) Smith, to reply. He picked up the gauntlet thrown down in the form of challenge messages, and solved them, learning a great deal about cryptology in the process.

In 1916, the Navy had three main codes: the old, ponderous, seldom-used Secret Code of 1887, the five-letter SIGCODE, which could be used only by officers and which had a variety of ciphers, some for flag officers, some for all Navy ships, and the four-letter radio code that was only confidential and that could be worked by enlisted men. But at the time of the Marine landing in Haiti, a State Department message was transmitted there in the SIGCODE; the plaintext was published; the code was assumed compromised, and Smith was designated to prepare a new one.

"It was," he recalled, "a colossal job. First, I simplified but expanded the context.... Now, a more difficult problem: five-letter code groups and the text were both arranged alphabetically. This would not do. Exhausting the possibilities of arranging the letters of the alphabet into mixed groups of five letters each,* I typed these in columns, scissored them, and dropped them into a bucket. After mixing, I drew the groups one at a time and typed them in double-spaced columns to be placed opposite the text words or phrases to be encoded. Tedious work." Also crude and time-consuming. Naval Code A-1 was not completed and printed by the Government Printing Office until after the United States had entered World War I.

While Smith was making up the code, the Navy set up a Code and Signal Section in naval communications to handle the cryptographic duties. In charge was Lieutenant Russell Willson, who devised a strip form of the Jefferson cylinder with fixed indices as a superencipherment system. The metal frame and strips on which the mixed alphabets were stamped were manufactured at the Naval Gun Factory in southeast Washington, and the device, called the "NCB" (for "Navy Code Box"), was used from 1917 on. (Congress awarded Willson $15,000 in 1935 for the Navy's use of the device, which was then still in service.) Meanwhile, Smith, who wanted to remain a line officer for future command and not become a deskbound specialist, sailed off to war in January, 1918, vowing never to return to communications duty—which he never did. An experience like his in code-construction would have conditioned anybody against cryptology. (He did, however, write one of the classic expositions of the solution of the Playfair cipher, which appeared in J. C. H. Macbeth's translation of André Langie's *De la cryptographie*.)

Naval participation in the war was too limited for much cryptanalytic development, but interest was stimulated. Accordingly, in January of 1924, Lieutenant Laurance F. Safford was ordered to set up a radio intelligence organization in the Code and Signal Section. When he left for sea duty two years later, a small, highly secret organization was functioning in Room 2646 of the "temporary" Navy Department building on Constitution Avenue. Lieutenant Ellis M. Zacharias, who trained seven months in 1926 with the cryptanalytic organization, told what it was like:

> My days were spent in study and work among people with whom security had become second nature. Hours went by without any of us saying a word, just sitting in front of piles of indexed sheets on which a mumbo jumbo of figures or letters was displayed in chaotic disorder, trying to solve the puzzle bit by bit like fitting together the pieces of a jigsaw puzzle. We were just a few then in Room 2646, young people who gave ourselves to cryptography with the same ascetic devotion with which young men enter a monastery. It was known to everyone that the secrecy of our work would prevent the ordinary recognition accorded

---

* Poetic license. There are actually 11,881,376 permutations of the 26 letters in groups of five, far more than any code has ever used.

to other accomplishments. It was then that I first learned that intelligence work, like virtue, is its own reward.

On completion of his apprenticeship, Zacharias took charge of an intercept post on the fourth floor of the American consulate in Shanghai to learn as much as he could from Japanese naval messages. Safford returned to cryptology in June, 1929, and, except for a four-year tour at sea from 1932 to 1936, stayed with the science from then on. He built up the communications intelligence organization into what later became OP-20-G and, by adding improvements of his own to Edward Hebern's rotor mechanisms, gradually developed cipher machines suitable for the Navy's requirements of speed, reliability, and security. His contributions to cryptanalytics were minor, since his talents lay more in the administrative and mechanical fields. But he is the father of the Navy's present cryptologic organization.

In the Munitions Building next door to the Navy Department, Friedman had begun tutoring his junior cryptanalysts, who had not the feeblest knowledge of codes and ciphers, in these arcane mysteries. They discovered an aptitude for them. In November, 1931, they and Friedman solved in a few hours a teletypewriter cipher machine offered for sale to the State Department by its inventor, Parker Hitt, then of International Telephone and Telegraph. In 1934 they prepared a paper on a general solution for the ADFGVX, and in 1935 Kullback devised the phi and chi tests, publishing them in an important monograph entitled *Statistical Methods in Cryptanalysis*. Friedman wrote *Elementary Military Cryptography*, *Advanced Military Cryptography*, and *Military Cryptanalysis*, the latter an expansion of his *Elements of Cryptanalysis*, as texts for Army extension courses. *Military Cryptanalysis*, which appeared in four parts, comprises the finest, most lucid exposition of the solution of basic ciphers that has ever been published.

Gradually, despite depression and isolationism, the Signal Intelligence Service expanded. In July of 1934, First Lieutenant W. Preston (Red) Corderman, who had studied in what was rather grandly known as the S.I.S. School (the faculty consisted of Friedman and his assistants), became an instructor in that school when it was formally constituted as a separate section. In August of 1935, Major Haskell Allison replaced Friedman as administrative head of S.I.S., though Friedman continued to direct the cryptologic activities. Its first sizable expansion came in the fiscal year 1938, when the number of civilian employees (clerks included) was raised from six to eleven on a personnel budget of $24,360.

During these years, Friedman further expanded his interests. He discussed the cryptologic abilities of Edgar Allan Poe and Jules Verne in scholarly articles, solved ciphers posed as challenges by earlier writers on cryptology, investigated historical problems such as the Zimmermann telegram and the field codes of the A.E.F. He got important works translated, and annotated them with his ubiquitous "W.F.F." He continued to patent inventions. Unfortunately, caught between the need for secrecy and a desire for fame, he tended to play the dog in the cryptologic manger—if he couldn't have the glory, no one else would. His usual tactic was to blacken amateur contributions, often quite worthwhile, as "unprofessional." His wife, who had solved the codes of rumrunners during Prohibition, continued her cryptanalytical activities for the Treasury Department. They even managed to raise two children, Barbara and John Ramsay.

In the late 1930s, as the crisis of war drew near, the Army accelerated its plans for mobilization. Of the entire War Department establishment, the S.I.S. was the first to be augmented in personnel, space, and facilities. On November 2, 1939, authorization was obtained for 26 more civilian employees. Selected civilians, enlisted men, and Navy reserve officers were allowed to take the extension courses previously given only to Army reserve officers; by June 30, 1939, a total of 283 students were enrolled. A few members of the American Cryptogram Association were recruited. The six Signal Service Companies in the field that had supplied intercepts to S.I.S. were centralized on January 1, 1939, in a 2nd Signal Service Company, with an authorized strength of 101 enlisted men.

The driving force behind this expansion was the Chief Signal Officer, that one-time cryptologist, Joseph O. Mauborgne, now a two-star general. As one of the first steps in the upgrading of S.I.S., he had established it on April 23, 1938, as an independent section in his office. It was he who directed it to bend its energies to the solution of the Japanese PURPLE system and, as an old and close friend of Friedman, urged him to lead the assault. Friedman did—and with that bright genius of a dark science blazing the way, the S.I.S. team struggled upward in one of the most arduous, grinding, extended, and ultimately triumphant cryptanalyses in history. The date was August, 1940; Friedman was 48. With the conquest of this Everest, the greatest career in cryptology reached its climax. A few months later, the captain of the team succumbed to the strain of the solution. He was admitted to Walter Reed General Hospital on January 4, 1941, for a nervous breakdown and was discharged March 24. He had to retire, with a permanent disability, from his lieutenant colonelcy in the Signal Corps reserve.

Afterward, his superiors refused to allow him to work more than a few hours a day, and then only in the less taxing area of communications security. Though he was still Chief Cryptanalyst of the War Department, he served as Director of Communications Research for the S.I.S. (under its various names, chiefly Signal Security Agency) throughout World War II. The post was a high one; military reviews were held for him when he visited intercept stations or other cryptologic posts. He spent most of the war at the Arlington Hall Station, located in suburban Virginia in what had been a girls' school. Not a few of the thousands who worked there remember with gratitude the natty, mustachioed man with the bow tie who picked them up as they stood shivering at the bus stop and gave them a lift into Washington.

Friedman retained his directorship when the agency was divorced from the Signal Corps on September 15, 1945, and placed under G-2 as the Army Security Agency. Upon the creation of the Armed Forces Security Agency in 1949, he became chief of the technical division. When this agency was supplanted in 1952 by the National Security Agency, which handles most of the cryptologic activities of the United States, Friedman became chief technical consultant, and two years later, special assistant to the director. He had also been, since 1947, the Cryptologist of the Department of Defense.

He retired in 1955, relinquishing all these posts but remaining as a consultant. In 1944, he received the Commendation for Exceptional Civilian Service, the War Department's highest civilian decoration, and, in 1946, President Truman conferred upon him the Medal for Merit, the highest award for civilian service that the United States government can give. The citations were necessarily vague, referring only (in the case of the Medal for Merit) to "exceptionally meritorious conduct in the performance of outstanding service, conspicuously above the usual." On October 12, 1955, at a ceremony before 500 people honoring his retirement, Allen W. Dulles, the Director of Central Intelligence, unexpectedly pinned the National Security Medal on Friedman's breast. A picture snapped just after the presentation shows Friedman standing overwhelmed with surprise, apparently fighting back tears, as Dulles, Sinkov, Kullback, and Major General Ralph J. Canine, director of N.S.A., applaud. The medal, the highest decoration for distinguished achievement relating to the national intelligence effort, was the sixth to be awarded since its creation in 1953.

As the pressure of his duties declined, Friedman and his wife returned to the cryptologic field that had gotten them started—the Baconian ciphers. They summed up the experience of a lifetime in a long and exhaustive report that won them the Folger Shakespeare Library literary prize in 1955. After his retirement, they collaborated in preparing this work for 1957 publication by the Cambridge University Press as *The Shakespearean Ciphers Examined*. While, as *The New York Times Book Review* accurately said, they buried "these pseudocryptograms beneath a mass of evidence as crushing as an avalanche," they also introduced their readers to a rogues' gallery of pseudo-cryptologists not to be met elsewhere in literature. The Friedmans here display a rather surprising—surprising to one who has perused only his technical writing—wit and talent for personality sketches.

In 1956, the 84th Congress voted to pay Friedman $100,000 in compensation for profits he had been unable to realize because security prevented him from marketing cipher machines that he had invented for the government. It marked the successful end of a battle that had begun six years earlier when his lawyers decided that under existing law he could not sue to recover his losses and that he must seek legislative relief. "The immeasurable stress of his work," they stated in a memorandum asking the Defense Department not to oppose the measure, "and the burden of responsibility imposed by the necessity for constant secrecy ever since 1921 were major factors in the impairment of Mr. Friedman's health which now makes his livelihood increasingly precarious. It is this last consideration which finally induced Mr. Friedman to permit us to bring the matter to the attention of the Department of Defense."

Involved were nine inventions made from 1933 to 1944, two with Rowlett's aid, though the bill was not limited to them. Two were so secret that no patent applications had ever been filed. Four are held in secrecy in the Patent Office: three of these pertained to the Converter M-134-C, a rotor machine, and one to the Converter M-228. Three have issued as patents: a strip form of the Jefferson cylinder; the Converter M-325, another rotor machine; and a facsimile enciphering system.

"Procurement by the United States of devices constructed in accordance with the principles of Mr. Friedman's inventions has approximated $10 million," the Secretary of the Army wrote to Congress in support of Friedman's case in 1953, "most of which occurred during the active phase of World War II, and has involved the use of substantially all his inventions.... Under the circumstances of his employment, it appears that the Government has at least a nonexclusive license in Mr. Friedman's inventions, Mr. Friedman retaining the right to otherwise exploit them. Because of security considerations, however, Mr. Friedman has been prevented from attempting to derive any gain from his inventions commercially or from foreign governments."

The legal question was fearfully confused, but the Secretary, Robert T. Stevens of Army–McCarthy-hearings fame, felt that Friedman deserved equitable redress—in the sum, however, of only $25,000. The following year, he changed his mind and agreed that $100,000 "would not constitute more than adequate compensation." This followed a reappraisal by N.S.A. Director General Canine, who observed that a large market existed among foreign governments for cipher machines and that the excellence of Friedman's inventions would have given him an important competitive advantage. The Bureau of the Budget questioned the award on the ground that it was inconsistent with government policy on secret inventions made by federal employees. It also put its finger on what appeared to be one of the chief motives for the award: Friedman's outstanding achievements. His lawyers were always careful to found their claims on the alleged financial loss—but they never failed to cite Friedman's record.

Two bills for Friedman's relief had died in committee during these prolonged negotiations. Finally, a hearing was held on the third bill before the Senate subcommittee on patents, trademarks, and copyrights. It was brief, mainly because Senator Joseph C. O'Mahoney, who was presiding, was in a great hurry to get to the Senate floor. The witnesses—notably Friedman's attorney and the lawyer for Swedish cipher-machine manufacturer Boris C. W. Hagelin, who had become a millionaire when Friedman had ordered his machines for the U.S. Army in World War II—discoursed eloquently on the glowing opportunities of commercial cryptography. The subcommittee approved the bill; Congress passed it; President Eisenhower signed it on May 10, 1956, and Friedman got his $100,000.

It must be stated that justice was not served thereby. In the case of the seven inventions that were filed in the patent office, at least five were derivative—mere improvements upon the basic creations of others. Such were the rotor machines, compensation for which should have gone to the estate of Edward Hebern, and the strip device, recompense for which should have been paid either to Jefferson's estate or to Parker Hitt, who first conceived the principle in strip form. (The other two were quite probably derivative as well.) Hebern's lawyer, in fact, tried to make this point at the hearing, but O'Mahoney cut him short. The Friedman award more rightfully belonged to others; it went to him because of well-situated friends, picayune mechanical differences, and a great but totally irrelevant record.*

This blot dims but little the luster of Friedman's escutcheon. He has ranged over more cryptologic territory than anyone else, and has mined it more deeply. Some of this was due to the accident of time and circumstance, which were more propitious for cryptology then than before or since. The era of radio had opened; mechanization had begun to transform cryptography; armies were becoming more mobile and larger and increasingly dependent upon control by communications; the United States had emerged as a major power, and politics were global. These currents gathered momentum, culminating in the Second World War; after a brief respite, the cold war renewed them. Friedman was lucky enough to come to maturity as this surge was swelling, and smart enough to see and seize the opportunity it presented. Yet environment alone does not explain the magnitude of his achievements; none of his contemporaries approached them.

His theoretical studies, which revolutionized the science, were matched by his actual solutions, which astounded it. Both are complemented by his peripheral contributions. He straightened out the tangled web of cipher systems and introduced a clarifying terminology for his arrangement. Words he coined gleam upon more than one page of today's dictionaries. His textbooks have trained thousands. His historical articles have shed light in little-known corners of the study, and the Shakespeare book has done much to quash one major area of a perennial literary nuisance. Singlehandedly, he made his country preeminent in his field. And finally, the vast American cryptologic establishment of today, with its thousands of employees, its

---

* The same remarks apply, though in a more attenuated degree in all respects, to the Congressional awards of an identical $100,000 on essentially the same basis of equity to Safford in 1958 and to Rowlett in 1964.

far-flung stations, its sprawling headquarters—this gigantic enterprise (except for the Navy branch started by Safford) is a direct lineal descendant of the little office in the War Department that Friedman started, all by himself.

This life's work, as extensive as it is intensive, confers upon William Frederick Friedman the mantle of the greatest cryptologist.

13

SECRECY FOR SALE

ON A MORNING in December of 1917, a rather handsome young man of 27 hurried through the colonnaded lobby of the American Telephone & Telegraph Company at 195 Broadway in downtown Manhattan. He rode the elevator up to the 17th floor, where he worked in the telegraph section of the company's development and research department. This section, composed of some of the brightest engineers in the company, was concentrating on the newest development in telegraphy, the printing telegraph or teletypewriter.

Gilbert S. Vernam was—if things were as usual—a little late that morning. He nearly always was, and, his boss said, "It used to burn me up to see him come sneaking in and, slink into his seat." The yearbook of his alma mater, Worcester Polytechnic Institute, had wondered "what would happen to Tech if 'Tau' should accidently get to class on time in the morning."

A native of Brooklyn, Vernam was graduated from the Massachusetts college, where he had been president of the Wireless Association and had been elected to Tau Beta Pi, the engineering honorary society, in 1914, after having spent a year working. He immediately joined A. T. & T. and, a year later, married a Brooklyn girl, Alline L. Eno. They had one child. Vernam was a clever young man—one of the stories about him has him stretched on his couch each evening wondering aloud, "What can I invent now?" He had the rare type of mind that can visualize an electrical circuit and put it down on paper without having to try it out with wires. He did so well in the telegraph section that its head, Ralzemond D. Parker, assigned him to a special secrecy project. And late though he may have been that winter morning, Vernam had brought a bright idea to work with him. Quiet and unassuming, though with a droll sense of humor, he probably put forth his suggestion with diffidence, but his co-workers on the secrecy project saw at once that he had something.

The project had begun during the summer, a few months after war had been declared, when Parker directed some of the telegraph section members to investigate the security of the printing telegraph. Would its very newness, the fact that the enemy might not have developed such means, guard its messages? The secrecy group soon found that it did not. The fluctuations of the current could be recorded by an oscillograph and the messages read with ease. Even multiplexing—sending several messages simultaneously in both directions

Secrecy for Sale

over a single wire—offered no real security. The engineers resolved the oscillograph undulation into its constituent curves and read the eight individual messages. The group discussed altering connections inside the printing telegraph mechanism. This would have the effect of enciphering one letter into another in a monalphabetic substitution. The engineers realized that this offered no real secrecy but, stymied, did not pursue the matter until Vernam bounded in with his idea.

It was based upon the Baudot code, the Morse code of the teletypewriter. In this code, named for its French inventor, J. M. E. Baudot, each character is allotted five units, or pulses. Each unit consists of either an electrical current or its absence in a given time. There are, consequently, 32 different combinations of marks and spaces, and a combination is assigned to each character—26 for the letters and one each for the six "stunts" (space between words, shift up to numbers and punctuation marks, shift back down to letters, return type-carriage to left side of paper, feed paper up a line, and idle). Through an electrical arrangement involving rotating commutators, the proper sequence of pulses is sent out when a character's key is struck on the keyboard. For example, *a* is *mark mark space space space*, *i* is *space mark mark space space* and the figure shift is *mark mark space mark mark*. At the receiving end, the incoming pulses energize electromagnets that, in combination, select the proper character and print it. In the punched paper tape which is frequently used to run teletypewriters, marks are represented by holes and spaces by leaving the tape intact. To read the tape, metal fingers push through the holes to make contact and thereby send pulses; where there is a space, the paper keeps the fingers from completing the circuit.

Vernam suggested punching a tape of key characters and electromechanically adding its pulses to those of the plaintext characters, the "sum" to constitute the ciphertext. The addition would have to be reversible so that the receiver could subtract the key pulses from the cipher pulses and get the plaintext. Vernam decided upon this rule: If the key and the plaintext pulses are both marks or both spaces, the ciphertext pulse will be a space. If the key pulse is a space, and the plaintext a mark, or vice versa—if, in other words, the two are different—the ciphertext pulse will be a mark. The four possibilities are these:

plaintext		*key*		*ciphertext*
mark	+	mark	=	space
mark	+	space	=	mark
space	+	mark	=	mark
space	+	space	=	space

Decipherment is unambiguous. For example, with ciphertext *mark* and key *space* only *mark* is possible for the plaintext. The whole system may be set out in a single, compact table. Using the convenient notation of 1 for *mark* and 0 for *space*, the rule would be tabulated as follows:

	plaintext	
	1	0
key		
1	0	1
0	1	0

key   ciphertext

In accordance with this rule, Vernam combined the five pulses of the plaintext character with the five of the key character to obtain the five pulses of the ciphertext character. Thus, if the plaintext is *a*, or 11000, and the key is 10011, which happens to be B, the encipherment is this:

plaintext	1	1	0	0	0
key	1	0	0	1	1
ciphertext	0	1	0	1	1

At the receiving end, the key pulses are applied one by one to the successive ciphertext pulses; the rule determines the plaintext pulses. With cipher pulses 10100, and the key pulses 00110, the plaintext would be:

ciphertext	1	0	1	0	0
key	0	0	1	1	0
plaintext	1	0	0	1	0, or *d*.

To combine the pulses electrically Vernam devised an arrangement of magnets, relays, and bus-bars. Since encipherment and decipherment were reciprocal, the same arrangement served for both. He fed the pulses into this device from two tape readers—one for a keytape, the other for the plaintext tape. The mechanism closed a circuit, resulting in a mark, when the two incoming pulses were different, and opened a circuit, resulting in a space, when they were the same. This output of marks and spaces could be transmitted just like an ordinary teletypewriter message to the receiver. Here the Vernam apparatus subtracted out the key pulses, which were supplied by an identical keytape, and recreated the original plaintext pulses. These it would channel into a teletypewriter receiver, which would print out the plaintext, just like a news ticker in a city room.

That was the beauty of it. No longer did men have to encipher or decipher a message in a separate step (though they still had to prepare keytapes, insert them in the apparatus, etc., since doing away with these would dispense with secrecy altogether). Plaintext went in and plaintext came out, while anyone intercepting the message between the two endpoints would pick up nothing but a meaningless sequence of marks and spaces. Messages were enciphered, transmitted, received, and deciphered in a single operation—exactly as fast as a message in plain English. The advantage was not the mechanical enciphering and printing of the message. That had been accomplished as far back as the early 1870s by two Frenchmen, Émile Vinay and Joseph Gaussin—though not with the speed and ease of a typewriter keyboard. Rather it was the assimilation of encipherment into the overall communication process. Vernam created what came to be called "on-line encipherment" (because it was done directly on the open telegraph circuit) to distinguish it from the old, separate, off-line encipherment. He freed a fundamental process in cryptography from the shackles of time and error. He eliminated a human being—the cipher clerk—from the chain of communication. His great contribution was to bring to cryptography the automation that had benefited mankind so much in so many fields of endeavor.

These values were immediately recognized, and Vernam's idea quickly kicked up a flurry of activity. He put it down on paper in a sketch dated December 17. A. T. & T. notified the Navy, with which it had worked closely in a communications demonstration the previous year, and on February 18, 1918, Vernam, Parker, Lyman F. Morehouse, equipment engineer of the telephone company, and Edward Watson explained the Vernam system, together with some other possibilities, to a Lieutenant Griffiths. On March 27, the engineers conferred with colleagues of the Western Electric Company, A. T. & T.'s manufacturing subsidiary, and began constructing a couple of Vernam devices, using as many standard parts as possible. They hooked them up to two teletypewriters and, in the Western Electric laboratory, ran the first tests of what the engineers called "automatic cryptography." The devices worked like a charm. A. T. & T. reported this to the Army. Major Joseph O. Mauborgne, then head of the Signal Corp's research and engineering division, came, saw and was conquered. Except for the problem of the keys.

In the first days of development, the Vernam keys took the form of loops of tape perforated with characters drawn from a hat, giving a random keytext. The engineers, who were rapidly learning about cryptology, probably from Hitt's *Manual*, soon spotted the flaw in this. The Vernam system is a polyalphabetic. A 32×32 tableau may be set up with the 32 characters of the Baudot alphabet across the top as plaintext and down the side as keys. Because the Baudot alphabet is public information, the composition of the 32 cipher alphabets filling the body of the tableau would be known. Secrecy in the Vernam system thus resides entirely in its keys. Looped keytapes would pass through the Vernam mechanism at regular intervals, permitting a simple Kasiski solution, even though the key recovered would be incoherent. The engineers made the keytapes extremely long to increase the difficulty of such a solution. But then the keytapes became too hard to handle.

Engineer Morehouse surmounted these difficulties by combining two short keytapes of different lengths in a Vernam device as if one were enciphering the other and using the extremely lengthy output—called the secondary key—as the key for plaintext. If one loop were 1,000 characters long and the other 999, the one-character difference would produce 999,000 combinations before the sequence would repeat. Thus two tapes each about eight feet long would breed a key that would extend 8,000 feet on a single tape. This was a major practical improvement.

But Mauborgne recognized that even this system was not immune to cryptanalysis. The future Chief Signal Officer, then 36, was an extraordinary cryptanalyst. He had studied the subject at the Army Signal School with Parker Hitt, was thoroughly conversant with its techniques, had devised a solution for the hitherto unsolved Playfair, and almost certainly knew of Friedman's Riverbank Publications, including No. 17 on solving running-key. cryptograms. He therefore saw that heavy traffic raised the possibility of a Kerckhoffs superimposition, even with the two-tape system. Moreover, probable words would enable the cryptanalyst to recover the secondary key. He could then test the various possibilities for the two primary keys at intervals of 999 and 1,000 letters, and so gradually build them up. Mauborgne demonstrated this to the A. T. & T. engineers with the keywords RIFLE and THOMAS.

Mauborgne had himself perhaps participated in work at the Army Signal School several years earlier that had concluded (before Friedman's solution) that the only safe running key was, in Parker Hitt's words, one "comparable in length with the message itself." Mauborgne's study of the A. T. & T. system brought this home to him more forcefully. Any repetition of any kind in the keys of cryptograms under analysis imperils them and perhaps dooms them to solution. It does not matter whether the repetitions lie within a single message or among several, arise from the interaction of repeating primary keys or from the simple repeating of a single long key. Repetitions in the key could not be permitted. At the same time, Friedman's work had demonstrated that running keys could not be intelligible. To avoid the Scylla of repetition and the Charybdis of intelligibility, keys would have to be, Mauborgne realized, both endless and senseless. He therefore welded together the randomness of the key, created, perhaps almost accidentally, by Vernam, and the nonrepetition of the key, discovered by the Army Signal School cryptologists, into what is now called the "one-time system." It consists of a random key used once, and only once. It provides a new and unpredictable key character for each plaintext character in the whole ensemble of messages ever to be sent by a group of correspondents.

And it is an unbreakable system. Some systems are unbreakable in practice only, because the cryptanalyst can conceive of ways of solving them if he had enough text and enough time. The one-time system is unbreakable both in theory and in practice. No matter how much text a cryptanalyst had available in it, or how much time he had to work on it, he could never solve it. This is why:

To solve a polyalphabetic cipher is essentially to gather all the letters that are enciphered in a single alphabet into a homogeneous group that may be studied for its linguistic traits. The techniques of this collection differ, as do the kinds of keys. Thus a Kasiski examination sifts out the identically keyed letters in a repeating key. A running key with a coherent text can be solved by reciprocally reconstructing the plaintext and the keytext. A running key with a random text used in two or more messages succumbs to a simultaneous reconstruction of the two plaintexts, one checking the other. Other polyalphabetics, such as the autokey and the two-tape system, engender specialized solutions that stem from their own peculiarities. The monalphabetically enciphered letters that are the goal of these techniques also exist in a Vernam one-time system cryptogram because the 32 available cipher alphabets are used over and over again. But the cryptanalyst has no way of sorting them out because the key in a one-time system neither repeats, nor recurs, nor makes sense, nor erects internal frameworks. Hence, his methods, all based in one way or another on these characteristics, all fail. The perfect randomness of the one-time system nullifies any horizontal, or lengthwise, cohesion, as in coherent running key or autokey, and its one-time nature bars any vertical assembly in Kasiski or Kerckhoffs columns, as in keys repeated in a single message or among several messages. The cryptanalyst is blocked.

How about trial and error? It seems as if brute testing of all possible keys, one after another, would eventually yield the plaintext. Success this way is an illusion. For while exhaustive trials would indeed bring out the true plaintext, they would also bring out every other possible text of the same length, and there would be no way to tell which was the right one. Suppose that the cryptanalyst deciphers a four-letter military message with every key, beginning with AAAA. He strikes plaintext at key AABI: *kiss*. Unlikely in this context. He presses on. Key AAEL yields plaintext *kill*. Better—but he wants to make sure. He continues through key AAEM, giving *kilt*, which might be an oblique reference to a Scottish maneuver, and AAER, *kiln*. Further down the line he reaches *fast* at GZBM and *slow* at KHIA, *stop* at HRIW and *gogo* at XSTT, *hard* at PZVQ and *easy* at RZBU. He finds when he ends at ZZZZ that he has merely compiled a list of every possible four-letter word— the hard way. He can no more pick the right solution from this list than he can from a dictionary of military terms. The key does not help in limiting the selection because, since it is random, any group of four letters is as acceptable a keytext as any other. The worst of it is that the possible solutions increase as the message lengthens. There are only three possible solutions for a one-letter cryptogram, but dozens for those of two letters, and zillions for those of 100.

A final hope flickers. Suppose that the cryptanalyst obtains the plaintext of a given cryptogram, perhaps through theft or the error of a radio operator. Can he use the key that he can recover to determine the system on which that key was built, and so predict future keys? No, because a random key has no underlying system—if it did, it would not be random.

These are empiric proofs. It is possible, however, to demonstrate a priori that the one-time system is unbreakable. This constitutes the proof that it is theoretically unbreakable.

In essence, the Vernam encipherment constitutes an addition—an addition based on the Baudot alphabet, but an addition nonetheless. Suppose then that the plaintext is 4 and the key is 5. The ciphertext will be 9. Now, given only this, the cryptanalyst has no way of knowing whether it results from the addition of $7+2$, or $6+3$, or $-2+11$, or $4+5$, or any other of the 32 possible combinations. Generalized, the situation is $x+y = 9$. Mathematicians call this an equation in two unknowns, and a single such equation has no unique solution. Two equations with the same two unknowns are required. The one-time system prevents the cryptanalyst from ever bringing two or more such equations together. The utter absence of any pattern whatsoever within its key precludes him from finding two occurrences of a given key character by reconstructing a pattern. And the tape's exhaustless novelty makes it impossible for him to locate these occurrences in any key repetitions. The cryptanalyst is thus denied any chance of getting additional information to delimit one of the unknowns; he is left with all 32 possibilities for the key character, and consequently all 32 for the plaintext. True it is that in the cryptanalytic case of an equation in two unknowns, some solutions are more probable than others. Thus, there is a 12 per cent chance that the plaintext unknown is *e*, an 8 per cent chance that it is *t*, and so on down the frequency table. But this does not answer the cryptanalyst's question, for it does not specify which of these probabilities is actually present in the individual case before him.

So the answers again evade the cryptanalyst. Formless, endless, the random one-time tape vanquishes him by dissolving in chaos on the one hand and infinity on the other. Here indeed the cryptanalyst gropes through caverns measureless to man. His quest is Faustian; who would dare it would know more than can be known.

Why, then, is this ultimate cipher not in universal use? Because of the stupendous quantities of key required. The problems of producing, registering, distributing, and canceling the keys may seem slight to an individual who has not had experience with military communications, but in wartime the volumes of traffic stagger even the signal staffs. Hundreds of thousands of words may be enciphered in a day; simply to generate the millions of key characters required would be enormously expensive and time-consuming. Since each message must have its unique key, application of the ideal system would require shipping out on tape at the very least the equivalent of the total communications volume of a war. In fact, however, considerable extra key material would have to be supplied. A group of subordinate units may possess some tape in common for intercommunication, but once one unit uses a roll of keytape, the others must cancel their identical rolls. In practice, this step is the most difficult. It is virtually impossible in the hubbub of battle to monitor the messages of a dozen other units to determine what keytapes they have used.

In general, the physical problems bar employing a one-time system in a fluid situation, such as military operations in the field. These difficulties do not hold for more stable situations, such as exist at high military headquarters, at diplomatic posts, or in a two-way spy correspondence—and in such situations one-time systems are practicable and are used. Even here, however, difficulties arise if traffic volume is heavy.

Such was the case when Mauborgne, in the first large-scale trial of the Vernam system, set up machines in Hoboken, Washington, and Newport News, and soon had as many as 135 messages a day flying between them with speed and reliability. Even with this relatively low volume, it apparently proved impossible to produce sufficient key for a one-time system. Consequently, Mauborgne fell back upon the Morehouse two-tape system as the next best thing. In May, 1918, he paved the way for the first cryptanalytic test of the several keying procedures of the Vernam system when he told Bancroft Gherardi, assistant chief engineer of the telephone company, about Fabyan's Riverbank Laboratories.

"I am not a cipher expert," Gherardi wrote Fabyan on June 11, enclosing seven test cryptograms, "and would not presume to say what can and cannot be done, but should you and Professor Friedman decipher messages Nos. 1, 5, 6, and 7, I shall feel that I owe you both a good dinner. I have no doubt that you can decipher Nos. 2, 3, and perhaps 4. These, however, as you understand, are not the arrangement which we propose." Friedman was overseas in G.2 A.6, but soon after his return he solved Messages 2 and 3, and part of 4. Since all three used the same portions of a single keytape of 2,000 random characters (except that 4 ran longer), a tentative recovery in one could be tested against the others by deciphering with the resultant key. Messages 5, 6, and 7 were enciphered with the two-tape system, started at different points, and though Friedman seems not to have broken these, owing to their brevity, he did solve the messages in the tri-city traffic, which used the same system. No. 1 was enciphered in the true one-time system. It shared its random keytape with no other messages. And it, of course, was never solved.

In September of 1918, Vernam himself went down to Washington to file his patent application on Friday the 13th. The war ended without any widespread application of the system before the patent—No. 1,310,719, and perhaps the most important in the history of cryptology—was granted on July 22, 1919. But A. T. & T. also saw possible peacetime profits in the invention. On October 21, 1920, the company demonstrated it before foreign postal officials at the Preliminary International Communications Conference by radioing Vernam-system cryptograms from New York to Cliffwood, New Jersey, and wiring them back again. On the afternoon of February 9, 1926, Vernam delivered a paper and ran his machine before the midwinter convention of the American Institute of Electrical Engineers in New York.

But though the device was an engineering success, it proved a commercial failure. Cable companies and business firms, which A. T. & T. hoped would buy cipher attachments for its teletypewriters, passed it over in favor of the old-fashioned commercial codes, which substantially shortened messages, thereby cutting cable tolls, and which gave a modicum of secrecy as well. The armed forces budgets had shrunk to their peacetime tightness; cryptologically, the physical difficulties forced Army communicators back onto the two-tape system, and the demonstrated solvability of this threw the whole Vernam arrangement into temporary limbo.

At about the same time on the other side of the Atlantic, cryptologists saw things differently. Three experts in the German Foreign Office—Werner Kunze, who was strongly mathematical in his approach; Rudolf Schauffler, an all-round cryptologist who specialized in East Asian languages and later received a doctorate in mathematics; and Erich Langlotz, who had been educated as a chemist and was more involved in the practical problems than the others—were given the task of providing security for their own diplomatic communications. Enciphered code was then the customary method for diplomatic communications. Often the encipherment took the form of an additive. The numerical codegroups of a diplomatic or military code were disguised by adding to them a numerical key, usually fairly long. For example, to the placode 3043 9710 3964 3043 . . . , the code clerk would add the key 7260 0940 5169 4174 . . . by noncarrying addition (tens digits are neither written down nor carried). The result, 0203 9650 8023 7117 . . . , effectively conceals the repeated 3043 in the original message. Kunze, at least, was well aware of the difficulties of affording secrecy: he was then scraping a nonadditive superencipherment from a French number code that employed 40 or 50 two-digit encipherment tables.* The trio studied ciphers with longer and longer additives and they eventually concluded that the only system that is absolutely unbreakable is the one with a random, nonrepeating additive key—the equation in two unknowns. Some time between 1921 and 1923 they instituted the system in the German diplomatic establishment.

It took the form of pads of 50 numbered sheets of legal-size paper, each with 48 five-digit groups distributed in eight lines of six groups each. The 240 digits were random, and no sheet duplicated any other. Each pad was entirely different from every other (except for its mate for deciphering purposes). The digits constituted the key that was added to the number groups of the German codes. Langlotz supervised the distribution of the pads, giving the embassy at Washington, say, one set for outgoing and another for incoming messages to

---

* The code used four-digit groups, but the French divided the codetext into clusters of five figures, and divided each cluster into two pairs, which were enciphered by the tables, and a single figure, which was left unenciphered. The encipherment thus straddled from one codegroup to another. The French furthermore cut the clusters in three ways: with the single figure at the beginning, with it between the two pairs, and with it following them. Kunze began working on the superencipherment in 1921 and had reconstructed it by 1923. He returned to the system in 1927–28 and solved the code, which the French were still using. By then they were combining the single digit of one cluster with that of another and enciphering them as a pair. For instance, the imaginary codetext 8975 4263 . . . would be divided 8 97 54 2 63 . . . , and the 8 and 2 would be enciphered together, as well as the 97, the 54, etc. Kunze solved that variation as well.

and from Berlin, and similar double sets for communicating with all German legations. The code clerks used a different sheet for every message, tearing it off when they were through, and never using the same sheet twice. Thus, though the addition was done by hand and involved numbers as opposed to the Vernam electrical addition of pulses, the principle—and the unsolvability—was the same. It soon became known as the "one-time pad" system, the name by which systems using random, nonrepeating keys are now generally known, though the mechanical embodiment is sometimes called a "one-time tape" system. For the first time in history, the official communications of a government were absolutely secure against the prying eyes of others.

Not those of the United States, however. Though the system was invented in America, though an article by Vernam headed a convention issue of the important *Journal of the American Institute of Electrical Engineers*, though his talk was picked up by the mass-circulation *Literary Digest* and the general scientific weekly *Science*, though Yardley brought Vernam's device to the attention of a high State Department official, mentioned it in his sensational book, and later tried to embarrass the department into using it in a needling magazine article—despite all this, the United States remained blind to the unbreakable system.

The Army revived it in a hurry as SIGTOT when World War II loomed, but by then Vernam was well out of it. He had continued developmental work at A. T. & T. for several years. He improved his own system,* invented a device for enciphering handwriting during telautograph transmission, and came up with one of the earliest forms of binary digital encipherment of pictures—another precocious development. He was so good that he was grabbed off at a substantial raise by International Telephone and Telegraph Corporation's cryptographic subsidiary, International Communication Laboratories, where Parker Hitt was vice president. Four months later the stock market crashed. Vernam, with no seniority, was soon out. He went to Postal Telegraph Cable Company, which merged with Western Union. His inventive spark flared from time to time, and he was granted 65 patents in all, among them such important noncryptologic items as the semiautomatic torn-tape relay system, the push-button switching systems, and finally the fully automatic telegraph switching system, all for the Air Force's 200,000-mile domestic network.

But the reversal in his personal fortunes seemed to depress him. Each night he sank deeper and deeper into the newspaper. Finally, on February 7, 1960, after a long bout with Parkinson's disease, the man who had automated cryptography died in obscurity in his home in Hackensack, New Jersey.

* In its original form, the ciphertext included the stunt characters. This made it difficult to record the ciphertext on paper. The sudden appearance of a figure shift would abruptly convert a literal cryptogram into one of numbers and punctuation marks. A carriage return without a paper feed would result in an overline. To prevent this, Vernam added some circuits that would cause the stunts to print as two-letter groups.

It is self-evident that, as the number of plaintext elements increase, so does the security of a cryptosystem. Thus a large code is harder to solve than a small one. Similarly, among cipher systems in which only a single set of plain-to-cipher equivalents is used (that is, nonpolyalphabetic systems), those enciphering two letters at a time offer more resistance than those enciphering just one at a time, all other things being equal. In other words, a digraphic substitution such as the Playfair is stronger than a monographic substitution. The reason is that digraphs are harder to identify than single letters—partly because there are more to choose from, partly because their characteristics are less sharply defined. These problems would be aggravated for trigraphic substitutions, and would rapidly approach insuperable proportions for tetragraphic, pentagraphic, hexagraphic, and even larger polygraphic substitutions.

Such substitutions have always been possible in principle simply by listing plaintext polygraphs opposite their ciphertext polygraphs. The first such list was constructed for digraphs when Porta set one up as a tableau, using distinctive symbols for each plaintext digraph. Many digraph lists using letters have been compiled, usually in big 26×26 tables. But such lists have almost never been produced for trigrams, and never for tetragrams or larger polygram substitutions. Their bulk (26^3 or 17,576 entries for the trigraphic, 26^4 or 456,976 for the tetragraphic, and so on) is prohibitive, and much of the labor would be wasted on useless polygrams, as *jgt* or *wqh*.

Ever since Wheatstone's Playfair showed how a digraphic substitution could be achieved compactly and without a lengthy list, other cryptographers have tried to extend his geometrical technique to trigraphic substitution. Nearly all have failed. Perhaps the best known effort was that of Count Luigi Gioppi di Türkheim, who in 1897 produced a pseudo-trigraphic system in which two letters were monalphabetically enciphered and the third depended only on the second. Finally, about 1929, a young American mathematician, Jack Levine, used six 5×5 squares to encipher trigraphs in an ingenious extension of the Playfair. But he did not disclose his method.

This was the situation when a 38-year-old assistant professor of mathematics at Hunter College in New York published a seven-page paper entitled "Cryptography in an Algebraic Alphabet" in *The American Mathematical Monthly* for June–July 1929. He was Lester S. Hill, a five-foot-six, blue-eyed, black-haired native of New York and a Phi Beta Kappa graduate of Columbia College who had taken his Ph.D. in mathematics at Yale in 1926. Hill had taught mathematics at the University of Montana, at Princeton, at the University of Maine, and at Yale before coming to Hunter in 1927. While at Yale, he had written three articles for *Telegraph and Telephone Age* dealing with mathematical means of checking the accuracy of telegraphed code numbers. He hoped to make some money from his checking scheme, which he was seeking to have patented. This did not go anywhere, but it sparked in Hill an interest in secret communications. Later in the summer in which his

Secrecy for Sale

paper on algebraic cryptography appeared, he expanded the topic before the American Mathematical Society at Boulder, Colorado. This lecture was later published in *The American Mathematical Monthly* as "Concerning Certain Linear Transformation Apparatus of Cryptography."

Hill successfully used algebra as a process for cryptography. Probably many mathematicians had toyed with this idea; two proposals had even reached print—one by a German, F. J. Buck, as far back as 1772, the other by the young mathematician Jack Levine in a 1926 issue of a detective magazine. But Hill alone devised a method of power and generality. In addition, his procedure made polygraphic cryptography practical for the first time.

It employed equations in which the keys and plaintext letters had numerical values. Encipherment consisted of solving the equations. There were as many equations as letters in the polygraph. Since there are 26 letters in the alphabet, and since he had to make decipherment possible, Hill performed his computations modulo 26. This means that the mathematician uses only the integers from 0 to 25. Any number higher than 25 must be reduced by dropping out as many multiples of 26 as possible; the remainder equals that number modulo 26. Thus 28 is 2 modulo 26, because 28 minus 26 leaves 2. Likewise, 68 is 16 modulo 26, for 68 minus 2 times 26, or 52, leaves 16.

To demonstrate a tetragraphic substitution, Hill framed the following set of simultaneous equations. The x's represent the plaintext letters, x_1 being the first, x_2 the second, and so on; the y's represent the ciphertext letters:

$$y_1 = 8x_1 + 6x_2 + 9x_3 + 5x_4$$
$$y_2 = 6x_1 + 9x_2 + 5x_3 + 10x_4$$
$$y_3 = 5x_1 + 8x_2 + 4x_3 + 9x_4$$
$$y_4 = 10x_1 + 6x_2 + 11x_3 + 4x_4$$

In the first step of actual encipherment, Hill converted the letters of his plaintext—*Delay operations*—into numbers according to the following arbitrary alphabet:

a	b	c	d	e	f	g	h	i	j	k	l	m	n	o	p	q	r	s	t	u	v	w	x	y	z
5	23	2	20	10	15	8	4	18	25	0	16	13	7	3	1	19	6	12	24	21	17	14	22	11	9

Then he inserted the numerical values for the first four-letter group—*dela*, or 20, 10, 16, 5—into the equations as x_1, x_2, x_3, and x_4, resulting in the following:

$$y_1 = (8 \times 20) + (6 \times 10) + (9 \times 16) + (5 \times 5)$$
$$y_2 = (6 \times 20) + (9 \times 10) + (5 \times 16) + (10 \times 5)$$
$$y_3 = (5 \times 20) + (8 \times 10) + (4 \times 16) + (9 \times 5)$$
$$y_4 = (10 \times 20) + (6 \times 10) + (11 \times 16) + (4 \times 5)$$

Hill then carried out the multiplications and additions in each equation modulo 26. For example, solving for y_1 gave: $8 \times 20 = 4$, $6 \times 10 = 8$, $9 \times 16 = 14$, and $5 \times 5 = 25$. They summed to 25. Reverting to literal values,

25 became J, the first cipher letter. The others were found in the same way, and the full ciphertext for *dela* became JCOW. The completed cryptogram is JCOW ZLVB DVLE QMXC.

Suppose, now, that the plaintext message had begun *Demand*..., which would alter only the third letter of the first tetragram from an *l* to an *m*. The replacement in the four equations of the 16 of *l* by the 13 of *m* would change the products of the third elements in each equation, thereby modifying the sums. Consequently the ciphertext for *dema*, which is CMZQ, appears entirely different from JCOW of *dela*. Such a system is genuinely polygraphic, and its cryptographic security is substantial.

The fixed values in the equations—the numbers that multiply the plaintext numbers—cannot be selected at random if the system is to work in reverse. Hill specified the requirements and derived the deciphering equations. For the above key, they are:

$$x_1 = 23y_1 + 20y_2 + 5y_3 + 1y_4$$
$$x_2 = 2y_1 + 11y_2 + 18y_3 + 1y_4$$
$$x_3 = 2y_1 + 20y_2 + 6y_3 + 25y_4$$
$$x_4 = 25y_1 + 2y_2 + 22y_3 + 25y_4$$

Hill eliminated separate deciphering equations by constructing "involutory transformations." A single set of these equations serves both to encipher and decipher. Involutory transformations are constructed according to a special formula, which limits their number compared to noninvolutory ones. In theory this also reduces the cryptanalytical resistance. But the security loss is negligible, especially when measured against the increased facility of operation.

Hill further simplified the cipher's operation by introducing matrices. A matrix is simply a square of numbers. Matrices can be added and multiplied together under their own rules. The numbers in a matrix may represent plaintext letters. And since each matrix may be handled arithmetically as if it were a single number, two equations serve for the encipherment of two matrices, no matter how many numbers each contains. Thus, by disposing plaintext in matrices, more letters can be handled with fewer equations. Thus two 3 × 3 matrices will encipher 18 letters at a time with only two equations instead of the 18 that would be needed for the so-called linear encipherment. Hill gave an example of this massive polygraphic encipherment in his second article. His plaintext was *Hold out. Supporting air squadrons en route*, and, using a different numerical alphabet than in his first example, he prepared his first two *x*, or plaintext, matrices as follows:

$$x_1 = \begin{pmatrix} h & o & l \\ d & o & u \\ t & s & u \end{pmatrix} = \begin{pmatrix} 5 & 6 & 22 \\ 2 & 6 & 7 \\ 12 & 19 & 7 \end{pmatrix} \quad x_2 = \begin{pmatrix} p & p & o \\ r & t & i \\ n & g & a \end{pmatrix} = \begin{pmatrix} 21 & 21 & 6 \\ 23 & 12 & 17 \\ 24 & 16 & 4 \end{pmatrix}$$

Secrecy for Sale

These he inserted into the equations, which are involutory and have an extra arbitrary matrix to be added in to further complicate the encipherment:

$$y_1 = \begin{pmatrix} 3 & 6 & 2 \\ 16 & 23 & 8 \\ 2 & 16 & 13 \end{pmatrix} \begin{pmatrix} 5 & 6 & 22 \\ 2 & 6 & 7 \\ 12 & 19 & 7 \end{pmatrix} + \begin{pmatrix} 2 & 6 & 14 \\ 8 & 24 & 4 \\ 14 & 16 & 20 \end{pmatrix} \begin{pmatrix} 21 & 21 & 6 \\ 23 & 12 & 17 \\ 24 & 16 & 4 \end{pmatrix} + \begin{pmatrix} 18 & 6 & 6 \\ 24 & 20 & 22 \\ 2 & 2 & 16 \end{pmatrix}$$

$$y_2 = \begin{pmatrix} 18 & 14 & 22 \\ 20 & 4 & 10 \\ 22 & 20 & 24 \end{pmatrix} \begin{pmatrix} 5 & 6 & 22 \\ 2 & 6 & 7 \\ 12 & 19 & 7 \end{pmatrix} + \begin{pmatrix} 15 & 16 & 20 \\ 4 & 13 & 2 \\ 20 & 8 & 11 \end{pmatrix} \begin{pmatrix} 21 & 21 & 6 \\ 23 & 12 & 17 \\ 24 & 16 & 4 \end{pmatrix} + \begin{pmatrix} 2 & 16 & 14 \\ 8 & 12 & 4 \\ 18 & 8 & 20 \end{pmatrix}$$

When he performed the appropriate matrix multiplications and additions modulo 26, y_1 and y_2 were found to be:

$$y_1 = \begin{pmatrix} 13 & 20 & 12 \\ 22 & 16 & 23 \\ 16 & 19 & 23 \end{pmatrix} = \begin{pmatrix} Y & K & T \\ L & G & R \\ G & S & R \end{pmatrix} \quad y_2 = \begin{pmatrix} 13 & 23 & 12 \\ 17 & 20 & 15 \\ 20 & 4 & 20 \end{pmatrix} = \begin{pmatrix} Y & R & T \\ I & K & W \\ K & A & K \end{pmatrix}$$

Such an encipherment virtually obliterates ciphertext repetitions. Even if an exact 18-letter plaintext group recurs, it must begin at exactly the same point in the encipherment equation to produce a ciphertext repetition—and there is only one chance in 18 of this happening. More importantly, a polygraphic encipherment of this magnitude is possible only with a Hill transformation. The more than 40 quintillion 18-letter groups, printed 100 to each side of a page with their ciphertext equivalents, would fill a codebook thicker than the distance from the sun to Pluto.

Mathematically, there is no limit either to matrix size or to the number of equations. A cryptographer may use matrices ten letters square in five simultaneous equations to catapult 500 letters into cipher at once. Or he may set up 500 simultaneous linear equations each with 500 terms to encipher that regiment of letters together. From a practical standpoint, the matrix method is superior because it enciphers more letters for a given amount of work than the linear method, and larger polygraphs resist cryptanalysis more strongly than smaller ones. But from a purely theoretical standpoint, the matrix encipherment is less secure than a linear encipherment of the same number of letters. This is because the linear encipherment employs a greater number of arbitrary key constants in its equations. Many of the matrix constants reduce to zero when the matrix equations are written out in their linear equivalent. These play no role in the arithmetic. As a result, while the change of a single plaintext letter in a linear encipherment will affect every ciphertext letter, such a change will affect only every second ciphertext letter in a 2×2 matrix, every third in a 3×3 matrix, and so on. Conversely, an error in a linear ciphertext will garble the entire plaintext group, whereas an error in a matrix ciphertext will garble only every second letter, or every third, or fourth, and so on, depending on the size of the matrix.

In general, the Hill system defends itself well against the direct onslaughts of cryptanalysis. Without a knowledge of the basic letter-to-number conversion alphabet, the cryptanalyst may not even be able to start. Even with it, a straightforward frequency-analysis attack is out of the question: octogram frequencies, for example, are hard to collect and even harder to differentiate. Probable words require tedious testing for possible locations and then much mathematical juggling to determine the correct equations; even so, only the relatively trivial trigraphic encipherments have been solved. The cipher has, however, at least one curious chink in its armor. If a cryptanalyst obtains two ciphertexts resulting from a single plaintext enciphered with different involutory equations (of the same type and polygram size), and if he knows the conversion alphabet, he can, in general, recover the equations fairly easily.

The real obstacle to practical use of the Hill system is, of course, its ponderousness. Hill sought to minimize this by patenting a device that will encipher small polygrams (up to hexagrams). It consists of a series of geared wheels connected by a sprocketed chain so that the rotation of one wheel will turn all the others, but the range of its keys appears to be limited. Mechanisms could also be built to compute the encipherments of large polygrams, which give the best security, but they would be so complicated that they could not compete on a practical basis with simpler, though possibly less secure, cipher machines. For such reasons, the Hill system has served as a U.S. governmental cryptosystem in only one minor capacity—to encipher the three-letter groups of radio call-signs.

Hill never published any further papers on cryptology, but he kept writing them, turning over most of his studies to the Navy (probably because he was a lieutenant in that service in World War I). They mostly concerned further variations on the polygraphic scheme or elaborate complications on Vigenère-type systems. But though none ever approached his first publications in significance, the Navy welcomed his suggestions. In 1955, Rear Admiral H. C. Bruton, director of naval communications, wrote him: "I am pleased to acknowledge that you furnished material to naval communications during World War II, and that the ideas presented were ingenious, detailed, and complete. The cryptographic system which you proposed at the time demonstrated competence and inventiveness of a high order in the application of advanced mathematical concepts to the field of cryptography. May I again express to you the appreciation of naval communications. . . ." Hill retired from Hunter in 1960, and on January 9, 1961, died in Lawrence Hospital in Bronxville, New York, after a long illness.

Although Hill's cipher system itself saw almost no practical use, it had a great impact upon cryptology. When he published his articles in 1929 and 1931, cryptology, like other applied sciences, was beginning its drift toward a widespread application of mathematics to its problems. Friedman had just linked cryptanalysis to statistics. Two of the junior cryptanalysts he hired were mathematicians. Kunze, in the German Foreign Office, a Ph.D. in

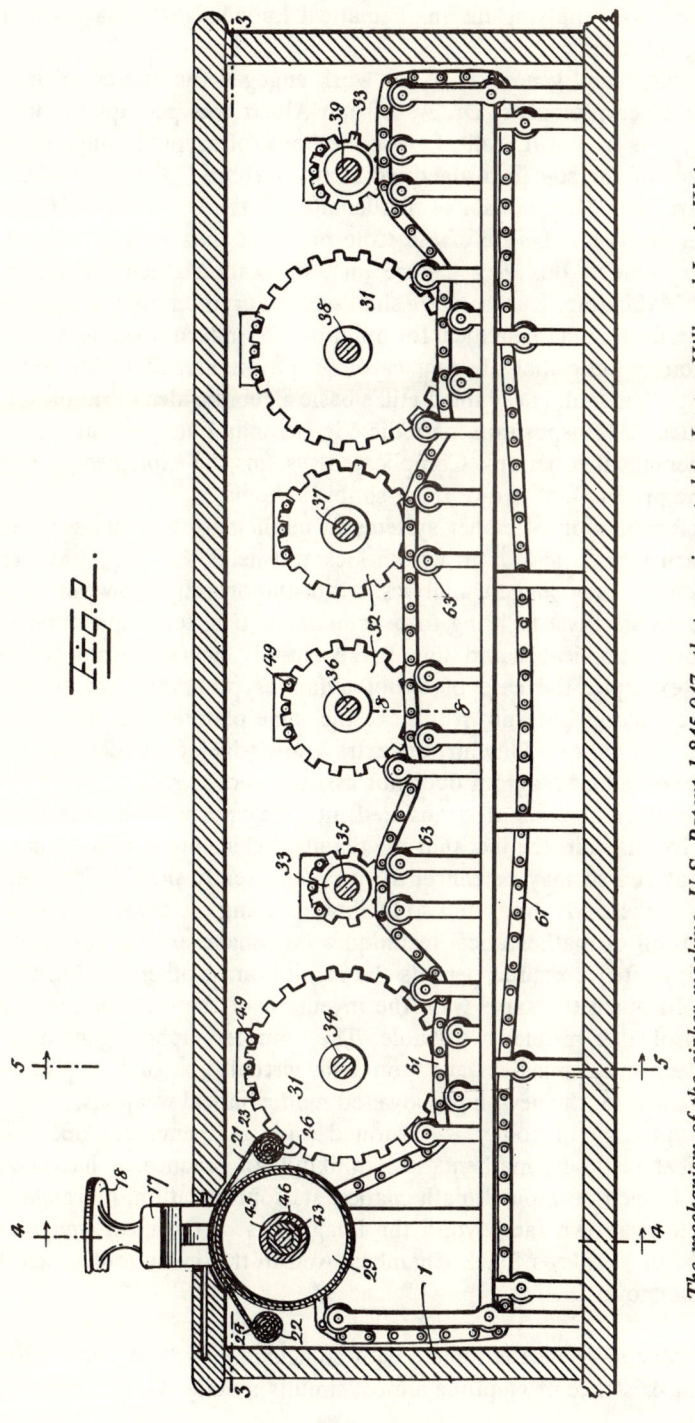

The mechanism of the cipher machine, U.S. Patent 1,845,947, that was invented by Lester Hill and Louis Weisner, for polygraphic substitution

mathematics, was applying his mathematical knowledge to his work. Hill accelerated this trend.

The elegance and generality of his work engaged the interest of mathematicians and cryptologists. Dr. A. Adrian Albert was perhaps the first to observe that, as he put it, "all of these methods [of cryptography] are very special cases of the so-called algebraic cipher systems." On November 22, 1941, Albert, then 36, professor of mathematics at the University of Chicago and winner two years before of the Cole prize for outstanding research in algebra, expounded this view before an American Mathematical Society meeting at Manhattan, Kansas. "We shall see that cryptography is more than a subject permitting mathematical formulation, for indeed it would not be an exaggeration to state that abstract cryptography is identical with abstract mathematics," he said. He adapted Hill's basic algebraic idea to simple cipher systems, such as transposition, periodic Vigenère, and autokey, and derived their mathematical equations. Complicated systems, he explained, are often merely "the product" of two of these simple systems.

This reformulation of cipher systems in mathematical terms bares their essential structure. It shows up weaknesses and helps the cryptographer to correct them. It may suggest analyses. More importantly, however, it may enable the cryptanalyst to bring to bear mathematical techniques that were not previously applicable and that make entirely new solutions possible. Take, for example, the case of two Playfair cryptograms, enciphered in different keysquares but known to have the same plaintext. In the ordinary geometrical solution of a Playfair, the extra knowledge of the identical plaintext in the second cryptogram does not assist in reconstructing the first key. But if the two ciphertexts are translated into the appropriate mathematical equations for Playfair, the fact that the plaintext elements in these equations are identical and so may be cancelled out may greatly simplify finding the unknowns in these equations and so facilitate solving the cryptograms. Thus the application of mathematical techniques that make explicit fundamental relationships often obscured permits the resolution of otherwise intractable problems. In much the same way, the invention of the calculus made previously unsolvable problems solvable. The complex ciphers generated by modern electromechanical means would lie virtually beyond cryptanalysis without the help of the new, high-powered mathematical weapons.

The cryptology of today is saturated with mathematical operations, mathematical methods, mathematical thinking. In practice, it has become virtually a branch of applied mathematics. Its sophistication, its range, and its power have grown far beyond the imaginings of the most imaginative cryptologist in Yardley's Black Chamber. And in this evolution, Lester Hill was a prime mover.

The history of science is replete with coincidence. Adams and Leverrier deduced the existence of Neptune almost simultaneously. While Darwin was elaborating his theory of evolution, Wallace sent him a short paper that succinctly set it forth. Five years after Morse invented his telegraph, Wheatstone independently invented another. So it is not surprising that coincidence brushed cryptography in the crucible years of the First World War and just after. Its fabled long arm reached out and tapped four men in four countries. Spurred by the vast wartime use of secret communications, and beckoned by the new age of mechanization, they independently created the machine whose principle is perhaps the most widely used in cryptography today. This principle is that of the wired codewheel, the rotor.

The body of a rotor consists of a thick disk of insulating material, such as Bakelite or hard rubber, commonly two to four inches in diameter and half an inch thick. Embedded around the circumference of each face are 26 evenly spaced electrical contacts, often of brass. Each contact is connected at random by a wire to a contact on the opposite face. Thus a path for an electric current is set up that starts at one point on the circumference of one side and ends at another point on the other.

The contacts on the starting, or input, face represent plaintext letters and those on the output face ciphertext letters. The wire connections between the two then provide a way of converting plaintext letters to ciphertext. To encipher, one need only fire a burst of current into the rotor at the input contact of the desired plaintext letter, say, *a*; this current then courses along the wire to emerge at an output contact representing the ciphertext letter, say, R. If a list be drawn up of all the rotor's wire connections from the plaintext to the ciphertext face, it will constitute a monalphabetic substitution alphabet. The rotor thus embodies a cipher alphabet in a form suitable for electromechanical manipulation.

To carry out this manipulation, the rotor is placed between two fixed plates, each also of insulating material and with 26 contacts studded in a circle to match those on each face of the rotor. Each contact on the input plate is connected to a typewriter key that represents a plaintext letter. Each contact on the output plate is connected with some kind of device to indicate the ciphertext letter, such as a lamp or a typebar. When the encipherer strikes the key representing the plaintext letter *a*, he allows electricity to flow from the power source, into the input plate contact for *a*, across the junction into the rotor at the input contact for *a*, through the wire heart of the rotor to the output contact for ciphertext R, across to the output plate contact for R, and to the bulb that lights up the letter R as the ciphertext letter.

If this were all there was to it, the rotor would not be so remarkable a device. Each time the *a* key was pressed, the current would trace the same path through the rotor to indicate R. This would be nothing more than a fancy and extremely expensive way of performing a monalphabetic substitution.

But there is much more. The rotor does not remain stationary. It turns. Suppose that it clicks forward one step. The current that formerly emerged at R after starting at input plate contact *a* will now exit at an entirely different letter because a new rotor contact, with a different wire path, now stands opposite input plate contact *a*. Similarly, all the other plaintext letters will have cipher letters different than before. This creates a new ciphertext alphabet. Each time the rotor moves forward a space, a new alphabet comes into play. A list of these alphabets can be made, and, since they are all based on the primary alphabet of the rotor, they will form a 26 × 26 tableau with a single mixed alphabet shifting one space forward in each successive line. If the machine is so constructed as to nudge the rotor forward one space each time a letter is enciphered, the result will be the same as using the tableau line after line, from top to bottom, and then repeating. This constitutes, of course, nothing more than a progressive-key polyalphabetic substitution with a mixed alphabet and a period of 26.

This is likewise not worth the expense of a machine. If, however, a second rotor be added by the side of the first, a great stride is taken. Two successive encipherments are produced. If the rotors move together, the result will still be a mixed-alphabet polyalphabetic with a period of 26, though with a tableau that represents their combined encipherments. But if the second rotor shifts a space only after the first rotor has completed its revolution, the change will vary the total encipherment: for though the first rotor is back in its original position with regard to the fixed plates, the second has moved. This new displacement brings into play a new cipher alphabet, the 27th. Each new variation in position between the two rotors and the plates creates a new alphabet. If the machine is so constructed that the second rotor moves forward a space only as the first is returning to its starting point, then it will take 26 revolutions of the first rotor to drive the second through one full revolution so that both return to their original stations. Since the second rotor assumes 26 positions, and the first rotor assumes 26 positions for each one of the second rotor's, the two combined assume 26 × 26, or 676, different positions with regard to the fixed plates.

Each of these 676 different positions produces a different wire maze inside the pair of rotors, and each different maze means a different ciphertext alphabet. For imagine that both rotors are held steady in one position while each letter from *a* to *z* is tapped out on the keyboard. The bulbs that light up comprise the ciphertext equivalents for these letters, and those ciphertext equivalents taken as a whole comprise the ciphertext alphabet representing that particular maze. Let one rotor turn one space and the process be repeated, begetting another ciphertext alphabet. These two alphabets are brothers under the skin but superficially they differ. The substitute for *e* may be x in one and z in the other. Consequently, the two-rotor machine produces a polyalphabetic substitution with a period of 676.

The addition of a third rotor multiplies that figure by 26, since all three rotors will not return to their starting position for 26 × 26 × 26, or 17,576, successive encipherments. Fourth and fifth rotors result in periods of 456,976 and 11,881,376 letters, respectively.

Each of those letters, moreover, is enciphered with a different ciphertext alphabet. In that lies the strength of the rotor system. The case differs from one in which an 11,881,376-character Vernam tape keys a message. The period is the same in both cases, but the Vernam employs only 32 different alphabets. Secrecy resides in the nonpattern in which they serve. Rotors, however, unfailingly turn one space per letter (barring gears to vary this), and consequently its alphabets succeed one another in the most rigid order, whose predictability hardly adds to the system's security. When all have been used the sequence repeats. This is a progressive-key system and, considering that it was originated by the Abbot Trithemius, it is hardly new. But the rotor device carries the process to such astronomical lengths that a difference in degree becomes a difference in kind. The special merit of the rotor system springs from its outpouring of cipher alphabets in such hemorrhaging profusion as to provide a different alphabet for each letter in a plaintext longer by far than the complete works of Shakespeare, *War and Peace*, the *Iliad*, the *Odyssey*, *Don Quixote*, the *Canterbury Tales*, and *Paradise Lost* all put together.

A period of that length thwarts any practical possibility of a straightforward solution on the basis of letter frequency. This general solution would need about 50 letters per cipher alphabet, meaning that all five rotors would have to go through their combined cycle 50 times. The cryptogram would have to be as long as all the speeches made on the floor of the Senate and the House of Representatives in three successive sessions of Congress. No cryptanalyst is likely to bag that kind of trophy in his lifetime; even diplomats, who can be as verbose as politicians, rarely scale those heights of loquacity.

Consequently the cryptanalyst must fall back on special cases. They furnish him with what he must have for a practicable rotor solution: the plaintext for a length of ciphertext. He can get this in several ways. A Kerckhoffs superimposition is possible when several messages begin at the same rotor setting, or with settings so close to one another that the cipher-alphabet sequence overlaps among messages. The kappa test will reveal these. Sometimes two cryptograms have the same plaintext: one was sent in the wrong key, or identical orders are being sent to several units. Probable words or stereotyped beginnings will sometimes provide good clues. And sometimes the plaintext itself becomes available, through wireless queries, a cipher clerk's carelessness, published diplomatic notes, and the like. All of these situations have occurred often enough for the cryptanalyst to exploit them.

That exploitation entails resolving the millions of secondary alphabets into the few primary ones. It calls upon the resources of higher mathematics, especially group theory, whose techniques are particularly suited to handle the many unknowns involved in a rotor solution. Basically these unknowns are the paths taken by the wires of each rotor from one face to the other. The cryptanalyst-mathematician quantifies them by measuring the distance, or displacement, between the input and the output contacts. For example, a wire from input contact 3 to output contact 10 marks a displacement of 7. Similarly, letters are given numerical values, usually $a = 0$, $b = 1, \ldots z = 25$. Using his known or assumed plaintext values, the cryptanalyst sets up equations in which the displacements of the several rotors constitute the unknowns, and then solves the equations for them.

For example, the cryptanalyst may find two identical ciphertext letters in the first 26 letters of the cryptogram. Only the first rotor is turning; the last four have not moved. Since the two electrical impulses emerged at the same ciphertext lamp, they had to trace the same course through the maze of the last four rotors. Their paths differed only in the first rotor. The cryptanalyst can set up two equations. In each, the ciphertext's numerical value equals the known plaintext value plus the unknown displacement on the first rotor plus the unknown displacement on the last four together. He takes into account by a correction the first rotor's having turned several spaces. He subtracts one equation from the other in the standard algebraic process for solving simultaneous equations. This will reduce the substitutive effect of the last four rotors to zero. It will also give the cryptanalyst a numerical value that equals the difference between the two displacements in the first rotor. By repeating this process, the cryptanalyst can list the differences between many of the displacements on the rotor. He can then seek an arrangement of wires having these differences that will reproduce the known cryptographic effects.

In similar fashion, he will reconstruct another rotor. To isolate it, he must neutralize the movement of its fellows. Thus the first rotor will return to its original position at the 1st, 27th, 53rd, 79th, and so on, letters of the cryptogram. The second rotor remains in its first position for the first 26 letters of the cryptogram, in its second position for the second 26, and so on, not resuming its starting position until the 677th letter, when it again remains fixed for 26 letters. The other rotors likewise stand and turn in their own rhythms. By selecting letters at the proper intervals, the cryptanalyst can "stop" the revolution of a rotor much as stroboscopic flashes do.

Such are the basic principles of the rotor solution. But their practice wracks the cryptanalyst with some of the most excruciating mental torture known to man. The equations seem to stretch from here to the moon and to involute their parts as confusingly as the Gordian knot. In part, this complexity results from the need to index all displacements against the fixed input and output plates, which, after all, represent the plain- and ciphertext components, and the consequent continual corrections that must be made. In part, it results from the frequent necessity of expressing one displacement difference in terms of several others. A difference on the third rotor may only be known as the sum of differences on the first and fourth rotors, and the difference on the fourth may, in turn, be known only as the sum of differences on the second and fifth. Thus one unknown may be represented by four or five terms. Group theory is particularly fitted to handle this sort of problem, but it is also peculiarly prone to error. A false assumption will spread and grow like a malignant fungus over the treelike branches of these equations. Finally, the pattern of displacements that the cryptanalyst reconstructs may be correct only in a relative sense and may require permutation to the absolute form. These inherent problems are aggravated by external ones. The enemy cryptographers seldom oblige by beginning all their messages with the rotors in their starting position. The cryptanalyst is forced to determine first when the several rotors change positions. This problem, in turn, is made more difficult by the use of devices that impart an irregular movement to the rotors. Furthermore, the cryptographer can alter his substitution just by changing the order of the rotors.

All in all, the rotor system produces an extremely complex and secure cipher from simple elements in a simple construction. Who are the four contrivers of this miniature labyrinth, the four modern Daedaluses of cryptography?

The inventor of the first machine to embody the rotor principle gave the best efforts of his life to it. Edward Hugh Hebern was born April 23, 1869, in Streator, Illinois, and was raised in the Soldiers' Orphan Home in Bloomington. When he was 14 he began living and working on a farm near Odin, where he got a high school education. He headed West at 19, and, after selling a timber claim in California to a sawmill where he worked for a time, he turned to carpentry and built and sold houses in Fresno. Soon after he turned 40, he somehow became interested in cryptology. Hebern was at this time a blue-eyed, brown-haired man of medium height and build, mustachioed, quiet, a great reader, kind, and even-tempered.

From 1912 to 1915, he filed for patents for cryptographic check-writing devices, cipher keyboards for typewriters, movable letter blocks to form mixed reciprocal monalphabets, and a ciphering typewriter. In 1915, he devised an arrangement in which two electric typewriters were connected by 26 wires in random fashion; thus when a letter was struck on the plaintext keyboard, it would cause a ciphertext letter to print on the other machine. Since the wires remained plugged into the same jacks during an entire message, the cryptogram would be monalphabetic—but it would have been electromechanically enciphered.

The wire interconnections comprised the germ of the rotor—a means to vary the monalphabetic encipherment. In 1917, Hebern reduced his ideas to the first drawings made of a rotor system, which, a year later, grew into actual apparatus.

Early in 1921, he advertised an "unbreakable" cipher in a marine magazine, but Miss Agnes Meyer, a cryptanalyst in the Navy's Code and Signal Section, solved the sample message. When Commander Milo F. Draemel, the officer in charge, sent Hebern the solution, he came at once to Washington and showed the Navy his machine, filing his first rotor patent while he was there. The Navy had been looking, a director of naval communications later recalled, for "something radically better [in secret communications].

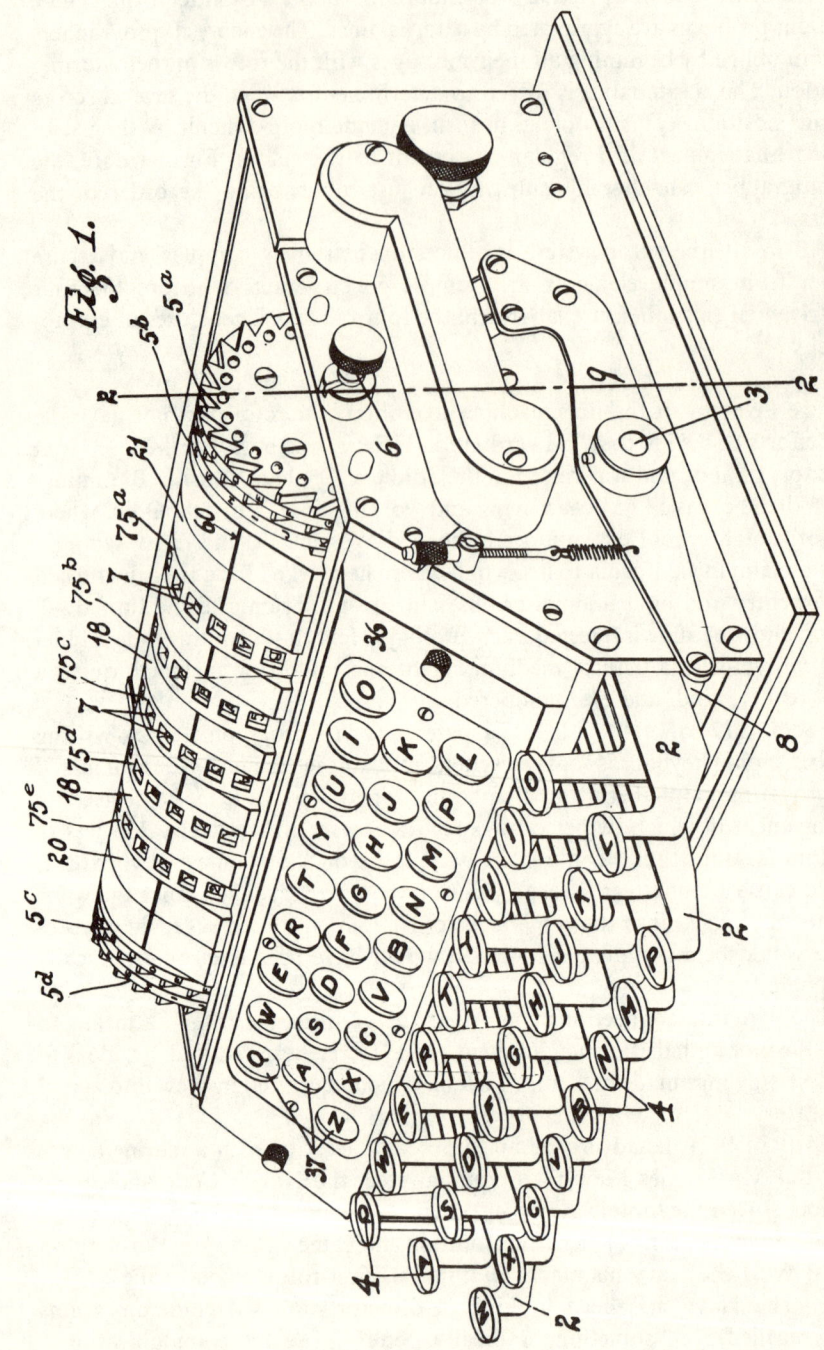

Edward Hebern's "Electric Code Machine," U.S. Patent 1,683,072. Rotors are 75a–e; plates, 18, 20, 21; the output letters glow behind the imprinted windows 37

Something automatic came into our minds, and it had been in the back of our heads for some time. Along came Mr. Hebern from the West Coast with the Hebern machine. He made one, as I recall, and we were very thrilled when he showed us what it could do.... I remember we wanted to get some right away for the whole Navy."

Hebern had, in 1921, incorporated Hebern Electric Code, the first cipher machine company in the U.S., and with this kind of encouragement from the Navy, and believing—rightly—that his new rotor device was the cipher machine of the future, he began selling shares in his firm to raise capital. Since it controlled scores of patents in the United States and abroad, not only on the cipher machine but on such other pioneering devices as electric typewriters and directional indicators for cars, he had no trouble selling about $1,000,000 worth of stock to 2,500 shareholders, mostly from Oakland, where he then lived.

On February 5, 1922, Hebern bought a machine works to help his production facilities make cipher machine dies, molds, and patterns. Then, thinking that "we are very close to a great financial success with our code inventions and that it is sensible to be prepared to take care of a big business in a permanent way," he decided to erect a plant large enough to house a 1,500-man factory. A steam shovel, with Hebern at the controls, broke ground on September 21 for a three-story neo-Gothic building occupying half a square block on the west side of Harrison Street between Eighth and Ninth Streets in Oakland. Plans called for a buffing-and-polishing room, a plating room, a 200-foot-long assembly room, a tool-and-die room, and numerous other facilities, including a corner office with fireplace for the president. In February of 1923, he hired Agnes Meyer (by now Mrs. Driscoll) for cryptologic help and liaison with the Navy.

While the building was going up, Hebern sold more stock in the company ("Remember, your stock is participating stock, and has the same chance to advance as the original stock of the telephone, wireless and other great inventions"), inundated his stockholders with optimistic reports, and kept his offices open until 9 p.m. every night, including Sundays, so that stockholders could examine the wonderful device. His handiwork filled Hebern with such awe that he extolled it in what may be the first ode to a cipher machine:

> Marvelous invention comes out of the West
> Triumph of patience, long years without rest
> Solved problem of ages, deeper than thought
> A code of perfection, a wonder, is wrought
>
> Of international scope, is the code electric
> With merit so obvious, no nation can reject it
> Result of deep study, when necessity goads
> Hebern Electric, is the peer of all codes

> Sphinx of the wireless, guardian of treasure
> Brain of a nation, safety beyond measure
> Heart of a battleship, preserver of lives
> When brute force, against intellect strives
>
> Keeper of secrets, of state and alliance
> Inscrutable, wonderful, a mystery to science
> Of depth so profound, brainy traitors, beware
> Invisible around you, is the genii's snare
>
> Conceived of the world war, in desperate need
> Brains of all nations, competing in speed
> Trained minds of the highest, seeking for might
> An American achievement, is now brought to light

Overlooking this, the Chief of Naval Operations convened a board in 1923 to look into the Hebern machine. On it were Commander R. E. Ingersoll, later Commander in Chief Atlantic Fleet, Commander Russell Willson, and Lieutenant Commander W. W. Smith. It recommended the machine's adoption when perfected, and when the Secretary of the Navy approved the report, the Navy felt committed to the Hebern machine. None of this, however, had resulted in any cash sales by the time the grandiose factory was completed late in 1923 at a cost of $380,000—half again as much as the original $250,000 estimate. This lack of income made it impossible for Hebern to bear the burden of its overhead, and, in the spring of 1924, the firm defaulted on the interest on its $100,000 mortgage. In the subsequent reorganization, Hebern was removed as president, though he remained in control. On April 30, an angry group of stockholders, at a stormy meeting that attracted newspaper coverage, protested a 10 per cent assessment levied by the firm to pay the interest. They prompted a state investigation into charges that Hebern had sold stock in the firm at $3 and $5 a share instead of at the legally authorized $1 par value. In the summer Mrs. Driscoll returned to the Navy Department.

The investigation—largely under Alameda County District Attorney Earl Warren, later Chief Justice of the United States—continued through 1924 and 1925 and into 1926. During that time the U.S. Navy ordered two Hebern machines at $600 each, and the Army paid him $500 for two that he had already delivered. The Pacific Steamship Company bought seven at $120 (the difference in price was due to the variation in the number of rotors in the machines offered for sale) for use aboard four ships and in three shore offices. The Italian government purchased a machine, and Britain's Admiralty was studying one.

But shareholder pressure was mounting. Only twelve machines had been sold, they complained. As many as 500 stockholders thronged the protest meetings, and 150 crowded the Oakland Police Court at preliminary hearings of Hebern's case, which attracted considerable public notice. Hebern was finally brought to trial March 1, 1926, in the Superior Court on a charge of violating California's corporate securities act. After four days—during which such witnesses as 74-year-old Mrs. Caroline Gowdy testified how she had purchased 200 shares at $5 apiece—the jury retired. Twelve minutes later it returned, having found Hebern guilty. Though this verdict was later set aside and the charge dismissed for lack of evidence, it killed Hebern's chances of attracting large amounts of capital. Three months later, Hebern Electric Code, Inc., went into bankruptcy.

Hebern refused to give up. Pinning his hopes on the Navy, he incorporated the International Code Machine Company in Reno, Nevada. Things started to look up in 1928 when he sold four five-rotor machines to the Navy at $750 for each machine and $20 for each rotor. Hebern and a handful of employees had built them by hand, and he himself then drove them to the 12th Naval District Office in San Francisco. One machine stayed there; the others were sent to the Navy Department and to the commanders in chief of the United States Fleet and the Battle Fleet for field tests. The Navy wanted to determine their mechanical reliability rather than their cryptographic capabilities, which were regarded as satisfactory, even though Friedman had made a cryptanalytic breakthrough and solved the first rotor system. During 1929 and 1930 these machines handled a considerable portion of the Navy's official high-command communications. Things looked even better for Hebern in 1931, when the Navy purchased 31 machines for $54,480. These were not experimental machines, but were issued to the more important flag officers as the top cryptographic system in the United States Navy. In 1934, Hebern, who was continually trying to improve his machines, submitted one that proved a complete failure. The officer who had dealt most with him, Safford, was on sea duty, and some Navy man who did not know Hebern sent him an abrupt and discourteous letter, discontinuing business with him. As Safford later put it, "They pulled the rug out from under Hebern and were not even polite about it."

That virtually ended Hebern's chances, for although his machines were still in service, when they wore out in 1936 after carrying heavy loads of traffic they were replaced by another, non-Hebern cryptographic system. Interestingly, the Hebern machines themselves were renovated and sent to shore stations, where some remained in use until 1942. Two were, in fact, captured by the Japanese during World War II.

During this time, Hebern was living on income from properties left by his wife's sister. He continued to improve his machines and to take out patents, despite the setback of losing a patent interference case against International Business Machines in 1941. In 1947, convinced that the armed forces had used his basic ideas throughout the war without compensating him for them, he filed a claim of $50,000,000 against the three services. In the six-year period that this remained entangled in bureaucratic red tape, Hebern died. He was 82, and had suffered a heart attack on February 10, 1952, while trying to lift a box that was too heavy for him.

Early in 1953, the departments of the Army, Navy, and Air Force rejected his claims, and a few months later his estate sued the government for the $50,000,000. On the basis of legal technicalities, the United States Court of Claims limited the period of recovery to 1947-1953 and the infringement question to the exceedingly narrow one of a particular dog arrangement for turning the rotors. Ignored was the basic question of whether the armed forces had adopted the rotor principle from Hebern and used it without just compensation in hundreds of thousands of high-security machines in World War II and in the cold war—which they had unquestionably done. Ignored were the ethics of having obtained Hebern's best developmental efforts on the implied promise of large production contracts, which were awarded instead to the Teletype Corporation.

The government, taking refuge from the spirit of justice in the letter of the law, fought to keep from giving him a penny. In 1958, it finally settled for the pittance of $30,000—and not out of a sense of fair play, but because it feared that the court's sense of right would compel it to bare some cryptographic secrets. The payment was disproportionate to Hebern's contribution, which was worth, not $50,000,000, to be sure, but $1,000,000 at the least. Hebern deserved better. His story, tragic, unjust, and pathetic, does his country no honor.

At 2:55 p.m., Tuesday, October 7, 1919, the man who viewed the rotor most comprehensively filed what was to become Netherlands patent No. 10,700 for a "Geheimschrijfmachine" ("secret writing machine"). Hugo Alexander Koch, then 49, a native of Delft, had apparently devised it as an outgrowth of his engineering hobbies. He foresaw some commercial value for the system, for he set up a corporation, the Naamlooze Venootschap Ingenieursbureau "Securitas," in whose name the patent was issued. Koch pointed out in this patent that steel wires on pulleys, levers, rays of light, or air, water, or oil flowing through tubes could transmit the enciphering impulse as well as electricity did. He also observed that this impulse did not have to flow through a rotor, but could move through tubes drilled through bars that slid between plates, or from an interior disk to a circumjacent ring. He favored the rotor mechanism, but no machine ensued in any of the forms. In 1927, he assigned the patent rights to the German inventor of a rotor device, and the following year he died in Düsseldorf.

The German was Arthur Scherbius. Little more is known of him than that he was an engineer, had a doctorate, held a number of patents involving such far-from-cryptologic materials as ceramics, and lived in Wilmersdorf, a suburb of Berlin. His first cryptologic device enciphered codenumbers into pronounceable codewords, which were then favored by international telegraph conventions. It did this by feeding the placode numbers alternately to

Secrecy for Sale

vowel and consonant encicode equivalents. The device included "multiple switch boards which connect each arriving lead with one of the outgoing leads and which are adapted to interchange this connection with great facility of variation." Though Scherbius did not describe this device further, it was the basis of a rotor system. Such appeared full-blown in his next patent. The rotors served only for numeral encipherment in this device, but in subsequent ones they expanded their contacts from 10 to 26 and so could be used for standard literal encipherment.

He called his machine the Enigma. Model A, a monster about the size and shape of a cash register, was soon discarded for Model B, which stuck the enciphering mechanism on the right side of an ordinary typewriter. Model C was a portable, nonprinting device in which the letters were indicated—as in the early Hebern models—by lamps. All models had typewriterlike keyboards. The Enigma differed in two important ways from the other rotor conceptions. Its final rotor was a half-rotor: it had contacts on one face only and these were interconnected. An impulse coming to this rotor would thus be reflected back through the rotors through which it had just come. This doubly enciphered each letter, but it also made the encipherment reciprocal (if plaintext *e* became x, then plaintext *x* had to become ciphertext E), which is a weakness. The second difference was that the rotor progression was governed by gears to make it irregular. Unfortunately, the gears had so low a pitch that their period came to only 53,295 letters. Later machines improved this.

Scherbius seems to have formed a little company of his own, Gewerkschaft Securitas, to promote his machine. Evidently some businessmen saw possibilities in the mechanism, for in July of 1923 a corporation was set up to manufacture and sell it. Chiffriermaschinen Aktiengesellschaft ("Cipher Machines Corporation") was capitalized during Germany's disastrous postwar inflation at 500,000,000 marks, distributed in 50,000 shares of 10,000 marks par value. It paid Gewerkschaft Securitas 300,000,000 marks for a controlling share of the company and its patents, models, drawings, and tools. Scherbius sat on the six-man board of directors.

Chiffriermaschinen Aktiengesellschaft began operating on August 24, 1923, at 2 Steglitzerstrasse, Berlin, and worked hard to create a demand for its product. It exhibited the Enigma before the 1923 congress of the International Postal Union, and the following year got the German post office to exchange Enigma-enciphered greetings with the congress. It got some publicity in *Radio News* and extensive coverage in a book on cipher machines by Dr. Siegfried Türkel, scientific director of the Criminological Institute of the Vienna police. It printed flyers in German and illustrated brochures in English: "The natural inquisitiveness of competitors is at once checkmated by a machine which enables you to keep all your documents, or at least their important parts, entirely secret without occasioning any expenses worth mentioning. One secret, well protected, may pay the whole cost of the machine...."

But nothing helped. A few machines were bought for study purposes by the armed forces of various nations and communications companies, but mass sales never materialized. Production constantly declined. In 1924, the first full year of operation, Chiffriermaschinen Aktiengesellschaft spent 102,812 reichmarks (the new monetary unit) for expenses, salaries, and wages. In 1929 it disbursed only 56,345. By then Scherbius' name was no longer listed among the directors, most probably because he had died. After ten full years of operation, the firm had still failed to pay a dividend. So on July 5, 1934, it dissolved and transferred its assets to Chiffriermaschinen Gesellschaft Heimsoeth und Rinke, a new cipher machine firm organized by Dr. Rudolf Heimsoeth and Frau Elsbeth Rinke, both directors of the old firm.

Soon Hitler began rearming Germany, and the cryptologic experts of the Wehrmacht, deciding that the Enigma offered satisfactory guarantees of security, began supplying their expanding forces with it. Whether Heimsoeth and Rinke enjoyed this new prosperity, or whether the Nazis nationalized their business or merged it into others, is unknown. During World War II, the portable glowlamp Enigma, battery-powered, and, in its wooden box, about the size and weight of a standard typewriter, served as the top German Army, Navy, Air Force system. Signal officers regarded it as very dependable and believed it to be secure. Its only disadvantage was that it did not print, and speedy operation required three men—one to read the incoming text and press the keys, one to call out the letters in a loud voice as they lit up, one to write down the text.

Oddly enough, the fuzziest of the four original rotor conceptions reached a patent office only three days after the clearest. Koch had filed for his patent in Holland on a Tuesday, and on Friday of that same week in October, 1919, Arvid Gerhard Damm applied in Stockholm for what was to become Swedish patent No. 52,279.

Damm's device employed a kind of double rotor arrangement. Two circular flat plates, both wired like rotors, turned above and below a horizontal intermediate plate. Gears moved the rotors an irregular number of spaces at each plaintext letter. Damm, however, regarded the rotor as only an auxiliary feature of the enciphering mechanism, which was so extraordinarily clumsy and complicated that it seems never to have been built. And though Damm's conception of the rotor accords him a listing in the honor roll of cryptologic inventors, his real impact on cryptology comes from his having established a cipher machine company that eventually became the only commercially successful one in the world.

Damm is one of cryptology's "characters." He was originally a textile engineer. While engineering manager of a cloth-making factory in Finland, he became enamored of a Hungarian equestrienne in a traveling circus. Unable to overcome her virtue, he had a chum dress up like a clergyman and "marry"

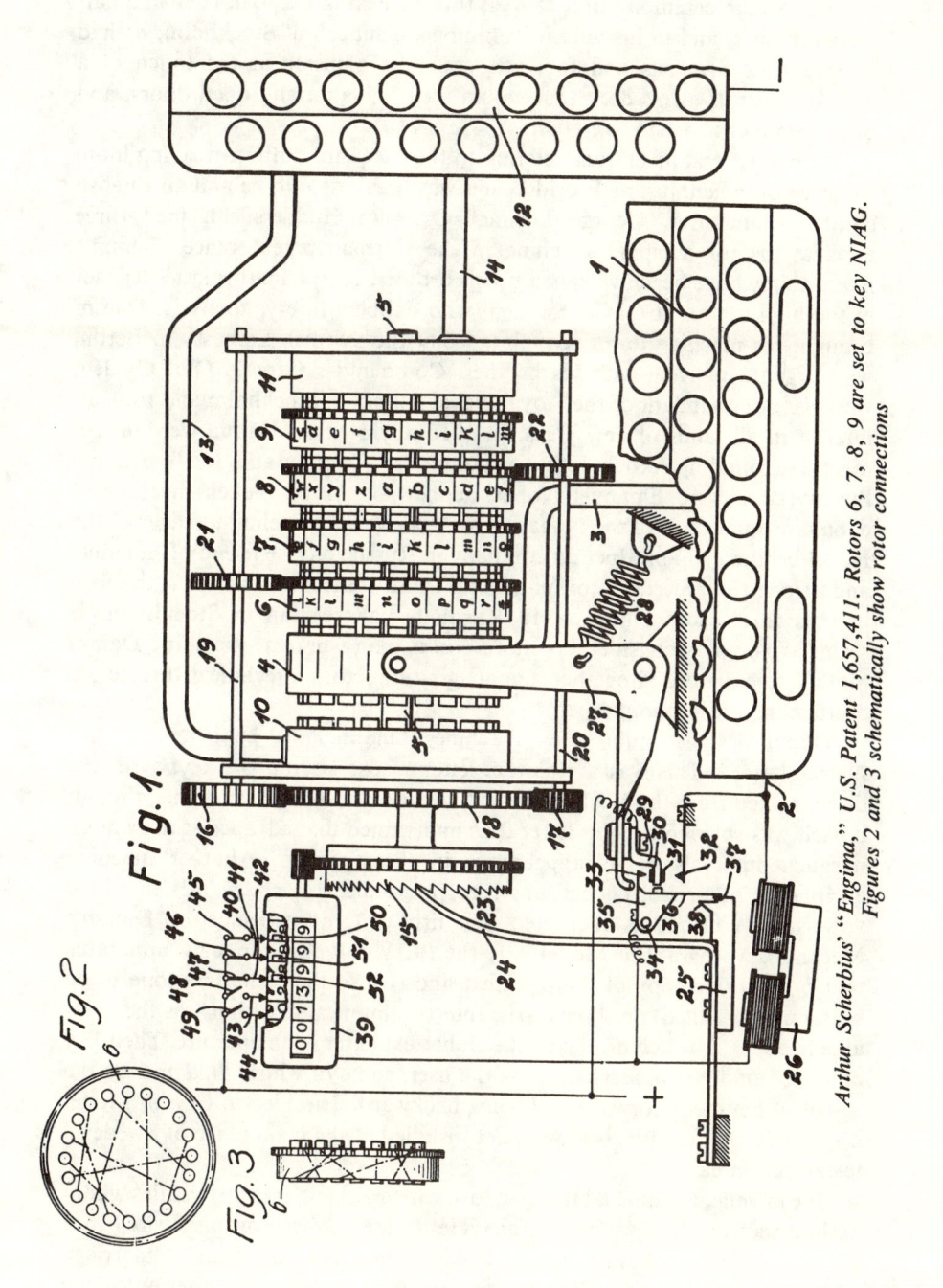

Arthur Scherbius' "Engima," U.S. Patent 1,657,411. Rotors 6, 7, 8, 9 are set to key NIAG.
Figures 2 and 3 schematically show rotor connections

them in a fake ceremony in a chapel, thus achieving his goal. He had a flair for mechanics, and in his villa in Rönninge, a suburb of Stockholm, he had chairs whose armrests and footrests could be adjusted at the touch of a button, controls at his desk that would flick lights on and open doors, and other gimmicks to astonish guests.

He had several inventions relating to the Jacquard pattern-weaving loom to his credit when, just as World War I was breaking out, he and an English cloth manufacturer, George Lorimer Craig of Huddersfield, filed three applications for a cipher machine in the German patent office. Damm's interest may have been awakened by his brother, Ivar, a mathematics teacher in the high school at Gävle, Sweden, who dabbled in cryptanalysis. Damm brought his machine to an acquaintance at the Swedish Embassy in Berlin, who urged a meeting with his brother, Commander Captain Olof Gyldén, who was commandant of the Royal Naval School in Stockholm and took an interest in all kinds of new ideas. In 1916, Gyldén and Damm were instrumental in founding Aktiebolaget Cryptograph ("Cryptograph, Inc."). Among the investors were Emanuel Nobel, nephew of Alfred Nobel, inventor of dynamite and donor of the Nobel prizes, and K. W. Hagelin, manager of the Nobel brothers' oil production company in Russia, a close friend of Emanuel and at one time Swedish consul-general in St. Petersburg. In 1921, the firm had its three-room offices at 19 Karduansmakaregatan in Stockholm. It seemed to employ considerably more bosses than workers: excluding Damm himself, there were altogether a managing director, a technical director, a draftsman, and a bookkeeper.

Damm designed quite a few machines. One included his ingenious "influence letter." This was a plaintext letter whose key on the keyboard was disconnected from the mechanism that advanced the cipher elements, though it itself was enciphered; this letter thus interrupted that advance at the wholly irregular intervals of its appearance in the plaintext. Another machine enciphered numerical codegroups into pronounceable codewords in which vowels and consonants alternated. The firm concentrated most on Damm's Mecano-Cryptographer Model A 1, the "Cryptotyper," an ugly apparatus that printed one copy of the plaintext and two of the ciphertext (one to be sent, one to be filed) on three tapes. Intercommunicable with it was the portable Model A 2, which displayed the ciphertext letter in an aperture. Their key consisted of a chain, assembled by the user, some of whose links moved the so-called key-body forward and some backward. The Electro-Crypto Model B 1, handsome but massive, was later installed at the main office of Sweden's telegraph bureau.

Meanwhile, Damm had fallen in love with a girl in her early twenties whom he had met on the commuter train. He decided to jettison his "wife" in a divorce proceeding that he thought would be no more valid than the marriage and, taking no chances, by a denunciation of her as a spy, to get her out of the country. He was severely embarrassed in court, however, when his partner

Gyldén revealed the phony wedding as well as the spy gimmick. Damm rewarded Gyldén for this bit of candor by giving the managing directorship to someone else when it later became available. But he got what he wanted, and his new fiancée, Miss Spång, accompanied him to Paris on his business trips, living with him at the Hotel Périgord. Unfortunately, this saga ended sadly for him when she jilted him—doubly sadly, since he had given her his villa, though it was mortgaged, as the Swedes say, to the chimneys.

Damm had won orders for a single test Model B 1 from several major wireless companies. He hoped they would adopt it to safeguard the world's commercial wireless traffic. But the machines proved erratic. In tests in France in 1925, sometimes 1,000 letters could be deciphered correctly, and sometimes none at all. The following year the firm demonstrated its machines at The Hague for the Japanese military attaché. Difficulties abounded. Direct current was used where alternating current was needed; parts were too heavy to respond quickly; numerous malfunctions and cryptographic errors occurred. Sales were not spectacular.

By then, however, a new personality was asserting himself in the company. This was Boris Caesar Wilhelm Hagelin, son of the consul-general and investor in the firm. Born on July 2, 1892, in the Caucasus, where his father was working, he studied for three or four years in St. Petersburg, then returned to Sweden and was graduated from the Royal Institute of Technology in Stockholm in 1914 with a degree in mechanical engineering. After six years of working for ASEA, Sweden's General Electric, and one in the United States for the Standard Oil Company (New Jersey), in the expectation of returning to Russia for the Nobel interests, he and the Nobels realized that the Communist regime was not going to fall as they had hoped. Accordingly, his father and Emanuel Nobel put him into the Damm firm in 1922 to represent their investment.

Three years later, while Damm was in Paris, young Hagelin learned that the Swedish military was considering buying the Enigma. He simplified one of the Damm mechanisms, giving it a keyboard and indicating lamps like the Enigma's, and making it more suitable for field use. Its operation was based on the checkerboard. It electrically altered the row and column assignments to convert a plaintext letter to ciphertext. These alterations were controlled by a group of keywheels, each with pins near its rim that could be made active or inactive by extending or retracting them. Each wheel had a different number of pins. The machine produced a polyalphabetic substitution whose period was the product of all the pin numbers. Hagelin offered this machine, the B-21, to the Swedish Army. Damm criticized it but the Army liked it, and, in 1926, placed a large order.

On the verge of success, Damm, early in 1927, died. Aktiebolaget Cryptograph, which was in poor financial shape but which had a big order in its pocket, was purchased at a good price by the Hagelin interests and reorganized as Aktiebolaget Cryptoteknik, 14 Luntmakaregatan, Stockholm. Boris Hagelin ran the firm. He saw that printing cipher machines were faster, more accurate, and more economical in terms of manpower than indicating mechanisms like the Enigma. He first hooked up the Type B-21 to an electric typewriter and found it unacceptably bulky. So he merged the printing mechanism with the cryptographic in a single unit, producing the Type B-211. It weighed 37 pounds, operated at 200 characters a minute, and could be carried inside a case about the size of an attaché case.

This was the most compact printing cipher machine available in 1934, when the French general staff asked Hagelin for the impossible: a pocket-sized cipher machine that would print the ciphertext and so permit one-man operation. He first whittled a piece of wood that would fit into a pocket to mark the limits of his dimension. While trying to concoct a mechanism that would fit inside such space and also produce an effective cipher, he bethought himself one day of a construction that he had conceived three years before for the inventors of a vending machine. It was an adding device that would accept different amounts of money, and it consisted of bars arranged in a cylindrical cage with lugs projecting from them in rows. There were 10 lugs in one row, 8 in the second, 4 in the third, 2 in the next, and 1 in the last; by combining these rows in various ways any number from 1 to 25 could be produced. This was just what he needed. The inventors had given him the rights to it when they could not pay for the prototype that he fabricated. He now adapted it so that the rows would shift a cipher alphabet to any one of 25 positions, thus giving a plaintext letter any one of 25 ciphertext equivalents. And to produce the combinations of numbers for these shifts, he could employ the keywheels with the variable number of projecting pins that he had used in his B-21.

Hagelin shrank the device to $6 \times 4\frac{1}{2} \times 2$ inches—smaller than the base of a standard telephone set—and to under three pounds, or about the weight of a dictionary-sized codebook. To operate it, the encipherer, after first setting the key elements, twirled a knob at the left to the plaintext letter, and revolved a handle at the right. The mechanism spun, and a little typewheel printed the output on a gummed tape. Hagelin even managed to have it print the ciphertext in five-letter groups and the plaintext in normal word-lengths (by using a rare letter as a word-spacer). Its speed averaged 25 letters per minute.

This was the Type C-36, and when the French saw it, they snapped it up. Their 1935 order for 5,000 machines proved the turning point in the firm's fortunes. Looking back, Hagelin realized that Damm and the other cipher machine companies had not failed because of any intrinsic flaws in their machines, but only because the time was not ripe for them in the 1920s. Not until the war-weariness of that decade had worn off and the rearmament of the 1930s had begun did a substantial market appear. In 1936, Yves Gyldén, the son of Damm's early partner, analyzed the machine's cipher and recommended some important improvements, which Hagelin adopted, substantially strengthening its cipher.

That same year, Hagelin began corresponding with American cryptologic authorities about the C-36. He went over himself in 1937, and again in 1939 when war broke out in Europe. Now the United States was considerably more interested. Friedman suggested improvements, and Hagelin returned to Sweden to incorporate them and to streamline the machine for mass production. On April 9, 1940, he was in his cabin in Dalecarlia when he heard a radio announcement that the Germans had invaded Norway. His wife told him that if he wanted to do anything with his machine in the United States, he ought to go there at once.

"A normal visa was unobtainable," he has recalled, "so I induced the Swedish foreign office to send me as a diplomatic courier. My wife and I sent our luggage off in advance and took the train up to Stockholm. There we learned that the travel bureau had cancelled all trips to the United States, as the Germans had by now invaded France, Holland, and Belgium. We decided to take a chance and try to sail from Italy.

"With the blueprints in my briefcase and two dismantled ciphering machines in a bag, we boarded the Trelleborg-Sassnitz-Berlin express. Our luck held. We rattled right through the heart of Germany and arrived unmolested three days later in Genoa. That night the windows of our hotel were smashed—because we had innocently chosen to stay at the Hotel Londra and Italy was now at war with Britain. But we reached New York on the last outward-bound voyage of the *Conte di Savoia*."

This breathless escape proved worth it. The U.S. Army liked the machine, though it insisted on further tests. Hagelin got 50 machines flown out secretly from Stockholm to Washington for final exhaustive trials. They passed, and after long contract negotiations, the Army accepted the improved device as its medium-level cryptographic system. Under the U.S. military designation of Converter M-209, the Hagelin machine served in military units from divisions down to battalions. In 1942, L. C. Smith & Corona Typewriters, Inc., began turning out about 400 olive-drab Hagelin machines a day (compared to its output of about 600 typewriters a day) in its 900-man factory at Groton, New York. More than 140,000 were produced. (Ironically, the Italian Navy also used it.) Hagelin's royalties ran into the millions of dollars. He became the first—and the only—man to become a millionaire from cryptology.

What is this little jewel of a cipher machine like? What is this infant Hercules of cryptography, which raised its inventor to such financial heights?

In essence, it is a gear with a variable number of teeth. These turn a cipher alphabet through as many positions as there are teeth for that particular encipherment. The various parts of the mechanism interact to produce an incoherent running key with a very long period. The machine consists of four main operating elements:

(1) The cage, in which 27* bars are disposed in the form of a horizontal cylinder, which revolves. The individual bars can slide to the left. The ends of those bars that are slid to the left comprise the cogs of the variable gear. The bars that are not slid comprise its gaps. Each bar carries two lugs, or projecting members, that can be set to two of eight locations on the bar. Six of these are operative, two nonoperative. As the cage turns toward the operator, it will bring the lugs in eight columns up over the top, down, and around.

(2) Six flat vertical rods called "guide arms" to contact these projecting lugs. Each of the six guide arms is matched with one of the six operative locations. The guide arms can rock forward into an operative position of their own or back into a nonoperative position. In the operative position a guide arm will contact lugs, but if either lugs or guide arms are nonoperative no contact will take place. Each guide arm has its upper end angled to the right so that, when the cage is turning and bringing an operative lug down onto an operative guide arm, the slant will push the lug to the left. This will carry the lug's bar to the left, adding a tooth to the variable gear.

(3) Six keywheels, each controlling a guide arm. The keywheels have 26, 25, 23, 21, 19, and 17 indicator letters on their rims and a pin underneath each letter. Each pin can project either from the right or the left side of its keywheel, the right-hand position being its operative position. When an operative pin reaches a certain point in the revolution of the keywheel, it will move the guide arm into an operative position. When a nonoperative pin reaches that point, it will pull the guide arm back into a nonoperative position. Thus the succession of operative and nonoperative pin positions around the circumference of a keywheel will bring its guide arm into and out of operating position. This determines whether lugs will be contacted, and hence whether teeth will be added to the variable gear.

(4) The displacement and printing mechanism. A knob at the left of the machine turns an indicating disk with the 26 plaintext letters. It also turns, on the same axis, a typewheel that prints the machine's output on paper tape, and a typewheel gear that connects, through an intermediate gear, with the ends of the slide-bars that are serving as the teeth of the variable gear. At the start of an encipherment, before the slide-bar ends begin to engage the intermediate gear, these three elements can revolve freely (as a unit, not separately), permitting the setting of any plaintext letter opposite a benchmark.

To encipher, the lugs on each bar must be set in prearranged key locations, and the pins on each wheel must also be set in prearranged key positions. The deciphering machine must naturally be set identically. The encipherer then

---

* In the original C-36, only 25. The machine described here is the M-209. Similarly, where the M-209 had six keywheels and moveable lugs, the C-36 had only five keywheels and fixed lugs. The increase in the number of keywheels and the number of bars, and the moveability of the lugs, is due to Yves Gyldén. The operation of the two models is the same, however.

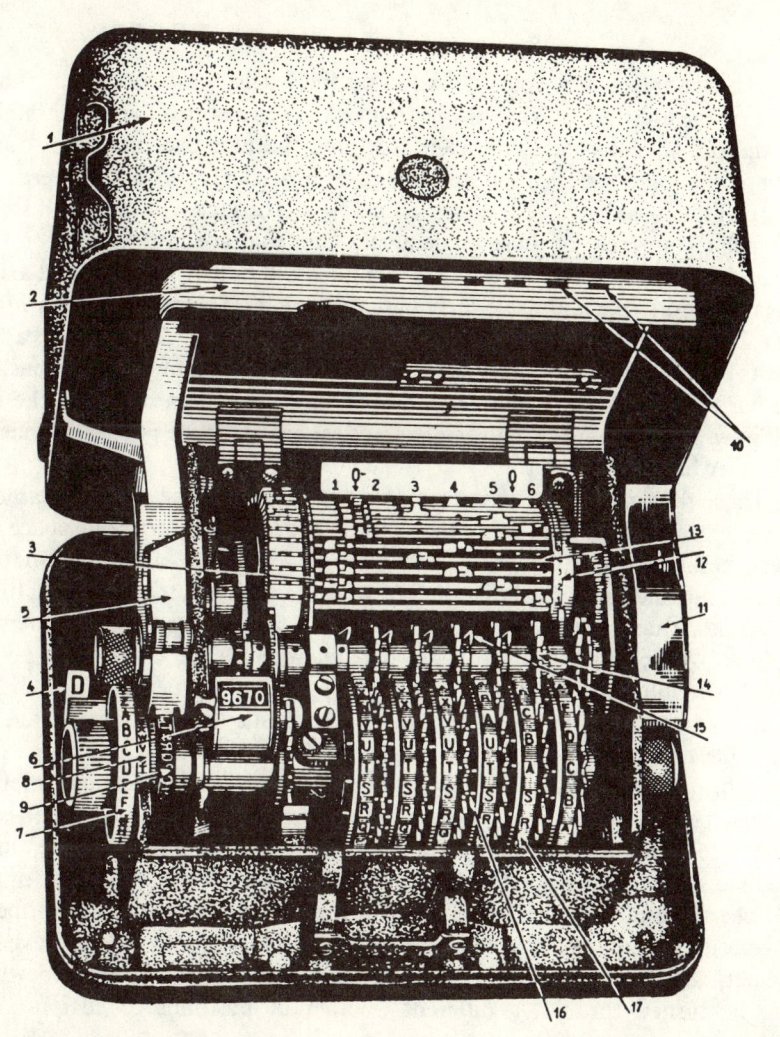

Boris Hagelin's M-209. *1* Outer cover *2* Inner cover *3* A lug *4* Encipherdecipher knob, set at D for decipher *5* Paper tape *6* Letter counter *7* Indicating disk, on which input letters are set *8* Reproducing disk, on which output letters are shown *9* Typewheel, which prints output letters *10* Windows to display keyletters on keywheels *11* Power handle *12* Cage disk, numbered for each slide-bar *13* A slide-bar, which moves left to become a tooth of the variable gear *14* Keywheel advance gear *15* Upper part of angled face of guide arm of keywheel 4; lugs in column 4 will strike it as cage rotates forward, driving slide-bars to the left *16* Pin for S on keywheel 4, in ineffective position *17* Keywheel 5

turns the six keywheels to any random position, which he records by the letters on the rims. The position changes from message to message; hence the letters—PQFPHJ, for instance—are inserted at a prearranged point in the cryptogram to permit the decipherer to set his machine to the same starting position.

The encipherer now spins the knob on the left to bring his first plaintext letter on the indicating disk to the benchmark. Then he turns the power handle on the right. This rotates the cage, carrying the lugs over and then down toward the guide arms. Suppose that guide arms 1, 3, and 5 are operative. Then all the lugs that have been set in operative locations 1, 3, and 5 will strike the inclined surfaces of those guide arms. Lugs that are in the nonoperative locations or in operative locations 2, 4, and 6 will not strike any guide arms. Lugs that do strike will drive their bars to the left. (Since there are two lugs on each bar, there may be some duplication of effort, if, for instance, a bar has its lugs in locations 1 and 5. The result is the same as if only one lug pushed the bar to the left.) The ends of those bars that have been driven to the left will now be able to mesh with the teeth of the intermediate gear. The ends of the other bars will miss it.

Those that mesh will transmit the turning motion of the cage to the intermediate gear, which then turns the typewheel gear. This turns one space for every meshed bar-end, or tooth of the variable gear. Thus, if the combination of lugs and guide arms pushes a total of 15 bars to the left, the typewheel turns 15 spaces, thus shifting the plaintext letter 15 positions in the ciphertext alphabet (which is the alphabet on the typewheel). The end of the power handle's revolution presses the paper tape against the typewheel (which has been inked by running over the inkpad) and prints the ciphertext letter. At the same time, the power handle advances all six keywheels one space forward, bringing into play a different set of pins, which in turn creates a different arrangement of operative and nonoperative guide arms. The slid-out bar-ends retract to their original neutral position after disengaging from the intermediate gear. This completes the cycle, and the device is now ready for the encipherment of the next letter. Since different guide arms are now in operative positions, different lugs will contact them, different bars will be shoved to the left, different bar-ends will make up the variable gear, and the typewheel will be turned through a different number of positions to encipher the letter.

The cipher that the M-209 produces in so intricate a fashion is a polyalphabetic. Only one primary ciphertext alphabet is employed, and that the normal reversed alphabet. Thus the encipherment may be reproduced by a St.-Cyr slide with a direct normal alphabet for the plaintext and a reversed alphabet for the cipher. The variable gear shifts this ciphertext alphabet in a highly irregular sequence to its 26 possible positions. Because this sequence cannot repeat until the guide arms repeat their successive positions, because they cannot repeat until the keywheels do, and because the keywheels have no factor in common, the sequence will not recommence until $26 \times 25 \times 23 \times 21 \times 19 \times 17$ letters have been enciphered. This gives the M-209 a period of 101,405,850 letters.

This figure, nearly ten times greater than that of a five-wheel rotor machine, discourages a straight Kasiski solution. But, as with a rotor system, heavy traffic may produce two settings of the keywheels close enough together to cause two messages to overlap portions of that long sequence. A kappa test can sound out these overlaps. Then, since the cipher alphabet is known, the cryptanalyst can solve these two identically-keyed ciphertexts by seeing whether a plaintext assumption in one message produces intelligible text in the other.

With the plaintext for a length of ciphertext, the cryptanalyst can then recover the machine's lug and pin settings. He begins from the observation that each lug can cause a shift of one space in the position of the cipher alphabet. If operative, it will kick this alphabet forward one space. Thus, if the ciphertext letter B would have occurred without this lug, its operation will produce an A (the alphabet is reversed). Conversely, if the cryptanalyst tries a lug in a nonoperative location when in fact it should be operative, it will subtract a kick, producing a B instead of an A. A lug in the wrong operative location will add some kicks and subtract others. These effects will occur at nonperiodic intervals.

The effects of keywheel pins, on the other hand, will show up at periodic intervals. If, for example, an encipherer has set a pin on the 19-letter keywheel incorrectly, the decipherer will find a wrong letter appearing every 19 letters. This letter will be many kicks removed from the correct one since the guide arm will have wrongly activated many lugs. On the basis of these principles, by considering the lugs in a column as a group, by setting up algebraic equations in from six to four unknowns, and by repeated cross-corrections, the cryptanalyst can determine the key settings. Usually 150 letters will suffice, and, if he is lucky, as few as 35. The required plaintext may be obtained by probable words or stereotyped beginnings in a single message, and even if a complete recovery cannot be made, a partial one can be and then expanded later.

The machine's handicap of mediocre security is partially overcome by the ease of changing the internal settings, of which there are, literally, vigintillions. And it presents many operational advantages. It prints the output, properly spaced—ciphertext in groups of five, plaintext in word-lengths (usually z is used as a spacer, so that *minimize* will come out *minimi e*). A counter that shows the number of letters enciphered or deciphered allows easy checking of errors. A reset button permits turning the keywheel assembly back to a previous position. If the machine runs out of tape, the ciphertext letters can be read off an indicating disk. Packed within the $3\frac{1}{4} \times 5\frac{1}{2} \times 7$ inches of its housing are paper tape, oil, extra inkpads, tweezers, and screwdriver. It weighs about six pounds and is extremely rugged, able to survive jolts, dust, sand, tropic humidity, and arctic chill. Actual operation could hardly be simpler, requiring only the turning of a knob to bring the plain- or ciphertext letter opposite a mark, then the flipping of the power handle to revolve the mechanism. Encipherment runs at from 15 to 30 letters a minute.

From a purely mechanical point of view the device is an absolute marvel. Hagelin has engineered a mechanism that spouts an extremely long key from relatively few elements in an astonishingly compact format, which also permits of practically unlimited key changes. It is the most ingenious mechanical creation in all cryptography.

In 1944, Hagelin, now a multimillionaire, returned to Sweden on a safe-conduct vessel that took 30 days to cross the Atlantic. "With my earnings," he said, "I bought myself a 2,000-acre estate with a brick factory 30 miles south of Stockholm, outside Södertäge, as I thought that the cipher machine business was finished." How wrong he was! First came the cold war. As the two great powers built up their military might and those of their satellites in mutual fear and mistrust, a new market came into being for cipher machines. Then the old colonial empires broke up. The dozens of new nations that emerged from the ruins created a market for cipher machines far wider than any that had yet existed. To safeguard the communications of their little armies and of the diplomatic posts that they established all over the world, these countries turned to Hagelin.

At first his entire Aktiebolaget Cryptoteknik organization was concentrated in Stockholm. But a Swedish law enabling the government to appropriate inventions that it needed for national defense compelled him to take his developmental work to Zug, Switzerland, in 1948. Zug proved so attractive—not least because of its tax benefits, for which it is widely known—that in 1959 Hagelin moved the rest of the firm there, incorporating it as Crypto Aktiengesellschaft.

The corporation is housed in a four-story tan stucco factory building at 10 Weinbergstrasse on a hillside in the middle of a residential section. It looks out at the sparkling Lake of Zug and beyond to the distant bluish Swiss Alps —probably the loveliest setting in which cryptology has ever been practiced. From inside come the humming, buzzing sounds typical of any light industry. The 170 employees mostly just assemble parts that Hagelin has purchased from manufacturers in Switzerland and Germany; if he made all his own parts, he would need a work force of 300. The building's top floor holds the drafting offices, and the third floor the administrative, where Hagelin has a two-shelf "museum" of cipher machines. Tool-making occupies the first floor, together with some die-stamping; assembly takes place on the second floor, where stacks of parts stand next to a tiny watchmaker's lathe and where workmen solder ultrasonically. In a laboratory, engineers create and test new mechanisms, such as electronic devices that simulate mechanical operation to attain very high-speed operation. Hagelin does not attempt to cryptanalyze his own machine ciphers, however, probably because he fully understands the principles of solution and realizes that the success of his machines depends on proper usage. Instead he draws upon the reactions of his users for improvement ideas.

The firm sells three basic machines. The C-52 is a vastly improved form of the C-48, the firm's designation for the M-209. Though it employs the same basic mechanism, its keywheels have 47, 43, 41, 37, 31, and 29 pins on them, whose period of 2,756,205,443 reduces the likelihood of overlap. The keywheels can be removed and reinserted in a different order. The typewheel carries a mixed alphabet. The indicating disk appears as a dial that shows all letters at once and is easier to operate. With some modifications, it is cryptographically compatible with the older C-48's, a thoughtful arrangement that enables countries that have bought the older ones to use them with the newer ones until they wear out, thereby easing the strain on the communications budget. Price: $600.

The CD-55 is a pocket machine, 5 × 3 × 1½ inches, or slightly larger than a transistor radio. It weighs only 22 ounces. Its mechanism differs from the C-52 but produces the same cipher. A power lever that springs out from the side of the machine is pressed in and released by the thumb. This turns the inner ring of the two circular alphabets—one plain, one cipher—displayed on the face of the machine. This midget sells for $200.

The T-55 is an on-line device that enciphers teletypewriter pulses instead of letters, either by an appropriate modification of the Hagelin cage principle or by a straightforward one-time tape Vernam principle. To make sure that the tape is truly one-time, this machine slices it in half after use! It is much larger and heavier than the other machines.

In addition, Hagelin tempts his customers with a full line of accessories, which in their way are not unlike those that hi-fi addicts or yachtsmen find so hard to resist. A base with a keyboard and an electric motor fits under the C-52 to convert it to rapid, typewriter-like operation—for $1,000. (This gadget replaces the wholly separate electrical printing machines that the firm used to manufacture.) Attachment PE-61 will perforate a teletypewriter tape with the C-52's ciphertext. To facilitate setting the keywheel pins, the pin-setter SRP-58 is available. Arabs, Burmese, Thais, and other users of non-Latin alphabets may purchase machines with their own scripts; these usually serve only for the plaintext, the ciphertext using the Latin letters which are more acceptable in international communications. Units to produce one-time tapes may also be purchased. (These usually generate the random keys required from one of the most random processes known: the decay of a radioactive element. A Geiger counter causes the unit to punch a hole in the tape whenever the disintegration exceeds a certain level in a given period of time; it leaves a blank when the rate falls below this level. Thermal noise, which is equally unpredictable, is also used.)

Nearly all Crypto Aktiengesellschaft's production goes to its approximately 60 governmental customers, whose military services buy substantially more than their diplomatic. Complete installations typically cost from between $30,000 and $50,000. When the purchasers squawk about the price, as they invariably do, Hagelin's representatives ask them whether they ever send messages whose value is much greater than that. This quiets them. A minute portion of the firm's output goes to commercial users, nearly all of whom have international interests, usually highly competitive, such as oil and mining, or highly confidential, such as finance.

The firm explains that the "tremendous number of variable elements"—more than 24 quintillion quintillion quintillion quintillion—enables each customer to select an individual set of keys. It advises which key procedures are good and which bad, but carefully refrains from recommending specific keys because it does not want one customer to think that it is giving them instructions that it could also give to others. "It is not good business practice for us to be knowledgeable of the details of the customer's machine and usage, which should be truly national secrets," says the company in its instruction brochure, "any more than it would be for the safe manufacturer to know the combination of his customer's safe."

Hagelin, whose house in Zug stands a few dozen yards behind his factory, has retired only partially. He does not spend all day at his unique operation, but he still does most of the firm's development work. He says, "I don't understand electronics but I know what it can do." He handles his old customers, though he leaves the new ones and many administrative details to his general manager, Sture Nyberg. A white-haired man of greater than average height and of average build, with firm, pleasant features, Hagelin has a quiet humor and a gentleness about him. Is it true that he speaks five languages fluently? "Only one at a time," he smiles. In his pockets he carries peanuts to feed the birds that fly to his window; one day one perched on his head and another on his arm as he was walking up the steps from his office to his home. At night they leave their "calling cards" on his bedroom light.

His interests are wide. He discusses food like a gourmet, takes good amateur photographs, enjoys sailing, and talks knowledgeably about the flowers in the beds behind his house cultivated by his wife, the former Annie Barth, a distant relation of theologian Karl Barth. He lives very well. Twice a year he returns to Sweden, either to his estate outside of Stockholm or to a log cottage in the north. A soufflé served at luncheon by his cook will be as high and fluffy and tasty as any in a fine restaurant in New York or Paris. The smell of the tan leather upholstery in the white Mercedes-Benz that he drives is almost overpowering. His guest book contains signatures from all over the world—the United States, France, Egypt, Iran, Germany—and he himself is an extremely gracious and considerate host. Hagelin has enjoyed greater material rewards from cryptology than any other person in the world, and it might well be said that it couldn't have happened to a nicer guy.

14

DUEL IN THE ETHER: THE AXIS

SHORTLY AFTER NOON on the tense 31st of August, 1939, the last day of peace that the world was to know for six years, Swedish businessman Birger Dahlerus met with Hermann Göring at the Nazi leader's large and richly furnished town house at 2 Leipzigerstrasse in Berlin. Dahlerus had been trying desperately to avert the onrushing cataclysm of war by flying between England and Germany as Göring's unofficial mediator. Britain had pledged to aid Poland if Hitler attacked her, and, in an effort to stave off actual warfare had proposed to both Germany and Poland that they negotiate their differences directly. At a few minutes past one, as Dahlerus and Göring were discussing the situation, an adjutant brought in a red envelope of the kind used for especially urgent affairs of state. Göring ripped it open. When he read its contents, he leaped from his chair and, striding angrily up and down, raged at Dahlerus that he had in his hands proof that the Poles were sabotaging every move toward negotiation.

After a few minutes he calmed down enough to tell the Swede what had been in the envelope. It was a telegram from the Polish government in Warsaw to its ambassador in Berlin. It was in code, of course, but the cryptanalysts of the German Foreign Office, who had long ago cracked the Polish diplomatic code, had reduced it to plaintext at once, translated it into German, and sent a copy to Göring via messenger. The entire process had taken less than an hour.

At the end of the telegram came a "special and secret message" to the ambassador: "Do not enter under any circumstances into any factual discussions...." To Göring this proved so conclusively that the Poles had no intention of negotiating in good faith that he copied the translation in his own hand for Dahlerus to show the British ambassador. The German Air Minister told Dahlerus that he was taking a great risk in doing this—he undoubtedly meant jeopardizing Germany's possession of the Polish code—but felt that Britain should know how faithless the Poles were.

In fact this was not a reason for going to war, but just another excuse to do so. The Germans were using Dahlerus as a cat's-paw, for at the very moment that Dahlerus entered Göring's home, Adolf Hitler was signing his "Directive No. 1 for the Conduct of the War." At daybreak the next morning

German troops invaded Poland. And although the Foreign Office solution of the Polish message had no role in that attack except to confirm the Nazis in their perfidy, it did demonstrate the keenness and efficiency of one of Germany's major intelligence weapons as she embarked upon what she fondly thought would be her blitzkrieg of conquest.

The cryptanalytic service of the German Foreign Office was created early in 1919, apparently at the suggestion of Kurt Selchow, a 32-year-old former captain in the Army intercept service. Selchow became its administrative chief and staffed it with cryptologic acquaintances from the war. His organization was at first known as Referat I Z, the z section of Division I, Personnel and Budget, of the Foreign Office. It included both the cryptanalytic service (the Chiffrierwesen) and the cryptographic (the Chiffrierbüro), the latter twice as large as the former. Around 1936 a reorganization of the Foreign Office renamed I Z as Pers z (pronounced "pers-zed"), the z section of the Personnel and Administrative Division. The z meant nothing—the division did not have 26 sections—and it may have been chosen because it seemed appropriate to cryptology. Much later, Foreign Minister Joachim von Ribbentrop took the Chiffrierbüro under his own office, presumably to restrict access to his own coded telegrams.

By 1939, Pers z had divided the Chiffrierwesen into two groups—one that dealt with ciphers, either as primary systems or as superencipherments, and that was heavily mathematical in personnel and approach; and one that dealt with codes and emphasized the linguistic.* Three senior cryptanalysts headed them—Rudolf Schauffler and Adolf Paschke as joint chiefs of the linguistic section, Dr. Werner Kunze as chief of the mathematicians. All were veterans of the military cryptanalytic bureaus that Germany had belatedly started in World War I; all joined the Foreign Office in 1919 when they were close to 30. Schauffler and Kunze participated in the development of the one-time pad.

Kunze had his doctorate in mathematics from the University of Heidelberg, where he also studied physics and philosophy. A cavalryman for most of World War I, he began cryptanalysis in January of 1918, solving some English ciphers but working for several months without success on a British code. During his first years in the Foreign Office, he studied cryptanalysis, emphasizing theory and applying his mathematical knowledge. Kunze may well have been the first mathematician employed in a modern cryptanalytic office. About 1921 he opened his first major assault—on the superencipherment of a French diplomatic code. He solved it in 1923, thus learning early the need for persistence and patience in cryptanalysis. His theoretical studies helped him in the joint development of the one-time pad for German diplomatic systems.

* This division carries into the practical sphere the distinction that codes operate upon texts linguistically whereas ciphers operate nonlinguistically.

In the spring of 1936, he undertook his finest work: ascertaining the system of and ultimately solving a Japanese machine cipher, apparently known to the Americans as the ORANGE system that preceded the RED machine that preceded PURPLE, the same system solved by the U.S. Navy's Lieutenant Jack S. Holtwick, Jr. Kunze thought that the solution would take only six weeks, but it was not until the day before he went on his vacation in July that he made his entry. The machine enciphered vowels into vowels and consonants into consonants by separate sets of rotors, and by September Kunze had recovered all the alphabets used in the machine. He also solved the later RED, in which vowels and consonants were enciphered indiscriminately through the two rotor arrays. But neither he nor anyone else in Pers z ever solved the final system of this development, the PURPLE machine.

Paschke and Schauffler served as joint heads of the linguistic group because it was so large. Paschke was the nominal head, handled more of the administration, and was in charge of European languages; Schauffler, an expert in Asiatic languages who was in charge of them, also had a good grounding in mathematics. He concentrated more on the substantive work. As one colleague described it, "Paschke said he was in charge and Schauffler was modest and didn't object." Paschke, a slight, erect man, with a little mustache and a small smile, was sensitive and touchy, but courteous and a good family man. Born in St. Petersburg, he got into cryptology in 1915 because of his expertise in Russian. Though he was a lawyer, he liked cryptology so much that he stuck with it, working on Russian, British, and Italian codes. He was a natural linguist. One of his specialities was to establish the meanings of the first 500 or so codegroups of a code and then to turn it over to a less able cryptanalyst for the much easier task of completing the solution.

Schauffler, a nervous and high-strung man who had studied at Tübingen and Munich, and had taught school before the war, started his cryptanalytical career at Army headquarters in 1916. A thorough student who felt that a comprehensive theory would pay off in practice, he probed much more deeply into the core of cryptology than the others, who mostly limited themselves to practical results. Thus he tried to systematize the science, sought to impose a uniform terminology, kept up with the work going on in all areas, and either wrote or encouraged the writing of reports on important topics. Pers z's theoretical investigations into the mathematical structure of the Enigma and into the regularities in a stack of codewords that are necessary to correct garbles but that correspondingly help cryptanalysts were probably inspired by Schauffler, as well as its texts on cryptology, its "Introduction to Probability Theory" with applications to cryptanalysis, and its preparation of graphs and nomograms. Schauffler bridged the linguists and the mathematicians—he knew the main Asiatic languages well enough to provide the linguistic data to help Kunze reconstruct the alphabets of the Japanese cipher machines. After the war he got his doctorate in mathematics.

These three were chiefly assisted by three other old-timers, Erich Langlotz, the third inventor of the one-time pad; Ernst Hoffmann, who held the title of Counsel for the High Cipher Service; and Hermann Scherschmidt, a specialist in Polish and other Slavonic codes. All usually held the same rank of Regierungsrat that Kunze, Schauffler, and Paschke did. In 1933, when Hitler came to power, Pers z employed about 30 civil servants. As Germany rearmed, Pers z expanded, though slowly at first. Recruiting was subtle: prospective recruits did not know that they were being considered for the highly secret work of cryptanalysis. One woman, Asta Friedrichs, who had taught school in Bulgaria and knew that language, which Pers z needed, was simply asked if she would like to learn Serbo-Croatian and do some work involving it; she accepted, and not until after a probationary period was she told about the codebreaking. She began solving Serbo-Croatian codes, then some Bulgarian, then helped with others.

With the outbreak of war, Pers z's growth became explosive. Among the brightest of its new members was Dr. Hans Rohrbach, a 37-year-old mathematician who later became editor of the oldest mathematical journal in the world, the *Journal of Pure and Applied Mathematics*. Another mathematician was Dr. Gottfried Köthe, later rector of Heidelberg University. The agency needed people and it made exceptions. Ottfried Deubner, whose father, Ludwig, had solved Russian military cryptograms for Germany in World War I, was partly Jewish, but he was allowed to join and work on Italian cryptograms because of his father's earlier contributions; the Nazis made him an honorary Aryan.

For several years, Pers z had been situated on the top floor of the library building just behind the Foreign Office main building in Berlin's Wilhelmstrasse. But by early 1940, it had burst out of these quarters. The mathematicians moved out first, into several flats in an apartment house at w-8 Jaegerstrasse that had been entirely taken over by the Foreign Office. Their departure relieved the crowding in the original office only temporarily, and soon the linguistic codesolvers found new offices, first in an anthropological museum, where they were surrounded by artifacts from Siam, and then in Dahlem, a suburb of Berlin. Here some worked in a garden apartment on a street called ImDol, some in a nearby girls' boarding school, where they were joined in 1943 by the mathematicians. The combined group, the Chiffrierwesen arm of Pers z, called itself the Sonderdienst Dahlem ("Dahlem Special Service"). While there, during the middle period of the war, it consisted of about 200 staff members—20 to 25 mathematical cryptanalysts, probably the same number of linguistic cryptanalysts, the rest clerks and support staffers. Later it grew to 300.

Heavy bombings—the workers had to spend nearly every night in air-raid shelters—forced still another move in the summer of 1944. The linguistic branch moved 150 miles southeast to Hirschberg in Silesia, where they installed themselves in another school; the mathematicians moved to the nearby town of Hermsdorf. The odyssey of Pers z did not end even there, however. In February, 1945, the advance of the Russians compelled each group to move about 150 miles west. The mathematicians evacuated to Zschepplin Castle, near Eilenburg, about 80 miles south of Berlin. The linguists, joined by a few mathematicians to strip current superencipherments, moved into a wing of Burgscheidungen Castle near Naumburg, northwest of Wiemar. Here, as wartime guests of the Count von der Schulenburg and his five daughters, the 90 cryptanalysts, some with their wives, lived and worked amid art treasures and ancient furniture, handicapped by the almost total lack of liaison with the mathematicians, about 50 miles away.

The ever-present problems of security added to the difficulties of Pers z. Ink was not permitted because it required blotting paper. Each night all papers had to be locked away. Waste paper had to be burned, and the ashes broken up to make sure that no cinder would float away. Later Pers z got a machine to shred the paper before it was incinerated. None of the codesolving groups was allowed to know what the others were doing— but these artificial barriers dissolved in the camaraderie of the Dahlem bomb-shelter.

Security also meant political security, and even before the war the Nazis planted a spy in Pers z to watch for any signs of anti-Hitler activity. In 1942 Selchow became a Nazi. He took the honorary rank of Sturmführer, which gave him access to three or four cars. The next year he became an Obersturmführer because this gave him "a certain authority with the drivers." However, he insisted, he never wore the uniform. Among the cryptanalysts, Paschke, Schauffler, and Kunze, at least, also joined the Nazi party.

The cryptanalysts' raw material was intercepted by either military radio stations or the post office telegraph bureau. In Silesia, it came in by courier about noon. Most of the diplomatic messages bore address and signature, so few traffic-analysis problems of discovering language, cryptographic family, and the like, arose. The cryptanalyses required enormous volumes of text and corresponding quantities of statistics. The army of clerks, mostly women, compiled these, but it usually paid the cryptanalysts to work up a few statistics themselves. The solutions took a heavy toll of nervous energy. "You must concentrate almost in a nervous trance when working on a code," Miss Friedrichs recalled. "It is not often done by conscious effort." The solution often seems to crop up from the subconscious.

The subconscious got considerable help, however, from an information group headed by Pastor Joachim Ziegenrücker. The group collated information from radio broadcasts, Foreign Office memoranda, Allied newspapers (it read *The Times* throughout the war), and the Pers z output so that, as Miss Friedrichs said, they could give the answer when the cryptanalysts asked them "Who beginning with w spoke with somebody ending with n in a place with a kind of *po* on Thursday?"

More help came from the financial bonuses that kept up the codebreakers' knowledge of foreign languages. The amount depended upon the difficulty of the tongue; nothing was paid for English and French, which they were expected to know anyway. The codebreakers had to take an examination in the language every four years to prove their continued competence, and many of them learned four languages, taking an examination each year and brushing up at the local Berlitz school for a month before the test. Pers z had experts in the language of almost every country large enough to maintain a diplomatic corps. One Olbricht attacked the difficult problems of breaking Chinese codes. A man named Benzing took such delight in the Turkish language and Turkish cryptanalysis that his confrères regarded him as a veritable Turcomaniac.

The cryptanalysts received some of their greatest help from robots—mechanisms that speedily performed some of the highly repetitious tasks required, or that simplified the handling of many items. Many were tabulating machines that used punched cards in ordinary ways. But many others were assembled out of standard parts for special purposes by Hans-Georg Krug, a former high school mathematics teacher who possessed a positive genius for this sort of thing.

Messages were punched onto the cards (or sometimes, in the case of some Siemens machines, onto paper tape) and run through the mechanism to tabulate frequencies, to search for repetitions or interrupted (partial) repetitions and calculate the intervals between them, to sort texts. One arrangement of the machines, called the special comparer, automatically solved single columnar transposition. Using the punched cards, it extracted a portion of the ciphertext of the probable length of a column of the transposition tableau. Then it paraded the rest of the ciphertext past this fixed portion, calculating the frequency of digraphs at each juxtaposition. The match that yielded the highest frequency probably represented two adjacent columns of the tableau. The process was then repeated with the new column to extend the reconstruction. Since the device could compare the digraphs against any set of frequencies stored in it, it may have been adapted to solve transposed code, if the underlying code were known.

The machines were ideal for what was probably the single most common cryptanalytic procedure of the war—the stripping of a numerical additive from enciphered code. Axis, Allied, and neutral cryptanalysts employed the identical technique, which each major power apparently developed independently, probably between the wars. Military cryptanalytic units in the field employed it on a manual, pencil-and-paper basis.

It is generally called the "difference method." The cryptanalyst first identifies, by indicators or traffic analyses or other information, a group of encicode messages that he believes used the same basic code and portions, at least, of the same long additive key. Using repetitions or clues from indicators as anchor points, he places the messages one under another so that the identical portions of the additive key will stand in vertical alignment. (If no information suggests an alignment, the cryptanalyst may have to try one after another to see if any produces results.)

He subtracts every encicode group in a column from every other. He subtracts the first group from itself, from the second, third, fourth, and so on, encicode groups, the second group from itself, from the third, fourth, and so on. The differences resulting from these "runs" are listed in a difference book, which also gives the location of the two encicode groups that produced each difference. The cryptanalyst repeats the subtractions for every column and indexes all differences in the difference book. He then examines this book for two columns that have a difference in common. This common difference indicates that the two columns include the same placode group, which each column has enciphered with its own additive.

The identity makes it possible for the cryptanalyst to reduce the two columns to an equivalent form. In the first column, he simply subtracts the encicode group whose run produced the same difference as the second column from every other encicode group in the first column—or, in other words, he just picks up the figures for that run. He does the same for the second column with its encicode group. This produces a relative placode in both columns. All groups in the two columns that were identical in the original placode will emerge as identical in this relative placode. They will, however, differ from the original absolute placode by a constant factor. The cryptanalyst repeats this process with other columns having a common difference, thus reducing as many columns as have such a difference all to the same relative placode. He then solves the code. If it is a one-part code, he can quickly determine the constant factor and obtain the absolute placode; if it is a two-part code, this step is usually neither possible nor necessary.

Take, for example, the following five cryptograms, presumed selected from a day's intercepts. Experience has taught the cryptanalyst that the first group of each message, the indicator, designates the starting point for the additive sequence contained in the enemy keybook. Thus, 6218 means to begin with the group on page 62, line 1, column 8. Three of the messages have this indicator, and therefore overlap from their very first groups. But the second message, with indicator 6216, begins in column 6 of the same line. Consequently, its third group would have been enciphered with the same additive group as the first group of the three other messages, and it is so aligned. The same procedure aligns the message that has indicator 6217. When all five are brought into position, each column of encicode groups will share the same additive key.

	indicator			A	B	C	D	E	F	G	H	I	J	
1	6218			6260	7532	8291	2661	6863	2281	7135	5406	7046	9128	...
2	6216	3964	3043	1169	5729	3392	1952	7572	2754	7891	6290	6719	7529	...
3	6218			4061	6509	4513	1881	0398	3402	8671	4326	8267	6810	...
4	6218			5480	9325	3811	4083	5373	4882	8664	8891	6337	5914	...
5	6217		7260	8931	8100	5787	6807	2471	0480	9892	1199	8426	1710	...

The cryptanalyst makes his runs in each column (temporarily by-passing the short ones). He sets out the results in ten tables, of which those for columns A and E are:

A	6260	1169	4061	5480	8931	E	6863	7572	0398	5373	2471
6260	0000	5909	8801	9220	2771	6863	0000	1719	4535	9510	6618
1169		0000	3902	4321	7872	7572		0000	3826	8801	5909
4061			0000	1429	4970	0398			0000	5085	2183
5480				0000	3551	5373				0000	7108
8931					0000	2471					0000

Table A shows, for example, that 6260 has been subtracted from itself, leaving a difference of 0000; from 1169, leaving 5909; from 4061, leaving 8801; and so on. (Subtraction, like the addition, is noncarrying.) Each horizontal line records a run.

A portion of the difference book for these five messages would show that columns A and E share the differences 8801 and 5909. It would also show other columns with differences in common:

difference	column	messages	run group
....	...	....	....
8736	F	1, 5	2574
8801	A	3, 1	6260
8801	E	4, 2	7572
9077	B	3, 1	7532
9106	J	4, 3	6810
9220	A	4, 1	6260
9220	D	3, 1	2661
9308	C	4, 3	4513
9391	D	2, 1	2661
9391	I	4, 1	7046
9391	J	3, 2	7529
9510	E	4, 1	6863
....	...	....	....

Since encicode group 6260 produced in column A the difference 8801 that column A shares with column E, the cryptanalyst subtracts 6260 from every encicode group in column A. He does the same with 7572 in column E. Likewise, 9391 constitutes a difference common to columns D, I, and J and permits them to be reduced to equivalent form in the same way—by subtracting in each column the encicode group whose run produced the common difference. These five reductions yield relative placode in five columns:

	indicator	A	B	C	D	E	F	G	H	I	J	...
			6260	....	....	2661	7572	....	....	....	7046	7529	} relative key
1	6218		0000	....	....	0000	9391	....	....	....	0000	2609	
2	6216	3964 3043	5909	....	....	9391	0000	....	....	....	9773	0000	
3	6218		8801	....	....	9220	3826	....	....	....	1221	9391	} relative placode
4	6218		9220	....	....	2422	8801	....	....	....	9391	8495	
5	6217	7260 2771	....	....	....	4246	5909	....	....	....	1480	4291	

It is easy to see the numerous repeated relative-placode groups—0000, 5909, 9391, and so on. Because this is a contrived example, the entire message (except for the two short columns) can be reduced to this relative form. In practice, however, it is not always possible to reduce messages fully, and partial solutions result. Accidental common differences will occur occasionally. In this series, 1480 results in columns F (4882–3402) and I (8426–7046). If 3402 were used as the relative key for column F, it would produce a false relative placode that would be corrected in the cryptanalysis of the code itself. Here, however, a preponderance of correct common differences outweighs this accident. If the underlying code proved to be one-part, the cryptanalyst would discover that the relative placode differs from the absolute placode, or base, by a correction factor of 2371.

The thousands of repeated subtractions, first to find differences and then to reduce to relative placode, and the routine compilation of the difference tables, furnish an almost ideal subject for the mechanical operation of the tabulators, and it was for this that similar machines were most frequently used in cryptanalytic offices throughout the world. In addition to these punched-card machines, Pers z invented or adapted several special-purpose devices.

One of them employed translucent paper and light to strip a new additive from a base code that had been previously solved. By indicators or repetitions, the cryptanalyst lined up messages so that a column of encicode groups represented encipherments of the same additive group. If the code used four-digit groups, the cryptanalyst reached for a sheet of translucent paper imprinted with a square 200 cells by 200. The top and the side were indexed with coordinates that ran from 00 to 99 twice. Thus the four cells at the intersections of the two side coordinates 31 and the two top coordinates 50 represented the codegroup 3150, repeated four times.

The cryptanalyst's previous solution of the code had told him that the most frequent placode groups were, say, 6001, 5454, 5662, and 7123. (If the code were two-part, these could be relative placode; if one-part, they would probably be absolute.) The cryptanalyst punched holes in several sheets for all five placode groups at each one's four locations. He inked out the four cells of the first encicode group of the column on one sheet, of the second on another, and so on, and positioned the sheets over a source of light so that the marked encicode cells lay one atop the other. The brightest spot of light then represented the greatest congregation of punched-out placode holes, and the numerical difference between the coordinates of this light spot and those of the dark pile of encicode cells constituted the additive for that column of encicode messages. The difference was usually measured on the top sheet. Thus, if the encicode on that sheet were 8808, and the light spot were at 6001, the additive for that column would be 2807, and the placode for that particular encicode group would 6001, one of the common ones.

The method is analogous to determining which of the 26 possible decipherments of a column of letters in Vigenère (a column enciphered by a single keyletter) is correct by virtue of having the most high-frequency letters. Often these tests are made with alphabet strips on which the high-frequency letters are printed in red; the strips are aligned so that the ciphertext letters stand under one another, and the columns out to the right are scanned to see which is the reddest and therefore most probably the correct set of plaintext letters. In both this case and the Pers z device, the high-frequency elements that underlie the cipher are known (plaintext in Vigenère, placode in enciphered code), and the cipher alphabets are known (normal alphabet in Vigenère, ordinary noncarrying addition in enciphered code). Since a strip thousands of cells long would be unwieldy, the Pers z device uses two dimensions instead of one, but it must repeat its coordinates just as the Vigenère strip must repeat its alphabet. In both cases, all possible solutions are tested simultaneously. The high-frequency elements concentrate to make the brightest spot in one, the reddest column in the other.

These Pers z robots helped solve codes of France and Italy, both of which used at times four-digit codes with additive superencipherments. One English code, however, remained invulnerable, because the 40,000-group length of her additive key prevented enough material from accumulating. At the start of World War II, most countries probably employed the additive system of enciphered code in a hierarchy of codes for their foreign services. Germany herself did, using sometimes a four-digit, sometimes a five-digit code, only her additive was the one-time pad. Despite all the mechanical help, however, solution of most codes came right down to pencil-and-paper work by individual cryptanalysts.

Such was the solution of the superencipherment of the Japanese TSU diplomatic code—the columnar transposition with blank spaces in the transposition blocks that American cryptanalysts called the K9 transposition to the J19 code. The Japanese embassy in the Soviet Union began relying heavily on this code in October of 1941, when the Soviet government moved its capital eastward from threatened Moscow to Kuibyshev. The diplomats had to stay close to the seat of government, and the Japanese may have junked their heavy cipher machine instead of moving it, using their paper codes instead. Pers z made its first break by spotting two messages which had patches of identical letters separated by nonidentical sections. Deducing that these differing portions represented the same placode text, the cryptanalysts compared the two messages until, in a single afternoon, they found a transposition and blank arrangement that yielded the same texts in a form that resembled legitimate codewords. In one of their greatest technical successes, the mathematical cryptanalysts cracked the approximately 30 transposition and blank patterns; the linguists read the code, and the subsequent solutions provided the Germans with information about Russian war production and army activities.

It would, of course, be embarrassing for the Germans to admit that they were reading the code messages of their allies, and this led to a touchy situation early in 1941. Franz von Papen, ambassador to Turkey, reported on February 4 that the Iraqi minister to Turkey had told him "that the English can plan with a full knowledge of Italian intentions because they can read the Italian cipher." Ernst Woermann, director of the Foreign Ministry's political department, undertook inquiries. By the end of March he learned from Selchow that "the Italians make use of three groups of ciphers, of which the first group is easily readable, while the second is harder to solve. Of the third group, it is considered probable, though not certain, that into that complicated system the English cannot break. Even this cipher can be read by our offices. . . . The Rome-Bagdad cipher belongs to the second group."

Woermann suggested various ways of getting the word across to the Italians, one of them Germanically subtle: "We could say that the information from Ankara led us to try our hand at decrypting a radiogram from the Rome–Bagdad traffic, and we have just succeeded." The Italians were duly warned, though it is unknown whether the hint of German diplomat Prince Otto von Bismarck to an Italian Foreign Office official a few months later that the Germans had the Italian codes (without mentioning the English) was how it was done or whether that was merely an indiscretion. The Italians were the despair of the Germans in this, as in everything else; they did not change their codes and Pers z continued to read them. But they were not quite as shiftless as the Germans thought. Count Galeazzo Ciano, the Foreign Minister, commented in his diary when he heard that the Nazis were reading his messages: "This is good to know; in the future, they will also read what I *want* them to read."

The codes of small countries are usually simpler to solve than those of large, and not only because of intrinsic qualities as smaller code size and fewer codes and additive tables. Their personnel is less well trained, and so they often ask for repeats if, as happens more often than with major powers, they cannot decode a message. Moreover, not having the courier services or communications of larger and richer countries, they cannot get new codes to distant outposts as often as the large countries and so continue using the older codes too long. While their messages usually do not contain the crucial portents of those of great powers, their diplomats are sometimes well situated and can provide information of value. Yet even these small nations sometimes seem to have a feel for knowing when their codes are broken. "You just get to a point where you are reading a good part of the traffic when one morning you come in and it's all changed," said Miss Friedrichs.

The Pers z solutions, typed up, went to Selchow. He submitted them to the state secretary of the Foreign Office before Ribbentrop became Foreign Minister, and afterwards to both the state secretary and the Foreign Minister's office, at Ribbentrop's order. Those for the Führer were marked with a green "F." He did not always see them, since Ribbentrop did not dare give him bad news. Those that he did see, he did not always appreciate. Across the face of one long dispatch that gave considerable information on agricultural conditions in Russia, which bore importantly upon military possibilities, Hitler scrawled "Kann nicht bir stimme" ("This cannot be"). Nazidom preferred its own lies and propaganda to unpalatable truths, and so, as Miss Friedrichs said, "Even if we had a plum, it was not considered as one."

In April of 1945, the American front engulfed the cryptanalysts at Burgscheidungen Castle and swept past. A few days later, Haskell Cleaves, a Signal Corps officer from Maine, discovered what they were doing. Headquarters sent out a mixed commission of American, British, and French experts to interrogate them. On May 8, while the world was celebrating V-E Day, 35 of them were flown to London for several months of questioning; among their interrogators was a "Major Brown," who was really William P. Bundy, later U.S. Assistant Secretary of State for Far Eastern Affairs. For the cryptanalysts of the German Foreign Office, the war had ended.

What had they accomplished? They had achieved some remarkable technical successes, and for some that was enough. Kunze and the other mathematicians usually lost interest in a problem after its cryptanalytic difficulties had been surmounted. Even the codebreakers who were interested in their influence on their country's policy could rarely learn anything about it: the diplomats seldom told them, and Selchow stood between them and the users. Moreover, the effects were diffused over many messages, commingled with other sources of information, distorted by Nazi preconceptions, so that it was virtually impossible to single out cryptanalyzed information as critical in a specific event. Finally, and most important, Germany lost the war, reducing all the Pers z efforts in the final analysis to nullity. "As I am accustomed to say," said Schauffler, "a bridge builder can see what he has done for his countrymen, but we cannot tell whether our life was worth anything."

Yet they read the secret communications of the British Empire, Ireland, France, Belgium, Spain, Portugal, Italy, the Vatican, Switzerland, Yugoslavia, Greece, Bulgaria, Rumania, Poland; Egypt, Ethiopia; Turkey, Iran, China, Japan, Manchukuo, Thailand; the United States, Brazil, Argentina, Chile, Mexico, Bolivia, Colombia, Ecuador, Peru, the Dominican Republic, Uruguay, Venezuela. Not every code of every country was always read, but the solution of the codes of 34 nations of the earth suggests that, whether or not the the Pers z cryptanalysts' life was "worth anything," the reckoning cannot involve whether they had done their duty. That they had.

In the nightmare totalitarian jungle that was Nazi Germany, the bigwigs of National Socialism consolidated their positions by building up personal power structures. Extra power could come from the knowledge obtainable through intercepting communications. Thus it was that a few weeks after Hitler appointed Hermann Göring as Air Minister in his new government in 1933, the fat ex-air ace established an eight-man unit in his Air Ministry to do as much intercepting as possible. He called it the Forschungsamt ("Research Office"), but its research was highly specialized. Apparently attached to the minister's office, it bore no relation either to the research division of the Luftwaffe's technical office or to the Luftwaffe's own military intercept and cryptologic unit.

Göring installed the Forschungsamt in a requisitioned building on the Behrendstrasse, Berlin, but moved it at the end of 1933 to the Hotel am Knie in the suburb of Charlottenberg. He named as its first chief an old friend and loyal party member named Hans Schimpf, a former naval lieutenant who had once served as liaison between the Army and the Navy cryptologic organizations. In 1934 the unit did exactly what Göring expected it to do when it supplied him with information that helped him win Hitler to his side in the first great power struggle of the Third Reich—that between Hitler's oldest friend and closest associate in the Nazi movement, the homosexual Ernst Roehm, on the one hand, and Göring, Heinrich Himmler, head of the S.S. and the Gestapo, and the Junkers on the other. Roehm was shot, and soon thereafter Schimpf suffered the same fate, presumably because he had done his job so well that he knew too much. Göring replaced him with Prince Christoph of Hesse, younger brother of Prince Philip of Hesse, one of Göring's friends since the late 1920s. Christoph, then in his mid-thirties, was the fourth and youngest son of the Landgrave of Hesse, former ruler of that principality and a member of one of the oldest traceable families in Christendom (to Charlemagne). Christoph became a ministerial director in the Air Ministry and also had the title of Oberführer of the S.S. on the staff of the S.S. Reichsführer, who was Himmler. He died in Italy in 1941.

The Forschungsamt tapped telephones, opened letters, solved encoded telegrams. Its reports were called Braune Blätter ("Brown Sheets"). A typical one, of March 19, 1945, which was passed to the economic division of the armed forces, reported that on March 14 the Swiss political department informed the Swiss embassy in Lisbon about an agreement reached with the Allies concerning railroad operations from southern France. The Forschungsamt also recorded the conversations of Göring and Hitler. These were passed to the appropriate government department for action or reference, if necessary. In its most famous case, it transcribed 27 conversations from Göring's office with various officials in Rome and Vienna that settled Austria's fate in the hours before the Anschluss. Ironically, one of those whose subservient words to an overjoyed Hitler were recorded for posterity was Prince Philip, emissary of the Führer and brother of the chief eavesdropper.

Christoph's membership in the S.S., or Schutzstaffel ("Protection Staff"), the notorious blackshirted strong arm of the Nazi party, pointed to a close relationship between the Forschungsamt and the S.D., or Sicherheitsdienst ("Security Service"), the branch of the S.S. that served as the ideological watchdog for the Nazis. The S.D., for example, determined who voted the wrong way in German plebiscites by numbering the back of the ballots with milk, a simple but effective secret ink. Its efforts were primarily internal, and since private citizens, even conspirators, seldom use complicated code or

Geheime Reichssache!

1. Dies ist ein Staatsgeheimnis im Sinne des RStGB. (Abschnitt Landesverrat) in der Fassung des Gesetzes vom 24.4.1934.
2. Nur für die vom FA verpflichteten und zum Empfang berechtigten Personen bestimmt und diesen gegen Empfangsbescheinigung auszuhändigen.
3. Beförderung nur in doppeltem Umschlag und durch Kurier oder Vertrauensperson.
4. Vervielfältigung jeder Art, Weitergabe im Wortlaut oder Herstellung von Auszügen im Wortlaut verboten.
5. Empfänger haftet für sichere Aufbewahrung im Geheimschrank, Nachweisbarkeit und Rückgabe. Verstoß hiergegen zieht schwerste Strafen nach sich.

(12A) v.Hae./Ry.   **Forschungsamt**   19. März 1945.

N450237

Abkommen der Schweiz mit den Alliierten über die Regelung
schweizerischer Verkehrsfragen.
==

Einsatz von täglich 3 schweizerischen
Zügen zwischen Cerbère und Genf.
Benutzung des Hafens von Toulon durch
schweizerische Schiffe.

     Das Politische Departement in Bern verständigt am 14.3.45 die schweizerische Gesandtschaft in Lissabon, dass das mit den Alliierten getroffene Abkommen den Betrieb von täglich 3 Zügen zwischen Cerbère und Genf mit je 600 t Ladung vorsehe. Die schweizerischen Schiffe könnten in Zukunft den Hafen von Toulon benutzen, doch seien die Umschlagsmöglichkeiten auf 400 t täglich beschränkt. Der Eisenbahnverkehr in Frankreich werde mit schweizerischen Waggons und Lokomotiven durchgeführt werden. Die alliierten Regierungen gewährten der Schweiz weiterhin das Kontingent und die Navicerts für Lebensmittel im Rahmen der früher bezogenen Mengen. Ferner habe die Schweiz für verschiedene industrielle Rohstoffe neue Quoten erlangt. Da die Transportmittel im Augenblick nicht ausreichen, werde für den Transport von Waren nach der Schweiz eine Vorrangliste aufgestellt.

     Das mit den Alliierten getroffene Abkommen erstreckte sich ausserdem auf verschiedene Finanzangelegenheiten und Fragen bezüglich des Warentransits durch die Schweiz nach Deutschland, Italien und umgekehrt sowie auf die wirtschaftlichen Beziehungen zum Reich.

(Vergl. E 8/209/ 3.45 Eing.:17.3.)

A "Brown Sheet," or cryptanalytic report of the Forschungsamt cipher systems, its cryptanalytic organization—if it even had one—was small and nameless. This is not to say that the S.D. was not interested in other people's conversations: it probably did its share of telephone tapping and mail opening.

After 1936, the S.D. extended its watchdog duties from just the party to the government as well, with a domestic branch and a foreign branch that would nullify dangers before they could be launched against the sacred soil of the German Reich. Probably the S.D. also broadened its communications activities somewhat. It filched a diplomatic telegram here and there, and listened in to diplomatic telephone conversations, even one, on May 7, 1940, between Prime Minister Neville Chamberlain of Britain and Premier Paul Reynaud of France—Chamberlain and Reynaud could certainly be considered enemies of Germany and the Nazi party. But the S.D. probably got most of the external communications intelligence that it needed from the Forschungsamt, which was quite as interested as the S.D. in preserving the Nazi regime.

Himmler headed the S.S. as a party official; as a government official he headed the two Reich police organizations: the Gestapo, which handled political crimes, and the Kripo, or Kriminalpolizei, which dealt with ordinary crimes. Both had communication intelligence sections, but, as with the S.D., these probably concentrated primarily on telephones and mail and had but little cryptanalysis to do.

In 1939, the party and government police organizations were merged as the R.S.H.A., the Reichssicherheitshauptamt ("Reich Central Security Office"). The Gestapo became Amt IV of the R.S.H.A., the Kripo Amt V. The government domestic watchdog branch of the S.D. evolved into the R.S.H.A. Amt III, Domestic Intelligence, and the foreign branch into Amt VI, Foreign Intelligence. Amt VI was charged with the production of secret information about enemy countries.

It apparently directed its thoughts mainly to the more traditional methods of gathering such intelligence. But shortly after the Anschluss, Walter Schellenberg, a young S.D. official, seized the files of the Austrian secret service and found that among the most interesting documents were those on cryptanalysis. This find may have soon thereafter recalled to the mind of Wilhelm Höttl, a youthful Austrian staff member of the new R.S.H.A., the World War I deeds of the Austro-Hungarian cryptanalysts, which General Max Ronge had detailed in an exciting book. Höttl discovered that General Andreas Figl, former head of the Austrian Dechiffrierdienst, had been arrested by the Gestapo in 1938. Höttl got Heinz Jost, then head of Amt VI, to free Figl and to install him as an instructor in cryptology in a villa in the Wannsee section of Berlin. Here he passed on his experience to a new generation.

But such training takes time, and any intelligence that the R.S.H.A. obtained from communications continued to come to it from other sources. It seized an occasional plaintext telegram and somehow acquired a one-part

Spanish code and used it to read intercepts. It also was granted what must have been the first opportunity in history to get codes wholesale. Yamato Ominata, Japan's intelligence chief in Europe, offered to deliver the Yugoslav general staff and Turkish, Vatican, Portuguese, and Brazilian codes for 28,000 Swiss francs, or about $20,000. The offer may well have been accepted, for all those codes were read at one time or another by various German agencies.

In addition, the R.S.H.A. depended upon the military and the Forschungsamt for communications intelligence. Thus, in the autumn of 1941, Schellenberg, who had become deputy chief of Amt VI, asked Reinhard Heydrich, head of the whole R.S.H.A., to contact both the Forschungsamt and the military. Schellenberg wanted them to concentrate their intercept posts and cryptanalysts on Vichy and Belgrade traffic for some information he needed. At about the same time, Heydrich called the chief of the Wehrmacht signal organization and asked him to send Schellenberg any information about American-Japanese negotiations that he might obtain.

Himmler disliked such dependency and in March of 1942 he sent Schellenberg to Göring's beautiful country house, Karinhalle, to urge that the Forschungsamt be incorporated into Amt VI. Göring greeted him in a Roman outfit, toga, sandals, and all, carrying his Reichmarschal's baton, and, after hearing Schellenberg, said vaguely, "Well, I will have a word about it with Himmler." Nothing happened, of course, and Schellenberg, who at this time became head of Amt VI, set up a well-funded department, to carry out research in secret communications including invisible inks and microfilms as well as cryptography and cryptanalysis. Figl may well have been the nucleus of this group. It may have provided the digraphic cipher—ten tables 26×26, one of which was selected to encipher each message—that one R.S.H.A. radio net was using much later in the war. This system may have been adapted from the Army, which at one time used digraphic substitution as a field cipher. For internal communications, the R.S.H.A. used cipher machines supplied by the military.

The new department did not, in any event, produce a great deal of communications intelligence, for Schellenberg continued to get most of his from the outside. Starting in 1942, he said, "Every three weeks or so I gave a dinner party at my home where the technical heads of the three services, Defense Ministry, Post Office [which unscrambled transatlantic telephone conversations], and Research Stations [Forschungsamt] discussed new developments and helped each other with their problems.* These meetings were perhaps more than any other single factor responsible for the high standard of the scientific and technical side of my service. It was the cooperation and interest

---

* No Pers z representative appears to have attended—probably a reflection of the high-level personal dislikes and power struggles between Göring and Himmler on the one hand and Ribbentrop and the military on the other. At one point Göring tried to bring Pers z within the ambit of the Forschungsamt.

Duel in the Ether: The Axis

which these people showed to me personally which made most of my success in Secret Service operations possible"—an unexampled acknowledgment of indebtedness to communications intelligence by a cloak-and-dagger man.

The R.S.H.A. repaid some of this generous help with the products of the greatest spy coup of World War II—Operation Cicero. "Cicero" was Elyesa Bazna, an Albanian working in Ankara as the valet to Sir Hughe Knatchbull-Hugessen, British ambassador to neutral Turkey. Bazna had taken wax

Encipherment table H-1 for a digraphic cipher of an R.S.H.A. radio net in Norway

impressions of the keys to the black dispatch box which Sir Hughe kept beside his bed for the secret papers that he liked to pore over late at night. The valet would open the box, photograph the documents, and sell the rolls of film to the R.S.H.A. agent in Turkey, L. C. Moyzisch. Cicero received £15,000 a roll—in counterfeit notes.

The documents consisted largely of cables to Sir Hughe. They were of the highest importance—reports of Stalin-Roosevelt-Churchill conversations, for example. But when this information began streaming into Berlin in November and December, 1943, Hitler and other top officials refused to believe that it was genuine. "Too good to be true," Ribbentrop told Moyzisch. The fact is that he did not want to read therein the impending doom of the German Reich.

The messages, which bore date-time notations, could help in breaking the British diplomatic codes, and though Pers z would seem to have been the logical recipient, Schellenberg gave the photographs to his communications-intelligence friends in the military. They cooperated fairly closely with Pers z, however, and they probably passed the material to it. Pers z may also have gotten copies from Ribbentrop. Kunze and Paschke both saw Cicero documents and were unimpressed. For the British were by then superenciphering their most secret messages in a one-time pad. Though the Cicero messages may have contributed to the solution of some lesser British systems and so helped produce some minor information, they could not make possible the recovery of the one-time keys of any other messages. Operation Cicero, so complete a success in one sense, was thus an almost total failure in another.

At about this time, Höttl, the young man who had discovered Figl, became, at age 28, the head of Amt VI E—the Amt VI section for southeast Europe. He soon grew friendly with Hungarian Army intelligence, whose chief one day showed off his communications-intelligence unit. The Hungarians did indeed have a fine organization, and it very much impressed Höttl. He thought that it did relatively more with its poor resources than did Pers z, the Forschungsamt, the German military cryptanalysts, and the police eavesdroppers all put together. In the middle of 1944, he convinced the pro-Nazi Hungarian Premier, Andor Sztojay, to have the unit furnish him with its results. The unit's commander, Major Bibo, who lived only for his work, agreed to concentrate on the traffic that Höttl wanted when Höttl promised him more men, better equipment, and extra money.

Höttl went from room to room in Bibo's offices and picked out the choicest of the copious solutions. A few days later, he laid the sheaf before Schellenberg and said: "Please read this, and if you would like to have it regularly, give me a credit for the first 100,000 Swiss francs." But Schellenberg feared that Hitler, who distrusted the Hungarians because of their marked lack of enthusiasm for being an Axis partner, would not like the idea if he heard of it. He gave Höttl only a nominal sum. But Höttl wangled the francs out of the R.S.H.A. financial wizard, Friedrich Schwend—not too difficult a task, since the money was bogus.

Within six months, the unit exceeded even Höttl's sanguine hopes by reading a goodly portion of the secret radiograms of embassies in Moscow. Figl seems to have joined it and become one of its star cryptanalysts, performing some minor miracles in his room with pots of black coffee and packs of cigarettes whenever the unit was stumped. Bibo's interceptors and cryptanalysts had become the R.S.H.A.'s first major source of its own of foreign communications intelligence. It could read some American and British messages, especially in 1945, when it acquired a cryptanalyst "who could sift the unimportant from the important with the sureness of a sleep-walker." It read almost all the radio traffic of the Turkish embassy, learning that Stalin deeply suspected his Anglo-American allies and feared that they might conclude a separate peace with Germany. The reports of the Turkish military attaché, Höttl was told by General Alfred Jodl, chief of the Wehrmacht operations staff, contained the most valuable information about Russia that the high command then had. By this time, about the end of 1944, the advancing Russians forced the unit to retreat from Budapest to the Odenburg hills and, three months later, to an Alpine redoubt. These disruptions did not choke off the flow of intelligence, which ended only when the war did.

"I do not want to exaggerate the importance of what we achieved, although in this one year of my collaboration with the Hungarians there were at least a hundred successes such as seldom fall to the lot of a Secret Service working in the ordinary ways," Höttl wrote. His impressive tribute, which independently seconds the praise that Schellenberg offered to other cryptanalysts, confirms the overwhelming supremacy that communications intelligence attained in both quantity and quality over almost any other form of secret intelligence in World War II.

Long before the S.D. or the R.S.H.A. came into existence, a military organization handled Germany's intelligence and counterespionage functions. This was the Abwehr. The name means "counterespionage," and that was the original function of the six-officer Abwehr unit permitted Germany under the 1919 Treaty of Versailles. As the German Army grew, so did the Abwehr's functions, until it encompassed foreign "counter" intelligence and standard military intelligence. The name, however, stuck.

In 1934, Hitler merged the Army, Navy, and Air Force into the Wehrmacht, with a single general staff for all the armed forces—the O.K.W., or Oberkommando der Wehrmacht. To this the Abwehr was attached, and in 1935 a naval officer, Admiral Wilhelm Canaris, took over as Abwehr chief. He was a sensitive, white-haired, mufti-garbed, mysterious personage. He hated Hitler, and his organization abominated the Nazi-spawned S.D. and R.S.H.A. that reduplicated Abwehr functions. The feeling was reciprocated, but the rivals reached an uneasy truce in which the Abwehr handled military matters and the others nonmilitary. However, in February of 1944, Hitler dissolved the Abwehr headquarters and merged it into the R.S.H.A., where it became Amt VI/Mil under Schellenberg.

The Abwehr had three headquarters sections: Abwehr I, for secret intelligence, whose Group G produced invisible inks and forged passports and other documents for secret agents, and whose Group I maintained wireless contact with Abwehr secret agents; Abwehr II, for sabotage and special duties; Abwehr III, counterespionage, whose Group N, added in wartime, secured communications organizations. Among the Abwehr radio stations for agent contact were those at Hamburg, where 20 transmitters were installed in separate concrete dugouts in an open field and were remote-controlled from the receiving center a few kilometers away, and at Ulm, where 19 transmitters radioed agents from a small wooden building constructed in 1938 on a hill just outside the city.

The Abwehr did not have its own codebreakers. For such intelligence it relied, as part of the Wehrmacht, upon the military cryptanalytic agencies.

Of these there were four: one in the Oberkommando der Wehrmacht for the armed forces as a whole, and one each for the high commands of the Army (O.K.H., or Oberkommando des Heeres), the Navy (O.K.M., or Oberkommando der Kriegsmarine), and the Air Force (O.K.L., or Oberkommando der Luftwaffe). They traced back to an intercept and cryptanalytic service established in the Army in 1919 by one Lieutenant Colonel Buschenhagen, who had worked in the intercept service in the war. He called it the "Volunteer Evaluation Office" and installed it on the Friedrichstrasse. In February of 1920, its twelve-man staff moved to the Defense Ministry Building on the Bendlerstrasse, where it became Group II of the Abwehr. Since the unit's work was much more closely allied with communications, however, it reverted a few years later to the administrative control of the chief of signal troops.

Even before that, it had moved out to nearby Grunewald, disguising itself as a newspaper translation and study group to avoid the Inter-Allied Military Control Commissions, which had proscribed intercept and codebreaking activities for the postwar German Army and had very nearly discovered the unit's real activity. The unit further evaded both the letter of the Commissions' directives and the spirit of the disarmament clauses of the Versailles Treaty when it began to prepare itself for any sudden demand for cryptanalysts that might arise—as in the case of a war. On October 31, 1921, the Army high command sent out a secret circular:

> In order to cultivate and develop further the study of cryptography and the utilization of the results of the Intercept Service [Horchdienstes], it is necessary to train suitable officers for this special service branch.
>
> Such officers are required to have a good knowledge of radio technique and mathematics, as well as geography, and some knowledge of a language (English, French, or an Eastern language).
>
> The officers concerned are not to be detached. At first it is intended that instruction will be by correspondence only, using problems given by the Army command for the winter half-year.
>
> Officers who distinguish themselves by especially good performance will be considered for service in evaluation stations of the higher commands and of the Army command; in addition there are expected to be prizes in the form of books on special branches of science.

The communications-intelligence unit stepped up its activities as Allied supervision waned. Part of its work consisted of picking up press association messages and news broadcasts and distributing a digest of them to government officials. By 1926, it had intercept stations in six major cities of Germany. In

1928, it began following the military maneuvers in which neighboring countries were once again engaging. It sneaked its intercept units into the demilitarized zone along the Rhine by disguising them as technicians for the German broadcasting or postal organizations. Much of its success resulted from traffic analysis—in 35 of the 52 major maneuvers between 1931 and 1937, the foreign forces were reconstructed completely. But it also solved some cipher systems.

When in 1934, Hitler pointed Germany toward its eventual war of revenge and conquest, he swelled the ranks of the armed forces and intensified military activities. But though the cryptologic agencies likewise grew in size, they did not necessarily grow in effectiveness. There were too few specialists in this recondite field to fill the need created by the proliferating military and party organizations. Some of the Army cryptanalysts were siphoned off to serve in the Forschungsamt, others, the Luftwaffe. Some of the intercept people moved over to Josef Goebbels' Ministry of Propaganda, where their news-eavesdropping could help. About 1937, the O.K.W. created its own communications and cryptologic staff, thereby draining off more of the experts and further splintering the effort in the field. These new agencies were staffed by World War I veterans who were now rejoining the German Army; most had been officers in the signal corps but had no great experience in or aptitude for intercept or cryptologic work. By mid-1939, the German communications-intelligence services had 18 times as many people in them as they had had in 1932, but useful results had in no way kept pace.

Six days before Hitler fell upon Poland, Major General Erich Fellgiebel, 52, who had been in communications since he joined a telegraph battalion upon enlisting in 1905, was named head of the O.K.W. communications organization. His title was Chef, Wehrmachtnachrichtenverbindungen ("Chief, Armed Forces Signal Communications"), or Chef W.N.V. His superior was the O.K.W. chief, Field Marshal Wilhelm Keitel, whose only superior was Hitler. Keitel wrote in Fellgiebel's fitness reports: "In his field a pronounced leader type with foresight, a gift for organization, full energy and dedication.... In his attitude towards National Socialism an inclination to unconsidered overcriticism...." The W.N.V. supervised communications, including communications security, and intercept operations;* it served as a kind of staff, an advisor and controller, for the service branches that largely operated the communications and intercept networks for the Army, Navy, and Air Force, much as the O.K.W. itself advised and directed the service commands.

Under the Chef W.N.V. came the Amtsgruppe W.N.V. Its chief was Major General Fritz Thiele, 48, a close colleague of Fellgiebel's who had previously headed the O.K.H. communications and intercept organization. He became Chef, Amtsgruppe W.N.V. the day the war began. The unit

* The term "Nachrichten" reflects this, since it means not only "communications" or "signals" but also "intelligence." In nonmilitary contexts, it means "news" or "information."

comprised radio and wire branches, which maintained communications between the headquarters of the three armed forces high commands, a technical equipment office, an administrative office, and the Chiffrierabteilung ("Cipher Office"), usually abbreviated "Chi." Colonel Siegfried Kempf assumed command of Chi on the same day that Fellgiebel became Chef W.N.V. Then 43, he was a career communications officer, a martinet disliked by his subordinates. He was succeeded in October, 1943, by Colonel Hugo Kettler, 48, who had had considerable intercept experience and who brought out the best in his men.

In 1944, the Chiffrierabteilung was divided into eight groups. Four came directly under Kettler; the other four were combined into two supergroups, Gruppen II and III into Hauptgruppe A for cryptography, Gruppen IV and V into Hauptgruppe B for cryptanalysis, each with its own head who reported to Kettler. This was the organization:

Gruppe Z (Zentralgruppe): personnel; pay, administration; office space and furnishings; Nazi ideological supervision.

Gruppe I: Organization and Control. Referat Ia: direction of the international monitoring service (Chi had intercept posts in Madrid and Seville as well as Lörrach and Tennenlohe, with main posts in Lauf and Treuenbrietzen). Referat Ib: study of foreign communications systems. Referat Ic: provision of teletype communications for Chi and R.S.H.A./VI/Mil (former Abwehr).

Gruppe II: Development of German Cipher Methods and Control of Their Use. Referat IIa: camouflage methods for telegraph and radio messages; intercept and wiretapping techniques; cryptographic policy; supervision of cipher employment; cryptographic compromises. Referat IIb: development of German cipher systems (camouflage methods, secret writing, secret telephony); supervision of and instruction in cipher production. Referat IIc: cryptographic systems for radio agents.

Gruppe III: Cipher Supply. Control of production, printing, and distribution of ciphers and keys; operation of the distribution posts (headquarters at Dresden with depots in Halle, Zwickau, Chemnitz, Leipzig, Frankfurt-am-Oder, Bischofswerda, Magdeburg, and Reichenbach).

Gruppe IV: Analytical Cryptanalysis. Referat IVa: testing of suggested German military cryptosystems and telephone scramblers for resistance to cryptanalysis: examination of inventions. Referat IVb: development and construction of cryptanalytic apparatus for Wehrmacht cryptanalytic units; operation of the equipment at Chi. Referat IVc: development of cryptanalytic methods; stripping of superencipherments for Gruppe V. Referat IVd: instruction.

Gruppe V: Practical Cryptanalysis of the Messages of Foreign Governments, Military Attachés, and Secret Agents. Referate V 1-22: national offices. Referat Va: Wehrmacht codewords.

Gruppe VI: Interception of Broadcast and Press Messages. Referat VIa: radio reception technique; administration and control of the listening posts at Ludwigsfelde, Husum, Münster, and Gleiwitz. Referat VIb: interception of radioed press and teletype transmissions and of international radio traffic. Referat VIc: surveillance of transmissions from within Germany to the outside. Referat VId: evaluation of broadcasts and press communication; issuance of the Chi-Nachrichten (a 10- to 20-page daily summary of the noncryptographic intercepts); special reports.

Gruppe VII: Referat VIIa: evaluation and distribution of output. Referat VIIb: chronicles of events (perhaps serving as an information unit).

In addition to these eight sections, a working committee for the testing of German cryptographic security reported directly to Kettler, and half a dozen intercept companies worked for Chi. The office was expected to maintain liaison with the communications units of the Army, Navy, and Air Force; with the chief of army equipment and commander of the replacement army, under whom there was an inspector of signal troops; with the R.S.H.A., the Foreign Office, the Propaganda, Post, Air, Trade, and War Production ministries and, of course, with the party.

(By 1945, the Chiffrierabteilung had been reorganized into seven groups, with functions apparently as follows: Gruppe Z, administration; Gruppe I, organization and control; Gruppe II, Chi-Nachrichten; Gruppe III, broadcast and press interception; Gruppe IV, cryptanalysis; Gruppe V, teletype for Chi and R.S.H.A./VI/Mil; Gruppe X, evaluation, distribution and information services. This downgrading of cryptanalysis and upgrading of the noncryptanalytic results may reflect a drop in the cryptanalytic results late in the war.)

Chief of Hauptgruppe B, in which the cryptanalytic functions reposed, was Ministerial Counselor Wilhelm Fenner, 48 when the war started. A German born and raised in St. Petersburg, he had headed German military cryptanalysis since 1922. He was a brilliant organizer who oversaw the expansion of the group from a handful to more than 150, but he handicapped himself by his egocentricity and by his superciliousness with regard to the noncryptanalytic aspects of communications intelligence. His right-hand man was a Russian emigrant, Professor Novopaschenny, who under the Czar had been attached to an astronomical observatory in Pulkovo, outside St. Petersburg. He developed much of the technical aspects of the work, but seems to have held only a relatively subordinate post as a chief cryptanalyst in one of the national offices, apparently Referat V 9, which was probably Russia.

Head of Analytical Cryptanalysis (Gruppe IV) was Dr. Erich Hüttenhain, who also directed that group's instructional activity (Referat IVd). Referat IVa, which tested German cryptosystems, frequently with mathematical tools to calculate theoretical limits of security and to find improvements, was headed by mathematician Dr. Karl Stein, who held the rank of lieutenant, surprisingly low for so lofty a position. Referat IVb, headed by Engineer Wilhelm Rotscheidt, used tabulating machines and special-purpose devices. It invented the prototype of the translucent-sheet-and-light device used by Pers z to strip additives from a known code. The unit first worked out the device for two-digit codes and then extended it to four. Instead of punching out holes corresponding to the most frequent groups, however, Referat IVb marked them with small crosshatched disks, and looked, not for the brightest spot, but for the darkest. Stein's mathematicians extensively investigated the question of how a codegroup stock could be constructed so that this method would not work against it. Referat IVc's chief was Professor Dr. Wolfgang Franz, and Ministerial Counselor Dr. Victor Wendland was head of Gruppe V (Practical Cryptanalysis) and so Fenner's immediate subordinate.

Early in the war, the O.K.W. cryptanalysts worked in a former town house on one of the streets that run off the Tirpitzufer, not far from O.K.W. headquarters on the Bendlerstrasse. About 1943 they moved to much larger quarters in a modern semicircular concrete office building at 56 Potsdamerstrasse called the Haus des Fremdenverkehr—a name that gave rise to many bad jokes because "fremdenverkehr" ("tourist traffic") is German slang for "fornication."

On July 21, 1944, Fellgiebel's sudden removal from command rocked the whole W.N.V. It seemed to be connected with the bomb attempt on Hitler's life of the day before—and it was. Fellgiebel, whose anti-Nazi proclivities had been noted in his fitness report by Keitel, had in fact been a key figure in the plot. He was replaced by Thiele, who became head of both the O.K.W. and the O.K.H. agencies. He served for exactly a month. Then he was arrested as a co-conspirator, his personnel file crossed out with a giant X, and the entry made under his name, "stricken from the honor roll of the German Army and the Wehrmacht!" Fellgiebel had been executed on August 10; Thiele soon followed. Lieutenant General Albert Praun took Thiele's place in both offices and retained them to the end of the war.

The oldest, most experienced, and closest to O.K.W. of the other cryptanalytic agencies was the Army's Heeresnachrichtenwesens ("Army Communications System"), or H.N.W. The Chef, H.N.W., served on the Army general staff. Like the U.S. Army's Signal Corps during World War II, it had both communications and intercept-cryptanalysis duties; like the Signal Corps, it turned over its solutions to Army intelligence for evaluation and use.

Under Chi's watchful eye, it issued cryptosystems for the troops. For high-level communications, from the O.K.H. down to regiments, the Army used the glowlamp Enigma cipher machine. It was reliable, working well in the Russian winter and the Libyan summer. Signal officers thought it cryptanalytically secure if—as ordered by 1942—keys were changed three times a day. Its chief disadvantage was that it did not print its output. Battery-powered and portable, it could be operated in a moving truck and was well adapted to radio work.

Nevertheless, in 1943 a new machine began replacing it in some areas. This was a printing machine, produced by the Wanderer Werke firm, which copied the Hagelin variable-gear principle. There is a story that one of these was found in Norway at the end of the war with a message still in it, obviously abandoned by an operator who disagreed with what he had deciphered: *Der Fuehrer ist tot. Der Kampf geht weiter. Doenitz* ("The Führer is dead. The war goes on. Dönitz").

For wire teletypewriter communications from the O.K.H. to army corps and a few divisions, the Germans used an on-line machine produced by Siemens & Halske Aktiengesellschaft. Its heart was a set of ten keywheels, similar to those on a Hagelin machine, rimmed with pins that could be made either operative or inoperative. Each wheel had a prime number of pins, ranging from 47 on the smallest to 89 on the largest. Five of these wheels enciphered the five teletypewriter pulses, transforming a mark into a space or vice versa if the pin then in position was operative, or leaving the pulse unchanged if it was inoperative. The other five wheels effected a transposition of the pulses. The machine enciphered and transmitted in a single operation, and likewise deciphered and printed out the message automatically.

Beginning in June, 1942, regiments, battalions, and companies enciphered with the double transposition, with the same keyword for both blocks—the same system, interestingly, as the German Army used at the start of World War I. (This system also backed up the Enigma.) Each division produced at least three keys for its subordinate units. The troops heartily disliked the double transposition, however, and cleartext messages showed a noticeable upsurge. For intelligence and combat reports, these units used small three-letter or three-digit codes, which were likewise published by their divisions. Many cipherers preferred their simplicity to the complexity of the double transposition, and often used them for orders and other unauthorized messages. A signal officer complained bitterly of this practice: "Tarntafeln sind kein Schlüsselersatz!" ("Code tables are not cipher substitutes!"), he wrote in a report. Later in the war, a bigraphic substitution replaced the double transposition as a front-line cryptosystem, and in 1944 a modification of the grille replaced that. In addition, the signal troops used numerous special ciphers—for call-signs, numbers, and so on.

The H.N.W. communications-intelligence service operated as a separate organization within an army or an army group, though parts of it were sometimes specially assigned. In 1943, for example, the commander of Fernmeldeaufklärung 7 ("Radio Intelligence 7"), reported to Field Marshal Albert

Kesselring. Fernmeldeaufklärung 7 consisted of radio intelligence companies and platoons and direction-finding stations widely scattered over the central Mediterranean area—in western Crete, southern France, northern Africa, Sicily, Sardinia, and Italy. These units reported their intelligence results via their own radio net to the headquarters at Rocca di Papa, south of Rome; the original intercepts were then forwarded to headquarters for more comprehensive evaluation. Fernmeldeaufklärung 7 distributed radio intelligence of tactical importance to the lower commands by broadcasting it in a special cipher. While much of this intelligence came from conversations or radio messages in plaintext or from traffic analysis, much also came from cryptanalysis. Similar units on other fronts also provided valuable material.

Thus when Hitler, in a fit of rage, fell upon Yugoslavia, his armed forces overran that tough little nation across mountainous terrain formerly considered blitzproof with a speed that could not be fully accounted for even by their overwhelming strength. And in fact the Germans could exploit the Yugoslav military messages to tell their Panzer commanders where and how their armored columns might best spear down toward Zagreb, Sarajevo, and Belgrade. For since January, 1940, German Army intercept personnel, wearing civilian clothes, had monitored Yugoslav emissions from an intercept station in Sofia and had broken the Yugoslav military cryptosystem.

After the conquest, a radio intelligence platoon cryptanalyzed the ciphers of the partisans under General Draja Mikhailovich and his Communist rival, Tito. The results enabled the occupation troops to forestall many guerrilla depredations. Tito, finding some of his efforts frustrated, at first suspected treachery and purged some of his underlings. Soon, however, he guessed the truth and changed his ciphers with great frequency but with no success. In the spring of 1943, for example, the Germans picked up a series of messages from which it became clear that Tito's relations with his Anglo-American allies had deteriorated. Others spoke of a proposed Anglo-American landing on the Adriatic coast—but this never came off.

German Army cryptanalysts solved American M-209 messages almost from the days late in 1942 when the two armies first clashed in North Africa. They picked up such tidbits of information as that the 72nd, 45th, and 29th Light and the 71st Heavy Anti-Aircraft Regiments were placed under the 52nd Anti-Aircraft Brigade, which is part of the order-of-battle intelligence basic to a field commander, that on April 1, 1943, the 3rd Infantry Regiment was located at grid square 43835, or 37 kilometers from Gafa, that American forces were forbidden to fire upon airplanes unless the airplanes attacked them (to prevent shooting down Allied planes). All these details were fitted together to give the German command a picture of the troops facing them, their state of mind, their preparation.

Occasionally, a single solved message produced strikingly dramatic results. During a conference at the headquarters of the Commanding General,

Southwest, in 1943, Colonel Karl-Albert Mügge, commander of Fernmeldeaufklärung 7, brought Field Marshal Kesselring a British intercept that had just been cryptanalyzed. It reported that in North Africa several troop columns were caught in a traffic jam of their own making by crowding into a wadi at—and here the cryptogram was garbled so that the exact location could not be read. Kesselring called for an immediate air search; the jammed wadi was discovered while the Germans were still in conference. Kesselring promptly ordered an air attack, which wreaked considerable destruction upon the concentrated British forces.

Early in February, 1944, during the Italian campaign, the American 5th Army attempted to recapture the Carrocetto factory, a pivotal point which the Germans had taken in a counterattack. "It was important for VI Corps not only to regain the Factory area but also to effect the relief of at least a major part of the I Division," the 5th Army historian wrote. "Aided by the 191st Tank Battalion, men of the 1st Battalion made their way into the Factory in the afternoon, only to be driven out. Though our artillery and tanks converted the buildings into a blazing mass of ruins, the enemy held; prisoners reported that an intercepted radio message had given them foreknowledge of the attack. Another attack before dawn on the 12th likewise failed, and the 45th Division gave up the effort to regain the Factory."

As the Allies gained air superiority and the Germans could no longer reconnoiter by air, they depended more and more on radio intelligence. This was especially true after the Normandy invasion. But this means was not omniscient. In the fall of 1944, when General George Patton's army was preparing to bite out the fortress of Metz, the German forces detected his preparations, largely through radio. "Yet," wrote a German staff officer, "the actual attack on 8 November came as a surprise to the front line troops."

In the field, the German Army's communication intelligence unit worked closely with the Luftwaffe's Funkaufklärungsdienst ("Radio Reconnaissance Service"). This was the intelligence side of the Air Force's Nachrichten-Verbindungswesen, or N.-V.W. ("Intelligence and Signal System"), whose chief served on the staff of the O.K.L. He also prescribed secret communications systems for the Luftwaffe. Air-to-air communications, which were mostly by voice, employed simple codewords to disguise unit names, much as American pilots referred to one another as EASY RED or GREEN ARROW in the style made familiar by war movies. Air-ground communications were encoded in small three-digit or three-letter codes. Luftwaffe ground-to-ground cryptography used the Enigma.

The Funkaufklärungsdienst employed more than 10,000 men. Its largest subdivision was Luftnachrichten ("Air Intelligence") Regiment 351, with 4,500 men, which intercepted, solved, and evaluated the radio traffic of Allied light and heavy bombers, fighters, transports, and air staffs in Western Europe. An additional unit of 1,000 provided further detailed information on the heavy bombers. Smaller regiments covered other theaters. Luftnach-

```
- 3 -

v a r    Abstimmspruch wird getastet um ... Uhr
v i s    Geben Sie zur Abstimmung Wettermeldung
         um .... Uhr
v w L    Befehlswelle
x d n    Schlüsselmittel und Nachrichtenunter-
         lagen wegen drohender Gefahr des Feind-
         verlustes vernichtet
x v o    Bis auf weiteres Wettermeldung gemäß
         Funkbefehl tasten
y d e    Prage
s L k    Befehl


f i n    beendet
e o m    eigene Maschinen
s u b    Suchbefehl
g r t    Es folgt Leuchtfeuer-Schaltbefehl
```

A three-letter code of the Luftwaffe, used in 1945

Duel in the Ether: The Axis

richten Battalion 350, with 800 men, served as the Luftwaffe center for basic cryptanalysis and traffic analysis, as well as for the study of new enemy radars and radio navigation systems to find the best means of jamming or deceiving them. It also covered the Allied transatlantic air transport service. It was attached to the main headquarters of the Funkaufklärungsdienst.

Other cryptanalysts served in outlying Funkaufklärungsdienst units, solving messages in systems whose basic solution had been worked out at headquarters. They had reportedly tried to use women in teams for solving a widely used Allied air-ground system, called SYKO, but switched to male students when the women did not produce satisfactory results. They tested the youths by crossword puzzles and sent the 10 per cent doing the best to a training school for about a month. Here they were trained in SYKO cryptanalysis and nothing else. As an incentive, the Nazis told the trainees that

Training card for Allied air-ground cipher SYKO

the lower 90 per cent of the class would be shipped off to the Russian front.

Early in the war, SYKO consisted of 30 unrelated, mixed cipher alphabets printed on a card. The alphabets were to be used in succession to encipher a message, the encipherer using an indicator to define the one he was using first. The cards were changed every midnight. Later, SYKO took the form of a hinged frame holding a card on which 32 mixed alphabets of letters and numbers were printed vertically. The frame also supported 32 sliding strips, each also with a mixed alphabet, each of which uncovered and covered one of the card alphabets as it moved up and down. The encipherer slid the strips to align the plaintext message on them horizontally at the foot of the frame, and read the ciphertext from the letters of the card showing immediately above the tops of the strips. The alphabets were reciprocal, so that decipherment followed the same procedure. It produced the same cipher as the older version: a periodic polyalphabetic with mixed alphabets, whose period, moreover, was known—rather like the Für GOD of World War I. An *e* in the first column was always represented by the same ciphertext letter while that card remained in use, which was for 24 hours. The Allies apparently used SYKO because it was light, fast, and simple, but its insecurity meant that on days of heavy traffic the Axis SYKO teams were reading Allied air messages by 10 or 11 a.m.

It was probably not SYKO that enciphered the message that gave the Funkaufklärungsdienst one of its greatest triumphs, since the message originated in a high-echelon ground command and was directed to other ground commands, while the planes themselves maintained radio silence. These were 178 four-engined Liberators, heading for the Rumanian oil fields at Ploesti, Hitler's chief source of oil for his thirsty war machine, in one of the longest-range and potentially one of the most important air strikes of the war. As they lumbered into the air at Bengazi on the morning of August 1, 1943, for their 1,200-mile flight, the 9th Air Force spread a short message to Allied forces in the Mediterranean area announcing that a large mission was airborne from Libya. This was necessary because only a few weeks before, in the invasion of Sicily, the U.S. Navy had shot down dozens of American troop planes in the tragically mistaken belief that they were German bombers.

The message was picked up by a Funkaufklärungsdienst unit recently posted near Athens. Soon its cryptanalysts had reduced it to plaintext. Lieutenant Christian Ochsenschlager then passed to all defense commands "interested or affected" a message stating that a large formation of four-engined bombers, believed to be Liberators, had been taking off since early morning in the Bengazi area. This gave the antiaircraft defenses at Ploesti, the heaviest in Europe, plenty of time to get ready. When the bombers roared at derrick-top height over the Rumanian oil field, with its wells, refineries, and tanks, they were met with the worst flak encountered by American bombers during the war. Of the 178, 53, or almost every third plane, were downed, and dozens of Americans died.

The German cryptanalytic agency that probably had the greatest effect upon the course of the war was also the smallest and least known. It belonged to the O.K.M., and Grand Admiral Karl Dönitz, commander of the German Navy during the latter half of the war, called it his "B-Dienst," for "Beobachtung-Dienst" ("Observation Service"). The B-Dienst had little contact with the other codebreaking agencies. Yet its successes were more far-reaching than any of theirs, and it participated in some of the most unusual activities of the cryptanalytic war.

Stung in the 1920s by revelations of Room 40's readings of German naval traffic, the O.K.M. built up so effective a cryptanalytic unit that by the start of World War II the B-Dienst had solved some of the most secret Admiralty codes and ciphers. The penetration of British naval messages enabled German surface raiders to elude the British Home Fleet, spared German heavy ships from many a chance encounter with stronger British forces, permitted surprise attacks on British warships, and helped sink six British submarines in the Skagerrak area between June and August of 1940.

Perhaps its greatest feat came in the Norway invasion. On March 1, Hitler approved the plan to invade Norway, but set no date for it. Soon thereafter, the B-Dienst solved British naval messages that revealed a British plan to mine the entrance to Narvik, far in the north of Norway, and to occupy that port; Britain intended to block German ore shipments. This information enabled the German high command to shape a strategy for surmounting the greatest difficulty in its Norway invasion: how to move its weakly guarded transports from Germany to Norway without interference by the powerful British fleet. When the British Narvik expedition was under way, the high command plotted, Germany would send out a decoy force which the British would think was heading to attack their expedition at Narvik. To protect it, Britain would send the rest of its naval forces away to the north. As soon as this happened, the transports would cross the Skagerrak without fear of major sea attack.

The scheme worked to perfection. Late in March the B-Dienst showed British vessels en route to Narvik. On April 2 Hitler set the invasion for the 9th. The decoy force put out to sea and was spotted on the 7th by the British. As the Germans expected, the Admiralty ordered the Home Fleet and the 1st and 2nd Cruiser Squadrons to head for Narvik. As they raced away from where the action was, the German transports completed their voyage undisturbed by the nation that supposedly rules the waves and landed their occupation troops without a hitch. Even Winston Churchill admitted that Germany had "completely outwitted" Britannia.

The B-Dienst may have gained a great deal of help from some spectacular coups by the German merchant raider *Atlantis*. This specially fitted high-speed freighter, whose heavy armament was carefully camouflaged, was one of several that cruised the oceans and harassed Allied shipping. On July 10, 1940, in one of her first actions, *Atlantis* fired a few shots into *City of Baghdad* in the Indian Ocean and captured the vessel almost intact when her crew hastily abandoned ship. A boarding party reached the officers' cabins just in time to point a pistol at the captain and stop him from throwing overboard most of the ship's secret papers. Among them was the Allied *Merchant Ships' Code*, a two-part code issued by the Admiralty for messages via the Broadcasting for Allied Merchant Ships, or BAMS, commonly called the "BAMS code."

Also recovered were several superencipherment tables, though not the current ones. *Atlantis*, however, had aboard in her special crew a wireless operator named Wesemann who had served for three years in one of the German cryptanalytic services. Wesemann achieved what might be the first nautical cryptanalysis on record when, on the basis of the captured code and several merchant messages that he had intercepted, he succeeded in reconstructing about one third of the superencipherment table then in use. As a result, *Atlantis* could read much of the Allied merchantmen's traffic and could await her victims at likely spots.

When the tables were changed, Wesemann partially reconstructed the new ones with the help of some messages found in the wastebasket of the radio shack of another captured vessel, *Benarty*. The work was completed for him by the B-Dienst, which deduced from his radio queries that he had obtained the BAMS code and consequently sent him the interpretations he needed. Since *Atlantis* and Berlin were then almost at antipodes from one another, this must rank as the longest-distance cryptanalytic collaboration known. A few months later, on November 11, 1940, the crew of the German raider found aboard *Automedon*, the 13th ship she had sunk, another copy of the BAMS code and superencipherment tables 7, 8, and 9. All the cryptanalyzed information contributed to *Atlantis*' record as the war's deadliest sea raider.

She may have sent the B-Dienst photographs of the captured codebooks when one of her prize ships returned to Germany, or the B-Dienst may have obtained a copy elsewhere. Either way, the German knowledge of merchant messages vastly improved U-boat attacks. And, wrote Churchill, "The Battle of the Atlantic was the dominating factor all through the war. Never for one moment could we forget that everything happening elsewhere, on land, at sea, or in the air, depended ultimately upon its outcome." More than once, the B-Dienst placed in the hands of the U-boat commanders the knowledge that brought them to the edge of victory.

In 1941, for example, the B-Dienst read messages to convoys from the Commander in Chief, Western Approaches, that directed those convoys from the danger zones just west of the British Isles. With this intelligence, the U-boat command had no difficulty in deploying its submarines to the maximum effectiveness. Allied losses mounted steeply. In March, April, and May, U-boats sank 142 vessels, or more than one every 16 hours. In January and February of 1943, the B-Dienst mastered British naval cryptosystems so fully that it was even reading the British "U-Boat Situation Report," which was

62969	**Q U A Q**	British Honduras	63320	**Q W A O**	Submarine submerged
970	B P	Gauntlet	327	B N	188°
981	C O	Unzen	338	C M	Close port
990	D N	Savoia	340	D L	No
992	E M	Mainmast-s, *of*	349	E K	HOM
			350	F J	Plate
63003	F L	Assisted, *the*	356	G I	
010	G K	Buoy-s formerly situated in (*position-s*) is (are) no longer there	365	H H	EX
			371	I G	Rockhampton
015	H J	ETICS	376	J F	Cannot arrive, *at*
026	I 'I	Cement-s-ed-ing,´*for*	382	K E	
031	J H	String-s	391	L D	Taku
048	L F	08	393	M C	For REPAIR, AT, BY
050	M E	Bridgewater			
059	N D	Mention-s-ing, *the*	**63401**	N B	Standard Time of Zone [+10
064	O C	Suva			
068	P B	Negotiat-e-es-ed-ing-[ion	413	O A	DUKE
			420	P Z	Caus-e-es-ing, *the*
070	Q A	Substituted	424	Q Y	Search-es for, *the*
081	R Z	BA	435	R X	Farne Is.
089	S Y	Nót have	442	S W	Submerged
092	T X	Trafalgar, *Cape*	446	T V	GRA
			457	U U	198°
63100	U W	Barclay-'s	461	V T	Trinidad
109	V V	Larger, *than, the*	462	W S	JN
112	W U	9 feet	478	X R	CW
127	Y S	Possibilit-y-ies, *of, the*	482	Y Q	Sunk by
134	Z R	SPA	489	Z P	Honan
			494	**Q X B M**	Bunbury
145	**Q V A P**	Irrawaddy			
150	B O	Caledonian Canal	**63508**	C L	Convoy arriv-e-es-ing, [*at, on*
156	C N	& ¼			
161	D M	Anxious-ly, *that, the*	510	D K	Plot-s-ted-ting, [*against, the*
174	E L	Upper wind			
177	F K	Take-s your	517	E J	Williamstown
188	G J	Esquimalt	521	F I	241°
189	H I	Tweed	541	H G	Solent
199	I H	Edge-s, *of, the*	543	I F	012°
			554	J E	Prevent-s, *any*
63207	J G	Number-s-ed-ing	559	K D	Flat-s
211	K F	Cat Island	569	L C	RRY
219	L E	NO	575	M B	Peiping (Peking)
231	N C	EEN	580	N A	Unlikelihood, *of, the*
238	O B	Kribi	586	O Z	166°
242	P A	Given for	592	P Y	Connecting up, *the*
253	Q Z	5th October	597	Q X	No one-s
260	R Y	What ship-s, *is, are*			
268	S X	Santa Isabel	**63605**	R W	Monchair Carré
274	T W	S.S.E. ¼ E., *from, of*	610	S V	Unaware-s, *that, of*
281	U V	Universal-ly	617	T U	MU
285	V U	062°	628	U T	NAN
292	W T	São Thomé	633	V S	121°
296	X S	Major-s	639	W R	August
			640	X Q	Port Convoy Officer-s, [*at*
63304	Y R	Petropavlovsk	646	Y P	Muscat
316	Z Q	Adoption, *of, the*	651	Z O	

Page of decoding section of British BAMS *merchant ships' code* regularly broadcast to the commanders of convoys at sea, telling them the known and presumed locations of U-boats! "These 'Situation Reports' were of the greatest value to us in our efforts to determine how the enemy was able to find out about our U-boat dispositions and with what degree of accuracy he did so," wrote Admiral Dönitz.

The following month, March of 1943, saw the climax of the Battle of the Atlantic. And the climactic action, the greatest triumph of the U-boats, in which they very nearly severed Britain's lifeline, stemmed directly from a series of B-Dienst solutions.

The first came on March 9. A B-Dienst report gave the precise location of the eastbound convoy HX 228. (The HX stood for Halifax, Nova Scotia, assembly point for all fast convoys. Slow convoys, which started at Sydney, Cape Breton Island, Nova Scotia, were designated SC.) Shortly thereafter, the B-Dienst reported that the next fast convoy, HX 229, was southeast of Cape Race, steaming on a course of 89 degrees. On the 14th, another solution revealed that a third convoy, SC 122, had received orders at noon the day before that on reaching a given point it was to steer 67 degrees. The U-boats, then operating in wolf packs of two or three dozen, were ordered to search for the convoys. On the morning of March 16, they sighted a convoy which turned out to be HX 229, and in the next two days, 38 U-boats sent 13 ships to the bottom. Meanwhile, HX 229 overtook the slow-moving SC 122, forming a large mass of shipping in a small space of ocean. The wolf pack nipped at its edges and sank eight more vessels, making a total of 141,000 tons sunk in the three-day battle, at a cost of only a single U-boat. Dönitz exulted: "It was the greatest success that we had so far scored against a convoy."

The Admiralty despaired. They considered abandoning the convoy system as ineffective, which was tantamount to an admission of defeat, since no alternative existed, the loss rate of single vessels being double that of ships in convoy. "The Germans never came so near to disrupting communications between the New World and the Old as in the first twenty days of March, 1943," the naval staff later recorded. It marked the darkest hour of the longest, most crucial battle of the war. And in large measure German cryptanalysts had cast this pall upon Britain by—paradoxically—throwing light upon British communications.

Italy relied for her communication intelligence upon her Army and her Navy. The Navy's cryptanalysts formed the B section of the Servizio Informazione Segreto, or naval intelligence. Early in 1942, they had penetrated the British naval ciphers in the Mediterranean—these were so poor that Admiral Sir Andrew Cunningham reportedly threatened after the invasion of Crete to transmit entirely in clear if he were not given better ciphers. The Italian solution of a British scout plane report enabled the Italian high command to warn one of its task-force commanders at 6 p.m. March 27, just before the

Battle of Cape Matapan, that the English had sighted him soon after he had put to sea. Next day the reading of an order to Cunningham from Alexandria made the Italians certain that British torpedo planes would attack. They did, and so prepared were the Italians that the intensity of their antiaircraft defense made it almost impossible for the English to identify their targets or observe the results of the attack.

The Italian Army's security and intelligence organization, the Servizio Informazione Militare, or S.I.M., had a large and well-organized cryptologic section which solved diplomatic as well as military cryptograms. This was its Sezione 5, headed by General Vittorio Gamba, an old Alpine warrior with austere features. A long-time student of cryptology and author of an excellent article on the subject in the *Enciclopedia Italiana*, Gamba was a noted linguist who reputedly knew 25 languages. He came to public attention in 1911 when he translated a series of proclamations into Arabic during the Italo-Turkish conflict over Tripoli. The 50 members of Sezione 5 were housed in a large apartment house in Rome far from S.I.M. headquarters but connected by teletypewriter with it and with the extensive intercept unit, Sezione 6, located on the Forte Bocea, a hill behind the Vatican. Gamba's cryptanalysts maintained close liaison with the chemical section, which worked with secret inks and other means of steganography, with the censorship section, and with the phototypographic section, which rapidly reproduced stolen documents.

Also under Gamba was a subsection headed by the elderly Colonel Gino Mancini that produced codes and ciphers for the Italian Army. At the higher levels, these were enciphered codes, also used by the Italian Navy (which at other times used the Hagelin machine). The Italians liked superencipherments that combined transposition with substitution—a preference that can be seen as far back as the Panizzardi telegram of Dreyfus case fame, in which the first placode digit became the second encicode digit and vice versa. In one of their World War II encipherments, for example, with placode groups 12345 67890, the encipherer would pick out 1 and 6, find the encicode for 16 in a 10×10 table, and, assuming it to be 38, would set down 3 as the first digit of the first encicode group and 8 as the first digit of the second. He would repeat this with 2 and 7, using, however, a different 10×10 table. At first the Italians used five such tables; later, they used ten.

Like their O.K.W. colleagues, the Sezione 5 cryptanalysts had solved the military ciphers of Yugoslavia, with whom Italy's relations had been strained over Fiume and Trieste practically since Yugoslavia was created after World War I. The Germans used the solutions for a blitzkrieg from the north. The Italians exploited them in a crafty deception that helped avoid a possible debacle in the south.

Almost up to the moment of the Axis invasion, the Italian armies that had occupied Albania had exposed what Churchill picturesquely called their "naked rear" to Yugoslavia in the north. Yugoslavia had no chance against the Wehrmacht, but both Axis and Allies realized that if she struck forcefully against the rather disorganized Italians, she could win a major victory, embarrass Mussolini, delay the Axis conquest, and acquire the munitions and supplies for a large-scale guerrilla harassment of the Nazi occupiers. Thus, when two Yugoslav divisions drove southward on April 7—one from Cetinje toward Shkoder, the other from Kosowska Mitrovica toward Kukes—it was regarded as a serious business. Especially when, by April 12, the Cetinje division had shoved the Italians back to the gates of Shkoder and was pummeling them with attacks of increasing intensity.

At this juncture the Servizio Informazione Militare got an idea. It drafted two telegrams in Yugoslav military style and affixed the signature of General Dusan Simovič, head of the new government. One read:

> To the Cetinje divisional headquarters:
> Subordinate troops will suspend all offensive action and retire in the direction of Podgorica, organizing for defense.

And the other:

> To the Kosowska Mitrovica divisional headquarters:
> Withdraw immediately with all subordinate troops back towards Kosowska Mitrovica.
>
> Simovič

Both messages were enciphered in the Yugoslav Army system, and at 10 a.m. on April 13, an S.I.M. station, observing all Yugoslav radio regulations as to wavelength, transmission times, and subordinate stations, contacted the two divisional stations and passed the messages, both of which were receipted for. The drive toward Kukes slackened immediately. The Cetinje division, however, requested confirmation. None came.

Next morning, the confused divisional command, not having received any disavowal of the enciphered orders, and consequently believing that they were valid though incomprehensible, lifted its attacks at Shkoder and began retreating northward. The Italians hastened to fill the military vacuum that was created, and marched the 10 miles from Kotor to Cetinje in a day. Next day the Yugoslav headquarters replied that no retreat had been ordered, but by then it was too late. It only told the Yugoslavs that their ciphers were compromised, and, unable to issue new ones in the fluid situation, they attempted to assure the legitimacy of their communications through onerous controls. Instead they gummed their command machinery at a time when every hour counted. A few days later it was all over. The S.I.M.'s fake messages had saved Italy from a crippling defeat.

In a typical month during the war the S.I.M.'s Sezione 6 intercepted 8,000 radiograms. About 6,000 were considered worthy of study, and of these, Sezione 5 reduced 3,500 to plaintext. So great was the flow that General Cesare Amè, head of the S.I.M., began to publish a daily Bulletin I, which summarized the most significant information. Its three copies went to

Mussolini, to the chief of the general staff, and to the king, through his aide-de-camp. The S.I.M. distributed other important solutions individually to the proper parties.

Diplomatic traffic naturally went to Count Galeazzo Ciano, the Foreign Minister, whose many mentions of the solutions in his famous diary testify to their importance. According to the diary, Sezione 5 read British, Rumanian, and Turkish traffic. The Italians drank as deeply of the stream of that neutral's messages as the Hungarian group that worked for Höttl was to do. For more than two years, Turkish cryptograms told the Italian government of rumored Allied war plans, of Allied views, of an uncommitted observer's comments on Axis programs and prospects. On January 4, 1943, Ciano jotted in his diary: "The Duce asked me to give [Hans Georg] von Mackensen [German ambassador to Italy] a copy of a telegram the Turkish ambassador Zorlu sent to his government from Kuibyshev. It is a description of the Soviet situation. It seems impartial and quite informative. According to him, the war weighs heavily on the Russians, but Russia is still strong, and, in the judgment of the diplomatic corps in Kuibyshev, Axis stock is falling."

One entry may indicate the Italian solution of an English solution of a German telegram: "Then, too, he [Mussolini] is angry at Rommel, who, according to English sources, has telegraphed accusing several of our officers of having revealed some of his future plans to the enemy. As always, victory finds a hundred fathers, but defeat is an orphan." Two and a half months later, on December 24, 1942, another British intercept enabled Mussolini to ready a reply to a planned British move: "We are at loggerheads again on the question of the bombing of Rome. From an intercepted British telegram we learn that in addition to the departure of the Duce and the commands from Rome, [British Foreign Minister Anthony] Eden also wants that of the King and of the whole government, with Swiss officers controlling the evacuation. Naturally Mussolini reacted vigorously and is preparing to refuse." Six days later, Ciano noted: "A good point on the question of the bombing of Rome: from an intercepted telegram we learn that the Americans have said no to Eden's Draconian request, declaring that they do not intend to bomb the city of St. Peter because there would be more disadvantages than advantages for the Allies. Thus it seems to me that the matter can be tabled. At least for the time being." And the following month Mussolini ordered Ciano to give von Mackensen yet another British intercept. This one reported a conversation between General Bernard Montgomery and the captured German commander in Africa, General Ritter Wilhelm von Thoma, in which "von Thoma said that the Germans are convinced that they have lost the war, and that the Army is anti-Nazi because it holds Hitler completely responsible."

These were only the telegrams that Ciano thought outstanding enough to note. How many more must have fluttered onto Fascist desks without his mentioning them, and how much knowledge of Allied plans must Italy have obtained from the continuous flow!

Though Sezione 5 solved many cryptograms, many of its successes came, not from cryptanalysis, but from the S.I.M.'s theft of cryptologic documents. In 1941 alone, the S.I.M. obtained possession of about 50 such items, or about one a week. Some of these probably were only plaintext versions of coded telegrams. But many were the codes or ciphers themselves, and one of them, which led to probably the greatest Axis communications-intelligence results of the war, was a secret code of the United States of America.

The spy who stole it appears to have been Loris Gherardi, a messenger in the office of the American military attaché in Rome. An Italian national just turned 40, he had worked for the Americans since about 1920. His duties included the carrying of telegrams from the attaché's office to the Italian telegraph bureau. In August of 1941 he apparently obtained for the S.I.M. the key or an impression of the key or the combination to an embassy safe. This enabled the Italians surreptitiously to open the safe, remove and photograph the BLACK code and its attendant superencipherment tables, and then replace them. Neither his boss, the military attaché, Colonel Norman E. Fiske, nor the ambassador ever suspected a thing. Loris continued on the job.*

The BLACK code, so called for the color of its binding, was a relatively new and secret military attaché code, with its own superencipherment tables. Ambassadors may also have used it. Thus Ciano gloated in his diary on September 30, 1941, shortly after the theft: "The military intelligence service has come into possession of the American secret code; everything that [U.S. Ambassador William] Phillips telegraphs is read by our decoding offices...."

Soon after the S.I.M. acquired the code, it gave a copy to Germany's Canaris. From that moment, the Axis powers—subject only to their ability to strip the superencipherments—were enabled to peer into the secret messages of the diplomats and the military attachés of a great power that their enemies were seeking desperately to win over. And the messages came from all over the world, not only from Axis capitals, but also from Allied capitals where the American attachés had access to some of the most intimate secrets of the Axis' foes. "I handed Mackensen," Ciano noted on February 12, 1942, "the text of a telegram from the American military attaché at Moscow, addressed to Washington. It complains about failure to deliver arms promised by the United States, and says that if the U.S.S.R. is not aided immediately and properly she will have to consider capitulating."

But the most valuable material dealt with the battlefronts, where the issue of victory or defeat was being decided. In the fall of 1941, the Germans were driving eastward on two fronts, Russia and North Africa, intending to link them up in the Near East, make the Mediterranean an Axis lake, march

---

* Gherardi stayed on until Italy's declaration of war upon the United States closed the embassy. After the war, he coolly asked for his old job back—and got it! He held it until the secret finally leaked out; then, after several interrogations, he resigned, in August, 1949.

on to India, and meet the Japanese in Asia, thereby ruling the world and fulfilling Hitler's dream of out-conquering Alexander the Great.

The American military attaché in Cairo had much better opportunities to observe military action than his colleague in Moscow, owing to factors of distance, language, and politics, and he took full advantage of these opportunities to do his job. He was Colonel Bonner Frank Fellers, a West Pointer with a varied peacetime experience, including two years as assistant to General Douglas MacArthur. Fellers had been posted to Cairo in October, 1940. He industriously toured the battlefronts and studied the tactics and problems of desert warfare. He asked questions. He kept his eyes open. The British let him in on some of their secrets, hoping that this would improve American equipment lend-leased to Britain's desert forces, but probably withheld some because of his anti-British predilections. Fellers soaked up this great quantity of information and poured it out to Washington in voluminous and detailed reports.

He discussed the British forces at the front, their duties, capabilities, and effectiveness; he told of reinforcements that were expected and supply ships that had arrived, explained morale problems, analyzed the various tactics that the British had under consideration, even reported on plans for local military operations. He carefully encoded his messages in the BLACK code and radioed them to Washington, usually addressed to MILID WASH (*Mil*itary *I*ntelligence *D*ivision, *Wash*ington). And as his transmissions flashed through the ether, listening Axis radio stations—usually at least two, so that nothing would be missed—took down every word. The intercepts were transmitted by direct wire to cryptanalysts, where they were reduced to plaintext, translated, reenciphered in a German system, and forwarded to General Erwin Rommel, commander of the Afrika Korps. He often had the messages only a few hours after Fellers had sent them.

And what messages they were! They provided Rommel with undoubtedly the broadest and clearest picture of enemy forces and intentions available to any Axis commander throughout the whole war. In the seesaw North African warfare, Rommel had been driven back across the desert by the British under General Claude Auchinleck at the end of 1941, but beginning on January 21, 1942, he rebounded with such vigor that in seventeen days he had thrown the British back 300 miles. During those days he was getting information like this from the Fellers intercepts:

January 23: 270 airplanes and a quantity of antiaircraft artillery being withdrawn from North Africa to reinforce British forces in the Far East.

January 25–26: Allied evaluation of the defects of Axis armor and aircraft.

January 29: Complete rundown of British armor, including number in working order, number damaged, number available, and their locations; location and efficiency ratings of armored and motorized units at the front.

February 1: Forthcoming commando operations; efficiency ratings of various British units; report that American M-3 tanks could not be used before mid-February.

February 6: Location and efficiency of the 4th Indian Division and the 1st Armored Division; iteration of British plans to dig in along the Acroma–Bir Hacheim line; recognition of the possibility that Axis forces might reach the Egyptian frontier once the armored divisions had been regrouped.

February 7: British units stabilized along the Ain el Gazala-Bir Hacheim line.

These only highlight the outstanding tesserae of the abundantly detailed mosaic which Rommel had available and which helped him win his epithet, "the Desert Fox." And when in May of 1942 his Panzer divisions rolled forward in his supreme effort to conquer Egypt and punch through Palestine to join the Wehrmacht forces from Russia, the intercepted American messages again brought him information of the highest importance. They first told him that the British were planning to anchor their defense line on Mersa Matruh, a town on the Mediterranean coast about 200 miles west of Alexandria; then, when Auchinleck decided that this position was untenable, the intercepts kept Rommel up to date with the British changes of mind.

But even Rommel could not do much without gasoline for his tanks and troop-carriers, and of this he never had enough. The thorn in his side was Malta. This tough little island, a British bastion lying in the Mediterranean between Sicily and the Axis bases in North Africa, served as the base from which Allied ships, planes, and submarines wreaked havoc on Axis convoys carrying men and supplies to Rommel. Thus Germany and Italy sought to batter it into submission with air raids night and day, while England sought to strengthen and arm it by driving convoys through to her port of Valletta. When the Axis supply line was flowing freely, Rommel scored one victory after another; when the Allies choked off his supply line and his tanks thirsted for petrol, Rommel's mobility in this highly fluid war of movement was seriously restricted, giving the Allies a considerable advantage.

Hence in June of 1942 the British determined to make a large-scale attempt to relieve Malta. They planned to pass convoys through from the east and from the west simultaneously, thus preventing the Axis from concentrating all its might on either movement. To paralyze Italian surface forces, Britain heavily bombed the Taranto naval base, and to minimize Axis air attacks on the convoys, the British planned to destroy Axis airplanes just before the convoys sailed. This they would accomplish by bombing, by swift strikes of motorized forces on airfields near the front, and by sabotage from commandos parachuted onto other airfields deeper within the German lines. Fellers, who was in close touch with the situation, knew of these plans, and on June 11—the day the eastern half of the convoy sailed from Alexandria—he drafted message No. 11119:

Nights of June 12th June 13th British sabotage units plan simultaneous sticker bomb attacks against aircraft on 9 Axis airdromes. Plans to reach objectives by parachutes and long range desert patrol.

This method of attack offers tremendous possibility for destruction, risk is slight compared with possible gains. If attacks succeed British should be prepared to make immediate use all R.A.F. [Royal Air Force] to support co-ordinating attacks by army.

Today British making heavy troop movement from Syria into Lybia.

Fellers

He encoded it and filed it with the Egyptian Telegraph Company in Cairo for radio transmission to MILID WASH. The O.K.W. intercept station at Lauf snatched it from the ether at about 8 a.m. June 12. By 9 a cryptanalyst was working on it to strip the superencipherment; by 10 it had been decrypted; by 11:30 Rommel had it in plenty of time to warn his airfields. On the night of the 13th, as expected, commandos dropped from the sky and strike forces roared in from the east.

The waiting German and Italian forces massacred them. The carefully planned operation failed almost completely. At the three North African airports of Martuba, El Fetejak, and Barce, not a plane was touched; at the K2 and K3 airfields, the British succeeded only in slightly damaging eight craft, all of them repairable in a few days. At three other airfields (Benina in North Africa and Heraklion and Castelli in Crete), where the warnings were either not received or ignored, the British destroyed a total of 18 planes and burned two hangars.

Next day, airplanes that had been saved from destruction by the timely warning delivered heavy attacks upon the convoy from Alexandria, sinking three destroyers and two merchant ships. A U-boat got a heavy cruiser, and when heavy Italian forces sortied from Taranto, the convoy turned back under this threat and the entire operation failed. "The approach to Malta from the eastward remained sealed, and no convoy again attempted this passage until November," wrote Churchill. "Thus, in spite of our greatest efforts, only two supply ships out of seventeen got through, and the crisis in the island continued." And Rommel's pipeline remained open.

With his gasoline supplies assured, at least temporarily, the Desert Fox swept forward in the onslaught he had begun on the moonlit night of May 26–27. Complementing the strategic intelligence that the Fellers intercepts were providing was the tactical intelligence from his highly efficient Fernmeldeaufklärung Company under Captain Alfred Seeböhm. This mobile outfit tuned into every British 8th Army radio station, picked up every scrap of chat, ascertained troop and tank concentrations and movements by direction-finding, learned which units were where by analyzing call-signs, studied British cryptograms, and in general provided Rommel with much of the raw data by which he could sniff out the enemy's intentions.

During the drive to isolate Tobruk, for instance, the Fernmeldeaufklärung

Company overheard a radiotelephone conversation in clear at 10:30 a.m. June 16, 1942, between the 29th Indian Brigade and the 7th Armored Division. From this it appeared that the garrison of the El Adem box, or strong point, intended to attack the Germans that night. The information was passed to Rommel and his intrepid 90th Light Division, who attacked at once, catching the British so off balance that instead of their pummeling the Germans, Rommel captured El Adem. This enabled him to surround and isolate Tobruk, which unexpectedly capitulated on the 20th, allowing enormous quantities of stores to fall into German hands and giving the daring Panzer leader his opportunity to strike immediately for Suez. It was aid of this sort that prompted Rommel's intelligence officer to call Seeböhm's Fernmeldeaufklärung Company "a very important factor in Rommel's victories." The company could also have independently read the Fellers messages with a furnished copy of the BLACK code to save time in getting the information to Rommel.

On July 10, the swirling desert warfare brought the Afrika Korps staff headquarters directly into the path of a British armored thrust. In a brief, fierce spurt of action, the brilliant Seeböhm was killed and most of his unit wiped out or captured. Many of their records fell into British hands. This loss deprived the company's replacements of a great deal of necessary information, and at the same time enabled the British to correct many radio-security mistakes. Rommel thus lost the microscope that scrutinized the enemy lines and presented to him so many bits of information.

At about the same time he lost his telescope. The United States appears to have had some suspicion of the leak earlier in the spring, when two officers came out from Washington to check on Fellers' security measures. They cleared him, and perhaps this lulled their fears until new information reached the Allies. Apparently a prisoner of war told the British of the intercepts, and the British, who had themselves broken the BLACK code and its superencipherment, using it to read other traffic, now began to pick up Fellers' messages within an hour after he filed them. After ten days of studying his "long, detailed, and extremely pessimistic" reports, they notified American authorities late in June of the leak and perhaps of Fellers' attitude. Fellers himself was never told of the German solutions, but was recalled to Washington, returning in July.* Later messages from Cairo still contained some noteworthy observations but no broad view of the situation. And when the new military attaché there began using the M-138 strip cipher, which defied all Axis attempts at solution, it cut Rommel off from the strategic intelligence on which he had so long depended.

The loss occurred just as he was crossing the frontier into Egypt and seemed to have the Pyramids and victory almost within his grasp. The British

---

* Later in 1942 he was awarded the Distinguished Service Medal for his work as military attaché, which "contributed materially to the tactical and technical development of our Armed Forces." The citation also stated that "His reports to the War Department were models of clarity and accuracy."

8th Army fell back to its fortified positions at El Alamein, and on July 2 Auchinleck jabbed out with the first of a series of counterattacks. Rommel, deprived of his most valuable source of information, could no longer take the expeditious measures for defense and offense that he was previously enabled to. On July 4, he reported that he was going over to the defensive. Meanwhile, Britain succeeded in reinforcing Malta, and attacks from there pinched the Axis pipeline. Rommel clamored in vain for fuel.

At the same time, the 8th Army built up a powerful force in secrecy, and concealed not only the date but the direction of its main thrust. Two divisions arrived with 240 guns and 150 tanks. In the old days, the Afrika Korps would have learned of it from Fellers' messages; this time they never knew the two were there. The British had profited from their capture of the Fernmeldeaufklärung files to institute an improved call-sign procedure, tauten cryptographic discipline forward of divisional headquarters, introduce radiotelephone codes, impose rigid wireless silence on reserve formations, pad out real messages with dummy traffic, and create an entire fake signals network in the southern sector. The new Fernmeldeaufklärung staff had neither the talent nor the experience to penetrate these disguises and sift the true from the false. The Germans, who had been used to the constant flow of information from Seeböhm's men, had to depend almost exclusively upon air reconnaissance, without any radio-intelligence corrective. And camouflage fooled it. Hundreds of tanks and guns were hidden beneath dummy trucks; large supply depots were created so slowly in the south that it looked as if they could not be ready for several months.

So when General Bernard Montgomery opened fire with a thousand cannon on the German positions at Alamein on October 23, it came as a complete surprise to the Afrika Korps. Rommel had been so certain that nothing would happen for a while that he had gone to Austria to convalesce. He flew back at once to take personal charge of the battle, but by the time he arrived it had already been lost. Hampered by shortages of oil, men, and armor, he could only shift his divisions about in desperate but futile attempts to recover. The defeat became a rout, and the Afrika Korps fled west across the desert, leaving a battlefield littered with hundreds of destroyed or useless tanks and troop-carriers. A few months later the Germans were driven out of Africa, then out of Crete, then up the boot of Italy—always retreating, never again advancing. The Battle of Alamein marked the turning of the Allied hinge of fate. "Before Alamein we never had a victory," Churchill said. "After Alamein we never had a defeat."

That change in fortune had revolved, to no small degree, upon cryptology.

15

DUEL IN THE ETHER: NEUTRALS AND ALLIES

THE BELLIGERENTS were not the only ones who availed themselves of the valuable intelligence of cryptanalysis. Vichy France, for example, installed about 50 cryptanalysts and clerks in a villa outside Lyons. Their success seems to have been limited. A newspaper story reported their 1941 failure to solve the systems of former French Minister of the Interior Georges Mandel, Churchill's friend, then in Vichy custody for his attempt to set up a resistance government in North Africa with himself as premier after the fall of France. At least part of their work was directed at the Free French and the underground, but they never communicated any of their results to the Germans. In fact, one member of the bureau, Charles Eyraud, later known as the author of a fine modern work on cryptanalysis, himself burned all the bureau's papers when the Germans occupied all of France.

Almost certainly the best of the nonbelligerent cryptanalysts, and perhaps one of the best in the war, was that of the precarious neutral, Sweden. At first she used codebreaking primarily to see whether Hitler planned to grant her the same sort of military protection that he so generously accorded Norway and Denmark. His preparation for occupying those two countries was one of the best-kept secrets of the war, and Sweden did not want to be caught napping. Later she used the intelligence to keep abreast of a variety of political events.

Except for a brief interlude back about the turn of the century, when R. Torpadie so impressed the Swedish authorities by solving a nomenclator of 1632 for a historical study that they commissioned him to set up a cryptologic bureau called Room 100, Swedish cryptology got its real start with Yves Gyldén. His father, Olof, the head of the Royal Naval School, had been financially interested in Arvid Damm's cipher machines. Yves, who got his un-Swedish first name from his French mother, became cryptologically interested and subjected them to every possible cryptanalytic test. The interest thus kindled in cryptology remained with him throughout a business career with the pharmaceutical firm of Astra, founded by his grandfather. In 1931, a tall, grave man of 36, Gyldén published his *Chifferbyråernas insatser i världskriget till lands*, a keen, perceptive study of World War I cryptology and its effects. Its 139 pages were later translated into English by the U.S. Army Signal Corps as *The Contributions of the Cryptographic Bureaus in the World War*, and portions were published in the *Revue Militaire Française*. This book demolished the lingering myth of chamber analysis, demonstrated the crucial role of errors and of torrents of ciphertext, and generally crystallized the lessons of World War I and catalyzed the evolution of the cryptology of today.

Five years after the influential little book was published, Sweden set up a cryptologic bureau. It was headed by Colonel C. G. Warburg, a gentleman who had fallen off a horse, broken both arms and legs, and needed a sinecure. He proved as incompetent in cryptology as in equitation, and was replaced by a naval officer who won the respect of the experts who later served under him. During the late 1930s Gyldén gave many talks on cryptanalysis to Swedes. He also sowed the seeds of a valuable cooperation with the other Scandinavian countries when he lectured in Oslo and stimulated a Captain Rocher-Lund to set up Norway's first cryptologic office. In 1939, during a 12-hour war game, Gyldén headed the cryptanalytical office that solved 38 of the 56 rather simple cryptograms transmitted by the "invaders." Sweden's preparations extended to recruiting talks at Uppsala University, where coeds were entertained with the intrigues of cryptology and sold on the idea that they could become good codebreakers. Other personnel were drawn from the winners of cipher-solving contests which the cryptanalysts got the newspapers to run.

When war broke out, the Swedish cryptanalysts numbered 22. All were paid the magnificent sum of half a crown a day (raised later by stages to two crowns), as a result of which most of them engaged in a kind of part-time cryptanalysis—working for the government in the morning and at regular jobs to get money to live on in the afternoon. They were installed first in the Gray House, Sweden's Defense Ministry building, and afterwards in an old house at Carlaplan 4, since demolished and replaced by Sveriges Radio; they finally settled down in an old, drafty, noncentrally-heated apartment house at Styrmans-gatan 2. (A branch was also established in a modern apartment house in Strandvagen in 1943.)

In 1940 the cryptanalysts were divided by language, though some of the mathematicians shifted from group to group. The four units were: No. 1, for Romance languages, primarily French and Italian, headed by Gyldén, who had spent ten years in France and was fluent in that language; No. 2, for German, in which one of the brightest workers was Carl-Otto Segerdahl, a young mathematician; No. 3, for English, which attacked American and British systems and was headed by Dr. Olof von Feilitzen, 32, a librarian whose English is better than that of many Americans; No. 4, for Russian, headed by Dr. Arne Beurling, 35, a big, slow-talking, quietly handsome professor of mathematics at Uppsala University, who in 1952 became a member of the Institute for Advanced Study at Princeton. Beurling, one of the war's finest cryptanalysts, also determined the unknown ciphers of other countries and made the initial breaks. Gyldén, as the founder, was a kind of first among equals; he also taught new recruits. These came in at such a pace that by the time he left in 1941 the group had grown to 500, and by the end of the war to 1,000.

Messages, too, poured in. Teletypewriters, cut directly into Swedish post-office circuits, duplicated messages sent over those wires. Norway, Denmark, and Finland forwarded their intercepts to Sweden, which had the only effective cryptanalytic center among them, and these messages enabled Sweden to make very fruitful comparisons between the same text enciphered in different keys. She paid her Nordic associates back with the information gained in the resultant cryptanalysis—sometimes with valuable results.

Early in 1940, just before the German occupation of Norway, Nazi agents there, who were concentrated in the German-Norwegian shipping lines and in the large fishing and fish-processing firms, were ordered to pass back information on ship movements and weather. They disguised the data as sales prices, offers, and tonnage reports on fishing, and transmitted by telephone and radio. But the Norwegian authorities had intercepted the telephone calls, which dealt with prices in a highly suspicious manner. They sent recordings to Sweden, where Segerdahl discovered that the five-digit "prices" actually represented the transposed and monalphabetically enciphered numbers of ships in *Lloyd's Register*. The solutions enabled Norway to break up at least one of the rings in February, though others continued to operate.

The Swedes not only used cryptology against foreign espionage, they sometimes used espionage against foreign cryptology. In one case, they tapped a telephone call between the Italian military attaché in Stockholm and his colleague in Oslo. The recording sounded absolutely unintelligible, and the Swedes at first thought that the Italians had used a telephone scrambler. When they determined that they had not, the recording was sent to the language department at Uppsala, where it was found to be a Sicilian dialect rendered incomprehensible by the attaché's over-liberal use of cursewords. Eventually the sense was sorted out, and the conversation proved to comprise the Stockholm attaché's explanations of how to use the military attaché code, which the Oslo man—who was railing at the idiots in Rome who would send him such a code—could not fathom. Between the explosions of the colorful Sicilian equivalents for "dunce" and "jackass" and still other expletives were references to operating procedure, meanings of specific codewords, and so on. Needless to say, it proved a great help to Gyldén in his Italian-code solutions.

The Swedes also obtained much help from their own Foreign Office in the form of diplomatic notes sent and received, reports of notes verbales, aides-mémoires of conversations with various ambassadors, and other memoranda. This is common practice in all countries, but the Swedish cryptanalysts carried it to a peak of perfection by using as their liaison man a former foreign minister. Rickard Sandler, 56, had served in that post from 1932 to 1939; he had also filled in as premier for 18 months in 1925 and 1926, and in 1934 had been elected president of the League of Nations Assembly. Spare and round-faced, Sandler had been bitten by the cryptology bug, and in 1943 he wrote a book on famous ciphers. But he proved inept as a cryptanalyst, unable to solve what the Swedes regarded as the simplest of practical problems—Norwegian one-part codes. However, he was a great success in making sure that the Foreign Office reported every scrap of information promptly to the cryptanalysts. So well did he have his contacts trained that the Foreign Office even reported the time of departure of an ambassador's car from the Foreign Office building. With this little datum, the cryptanalysts—knowing the message he had been given and estimating how long it would take the ambassador to drive to the embassy and have a message of that length encoded and sent to the telegraph office—could more easily pick out the cryptogram corresponding to that message from the embassy's daily file.

As usual, the Swedish cryptanalysts were greatly helped by lazy or stupid encoders. Clerks repeatedly violated the most elementary rules by failing to superencipher and forgetting to bisect messages. The worst bungler the Swedes came across was the German consul at Stavanger, whose numerous blunders became the vulnerable heel of many a German message. His name—almost too fittingly—was F. W. Achilles. The Swedes appreciated his help so much that they hung a large photograph of him in their office. "He was very fat and he looked like a gorilla," Segerdahl said. "I never met the man personally, but I considered him my best friend in the German diplomatic service!"

The Swedes also read messages in other German systems—a double transposition for the military attaché and two substitution systems for the troops. The latter gave them an unexpected peek into the sex habits of German soldiers. The Wehrmacht provided women from the Baltic states and concentration camps as prostitutes for the occupation forces in Norway, and the vessels were naturally awaited with great eagerness. Their arrivals and departures formed the subject of excited communication between units, and not infrequently a radioman in a port from which a ship had just sailed would recommend one of the girls to a fellow signalman in the port to which the ship was headed. The reasons were sometimes quite specific, and the Swedes came to think that they knew the girls almost as well by cryptologic means as the soldiers did by carnal.

But errors, circular messages, and all the other aids would not have helped the Swedes much if they were not as clever as they were. They became so attuned to French procedure in regard to a multiplicity of codes—at one time the French had eleven in simultaneous use—that they could tell when the French regarded them as compromised (after about four years) and began sending material in them that they wanted others to read. Usually this tried to implant the idea that the French were acting only out of the most moral considerations in a given situation, probably to distract attention from their real motives. Many phrases from the messages in these compromised codes later showed up in the French Yellow Books, the official governmental statements of their positions. The Swedes also solved an American-British code in which U-boat warnings were transmitted—probably the same that Germany's B-Dienst read—and thus got a free ride in safeguarding their own merchantmen.

Quite possibly the finest feat of cryptanalysis performed by the Swedes, and the most far-reaching, was Arne Beurling's solution of the German Siemens machine. Since German messages passed over Swedish wires just as German soldiers passed over Swedish rails, both the Wehrmacht in Norway and the German embassy in Stockholm took advantage of the machine's on-line capabilities to wire messages directly to Berlin. The German Foreign Office called the machine the Geheimschreiber ("secret writer"). The teleprinters in the Swedish cryptanalytic bureau rapped out the German correspondence, and it was given to Beurling for an attempt at solution.

He observed at once that the ciphertext consisted of the 26 letters and six digits, a total of 32 characters, or 2^5. This suggested a cipher based on a teletypewriter to him, since he knew that teletypewriters used a five-hole punched tape. That was about all he knew, though, and he had to get a book on them to see how they worked. His studies—perhaps aided by an examination of patents—led him to the conclusion that a machine based on the Baudot code would encipher by shifting the positions of the five contacts, that each of these positions would very likely be controlled by a keywheel of its own, and that the number of control pins on the circumference of these wheels would vary from wheel to wheel to make the period as long as possible.

Since the key probably changed daily, Beurling selected the traffic for a single day, May 25, 1940, to work on. It covered the equivalent of two large sheets of paper. His analysis soon showed that his preliminary suppositions were correct, except that the substitution of the Baudot pulses was followed by a transposition. Very often the transposition had no effect. If, for example, pulses 1 and 2 were the same, the transposition of 1, 2, 3, 4, 5 into 2, 1, 3, 4, 5 would leave the character unchanged. Beurling took full advantage of these peculiarities to reconstruct the mechanism. He checked his work with new data from the traffic of May 27, found it was correct, and within two weeks of undertaking the job had solved the cipher. A Swedish mechanic constructed an apparatus to Beurling's specifications, and though it looked monstrous and made a terrific racket, it printed out the German messages that the Swedes wanted to read.

To recover the daily keys, the cryptanalysts would work through the night, and in the morning, when the Swedish commander, Lieutenant General Olov Thornell, came in to ask, "What's the news from the Germans today?" they were usually able to tell him. Twice when the Germans made threatening moves with their troops in Norway toward Sweden, Swedish troops, alerted by cryptanalyzed messages, moved swiftly into position and blocked the Germans. Their commander, General Niklaus von Falkenhorst, later extended congratulations to Thornell on the brilliance of his tactics. Thornell passed the felicitations on to the cryptanalysts.

In the spring of 1941, the Swedes cryptanalyzed other German military messages that, put together, spelled an invasion of Russia between June 20 and 25. Erik Bohemann, secretary general of the Swedish Foreign Office, passed the information to Sir Stafford Cripps, British ambassador to the Soviet Union, at a dinner in Stockholm while Cripps was passing through. This may not have come as news to Cripps, who may have known of the invasion from other sources, but it certainly reinforced any knowledge he had. Unfortunately, Stalin did not believe the British.

The dozens of diplomatic messages that clattered out of the Beurling mechanism told the Swedish Foreign Office what the Germans were really doing and thinking. They gave Foreign Minister Christian Günther advance warning of diplomatic notes that the German embassy was ordered to submit to him. The cryptanalysts tell a story that, after reading a particularly demanding note, they took the unusual step of notifying Günther of its contents by telephone, which they rarely used. (Later they sent it over by the regular messenger, who wore two shoulder holsters.) Günther promptly went on a "hunting trip," and the German diplomat could not serve his demand until after the weekend. By then the Swedes had formulated a policy that enabled them to tell the Germans, with suitable regret, that they were unable to fulfill the requests.

And so Sweden's cryptanalysts helped her navigate the perilous waters of neutrality while all about her raged the war.

Great Britain's main cryptanalytic agency lay within her Foreign Office, which had taken over the personnel of the Admiralty's Room 40 at the end of World War I. The Reverend William Montgomery, one of the solvers of the Zimmermann telegram, for example, joined the Foreign Office. Early in the 1920s, in a circular urging its diplomats to be more careful in the use of their codes, the Foreign Office told them that it was spending £12,000 a year, or almost $60,000, both in keeping British codes secret and in solving those of foreign governments, and that carelessness in handling codes was wasting much of this (or at least much of the part spent for British cryptography). The usual legends circulated among the diplomats about their code experts, some of whom had "made a life-long study of the work." One story credited one of these wizards with solving a Turkish code during the war in less than five months, though he himself could not speak Turkish and had had to call in experts in the language to translate the messages. The Foreign Office reportedly considered no code as fully secret after it had been used for six months; consequently it changed all highly confidential codes every four months.

In 1939, the Foreign Office moved what it euphemistically called its Department of Communications to Bletchley Park, an estate and mansion in Bletchley, a town in Buckinghamshire about 50 miles northwest of London. It is far and away the most history-redolent black chamber of all. The British, of course, trace the land from a Roman encampment, through its award by William the Conquerer to Bishop Geoffrey of Constance for services rendered at the Battle of Hastings, down on through the ownership of various lords (most notably the two George Villierses, first and second dukes of Buckingham) and rich men of decreasing interest. A mansion was first built on the land in the 1870s and added to repeatedly; the Foreign Office, finding this too small, added many buildings, including a cafeteria and a large hall. Eventually 7,000 worked and trained there, including members of the armed services.

Britain urges cryptographic discipline

The War Office expanded its M.I. 1(b), the cryptanalytic agency started in World War I under Major Hay, to M.I. 8—the same name, coincidentally, as that held by Yardley's organization. The Admiralty and the Air Ministry presumably had cryptologic agencies of their own. One of the first victories of the Admiralty's unit was, surprisingly, in the domain of cryptography.

Since the beginning of the war, Admiralty secret communications had been read by the B-Dienst, with such disastrous results as the loss of Norway almost by default. The Germans continued to listen in to Admiralty messages during the critical summer of 1940 as Hitler prepared for Operation SEALION— his invasion of England. The cryptanalytic intelligence had long been entering into operational planning, and the Oberkommando der Kriegsmarine had come to depend on it. Suddenly, on August 20, as all England was bracing itself in its finest hour, and the sky above was streaked with contrails as the few earned their tribute from the many, the Admiralty, which had finally tumbled to the German cryptanalysis, changed its codes and ciphers. O.K.M. went deaf. The abrupt cutting off of quantities of information about British plans and dispositions caused, a German said, "a great setback for German naval strategy." No longer could German vessels strike out at the greater British forces with foreknowledge or move deftly out of their way. British sea power rapidly gained its normal ascendancy. English ships shelled the invasion fleet in Channel ports. Air reconnaissance alone could not tell the Germans enough. The O.K.M., never very warm for SEALION, chilled still further. Eventually its coolness spread throughout O.K.W., and then to Hitler. It contributed to his ultimate decision to postpone SEALION indefinitely, and hence forever.

All of Britain's cryptologic work seems to have been coordinated by the

A British naval officer demonstrates the proper codebook security for when capture threatens

Foreign Office's Department of Communications, which apparently handled strategic and primary cryptosystem solutions. All over the world, Britain had about 30,000 persons in communications intelligence. Deputy director of the Department of Communications was a man who had already made a mark in the world by his cryptanalytic efforts. He was Nigel de Grey, who in 1917 had solved the Zimmermann telegram.

The department turned out solutions at a fairly rapid rate. On November 21, 1941, a Japanese diplomatic solution was given number 097975; on December 12, another Japanese diplomatic solution was numbered 098846; —indicating almost 300 solutions a week at that time (not Japanese alone, of course). A typical distribution of these solutions would send three copies each to the director of the department, the Foreign Office, and the War Office, two to the India Office, and one each to the Admiralty, the Air Ministry, the Colonial Office, the Dominion Office, M.I. 5 (counterintelligence), and Sir

Edward Bridges, secretary to the Cabinet. The appearance of Bridges' name on the list suggests that some of the British intercepts may have been read aloud at Cabinet meetings. In addition, Churchill, on August 5, 1940, ordered that a daily selection of original intelligence documents be submitted to him personally "in their original form," which almost certainly included intercepts. Much of the cryptanalytic output must have gone to the Joint Intelligence Committee, which evaluated all intelligence. It was always chaired by a Foreign Office representative, who was Victor F. W. Cavendish-Bentinck throughout most of the war, and included the directors of military, naval, and air intelligence.

The intelligence from these solutions went also to the United States, but so closely did Britain guard her cryptanalytic capabilities that for more than a year she would give the United States information based on the cryptanalyses but would not name the source. In January, 1941, however, a four-man American cryptanalytic mission accompanied a PURPLE machine to England to establish technical cooperation with British cryptanalysts. Britain had not cracked the PURPLE machine, but they had more in the way of cryptanalyzed intercepts than the United States, and this was the quid pro quo. This cooperation between the two English-speaking nations in the most sensitive of areas tells the depths of their friendship. The American Signal Intelligence Service and OP-20-G radioed the PURPLE keys to London daily. Cooperation extended to the small Australian communications-intelligence unit and to the unit at Singapore, and Canada assisted in making sure that all got all Japanese intercepts.

Some of the most important British communications intelligence resulted, however, not from the scribblings and quiet cogitations of reticent cryptanalysts, but from the explosive sexual charms of a British secret agent in America. Her unlocking of several hearts gave Britain access to vast treasuries of intelligence. She was an American, the daughter of a Marine Corps Major. Her real name was Amy Elizabeth Thorpe but she was known in espionage by her codename, CYNTHIA. She had had her first sexual experience at 14, and was pregnant when, at 19, she married a junior British diplomat, whom she later divorced; at the start of her espionage work she had just turned 30. A moderately attractive blond, tall and with prominent features, soft-voiced, a good listener, and with a sensuality that was indefinable but very much present, she served British Security Coordination, Britain's intelligence organization in the United States, not for money, but for thrills.

In the winter of 1940–1941, B.S.C. assigned CYNTHIA the task of obtaining the Italian naval cryptosystem. She managed an introduction to the Italian naval attaché in the embassy at Washington, Admiral Alberto Lais. Within a few weeks he was infatuated. When she was certain of her power over him, she told him directly that she wanted the naval code. Lais, despite his age and experience, agreed without any protest to betray his country for a woman. He arranged for her to meet his cipher clerk, who produced the codebook (and, presumably, any superencipherment tables for it) for a fee. It was promptly photostated and returned to the safe; the photostats went to London.

A few months after the English cryptanalysts received them, CYNTHIA's feat paid off. As Churchill obliquely put it, "Towards the end of March [1941] it was evident that a major movement of the Italian Fleet, probably towards the Aegean, was impending." Admiral Cunningham, commanding in the Mediterranean, whose cryptanalytic unit probably had been given copies of the Italian code and superencipherment, sensed by March 25 the Italian sortie against British convoys carrying troops to aid Greece. Two days later he slipped out of Alexandria after dark and set his course so foresightedly that at dawn a scouting plane contacted the enemy squadron. Though the Italians were also reading Cunningham's messages and so took action that increased the difficulty of his attack, he destroyed the cruisers *Pola*, *Fiume*, and *Zara*, and damaged the battleship *Vittorio Veneto* in the Battle of Cape Matapan. The victory, Churchill said, "disposed of all challenge to British naval mastery in the Eastern Mediterranean at this critical time."

A few days later, the State Department declared Lais persona non grata as a result of sabotage plans that he had disclosed to CYNTHIA, who had maintained profitable contact with him. At dockside, he spent his last few minutes with CYNTHIA, ignoring his weeping family. His departure enabled her to turn to her next assignment, at the embassy of Vichy France.

She gained entrance by posing as a newspaperwoman. During the wait to interview the ambassador, she chatted for an hour with the press attaché, Captain Charles Brousse—and captivated him. By July of 1941, after allowing him to seduce her, she "confided" that she was an American agent and urged him to work for the real France against the Laval government. Soon she was getting a plaintext copy of every incoming and outgoing telegram of the embassy, plus a daily report that Brousse wrote to fill in the missing details.

The plaintext undoubtedly enabled the British to reconstruct French diplomatic codes, if they had not already done so.* But in March of 1942, London asked British Security Coordination to obtain the French naval code, which was used both by naval attachés and fleet commanders. This might have stemmed ultimately from an order by Churchill himself. He was then mounting a force to seize French-owned Madagascar to keep it from becoming a Japanese submarine base and he feared that Vichy might reinforce the island from Dakar just on the possibility that England might attempt such a seizure. "I therefore asked for extreme vigilance about any convoys or

---

* The British also read Spanish diplomatic traffic between Washington and Madrid from early 1942 to the end of the war, thanks to B.S.C.'s photographing of Spain's diplomatic code. This it accomplished with the help of a Basque leader who had exiled himself after the Falangist victory, and a Basque janitor and an anti-Franco typist at the Spanish embassy in Washington. B.S.C. also photographed Spanish codebooks in Caracas in October, 1942.

shipping which might pass from Dakar to the island, toward which our forces were already about to start," he wrote. Supervision of Vichy naval signals constituted, of course, one aspect of this vigilance.

CYNTHIA first asked her lover to get the code for her, but he replied that it was an impossible task, since only the chief of the code room, one Benoit, and his assistant had access to that tightly guarded sanctuary. CYNTHIA approached them, but failed with both.

Undaunted, she switched tactics. She and Brousse—who was now totally infatuated and willing to assist her in any of her plans—arrived late one night at the embassy. They explained as tactfully as possible to the watchman the difficulty of obtaining hotel rooms in wartime Washington and, smoothing his qualms with a tip, went in to spend the night on a divan on the first floor. They repeated this several times, until the watchman became used to it. One night in June, 1942, they clambered out of their taxicab in festive mood with a bottle of champagne, which they invited the watchman to share. He was happy to do so. A few minutes later, he had sunk into a drugged slumber. The "cab driver," an expert locksmith working for B.S.C., worked three hours and discovered the combination of the safe in the code room. But he did not have enough time to take the codebooks for photostating, and CYNTHIA and Brousse had to return two nights later.

It would be almost impossible to drug the watchman again; and furthermore it was inadvisable, for CYNTHIA felt that he was growing mistrustful of their repeated visits. She sensed that he would look in on them that evening, and so she prepared a counterstratagem that would allay his suspicions. When, as expected, the watchman walked into the room twenty minutes later, she was totally nude. It was utterly convincing. The watchman retired in confusion and did not bother them again.

They let the locksmith in through a window; he removed the codebooks and their accompanying tables of encipherment and handed them to another agent outside, who had them photostated in a nearby house by other B.S.C. operatives. By 4 a.m. they were back in their safe with no sign that they had ever been abstracted; 24 hours later the photostats reached England.

It was by then too late to help with the capture of Madagascar, which had gone off without a hitch the previous month. But plans were now afoot for the Allied landing in North Africa, and the photostated code helped keep the Anglo-American forces informed of the movement—or, rather, nonmovement—of the units of the Vichy French fleet at Toulon, Casablanca, and Alexandria during the invasion. Thus was England once again helped by a Lady Godiva.

No such dramatic feats were required by the British or by anyone else to read American diplomatic codes. The cryptanalysts who worked on them did not even have to furrow their brows excessively. For these codes of a great power were, from before World War I to the middle of World War II, as puny as those of many smaller nations. The United States must have been the laughingstock of every cryptanalyst in the world. And during World War I, the twenties, and the thirties, American diplomacy must have been conducted largely in an international goldfish bowl.

During that period, the Department of State entrusted its code compilation to the chief of its Bureau of Indexes and Archives, later the Division of Communications and Records, which handled both the code-making and the coding. For nearly all those years, the post was held by David A. Salmon, a career employee whose knowledge of cryptology was limited to what he had learned on the job.

He inherited from his predecessor, John R. Buck, the practice of designating American diplomatic codes by the color of their binding. Thus, since before World War I, the United States had had a RED and a BLUE code, both using five-figure groups. The RED was the older of the two, and State had given the Navy some copies of it for communication at outposts between diplomats and naval officers. In 1912, soon after Woodrow Wilson took office, the President's Commission on Economy and Efficiency asked the State, War, and Navy departments to consider a standard interdepartmental code and "better and less expensive methods of enciphering cablegrams." The RED code had by then become, in Salmon's unconscious pun, an "open book." Nearly a year later, the three departments finally agreed to use, as an emergency cryptosystem—the Vigenère! They knew it in a slightly different arrangement, called the Larrabee, in which the plaintext alphabet was repeated above each ciphertext alphabet and the keyletter was printed in large type at the left. Cryptographically, however, it was identical with the system that Kasiski had demolished half a century before. Not only did they merely contemplate using the system, which was bad enough; they actually did use it. And making things as easy as possible for foreign cryptanalysts were the short keywords: State used PEKIN and POKES in 1917.

Even though the alphabet card on which the Larrabee was sent to American diplomatic and consular offices, with instructions to paste it inside the cover of departmental codebooks, would not help much in solution, one nation was taking no chances. Vice Consul General Alfred V. Smith wrote on September 13, 1913: "In reference to Circular Instruction 'Larrabee Cipher' of March 8, 1913, received at this office on April 3rd last, I have the honor to inform the Department that the 'Larrabee Cipher Code' referred to in the above instruction as being 'transmitted herewith,' was not to be found in the envelope." Smith was in charge of the consulate general at Moscow.

In October it was learned that there were no funds available for the proposed interdepartmental code, and so the United States government persisted in the amazing cryptographic imbecility of using the Larrabee throughout World War I. For strictly diplomatic messages, State continued to use RED and BLUE, relying increasingly on the latter as the former declined in security. In 1915, Mexicans somehow obtained the RED code at Vera Cruz. Across the

Atlantic, the American minister to Rumania, a former politician, found it easier to keep his one copy under his mattress than to fiddle with the safe-combination. It disappeared one day, reportedly finding its way to St. Petersburg. The minister never troubled to report this loss. He solved the potentially embarrassing problem of not being able to read incoming messages by letting the relatively light coded traffic pile up, then hopping a train to visit the embassy in Vienna, where he decoded the messages which, he said, had arrived just as he was leaving. At the same time he composed and encoded his replies. When the war came, however, traffic increased, the artifice no longer applied, and he admitted his dereliction and returned to politics.

The need for security penetrated the departmental bureaucracy and in 1914 it instituted a "special cipher," probably a superencipherment of the existing codes. The London embassy gleefully hailed it as a success and an ensurer of secrecy. It was probably only a stopgap until the State Department could compile and place in service a new code—the GREEN. This one-part code used five-letter codegroups of the form CUCUC (C = consonant and U = vowel); thus *department* was FYTIG, *message* was MIHAK, *secured from* was PEDEK, *secured the*, PEDIV.

Nevertheless, by the time the United States entered the war, every major European power must have had copies of one or more American diplomatic codes. Foreign employees had the run of the embassies, and it would have been little trouble for them to get hold of the books. (One of the first German spies arrested was the clerk to the commandant at Pearl Harbor, who had access to the Navy's most secret code.) The Germans even returned a State Department codebook that had been used by the American consulate in Leipzig. If England's Room 40 could solve German two-part codes, it could certainly read the simpler American ones, and in fact rumors that Britain was doing so even reached the newspapers. During the war, the London embassy reported that German authorities in Spain obtained a copy of an American cablegram to Valencia, radioed the codetext to Germany, and promptly got back the plaintext. The State Department attempted to counter such embarrassments by enciphering the GREEN code with a key that changed monthly and by producing a new code ("I never realized until now what an arduous task it is to prepare a wholly new cipher," sighed Under Secretary William Phillips.)

In 1919, the United States, which Will Rogers said never lost a war nor won a peace, may have been assisted in losing the current peace by its cryptographic practices. The American Commission to Negotiate Peace furnished its field agents, who reported to it on the conditions and aspirations of the little peoples of Europe, with a publicly available commercial code, the *Universal Pocket Code*! No doubt the French cryptanalysts were pleased to see their work thus facilitated.

The new code that Phillips had sighed over was the GRAY code, destined to become the best known and longest lived of American diplomatic codes. In theory it was a confidential code: when a telegram from Mexico reported a rumor that that country had obtained an American code (not the same as the RED stolen earlier), the department replied that GRAY could be used for confidential messages. But a truer picture might be that drawn by former code clerk James Thurber, who served with the peace mission:

> All our code books except one were quaint transparencies dating back to the time when Hamilton Fish was Secretary of State under President Grant, and they were intended to save words and cut telegraph costs, not to fool anybody. The new code book had been put together so hastily that the word "America" was left out, and code groups so closely paralleled true readings that LOVVE, for example, was the symbol for "love."
>
> Whatever slight illusion of secrecy we code clerks may have had was dispelled one day by a dour gentleman who announced that the Germans had all our codes. It was said that the Germans now and then got messages through to Washington taunting us about our childish ciphers, and suggesting on one occasion that our clumsy device of combining two codes, in a desperate effort at deception, would have been a little harder if we had used two other codes, which they named. This may have been rumor or legend, like the story, current at the time, that six of our code books were missing and that a seventh, neatly wrapped, firmly tied, and accompanied by a courteous note, had been returned to one or another of our embassies by the Japanese, either because they had finished with it or because they already had one.
>
> A system of deception as easy to see through as the passing attack of a grammar-school football team naturally produces a cat's-out-of-the-bag attitude. In enciphering messages in one code, in which the symbol for "quote" was (to make up a group) ZOXIL, we were permitted to use UNZOXIL for "unquote," an aid to perspicuity that gave us code clerks the depressing feeling that our tedious work was merely an exercise in block lettering. The Department may have comforted itself with the knowledge that even the most ingenious and complex codes could have been broken down by enemy cipher experts. Unzoxilation just made it a little easier for them.

So did the continued use of the Larrabee. In 1921 the Navy awoke to the danger. Commander Milo F. Draemel conferred with Salmon, and the two agreed that a double transposition cipher would afford sufficient security for the limited State-Navy communications. But not until almost a year later did the State Department finally distribute it to 16 legations and 59 consulates around the globe.

What also made the work of foreign cryptanalysts easy was America's continued use, year after year, of the old codes. The GRAY code especially became so familiar to American foreign service officers that when colleagues tendered a senior consul at Shanghai his retirement dinner late in the decade, he responded with a farewell speech in GRAY—which the old-timers followed with ease. By then, superenciphered codes called A-1 and B-1 had been introduced. In 1925, the chargé d'affaires at San Salvador, pointing out that the GRAY and the GREEN codes were too old to be secret but that they were still being used for confidential messages, suggested that the department mandate the A-1 for ordinary confidential messages and the newer B-1 for highly confidential ones. The department seems not to have adopted this sensible suggestion. Instead it continued to use what Herbert Yardley, then its quasi employee, bitterly and accurately called sixteenth-century codes.

From time to time Salmon's office would test a new system, as it did with the Hitt cipher machine that Friedman so promptly broke. But more often Salmon would send out—without even examining the system—a stock, smug reply to each of the dozens of proposals that poured in on him from inventors: "The Department is in receipt of your letter of the 25th instant making reference to the creation by you of a new code system and inquiring if there is a usage for such a code. I beg to inform you in reply that the codes and ciphers now in use are adequate to the present needs of this Department."

Why did the Department of State not introduce improved methods of cryptography—perhaps the Vernam machine or the one-time pad—at least for its more secret messages? Apparently nothing more than bureaucratic inertia, probably compounded with some budgetary tightness. As Yardley said: "There is only one indecipherable means of communication, and its adoption would require the Department to revolutionize its antiquated methods." His conference in the late 1920s with a high department official, who had summoned him to discuss the problem because the official had heard that Mexico was reading American code messages, ended on that note.

> Nothing less than an international scandal would wake up the government to the fact that the very basis of all successful diplomacy is safe and secret lines of communication. But my whole life had been devoted to destruction. I should like to leave a monument to constructive cryptography.
>
> As I walked through the wide high corridors on my way to the entrance, I mused how proud one might be to leave to the United States Government a method of communication that would insure the secrecy of her dispatches throughout the ages. Aside from this, of course, was professional pride. Then too it would be fun to laugh at foreign cryptographers as in my mind I saw them puzzling over our secret telegrams, striving in vain for a solution.
>
> But why dream? After all, weren't all diplomatic representatives just funny little characters on a stage, whispering, whispering, then yelling their secrets to the heavens as they put them on the cables!

American cablegrams certainly yelled. In 1929, Charles G. Dawes, ambassador to the Court of St. James's, found it necessary to wire the State Department: "Suggest telegrams contents of which under instruction are to be conveyed to the British Government should not be coded in such confidential code." In 1931, Stanley K. Hornbeck of the Division of Far Eastern Affairs minuted to Secretary of State Stimson: "Mr. Secretary: I have the feeling that it is altogether probable that the Japanese are 'breaking' every confidential telegram that goes to and from us, in Japan and in territory controlled by Japan. It is not impossible, but less likely, that the Chinese are doing the same thing. Whatever may be the facts, I feel that we should have the possibility constantly in mind." A few months later, as if in confirmation, the chargé d'affaires at Tokyo reported that the American consul general at Seoul, Korea, then a part of the Japanese Empire, had received new A-1 cipher tables with wax seals broken. By this time, the insecurity of American codes seemed almost to be taken for granted. "I could not help wondering," Ambassador to Japan W. Cameron Forbes cabled Stimson on February 16, 1932, "whether in view of the imperfection of our codes, this [aforementioned dispatch] might not be read off by the Chinese secret service people"—a reading which, he thought, "would immediately put the Chinese against the proposition."

This disquieting state of affairs remained pretty much in effect during the thirties. State basically continued to use the same old codes. Ambassadors still had to decode especially secret messages intended for them alone. For at least one, Harry F. Guggenheim in Cuba, the excitement of knowing that the message would be important mitigated the onerousness of the task. Under the prodding of President Roosevelt, who had learned to pay attention to communications security as an Assistant Secretary of the Navy in World War I, State produced several new codes, among them the BROWN. The BROWN was stolen from the American consulate at Zagreb by a gang of Ustachi bandits as a by-product of a safe-cracking raid, but it continued to be used elsewhere in the world. In addition, C-1 and D-1 codes had been added, each—like the A-1 and B-1—with its own tables for superencipherment. These tables served for irregular periods ranging from two to five months. They added slightly to the security of the codes but greatly to their cumbersomeness: during the Munich crisis, half the vice consuls in Berlin had to work in the code room.

Late in the 1930s, the department adapted as its most secret method of cryptography the system invented a century and a half earlier by the first Secretary of State, Thomas Jefferson. This was the strip cipher, the M-138, the flattened-out Jefferson wheel cypher–Bazeries cylinder, first constructed in strip form by Parker Hitt in 1914. Each M-138 set had 100 strips. In enciphering, 30 at a time were used, with the ciphertext being read off, not from one generatrix, but from two in groups of 15 letters each. So long as the strips were kept secret and were changed often enough, the strip system apparently secured important American diplomatic correspondence. State used it, for example, to encipher a triple priority message from Roosevelt to Churchill just after the Atlantic Conference.

President Roosevelt, however, distrusted State Department codes on principle. So when war broke out in Europe, he communicated with his ambassadors in London, Paris, and Moscow via Navy Department cryptosystems for "matters of utmost secrecy." This annoyed the State Department, which felt that diplomatic matters were being kept from it. "But," William C. Bullitt, ambassador to France, later wrote, "I should regret to have the impression prevail that this was due to a desire to conceal anything from the Secretary of State, Mr. Hull, for whom I always have had high respect. It was due to lack of security in the Department of State. The codes of the department were so antiquated that, in the opinion of the President, they had been broken by all the totalitarian powers." Admiral W. H. Standley, ambassador to Moscow, said that "It was also common gossip that the State Department codes were insecure." The American embassy in Madrid received its most secret instructions in a British code!

Both Bullitt and Standley also mentioned leaks in the State Department as another reason for using Navy codes. Leaks there were—and from the very heart of State's communications. On April 30, 1940, Hans Thomsen, Germany's chargé d'affaires at Washington, cabled home: "A reliable and tried confidential agent who is very friendly with the director of the code room of the State Department reports as follows after having seen the relevant telegraphic reports." On September 30, Thomsen relayed to Germany intelligence that the same reliable informant had obtained from a cablegram sent to Roosevelt by the American ambassador to Britain, Joseph P. Kennedy. On December 29, the German ambassador to Spain wired home about "a code telegram from Cordell Hull to the United States ambassador here on December 18, the text of which has become known to me." All these helped Germany in shaping her foreign policy. The message to Madrid, for example, showed that the Spanish Foreign Minister was lying to Germany when he insisted that Spain would not receive needed grain if she stayed neutral.

The worst of the leaks took place in London, where Tyler Kent, a bright, handsome, but twisted young man, worked in the code room of the American embassy. Convinced that a vast Jewish conspiracy was pushing the United States into an unwanted war, and that to help the enemy of the Jews was to help his own country, Kent took telegrams from the embassy and passed them to a pro-Nazi group. By various channels they reached Germany. The German ambassador in Italy wired home a report of Roosevelt's reply to Churchill's request for 50 destroyers only seven days after it was received in London. On May 20, however, Scotland Yard plugged the leak. It arrested members of the pro-Nazi group for espionage and, with State Department approval, searched Kent's rooms.

There police agents found copies of more than 1,500 embassy papers, many of them telegrams, as well as two newly made duplicate keys to the index bureau and the code room of the embassy. When the stunned ambassador asked him why he would betray his country this way, Kent explained that giving the documents to Germany would help keep America out of war. He was instantly dismissed, and then, having lost his diplomatic immunity, was arrested, tried, and convicted by the British for violating the Official Secrets Act and sentenced to seven years in prison.

But the damage had been done. "The removal of so large a number of documents from the Embassy premises," the State Department later declared, "compromised the whole confidential communications system of the United States, bringing into question the security of the secret ciphers." Kennedy said: "Because of his [Kent's] treachery, all diplomatic communications of the American diplomatic service were blacked-out at a most critical moment in history—during the days of Dunkirk and the fall of France. The blackout, which concerned the American embassies and missions throughout the world, lasted from two to six weeks until scores of special couriers had reached the embassies with new codes from Washington."

On the other side of the globe, meanwhile, poor American cryptography gave aid to a potential enemy and injured the cause of peace. Within the cable section of Japan's Foreign Ministry was hidden a small cryptanalytic group, the Ango Kenkyu Han ("Code Research Section"). About five of its members worked on English and American codes. Each morning a messenger from the Foreign Ministry (and others from the Army and Navy) picked up copies of foreign diplomatic telegrams from the Communications Ministry's censorship department. Of the main codes then in use by the American embassy—GRAY, BROWN, A-1, B-1, C-1, D-1, and M-138—the Ango Kenkyu Han could read three or four of the lower grade. Ambassador Joseph C. Grew may have inadvertently helped them. "One of the high officials of the Japanese Government wanted to send a secret message to our Government which they did not want the Japanese military to see and in passing this message on they asked me to please put it in our most secret code. I said of course I would do so." Even so, the Japanese failed to penetrate the M-138 and the higher-grade codes.

The nonsecrecy of the State Department codes inhibited negotiations with the moderates in Japan. Noted Grew in his diary on August 1, 1941: "Prince Konoye [the Japanese premier] knows that I would like to talk with him oftener, just as the President does with Admiral Nomura, but it is the fear of leakages and publicity which has prevented such interviews. It was indicated that any reports which our Embassy might send to Washington would of course become known to the Japanese authorities, although our informant said that he understood that we did have 'one confidential code' (highly significant, but I feel perfectly safe in the use of the one confidential code referred to)."

On December 6, 1941, President Roosevelt dispatched his personal appeal for peace to the Emperor of Japan. He sent it to the State Department accompanied by a handwritten note on White House stationery: "Dear Cordell Shoot this to Grew—I think can go in gray code—saves time—I don't mind if it gets picked up FDR." His message was delivered to the embassy in Tokyo ten hours after it had been received in the Communications Ministry in Tokyo, and it is interesting that Grew, though he did not know of Roosevelt's note, long thought that the use of the GRAY code had not saved but cost time because Japanese militarists had picked up the message, solved it, and deliberately detained it to frustrate any peace efforts. However, this was not so; the delay resulted from an embargo placed by the military on all incoming diplomatic messages.

Among the interested readers of coded American diplomatic messages was the Reich Foreign Minister. Pers z served him well. As early as 1925, it had

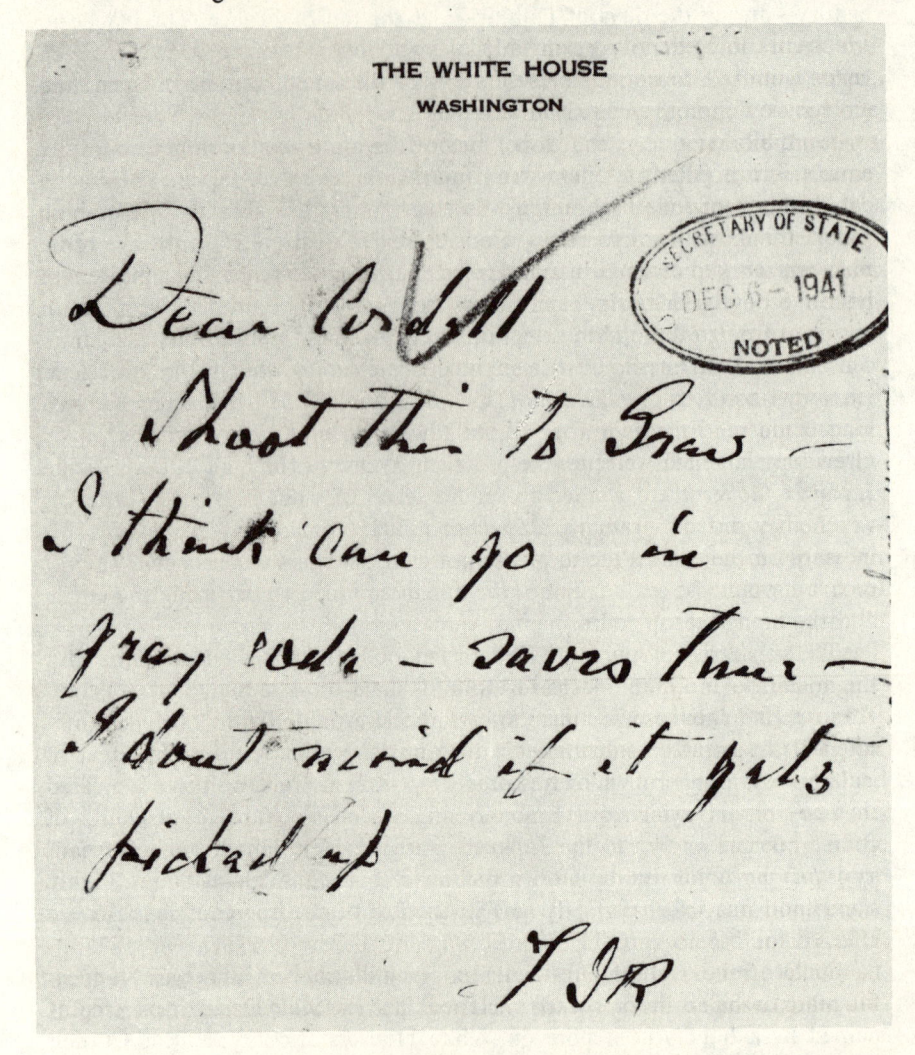

> **THE WHITE HOUSE**
> **WASHINGTON**
>
> *Dear Cordell*
>
> *Shoot this to Grew —*
> *I think can go in*
> *gray code — saves time —*
> *I don't mind if it gets*
> *picked up*
>
> *FDR*

President Roosevelt prescribes to the Secretary of State the code to be used to speed his personal appeal for peace to the Emperor of Japan the night before Pearl Harbor

studied the American system of superencipherment. The codewords were only of the CUCUC and CUCCU types; to encipher them, the code clerk split them into a single consonant and two CU or UC groups, then replaced these segments with substitutes from the appropriate tables. This superencipherment left the

Duel in the Ether: Neutrals and Allies 497

CUCUC and CUCCU configuration of the codegroup unchanged, and this regularity enabled the Pers z mathematicians to break first into this original system and, in 1940, into a modification of it. Ironically, changes of superencipherment within a message, intended to provide greater security, furnished the German cryptanalysts with isomorphic repetitions that helped them reconstitute the superencipherment substitution. With the superencipherment stripped off, the linguistic group solved a big 72,000-group code with not too much trouble. Dr. Hans-Kurt Müller was instrumental in this; he had an

```
Abschrift                    Geheime Reichssache

Von Algier nach Washington. 21.7.
An das Staatsdepartement in Washington: 338.

Dreifacher Vorrang Persönlich für den Stellvertretenden
Staatssekretär. Von Murphy. Unter Telegramm Nr. 184 vom
17.7. 22.00 Uhr.

    Ich sah vor einigen Minuten Weygand allein und un-
terrichte ihn von Ihrer Botschaft. Ich wiederholte sie in
der Übersetzung und erklärte, daß ich ermächtigt sei,
sie nur mündlich zu übermitteln. Nun war die erste Ge-
legenheit, mit ihm seit seiner Rückkehr von Marokko
Sonnabend abend zu sprechen.

    Weygand hörte mit dem größten Interesse zu. Seine
erste Bemerkung war ein Ausdruck offensichtlicher Freude
und Genugtuung über die persönlichen Höflichkeitsbezeu-
gungen des Präsidenten ihm gegenüber. Er sagte lächelnd,
```

Pers z solution of an encoded message of Robert Murphy to the State Department dealing with highly secret negotiations with General Weygand in North Africa in 1941

uncanny gift for seeing the outlines of the whole plaintext in the murk of the partial solutions. Miss Friedrichs assisted.

They were greatly helped in their work by their knowledge of the activities of diplomat Robert Murphy, who in 1941 and 1942 was in North Africa, handling delicate negotiations with the Vichy French and paving the way for the Allied invasion of North Africa. Murphy insisted upon using the State Department codes to preserve his autonomy, even though American officers in Eisenhower's command pointed out their insecurity. He was certain that the Germans had not broken his codes. In fact, however, the Pers z cryptanalysts had broken them enough to recognize the groups meaning *For Murphy* or *From Murphy* that recurred at the head of so many telegrams. "We knew what he was interested in, and this gave us clues," Miss Friedrichs said. These rapidly helped complete the solution of the big code. Murphy's communications so facilitated her work, she said, that when she saw him drive by one day after the war while she was interned in Marburg, "I wanted to stop him and shake his hand."

Thus, as early as August 12, 1941, the state secretary of the Foreign Office could hand to von Ribbentrop fully solved copies of Murphy's telegrams of July 21 and August 2. The first reported that Murphy had transmitted Roosevelt's views on French North Africa to General Maxime Weygand, commanding there. The second transmitted a Weygand aide's request for an American promise of military assistance. The Nazis knew Weygand was no friend of theirs, but it was not until they had what a Vichy source called "documentary proof" of his dealings with the United States that they forced Vichy to dismiss him. Thus the solution of an American diplomatic code cost the United States much valuable time and work that it was forced to recommence with the new leaders of French North Africa, and it may ultimately have prolonged the war and cost the lives of American soldiers who fought in that theater.

A year later, the still-continuing German reading of coded American dispatches endangered the work of Allen W. Dulles, nominally a diplomat attached to the Bern legation but actually chief American spymaster in Europe. Dulles, who had recently begun to plot with anti-Nazis in Germany to overthrow Hitler, was unusually sensitive to the possibility of broken codes. In his cables, he referred to agents by codenames, which he changed frequently. He called the conspirators planning to assassinate Hitler BREAKERS. In February of 1943, one of them, Hans Bernd Gisevius, an official in the German consulate at Zurich, told Dulles that Germany had broken one of the American codes. Producing a little black notebook, he recited the gist of numerous telegrams from Bern to Washington. "Fortunately," Dulles wrote, "it was not my own code and I had not used it for sending any operational messages, but as I was then short of code clerks I occasionally had fallen back on this particular code to send general political reports."

One of the messages that Gisevius read off had contained a fairly accurate portrait of the anti-German group in Italy. Even early in 1943, this was solidifying around Marshal Pietro Badoglio, who in July deposed Mussolini and formed a new anti-Fascist government, and around the prolific diarist Count Galeazzo Ciano, Mussolini's son-in-law and Foreign Minister. Gisevius told Dulles that the American telegram had been laid on Hitler's desk and then sent by the Führer to Mussolini with his compliments. A few days later Ciano was dismissed as Foreign Minister. "I never was able to discover," Dulles wrote, "whether this was coincidence or whether this cable was the cause."

After Gisevius' disclosure, Dulles, displaying great delicacy in intelligence operation, used the code "only for messages which we were quite willing or even anxious to have the Germans read, and over the months we discarded it entirely. To have stopped using it immediately would have told the Germans that we knew they had broken it." Gisevius had feared that the intelligence the Germans might have obtained from the cryptanalysis would spoil the anti-Hitler program. But Dulles convinced him that he took every precaution in handling this information. The incident actually strengthened their collaboration, which culminated in the bomb plot of July 20, 1944, in which Hitler narrowly escaped with his life.

Dulles thought that, after abandoning use of the broken code, "the Germans never succeeded in deciphering any of the messages I sent, and I had the satisfaction of knowing that no one who worked with me was ever jeopardized through deciphered telegrams. It was worrisome business, however, and I never put a cipher message on the air which gave specific facts about the underground without a feeling of apprehension." His apprehensions were justified. For although the Germans may not have solved his cryptograms, the Hungarian Army unit under Major Bibo had. It fed its information to the R.S.H.A. through Wilhelm Höttl, but no concrete anticonspirator results seem to have been achieved, perhaps because of Dulles' care in always using codenames.

During these midwar years, President Roosevelt, still distrusting State Department codes, continued to rely on naval cryptosystems for his most secret messages. He exchanged hundreds with Churchill, who, signing himself "Former Naval Person" in recollection of his having been First Lord of the Admiralty (and no doubt with Roosevelt's former assistant secretaryship of the Navy well in mind), said that "I sent my cables to the American Embassy in London, which was in direct touch with the President at the White House through special coding machines." These machines were naval; they were very probably one-time tape devices manufactured by the Teletype Corporation.

As the war progressed, the State Department gradually took the old solved codes out of service and replaced them with new cryptosystems. It thus choked off the German sources of information. To get them flowing again, Pers z launched, in 1944, a major effort to break the M-138. The work was primarily mathematical, with Hans Rohrbach, a 37-year-old doctor of mathematics, playing a leading role. Rohrbach and Müller first divided the messages into "families" enciphered with the same strip arrangement, using repetitions as family resemblances. This meant that, in a given family, the first strip was always the same, the second was always the same, and so on. Stereotyped beginnings gave the cryptanalysts many plaintext assumptions—Müller was as adept at spotting words here as with the code. On each strip, the plaintext stood an unknown distance from the ciphertext. By comparing many such equivalents, both within a single strip and with the help of information from neighboring strips, the cryptanalysts mapped the letters on the strips to reproduce the original alphabet. Collaboration among the half-dozen cryptanalysts was extremely close. Each man looked after his own families, but they conferred frequently so that each could try on his own sequence of strips the possibilities found by others. Helping them in their work

NAVAL MESSAGE		NAVY DEPARTMENT	
DRAFTER	EXTENSION NUMBER	ADDRESSEES	PRECEDENCE
FROM ALUSNA LONDON	FOR ACTION	OPNAV	PRIORITY / ROUTINE / DEFERRED
RELEASED BY			
DATE 3 JANUARY 1943			
TOR CODEROOM 1843	INFORMATION		PRIORITY / ROUTINE / DEFERRED
DECODED BY J ALLEN			
PARAPHRASED BY			

INDICATE BY ASTERISK ADDRESSEES FOR WHICH MAIL DELIVERY IS SATISFACTORY.

031730   NCR 54008

UNLESS OTHERWISE INDICATED THIS DISPATCH WILL BE TRANSMITTED WITH DEFERRED PRECEDENCE.

| ORIGINATOR FILL IN DATE AND TIME | DATE | TIME | GCT |

TEXT

FROM THE FORMER NAVAL PERSON TO PRESIDENT ROOSEVELT.
MOST SECRET AND PERSONAL NUMBER 253.

YOUR 252

1. YOUR PARAGRAPH 1 WILL BE DONE.

2. YOUR PARAGRAPH 2. HOWEVER DID YOU THINK OF SUCH AN IMPENETRABLE DISGUISE? IN ORDER TO MAKE IT EVEN HARDER FOR THE ENEMY AND TO DISCOURAGE IRREVERENT GUESSWORK PROPOSE ADMIRAL Q. AND MR P. (N B) WE MUST MIND OUR P'S AND Q'S

DISTRIBUTION: ACTION.....P1A

| No. 1 ADMIRAL. | No. 2 FILE. | No. 3 F-I OR CHARTROOM. | No. 4 SPECIAL. |

SEALED ~~SECRET~~

Make original only. Deliver to communication watch officer in person. (See Art. 76 (4) NAVREGS.)

Churchill expresses amazement at Roosevelt's cryptographic subtlety in proposing to call himself "Admiral Q" was a mechanism that moved the strips up and down to align them quickly. Eventually Pers z recovered all the M-138 strips and read nearly all the messages. But by then they had lost much of their intelligence value, and any hopes that the solution would help in the future vanished when the strips were changed.

The M-138 was, by then, no longer the topmost American diplomatic cryptosystem. The armed services had given the State Department cipher machines, including Vernam-system machines called SIGTOT, which the diplomats used for their most secret messages, though they still used codes for economy. American Army and Navy cryptanalysts taught State some of the practical lessons in cryptology that they had learned through their solutions. On June 3, 1944, Captain Lee W. Parke, the Navy cryptanalyst who had been senior watch officer in OP-20-GY at the time of Pearl Harbor, was detailed to the State Department, and on November 1 he became chief of the new Division of Cryptography. Under the direction of an expert cryptologist, the State Department communications at last took on a strength commensurate with that of the nation itself. The days of easy-to-break codes were ended. The era of American diplomatic cryptosecurity had begun.

Among the characteristic features of World War II was the extensive use of codenames to designate important operations or secret projects. Codenames had been used before—the words "tank" and "blimp" themselves derive from World War I codenames—but never so frequently. They aimed both at security and brevity: obviously it was easier to say "Operation TORCH" than "the Anglo-American invasion of North Africa," and solvers of any messages would still have to determine the meaning of the codenames.

Selection and assignment of the codenames was, in the United States, a duty of the Current Section of the Army's Operations Division. Men of the unit culled the unabridged dictionaries for suitable words—chiefly common nouns and adjectives that did not imply operations or localities. They avoided, as confusing, personal and ships' names and geographical terms. Of the dictionaries' 400,000 words, they compiled about 10,000 in scrambled order in a classified book. They cross-checked these to eliminate any conflicts with British codenames. Then they assigned blocks of codenames to theater commanders.

In theory the codenames bore no relation, either by denotation or connotation, to what they stood for. In the majority of cases this held in practice. FLINTLOCK meant the Allied attack on the Marshall Islands in 1944; AVALANCHE, the amphibious attack on Salerno; ANVIL, later DRAGOON, the Anglo-American landings in the soft underbelly of France. Even relatively small operations were dubbed: the relief of Australians trapped in Tobruk was SUPERCHARGE, the occupation of the Canary Islands was PILGRIM. Some codenames were written in blood: OMAHA, UTAH, GOLD, SWORD, and JUNO, for the Normandy beaches of D-Day.

Five of the codenames assigned for that cross-channel operation—themselves highly secret, as were their referents—inexplicably appeared in the crossword puzzles of the London *Daily Telegraph* in the month before June 6. Alarmed counterintelligence officials, fearing a Purloined-Letter type of concealment in what might be a warning to Germany, investigated—and found that the cause was merely an incredible coincidence.

For minor operations the Germans usually selected Decknamen ("covernames") that did not suggest the operation: MERKUR ("Mercury") for the seizure of Crete and FISCHREIHER ("Heron") for Stalingrad. But in major operations they violated this precept. The Decknamen SEELÖWE ("Sea Lion") for the invasion of England and HERBSTREISE ("Autumn Pleasure Voyage") for the simultaneous feint of seaborne troops from Norwegian ports to northern England hardly obscured the secrecy of the operations they named. Least subtle of all was BARBAROSSA for the invasion of Russia. To be sure, "Barbarossa" was the nickname of the great medieval German king, Frederick I, but not only does it mean "Red Beard" in Italian, it also calls to mind one of Frederick's greatest achievements in extending German authority over Slavs to the east.

The Allies never were as obvious as that, but their selections were sometimes constrained by principles that that master of English, Winston Churchill, laid down in a memorandum of August 8, 1943:

> I have crossed out on the attached paper many unsuitable names. Operations in which large numbers of men may lose their lives ought not to be described by code-words which imply a boastful and overconfident sentiment, such as "Triumphant," or, conversely, which are calculated to invest the plan with an air of despondency, such as "Woebetide," "Massacre," "Jumble," "Trouble," "Fidget," "Flimsy," "Pathetic," and "Jaundice." They ought not to be names of a frivolous character, such as "Bunnyhug," "Billingsgate," "Apéritif," and "Ballyhoo." They should not be ordinary words often used in other connections, such as "Flood," "Smooth," "Sudden," "Supreme," "Fullforce," and "Fullspeed." Names of living people—Ministers or Commanders—should be avoided, e.g., "Bracken."
>
> 2. After all, the world is wide, and intelligent thought will readily supply an unlimited number of well-sounding names which do not suggest the character of the operation or disparage it in any way and do not enable some widow or mother to say that her son was killed in an operation called "Bunnyhug" or "Ballyhoo."
>
> 3. Proper names are good in this field. The heroes of antiquity, figures from Greek and Roman mythology, the constellations and stars, famous racehorses, names of British and American war heroes, could be used, provided they fall within the rules above. There are no doubt many other themes that could be suggested.
>
> 4. Care should be taken in all this process. An efficient and a successful administration manifests itself equally in small as in great matters.

Churchill himself had always manifested an interest in these matters, particularly where they involved nuances of meaning. "The name 'Round-up' has been given to the 1943 operation [proposed invasion of Europe]," he cabled to Roosevelt on July 6, 1942. "I do not much like this name, as it might be thought overconfident or overgloomy, but it has come into considerable use. Please let me know whether you have any wishes about this." He complained to the chiefs of staff that it was "boastful, ill-chosen," and hoped that "it does not bring us bad luck." The codeword died a natural death (for a codeword) when the plan it designated was replaced by Operation GYMNAST, whose possible variations were indicated by appropriate modifications of the codeword. Churchill had strongly urged this operation, which was the invasion of North Africa, and after the Allies decided to go ahead with it, he "hastened to rechristen my favourite. 'Gymnast,' 'Super-Gymnast' and 'Semi-Gymnast' vanished from our code-words. On July 24 in an instruction from me to the Chiefs of Staff 'Torch' became the new and master term."

The Americans demonstrated a like sensitivity when they codenamed the crowning operations of the Pacific War, the invasion of Japan, CORONET and OLYMPIC. But it remained for Churchillian eloquence to find the great codename of the war for the greatest operation of the war. The name evoked a sense of majesty and patriarchal vengeance and irresistible power for the supreme Allied effort to enter the continent of Europe and crush forever the wicked Nazi conspiracy. The master wordsmith himself consecrated that crusade with the codename Operation OVERLORD.

Before that vast offensive could be mounted, the Allies had to win the Battle of the Atlantic. In this, communications intelligence played a role of high importance. Indeed, in some respects the Battle of the Atlantic might be viewed as a duel between the Axis and the Allied cryptanalytic organizations. And while Dönitz' B-Dienst had its successes, the Allied communications-intelligence agencies enjoyed the advantage of access to the extremely heavy traffic of the U-boat fleet.

In part, this stemmed from Dönitz' insistence on maintaining tactical control of his submarines so as to concentrate them in wolf packs on the richest prizes. He was aware of the danger in all the talk, but, he contended, "The signals from the U-boats contained the information upon which was based the planning and control of those combined attacks which alone held the promise of really great success against the concentrated shipping of any enemy convoy." His encouragement of communication led to an almost complete relaxation of radio discipline. U-boats went on the air to report a toothache on board or to congratulate a friend at headquarters on a birthday. U-boat command became "the most gabby military organization in all the history of war."

Thanks to Commander Laurance F. Safford, head of OP-20-G and father of the Navy's communications-intelligence organization, the United States had, upon its entrance into the war, an Atlantic arc of high-frequency direction-finders to exploit the U-boat garrulity. Stations reported their bearings to their net control center in Maryland, whence they were flashed to the naval communications-intelligence organization at 3801 Nebraska Avenue, North West, in Washington. Commander Knight McMahon and his staff combined them into fixes and flashed these to the Atlantic Section of the Navy Commander in Chief's Combat Intelligence Division. From here they sped to antisubmarine forces.

How fast this net—called "huffduff" from the HF/DF abbreviation of "high-frequency direction-finding"—could work was shown by the episode of June 30, 1942. That morning, *U-158* went on the air to report to Dönitz that he had nothing to report. Huffduff stations at Bermuda, Hartland Point, Kingston, and Georgetown heard him. McMahon plotted his position as latitude 33 degrees north, longitude 67 degrees 30 minutes west. This information raced down through channels until it reached Lieutenant Richard E. Schreder, U.S.N., flying an antisubmarine patrol out of Bermuda. Ten miles from the spotted location he found *U-158* loafing on the surface, its crew sunbathing. One of Schreder's depth charges landed on the submarine's superstructure just as it was trying to dive. It went down all right, but it never came up.

In another case, huffduff hounded a U-boat to death. The net first heard a transmission of *U-66* on April 19, 1944, and followed her successive messages in her attempts to rendezvous with a supply submarine. Allied ships, told where to go by huffduff, repeatedly frustrated these efforts, and on May 5 her commander wirelessed home: "Refueling impossible under constant stalking. Mid-Atlantic worse than Bay of Biscay." Her "spurt" transmission—made by tape-recording the message and then radioing the tape at high speed—lasted less than 15 seconds, but no fewer than 26 huffduff stations got bearings on it, probably as a result of improved equipment that scanned the horizon 20 times a second and zeroed in accurately and semiautomatically on any emission. Three hours later, an American plane spotted the U-boat; an hour after that an American ship began to attack it, and within 25 minutes the submarine had gone down.

In addition to huffduff, an intercept network eavesdropped on the text of the German messages. The Navy monitors could often tell one U-boat from another by the sending characteristics of their radio operators, and sometimes could ascertain the number of U-boats in a wolf pack. They grew so familiar with the submarine signals that they sometimes knew simply from external characteristics that a given message was a convoy contact report or a signal that attack had begun.

Help was obtained from the most exciting code theft of World War II. It took place on the high seas with lightninglike speed under conditions of great peril.

Early in 1944, Captain Daniel V. Gallery, U.S.N., commanding the antisubmarine Task Group 22.3, conceived a daring plan for boarding a U-boat

Messages in plaintext from Radio Logbook No. 6 of the captured U-505

and capturing it if, as sometimes happened, it surfaced after depth-charge damage to allow its crew to escape. Even though the plan as a whole might fail, he might pirate the submarine's cryptographic equipment, which alone would make such a venture worthwhile. So he trained a team of volunteers in dismantling booby traps, closing sea cocks, and handling a U-boat.

On May 31, 1944, he began tracking *U-505*, which huffduff had discovered was apparently heading for its home port at Brest. At 11 a.m. Sunday, June 4, a clear day with a light breeze, he made sound contact with the U-boat about 150 miles west of Cape Blanco, French West Africa. Its captain was at lunch when a salvo of depth charges slammed the peacefully gliding vessel, holing the outer hull and convincing him that his ship was mortally stricken. He blew his tanks and surfaced, and as his crew boiled out of hatches and the conning tower and leaped into the sea, U.S.S. *Pillsbury* was lowering a whaleboat carrying the boarding party.

A few moments later, it reached the abandoned sub, rocking gently in the long Atlantic swells. Lieutenant (j.g.) Albert L. David, leading the boarding party, and petty officers Arthur K. Knispel and Stanley E. Wdowiak slipped through the hatch, raced forward to the radio room, smashed open a couple of lockers, and grabbed the cryptographic equipment—the current codebook with superencipherments, the cipher machine and its list of keys, and hundreds of messages with parallel plaintexts and ciphertexts. The Germans had apparently never considered the possibility of a boarding and so had not bothered to jettison the material. The three Americans hastily passed the items up on deck so that the team would have something to show for its efforts even if it lost the sub.

But within fifteen minutes, the team had disconnected demolition charges and shut off an eight-inch stream of water, and *U-505* had become the first enemy warship captured by a U.S. Navy boarding party since the War of 1812. Gallery put a line on her and towed her back to the United States, where she eventually wound up as a permanent display outside Chicago's Museum of Science and Industry. David received a Congressional Medal of Honor for his heroism; his helpers were awarded Navy Crosses. The cryptographic material went to Nebraska Avenue. The crews of Task Group 22.3 maintained a discreet silence about their feat, and U-boat command, thinking that *U-505* had been sunk, since no contact had been made after June 3, never suspected the truth and did not change its ciphers. Writer Ladislas Farago called the seizure "the climactic single episode of the American antisubmarine effort in the Atlantic."

The Allies now read U-boat operational traffic. For they had, more than a year before the theft, succeeded in solving the difficult U-boat systems and—in one of the finest cryptanalytic achievements of the war—managed to read the intercepts on a current basis. For this, the cryptanalysts needed the help of a mass of machinery that filled two buildings.

What all this did to the submarines was graphically described by the German naval officer Harald Busch: "In the latter half of 1944 no U-boat commander would incur the ordeal of refueling if he could possibly avoid it. ... on a suspiciously large number of occasions, enemy aircraft had made their appearance at the very moment when the pipeline was stretched between the two boats and neither was able to dive, with the result that many U-boats had been destroyed in the act of refueling.... Evidently U-boat commanders were right in their suspicions: the enemy could and did decipher the signals transmitted by Admiral Dönitz' headquarters in Berlin."

In the eleven months remaining before the end of the European war, the Allies, greatly aided by the information that told them where to send their now powerful air and naval forces, sank nearly 300 U-boats—almost one a day—and greatly reduced their shipping losses. "Battles might be won or lost," Churchill wrote, "enterprises might succeed or miscarry, territories might be gained or quitted, but dominating all our power to carry on the war, or even keep ourselves alive, lay our mastery of the ocean routes and the free approach and entry to our ports." These the Allies mastered. "Reduced to the simplest terms," wrote Farago in his study of the Battle of the Atlantic, "the Allies won the U-boat war and Germany lost it because Dönitz talked too much."

Final victory over the Nazi evil could come only by driving a military stake through its heart, and in this mission communications intelligence played an important role. The march actually began in North Africa in 1942 under the pressure for a "Second Front Now." Communications-intelligence units were there—though not exactly in the role assigned them. Radio-intelligence companies of the American Army charged ashore as assault troops! They soon resumed their proper duties, however, and, equipped with intercept receivers and direction-finders, began to eavesdrop on the Axis messages. During the Tunisia campaign, the 128th, 117th, 122nd, 123rd, and 849th Signal Companies (Radio Intelligence) tracked the Germans all over North Africa and, by monitoring American communications, plugged leaks in Allied radio security. The 128th first discovered that the Germans were withdrawing from the Kasserine Pass, which they had taken a few days earlier in America's first blooding in Europe. Later the 128th gave advance warning of several enemy attacks. In Italy, the VI Corps intelligence officer said that his radio intelligence platoon had done "outstanding" work during the march on Rome and had supplied information second in value only to battle reconnaissance. Thus, even though the manning and equipping of radio intelligence companies did not get under way until relatively late in the war, officers in the field soon declared their product to be "of material value ... at times vital" and praised the units as among the "most constantly profitable sources" of intelligence on German plans and movements.

Strategic communications intelligence about German intentions in the European war mainly came, however, from Japanese sources. This should not be surprising. The Wehrmacht had the advantage of interior communications throughout occupied Europe and so could use wire networks, which offer very little opportunity for interception. But the Japanese diplomats in Berlin, Rome, Madrid, Lisbon, Sofia, Budapest, and Moscow had no way of getting messages back to Tokyo but by radio. These the Allies intercepted.

The messages of the Japanese military attachés, whose code the United

States had broken, yielded quantities of information. This source was lost to the Allies in 1943 in an ironic development that demonstrates the superiority of cryptanalysis over theft as a secret source of information. The Office of Strategic Services, America's new spy outfit, in a laudable attempt at espionage, penetrated the offices of the Japanese embassy in Portugal. They did not disclose their plans to the Army, whose Signal Security Agency (formerly the Signal Intelligence Service) had broken the code; nor did the Army warn the O.S.S. against doing anything that would jeopardize its cryptanalyses. The upshot was that the Japanese discovered traces of the search, decided that their military attaché code might have been compromised, and changed it. The Allies, who had been comfortably reading the messages without benefit of espionage, still had not broken into the new code by the fall of 1944. Thus the attempt to gain information by cloak-and-dagger methods deprived the United States of information that it had been obtaining by the traceless means of communications intelligence.

Bulky cipher machines such as the Japanese diplomats used could not be shipped or smuggled into blockaded Europe very easily, and so PURPLE remained in service throughout the war. Quite probably the Japanese considered the system secure. But even before Pearl Harbor American cryptanalysts were reading Japanese PURPLE messages from Berlin, and they preyed upon them even more avidly after the United States entered the war. Thus William F. Friedman's solution of PURPLE reverberated throughout the war, leading to major effects and making it one of the world's great cryptanalyses not only in technique but in importance as well.

The Germans granted the Japanese ambassador, Baron Hiroshi Oshima, the intimacies of an ally, and, as a former military attaché, he took considerable interest in the military sphere. Toward the end of October, 1943, when it became evident that the Allies would invade Europe and the Wehrmacht had begun to stiffen its defenses, Oshima toured the Westwall and the Siegfried Line. He reported on these preparations in great detail in a long radiogram of between 1,000 and 2,000 words.

As a powerful German station pumped it into the ether for the 5,000-mile leap to Tokyo, a new American intercept post at Asmara, in the former Italian colony of Eritrea bordering the Red Sea, picked it up. Back the cryptogram went to the Signal Security Agency. It proved to be in PURPLE, which the American cryptanalysts read with relative ease. The solution went to General Dwight D. Eisenhower's headquarters, where its intelligence helped shape basic strategy for the conquest of Germany.

The success of the invasion stemmed in part from its geographical surprise, and that surprise stemmed largely from an elaborate deception by the Allies, in which radio played the major role. To distract German attention from the real landing area in Normandy, Eisenhower's headquarters cooked up a complete cover-plan codenamed FORTITUDE. Parts of it had gone into operation more than a year before the invasion. Field Marshal Montgomery's radio messages were not broadcast from his actual location in the south of England, but were led by land line to a spoof headquarters near Dover and transmitted from there. Dummy ships were concentrated in the Cinque Ports to help the illusion. A very busy signals staff contrived, by sending out the right sort of dummy wireless traffic, to "assemble" a fictitious 4th Army in Scotland. The "wireless training" of this army contained some purposeful indiscretions. By these furtive, impressionistic, and devious indirections, FORTITUDE sought to let the Germans convince themselves of what they had always wanted to believe anyway—that the invaders would pour across the Channel at the narrowest point, from Dover to the Pas de Calais; the build-up in Scotland suggested a preliminary feintlike assault on southern Norway. 'The final result was admirable," Churchill wrote. "The German High Command firmly believed the evidence we obligingly put at their disposal." In fact, so conclusive did the evidence seem to be that more than a month after the invasion in Normandy, Hitler declared that "the enemy will probably attempt a second landing in the 15th Army's sector"—which was the Pas de Calais!

On the Normandy beachhead, the solution of a German message enabled General Omar Bradley's 12th Army Group "to meet a very strong attack against one of our weaker positions," he said. His cryptanalytical unit was the 849th Signal Intelligence Service (formerly the radio intelligence company of the same number). Though attached to the army group, it worked not at headquarters but in the field, intercepting and cryptanalyzing German messages from the level of the army group down to company. The material was tactical and of great value in day-to-day operations.

In the fall the 849th moved into winter quarters in a building in Luxembourg. About the first of December it began to read German messages indicating the movement of armored divisions behind the Ardennes forest. These increased from day to day, but G-2, the recipient of this information, appeared to take no notice whatever. Finally, on the Sunday morning of December 17, the unit solved messages that confirmed what the cryptanalysts had long dreaded: the German Panzer attack. Why had the army commanders not heeded the intelligence—which included a great variety of other indications? They did not believe that the Germans would or could attack with armor through so heavily wooded, so hilly, and so generally unfavorable a terrain for tanks. The Battle of the Bulge has long been cited as a failure of intelligence. It was not the intelligence that failed, however. The Bulge was a failure of evaluation.

Attached to Lieutenant General George S. Patton Jr.'s 3rd Army was a similar radio intelligence unit, commanded by Major Charles Flint, regarded by one fellow officer as "a young, trigger-smart expert." Flint's outfit was particularly valuable in fluid situations when the Germans were on the move and had to use radio. At Bastogne, it solved a message that enabled Patton to inflict heavy losses on the redoubtable 5th Para Division. Like other S.I.S.

units, Flint's monitored American traffic; it once warned a mechanized-cavalry transmitter of a communications-security violation that might have revealed important information to the enemy.

How highly the Allies regarded communications intelligence was demonstrated in a left-handed fashion in the closing days of the war by the case of the missing SIGABA. Also known as the M-134-C, the SIGABA, which had been devised by William Friedman, was a rotor machine like the German Enigma and British TYPEX; like them, it protected top-level communications—an interesting case of parallel evolution and an indication of the cryptographic success of the rotor. And it protected them exceedingly well. The branch of the Army's Signal Security Agency charged with testing American cryptosystems had failed in all its efforts to break down messages enciphered in M-134-C. And, though the United States did not know it at the time, German cryptanalysts had, despite prolonged efforts, likewise found it impossible to read these cryptograms.

But all the cryptographic ingenuity built into the machines would have been expended in vain had only one of them fallen—even briefly—into the hands of the enemy. As a result, probably nothing in the war zones were guarded as closely as the ABA's, as they were called for short. Some units close to the front moved them to the rear each night. Heavy safes protected them when not in use—one safe for the basic mechanism, another for the rotors (for additional key changes, the machine came equipped with more rotors than the five it used at a time), a third, apparently, for the key lists. Armed guards watched over them continuously. The precautions seemed to be paying off, for to the Army's knowledge, not one ABA had ever been compromised.

But on the night of February 3, 1945, two ABA guards, sergeants of the 28th Division, parked the truck in which they were transporting the three safes of a divisional ABA outside a house in Colmar, France, and paid a brief visit to some friendly ladies. When they emerged, the truck and its safes were gone. Counterintelligence began at once to search for it. On the side of a road near Colmar, agents found a trailer that had been attached to the truck—but no truck, no safes, and no ABA.

Panic struck. At Eisenhower's headquarters, security and cryptologic officers went frantic. Ike himself was concerned. Colmar, which had just been liberated, was still close enough to the front for German collaborators or agents planted by the retreating Wermacht to have stolen the ABA's. Somehow they might have gotten through the fluid front lines and so to German cryptanalysts. These would then be in a position to do what they had not been able to do before. For with a knowledge of the wiring of the ABA rotors, the heart of the system, and with a working mechanism to complete their understanding, all the German cryptanalysts would have to do would be to determine which rotors in the set had been used for a particular message and their initial setting. This would not be easy, but it certainly could be done.

The danger to the Allies did not come from any possible future solutions, since new sets of rotors were issued almost immediately. Rather it came from the past. Eisenhower and his high subordinates had been directing the greatest campaign in all history by streams of ABA-sheathed messages. These were all based upon the well-matured plans of high strategy. The past traffic dealing with supplies alone would tell the Germans a great deal about Allied potentialities, since modern war is, to a very considerable degree, a conflict of logistics. If the Germans could translate their back files of intercepts with the missing ABA, they could obtain a profound insight into the broad guidelines on which the Allies were conducting the war in Western Europe. Nor could the Allies easily reshape these plans, for mountains of supplies and millions of men had been moved to conform with them. Thus, given intelligence of this high order, and the massive irreversible momentum of modern war, the Germans might well counter Allied moves so effectively as to add months to the war and thousands of lives to its toll.

None of this was lost on Eisenhower. He personally pressed the commander of his 6th Army Group, General Jacob L. Devers, to find the missing safes at all costs, and Devers assigned the task to his group's chief counterintelligence officer, Colonel David G. Erskine.

Erskine began by sending out feelers to anti-Nazi German spies in Switzerland to find out if the Nazis had been congratulating themselves on some extraordinary feat recently. Then he spread discreet queries through the 6th Army Group's area to determine if anyone knew anything about a missing truck bearing three safes containing "highly classified documents." Perhaps a French civilian or an American soldier had appropriated the truck without knowing of its precious cargo. Any American finding the truck, or the safes, or both, Erskine announced, would get that coveted reward: home leave. No one claimed it.

Erskine sent L-5 liaison planes skimming low over Alsace, but their pilots spotted no abandoned trucks. So every unit commander in the 6th Army Group was ordered to personally check the serial numbers of every one of his vehicles against that of the missing truck. Nothing. The search was extended over most of the front. Military policemen checked vehicles at roadblocks; canals were drained; informants were checked. The mystery just deepened. Repeatedly, Eisenhower asked Devers, and Devers daily asked Erskine, whether the missing ABA had been found.

After three weeks of intensive but fruitless search, a special squad of American and French counterintelligence agents was formed to concentrate solely on the loss. In charge was Lieutenant Grant Heilman, a tall, blond Pennsylvanian. His operation got off to an embarrassing start when two jeeps parked outside his headquarters disappeared as mysteriously as had the truck. But it picked up when Eisenhower sent a two-star general, Fay B. Prickett, to Colmar to lend authority to the search. Heilman checked everything, including shelled trucks abandoned at the bridge over the Rhine. Erskine's Swiss spies returned negative reports, and his hunch that French intelligence might have taken the ABA to improve their own cryptology—checked with no less a personage than General Charles de Gaulle, head of the provisional government—did not pan out.

Suddenly, when no more clues could be discerned, Erskine got a tip from a French source. Rushing to a sizable creek called the Giessen River near the town of Sélèstat, not far from Colmar, he saw, lying in the mud, two of the missing 300-pound safes. It seemed likely that they had been dumped into the Giessen from a masonry bridge about a hundred yards upstream from where they had been found and had been rolled downstream by the strong current. Erskine immediately ordered a search of the banks for the third safe. They were barren.

Divers were brought in from Cherbourg to examine the stream bed. They found nothing. Erskine decided to dam the stream and dredge the bottom with a bulldozer. In three days the dam was built and the bottom scoured—with no luck. Heilman, feeling hopeless, began to search the muddy portion of the bed that the falling waters had exposed. Suddenly something metallic glinted in the sun. He rushed over—and found his own buried treasure. It was the missing safe. Both its handles had been knocked off by rocks, but otherwise it appeared, on checking by Signal Corps officers, to be intact.

Thus, on March 20, the search for the missing SIGABA ended, six frantic weeks after it had begun. Erskine, checking again with the French, this time on an I-don't-want-anyone-punished basis, discovered that a French military chauffeur who had lost his truck in Colmar "borrowed" the American one while the sergeants were in the brothel, and, afraid that he might be accused of stealing the safes, pushed them off the bridge into the Giessen. This ruled out the possibility that the secret mechanism had ever been in the hands of the enemy.

Heilman was promoted to captain. Both he and Erskine were awarded the Bronze Star. Uncounted man-hours had been squandered in the search and an unknown toll of nervous energy taken. But the precious messages were safe, and with them the plans that within a few more weeks directed the Allies to victory.

16

CENSORS, SCRAMBLERS, AND SPIES

CIPHER IS THE LANGUAGE OF SPIES—and usually they must talk in whispers. A spy's success, his very existence, depends on his not being seen or heard. Sending messages in obviously cryptographic form would alert counterespionage to him as effectively as wearing a cloak and dagger. Yet he must transmit, else he is useless. So he eschews the overt methods of secret communications for the covert. He resorts to open codes, hollow heels, invisible inks, microscopically small missives—the steganographic methods that conceal the very fact that a message is being sent. He seeks to communicate unnoticed.

And to block this very attempt and root out the enemy within, governments erect great filters at their mail and cable ports of entry to prevent and detect these clandestine communications. These sieves, which let innocent messages flow through, are the censorship organizations.

Descended in a sense from the black chambers of the 1700s, they are creatures of war in democracies and of tyranny in dictatorships. Censorship first sprang up on a major scale in World War I, and the lessons that Britain learned then she put to good use twenty years later when she again filtered communications. Even before the United States entered the war, British censorship had caught two major German spies in the United States and its protectorate of Cuba.

In December, 1940, one of the 1,200 examiners that British censorship had installed in the commodious Princess Hotel in Bermuda stopped a letter addressed to Berlin from New York. He suspected it because it described a list of Allied shipping and used several expressions—such as "cannon" for "guns" in describing the vessels' armament—that suggested the writer might be German and a possible Nazi agent. The letter was signed "Joe K." A watch set up for more letters with his handwriting soon picked out quite a few more, mostly to Spain and Portugal. Their language seemed slightly forced, and a team began studying the letters to see whether this indicated an open code and, if so, what the real meaning was.

One member of the team was a persistent young woman named Nadya Gardner, who became convinced that the letters contained invisible writing. The usual strip tests with chemicals that bring out the ordinary secret inks gave negative results, but Miss Gardner persisted. Finally the chemists, under Dr. Enrique Dent, applied the iodine-vapor test invented back in World War I—and to their surprise secret writing did appear on the back of the typed sheets. The letter of April 15, 1941, addressed to Mr. Manuel Alonso, Apartado 718, Madrid, carried on the back of its two pages a list of ships then docked at New York: "On April 14 was at pier 97 (Manhattan) the Norwegian M. S. *Tain Shan*—6601 tons—gray superstr # at pier 90 was a Dutch freighter . . . ." A letter of six days later, addressed to a Miss Isabel Machado Santos in Lisbon, reported in invisible ink that "British have about 70,000 men on Iceland # The S.S. *Ville de Liege* was sunk about April 14—many thanks # Types of airplanes flown to England (continued from letter 69)—3. Boeing B-17C (model 299T) twenty were released by the U.S. Army to Britain on Nov 20 . . . ." These little billets-doux were written in a solution of pyramidon, a powder often used as a headache cure and readily obtainable at most pharmacies.

But there was still no clue as to the sender. The letters bore no return address, and it was rather unlikely that "Joe K" was the spy's real first name and last initial. Finally, British censorship picked out another Joe K letter that reported that "Phil" had been fatally injured in a New York traffic accident on March 18 and had died at St. Vincent's Hospital. F.B.I. agents found that the man in the accident was known as Julio Lopez Lido, and that witnesses had seen that a man with Lido had grabbed his briefcase after the accident and hurried away. Eventually, the agents learned that Lido's true name was Ulrich von der Osten and that the writer of the Joe K letters was Kurt Frederick Ludwig. Ludwig, born in Ohio but raised in Germany, had come to the United States in March of 1940 to organize a spy ring, which he had done with moderate success.

When captured, he had several bottles of pyramidon in his possession. The odd tone of the open text of his letters was accounted for by its double meanings. "Your order 5 is rather large—and I with my limited facilities and funds shall never be able to fill such an immense order completely," he wrote to one of his addressees—all of them, incidentally, cover addresses for Himmler. This message really meant that he would have difficulty fulfilling the instructions sent him in communication No. 5 because of too few agents and too little money. Ludwig was convicted in the U.S. District Court at Brooklyn.

The second spy trapped by the alert Bermuda station went to his death. On a November day in 1941, an alert censor detected a rather Germanic cast to the handwriting in a Spanish-language letter from Havana to Lisbon and sent it over for a routine test for secret ink. His intuition was confirmed when a long missive appeared, listing ships being loaded in Havana harbor and discussing an airfield being constructed. The examiners were alerted to watch for similar handwriting. The next letter turned up a few days later. Censorship continued picking out these letters, which recited details of merchant

Censors, Scramblers, and Spies

shipping in Cuban waters and of the enlargement of the U.S. Navy's base at Guantánamo Bay, until the writer's real Havana address showed up in secret ink. Letters posted to this address were watched, and on September 5, 1942, after sufficient evidence had been amassed, police arrested "R. Castillo," who proved to be Heinz August Luning. He had been sent to Havana from Germany in September, 1941, and of the 48 letters he had sent to Europe, the Bermuda censors had intercepted all but five. On November 9, 1942, he went before a firing squad at Principe Fortress, the first man in Cuba to be executed as a spy.

Soon after Pearl Harbor, the United States built up a censorship service that began in the borrowed office in which Byron Price went to work as Chief Censor and grew to an organization whose 14,462 examiners occupied 90 buildings throughout the country, opened a million pieces of overseas mail a day, listened to innumerable telephone conversations, and scanned movies, magazines, and radio scripts. Millions became familiar with the "Opened by Censor" sticker and the scissored letter.

To plug up as many steganographic channels of communication as possible, the Office of Censorship banned in advance the sending of whole classes of objects or kinds of messages. International chess games by mail were stopped. Crossword puzzles were extracted from letters, for the examiners did not have time to solve them to see if they concealed a secret message, and so were newspaper clippings, which might have spelled out messages by dotting successive letters with secret ink—a modern version of a system described more than 2,000 years earlier by Aeneas the Tactician. Listing of students' grades was tabooed. One letter containing knitting instructions was held up long enough for an examiner to knit a sweater to see if the given sequence of knit two and cast off contained a hidden message like that of Madame Defarge, who knitted into her "shrouds" the names of further enemies of the French Republic, "whose lives the guillotine then surely swallowed up." A stamp bank was maintained at each censorship station; examiners removed loose stamps, which might spell out a code message, and replaced them with others of equal value, but of different number and denomination. Blank paper, often sent from the United States to relatives in paper-short countries, was similarly replaced from a paper bank to obviate secret-ink transmissions. Childish scrawls, sent from proud parents to proud grandparents, were removed because of the possibility of their covering a map. Even lovers' X's, meant as kisses, were heartlessly deleted if censors thought they might be a code.

Censorship cable regulations prohibited sending any text that was unclear to the censor, including numbers unrelated to the text or a personal note in a business communication, and that was not in English, French, Spanish, or Portuguese plain language. To kill any possible sub rosa message, censors sometimes paraphrased messages. This practice gave rise to Censorship's classic tale, which dates back to World War I. Onto the desk of a censor was placed the cablegram *Father is dead*. The censor considered it briefly, changed it to *Father is deceased,* and forwarded it. Soon thereafter the reply appeared on his desk: *Is Father dead or deceased?*

Cables ordering flowers—"Deliver three white orchids to my wife Saturday"—offered so blatant an invitation to clandestine communication that the censors forbade naming the kind of flower and the date of delivery, leaving both up to the individual florist. Later in the war, all international flower messages were prohibited by the United States and Great Britain because of the danger of their masking signals. Only those between the U.S. and her territories and between the U.S., Canada, and Mexico were permitted. The censorship permitted only nine of the most widely used commercial codes, and every coded message had to include an indicating abbreviation in its preamble. A firm could not use its private code without a special license from the director of censorship, who required that fifteen copies of the codebook be furnished for use by the censors.*

Precautions were taken with the mass media, too. Newspapers were warned to be careful in taking want ads. Prevention was directed mainly at commercial radio, which could instantaneously deliver open-code secret messages to listening submarines or enemy agents with the greatest of ease. Such possibilities had been driven home forcefully to the broadcasting industry a year before Pearl Harbor in a test conducted by a military intelligence officer. By having an announcer mention England's Queen Elizabeth, the officer wove into an interview with former heavyweight champion Max Baer the hidden message: *S-112: Queen Elizabeth sails tonight with hundreds of airplanes for Halifax.* What was disturbing was that neither the announcer, the station manager, Baer, nor any of the thousands of listeners on the nationwide hook-up except those who had been initiated into the secret were aware that the message had been broadcast. With this in mind, the Office of Censorship ruled that telephone or telegraph requests for phonograph records were not to be honored, and that mail requests must be held for an irregular, unspecified time before playing. This would defeat any attempts to have "Jersey Bounce" tell a waiting U-boat that *Convoy sails today.* The same situation applied to

---

* At the start of the war in September, 1939, the Allies prohibited the use of any codes at all. But pressure of business houses and realization that commercially coded messages were only a step up from plaintext forced them to relent, and at the end of December they permitted the use of *Bentley's Complete Phrase Code, Bentley's Second Phrase Code,* the *ABC Code* (6th edition), and *Peterson's Code* (3rd edition). In April, 1940, they admitted five more codes: *Acme Code and Supplement, Lombard General Code, Lombard Shipping Code and Appendix, New Standard Half Word Code,* and *New Standard Three Letter Code.* These were the nine later allowed by the United States and most of the Latin American nations. Under pressure from the Allies, Argentina, which had not severed diplomatic relations with the Axis, halted all code communications—but the first code message stopped was one from the Vatican! During the war, even neutrals such as Spain and Sweden demanded copies of the codes used and prohibited the use of (secret) cipher. Only Switzerland placed no restrictions on either code or cipher communication.

the personal ads, such as for lost dogs, that local stations broadcast. Halted completely were man-in-the-street interviews and Santa Claus lists of toys that children wanted.

Preventive censorship like this was only half the job, however. It could not be expected that spies would limit themselves to such easily confounded methods of communication. The other half of the job was the detection of the other methods that they might use. To sharpen Censorship's spy-catching tools by coordinating and assisting the field stations that spotted the hidden messages and by improving liaison with counterespionage agencies like the F.B.I., Price in May of 1943 established the Technical Operations Division at headquarters, appointing Lieutenant Colonel Harold R. Shaw as its chief and an assistant director in the Office of Censorship. Shaw, 39, son of a Regular Army officer, had been commissioned in the Army Reserve upon his graduation from the University of Hawaii. He maintained a strong interest in military intelligence while working in soil physics and chemistry and hydraulics as irrigation superintendent of a large sugar plantation on Oahu. In the fall of 1941, after being called to active duty, he had taken an intensive two-month course with 14 other reservists who would serve as the nucleus of a postal censorship in case of war. The training was conducted by Major W. P. (Red) Corderman in a three-story brick office building in Clarendon, Virginia, a sleepy suburb of Washington; one of the most frequent lecturers was William F. Friedman. Across the street a group of Navy Reserve officers under Captain Herbert K. Fenn was similarly planning the details for cable and radio censorship. Fenn, a World War I base censor and a Navy communications expert, later became Chief Cable Censor. One of Shaw's classmates, Norman V. Carlson, president of a San Francisco movie-camera firm, early in the war replaced Corderman as Chief Postal Censor. With the outbreak of war, Shaw rushed back to Hawaii to become District Postal Censor and Chief Military Censor. Price recalled him from there to head the Technical Operations Division.

T.O.D. was quartered in the Federal Trade Commission Building, the three-sided structure that housed the Office of Censorship at Pennsylvania and Constitution avenues in Washington. Shaw administered it from Room 509 with three assistants and a secretarial staff. Two technical sections operated under maximum security in a windowless, guarded area on the seventh, or top, floor. The laboratory was headed by Dr. Elwood C. Pierce, a biochemist at the University of Indiana who had joined Censorship at the start of the war. He and his assistant, Dr. Willard Breon of the University of Maryland chemistry faculty, had prepared a manual on detection of secret inks, trained key personnel of the censorship field stations in laboratory operation, and handled some of the more active and difficult cases themselves. From Hawaii Shaw imported his trusted cryptanalytic expert to form a unit "capable," he said, "not only of cracking codes and ciphers but also of building the intricate dossiers of personal history, contacts, handwriting peculiarities, and correspondence habits of each actual and suspected espionage agent." The man who could do it was Armen Abdian, a former New Englander who had come to Hawaii in the prewar Army, had taught a cram course for prospective West Pointers, and had gone into business in Honolulu.

T.O.D. also drew upon the pool of scientific knowledge of the Office of Scientific Research and Development. Each month, Shaw and his technical aides met with a bevy of physics and chemistry Ph.D.'s in the board room of Harvard's Mallinckrodt Chemical Laboratory. Arthur B. Lamb, professor of chemistry at Harvard and editor of the *Journal* of the American Chemical Society, presided over a group that included Robley D. Evans, a physicist at the Massachusetts Institute of Technology, Harris M. Chadwell, a physical chemist at Tufts University, Warren C. Lothrop, an organic chemist at Connecticut's Trinity College, S. Edward Eaton, a chemist at Arthur D. Little, Inc., and George Richter, an expert in inks and papers with the Eastman Kodak Company. In addition, Sanborn C. Brown, a young faculty member of M.I.T. who worked as a "free physicist" for the O.S.R.D.'s National Defense Research Committee, unraveling puzzlers that had baffled other agencies, such as ways of de-arming booby traps and the causes of mysterious accidents to dive-bomber pilots, attacked some of the toughest technical problems faced by Censorship.

The primary detection of clandestine communications took place in the censorship field stations. Largest of all was New York's, filling a huge building on lower Eighth Avenue. About 4,500 postal examiners scanned the snowdrifts of mail that piled onto their desks each day. They excised all matter that might have injured the Allied war effort, and they looked closely for traces of hidden messages. Censorship had catalogued the occupations and hobbies of its examiners. A balance sheet would be given to an accountant to see whether it made financial sense; an amateur horticulturist could tell whether a discussion of tulip beds rang true. Once an examiner in New York was perturbed by a letter from Germany to a prisoner of war in the United States, saying that Gertrude was developing into a swimming champion and listing the times of her victories. He consulted an amateur swimmer in the office, who reported that the speeds were impossible. Further investigation revealed that the times actually indicated the speed of a new fighter plane, given by a war worker who could not resist bragging. The factory was later bombed. Censors in a political section looked for clues to hoards of vital material that might be bought by the Allies to preclude the Axis from getting it. An economic section extracted remarks about shortages and living conditions to help build up pictures of national economies. Letters in uncommon languages went to a language identification section, which obtained translators for such esoteric tongues as Ladino, a mixture of Hebrew and 15th-century Spanish spoken only by the 30,000 Sephardic Jews in colonies in Spain, the Balkans, and Latin America.

Floor examiners passed all messages with peculiar wording, odd-looking marks, or other suspected indications to the security division, which had two sections to examine steganograms concealed in the two basic ways—linguistically and technologically. These were the code and cipher section for the linguistic steganograms and the laboratory section for the technological. Both were linked to T.O.D. by a security assistant who implemented T.O.D.'s instructions and passed the more recalcitrant problems back to Washington. The 70 examiners in the New York code and cipher section occupied about half the 14th floor, with some of the more expert people constituted as a specialist group. About 30 technicians tested for secret inks in the laboratory next door.

Linguistically concealed messages fall into two general categories, the semagram and the open code. There are three kinds of open code: the jargon code, the null cipher, and geometrical systems like the Cardano grille. In the jargon code, an apparently innocuous word stands for the real term in a text contrived to seem as bland and as innocent as possible. Jargon codes can range from the most informal sort of code to a full code list. They begin with mere allusions to mutually known events and persons—"I visited the man you had dinner with last week." They continue through double meanings that would be easily understood by the recipient, as one criminal's referring to another's arrest by saying "Joe went to the hospital." They culminate in a prearranged table of artificial meanings. Jargon has been popular since the dawn of cryptography. The Chinese employed it; the oldest papal code is the 14th-century use of EGYPTIANS for *Ghibellines* and SONS OF ISRAEL for *Guelphs*; in the 17th century a French code consisted entirely of such jargon expressions as GARDEN for *Rome*, ROSE for *the pope*, PLUM TREE for the *Cardinal de Retz*, WINDOW for *Monsieur the king's brother*, and STAIRCASE for the *Marquis de Coeuvres*. It is clear that skillful application of jargon's literary veneer requires no little finesse!

Censorship defends itself against this ruse by a feel for stilted or heavy-handed language and by a healthy skepticism concerning subject matter. The standard story about jargon comes from World War I. A British censor grew suspicious of the enormous orders for cigars wired each day—mostly from port towns—by two "Dutch businessmen." One day Portsmouth called for 10,000 Coronas; the next day Plymouth and Devonport craved large quantities of stogies; then Newcastle succumbed overnight to the tobacco habit. It seemed as though all the males in the coastal population of England had suddenly and simultaneously developed an irresistible addiction to the weed, so inexhaustible was the demand for cigars. At the suggestion of the censor, a check was made; the two businessmen proved to be German spies, and their orders an open code, in which, say 5,000 Coronas for Newcastle meant five cruisers lying in that port. On July 30, 1915, the two—Haicke P. M. Janssen and Wilhelm R. Roos—were executed at the Tower of London by a firing squad whose triggers were really pulled by an alert censor.

So long as jargon codes can pass unnoticed, they are, naturally, safe. But they nearly always give up their secrets soon after detection. Paradoxically, the less suspect they are, the easier they are to solve when discovered: because the more they throw the burden of communication on the context, the more information the context contains that may be used as a lever to pry out the secret meaning. Thus in World War II, a series of letters evidencing a legitimate if somewhat neurotic concern for dolls apparently eluded censorship. Suspicion was drawn to them when one was returned from Buenos Aires, marked "Unknown at this address," to the person marked as the sender, a woman in Portland, Oregon. Not having sent it, she brought it to the F.B.I. "I just secured a lovely Siamese Temple Dancer," the letter said in part, "it had been damaged, that is tore in the middle. But it is now repaired and I like it very much. I could not get a mate for this Siam dancer, so I am redressing just a small ordinary doll into a second Siam doll. . . ." Then other doll letters, all in the same disconnected feminine style filled with typographical errors, were intercepted by censors. "A broken doll in a hulu grass skirt will have all damages repaired by the first week of February," and "The broken English dolls will be in a doll hospital for a few months before repairs can be completed. The doll hospital is working day and night."

T.O.D. and F.B.I. cryptanalysts soon determined that the dolls represented warships in a jargon code, each kind a specific type of ship. The innocent chatter assumed sinister overtones: "Light cruiser *Honolulu* will have all damages repaired by the first week of February." "The damaged English warships will be in a shipyard for several months before repairs can be completed. The shipyard is working day and night." "I just secured information of a lovely aircraft carrier, it had been damaged, that is torpedoed in the middle. But it is now repaired [the "and I like it very much" just adds to the air of innocence]. A second carrier could not be obtained, so another ship is being converted to an aircraft carrier." But no clue as to the writer emerged until she used as a return address a woman with whom she had had a spat. When an F.B.I. agent checked with this woman to ask if she knew who might have been using her address, she named Mrs. Velvalee Dickinson, who ran an exclusive doll shop on New York's Madison Avenue. A Japanophile and friend of prominent Japanese, she was later found to have received thousands of dollars from Japanese officials. She was charged with espionage, which could have brought the death penalty, but was allowed to plead guilty to the lesser charge of violating wartime censorship regulations by illegally using codes in international communications and was sentenced to ten years in jail and a $10,000 fine.

A second type of open code is the null cipher. Only certain letters or words of a null cipher's text are significant; for example, every fifth word or the first letter of every word, with all the other letters and words serving as nulls to produce the disguise. These usually sound even more strained than the jargon code. Even two of the better examples, sent by the Germans during

Censors, Scramblers, and Spies

World War I, have that "funny" sound that invariably accompanies them. The first, disguised as a press cable, read:

PRESIDENT'S EMBARGO RULING SHOULD HAVE IMMEDIATE NOTICE. GRAVE SITUATION AFFECTING INTERNATIONAL LAW. STATEMENT FORESHADOWS RUIN OF MANY NEUTRALS. YELLOW JOURNALS UNIFYING NATIONAL EXCITEMENT IMMENSELY.

The initial letters spell out *Pershing sails from N.Y. June 1*. The second message, apparently sent as a check on the first, beaded the same content on the second letters of each word:

APPARENTLY NEUTRAL'S PROTEST IS THOROUGHLY DISCOUNTED AND IGNORED. ISMAN HARD HIT. BLOCKADE ISSUE AFFECTS PRETEXT FOR EMBARGO ON BYPRODUCTS, EJECTING SUETS AND VEGETABLE OILS.

Whoever the sender was, his ingenuity was expended in vain, since Pershing actually sailed May 28.

Most null ciphers in World War II were used not by spies, but by otherwise loyal Americans who could not resist trying to "beat the censor." Servicemen in particular attempted to sneak information about their whereabouts to families who otherwise would quite literally not know where in the world their soldier boy was—even though such attempts endangered the serviceman's own life.

One such system, though elementary, brought deserved bewilderment instead of clarification to its intended recipients. A young GI, following a prearranged system with his parents, tried to tell them he was in Tunis by using first T, then U, then N, I, and S as his father's middle initial in successive letters home. Unfortunately, he forgot to date them and they arrived out of order. The frantic parents wrote that they had looked and looked through their atlas but couldn't find *Nutsi* anywhere! Attempts of this sort grew so frequent by 1943 that the Navy had to warn its sailors that these "family codes," which were usually solved quite easily, could lead to severe penalties for the users.

The third kind of open code is the geometrical. A Cardano grille places the message-bearing words in fixed positions on a page. The significant words can be placed at intersections of the lines of a geometrical diagram of specified dimensions. In the 1600s, Sir John Trevanion, a Cavalier awaiting trial and almost certain execution by Cromwell's forces, noted the third letter after each punctuation mark in a letter that his jailers had scrutinized before giving him and learned that *Panel at east end of chapel slides*. He disappeared during vespers. And in World War II, captured U-boat officers spelled out secret messages in their letters home by breaking the flow of script after each significant letter. An alert censor noticed that the minute gaps did not occur in natural places, as after syllables. The hidden messages described Allied anti-submarine tactics and technical U-boat faults. Some outlined escape plans—which were, of course, foiled.

The second category of linguistically concealed messages is the semagram (from the Greek "sema," for "sign"). A semagram is a steganogram in which the ciphertext substitutes consist of anything but letters or numbers. The astragal of Aeneas the Tactician, in which yarn passing through holes representing letters carried the secret message, is the oldest known semagram. A box of Mah-Jongg tiles might carry a secret message. So might a drawing in which two kinds of objects represented the dots and dashes of Morse Code to spell out a message. The New York censorship station once shifted the hands and altered the positions of the individual timepieces in a shipment of watches lest a message be concealed in it.

The examination of the linguistically concealed messages—or, more correctly, those suspected to be such—was largely a frustrating experience. Often the examiner could not tell whether or not a message was hidden beneath the awkward or illiterate or misspelled writing. And even if he felt certain, solution often eluded him. He usually had only one message to work on, and no probable words. Early in the war, censorship practice even forbade working on a suspected cryptogram more than half an hour, on the theory that if the cryptanalyst hadn't gotten it by then, he'd never get it. These unsolved messages posed a difficult problem to the censors. Presumably they were carrying contraband information and so should be banned. But, in the absence of solution, no proof of this existed, and so the letter could not be mutilated. Sometimes this was done anyway, to destroy the suspected code.

Technological steganography early in the war consisted almost exclusively of invisible inks. This is truly an ancient device. Pliny the Elder, in his *Natural History*, written in the first century A.D., told how the "milk" of the tithymallus plant could be used as a secret ink. Ovid referred to secret ink in his *Art of Love*. A Greek military scientist, Philo of Byzantium, described the use of a kind of ink made from gall nuts (gallotannic acid), which could be made visible by a solution of what is now called copper sulfate. Qalqashandi described several kinds of invisible ink in his *Ṣubḥ al-aʽ shā*. Alberti mentions them. The Renaissance employed them in diplomatic correspondence. About 1530 a book was printed with panels in invisible ink; if these pages were dipped in water, the message would appear; this could be repeated three or four times. Porta devoted Book XVI of his *Magia Naturalis* to invisible writing.

The common inks are of two kinds: organic fluids and sympathetic chemicals. The former, such as urine, milk, vinegar, and fruit juices, can be charred into visibility by gentle heating. Despite their antiquity and their minimal protection, they are so convenient that they were used even during World War II. Count Wilhelm Albrecht von Rautter, a naturalized American who was spying on his adoptive country for his native Germany, ran out of his good secret ink and had to use urine.

Sympathetic inks are solutions of chemicals that are colorless when dry

Censors, Scramblers, and Spies

but that react to form a visible compound when treated with another chemical, called the reagent. For example, when a spy writes in iron sulfate, nothing will be visible until it is painted over with a solution of potassium cyanate, when the two chemicals will combine to form ferric ferrocyanide, or Prussian blue, a particularly lovely hue. The colorless writing of lead sub-acetate will turn into a visible brown compound when moistened with sodium sulfhydrate. Copper sulfate can be developed with ammonia fumes, and it may have been this chemical that was used for the secret writing on the handkerchief of

A drawing of the San Antonio River that conceals a secret message (solution in Notes)

George Dasch, leader of the eight Nazi spies who landed by submarine on Long Island in 1942 to blow up American defense plants, railroad bridges, and canal locks. The red letters that appeared as if by magic when the pungent ammonia reached it spelled out the names and addresses of a mail drop in Lisbon and of two reliable sources for help in the United States. Each of the eight saboteurs had also been given a watertight tube containing four or five matchsticks tipped with a grayish substance that served as a ready-made pen-and-secret-ink. The trick in concocting a good secret ink is to find a substance that will react with the fewest possible chemicals—only one, if possible, thus resulting in what is called a highly "specific" ink.

To test for secret inks, censorship stations "striped" letters. The laboratory assistant drew several brushes, all wired together in a holder and each dipped in a different developer, diagonally across the suspected documents. The developers were wide-spectrum, picking up even such substances as body oils, so that fingerprints and sweat drops often showed up. On the other hand, they missed some specific inks. A bleaching bath removed the stripes. Letters were also checked by infrared and ultraviolet light. Writing in starch, invisible in daylight or under electric light, will fluoresce under ultraviolet. Infrared can differentiate colors indistinguishable in ordinary light and so can pick up, for example, green writing on a green postage stamp. The censorship field stations tested all suspicious letters and a percentage of ordinary mail picked at random, and sometimes all letters to and from a certain city for a week to see if anything suspicious turned up. During the war, about 4,600 suspicious letters were passed along to the F.B.I. and other investigative agencies; of these 400 proved to be of some importance.

Problems that would not yield to the crude approach of the field stations went back to the T.O.D. laboratory. Here, amid Bunsen burners and retorts, Pierce and Breon, aided by an expert photographer and laboratory technicians, cooked up reagents that would reincarnate the phantom writing. Better equipped and more deeply versed in the nuances of sympathetic inks than the mass-production workers of the field stations, they had received a great stimulus from contact with one of the great secret-ink experts of the world, England's Dr. Stanley W. Collins, who had conducted this battle of the test tubes in two World Wars; he spoke at the Miami Counter-Espionage Conference in August, 1943. T.O.D. soon learned that Nazi spies were taking countermeasures to frustrate the iodine-vapor test and the general reagent.

One was to split a piece of paper, write a secret-ink message on the inner surface, then rejoin the halves. With the ink on the inside, no reagent applied to the outside could develop it! The technique came to light when one German spy used too much ink and the excess soaked through. Sanborn Brown, the M.I.T. physicist, got two inmates of a local jail to explain how two sheets of parchment could be used to do the splitting. They had been caught misapplying the talent to one- and ten-dollar bills, pasting one half of the tens to one half of the ones and passing them with the ten-dollar side up. The method is more an art than a science, for if the sudden tear is not done just right, the paper will shred. To read the message, the paper must be resplit, but it comes apart much more easily the second time.

Another antidetection measure was transfer. German agents would write their message in invisible ink on one sheet of paper, then press this tightly against another sheet. Moisture in the air would carry some of the ink to the second sheet without the telltale differential wetting of the fiber papers on which the iodine test relied. This compelled T.O.D. to find the specific reagent required.

Perhaps the most interesting development of the secret-ink war was the German instrument discovered by Shaw, Pierce, and Richter in 1945 and dubbed the "Wurlitzer Organ" because of its resemblance to that musical instrument. They found a burned-out shell of one "organ" in the bombed remnants of the Munich censorship station, and an undamaged one in the censorship station on an upper floor of the Hamburg post office. It examined suspected letters on an assembly-line basis by ingeniously exploiting some principles of physics to make the invisible ink glow. It first exposed the paper to ultraviolet light. This pumped energy into chemicals of the ink, boosting their electrons out of their normal orbits into higher ones. The chemical was then in a metastable state. The heat from a source of infrared then nudged the electrons from their higher orbits back into their regular ones. As they did so, the substance would give up, in the form of visible light, the energy that it had absorbed from the ultraviolet. Since this phenomenon will occur for nearly all substances, even common salt, though some will naturally shine more brightly than others, the Germans had a system that would develop a good many inks.

The chief difficulty with secret inks was their inability to handle the great volume of information that spies had to transmit in a modern war. One way of channeling large amounts was to dot the meaningful letters in a newspaper with a solution of anthracene in alcohol. This was invisible under normal circumstances but glowed when exposed to ultraviolet light. But with newspapers being carried as third-class mail, this was hardly the fastest method of getting information to where it was going.

The Germans then came up with what F.B.I. Director J. Edgar Hoover called "the enemy's masterpiece of espionage." This was the microdot, a photograph the size of a printed period that reproduced with perfect clarity a standard-sized typewritten letter. Though microphotographs (of a lesser reduction) had carried messages to beleaguered Paris as far back as 1870, a tip to the F.B.I. in January of 1940 by a double agent, "Watch out for the dots—lots and lots of little dots," threw the bureau into a near panic. Agents feverishly looked everywhere for some evidence of them, but it was not until August of 1941 that a laboratory technician saw a sudden tiny gleam on the surface of an envelope carried by a suspected German agent—and carefully pried off the first of the microdots, which had been masquerading as a typewritten period.

At first the microdot process involved two steps: A first photograph of an espionage message resulted in an image the size of a postage stamp; the second, made through a reversed microscope, brought it down to less than 0.05 inches in diameter. This negative was developed. Then the spy pressed a hypodermic needle, whose point had been clipped off and its round edge sharpened, into the emulsion like a cookie cutter and lifted out the microdot. Finally the agent inserted it into a cover-text over a period and cemented it there with collodion. Later, one Professor Zapp simplified the process so that most of these operations could be performed mechanically in a cabinet the size of a dispatch case. The microdots, or "pats," as T.O.D. called them, were photographically fixed but were not developed; consequently, the image on them remained latent and the film itself clear. In this less obtrusive form they were pasted onto the gummed surface of envelopes, whose shininess camouflaged their own. The pats could show such fine detail because the aniline dye used as an emulsion would resolve images at the molecular level, whereas the silver compounds ordinarily used in photography resolve only down to the granular level.

The microdots solved the problem of quantity flow of information for the Nazis. Professor Zapp's cabinets were shipped to agents in South America, and soon a flood of material was being sent to Germany disguised as hundreds of periods in telegraph blanks, love letters, business communications, family missives, or sometimes as a strip of the tiny film hidden under a stamp. The very first discovered, and the most frightening, was one in which a spy was asked to discover "Where are being made tests with uranium?" at a time when the United States was fighting to keep secret its development of the atom bomb. The "Mexican microdot ring," which operated from a suburb of Mexico City, microphotographed trade and technical publications that were barred from international channels—a favorite was *Iron Age*, with statistics on American steel production—and sent them to cover addresses in Europe on a wholesale basis, with as many as twenty pats in a single letter. Technical drawings also went by microdot. Other microdots talked of blowing up seized Axis ships in southern harbors, the deficient condition of one of the Panama Canal locks, and so on. Censorship discovered many of these, now that it knew what to look for, and this enabled the F.B.I.'s wartime Latin American branch to break up one Axis spy ring after another.

With mail and cable routes being screened so closely and subject to unpredictable delays, it was not unlikely that Axis agents would take to the ether to gain speed and avoid censorship. But here, too, the United States was ready for them.

The Radio Intelligence Division of the Federal Communication Commission had the job, in peacetime, of policing the airwaves, which are public property, for violations of federal radio regulations. During the war, its 12 primary and 60 subordinate monitoring posts and about 90 mobile units patrolled the radio spectrum for enemy agent radios. Teletype linked them into a direction-finding net coordinated from Washington. R.I.D. employed the latest radio equipment, including an aperiodic receiver that would give an alarm whenever it picked up a signal on any of a wide range of frequencies, and the "snifter," a meter that a man could carry in the palm of his hand while inspecting a building to see which apartment a signal came from.

> In the routine day-and-night operation of a monitoring station [wrote George E. Sterling, R.I.D.'s chief], the patrolman of the ether would cruise his beat, passing up and down the frequencies of the usable radio spectrum, noting the

landmarks of the regular fixed transmission, recognizing the peculiar modulation of a known transmitter or the characteristic fist of a familiar operator, observing an irregularity in operating procedure and pausing long enough to verify the call letters, or finding a strange signal and recording the traffic for close examination, and then sometimes alerting the nation-wide net to obtain a fix on the location of its source. More than 800 such fixes would be made in an average month, requiring the taking of some 6,000 individual bearings.

This sort of efficiency, built up during the long prewar years, so terrified the Japanese that when an agent requested permission to set up a transmitter, he was turned down on the ground that the F.C.C. would nab it as soon as he went on the air. It evidently made its impress on the Nazis as well, for only one bona-fide Axis station was ever heard in the United States. It was the German embassy in Washington which, using the call letters UA, tried to make contact with Berlin in the few days after Pearl Harbor. They never succeeded—nor did any other Nazi agent.

But R.I.D. did not live up to its acronym only within the United States. It insinuated its supersensitive antennae into the furtive Morse whisperings between other continents and thereby made an unexpected contribution to the Allied war effort. This began even before Pearl Harbor, when monitors at Miami heard station UU2 using irregular procedures. R.I.D. antennae swung silently, and the station was soon pinpointed in Lisbon. After a month of listening, monitors in Pittsburgh and Albuquerque finally picked up its correspondent: station CNA in South America. Then Lisbon station BX7 was identified from characteristics of its signal as being UU2 with different call letters, and a week later BX7's correspondent, NPD, was discovered in Portuguese West Africa. Sterling's men continued monitoring the little network, and two staff members who had become interested in cryptanalysis, Albert McIntosh and Abraham Checkoway, solved the transposition cipher in which the traffic was enciphered. The decrypted messages disclosed German agents in the neutral colonies and countries of Africa reporting on all manner of things—ship sailings, troop movements, political conditions. When McIntosh and Checkoway solved a message from Lisbon, indiscreetly ordering an agent codenamed ARMANDO in Portuguese West Africa to have one of his assistants "deliver letters personally to Porter Hotel, Duas Hacoes, Victoria Street, for Mr. Merckel," the fate of the German ring was sealed. Several weeks later, Allied counterintelligence cleaned it out.

Following this demonstration of its ability, R.I.D. was asked early in 1942 by its British counterpart, the Radio Security Service, to cooperate in watching German diplomatic and espionage networks. The two agencies discovered that many clandestine Nazi transmitters changed call-signs every day in a rota that ran for a month and then repeated. They catalogued the characteristics of individual transmitters and operators so that they could be recognized on different circuits. Counterespionage services told them how Nazi radio spies were trained in a school near Hamburg, how each agent's "fist" was recorded to make radiotelegraph forgery by the Allies that much more difficult, how the spies set up their suitcase-sized transmitter-receivers and connected them to directional antennae that focused maximum signal power on Germany and minimized dispersion. As the war in Europe mounted toward its climax, R.I.D. found itself monitoring 222 frequencies used in clandestine European traffic, breaking most Axis radio-spy codes and ciphers, and reading nearly all the messages of nearly all German networks.

Some of its most spectacular results came in Latin America, where its interceptions of the numerous Axis radios enabled the F.B.I. to help local authorities weed out these infestations. R.I.D. gathered in the transmissions of the three main agent networks in Brazil, centered on transmitters LIR, CEL, and CIT. Solutions of the columnar-transposition cryptograms enabled R.I.D. to feed information to the F.B.I.'s wartime Latin American branch; its agents then gumshoed these leads until it ferreted out the members of the rings.

Such was the story of the CIT ring. In April of 1941, Josef Jacob Johannes Starziczny, an engineer who had been trained at the Nazi spy school, arrived in Rio de Janeiro as Niels Christian Christiansen, smuggling ashore a black leather bag containing a transmitter, four coding books, and microfilmed instructions. A month later CIT went on the air. It and two associated transmitters poured quantities of information into the ether, mostly directed at the Hamburg control station that used call-sign ALD for this operation and the signature *Stein* in many of its plaintext messages. The information was usually of high quality, and the agent radios reached a frenzy of activity early in March, 1942, when the liner *Queen Mary* arrived in Rio with 10,000 troops aboard. Sinking her would be a tremendous blow to the Allies, both in terms of the actual loss of the troops and the transport capacity of the vessel and in terms of morale. Because of her speed, she traveled without a convoy, and the agents in Brazil pounded out message after message to Germany in an attempt to enable the U-boat wolf packs to get on her trail.

"*Queen Mary* arrived here today at 10:00 . . . she must [go] to cellar," wirelessed CIT on March 6, 1942. Two days later, CEL flashed: "*Queen Mary* sailed on March 8, 18 o'clock local time." The next day, CIT tapped out, "With *Queen Mary* falls Churchill . . . Good luck." Unknown to the operators, however, R.I.D. was eavesdropping. And when, on March 13, LIR sent a slow hand-keyed message on 11,220 kilocycles, an R.I.D. operator at Laredo, Texas, copied it with ease:

```
VVVV EVI EVI EVI
IWEOF  WONUG  IUVBJ  DLVCP  NABRS  CARTM  IELHX  YEERX
DEXUE  VCCXP  EXEEM  OEUNM  CMIRL  XRTFO  CXQYX  EXISV
NXMAH  GRSML  ZPEMS  NQXXX  ETNIX  AAEXV  UXURA  FOEAH
XUEUT  AFXEH  EHTEN  NMFXA  XNZOR  ECSEI  OAINE  MRCFX
SENSD  PELXA  HPRE
```

From one of LIR's first messages, R.I.D. had discovered that the group based its calls and its transposition cipher on Axel Munthe's *The Story of San Michele*, using an edition excluded from the United States and the British Empire. The agent determined the page to be used by adding his personal keynumber to the number of the month and the date. The last line of that page furnished the call letters that LIR was to use that day—the first three letters reversed for the station in Germany and the last three letters reversed for the agent post. From analysis of previous messages, R.I.D. knew that the LIR operator's keynumber was 56. Added to 3, for the month, and 13, the day, this would total 72. The last word on page 72 was "give," so EVI was the proper call-sign for the sender. The repeated v stood for *von* ("from").

The message had been sent in the early hours of the 13th, but had actually been enciphered on the 12th with the key for that date, which would be found on page 71, from 56+3+12. The first line on this page began, "I would have known how to master his fear," and R.I.D., like the agent, assigned numbers to the first nine different letters:

```
          I  W  O  U  L  D  H  A  V
          1  2  3  4  5  6  7  8  9
```

This key deciphered the first four groups, with other letters acting as nulls:

```
     I W E O F      W O N U G      I U V B J         D L V C P
     1 2   3          2 3   4      1     4 9         6   5 9
```

which meant "12 March, 2304 hours, 149 letters, 659th message." The next group, NABRS, identified the agent, and the 149 remaining letters were then inscribed into a columnar transposition block in accordance with a key derived by taking the initial letters of the first twenty lines on page 71 (skipping indented lines) and forming a numerical key from them. The result was:

initials	I	B	M	R	A	A	T	M	A	T	S	U	N	E	U	F	F	N	P	T
key	8	4	9	14	1	2	16	10	3	17	15	19	11	5	20	6	7	12	13	18
	S	P	R	U	C	H	X	S	E	C	H	S	N	U	L	L	X	V	O	N
	V	E	S	T	A	X	A	N	X	S	T	E	I	N	X	X	Q	U	E	E
	N	X	M	A	R	Y	X	Q	U	E	E	N	X	M	A	R	Y	X	A	M
	X	E	L	F	T	E	N	X	E	I	N	S	A	C	H	T	X	U	H	R
	M	E	Z	X	M	E	Z	X	V	O	N	D	A	M	P	F	E	R	X	C
	A	M	P	E	I	R	O	X	C	A	M	P	E	I	R	O	X	A	U	F
	H	O	E	H	E	X	R	E	C	I	F	E	X	R	E	C	I	F	E	X
	G	E	M	E	L	D	E	T	X											

This single transposition, with x's as word-dividers, sufficed, and the text can be read directly from the tableau. In English, and without the repetitions: "Message six zero from Vesta to Stein. *Queen Mary* reported off Recife by *Campeiro* on eleventh at one eight hours MEZ [Middle European zone time]."

But all the German effort that went into the collection and transmission of this intelligence was frustrated when the *Queen Mary*, perhaps alerted by these solutions, dashed across the Atlantic, eluding the submarines and making port safely with her 10,000 men. The *Queen Mary* messages were, in fact, the last the three Nazi radio rings ever sent. Brazilian police, tipped off by the F.B.I. and helped by an R.I.D. agent, swooped down on Starziczny on March 10 and on the other two rings soon thereafter. Two hundred agents and sympathizers were arrested and the spy nets destroyed.

The stupidity of sending a key so that anyone could understand it was not confined to LIR. The best-organized Nazi espionage apparatus in South America, which had transmitted its messages to Germany via stations PYL and PQZ in Chile, was finally smashed in February of 1944, largely through R.I.D. and F.B.I. information. Afterwards, its chief, Major Ludwig von Bohlen, set down his "Experiences Gained from the Valparaiso Process," and his very first item read: "The cardinal mistake was the insufficiency of the original key, and the transmission of the second key together with the first. If the communication identification word had not been deciphered, the code would not have been broken."

There were, however, two stations communicating with Hamburg which R.I.D. left undisturbed—even though both were operating on American soil. The first used the call CQ DX V W2—CQ being the general call to anyone to listen, DX meaning that a long-distance contact was desired, V meaning "from," W2 being the prefix assigned to amateur radio operators' stations in the second call area, which embraced Long Island. The two or three letters that should follow the W2 prefix were not used. This station began operating at 6 p.m. on May 15, 1940, trying to reach the Hamburg station on a wavelength of 14,300 to 14,400 kilocycles from a small house at Centerport, Long Island. After several tentative contacts, AOR in Hamburg flashed back on May 31 with the first full-length coded message, demanding information on monthly airplane production, how many were exported to all countries, especially England and France, whether they were delivered by ship or air, and whether payment was credit or cash and carry. The messages were enciphered in a transposition cipher like LIR's, keyed on Rachel Field's best-selling *All This, and Heaven Too*. This seems to have been the standard Nazi spy cipher, since it was still being used in 1943 by two German agents caught in Newark. The F.B.I., however, was able to read the Centerport messages without cryptanalyzing them—not because the G-men were clairvoyants or miracle-workers, but because they had made them up in the first place.

The ostensible operator of the Centerport set was William G. Sebold, a German-born American citizen secretly working for the F.B.I. When, in the summer of 1939, Sebold returned to his native Mulheim for a visit, the Gestapo had stolen his passport and threatened to harm his Jewish grandfather unless Sebold promised to become a spy for Germany in America. Sebold, who had meanwhile contacted American authorities in Cologne, pretended to agree. After a course at the Hamburg spy school, he returned to the United States on February 8, 1940, contacted the Nazi agents whose names he had been given, and set up the radio station to transmit their information to Germany.

Two F.B.I. agents were in fact manning the Centerport set, enciphering and sending messages whose contents had been carefully screened to include enough true information to seem authentic and enough false data to be misleading. At the same time other F.B.I. agents were using the contact to build up evidence against Frederick J. Duquesne and other Nazi agents. On June 28, 1941, the F.B.I., in a sudden series of raids, smashed the largest spy ring to be uncovered before Pearl Harbor.

Even more successful in tricking the Nazis was the double-agent ND98. An importer-exporter when the Nazis recruited him for espionage, he sold out to the Americans as soon as he arrived in the Western Hemisphere to carry on his spy activities for Germany. Like Sebold, he established a radio station on Long Island under F.B.I. supervision and began feeding the Nazis with a careful mixture of true and false data. For example, he hinted that the United States planned a major operation against the northern Kurile Islands in the Pacific. In fact this was to be merely a feint for the real assault, on the Marshall Islands. As hoped, Germany relayed the information to Japan, and later the Joint Chiefs of Staff advised the F.B.I. that ND98's information may well have contributed to the success of the invasion of the Marshalls in February of 1944. The Nazis liked ND98's information so much that they paid him $55,000 for it and maintained contact with him from February 20, 1942, when the first of hundreds of messages was sent, right up to the very end of the war. They only stopped communicating on May 2, 1945, when the Hamburg station was captured by the advancing British.

But this was child's play in comparison with the greatest radio deception of them all.

The Germans called it a "Funkspiel," and they could not have named it better. "Funk" means "radio," while "Spiel" means "play" or "performance," with secondary meanings of "game," "sport," and "match." Even all these together do not fully express the connotation of the German. As one writer put it, "The word implies a mysterious carillon that rings out in the ether, sounding a Lorelei tune to mislead or entrap men who listen to it."

Director of the funkspiel that achieved more spectacular results than any other in World War II was Major Herman J. Giskes, 46, a Rhinelander who had spent most of his adult life in the German Army. Giskes was chief of the Netherlands branch of Section III F (counterespionage) of the Abwehr, but though the Abwehr had its own efficient mobile radio-intelligence units, Giskes came to use the radio-intelligence section of the Ordnungspolizei, an occupation police force, for this funkspiel.

The Germans began tugging on the rope of the great carillon when they recruited a bloated, lame, perspiring Dutchman named George Ridderhof as a V-man. The V-men, posing as patriots, wormed into the Dutch underground and fed information to the Nazis. For a few months, Ridderhof, who was called F2078 by Giskes, registered little progress in his reports as he sought to gain the confidence of a cluster of Dutch agents working in The Hague.

Meanwhile, the Abwehr radio-intelligence units had been intercepting and solving messages sent five times a week from an underground transmitter with call letters UBX. Gradually the direction-finders closed in, and suddenly, at 8 o'clock one morning, UBX was raided. Captured were the operator, his assistant, their ciphering material, the transmitter, and espionage material.

This was Section III F's first major success in Holland, and Giskes immediately began bending his thoughts to see whether UBX could be "played back" in a funkspiel. The advantages of a funkspiel are great. With the Germans operating a radio set that the Allies believed to be still in the hands of the underground, the Abwehr would be able to learn a great deal about enemy intentions from instructions sent out by London. It could exploit this information to frustrate Allied military excursions and to break up other Resistance groups. It could lace Allied intelligence with false information in the expectation that when plans based on this data miscarried Allied commanders would lose confidence in their intelligence. A funkspiel works in the ether precisely as a double-agent does in person. Because of its value, the Abwehr subordinated all other considerations to the possibility of reversing a Resistance station. The underground, on its part, was well aware of the danger of a funkspiel, and, to discourage the Germans, would booby-trap doors and radios and leave half-emptied bottles of poisoned brandy standing about.

But UBX was not reversed. Some details necessary to make the playback sound authentic were missing, and the operator refused to divulge them under interrogation. Two other afus—as the Germans sometimes dubbed the agent radios, from their own highly compact but powerful clandestine transmitter—were captured, but attempts at reversing them also failed. These failures whetted Giskes' appetite for a success.

The possibility of one began glimmering in January, 1942. Ridderhof reported that the network that he had penetrated was about to receive equipment from Britain via a parachute drop that had been arranged by radio. "Go to the North Pole with your stories," Giskes wrote angrily on the report. "There is no radio communication between Holland and England." A few days later, however, the FuB, or intercept station, of the Ordnungspolizei heard a new radio link between station RLS in south Holland and PTX in England, north of London—a location that communicated with many of Europe's underground radio stations. Ridderhof confirmed that his network

Censors, Scramblers, and Spies

was operating RLS, and his Abwehr contact man, in reporting this to Giskes, referred slyly to "Operation North Pole." Giskes laughed, and Funkspiel NORDPOL got its name.*

Close surveillance of RLS began at once. The FuB soon established its transmission routine, and direction-finding pinpointed the afu in an apartment house on Fahrenheitstraat, The Hague. Ridderhof dribbled information into the net, items both false and true, one of which, for example, confirmed that the cruiser *Prinz Eugen* was undergoing repair at Scheidam. Within a month, Section III F had gained enough knowledge of RLS to attempt a funkspiel. A raid was set for the next regular transmission period, with a virtually simultaneous roundup of the other agents, as much to keep them from disclosing the funkspiel as to quash the network.

At 6 p.m. Friday, March 6, 1942, four disguised police cars blocked off Fahrenheitstraat. In the back seat of one, a man in plain clothes heard the key-clicks of a nearby transmitter as he sought the exact frequency. RLS was trying to raise London. Giskes planned to burst in before the radio operator made contact, to prevent his warning London. But the operator, tipped off by the owner of the apartment house that several cars filled with men were outside, broke off his transmission, gathered his three enciphered messages, and fled. He was apprehended a few yards away, and the police, breaking into the flat, discovered a small trunk, with the radio set and various papers in it, resting across two lines of washing in the rear garden, where the wife of the apartment house owner had dropped it.

The cat-and-mouse game now began. The radioman, Hubertus M. G. Lauwers, had been prepared for just such a situation in the spy school he had attended while training in England as an underground agent. The Nazis, he had been told, would try, first through persuasion and then through torture, to win the cooperation of the radioman on the key so that no change of fist would become apparent to England. And since it was desirable for an agent to avoid torture, to prevent his spilling really important secrets, such as names of other members of the ring, the agent was directed to pretend to cooperate—warning England, however, that he had been captured and his radio compromised. He was to sound a silent alarm by omitting his security check from his compromised transmissions.

---

* The R.S.H.A., whose Section IV E was charged with domestic counterespionage and frequently clashed with the Abwehr's Section III F over their differing views of their almost indistinguishable responsibilities, called it the ENGLANDSPIEL, the name by which it is perhaps more widely known. The R.S.H.A. felt it more important to uproot an underground network than to play back its afu and this led to several conflicts with the Abwehr. Giskes finally agreed with his opposite number in Section IV E-Netherlands, Sturmbannführer Joseph Schreieder, that the Abwehr would handle matters in the ether while the R.S.H.A. would make arrests on the ground. The rivalry between the two, which hampered German counterespionage, reflected the high-level power struggle between Himmler, the R.S.H.A. overseer, and Admiral Wilhelm Canaris, chief of the Abwehr, which Himmler eventually won when the R.S.H.A. absorbed the Abwehr.

The security check was an authenticator that the agent was to include in every one of his messages to prove their validity. It might consist of a number group, inserted at a prearranged point in the ciphertext, that had been obtained by adding together the date and a special number belonging to that agent alone. It might consist of the insertion of an x after every tenth letter of plaintext. It could take many forms. When a message came in without this check, or with what appeared to be a wrong security check (for the Germans could be expected to be as familiar with the technique as the Allies), a tocsin was to ring in London.

Then the Allies would be able to funkspiel a funkspiel. While the Germans thought that they were tricking London, feeding it false information and milking it of true, London would have turned the tables on them and engorged the Germans on false data while deducing, by contradiction, the Germans' real plans from the phony ones they sent London. And the Abwehr's respect for funkspiel information as being especially accurate and valuable promised the Allies commensurate rewards for contaminating it. This outfoxing of the foxes, this reversing of a reversed radio and double-crossing a double-crosser —all these spymasters' dreams of glory entered the realm of possibility with the recognition of the missing security check.

Thus, so long as the true check was kept secret, Lauwers had little to fear, and even much to gain, from disclosing his method of operation. And, as he had been told in security school, the Nazi soft-sell began first, starting even before he had been taken from the Fahrenheitstraat. The head of the FuB unit, Lieutenant Heinrichs, stated that he could cryptanalyze the three messages found on Lauwers. However, Lauwers recalled, "He wanted to give me an opportunity of saving my skin by handing over the particulars of my code voluntarily, and he added that I could save him a lot of trouble by doing this. To me it seemed reasonable to meet this proposal, and I promised that I would fall in with his wish if he were to succeed in deciphering one of the three messages which had been found on me. To my surprise he agreed at once. He sat down at a table, seemingly immersed in his 'game of patience,' and after about twenty minutes declared triumphantly, 'I see—*the cruiser Prinz Eugen is lying at Schiedam*—eh?'" This was the message that Ridderhof had planted and that Heinrichs had used as a crib to crack the system.

Lauwers, astounded at this demonstration of omniscience, kept his word to hand over the details of the cipher, which consisted of a double transposition with a group of nulls at the head and tail. He kept silent about his security check, however, until Giskes shocked him at the end of one interrogation by asking, "And what kind of mistake do you have to make?" For Lauwers' security check consisted precisely in making a deliberate error in the sixteenth letter of the plaintext. The error had to be one that could not occur by the accidental addition or omission of a single dot or dash in the letter's International Morse equivalent. Thus, an s (· · ·) was not to be transformed to an i (· ·) or an h (· · · ·), but to, say, a t (–).

Censors, Scramblers, and Spies

As it happened, however, the sixteenth letter in two of the three captured messages was the *o* of *stop*. Lauwers had accordingly changed one *o* (– – –) to an *i* (· ·) and the other into an *e* (·). This fortunate coincidence enabled him to produce a false security check that agreed with what Giskes appeared to know. He told the Germans that his security check consisted of changing the word *stop* once in every message into *step* or *stip*. The Germans accepted this,* and Lauwers agreed to work the RLS transmitter for them, contriving to do the enciphering himself to perpetuate the false security check. He was confident that the Dutch section of Special Operations Executive, the British organization that managed underground activities in Europe, would spot the warning and take the proper measures.

The first regular transmission period after the capture on March 6 came at 2 p.m. on March 12, and Lauwers sent the messages that he had not sent the night of the raid, which, of course, had the correct security check but also the information he was going to send anyway. In subsequent messages, RLS, directed by Giskes, asked that the drop point for an already arranged parachute drop be shifted from near Zoutkamp, which RLS now said was too isolated, to a moor near Steenwijk. On the 25th, S.O.E. acquiesced and, two days later, broadcast the signal for the drop itself. This was the crucial test. S.O.E.'s own security check and encipherment details seemed to be all right, but perhaps S.O.E. was itself planning a trap. Would the plane deliver bombs instead of supplies, blowing up not only the Abwehr's hopes for a funkspiel but also part of the Abwehr itself? Lauwers, who expected that S.O.E. would detect his false security check, hoped so. Giskes, though unaware of Lauwers' silent alarm, could nevertheless not be absolutely confident of success.

On the 27th, Giskes and the German team huddled in the juniper bushes on the moor, and soon after midnight they heard the drone of aircraft engines. The plane headed for the triangle of red and white lights that the Germans shone upwards, and suddenly in its wake five large black shadows blossomed and rushed earthward. From the parachutes swung heavy black containers, which hit the ground with a dull thud. The plane blinked its navigation lights and disappeared westward into the mist. The Germans, scarcely able to believe their luck, pressed one another's hands in dumb joy. The first of many echoes had come back from the pealing of the great carillon.

And the security check? Why had its alarm not gone off? Because of stupidity and incompetence within S.O.E., with a single factual condition as an alibi. This condition was the weakness of the agents' radios and the agents' poor abilities as operators. Consequently, messages seldom arrived with perfect accuracy. In some cases, the decipherers in the Dutch section of S.O.E. could not tell whether an error was a deliberate one to conform to the

---

* Apparently they never noticed that neither the third captured message nor the previously intercepted ones fitted this pattern, or perhaps they thought that Lauwers had made some errors.

security check or just an ordinary garble. From 5 to 15 per cent of the messages were so unclear that the decipherers were happy if they could just read the text—with these, they were not concerned with security checks. But even granted this, the negligence of S.O.E. bordered on the criminal. The vast majority of messages in which there was no question but that the crucial security check was missing were regarded as bona fide by the organization. Some messages were even marked "Identity check [same as security check] omitted"; S.O.E. did not reject them. Thus, by disregarding the precautions which it had itself instituted, S.O.E. fell headlong into a funkspiel.

NORDPOL's first success was followed by others. A succession of air drops took place, each one increasing Giskes' confidence in the success of his funkspiel. Then, at the beginning of May, 1942, a series of Resistance mishaps, skillfully exploited by the Germans, delivered into their hands the radio links, and hence the control, of all underground networks in Holland. Two two-man rings, called TURNIP and HECK by the S.O.E., had been parachuted into Holland; their radios had been damaged in the drop, and they contacted group LETTUCE to report their problems to London. Meanwhile, the NORDPOL group, which was known as EBENEZER to S.O.E., was directed to contact LETTUCE to help an agent of still another ring, POTATO. The Nazis rounded up these agents before they could warn London, and on May 5, Giskes began operating the LETTUCE transmitter in a second funkspiel. In this one, a captured agent, Hendrik Jordaan, betrayed his security check.

Eventually the Giskes-Schreieder combine was running fourteen funkspiels with S.O.E. Hitler himself was regularly reading reports on it that gave the texts of many of the messages; these were submitted by Himmler. The all-important security check continued to be omitted from many of the transmissions—Lauwers alone transmitted checkless messages for seven months. S.O.E. actually bestirred itself a few times to wonder whether the Dutch operations had been penetrated and should therefore be terminated. Each time it decided to continue them because it felt that the security checks were "inconclusive as a test." The full scale of the Dutch section's bungling is displayed in the fact that the fourteen transmitters were operated by only six FuB radiomen, who were so overworked that Giskes sought to eliminate some sets by reporting that they had been knocked out by German action. S.O.E. had obviously either never recorded its agents' fists before sending them out or never bothered to check their supposed transmissions against any transcriptions that they might have made. On the other hand, many of the messages did have the correct security check. Credit for much of the authenticity of many of these messages must go to Schreieder's cryptologic specialist, Ernst Georg May, a corpulent, crew-cut Prussian in his late thirties, who thoroughly studied the Resistance cipher systems and the recurrent "mistakes" therein.

Keeping NORDPOL going involved a good deal more than thinking up fairy tales to put on the air. What was to be done about orders received from S.O.E.?

How could the Abwehr maintain S.O.E.'s confidence that its underground networks were all operating healthily? Giskes resorted to a variety of elaborate charades, excuses, and, in a few cases, actual aids to the Allies. Most of the latter involved helping downed airmen escape to Spain. When these reached England, they extolled the help given them by GOLF, one of the Dutch Resistance groups. They never realized that GOLF's extraordinary success was due to its direction by a German officer, and S.O.E., confronted by proof positive of GOLF's efficacy in the form of living Allied airmen, suspected nothing. In another case, when S.O.E. ordered EBENEZER to blow up an Occupation antenna complex, Giskes reported that a minefield had thwarted their attempt. S.O.E. accepted the excuse, saying that the defense was unforeseeable. When one new agent parachuted into Holland and found himself in the Abwehr's arms, he told his captors that unless he sent the code message THE EXPRESS LEFT ON TIME by 11 a.m. S.O.E. would know that he had been nabbed. Giskes, thinking fast, signaled London through another *funkspiel* that the agent had landed heavily and was unconscious. Four days later, S.O.E. was told that he had died without gaining consciousness. Giskes even went so far as to sabotage a barge in Rotterdam harbor before an audience of thousands of cheering Dutchmen—and then, after reporting it as a Resistance coup, planted stories in the German-controlled newspapers in the hope that they would get to England and corroborate his reports.

Lauwers, on the other hand, was going frantic. After thinking at first that London had reversed the Abwehr radio, he finally realized that there had been a serious slip, and he began to look for other means of alerting S.O.E. He first sent the word *caught* by altering the Morse equivalents of the radioman's standard Q-code signal QRU (– – · –   · – ·   · · –), meaning "I have nothing further for you," to *cau* (– · – ·   · –   · · –), and the Morse of his call-sign, which he himself could select and which followed QRU, to *ght*. Though he slipped this past the German operators, developments gave no indication that London had recognized the cue. He then tried to spell out *caught* by altering a likely five-letter ciphertext group and adding on the single dash for a *t*; to increase the chance of a suitable group appearing, he used C, G, and H almost exclusively as his nulls. He then transmitted CAUGHT as if it were an error, repeating this error several times in pretended self-irritation so that it would be picked up several times in England, and finally sending the text correctly. No response.

With agents falling like flies into the hands of the Nazis, Lauwers and his cellmate, Jordaan, the operator who had betrayed his check, determined to try once more with a scheme that was more difficult but that might show up more clearly in England. They would make a warning message out of the nulls at the head and tail of two messages. The Germans prohibited the use of vowels in the nulls at the head and tail of their plaintexts, so the Dutchmen had to use consonants in place of the vowels of their clandestine message, follow these consonants through the two transposition blocks, mentally reconvert them to vowels in the cryptogram, and then transmit these vowels as if they were errors for the consonants. The two practiced this difficult process in their cell and managed to pass the first part of their message. But then Giskes changed procedure: a German operator read the cryptogram off letter by letter, perhaps to prevent just such tricks, and the second half was never sent. It probably didn't matter anyway: the first part went unheeded.

As a result, Giskes managed to keep NORDPOL going effectively for the unprecedented period of twenty months. No other funkspiel had ever lasted more than three. Agent after agent parachuted into captivity. The beginning of the end came when two agents escaped from the prison at Haaren and made their way to Dutch authorities in Switzerland, where they told the story. Even then the resourceful Giskes staved off defeat by smearing them through a NORDPOL link as having escaped with German aid to infiltrate S.O.E. But with the escape of three more agents on November 23, 1943, the radio game was finally over. Giskes realized this when the messages from England, usually packed with information, came in leached of anything solid.

NORDPOL dragged on for a few more months as both sides fenced for advantage by sending meaningless messages, until the Abwehr decided to end the pointless exercise. Giskes thereupon composed a plaintext message to be sent to the men heading the Dutch section of S.O.E.

> To Messrs. Blunt, Bingham & Co., Successors Ltd., London. We understand that you have been endeavoring for some time to do business in Holland without our assistance. We regret this the more since we have acted for so long as your sole representatives in this country, to our mutual satisfaction. Nevertheless we can assure you that, should you be thinking of paying us a visit on the Continent on any extensive scale, we shall give your emissaries the same attention as we have hitherto, and a similarly warm welcome. Hoping to see you.

With malice aforethought, Giskes ordered it passed on April 1, 1944. All ten remaining funkspiel links sent it; four British stations receipted for it as usual; six did not answer the calls. More than two years after it had begun, NORDPOL finally ended.

It had arranged for 190 parachute drops and received 95 of them, containing 30,000 pounds of explosives, 3,000 Sten guns, 5,000 revolvers, 2,000 hand grenades, 75 radio transmitters, 500,000 cartridges, and half a million Dutch guilders in cash—all of which had fallen into German hands. It had captured 54 agents, 47 of whom were shot without trial that autumn at the Mauthausen concentration camp. The great NORDPOL carillon tolled not only their deaths, but those of the hopes of the Allies to establish a viable underground in Holland. It had kept German defenses in the Netherlands intact and untroubled by saboteurs, and had deceived the Allies as to the capabilities of German forces there: The Hague was not liberated until an amazing seven months after D-Day.

It was the worst Allied defeat in the espionage war.

That clandestine struggle bred a surprising variety of systems of clandestine communication. Perhaps the most common one was double transposition. Like the Dutch Resistance groups, the French Maquis often used it. A group led by Gilbert Renault picked a key from 15 to 20 letters long at random from a book held both by the group and its London radio correspondents. The same key served for both transpositions. About half a dozen nulls began and ended each plaintext; the security check often involved inserting a specified letter among these. The encipherer told London what passage had been used as the key by a series of numbers. For example, 05702 01837 would mean page 57, line 2, with 18 letters taken from that line to generate the numerical transposition key, and with the message text 37 groups long. The encipherer then added his personal keynumber to these digits, converted them into two groups of five letters by a homophonic substitution, converted them a second time into two other groups of five letters in case the first pair was garbled in transmission, placed them at prearranged places in the message, and gave it to his radio operator.

Renault's network used this system from August, 1940, to the summer of 1943, when, while in London, he compiled a code of five-letter groups representing whole phrases in an attempt to reduce his dangerously long radio transmissions. He drew his vocabulary from a study of a commercial code and his network's messages. He had planned to encipher the codetext by double transposition, but an elderly English cryptologist with bulging eyes, glasses on the end of his nose, and a gold chain across his vest advised him to change his five-letter groups to five-digit ones so that they could be enciphered by one-time pads, which London produced by machine and would give him. The destruction of each sheet after use would prevent the Nazis from reading his back intercepts even if the unused portion of the pad were captured. Renault took the advice. Back in France, he had the satisfaction not only of seeing his transmission times drop from half an hour to five minutes but of knowing that his cryptograms were perfectly secure.

Agents of the American Office of Strategic Services also used double transposition. They often keyed their messages with their school songs, using lines 1 and 2 as keys for the first message, lines 1 and 3 for the second, and so on, to prevent the multiple anagramming of two messages with identical keys. One agent, Peter Tompkins, who at 23 was slipped into Rome in January, 1944, to organize a spy ring, employed as keys two passages from Dante that he had memorized but could easily obtain anywhere in Italy if they slipped his mind. Nulls were sprinkled about freely. Interestingly, O.S.S. did not use a security check, but relied instead on "electronic fingerprinting"—taperecording an agent's fist before he went into the field. Double transposition was simple and quite secure, but it was occasionally solved. A contributory reason may have been such practices as that of the Resistance group codenamed MARCO POLO, which time after time used the word *tobacco* as a group of nulls in its transposition blocks in (successful) attempts to get the British to supply that necessity in their parachute drops.

The O.S.S. employed a variety of other cryptographic systems for intercommunication among its branches in London, Chungking, Karachi, Burma, North Africa, and other places around the world. It had one-time pads, with random numbers generated by I.B.M. machines, SIGABAS, which it called "Berthas," M-209s, and strips. Its headquarters message center was in the basement of the O.S.S. administration building at 26th and E streets, North West, in Washington, and was run by New York socialite lawyer John W. Delafield. It included a specialist department of five or six men, headed by bridge expert Alfred Sheinwold, whose task it was to untangle badly garbled messages, to make sure that O.S.S. ciphers were secure and that keys were not being used too long, and to train cryptographers for the branches.

Individual agents sometimes developed systems of their own for special-purpose use within the networks of spies that they recruited. In Rome, for example, Peter Tompkins employed a Vigenère with a tableau based on the 21-letter Italian alphabet (j, k, w, x, y omitted); one keyphrase was AVANTI TORINO. Another was a one-page code of five-letter groups for communication with a group in the mountains near Visso whose radio signal was very weak; the codegroups were so designed that if either the first or the last letter (which were the same) and any of the intervening three letters were received correctly in proper position, the group was known unequivocally. Thus, in the weather section, the first three groups were *sereno* ("clear") = TABCT, *pioggia* ("rain") = TBCDT, *nebbia* ("fog") = TCDET.

The governments-in-exile, who abhorred any semblance of collaboration with the Nazis and who directed their resistance from their headquarters in London, received information from the legations they maintained in neutral and Allied capitals. The Czech counselor in Stockholm, Dr. Vladimir Vanek, sent about 500 messages to his chief between August, 1941, and March, 1942, when the Swedes arrested him on espionage charges, probably under German pressure. Vanek's messages, sent to the cable address MINIMISE LONDON through the British embassy, were enciphered in a combined transposition-substitution system. It began with a monalphabetic substitution into a numerical alphabet whose first digit always matched the date. Thus, for the 8th of the month, the alphabet was this, with the * used as a word-divider:

```
a   b   c   č   d   e   ě   f   g   h   i   j   k   l   m   n   o   p   q   r   ř   s   š
08  09  10  11  12  13  14  15  16  17  18  19  20  21  22  23  24  25  26  27  28  29  30
t   u   v   w   x   y   z   ž   .   ,   *   0   1   2   3   4   5   6   7   8   9   0
31  32  33  34  35  36  37  38  39  40  41  42  43  44  45  01  02  03  04  05  06  07
```

The transposition keys were derived from one of the bibles of Czech nationalism, Tomáš Masaryk's *Svetová Revoluce*. (His son, incidentally, who was Foreign Minister of the Czech government-in-exile, was the recipient of many messages keyed through his father's book.) The pages used were selected apparently at random: page 74 for August, page 391 for September, 25 for October, and so on. For the 8th of September, the eighth line on the page would be taken. The first 18 letters of the line—"pakani profesors tvi . . ."— bred a numerical key for a transposition block for the substitution. The result of this transposition was inscribed into a second block whose key was derived from the last 19 letters of the same line ("politicky aneskodilo . . ."). The plaintext sent by Vanek on that date was: *Sudar.Pachatel*atentatu*na* něm.Muniční*vlaky*ve*švedsku*je*německy*konsul*v*malmoe*nolde. Mame* duvěrně*od*noru.Jlnas37*, plus 0 as a null. The ciphertext began: 34232 21333 19293 11121 33020 10121. . . .

Sweden's Arne Beurling solved it when he saw "a shadow of the system" in the cryptograms. He noticed that 0's, 1's, 2's, and 3's, which stood out because of their much greater frequency, appeared at approximately regular intervals in the cryptograms. He deduced that this resulted from a preliminary encipherment in an alphabet of the type actually used, followed by a first inscription into a transposition block with an even number of columns. This would columnize all the 0's, 1's, 2's, 3's, and 4's that formed the first digits of the two-digit substitutes. In the second transposition block, this stack of digits would form a row, and as the approximately equal columns of this block were transcribed, the digits of that row would appear in the cryptogram at approximately equal intervals. Beurling called it one of the best hand systems he ever faced. A linguist disappointed him in not recovering the literal key from the numerical and so culminating the solution by finding the keybook. The solved messages played a role in convicting Vanek as a spy. The Germans also solved the system. By reading Czech exile messages from various capitals, they learned so much about the uprisings in Czechoslovakia in 1944 that they were able to quell them with relative ease.

Most widely used of the spy systems were the jargon codes. A phrase intoned in French, Dutch, Norwegian, or Italian in the imperturbable voice of a British Broadcasting Corporation announcer would detonate explosions at a German radio station, cause machine-gun bullets to rattle in a wild raid, ignite a wooden railway trestle. For these innocent-sounding "personal messages" were, in large measure, signals to Resistance groups for an imminent operation. Peter Tompkins has evoked the atmosphere of a group listening for one of these messages: "Thus, on the night of our first expected drop we sat tensely round the radio listening to the news in Italian, waiting for the announcer slowly to enunciate his special messages: 'Catherine is waiting by the well,' 'The sun will rise at dawn,' 'Johnny needs sandals,' then, like a stab of light, our own special message: 'William waits for Mary'! The drop was on, due about midnight."

Other jargon codes acknowledged receipt of messages and information. The MARCO POLO Resistance group, which sent its 20- or 30-page answers to such requests as "What is the diameter of the pebbles on the beaches of

France?" and "Provide a calendar of fair days in the towns of France" to England by airplane in unenciphered form because of their length, heard that the information had gotten safely to England when the B.B.C. broadcast the Alexandrine verse ET LE DÉSIR S'ACCROÎT QUAND L'EFFET SE RECULE ("And desire grows when the result recedes"). Still other code messages were in the nature of authenticators. When a Russian engineer came to work with MARCO POLO to help dig out information about Peenemunde, where the Germans had constructed their secret V-weapon launching sites, the B.B.C. confirmed his identity with the phrase LES ÉLÉPHANTS MANGENT LES FRAISES ("The elephants are eating the strawberries"), which is nothing if not unmistakable.

Among the most dramatic of the jargon-code messages were the two that set in motion all across France a massive underground sabotage of German transportation and communications. When the B.B.C. broadcast, in French, "It is hot in Suez," the Resistance was to put into effect the Green Plan, which called for the sabotaging of railroad tracks and equipment. "The dice are on the table" would institute the Red Plan for the cutting of telephone lines and cables. Throughout France Resistance leaders listened tensely for these code-phrases on their hidden radios. As D-Day approached, the number of messages rose into the scores. Finally, at 6:30 p.m. on June 5, 1944, the two crucial messages were broadcast, followed by hundreds of others, such as "The arrow pierces steel." And, as the underground leaders mentally interpreted them, they were stunned by a blinding realization that the liberation for which they had worked and waited and hoped throughout four dark years of Nazi oppression was now at hand. For many of them, their hearing of a jargon-code message would remain one of the unforgettable moments of their lives.

The most famous of these jargon-code messages was the one announcing D-Day which the Nazis intercepted, recognized—and ignored.

Abwehr headquarters had discovered that the great Allied invasion of Europe would be signaled to the underground by the first stanza of Paul Verlaine's melancholy "Chanson d'Automne." The first half of the stanza, when broadcast on the first or the fifteenth of a month, would warn of the imminence of the Anglo-American invasion. The second half would mean: "The invasion will begin within 48 hours . . . the count starting at 0000 hours of the day following the transmission."

In January, 1944, Canaris had passed the details to German intelligence units, with orders for them to listen for the two messages. Among the units that had been straining for months to pick them up was that of Lieutenant Colonel Hellmuth Meyer, intelligence officer for the German 15th Army, whose information came largely from his 30-man interception crew. In their concrete bunker at army headquarters near the Belgian border, filled with sensitive equipment, these experts—each of whom could speak three languages fluently—captured virtually every wisp of radio emanation from Allied sources. They had heard many of the jargon messages, which irritatingly eluded their comprehension. They had even intercepted the calls of military policemen using transmitters in jeeps to direct convoys in England, more than 100 miles away. This information had enabled Meyer to learn the names of many of the outfits preparing for the invasion. Recently, however, these calls had stopped. Radio silence had descended upon England, another bit of evidence that the invasion of the Continent was close at hand. Meyer thereupon redoubled his efforts to pick up the fateful Verlaine message.

On June 1, Sergeant Walter Reichling of Meyer's team was monitoring the messages in French that followed the 9 p.m. B.B.C. news. "Kindly listen now to a few personal messages," said the announcer. Reichling switched on a wire-recorder. After a brief pause there followed the first half of the first stanza:

> LES SANGLOTS LONGS
> DES VIOLONS
> DE L'AUTOMNE

("The long sobs of the violins of autumn"). Reichling rushed to Meyer's office, and the two listened to the recording. Meyer immediately informed the chief of staff, who alerted his own 15th Army, then teletyped the notification to O.K.W. and telephoned the two German headquarters charged with defending against the invasion. But though the message gave clear warning that the invasion was to be launched within two weeks, at the most, nothing was done about it. O.K.W. thought that one of the invasion headquarters had ordered an alert, and that headquarters thought that the other one—headed by Rommel—had done so. But though Rommel must have known about the message, he apparently discounted it, for on June 4 he left for a much-needed home leave.

Meyer, who knew nothing of this, strained to hear the second half of the stanza. "Its awesome significance overwhelmed Meyer," wrote Cornelius Ryan. "The defeat of the Allied invasion, the lives of hundreds of thousands of his countrymen, the very existence of his country would depend on the speed with which he and his men monitored the broadcast and alerted the front. Meyer and his men would be ready as never before."

There were at least 15 other D-Day messages which the Germans intercepted and interpreted. On June 2, for example, O.K.H. teletyped to an invasion defense headquarters detailed information received from the R.S.H.A. about jargon messages. Within three days after hearing MESSIEURS, FAÎTES VOS JEUX ("Gentlemen, place your bets"), L'ÉLECTRICITÉ DATE DU VINGTIÈME SIÈCLE ("Electricity dates from the 20th century"), or some other messages, O.K.H. warned, "die Invasion rollen." But the Germans placed most credence in the Verlaine message.

It came at 9:15 p.m. June 5:

> BLESSENT MON COEUR
> D'UNE LANGUEUR
> MONOTONE

("Wound my heart with a monotonous languor"). Meyer hurried out of his office with what "was probably the most important message the Germans had intercepted throughout the whole of World War II." In the dining room of headquarters, he breathlessly told General Hans von Salmuth, the 15th Army

Tag Uhrzeit Ort und Art der Unterkunft	Darstellung der Ereignisse (Dabei wichtig: Beurteilung der Lage [Feind- und eigene], Eingangs- und Abgangszeiten von Meldungen und Befehlen)
5.6.44	Am 1., 2. und 3.6.44 ist durch die Nast innerhalb der "Messages personelles" der französischen Sendungen des britischen Rundfunks folgende Meldung abgehört worden : "Les sanglots longs des violons de l'automne ". Nach vorhandenen Unterlagen soll dieser Spruch am 1. oder 15. eines Monats durchgegeben werden, nur die erste Hälfte eines ganzen Spruches darstellen und ankündigen, dass binnen 48 Stunden nach Durchgabe der zweiten Hälfte des Spruches, gerechnet von 00.00 Uhr des auf die Durchsage folgenden Tages ab, die anglo-amerikanische Invasion beginnt.
21.15 Uhr	Zweite Hälfte des Spruches "Blessent mon coeur d'une longeur monotone" wird durch Nast abgehört.
21.20 Uhr	Spruch an Ic-AO durchgegeben. Danach mit Invasionsbeginn ab 6.6. 00.00 Uhr innerhalb 48 Stunden zu rechnen. Überprüfung der Meldung durch Rückfrage beim Militärbefehlshaber Belgien/Nordfrankreich in Brüssel (Major von Wangenheim).
22.00 Uhr	Meldung an O.B. und Chef des Generalstabes.
22.15 Uhr	Weitergabe gemäss Fernschreiben (Anlage 1) an Generalkommandos. Mündliche Weitergabe an 16. Flak-Division.

The German 15 Army detects the open-code message to the French Underground that warns that the invasion of Europe will start within 48 hours

commander, who was playing bridge, that the second half of the vital message had arrived. Von Salmuth considered a moment, ordered the 15th Army on full alert, then returned to his cards. "I'm too old a bunny to get excited about this," he remarked to the other players.

Meanwhile, Meyer telephoned his headquarters, and later dispatched

"Teletype No. 2117/26 urgent to 67th, 81st, 82nd, 89th Corps; Military Governor Belgium and Northern France; Army Group B; 16th Flak Division; Admiral Channel Coast; Luftwaffe Belgium and Northern France. Message of B.B.C., 2115, June 5, has been processed. According to our available records it means 'Expect invasion within 48 hours, starting 0000, June 6.'" It was then only about three hours until 18,000 paratroopers would drop into the hedgerows of Normandy to begin the invasion, only about eight hours to the H-Hour landing on Omaha, Juno, Sword, and the other beaches. All the German commands were notified—except one. For reasons that have never been fully explained, the German 7th Army, the one on which would fall the brunt of the cross-channel attack, was never alerted to D-Day.

In the United States, a great battle to wrest almost infinite power from the infinitesimal atom was plunged in secrecy as deep as nature's own. Congress did not know about it: the two-billion-dollar cost of creating the atomic bomb was appropriated from a special presidential emergency fund. References to uranium were kept out of the newspapers. The huge plants and laboratories necessary were built in sections of the country as remote as possible—Oak Ridge, Tennessee; Hanford, Washington; atop a mesa at Los Alamos, New Mexico. And everybody and everything had a codename, beginning with the very name of the project: the MANHATTAN ENGINEERING DISTRICT. Even before it came into being, the bomb was being called THE GADGET, THE DEVICE, S-1, THE THING, THE BEAST, or simply IT. Later, after its probable dimensions had evolved, the scientists called the uranium bomb, which would bring the two masses of uranium into one of the critical size by shooting one into another down a gun barrel, the THIN MAN after President Roosevelt. The plutonium bomb, which would implode a sphere of plutonium and thus would require a bulkier casing, was called, in contradistinction, the FAT MAN after Churchill. When the THIN MAN's gun barrel was shortened, it became known as the LITTLE BOY.

The man in charge of the project, Brigadier General Leslie R. Groves, was sometimes called RELIEF, sometimes 99—from the way his secretary wrote "G.G." for "General Groves." In fact, some of the scientists who were less bemused than most by the secret-club nature of the project simply referred to him as "G.G." A special operation to ascertain German atomic capabilities was called ALSOS, a Greek word meaning "groves." Dr. Arthur Holly Compton became A. H. COMAS or A. HOLLY. Niels Bohr, one of the top atomic scientists, was rechristened NICHOLAS BAKER, and Enrico Fermi became HENRY FARMER. The Los Alamos laboratory was SITE Y; K-25 was the gaseous diffusion plant at Oak Ridge and Y-12 the electromagnetic plant there. For Manhattan District purposes, the University of Chicago was known as the CHICAGO METALLURGICAL LABORATORY, and the first man to take charge of the atom-splitting work there, Gregory Breit, was rather uninhibitedly referred to as the COORDINATOR OF RAPID RUPTURE.

Though telegraphic messages were handled by the Signal Corps with its own cryptographic equipment, a need arose for secrecy in telephone conversations in the nationwide project, which frequently sent key officials into the field far from any cipher machines. The first telephonic cipher was devised on an impromptu basis by Groves's secretary, Mrs. Jean O'Leary, when she had to telephone some secret information to him. "Go get what you always see me using," she said. Groves bought a pack of her favorite cigarettes and spelled out the message as she gave each letter by its position in the words on the pack. A few days later, Groves himself made up what he called a "quadratic code" for use with a "number of people with whom I might have had to talk over the phone on matters of high secrecy. Each one was different and as far as I can recall I was the only one who had all the codes. Possibly Mrs. O'Leary kept them all in one of the top-secret safes. People were instructed to carry them in their billfolds and report instantly if they were lost." The quadratic code was actually a 10 × 10 checkerboard, like this one, a typewritten square about 3½ × 4 inches that Groves used with Lieutenant Colonel Peer da Silva, chief of security at Los Alamos:

	1	2	3	4	5	6	7	8	9	0
1	I_8	P	I		O	U	O		P	N
2	W	E	U	T	E	K_6		L	O	
3	E	U	G	N	B_4	T	N		S	T
4	T	A	Z_2	M	D		I	O	E	
5	S_9	V	T	J		E		Y		H
6	N_7	A	O	L	N	S	U	G	O	E
7		C	B	A	F	R	S_5		I	R
8	I	C	W	Y_3	R	U	A	M		N°
9	M	V	T		H_0	P	D	I	X	Q
0	L	S	R_1	E	T	D	E	A	H	E

Censors, Scramblers, and Spies

Teller might be enciphered 93, 31, 64, 28, 07, 70, and *U-235* as 23, 80, 43, 84, 77. No key pattern is apparent, and the square provides a satisfyingly sufficient complement of plaintext letters to suppress frequency: nine *e*'s, seven *t*'s, six *i*'s, six *o*'s, and so on. All letters are represented. "The codes were not used to spell out an entire message," Groves has written, "but rather one or, at most, a few key words. . . . Even in spelling out the key words, it was not usual to spell them out in their entirety. Between [J. Robert] Oppenheimer and myself, only the first two or three letters would normally be needed." A checkerboard is hardly a high-security cipher, but in view of this brevity, of Groves's assurance that "all codes were constantly changed, as we recognized how easily any code could be broken if enough messages were available," and of a spy's difficulty in tapping just the right telephone wire to intercept one of these messages, it seems adequate to its purpose. In any event, there is no record of anything having been compromised through its interpretation.

"Most of our telephone calls included a great deal of double talk and references to things and individuals which no one else would easily spot," Groves has noted. One of these spur-of-the-moment jargon codes was employed by Arthur Compton when, on December 2, 1942, he telephoned James B. Conant, president of Harvard, to report on Enrico Fermi's unexpectedly early success in producing man's first controlled chain reaction in a squash court at Stagg Field, Chicago.

"Jim, the Italian navigator has just landed in the new world," said Compton, who composed one of the more felicitous jargon expressions in history when he equated atomic fission with a new world and made Fermi the Christopher Columbus of nuclear physics. "The earth was not as large as he had estimated," Compton continued, indicating to Conant that the size of the atomic pile was not as large as originally thought necessary, "and he arrived sooner than expected."

"Were the natives friendly?" asked Conant in oblique reference to possible problems.

"Yes. Everyone landed safe and happy."

This quick resort to indirection sometimes partook, in the heavily intellectual Manhattan District atmosphere, of a somewhat exotic nature. Compton once had to discuss the problem that the by-products of fissionable material might pollute the water supply. He succeeded in conveying this message about this most modern of difficulties through fairly obscure references to ancient Greek mythology. At the other end of the long-distance wire, Crawford H. Greenewalt of du Pont not only understood but replied in kind.

When the first atomic bomb was exploded near Alamogordo, New Mexico, the test was given perhaps the least felicitous codename in history: TRINITY. Details of its success were reported to Secretary of War Stimson, then at the Potsdam Conference, in still another informal jargon code. To give Stimson some idea of the immensity of the blast, the originator of the message, special consultant George L. Harrison, related its visibility to the 250-mile distance between Washington and Stimson's Highhold estate on Long Island and its thunderousness to the 60 miles between Washington and Harrison's farm at Upperville, Virginia. The LITTLE BOY in his message referred, not to the uranium bomb, but to the plutonium bomb just detonated; his BIG BROTHER referred to the uranium bomb that all Manhattan District people now felt confident would explode. DOCTOR harkened back to a previous telegram, in which Groves was referred to as a physician and the TRINITY test as an operation. Harrison's message read: DOCTOR HAS JUST RETURNED MOST ENTHUSIASTIC AND CONFIDENT THAT THE LITTLE BOY IS AS HUSKY AS HIS BIG BROTHER. THE LIGHT IN HIS EYES DISCERNIBLE FROM HERE TO HIGHHOLD AND I COULD HAVE HEARD HIS SCREAMS FROM HERE TO MY FARM. Stimson understood it all without trouble and interpreted it to President Harry S Truman. But the young signal officers who deciphered it at the Potsdam message center had no inkling of its real meaning, and they speculated irreverently on whether the 77-year-old Stimson had become a father and whether the Big Three would adjourn for a day in respectful tribute.

The mission of dropping the atomic bomb on Japan was given the codename CENTERBOARD, but so secret was the project that the officer in charge of assigning codenames was not told what it was for. The transportation of uranium to Tinian, the Pacific Island where the bomb would be finally assembled and from which the plane would take off for the strike, was referred to as BOWERY shipments. Those who had codenamed the atomic bomb LITTLE BOY had severely underrated it: LITTLE BOY stood 14 feet tall, measured five feet in diameter, and weighed just under five tons.

When the *Enola Gay* took off toward Hiroshima on that meteorologically beautiful morning of August 6, 1945, with LITTLE BOY in her bomb bay, she carried also a special code for reporting the bomb's effects. It was in the hands of Captain William S. Parsons, the atomic expert who flew the mission. He had made it up two days earlier with Brigadier General Thomas F. Farrell, Groves' personal representative on Tinian. It consisted of 28 items covering every eventuality that they could think of for the drop. Each item had been placed on a separate line, and to transmit the strike report all that Parsons had to do was to read off the number of the appropriate line. In addition, the code was divided into three sections, ABLE, BAKER, and CEDAR, for good, medium, and bad results. One of these words was to be transmitted first as a general indication of what was to follow. Farrell had practically memorized it:

ABLE Line 1. Clearcut, successful in all respects.
2. Visible effects greater than TRINITY.
3. Visible effects about equal to TRINITY.
. . . . . .
6. HO [Hiroshima, the primary target].
7. KQ [Kokura, a secondary target].
8. NA [Nagasaki, a secondary target].

Censors, Scramblers, and Spies

> 9. Conditions normal in airplane following delivery, proceeding to regular base.
> ... ...
> BAKER Line 11. Technically successful but other factors involved make conference necessary before taking further steps.
> 12. Doubt as to whether delivery was made to planned target.
> 13. Apparent functioning in an unprofitable portion of target.
> ... ...
> CEDAR Line 21. Apparent technical failure.
> 22. Returning with unit to indicated place due to weather.
> ... ...
> 27. Iwo Jima.
> 28. Destination.

At 8:16 a.m., the incongruously named LITTLE BOY, the most awesome weapon that mankind had ever built, obliterated Hiroshima in a blast of fire and destruction that killed 60,000 Japanese, made the very name of the city a synonym for horror, and changed the face of war. A few minutes later, as the *Enola Gay* headed back to Tinian, Parsons reported the bare facts of the holocaust in a brief code message: ABLE, LINE 1, LINE 2, LINE 6, LINE 9. Farrell translated it aloud to a small group of observers without looking at his codesheet, and immediately passed the word to Washington. Sixteen hours later, a stunned world learned that it had entered the atomic age.

Telephoning is an exceedingly convenient way to communicate. How delightfully simple to pick up a phone, talk with the other party, and get everything settled in one conversation! Much easier than sending written messages back and forth. But the telephone is notoriously insecure—and its offspring, the radiotelephone, even more so. A single wiretap grants access to a telephone conversation, and only a radio set is needed to overhear radiotelephone talk. And the Axis did not hesitate to grasp these opportunities at the highest diplomatic levels.

The most obvious protective measure against eavesdropping is to make up codes for conversation, and this has of course been done at one time or another by almost anyone who has spoken over the telephone. The codes range from mere oblique references and the most impromptu cant to elaborately prepared lists of jargon. Less frequently, a message might be enciphered in a prearranged system and the ciphertext read off letter by letter, as with the Manhattan District checkerboard. Or the speakers may resort to a foreign language.

The United States raised the latter device to the level of a full-scale system in both World Wars by making use of a resource that virtually no other combatant had: pools of tongues so recondite that almost no one else in the world understood them. These were the American Indian languages, which are isolated both geographically and linguistically. In 1918, eight Choctaws of

Company D, 141st Infantry, transmitted orders by field telephone; this was the idea of Captain E. W. Horner, who named Solomon Lewis as the chief of the detail. Other Indian tongues were also used. During preparations for World War II, the Signal Corps tested Comanches and Indians from Michigan and Wisconsin in war games, but most of the codetalkers in the combat itself were Navaho. One reason probably was that the tribe was large enough (more than 50,000 persons) to furnish a goodly number of speakers; another, that reportedly only 28 non-Navahos—mainly anthropologists and missionaries—could speak the language, and none of these were German or Japanese; a third reason was the extreme difficulty of the tongue and the near impossibility—even if someone did learn it—of counterfeiting its sounds.

"Sounds [in Navaho] must be reproduced with pedantic neatness ... almost as if a robot were talking," wrote anthropologist Clyde Kluckhohn. "The talk of those who have learned Navaho as adults always has a flabby quality to the Navaho ear. They neglect a slight hesitation a fraction of a second before uttering the stem of the word." A hint of its complexity may be seen in some of its verb forms, on which it insists. The stems of many Navaho verbs differ with the object acted upon. Thus one stem must be used with long objects (pencils, sticks), another with slender flexible objects (snakes, thongs), and still others with granular masses (sugar, salt), things bundled up (hay, bundles of clothing), fabrics (paper, blankets), viscous objects (mud, feces), bulky round objects, container-and-contents, animate objects, and so forth. An entirely different verb form concerns itself with the manner of knowing an event. For example, a Navaho must use one form if he himself is aware of the actual start of rain, another if he believes that rain was falling for some time in his locality before he noticed it, and so on. "Because so much is expressed and implied by the few syllables that make up a single verb form, the Navaho verb is like a tiny imagist poem." Thus "ná'íldil" means "You are accustomed to eat plural separable objects one at a time."

A cryptosystem like that boasts considerable security, and it is not surprising that the dark-skinned, black-haired Navaho became a familiar sight in Marine regimental, divisional, or corps command posts, translating a message into a conglomeration of Navaho, American slang, and military terminology as he huddled over a radio set in the Pacific combat zone. Close friends usually worked together. The number of Navaho codetalkers in the Marines rose from 30 at the start of the war to 420 at the end. They relayed operational orders with a secrecy that helped the United States advance from the Solomons to Okinawa.

Linguistic codetalking, jargon codes, or double meanings all use the human speaker as the coding machine. But this job may be delegated to a real machine—the scrambler. These two modes of oral secrecy, the human and the mechanical, correspond to the two basic forms of cryptosystems. Human coding transmutes words, syllables, and sounds (as in Pig Latin)—the linguistic elements of speech—into secret forms and so parallels code. Both ciphers and scramblers, on the other hand, work upon particles of a text cut up without regard to linguistic functions. From this analogy, scrambler methods of modifying speech are called "ciphony" (from "cipher" plus "telephony"). The field of secret voice communication as a whole may be termed "cryptophony."

Though it was only in World War II that scramblers came into widespread use, and only in that war that serious attempts began to be made to solve scrambled speech, devices to assure telephonic secrecy had been in existence almost as long as the telephone itself. The granddaddy of these was patented on December 20, 1881, only five years after Bell obtained his patent on the telephone. Its inventor, 25-year-old James Harris Rogers, an American electrical pioneer who was then chief electrician for the Capitol, wrote: "My invention consists in throwing a message sent from any transmitting instrument through two or more circuits alternately in rapid succession . . . in such a manner that anyone tapping but one of the circuits is unable to obtain anything but a confused and unintelligible series of signals. . . . The two or more lines on which a signal is transmitted according to my plan may be carried to a common terminus by widely different routes, and thus it will be impossible for any person wishing to do so to . . . or tap both lines at the same time."

Later methods operate more directly on the speech itself, often in ways that resemble transposition, substitution, and null ciphers. In most of the substitution systems, ciphony selects one component out of the many that make up the complex phenomenon of speech and alters it. It usually chooses frequency, though some scramblers distort volume. Frequency here refers to the number of times the vocal chords vibrate; it is usually stated in terms of cycles per second, or c.p.s., so that a frequency of 500 c.p.s. means that the vocal chords are vibrating 500 times a second. Because of the resonance of the vocal organs, most sounds in speech combine several frequencies, and each sound has its distinctive combination of frequencies. The main frequency of the /ē/ sound in "feel," for example, is much higher than that of the /ü/ sound in "fool." Naturally, the absolute frequencies will differ somewhat from person to person, but it is the relative variations within an individual's speech that carry much of its information content.

Ciphony seeks to conceal this content by shifting the frequencies of the sounds of speech. It can do this because the telephone first converts these sounds into a fluctuating electrical current, which the tubes, switches, filters, and circuits that comprise a scrambler then modify according to well-known principles of electricity.* Though this current may be transformed in a great

---

* It does not seem possible to devise a scrambler that distorts the sound itself (i.e., the vibrations in the air) because, once the waves were degraded by, say, some kind of baffle, they could not be restored to their original form. Transposition systems, on the other hand, might be possible in a very crude form by means of mechanical phonographs. From a practical point of view, however, nonelectrical scramblers may be ruled out. None ever seems to have been constructed.

variety of ways, many affect the voice essentially alike, so that there are relatively few basic scrambles.

The simplest is inversion. This turns the voice upside down. Though normal speech ranges from about 70 to about 7,000 c.p.s., the telephone, for engineering reasons, responds only to sounds from about 300 to 3,300 c.p.s. It is this frequency band that is inverted. A voice tone of 300 c.p.s. will emerge from the inverter at 3,300 c.p.s., and vice versa. A tone of 750 c.p.s. will become 2,250 c.p.s., and again vice versa. It is the equivalent of $a = z$, $b = y, \ldots, z = a$, a phonetic atbash. Inverted speech sounds like a thin high-pitched squawking, ringing with bell-like chimes. The word *company* resembles CRINKANOPE, *Chicago*, SIKAYBEE. The inversion pivots in the middle of the frequency band, which means that tones in this area somersault through a narrow range. A frequency of 1,625 will become 1,675. This relative lack of change results in the phenomenon that the word *inverter* itself, which is composed largely of such tones, emerges from the enciphering process that it describes almost unchanged!

Another simple technique is the band-shift. This is a kind of telephonic Caesar substitution, in which all the frequencies are shoved upwards or downwards a certain distance, with the portion pushed out of the frequency band reentering at the bottom or the top. For example, a factor of 1,000 might be added to all frequencies in the 300-to-3,300 band, so that a tone of 500 c.p.s. would be shifted to 1,500. One of 2,800 c.p.s. would then be enciphered to 800.

Band-splitting splits the frequency band into several smaller bands and interchanges these. Filters can divide a 250-to-3,000 band into five subbands of 550 cycles each: subband A of 250 to 800, subband B of 800 to 1,350, subband C of 1,350 to 1,900, subband D of 1,900 to 2,450, and subband E of 2,450 to 3,000. Then the scrambler's switches and circuits may replace A by C, B by D, C by E, D by A, and E by B, thus jumbling the normal tones. The better band-splitters shift these substitutions every few seconds or milliseconds. The result sounds something like a recording of a Mah-Jongg game played too fast.

Masking systems bury the voice signal in noise. The music from a phonograph record can be electrically superimposed on the voice, drowning it out. The descrambler, which must have an identical disk precisely synchronized with that of the scrambler, subtracts the phonograph signal out, leaving the voice. These systems resemble null ciphers, which interlard the true message within a welter of spurious symbols. Another system is wave-form modification. A fluctuating electrical current operates upon the voice current to produce rapid and extreme variations in the amplitude of the transmitted speech. This sounds rather like a radio whose volume control is being turned up to full blast one instant and then down to a whisper the next. In the descrambler, an identical synchronized current reverses these effects.

All these encipherments transform the speech only in the frequency dimension, along the vertical axis, as it were. None extends horizontally along the time axis. Systems that encipher by changing the temporal relationships of

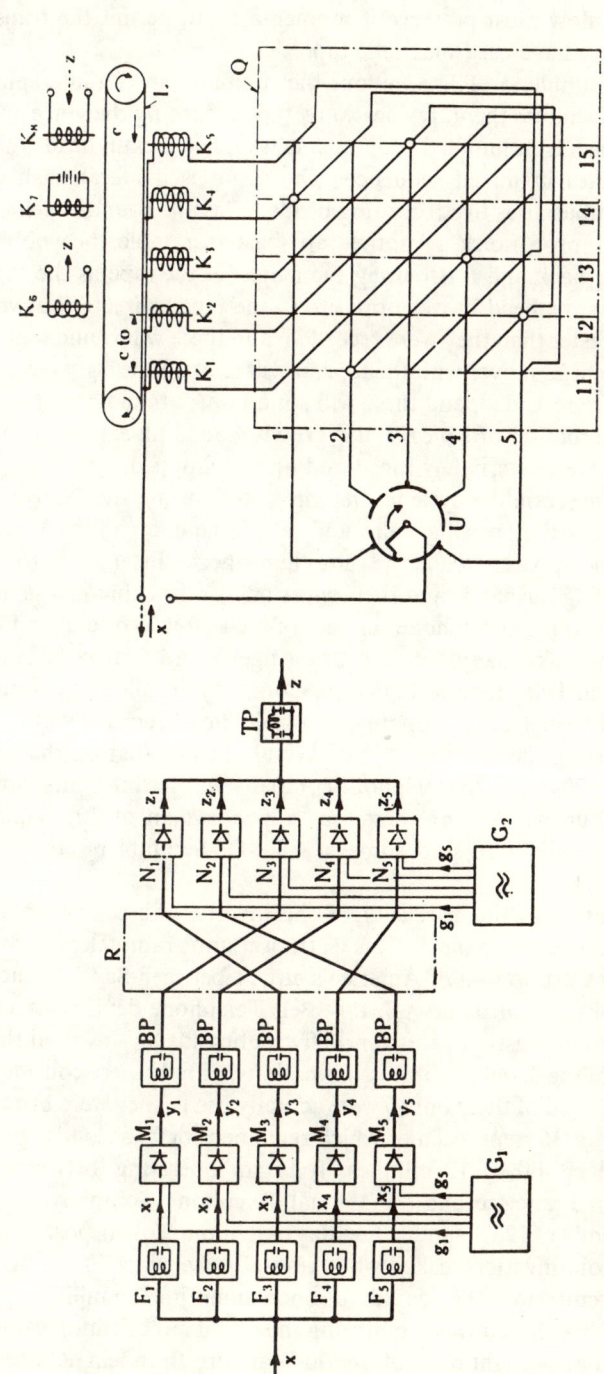

Voice scramblers. Left, band-splitting. Voice signal, x, enters, is split into five frequency bands by filters F, modulated by modulators M with auxiliary frequency from generator G, passed through band-filters BP to coding device R, where the bands are shifted, passed through modulators N and combined at filter TP into scrambled signal, z. Right, time-division scramble. Voice signal, x, enters commutator U, which divides it into five portions and sends them through the coded connections Q in scrambled order to the five recording heads K_{1-5}. Segment 1 goes to head K_4, for example. These record the signal portions on the endless tape L. Pick-up head K_6 sends out the jumbled signal, z; magnet K_7 erases tape. In decoding, head K_8 places incoming scrambled signal z on tape and process is reversed speech's continuous flow must preserve it momentarily to permit the transposition. Usually they have used magnetic tape.

Time-division scramble, or T.D.S., chops the stream of speech into split-second portions and shuffles them. It does so by tape-recording the voice and then picking off segments in jumbled order, using, say, five pickup heads that a mechanism activates in mixed sequence. The result is a literal hash of sounds. The descrambler uses five recording heads to lay the sounds back on a moving tape in their proper order. Another tape-based scramble, the wobble, slides a pickup head back and forth along the length of the tape as the tape passes beneath it. As the head moves opposite to the tape's direction, it will read off the signals faster than they were recorded, and these will sound higher than normal. As the head moves with the tape, it will read off the signals more slowly than they were recorded, and these will sound lower than normal. The result will be an alternation of squeaks and growls, sounding exactly as if a phonograph record were alternately raced and almost stopped.

Most of the basic scrambler systems were invented during the 1920s and 1930s by engineers for the growing radio and telephone companies. A need for them first became apparent when the radio hams began listening in to the conversations of erring husbands and their wives and on stockbrokers giving tips on the first public radiotelephone service, offered after World War I by the Pacific Telephone Company between Los Angeles and nearby Catalina Island. The American Telephone & Telegraph Company installed an inverter. While it prevented casual eavesdropping, it would not keep a determined amateur from inverting the inversion. And several did just that on the East Coast in the latter 1920s when the telephone company was setting up its radiotelephone link to Europe. Among them was a young man of 20, William Roberts of Trenton, who even sold some of his "De-Scramblers" to Latin American countries.

Growing realization of the insecurity of the inverter caused its replacement by band-splitters on both the A. T. & T. transatlantic radiotelephone circuit and the Radio Corporation of America's circuit between San Francisco, Honolulu, and Tokyo. Called the A-3, this Bell Telephone device not only switched the substitution assignments for its five subbands but inverted them as well. However, of the 3,840 possible combinations, only 11 were considered suitable for privacy, and of these only 6 were actually used. They were brought into play in a cycle of 36 steps, each of which remained for 20 seconds, giving the A-3 an overall period of 12 minutes. It began operating between the R.C.A. post in San Francisco and the Mutual Telephone Company post in Honolulu in December, 1937—and a few days later the Tokyo post, which was still using the old inverters, asked what kind of system was in use on the other leg of the circuit, since they could not understand it. The military took the query as proof that Japan was monitoring the mainland communications.

It was the A-3 that brought news of World War II to President Roosevelt, who was awakened early on the morning of September 1, 1939, by a call from

Censors, Scramblers, and Spies 555

the American ambassador in Paris, William C. Bullitt. As the United States was drawn closer and closer to war, the President conferred with his emissaries abroad more and more by scrambler radiotelephone. During the Battle of France he sometimes spoke with Bullitt several times a day. Characteristically, Roosevelt liked the telephone because it cut through the red tape of diplomatic routine and the delays of coding and cabling and because it gave him personal contact with the speaker. Occasionally he spoke with Premier Paul Reynaud, and frequently and increasingly with Churchill.

The President's words sped from the White House to the overseas switchboard in an A. T. & T. building at 47 Walker Street, New York. In common with all other transatlantic conversations, the nasal Roosevelt drawl then entered a special locked room, barred to all except government-licensed employees, where the A-3 equipment mangled it. Here engineers watched dials and listened to the sound to make sure that the speech was properly scrambled. At the transmitter, channel mixers continually shifted the transmission from one frequency to another, so that anyone listening on one circuit would hear it go suddenly blank.

And someone was indeed listening. The Deutsche Reichspost—which, like other European post offices, handled telephone and telegraph traffic as well as mail—realized that the only telephone link between England and the United States was the radio circuit, and it reported "The special national political importance of this communication connection has caused the D.R.P. to try with all available scientific means to decipher the conversation carried on this connection." A task force under Postal Counselor Graduate Engineer Vetterlein of the D.R.P.'s Forschungsanstalt ("Research Bureau") set to work on the problem. The engineers soon learned the nature of the A-3 system and found that they had to wire circuits for only the six different combinations of subband substitutions. Naturally, they had to experiment to find the exact subband divisions and the sequence in which the six combinations were used, but from start to finish the solution took only a few months. They completed it by September, 1941. Within a few more months the D.R.P. had established an intercept and voice-cryptanalysis station on the Dutch coast. Its elaborate equipment instantaneously unscrambled the conversations, losing only a syllable or two after a key change until the proper one was found. When this was in operation, the German Postal Minister, Wilhelm Ohnesorge, notified Adolf Hitler:

THE REICHSPOST MINISTER	BERLIN W 66, 6 March 1942
	LEIPZIGER STR. 15
U5342–1/1 Bfb Nr. 23 gRs	SECRET REICH MATTER
Decipherment of the U.S.A.-England telephone connection	

Mein Führer!

The Forschungsanstalt of the Deutsche Reichspost has completed as the latest of its enterprises an intercept installation for the telephone traffic between the U.S.A. and England, which has been made unintelligible using all present knowledge of communications technology. Thanks to the devoted work of its scientists, it [the D.R.P.] is the only place in Germany that has succeeded in making the scramble, which had been made unintelligible with the best methods, again understandable at the instant of its reception.

I will give the results of our interceptions to the Reich Leader of the S.S., Party Comrade Himmler, who will submit them on March 22.

I will limit the circulation of this communication pending higher decision in view of the fact that if this success were to come to the knowledge of the English, they would further complicate the problem of telephone traffic and cause it to be sent on the telegraph cable.

Heil mein Führer!

(*signed*) Ohnesorge

To the
Leader and Reich Chancellor
of the Greater German Reich
Berlin W8

Dr. Ohnesorge appended a concrete example of the intercept station's success: a cryptanalyzed and translated conversation plucked from the ether at 7:45 p.m. September 7, 1941. A Briton who had just arrived in the United States was talking with a colleague back in England about the need for a man named Campbell to have an assistant and about their propaganda bureau.

The group continued to send transcripts to Hitler's desk, including a 1942 chat between Churchill (at Whitehall 4433) and a Mr. Butcher in New York, and one between Major General Mark Clark and the Inspector General's office in Washington. At 1:00 a.m. July 29, 1943, they hit the jackpot: a radiotelephone conversation between Roosevelt and Churchill. They were discussing the coup in Italy that had just ousted Mussolini's government:

"We do not want proposals for an armistice to be made before we have been definitely approached," said Churchill.

"That is right," agreed Roosevelt.

"We can also wait quietly for one or two days."

"That is right," said Roosevelt again.

Churchill said that he would contact the king of Italy, and Roosevelt replied that he too would get in touch with "Emmanuel." "I do not know quite how I shall do this," he admitted. The Germans took the conversation as evidence of the treachery and complicity of the Italians: "This is complete proof that secret negotiations between the Anglo-Americans and Italy are under way," the war diary of the O.K.W. noted. This does not seem to have been the case; in any event, the Allies were cool to the coup.

Later the Forschungsanstalt again picked up a Roosevelt-Churchill conversation—Churchill was practically addicted to the telephone, calling Roosevelt at all hours from his bombproof shelter in Whitehall, and placing

Censors, Scramblers, and Spies

great faith in the scrambler. This conversation, early in 1944, "lasted almost five minutes," wrote Walter Schellenberg, the Himmler aide who studied it, "and disclosed a crescendo of military activity in Britain, thereby corrobora-

Transcript of a German descrambling of an intercepted Churchill transatlantic conversation

ting the many reports of impending invasion." Soon thereafter the A-3 was replaced by a more secure system, and English became Greek to the listening Germans.

Similar activities had, rather surprisingly, been started in the United States even before the D.R.P. project began. Early in October, 1940, the communications division of the National Defense Research Committee set up a group on speech secrecy. It would concentrate on cryptanalysis, partly to eavesdrop on enemy radiotelephone talk, partly to evaluate proposed Allied scramblers. The N.D.R.C. contracted with A. T. & T.'s Bell Telephone Laboratories for these studies, and during World War II the laboratories handled most of the American speech-scrambling work. It was done in two small workshops in the vast pile of stone at 463 West Street, New York, that housed Bell Labs. Though the shops faced on an inside courtyard, both had their windows painted black because of the secret nature of their work. In charge was Walter Koenig, Jr., a short, reticent engineer then turning 40 who had gone to work for Bell right after being graduated from Harvard with an A.B. in chemistry and physics. Much of his work dealt with acoustics, in which the telephone company had a natural interest, and he slid into descrambling because he had helped develop an instrument that was to play an important role in scrambler cryptanalysis.

Before his device came into widespread use, however, a much easier-to-operate and more common instrument proved to have unsuspected capabilities as a tool for solving ciphony. This was the human ear. Anyone who has managed to converse at a noisy cocktail party should not be surprised at the ear's ability to pick out speech—and the right speech—from amidst a babble of noise. Nevertheless, wrote Koenig:

> Beginners in the study of privacy systems never fail to be amazed at the difficulty of scrambling speech sufficiently to destroy the intelligence. The ear can tolerate or even ignore surprising amounts of noise, nonlinearity, frequency distortion, misplaced components, superpositions, and other forms of interference. We can therefore very often obtain partial or even complete intelligence from a privacy system by partial or imperfect decoding. . . . These non-cryptographic methods are very important, because they may reduce the delay in obtaining the intelligence substantially to zero. . . . Some of them, of course, result in poor quality, but the saving of time, labor and equipment may be very great.

With some experience in hearing how words sound when scrambled, with some practice in trying to make out scrambled speech, and with repeated listenings to a scrambled conversation, one can understand a goodly portion of what has been said even without electrically cryptanalyzing the scramble. As a not-at-all extreme example, some Bell Telephone Laboratories engineers recovered an average of 47 per cent of the words scrambled by the A-3 simply by listening to it several times. This means that almost half the intelligence leaked through. In one test, intelligibility rose to 76 per cent, or three quarters of what was said. This is enough to give an eavesdropper the gist of a conversation.

This weakness results from the large safety factor with which the system of oral communication is invested. Speech contains many more elements than

William Frederick Friedman, about 1930

J. Rives Childs and Herbert O. Yardley on duty in the Hotel Crillon at the Paris Peace Conference, 1919

Herbert O. Yardley, head of the American Black Chamber, in 1931

William Powell, at left, plays a codebreaker in the movie Rendezvous, *based on one of Herbert O. Yardley's books*

The second generation of American cryptologists: from left, *Abraham Sinkhov, Frank B. Rowlett, Solomon Kullback, all in 1941 or 1942*

William F. and Elizebeth S. Friedman in 1958, with part of their collection of cipher machines

Left, *Gilbert S. Vernam*, who invented the first on-line cipher machine, about *1914;* right, *Major Joseph O. Mauborgne*, who welded several pre-existing elements into the unbreakable cipher, in World War I.

Edward H. Hebern, inventor of the rotor

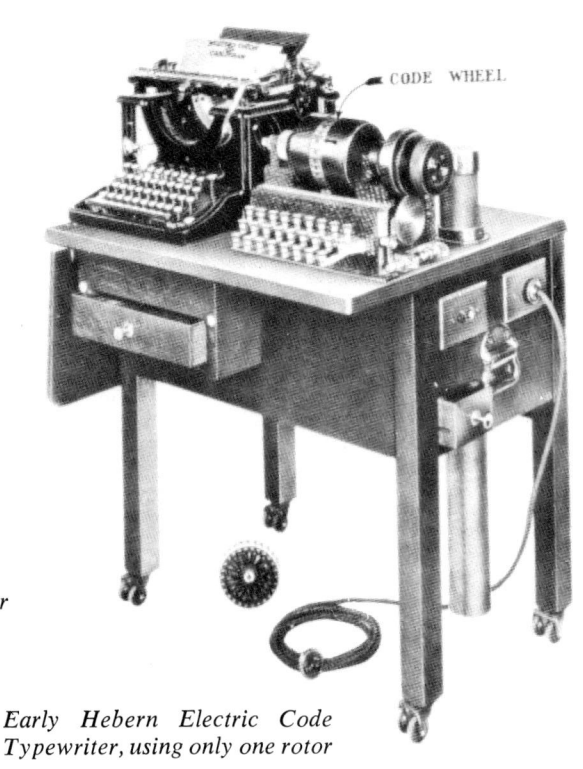

Early Hebern Electric Code Typewriter, using only one rotor

Left, *inventor Boris Hagelin examines the cipher machine that made him rich;* upper right, *Lester S. Hill, inventor of algebraic cryptography;* lower right, *Arvid G. Damm, unsuccessful cipher machine inventor*

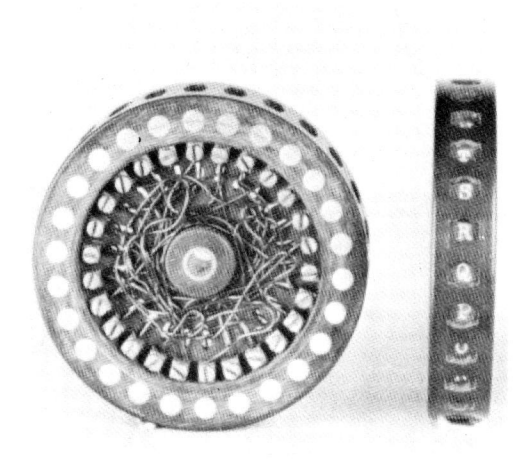

Left, *cryptographic rotor from one of Hebern's machines showing wiring;* right, *Hagelin's* M-209, *used by U.S. Army in World War II, showing mechanism*

Left, *Adolf Paschke*, and, center, *Werner Kunze, head cryptanalysts of Pers Z of the German Foreign Office;* right, *Yves Gyldén, mentor of Swedish cryptology, all in 1962*

Left, *Captain Alwin D. Kramer, who delivered* MAGIC *intercepts before Pearl Harbor;* center, *Captain Laurance F. Safford, founder of U.S. Navy cryptologic organization;* right, *Captain Joseph J. Rochefort, head of the Navy cryptanalytic unit that read pre-Midway messages, all in 1946*

Left, *Captain Thomas H. Dyer, chief cryptanalyst of Rochefort's unit, about 1946;* center, *Colonel Harold R. Shaw, head of Technical Operations Division, Office of Censorship, about 1944;* right, *Walter Koenig, Jr., Bell Telephone Laboratories expert in breaking scramblers, in 1964*

The fruits of cryptanalysis: a Japanese cruiser after Midway

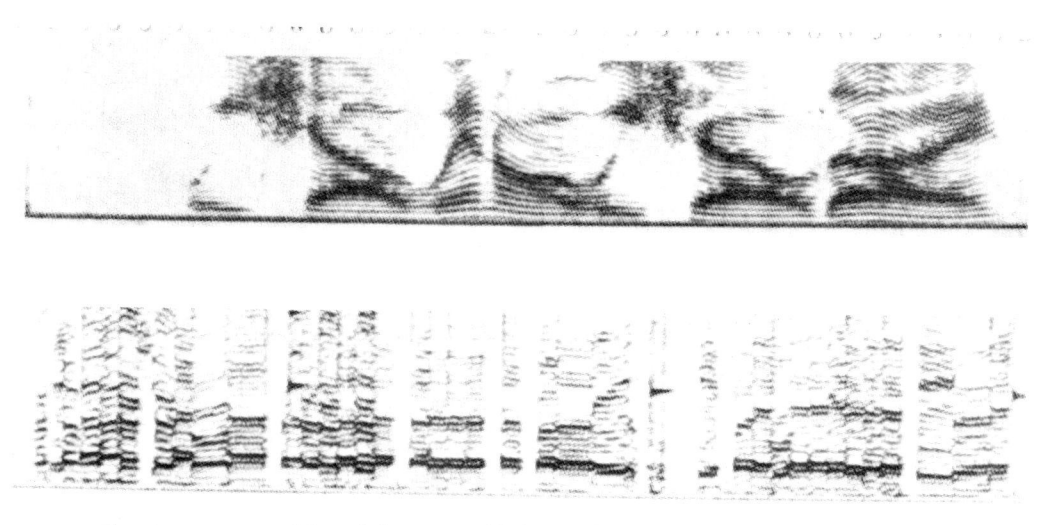

Spectrograms used in solving scrambled speech: above, *spectrogram of "We shall win or we shall die";* below, *spectrogram of a time-division scramble*

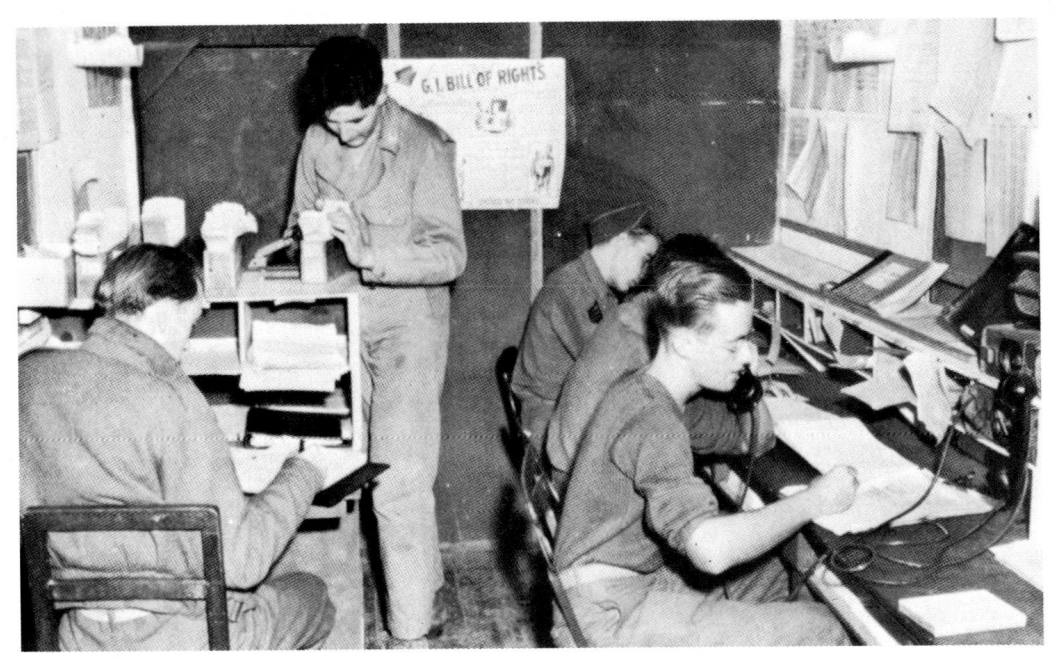

Traffic analysts of the U.S. 7th Army work in a van in France in 1944

Old Glory waves triumphantly from U-505, just captured, codebooks and all, by a Navy boarding party, as its captors secure a towline

it actually needs to be understood. Psychologists and communication engineers have demonstrated this in a great variety of tests—which, interestingly, employ scramblerlike equipment. One test, for example, eliminated (by electrical means) all sounds below 100 c.p.s. in a series of nonsense syllables. Subjects missed less than 10 per cent of the syllables, and in running speech probably would have lost nothing. Why, then, does speech include these low-frequency sounds? Because low frequencies get around the objects and corners of everyday life much better than high frequencies; without them, oral communication would be reduced much more to the line of sight and would lose many of its present advantages. The excess of detail defends speech against the noise and accidental distortion of ordinary activities by ensuring that, even if one component is eroded, the others will sustain the message. This superabundance resists the deliberate deformations of scrambler systems just as strongly. Thus, only 1,000 c.p.s. of the full speech-band of about 7,000 c.p.s. will allow a listener to hear 45 per cent of a series of nonsense syllables. This helps explain why the Bell engineers could understand 47 per cent of the A-3's scrambled speech even without cryptanalysis.

"The fact that the ear is such a good decoding tool," wrote Koenig, "makes the production of privacy systems very difficult. Scrambling systems which look very effective on paper sometimes turn out on trial to degrade the intelligibility very little, although the scrambled speech usually sounds unpleasant. Most methods if they are pushed to the point where they do succeed in hiding the intelligibility are impossible to restore with good quality. There are in fact very few speech privacy systems which achieve a high degree of privacy with acceptable quality."

The ear, however, cannot reconstruct the specific nature of the scrambler. This calls for precise differentiation of frequencies and for a kind of total recall of the order of many minute speech segments. These matters were best handled with the sound spectrograph, an instrument that portrayed sound pictorially. Ralph K. Potter of Bell Labs had devised it—with some later help from Koenig—purely for research, but its applications to cryptanalyzing scramblers soon became evident. They were even demonstrated to Dr. Vannevar Bush, the highly respected head of the Office of Scientific Research and Development, N.D.R.C.'s parent body.

Bush saw how the spectrograph, by laying down a permanent visualization of scrambled speech, enabled the scientists to compare this with normal speech, to deduce from the difference the type of scrambling employed, and so to crack it. The device records the voice sounds on paper as a series of horizontal lines representing the main frequencies. In normal speech, these lines appear and disappear, rise and fall in flowing patterns as the frequencies do. Sounds loaded with low frequencies, like /fül/, show up in the spectrograph record as a heavy concentration of lines near the bottom of the paper. The lines for /fēl/ are much higher. In scrambled speech, the normal patterns are distorted. Inversion has the dark lines of the more powerful middle-to-low frequencies near the top of the spectrogram. Inflections which normally climb slope. A band-splitter shows the long horizontal divisions of the subbands. T.D.S. consists of disjointed segments divided by sharp vertical boundaries.

Mere examination of the spectrogram will thus disclose the type of scramble; solution then becomes the jigsaw-puzzlelike task of cutting apart the spectrogram along the boundaries of the scramble and reassembling it to re-create the flow-pattern of normal speech. This reconstruction will suggest the key used in the scramble, and the cryptanalyst will set up his own apparatus to this key and run the recording of the scrambled message through. Koenig and his associates perfected spectrographic cryptanalysis to the point where, in field tests at Camp Coles in 1943, four people working in a laboratory set up in an Army van truck solved T.D.S. test-scrambles within 15 to 18 minutes of the time of transmission. As a result, eight spectrographs suitable for field use were built and delivered—three to the Army, three to the Navy, and two to the British—between January and May 1944. Some of these were apparently used in cracking a new Japanese scrambler intercepted by the Army at Point Reyes and later at Two Rock Ranch, California. The results sometimes yielded valuable information about forthcoming Japanese moves.

Much of Bell Labs' expertise was developed in testing Allied scrambles, particularly a highly regarded combination of band-splitting and T.D.S. This was called a 2-dimensional, or 2-D, scramble because it operated along both the vertical (frequency) and the horizontal (time) axes. With its trusty spectrograph, the Bell Labs defeated even the best of these, the British 2-D privacy system. The reconstitution of speech patterns from the many little rectangles in the spectrogram was a tedious job but surprisingly quick—a crew of six men would take from two to three hours to do it. The experience suggested some humble but effective ways of increasing privacy: speaking in a low-pitched monotone to diminish speech patterns, varying the length and cycle of T.D.S. elements to eliminate periodicity, and adding noise after scrambling the speech. The noise would not bother the ear, but it would spatter the spectrogram with false lines that would mislead the solver. In fact, noise of the right kind might make T.D.S. or 2-D spectrograms appear more continuous in their scrambled order than in the order that unscrambles the speech but scrambles the noise!

Ciphony never attained the security of written communications. Cryptologic terminology reflects this difference by calling scramblers "privacy" systems and not "secrecy" systems. Late in the war, Roosevelt and Churchill recognized this gauzelike security and switched from the telephone to teletype talks, enciphered by a little box called "Telekrypton" that was almost certainly the one-time tape. Nevertheless, ciphony made such great strides during the conflict that General George C. Marshall, whose fear of using a scrambler had had such dire effects on December 7, 1941, could say three years later, "We have the very finest equipment now."

17

THE SCRUTABLE ORIENTALS

FROM THE SUNDAY MORNING when Commander Mitsuo Fuchida, in his bomber high over Pearl Harbor, radioed "TORA, TORA, TORA!" to indicate that his attack force had achieved complete surprise, the gods of war had smiled without surcease upon the armed forces of imperial Japan. The strike at Pearl Harbor had decimated the United States fleet. Unhindered, the Greater East Asia Co-Prosperity Sphere expanded rapidly and uninterruptedly. Guam was captured on December 10, Wake on the 23rd. Two days later Hong Kong fell. Japanese aircraft sank *Prince of Wales* and *Repulse*, giving Winston Churchill his worst shock of the war and leaving the whole western Pacific, the Indian Ocean, Oceania, and even Australia virtually undefended by naval forces. Tojo's armies overran Singapore and Malaya with its rubber plantations, then the Dutch East Indies with its great oil fields. Siam and the Solomons were in their hands. China was under blockade. In May the Philippines surrendered. Within six stupefying months, the Rising Sun shone upon nearly a tenth of the globe's surface. Nippon's enemies had been wiped from the seas. Her troops raped and pillaged from bustling Rangoon to the languorous South Sea islands. It was the most rapid conquest in history.

It amply fulfilled the Japanese war plan. Japan did not intend to invade the United States. Rather, she planned to feed upon the riches of the conquered territories behind a ring of impregnable defense positions, from which she would beat off any attacker. But the high command, bedazzled by success and greedy for more, decided instead to continue the sweep before its momentum was lost. The admirals and generals pointed out that naval losses, which they had anticipated at 25 per cent, had been infinitesimal. The largest ship sunk had been a destroyer, and so more than adequate forces remained for the new drive. Furthermore, they reasoned, the defense perimeter would be protected as much by greater depth as by greater consolidation. They therefore set in motion two ambitious plans. One was an amphibious assault southward to Port Moresby, a town on the southeastern tip of New Guinea only 400 miles from Australia. The other pivoted on Midway, a tiny atoll in the middle of the Pacific that stood as a sentinel to Hawaii.

This second plan had two parts. The first part aimed at the atoll's capture. Its two coral islets—the larger barely two miles long—possessed no intrinsic worth but great strategic value, for whoever held them controlled the central Pacific and hence the approaches to either end of the oceanic basin. The second and more important part of the plan sought to lure out the remainder of the American fleet and destroy it. Admiral Isoroku Yamamoto, Commander in Chief of Japan's Combined Fleet, appreciated America's industrial might and realized that Japan had to win quickly—before America could bring it to bear. He also knew that the United States could not let Midway go by default, as it had Wake and Guam. When the Pacific Fleet, enfeebled by the losses at Pearl Harbor, steamed out to defend the atoll, he would fall upon it with his vastly superior forces and annihilate it. This final disaster would convince Americans that Japan could not be beaten. They would therefore quit a pointless struggle and leave Japan master of the western Pacific. Or so the warlords purposed.

They did not know that the United States had fashioned a secret weapon of such potency that it could alter the balance of power in the Pacific. It was located in the long, narrow, windowless basement of the 14th Naval District's Administration Building in the Navy yard at Pearl Harbor. Vaultlike doors protected its secrets; steel-barred gates at the top and bottom of the stairs kept out visitors; guards stood a round-the-clock watch. This office was staffed, when the war broke out, with about 30 officers and men. It was equipped with International Business Machine Corporation tabulators, which were partitioned off in a separate section because of the racket they made. Its raw material came in by courier from the radio intercept station at Wailupe. This was the so-called Combat Intelligence Unit, the radio intelligence organization that served the Pacific Fleet.

Lieutenant Commander Joseph John Rochefort had commanded it since May of 1941. Before Pearl Harbor, the bulk of its personnel worked on interception, direction-finding, and traffic analysis; the unit fed these results to the fleet intelligence officer. Though one of its young cryptanalysts, Chief Radioman Farnsley C. Woodward, had attacked the Japanese diplomatic systems in use by the Honolulu consulate as a favor for counterintelligence, the unit's main cryptanalytic duties before Pearl Harbor involved the solution of the Japanese flag officers' system and miscellaneous administrative, personnel, and meteorological codes. It had only three real cryptanalysts to handle this workload, Rochefort and Lieutenant Commanders Thomas H. Dyer and Wesley A. Wright. The others were trainees, aides, clerks, and translators. Since August of 1941 it had been working a seven-day week; in October it went to a night watch as well—the only unit in Pearl to do so.

Three days after Pearl Harbor the unit was given a major change in assignment. It was to discontinue work on the flag officers' system (which was to be analyzed in OP-20-G in the Navy Department in Washington) and to join in the attack and breakdown of the Japanese fleet cryptographic system, dubbed JN25 by OP-20-G. This most widely distributed and extensively used of Japan's naval cryptosystems, in which about half her naval messages were transmitted, was already the target of three other cryptanalytical units—a 16th Naval District group under Lieutenant Rudolph J. Fabian on Corregidor, a British group at Singapore, and OP-20-G. They had determined that it was a two-part code of about 45,000 five-digit groups, enciphered by two volumes of 50,000 five-digit additives each. The b, or second, edition had come into force on December 1, 1940, and by the following November messages in it were partly readable. At 6 a.m. on December 4, 1941, new additive books came into effect, together with new indicators. Fabian's group broke into this new encipherment four days later, and by Christmas messages were again being read as before. But these readings were tantalizingly fragmentary, and much remained to be done.

The commencement of hostilities generated an enormous increase in radio traffic and consequently in the workload of the Combat Intelligence Unit. To handle it, the unit dragooned personnel from every possible source. It first acquired the band of the U.S.S. *California*, which had been badly damaged in the first few minutes of the air attack. Dyer threw up his hands when he heard about it, but music and mathematics and cryptanalysis seemed to go together,* and nearly all the bandsmen proved above average and some exceptional in their new tasks. By May, the basement office contained about 120 persons. Of these, perhaps half a dozen were by then fairly competent cryptanalysts, 50 were beginning to get the feel of the work, and the remainder were clerks. Work went on round the clock in the air-conditioned basement, but the unit was woefully understaffed.

Rochefort virtually lived in that cellar for the first three months. He supervised the entire operation—interception, traffic analysis, cryptanalysis, translation. Dyer, his immediate subordinate, was in charge of the cryptanalytic section. A slender man just turning 40, with a mild, friendly personality but a tough and unrelenting mind, Dyer had come to the Islands in 1936 and had begun cryptanalytical work largely on his own initiative. He had become interested in the field soon after his graduation from Annapolis in 1924. Assigned to *New Mexico* as an assistant radio officer, he began doing the cryptograms in the naval communications bulletins, which intrigued him, and then read Friedman's *Elements of Cryptanalysis*, which hooked him. In 1931, he succeeded Safford as head of the Research Desk in the Code and Signal Section of Naval Communications, commanding the entire U.S. Navy cryptanalytical group of four people, clerks included.

The following year, Dyer became the father of machine cryptanalysis when he installed I.B.M. machines to speed up solution. (The Army did not begin using the machines for cryptology until 1936.) In 1937, after he had been in Hawaii for a year, the Navy sent some I.B.M. machines out to him and assigned him a yeoman to expand, in a modest way, the cryptanalysis that he had been doing. Those machines were his baby. While other cryptanalysts used

---

* As corroboration, it might be noted that Painvin won a prize as a young 'cello player, that Mauborgne and Kunze both play the violin at least passably, and that Hitchings taught music.

pencil and paper to test assumptions, Dyer tried them out directly on the machines—and worked more quickly that way than he could have by hand. He stayed in cryptanalysis all during the war, winning the Distinguished Service Medal, and even afterward, rising to a captaincy. On his retirement from the service in 1955, he started teaching mathematics at the University of Maryland.

His chief assistant was Wright, who handed out the work that Dyer wanted done and then pitched in himself. In 1929, three years after he graduated from Annapolis, he found himself with his crew on a rifle range shared by Safford, a fellow officer in a destroyer division. Like Dyer, he had solved the ciphers in the communications bulletins, and Safford, in a sales campaign that began to the crack of musketry, convinced him that he should specialize in cryptology. But it was not until June of 1933 that Wright began his first tour in communications. Sea duty alternated with cryptologic work until, in March of 1941, he went to Pearl Harbor with Admiral Kimmel as the cryptanalyst in a fleet security unit. He immediately began working with the Combat Intelligence Unit and in February of 1942 was formally transferred to it. He was then 39, a broad-shouldered redhead with craggy features and big hands whose strong resemblance to a tugboat captain—his nickname is "Ham"—belies his gentle manner and his courtesy. He too remained in cryptology throughout the war, winning the Legion of Merit; like Dyer he stayed in it afterwards, winning a gold star to his Legion of Merit. He retired in 1957.

With the entrance of the Rochefort group into the fray against JN25b, the three Allied cryptanalytic units in the Pacific and OP-20-G in Washington began working in the closest possible cooperation. Positive or tentative codegroup recoveries were flashed from unit to unit via the COPEK channel for MAGIC. Each unit intercepted messages that the others might not have picked up, and so could make new assumptions or confirm or disprove old ones. Washington, which had the most equipment and the largest staff, seems to have led in the work of stripping the additive groups. The Singapore and the Philippines units had made the difficult initial entries, but their work was interrupted when the British had to move to Colombo and Fabian was evacuated by submarine from Corregidor in February, 1942, several weeks before MacArthur. Aside from a few such generalized observations, it is almost impossible to say which group, much less which individual, deserves the major share of credit for solving the edition of the fleet cryptographic system then in force. Collaboration was too intimate. A possibility raised in a discussion between Dyer and Wright might be developed into a probability by a check of messages in Washington and verified by a new intercept at Colombo.

Meanwhile, the Japanese—who had no suspicion of all this activity—felt a vague unease at the extreme length of service of this code. A new edition, which would be called JN25c by the Americans but was called the Naval Code Book D by the Japanese, was to be placed in service April 1. But administrative confusion in the Navy libraries, which had custody of the codebooks, plus difficulties in physically distributing the books by destroyer and airplane to moving ships and widely dispersed installations, forced a postponement to May 1. Consequently, the American cryptanalysts could tunnel ever more deeply into JN25b.

Gradually the isolated fragments of plaintext that they were recovering grew denser, enlarged, touched, made sense. Parts remained unread, but the large patches of coherence offered clues to Japanese thoughts and plans. Hence it was that by April 17 the cryptanalysts smoked out the gist of the Japanese plan to seize Port Moresby and threaten Australia. The new Commander in Chief of the Pacific Fleet, Admiral Chester W. Nimitz, dispatched two carriers, *Lexington* and *Yorktown*, to spoil it.

This task force, commanded by Rear Admiral Frank Jack Fletcher, began cruising the lovely waters of the Coral Sea off the northeast coast of Australia in search of the enemy. At 8:15 a.m. May 7 a message from a *Yorktown* search plane was decoded as reporting the discovery of "two carriers and four heavy cruisers" 175 miles northwest of the American force. Fletcher thought that this was the main Japanese force covering the amphibious landing and flew off two deckloads of planes to attack it. When the search pilot returned, it was discovered that the "two carriers and four heavy cruisers" had resulted from a disarrangement of his codepad; they should have been reported as "two heavy cruisers and two destroyers." But another contact report alerted the fliers to the presence nearby of the landing force itself, escorted by the light carrier *Shoho*. They swarmed over *Shoho* and sank it in ten minutes—a record for the war. "Scratch one flattop!" exulted one pilot. The transports, shorn of their air cover, retired to the northward. This accidental attack on the wrong force thwarted the main Japanese objective and, since the transports never again entered the Coral Sea, lifted the threat of invasion from Australia.

Fletcher could hardly foresee this, however, and next day he located the main Japanese force of two big carriers and attacked them at the same time that they spotted and attacked him. It was the first naval battle in history which was fought entirely by air and in which the opposing ships never even sighted each other. One Japanese carrier was put out of action; the other had its flight deck bent so that it could not recover all its planes, many of which had to be jettisoned. But *Yorktown* was scarred and the beloved *Lexington* so badly damaged that, after futile attempts to save her, she had to be torpedoed by an American destroyer. Though this gave the Japanese a tactical victory in the Coral Sea, they had lost strategically. More important, their two damaged carriers would not be present at the Midway battle. For the check at the Coral Sea had not altered Japan's grandiose plans for winning the war against America.

During these hectic spring days, the cryptanalysts strained under high pressure. Rochefort and Dyer alternated 12 hours on, 12 hours off. Speed was emphasized. As the meaning of a codegroup became known in the Combat Intelligence Unit, whether through its own efforts or by a COPEK message from another unit, the codegroup and its meaning were punched on an I.B.M. card and stored in the machine. When an intercept came in, a clerk would punch its codegroups on I.B.M. cards and feed them in. The machine automatically made the run of repeated subtractions and the check of its mechanized difference "books" necessary to find the identical remainders, and then, with human guidance, the runs to reconstruct the relative additive sequence, correct it to the absolute sequence, and strip it from the encicode message. The machine would then compare the placode groups with the decode cards in its storage and print out the plaintext for whatever decode cards it had. Presumably it would also print out the various possibilities in the case of garbled or partial codegroups. It could also make frequency counts and contact counts and on command could disgorge a desired set of statistics—all codegroups preceding and following a given codegroup, for example. Head of the I.B.M. room, which was constantly being enlarged, was Lieutenant Commander Jack S. Holtwick, Jr., a 1927 Annapolis graduate who had done cryptologic work at the Navy Department, the 16th Naval District, and the Asiatic Fleet from 1934 to 1939; he had reported to the Hawaiian unit in June of 1940.

Not every cryptogram was decrypted. Japanese traffic was too heavy for the undermanned Combat Intelligence Unit. All major and most minor Japanese fleet circuits were monitored, and the messages that were driven down by car from the intercept stations were scrutinized by traffic analysts. From such indications as the length of a message, its originator, the time of day at which it was sent, the circuit used, the addressees, and stereotypes in the text of the cryptogram itself, plus an intuitive "feel" based on day-in, day-out listening-in to Japanese communications, these "scanners" could pick out the important messages. The cryptanalysts concentrated on these, filling in missing additives and conjecturing the meaning of new codegroups. They seldom read messages "solid"; even the translators—who were half cryptanalysts—did not fill in all the holes.

As these translations were written up, Lieutenant Commander W. J. (Jasper) Holmes brought them, blank spots and all, together with some that were very sketchy indeed, to Nimitz' chief of staff, Rear Admiral Milo F. Draemel, who took the important ones in to Nimitz himself. Holmes had retired in 1936 with an arthritic back but had returned to active service after Pearl Harbor. He was a good enough writer to have sold several pieces on naval subjects to *The Saturday Evening Post*, the toughest magazine market in America, and he used this literary ability in collaborating with the fleet intelligence officer in pulling together information from sightings by U.S. submarines, traffic analysis, and comparison of many intercepts into an intelligence compendium that went to the higher-ups.

On May 5,* Imperial General Headquarters issued Navy Order 18: "Commander in Chief Combined Fleet will, in cooperation with the Army,

---

* All times are local times. This would be May 4 in Hawaii.

invade and occupy strategic points in the Western Aleutians and Midway Island." Wireless traffic subtly changed its character. More than 200 ships would take part in the operation, and though most were already in the Inland Sea, many of the carriers, battleships, submarines, minesweepers, transports, and supply vessels had to be summoned from missions at sea. Some had to be refitted, and messages crackled to and from the naval base at Kure. The magnitude of the supply problem alone was indicated by the fact that this one operation would consume more fuel and cover a greater mileage than the entire Japanese Navy had done in any previous peacetime year. The battle preparations called for the ships to assemble in Hiroshima Bay and then to sortie in five main forces over a four-day period according to a precisely calculated schedule. The directives, queries, and responses involved in organizing so complex an operation filled the airwaves. Coded messages streamed out of Yamamoto's headquarters aboard *Yamato*, the world's largest battleship. And not only the legitimate recipients were reading them.

For the effective date of the new edition of the fleet cryptographic system, whch had been postponed once from April 1 to May 1, had to be again set back another month, to June 1. Perhaps the very extent of the Japanese conquests defeated their distribution efforts. These may not have been very energetic in any case, for the Japanese, while paying lip service to the need for communication security, seemed to believe, on the evidence of their military successes, that their codes were not being broken and that timeliness in their replacement was not really necessary. By early May, Allied cryptanalysts, who had recovered about a third of the JN25b lexicon, could read about 90 per cent of an ordinary cryptogram (because the recovered codegroups were the most frequently used). Had Japan changed her main naval code on May 1 as scheduled, she would have blacked out Allied cryptanalysts for at least several weeks—weeks that, as it turned out, were to be crucial to history.

Her failure to do so meant that she was masking her Midway preparation messages behind a cryptographic smoke screen that American cryptanalysts had almost entirely blown away. And as solutions of these messages drifted into Nimitz' office in the first weeks of May, that old sea dog scented a major offensive. Hastily, he recalled carriers *Hornet* and *Enterprise*, which had headed for the Coral Sea after launching Jimmy Doolittle's raid on Tokyo, and *Yorktown*, to be ready for any eventuality. But what eventualities were possible? The Fleet Intelligence Summary of May 15 warned of an enemy raid or seizure of Dutch Harbor in the Aleutians some time between May 30 and June 10. This was almost certainly a diversionary move. But where would the main Japanese attack fall—and when? There was no clear-cut answer. Several Japanese strategies appeared possible. Nimitz himself thought Midway was the target, but in Washington Admiral Ernest J. King, Chief of Naval Operations, who was working from essentially the same information, concluded that Oahu was.

Yamamoto was well aware of the inestimable advantage of surprise, that element of warfare which so often decides the course of battle. He felt confident that the United States, unable to defend all points, would have to counterattack at a time and place governed by the Japanese moves, giving Yamamoto control of every situation. In addition to this tactical initiative, he had an overwhelming preponderance of forces. To his 11 battleships, 5 carriers, 16 cruisers, and 49 destroyers, Nimitz could oppose no battleships and only 3 carriers, 8 cruisers, and 14 destroyers.

On May 20, Yamamoto issued an operations order that spelled out in detail the tactics to be used in the Midway assault. It was to begin on June 3 with a diversionary attack on the Aleutians. With Nimitz' forces thus pulled off balance, the softening-up would begin on the Midway defenders, to be followed on June 6 by a dawn assault. When the Pacific Fleet either hurried south from the Aleutians or sallied forth from Pearl Harbor to defend Midway, the numerically superior bombers and torpedo planes of the Japanese force would cripple it. Then Yamamoto's battleships and heavy cruisers would move up to sink its remnants by gunfire. The work of December 7 would be completed; a Japanese Midway would rule the Pacific, threatening Hawaii itself; and the war would be as good as won.

Unknown to Yamamoto, his order was also picked up by the Allied listening posts that ringed the Pacific. Its extreme length indicated its importance, and Fabian's unit, by this time in Melbourne, may have first suggested that it might be an operations order. But the Hawaii unit put out the first fragmentary solution. The I.B.M. apparatus rapped it out in a mechanical cryptanalysis for as much of the intercept as codegroups and additives were available in storage. Only about 10 to 15 per cent of the message was lacking, and the unit began a massive effort to fill in these holes. This task lasted more than a week. Dyer pushed cards through the clacking machines. The fledgling cryptanalysts drove pencils furiously across sheet after sheet of paper. The clerks scurried among the desks. Overworked language officers sucked in Japanese through their eyes and spouted English at their fingertips. Gradually additives were recovered and stripped and the plaintext of the uncovered codegroups was revealed or inserted. As each new portion came to light, adding another scrap of information, it was rushed upstairs to Jasper Holmes. He would write it into its proper place in the picture and send it along to Commander Edwin T. Layton, the fleet intelligence officer, for transmission to Draemel and Nimitz. The operations order was so long and so detailed that dozens of such fragments rustled across the commander's desk.

Still in doubt, however, were its most important parts: the dates, the times, and the places of the various operations. The date-time information had been superenciphered in what appeared to be a polyalphabetic system. This had never been solved because it had been observed only three times before, and one occasion had a garble that threw sand in the gears of every attempted reconstruction. The cryptanalysts had considered that they could not do anything with this, and so, rather than waste a man on a fruitless endeavor, all hands concentrated on the body of the message. Additives and codegroups recovered there would be of value in later solutions. Consequently, the question of when was left to other branches of naval intelligence, which applied ship speeds and similar data to estimate the date and time for the attack.

The question of where was answered fairly quickly by the Combat Intelligence Unit. The Japanese indicated geographic locations by maps with coordinates in code; they called these their CHI-HE systems, and they served as much to avoid error in transliterating kata kana as to conceal. The cryptanalysts had partly recovered one such map; they knew the designators for Pearl Harbor, for example. Several weeks earlier, they had discovered the code coordinates AF in a message sent from two scout planes over Midway. Context suggested that AF meant *Midway*. When they checked this against their partially solved map grid, they found that A's representing one coordinate of Midway's position and F's representing the other fit into it perfectly. So when they saw that AF was the codegroup for the locus of the main attack, they felt quite sure that Midway was the target.

But the top brass squinted at this identification. On it rode the very existence of the American fleet and the future course of the whole Pacific war. They demanded confirmation.

Rochefort decided to trick the Japanese into giving him the proof. He cooked up the idea of having the Midway garrison broadcast a distinctive plain language message which would presumably be picked up by Japanese monitors. Their coded report would be intercepted and solved by Americans, and the geographic indicator that they used in this telltale dispatch would have to mean *Midway*. Layton liked the idea, and the two men drafted a message in which Midway reported that its fresh-water distillation plant had broken down. They cabled it to the atoll with an order to radio it back to Pearl in clear. Midway complied. The cryptanalysts waited. Two days later there appeared in the harvest of Japanese intercepts one stating that AF was short of fresh water.

By about Wednesday, May 27, Nimitz knew almost as much about the Midway operation as many of the captains of Japanese warships who were to take part in it. In all respects but one his information was solid: it had come from the Japanese themselves and had even been verified. The one point was the when. His intelligence staff had erected an elaborate scaffolding of estimates, deductions, probabilities, and predictions to date the operation as beginning against Midway June 3. The reasoning was shrewd, but its hypothetical framework could hardly have comforted Nimitz in so weighty a matter as much as the repeatedly confirmed perceptions of the cryptanalysts.

Meanwhile, in the basement office, nearly everything that could be done to the body of the Yamamoto operations order had been done. Hardly any gaps remained, and only an occasional paper went upstairs. Intercept importance had fallen off with the sortie of the Japanese fleet under radio silence. Late one afternoon in this comparative lull, Lieutenant Commander Joseph Finnegan, a 1929 Annapolis graduate who had served as a language officer in Japan from 1934 to 1937, brought the section with the untouched internal date-time cipher over to Wright.

"Ham," he said, "we're stuck on the date and time."

Wright had already stood his 12-hour watch and was about to go home before returning in 12 hours for another. Instead, he went with Finnegan to an empty desk in the traffic analysis section. Finnegan gave him the three previous uses of the cipher—one of them in a message that had led to the Coral Sea battle, another the garbled text. Wright put four people on a search for other instances of the cipher, and he and Finnegan set to work. For a good while the flaw in the one corrupt cryptogram frustrated their efforts, but as the night wore on Wright worked it out. He discovered that the date-and-time cipher comprised a polyalphabetic with independent mixed-cipher alphabets and with the exterior plain and key alphabets in two different systems of Japanese syllabic writing—one the older, formal kata kana, the other the cursive hira gana. Each has 47 syllables, making the polyalphabetic tableau a gigantic one of 2,209 cells, more than three times as extensive as the ordinary Vigenère tableau of 676 cells.

Nevertheless, by about 5:30 the next morning he had a solution. His inability to apply symmetry of position to the unrelated alphabets gave it a certain amount of slack, but he regarded it as essentially sound. He showed it to Rochefort. That expert noted the weak spots and said to Wright in mock rebuke:

"I can't send this out."

"If you don't," Wright replied firmly, "I will."

Rochefort laughed. He had only been testing Wright's faith in the solution, and Wright knew it. "Go ahead," he said.

Wright took it up to communications for transmission via the COPEK channel to the other communications intelligence units. He then headed once again for home, and on the way saw Layton about 7:45 and told him about it. Within hours, Nimitz knew that the Japanese had ordered that the Midway operation was to commence June 2 against the Aleutians and June 3 against the atoll. His intelligence staff had forecast correctly—but what a relief it was to know for sure, to work on fact instead of on theory.

By this time—the middle of the week before the attack was due—*Enterprise* and *Hornet* had reached Pearl after racing up from the southwest. *Yorktown* limped in the next day, her bowels torn by a Coral Sea bomb. Peacetime structural repairs would have taken 90 days; now the Navy yard, goaded by Nimitz, who knew how soon the hammer would fall, did the impossible and patched her up in two. On the 27th, Nimitz had issued his Operation Plan 29-42, stating that "The enemy is expected to attempt the capture of Midway in the near future" and setting forth his dispositions for the counterattack.

He ordered his carriers to a position codenamed POINT LUCK about 350 miles northeast of Midway. Here, on Yamamoto's flank, where they were not likely to be scouted, they were to await his advance. Then, with the advantage of the surprise that the American cryptanalysts had wrested from the unsuspecting Yamamoto, they were to spring on him, repulse the Midway invasion, wreak havoc on his carriers, and finally cheat him of the naval victory on which his war-winning strategy depended.

The three carriers took up station at POINT LUCK on June 2. By then the Japanese had succeeded in effecting their long-desired code change. It completely blacked-out the cryptanalysts of the Combat Intelligence Unit. They began chipping away at what they called JN25c, but they got only a few glimmers of light before edition d came into force, unexpectedly soon, in August. Had the June change been made in April as the Japanese had originally wanted, the cryptanalysts, Dyer said, "could not have gotten back in in time to do any good. May 1st would have been impossible. Midway was therefore a very close thing." But the June change did not affect the course of events, since all plans had been made and the great operation had already been set in motion.

According to program, the Japanese Aleutian force struck first. Nimitz had sent a North Pacific Force of cruisers and destroyers to protect his flank. Like some other officers, its commander, Rear Admiral Robert A. Theobald, suspected that the Japanese had "planted" the information on which U.S. intelligence estimates were based. They were probably thinking of dummy radio activity to fool the traffic analysts, for Nimitz never mentioned the supersecret cryptanalytic successes to his force commanders—not even in the briefings just before the battle. The suspicions of the doubters may have been reinforced by an intercepted plaintext request of a Japanese Army officer that all mail for his unit be addressed to Midway after June 5; as General Marshall later said, "that seemed a little bit too thick." Furthermore, Nimitz himself warned of Japanese trickery when arranging for identification by radio in his Operation Plan 29-42: "The Japanese are adept at the practice of deception. Have authenticators ready for use when needed. Small craft and aircraft except patrol planes use two alternate letters from the expression: 'Farmer in the dell.' Example: RE or EL or NH." Hence Theobald disbelieved the intelligence supplied him that the Japanese were going just to bombard Dutch Harbor but to seize Attu and Kiska. He deployed his force to prevent what he was convinced would be an invasion of Dutch Harbor. Unfortunately, this disposition deprived him of any opportunity to fight when, on the morning of June 3, right on schedule, the Japanese did just what the cryptanalysts had said they would do and bombed Dutch Harbor, inflicting considerable damage. They escaped unmolested.

The same morning an American search plane from Midway spotted the enemy. It was the troop-carrying invasion force, which Midway-based planes promptly but ineffectually attacked. The main striking force of four big carriers—*Akagi, Kaga, Hiryu,* and *Soryu,* veterans of the Pearl Harbor attack—remained hidden by clouds until the next morning, June 4. Again a Midway scout discovered the vessels. The American carriers sped toward them to launch planes for an attack. Meanwhile, American bombers from Midway and Japanese bombers from the carriers were mounting simultaneous attacks. Neither did much damage. Returning Japanese planes told of the need for further attacks.

So far the Japanese had sighted no American ships. They had not been diligently looking for them because, according to their expectations, no major enemy forces should have been in the vicinity: they should have been in Pearl, waiting to find out where the Japanese would strike. Admiral Chuichi Nagumo therefore struck below the 93 planes he had prudently held to counter even the highly unlikely enemy naval attack and ordered them rearmed for land bombardment. Thirteen minutes later he was dumfounded to receive a report of the sighting of enemy ships to the northeast. What should he do? For a precious quarter of an hour he mulled it over. Finally he canceled his order and directed the planes readied to attack ships. The incendiary and fragmentation bombs that the crews had just sweated into the bomb bays had to be replaced with the original torpedoes and armor-piercing bombs. Before this work was completed, his airplanes began returning from Midway, and his carriers had to recover these before launching the others.

It was at this most vulnerable of moments—with all planes aboard, with fueling in process and bombs and ammunition stacked in the open on the hangar and flight decks—that American planes attacked. Three waves of torpedo-bombers, one each from *Hornet*, *Enterprise*, and *Yorktown*, swept in, suffered heavy losses under Zero attacks or antiaircraft fire, and scored not a single hit. The last plane zoomed away at 10:24 a.m. This moment marked the high tide of Japan's fortunes in World War II. Jubilant officers cheered what they thought was victory at Midway, and in the war. Within six minutes, the tide was ebbing.

Dive-bombers from *Enterprise* screamed down on *Akagi*, *Kaga*, and *Soryu*. One hit set off *Akagi*'s torpedo storage, another exploded amid planes being rearmed on her flight deck; flames swept her, and within 24 hours she had been sunk. *Kaga* took four hits in rapid succession and sank that evening. *Yorktown* dive-bombers pummeled *Soryu* with three half-ton bombs; within 20 minutes she had to be abandoned, and a few hours later was torpedoed by an American submarine. The work of December 7 had not been completed, but avenged.

The rest was anticlimax. Later in the day *Hiryu* was sunk, and the Japanese in turn got *Yorktown*. Yamamoto next day realized that he was beaten. He called off the invasion of Midway and retreated, keeping close to his cabin on the homeward voyage. The samurai chieftains canceled plans for further advances and shifted from offense to defense. The failure to destroy the American Navy knocked the keystone from Yamamoto's strategy, and his words to Prince Konoye before the war haunted him: "I must also tell you that, should the war be prolonged for two or three years, I have no confidence in our ultimate victory." And not only did American industrial strength rise up like a specter. Japan's lack of it meant that she would never recover from the loss of four big carriers. The 4th of June had doomed her.

"Midway was essentially a victory of intelligence," Nimitz has written. "In attempting surprise, the Japanese were themselves surprised." General Marshall was even more specific. As a result of cryptanalysis, he declared, "We were able to concentrate our limited forces to meet their naval advance on Midway when otherwise we almost certainly would have been some 3,000 miles out of place." The surprise, the concentration, were engineered days before in a basement office a thousand miles from the scene of the action, where the solution of messages in JN25b (abetted by the recoveries of the other cryptanalytic units) and its internal time and place ciphers forged effects more crucial to the course of history than any other solution except that of the Zimmermann telegram. The codebreakers of the Combat Intelligence Unit had engrossed the fate of a nation. They had determined the destinies of ships and men. They had turned the tide of a war. They had caused a Rising Sun to start to set.

There was no single moment when the Battle of Midway was suddenly and decisively won, and so there was no burst of wild cheering in the basement office. The cryptanalysts reacted prosaically. The unit went on a watch in three instead of a watch and watch. It was also expanding rapidly. By the next year, it had changed its name to Fleet Radio Unit, Pacific Fleet—FRUPAC, in the Navy's interminable list of acronyms. Rochefort had departed in October, 1942, for two years of noncryptologic duties. He was replaced by Captain William B. Goggins, 44, a 1919 Annapolis graduate with long communications experience. Goggins, who had been wounded in the Battle of the Java Sea, remained as head of FRUPAC to January, 1945. Dyer continued to head cryptanalysis. Eventually FRUPAC comprised a personnel of more than 1,000. Much of the work was done in the new Joint Intelligence Center, housed in a long narrow building across Midway Drive from Nimitz' headquarters perched atop a cliff overlooking Pearl Harbor. Fabian, in Melbourne, directed a field unit similar to FRUPAC. He was on the staff of the Commander in Chief, 7th Fleet, which was attached to MacArthur's South West Pacific Area command.

FRUPAC's growth mirrored that of all American cryptanalytic agencies. This expansion compelled OP-20-G to reorganize as early as February, 1942. The workload had become too heavy for one man (Safford). The outfit was split up into sections for its three major cryptologic functions: (1) the development, production, and distribution of naval cryptosystems, headed by Safford; (2) policing of American naval communications to correct and prevent security violations; (3) cryptanalysis, headed by Commander John Redman. In September the development function was separated from the production.

Safford retained control of the development work until the end of the war, devising such new devices as call-sign cipher machines, adapters for British and other cryptographic devices, and off-line equipment for automatic operation. About June, the Navy ceded Japanese diplomatic solutions to the Army, giving over its files as well as its PURPLE machine. So rapidly was the workload expanding, however, that this diminution of its responsibility did not prevent the cryptologic branch from bursting the seams of its Navy Department building offices. In 1942, it moved into the brick buildings of a former girls' school at 3801 Nebraska Avenue, at the corner of Massachusetts Avenue, in a quiet section of northwest Washington. In the fall of 1941, about 700 persons, including 80 officers, had been doing communications intelligence in the entire Navy; two thirds of them were intercepting, direction-finding, or training for that work; the others, including most of the officers, were solving and translating. By the end of the war, there were 6,000.

The Army's growth was even more spectacular. It multiplied its communications-intelligence manpower thirtyfold from its strength December 7, 1941, of 331—44 officers and 137 enlisted men and civilians in Washington, and 150 officers and men in the field. Ever-growing requirements quickly dwarfed early estimates, such as the one early in 1942 that a staff of 460 would suffice, and kept up a relentless pressure for more and still more workers. Yet the agency faced stiff competition for them in manpower-short Washington. Moreover, the necessity for employees to be of unquestioned loyalty and trustworthiness, because of the sensitive nature of cryptanalytic results, and the importance of their being temperamentally suited to the highly specialized nature of the work, greatly reduced the number of prospects. To fill its needs, the agency launched a series of vigorous but discreet recruiting drives. It snatched people out of its school even though they were only partially trained: during the school's entire time at Fort Monmouth, New Jersey, not one student completed the full 48-week course. It brought in members of the Women's Army Corps—almost 1,500 of them. These measures enabled the agency to grow to a strength of 10,609 at its peak on June 1, 1945—5,565 civilians, 4,428 enlisted men and W.A.C.'s and 796 officers. (This figure excludes cryptologic personnel serving under theater commanders overseas.) Nevertheless, the personnel supply never caught up to the demand. In April, 1944, for example, the agency had more than 1,000 civilian positions empty.

But its growth soon made more space necessary. Like the Navy, it found a former girls' school ideal for its purposes. During the summer of 1942, it moved from the Munitions Building to Arlington Hall, whose brick buildings stood on 58 wooded acres fronting on Glebe Road in Arlington, Virginia, about three miles from downtown Washington and away from the eyes of enemy agents. The agency soon outgrew even this, and in the late fall of 1942 began expanding into Vint Hill Farms, an old estate in the Virginia horse country about 50 miles from Washington. Giant intercepting towers and half a dozen ugly barracks-like buildings soon disfigured the lovely

The Scrutable Orientals

Blue Ridge foothills, and here, in rooms filled with desks with tilted tops, most of the Army's traffic analysis was done. In addition, the agency taught most of its cryptology here, with the removal of its school from Fort Monmouth in October, 1942.

In June of 1942, owing to a reorganization in the Office of the Chief Signal Officer, the outfit shed its old name of Signal Intelligence Service and gained and lost three new ones within two months. Then from July, 1942, to July, 1943, it was called the Signal Security Service, and from July, 1943, to the end of the war, the Signal Security Agency. Lieutenant Colonel Rex Minckler, chief since before Pearl Harbor, was replaced in April, 1942, by Lieutenant Colonel Frank W. Bullock. In February, 1943, Lieutenant Colonel W. Preston (Red) Corderman, tall, husky, quiet, pleasant, who had studied and then taught in the S.I.S. school in the 1930s, became chief. He remained in the post to the end of the war, rising to a brigadier general in June, 1945.

Its population explosion and its voluminous output strained its administrative structure, and this was realigned several times. As of Pearl Harbor it was divided into four sections: the A, or administrative; the B, or cryptanalytic; the C, or cryptographic, and the D, or laboratory.

The C, or cryptographic section, devised hundreds of codes and ciphers during the war and produced thousands of key lists. It printed 5,000,000 classified documents, some running to many pages each, and distributed them in a carefully guarded manner throughout the world, accounting for each one. It tested the security of Army cipher machines (mainly Friedman's M-134 SIGABA) by attempting to solve them—and found that they generally proved impregnable. It supervised the mechanization of Army cryptography —the increasing replacement of strip cipher and M-209s and similar slow systems with typewriter-keyboard cipher machines, often with an on-line capacity. Only such mechanization enabled Army cryptographers to keep up with the ever-rising flood of traffic: the 23,000 codegroups a day that the 5th Army headquarters processed during its Sicily campaign strained even the machines to their limit—and by the time that army was marching on Rome, its headquarters was handling 40,000 groups a day. Traffic volume passed belief: in Hollandia, a million groups a day in November, 1944; at the Army's European Theater of Operations headquarters even before OVERLORD, 1,500,000 to 2,000,000 groups a day, or the equivalent of a shelf of 20 average books. The biggest message center of all, the War Department's in Washington, handled its peak load on August 8, 1945: nearly 9,500,000 words, the equivalent of almost one-tenth the total of French intercepts in all of World War I.

In August of 1942, subsection 6 (traffic) of the cryptanalytic section was upgraded to an E, or communications, section, to disseminate the solutions and to send directives to the field intercept units. In December, the shop of the cryptographic section was set up as the nucleus of the F, or development, section, for cryptographic equipment. In March of 1943, all six sections were elevated to branches, and by the following year two more had been added: the machine and the information and liaison branches. The Army had begun to use machines for cryptology in 1936, when Hollerith tabulating machines facilitated the compiling of codes. Their cryptanalytic potential had also been noted in that same year. By Pearl Harbor, 13 I.B.M. machines tended by 21 operators were working on S.I.S. projects. The personnel-short agency converted as many tasks as possible to mechanical operation, and the G, or machine, branch grew to enormous proportions. The 407 machines and 1,275 operators that it had by the spring of 1945 handled accounting and cryptologic tasks that would otherwise have required the hand labor of impossible numbers of clerks.

The cryptanalytic branch, then headed by Solomon Kullback, one of the three original cryptanalysts hired by Friedman in 1930, was much the largest, with 2,574 people in July of 1944, 82 per cent working on Japanese Army messages. To balance the agency and reduce the number of branch chiefs reporting to its commanding officer, the agency was reorganized the following month into four divisions: intelligence, which did traffic analysis and cryptanalysis; security, which handled cryptography and radio countermeasures and formulated and executed policy and technical doctrines; operating services, which provided services for the intelligence and security divisions and ran the secret-ink laboratory; and personnel and training.

Though this set-up held until the war ended, operational control of the agency passed on December 15, 1944, to G-2, the military intelligence section of the War Department General Staff, which was the agency's major customer and which, as such, for many months had indirectly guided its activities. The Signal Corps merely retained administrative control. This confusing arrangement—complicated further by the agency's having both staff and command functions—ended in August, 1945, when the War Department transferred all signal intelligence units to agency control. On September 6, four days after the war ended, the War Department ordered the creation within G-2 of a new cryptologic organization by merging the Signal Security Agency, the field cryptanalytic units, and Signal Corps cryptography. This was the Army Security Agency, which came into existence September 15, 1945.

Throughout the war, most of the intercept material for Signal Security Agency headquarters was supplied by the 2nd Signal Service Battalion. It had been created as the 2nd Signal Service Company on January 1, 1939, by Major General Joseph Mauborgne, the chief signal officer, out of the 1st Radio Intelligence Company at Fort Monmouth, plus the radio intelligence detachments of signal companies in the Canal Zone, Fort Sam Houston, Texas, the Presidio, San Francisco, Fort Shafter, Hawaii and Fort McKinley, Philippine Islands. Commanding its 101 enlisted men was First Lieutenant Earle F. Cooke. It grew rapidly—in October, 1939, a detachment under First Lieutenant Robert E. Schukraft arrived at Fort Hunt, Virginia, to install and operate a new Army intercept station. With the onset of war, the imperative demands for manpower compelled the Army, on April 2, 1942, to increase the company to battalion strength. Eventually it expanded to an enormously oversized company of 5,000 men. From April, 1942, to the end of the war, its commanding officer was the Signal Security Agency chief. When G-2 took operational control, the battalion was redesignated the 9420th Technical Service Unit, which at the end of the war became part of the Army Security Agency. By that time, the original four radio circuits on which it was sending intercept material back to Washington at the time of Pearl Harbor had swollen to 46 full-time radioteletypewriter channels.

The Army, like the Navy, established cryptanalytic units in the several theaters of war. Their organization varied from one theater to another. The South West Pacific Area, under MacArthur, had at its headquarters a communications-intelligence unit called the Central Bureau and in the field a number of subordinate units. Central Bureau, or simply C.B., had been founded in August of 1942 by Lieutenant Colonel Joe R. Sherr, who had been head of the 18-man 2nd Signal Service Company detachment in the Philippines and who had accompanied MacArthur to Australia. Later, Abraham Sinkov, who had been another of Friedman's original cryptanalysts, went out to take charge. C.B. was quartered in a rambling wooden house—which local legend said was a former whorehouse—close to the Ascot racetrack in Brisbane. A guard stood in front. A small air-conditioned brick building at the track itself housed the I.B.M. machinery. Sinkov worked wonders: when a downed Japanese bomber yielded an air-to-ground codebook, it was discovered that Sinkov had already recovered nearly all of it. His title at the end of the war was Cryptanalytic Officer, Signal Intelligence Service, U.S. Army Forces, Far East; his rank by then was colonel. A sweet and unmilitary man who seemed slightly embarrassed by the eagles on his shoulders, he was unable to return a salute without blurting out a "Good morning." He was awarded a Legion of Merit and an Oak Leaf Cluster to it for his work.

Some elements of the Central Bureau were—despite the name—attached to widely scattered units. MacArthur's chief signal officer, Brigadier General Spencer B. Akin, who enjoyed more authority than any other theater signal officer, attached communications-intelligence units to major headquarters so that the intelligence would be promptly available to officers who could act upon it. He even assigned one such detachment to Admiral William F. Halsey, Jr.'s flagship, while Admiral Spruance found the Army service so valuable, when he took command of the 5th Fleet, that he kept the communications-intelligence specialists with him.

In addition, Signal Corps radio intelligence companies provided tactical, combat-level communications intelligence. One of the first, the 101st Signal Company (Radio Intelligence), replaced Hawaii's old Monitor Post 5 in July of 1942, vastly improving the quantity and quality of the work. Typical, perhaps, of these companies was the 138th. Trained in Spokane for Europe and then transported to the East Coast, it was loaded aboard a transport and promptly shipped through the Panama Canal to Australia, landing there in June of 1943. The 299-man company was mobile and self-contained so that it could operate in isolation: it was mountable within two hours and had its own truckdrivers, cooks, repairmen, and so forth. The men lived in tents.

The company's mission was to determine the Japanese order of battle and ascertain military concentrations and movements. Most of its work involved air-to-ground messages. To pick up these low-power transmissions, it had to move forward from island to island as the Allies advanced. Its first position, early in 1944, was at Nadzab, an airstrip in the Markham Valley of New Guinea. One subordinate direction-finding group was over a hump at Gusap; another was on an abandoned ranch near Darwin, Australia, where it enjoyed fresh meat daily. In the middle of the year it advanced to Biak, a small island north of New Guinea, where it was nearly strangled by the thick jungle, and it went ashore on Leyte about five days after the first wave of invasion troops. By then its direction-finding groups were scattered all over the South Pacific.

The unit worked near the front lines so as to get as many intercepts as possible. So close were they that on Leyte late in 1944 Japanese paratroops dropped on the unit, apparently having mistaken it for a command post because of its numerous antennae. One startled radioman, isolated in a direction-finding booth in the middle of a clearing, suddenly heard bullets whizzing all around him. The codebreakers dropped their pencils, grabbed their rifles, and engaged in rather more direct action against the enemy than that to which they were accustomed. The paratroopers were driven off, but not quickly enough to save the unit's documents from the flames.

Its radio operators, specially trained in Japanese Morse, listened in 24 hours a day on at least some of its two dozen receivers. Sometimes just the circuits being used would give Japanese intentions away. On Biak in 1944, the unit quickly learned that messages on a certain frequency invariably preceded an evening air raid—a bit of foreknowledge that enabled one member to collect regularly on sure-fire bets with a sergeant from a nearby outfit. Other times the 20-odd nisei in the unit intercepted Japanese cleartext. Usually, however, the radiomen typed out the coded intercepts and handed them to a traffic analyst. Most of the messages reported planes flying from one point to another, and the analyst, by a study of call-signs, could tell which unit and which points were meant. The 15 cryptanalysts had the mechanical task of stripping the additive from codes that had been solved at C.B. Each day a report summing up the unit's conclusions went rearward to 5th Air Force headquarters, to which the unit had been attached, switching from the Signal Corps under C.B. to the Army Air Corps and receiving the new name of 1st Radio Squadron, Mobile.

Success usually came in the humble form of an early warning of an air raid that probably saved American lives, or as some insight into a Japanese move that enabled an American commander to neutralize it. Late in the war, the unit's solution of Japanese meteorological codes told American bombing commands what they wanted to know most—weather conditions over target. The outfit alerted the Allies to a major Japanese build-up when it solved a message reporting the presence in an airplane of two high-ranking officers of Japan's 4th Air Army, which up to that time had been thought to be in northern China. But its greatest feat was the discovery of a huge concentration of Japanese air strength at Hollandia. The 5th Air Force launched massive raids and destroyed more than 100 enemy planes. Consequently they were not present to attack the American invaders, who splashed ashore with virtually no opposition.

The Imperial Japanese Navy had commenced its cryptanalytic efforts in 1925 with the creation of an ultra-secret Tokumu Han ("Special Section") in the 4th, or communications, Department of the Naval General Staff. It then numbered six persons, including clerks, and was located in the red brick Navy Ministry building in Tokyo. Among its early members were the young naval officer Hideya Morikawa, nephew of Chief of Staff Admiral Kanji Kato, and Morikawa's former superior, First Lieutenant Kamisugi, who had handled cryptography aboard the flagship *Nagato*. Captain Kowalefsky, the Polish cryptologist who had improved the codes that Yardley had solved, lectured on cryptanalysis, and the neophyte codebreakers cut their eyeteeth on the GRAY code of the U.S. Department of State, making their entry through the classic technique of identifying NADED as *period*.*

They also solved Chinese cryptograms during the Manchuria incident, primarily because these were based on a commercial codebook that transformed the Chinese ideographs to four-digit numbers for telegraphic communication. After the Japanese seizure of Shanghai early in 1932, Morikawa was sent there as chief of a cryptanalytic unit attached to the 3rd Fleet. He solved a Chinese message that corroborated a slightly doubtful Tokumu Han solution of an American GRAY message reporting Chinese plans to use its Air Force to attack Japanese troops. Instead the Japanese struck first, catching most of Chiang Kai-shek's Air Force at Hangchow.

The Tokumu Han failed, however, to break two-part codes, such as the State Department's BROWN code, those used by the American Navy, and those introduced by Yardley into Chinese communications when he was Chiang's cryptologist—except in extraordinarily favorable circumstances. One such occurred on February 26, 1936, when two regiments mutinied in Tokyo and several statesmen were assassinated in an attempted coup d'état. This furnished the cryptanalysts with an ocean of text and plenty of probable words to go fishing with. For a short time they read most American communications, including those of the naval attaché. Then the United States changed systems,

* Whether this solution was made in cooperation or in competition with the Ango Kenkyu Han, the Foreign Ministry's cryptanalytic section, is not known.

and the skill of the Tokumu Han again proved unequal to its task. Its resourcefulness made up for this: near the end of 1937, Morikawa, accompanied by a locksmith, a photographer, and some lookouts, broke into the American consulate at Kobe and photographed the BROWN code and the M-138 cipher device, which the Japanese had never seen before.

Soon thereafter, as part of Japan's preparation for war, the naval shoguns built their first big intercepting post at Owada, a village about fifty minutes by car from Tokyo. During American naval maneuvers, its direction-finding and traffic analysis helped the general staff analyze American forces and tactics. The Tokumu Han also added cryptanalysts, all of whom were officers. By Pearl Harbor there were ten working full time and ten part time. They had still not succeeded, however, in reading American cryptograms.

After Pearl Harbor, the rampant growth of Allied communications compelled the Tokumu Han to expand still further. The first batch of recruits—60 of them—were drawn from foreign-language schools and commercial colleges to become the first civilians in the Tokumu Han. The second batch consisted of about 70 reserve officer candidates selected from about 500 in basic training on the basis of their competence in foreign languages. (These signal intelligence groups differed from classes learning cryptography.) During a five-month course at the Naval Communication School at Kurihama near Yokosuka—hard by the Commodore Matthew Perry monument—they practiced International Morse, studied the elementary Oriental Tenji and Tenchi ciphers as well as the Occident's more advanced Porta and Vigenère, and learned how to break codes and ciphers. Six classes, each larger than its predecessor, were trained during the war. Some graduates were assigned to communications intelligence in the intelligence units of fleet and force headquarters. In November of 1943, for example, the 3rd Fleet employed three officers and six enlisted men to monitor enemy messages. But most went straight into the Tokumu Han proper.

A torrent of intercepts was pouring into it. Most came from the hundreds of radio receivers and direction-finders of the Owada Communications Unit. Some were picked up by the 20 Americans and Australians pressed into service with the Kanagawa Communication Force near Hiyoshi, and a few messages trickled in from fleet radio units. Near the end of the war a unit was set up in a radish field at Yokosuka. The entire Tokumu Han had swollen to several thousand men by the end of the war, most engaged in intercepting. So hungry was it for competent personnel that it did something almost unheard-of in misogynistic Japan: it employed women—putting about 30 nisei girls to work eavesdropping on American radiotelephone conversations. By the middle of 1943 it had outgrown its quarters, and the traffic analysis section moved to the third floor of the Naval War College in Tokyo, leaving only the cryptanalysts at the Navy Ministry

They comprised the 2nd Branch of the Tokumu Han's three. In charge was Captain Endo. Under him were several national sections: United States and

The Scrutable Orientals 581

Britain, with about 50 officers under Lieutenant Commander T. Satake; China, with about 20 officers under Lieutenant Commander Nakatani; Russia under Lieutenant Commander Masayoshi Funoto; and Italian, German, French, and others, about 10 officers. The 3rd Branch handled traffic analysis. It was likewise organized on a national basis, subdivided into areas,

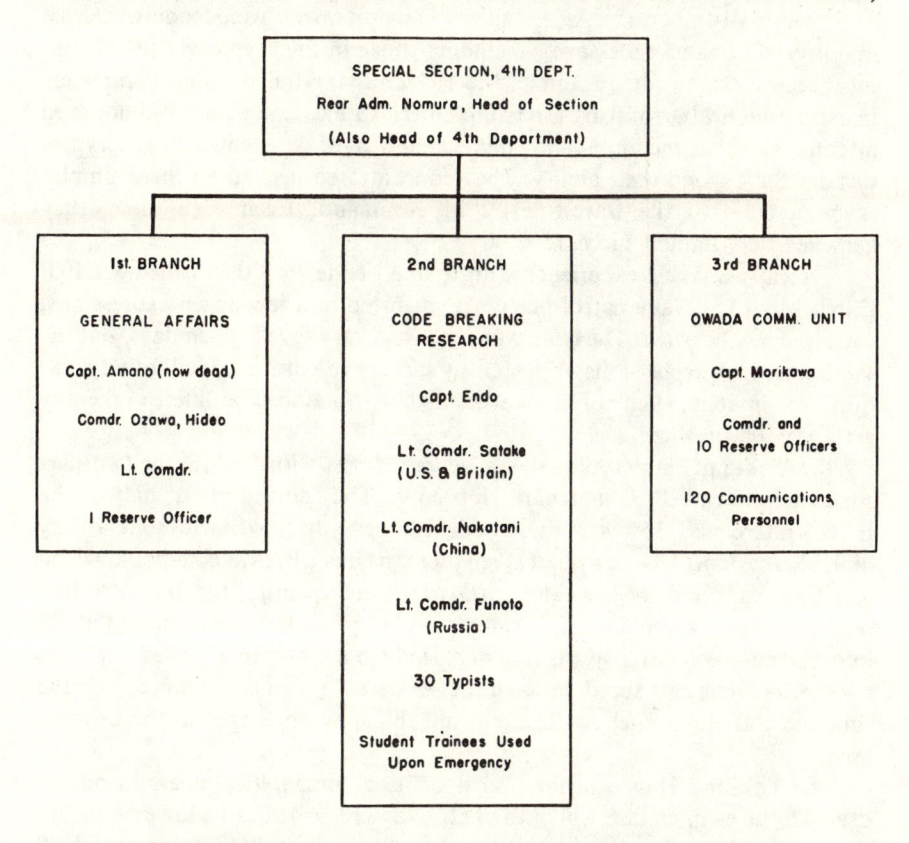

```
                 SPECIAL SECTION, 4th DEPT.
              Rear Adm. Nomura, Head of Section
                (Also Head of 4th Department)
                            │
        ┌───────────────────┼───────────────────┐
   1st. BRANCH          2nd BRANCH          3rd BRANCH

  GENERAL AFFAIRS      CODE BREAKING       OWADA COMM. UNIT
                         RESEARCH
  Capt. Amano                              Capt. Morikawa
  (now dead)           Capt. Endo

  Comdr. Ozawa, Hideo                      Comdr. and
                       Lt. Comdr. Satake   10 Reserve Officers
  Lt. Comdr.           (U.S. & Britain)
                                           120 Communications
  1 Reserve Officer    Lt. Comdr. Nakatani Personnel
                       (China)

                       Lt. Comdr. Funoto
                       (Russia)

                       30 Typists

                       Student Trainees Used
                       Upon Emergency
```

(THE OWADA COMMUNICATIONS UNIT WAS AN INDEPENDENT UNIT CAPTAIN MORIKAWA HAD TWO DUTIES — COMMANDING OFFICER OF THE OWADA COMMUNICATIONS UNIT, AND HEAD OF THE THIRD BRANCH OF THE SPECIAL SECTION.)

The Imperial Japanese Navy radio intelligence organization (Tokumu Han) of the 4th Department (communications), Naval General Staff

with an average of two officers and a handful of enlisted men working on each area. This was fluid, however, and sometimes as many as ten officers would be working on a single area. The branch was commanded by Morikawa, now a captain, who, in a separate capacity, also headed the Owada Communications Unit. The 1st Branch planned, made policy, and distributed the results of the two operating branches. In charge was Captain Amano, with

Commander Hideo Ozawa his executive officer. Command of the entire Tokumu Han was vested in the chief of its parent body, the 4th Department; in effect, this gave the Tokumu Han a seat on the Naval General Staff. In 1943 the head of the 4th Department was Rear Admiral Gonichiro Kakimoto, and at the end of the war, Rear Admiral Tomekichi Nomura.

In sharp distinction to American cryptanalysts, who were reading the vast majority of Japanese messages, including those in the cryptosystems of topmost security, the codebreakers of the Tokumu Han failed almost completely in extracting usable information from American messages. They did not even attempt to solve medium- and high-echelon messages, couched in cryptosystems far beyond their ability. They concentrated instead on three simpler cryptosystems of the lowest levels of command. Even with these, they achieved only limited success.

Typical was their experience with a small code that they called AN 103. Carried by U.S. Navy patrol planes, it consisted of a few dozen expressions, such as *enemy sighted*. The code was changed every seven to ten days, but the same plaintext expressions appeared in successive editions, facilitating solution. Fortunately, such solutions were usually obtained too late to take any action based on them.

The Tokumu Han cryptanalysts succeeded best with BAMS, the two-part superenciphered Allied merchant ship code. They solved about half of the BAMS intercepts. How were they suddenly able to do so well with so relatively difficult a system? Germany had given them the basic BAMS codebook, which had been captured by her raider *Atlantis*. Consequently, the Japanese had only to remove the superencipherment. BAMS provided occasional tidbits of information—three transports had departed from California, for example, or a vessel's course and speed data—but even here, Ozawa complained, "By the time the code [message] was broken, the ship was no longer in the original area."

The Tokumu Han expended most of its cryptanalytical energies on the CSP 642, the strip cipher, which the U.S. Navy regarded as its lowest-echelon system. The Navy complicated it by not using the full complement of 30 strips every time. Instead it eliminated from zero to five strips from one day to another. Thus one day's messages might use only 25 strips, the next day's, 27, the next, 30.

Japan had captured strip ciphers on Wake and Kiska, and with these she attacked the intercepts. Her methods mixed sophistication and naïveté. To determine how many strips had been eliminated, the Tokumu Han used I.B.M. tabulators of the First Life and the Meiji Life Insurance companies of Tokyo. These took frequency counts at intervals of 30, 29, 28, ..., 25 and compared them; the interval that showed the most repetitions indicated the correct encipherment length. Many of the strip messages were sent by American submarines; these were identifiable by their indicators—BIMEC or FEMYH—and by their transmission from close to the Japanese coast. The

Tokumu Han could know that at that position a merchant ship had been sunk, or that certain units of the Japanese fleet near there were steaming at such-and-such a course and speed, and that the submarine was reporting this. With this as a lead, two first lieutenants who had majored in English in college, Shimizu and Oda, composed what they thought the plaintext intercept was. They varied expressions, word positions, guesses of latitude and longitude until they had a supposed plaintext that matched the cryptogram in length and whose letters all differed from their ciphertexts—since in the strip system no letter can represent itself. Then they arranged and rearranged the strips until they had reproduced the ciphertext on one line and the presumed plaintext on another; the sequence of strips almost certainly represented that day's key. With it they decrypted other intercepts.

This tortuous method—for some reason they did not heed the lessons of de Viaris and Friedman on solving this system—suggests why so little information was extracted from the strip cipher. The Tokumu Han kept increasing the size of the section in its American branch that handled strip messages until there were about 40 officers, 10 enlisted men, a dozen typists, two dozen women clerks, Professor Yamanashi of the Navy War College, and a mathematician, Ozaki. Though efforts were continued up to the end of the war, the life had long since gone out of them; the Tokumu Han, considering the strip cipher unbreakable for all intents and purposes, vacated its hopes for cryptanalysis and looked instead to traffic analysis as its chief source of information.

The difficulty with this, as Lieutenant Commander Satake put it, was that "Our whole analysis was based on probabilities; there was nothing of a definite nature." The 3rd Branch graphed the volumes of urgent, priority, routine, and deferred messages transmitted from each major American station. It charted the traffic flow among the various call-signs. It located the transmitters by a widespread direction-finder net of a dozen linked stations situated from Kiska to Rabaul, from Wake to Manila. By following the bulge in BAMS transmissions from California to Hawaii to, say, Guam, the traffic analysts could predict the general area in which the next American assault would come. Messages from reconnoitering submarines or airplanes reinforced the estimate. The time of the attack was often gauged by noncommunications means—such as guesses based on previous movements—but sometimes by such communications intelligence as the imposition of radio silence or an increase in the urgency of reconnaissance messages. None of these methods, however, enabled the 3rd Branch to pinpoint time or place. The Japanese knew in advance, for example, that the United States was mounting an invasion of the Philippines, but when it would come they could tell no more closely than within a month, and upon which island the assault would fall, they never knew until it happened. Compared to the crystalline precision of America's Midway intelligence, Japanese intelligence floundered in a miasma of vaporous generalities. Only once in four years of war—at the

Marshalls—did it get word to a garrison early enough to help it prepare for an impending attack.

The Japanese Army, personified by the combined War and Prime Minister General Hideki Tojo, had panted for this war much more than the Navy, and so might have been expected to produce striking communications-intelligence results when the desired hostilities broke out. The woeful actuality was summed up in one sentence after the defeat of Nippon by Lieutenant General Seizo Arisue, chief of Army intelligence: "We couldn't break your codes at all."

It was not for lack of trying. The Army centered its communications-intelligence work at Tanashi and dispersed seven intercept and direction-finding units through the home islands alone. Runners, telegraph, and radio brought the average of 250 diplomatic and press messages and 800 military dispatches intercepted each day to the cryptanalysts. Headed by Major Machida, they worked in an old folks home named Yofuen in Tokyo, with two unimportant subordinate groups in the villages of Ono and Itakura. They failed utterly with the diplomatic traffic. Not until 1944 did they begin work on the military strip ciphers, and though they drafted some mathematics students, brought in an I.B.M. tabulator, and consulted with the Navy, they had no more luck than did the Tokumu Han.

Field units were attached to Army staffs. They listened in to American radio messages and even sent out special wiretapping patrols. Results were disappointing, mainly because few men at the front could understand English. And since the soldiers' war in the Pacific comprised a series of brief, individual battles for small islands, the Army had little opportunity to build up an enemy order of battle or to predict attacks by traffic analysis. As for field cryptanalysis of Allied messages, Arisue's mournful plaint was echoed by a colonel on the staff of the 25th Army: "We did not break your codes." How debilitated their intelligence must have been—for the Japanese rated communications intelligence as their most valuable source of information on the enemy!

The Arisue concession must be qualified somewhat. In occupied Manila, cryptanalysts in a staff section monitoring squad of the 14th Army frequently solved the messages of Filipino and American guerrillas. These jungle warriors wirelessed information on Japanese activities to MacArthur's headquarters in Australia and direct to San Leandro, California. At first they enciphered with whatever was at hand. One of the first guerrillas, an unsurrendered American soldier on Luzon, employed the venerable U.S. Army Cipher Disk. Some used M-94s, at least one of which was captured by the Japanese. When Colonel Wendell Fertig on Mindanao finally contacted Australia early in 1943, he was instructed: "If you know double transposition use as key first name of second next of kin [which would be his first-born child, Patricia] and city of residence second next of kin [she was then living in Golden, Colorado] and encode the following information . . ." as an authentication. Later in the war, the guerrillas employed new ciphers smuggled in on the supply submarines. One such system, comprising seven closely typed pages and intended for a special operation, was microfilmed and concealed in the ankle patch of a pair of sneakers for transportation to another leader, Macario Peralta, Jr., on Panay.

The cryptanalysts in Manila seemed to do best in the first half of 1943—after volume from the guerrilla stations had built up but before the improved systems appeared. From February through April they read messages in a number cipher emanating from Cebu and used to report shipping movements, though they failed to solve "a special code . . . used by one part of the Cebu system"—probably the guerrilla units under Colonel Harry Fenton. In March and April they broke the system used by Peralta's units on Negros, as well as various double transpositions, until their keywords were changed in April. Solution of the system used by the headquarters station DKZ provided information "on the general organization of the enemy guerrillas over all of Negros, Siquijor, and Mindanao," boasted the cryptanalysts in their report for the last ten days of April. Next month they had to confess that "deciphering is at a standstill," but in July—perhaps as a result of an increase of traffic, since 214 messages were sent in just ten days by only two stations, KML and WZE—they broke through to their last big success. They cracked the Fenton system that had rebuffed them before, as well as Fertig's messages, enabling them to read both leaders' back files since March. A few days later, interrogation of a captured American yielded keywords used for communication with Australia and America.

The information produced by the cryptanalysts and the direction-finding units with which they were affiliated enabled Japanese Army units to raid guerrilla posts, often with success. But this was defensive; it removed a thorn in the Japanese side, but it did nothing positive for their war effort. And even this declined steeply in the fall of 1943. "Although enemy wireless stations in the Philippines were disturbed by the strength of our punitive activities," a September report said, "they avoided punishment by skillful concealment, and they are maintaining communication between themselves as well as with America and Australia." In November, after some empty bragging about "a fatal blow to the guerrillas," the Japanese admitted that "As always all the systems were very active and communication was carried on extensively within the Philippines and with outside stations." And at these stations, notably Heindorf House, the Brisbane headquarters of MacArthur's Allied Intelligence Bureau, where the cryptographic section, under Lieutenant C. B. Ferguson, deciphered the incoming traffic with quiet efficiency, the producers of intelligence for the strategic planners noted with satisfaction that as 1944 arrived the stream of information from the Philippines was assuming impressive proportions. Thus the only Japanese cryptanalyses that might be considered to any degree successful turned out in the end to be short-lived, limited, and utterly inconsequential to the greater course of the war.

Japan's cryptography was as poor as her cryptanalysis, though it looked good on paper. Codes were numerous, with different users having their own; they were also changed regularly and varied from one geographical area to another. But the system did not work out well. Poor administration, distribution troubles, and lax security vitiated the theory.

Admittedly, the Japanese faced a difficult situation. Just getting codebooks to the thousands of ships and island garrisons scattered over the 20,000,000 square miles that they had conquered posed a staggering physical problem. Indeed, this problem had defeated them twice before Midway. Furthermore, the problem was magnified by the great numbers of codebooks that had to be distributed. Exactly how many codes Japan employed throughout the war may never be known. Probably the figure would reach several hundred, if every edition of the small codes carried by airplanes and auxiliary vessels were counted. An outline of Japanese naval cryptosystems—all of which were codes—will give an impression of the bristling panoply employed by a modern nation, as well as of Japanese distribution difficulties. Probably not all were in use together. In each case, the letter or the kana names the codebook.

I. Strategic and Administrative
   A. KO—the flag officers' system, a four-numeral code superenciphered by transposition; called AD by Americans; abandoned in 1942 or 1943 because of excessive garbles
   B. D, later called RO—the fleet cryptographic system, the most widely used; called JN25 by Americans; a superenciphered two-part code
   C. SHIN—a special logistics code, in practice usually replaced by D

II. Tactical
   A. OTSU—for tactical communications of surface forces
   B. BO—for local actions
   C. F—for air; revised every two months
   D. C—for air and miscellaneous
   E. H—for air in China; a simple, easy-to-revise code
   F. KI—for land combat in China; widely used during the China Incident, but generally neglected after Pearl Harbor in favor of OTSU
   G. Joint Army-Navy codebook—suspended after the Army compromised it
   H. A—combined fleet special code phrases

III. Attaché and intelligence
   A. J—for attachés in Europe and the Americas
   B. IC series—for intelligence agents
      1. IC-A—in Great Britain, France, Italy, Spain, Portugal, Turkey, Soviet Union
      2. IC-B—in China
      3. IC-C—in Korea and Manchuria
      4. IC-D—in the Americas
      5. IC-E—in Burma
   C. HEI—for intelligence in the China area
   D. "The New Code Book"—for intelligence officers on the western coast of America

E. Overseas Secret Telegraph Code Book—in reserve for attachés
IV. Extra-naval
   A. HATO—for joint use of the three ministries of Foreign Affairs, Army, and Navy; superenciphered by additive
   B. s—for merchant ships of more than 1,000 tons
   C. [no name given]—for fishing boats
   D. w—for reporting foreign vessels clearing Japanese ports; distributed to custom houses, harbormasters, and resident officers

Many special systems also served. The polyalphabetic date-time cipher that Wright solved before Midway and the CHI-HE map grid code were two examples. There were, in addition, a primary signal book for visual signals, lists of standard and special abbreviations, and call-sign tables for both strategic and tactical communications.

Once the Japanese introduced a special code for extra secrecy. The effects were disastrous. On June 15, 1944, when they set in motion their big A-Go operation to ambush the Allied fleet, the carrier *Taiho*, flagship of their 1st Mobile Fleet, carried this highly secret code for communications with Combined Fleet headquarters. Four days later, an American submarine torpedoed it, and a delayed gasoline explosion destroyed all communications facilities, including the special code. Urgent messages from headquarters piled up until other ships reported the loss. Among them was one reporting that the fleet was being trailed by an enemy task force, which attacked and sank another carrier. The A-Go operation ended in failure and the Marianas were lost.

The Japanese Army encoded its messages with four-figure codes that were superenciphered with the usual additives. For example, in the code used by the 6th Division around Bougainville late in 1943, 9019 stood for *23rd Infantry*, 9015 for *division headquarters*, 9022 for *6th Cavalry*, and so forth. The cipher section of the Kwantung Army in Manchuria compiled a 100-page geographical supplement to Army Codebook No. 3, listing codenumbers for places across the border in Siberia as preparation for a possible attack. The Army convened an annual conference in Tokyo for the chiefs of cipher sections of its various Army headquarters.

The wartime increase in communications naturally accelerated the Japanese Navy's prewar schedule of changing a code every few years. The new standard called for changing the fleet system every six months to a year, its additives every month to six months, and the tactical code every month. In general this was met, except for the tactical OTSU, which was revised only once or twice a year. JN25, for example, went through about a dozen editions during the war—JN25b, c, d, and so on.

The numerous codes, and the frequent revisions of the most important ones, overburdened the Navy's distribution system. To ease the strain, the Navy divided its whole theater of operations into eleven "code areas." Distribution to one area would not depend upon distribution to another, and failure to get a code to an outpost would not compromise the entire system. The plan was for each area to have its own code, called HA-1, HA-2, and so on, according to the area. But the HA codes were not compiled in time, code TEN had to be used instead, and, as it worked out, all areas got the same code anyway with only the additive tables differing from one code area to another. High commands additionally held the RO code (JN25) for communications with other code areas.

This snafuing seems to have resulted from an administrative arrangement that was both unnecessary and unintelligent. Communications security in the Imperial Japanese Navy was basically the job of the 10th Section of its 4th Department (communications, whose Special Section was the Tokumu Han). The 10th Section planned cryptographic procedures, outlined the training of code clerks, compiled codebooks and additive tables, and supervised production. At first the printing of codebooks was done by the Printing Bureau of the Japanese Cabinet, later by the Navy Ministry's printing office. Volume increases brought the presses of the Naval Torpedo and Communications Schools into service. Still later, most of the cryptographic printing was transferred to the Navy-controlled Bunjudo Printing Office in Yokohama, and in 1944 the 10th Section moved onto the firm's premises. (This followed the transferral in September, 1943, of routine encoding and decoding of headquarters messages from the 10th Section to the Tokyo Communications Unit, thereby relieving a staff of a line function. Headquarters now conformed to the Navy-wide arrangement, in which local communications units encoded and decoded for their commands.)

After being printed under the control of the 10th Section, the codebooks were physically taken to, and passed into the custody of, the Navy Library, which distributed all naval publications. This main library in turn sent the codebooks out to the district libraries, under the escort of librarians. District staff officers then carried the codebooks en masse to their area's commands, where they were handed out to individual ships and units. Minor recipients picked up their codebooks themselves at the district library, or sometimes received them by registered mail. The Japanese sought to disseminate to combat units not only the new code, but a reserve code that was to supplant the new one. In addition, another back-up code was held at the district libraries. Canceled codebooks were at first returned to Japan, but later in the war they were simply burned and notification filed in writing.

The severance of the distributive function from the productive, and its bestowal on personnel less alive than the 10th Section to the imperatives of communications security, endangered Japanese cryptography. The librarians sometimes lost codebooks; sometimes they simply failed to observe the proper precautions. In 1943, a box of cryptographic publications en route from Kure to the Tsingtao Base Force in China was inadvertently opened. This was specifically charged to failure to provide a responsible escort aware of the publications' importance. When a freight car carrying codebooks from the Yokosuka Naval District Library arrived at the Ominato Ship and Ordnance

Department in 1943, its door lock was found to be missing. Investigators could not ascertain whether it had fallen off or been knocked off, but since the packing appeared undisturbed, they assumed that no compromise had occurred. In 1944, a whole load of codebooks disappeared during their rail trip from the Chinhae Communications Unit to one of its detachments. The unit was simply issued replacements.

Part of a page of the encoding section of a 1943 edition of the main Japanese Navy code

The Japanese stiffened this rather lax attitude when it came to losses in the combat zone. A submarine unloading cargo at Salamaua, New Guinea, crash-dived to avoid air attack and some codebooks were washed off deck. "Emergency measures"—whatever they were—were taken. They were also taken in

1943, when a transport plane jettisoned some cargo because of motor trouble between Truk and Rabaul. Included was a tightly packed box of codebooks which might have floated to nearby land. When the Allies assaulted Biak in May, 1944, a radio crew carrying codebooks to a safer location encountered an Allied patrol, and during the skirmish the codebooks were lost. The responsible officer did not report it for three weeks. Prompt investigation showed that only one or two lesser codes were missing, but since the loss took place while the Japanese were planning their A-Go operation, they changed codes wholesale. A new edition of JN25 was issued. Ironically, one of the main effects of the changes was to hamper Japanese communications on the eve of the operation.

But their remedial steps could not always prevent serious breaches of their communications security. One unavoidable case was that of the submarine *I-1*.

On the night of January 29, 1943, the cargo- and troop-carrying *I-1* had the misfortune to surface near the New Zealand corvette *Kiwi*, commanded by Lieutenant Commander G. Bridson. He, his chief engineer, and his medical officer were famed throughout the South Seas for their mastodonic bulk and their practice of parading through Nouméa playing on a dented trombone, a jazz whistle, and a concertina. Upon spotting *I-1*, Bridson put his helm over and rang up full speed to ram. When the chief questioned this, he was told: "Shut up! There's a weekend's leave in Auckland dead ahead of us." Ram they did, though *I-1* was half again as big as *Kiwi* and had twice the firepower. With all guns from 20-millimeter to 4-inch blasting away at a range never exceeding 150 yards, *Kiwi* backed off and charged again—this time for "a week's leave." A third time she rammed, "for a fortnight"; this time she climbed right onto *I-1*'s deck. At 11:20 p.m. the submarine grounded on a reef at the northwest tip of Guadalcanal, ending the battle.

Among other things, she was carrying 200,000 codebooks. The crew buried some of these on the enemy-held shores, and when word of the action got back to Japanese headquarters, aerial bombardment and submarine torpedoing was ordered in an unsuccessful attempt to destroy the documents still aboard. But the Allies had already recovered the codebooks, which included both current and reserve codes. The Japanese ordered some new codebooks and additive tables to be used, but JN25 remained unchanged, and the documents as a whole were of great value. Bridson and his chief were awarded the Navy Cross.

So even the best of Japanese intentions proved to be too little and too late. Their communications security was as bad as their communications intelligence. Sometimes it seemed as if they didn't care. The Navy attempted to find a water-soluble ink for codebooks to dissolve the printing when the books were jettisoned or the ship sunk, but when the Technical Research Laboratory reported that it could not find one that would fully obliterate the writing when immersed and yet would not run when splashed with rain, sea spray, or sweat, this worthy effort simply petered out. Certainly a lackadaisical attitude blighted their communications security. Instructions for a new Army code complained that "in certain situations, the use of the National Army Code was terrifying." Though these instructions pointed out that sometimes code messages were sent to units which do not have the codebook for them, and urged that "The nature of the B Supplement [of Army B Code, No. 3] will be studied carefully and precautions taken so that such things will absolutely never happen in the future," they also admitted with refreshing candor that "the time for the compilation being short, printing presses being busy and lacking the materials for one edition of the codebook, it may not be possible to fulfill the needs of each unit." For communications security, they seemed to depend, not on training or on adequate cryptosystems, but on patriotic exhortation: "Even if there are any blunders, it is necessary that an endeavor be made to decipher the [garbled] message ... even though it is just a trivial matter in the use of the general code of the National Army ... so that flaws will not be exposed and earnest prayers will be offered for the glorious progress of one phase in the fulfillment of the sacred duties in the Great East Asia conflict."

In part, the Japanese trusted too much to the reconditeness of their language for communications security, clinging to the myth that no foreigner could ever learn its multiple meanings well enough to understand it properly. In part, they would not envision the possibility that their codes might be read; the success of the Kiska withdrawal—in which they sneaked 5,000 troops off the Aleutian island in mid-1943, leaving only three yellow dogs to defend it against a powerful American force—"proved" to them that their secrets were still intact. Perhaps the cryptographers simply grew tired of printing the 2,000,000 codebooks needed to replace those jeopardized in the course of war. Perhaps their own failures with American ciphers convinced them that cryptanalysis was a practical impossibility. In any event, they hypnotized themselves into the delusion that their codes were never seriously compromised.

An incident of 1943 epitomizes Japanese incompetence in this whole field. It involved a future President of the United States, who, with his crew, formed the subject of a series of dispatches the Japanese apparently never solved.

These messages were transmitted by three brave Australian coastwatchers, part of a widespread network whose members observed enemy activity from the peaks and cliffs of enemy-held islands, collected tidbits from native allies, and radioed their information to Allied military commands. They frequently gave valuable early warning of Japanese bombing raids and ship movements, and they assisted in the rescue of downed Allied airmen.

In the early morning hours of August 2, 1943, coastwatcher Lieutenant Arthur Reginald Evans of the Royal Australian Naval Volunteer Reserve saw a pinpoint of flame on the dark waters of Blackett Strait from his jungle ridge on Kolombangara Island, one of the Solomons. He did not know then that the Japanese destroyer *Amagiri* had rammed and sliced in half an American patrol torpedo boat, *PT 109*, Lieutenant John F. Kennedy, United States Naval Reserve, commanding. But at 9:30 that morning he received a 20-group message enciphered in Playfair, the coastwatchers' cipher system. He deciphered it with key ROYAL NEW ZEALAND NAVY and learned, *PT boat one owe nine lost in action in Blackett Strait two miles SW Meresu Cove X Crew of twelve X Request any information X*. He reported back to the coastwatcher near Munda, whose call-sign was PWD, that *Object still floating between Meresu and Gizo*, and at 1:12 p.m. he was told by the coastwatcher station KEN on Guadalcanal that there was a possibility of *survivors landing either Vangavanga or islands*.

Arthur Evans' decipherment of the message of 9:30 a.m., August 2, 1943, that reported the sinking of John F. Kennedy's PT 109

This was just what Kennedy and his crew had done. They had swum to Plum Pudding Island, one of a group that hangs from the southeastern tip of Gizo Island. This group was behind enemy lines, and Gizo itself, only three or four miles away, was garrisoned by Japanese troops. Though messages about the missing crew continued to stream for the rest of the week between PWD, KEN, and GSE, as Evans called his station (after his wife, Gertrude Slaney Evans), the Japanese made no attempt to capture them. Yet the importance of the crew should have been obvious to the Japanese from the many messages concerning it and from the search mission flown by P-40s, and a capture could not have caused them too much trouble, since on one occasion a Japanese barge chugged right past the island hideout of Kennedy and his crew. Even if they had been intercepting and reading the cryptograms, however, the Japanese may not have wanted to waste time looking for the Americans, since none of the messages specified their location.

This excuse vanished at 9:20 a.m. Saturday morning, August 7. Two natives had found the sailors, who had moved to Gross Island, and had reported the find to Evans. He wrote a brief message: *Eleven survivors PT boat on Gross Is X Have sent food and letter advising senior come here without delay X Warn aviation of canoes crossing Ferguson RE.* He drew up a square based on the current key of PHYSICAL EXAMINATION,

```
P H Y S I
C A L E X
M N T O B
D F G K Q
R U V W Z
```

and enciphered the message, departing from traditional Playfair only by leaving doubled letters unenciphered, as the *s*'s in *Gross* and *crossing*: XELWA OHWUW YZMWI HOMNE OBTFW MSSPI AJLUO EAONG OOFCM FEXTT CWCFZ YIPTF EOBHM WEMOC SAWCZ SNYNW MGXEL HEZCU FNZYL NSBTB DANFK OPEWM SSHBK GCWFV EKMUE. A message of this length would alone suffice for the solution of a Playfair, and there were four others in the same key, including one of 335 letters, beginning XYAWO GAOOA GPEMO HPQCW IPNLG RPIXL TXLOA NNYCS YXBOY MNBIN YOBTY QYNAI . . . , for *Lieut Kennedy considers it advisable that he pilot PT boat tonight X* . . . .

These five messages detailed the rescue arrangements, which offered the Japanese a chance to get not only the shipwrecked crew but the force coming out to save it. All of them could have been solved within an hour by even a moderately experienced cryptanalyst. Yet at 10 p.m. the operation went off without the least hint of enemy interference. It seems likely that had the Japanese solved these elementary enciphered messages, they would have taken some action against the rescuers or the rescued or both. They did nothing. If their communications intelligence had been better, how might contemporary history have been changed!

Their failure sharpens the contrast with Allied successes. For Allied cryptanalysts—which in the Pacific meant mostly Americans—galloped like Tartars through the phalanxed ranks of a legion of Japanese cryptosystems. They ravaged and plundered with a prodigality that did not trifle with petty matters. One system, when solved, proved to be used by direction-finding teams; though this might have afforded some indirect clues to Japanese attacks, it was cast aside for richer treasure. Commander Dyer estimated that American cryptanalysts demolished 75 Japanese naval codes during the war.

Among them was the four-digit code used by the marus, or Japanese merchant vessels—the s code. Presumably this was attacked after the more important combat codes had been resolved. From about 1943, it yielded information of the greatest value: the routes, timetables, and destinations of Japanese convoys. Japan's conquests consisted almost entirely of islands which could be supplied and reinforced only by sea, and Nippon itself was an island empire. American submarines therefore undertook in the Pacific what U-boats were attempting in the Atlantic, and, as with the U-boats, cryptanalysis helped them achieve their greatest successes.

A direct line led from FRUPAC to the office of Captain R. G. Voge, operations officer of the Commander, Submarines Pacific Fleet. The Japanese convoys radioed the positions where they estimated they would be as of noon on the next few days. This was to inform their own forces of their locations, but FRUPAC solved the messages, and Jasper Holmes, an ex-submariner himself, relayed them to Voge, who broadcast them to the American submarines. This fattened their kill. Vice Admiral Charles A. Lockwood, Jr., who was COMSUBPAC during most of the war, estimated that cryptanalytic information stepped up American sinkings by about one third on the trade routes to the Philippines and the Marianas. Eventually the submarine commanders received it so regularly that they complained if a convoy reached its noon position half an hour late!

The pigboats accounted for nearly two thirds of Japanese merchant tonnage sunk during the war. Their torpedoing of 110 tankers from the East Indies resulted in oil shortages in the homeland that prevented the training of badly needed pilots and forced a split-up of Japan's Navy, with serious tactical results. Starvation at home caused Japan to make surrender overtures even before the islands were invaded, before the atom bombs exploded. After the war, Tojo said that the destruction of the merchant marine was one of the three factors that defeated Japan, the others being leapfrog strategy and fast carrier operations. This is why Dyer, looking back, regarded FRUPAC's solution of the maru code as one of its primary contributions to victory.

American cryptanalysts scored some long-range combat triumphs as well. Shortly after MacArthur invaded Leyte, they discovered from their reading of coded enemy messages that 40,000 soldiers were on their way to reinforce Japanese troops in the Philippines. American air and sea power met and destroyed this force, and not a man reached Leyte. During the Okinawa campaign, the sharp ears of the cryptanalysts overheard the orders that directed the superbattleship *Yamato*, a 72,000-ton monster with 18-inch guns that could hurl a projectile 22 miles, to sortie in a last-ditch defense effort. They passed this news to the American commanders on the spot. Thus alerted, the commanders prepared to attack her, and after a picket submarine reported her position, flung wave after wave of carrier-based planes at her. They struck her at 12:32 p.m. April 7, 1945, and after less than two hours of repeated bomb-hits and torpedoings, the world's largest battleship slid to the bottom, rumbling and exploding, and taking with her 2,488 officers and men of her complement of 2,767.

FRUPAC also engendered what is probably the most spectacular single incident ever to result from cryptanalysis.

In the spring of 1943, Admiral Isoroku Yamamoto came down to Rabaul to take personal charge of the deteriorating situation in the Solomon Islands. Japan had just been pushed off Guadalcanal and her supply lines were being snarled by Allied air attacks. Yamamoto welded together the biggest Japanese air armada of the war and sent it against the Allies, achieving some tactical successes. In preparation for further aerial offensives, the stocky, black-browed seaman decided to make a one-day morale and inspection tour of bases in the upper Solomons. Those bases would have to be alerted, together with several other units, so that they could make the many preparations needed for an inspection by the Commander in Chief Combined Fleet. At 5:55 p.m. on April 13, 1943, the commander of the 8th Fleet broadcast Yamamoto's itinerary of five days hence to the 1st Base Force, the 26th Air Flotilla, all commanding officers of the 11th Air Flotilla, the commander of the 958th Air Unit, and the chief of the Ballale Defense Unit. The great variety of addressees, plus the need to safeguard the person of the head of the Navy, makes it almost certain that the Japanese communicator selected the current edition of JN25—the most widely distributed high-security code—in which to armor this information.

Unfortunately for the Japanese, this armor plating had been dissolved in the acid of Allied cryptanalysis. As with the pre-Midway solution, the scattered codebreaking units had exchanged their results—possibly augmenting them this time with documents salvaged a few weeks previously from the grounded submarine *I-1*. Though the additive had been changed only two weeks before, on April 1, large portions of it had been recovered. At FRUPAC, these results had been punched onto cards for the I.B.M. machines. FRUPAC's monitors had intercepted the message that the 8th Fleet commander had spread on the airwaves, and when this was fed to the robot cryptanalyst in a form palatable to it, it swallowed it, digested it to the accompaniment of horrendous clickings and rattlings, and disgorged the Japanese plaintext.

Because of the many addressees, the "scanners," or traffic analysts, had probably flagged the message as one of more than ordinary importance. Hence the plaintext went to a translator of more than ordinary competence, a 38-year-old Marine Corps lieutenant colonel, Alva Bryan Lasswell. He had studied Japanese as a language officer in Tokyo from 1935 to 1938 and had helped with communications-intelligence activities in Hawaii since May, 1941. The message was essentially complete, but he helped fill in some holes, while Dyer recovered some additives and Wright determined the meaning of internal geographical codegroups: RR for *Rabaul*; RXZ for *Ballale*, a small island in the Solomons group, just south of Bougainville; RXE for *Shortland*, another of the Solomons, also south of Bougainville and west of Ballale; and RXP for *Buin*, a base on the southern tip of Bougainville. When this work was completed, Lasswell translated the message.

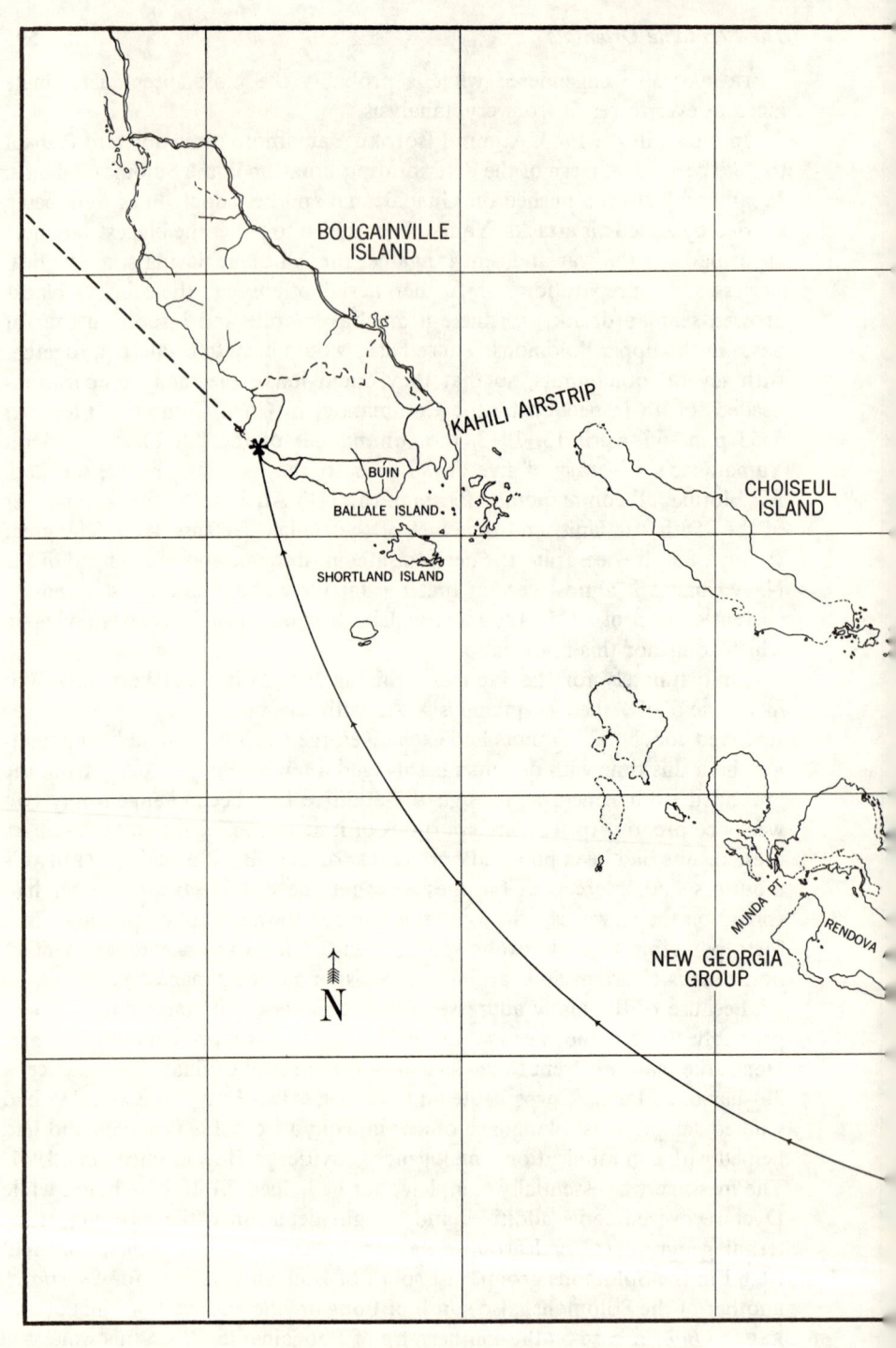

Routes followed by American airplanes (solid line) and by Japanes

SOUTH PACIFIC OCEAN

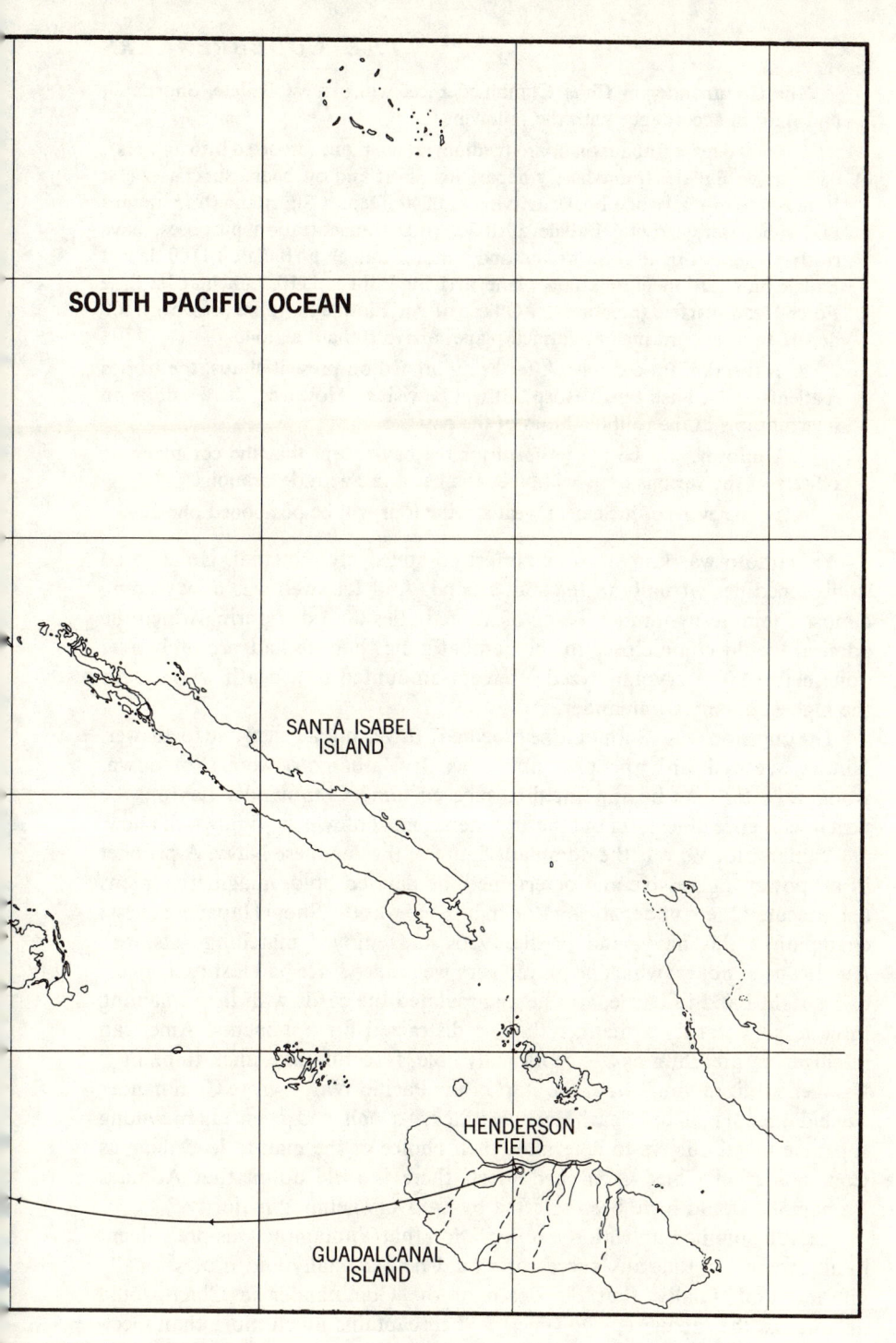

SANTA ISABEL ISLAND

HENDERSON FIELD

GUADALCANAL ISLAND

(dotted line) on mission to shoot down Admiral Isoroku Yamamoto

The Commander in Chief Combined Fleet will inspect Ballale, Shortland, and Buin in accordance with the following:

1. 0600 depart Rabaul on board medium attack plane (escorted by 6 fighters); 0800 arrive Ballale. Immediately depart for Shortland on board subchaser (1st Base Force to ready one boat), arriving at 0840. Depart Shortland 0945 aboard said subchaser, arriving Ballale at 1030. (For transportation purposes, have ready an assault boat at Shortland and a motor launch at Ballale.) 1100 depart Ballale on board medium attack plane, arriving Buin at 1110. Lunch at 1st Base Force Headquarters (Senior Staff Officer of Air Flotilla 26 to be present). 1400 depart Buin aboard medium attack plane; arrive Rabaul at 1540.

2. Inspection Procedures: After being briefed on present status, the troops (patients at 1st Base Force Hospital) will be visited. However, there will be no interruptions in the routine duties of the day.

3. Uniforms will be the uniform for the day except that the commanding officers of the various units will be in combat attire with decorations.

4. In the event of inclement weather, the tour will be postponed one day.

Yamamoto was known to be almost compulsively punctual. He adhered to his schedules virtually to the split second. And Lasswell was now reading almost a minute-by-minute listing of his activities on a day during which the admiral would come closer to the combat zone than he had probably ever done before! The cryptanalyzed intercept amounted to a death warrant for the highest enemy commander.

The question was: Should it be executed? It was not an easy one to answer. Nimitz wrestled with the pros and cons. If Yamamoto were shot down, would a better man be appointed to succeed him? Commander Layton, the fleet intelligence officer, set out the arguments, most of which Nimitz well knew.

Yamamoto, 59, was the dominant figure of the Japanese Navy. A prophet of air power, aggressive and determined, he devised bold, imaginative plans and executed them under strong leadership. He was the Shogi (Japanese chess) champion of his navy, and in the 1920s had enjoyed matching wits with Americans at poker, which he played very well indeed. He had lost two fingers of his right hand in battle, and he manipulated the cards with the remaining three in so wizardly a manner that he distracted his opponents. American intelligence rated him as "Exceptionally able, forceful, and quick-thinking." His men idolized him. "If, at the start of the Pacific War," wrote Commander Fuchida, leader of the Pearl Harbor attack, "a poll had been taken among Japanese naval officers to determine their choice of the man to lead them as Commander in Chief Combined Fleet, there is little doubt that Admiral Yamamoto would have been selected by an overwhelming majority."

Layton summed up with the observation that Yamamoto was preeminent in all categories, that any successor would be personally and professionally inferior, and, finally, that the death of the Commander in Chief would demoralize the Japanese, who venerate their captains much more than Occidentals do. Nimitz concurred. He realized that the shock of such a leader's death, combined with the elimination of the finest strategist of the enemy war machine, would equal a major American battle victory. He was furthermore probably influenced by the general American hatred of Yamamoto. Naval officers knew that he had conceived the treacherous strike at Pearl Harbor that had slaughtered their shipmates and wrecked their ships. He had, they thought, arrogantly boasted that he would dictate peace in the White House.* This was why Admiral William F. (Bull) Halsey made him "No. 3 on my private list of public enemies, closely trailing Hirohito and Tojo."

By chance, the Ballale-Shortland-Buin area was in Halsey's theater of operations. Consequently Nimitz sent him a top-secret command-level communication referring to the Yamamoto itinerary and authorizing him to shoot down the Japanese planes if his forces had the capability of doing so. Halsey was in Australia; his deputy, Vice Admiral Theodore S. Wilkinson, reported that he could do it, but invited Nimitz' attention to the danger of making the Japanese suspicious that the Allies were reading their codes. If they changed them, might not this deprive the Allies of possibly even more valuable intelligence in the future?

Nimitz felt that this bird in the hand was well worth any two in the bush. Nevertheless, he sought to minimize the danger by following Layton's suggestion of a cover story. This was to the effect that Australian coastwatchers had radioed in the Yamamoto flight information, probably getting it from friendly natives around Rabaul. The coastwatchers enjoyed a superexcellent reputation among airmen and so the story would ring true. If it got back to the Japanese, they might never even think about codes. Even if they did realize that the Allies were reading their codes, either by capture or by cryptanalysis, they could probably do no more than issue a new edition of JN25 and perhaps tighten cryptographic security. But this had happened before, and Allied cryptanalysts had broken the new codes. The most realistic assessment predicted that the Yamamoto mission might temporarily dim Allied communications intelligence while cryptanalysts sought entry into the new code.

Such a loss of information is never good, but it would be less unfortunate now, when the Allies were resting and consolidating their positions, than during a major operation. No such advance was planned for two and a half months. Hence if the Japanese changed their code immediately after Yamamoto's death, the cryptanalysts would have ten weeks of relative quiet to break back in. In his reply to Wilkinson, therefore, Nimitz ordered him to brief all personnel on the cover story, iterated his authorization, and added a personal "good luck and good hunting" to the message.

The death warrant was now signed, sealed, and delivered.

On the afternoon of April 17, Major John W. Mitchell and Captain Thomas G. Lanphier, Jr., both of the Army Air Corps, walked into a dank and musty Marine dugout on Henderson Field, Guadalcanal. An operations

---

* This was later proved to be a canard, but its authenticity was accepted at the time.

officer handed them a cablegram on blue tissue—the kind used for top-secret dispatches. It detailed Yamamoto's itinerary, including times of arrival and departure from each place. The airmen vetoed a suggestion to strafe him while crossing from Ballale to Shortland in the subchaser because of the difficulty of identifying the right craft. Instead they decided to intercept him in the air.

Their plan depended upon Yamamoto's punctuality and required careful timing of its own: Ballale was near the limit of range of the twin-engined P-38 Lightnings that the pilots flew, so there would be little fuel for waiting. Though the Japanese message specified arrival at Ballale at 8 a.m. after a two-hour flight from Rabaul, calculations showed that the two-motored Mitsubishi (Betty) attack bombers would reach Ballale in an hour and 45 minutes; this was partially confirmed by the estimated hour-and-40-minute return time from the slightly closer Buin. This meant that Yamamoto would arrive at Ballale about 7:45 a.m. Though he would be escorted by six fighters, Mitchell and Lanphier decided to attack him about 35 miles up the Bougainville coast to avoid the planes that buzzed around Kahili airstrip not far from Buin. This pushed the time of interception back ten minutes to 7:35 a.m.—or 9:35 a.m. American time.

Next morning, 18 P-38s of the 12th, 339th, and 70th Fighter Squadrons lifted off the Henderson runway at 7:25 (American time). Thirty-five minutes later and 700-odd miles away, Yamamoto's flight took off right on schedule. Radios silent, the Americans flew a semicircle of 435 miles around Munda, Rendova, and Shortland at wave-top height to avoid radar detection. Mitchell navigated by compass and airspeed indicator, and two hours and nine minutes after take-off was skimming the waves toward the Bougainville coast. He had timed the flight to the split second, and suddenly, as if the entire affair had been rehearsed to perfection, the black specks of Yamamoto's squadron appeared five miles away.

"Bogey. Ten o'clock high," called out Lieutenant Doug Canning, breaking radio silence. Mitchell led 14 fighters up to 20,000 feet as cover and to engage the fighters. Lanphier dropped his belly tanks, and, with his wing man, Lieutenant Rex T. Barber, climbed to within two miles of Yamamoto's right and a mile in front of him before his escorting Zeros saw them and turned to attack. Lanphier disintegrated one of them, then kicked his ship on its back and looked down for the lead bomber. He spotted it dodging away at tree-top level. As he spun toward it, two Zeros dived at him. But, he said, "I remember suddenly getting very stubborn about making the most of the one good shot I had coming up. I fired a long steady burst across the bomber's course of flight, from approximately right angles. The bomber's right engine, then its right wing, burst into flame. . . . Just as I moved into range of Yamamoto's bomber and its [tail] cannon, the bomber's wing tore off. The bomber plunged into the jungle." The Zeros screamed helplessly overhead. Barber, meanwhile, exploded the other Mitsubishi. Lanphier shook his pursuers in a speedy climb to 20,000 feet, and he and all other members of the mission except one returned safely to Henderson.

Deep in the Bougainville jungle, Yamamoto's devoted aide found his admiral's charred corpse still in its seat, its chin on a samurai sword. The body was extricated with care and solemnly burned. On May 21 a Japanese newscaster announced, in tones heavy with sorrow, that Yamamoto, "while directing general strategy on the front line in April of this year, engaged in combat with the enemy and met gallant death in a war plane." Toward the end of the communiqué his voice became choked, as if through tears. As Layton and Nimitz had foreseen, Yamamoto's death stunned the entire nation. On June 5, his ashes were interred with great pomp in Tokyo's Hibiya Park in the presence of the government and an immense and silent crowd. The death of the great popular hero disheartened Japanese soldiers, sailors, and civilians. "There was only one Yamamoto, and no one is able to replace him," said the man who succeeded him. "His loss is an insupportable blow to us." Cryptanalysis had given America the equivalent of a major victory.

In forwarding a report of the Yamamoto operation to Admiral King, Nimitz noted that it took place "on a particularly high plane of secrecy" and recommended that "no publicity of any kind should be given this action." The main reason was to keep Japan's curiosity from being drawn to how the United States knew that Yamamoto was in a certain airplane. A secondary reason was that Lanphier's brother was a Japanese prisoner of war and reprisals were feared. Thus Americans only learned of the admiral's death from news stories based on the Japanese newscast.

Many wondered how it had happened. No major combat activity extensive enough to cause such a death had occurred in April. The armed forces, following Nimitz' advice, blankly disclaimed any knowledge of the incident. One rumor speculated that Yamamoto had died in an air accident, another that he had committed hara-kiri because of increasing Allied successes. But the real story filtered into wider and wider circles, until soon much of official Washington was whispering at cocktail parties and dinners—probably right under those ubiquitous "The walls have ears" posters—about how cryptanalysis killed Yamamoto. So widespread did the talk become that one responsible citizen telephoned General Marshall and told him about it.

For Marshall, it was the latest headache in a long series. Security was always his most difficult problem in dealing with intelligence from cryptanalysis—MAGIC, or ULTRA, as it was sometimes called. Codebreaking successes are especially vulnerable to betrayal because of the ease with which a change of code can nullify them. The problem had existed since well before Pearl Harbor, when in his concern Marshall had ordered special zippered briefcases with padlocks, restricted the number of recipients, and generally tightened security on MAGIC. War aggravated the problem. The cryptanalytic agencies burgeoned, their output increased, the number of distributees rose.

Though the agencies insisted upon discretion as one of their prime recruiting criteria, the demand for personnel was so acute that some bad apples slipped into the barrel. Gossips, would-be big shots, and just plain thoughtless individuals bragged about how their work was winning the war. This reached a crescendo in the Yamamoto incident. Marshall had repeatedly sent oral requests through G-2 to F.B.I. Director J. Edgar Hoover to investigate the leaks, and particularly to nab some flap-jawed Army officer so that Marshall could make an example of him to discourage the loose talk. Hoover told Marshall that he was reluctant to probe another government agency for fear of being regarded as heading a Gestapo, but he did help. Unfortunately, the one strong case that they found was snagged by a legal technicality that would have prevented conviction.

The pre-Pearl Harbor policy of not indicating the source of communications intelligence disseminated to field commands was continued during the war. This extended to an ally, Russia. Related Marshall: "We have told them that we had good reason—not good reason—we had the best evidence that certain actions were going to be taken by the Germans against them, but we couldn't tell them why, and there was quite a long debate as to whether we should not go into the whole thing, but that was felt most dangerous from two points of view. One was, we were spreading the thing out, and we didn't know who all would become involved in it; and more particularly, they would probably get infuriated because they hadn't had it from the start."

This extreme caution cloaked MAGIC as far as it could go—to its very effects themselves. The third of four alternating red and black paragraphs printed on the cover of the Top Secret MAGIC summaries for European, Far Eastern, and diplomatic traffic stated: "No action is to be taken on information herein reported, regardless of temporary advantage, if such action might have the effect of revealing the existence of the source to the enemy." This, of course, was a dilemma of the Yamamoto mission. So precious was MAGIC that the Allied command on occasion let convoys sail into the jaws of U-boat wolf packs rather than chance the Germans' surmising that the Allies had a way of avoiding them. In the Pacific, American submarines were allowed to depredate Japanese merchant vessels on an ULTRA basis so uninterruptedly only because other intercepts showed that the Japanese thought that the vessel movements were reported to the Allies by coastwatchers; had they suspected cryptanalysis, the submarines would have had to hold off somewhat, for fear of losing long-term advantages.

In general, American security problems proceeded from MAGIC's embarrassment of riches and its existence within a democracy. The first of these produced one of the three great security crises that plagued MAGIC during the war—the buzzing about the dramatically successful Yamamoto shooting. Democracy engendered the other two crises—one at the time of Midway, the other during a presidential campaign.

The Scrutable Orientals

On the morning of Sunday, June 7, 1942, while *Yorktown* was still afloat and the Battle of Midway still, in a sense, in progress, the *Chicago Tribune* appeared on the streets with a column-long front-page story, headlined "Navy Had Word of Jap Plan to Strike At Sea." Datelined "Washington, D.C., June 7," it began:

> The strength of the Japanese forces with which the American navy is battling somewhere west of Midway Island in what is believed to be the greatest naval battle of the war, was well known in American naval circles several days before the battle began, reliable sources in the naval intelligence disclosed here tonight.
>
> The navy learned of the gathering of the powerful Japanese units soon after they put forth from their bases, it was said. Altho their purpose was not specifically known, the information in the hands of the navy department was so definite that a feint at some American base, to be accompanied by a serious effort to invade and occupy another base, was predicted. Guesses were even made that Dutch Harbor and Midway Island might be targets.

The story went on to describe the split-up of the Japanese armada into three forces and to give, in the greatest detail, the composition of these forces. It named the four carriers of the striking force and even went so far as to list—correctly—the four light cruisers that supported the occupation force. Near the bottom of the page, it asserted: "When it [the Japanese fleet] moved all American outposts were warned. American naval dispositions were made in preparation for the various possible attacks the Japs were believed to be planning." The dispatch, which carried no byline, had been written by Stanley Johnston, a *Tribune* war correspondent who later authored *Queen of the Flattops*. Despite its dateline, he had written it in the Pacific.

At no point did the story refer in any way, even obliquely, to Japanese codes or to American communications intelligence. But the Navy feared that the Japanese would realize that its details could have come only from a reading of their coded messages. In August, the Justice Department appointed former Attorney General William L. Mitchell to direct a Chicago grand jury in determining whether the disclosure of confidential information violated the Espionage Act of 1917. The *Tribune* complained that it was being persecuted because the Secretary of the Navy, Frank Knox, published the rival *Chicago Daily News*. After a five-day closed inquiry, during which Johnston and the *Tribune*'s managing editor testified, the grand jury returned no true bill. None of *The New York Times* accounts of the investigation mentioned codes or suggested any reason for the nonindictment beyond Mitchell's statement that "no violation of the law was disclosed." However, it was widely recognized that the grand jury declined to indict because a trial would have called attention to something that, the authorities hoped, the Japanese might have missed. Their hope was fulfilled. The Japanese never saw it and never tumbled to the solution. Their switch to JN25d in August appears to have been unrelated.

After everything had been sewn up, a public indiscretion threatened to rip it open again. Representative Elmer J. Holland of Pennsylvania made a speech about the episode on the floor of Congress on August 31 which was carried far and wide by news stories. He was castigating the *Tribune*'s "unthinking and wicked misuse of freedom of the press." "American boys will die, Mr. Speaker, because of the help furnished our enemies" by the *Tribune*, he declaimed. But in stating what this help was, he disclosed what the *Tribune* had not and trumpeted loud and clear what everyone was trying to hush up: "that somehow our Navy had secured and broken the secret code of the Japanese Navy."

Fortunately, the Japanese missed that one too.

Potentially the most explosive situation stewed in the cauldron of national politics in the late summer of 1944. Republicans were preparing to run Thomas E. Dewey for President. High among their issues was the charge that inexcusable administration laxity had permitted the Japanese attack at Pearl Harbor to succeed so cruelly; there were even hints that President Roosevelt had deliberately invited the attack to get the country into "his" war over strong isolationist sentiment. Buttressing the charge was the knowledge, circulating secretly among many high officials, that the United States had cracked Japanese codes before Pearl Harbor. From this, many Republicans concluded that the decrypted messages had warned Roosevelt of Pearl Harbor and that he, with criminal negligence, had done nothing about it. This was false, but evidence to the contrary was not available and many men believed it.

As the campaign warmed up, bits and hints about MAGIC began to appear in political speeches. Representative Forest A. Harness of Indiana, for example, told the House on September 11 that "the Government had learned very confidentially that instructions were sent out from the Japanese Government to all Japanese emissaries in this hemisphere to destroy the codes." The chief of Army intelligence, Brigadier General Clayton L. Bissell, reported these incidents to Marshall, who saw the danger of further revelations in the heat of contention for the greatest office of all. Bissell suggested that Marshall go to the President for help in squelching the talk. Marshall didn't think that would do, and slept on it. Next morning he dictated a three-page, single-spaced letter to the Republican candidate pointing out the extreme danger of disclosing the MAGIC information. Because he felt that the success of his appeal depended on Dewey's conviction that it was nonpolitical, he did not discuss the matter with either the President or the Secretary of War, and he began his letter, "I am writing you without the knowledge of any other person except Admiral King (who concurs)."

An Army security officer, tall, slim Colonel Carter W. Clarke, flew out West in a B-25 bomber to deliver the letter to Dewey, who had just given his first campaign speech devoted entirely to an attack upon the national administration. Clarke gave the sealed letter to Dewey on the afternoon of September 26 in a hotel in Tulsa, Oklahoma. Under "Top Secret" and "For Mr. Dewey's eyes only," its second paragraph stated: "What I have to tell you below is of such a highly secret nature that I feel compelled to ask you either to accept it on the basis of your not communicating its contents to any other person and returning this letter or not reading any further and returning the letter to the bearer."

From a paragraph lower down, the word "cryptograph" leaped to Dewey's vision. At once he guessed the subject of the letter, and since he had already learned the basic codebreaking secret from a number of individuals, and felt in any case that as a presidential candidate he was "not in a position to make blind commitments," he stopped reading and returned the letter to Clarke.

When Clarke got back to Washington, Marshall discussed Dewey's rejection with him and Bissell. They decided that the matter was so important that they had to try again, so after redrafting the first part of the letter, he sent Clarke—in civilian clothes this time—to Albany. Dewey, who was then governor of New York State, received him in the Executive Mansion on September 28, but declined to discuss the subject or read the letter except in the presence of one of his closest advisors, Elliott V. Bell, State Superintendent of Banks. He wanted to have corroboration of the occurrence in case something happened to Marshall, and for the same reason insisted upon keeping the letter, though Marshall had asked to have it returned. Clarke telephoned Marshall, who agreed to these conditions, and Dewey then came on the wire and promised to keep the letter locked up in his most secret file. He then read the most revealing single document in the annals of cryptology:

TOP SECRET

For Mr. Dewey's eyes only.

27 September 1944.

MY DEAR GOVERNOR: Colonel Clarke, my messenger to you of yesterday, September 26th, has reported the result of his delivery of my letter dated September 25th. As I understand him you (a) were unwilling to commit yourself to any agreement regarding "not communicating its contents to any other person" in view of the fact that you felt you already knew certain of the things probably referred to in the letter, as suggested to you by seeing the word "cryptograph," and (b) you could not feel that such a letter as this to a presidential candidate could have been addressed to you by an officer in my position without the knowledge of the President.

As to (a) above I am quite willing to have you read what comes hereafter with the understanding that you are bound not to communicate to any other person any portions on which you do not now have or later receive factual knowledge from some other source than myself. As to (b) above you have my word that neither the Secretary of War nor the President has any intimation whatsoever that such a letter has been addressed to you or that the preparation or sending of such a communication was being considered. I assure you that the only persons who saw or know of the existence of either this letter or my letter to you dated September 25th are Admiral King, seven key officers responsible for security of military communications, and my secretary who typed these letters.

I am trying my best to make plain to you that this letter is being addressed to you solely on my initiative, Admiral King having been consulted only after the letter was drafted, and I am persisting in the matter because the military hazards involved are so serious that I feel some action is necessary to protect the interests of our armed forces.

I should have much preferred to talk to you in person but I could not devise a method that would not be subject to press and radio reactions as to why the Chief of Staff of the Army would be seeking an interview with you at this particular moment. Therefore I have turned to the method of this letter, with which Admiral King concurs, to be delivered by hand to you by Colonel Clarke, who, incidentally, has charge of the most secret documents of the War and Navy Departments.

In brief, the military dilemma is this:

The most vital evidence in the Pearl Harbor matter consists of our intercepts of the Japanese diplomatic communications. Over a period of years our cryptograph people analyzed the character of the machine the Japanese were using for encoding their diplomatic messages. Based on this a corresponding machine was built by us which deciphers their messages. Therefore, we possessed a wealth of information regarding their moves in the Pacific, which in turn was furnished the State Department—rather than as is popularly supposed, the State Department providing us with the information—but which unfortunately made no reference whatever to intentions toward Hawaii until the last message before December 7th, which did not reach our hands until the following day, December 8th.*

Now the point to the present dilemma is that we have gone ahead with this business of deciphering their codes until we possess other codes, German as well as Japanese, but our main basis of information regarding Hitler's intentions in Europe is obtained from Baron Oshima's messages from Berlin reporting his interviews with Hitler and other officials to the Japanese Government. These are still in the codes involved in the Pearl Harbor events.

To explain further the critical nature of this set-up which would be wiped out almost in an instant if the least suspicion were aroused regarding it, the battle of the Coral Sea was based on deciphered messages and therefore our few ships were in the right place at the right time. Further, we were able to concentrate our limited forces to meet their naval advance on Midway when otherwise we almost certainly would have been some 3,000 miles out of place. We had full information of the strength of their forces in that advance and also of the smaller force directed against the Aleutians which finally landed troops on Attu and Kiska.

Operations in the Pacific are largely guided by the information we obtain of Japanese deployments. We know their strength in various garrisons, the rations and other stores continuing available to them, and what is of vast importance, we check their fleet movements and the movements of their convoys. The heavy losses reported from time to time which they sustain by reason of our submarine action, largely result from the fact that we know the sailing dates and routes of their convoys and can notify our submarines to lie in wait at the proper points.

* Actually December 11. Marshall was referring to Yoshikawa's message of December 3, Honolulu to Tokyo, setting up Kühn's signalling system.

> The current raids by Admiral Halsey's carrier forces on Japanese shipping in Manila Bay and elsewhere were largely based in timing on the known movements of Japanese convoys, two of which were caught, as anticipated, in his destructive attacks.
>
> You will understand from the foregoing the utterly tragic consequences if the present political debates regarding Pearl Harbor disclose to the enemy, German or Jap, any suspicion of the vital sources of information we possess.
>
> The Roberts' report on Pearl Harbor had to have withdrawn from it all reference to this highly secret matter, therefore in portions it necessarily appeared incomplete. The same reason which dictated that course is even more important today because our sources have been greatly elaborated.
>
> As another example of the delicacy of the situation, some of Donovan's people (the OSS) without telling us, instituted a secret search of the Japanese Embassy offices in Portugal. As a result the entire military attaché Japanese code all over the world was changed, and though this occurred over a year ago, we have not yet been able to break the new code and have thus lost this invaluable source of information, particularly regarding the European situation.
>
> A further most serious embarrassment is the fact that the British government is involved concerning its most secret sources of information, regarding which only the Prime Minister, the Chiefs of Staff and a very limited number of other officials have knowledge.
>
> A recent speech in Congress by Representative Harness would clearly suggest to the Japanese that we have been reading their codes, though Mr. Harness and the American public would probably not draw any such conclusion.
>
> The conduct of General Eisenhower's campaign and of all operations in the Pacific are closely related in conception and timing to the information we secretly obtain through these intercepted codes. They contribute greatly to the victory and tremendously to the saving in American lives, both in the conduct of current operations and in looking towards the early termination of the war.
>
> I am presenting this matter to you in the hope that you will see your way clear to avoid the tragic results with which we are now threatened in the present political campaign.
>
> Please return this letter by bearer. I will hold it in my most secret file subject to your reference should you so desire.
>
> Faithfully yours,
>
> (Sgd) G. C. MARSHALL.

This extraordinary missive put Dewey in a grave predicament. He felt that the Japanese simply could not be using the same code in September, 1944, as they had been in November, 1941. Profoundly convinced of the rightness of his cause and of the "dreadful incompetence" of the Democrats, both in the country and the world as a whole and at Pearl Harbor in particular, he—and many Republicans—might well have thought that true patriotism actually called for exposing some three-year-old secret about prewar codes to prove his point and elect the right man and the right party to control the destinies of a whole nation. For with that exposure furnishing apparently solid evidence, the Pearl Harbor charge might have propelled him into the White House.

Dewey talked the matter over in detail with Bell and with Herbert Brownell, his two closest advisors. He weighed these arguments and the prize at stake—leadership of the most powerful country in history—against the possibility of prolonging a war in which hundreds of Americans were dying daily and against his regard for Marshall as an utterly truthful and honorable man. After two days of intense deliberation, he decided not to mention the codebreaking.

Marshall had never actually asked him for any assurances, and Dewey never communicated his decision to the chief of staff. But, Marshall acknowledged, "there seemed to be no further reference to the matter in the campaign." Dewey lost, heavily. Afterwards, as a gesture of appreciation, Marshall sent Bissell to Albany with copies of the current MAGIC to show Dewey how it was helping in the Pacific. Dewey told Bissell that he had heard that a debate on Pearl Harbor was going to be held in Congress, and he asked whether Marshall wanted him to intervene and suppress it. When Bissell returned, Marshall had him call Dewey and say that Marshall had already embarrassed him with requests which had affected his personal actions and that he would not make any further requests. Dewey replied that it wasn't a matter of personal embarrassment but of the progress of the war. Bissell told the governor that Marshall had anticipated that reply and still had no request to make. Nevertheless, the debate never materialized. The episode had a final echo at Roosevelt's funeral, when Dewey was thrown in with Marshall, "I asked him to come to the War Department with me. He did and we showed him the situation out in the Pacific. Showed him also the current MAGIC, giving the Japanese movements at that time, and made as plain as we could to him just what the importance of these matters were. His attitude was very friendly and very gracious."

So ended the last and most serious threat to the security of American cryptanalysis. The Japanese never realized the ludicrous transparency of their codes. They never suspected the truth behind the Yamamoto incident. And cryptanalysis went on to play a role in the struggle against Japan even beyond its formal end.

The cipher war in the Pacific drew to its conclusion not with sagas of high drama but rather with a foam of poignant vignettes. There was, for instance, the time when a junior communicator's wise-guy thoughtlessness robbed Halsey of the classic gun duel between battleships for which he had always yearned.

It happened on October 25, 1944, during the Battle for Leyte Gulf. Halsey had organized within his 3rd Fleet a Task Force 34, consisting of most of his battleships and cruisers. Since it stayed with his main force, it was largely a paper organization, but owing to a syntactical ambiguity in a message, Nimitz and others thought it was a separate body. The battle ranged over an enormous area, and while Halsey's carriers were attacking the four battleships and

The Scrutable Orientals

two carriers of the Japanese Northern Force, Admiral Thomas C. Kinkaid sent, in clear, a desperate call for the gunfire of Task Force 34 ships. While Halsey was speculating over the effect its possible interception by the Japanese might have had, Nimitz, who had been following the battle by radio, sent him a query: "Where is Task Force 34?"

Naval communication procedure called for the head and the tail of messages—their most vulnerable points—to be concealed by nulls consisting of meaningless words. This "padding" was supposed to be totally alien to the text, but the enciphering ensign in Pearl Harbor violated this rule when he used a phrase that was "just something that popped into my head." Though he correctly set the padding off from the text by doubled letters, communicators on Halsey's flagship decided against removing it on the chance that it might be part of the message. Thus, the decipher tape that they rushed to Halsey read:

From CINCPAC [Nimitz] action Com Third Fleet [Halsey] info Cominch [King] CTF seventy four [Kinkaid] X Where is repeat where is Task Force thirty four RR the world wonders

When Halsey read this, he said, "I was as stunned as if I had been struck in the face. The paper rattled in my hands. I snatched off my cap, threw it on the deck, and shouted something that I am ashamed to remember.... I was so mad I couldn't talk." The more he thought about this apparent insult, the more furious he became, and, a little before 11 a.m., he angrily turned Task Force 34 from due north to due south to go to Kinkaid's aid. "At that moment," he said, "the [Japanese] Northern Force, with its two remaining carriers crippled and dead in the water, was exactly 42 miles from the muzzles of my 16-inch guns." Though the carriers were later finished off, the misunderstanding cleared up, and the enciphering ensign chewed to bits by Nimitz, Halsey had lost "the opportunity I had dreamed of since my days as a cadet."

Bitterest of the vignettes depicts a negation of America's total communications-intelligence mastery near the end of the war—with tragic consequences. At about 3 a.m. on July 30, 1945, the Japanese submarine *I-58* encoded a dispatch reporting that three hours earlier it had "released six torpedoes and scored three at battleship of *Idaho* class ... definitely sank it." He addressed it to 6th Fleet and to Combined Fleet headquarters and transmitted it on a standard Japanese naval frequency.

Americans intercepted it; FRUPAC read it; and within 13 hours of its transmission had the report in Nimitz' Advance Headquarters, on Guam. The position given was approximately that of the heavy cruiser *Indianapolis*, which on July 26 had delivered a chunk of U-235 to Tinian for the first atomic bomb. But nobody at Advance Headquarters checked to see if any American battleships, or cruisers, or other heavy vessels, were missing. Why, nobody knows. As a result of this and other blunders, no search was instituted for the swimming crewmen for nearly a week; in the meanwhile, nearly 900 American sailors died uselessly—the greatest disaster at sea in the history of the United States Navy.

American cryptanalysts, who usually strove to win battles, worked to make peace when they solved Japanese messages that indicated Japan's desire to quit the war before the atomic bombs had devastated her and opened the era of nuclear war. Though the formation of a new cabinet in April, 1945, implied a mandate to seek peace, the United States obtained the first concrete evidence of this desire on July 13. On that date, President Truman and other high American officials read an instruction of Foreign Minister Shigenori Togo to his ambassador in Moscow, Naotake Sato. Togo urged Sato to see the Soviet Foreign Minister before the Big Three conference at Potsdam and tell him of the Emperor's strong desire to end the war. Explain, Togo said, that the only real obstacle to peace was the Allies' demand for unconditional surrender. If this were insisted upon, he said, Japan would have to continue the fight. The implication was that another surrender formula might bring peace.

In the next few days additional messages were intercepted and read that threw further light on Japanese intentions. They verified the view of many experts on Japan that a promise to preserve the Emperor would open the way to a surrender which in most other respects would be unconditional. Probably as a result of this cryptanalyzed information, America, Britain, and Russia at Potsdam moderated their demands from an unconditional surrender of all Japan—which would have threatened the throne in which each Japanese rooted his very claim to being Japanese and which Togo had therefore said would be unacceptable—to an unconditional surrender of merely the military. The Big Three hoped to end the war without having to use the atom bomb, but they would do so if necessary. Hence the Potsdam Declaration on July 26 offered Japan a choice between "unconditional surrender of her armed forces" and "prompt and utter destruction." But Japan, unable to accept the former because it did not positively promise the retention of the Emperor, embraced the latter.

The fatal glare spread first over Hiroshima. The traffic analysts of the Tokumu Han, who had learned how to predict the B-29 bombing raids launched from Tinian, listed the special signal of the single bomber that preceded Hiroshima's obliteration. Three days later, they heard the signal again. Japan had no air force to alert, and the analysts could not tell that the plane was heading for Nagasaki. But they knew what the beeps meant. As they mechanically plotted it, they were, in the Japanese phrase, swallowing their tears.

For Americans, however, MAGIC extended its efforts even beyond the conclusion of hostilities. The United States, fearing a possible banzai suicide resistance by Japanese troops in Korea, like that encountered on some island garrisons, had not planned to occupy the peninsula until September 23, and then only with an entire army corps. But American cryptanalysts disclosed that the Japanese commander there was appealing to his own government to hasten the movement of American troops into Korea. This proved rather conclusively that no adverse reaction need be expected, and so a mere regiment took control of the country on September 3—three weeks early. Similar considerations aided the disarming of Japanese troops in China and Manchuria, and finally expedited the peaceful occupation of the islands of Japan itself.

What happened to cryptology during World War II?

The war worked no changes as basic as those of telegraphy, which revolutionized the structure of cryptography, or of radio, which ushered cryptanalysis into the world as a factor of importance. Rather it enlarged, accelerated, intensified what was already there. This held true even in the two most noteworthy cryptologic developments of the war. One was internal, in which the changes were so great as to be qualitative: the evolution in the operations of cryptography and the techniques of cryptanalysis, and one external: the elevation of cryptanalysis from just one among many sources of intelligence to the principal one.

All this resulted, of course, from the immense increase in the use of radio. Blitzkrieg required the closest coordination between motorized spearheads, air support, and consolidating infantry. Global conflict demanded global communications. Unprecedented volumes of traffic streamed through radio channels. To handle it, huge agencies sprang into being.

In World War I, the U.S. Army and Navy had about 400 persons in cryptology (excluding cipher clerks), or about one person in every 10,000 under arms. In World War II, there were 16,000 in cryptology—40 times as many—and the ratio was one person in every 800. In World War I, a handful of officers and enlisted men in the Code Compilation Section had produced codes for the whole A.E.F. In World War II, hundreds of privates at Arlington Hall did nothing but draw up key patterns for the tens of thousands of M-209s all over the world which devoured a new pattern once every eight hours. (Eventually, a linguist on the Hall's think squad devised a mechanism that produced the patterns automatically.) In 1918, a few men had carried the packages of codebooks to the American headquarters that received them. In 1942, Japan was faced with a major logistics task in distributing new codebooks to her far-flung forces. Her disastrous pre-Midway failure to do the job in time showed that codes had become cargo almost as essential as food or ammunition. Codes and ciphers cloaked even more secondary forms of messages—meteorological, direction-finding, airplane, merchant ships'. Intercept stations covered the globe. Branches and subsections sprouted that the science had never known: the Signal Security Service had a special section just to distribute its solutions, another one just to improve and develop cryptographic mechanisms. Brass hats abounded. Recruiting drives were mounted. The whole paraphernalia of large organizations materialized. Cryptology became big business.

At the same time, cryptology completed an evolution in the two core areas of cryptographic operations and cryptanalytic techniques. World War I had left both of them depleted and inadequate. Hand encipherment had barely coped with the message load, even though codes furnished a primitive mechanization. Brute frequency analysis had barely sufficed for the ADFGVX, even though it was handled by a master. The 1920s began to furnish the tools and ideas for which this lack cried out. In cryptography, Vernam, Hebern, Scherbius, Damm, and Hagelin invented practicable cipher machines—secure, portable, rugged, printing. Governments gradually introduced them into service, replacing the old pencil-and-paper methods. In cryptanalysis, Friedman pioneered with statistical methods. Hill opened a window on the new vistas of mathematics. Cryptologic agencies hired mathematicians like Kunze and Kullback and Sinkov as cryptanalysts and purchased tabulating machines to make more calculations. Mathematics generated analytical techniques of great precision and power. These trends, which were still just getting under way in 1939, accelerated with a rush during the war and culminated by 1945. This evolution transformed both cryptography and cryptanalysis and gave each a characteristic it still has. World War II mechanized cryptography and mathematized cryptanalysis.

This development of cryptology's substance, like the growth of its administrative organization, was paralleled by the enormous amplification of its effects. In World War I, cryptanalysis played a central role in one event of high significance—the American declaration of war following the Zimmermann telegram disclosure. In World War II, cryptanalysis helped make possible at least four critical events—Midway, Yamamoto, the rapid cutting of Japan's lifeline, the defeat of the U-boats. Cryptanalysis was not just a tangential and merely helpful factor; it was a vital one.

Indeed, the higher in the politico-military realm are the events, the more important becomes cryptanalysis. At the front, it probably stands equal with prisoner-of-war intelligence or aerial reconnaissance. But neither of these can match it for providing insight into the strategic plans of top generals or the basic diplomatic policy of a whole country. A spy may occasionally pluck forth a richer nugget, but he cannot refine the quantity of ore that a cryptanalyst can, nor can he command the credibility. The ungrudging tributes of the two German spymasters attest to this superiority: Walter Schellenberg's acknowledgment that the assistance rendered him by the communications-intelligence chiefs "made most of my success in Secret Service operations possible," and Wilhelm Höttl's boast that his Hungarian cryptanalysts provided him with "at least a hundred successes such as seldom fall to the lot of a Secret Service working in the ordinary ways." General Amè, chief of Italy's Servizio Informazione Militare, listed three succinct reasons why intelligence chiefs like cryptanalysis: it is usually the cheapest, the latest, and the truest source of information.

After the war was over, an American official familiar with the wartime value of codebreaking said that it had shortened World War II by a year. The estimate may be conservative: a Japanese victory at Midway would probably have cost the United States more than a year to come back. When asked about the value of the wartime codebreaking, Vice Admiral Walter S. Anderson, a former Director of Naval Intelligence, exclaimed "It won the war!" Hyperbole, to be sure, but indicative nevertheless. In fact, the letter of General Marshall, who was certainly in a position to know, tends to support the hyperbole. It was this vital importance of cryptology that was new in the world. No one could have articulated in 1919 the tribute that Representative Clarence B. Hancock offered at the end of 1945 on the floor of the Congress of the United States: "I believe that our cryptographers [cryptanalysts] ... did as much to bring that war to a successful and early conclusion as any other group of men."

For in World War II cryptology became a nation's most important source of secret intelligence.

18

РУССКАЯ КРИПТОЛОГИЯ*

ALTHOUGH SECRET WRITING appears in Russia in the simple letter-substitutions of 12th- and 13th-century manuscripts, akin to those of medieval France and Germany, political cryptography seems to have first come to the country under the Westernizing influence of Peter the Great.

The most direct evidence outside the nation's archives lies in the records of England's Decyphering Branch, whose first Russian solution is dated 1719 —the 37th year of Peter's reign. This accords well with what one might expect. Peter was fascinated by technical arts of all kinds; he not only studied them but picked up their tools and worked at them. He perhaps heard about codes and ciphers during his visits to Holland and England in 1697–98 and Paris in 1717. It was a time when official nomenclators were formally employed by the emergent nations of Europe—and when cryptanalysts were paid to solve them. If he himself did not import cryptography to Russia, the seeds might have been planted by the foreigners that Peter imported for the governmental reforms that began in 1712. The new structure was modeled on Sweden's, and perhaps included a cipher office, for by that time Sweden had had more than a century and a half of cryptographic experience—employing, for example, a one-part code of almost 4,000 groups in 1700. Secret writing thus might well have been among the new and useful practices that Peter adopted in transforming Russia from the semibarbarism of Ivan the Terrible to a modern state.

The first ciphers used by Peter's ambassadors in London were as primitive as his country then was, and had no more security than first ciphers usually possess: they were monalphabetic substitutions. The plaintext was replaced with secret symbols hardly less bizarre to the insular English eye than the original Cyrillic letters themselves. Such systems served at least until 1728. In the reign of Peter's strong-willed daughter, Elizabeth, Russian cryptography suddenly blossomed forth with all the maturity of Europe's best. In 1754, the Russian ambassadors to England employed a two-part nomenclator of 3,500 elements, including homophones. It was in French, which was then not only the language of diplomacy but also the tongue cultivated in most of the courts of Europe, nowhere more slavishly than in Russia's. (Sweden, too,

* Russkaya Kriptologiya ("Russian Cryptology").

Русская Криптология

was using French-language codes.) Other, smaller two-part nomenclators followed at frequent intervals: one of 900 elements appeared in 1755, and still another of 1,000 in 1761.

Russian monalphabetic key, recovered by England's Decyphering Branch, 1728

The next year Catherine II—she who was to make her country the chief continental power of Europe and to become known as "the Great"—ascended the imperial throne. Six years later, the codemakers of St. Petersburg experimented with Russian for a two-part nomenclator of 1,500 elements. By 1780 they had returned to French. It was on a worksheet for this code that an English decypherer noted "many nulls beginning and ending sentences"—authoritative testimony to the craft of the Russian cryptographers. In 1784 they tried something new: a kind of voluntary superencipherment in which the initial numbers 1, 2, 3, or 4 of a codegroup could be replaced at will by 6, 7, 8, or 9, respectively, or left unchanged. Thus *que* was represented by either 3126 or 8126. This may have been some kind of an economy move, for the underlying nomenclator was one-part; if so, the Russian experts saw quickly that it was a false economy, for the system could not provide enough security, and they discarded it the very next year for a new two-part nomenclator.

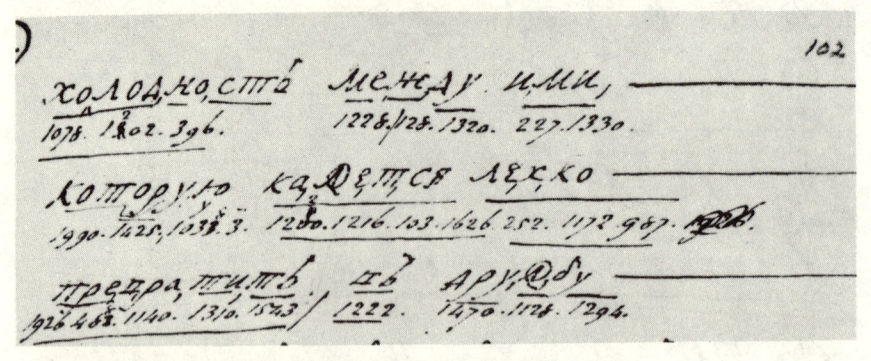

Part of English solution of Russian dispatch encoded with full nomenclator, 1700s

Annual changes, in fact, may have been routine. One French-language chiffre général existed for 1798 and another for 1799; the presence of a Russian-language general cipher for 1798 in addition indicates the open-handedness of the Foreign Ministry in cryptography. Sometimes nomenclators were changed or canceled before the year was out if they were suspected of being compromised. On January 22, 1800, the Foreign Minister, Count Nikita Petrovich Panin, ordered his ambassador in Berlin not to use the 1799 general cipher, which was thought to have been carried off by the enemy with the baggage of a Russian general during the French revolutionary wars. A similar suspicion may have caused the Foreign Ministry to discontinue a code used by their ambassadors in Madrid and Lisbon after only about ten months of use.

The Russians exercised great cryptographic prudence. Panin warned the Berlin ambassador: "Your confidential reports must always be ciphered with one of the new keys, even when you use a courier." As an added precaution, he wrote many of his own dispatches in invisible ink beneath a cover-text. This also had the advantage that development of the ink would indicate rather pointedly that the letter had been tampered with. Once he wrote to Berlin that "Not having at hand the sympathetic ink that I have been using, I used lemon juice today in the attached confidential letter; consequently, instead of dipping it into aqua fortis, it must be heated." All this sophistication suggests that the Czarina's cryptographers learned their techniques in the only way they really can be learned—through cryptanalysis.

For among the Western innovations that had come to the new Russia was the exceedingly valuable one of black chambers. Situated, like those of England, France, and Austria, in the post offices, they employed the full battery of expert openers, seal-forgers, translators, and cryptanalysts. At least some of the latter appear to have been German, probably hired by Peter, and their descendants seem to have maintained a monopoly in this field for generations.

The black chambers were in operation as early as Elizabeth's reign, and the French ambassador, the Marquis de la Chétardie, knew full well that they were opening his dispatches. But they were enciphered, and, in the manner of diplomats everywhere, he felt safe because he thought that the Russians were too dumb to break his cipher. He may have been right about Russians, but three Germans in the black chamber were making mince pie out of it. He erred in writing home with a deplorable lack of gallantry about the Czarina, remarking that she was "given entirely to her pleasures" and was "so frivolous and so dissipated." The interceptions were seen as a matter of course by Count Aleksey Bestuzhev-Ryumin, grand chancellor of the imperial court. He had been waiting to strike back at Chétardie, who had organized a cabal against him because of his Anglophile tendencies. He showed the solutions to Elizabeth, who, blinded by her own French leanings, refused to believe them until he deciphered them in her presence. The next day, June 17, 1744, as Chétardie entered his residence, he was handed a note ordering him to leave Russia in 24 hours. He protested; a Russian began reading him his dispatches. "That's enough," he said, and started to pack.

At the turn of the century, cryptanalytic information was still informing Russian foreign policy. Foreign Minister Panin wrote on March 26, 1800, from St. Petersburg to his ambassador in Berlin: "We possess the ciphers of the correspondence of the king [of Prussia] with his chargé d'affaires here: in case you suspect [Prussian Foreign Minister Count Christian von] Haugwitz of bad faith, it is only necessary to get him to write here on the subject in question under some pretext, and as soon as his or his king's dispatch is deciphered, I will not fail to apprise you of its content."

Twelve years later, Russian cryptanalysis played an obbligato to the grand symphony of the Russian winter in inflicting the first defeat on the hitherto unconquerable Napoleon. That military genius, though not quite the cryptologic moron that it has been the fashion to portray him as being, certainly did not fully appreciate the importance of a tough cryptography. He depended upon a single, easy-to-solve system during most of his campaigns, including the Russian; this was his petit chiffre, a nomenclator of about 200 groups. Even without his generals' predilection for partial encipherments, the Napoleonic cryptograms must have crumpled before the assault of the Russian cryptanalysts. How the solutions helped the Russians is not known, but that they must have been of some assistance is indicated by the fact that the victorious Czar, Alexander I, cited them himself when reminiscing about the war. At a state dinner that he gave in Paris years later for the marshals of France, he mentioned having read secret French dispatches. Marshal Macdonald, who had commanded a corps for Napoleon, recalled that one of the French generals had defected and said, "It is not surprising that Your Majesty was able to decipher them; someone gave you the key." Alexander denied it. "He assumed a serious air," Macdonald related, "placed one hand on his heart and raised the other. 'No,' he replied, 'I give you my word of honor.' " His cryptanalysts would have been proud of so stout a defense of their honor.

During the nineteenth century, cryptanalysts functioned as one of the Czar's chief tools of despotism. Libertarian movements were growing increasingly restive and radical. One way in which the Okhrana, the notorious secret police, kept tabs on underground workers was to have the black chambers read the letters and telegrams of suspects—as well as most foreign mail and a random selection of the domestic post, too.

Permanent black chambers were established in the post offices of St. Petersburg, Moscow, Warsaw, Odessa, Kiev, Kharkhov, Riga, Vilna, Tomsk, and Tiflis; temporary ones were set up elsewhere when needed. Most of the experts were foreigners, though Russian subjects; a fair number were Germans who spoke Russian with a heavy accent, apparently because they secluded themselves for security's sake from their neighbors. Though they mostly worked from watch lists, they became so sensitive to the nuances of clandestine correspondence that they could detect a suspicious letter from an insignificant blot on an envelope, a line under a name, the odd formation of an address. Letters were usually opened with steam or a hot wire or blade under the wax seal, but one dedicated employee, Karl Zievert, in charge of the Kiev office (and later convicted of being an Austrian spy), invented a device that eliminated all possibility of telltale wrinkles or scorches. It consisted simply of a thin round, polished, flexible stick about the size and diameter of a knitting needle, split down half its length. Zievert would slide this under the flap of an envelope at the corner, catch the letter in the slit, furl the paper around the needle, and then draw it out without noticeably distending the envelope!

Ciphers posed few problems for the official meddlers. The black chambers forwarded the cryptograms they had light-fingered to the Okhrana, whose specialist in cryptanalysis, Zybine, displayed almost uncanny powers. The former Okhrana head in Moscow, P. Zavarzine, has given a vivid portrait of him: he was fortyish, tall, thin, swarthy, with long hair separated by a part, and with a lively and piercing look. "He was a fanatic, not to say a maniac, for his work. Simple ciphers he cleared up at a glance, but complicated ciphers placed him in a state almost of a trance from which he did not emerge until the problem was resolved," said the police chief.

Zavarzine had to send for him once in 1911 to solve an intercept, written in secret ink and consisting largely of fractions, which nobody in the Moscow section could make out (apparently the black chambers of Okhrana prefectures had staff members who could solve the simpler ciphers). Zybine arrived the next morning from St. Petersburg and barely greeted Zavarzine before asking for the letter. An official gave him a copy. He wanted the original. He instantly started for the post office to get it, but was told that it had already been sent on. Zavarzine lent him his desk, and soon Zybine was totally immersed in his work, scribbling rapidly on papers spread before him. When Zavarzine returned to invite the cryptanalyst to dinner, he had to call him twice before he answered, and to insist before he came. At table, Zybine, still in a trance, downed a bowlful of soup, then turned the plate over and tried to write on its back. When the pencil would not take, he started on his cuffs—all the time completely ignoring his hosts. Suddenly he leaped from his chair and shouted, "Tishe idiote, dalshe budiote!"

After which he sat down, relaxed, and ate his dinner like a normal man. He explained to Zavarzine that the repetitions of the letters had given him the clue. The proverb that he had shouted, meaning "Who walks softly goes far," served as the key for the cipher. The phrase was written vertically. Each of its letters headed a Caesar alphabet (in Russian) that extended out to the right; these rows were numbered. The ciphertext fractions that formed the ciphertext were composed by taking as numerator the number of the row of the plaintext letter and as denominator the position of the letter in the row. Thus 1/3 would mean the third letter in the first row; since this row was headed by т, 1/3 would represent ф. The cipher, a weak homophonic substitution, served the underground as one of its standard systems. The message told of sending some cardboard boxes, undoubtedly loaded with explosives, to Kiev when the Czar was planning a visit there. Zavarzine promptly slapped shadows onto the addressees of the letter and kept them from blowing up their Little Father.

Zybine said that he had been defeated by a cryptogram only once, in a letter sent by an Austrian spy. "But that was a long time ago," he told Zavarzine. "Today it wouldn't happen." The last head of the Okhrana, Alexei T. Vassilyev, also speaks of Zybine, though he does not give his name. In one case, a raid on a house in Sevastopol uncovered a sheet of paper covered with figures. Vassilyev gave it to Zybine, who suggested that the chief telegraph to Sevastopol for a list of all books found in the house. A short time after Zybine received it, he placed the solution before Vassilyev; it was based on *The Duel* by Aleksandr Kuprin—which was, appropriately, a novel of protest against the Russian military class. Zybine got a raise and a decoration for that job. On another occasion, he cracked another terrorist missive as soon as he had learned from Vassilyev the price of a pound of dynamite! Vassilyev, who seems to have been a little awed by Zybine's mysterious faculty, says that the cryptanalyst could pick out nulls and nonsignificant lines at a glance.

The most popular cipher of the Russian underground seems to have derived from the prisons in which so many of its leaders had to serve time.

Intercommunication among the inmates was strictly forbidden. But the prisoners, languishing in the tomblike solitude of their gloomy stone casements, with nothing to occupy their minds, had the patience, perseverance, and ingenuity to outwit their jailers. They knocked, using the number of taps to indicate the rows and columns of a simple checkerboard, like the original Polybius square, sometimes 6 × 6 to accommodate the 35 letters of the old Russian alphabet, more often five across and six down, with the alternate letter forms eliminated. In English, the checkerboard would take this form:

	1	2	3	4	5
1	a	b	c	d	e
2	f	g	h	ij	k
3	l	m	n	o	p
4	q	r	s	t	u
5	v	w	x	y	z

Thus *hello* would become 23 15 31 31 34. Prisoners quickly memorized the proper numbers and "talked" at from 10 to 15 words a minute. The system was universal in the penal institutions of Russia, with felons as well as political convicts employing it.

One of its advantages was that it afforded communication by a great variety of media—anything that could be dotted, knotted, pierced, flashed, or indicate numerals in any way could be pressed into service. It often concealed a message within an innocuous handwritten letter. The ciphertext numbers were indicated by the number of letters written together; breaks in the count were indicated by minute and almost imperceptible spaces, much as occur naturally in many persons' handwriting. Spaces between words were bridged by having the last letter of a word end in an upstroke if the count was to continue, in a downstoke if the end of the word coincided with the end of a count. This subtle means, in which the cover-text bears no relation to the underlying message, and so does not have to strain to make sense, frequently bootlegged secrets in and out of prisons, and undoubtedly past the noses of the black chamber experts, until they finally caught on.

The popular cipher that the checkerboard inspired is named for the Nihilists, the anarchistic opponents of the czarist regime, who may have invented it. The Nihilist cipher converts both the plaintext and a repeating keyword into numerical form via the checkerboard, and then adds them together to produce the ciphertext. If the keyword is ARISE, or 11 42 24 43 15, the plaintext *Bomb Winter Palace* would be enciphered like this:

literal plain	b	o	m	b	w	i	n	t	e	r	p	a	l	a	c	e
numerical plain	12	34	32	12	52	24	33	44	15	42	35	11	31	11	13	15
key	11	42	24	43	15	11	42	24	43	15	11	42	24	43	15	11
ciphertext	23	76	56	55	67	35	75	68	58	57	46	53	55	54	28	26

Occasional three-digit groups will occur, as $55 + 54 = 109$. The cipher is a kind of modified numerical Vigenère with additional weaknesses that simplify solution. It would not have baffled a Zybine very long. Yet this basic system—the adding of a key to a checkerboard substitution, though with important improvements—survived through the years to become the primary form of secret communication for Russian undercover agents.

Only one other department of Russian officialdom coddled cryptology as did the Ministry of the Interior's Okhrana: the Foreign Ministry. It employed six or seven codes, most of only 1,000 elements, the more important of which were superenciphered by a table of 30 number alphabets. Keys varied from day to day, and deliberate "errors" were reportedly made to muddy the statistics of enemy cryptanalysts; these naturally had to be eradicated by the cipher clerks before they could read their own messages. The wily Russians also employed a code that they knew had been solved by other nations to keep the foreign cryptanalysts happy and productive and away from the important codes. Still, Russian codes were read, either by bribery or by solution. At least one of the cryptanalyses of a Russian diplomatic code was made through the classic entry of guessing that a message ended with a full stop.

Inheriting, perhaps, the cryptanalytic service that had solved the dispatches of diplomats during the times of Elizabeth and of Catherine the Great, the Foreign Ministry impartially read the coded messages of friends and foes alike: Turkey and Austria-Hungary in the latter category, France and England in the former, and Sweden, a neutral, in neither. Just before World War I, the Foreign Office cryptologic organization was streamlined by Aleksandr A. Savinsky, chief of the ministry's cabinet from 1901 to 1910. He placed the cryptanalysts directly under the minister, introduced new codes, and promulgated strict regulations for their employment.

The Ministry of War, on the other hand, meant well, but outside factors defeated its efforts. In 1910, Major Cartier came from France to prepare signal and cryptographic liaison with Russia. The following year he came again with a supersecret codebook, complete with superencipherment, of which only eight copies had been printed by the French Army's geographic service. Four were retained by the French War and Marine ministries; Cartier smuggled the other four—for the corresponding Russian ministries—across the border in his luggage amid novels and Russian-French dictionaries. Soon thereafter he learned that the shifty-eyed Tartar officer to whom he had delivered the two books for the War Ministry had sold one of them to the Germans.

This typified the atmosphere of corruption that infected the entire Russian military establishment before World War I. The lover of the young wife of the elderly Minister of War dined with the Kaiser and held five German decorations; the not unnatural suspicions that he was a German spy were later confirmed. Russia had herself scored one of the most spectacular spy coups of modern times when it blackmailed the homosexual Colonel Alfred Redl into betraying the strategic plans that the Austro-Hungarian general staff had drawn up for use in the expected war against the Slavs. Fear of a Russian Redl had kept Colonel Andreiev, in charge of the Army's cipher bureau, from distributing copies of the new and secret cipher that he had drawn up for war use until the very last minute.

His caution bred disaster.

The Russian plan of campaign against Germany in 1914 called for an invasion of East Prussia by two armies. The 1st Army was to drive straight west into that province and grip the German defenders tightly in battle. The 2nd Army, to the south, was to circle around the Masurian Lakes, come up behind the Germans, block their retreat, and destroy them. This strategy naturally required careful timing and close collaboration between the two forces. Unfortunately, Russian communications were woefully inadequate. The 2nd Army had only 350 miles of wire all told to string during its advance across the plains of Poland; this pitiful supply contrasts sharply with the 2,500 miles of wire later used in a single day by an A.E.F. army on the Western Front. At the same time radios were issued only to the headquarters of both armies and the headquarters of their immediate subordinates—their corps. Division and lower headquarters lacked them. The several corps headquarters therefore used their wire to link up with their divisions. Since army headquarters had exhausted their meager wire supplies in stringing lines to the rear commands, this left wireless as the only means of communication among the several corps headquarters and between them and their army headquarters—the two highest echelons of field command.

Their messages lay naked to the enemy. The general inefficiency that crippled the Russian mobilization had fouled up distribution of the new military cipher and its keys. Within a single army (the 2nd), for instance, the XIII Corps did not have the key needed to read cryptograms from its immediate neighbor, the VI Corps. The war broke out August 4. Before a fortnight had passed Russian signalmen were no longer even trying to encipher messages, but were passing them over the radio in the clear.

In accordance with the Russian strategy, General Pavel Rennenkampf, commanding the 1st, or northern, Army, began moving into East Prussia on August 17. The German general staff had long foreseen the two-pronged attack—the terrain made it obvious. They had left only one army to defend East Prussia because their strategy called for a quick and decisive victory against France first. This single force was approximately as strong as either Russian army but desperately weaker than both combined, and the general staff had dictated as its strategy to strike with all possible strength at the first Russian force within reach, then to turn and attack the second. East Prussia was the homeland of the Junkers. The Germans preferred not to yield it to the hideous trampling of the Slav.

They gave battle to Rennenkampf at Gumbinnen. Under a hammering

Russian artillery barrage, the German troops broke and fled 15 miles to the rear before they could be halted. The frightened German commander prepared to fall back to the Vistula River and abandon East Prussia. He reported his intentions to the German high command, which promptly began looking for a replacement. But his brilliant First Chief Staff Officer, Colonel Max Hoffmann, pointed out that the southern Russian army had already invaded so far that its left wing was actually closer to the Vistula than the German rear and so was in a position to cut off the German retreat. He convinced his chief that he had to strike against this wing to give the German army freedom to maneuver, if only to reach the safety of the Vistula. The Germans had somewhat mauled the Russian bear before their rout, and Rennenkampf, instead of pursuing to turn victory into triumph, had paused to lick his wounds. Hoffmann was confident that he would rest another day or two. He proposed, and his general agreed, to disengage two German corps from the front against Rennenkampf, switch them southward over the excellent network of German railroads, and fall upon the Russian southern prong with surprise.

The movement was in its early stages when the new German commander, Paul von Hindenburg, and his chief of staff, Erich Ludendorff, who really ran the show, arrived and confirmed it. The difficult entrainment process began. Ludendorff flung out a screen of cavalry along the northern battle line to conceal the withdrawal of his troops and to keep Rennenkampf under observation. The division of forces violated the German strategic doctrine of concentration, and the question arose as to whether all German forces should be thrown into the battle against the southern force, commanded by General Aleksandr Samsonov. To do so would almost ensure victory, but it would also leave the German rear entirely unprotected from an attack by Rennenkampf. While the German staff was discussing the pros and cons of this move on the evening of August 24, a motorcyclist brought in two Russian intercepts. They had been forwarded on the initiative of the head of the radio station at the German fortress at Königsberg. His operators, who had little traffic of their own to transmit, had begun listening in to the Russian transmissions as a diversion.

Both messages were from the headquarters of Samsonov's XIII Corps, which was communicating with army headquarters by radio because that was the only means the corps had. And both were in the clear because XIII Corps had never received the proper cipher key. They specified exactly where the corps was going, when it expected to be there, and what it would do next. Was it a trick? No, because these details were perfectly consistent with an overall Russian directive that had been found in the wallet of a dead Russian officer the day before. The intercepts did not answer the crucial question of Rennenkampf's intentions. But Ludendorff decided that, with this intelligence, the likelihood of overwhelming victory over Samsonov was worth risking defeat by Rennenkampf. The orders went out to march the remaining troops facing Rennenkampf across the short inner distance between the two pincers.

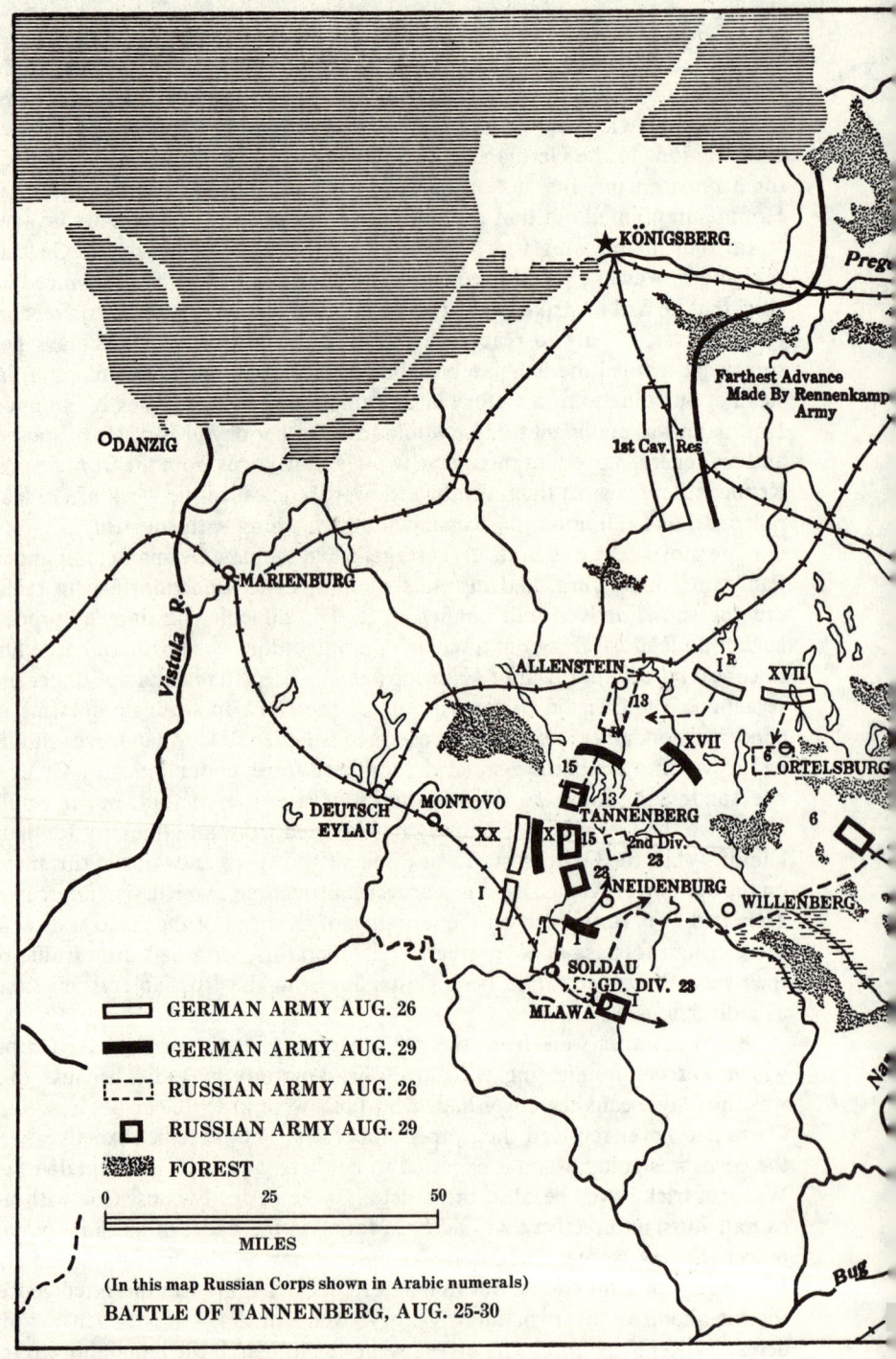

The Battle of Tannenburg, August 24 to 30, 1914

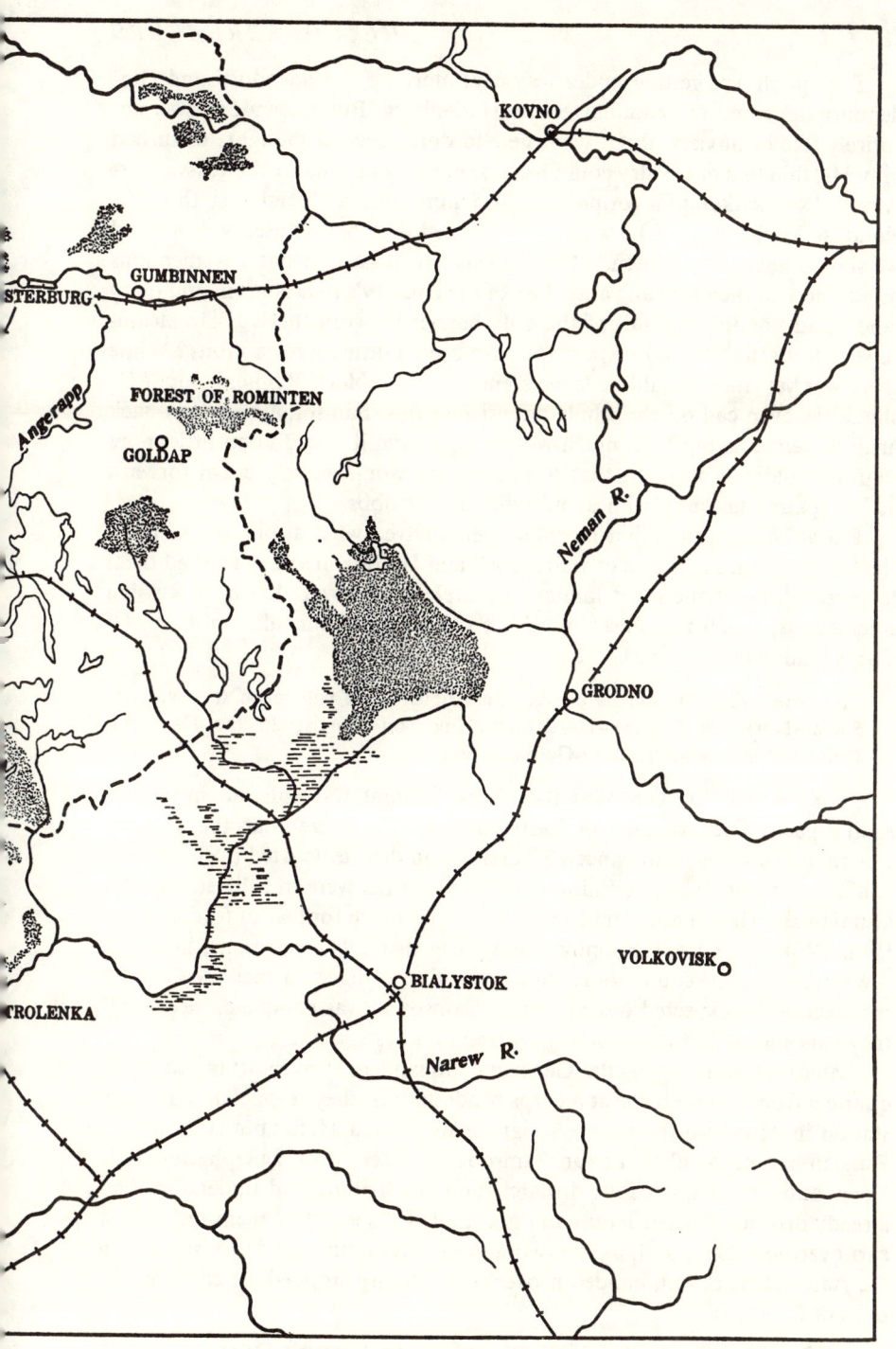

(Reprinted from *The Guns of August*, courtesy of Barbara W. Tuchman)

The march was getting under way next morning as Ludendorff and Hindenburg appeared at headquarters in Marienburg. But Ludendorff was not entirely free of anxiety about what he had done; second thoughts disturbed him. His thin line of cavalry could have been easily pierced by the Russian 1st Army. "Rennenkampf's formidable host hung like a threatening thundercloud to the northeast," he worried. "He need only have closed with us and we should have been beaten." Their defeat would have meant a tremendous moral blow to the German cause, loss of the country's richest grain and dairy lands, and possibly the fall of the only barrier between the Russian steamroller and Berlin. Should he perhaps have been a little more cautious? While there was yet time, should he leave some troops to block Rennenkampf? Or should he even call off the whole offensive against Samsonov and turn back against Rennenkampf? So much was at stake, and it rested upon little more than his soldier's intuition that Rennenkampf would merely crawl forward as he repaired his supply lines and refitted his troops.

But at headquarters that morning there arrived what at one stroke lifted the burden from the minds of Ludendorff and Hoffmann and permitted them to prepare one of the great military triumphs of the war. It was a Russian intercept. It, too, was in clear, but this one was from Rennenkampf to his IV Corps, and it read, in part:

> The army will continue its attack. On August 25 it will reach the Wiberln-Saalau-Norkitten-Potauren-Nordenburg line; on August 26 the Damerau-Petersdorf-Wehlau-Allenburg-Gerdauen line.

Their maps told the Germans that Rennenkampf was still moving at his snail's pace. The evidence of hasty German departure that the Russian general had seen as he advanced leisurely upon their evacuated positions had confirmed his erroneous opinion that the Germans were in full retreat after Gumbinnen. He did not want to press them too much for fear of forcing them to the Vistula before Samsonov could crush them. The Germans, however, saw at once that he could not reach any position in time to attack the German rear before the expected destruction of Samsonov was complete. Relieved, they concentrated at once on engineering that destruction.

Later that morning, as the German commanders were returning to headquarters from a conference at a corps headquarters, they stopped at a railway station in Montovo for news. A signalman handed Hoffmann still another Russian intercept—also in clear. Samsonov had sent it to the cipherless XIII Corps at 6 a.m. It was a long dispatch, and Hindenburg and Ludendorff had already driven off when Hoffmann got it all. He sped after them in his own car, overtook them, and, as the two automobiles jounced side by side along the rutted Polish road, handed it over. Hindenburg stopped his car, and the officers studied it:

> ... On 25 August the 2nd Army proceeds to the Allenstein-Osterode line; the main strength of the army corps occupies: XIII Corps the Gimmendorf-Kurken

line; XV Corps Nadrau-Paulsgut; XXIII Corps Michalken-Gr. Gardienne . . . .
The I Corps to remain in District 5, to protect army's left flank . . . .

It was, in fact, nothing less than a full roundup of the situation as Samsonov saw it, together with the most detailed and explicit moves to be followed by his army. It gave the Germans a knowledge of enemy intentions unprecedented in the whole of military history. It was like reading the mind of a chess opponent, like playing blindman's buff without the blindfold. It was almost impossible to lose.

The Germans formulated their plans to take advantage of the weaknesses of the Russian dispositions. They plotted a double envelopment of Samsonov, and it worked to perfection. General combat opened the next day, the 26th. One of the Germans corps marching down from Rennenkampf's front struck hard at Samsonov's right; during the night, that wing was turned. Before dawn on the 27th, a hurricane barrage of artillery demoralized the hungry, tired troops of his left flank, and before noon they had fled the field without a single serious German infantry assault. Soon the realization penetrated to Samsonov that instead of the Russians crushing a retreating German Army, that army had in fact almost enveloped him. His XIII and XV Corps, in the center, fought bravely in the confused, surging struggle, but the frantic orders and cries for help that their radios squealed in clear were all heard by the Germans who, fully informed, could exploit a gap here, a movement there. Bit by bit the Germans drove in behind the two corps from both sides; soon the Russians found themselves fighting both front and rear. By the 30th, the Germans had encircled the corps with a ring of steel from which only 2,000 Russians escaped. This ended the battle: there were no Russians left to fight. By then Samsonov was dead. He had shot himself in despair as he and his staff stumbled through the forest in the dark night of defeat.

Gradually, it became clear to the Germans that they had won, as Hoffmann wrote, "one of the great victories in history." Almost 100,000 Russians were taken prisoner. An estimated 30,000 were dead or missing. The Russian 2nd Army had ceased to exist. One of the few battles of the entire war that was a decisive victory, Tannenberg—as the Germans named it—demonstrated that the Russian steamroller was not quite the invincible machine that had terrorized central Europe. It catapulted Hindenburg to a popularity that carried him, later in the war, to supreme command, and, in peace, to the presidency of his country. Pro-German groups in Russia began to agitate for a withdrawal from the war. Russian morale sank.

Hoffmann, the architect of the victory, acknowledged its real cause. "We had an ally that I can only talk about after it is all over—we knew all the enemy's plans. The Russians sent out their wireless in clear." The case was clear-cut. Interception of unenciphered communications had awarded the Germans their triumph. Tannenberg, which gave Russia the first push on her long slide into ruin and revolution, was the first battle in the history of the world to be decided by cryptologic failure.

So inexhaustible were the manpower resources of Russia that not even a debacle like Tannenberg could cripple its war effort. "We are happy to make such sacrifices for our allies," replied the Grand Duke Nicholas, commander in chief of the Russian armies, when the French ambassador expressed his condolences. And even though the Germans turned on Rennenkampf and drove him out of East Prussia in the Battle of the Masurian Lakes, two Russian armies pounded the Austro-Hungarian forces back through Lvov with such force that they retreated almost to Krakow. Meanwhile, though still plagued with shortages of all kinds, including signal equipment, the Russians finally managed to distribute their cipher system to all commands by the middle of September. On the 14th, the Stavka, the Russian high command, prescribed its use for all military orders.

The system was a numerical polyalphabetic which negated most of the advantages of polyalphabeticity by enciphering several letters in succession in a single cipher alphabet. It resembled the feeble cipher used by Cornwallis in the American Revolution and solved with ease by James Lovell. Along the top of its tableau were listed 33 letters of the Russian alphabet; the tableau proper consisted of eight lines of two-digit numbers in mixed order. Each line differed from the others, and they were numbered at the left in mixed order. In enciphering, these cipher alphabets were used in rotation, the one numbered 1 first, the one numbered 2 second, and so on. Each alphabet enciphered several letters at a time. The number of letters to be enciphered in a given alphabet before the next came into play lay at the whim of the encipherer, who informed the decipherer of this number by writing it out five times and then placing this group at the head of the cryptogram. If he wished to change this number during a message, he simply repeated the new encipherment group length five times, inserted it into the body of the cryptogram, and used that length from then on.

Cryptograms in the Russian Army cipher thus consisted of groups of monalphabetically enciphered letters, with the length of the groups clearly indicated by the unmistakable appearance of, say a 99999 (the maximum length) or a 66666. Aside from being vulnerable to the usual techniques of frequency analysis, the cipher would often mirror the telltale repeated-letter pattern of an underlying plaintext word, such as *attack* or *division*, that had fallen entirely within a single encipherment group and so had been monalphabetically enciphered. Such a system does not interpose insuperable difficulties to the cryptanalyst, especially when, as with the Russians, it was poorly used, often with intermixture of plaintext. Mixed text was soon prohibited, but by then it was too late.

For the brilliant young Captain Hermann Pokorny, head of the Russian subsection of the Austro-Hungarian Dechiffrierdienst, had cracked the system and reconstructed all its alphabets by September 19. His first important solution, on September 25, disclosed General Novikov's lengthy report of his reconnaissance of Central Powers troops, with his additional note: "I took the decision of not crossing the Vistula." The message was dated 8:40 a.m.; by 4 p.m. the Austrian liaison officer had brought it to the attention of the German headquarters. Knowledge of Novikov's decision determined the initially successful Austro-German tactics of the battles of the Vistula and San rivers. Other intercepts were valuable in more local situations. A message of Prince Engalitschev, colonel of the 10th Russian Cavalry Division, warned of a strong attack on the fortress of Przemysl; the prepared commander easily warded it off until the Austrian advance forced the Russians to lift the siege in mid-October. During this advance, Pokorny's group solved as many as 30 cryptograms a day.

It was at about that time that the Russians made their first key change. It apparently consisted only of altering the order in which the cipher alphabets were to be used, the alphabets themselves remaining unchanged. Solution of this would have taken Pokorny at most a few minutes. Any difficulty that he might have encountered evaporated when a Russian station repeated in the old key a message already sent in the new.

Meanwhile, the Germans had, more by fortune than by foresight, developed a cryptanalytic service of their own. Ludwig Deubner, a professor of philology at the University of Königsberg who had enlisted in the Landsturm as an interpreter of Russian and who was stationed at the Königsberg fortress, began his radio-intelligence work by translating the cleartext intercepts that the fortress radio station picked up. As words in cipher began to appear, he undertook to solve them. Gradually he mastered the Russian system so that he could read messages entirely in cipher. At the end of September, he was called to headquarters and given charge of a group of interpreters who were to learn cryptanalysis. Soon he and an outstanding colleague—Hoffmann called them "quite geniuses in deciphering"—were, with their neophyte codebreakers, sending a stream of solutions to Ludendorff each night about 11. The chief of staff waited for them impatiently, barking, "Any radiograms?" at his subordinates. He based his orders for the next day in large measure on the intelligence the intercepts gave. When they were late, he would stalk into the cryptanalytic section to find out what the delay was. And if for a time nothing of importance appeared in the messages, he would growl that the intercept service had not been paying attention.

Such occasions were rare. Direct telegraph connections were soon established between Pokorny's group and Deubner's; together they laid open virtually every Russian cryptogram that their posts intercepted. And they were guaranteed a good harvest when the headquarters of a Russian army was given permission to use radio for its front-line activities because its linemen were busy with repair work.

Thus it was that the Central Powers learned from Russian wireless that the Grand Duke Nicholas was forming a huge phalanx of seven armies to rumble into the industrialized heart of Silesia in east-central Europe. By the end of October, the picture of the composition, disposition, and strength of the

Russian forces that Hindenburg and Ludendorff had before them could not have differed much from the official one at Stavka. Only the date of the advance was unknown, but the Germans assumed that it would take a little time before this ponderous Russian steamroller could get up momentum. They determined to seize the initiative and attack first in the hope of throwing a monkey wrench into the steamroller's mechanism.

Ludendorff's plan was characteristically bold. He removed a German army from the defenses blocking the invader and poised it in the north for a plunge downwards into the right side of the Russian wedge. On November 11, the point of this dagger—an army under Mackensen—began to pierce the Russian flank. At 2:10 p.m. the next day, the chief of staff of one of the Russian armies under attack transmitted a long radiogram which the Central Powers intercepted. In addition to mentioning the date of the projected Russian advance, it specified the line of demarcation between his army and a neighbor—always a zone of weakness. This message lay, cryptanalyzed and translated, on the desks of the German headquarters for the Eastern Front at Posen by the next afternoon.

It was immediately forwarded to Mackensen. At 7:30 p.m., with this picture of the Russian dispositions before him, he telephoned his order for the next day to his subordinates. It called for an all-out attack, concentrating on the meeting line of the two armies in the hope of driving them apart and breaking through.

He achieved a massive success. The Russian forces were split; they pulled back hastily to the south. Mackensen shoved the dagger in up to the hilt. At the same time, Ludendorff pinned the front Russian armies in combat and sent a corps to turn the Russian left flank. He hoped to effect another Tannenberg—a double envelopment. In sharp fighting around Lodz, the German forces drove their enemy back, abetted by a constant stream of cryptanalyzed intelligence. On November 15, for example, the German command learned that four corps were to reinforce Russian troops at the Ner and Bzura rivers and that another corps was to cross to the left bank of the Vistula at Plozk. These details enabled the Germans to maneuver each day as if in a war game.

By now the Russians were changing the key to the order of the cipher alphabets—not the alphabets themselves—each day. The cryptanalysts kept pace. On November 18, it appeared that the Germans had won their victory when the cryptanalysts solved a message ordering a Russian retreat from Lodz. But the rejoicing at headquarters was cut short when the codebreakers read a message from Grand Duke Nicholas countermanding the order and directing his forces to fight on despite their difficult position. The flow of radio intelligence continued unabated, and on the 19th Mackensen even delayed giving an order until intercepted information was received.

The next day a premonitory fear chilled the intercept services when they picked up a message from a liaison officer of the Russian 4th Army to a colleague, warning that the Germans had the Russian cipher key. The Russians had captured a German cipher key, and they apparently assumed that one of theirs had likewise fallen into German hands. A new key was instituted—and this time the entire set of cipher equivalents was changed. A curtain of silence descended upon the Eastern Front.

Feverishly, Deubner and Pokorny, who was assisted by Lieutenant Colonel Heinrich Zemanek and Lieutenant Viktor von Marchesetti, grappled with the new key as the intercept posts sucked in every scrap of Russian wireless. The moment could not have been worse. The battle around Lodz raged at its peak, and just as Ludendorff was about to consummate his envelopment with his inferior forces but his superior intelligence, that intelligence was abruptly blanked out. Deprived of his eyes and ears, he did not know of the Russian reinforcements that began to cut off the deeply sunk point of Mackensen's dagger. By the 21st, the point had been isolated, and the envelopers were themselves enveloped. A guards division and two cavalry corps were encircled by Russian forces with no apparent hope of escaping. The Russians exultantly ordered up trains to carry off the prisoners.

But the next day, Pokorny's group finally subdued the new Russian alphabets, and the intelligence once again began streaming into German headquarters. Intercepts soon revealed a weak spot at Brzeziny in the ring of Russians. Ludendorff's headquarters radioed this information to the trapped commanders, who, grouping their forces densely and fighting hard, broke out on the 25th and reached safety, bringing with them 10,000 prisoners. General Lietzmann, commander of the guards division, won the title "Lion of Brzeziny" for the brilliant escape; the cryptanalysts who had showed him how best to use his fangs and claws purred with amusement in their secret lairs.

This harrowing episode, resulting from a fortuitous change of key, balked the Germans of a decisive victory, but they had succeeded in throwing the vaunted Russian steamroller out of gear. Never again did it threaten German soil. The Central Powers pressed forward, still reading Russian cryptograms, and on December 6 the soldiers of the Czar evacuated Lodz, the second city and the industrial capital of Poland. Eight days later they again made a wholesale change of alphabets in their digit cipher. Solution again required several days, and when it was completed the Austro-German command learned that the Russians planned to dig in for the winter along the Nida River. Soon thereafter they gave up the old cipher altogether.

When activity quickened in the spring of 1915, the Russians were using a simple Caesar cipher.* The multiplicity of tables used by different armies in the old cipher, the daily shift of keys, had evidently proved too difficult to handle for the half-illiterate muzhiks. The Austrian and German cryptanalytic organizations saw right through this transparent new cipher and

* During the Second Battle of the Masurian Lakes in February, in which the Russians were defeated, they used a service code called the RSK, which the Germans solved. Its nature is unknown.

read the indications of a projected Russian invasion of East and West Prussia. Then began what Colonel Max Ronge, head of Austro-Hungarian intelligence, called "the most brilliant period of our interception services." Enormous quantities of intelligence were sluiced from the Pokorny and Deubner groups into the offices of the operations staffs of the German and Austro-Hungarian commands. Helped by this, they parried the first tentative Russian advances, and then themselves swept through the whole enemy line in a rapid onslaught that penetrated 80 miles in two weeks.

Time after time, their solutions enabled the Central Powers to take steps which were so perfectly the right thing to do in each tactical situation that the Russian general staff was mystified by its opponents' apparent clairvoyance. Once the Germans fell back just two days before an overwhelming assault was to be launched; had they remained in place, their position would quickly have become critical. After the Germans captured Lodz, the Russians pondered the precision of the enemy moves and decided that the Germans must have obtained intelligence from air reconnaissance.

Eventually, however, the conviction grew that the foe must be reading their ciphers. They did not suspect cryptanalysis. Spies, they thought, must have sold them to the Austrians, and in a wave of spy-mania they persecuted officers with German names—none of whom, Ronge said, had ever given anything to him. The Russians changed their cipher at the height of the enemy's spring offensive, but this caused the cipher clerks more trouble than it did the cryptanalysts, for almost all messages of May 15 were unintelligible to their recipients and most of those of the 16th as well.

The summer-long Russian retreat finally came to a halt at the end of September on a defensible position deep within their own territory. By then Russia had lost 750,000 men as prisoners and untold hundreds of thousands more as casualties. She simply threw more men into the war. She seemed to adhere to the same policy in cryptography—and with the same lack of success. On December 20, 1915, she put her 13th cipher into operation. The Austrian and German cryptanalysts recognized it at once as having been used elsewhere on the front, and during the inconclusive battles before and after New Year's Day kept up with the enemy situation hour by hour. On June 16, 1916, the Russians began using their first code, a small one of about 300 groups. This development may have been influenced by the French, who had learned about the German solution of Russian messages from their own cryptanalyses and had passed the news to their allies. Or it may have resulted from Russia's own intercept service; just how well Russia did in military cryptanalysis is not known, but she did set up direction-finding stations in mid-1916 and started an intercept school at Nicolaieff.

The travail of the Central Powers cryptanalysts, who were unused to code, was simplified when some Russian commands, who were equally unfamiliar with it, continued using the old system. And their work was made almost mechanical when the headquarters of a Russian guard detachment that was

Русская Криптология 633

being joined to the 8th Army compromised the new system by a message in clear. A great hubbub arose in the 8th Army; a new code was instituted; this one cryptanalysts solved without much trouble. By then they were reading up to 70 Russian dispatches a day. The German solutions seem to have been made in the radio stations of the various fortresses, to which Deubner communicated the keys as he solved them. Some of the Austrian cryptanalysis was done at Ronge's Austro-Nord Penkala under the command of Captain Karl Boldeskul. Later in the war, when Pokorny was promoted to head of the whole Kriegschiffregruppe, the Russian subsection of the Dechiffrierdienst at headquarters was taken over by von Marchesetti; in 1918 Rudolf Lippmann succeeded him.

On November 6, 1916, the Russian Army of the Danube suppressed the radio use of cipher No. 14 as known to the enemy, and on December 17 another cipher was called out of service because the radio station of the 1st Cossack Division had been captured. Four days later they returned to the air with a code that proved to be merely a slightly shifted version of one that had been instituted a week earlier. All these changes the cryptanalysts followed with contemptuous ease. The increasing disorganization of the Russian armies contaminated the radio services, and as discipline relaxed, garrulity increased. One day early in 1917, the Dechiffrierdienst solved 333 radiograms, from which it inferred that the Russian secret communications were rapidly disintegrating. In March the Czar was overthrown, in July an all-out offensive by the Russian armies collapsed, and in October the Bolsheviks, using the people's overwhelming desire for peace, seized power and took Russia out of the war.

The way to this situation was opened primarily by Russia's military failure. While this resulted largely from the lack of munitions, food, and supplies that the underindustrialized country could not supply, the tactical defeats inflicted by the Central Powers obviously played a conclusive role. And these victories of a David over a Goliath, though aided by superior German equipment, discipline, and logistics, were mainly engendered by cryptanalysis.

"We were always warned by the wireless messages of the Russian staff of the positions where troops were being concentrated for any new undertaking," wrote Hoffmann. So complete was the intelligence that he could say: "Only once during the whole war were we taken by surprise on the Eastern Front by a Russian attack—it was on the Aa in the winter of 1916–17." This dramatically underlines the importance of cryptanalysis in the outcome of the war in the East and in all that that entailed. Indeed, it may not be too much to claim that the establishment of Communist power, perhaps the supreme fact of contemporary history, was made possible to a significant degree by the cryptanalysis of czarist secret communications.

The consolidation of the Soviet regime permitted Lenin and his colleagues to turn not only to the difficult problems of running the world's first socialist state but also to the traditional Communist activity of fomenting class struggle and the revolution of the proletariat. They felt justified in using subversion as well as the more orthodox methods of propaganda and political agitation in advancing Marxism in countries that had not yet reached Russia's stage of historical development.

Some of their agents were mere mercenaries, some were Russians planted as spies, but many were native members of Communist parties who placed their quasi-religious dedication to that ideology above allegiance to country. These spies were soon sending quantities of information to, and receiving instructions from, Moscow, whence the impetus and control for the world revolution would come. In doing so during these early years before Communist espionage had stabilized itself they employed a wide variety of cipher systems.

In 1919, German Communists employed an irregular columnar transposition. One key was the second line of Heinrich Heine's "*Die Lorelei*": DASS ICH SO TRAURIG BIN: another was ACH, WENN DAS DER PETRUS WÜSSTE (Oh, if Peter only knew it). Three messages so enciphered were discovered in an airplane en route to the Soviet Union from Germany that was forced down in Latvia. The Latvian government, after failing to solve them, had turned them over to the American consul at Riga for help, and from him they eventually found their way to Yardley's Black Chamber, where they were quickly solved. They began with a plea to *Sendet geld* ("Send money"), discussed the fiasco of a Communist conference in Holland, reported the arrest of the fiery German Communist Klara Zetkin, pleaded that "[Karl] Radek or [Nikolai] Bukharin [both intimates of Lenin] is absolutely needed here," disclosed that "Radio station finally ready to send. Expert engaged . . . Guralski arrived here with money on his way to America," and cautioned that "My name is now JAMES." The solutions caused a stir in Washington, for they were among the first authentic documents dealing with Soviet international activities that came into the American government's hands.

At about the same time, the U.S. Department of Justice began what must have been one of its first infiltrations into the Communist party, U.S.A. Undercover agent Francis A. Morrow of Camden, New Jersey, sent a steady stream of reports to the department while rising in the party to become secretary of a district committee. He got on close terms with the district organizer, and one day the latter, when a little tipsy, let Morrow help him in deciphering a message. The cipher that Morrow thus reported to the Justice Department was used by the party's leadership to communicate with its organizers. It was based upon a United States postal money order, possession of which would not incriminate anyone. Its ciphertext appeared as a series of arithmetical fractions, whose numerator represented the line of type on the back of the money order blank, and the denominator the letter in that line. The system recalls the fractional one used by the Russian revolutionaries in czarist days, and was, in fact, probably taken over from that time, as were many Communist underground practices. For example, the use of the term "dubok," which literally means "little oak," to mean a hiding place for messages, and of "illness" to mean an arrest, originated before the Revolution.

This simple system vanished with the advent of a more highly organized Soviet intelligence apparatus. Russia's Amtorg Trading Corporation, which set up offices in New York in 1924, controlled the first real Soviet espionage effort against the United States. Communications with the Soviet Union were naturally carried on in code, and, whatever system was used, it effectively protected the secrets of their American spies. Representative Hamilton Fish, Jr., of New York, chairman of a committee investigating Communist activities in the United States, subpoenaed 3,000 coded Amtorg telegrams in 1930 in the hope of learning more about those activities. The cryptanalysts of the Navy's Code and Signal Section, to which he had submitted the cryptograms, reported that "the cipher used by the Amtorg is the most complicated and possesses the greatest secrecy within their [the Navy cryptanalysts'] knowledge." Fish then gave the cablegrams to the War Department for solution; two years later, he complained on the floor of Congress, "Not one expert—and they had from six months to a year—succeeded in decoding a single word of those cablegrams, although they had assured me they could decode them."

In Copenhagen in 1934, a cipher disk with seven rings of digits around a mixed plaintext alphabet guarded the messages of the Danish Communist party. This key was captured in a police raid, however, after which the messages yielded rather easily to the cryptanalytic ministrations of Yves Gyldén, who was summoned from Stockholm.

It was during the Spanish Civil War, in which Russia actively aided the Loyalists, that a cryptographic element that had served the revolutionary predecessors of Lenin & Co. reappeared in a form both streamlined and more secure. This was the straddling checkerboard. Its straddling feature makes use of cipher equivalents of two different lengths—lengths usually of one digit and two digits; the two sets of equivalents are so constructed that the cryptographer can unambiguously separate them when they are run together. The cryptanalyst, however, not knowing which digits are singletons and which form pairs, may divide the ciphertext incorrectly, thereby "straddling" many of the true pairs and combining two singletons into a false pair. The device also reduces the length of the numerical text as compared with checkerboards in which all letters are replaced by numerical pairs. Straddling was first employed by the Argentis in some of their 16th-century papal ciphers (one wonders whether the atheistic Communists knew!).

The straddling checkerboard produces single-digit equivalents by leaving the side coordinate off one of the rows of the checkerboard. A letter in this row is enciphered by just the single coordinate above it. If ambiguity is to be avoided, none of these singletons can start a two-digit group. Hence none can be used as a side coordinate (which is read first). Using eight digits of the ten as singletons leaves two digits as side coordinates; each of these two side coordinates can then pair with the ten top coordinates (the singletons may serve in second position) to produce 20 two-digit groups. This configuration makes 28 ciphertext equivalents available for plaintext elements.

It was used in 1937 with keyword M DEL VAYO, the M the initial of the agent, the DEL VAYO the name of a Spanish Communist. The two extra spaces were used for a period and a letter-number shift sign:

```
    0 9 8 7 6 5 4 3 2 1
   |
   | m d e l v a y o
 1 | b c f g h u j k n p
 2 | q r s t u w x z . /
```

With this, $e = 8$, $a = 5$, $b = 10$, $t = 27$, and so on. There will be no single 2 or 1. The decipherer takes all 1's and 2's as the first digits of a two-digit group, and joins to it whatever digit follows. He takes any digits from 3 to 0 as individuals if they are not already part of a pair. Thus the ciphertext 828115125 can be unambiguously divided as 8 28 11 5 12 5 and deciphered to *Espana*.

Other configurations are possible. Seven single digits will permit three side coordinates, for a total of 37 cells in the checkerboard. Six singletons will produce 46 cells; five, 55, and so on down to one singleton, 91 cells. The arrangement with 28 equivalents has been widely used for Latin-alphabet texts, that with 37 for Cyrillic texts.

Although the M DEL VAYO checkerboard was used by the Swedish fellow traveler Dr. Per Meurling only to teach his fiancée secret writing, his knowledge of it testifies to its use at that time by the Communists. He subjected the numerical text resulting from the checkerboard to a multiplication, and then reconverted the product to letters in another checkerboard. The system resembled but was much weaker than Pliny Earle Chase's of 1859, and it is unlikely that the Russians would have used it in that form.

The Spanish Civil War, a prelude to World War II, furnished the Fascist-Nazi and the Communist dictatorships with a testing ground for the weapons they would use in the later conflict. Perhaps this extended—for the Communists, at least—to the cryptologic arena as well. Red ciphers of World War II had purged themselves of whatever weaknesses were discovered in Spain and had erected upon their strengths an impregnable structure.

The Soviet Union was not so totally immersed in the task of improving its own ciphers that it could not heed what other nations were doing to theirs. On the contrary, it engaged in the constant tug-of-war of "practical cryptanalysis." This is more prosaically known as stealing codes. It is speedier and easier on the cryptanalysts' brains than pure analytical cryptanalysis, or solving, but it costs more and risks loss of the information if the theft is discovered.

Victories in this tug-of-war went now to one side, now to the other. In 1926, a French Communist was arrested in Marseilles with the French Army code AFNO in her possession. Both it and an Interior Ministry code had been smuggled out of the prison at Melun, where French codes were printed, by a convict named Bultez, who concealed them in the pages of an English grammar on his release. The following year, Russia recruited the "cipher expert" of the Persian Council of Ministers, who promptly became Agent No. 33. Also serving the Communist cause was the cipher clerk of a Persian Army brigade near the Russian border. Somehow the Soviet espionage organization, the O.G.P.U., had obtained the cipher key of the Dachnaks, an anti-Communist party in Soviet Armenia. Dachnak activity was directed from Tabriz, across the border in Persia. The O.G.P.U. resident in Tabriz made certain arrangements with a Persian postal official, and soon the O.G.P.U. knew enough to block any Dachnak move, if necessary, with a swift series of arrests and raids. In 1930, a Rumanian police official expressed his displeasure over a demotion by presenting his country's secret code to the Soviets.

The shoe was on the other foot in 1925, when code documents disappeared from the Soviet embassy in Shanghai. The White Russian suspected of the theft disappeared overboard on his way to Vladivostok. Ten years later, a Soviet employee stole codes from his embassy in Prague; their subsequent recovery and courteous return by Czech police could hardly have convinced the Russians that they had not been compromised.

In the summer of 1936, Russian military intelligence gained access to the coded correspondence of the Japanese military attaché in Berlin with his home office in Tokyo. Photostats of the telegrams were rushed to Haarlem, where a Japanese-language expert from Moscow decoded them—with a Japanese codebook that the Russians had obtained—and then translated them. They proved to be messages relating to the Anti-Comintern Pact, which was of the greatest interest to the homeland of the Third Communist International. In 1937, the Russians were on the losing end again, when the code employed between Moscow and the Spanish Loyalist Ministry of National Defense, which was receiving help from Russia in the struggle against Franco, was reported stolen. The Russians again lost in 1938, when General G. S. Lyushkov, a secret police official in the Soviet Far East Army, defected to Japan and revealed details of his army's secret communications—though Soviet agents mitigated the damage by telling Moscow what he was telling the Japanese. A victory ended the following year, when another defector disclosed the presence of a Soviet spy, Captain John Herbert King, in the code room of the British Foreign Office. England sentenced him to ten years.

All this thievery back and forth reached a ludicrous climax of sorts in a 1939 lawsuit. Two Russian emigrés, Vladimir and Maria Azarov, had bootlegged out of the Soviet Union in 1939 a "certain Code Book containing the code for the transmission of messages, then in use by the Union of Socialist Soviet Republics, which Code Book was of a secret nature." The Cunard steamship line had shipped their goods, the codebook included, aboard the freighter *Baltabor*, which had grounded in the harbor of Riga, resulting in the loss of all the Azarovs' property. Whereupon they sued the steamship company for $511,900—$11,900 for clothes and house furnishings and half a million for the code, a figure which Azarov said represented the "value of the Code Book in the open market at the time of its loss." The matter was settled out of court, and how much cash the Azarovs finally accepted for this almost-impossible-to-price article has never been revealed.

Soviet cryptologic espionage extended beyond the simple theft of codes. It included, apparently, lifting plaintexts that might help Soviet cryptanalysts solve codes or ciphers. In this category fall the famous "pumpkin papers," which ex-Communist Whittaker Chambers accused Alger Hiss of giving to him for transmission to Soviet agents. Though Chambers never gave the particular rolls of film that constituted the actual "pumpkin papers" to the Russian Colonel Boris Bykov, they were representative of many other, similar photographed documents, allegedly from Hiss, that he did pass on. They included, for example, a cablegram from the American embassy in Paris of January 13, 1938, marked "Strictly Confidential, for the Secretary." Though parts of some of these messages were sent in the nonconfidential GRAY code, others, stated Sumner Welles, who was Under Secretary of State in 1938, "would presumably be sent in one of the most secret codes then in our possession." When he was asked, "Would the possession of the document as translated, along with the original document as it appeared in code, furnish an individual with the necessary information to break the code?" he replied: "In my opinion, decidedly yes." And at least one Russian expert (Isaac Don Levine, the Russian-born journalist who specialized in Soviet affairs) became convinced by mid-1939 from numerous conversations he had with General Walter Krivitsky, the defected head of Soviet military intelligence for Western Europe, that the Communist cryptanalysts were reading American codes.

Questions of the security of Soviet communications naturally interested their secret agents. One day during World War II, Lauchlin Currie, an assistant to President Roosevelt and allegedly an informer for Russia, reportedly burst into the house of George Silverman, a member of a Soviet spy ring, and told him that the United States was about to break a Soviet code. When Communist courier Elizabeth T. Bentley passed this news on, her Russian superior asked, "Which code?" Miss Bentley was unable to find out. (Currie has denied ever making such a statement to anyone, saying that he knew nothing about any American cryptanalytic attempts or successes, and that he was not a Soviet agent.)

Soviet espionage, finally, did not disdain the least tidbit of information that might be of help to its cryptanalysts. In the winter of 1945, when agents of the O.S.S. broke into the New York office of a Communist-linked magazine called *Amerasia*, they found therein, among approximately 1,800 confidential U.S. official documents, a top-secret report revealing the American breakdown and mastery of Japanese codes.

The Soviet Union expressed its intense interest in the codes and ciphers of other countries primarily through the clandestine activities of two agencies—the secret police and military intelligence.

The secret police, through which the Communist government enthralls the people of Russia, is more than just a Gestapo. It gathers external intelligence as well as guarding internal security. It thus encompasses the functions of a C.I.A. as well as an F.B.I. This seemingly unusual situation began under the czars, when revolutionary agents were very numerous outside Russia. The Okhrana infiltrated their conspiracies outside Russia, and its successor under Communism did the same to the exiles who sought to undermine Soviet power. Soon it extended these activities to capitalistic Western countries as a means of defending the Marxist regime, and in this way it developed into a political intelligence service. Created by Lenin only a month after he founded his government, the secret police has had an extremely tangled history. Its various reorganizations, mergers, and separations are reflected in its various names—Cheka, G.P.U., O.G.P.U., N.K.V.D., M.G.B., M.V.D., and K.G.B. After Stalin, it was divided into two agencies, the K.G.B. or Komitet Gosurdarstvennoi Bezopasnosti ("Committee for State Security"), responsible for external espionage and high-level internal counterespionage, and the M.V.D., or Ministerstvo Vnutrennykh Del ("Ministry of Internal Affairs"), for the more routine domestic policing functions.

The other Soviet intelligence agency is an arm of the Red armed forces, rather corresponding to the American Defense Intelligence Agency. Founded by Leon Trotsky, the first Soviet Minister of War, it, like the secret police, has changed its name and organization during Russia's administrative upheavals. In theory, it attends to military matters whereas the K.G.B. handles political espionage, but this line has often been blurred—perhaps intentionally. The two were even merged briefly. Military attachés belong to it, and contacts with foreign governments on intelligence matters are made through it. Its present title is G.R.U., for Glavnoye Razvedyvatelnoye Upravlenie ("Chief Intelligence Directorate").

One of the tasks of the secret police is to protect the dictatorship of the proletariat from the proletarians who are unhappy with the dictators. Soon after Lenin founded it, the Cheka resumed the czarist black-cabinet practices of opening mail and reading telegrams. The practice has gone forward uninterruptedly, altered only by improvements in techniques. By the 1950s, the M.V.D. was confiding this activity to an entire section—the 3rd, or Individual, Division of the M.V.D.'s 2nd Special Directorate, the Directorate for Positive State Security. This division ensures the reliability of the Soviet citizenry by the most modern methods of communications surveillance, such as electronic room-bugging, as well as by the most pedestrian methods of shadowing, using informers, and reading letters. Representatives of the secret police's Information Administration, stationed in postal-telegraph stations, have long opened foreign mail, letters to suspected persons, and a percentage of the rest of the mail at random.

They turned over any suspicious letters to the chief cryptologic agency of the Soviet Union, the quasi-independent Spets-Otdel ("Special Department"), whose primary task was reading the coded messages of other nations. Though attached to the foreign directorate of the secret police, it was actually responsible to the Central Committee of the Russian Communist party, the Soviet Union's real ruling body, whose chairman was first Lenin and then Stalin. In 1938, it appears to have been renamed and reorganized into the 5th Directorate of what was then the N.K.V.D.

Up until that time, and beginning, apparently, around 1927, its chief was Gleb I. Boki, an old Bolshevik and friend of Lenin, who, at the same time, sat on the Supreme Court of the Soviet Union! Born in 1879, he had taken part in prerevolutionary activities and had gained the Communist badge of honor by being arrested many times and winning a three-year sentence in Siberia. At the time of the Revolution, he was secretary of the Bolshevik cell in the capital, St. Petersburg. In the early 1920s, he headed the Cheka in Turkestan, where he so terrorized the country that legends about him remained alive long after he had gone: that he ate dog meat (especially execrable to the Moslem population), even that he drank human blood. It seems true, however, that as head of the Spets-Otdel Boki held wild parties, if not actual orgies, with a group of carefully selected guests at his rented dacha near Batumi during his vacations. He kept his office door always closed and used a peephole with one-way glass to examine visitors. Tall and stooped, with a sinister expression and cold blue eyes that gave one the impression that he hated the very sight of you, he gave at least one girl worker the shivers whenever he emerged from his sanctum and spoke to her when she was alone in the office on night duty. Never with a hat and always with his raincoat, which he wore in all seasons, Boki seems to have been an administrator rather than a cryptologist. He was executed in 1938 in the great Stalinist purges. Afterwards, it was discovered that he had, most unsocialistically, hoarded gold and silver coins.

The Spets-Otdel handled both cryptography and cryptanalysis. In 1933, the cryptographers worked in a big room on the fourth floor of a former insurance building that the O.G.P.U. occupied at 6 Lubyanka Street. The cryptanalysts were then on the top floor of a former Ministry of Foreign Affairs building at the corner of Lubyanka Street and Kuznetsky Bridge Street. The comings and goings of ordinary tenants on the lower floors and of the members of a diplomats' club disguised the presence of the office. In 1935, both cryptographers and cryptanalysts moved into the new building of what was now the N.K.V.D. at 2 Dzerzhinsky Street (named for the first head of the secret police, Felix Dzerzhinsky).

The cryptographic division was subdivided into several sections. There were separate sections, for example, for the N.K.V.D. network inside Russia, for the border patrols (under N.K.V.D. jurisdiction) and uniformed N.K.V.D troops, for Gulag, the prison administration, for clandestine agents abroad, and for the "legal" N.K.V.D. residents abroad. This last section was No. 6. Its chief, Koslov, was dismissed during the purges, and after his successor was sent to the United States as a cipher clerk, the section was headed by a man not unknown to later fame—Vladimir M. Petrov, who defected in 1954 and was granted asylum in Australia.*

The growth of Section 6 may measure that of Soviet espionage. When Petrov joined in 1933, there were only 12 workers; in 1951, there were 45 or 50. As cipher clerks in the N.K.V.D., entrusted with the deepest secrets of the most secret agency in Russia, these people were among the elite of the Soviet Union, yet their jobs in this workers' paradise were anything but heavenly. Ciphering was done by hand, and early in his career Petrov often worked until midnight to clear up the day's backlog of telegrams. Later, as deputy section chief, Petrov did no actual enciphering or deciphering, but read the telegrams, corrected them, and signed them. Sometimes the clerks were given noncryptographic assignments, as in the case of Bokov, a tall, taciturn, unusually strong staff member. He was selected to kill the Soviet ambassador in a Middle Eastern country, which he did with a single blow of a short iron bar that split the ambassador's skull in his office one day. Bokov stayed on for a year as a cipher clerk in the embassy to throw off suspicion, and then returned—with the order of the Red Star.

The cryptanalysts were divided into geographical and linguistic subsections—Chinese, Anglo-American, and so on.† The future Mrs. Ekdovia Petrov, who had studied Japanese for two years at a language school in Moscow, was assigned to the Japanese section. Among her co-workers were Vera Plotnikova, daughter of a professor of Japanese and a long-time resident of Japan; Galina Podpalova, who liked things Japanese so much that she

---

* Petrov named three men who were his bosses at different times while he was section chief—Ilyin, Degtjarov, and Shevelev. Whether these were the heads of the entire, then newly formed N.K.V.D. 5th Directorate, or whether they were department heads (a possible administrative level between the section chiefs and the directorate's chief), is not known. The former may be more likely in view of the fact that Boki's successor, Shapiro, lasted only a month or two before he was arrested, and three or four of Shapiro's successors were also arrested.

† In 1933, it also had a military intelligence group, headed by a Colonel Kharkevich, a solid, impressive man who reported to both Boki and the general staff. This group appears to have later been abolished or transferred to the Army; Kharkevich himself was purged in 1938. The head—under Boki—of the O.G.P.U. group of cryptanalysts was one Gusev, possibly Sergei I. Gusev, an old revolutionary, active in secret printing, a member of the Central Committee of the Russian Communist party since 1922, and on the Praesidium of the Comintern from 1930. He too was purged in 1938.

wore kimonos at home; Ivan Kalinin, who came in occasionally as a consultant; and Professor Shungsky, old, distinguished, vigorous, the section's supreme authority on Japanese. He gave Doosia (the future Mrs. Petrov's nickname) an affectionate kiss on the cheek when, after four years of his tutoring, she translated a difficult sentence to his liking at her final examination.

Shungsky had served in the czarist Army, and many others in the cryptanalytic section were elderly former Russian aristocrats, including counts and barons. This shocking breach of Bolshevik polity resulted from a serious shortage of linguists, who were needed in codebreaking. Cryptanalysts themselves were so excessively scarce that even when they were jailed they continued to work. Vladimir Krivosh, the father of Doosia's first love and de facto husband, Roman Krivosh, had held a high post in the Okhrana; he was alternately arrested and released, but worked for the Spets-Otdel even while he was in the Butirskaya Prison in Moscow. Eventually the police took Roman away to the same prison, but the head of his section in what was then the 5th Directorate brought him his work.

There was, of course, no security problem with inmate-cryptanalysts. But security was impressed on the others. They were not allowed to tell anyone the department in which they worked nor even where the office was. Doosia never even told her parents. They also had to keep out of restaurants, presumably because their conversations might be overheard.

Did their work prosper? It did, and very well indeed. In 1929 or 1930, the Spets-Otdel compiled a weekly précis of foreign telegrams that it had solved and sent it to O.G.P.U. department heads and to the Central Committee. By 1938, the pace seems to have accelerated, for by then Doosia had the job with a Madame Moritz of checking the typed fair copies that represented each day's output against their handwritten originals. One former O.G.P.U. official stated that the Spets-Otdel "carries on the work of reading codes splendidly" and praised Boki's staffers as "a first-class lot, often cited for emulation."

The Soviet military establishment seems to have had neither the tradition, the work force, nor the success in cryptanalysis that the secret police enjoyed. The inclusion of a military unit within the Spets-Otdel in 1933 testifies to this subordination. In any event, much less has been heard of it. Probably this is because each branch of the Soviet armed forces restricts itself to the cryptosystems of its opposite numbers—the Red Army to the secret communications of the German, Japanese, British, American, and other armies, and similarly for the Red Navy and Air Force. Cryptanalysis naturally constitutes a part of intelligence, and in 1941, the G.R.U., the Army's Chief Intelligence Directorate, had its cryptanalytic group as Section 8 of the eight sections of its operations branch: (1) Europe, (2) Near East, (3) Western Hemisphere and India, (4) advanced technical information, (5) terroristic activities, (6) production of false documents, (7) frontiers, (8) cryptology. What these had in common was the production of raw military intelligence by both clandestine and open methods. (In addition to operations, the G.R.U. had three other branches: information, which evaluated and disseminated operations' output; training; and auxiliary, which handled the housekeeping duties.)

In 1943, when Soviet military intelligence was reorganized into strategic and tactical branches, it expanded into a block-square baroque palace at 19 Znamensky Street, while retaining its former quarters in a building on the square at the Kropotkin Gate. There were also several auxiliary buildings, including a factory for photographic paper outside of Moscow, nearly all of whose output was consumed by a white two-story building in a yard of the intelligence complex. This was the photographic laboratory that produced and developed the films used by Soviet military intelligence for much of its mail communication with its agents abroad. What appeared to be a gold research institute on the Vorobiovy Gory was actually the Osobyi Radio Divizion ("Special Radio Division"), by which the G.R.U. maintained radio contact with its secret agents around the world. When Soviet spies tapped out their messages to the impersonal "Centre" in Moscow, an O.R.D. radioman received and acknowledged them. And when the agents received their orders, curtly signed "Director" (of Soviet military intelligence), the O.R.D. transmitted them. It was their only link with the agency for which they risked their lives. The O.R.D. was also staffed with radio technicians, who assigned wavelengths and schedules that would provide optimum reception from various points on the globe, and with clerks who allocated call-signs.

Cryptography was handled in a separate G.R.U. branch headed by Lieutenant Colonel Kravchenko. Among its clerks was another man not unknown to future fame—Igor Gouzenko. "I well remember the first telegram I was given to decipher at Intelligence Headquarters," he wrote. "It came from Harbin [in Manchuria] .... The telegram sounded like a page from a novel, giving minute details of the hiding place [of an agent's radio] in the vicinity of the Governor-General's palace, and described habits of the people living in that district.... The follow-up telegram was then given me for coding. It gave instructions for meeting the pick-up man in Harbin. The actual street corner and the alternative street corner were named together with the time, the day, tokens of recognition and passwords to be used." Gouzenko and his fellow clerks, among them his friend Lieutenant Burukin, sometimes followed agents day after day, living in imagination all the thrills and danger of a spy's life as they routinely deciphered his messages.

Soviet cipher clerks learned their trade at a number of schools. Gouzenko took the basic course at the Kuibishev Military Engineering Academy, where the political director was an owl-eyed former cipher clerk named Maslennikov, nicknamed Kriptus; despite his twisted body and rather pathetic personality, he was a good teacher and knew a lot about cryptography. Gouzenko got advanced training at the Higher Red Army School, generally known as the Intelligence Academy. Cryptography was among the courses taught at the

Red Navy's Electric Mine School at the big base at Kronstadt; here, Petrov, as a young recruit, first studied it two winters and two springs, going to sea during the summers and autumns. The course included some cryptanalysis. Afterwards, he served for two years as senior cipher rating aboard the destroyer *Volodarsky*, where he lived and worked in a small cabin under the bridge. His military service completed, he left the Navy and joined the O.G.P.U. as a cipher clerk. Cryptography may also have been taught in the Red Army's Military School for Signal Communication in Leningrad; this would be for use with the troops. The Army also ran a research institute for communications at Sokolniti in Moscow, which, since it encompassed such exotic studies as cosmic rays, almost certainly included cryptography. In 1937 it merged with another institute into a central scientific research institute for the Red Army.

The strides that the Russian Army had made in cryptography after the traumatic experiences of World War I were dramatized by an interchange of messages between incredulous Russian units at the very start of the Russo-German War. Moments after the Nazis launched their sneak attack at 3:30 a.m. June 22, 1941, a Red outpost wirelessed frantically, "We are being fired on. What shall we do?" Back came the stern reply, "You must be insane. And why is your signal not in code?"

Red Army cryptography rested in World War II upon the enciphered code. The system appeared in four series: 5-digit codes for strategic messages, 4-digit for high-level tactical communications, perhaps of the rank of army headquarters, 3-digit for medium-level tactical, as of brigade rank, and 2-digit for the front. The Soviets replaced their tactical codes frequently, although sometimes a code that had been used in one sector of their thousand-mile front reappeared later in another. The 4-digit codes were enciphered by 10 × 10 tables, one table for the first 2 digits and another for the second pair. The 5-digit codes were enciphered by additive tables of 300 groups changed daily. The Army and Navy shared the 5-digit strategic system; border patrol and N.K.V.D. units had their own systems, usually 4-digit. In addition, the Soviets got some Hagelin M-209s in Lend Lease, which they apparently used as models for their own constructions, though it is not known where these were used.

With enough traffic, enciphered code can of course be read. One of the first to do so in the case of the Russian military was the Swedish expert Arne Beurling. During the bitter struggle of Finland against Russian aggressors in the Winter War of 1939–1940, Sweden fed intelligence based on cryptanalysis to her neighbor. Beurling attacked the top system, the 5-digit strategic, which was actually a 4-digit code with an extra digit added as some form of check. In several of the codes, the page digit—the second—was repeated, so that the groups would look like 52217, 88824, and so on. In others, the fifth digit gave the unit total of the preceding four digits, so that 6432 would have a check digit of 5, making the codegroup 64325. Beurling wrote the cryptograms on a sheet of graph paper with five-millimeter squares that was so large—about 3 × 4 feet—that he had to order it specially. He would make his runs, and, if messages overlapped, he would be on his way.

Soviet strategy against Finland called for a five-pronged invasion along their north–south border. The middle force drove for the tiny village of Suomussalmi to cut Finland at her waist; the force just north of that one rolled on another little village, Salla, in a secondary cut-off. But intelligence developed in the Swedish cryptanalytic office helped the Finns to repulse both Russian attacks.

Crucial to Marshal Mannerheim's victory at Suomussalmi was the information that the Russian 44th Division, a crack motorized outfit from Moscow, was advancing from Raate. He immediately sent reinforcements to Suomussalmi. Two days after his five battalions reached there, the Finns, dressed in white and moving like the ghosts of the north, attacked the Russian forces in the village, broke their resistance, and forced them to flee across frozen Lake Kiantajärvi. The skiing wraiths then cut off the retreat of the 44th Division, severed its column and destroyed it section by section in fighting that continued into the first week of 1940. Large quantities of stores were captured, but, Mannerheim wrote, "The enemy's casualties could not be estimated, as great snowdrifts over a large area covered the fallen as well as the wounded who were frozen to death."

Temperatures during the battle dropped to 56 degrees below zero, and it was under such conditions that the Swedes solved some pitiful messages from isolated Russian units. One encircled group radioed that they were burning their papers and were going to shoot their last horse for food, and that this was their final message. Silence followed, and soon thereafter the Swedish cryptanalysts learned that the Finns had crushed them. Another Russian battalion sent a coded message that they were desperately short of supplies and would build three fires in a triangle to show the Red Air Force where to parachute desperately needed food and ammunition. The Swedes solved it and gave it to the Finns, who built a triangle of fires and watched with bitter satisfaction as the packages floated down into it.

Swarms of Russian Air Force cryptograms were downed by the Swedish codebreakers. Many were orders to bomb Helsinki, and often these were solved before the bombers took off from airfields in Latvia and Estonia for the 20-minute flight to their target. Finnish authorities thus had ample time to sound air-raid alerts; as a result the capital suffered exceptionally light civilian casualties considering the number of bombs dropped.

But little Finland was no match for the colossal U.S.S.R. despite her cryptologic advantages, and in March she signed a peace treaty. When the Germans invaded Russia a year later, Finland declared war against her harasser and later exchanged cryptographic intercepts with her new ally.

German radio intelligence against the Soviet Union appears to have been characterized by a severe split. Strategically it enjoyed no success at all. The Germans did not solve the cryptosystems of the top Soviet military commands —primarily the 5-digit codes. Perhaps by 1941 the Russians had corrected their cryptographic technique enough to keep the Germans from repeating the 1939 Swedish successes. Whatever the reason, cryptanalysis contributed little to O.K.W.'s overall picture of Russian strategy.

Tactically, however, the Germans reaped rich harvests of intelligence. In mid-1940, when Hitler first decided to attack the Soviet Union, Germany had no radio-intelligence service of any kind in the East; a year later, when Hitler struck, the new intercept service had already provided him with good information on Russian order of battle. In July, a captured Russian Air Force captain betrayed one of the Air Force systems. This intelligence windfall helped the Luftwaffe destroy hundreds of Soviet airplanes on the ground and another hundred in a great air battle over Minsk.

The resultant air superiority, plus surprise, momentum, armor, and speed, carried the Wehrmacht forward in a surge of victories. In 1941 and again in 1942 Germany mounted massive offensives and overran vast areas of Russia. But in the winter of 1942-43, Stalingrad held and the German 6th Army capitulated; at the same time, Germany lifted the two-year siege of Leningrad. By next summer, it had become evident that Nazidom could not win its great victory over Bolshevism, but the troops hoped at least for a stalemate that would stabilize their conquests. The high command decided on some limited attacks to cripple Soviet offensive power. With the waning of Luftwaffe air mastery, Nazi intelligence had to depend less upon aerial reconnaissance and more upon wireless surveillance. In tactical operations during the Battle of the Dnieper in October, 1943, the chief of staff of the 48th Panzer Corps declared, "The best and most reliable source of intelligence was our Wireless Intercept Service."

A few months later, that corps participated in one of the attacks that Army Group South, one of the three major German groupings on the Eastern Front, mounted to flatten the Kiev salient and further forestall Soviet offensive propensities. The 48th Panzer Corps had as its objective the disruption of the Russian 60th Army. Air reconnaissance produced no information, and the corps decided not to send out ground scouts for fear of alerting the Russians. The attack at 6 a.m. December 6 completely surprised the Russians, who recoiled in confusion.

> In those days [wrote the corps' chief of staff, Colonel F. W. von Mellenthin] we were really good at intercepting Russian wireless traffic; enemy messages were promptly deciphered and passed to Corps in time to act on them. We were kept well informed of Russian reactions to our movements, and the measures they proposed to take, and we modified our own plans accordingly. At first the Russians underestimated the importance of the German thrust. Later a few antitank guns were thrown into the fray. Then slowly the Russian Command

got worried. Wireless calls became frantic. "Report at once where the enemy comes from. Your message is unbelievable." Reply: "Ask the Devil's grandmother; how should I know where the enemy comes from?" (Whenever the Devil and his near relations are mentioned in Russian signals one can assume that a crack-up is at hand.) Towards noon the Russian 60th Army went off the air, and soon afterwards our tanks overran the army headquarters.

By that evening the Germans had rolled up the Russian front for 20 miles, and by the night of December 9 the Soviets' projected offensive was jolted thoroughly off balance. In the next few days additional blows punished them further. "The Russians were certainly flabbergasted by these ghost-like thrusts, which seemed to come from nowhere, and their wireless traffic provided abundant evidence of their bewilderment and anxiety," Mellenthin wrote.

This German victory at the Battle of Radomyshl delayed but did not prevent the Russian offense. At Christmas, Army Group South began its retreat from the Ukraine. Several months later the Russians had driven the Germans back 650 miles from their farthest penetration.

Mellenthin has remarked that "The Red Army of World War II was vastly different from the Imperial Russian Army of 1914–17, but in two important respects the Russians have not changed. They are still addicted to mass attacks, and they still show an extraordinary indifference to wireless security." This comment seems to hold true only in a tactical sense, and the adjective "extraordinary" is probably justified only under conditions of retreat and its accompanying confusion.

Army Group North, for example, read 5-digit code messages very rarely. Of the intercepts in 2-, 3-, and 4-digit codes, it read 28.7 per cent—13,312 messages out of 46,342 from the beginning of May, 1943, to the end of May, 1944, a year in which the Russians pushed back the northern sector of the front slightly, though not nearly as much as the southern. A month-by-month and system-by-system breakdown of the cryptanalytic success of Army Group North (excluding 5-digit codes) is shown in the table on p. 648.

As might be expected, the 2-digit systems, being the simplest, succumbed the oftenest. However, fewer 3-digit than the presumably more difficult 4-digit enciphered codes were solved, even though more 3-digit messages were picked up. The reasons for this seem to lie partly in the probable concentration on the information-rich 4-digit messages, partly in the many more 3-digit systems in use and the consequent difficulty of finding overlaps to strip off the additive and of getting sufficient text for solutions. This multiplicity of 3-digit systems can be seen in the number of new 3-digit systems reported solved each month by the cryptanalysts, which is invariably greater than the number of new 4-digit systems. In November, 1943, for example, Army Group North solved 15 new 3-digit systems as compared to one 4-digit; in December, the figures were 8 and 4, in January, 1944, 15 and 8. The cryptanalysts do not give the number of new systems introduced by the Soviets that the Germans did not solve.

Germany's Army Group North solutions of Russian Army messages, May 1943 to May 1944

month	daily average intercepts	overall messages intercepted	overall messages solved	overall % solved	4-digit messages intercepted	4-digit messages solved	4-digit % solved	4-digit new systems solved	3-digit messages intercepted	3-digit messages solved	3-digit % solved	3-digit new systems solved	2-digit messages intercepted	2-digit messages solved	2-digit % solved	2-digit new systems solved
May 1943	153	4,732	1,629	34	1,813	760	42		1,873	201	11		1,046	668	64	
June	120	3,603	1,330	37	1,530	789	52		1,422	154	11		651	387	59	
July	102	3,178	1,349	42	1,114	498	45		1,396	449	32		668	402	60	
August	67	2,079	909	43	619	286	46	6	1,163	409	35	8	297	214	72	
September	60	1,789	269	15	655	150	23	3	1,009	80	7	5	125	39	31	
October	78	2,404	467	19	931	252	27		1,356	162	11	5	117	53	45	
November	78	2,182	398	18	850	144	17	4	1,210	196	16	8	122	58	46	2
December	91	2,810	482	17	1,174	242	21	1	1,536	194	14	15	100	46	46	6
January 1944	152	4,724	1,074	23	1,593	467	30	4	3,005	528	18	8	126	79	63	3
February	178	5,175	1,217	24				8				15				
March	179	5,563	1,833	33	no figures available				no figures available				no figures available			
April	130	3,897	1,000	26												
May	136	4,206	1,355	32												
TOTALS	117	46,342	13,312	28.7	10,279	3,588	34.9		13,970	2,373	16.9		3,252	1,946	59.8	

Blanks in "new systems solved" columns mean that no data were given, not that no new systems were solved

Русская Криптология

Solved messages, said the cryptanalysts' report for February, 1944, "contain operational combat reports, statements about assembly areas, command posts, loss and replacement reports, reports about chain of command and positions prepared for the attack (e.g., messages of the 122nd Armored Brigade on February 14 and 17). Besides these reports, the plaintexts of the messages made possible the identification of seven armored units, including their numerical designations, as well as confirmation of twelve armored units. With few exceptions the material could be worked up in good time and put to use."

A Russian World War II military message partially solved by German cryptanalysts

These tactical solutions could, at best, produce local successes. The apparent failure of German cryptanalysts to solve Russia's strategic cryptosystems, with the valuable information that they concealed, led one German cryptanalyst to adjudge that Russia lost World War I in the ether and won World War II there.

A truth he never suspected may lurk in his apothegm. For the Russians may have done as well in solving German cryptograms as in protecting their own. By 1942 they had cracked messages in the Enigma, a rotor machine. And the Germans themselves paid a left-handed tribute to Soviet cryptanalytic perspicacity when a 1943 conference of signal officers ruefully ordered: "It is forbidden to mark the Führer's radio messages in any special way."

At the same time, the Soviet Union guarded her diplomatic flanks by the one-time pad, a practice she had begun in 1930. Consequently her crucial Foreign Office messages were read by neither foes, nor neutrals, nor allies. Any schemes that she may have instigated against those who, at the end of the war, were to become either her puppets or her adversaries remained among the most inviolate of her secrets.

During World War II, the secret prospectors of the G.R.U. and the N.K.V.D. drilled for information in scores of places all over the world. Three of the spy crews struck gushers of it. The fabulous "Lucy" network in Switzerland, the Rote Kapelle in Germany, and the Sorge ring in Japan pumped a continuous stream of the most detailed and precise intelligence into the Kremlin. And this they did through a pipeline that, despite the most strenuous bangings and poundings of counterintelligence, remained hermetically sealed against cryptanalysis. All three rings employed the then-standard Soviet espionage cipher. It achieved a triumph of encipherment, for it is a system that the spymasters of the Soviet Union rightly regarded as unbreakable.

It brought the old Nihilist substitution to a peak of perfection. It merged the straddling checkerboard with the one-time key.

It increased the efficiency of the checkerboard by specifically giving the high-frequency letters the single digits. This cut down the length of the cryptograms and hence time on the air. Both Max Clausen, radio operator for the Sorge net, and Alexander Foote of the Swiss ring, enciphered in English, and consequently they used the eight most common letters of that language. They memorized them by the rather ominous phrase "a sin to er(r)." However, the sequence of those letters played no part in the construction of the key alphabet.

For that construction, a keyword was selected. Clausen used SUBWAY. The encipherer wrote this out, followed by the rest of the alphabet in rows beneath it, with a full stop and a letter-number switch sign at the end. Then the digits 0 to 7 were assigned to ASINTOER as they occurred vertically in columns from left to right. Finally the two-digit groups from 80 to 99 were assigned to the remaining letters and symbols, also vertically:

```
 S  U  B  W  A  Y
 0 82 87 91  5 97
 C  D  E  F  G  H
80 83  3 92 95 98
 I  J  K  L  M  N
 1 84 88 93 96  7
 O  P  Q  R  T  V
 2 85 89  4  6 99
 X  Z  .  /
81 86 90 94
```

These equivalents can be placed into the more compact checkerboard:

	0	1	2	3	4	5	6	7	8	9
	s	i	o	e	r	a	t	n		
8	c	x	u	d	j	p	z	b	k	q
9	.	w	f	l	/	g	m	y	h	v

The encipherer next replaced his plaintext with his checkerboard equivalents. For numbers, he enciphered the switch sign, then repeated the digits twice, then enciphered the switch sign again to indicate a return to letters:

```
w  h  e r i s / 1 0 6 / d i v i s i o n
91 98 3 4 3 1 0 94 11 00 66 94 83 1 99 1 0 1 2 7
```

The next step enshrouded this simple text by adding a numerical key—an operation called "closing." Clausen and Foote took their keynumbers directly from a common reference book with many tables, like the *World Almanac*, possession of which would not necessarily be suspicious. Foote used a book of Swiss trade statistics, Clausen the 1935 edition of the *Statistisches Jahrbuch für das Deutsches Reich*—the main section, on white pages, for enciphering, the international survey section, on separately numbered green-tinted pages in the rear, for deciphering.

The message requesting information about the 106th Division resembles one actually sent to the Sorge ring on March 3, 1940. Since Clausen would be deciphering it, it was enciphered in Moscow with an additive from the green pages of the *Statistisches Jahrbuch*. The encipherer picked at random the group at the 11th row in the 3rd column of page 171. That group happens to give the thousands of metric tons of foundry products fabricated for railroad construction in Luxembourg in 1931, which was 113. The encipherer began, as an enciphering rule required, with the third digit, 3, and then ran along that line in the table, taking his other keydigits from the production figures for Belgium, France, Great Britain, and so on for 1931 and succeeding years: 134, 534, 517, and so on. These digits he wrote beneath the checkerboard encipherment and added them with noncarrying addition to produce the cipher:

```
checkerboard "plain"  9 1 9 8 3 4 3 1 0 9 4 1 1 0 0 6 6 9 4 8 3 1 9 9 1 0 1 2 7
key                   3 1 3 4 5 3 4 5 1 7 1 8 3 1 2 8 1 1 9 5 1 1 0 4 1 8 8 4 7

cipher                2 2 2 2 8 7 7 6 1 6 5 9 4 1 2 4 7 0 3 3 4 2 9 3 2 8 9 6 4
```

The encipherer divided this into groups of five, 22228 77616 59412 47033 42932 8964, with perhaps a 0 at the end to fill out the group. He then composed an indicator group to tell the decipherer where to find the key: 11 for the row, 3 for the column, 71 for the page (hundreds figures were omitted; presumably the decipherer would have to try page 71 or 271 if page 171's key did not make sense). To conceal this indicator group, 11371, the encipherer added to it, by noncarrying addition, the fourth group from the beginning of the message, 47033, and the fourth group from the end, 59412, to give 07716. He placed this group at the head of the message and gave it to the radioman to send.

This was the standard Soviet spy cipher of World War II. Later in the war, when Foote was enciphering, a few minor improvements had been made to improve reliability and security. Numbers were repeated three times instead of twice. Instead of just one enciphered indicator group, two were used. Foote composed them by adding the plain page-column-line indicator to a fixed group (his was 69696) and then, for the first enciphered indicator, he added this sum to the fifth ciphertext group from the beginning, and, for the second, to the fifth ciphertext group from the end. He then inserted these enciphered indicator groups as the third group and the third from last group of the final cryptogram.

Other Soviet spies, however, used a variation of this basic system that was both more complicated and less secure. It generated the key digits from the text of an ordinary book by enciphering that text in a checkerboard. The Rote Kapelle used this variation (when the Germans discovered one of the keybooks, a unit of the Rote Kapelle wirelessed, "Klaus has the Bible"). So did some members of Foote's Swiss ring, who used *Es geschah im September* ("It Happened in September"), and Bertil E. G. Eriksson, a Soviet spy arrested in Sweden in 1941, who used a 1940 Swedish edition of Jaroslav Hasek's *The Good Soldier Schweik*.

The first words of Eriksson's keytext also served to construct his keying checkerboard. For one such construction, Eriksson chose to begin at page 12, line 3, word 4: "PAUS, SOM SVEJK SJÄLV AVBRÖT...." He inscribed the first ten different letters into a straddling checkerboard as its first line and followed them on other rows with the remaining letters of the alphabet. He then produced a numerical key for the top coordinates by numbering the letters in the top row from 0 to 9 according to their alphabetical position. The first line was given no side coordinates; the two other lines got their coordinates from those standing above the first and last blank spaces in the last line. The result:

```
    6 0 8 7 5 4 9 1 2 3
    P A U S O M V E J K
  9 B C D F G H I L N Q
  3 R T W X Y Z
```

He then began his keytext with the third letter of the first word of the keyline, and enciphered Hasek's words to produce his additive: "[DE]T BLEV EN PAUS, SOM SVEJK SJÄLV AVBRÖT MED..." became 30 96 91 1 9 1 92 6, 0 8 77 54 79 1 2 3 72 0 91 9 0 9 96 36 5 30 4 1 98.... Eriksson added this to

Soviet spy Bertil E. G. Eriksson enciphers a message for Moscow in 1941. The upper line is the additive key, produced by enciphering through a straddling checkerboard a text beginning at page 12, line 3, word 1, letter 3, of a 1940 Swedish edition of Jaroslav Hasek's The Good Soldier Schweik; *the lower line is the plaintext, in Russian, based on a straddling checkerboard with key GAMBUSIA* a numerical plaintext produced via a Russian straddling checkerboard of 35 cells based on the keyword GAMBUSIA (a genus of minnows) and with seven high-frequency Russian letters given single digits.

This variant of the standard system is not unbreakable. The use of a coherent keytext gives the cryptanalyst a leverage which enables him to mutually recover both it and the plaintext. The straddling feature, the irregular lengths of the plain and key elements, destroys the ordinary one-to-one correspondence between plain, cipher, and key and makes his work more difficult than if an ordinary checkerboard had been used; nevertheless, solution is possible. It is probably not possible analytically with trade statistics as a key. Though such keys are not ideal because they may contain certain regularities owing to recurrent annual figures and because they are public, they certainly offer adequate security.

How did this standard Soviet system, so simple but so strong, serve Russia during World War II?

Dr. Richard Sorge, a tall, stocky man with malevolent eyes, worked in Japan as a correspondent for Germany's finest newspaper, the *Frankfurter Zeitung*. A member of the Nazi party, he was an intimate of the German ambassador, Eugen Ott, with whom he had been friends since Ott had been assistant military attaché. Sorge even served as press attaché for the German embassy, and, while breakfasting with Ott, read and discussed papers and policies with him. Then he passed this high-level intelligence to Germany's avowed enemy, the Soviet Union. For the efficient Germans had somehow failed to discover that Sorge's grandfather had been secretary to Karl Marx and that he himself was a dedicated Communist.

Sorge had directed a Soviet spy ring in Shanghai from 1929 to 1931, and the ability he had demonstrated, plus his interest in the Far East, caused the G.R.U. to send him to Japan two years later under his journalistic cover. His assignment was to ascertain the intentions of Japan, Russia's former enemy and only rival in the Western Pacific and holder of an Oriental dagger that she could plunge into Russia's back. Sorge painstakingly built up his own contacts and recruited agents among the Japanese. His most important catch was Hotsumi Ozaki, who was a kind of Harry Hopkins to Prince Konoye, thrice premier of Japan. Sorge thus had a direct pipeline into the highest councils of the Japanese government, while he himself had access to the best information and opinions of Japan's ally. In addition, more than two dozen other Japanese supplied important bits of military and economic intelligence.

Sorge sent this information to Russia by film through couriers and by radio. His radio operator was Max G. F. Clausen, a heavy-set German with pleasant features and curly hair who had served as a radioman in the German signal corps during World War I and had worked with Sorge in Shanghai. As cover, he sold machinery for blueprint reproduction in a private enterprise that was so phenomenally successful that it severely shook his faith in

Communism: in 1941, he sent only a third of the messages that Sorge gave him. But at first he performed miracles in establishing and maintaining radio contact over very long distances with a portable transmitter that he had built himself. He set it up for sending, and dismantled it and carried it away in a large briefcase after each transmission. This almost backfired one night when he and another agent had the radio in its case with them and were stopped by a policeman. "My heart jumped at the thought that we had been discovered," he wrote. "For some reason or other, the policeman merely remarked, 'Your headlights are out; be careful,' and walked away without examining our baggage or searching us."

With the approach of war, the Sorge ring accelerated its communications. Transmissions, which had been made irregularly, began in 1938 to be made regularly: on odd days and Sundays at 3 p.m. and the following mornings at 10. Clausen sent to a Russian station codenamed WIESBADEN, which he thought was probably in Vladivostok, possibly in Khabarovsk or Komsomolsk; the messages were relayed from there to Moscow. At first Clausen merely transmitted already coded messages, but after Sorge was in a motorcycle accident in 1938, he obtained permission from Moscow to teach Clausen the cipher system.

"I always encoded and decoded at my home in a room used only by myself," the radio operator wrote. "Usually I was warned of visitors by the ring of the doorbell so that I could clean up my papers before receiving them. On three occasions, my Japanese employees saw the code but did not seem to pay any attention to it. Once, when I was in bed [this appears to refer to his being bedridden from April to August, 1941, by a heart ailment] and encoding a message (employing a special board which enabled me to work in a reclining position), Dr. Wurtz, who was always shown in by the maid, suddenly appeared at my bedside alone. He glanced down at the code chart suspiciously but merely said, 'You must not do any writing until you get well,' went through a routine checkup, and departed. For several days I was afraid that he might have informed the police, but nothing came of it." His messages went out in English, sometimes German, never Russian—to conceal the true allegiance of the ring.

Sorge had discovered not only that Germany was planning to attack Russia, but also the approximate date. Stalin ignored the information, as he had other invasion tips, and was taken by surprise. With the war on, the moment for which Sorge and his ring had prepared ever since their arrival in Japan was at hand. They bent every effort to discover the one piece of information that both Sorge and the Soviet government considered the most vital to Russia's conduct of the war, perhaps, in fact, to her very existence: Would Japan attack Russia at this moment of weakness and "shake hands with Hitler in the Urals," or would she pursue her already well-laid plans to conquer Malaya and the Dutch East Indies with their rubber and oil? Japan made her decision in deepest secrecy at a cabinet meeting of July 2 in the presence of the Emperor. As hints and portions of it leaked out, the ring sent Russia increasing amounts of information.

In 1939, Clausen sent 23,139 cipher groups, in 1940, 29,179, and though, in 1941, increasingly disillusioned with Communism, he sent only 13,301, Sorge more than took up the slack, himself sending 40,000 groups. Much of this traffic was intercepted by Japanese counterespionage police. The Communications Ministry, the Tokyo Metropolitan Communications Bureau, the Osaka Communications Bureau, and the Communications Bureau of the Governor General of Korea had all been aware since at least 1938 that an illegal radio was transmitting from the Tokyo area. Japanese cryptanalysts failed utterly to solve the messages, and their radio policemen failed equally to locate the clandestine transmitter. These two failures precluded the Japanese both from rounding up the ring and from feeding it false information.

Various political considerations made it gradually clearer to Sorge that Japan had decided against marching to meet Hitler. Throughout the summer, as German columns rolled across the steppes, he communicated these developments to Moscow. Finally, Ozaki confirmed the decision for the southward advance and against war with Russia, and, early in October, Sorge reported his final sober conclusion: "There will be no attack until the spring of next year at the earliest." The Soviet Union had begun drawing troops from its eastern reservoirs of manpower as Sorge's reports grew increasingly optimistic. Now, just as his definitive message was reaching Moscow, the Germans launched an all-out two-pronged attack to capture the Russian capital before winter.

The Red command, no longer fearing a Japanese stab in the back, reduced its Far Eastern garrison by 15 infantry and 3 cavalry divisions and by 1,700 tanks and 1,500 planes. It transported these troops, which Germany thought it could not possibly possess, across the biggest country in the world to its Western Front. These fresh troops, plus the worsening winter, slowed the German advance, but the Germans repeatedly punched holes in the horseshoe of the city's defenses with "fists" of massed armor. On December 2, they reached the suburb of Khimki: in the distance, the onion domes of the Kremlin cathedrals pricked the leaden sky! The next day, Marshal Georgi Zhukov flung his newly arrived reserves into a furious counterattack, and, aided by weather 13 degrees below zero, drove the half-frozen Nazis back. Within five days, Berlin announced the suspension of the eastern offensive. Moscow had not fallen. The ikon of Holy Russia still stood.

Not so Sorge. A Japanese who was not in his ring had been arrested on suspicion of Communist activities. To ingratiate himself, he told of suspicious activities by a woman who was a member of the ring. Her confession led, through a long chain, to the arrest of Ozaki on October 15 and of Sorge and Clausen on the 18th. Clausen broke down under interrogation and disclosed the cipher system; the Japanese, finally able to read the tantalizing messages, produced them as damning evidence in the trial. Clausen was sentenced to life imprisonment. Ozaki and Sorge were hanged 50 minutes apart on November 7, 1944. But, more than most men, they had fulfilled their missions.

Perhaps the most widespread of the Soviet networks was one the Germans called the Rote Kapelle (the "Red Orchestra"). Its tentacles slithered into the most secret tabernacles of Naziism, and its loose ramifications covered much of Germany and occupied Europe. It derived its name from the steady hum of the "music boxes"—Soviet term for radio transmitters—in Berlin, Paris, Brussels, Ostend, Marseilles and elsewhere that piped out the coded information of 300 agents. Its maestro was Harro Schulze-Boysen, a Luftwaffe lieutenant in the Forschungsamt who came from an impeccable German family that included Admiral von Tirpitz; he had himself moved gradually from a conservative anti-Naziism to pro-Communism. Concertmaster was the fortyish Arvid Harnack, nephew of the influential theological historian, Adolf von Harnack. And the manager was Leopold Trepper, "grand chef" of Soviet espionage in the West, a professional spy director who had established himself at Paris under the cover of the Simex Corporation.

The organization that he built up under Schulze-Boysen and Harnack remained latent until the Germans crossed the border on June 22, 1941. Instantly Moscow demanded information on German plans. The Rote Kapelle sprang to life. Soon the cricketlike chorus of its Morse transmitters filled the ether with their incessant chirpings of five-digit groups.

In Cranz, in East Prussia, the antennae of the Funkabwehr, the Nazi radio counterespionage, quivered. The first message was intercepted June 26. Attempts to solve it and those that followed failed. Tracking down the transmitters themselves was hindered by a shortage of equipment: the Funkabwehr then had only six long-range direction-finders. Not until October did it ascertain that Moscow was receipting for the messages. Not until December did it pinpoint its first Rote Kapelle station. On the night of the 13th, a troop of soldiers wearing socks over their boots silently climbed to the second floor of a villa at 101 Rue des Attrebates in Brussels. They broke into the radio room and arrested the cryptographer-radioman, Mikhail Makarov, a Russian Air Force lieutenant and a relative of Soviet Foreign Minister Vyacheslav Molotov, and two other agents. At this very moment, Trepper himself arrived. But with superhuman aplomb, he passed himself off as—of all things—a rabbit vendor, and was not apprehended.

The Germans also found in the fireplace of the villa a charred piece of paper covered with numbers; it was obviously an enciphering worksheet. German cryptanalysts immediately began to study it. Makarov refused to talk, and it was not until six weeks later that the first significant information emerged. It was part of a sentence in French that seemed more like a fragment of keytext than of plaintext, and it contained the word PROCTOR. The Funkabwehr questioned the landlady, a naïve elderly widow, who named eleven books that she had seen her tenants reading. In *Le miracle du Professeur*

Wolmar, a 286-page science-fiction novel by Guy de Teramond, the Nazis found PROCTOR.

Suddenly the Germans saw the magnitude of what they were faced with. The Teramond key unlocked 120 messages of what had been the busiest Rote Kapelle station. These had warned Moscow of Germany's spring offensive in the Caucasus, reported on Luftwaffe strength, provided data on army fuel consumption and casualties, and furnished similar other vital information. But all names were codenames; the three arrested agents either would not or could not give links to the rest of the network. The Funkabwehr redoubled its efforts.

Trepper, however, after his melodramatic evasion, had alerted the other members of the Rote Kapelle. Couriers brought them new keys. Soon the orchestra was playing with renewed volume. Many of the numbers were requests by Moscow:

> To GILBERT [codename for Trepper] from Director. Check whether Guderian [German panzer general] really at Eastern front. Are the 2d and 3d Armies under his command? . . .

> To GILBERT from Director. Report about 26 armored divisions being formed in France.

The intelligence came from informants throughout the entire Nazi regime. Schulze-Boysen himself was pivotally located in the Forschungsamt. Harnack held a high post in the Economics Ministry as an expert on the Soviet Union. The Rote Kapelle had sources in—among others—the Foreign Office, the Luftwaffe's counterintelligence, the labor and propaganda ministries, and, in the person of young Horst Heilmann, an apostate from Naziism, in the cryptanalytic office of the Army. The arrhythmic monotone of its radio transmitters made beautiful music to Moscow. They sang to the Russians of German plans to encircle Leningrad instead of occupying it, of exact times of German parachute raids, of monthly aircraft production, of a Soviet code found at Petsamo in Finland, Luftwaffe losses, Luftwaffe production, capabilities of a new Messerschmidt fighter, production of synthetic fuel, foreign policy developments, political opposition to Naziism, troop movements along the Dnieper. The Russian bear performed to these tunes, knowing just where and how to claw and slash the Nazi forces.

The Funkabwehr monitors listened as this symphony reverberated through the ether. To them, it was cacophony. The cryptograms remained impervious. But the transmitters could be tracked down, and on June 30, 1942, another Belgian group, headed by a veteran Communist agent, Johann Wenzel, whose thorough knowledge of radio techniques had earned him the sobriquet "The Professor," was raided in Brussels; Wenzel was nabbed in front of his set. The Gestapo took over, and what the most energetic mental thumping of an impersonal string of numbers had not done, a moderate physical truncheoning of human flesh did. The Professor's wide acquaintance with Soviet spy communications soon had the Funkabwehr translating its file of back intercepts. In one of them, almost a year old, they read the true addresses of Schulze-Boysen and Harnack. . . .

Of all Soviet networks during the war, by far the most important was the Swiss. It owed its supremacy in part to its location in neutral Switzerland, where it operated for a long time out of reach of the German Abwehr, and in part to having in the network the agent codenamed LUCY, whom many regarded as the greatest spy of the war. This was Rudolf Rössler, a small, quiet, bespectacled German publisher of leftist Catholic books whose codename came from his residence in Lucerne. His sources appear to have been ten World War I companions, all German officers, five of whom became generals and served at least part of the time in the Oberkommando der Wehrmacht. One was General Fritz Thiele, who had the O.K.W.'s Chiffrierabteilung under him and who, as No. 2 man in the O.K.W. signal organization, used its facilities to radio messages to Rössler. Thus he procured intelligence of exalted importance and precise accuracy with dazzling speed from the very heart of the German High Command itself.

Head of the ring was Alexander Rado, a cartographer whose maps appeared daily in the Swiss newspapers. A Hungarian Communist, he had been sent to Switzerland to set up a ring in 1936. Second in command and chief radioman was Alexander Foote, a bearlike, unperturbable Englishman in his mid-thirties who pretended to be living in Switzerland on independent funds to escape military service. Early in 1941 he installed in his flat at 2 Chemin de Longeraie, Lausanne, the radio station that was to be known as JIM. On March 12, after a thousand tappings of the call-sign FRX, he heard the Moscow Centre calling him through the crackle of static and the background noise of other transmissions: NDA NDA OK QRK 5, the latter meaning in the radio Q code that his signals were being heard very strongly.

The Swiss group produced results quickly. One night in the middle of June, Foote sent off to Moscow a brief but vital message:

> DORA [codename for Rado] to Director, via Taylor [a courier]. Hitler has definitely set June 22 for attack on Russia.

This had no more effect on Stalin than had Sorge's information, for Stalin evidently regarded the obvious community of interest between Hitler and himself in subduing England and dismembering her empire as outweighing information from two individuals. The incident spotlights one of the most difficult problems in the assessment of intelligence: credibility.

At first Foote contacted Moscow only twice a week. But when the Russo-German war broke out, he was informed that the Centre would be listening to him round the clock. Priorities were established: VYRDO for exceedingly urgent messages, RDO for urgent, and MSG for routine. Moscow was always in a hurry for information, and Foote, who operated as a sort of loner, transmitted most of the LUCY material and received the VYRDO messages pertaining to it.

For two years his life fell into a routine that indicates the unglamorous ways of a spy. After a night of enciphering and radioing, he rose about 10, spent the morning maintaining his pose of emigré Englishman and the afternoon journeying to meet a cut-out, or courier, at some unobserved place. "Having returned," he wrote, "I usually had a long evening's ciphering before me. According to the rules, all ciphering should have been done after dark and behind locked doors. But needs must when the Centre drove and in the more hectic times I was enciphering in all my spare moments." During his active period, Foote sent 2,000 messages, or about six a day. They averaged 100 words each.

Contact with the Centre was made on a fixed wavelength. The Centre would reply on its fixed length. Both would then switch to another wavelength with a different call-sign for the evening's work. "My transmission time was usually about one in the morning," Foote wrote, "If conditions were good and the message short I was through in about a couple of hours. If, as frequently happened, I had long messages to send and atmospherics were bad I had to fight my way through and send when and as conditions allowed. Often on such occasions I was still at the transmitter at six and once or twice I 'signed off' at nine in the morning. . . . To be on the air for that length of time broke all the normal precautions against radio monitoring. But it was a chance which had to be taken if the intelligence was to be passed over, a risk which the Centre took despite frequent admonitions by Rado and me."

As the Germans approached Moscow, communications became increasingly difficult, and suddenly, at twelve hours' notice to the senior staff and none at all to its radio agents, the Centre was wrenched from its office and shifted 550 miles southeast to Kuibyshev. The move very nearly wrecked the Swiss ring. "On October 19," Foote wrote, "Moscow went off the air in the middle of a message. Night after night Rado and I called, and night after night there was no reply. Rado was in despair and talked of going over to the British. . . . Suddenly one night at the scheduled time—and six weeks after the break—the Centre piped up. As if nothing had happened, they finished the message that they had cut off halfway through, a month and a half before."

The information that the Centre's receivers pulled in from the Swiss network was valuable in the extreme. For Rössler provided the Russian general staff with nothing less than the day-to-day German order of battle. This told the Russians just which forces were opposing them. How heavily they relied on it can be demonstrated by a negative case in which Lucy's information was erroneous or falsified (just how this happened is not known). It dealt with troop dispositions, and, the Director told Foote after the war, it "cost us a hundred thousand men at Kharkov and resulted in the Germans reaching Stalingrad." Such total dependence suggests that many of the Russian war victories owed their success to Rössler's intelligence. Foote, in fact, believes that "Moscow very largely fought the war on Lucy's messages."

As with the Sorge network and the Rote Kapelle, the cipher in which this information was encapsulated could not be broken. The Funkabwehr and the Swiss police, the Bupo, intercepted hundreds of messages and read none. The Funkabwehr found that the transmissions were coming from Switzerland, where it had no power to make arrests, and the Bupo, which did have the power, at first was disinclined to do so in the case of an anti-Nazi group. For more than a year they left the ring alone, but German pressure finally compelled them to act. In October, 1943, two of the Swiss transmitters were raided by the Bupo, and at 1:15 a.m. on November 20, as Foote was taking down a long message from Moscow, "there was a splintering crash and my room was filled with police.... I was arrested and the last link between the Centre and Switzerland was broken." But its work was completed. Though another year and a half was to elapse before Germany surrendered, the issue was no longer in doubt; in the future shone the ultimate victory.

Russia's wartime allies had never ceased to be her espionage targets, and peace enabled her to concentrate on them again. Soviet espionage scored most spectacularly with the atomic spies Klaus Fuchs and Allan Nunn May, but it did not neglect lesser fry. As the Iron Curtain clanged down and the Cold War grew gelid, secret agents were planted here and there throughout the free and uncommitted worlds. The Soviet spy net covered the globe. To direct it, to protect it, and to harvest its catch, an elaborate system of secret communications was required. Often the node of a spy ring was the Russian embassy, and here security began with physical safeguards.

In Canada, the cryptographic keys used by cipher clerk Igor Gouzenko were kept in a sealed bag that was placed each night inside a steel safe that was within an eight-room suite, closed by double steel doors and with iron bars and steel shutters on the white-opaqued windows, that was on the second floor of a separate wing of the brick embassy building, which was surrounded by a fence. In Australia, where Vladimir Petrov handled the espionage cryptography, the key to the safe in which his cipher documents were stored was kept in an envelope sealed with wax and a signet and locked inside the general embassy safe. The cipher suite here consisted of four rooms, two outer ones, which served for general embassy purposes, and two inner sanctums, a kind of holy of holies, in which the clerks enciphered the espionage messages. In the desk of the chief cipher clerk in an outer room, Petrov saw four revolvers in a drawer. Both embassies had stoves in which to burn cryptographic worksheets and other secret documents. In the 1960s, the Washington embassy kept chemicals at hand that could eat through a thick stack of paper in seconds; in an emergency, this is much faster than trying to stuff wads into the incinerator. Just how seriously the Russians take their security is illustrated by the fact that on New Year's Day, 1956, they preferred to let flames gut the embassy in Ottawa rather than admit Canadian firemen to the grounds and, officials said, risk foreigners' seeing their codes and ciphers.

For transmission, documents are photographed and the films—undeveloped, so that a thief's illegitimate opening of them in the light would ruin them—sent in the diplomatic pouch. This procedure is followed for messages both to and from the embassy. When the 35-millimeter film arrives from Moscow, clerks develop it, make a single enlarged print from each frame, and destroy the negative. When Moscow acknowledges receipt of an embassy film, the embassy burns the original documents. The film for the secret police may come in a packet marked P.M.V., the initial letters of the Russian office of weights and measures. Late in the 1950s, the Russians began taking the precaution of using a locked container that automatically spilled acid onto the undeveloped film if anyone tampered with it. New cipher keys are sent by diplomatic bag; they are in an envelope, addressed to the secret police official, which is sealed inside an outer envelope addressed to the ambassador himself.

Those keys are one-time pads—in the old-fashioned manual form. Although the several branches of a Soviet mission—diplomatic, secret police, military, commercial, and political (Communist party)—all have their own keys and (in the larger embassies) cipher clerks, all probably use this system. All cables coming into the legation look alike: simple groups of five digits. The chief cipher clerk applies a key to the last group; it might decipher out as 66666, which on one day might mean that the message belonged to G.R.U., another day, K.G.B., another day, the trade section.

The one-time pads also play a role in the photographed letters. These are composed in plain Russian using the semisecret jargon of espionage—PACKING to mean *ciphering*, OPEN PACKING to mean *plaintext*, BANK for *hiding place*. In addition, specifically assigned codenames are used to cover real identities. For example, in Canada, Colonel Zabotin, the military attaché, was GRANT, and ALEK stood for Allan Nunn May. (How successfully such codenames work may be seen in Canada's *Report of the Royal Commission* on the Soviet spy ring, in which the commissioners conceded that "we have been unable to identify the following persons named under 'cover-names' in the documents and there definitely stated to have been members of Zabotin's ring: GALYA, GINI, GOLIA, GREEN, SURENSEN.") After codenames have been inserted, a code clerk copies the document, removing all sensitive terms and replacing the first with "No. 1," the second with "No. 2," and so on. The letter is photographed in this form. The terms themselves, with their numerical equivalents, are enciphered by the one-time pads. The numerical ciphertext is enclosed with the films in the diplomatic pouch on an ordinary sheet of paper.

Thus, when Vladimir Petrov developed a filmed letter from Moscow dated 25 November 1952, he found, in part:

> We request you to report to us by the next luggage all the information known to you concerning No. 42, who figures in the departmental files in connection with her No. 43, and about her No. 44 in Sparta. . . .

Русская Криптология

> Depending on the availability of full particulars concerning No. 42 and her No. 44 in Sparta, we shall weigh the question of No. 45 to Sudania one of our planners along No. 46 Novators, under the guise No. 44 of No. 42

Petrov knew that LUGGAGE meant *mail*, DEPARTMENTAL, *consular*, and PLANNER, *cadre worker* in the espionage jargon. He consulted a list of formal codenames and found that SPARTA meant *Russia*, SUDANIA, *Australia*, and NOVATORS, *secret agents*. Decipherment of the accompanying sheet of paper told Petrov that, in this letter, "No. 42—Kazanova; No. 43—last will and testament; No. 44—relatives; No. 45—sending; No. 46—lines. . . ." Thus, interpreted, decoded, and with the deciphered equivalents of the numbers inserted, the paragraphs read:

> We request you to report to us by the next mail all the information known to you concerning Kazanova [an old Russian woman living in Sydney], who figures in the consular files in connection with her last will and testament and about her relatives in Russia [whom she wanted to see]. . . .
>
> Depending on the availability of full particulars concerning Kazanova and her relatives in Russia, we shall weigh the question of sending to Australia one of our cadre workers along the lines of a secret agent, under the guise of a relative of Kazanova.

This system appears to be used instead of total encipherment because security has bowed to convenience. To encipher everything fully would take too long. Perhaps one reason is that the cipher clerks have to work by hand.

For its agents in the field, however, the Soviet Union uses the best. It takes no chances, cryptologically speaking, with them or their networks. It gives its agents the confidence that they need fear nothing from cryptanalysis. It will not jeopardize their radio links with Moscow by trusting to anything less than the one perfectly secure system of encipherment. The main Soviet spy cipher today employs the one-time pad.

Its form varies. It has been found as a thick, squarish booklet the size of a postage stamp and as a scroll about the size of a cigarette butt. It seems to be growing smaller. A pad captured in 1954 had 40 rows of eight five-digit groups. One captured in 1958 had 30 rows of ten. Pads captured in 1957 and 1961 had 20 rows of four and five groups, respectively. Columns, rows, and pages are numbered. One booklet had 250 pages of a material like very thin gold and silver foil (several scrolls are needed to provide an equivalent supply of key digits). Usually, one part of the pad is printed in red and the other in black, presumably to distinguish the enciphering keys from the deciphering. The "printing" seems to be simple photography—probably the best way to make the one accurate copy of the original key that the agent will need; extra evidence for this is that the Russian word *gamma* ("scale"), which appears to be the Soviet term for one-time pad, is used in photography. Furthermore, the "paper" of the pad is cellulose nitrate, which was used for film in the early days of the motion-picture industry. It is highly inflammable, and spies seem to have kept potassium permanganate at hand to turn an ordinary combustion into an almost explosive reaction to destroy the pads rapidly and completely. No latent image would remain.

Interestingly, some pads seem to be produced by typists and not by machines. They show strike-overs and erasures—neither likely to be made by machines. More significant are statistical analyses of the digits. One such pad, for example, has seven times as many groups in which digits in the 1-to-5 group alternate with digits in the 6-to-0 group, like 18293, as a purely random arrangement would have. This suggests that the typist is striking alternately with her left hand (which would type the 1-to-5 group on a Continental machine) and her right (which would type the 6-to-0 group). Again, instead of just half the groups beginning with a low number, which would be expected in a random selection, three quarters of them do, possibly because the typist is spacing with her right hand, then starting a new group with her left. Fewer doubles and triples appear than chance expects. Possibly the girls, ordered to type at random, sensed that some doublets and triplets would occur in a random text but, misled by their conspicuousness, minimized them. Despite these anomalies, however, the digits still show far too little pattern to make cryptanalysis possible.

One-time pads have turned up with a number of top Soviet spies. Rudolf Abel, the highest-ranking Russian agent ever captured in the United States, had the one in the form of a booklet and the size of a postage stamp—$1\frac{7}{8} \times \frac{7}{8} \times \frac{3}{8}$ inches. F.B.I. agents found it when they arrested him in his room in New York's Hotel Latham on June 21, 1957. Abel had wrapped it in paper and concealed it inside a hollowed-out block of wood covered with sandpaper like a sanding block (Abel posed as an artist) that he had tossed casually into the wastebasket. A Greek Communist, Gregory Liolios, had a one-time pad when he was arrested in 1954, as did another, Eleftherious Voutsas, picked up in 1958. In suburban London, early in 1961, half a dozen one-time pads in the scroll form were found hidden in the base of a Ronson cigarette lighter in the cottage of Helen and Peter Kroger, two Soviet spies who were actually two Americans named Lona and Morris Cohen. More pads were found in another lighter in the London flat of their chief, the Soviet Resident (agent in charge) for England, known only by his alias, Gordon Arnold Lonsdale. Later that year, Japanese police rounded up members of a North Korean Communist spy ring, and found among their effects some one-time pads. Atomic scientist Giuseppe Martelli, accused of espionage against Britain for the Soviet Union, was carrying two tiny packs of pads in a pack of cigarettes when he was apprehended at Southend Airport in 1963. Seven cigarettes were intact, but six others were glued together and partly cut away to form a recess for the pads. And a former spy for East Germany, who received his messages in an open broadcast of numerical codegroups and sent them by leaving them in a tin box hidden under a tree root, also enciphered with the one-time pad.

Messages so enciphered appear to have been radioed to Moscow. Abel had a shortwave set in his Brooklyn studio and a receiver in his hotel room. He told his lieutenant that he tape-recorded incoming messages, then took them down on paper and deciphered them. After his arrest, U.S. government agents listened in accordance with a broadcast schedule found in the tip of a hollowed-out pencil, also thrown into Abel's wastebasket, and twice picked up messages in five-digit groups. British security police found a signal plan with the one-time pads in the Krogers' lighter. They likewise listened in accordance with its instructions. At 12:32 a.m. January 9, 1961, tuned to 17,080 kilocycles, they heard the call-sign *dash dot dot*. Eighteen minutes later

```
39892 09897 07361 35736 38309     69801 56628 37254 61467 52308
33571 01448 63458 24848 30238     08098 14542 31851 07595 77970
27135 40220 47079 71707 80633     01536 97896 88209 71480 42063
49941 56035 48846 15111 59324     57188 83556 96509 08657 46851
10051 21816 63253 86240 99495     75643 56639 05326 97662 54705
40048 55040 17710 60896 94366     58493 69423 44744 07023 50651
11512 18996 91403 40539 50135     43896 70213 66610 65808 03001
74168 69956 53870 02897 18192     06724 13542 87558 11061 71468
20349 15133 12850 56853 47799     16904 59833 10280 50870 51183
20883 94649 78587 63065 94545     92600 10425 35051 98370 35554
51802 14552 07608 38392 22224     99718 57838 08540 62986 40799
20348 29842 76282 49048 51771     95196 30638 03983 76992 72652
98905 46438 78295 72769 07178     77170 45854 58100 40649 42651
53669 53304 18152 17691 54117     35868 60370 62207 91750 93298
08658 97627 93221 37250 66427     66368 08297 37727 99832 89892
52053 66220 87679 61332 81960     83742 23755 03930 41515 10297
54208 37131 32366 77519 57374     95762 25255 38703 20509 40545
06587 04827 18084 80286 29274     23049 07180 95128 34875 81629
54419 64469 20538 15087 89185     72724 98390 98735 09156 04417
52776 73748 01537 27259 51549 038 23888 63783 92325 29209 10390 038
```

A sheet of a one-time pad captured on Communist spies in Japan, 1961. One side may be for enciphering, the other for deciphering

they heard the same sign at 14,755 kilocycles. On January 18, at 6:38 a.m. at 6,340 kilocycles, they heard call-sign 277. Less than an hour later, they heard it again at 8,888 kilocycles. Direction-finders plotted the source of the signals as the Moscow area. Lonsdale had a high-speed transmission device that would send Morse at 240 words per minute; probably it recorded his message and then spewed it out in a spurt.

Communication seems to be fairly frequent. The Kroger signal plan provided for contact Tuesdays, Wednesdays, Fridays, and Saturdays. This frequency may explain why both Abel and Mrs. Kroger had enciphered messages on them when they were caught. Abel tried to stuff his up a sleeve. Mrs. Kroger asked to be allowed to stoke the furnace before leaving the house for a long period of questioning, but when an envelope containing a single sheet of paper with a block of typed numbers was removed from her handbag, "Mrs.

Kroger," a security officer said, "showed no further desire to stoke the boiler."

Radio was supplemented by microdots. Lonsdale hid a microdot reader in a can of talcum powder. Abel made his own microdots by reducing the 35-millimeter negative with a lens having a very short focal length. To preserve legibility in these great reductions, he used spectroscopic film, which is available at many camera stores and which can resolve 1,000 lines per millimeter. He undid the stapling of *Better Homes & Gardens* and *American Home*, inserted the thin strips of microdots between sections, rebound the magazines, and mailed them off to a prearranged general delivery number in Paris. For some reason the hidden messages were not received and Moscow told Abel to discontinue them. However, microdots brought the spies plaintext letters from home.

Though the one-time pad is the standard method for radio communication between top agents and Moscow, other systems serve the internal needs of secret communications within Communist spy rings. The rule here seems to be that where Russians have devised the systems, they are top-notch, and where local Communists who are natives of a country have done so, they can be solved—often with disastrous effect. In 1955, for example, Swedish counterespionage police noticed that a chauffeur at the Czech legation went to the Stockholm railroad station each night to buy copies of the newspapers *Kurier* and *Tidning*, both published in the provincial city of Karlskoga, where munitions are manufactured. Studying the papers, police noticed a number of oddly worded announcements. When they inserted similar advertisements, using the same identifying words, they received responses from several people who turned out to be Red agents. Eventually a ring that operated in five cities was broken up and four Communist satellite diplomats declared persona non grata.

The most catastrophic instance of the eggshell ciphers of local Communists took place in Iran. On the night of August 16, 1954, Iranian security police arrested Ali Abbasi, a former Army captain who had come under suspicion because of his activities in the Red Tudeh party. In the suitcase he was carrying as he came out of a house in Teheran, they found a complete plan of Shah Mohammed Reza Pahlevi's summer palace, showing guard posts and the number of men stationed at each, top-secret documents from Army files, reports on the disposition of artillery along Iran's Russian border, two notebooks in what were obviously cipher, and another with page after page of what appeared to be trigonometric equations, replete with the Greek letters beloved of mathematicians and the abbreviations for "secant," "cosine," "tangent," and "cotangent." The problem was that mathematically the formulas made no sense at all.

Colonel Mostafa Amjadi, chief of the intelligence directorate of the Teheran military governate, and another colonel in the Iranian Army went to work on the three notebooks. By August 30, they had cracked the two overt codes, but extracted only meager information from them. Meanwhile, Abbasi decided to talk. He revealed that the Tudeh party had riddled the Iranian Army with about 400 agents and that their names were listed in a mathematical cipher. This was the trigonometric system which Amjadi and his colleague were even then struggling with, but Abbasi warned that the system was so complex that it could be read only by its inventor, Lieutenant Colonel Jamsheed Mobasheri, an artillery officer regarded by his friends as something of a mathematical genius.

The imitation "trigonometric" cipher of Red agents in Iran

Mobasheri was picked up for questioning. Instead of revealing the key, he tried to puncture a vein with a rusty nail. The two colonel-cryptanalysts worked steadily 24 hours a day in overlapping shifts of 12 hours each. Mobasheri was again interrogated, and, now that the first shock of arrest had worn off, his pride of authorship in his cipher almost overcame his loyalty to Communism and he twice agreed to reveal the method—only to change his mind both times. The Iranian government quietly asked other countries if they would help in the solution. Meanwhile, one of the colonels formulated a theory as to Mobasheri's system and interviewed him, hoping to get some clues from the inventor's reactions. Mobasheri stubbornly insisted that the system could not be broken, but just as the colonel was leaving the cell Mobasheri's appreciation for an intelligent analysis broke through, and he admitted that the cryptanalyst was on the right track. On September 3, as an airplane was about to fly copies of the trigonometric notebook to an ally's cryptanalysts, the two haggard colonels cracked Mobasheri's cipher.

The roster proved to be as detailed as an official army register in describing the officers, making identification easy. But it was so extensive that it took several days to decrypt it and locate the conspirators. A week later all 400 were arrested. This enormous conspiracy, Iranian security police discovered, had not only obtained detailed information on the strength and disposition of Iran's entire armed forces, but had wormed into vital posts that would have enabled it to assassinate on a moment's notice members of the government from the Shah on down. It was ready either to pull a coup and set up its own Communist puppet government or to deliver the nation entire to the Soviet Union. Imperfect ciphers kept it from doing either. Instead, 26 of its leaders —including Mobasheri—were executed, and hundreds of run-of-the-mill plotters and sympathizers were jailed. A poisonous infection had been cleaned out; a year later Iran abandoned her traditional neutrality and, signing the Baghdad Pact, aligned herself with the West.

No cryptographic weakness imperils the operation of Russian spy rings. Perhaps the most striking example lies in the cipher used by Abel's lieutenant, Reino Hayhanen. For two years after the fat, lazy, and irresponsible Hayhanen landed in New York, he did not meet Abel in person, but communicated with him by messages hidden in prearranged "drops"—a crack in the cement wall that runs from 165th to 167th streets along Jerome Avenue in the Bronx, behind a loose brick under a bridge in Central Park, under lampposts in Prospect and Fort Tryon parks. The messages were on "soft" microfilm, which Abel made by dissolving the stiff film base; this left only the soft, image-bearing emulsion, which could be squeezed into tiny places. Abel and the couriers from Moscow used hollowed-out pencils, bolts, flashlight batteries, and coins as message-containers in his drops because they would be less likely to arouse suspicion if found by accident. A horizontal mark with blue chalk at various signal areas—park fences or subway stations—meant that a message had been placed in a drop, a vertical mark that it had been retrieved. These were to be checked daily. Soon after Hayhanen's arrival on October 21, 1952, he "posted" his first message. Moscow responded with an enciphered message on soft microfilm enclosed in a hollow 1948 Jefferson nickel. It read:

    1. We congratulate you on a safe arrival. We confirm the receipt of your letter to the address V and the reading of letter No. 1.

    2. For organization of cover we have given instructions to transmit to you three thousand in local [currency]. Consult with us prior to investing it in any kind of business, advising the character of the business.

    3. According to your request, we will transmit the formula for the preparation of soft film and the news separately, together with [your] mother's letter.

    4. [It is too] early to send you the one-time pads. Encipher short letters, but

do the longer ones with insertions.* All the data about yourself, place of work, address, etc., must not be transmitted in one cipher message. Transmit insertions separately.

    5. The package was delivered to [your] wife personally. Everything is all right with [your] family. We wish [you] success. Greetings from the comrades. No. 1, 3 December.

Somehow the hollow nickel went astray. Most probably Hayhanen, who was sloppy in his spy work, spent it. It circulated in the economy like millions of its fellows, with none of those who passed it from hand to hand aware of its secret cargo. Then one hot morning in the summer of 1953, newsboy James Bozart, who had just received it as part of 50 cents in change from a customer on his route at 3403 Foster Avenue in Brooklyn, dropped it with four other nickels and a quarter on the staircase. When he bent over to pick it up, he found that it had split in half. One of the hollowed-out halves held a piece of microfilm five-sixteenths of an inch square, wrapped in tissue paper. "It was a picture of a file card, or an index card," Bozart said. "There appeared to be a row of numbers on it." He turned it over to police, who gave it to the F.B.I., who must have immediately begun trying to crack it. They failed.

Four years later, Reino Hayhanen defected to the U.S. embassy in Paris as he was being sent back to the Soviet Union by the dissatisfied Abel for a "vacation." He disclosed the cipher system and the keys that he had used, and in the summer of 1957, F.B.I. Russian expert Michael G. Leonard applied them to the 207 five-figure groups of the microfilm that Bozart had found. At last the F.B.I. was able to read the nickel message.

Encipherment began with bisection: cutting the plaintext in half and putting the second part first, thus burying the vulnerable beginning (which was marked by a special indicator) deep within the body of the message. There followed a substitution by straddling checkerboard, based, in this case, on the first seven letters of the Russian word SNEGOPAD ("snowfall"). It was inscribed in the top line—there was no Russian equivalent of ASINTOER, though the seven letters s n e g o p a include the most frequent in Russian (o, at 11 per cent) and total to 40 per cent of normal Russian text. The rest of the Cyrillic alphabet and additional symbols followed below. This preliminary ciphertext was written horizontally into a columnar transposition block. It was transcribed vertically and written horizontally into a second transposition block. This one, however, had a series of steplike disruption, or D, areas. The first D area began in the top row under keynumber 1 and ran to the right side of that row. In succeeding rows it began one column to the right. When after several rows the starting point reached the right side of the block, a row was skipped and the second D area began under keynumber 2. It was constructed like its predecessor. Other D areas followed. The cipher digits being written into the second transposition block went first into the non-D area, and when this was filled the inscription continued in the steplike D areas. The final

---

* Probably as in the Petrov technique.

ciphertext was obtained by vertical transcription in keynumber order from this second block, in which transcription the D areas were disregarded.

The system dispensed with written keys such as Abel's one-time pad, which helped incriminate him. Hayhanen had to remember only four basic keys—SNEGOPA(D), the first 20 letters of a Russian popular song ("The Lone Accordion"), the date of the World War II victory over Japan (3/9/1945, in the Continental style), and his personal keynumber (13, changed to 20 in 1956). The latter three keys generated the keys for the transpositions and the coordinates of the checkerboard through a process that was extremely complicated but that possessed a kind of tractive logic, was meant to be memorized, and probably would be after two or three run-throughs.

This process injected an arbitrary five-digit number at the very beginning of the key derivation, strongly influencing the end result. (This number was also inserted in a predetermined position in the cryptogram so that the decipherer would have it. In Hayhanen's case, this position was the fifth group from the end, the position coming from the last figure, 5, of the victory date.) This group changed from message to message, so the enciphering keys, and consequently the ciphertexts of all messages enciphered in this system, would bear no exploitable relation to one another. Not only would the transposition keys differ, the very widths of the blocks would as well—this being a variable stemming from the key derivation. This kills any last hope of an analysis by comparing messages. The poor cryptanalyst would even be denied the consolation of discovering a common origin of the cryptograms through similarities in frequency counts, for the coordinates themselves would change. Any solution would thus have to be effected on the basis of a single message. It would require trying every sensible pattern of transposition until one was found that yielded a monalphabetic frequency count of the digits. The D areas significantly increase the difficulty of finding this pattern, just as the straddling effect increases the difficulty of getting a valid frequency count. The number of trials for a 1,035-digit message like the nickel one is astronomical, and, even with computers, it would probably take years. In theory the system is not unbreakable, but in practice it is. Its security could not have been more pointedly demonstrated than by the F.B.I.'s failure to solve it.

Such is the cryptology of the Soviet Union. It is interesting to contemplate its excellence. Russia herself remains "a riddle wrapped in a mystery inside an enigma." So, when she decrees it, do her communications. The one-time pad ensures this for the bulk of her spy messages and for a fair proportion of her diplomatic and secret-police messages. Complex rotor-type cipher machines, well-designed in themselves and handled with a sophistication that changes keys after foreign cryptanalysts have reconstructed part of the wiring and the rotation pattern but before they can read any plaintext, guard other high-level diplomatic and military messages of Soviet Russia. And even when she requires a cipher to be fully mnemonic, like Hayhanen's, she designs it so that it cannot be broken. She has solved, during the Cold War, ciphers in use at the American embassy in Moscow. Feats like these bear witness to knowledge that could only well up from a profound understanding of cryptography and cryptanalysis. Whether this comprehension springs from the scientific ability that has enabled Russia to orbit great artificial satellites, or from the decades-long experience of cryptology that the Communist dictators have had to practice for self-preservation and aggrandizement, or from the habits of secrecy and puzzling out the real meaning of things that are ingrained into every inhabitant of a totalitarian society, or from a dark-souled Slavic love of the mysterious, it has beyond question rocketed Red accomplishments in this black art to Sputnik height.

19
N.S.A.

IT HAS BEEN SAID that 90 per cent of all the scientists who have ever lived are living today. The remark applies to cryptology with even greater force. The age is one of communications and of Cold War. The titans that confront one another in Berlin and Vietnam and outer space owe much of their effectiveness as superpowers to the vast webs of communications through which they receive information and transmit commands. These networks, more extensive and more heavily used than any in history, furnish cryptologists with unparalleled opportunities. The Cold War gives them the impetus to exploit these opportunities—a stimulus that, in view of the dangers of national extinction, becomes almost an imperative. These two factors converge to produce more cryptology and more cryptologists than ever before.

The size and magnitude of modern communications are staggering. The Defense Communications System, a worldwide strategic network of the American armed forces, transmits well over a quarter of a million messages a *day*, or more than 10,000 messages every hour. Its 10,000,000-plus channel miles—enough to circle the globe 400 times—are distributed among 85 subordinate nets that provide 25,000 channels and pass through 200 relay stations and more than 1,500 tributary stations. Its plant is worth $2.5 billion and it costs nearly three quarters of a million dollars a year to run. Operating it are more than 30,000 soldiers, sailors, and airmen. The D.C.S. consists essentially of the strategic nets of the three service branches—the Army's STARCOM, or Strategic Army Network, the Navy's Naval Communications System, and the Air Force's AIRCOM, or U.S.A.F. Communications Complex—all welded into a compatible whole. The D.C.S. does not include the tactical, ship-shore, or air-ground facilities, all of which add to the communications volume. So heavy can the tactical volume become that the Navy has outfitted ships purely as communications vessels. The converted escort carrier *Annapolis* put to sea in the spring of 1964 with its cavernous aircraft storage space filled with a mass of radios, teletypewriters, and cipher machines. The Army talks over featherweight walkie-talkies and tiny helmet radios and observes the battlefield from rear command posts via portable field television sets.

But a few statistics, however overwhelming, and a few devices, however striking, cannot truly convey the volume, the variety, and the importance of communications in military affairs today. It can sink in only by enumerating one by one the at first interesting, then surprising, and finally numbing list of the various networks that a military force needs to send its many kinds of messages. Take, in this regard, the Air Force.

Its basic network for passing official traffic on a global basis is the radio and wire teletype AIRCOMNET, which handles the bulk of Air Force communications. AIROPNET, also teletype, provides communications among air bases to control worldwide flight movement. The Air-Ground Communications Network provides a voice link to airplanes from interconnected ground command posts and air bases for strike orders and traffic control. The Flight Service Network provides telephone service among military and civilian airports for flight safety. U.S.A.F. Weather Communications comprises the Weather Teletype Network, the Facsimile Network, and the Global Weather Intercept and Broadcast Network—all closely interrelated to provide worldwide meteorological information.

The Strategic Air Command alone employs six communications systems. Most vital is the Primary Alerting System, a wholly separate telephone system that connects the command post at Offutt Air Force Base in Omaha directly with all S.A.C. control rooms and major headquarters, even those in Alaska, Spain, and the United Kingdom. Its wires run solid from the famous red telephone at Offutt to loudspeakers and handsets at all control rooms. Over these circuits a commander would alert the major retaliatory forces of the United States. Backing this up is the all-radio Commander's Net, for the S.A.C. chief's exclusive use. The Teletype Net carries most S.A.C. traffic, and the Telephone Net, part wire and part radio, part commercial (through leases) and part military, supplements it. The Radio Telephone Network, within the continental United States, provides an emergency reserve for the Telephone Net. The High-Frequency Single Side Band Tactical Air-Ground Radio System sends messages to attacking S.A.C. bombers, including fail-safe messages.

The Tactical Air Command depends upon four networks—the Operational Teletype Circuits, Operational Telephone Circuits, Bomb Damage Assessment Reporting Circuits, and Reserve Forces Operational Telephone Network—as well as some mobile communications. The Air Defense Command relies upon its Alert No. 1 Teletype Network to transmit reports of possible attacking airplanes or missiles. It also has a Command Teletype Network and a Telephone Network. COMLOGNET transmits logistic data at high speed directly from punched tabulating cards. For verbal traffic concerning supplies, the Air Matériel Command employs SITECOMNET for operations, AMCOMNET for command and administration, LOGAIRNET for airlifting critical items, and LOGBALNET to supply ballistic-missile needs. Then the Military Air Transport Service has three networks—teletype, voice, and facsimile—and the U.S.A.F. Security Service enjoys a network of its own. In addition, the several theaters have independent networks for local traffic, such as the

Alaskan, Caribbean, and Pacific communications; the European–Near East web, with its high density of military installations and integration with North Atlantic Treaty Organization nations, is particularly complicated. U.S. Air Force traffic flows over all of these.

Even considering only the radio circuits, the possibilities for traffic analysis and cryptanalysis are enormous. The United States protects itself from these, and at the same time it exploits the opportunities afforded by the comparable Communist networks. The hugeness of this task has engendered the greatest cryptologic organization in history—the National Security Agency and the three armed service cryptologic agencies.

N.S.A. probably owes its existence, like the Central Intelligence Agency and the Department of Defense itself, to Pearl Harbor. Congress, after its investigation of the surprise attack, recommended "that there be a complete integration of Army and Navy intelligence agencies," and the record of the investigation contains a few anticipatory suggestions for cryptologic centralization as well. Major General C. A. Willoughby, MacArthur's G-2, complaining about Navy selection of cryptanalyzed information passed over to him, admonished: "The solution to this vexing and dangerous problem is a completely joint, interlocking intercept and cryptanalytical service, on the highest level, with the freest interchange of messages and interpretation." Colonel Henry Clausen, who investigated MAGIC in 1944, told the Joint Congressional Committee the following year: "I also think that the basic recommendation that can come from this committee is a very fine one if you make it that never again shall MAGIC, this information, be monopolized by one service or the other service, but have it distributed by one agency on an overall basis." Former Pacific Fleet intelligence officer Captain Edwin Layton may have had this in mind when, after deploring the publicity given to American cryptanalysis by the committee hearings, added that "it may serve a very fine purpose for the future." And in a memorandum concerning a proposed Central Intelligence Agency that Allen W. Dulles submitted to the Senate Armed Services Committee in 1947, the future Director of Central Intelligence noted that "An important balance [to intelligence obtained openly] must be supplied by secret intelligence which includes what we now often refer to as 'Magic,' " and that any Central Intelligence Agency should have access to "intelligence gained through intercepted messages, open and deciphered alike."

In the first postwar years, the cryptologic duties of the American armed forces reposed in the separate agencies of the Army, the Navy, and the Air Force. The Army, at least, charged its agency with maintaining "liaison with the Department of the Navy, Department of the Air Force, and other appropriate agencies, for the purpose of coordinating communication security and communication intelligence equipment and procedures." Presumably the Navy and the Air Force units were similarly charged. This arrangement, which relied on internal desire instead of external direction, prolonged the abuses hinted at by Willoughby. To rectify them and achieve the benefits of centralized control, the Defense Department in 1949 established the Armed Forces Security Agency. The A.F.S.A. took over the strategic communications-intelligence functions and the coordination responsibilities of the individual agencies. It left them with tactical communications intelligence, which can best be performed near the point of combat and not at a central location (except for basic system solutions), and with low-echelon communications security, which differs radically in ground, sea, and air forces. Even in these areas A.F.S.A. backed them up. A.F.S.A. drew its personnel from the separate departmental agencies, though it later hired separately, and housed itself in their buildings.

The merits of the unified approach to cryptology quickly manifested themselves. They warranted expanding that approach beyond the Defense Department to all cryptologic activities of the United States government, such as State Department cryptosystems. Accordingly, President Harry S Truman promulgated a directive that created the National Security Agency on November 4, 1952, abolishing A.F.S.A. and transferring its personnel and assets to N.S.A.

That directive was classified as security information, and for several years no government document publicly acknowledged the agency's existence. Finally, in 1957, the *United States Government Organization Manual* included a brief but vague description. Today the official description reads:

CREATION AND AUTHORITY.—The National Security Agency was established by Presidential directive in 1952 as a separately organized agency within the Department of Defense under the direction, authority, and control of the Secretary of Defense who was designated executive agent for the performance of highly specialized technical functions in support of the intelligence activities of the United States.

PURPOSE.—The National Security Agency has two primary missions—a security mission and an intelligence information mission. To accomplish these missions, the Director, National Security Agency, has been assigned responsibilities as follows: (1) prescribing certain security principles, doctrines, and procedures for the U.S. Government; (2) organizing, operating, and managing certain activities and facilities for the production of intelligence information; (3) organizing and coordinating the research and engineering activities of the U.S. Government which are in support of the Agency's assigned functions; and (4) regulating certain communications in support of Agency missions.

The unspecified nature of those two missions involves, of course, cryptology. In its security function, N.S.A. creates and supervises the cryptography of all U.S. government agencies. In intelligence, it intercepts, traffic-analyzes, and cryptanalyzes the messages of all other nations, friend as well as foe.

In its first years, A.F.S.A.–N.S.A. was scattered in offices throughout the Washington area, notably at Arlington Hall, home of the Army Security Agency, though its official address was 3801 Nebraska Avenue, North West, home of the Navy Branch. In 1953, however, the Defense Department called for bids on the preliminaries for constructing a single big building at Fort George G. Meade, Maryland, about half way between Washington and Baltimore. In July of 1954, the Charles H. Tompkins Company of Washington was awarded a $19,944,451 contract to construct one of the most costly buildings in the Washington area on an 82-acre site in conjunction with the J. A. Jones Company. It was essentially completed in the fall of 1957, but it was not until early in 1958 that the last of the employees had moved in. By then the total cost had risen to about $35,000,000 for the structure, for associated facilities such as parking lots, utility lines, electrical power substation, supply building, and barracks for the Marine Corps guards, and for moving in existing equipment and installing new.

The long, three-story structure, of concrete, glass, and steel, in the shape of a squared-off A, stands in a shallow bowl fringed with pine trees and surrounded by acres of asphalt parking lots. It faces south, fronting upon Savage Road, a narrow road that widens as it passes N.S.A. and then shrinks again. The Baltimore-Washington Expressway runs a few hundred yards to the west. This Operations Building is 980 feet wide by 560 feet deep, and along its full width runs the longest unobstructed corridor in the country, an honor previously claimed by the 750-foot central corridor of the United States Capitol.

In addition to dozens of offices and basement facilities for computers, the structure encloses a cafeteria accommodating 1,400 and an auditorium seating 500, eight snack bars, a post exchange, a dispensary with X-ray and operating rooms and dental chairs, a shoe-repair and clothes-cleaning shop, a barber shop, and a branch of the State Bank of Laurel. A system of "security conveyor belts" runs through the basement, carrying trays of documents to eight substations. A German pneumatic-tube system can whisk up to 800 containers an hour at 75 feet per second to interoffice destinations selected by a dial at each station. The building is fully air-conditioned. It has a public-address system. It is said to have more electric wiring than any building in the world. Its institutional, characterless offices, filled with metal desks, partitions, and lockable file cabinets, are the black chambers of today.

But although this cathedral of cryptology—far and away the greatest ever erected to that science—was the third largest building in the Washington area (after the Pentagon and the new State Department headquarters), and although its 1,400,000 square feet exceeded the C.I.A.'s 1,135,000, it proved too small after only five years. In May of 1963 the J. W. Bateson Co., Inc., was awarded a contract for $10,940,000 to construct a nine-story Operations Building Annex of boxy, modern style between the jutting arms of the square A. It added 500,000 square feet to the N.S.A. headquarters complex, 140,000 of it in a basement area almost certain to be used for computers. The annex was completed in late 1965.

This expansion was clearly made necessary by the rapid growth of the agency. In 1956, the director told a Senate committee, "We have almost 9,000 civilian employees here in the Washington area and around the world." In 1960, two former employees reported that 10,000 persons worked in the Operations Building. Based on a nationwide governmental average space-utilization of 150 square feet per worker, the two N.S.A. buildings would house more than 12,500 employees; based on the figure of 135 square feet per worker that modern buildings attain, the number of employees there would exceed 14,000. This is certainly greater than the number of C.I.A. employees in Washington, estimated at about 10,000, and even when the uncertain numbers of employees of both agencies in posts around the world are added to their totals, N.S.A. is still larger than C.I.A., making it almost certainly the largest intelligence agency in the free world. (At least a thousand N.S.A. employees are stationed overseas. Several hundred work in each of two branches, N.S.A. Far East in Japan and N.S.A. Europe in Germany. Others serve with N.S.A.'s worldwide intercept net, a few as radio operators, most as supervisors, since nearly all the intercept operators are armed forces personnel.) N.S.A.'s budget has also been reported to be twice as large as the C.I.A.'s.

Outside the agency but attached to it is a Scientific Advisory Board of leading figures in fields related to cryptology, such as mathematics and electronics. These experts are in business or at universities, but they bring outside experience and new insights to N.S.A. problems. The board, in turn, is advised by several panels of specialists. The agency also receives the results of the cryptologic research of an independent research organization. The Institute for Defense Analyses was formed in 1956 by five universities to offer academic evaluation of defense projects; it is supported by government contracts. In its fiscal year ending February 28, 1959, I.D.A. received a two-year contract for $1,900,000 to build and operate a laboratory for basic research into communication theory as it applies to Defense Department responsibilities. The institute created a Communications Research Division and constructed a brick building to house it, complete with a Control Data Corporation 1604 computer, on the campus of Princeton University. The division's first director was Dr. A. Adrian Albert, then 54, of the University of Chicago, one of America's outstanding mathematicians, with a long record of service to his country and his science, who had framed cryptologic concepts in algebraic terms as early as 1941, and who was an N.S.A. consultant. His task seems to have been to get the division off the ground, for he was succeeded by Dr. J. Barkley Rosser, and then by deputy director Dr. Richard A. Liebler, 47, who had worked for N.S.A. from 1953 to 1958 and was an old friend of N.S.A.'s deputy director, Dr. Louis W. Tordella (they had taught mathematics together at Illinois in 1937 and 1938).

The Communications Research Division interests bright mathematicians in the general field of communications and turns them loose on a project that interests them. Sometimes such a project bears directly on advanced practical problems, often dealing with rotor systems; sometimes it is more general, more basic, as how to get a computer to recognize actual English text instead of a collection of letters whose statistics resemble English text. Its policy has been to hire most mathematicians for a year only, to keep bringing fresh minds to bear. The size of the mathematical staff has remained in the neighborhood of the 24 of its first year. The division also encourages what amounts to basic research in its general field. It sponsors symposia, such as one on finite groups held in conjunction with the American Mathematical Society, and one on basic mathematical concepts in linguistics, as well as two summer campus projects, SCAMP and ALP, which introduce the academic world to cryptology. Though I.D.A. contracts with the Office of Naval Research, the cryptologic results are all sent to N.S.A.

Still other cryptologic agencies outside the American government with which N.S.A. cooperates are those of the North Atlantic Treaty Organization. The main ones are ECSA, the European Communication Security Agency in Paris, EUSEC, the Communication Security and Evaluation Agency, Europe, in London, SECAN, the Communication Security and Evaluation Agency, N.A.T.O., in Washington, EUDAC, the Signal Distribution and Accounting Agency, Europe, in London, and DACAN, the Signal Distribution and Accounting Agency, N.A.T.O., in Washington. In addition, N.A.T.O. has several communication agencies that use the security material provided by the cryptographic agencies.

None of these is a part of the American cryptologic organization, though all participate in its activities. That organization is not exhausted by N.S.A., its advisory board, and the agencies that feed it ideas and information. The creation of A.F.S.A. did not abolish the individual cryptologic agencies of the armed services. Though subject to N.S.A. in technical matters, they remain, as units of the Army, the Navy, and the Air Force, administratively separate from it.

Oldest, and probably the most direct ancestor of N.S.A. in view of its contributions to N.S.A. of the core personnel of Friedman, Kullback, Sinkov, and Rowlett, is the Army Security Agency. It can trace some functions back to G.2 A.6 and the Code Compilation Section, both of the A.E.F., but administratively it stems, though tortuously, from Yardley's MI-8 and his Black Chamber and from Friedman's two-man cryptographic bureau in the War Department. As a well-defined unit, it began with the creation of the Signal Intelligence Service in 1929. It continued through the war, changing its name first to the Signal Security Service, then to the Signal Security Agency. On September 15, 1945, a few days after the war ended, the War Department detached the agency from the Signal Corps and placed it within the Intelligence Branch (which had tried at least four times during the war to steal it).

It was renamed the Army Security Agency and was given authority over all Army cryptologic units, which had previously functioned independently under theater commanders and merely with the advice of the Signal Security Agency.

In February, 1949, Army Regulation 10–125 set forth these as some of A.S.A.'s responsibilities:

> ... the Chief, Army Security Agency, formulates and implements plans, policies, and doctrine on communication intelligence and communication security for the Army, and is specifically responsible for the following: ...
>
> *b.* Production of communication intelligence for the Department of the Army.
>
> *c.* Investigation of the means employed for clandestine communications; and the preparation, detection, and processing of secret inks, microphotographs, and open codes and ciphers.
>
> *d.* Technical supervision of communication security activities of the Department of the Army, including cryptocenter activities, programs of cryptographic instruction, and surveillance of friendly radio and wire traffic. ...
>
> *j.* Preparation, production, storage, distribution, and accounting of all registered cryptomaterial, together with the publication of instructions necessary for the use, handling, and safeguarding of such material, except in such cases where these duties may otherwise be specifically assigned.

Other responsibilities cover command of A.S.A. installations and units, liaison, preparation of publications, conduct of training programs, supervision of the Army Security Reserve, and advising the Department of the Army.

The establishment of A.F.S.A. and N.S.A. must have given these duties a restricted meaning. Nevertheless, so greatly had communications, and consequently cryptology, expanded, that on April 14, 1964, the Army redesignated the agency as a major field command. The published description is as uninformative as that of N.S.A.: "The Commanding General, United States Army Security Agency, is responsible for the operations, training, administration, services, and supply of all units, personnel, activities, and installations under his command throughout the world. He performs specialized technical functions relating to the national security."

Two of his chief customers must be the Assistant Chief of Staff for Intelligence (G-2), in whose hands are placed staff responsibility for "communications intelligence, electronic intelligence, communications security, and electronic security . . . ; Army cryptologic functions," and the Chief of Communications-Electronics (formerly the Chief Signal Officer), who advises the Chief of Staff on "communications, including pertinent communications security." The Chief of Communications-Electronics is assisted in his function of supplying cryptographic equipment to the Army by the United States Army Signal Communications Security Agency, which buys, distributes, registers, stores, and repairs that equipment. It follows each item from point to point with forms bearing titles like "Cryptomaterial Distribution Summary Record" and "Cryptomaterial Consolidated Flyleaf Receipt." Headquarters of the U.S. Army Security Agency remains at the Arlington Hall Station in Virginia.

The Navy's cryptologic agency remains buried in the Office of Naval Communications, and little more is known of it beyond its name—Naval Security Group—and its location at Nebraska Avenue. Presumably it feeds information to the Office of Naval Intelligence, and, like the other agencies, its radio stations do intercept work for N.S.A. On December 31, 1963, the Navy had 10,701 men performing cryptologic duties, both in the Navy itself and detached to N.S.A., or about 1 man in 70.

The United States Air Force Security Service, by contrast, actually issues a press kit. Activated in October, 1948, it is now a major command of the Air Force, headquartered in a spanking new three-story building in the shape of an inverted U at Kelly Air Force Base, San Antonio, Texas. It operates more than 50 units in 14 nations under four geographical subdivisions: European Security Region at Frankfurt, Pacific Security at Hawaii, the 6940th Security Wing at Goodfellow Air Force Base, Texas, and the 6981st Security Group at Elmendorf Air Force Base, Alaska. It also trains specialists at the U.S.A.F.S.S. Technical School at Goodfellow.

Its press kit describes its operations in this way:

> Foreign nations who cherish harmful designs against the Free World are constantly seeking useful information regarding the U.S. Aerospace forces. A prime target for such information seekers is the United States Air Force communications system.
>
> The primary responsibility for insuring that these nations are denied access to information transmitted over U.S.A.F. communications facilities is vested in the United States Air Force Security Service (U.S.A.F.S.S.). This mission is one of communications/electronic surveillance—or more simply stated "providing communications security for the Air Force."
>
> First of all, A.F.S.S. technicians attempt to develop and supply the necessary techniques and specialized equipment needed to safeguard classified information being transmitted by electrical means by the Air Force.
>
> Secondly, these technicians monitor and analyze unclassified Air Force electrical communications to determine the amount of information of intelligence value that can be derived from these communications.
>
> Finally, A.F.S.S. reports to the originator of such communications the information developed and any procedural discrepancies noted, and they make the necessary recommendations for securing these communications against exploitation by unauthorized agents or agencies.

All this is performed, of course, under the general guidance of the N.S.A. Thus the codebooks and the lists of authenticators that U.S.A.F.S.S. produces must conform to N.S.A. policy. And the *United States Government Organization Manual* adds to a one-sentence statement of the U.S.A.F.S.S. monitoring duties this second sentence: "Additionally, U.S.A.F. Security Service units occasionally conduct research in communication phenomena in support of various elements of the U.S. Government." That, of course, is a perfectly marvelous euphemism for interception. Some of the material must go to N.S.A., some to the Air Force Assistant Chief of Staff, Intelligence (A-2).

The Army Security Agency, and probably the other two service cryptologic agencies as well, maintains reserve components as a pool of cryptologic talent in time of mobilization or emergency. During the Berlin crisis of 1961, three Army Security Agency units were among the first reservists to be called up. They were stationed at the A.S.A. School at Fort Devens, Massachusetts —though one battalion had to come all the way from California. The others were the 197th A.S.A. Company from New York and the 324th A.S.A. Battalion, with members from Chicago.

The chiefs of the three military cryptologic agencies serve under the commanders of their own armed services, who also sit as the Joint Chiefs of Staff, which serves as the military staff of the Secretary of Defense. The staff of the Joint Chiefs includes a Directorate for Communications-Electronics (J-6), whose Security and Electronic Warfare Division prepares cryptologic plans. These must be individual programs for specific operations, presumably laid out under principles established by N.S.A. The Director of Communications-Electronics is assisted in his work by the Military Communications-Electronics Board, comprised of the chief communications officers of the Army, Navy, Air Force, and Marine Corps. Among its 11 part-time panels of military personnel is one on security and cryptography and another on electronic warfare. Also within the purview of the Joint Chiefs is the Defense Intelligence Agency, which undoubtedly receives, through the service intelligence units, information that has originated in the service cryptologic agencies as well as in the National Security Agency.

N.S.A., however, does not fall under the Joint Chiefs of Staff. Under an arrangement that became effective June 15, 1963, the N.S.A. director reports to that one of the Assistant Secretaries of Defense who serves as the Deputy Director of Defense Research and Engineering. He in turn reports to the Secretary of Defense, who sits on the National Security Council, which advises the President on domestic, foreign, and military policies relating to the national security. The other members of the National Security Council are the President, the Vice President, the Secretary of State, whose department is one of N.S.A.'s major customers, both for intelligence and for security policies, and the Director of the Office of Emergency Planning, which handles civil defense and civil mobilization. This office, which comes directly under the President, includes, as an assistant director, a Director of Telecommunications Management. As the President's Special Assistant for Telecommunications, he coordinates the telecommunication activities of the government and thus may be involved with cryptologic activities in a very general way.

Serving the National Security Council is the Central Intelligence Agency, which correlates information from the several branches of the intelligence community and presents it to the Council. There is a great interchange of this

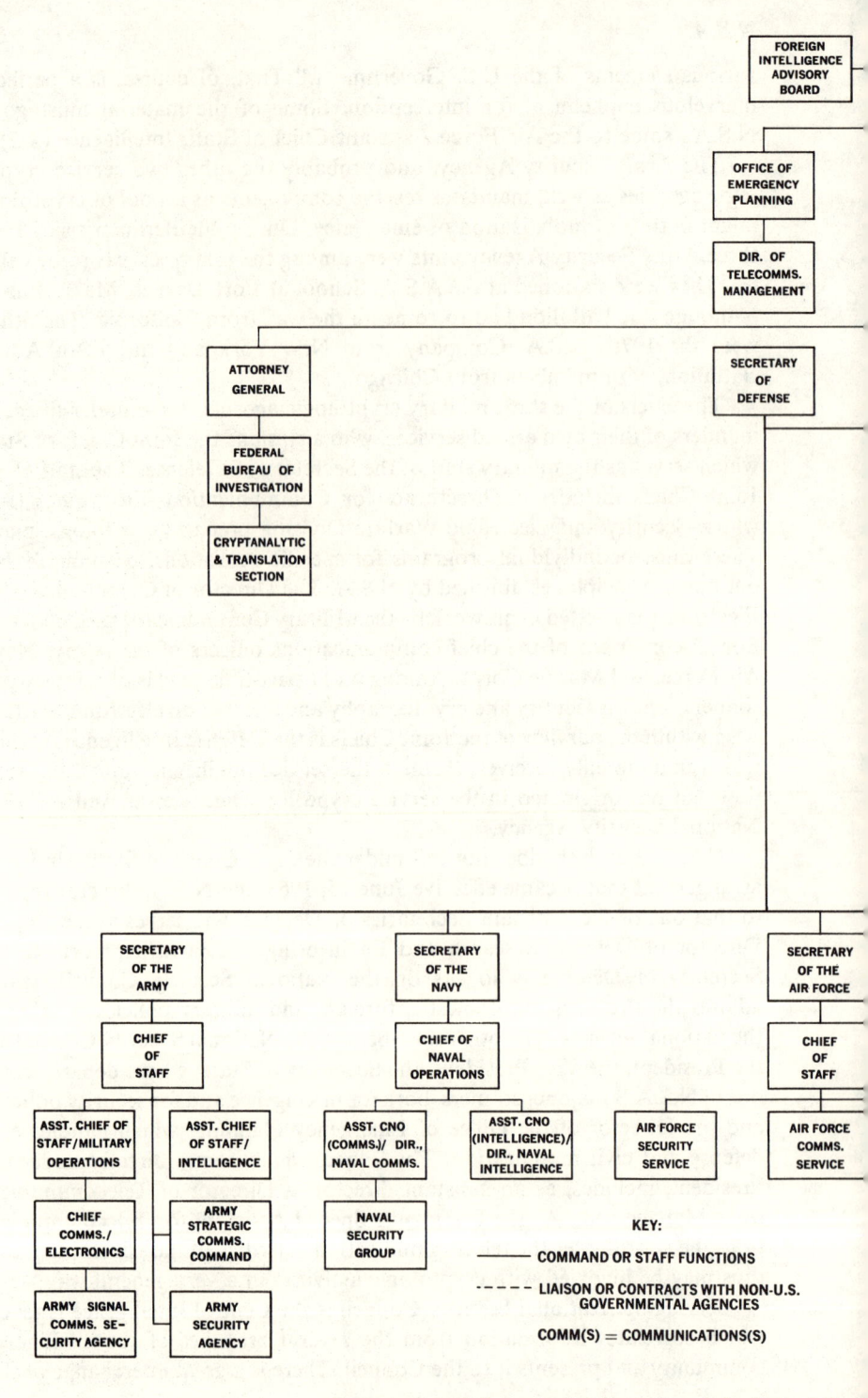

Organizational chart of chief agencies of the United State

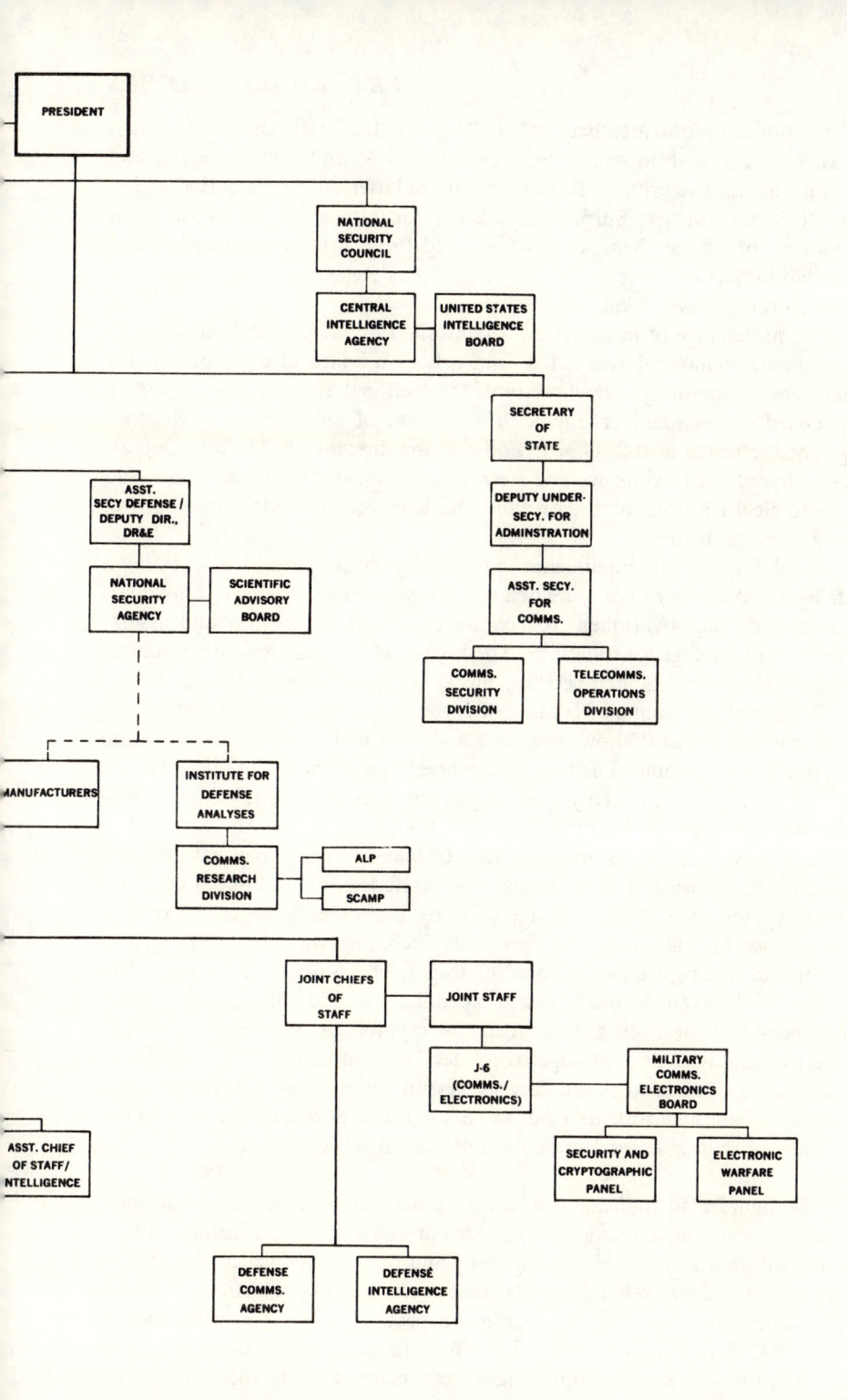

...involved in cryptology as producers, consumers, or critics

information among all members and at all levels of the intelligence community. Thus, N.S.A. may feed some intelligence to C.I.A. and some to State, and may in turn receive cribs to solution from the latter and some actual cipher keys from the former. Surprisingly, C.I.A. does some cryptanalysis itself (Rowlett worked for them for a while), and the F.B.I. Cryptanalytical and Translation Section attacks spy ciphers, such as Reino Hayhanen's message found in the hollow nickel.

The interchange of information is controlled by the United States Intelligence Board, which advises C.I.A. and acts as a board of directors for the intelligence community. The director of the National Security Agency sits on this board. Other members include the director of the Defense Intelligence Agency, the heads of G-2, O.N.I., and A-2, the director of the State Department's Bureau of Intelligence and Research, representatives of the F.B.I. and the Atomic Energy Commission, and the Director of Central Intelligence, who chairs the board.

Watchdog of the intelligence community is the President's Foreign Intelligence Advisory Board, created in 1961, with six experienced individuals from outside the government to "conduct a continuing review and assessment" of all intelligence functions. The board, which includes a communications expert among its membership, checks up specifically on N.S.A.

These multiple points of contact of cryptology with other elements of the American government show how vast and vital and complex an operation cryptology has become. The cost of the operation is enormous. In 1960, the United States was reportedly spending about $380,000,000 a year to maintain the far-flung N.S.A. intercept network and to forward the material to headquarters, and an additional $100,000,000 a year to pay salaries and operating expenses at headquarters. This excludes any additional costs incurred by the separate service agencies. By 1966, the figure had reportedly zoomed to $1 billion a year, probably including the cost of launching satellites to intercept other nations' messages. This amounted to about two per cent of the 1966 national defense expenditure of $50 billion, and it meant an expenditure of over $15 a year for cryptologic protection for each American family. This is a budget absolutely without precedent in the history of cryptology. It measures the distance cryptology has traveled just since the War and State departments paid out a total of a third of a million dollars over an entire decade for Yardley's American Black Chamber.

The figure also indicates the extraordinary value that the government places on cryptologic material—or, more precisely, on the information contained within the armor of cryptography and on the intelligence obtained by cryptanalysis. Great value demands great protection, and the effort to protect has shaped the characteristic external aspect of N.S.A.: imperviousness, blankness, silence, utter security. The efforts to attain this impregnability are not idle, for numerous attempts have been made by both the free and the

Communist worlds to penetrate each other's cryptologic secrets. This cloak-and-dagger work is the "practical cryptanalysis" which the Soviet Union has always engaged in, and which it has pursued with great vigor throughout the Cold War.

As early as 1946, Soviet agents obtained from cipher clerk Emma Woikin the gists of plaintext telegrams of the Canadian Ministry of External Affairs, and perhaps details of the ministry's cryptographic systems. Roy A. Rhodes, a married Army sergeant assigned to the motor pool at the American embassy in Moscow, went out drinking with some Russian "mechanics" around Christmas of 1952 and woke up in bed with a girl who later told him she was pregnant; threatened with disclosure of this episode to his wife, Rhodes revealed details of his earlier cryptographic work to the Russians. In 1954, a 27-year-old British ex-soldier named John Clarence was sentenced to five years' imprisonment for giving the Russians a codeword of "prime importance" for mobilizing Britain's northeastern air defense.

The incidents crowd one upon the other. At 7 p.m. on March 5, 1957, Dhanapolo Samarasekara, a Ceylonese, removed what was almost certainly the Ceylonese diplomatic code from the offices of the Ceylonese delegation to the United Nations in New York and delivered it to Vladimir A. Grusha, first secretary of the Soviet U.N. delegation. They met again an hour later and Samarasekara returned the red-bound book to the filing cabinets of the fourth-floor code room. On July 15, Prime Minister S. W. R. D. Bandaranaike told Ceylon's House of Commons that the code had been replaced "as a precaution." In 1959, Vadim A. Kirilyuk, a Russian working for the United Nations, urged an American who the Soviets knew from a scholarship application had worked on cryptographic machines to give information on them and to get a job with a vital U.S. agency, presumably N.S.A. The American strung him along for five visits, until, in January, 1960, Kirilyuk was declared persona non grata and sent home.

The care and thoroughness that Moscow lavishes upon this work, and consequently the importance with which it regards it, is nowhere better shown than in a letter to M.V.D. representatives in Australia. The Russians had been trying for two years to get information about French diplomatic cryptosystems from Mme. Rose-Marie Ollier, a second secretary doing cryptographic work at the French embassy in Canberra, but had made little progress. On January 2, 1952, M.V.D. headquarters wrote:

> In order that we should be able to make a maximum use of Mme. Ollier's agent capacities, Pakhomov must in the first place ascertain what type of work she carries out at the Embassy, her daily work routine: when she starts work, when is the lunch-hour break, where she lunches, when she finishes work, etc. It is particularly necessary to elucidate all the details connected with the fulfillment of her duties as cipher clerk, namely: in what room is she engaged on cipher work, where the cipher documents are kept, does she have access to the safe, where the ciphers are kept, and does she carry on her person the keys to the

safe, etc. It is also absolutely necessary to elucidate, at first orally, the actual technique of the enciphering and deciphering of cables. The elucidation of all these details is necessary to enable us to determine what would be the best way, least liable to exposure, of effecting the acquisition of deposits of ciphers of her embassy.

Pakhomov failed to get any information from Mme. Ollier, and was recalled in part because of this. Moscow then transferred the assignment to Vladimir Petrov (adding "ciphers of countries of Anglo-American bloc"), but he did not succeed either. The Australian Commission on Espionage that investigated this and other matters following Petrov's defection declared that "If they, the M.V.D., could, unknown to the French, get the key to their communications, the security not only of France but of the whole Western world might well be in jeopardy."

Strangely, this bitter possibility came partly true in 1954, when the Russians, having failed with France in Australia, succeeded in Paris. Communists in the message center of the French National Defense Committee stole a War Ministry cryptosystem and used it to read orders to the embattled bastion of Dien Bien Phu. This inside information may have contributed to the ultimate capitulation of that fortress, to France's consequent loss of French Indochina, and so to the miseries and warfare in Laos and Vietnam that, more than a decade later, still plagued the West.

The effort to get cryptologic material is not limited to the Russians. The Poles photographed Irwin W. (Doc) Scarbeck, 41, second secretary of the American embassy in Warsaw, naked in bed with his 22-year-old Polish mistress, who then urged him "to get for them the cipher." They also offered him 20,000 zlotys, or $833, for the cryptographic information, but he refused. On Formosa in 1957, organized rioters with axes concentrated on smashing their way into the American embassy code room during anti-American demonstrations. Failing to force the heavy iron door guarding the codes, they hacked through a six-inch concrete wall. The ambassador on the spot said that this would mean "some readjustment" of U.S. codes, but Secretary of State John Foster Dulles later reassured the nation that none had been compromised.

The free world engages in practical cryptanalysis too, and it has had its triumphs. In the nature of things, they are less publicized than the failures. Two former N.S.A. employees reported that "the United States Government gave money to a code clerk working in the Washington embassy of a United States ally [later identified as Turkey] for supplying information which assisted in the decryption of that ally's code messages." They also revealed that cryptanalytic "success in at least one case has also been facilitated by the fact that the United States supplied to other nations cipher machines for which it knew the construction and wiring of the rotors." Another ex-employee disclosed that "N.S.A. also obtains the originals of national ciphers from secret sources. This indicates that someone steals the ciphers of the Near East countries for the Americans. In N.S.A. I actually saw photocopies of ciphers of the Syrian

General Staff, and also instructions for using them." In Sofia in 1963, former Bulgarian Communist diplomat Ivan-Asen K. Georgiev pleaded guilty to charges of spying that included having disclosed the code of the Bulgarian mission to the United Nations to an American professor, who was probably a C.I.A. agent.

How lax security can be at some places is indicated by the experience of two American girls doing secretarial work for the Iranian mission to the United Nations. From time to time, when the mission's Hagelin machine jammed and the Iranians could not clear it, they called in the girls, who seemed to have a mechanical knack, to get it working again. The gross security blunder of letting two Americans—who might have been (but were not) reporting to the C.I.A.—examine so vital a secret seems never to have occurred to the Iranians.

Practical cryptanalysis has even been acknowledged at the highest level. The source is none other than Nikita Sergeyevitch Khrushchev. While sightseeing in Los Angeles with U.S. Ambassador to the U.N. Henry Cabot Lodge during his 1959 visit to the United States, the Soviet Premier boasted that he had seen a message that President Eisenhower had sent to Prime Minister Nehru of India about border troubles with Red China, as well as a message to Eisenhower from the Shah of Iran. Earlier, in Washington, he remarked to C.I.A. chief Allen Dulles that C.I.A. agents gave their codebooks to the Russians, which the Soviets used to feed false information to the C.I.A. and to demand and receive money. He suggested that the U.S. and the U.S.S.R. save money by pooling intelligence services.

It was no joke to American security officials, particularly those involved in cryptology. They go to extraordinary lengths to prevent security leaks. The United States channels cryptologic information through a separate security category of its own. Cryptographic equipment and documents are distributed, stored, and registered separately from other classified equipment and documents. Top-secret security clearances will not automatically permit their holders to see cryptologic information: this requires a special crypto clearance. Army Regulation 380-5 on military security accords cryptology an entire special section. President Kennedy's Executive Order 10964 on security exempts cryptologic material "from automatic downgrading or declassification," and adds: "Nothing in this order shall prohibit any special requirements that the originating agency or other appropriate authority may impose as to communications intelligence, cryptography, and matters related thereto."

Similarly, Congress in 1950 agreed with Defense Department contentions that neither the Espionage Law of 1917 nor the Yardley Law of 1933 (which covered only diplomatic codes) afforded sufficient protection to American cryptologic affairs. It enacted* Public Law 513, codified as Title 18, Section

* The Report from the Senate Committee on Armed Services recommending passage of the bill (S. 277) was submitted by Lyndon B. Johnson.

798, United States Code, which specifically made it a crime, punishable by a fine of $10,000 and a jail term of 10 years, to disclose classified information concerning American or foreign cryptosystems, "the communication intelligence activities of the United States or any foreign government," or material "obtained by the processes of communication intelligence."

This special protection stems in part from the extraordinary damage that betrayal of cryptosystems can do. Knowledge of a cipher system can give an enemy insight into quantities of information, whereas knowledge of, say, a particular weapon is limited to that item. In part, the protection is needed because of the special sensitivity of cryptanalytic intelligence. A nation can change its codes upon the merest suspicion that they are being read and can thus deprive its foe of an important source of intelligence. But to deprive the foe of intelligence obtained by a spy means first finding that spy in a large population.

The presidential directive that created the National Security Agency was and is classified as security information, and the veil thus thrown around the agency at its very birth has cloaked it to this day. N.S.A. is even more still, more secret, and more grave than the C.I.A., whose basic functions are set forth in the 1947 law that created it. C.I.A. officials have occasionally issued statements to the press and have more often leaked favorable publicity. N.S.A. officials never have. The National Security Agency thus remains the most reticent and least known organ of the entire hush-hush American intelligence community.

At N.S.A. security begins outside. Three fences ring the headquarters building. The inner and outer are Cyclone fences topped with V's of barbed wire. The middle one is a five-strand electrified wire. These are pierced by four gatehouses manned by Marine guards. When the gates are closed, a complicated electronic apparatus involving mirrors and lights buzzes warningly. Gatehouse 3, on the north side of the building, is open 24 hours a day.

Security permeates N.S.A.'s interior as well. Both the agency's organization and the physical arrangements that reflect this organization are highly compartmented, with numerous checkpoints, and employees are not permitted to enter areas in which they do not work without special permission. Colored badges limit them to their own areas. Pistol-packing guards block the entrance to specially restricted areas. The most secret documents must be locked in three-tumbler safes except when analysts are actually working on them—and these areas are also patrolled night and day. Offices that generate the least confidential documents in quantity may store them in desks or in file cabinets, sometimes unlocked, but these offices are under constant armed guard. When classified papers must be taken from N.S.A. to other agencies, employees must not go alone if they use a private car but must travel in pairs. They must keep the papers in a locked briefcase and must store them overnight in a safe stowage either at the other agency or at N.S.A.; they may not take them home.

Similar precautions are taken wherever cryptologic material is used. At the United States mission to the United Nations in New York, the code room is protected by a solid steel door three and a quarter inches thick. Guards patrol the corridor outside. Windows are frosted. White plastic domes on the ceiling emit ultrasonic rays that sound a warning if anyone moves in the room after hours. The cipher machines themselves stand in an alcove around a corner, hidden from the eyes of anybody at the door or admitted to the main message area. And to cut down on the number of times that the door has to be opened, the code room has its own pantry—and its own toilet.

N.S.A. security extends even to unclassified letters to private citizens. Unlike other government agencies, its envelopes are imprinted on the inside with markings that prevent anyone from reading the text of the letter through the envelope. And N.S.A. carefully words these letters to reveal as little as possible about itself. One minor slip-up gave away the agency technique. An amateur cryptologist offered N.S.A. his translation of a German doctoral dissertation in mathematics with cryptologic applications. He did not refer to it as a dissertation. N.S.A. declined the offer by saying that it "has no need of this dissertation"—a clear indication that the agency knew of the document and probably had it as well, but did not want to admit an interest in cryptology by saying so. N.S.A. supervisors tell new employees that this apparently obsessive preoccupation with security constitutes a large margin of safety: If the employee does not talk about even the obvious, he will not come close to talking about secret matters. In addition, this blanket coverage makes it much easier for N.S.A. to maintain security than a selective discrimination and release of items, such as textbooks, that are not really secret.

Among the agency's deep secrets is its annual budget. N.S.A. does not appear in the federal budget. All its funds, like those of the C.I.A., are cunningly concealed by adding a few million dollars to each of several line items in other parts of the budget. The chiefs of the agencies whose budget figures are thus padded know only that the money is for a classified project, but in many cases Congress is told in executive sessions what the figures are for these projects. The Secretary of Defense can legally shift the funds from one unit to another, within certain limits. Unlike the C.I.A., N.S.A. finances are audited by the Government Accounting Office. The results, however, have not been shown to Congress, G.A.O.'s boss.

The employees themselves must pass the strictest security standards in the Department of Defense. A prospective employee must pass the National Agency Check, in which several investigative agencies report any facts they have bearing on his loyalty. He must also pass a lie detector test.* He may then be hired for training, but final clearance depends upon a full Background Investigation. This involves verification of birth, education, and employment records, interviews with friends, neighbors, and former co-workers and

* This has led to abuses. One 17-year-old girl, trying to get a job as clerk-typist with N.S.A., was asked many over-intimate questions about her sex life.

employers on his trustworthiness and maturity, analysis of credit records, and a further check for membership in subversive organizations. No one who has close kin in an Iron Curtain country may be hired. Even after having passed these requirements and been hired, all employees undergo follow-up checks every four years to make sure that their security clearance should be maintained. All except some of the older employees must pass repeated lie detector tests. They must also periodically sign a certificate that they have read Public Law 513.

N.S.A. dins security security security security into its employees with remorseless persistence until it becomes more than habitual, more than second nature—it becomes virtual instinct. Many, perhaps most, N.S.A.ers never tell their wives and children just what their jobs are. "N.S.A.," they explain, stands for "Never Say Anything." The Security Education Program pulls out all stops: "Our job with N.S.A. is essential to the preservation of our American way of life. As part of that job, fulfilling our security obligations is equally essential to the success or failure of this Agency in the accomplishment of its mission." So thorough is the indoctrination that one employee wondered in a poem whether being not allowed to say what he did in this world would have dire effects in the next:

> But to St. Peter, must I say,
> "I learned my lesson well.
> You see, I worked at N.S.A.,
> So send me on to ——."

The bitter irony of all this is that, despite all the precautions, N.S.A. has been involved in security breaches more spectacular and more damaging to the free world than any others in the Cold War except those of the atomic spies.

The first involved Joseph Sidney Petersen, Jr. His arrest October 9, 1954, for taking classified documents from A.F.S.A.-N.S.A. made front-page news in both the largest U.S. daily—the New York *Sunday News*—and the most respected—*The New York Times*. Petersen, 39, a former physics teacher, had taken the Army correspondence course in cryptanalysis in 1940 and 1941 and had joined the Signal Intelligence Service in mid-1941. In his 13 years at Arlington Hall he worked on almost every problem and, on his own initiative just after the war, began giving sorely needed and "very successful" instruction in cryptology for new employees and for old ones who had become overspecialized. This training program was made official in 1953, becoming the basis for the present N.S.A. School. Petersen said he took two of the classified documents to help in preparing lessons. One was *Chinese Telegraphic Code SP-D*, with addenda and errata, dated July 1, 1945, and classified "secret"; this is the Ming commercial code in which 10,000 Chinese ideographs are assigned four-digit codenumbers so that they can be sent by telegraph, with some agency annotations. The other was A.F.S.A. 23 0763; KC 037, "Routing of North Korean Political Security Traffic as Indicated by Group A2," dated February 20, 1951, a traffic analysis classified "top secret."

During World War II, the tall, myopic Petersen had become friends with short, trim Colonel J. A. Verkuyl of the Royal Netherland Indies Army, one of Holland's finest cryptanalysts (with two others, he drew up the report on the cryptography of NORDPOL for the Dutch government). Verkuyl, a liaison officer, sat at the desk next to Petersen in Arlington Hall as together they solved Japanese diplomatic code messages—a field in which Verkuyl had had considerable prewar experience. Through Verkuyl, Petersen met Giacomo Stuyt, communications officer at the Dutch embassy. Their mutual interest in mathematics and in their work led them into discussions of cryptology.

After the war, when Verkuyl returned to Holland, Petersen mailed him ideas about instructional methods and other details helpful to his setting up of a cryptologic corps in Holland. Stuyt stayed in America and Petersen remained friendly with him. The Dutch at this time were using the Hagelin machine for their diplomatic communications, and in 1948 Petersen, for reasons that have never been explained, copied top-secret notes indicating American success in breaking Netherlands cryptosystems and removed a 1939 Signal Intelligence Service document entitled "Analysis of the Hagelin Cryptograph, Type B-211," and showed them to Stuyt. (The B-211 was not the M-209 widely used in World War II: it was the printing version of the machine that Hagelin had invented in 1925, nine years before he created the C-36, ancestor of the M-209.) Verkuyl thinks that Petersen was motivated, not by any intent to harm the United States' cryptanalytic effort, but to help secure the communications of his friends from other nations' prying.

When F.B.I. agents searched Petersen's apartment in the fall of 1954, they found the notes and documents. It was the first case to come under Public Law 513. Perhaps for that reason the Justice and Defense departments decided to prosecute instead of handling the matter administratively within N.S.A. to prevent publicity. Possibly they sought to make an example out of Petersen. But, as his lawyer said, "they had a bear by the tail after the decision was made," for the arrest attracted tremendous news coverage. The prosecution urged him to withdraw his plea of not guilty and to plead guilty to prevent the exposure of evidence that a trial would require. Petersen, filled with remorse, eager to repair the damage he had done to his country, and hoping to lighten his sentence, agreed. It seems likely that the government hinted at a light or suspended sentence. Federal District Judge Albert V. Bryan did dismiss two of the indictment's three counts. But, declaring that "The pith of this offense is not *what* the defendant withdrew, but *that* he withdrew, records from the National Security Agency," he sandbagged Petersen with a seven-year term. Petersen served four years before being paroled. The government thus managed to create an example for other potential offenders without the risks of a trial. How fair it was to Petersen remains an open question. But perhaps one should not argue with success: since Petersen, there have been no more prosecutions for leaking cryptologic information.

In the most spectacular of the security breaches, the only reason for the failure to prosecute was the venue of the potential defendants, well beyond the jurisdiction of federal authorities. They had gone to Soviet Russia. These were the turncoat American cryptologists, William Hamilton Martin and Bernon Ferguson Mitchell, who in 90 minutes of blabbing at a Moscow press conference in 1960 told more to a bigger audience in less time about any nation's intelligence effort than any other traitors have ever done.

Though much is known about these two young men, nothing is really known about why they betrayed their country. Both were West Coast boys, both extremely bright, both raised in an atmosphere as American as apple pie, and both "clean" enough to pass the rigorous Navy cryptologic clearance. Bernon Mitchell, born March 11, 1929, grew up in Eureka, California, where his father had a successful law practice. He concentrated on science in high school and engaged in such adolescent pranks as filling balloons with hydrogen and exploding them in airbursts that frightened the neighbors. When a teacher would lead him no further into the theory of relativity than he himself had gone, he abruptly quit Eureka High School and transferred to another school 80 miles north. He declared himself an agnostic, debated philosophy aggressively, played poker with a few close friends, read deeply in the philosophy of mathematics. A tall, lean youth with dark wavy hair and regular features, he seldom dated. In 1951, after a year and a half at the California Institute of Technology and under pressure from the draft, he enlisted in the Navy. He was cleared for cryptology and assigned to that work at the Yokosuka Naval Base.

There he met William Martin, a soft-faced youth who was born May 27, 1931, in Columbus, Georgia. The Martins had moved to Ellensburg, Washington, when Bill was 15. He was so brilliant a student in junior high school that a psychologist tested him to see if he should skip high school altogether and enter the University of Chicago in a program for gifted children. He was scholastically qualified for it, but his principal thought he was neither mature nor socially developed enough to bypass high school. Nevertheless, he finished three high school years in two. His interests lay in hypnotism, reading, psychology, and chess; at 17, he won the chess championship of the Northwest. He always wore a white shirt and tie but evinced no interest in girls. His personality was almost overbearing: he was quite capable of giving gratuitous and insulting advice to adults. He studied a year at Ellensburg's Central Washington College of Education—where he developed an interest in mathematics—before joining the Navy and meeting Mitchell in cryptologic work.

The two became firm friends during their four-year tours. After Mitchell returned to the United States to study mathematics at Stanford University, where he had a B average in the subjects that N.S.A. needed, Martin stayed on in Japan to do cryptologic work for the Army, then came back home to major in mathematics at the University of Washington. He had almost straight A's for his last two years. Both were separately approached by N.S.A. recruiters a few days apart in February and March, 1957, and offered employment. Both accepted and were hired as mathematicians, Civil Service grade GS-7, at about $6,000 a year, reporting for duty July 8, 1957, apparently under an interim security clearance. Later, under a lie detector examination, Mitchell admitted that he had engaged in sexual experiences with dogs and chickens when he was between 13 and 19; the agency's security office felt that this adolescent experimentation did not furnish sufficient basis for denying final clearance, which was eventually granted. Martin's investigation revealed that acquaintances considered him an insufferable egotist, slightly effeminate, not wholly normal, somewhat irresponsible, and susceptible to flattery. His superiors almost unanimously said that they would not want to have him work for them again, but all except one affirmed that he was loyal to the United States. Both men attended the N.S.A. School during the summer, then studied at George Washington University in the fall. Both reported to N.S.A.'s Office of Research and Development on January 27, 1958, for cryptologic duties. Mitchell's final clearance had come through four days earlier; Martin's was not granted until May 12.

They took separate bachelor apartments in Laurel, Maryland, not far from N.S.A. headquarters. Martin began picking up girls in Washington bars. Both joined the Washington Chess Divan, and Mitchell captained the N.S.A. chess team. Martin's work was so good that the head of Research and Development gave him a letter of praise and approved him for a N.S.A. scholarship. He later won an extension of this for another year—the first in N.S.A. to get a two-year scholarship. Under this, he went, in September, 1959, to the University of Illinois to take a master's degree in mathematics, while also studying Russian. Mitchell, in Washington, had an unhappy love affair with a married woman who was separated from her husband.

During this year, both men first expressed strong anti-American political feelings. Martin associated with a Communist at Illinois, and in December, 1959, he and Mitchell traveled to Cuba in violation of N.S.A. directives. It has been reported, however, that they had been members of the Communist party since at least February 4, 1958, when membership cards were allegedly issued to them. Both felt so strongly opposed to the then-secret U-2 flights over the Soviet Union, which they knew about through their work, that they visited Representative Wayne Hayes, an Ohio Democrat, to warn him of the "great dangers." In May, 1960, Mitchell, who worked out regularly with barbells and had posed for nude color slides seated on a velvet-covered stool, began visiting psychiatrist Dr. Clarence Schilt for intellectual discussions of homosexuality.

In June, soon after Martin had returned from Illinois, the two applied for annual leave for the two and a half weeks from June 24 to July 11. This was approved, and their supervisor also authorized them to extend their leaves to

July 18 in case they needed more time to visit their parents' homes on the West Coast. They never went there. Instead, they purchased one-way tickets to Mexico City on Eastern Air Lines Flight 305, leaving Washington's National Airport a little before noon on June 25. From Mexico City they flew to Havana on July 1. From there they apparently sailed on a Soviet trawler to Russia. For nearly a month nothing happened. On July 26, their chief tried to reach them at their Laurel apartments and at their parents' homes, and, when he could not, notified the personnel office. When a quiet investigation turned up the flight to Mexico, the Defense Department on August 1 announced their unauthorized absence, and four days later conceded that "there is a likelihood that they have gone behind the Iron Curtain."

They stepped back in front of it September 6 in the brightly lit theater of Moscow's House of Journalists. At a lavishly staged press conference, they read a long statement announcing that they had renounced their American citizenship and had received Soviet citizenship, and giving their reasons for their defection:

> Our main dissatisfaction concerned some of the practices the United States uses in gathering intelligence information. We were worried about the United States policy of deliberately violating the airspace of other nations, and the United States Government's practice of lying about such violations in a manner intended to mislead public opinion.
>
> Furthermore, we were disenchanted by the United States Government's practice of intercepting and deciphering the secret communications of its own allies. Finally, we objected to the fact that the United States Government was willing to go so far as to recruit agents from among the personnel of its allies.

They chose Russia, they said, because:

> In the Soviet Union our main values and interests appear to be shared by a greater number of people. Consequently we feel that we will be better accepted socially there and will be better able to carry out our professional activities.
>
> Another motivating factor is that the talents of women are encouraged and utilized to a much greater extent in the Soviet Union than in the United States. We feel that this enriches Soviet society and makes Soviet women more desirable as mates.

Following which double-talk, they proceeded to reveal American successes in cryptanalysis on an enormous scale. Their revelations caused many nations to change keys and systems, though, astonishingly, some of the very nations named took no action at all. The result was a partial dim-out of United States communications intelligence—and probably of Soviet Russia's as well. Some N.S.A. cryptanalysts went on double shifts, beginning the complex reconstruction of rotor wirings and lug and pin settings all over again. The first reaction of N.S.A.ers was shock; the second, anger: "The dirty bastards!" President Eisenhower branded them traitors. The Pentagon, stating that one was "mentally sick" and both "obviously confused," denounced the statements of both as "falsehoods"—itself a falsehood, in view of the Defense Department's own concession in its bill of particulars in the Petersen case that it had broken the code of its Dutch ally. The House Un-American Activities Committee and a special subcommittee of the House Armed Services Committee launched investigations, as did the Pentagon.

No one ever came up with a satisfactory explanation of why the two men had defected. It was suggested that they might have been homosexuals; but if they were, they would not have had to go to Russia to practice their perversion. On the other hand, there seemed no evidence of overt homosexual activities that might have subjected them to blackmail. The report of their being Communists does not say why they joined the party. Some have suggested that the immorality of codebreaking might have revolted them, which is what the pair hinted at in their Moscow statement; but why should this trouble only them so drastically and not other N.S.A.ers? One possible reason: a basic personality imbalance. Another theory for their defection involves the "syndrome of the labyrinth," in which the secrecy of the work precluded any external recognition. Here, too, this affected only Martin and Mitchell. Least satisfactory of all reasons was one of their own: that the United States spies on its allies. This displays a willful blindness to the duplicity of Soviet espionage and Soviet policy in general. A Freudian hypothesis has never been confuted, but never confirmed either: that the two were in unconscious rebellion against their fathers and had displaced this emotion onto the father figure of the government. The answer will probably never be known.

In its investigation, however, the House Un-American Activities Committee turned up some further violations of security in what it called "the most sensitive and secretive of all agencies established by the U.S. Government to protect the Nation's security and that of its people in a deadly cold war." Twenty-six sexual deviates were found to be employed by the agency; these were fired. Personnel procedures were shockingly lax. The agency habitually employed personnel before full clearances had been obtained. This practice, permitted under an emergency regulation, had begun in the manpower-short years of the Korean War, but remained in effect a decade later. N.S.A. often ignored derogatory information uncovered during background investigations. It relied too heavily on lie detector results. In at least one case, it hired a person denied employment by another government agency because he was strongly suspected of both homosexuality and Communist activities.

The most ironic violations involved the agency's directors of security and of personnel. The general counsel of the Defense Department had said piously: "A system of checks and balances has been established to protect the integrity of the Agency's security requirements. The authority to hire employees is delegated to the Director of Personnel, but the authority to grant security clearances is delegated to the Director of Security." When the House committee got through, the arrangement looked more like a mutual cover-up.

Maurice H. Klein, the personnel director, admitted that he had stated on his own employment forms that he had been graduated from Harvard Law School when in fact it had been from New Jersey Law School, and that he had tried to conceal this and a few other peccadilloes by retyping and falsely dating his records. The director of security, former F.B.I. agent S. Wesley Reynolds, knew of these discrepancies but concluded that they "did not have security significance." Both men resigned, Reynolds under a rule banning acceptance of favors from those doing business with the government.

A year after the committee issued its report, a former N.S.A. employee revealed more American cryptologic secrets in a letter in *Izvestia*. He was Victor Norris Hamilton, an Arab who had become a naturalized American citizen and changed his name from Hindali after coming to the United States with the American woman he had met in Libya and then married. A graduate of the American University in Beirut, he worked as a doorman and bellhop in Georgia because, he said, he was barred from teaching because he was an Arab. A retired American colonel recruited him for N.S.A., and he began work there June 13, 1957, as a $6,400-a-year research analyst—or cryptanalyst —solving the cryptosystems of Arab countries. Hamilton was forced to resign on June 3, 1959. According to him, officials became suspicious when he wanted to reestablish contact with relatives in Syria. According to the Defense Department, he was "approaching a paranoid-schizophrenic break." Whatever the reason, he sought asylum in the Soviet Union and presumably told that government of his work before writing his letter to denounce America's espionage practices.

Hamilton's letter appeared in *Izvestia* on July 23, 1963. On that very day, an N.S.A. clerk-messenger committed suicide by inhaling carbon monoxide in his car when he realized that the jig was up in his game of selling cryptologic secrets to the Russians. He was Sergeant First Class Jack Edward Dunlap, a decorated combat veteran with an unblemished record, a family man, an average Joe. He seemed to be an ideal security risk when he was assigned to N.S.A. in April, 1958, as part of an Army Security Agency unit. His first job was as chauffeur to Major General Garrison B. Cloverdale, N.S.A.'s assistant director and chief of staff. Later he was graduated to clerk-messenger duties.

The how and the what of Dunlap's treason have never been officially revealed. The why, however, has become abundantly clear: $60,000. He spent it on a 30-foot cabin cruiser, a world's-championship hydroplane skimmer capable of more than 100 miles per hour, a baby-blue Jaguar sports car, two late-model Cadillacs, rounds of drinks for the house at expensive resorts and yacht clubs from New Jersey to Florida, and a blonde mistress. He apparently began peddling his secrets in mid-1960, while Martin and Mitchell were planning their runaway, for in June of that year he bought the cabin cruiser with a $3,400 cash payment. He seems to have smuggled out the top-secret documents under his shirt (guards did not frisk personnel, though briefcases were spot-checked), and turned them over to the Russians, at first once a week, later once a month. His mistress knew only that he visited "the bookkeeper" regularly and returned with a large roll of bills. He told acquaintances various stories to explain his new wealth: that he owned land on which a mineral valuable for cosmetics had been discovered; that he had come into a little inheritance; that his father—actually a bridge-tender— owned a large plantation in Dunlap's native Louisiana. What he told and gave the Russians is unknown to Americans, but it may have included top-secret American estimates of the capabilities of the Soviet Army and Navy and nuclear forces, together with similar data on North Atlantic Treaty Organization forces.

Despite N.S.A.'s vaunted security programs, none of this was discovered —even though Dunlap drove to work in his Jaguar or one of the Cadillacs, took time off to race his hydroplane, began dating an N.S.A. secretary. Ironically, N.S.A. had sent an Army ambulance to return him to Fort Meade Army Hospital when he injured his back in a regatta, lest the local hospital give him sedatives which might make him talk—yet never once wondered how he could afford the yacht club in the first place. He was trapped, not by alert N.S.A. work, but by his own greed. Fearful that he might be transferred out of N.S.A. at the end of his duty tour, he applied in March, 1963, to leave the Army but keep his N.S.A. job as a civilian. This brought him into contact with a lie detector for the first time; service personnel assigned to the agency are not subjected to a polygraph test, but prospective civilian employees are. Two tests discovered evidence of petty thievery and immoral living.

For two months nothing happened. He continued his job and his thefts. Then further investigations disclosed that he was living beyond his pay, and he was quickly transferred to a routine job in a Fort Meade orderly room with no access to secret information. The investigation dragged slowly on, and it was not until a month after Dunlap killed himself—after two unsuccessful attempts—that the leisurely sleuths discovered that Dunlap's widow had found a sheaf of highly classified official papers among her husband's belongings. For the first time the F.B.I. was called in, but Dunlap's death ended all hope of learning exactly what he had peddled to the Reds. "To be safe," one authority said, "you have to proceed on the assumption that everything which passed through this section might be resting in a file in Moscow."

Episodes like these are bad in the short run, but in the long run their effects may be salutary. They shook the National Security Agency out of its smug self-complacency. For the agency had been so sure, so cocksure, so almost arrogantly certain that all cryptologic wisdom resided behind its triple fence, that its secrecy was hermetic, that, while improvement was always possible, there was very little room left for it at N.S.A.

Take, for example, the case of the road signs. When N.S.A. moved to Fort Meade, large white-on-green signs pointing to it blossomed on the

Baltimore-Washington Expressway. After employees became familiar with the new location, the signs were removed, presumably as a security measure. One can just hear the security staff congratulating itself for thinking of even that tiny detail. Yet at that moment the agency was harboring Martin, Mitchell, Hamilton, and Dunlap, as well as a dishonest director of personnel, a favor-taking director of security, and a couple of dozen sex deviates.

The agency impressed itself mightily. The Ming telegraphic code, which Petersen had taken, is a case in point. This is a public code which the agency republished with some annotations and classified "secret." An official explained that "It [the N.S.A. version] identifies it [the public code] with the agency, and therefore, indirectly it implies the work of the agency." But the legal criterion for classifying information "secret" is that its disclosure could "result in serious damage to the nation." One wonders whether in so grading the Ming code the agency does not exaggerate its importance a little.

The thick swaddling of secrecy insulated the agency from external examination and cauterization. As the Un-American Activities Committee wrote, "Past efforts by the Defense Department to investigate N.S.A. were ineffective for the most part because, when matters involving irregularities at the Agency were brought to the attention of the Department, it more often than not appointed as the investigators of the irregularities the very N.S.A. officials responsible for their existence." So strong was the agency's resistance to outside criticism that, the committee reported, "In 1960, when the investigation began, obstacle after obstacle was placed in the path of the committee." After Robert S. McNamara became Secretary of Defense in 1961, he cooperated much more closely with the committee than had his predecessor, Thomas S. Gates, Jr.

"The results," the committee said, "were rewarding." N.S.A. tightened its employment security practices. For example, it denied conditional employees access to sensitive material until they were fully cleared. It stopped delegating the director's authority to grant interim clearance for access to top-secret material. It appointed a board of psychiatric consultants to improve its psychological assessment program. It required supervisors to notify the personnel and security offices within two hours of any worker's unauthorized absence. It alerted supervisors to signs of undue mental strain. The agency also instituted some additional reforms, such as the expansion and reorganization of its Office of Security Services.

But perhaps the most important result was the improvement in N.S.A.'s attitude. It swallowed the bitter pill of Congressional criticism and cured itself of its infallibility syndrome. It discovered that there were things outside Fort Meade that it could learn with profit. Cooperation between the committee and N.S.A. "proved most beneficial to the committee's investigation and to the Agency's self-analysis of its programs and practices," the committee wrote. "The committee is confident that, through its efforts, N.S.A. has been helped and the national interest and security strengthened. It also believes that the N.S.A. and Defense Department have made a significant contribution to the national security by the manner in which they assisted the investigation and took steps to correct deficiencies pointed up in the course of the inquiry."

This return to reality was also marked by an increasing maturity in security matters. The agency is less hysterical about petty details, suggesting that it is more confident in essential points. For several years, N.S.A. recruiting pamphlets did not so much as mention the words "code" and "cipher," or any related words—presumably for the same reason that the Ming code was stamped "secret." But in 1964, a pamphlet for prospective employees declared: "N.S.A., as the Agency of the government responsible for the security of all U.S. communications systems, has need to recruit and develop specialists in cryptography." At about the same time, the agency declassified William F. Friedman's 1937 War Department publication on the Zimmermann telegram. These incidents imply that the agency has closed the gap that the case of the road signs epitomized—the gap between what the agency's preening self-esteem told it and what things were really like.

All this points up the value of Congressional surveillance of intelligence agencies. Yet Congress has shown an odd reluctance to put into practice the lessons of this case history. Subcommittees of the House and the Senate Armed Services and Appropriations Committees undoubtedly oversee N.S.A.'s operations, as they do those of the C.I.A., but these shadowy groups—they are not even listed in the *Congressional Directory*—appear to be less than vigorous in discharging these duties.

Though the Dunlap case came after reforms instituted as a result of the House Un-American Activities Committee investigation, both houses of Congress declined to look into it. "If a similar series of tragic blunders occurred in any ordinary agency of Government," wrote a journalist who had studied the Dunlap case in detail, "an aroused public would insist that those responsible be officially censured, demoted, or fired." Said Stewart Alsop: "The N.S.A. particularly could do with a bit of supervision. It has a horrible security record.... If the C.I.A. had been responsible for either case [Martin-Mitchell and Dunlap], there would have been a hullabaloo to make the Alger Hiss case seem tame." (To put the N.S.A. episodes into perspective: C.I.A. has not yet suffered a single known defection or penetration.) Even the Un-American Activities Committee used kid gloves. "The sensitive nature of the operation of the National Security Agency was recognized and respected by the Committee on Un-American Activities during its investigation and hearings. The committee did not attempt to learn the details of the organizational structure or the products of the Agency, feeling it had no need for knowledge in these areas." Yet greater knowledge may well have produced greater benefits.

Indeed, Congress behaves toward N.S.A. as if it is trying to propitiate the sorcerers who control the dark powers of cryptology. In 1956, the director,

Lieutenant General Ralph J. Canine, testified before a House committee in favor of a bill to increase the number of high-paying ($10,000 to $15,000) scientific jobs in the government, including N.S.A. Chairman Tom Murray later told the House that "The committee was so impressed with the need for adequately compensating people who have devoted a lifetime to this very important area, that at the request of General Canine we increased the amount from the original submission of 35 to 50 of these positions." In 1959, Congress passed Public Law 36 to exempt the N.S.A. from the legal requirement binding all government bodies to file a full description of each job in the agency with the Civil Service Commission.

In 1964, Congress gave the director of N.S.A. the power to fire at will any N.S.A. employee "whenever he considers that action to be in the interest of the United States." An identical bill had died in the Senate Judiciary Committee in the previous Congress. Both had been introduced by the House Un-American Activities Committee as a result of its Martin-Mitchell investigation. They wrote into law some of the stricter employment practices that the committee and the agency had agreed upon. In both Congresses, the summary discharge power was bitterly attacked as a violation of the Bill of Rights principle that no one shall be "deprived of life, liberty, or property, without due process of law." Liberals in the House quoted the Washington *Post*: "This [bill] is the very definition of arbitrariness. It means that an employee could be discharged and disgraced on the basis of anonymous allegations without the slightest opportunity to defend himself—without any hearing at all and without any administrative review or even any judicial review of the decision. This would put everyone working for N.S.A. at the mercy of any mischief-maker or malcontent or personal enemy who might call him a subversive or a homosexual or an alcoholic." Though the bill's sponsors did not rebut these arguments, the bill won an overwhelming 340 to 40 majority in the House and an easy voice passage in the Senate.

N.S.A. conjures up its biggest prizes from the legislative pocketbook. For Congress, which can treat some supplicants for funds very harshly, smiles beneficently upon N.S.A. In 1962, the House Armed Services Committee named a special three-man subcommittee to look into N.S.A.'s request for $10,000,000 for its nine-story annex and for money to hire more people. Since this plea came only a few years after Congress had given the agency some $35,000,000 for an enormous brand-new home, one might have expected it to encounter a rather cool reception. Instead: "After an exhaustive briefing and tour, I personally was convinced and have withdrawn all objection," said the financially conservative Republican member of the subcommittee, Durward G. Hall of Missouri. And of course N.S.A. got the money.

What is the potent spell that N.S.A. casts over Congress? Why this amazing haste to grant what appears to be the slightest whim of the agency? Much, no doubt, comes from the simple fact that, by and large, the agency does a good job. But part also comes from some razzle-dazzle by the agency's using the ultra secrets to which its work—unlike other agencies of the government—gives it access. Sometimes it lets key Congressmen take quick peeks at them, join the privileged fraternity of Those Who Know, and so champion the cause of their fraternity brother. "The members, and myself in particular," said Hall of his tour, "of the Armed Services Committee have probably seen more classified equipment and been exposed to more classified construction—from communications through telemetry—than most Members [of Congress]." More often the agency enshrouds its secrets in fearful gloom, awing Congressmen with sacred mysteries that are no more to be uttered than is the tetragrammaton. "The Agency is faced with enormous security responsibilities. The missions assigned to the Agency seek to fulfill basic requirements of our national security. All activities conducted by N.S.A. to carry out these missions are highly classified. Disclosure of the nature of these activities or portions of them could seriously impair the success of the Agency's efforts." So intoned the counsel of the Defense Department, and so an almost trembling House committee printed it in support of the summary-discharge bill.

This stratagem plays upon Congress' fear and ignorance. Unfamiliar with the complexities of modern cryptology, the legislators worry that a single slip could betray what they usually refer to as "the" American code system. They do not realize that there is not one but dozens or hundreds of such systems, and that a full compromise of even one would involve a detailed description of a complex mechanism, lists of hundreds of rotor wirings, and long schedules of keying arrangements. They regard cryptology not rationally as what it is but superstitiously as a potent magic—and the non-rational view of things has hardly advanced civilization.

N.S.A. exploits this attitude to withhold as much information as it can from Congress. Yet one may wonder whether the elected representatives of the American people may not be trusted with information handled daily by typists and technicians.

Although these N.S.A. tactics are improper and shortsighted, responsibility for Congressional supervision rests ultimately upon Congress. It should exercise its most jealously guarded prerogative—investigation—as vigorously in the intelligence field as it does elsewhere. The President's Foreign Intelligence Advisory Board cannot substitute for Congress, which is in a different branch of government from the intelligence agencies and which holds the pursestrings. Congressional surveillance would benefit both N.S.A. and the nation as a whole. It would, in the first place, help keep N.S.A. from reverting to its old, dangerous smugness; the Un-American Activities Committee investigation was the object lesson for this. It would, in the second place, make an essentially antidemocratic operation responsible to the processes of free men. The mail-opening activities of N.S.A. are repugnant to Americans, who tolerate them reluctantly only because of the Cold War. Its spyings can never be wholly reconciled with the ideals of a nation founded on a respect for the dignity of the individual. But they can be made accountable to those ideals, as embodied in the elected representatives of the people.

Furthermore, to the extent that N.S.A. produces knowledge, it produces power, and, Thomas Jefferson said, "whatever power in any government is independent, is absolute also." This problem is not as acute with N.S.A. as with C.I.A., because N.S.A. neither formulates nor executes policy, nor does it conduct actual operations, such as Cuban invasions. Nevertheless, N.S.A. should be energetically supervised by Congress to prevent abuse of power.

All this is a nuisance. So is democracy. It is much easier to hire a dictator than to bother with elections and all the other details. It is much easier not to bother with checking up on N.S.A. But it must be done. Otherwise the nation jeopardizes some of the very freedom that N.S.A. exists to preserve.

Since its organization in 1949, A.F.S.A.-N.S.A. has always been headed by a general or an admiral. The three services rotate the command. Terms have ranged from 18 months to more than four years. Six men have directed this silent agency: Rear Admiral Earl Everett Stone, U.S.N., July, 1949, to August, 1951; Lieutenant General Ralph Julian Canine, U.S.A., to November, 1956; Lieutenant General John Alexander Samford, U.S.A.F., to November, 1960; Rear Admiral Laurence Hugh Frost, U.S.N., to May, 1962; Lieutenant General Gordon Aylesworth Blake, U.S.A.F., to June, 1965; and Lieutenant General Marshall Sylvester Carter, U.S.A. The only thing they have in common seems to be their conspicuous absence from the public eye.

Stone, 53 when he assumed the directorship, had been in communications for virtually all his Navy career except sea tours. He holds a master of science in communications engineering from Harvard. His shore duty was entirely in naval communications, and as assistant director of naval communications from 1942 to 1944 he commanded the Navy's communications-intelligence unit. He served as director of naval communications from 1946 until his appointment to head the newly formed A.F.S.A. After his two-year tour, he commanded Cruiser Division 1 during the Korean War, bombarding shore installations, and then held two high naval training posts before retirement in 1958.

Canine was the only N.S.A. director not to have graduated from a service academy, and his cryptologic experience was limited to that obtained during a year's duty as part-time communications officer from 1919 to 1920; he also had very broad military experience. He was called to active duty as a second lieutenant of field artillery in 1917 after having graduated the previous year from Northwestern University. He served with the A.E.F., and in June, 1919, became communications officer and adjutant for the 7th Artillery Brigade at Camp Funston, Kansas, presumably handling some codes and ciphers. During the 1920s and 1930s, he taught military science at Purdue University, studied at the Field Artillery School, and served as a regimental supply and liaison officer, a trial judge advocate for courts-martial, a post exchange officer, a plans and training officer, student at the Command and General Staff School, professor of military science at Ohio State University, and as commander of the 99th Field Artillery Battalion. In August, 1942, he became an assistant chief of staff and then chief of staff of the XII Corps, the post in which he served through Normandy, the Battle of the Bulge, and contact with the Russians. After several command posts, he was appointed deputy assistant chief of staff for intelligence at Army headquarters in September, 1950, and ten months later, at age 55, took over A.F.S.A., which became N.S.A. during his four-year term. He was perhaps the best liked of N.S.A. directors.

Samford learned to fly at Kelly Field after his 1928 graduation from West Point, and spent the prewar years in routine duties at hot and dusty flying fields in Texas, Illinois, the Canal Zone, Virginia, and Florida, plus a four-year stint as a flying instructor at Kelly Field. He spent most of World War II in England as deputy chief of staff and then chief of staff of the 8th Air Force, whose Flying Fortresses pounded Germany. For two years, starting in 1944, he served as deputy assistant chief of staff for intelligence at Air Force headquarters in the Pentagon, and, after tours as commander of the Antilles Air Division in Puerto Rico and of the Air Command and Staff School, he became director of intelligence for the Air Force in October, 1951. In July, 1956, he became deputy director of N.S.A., serving for four months until he was named director at age 51. The end of his four-year term was marred by the Martin-Mitchell scandal.

Frost, who took a two-year postgraduate course in line and applied communications at Annapolis from 1933 to 1935, spent much of his naval service in communications. He handled presidential messages as communications officer of the U.S.S. *Indianapolis* when that cruiser took Franklin D. Roosevelt on a goodwill tour to Argentina in 1936. He was decorated for his command of the destroyer *Waller* in the Pacific in 1943, and then served in communications in the Solomons and in Washington to the end of the war. From 1945 to 1950, except for a year, he worked in intelligence, and after a year's study at the National War College and two years on sea duty, including command in Korean waters, he was assigned as N.S.A. chief of staff from 1953 to 1955. Following a year of sea duty he was named director of naval intelligence and then N.S.A. director, with temporary rank of vice admiral. He was 58. After a short 18-month term, during which he bore the brunt of the House Un-American Activities Committee investigation, he was named commandant of the Potomac River Naval Command.

Blake likewise spent nearly all his service career in communications, beginning with study at the Signal School at Fort Monmouth from 1933 to 1934. He held other communications posts in the 1930s, and during World War II commanded the Army Airways Communications System in the Pacific. He attended the Air War College and then headed research and development work at Wright-Patterson Air Force Base, Ohio, for four years. He was appointed Air Force Director of Communications in 1953 and, three years later, assistant deputy chief of staff for operations. From 1957 to 1959 he commanded the U.S.A.F. Security Service. After serving as chief of staff, Pacific Air Forces, and commander, Continental Air Command, he took over N.S.A. at age 51.

Carter, who had been deputy director of the C.I.A. for three years, had to be moved from that post when President Johnson assigned Admiral William Raborn as Director of Central Intelligence. The National Security Act of 1947 prohibits both top C.I.A. positions from being held simultaneously by military men. When Johnson moved Carter, 53, to N.S.A., the general remarked: "I've had some beauts, but this beats them all." Though he has had no specifically cryptologic experience, Carter is probably the best prepared of all N.S.A. directors in view of the great pervasiveness and importance of modern communications intelligence. A 1931 graduate of West Point, he spent his first ten years with various antiaircraft artillery units and teaching in West Point's Department of Natural and Experimental Philosophy. He spent most of World War II in the logistics group, Operations Division, War Department General Staff, and after a brief tour in China was named special representative in Washington for General Marshall, then on his China mission. When Marshall became Secretary of State, Carter became his special assistant in January of 1947, serving for two years and undoubtedly getting a good picture of American foreign policy. Between 1943 and 1949, he attended six international conferences, including the Big Four at Cairo and two U.N. General Assemblies. After brief tours in the American embassy at London, as a student at the National War College, and as commander of an antiaircraft group in Japan, he served from 1950 to 1952 as director of the executive office of the Secretary of Defense under General Marshall and his successor, here gaining an overall view of American defense. From November 1952 until his appointment to the C.I.A. ten years later, Carter held various command posts in infantry, antiaircraft, and air-defense units. His three years as No. 2 man in the C.I.A. must have given him vast experience in seeing where communications intelligence fits into the general intelligence pattern and, perhaps, many ideas for helping N.S.A. better fulfill its mission.

Such are the chieftains of history's largest cryptologic unit. Though their power dwarfs that of England's 18th-century Decyphering Branch, even on a relative basis, the directors probably do not possess even a tenth of Bishop Willes's cryptanalytic ability. Nor do they need it. They have cryptanalysts to handle that particular specialty among the dozens of specialized functions that modern cryptology entails. Their own task is directed outward, at Congressional committees, at the United States Intelligence Board, at the Secretary of Defense, at the heads of the service cryptologic agencies. For internal administration, they appear to lean on their deputy directors.

These deputy directors have come from backgrounds even more varied than their chiefs'. The first, Captain Joseph N. Wenger, U.S.N., who was named A.F.S.A. deputy director on July 15, 1949, had spent most of his naval career after graduation from Annapolis in 1923 in communications. He headed the Navy's cryptanalytic agency at Nebraska Avenue during most of World War II, rising to deputy director of naval communications. When N.S.A. was created, he became vice director, a post that seems to be no longer in existence; he left N.S.A. in August, 1953.

Deputy director for about four years, ending in 1956, was Joseph H. Ream, a lawyer who had worked his way up the corporate ladder of the Columbia Broadcasting System to become secretary, director, and executive vice president before going to N.S.A. Afterwards he returned to C.B.S., becoming vice president of its television network in 1959. His N.S.A. successor was the late Howard T. Engstrom, holder of a Yale Ph.D. in mathematics who had been vice president of Remington Rand, Inc., for three years when he was tapped for N.S.A. He had taught mathematics at Yale from 1926 to 1941, when he may have become a Navy cryptanalyst. After leaving N.S.A. in 1958, he became vice president of Sperry Rand, Inc.

Engstrom was succeeded by Louis W. Tordella, who, at 47, was the youngest to be named deputy director and who has held the post the longest. He taught mathematics at Loyola University in Chicago and at Illinois University from 1935 to 1942, where he obtained a Ph.D. in mathematics. He served in the Navy, presumably as a cryptanalyst, during the war; afterwards, he remained with the Defense Department. His mathematical specialties are algebra, group theory, and classical number theory. His appointment may represent a trend away from high-powered managers brought in from the outside and toward a policy of permanent career administrators to assure stability and continuity despite the political changes of the heads of the agency.

The agency that they run is divided into three operating divisions and a group of supporting administrative units. The three operating divisions are the Office of Research and Development, with about 2,000 employees, the Office of Communications Security, with about 1,500, and the Office of Production, with more than 7,500. The main supporting units are the Office of Personnel Services, which recruits and hires, the Office of Training Services, fourth largest unit in the agency, and the Office of Security Services, which maintains physical and personnel security, reviewing the background investigations of prospective employees, giving lie detector tests, and granting—or refusing, or revoking—security clearances. Smaller supporting units include the offices of the director, the comptroller, and the adjutant general, the inspector general, counsel, and the library, headed by Dr. John Sanford, which has a superb collection of works on cryptology and of up-to-date reference texts (needed by the cryptanalysts for probable words) and more than 600 mathematical publications in English, Chinese, French, German, Portuguese, Russian, and Spanish. At least once its copy of Shakespeare served a non-literary purpose when a cryptanalyst, cracking a spy cipher, recognized the first words of the key as a quotation from the Bard, rushed to the library, dug it out, and effortlessly reduced the cryptogram to plaintext.

Without people, of course, N.S.A. could not even exist, and getting and keeping personnel appears to be one of the chief continuing problems facing the agency. This is the task of the Office of Personnel Services.

The first part of the problem is getting them in. N.S.A. depends heavily on scientists and engineers. Their skills are in short supply, and competition for them is intense. Consequently, N.S.A. actively conducts a nationwide recruitment program, directed primarily at young college graduates because government salaries at their levels do not differ from industry's so markedly as with experienced men. Scientists in colleges throughout the country refer promising graduates to N.S.A. and recommend N.S.A. to them; their high professional caliber has been a major factor in the recruitment program's success. N.S.A. recruiters tell the prospective employees about opportunities to climb either a supervisory or a technical career ladder. As Canine put it, "There is a marshal's baton in each employee's knapsack when he starts out"—a metaphor that may be somewhat felicitous for cryptology in view of the story (though it is almost certainly apocryphal) that the skytale, which the Spartan commander always wore at his waist, became a symbol of authority that is today the swagger stick of the field officer and the baton of the marshal.

Applicants must pass the Professional Qualification Test and then the eagle-eyed scrutiny of a security check. So rigorous is this that, despite the agency's urgent need for scientific talent, five out of every six applicants are rejected. From the nation's college graduating classes of 1956, N.S.A. hired between 250 and 300 young men and women. Not all were scientific or engineering or even language personnel. N.S.A. also needs liberal arts graduates to work in its library and other support facilities. And the graduate's experience need not be directly related to his work, since the agency will train him for what it needs. Often it prefers to do this—taking a French major, for example, and teaching her Russian. Cryptanalysis, must, of course, be taught, and one member of the Office of Training Services, Lambros D. Callimahos, is revising the Friedman *Military Cryptanalysis* texts to bring them up to date.

As a consequence of this intensive recruitment, many N.S.A.ers are young. The agency regards all appointments as permanent, with no probationary or temporary positions, and it does its best to hold its hard-won new employees. It arranges excursions to New York. It stages hobby shows. In the evenings the sedate classrooms of the N.S.A. School, which during the day echo to the fricative paradigms of Russian verbs and dry-as-dust exercises in symmetry of position, resound to the hot rhythms of the rhumba and, perhaps, the twist, as N.S.A.ers take dance courses. Earnest young scientists, who cannot publish their highly classified work in the usual scientific publications, satisfy their yearnings for professional recognition by writing for the *N.S.A. Technical Journal*.

Yet personnel turnover is high. Young men and women who are just finding themselves change jobs. Industry offers more money. And always there is the oppressive atmosphere of security. Despite the picnics and the dances, the compartmentalization of offices and the restrictions of movement tend to limit the romantic aspirations of the girls in their early twenties. One girl blamed the omnipresent secrecy for keeping her from learning that a man with whom she had a love affair was married; while this was undoubtedly more her fault than the agency's, it does indicate the resentment that the security breeds. And the threat of sudden, instant dismissal, without recourse to a hearing or review and without any confrontation of any person who might have accused the employee, justly or unjustly, of something that the director feels might jeopardize N.S.A. security, cannot enhance morale.

The factors that outweigh all these, however, and that largely enable N.S.A. to retain its staff, are patriotism and the opportunity to serve. These provide spiritual satisfactions that money cannot buy.

The agency runs itself in accordance with modern principles of management. Its interne program seeks to develop civilian employees for high management posts. It promotes from within, and moves personnel from post to post to broaden them. It maintains a suggestion program that pays out hundreds of dollars for good ideas. It offers instruction in dictographs for supervisors, appraises its paperwork, and works hard at keeping itself as efficient and streamlined as possible.

The cutting edge of cryptologic progress in the United States is N.S.A.'s Office of Research and Development, or R/D. Solomon Kullback, one of the three cryptanalysts that Friedman hired in 1931, served as its head in the early 1950s. In 1957, Howard H. Campaigne, a Ph.D. in mathematics specializing in statistics and hypergroups, became head of the mathematical section at the age of 47. His assistant is Dr. Walter W. Jacobs, a mathematical statistician who had previously served in the Office of Production.

R/D is divided into three sections called REMP, STED, and RADE. REMP—the term stands for "Research, Engineering, Mathematics, Physics"—conducts basic cryptanalytical research. It ransacks the domains of statistics and higher algebra for ever more sensitive and more powerful tests to solve complex ciphers. It attacks difficult foreign cryptosystems to devise new techniques of solution; any intelligence obtained is, so far as R/D is concerned, a by-product of this search. It advises other N.S.A. divisions on problems involving new methods. It works intensively to improve computer applications to cryptology. Engineers and physicists seek increases in computer speed and data-handling capacity by transistor circuitry, short-pulse techniques, time-sharing, and magnetic memories. A recent effort involved eliminating speed-inhibiting factors from such memories. REMP uses computers to design computers, and engineers working on peripheral components, such as line printers and punched-card inputs, must strain to keep up with basic technology. N.S.A. leads even such firms as I.B.M. and Remington Rand in important areas of computer development, such as time-sharing, and industry has adopted many N.S.A.-designed features.

The second section, STED (for "Standard Technical Equipment Development") conducts basic cryptographic research. It looks for new principles of encipherment. It ascertains whether new developments in technology, such as the transistor and the tunnel diode, have cryptographic applications. Using such esoteric tools as Galois field theory, stochastic processes, and group, matrix, and number theory, it will construct a mathematical model of a proposed cipher machine and will simulate its operation on a computer, thus producing the cipher without having to build the hardware. Rotor principles have often been tested for cryptographic strength in this way. It devises audio scramblers, from the ultra-secure types for high officials to the walkie-talkies of platoon commanders, as well as video scramblers for reconnaissance television and for facsimile. Their development involves sciences from metallurgy to optics, as well as techniques—important in miniaturization—from printed circuits to ferro-resonance.

R/D's third section, RADE (for "Research And DEvelopment"), conducts basic transmission research, going deeply into such matters as the interaction of electromagnetic radiation and matter. It aims both at increasing the sensitivity of American intercepting receivers and the security of American transmission methods. N.S.A. radios operate at the extreme limits of radio frequencies and involve all types of electromagnetic emanations. Its listening posts require both panoramic receivers to scan the entire frequency spectrum and single-frequency receivers with a high degree of stability that will not drift off a signal. RADE strives constantly for antenna arrays that will accentuate the signal and eliminate atmospheric interference and circuit noise so as to pick up even the weakest radio messages. It improves direction-finding apparatus and devises radio fingerprinting apparatus. And it looks into new techniques of communication, such as methods that spread a transmission over so broad a frequency spectrum that anyone listening on one frequency band would hear only a faint crackle like static. These may themselves afford some security—at least until the enemy's technology catches up. Presumably it is investigating the possibility of sending messages by laser.

In addition, N.S.A. engages in some basic communications research in the broadest possible sense. The flow of impulses through a computer's circuits constitutes a study in communication, and N.S.A. mathematicians investigate it. They use the tools of the new field of information theory to look into other problems—compression of maximum information into a minimum bandwidth, expected percentages of errors, rates of transmission, pattern recognition. N.S.A. physicists study modern quantum theory of many-body systems, superconductivity, magnetic resonance, the electromagnetic properties of solids, and the scattering effect of the ionized region of the troposphere for possible application to communications. Language itself is dissected phonetically, phonemically, grammatically, logically, semantically, historically, statistically, and comparatively. These studies result in one of N.S.A.'s few unrestricted products: dictionaries and grammars of more recondite tongues, such as the 429-page *Vietnamese-English Vocabulary* issued by the Office of Training Services, the *Romanian-English Dictionary*, prepared by N.S.A.'s 762 Dictionary Unit, and *A Grammar of the Bulgarian Language*. R/D's research differs from that carried out by the Institute for Defense Analyses' Communication Research Division at Princeton in generally being rather more applied in nature. I.D.A. research is freer, more "far out."

Smallest of N.S.A.'s three operating divisions—and the only one whose duties are publicly acknowledged—is the Office of Communications Security, or COMSEC. It is responsible for the protection of secret American government communications. Consequently it prescribes or approves the systems each department must use and how they must use them. It furnishes some machines itself and lets contracts for the others. It promulgates the national crypto-security doctrine and supervises its execution.

"All cryptographic material (including cryptographic equipment, instructions, spare parts, and associated materials for the Armed Forces) is produced by, or procured under, the direction of N.S.A.," states an Air Force manual. The same must be true for the Army, the Navy, and the State Department. COMSEC standardizes as much of American cryptography as practicable, down to the short titles of communications security publications. Thus the Air Force Communications Security Manual 2, formerly known as AFCOMSECM-2, is now listed as AFKAG-2. COMSEC prepares courses of instruction for new cryptographic equipment and issues regulations for its operation, presumably mandating such matters as the when and how of primary and secondary key changes. For interdepartmental and presidential communications, it probably produces the keys—rotor wirings, lists of positions, one-time tapes. Keys for communications wholly within, say, the Air Force are presumably produced by its own cryptographic agencies.

COMSEC, drawing upon R/D's STED, devises new systems of encipherment and embodies them in new mechanisms. It works closely with potential users, such as the State Department, to make sure that the equipment fits the user's needs and at the same time provides adequate security. COMSEC engineers test this equipment for reliability in vibration machines and salt-spray chambers. They assure its compatibility with the user's existing equipment, and they cooperate with the manufacturer to get the best devices at the lowest cost.

In addition to the suggestions that contractors make for improving machines, COMSEC evaluates the hundreds of ideas for new "unbreakable" cipher systems that pour in upon the National Security Agency from amateur cryptographers. The agency gets at least one a day, often channeled to it from the Army or the F.B.I. or the State Department. Many are from professional men, such as doctors and lawyers, but one came in from a prisoner (it was forwarded by his warden). A good percentage include a challenge message, and the COMSEC experts can just visualize the devilish grin of the inventor as he finishes enciphering the message, and thinks, "They'll never get *that*!"

The inventors fall into two categories. One type has just read Edgar Allan Poe's dictum in "The Gold-Bug" that "it may well be doubted whether human ingenuity can construct an enigma of the kind which human ingenuity may not, by proper application, resolve," and has, in half an hour, invented an unbreakable cipher that disproves it. The other has just devised a cipher so simple that a 12-year-old can operate it (never a 13-year-old), and as a patriotic American is giving it to his government for a mere $100,000— a cheap price for assuring the security of information worth much more than that.

Few of the inventors have any idea of the volume of modern communications, of the conditions under which ciphering is done, of modern cryptanalysis, or that the unbreakable cipher, in the form of the one-time pad, already exists. Nearly all the systems are pencil-and-paper, which are all but useless today, and the chances are almost nil that even a tinkerer in a machine shop will come up with anything new and worthwhile. Nevertheless, COMSEC looks seriously at every proposal. It perhaps recalls that all the basic cryptographic principles now in wide use—the rotor, the Jefferson cylinder-strip system, the one-time tape, the Hagelin mechanism—were created by persons with no professional cryptologic background. The next letter may come from a new Hebern, submitting a valuable concept. Besides, it's fun to solve the challenge cryptograms—which COMSEC very often does, despite a brevity that would never be met with in practice.

In a way, however, the agency seems to take unfair advantage of these inventors. Their ideas disappear into the black maw of the N.S.A. and may even see service in American cryptography, but security prevents the inventor from ever knowing of this—and may enable the agency or its employees to utilize his ideas without compensation. Fear of this may keep some inventors from submitting potentially valuable ideas. The agency might attract more suggestions by a firm promise not to use ideas without payment; this might be of some value if the matter ever came to court. But the agency will not give such a promise. More incomprehensibly, it will not even say why it will not. It seems that here N.S.A. is being deliberately self-injurious.

COMSEC presides over a great variety of cryptosystems. The Army requires different methods for the differing needs of front-line, middle-echelon, and high-command communications. The Navy's needs may not vary quite so widely, but even it uses strip cipher for less important communications and rotor machines for more important ones. The Air Force probably uses small codes for its airborne communications and a host of systems for its ground communications, including those to the missile-launch centers.

Are American cryptosystems secure? Different agencies investigate this question in different ways. N.S.A. tests the theoretical limits of security of ciphers. For example, COMSEC mathematicians might calculate the maximum number of messages that could be sent with unchanged primary key (as the wiring in a set of rotors) before enough secondary-key overlaps could be expected to make solution likely. They use such information to prescribe key changes. The individual agencies probably test the practical security of their own systems by monitoring and actual cryptanalysis; the State Department, for example, employs half a dozen cryptanalysts. In addition, independent tests are made, as by the Institute for Defense Analyses. In one case, I.D.A. cryptanalysts were given 1,000,000 letters of error-free text in a top military cryptosystem. They put in the equivalent of six man-years on it—and finally gave up in defeat. The episode speaks well for the security of that cipher, and, by implication, for that of other American cryptosystems.

In a jet-age world, voice communications, with their speed, convenience, personal quality, and two-way nature, are essential. Scramblers keep the conversations private. COMSEC's functions extend to ciphony, though the Bell Telephone Laboratories also do a great deal of development work.

Scramblers today are vastly improved over the old World War II models, mainly because they employ a new form of telephony called "pulse code modulation." PCM converts the voice signal into a sequence of pulses and nonpulses, somewhat like a teletype signal. The number of pulses per second varies with voice frequency. This digital form permits the interlacing of many speech signals within a single circuit, thus increasing the capacity of a telephone network. While PCM alone affords some security, since PCM equipment is needed to reconvert it to voice form, its main cryptographic advantage lies in the ease and security of encipherment in the digital mode. The scrambler can encipher the sequence of pulses and spaces just as in the Vernam system. The millions of key pulses can be stored as magnetized spots on metallized tape, as light and dark spots on film, as holes in punched cards. Or a computer can generate them. (A million pulses will last for two and one half minutes of PCM encipherment at 8,000 pulses a second.) Though problems of synchronization afflict PCM systems, they are highly secure, since problems of the voice's resistance to distortion, which render the continuous-wave scramblers so vulnerable, do not arise.

Because of this security, the scrambler that the State Department and the Air Force use for their most secret and highest priority messages probably employs PCM. The price tag seems to confirm it: almost $100,000 per installation. This is the KY-9. Developed by the National Security Agency, it resembles a four-drawer file cabinet. State has seven in its headquarters, including one in its Crisis Center, which keeps a round-the-clock watch on world events; it has also installed two each in Paris and Geneva offices and one each in London, Bonn, Berlin, Rome, and the U.S. mission to the U.N. in New York. The Air Force carries KY-9's in the flying command posts that would control American retaliatory forces if its underground headquarters were wiped out in a nuclear missile attack.

Scrambler work goes hand in hand with speech compression, multiplexing (sending several messages simultaneously over a single channel), narrowing the bandwidth needed for radiotelephone, and spurt communication systems (in which messages are stored on tape or on a fluorescent scope and then read off and transmitted at high speed). Though these systems aim primarily at cramming more messages into the increasingly crowded electromagnetic spectrum, they also provide a measure of security because only special equipment can receive them. One Army system combines both economy and security. It sends teletype signals on a low frequency and voice on a higher one in the same transmission. The harmonics of the teletype signal spill over into the voice frequency, masking it. The result sounds something like a buzz saw with mutterings partly audible beneath it. The receiver uses a feedback circuit to subtract out the teletype, and with it its harmonics, leaving the speech clear.

Compression systems are no proof against real cracking, however; the teletype-voice system was broken by a radio ham. For use in tank battles, front-line combat, or raids on fast-moving guerrillas, actual scrambler equipment, employing transistors to make it lightweight, is probably being built into portable telephone or radio systems. Heavier and more complex scramblers, affording more security, will be incorporated into the extensive communications system of the dispersed command post of the future, in which functions traditionally centralized will be separated by miles to minimize the effects of an atomic strike. The Army is working actively on this problem in the Voice Security Branch of its Fort Monmouth signal laboratories.

One of COMSEC's chief customers is the Department of State. COMSEC supervises State cryptography and furnishes or approves State's equipment, but State pays for this equipment, does its own enciphering with its own personnel, composes its own keys, and checks on its own operation.

The cryptographic advances made during World War II, particularly in mechanization, benefited the State Department. The armed forces supplied the diplomats with surplus cipher machines needed for America's expanding interests. These machines handled larger volumes of traffic than codebooks could—a clerk operating a cipher machine can turn out 10 to 15 times as much work as one using a codebook. Some codebooks remained in use, however, particularly at isolated posts, for economy and brevity. In the postwar period, the Division of Cryptography (established in 1944) remained "responsible for providing for the security of telegraphic communications by means of cryptographic systems." By 1961, a Cryptography Staff of 31 administered and operated communications security. It was still headed by its first chief, Navy cryptanalyst Captain Lee W. Parke, by then a special assistant to the deputy assistant secretary for operations.

During these years, traffic volume skyrocketed. The telegraphic workload for all of 1930 amounted to 2,200,000 words. By January of 1960, State was sending and receiving that quantity every two weeks; 4,934,000 words were

N.S.A.

sent in that month alone. The department attempted to keep up with this flood by partial automation at its main communications center in the new State headquarters building. But the backbone communications and cryptographic equipment at the various U.S. embassies and missions remained of World War II vintage, subject to the mechanical problems of age and, in some cases, to suspicions about their security due to cryptanalytic advances. The tide of messages rose faster and faster. June of 1961 saw 6,929,000 words—an increase of 40 per cent in just 18 months.

In October of 1962, the Cuban missile crisis broke in full force upon the department's antiquated network. It barely coped. While Russian ships bearing missiles steamed toward blockaded Cuba, dispatches that should have passed between President Kennedy and Premier Khrushchev in minutes consumed precious hours in transit. Washington heard of some of Moscow's most important messages through Russian radio broadcasts hours before they were delivered at the White House. The situation glaringly revealed the inadequacies of American communication. That very month the President set up an inter-departmental committee to look into all aspects of the problem. It brought forth the National Communications System. Within the State Department, the communications organization was completely revamped and equipment was replaced in wholesale lots.

Early in 1963, the department established the post of deputy assistant secretary for communications to centralize and streamline all communications, including the diplomatic pouch and courier service. Under him a Communications Security Division

> prepares and executes a cryptographic program for the protection of classified and administratively controlled information electrically transmitted. To carry out this program there is involved the participation in the formulation of National Communications Security policy, development, issuance and maintenance of communications security controls, for both domestic and overseas communications facilities, participation in the design and development of cryptographic systems as to suitability for the Department's needs, determination of quantitative requirements, and ensuring an adequate supply of cryptographic material, maintaining the necessary records therefor, and serves [serving] as a primary point of contact with representatives of other governments on communications security matters.

Starting with seven persons when it was first created, the division nearly doubled to 13 in 1964, and increased to 17 the following year, thereafter staying that size. Its personnel includes cryptographers and cryptanalysts. The cryptanalysts, who may qualify for the job with experience in the physical sciences, presumably evaluate the department's cryptosystems. William H. Goodman, a former teacher who joined State as a cryptographer in 1945 after wartime cryptanalytic service in the War Department, became the first head of the division. Unlike the former Cryptography Staff, none of its personnel actually encipher or decipher the department's messages. That work is handled by $90-a-week code clerks in the Code Section of the Telecommunications Operations Division.

At the same time, State was replacing its outmoded cryptographic equipment—a move wholeheartedly approved by N.S.A. It began spending millions of dollars for new cipher machines and scramblers. It asked Congress for a supplemental $3,250,000 for fiscal 1964 for new communications security equipment. For fiscal 1965, its budget request of $4,500,000 for communications improvement made up almost a quarter of the $24,700,000 increase in the State Department budget. The cryptographic replacement program was substantially completed by 1965.

By far the largest part of the $3,250,000 went for 450 hw-28's. This device became State's basic cipher machine. It may serve either as a teletype or a "tape coding and decoding" mechanism—a one-time tape device—or, in an on-line capacity, as both. The Teletype Corporation of Chicago sells them to the department at $7,200 apiece, putting a price tag of well over $3,000,000 on the entire installation, which was to be spread over two or more fiscal years. Deliveries began about March of 1964.

To mechanize the manual one-time pad that must be used by consulates and embassies with no Marine guards to protect cryptographic equipment, the department budgeted $221,400 in 1964 for 50 kw-7's. These on-line transistorized devices, supplied by comsec, appear to be small enough to be locked up, like the pads, and so not to require guards. The per-item cost of $4,500 may be due in part to refinements to prevent inductive or galvanic interaction between the key pulses and the plaintext pulses, which wiretappers could detect in the line pulse and use to break the unbreakable system through its back door.

In 1963, State asked for $82,300 for a secure internal communications system that would replace the manual method of multilithing copies of "eyes-only" incoming telegrams and hand-carrying them to the offices of the Secretary of State and the assistant secretaries for the several geographic regions. Urgent messages were to be teletyped to their offices; ten kw-1's at $8,000 each provided on-line encipherment and decipherment for secrecy even though the messages never went outside the State Department building. The remaining $2,300 went for terminal switch gear.

In addition, the department spends tens of thousands of dollars each year "for the purchase of variable elements of cryptographic systems, elements which must be changed periodically in all Foreign Service posts to achieve the desired security." This expense has ranged between $50,000 and $100,000 in recent years.

The State Department employs leased cable circuits between Washington and regional communication centers abroad, such as its partially computerized center in Paris. This enables it to mix volumes of dummy traffic with the real cryptograms (at no extra cost) so that any interceptor will not easily separate the filler from the valid text. Indicators, of course, tell State's code clerks which is which. So thorough is the department's encipherment in some of its traffic—presumably the one-time tape systems—that green operators in the cable offices checking the traffic sometimes think the circuit is out of whack! All of this, together with additional personnel, is making it possible for the department to handle its telegraphic message load of 16,200,000 words a month—about three out of every five messages being in code—with speed and security.

More and better scramblers were part of the department's improvement program. The KY-9's were ordered before the program got under way, but older scramblers, costing $75,000 each, were to be junked and replaced with better ones. Their voice quality was not good on long-distance circuits, and they could not be used both to talk and listen at the same time: a push-to-talk button was used. As late as 1964, some posts—such as La Paz, Bolivia—had no telephone privacy at all. Presumably this was to be rectified in the $1,000,000 for voice equipment provided in State's supplemental budget for fiscal 1964. This figure included 48 KY-3's at $10,500 each (apparently a lower-security scrambler that was used primarily in Washington, including in the homes of a few high officials), ten KG-13's at $40,000 each, five KY-8's at $14,000 each, and a KY-9 spare-parts kit for $32,000. All were to be supplied by N.S.A. They would also make possible State's participation in an interagency system for a worldwide network of protected voice communication.

Another communications result of the Cuban missile crisis was the long-talked-about "hot line" between Washington and Moscow. At Geneva on June 20, 1963, the United States and the Soviet Union signed a Memorandum of Understanding that set up a duplex cable circuit routed Washington-London-Copenhagen-Stockholm-Helsinki-Moscow for primary communications and a duplex radio circuit routed Washington-Tangier-Moscow for service communications and as a back-up.

"In our negotiations," wrote Brigadier General George P. Sampson, deputy director of the Defense Communications Agency and chief technical member of the American negotiating team at Geneva, "it was obviously recognized early in the game that some steps had to be taken to insure the privacy of the communications; and quite as obviously the technique to be employed would have to be one generally known throughout the world. It was with this background that the method for privacy which was adopted was suggested and, if my memory serves me correctly, its first mention was by the U.S. side although the general subject had been alluded to by both groups." This method was the one-time tape. Section 4 of the annex to the memorandum stated:

> The U.S.S.R. shall provide for preparation and delivery of keying tapes to the terminal point of the link in the United States for reception of messages from the U.S.S.R. The United States shall provide for the preparation and delivery of

keying tapes to the terminal point of the link in the U.S.S.R. for reception of messages from the United States. Delivery of prepared keying tapes to the terminal points of the link shall be effected through the Embassy of the U.S.S.R. in Washington (for the terminal of the link in the U.S.S.R.) and through the Embassy of the United States in Moscow (for the terminal of the link in the United States).

As its one-time tape units, the hot line employs at the American end the ETCRRM II, or Electronic Teleprinter Cryptographic Regenerative Repeater Mixer II. One of many one-time tape mechanisms sold by commercial firms, it is produced and sold for about $1,000 by Standard Telefon og Kabelfabrik of Oslo, the Norwegian subsidiary of International Telephone and Telegraph Corporation, which installed the American terminal in the National Military Command Center deep within the Pentagon. It has four teleprinters—two with English alphabet and two with Russian—and four associated ETCRRM II's. The Moscow end is in the Kremlin, near the office of the Premier.

The hot line became operative August 30, 1963. So far, it has transmitted only hourly test messages: sometimes baseball game scores from the American side, excerpts from Ivan Turgenev's *Notes of a Hunter* from the Russian. No official substantive messages have passed over its wires, but it reportedly was used the day of President Kennedy's assassination. It remains in readiness, as President Kennedy said when inaugurating it, "to help reduce the risk of war occurring by accident or miscalculation." The keying tapes that help prevent insinuation of a false message and assure the privacy of delicate negotiations are almost certainly provided by N.S.A.'s Office of Communications Security.

COMSEC probably also supplies cryptographic protection for the one man who heads both the diplomatic and the military arms of American foreign policy. So awesome are the President's responsibilities that his messages must be concealed under the most profound secrecy. And so quickly can crises erupt in this tinderbox world that communications must accompany him wherever he goes.

The task of providing them falls to the White House Communications Agency, a unit of the Defense Communications Agency. Officers of the agency precede the President and set up communications facilities at his stop-over points. They also provide for him in transit. The presidential plane, Air Force One, is equipped with scramblers and a cipher machine that, with its cover on, resembles a closed typewriter. The President's automobile, a specially designed Lincoln Continental, has a scrambler attachment for its radiotelephone. A White House communications car follows a few places behind the President's in motorcades. During President Kennedy's visit abroad in 1963, a State Department official in Dublin was contacted by a colleague in Washington in the midst of the parade through cheering crowds. The President, of course, has a scrambler in his office—and its need is made clear by West German Chancellor Konrad Adenauer's report to his Parliament in 1962 that his telephone was being tapped.

In addition, a warrant officer carrying the most important codes in the United States—and perhaps in the world—in a slim black case inside a portfolio shadows the President day and night. Five officers alternate the duty, 24 hours a day, every day. When the President sleeps, they keep vigil in the hall outside his White House bedroom. When he works, they wait nearby. When he travels, they accompany him in civilian clothes. (On John Kennedy's yacht *Marlin*, the officer wore a deckhand's outfit.) They bear the codes that would be used to transmit the presidential command to launch nuclear missiles. Primarily authenticators, they assure the button-pusher that the order is bona fide, that it really does come from the President. So ubiquitous and essential is this warrant officer that when the one on duty merely flew in a separate airplane while accompanying Lyndon Johnson to Detroit on September 7, 1964, it made news.

These codes form part of the elaborate procedure to ensure that the firing command will get through at the critical moment and that no false message will trigger World War III. Robert S. McNamara has declared that he considered providing complete control over nuclear weapons to the President alone "my most solemn obligation as Secretary of Defense. I believe this has also been the view of every United States President, every Secretary of State and every Secretary of Defense in the nuclear era." To get at least one copy of the message through despite the fire, blast, radioactivity, and near-total devastation of an atomic attack, the Air Force disperses its communications centers, "hardens" (fortifies) some, makes others mobile (the flying command posts), multiplies the methods of transmission (solid-wire telephone, radio, teletype, perhaps even radio transmission through deep-rock strata), and provides alternate routes within each form of transmission.

Several layers of codes make sure that only a valid message gets through. On some circuits no messages may be transmitted until the receiver confirms by authenticating codes that the message really comes from the source it purports to be from. Both sides can challenge and counterchallenge by secondary codes. The President would forge the first link in this chain with codes provided by his briefcase-carrying officer. Though these are highly secret, their secrecy does not aim at protecting the content, for the message is, in effect, known. Rather the secrecy validates, assures, certifies.

The end link consists of a 3 × 5-inch card, sealed in clear plastic and framed in metal, which the two launch control officers wear on chains around their necks. They are forbidden to take them off while they are on duty in their concrete missile-control capsule deep underground. The message to go to war would come over the red telephone of the Primary Alert System, which rings with a high, warbling whippoorwill tone, in a crackly voice reciting letters in the phonetic alphabet: "TANGO MIKE PAPA YANKEE ROMEO . . . ," with a monotone "Break, break" after each group of five. Both officers must take down the message, decode it individually, and confirm each other's reading before commencing the countdown.

Further codes give the "Go" signal in the fail-safe system to manned airplanes. Should the alert be sounded, jet bombers of the Strategic Air Command would immediately streak toward preassigned targets. But they may not pass a certain point—the "fail-safe" point—until they receive positive instructions. The code for these instructions is kept in the "red box"—actually a beige box with a bright red door about 18 inches square on the wall of the S.A.C. headquarters at Offutt Air Force Base and in the flying command posts. It is changed at random intervals. The headquarters controller would remove the code documents, each covering a different contingency, from their sealed X-rayproof "unique device." The information, fitted into the proper context, is radioed to the planes, preceded by verification and acknowledgment. "They have separate pieces of the pie, and we have the whole pie," said an S.A.C. senior controller. "Until we send out the whole pie, their pieces mean nothing." Three members of each crew must individually copy down the go-to-war message, match this "whole pie" to the slices that each one carries, and agree with the others that it is the real thing. Only then, according to the system, can they "go." This is part of the overall control that, President Johnson has said, the nation has imposed to prevent accidental war. In it, COMSEC plays a vital role.

Far and away the largest of N.S.A.'s three operating branches is the Office of Production, or PROD, with a little more than half of N.S.A.'s entire headquarters personnel. What PROD produces is communications intelligence. The term must be taken in the broadest possible sense. For although it includes cryptanalysis, traffic analysis, and analysis of cleartext traffic, it is not confined to studies of man talking to man. Communications intelligence in the Cold War includes machines talking to machines—the self-interrogations of radars, the remote-control systems of guided missiles, the telemetry of artificial satellites, the I.F.F. or identification-friend-or-foe systems. All these are communications devices, usually radios modified in one way or another, and a great deal can be learned from their location and operation. N.S.A. entered this electronic field in the 1950s, and began monitoring Soviet missiles in 1958, the year after Sputnik, largely due to the initiative of PROD's Joseph P. Burke, a former traffic analyst.

PROD is always headed by a military man. The deputy at one time was Abraham Sinkov, one of Friedman's original three assistants. For many years the office was divided into eight sections. Four handled cryptanalysis and associated traffic analysis. ADVA (for "ADVAnced") attacked high-level Soviet cipher systems and diplomatic codes. GENS (for "GENeral Soviet") attacked Soviet military code systems and medium-level ciphers; its chief at one time was Francis A. Raven, who recovered the key-pattern of the Japanese PURPLE machine in 1941. ACOM ("Asian COMmunist") attacked the code and cipher systems of those nations, and ALLO ("ALL Others") attacked the cryptosystems of neutrals, Communist satellites, and the nations of the free world. A section called MPRO ("Machine PROcessing") provided computer services to the cryptanalysts. The section called Communications handled the intercept organization. The two other sections may have analyzed cleartext intercepts and studied the electronic material.

After Martin and Mitchell exposed this arrangement, however, PROD was reorganized into three big sections. These were set up on a geographical basis, and each analyzes all communications within its area, from human cleartext to coded mechanical "messages."

To gather the raw material for these sections, N.S.A. and the armed forces have cast a fine-meshed net over the world of electrical communications. Around the globe they have spotted more than 2,000 intercept positions (one man listening at one radio set). Most are on U.S. military bases overseas, but some are on planes or aboard ship. More than 8,000 soldiers, sailors, and airmen, accompanied and supervised by N.S.A. personnel, type out on four-ply paper the Morse code messages that peep incessantly in their earphones. Other personnel tend the equipment that intercepts radioteletype messages and the tape-recorders for voice communications. Still others forward the intercepts to Fort Meade. Interception goes on around the clock, at every wavelength, for every audible transmission, of every single country.

American electronic reconnaissance is carried out mainly by airplane. "Ferret" airplanes patrol the vast edges drear of the Communist world. Their guts are packed with complicated electronic gear for the use of their electronic specialists, called "ravens," in recording and analyzing radar signals. The ferret receivers pose interesting problems in design. On the one hand, they must be able to accept unexpected signals emitted by new Soviet radars. On the other hand, they must be able to measure the radar's pulse rate and its frequency with great precision. Ideally, they should always be ready to accept another signal and not dwell too long on the signal passing through their circuits. Since no one receiver can perform all these functions, the ferrets must carry many types of receivers. In addition to simply picking up the signals, the ravens try to locate their source: it is obviously more valuable to know that six new radars are operating around a region north of Moscow than just somewhere in Russia.

All signals are not always heard. The ferrets may not be in range. The ravens may not be operating the right equipment. The Russians may have turned some radars off so as not to show all their cards. To tease one another into turning on some of their silent and probably special ones, nations could direct a squadron of bombers at the enemy's territory on a mock raid. One can imagine the flurry of electronic activity that would be created if a dozen Soviet bombers headed toward the United States. Though this dangerous game is not played by the two great powers, a modification of it is. Individual six-jet RB-47 ferrets fly dangerously close to the Soviet frontiers and sometimes actually cross them—though such practices are of course denied by the United States government. Russian fighters and antiaircraft rockets attack and sometimes down them. Thus international incidents result.

Such was the case of the RB-47 shot down on July 1, 1960, in the arctic waters of the Barents Sea, killing four of its six-man crew. The Soviet Union protested in the United Nations that the aircraft had violated Russia's territorial rights—a charge that the United States denied. Later the newly elected President Kennedy negotiated the release of navigator Captain John McKone and co-pilot Captain Bruce Olmstead. Perhaps the best-known penetration flight of all was that of Francis Gary Powers, whose U-2, like all those that had preceded his, carried "black boxes" that recorded Soviet radar signals on magnetic tape for analysis by N.S.A.

The Soviets engage in electronic reconnaissance, too. They send their TU-16 Badgers day after day against the American radar picket fence in Canada's far north called the DEW (Distant Early Warning) Line. They depend more heavily, however, upon their trawlers. Most of the 3,000 ships of Russia's fishing fleet that regularly ply the waters of the North Atlantic are legitimate, but almost 90 during some major American exercises in 1961 were getting their best catch from the airwaves. The trawlers often roam the fish-poor but intelligence-rich waters off Cape Kennedy. Before a missile firing, tracking and guidance radars must be checked, communication links tested, telemetry circuits energized. All these give the Russian eavesdroppers a good picture of what is going on. The trawlers also lurk near the Army signal center at Fort Monmouth, New Jersey. Their appearance off the New England coast once caused a slowdown of experimental radar tests at M.I.T.'s Lincoln Laboratory in Lexington, Massachusetts.

The most sophisticated and most secret reconnaissance and intercept tools that serve N.S.A. are the satellites that eavesdrop upon communications. These are a subseries in the SAMOS (for "Satellite And Missile Observation System") satellites, other subseries of which photograph and televise the pictures of missile bases, encampments, and the like. The ferret satellite hears the faint whisperings of Communist radios and radars as it orbits high over the windy steppes. Its sensors, developed by Lockheed Aircraft Corporation and R.C.A., can tap microwave telephone links and can pick up the radio guidance signals of missile launch sites. When commanded by a signal from the ground, its tape recorders spew out these signals in what is probably an incredibly compressed spurt of information to a waiting ground station. With the attached second-stage Agena rocket, SAMOS satellites stand 22 feet tall and 5 feet in diameter; they weigh 4,100 pounds, and circle the globe upright like a giant cigar, carrying a 300-to-400-pound instrument package. The Soviets have their own COSMOS spy satellite, which probably includes a ferret series.

The information collected by ferrets constitutes electronic intelligence. The detection of a cluster of radars in a remote part of Siberia may indicate the presence of a Soviet rocket base. The operating parameters of a radar—its "electronic signature"—can disclose its function—a search, height-finder, or target-guidance radar, for example. Analysis of Russian telemetry signals may yield important details about rocket instrumentation. But most of this electronic intelligence is studied to find ways of thwarting Soviet radars that would detect and locate U.S. bombers or missiles and direct their destruction. These ways are called electronic countermeasures, or E.C.M.'s. The electronic security that defends against enemy E.C.M.'s comprises emission security, which defends against electronic reconnaissance, and electronic counter-countermeasures, or E.C.C.M.'s. In operation, E.C.M.'s and E.C.C.M.'s are so intimately intertwined and mutually reliant that the whole field of electronic security and electronic intelligence is usually considered under the general heading of "electronic warfare."

Electronic warfare began in World War II, when radar itself first emerged; in fact, the astonishing employment of electronics is one of the most notable features of that struggle. Winston Churchill, who was intimately involved with the warfare of these invisible radiations during the Battle of Britain, gave it the grandiloquent name of "The Wizard War." "This was a secret war," he wrote, "whose battles were lost or won unknown to the public, and only with difficulty comprehended, even now, by those outside the small high scientific circles concerned. No such warfare had ever been waged by mortal men." It was vital. "Unless British science had proved superior to German, and unless its strange sinister resources had been effectively brought to bear on the struggle for survival, we might well have been defeated, and, being defeated, destroyed." One of its battles was that of the KNICKBEIN, a German navigational beam whose two sections crossed over British cities and which the British scientists twisted so that the Luftwaffe bombers unloaded most of their high explosive during the Battle of Britain into empty fields and the Channel.

Later the British carried the Wizard War to the enemy. Radar, of course, operates by emitting pulses of radio energy which bounce off objects, such as airplanes, and return to the radar unit. The direction from which these echoes come gives the location of the object. And since radio waves travel at the constant speed of light, the radar unit can determine the distance of the object by measuring the interval between the transmission of the radar pulse and the reception of its echo. The British soon discovered that a strip of metal cut to half the length of a radar wavelength would return a much stronger echo than an untuned mass of metal, such as an aircraft. If these strips were dropped like chaff from airplanes, they would form an electronic smokescreen behind which British bombers could dispense death and destruction undisturbed by German night fighters and antiaircraft fire. Britain first tried this chaff, codenamed WINDOW, in a raid on Hamburg July 24, 1943. "Its effects surpassed expectations," Churchill said. "For some months our bomber losses dropped to nearly half."

After the war, as aircraft flew faster and guided missiles became common, radar, which alone could give sufficient warning of an attack, became increasingly important. So, then, did electronic warfare. Three technical developments intensified it: the transistor, which greatly lightened the reconnaissance equipment, giving planes greater range and allowing additional and more sensitive equipment to be carried; the traveling wave tube, which permitted rapid tuning over a broad frequency band; and the maser, which vastly increased receiver sensitivity. Today electronic warfare accounts for most of the huge defense electronics industry and costs the taxpayers well over half a billion dollars a year for research, development, and production—to say nothing of the operation of the equipment.

The tape recordings and the photographs of cathode-ray tubes that the ferrets bring back are subject in N.S.A. to intense analysis. This determines such radar operating parameters as frequency, type of modulation, pulse rate, pulse shape, power, type of scan, antenna rotation rate, and polarization. This information enables engineers to design techniques to blind or trick enemy radars.

The earliest and simplest E.C.M. was chaff. Modern radars winnow it out without much difficulty, largely because airplanes fly much faster than the drifting cloud of metal strips. To counter this, bombers fire rockets packed with chaff to explode well ahead of them to confuse the radars. Another E.C.M. uses decoys that enhance the radar echo, thus make the decoys appear larger on the radar scope than they really are, and so trick the operator into tracking them instead of the real bombers. One such device is the corner reflector. Its three metal plates are set at right angles to one another, and the corner formed by them returns a stronger echo than a flat surface. Another device is the Luneberg lens, a sphere that focuses a lot of radar energy onto a small surface that reflects it all back. One lens of 12 inches diameter produces a radar echo equivalent to a target with a cross section of 700 square feet. A swarm of them on decoy "penetration aids" accompanying an intercontinental ballistic missile could swamp out the enemy radar defense, making it almost impossible for it to discriminate the warhead and direct its antimissile missiles against it.

Diametrically opposed to the decoy technique are the materials that make an object invisible to radar. One kind is a two-and-a-half-inch thick sandwich of foam plastic. It absorbs and dissipates the radar energy, somewhat in the way that soundproofing material works. Since missiles can hardly be encased in this spongy material, they may use a special ceramic whose inner surface is lined with the radar-absorbent stuff.

These are all passive countermeasures. Active E.C.M.'s become much more sophisticated, although the simplest is crude—jamming. Jamming has the great advantage of disrupting much radar function. It does not require very much power, since the radar echo is so weak that it takes very little effort to overcome it. Modern radars can defeat jamming to an extent, however, by the E.C.C.M. called "integration." The returns from several sweeps of the radar beam are piled up on the scope until eventually the combined pips from the target become strong enough to stand out even against the background of noise. Jamming's real disadvantage is that it often disrupts one's own radars and radios and prevents interception of valuable enemy communications.

Another active E.C.M., the multiple-target generator, emits many fake returns. On the scope of the enemy radar will appear a whole flock of blips, confusing the operator, who will not be able to pick out the true return from the many false ones. A third active E.C.M. forces a precision radar that has locked on to a target to "de-acquire" it. The target transmits a false timing signal that disrupts the radar's function and prevents it from tracking him.

These three active E.C.M.'s are confusion techniques. They have the disadvantage that the enemy knows he is being confused. Subtlest of all E.C.M.'s are the deception techniques, which trick the enemy without his being aware of it. These usually rely upon two radar characteristics—that a target will sense that it is being "illuminated" by a radar long before the echoes are strong enough to return to the radar, and that radars usually follow the strongest echo. One deception technique sends out a strong fake echo timed to reach the radar earlier or later than the true echo. The radar will thus show a target much nearer or farther from it than the attackers really are. Another technique produces a false target moving at a false speed on the radar scope. Radars that depend on a Doppler shift to determine target speed can be tricked by E.C.M.'s that adjust their frequencies to indicate a false Doppler shift, showing a target moving more slowly than the real one is, or perhaps not moving at all.

Fighting these techniques are emission security and electronic counter-countermeasures, or E.C.C.M.'s. Radars can be made to respond only to a particular wave shape. They can shift frequency rapidly and irregularly, or change their pulse rates unpredictably. These constitute a kind of electronic code which the attackers would have to break. Electronic warfare has even invaded the infrared. Antimissile missiles that home in on their targets by the heat of the exhaust can be decoyed by extremely hot flares.

In an actual strike, a B-58 loaded with countermeasures equipment instead of explosives will convoy the attacking bombers to fight off the enemy with electronic bullets. The electronic warfare officer decides when to fire the varied weapons at his disposal. As he approaches the enemy radar limits and senses its illumination, he emits false range and speed data. With closer penetration, he launches chaff rockets and reflectors and generates multiple targets to deny information to the enemy. As the squadron nears the target area, he busily eyeballs his scopes and listens in his earphones for signal characteristics indicating that the precision radars have locked on to him. When they do, he pulls every trick in the book to nullify their threat. After determining their frequencies and pulse rates, he confuses the missile-control radars and jams their instructions to their missiles. He sends out small but big-looking decoys. In a few hectic minutes he must shelter his squadron under an impervious electronic canopy and shield it from the enemy radiations that can be as lethal to his mates as death rays. Upon him may rest the very success or failure of the mission.

Not all the human communications that N.S.A. studies are coded. Into the headquarters building at Fort Meade come recordings of the cleartext chatter between Soviet pilots. An N.S.A. section transcribes these, not into ordinary Russian writing, but into a phonetic representation that retains the pronunciation variations of the speakers. These transcription sheets go to analysts in another section. They compare the pilots' inflections with known dialectical pronunciations to determine where the men in a squadron come from. Long residence in one locality will sometimes shade an older pronunciation more toward the local one; the analysts can detect this and tell where the squadron is stationed. Slang and current phraseology assists in these determinations. When one pilot calls another "Ivan," and Ivan replies, the characteristics of his speech are carefully noted in an enormous file with all other Ivans so that future clues can be fitted into the original ones to add more details. Jokes, comments about superior officers, references to nearby units, remarks about the planes, all are catalogued. Sometimes an analyst will spend days on a single sentence, checking and cross-checking names and intonations. And just as the tens of thousands of points of pure color that Georges Seurat dabbed individually onto his canvas combined into the huge and stately "Sunday on the Grand Jatte," so the thousands of details elucidated by the analysts build up into a broad image of Soviet air power, fuzzier than the painting, of course, but with a great deal of collateral intelligence on capability, morale, equipment, and almost every subject which a potential adversary might find of interest.

But the National Security Agency produces its most valuable intelligence by breaking foreign codes and ciphers. And though "practical cryptanalysis" sometimes helps, most of the results come from true cryptanalysis. As Martin and Mitchell said: "Successes obtained by the National Security Agency in reading the code and cipher systems of other nations are due primarily to the skillfulness of cryptanalysts, frequently aided by electronic digital computers."

Who are the cryptanalysts, and how many does N.S.A. have? It is difficult to give an exact answer, because modern cryptanalysis is so specialized and so subdivided that many N.S.A. employees engage in partial or elementary cryptanalysis, or do the nearly mechanical task of filling in the holes after the "real" cryptanalysts have made the entry into a code or cipher and have thoroughly broken it. However, a rough guess might place the number of "real" cryptanalysts in N.S.A.—those who attack unknown or new systems—at about 200.

Despite the great secrecy surrounding their work, and the great events that can flow from it, the cryptanalysts' labors resemble those of any other office workers. At N.S.A., they arrive in one of three shifts, beginning at 7:20, 7:40, or 8:00 a.m. (and ending respectively at 3:50, 4:10, and 4:30 p.m.). Once in, the first order of business must be to finish reading the newspaper and shoot the breeze with one's officemates. When they get down to work, they write on cross-ruled paper with colored pencils, shuffle pages, look for significant patterns, look for plaintext, confer with colleagues, take coffee breaks. Sometimes a yelp of joy will pierce the concentration as a cryptanalyst breaks through. They have one advantage at least over workers in more ordinary fields: they cannot take their work home with them at night. But, in another sense, they cannot get away from it, for a problem in cryptanalysis grips the mind, teases and torments it more than other problems, and never seems to let go. If an idea occurs at home, the cryptanalyst may write a note to himself, or, if he lives close enough, he might perhaps drive down to the headquarters building to work on it.

As in other large white-collar organizations, they probably work in large open offices. Into them come the raw intercepts—no doubt, in most cases, the typewritten copies as made on four-ply paper by the intercept operators. Urgent messages are most likely forwarded by radio, as the MAGIC intercepts were sent to Washington from the Philippines. If several versions of the same message, picked up by several intercept operators, reach Fort Meade, editors will try to clear any garbles. Presumably traffic analysts then collate and compare sender location, routings, and indicators. This enables them to sort the messages into families of identical cipher systems for the cryptanalysts. And by studying traffic patterns, they can deduce tables of military organization and perhaps other information as well.

The cryptanalysts work in teams. Complex modern ciphers have rendered individual work as much a thing of the past in cryptanalysis as in other branches of science. Thirty-three atomic physicists signed the report announcing the discovery of the omega-minus particle; seemingly as many N.S.A. cryptanalysts would deserve credit for solving the rotor system of a sophisticated modern nation.

The head of the team apparently parcels out such assignments as different statistical tests, calls conferences, decides whether one attack is proving more fruitful than another. The cryptanalysts' work consists in essence of looking for textual patterns that deviate significantly from what could be expected by chance. These patterns are extremely tenuous, and the individual letters of which they are composed recur only at extremely long intervals. This results from the efforts of rotor systems, Hagelin machines, and computer-generated keys to make it as hard as possible for the cryptanalyst to assemble the monalphabetically enciphered letters that he must have to reach a solution. Only enormous quantities of text can make these faint patterns visible, and only huge data-processing computers can engorge the rivers of letters and test the innumerable possibilities to solve the system in real time, which is to say before it has lost its usefulness. For computer processing, key-punch operators very likely punch the messages on cards, and technicians feed the cards into the computers.

N.S.A. probably has more computer equipment than any other installation in the world. Some of those it reportedly has are general-purpose computers, such as the I.B.M. Stretch, one of the world's fastest and most powerful computers, the $2,898,000 I.B.M. 7090, which can perform 229,000 additions per second, and late-model Univacs; there is also the Atlas, which N.S.A. had built to its own specifications early in the 1950s, and probably several smaller general-purpose computers. The agency also has a great deal of special computer equipment. For example, a device may be built to run the kappa test instead of wasting a general-purpose computer on so restricted a task. N.S.A. may use its computers to determine which configuration of possible displacements on a rotor produces the group of letters that most closely resembles plaintext. The giant calculators may solve or partially solve the equations of group theory needed in analyzing a rotor machine. They may run test decipherments, simulating rotors wired in various ways and turning in various periods, and print out the test solutions at rates up to 600 lines per minute, starring those solutions that statistically most resemble plaintext. Undoubtedly the agency has prepared and debugged programs for common routines and holds them in readiness for immediate use.

The computer has in no way conferred total victory upon cryptanalysis in its unending struggle with cryptography, for cryptography has kept pace with countervailing developments of its own. Nor has the computer automated the cryptanalyst out of a job. The computer has relieved him of much drudgery, but modern cryptosystems involve much more work than older ciphers. Computers could be programmed to recognize plaintext by stocking their memories with letter frequencies, 10,000 common words, and basic grammatical rules. But it could not do so as quickly as a human being. Furthermore, the computer would have to run through all of even the better possibilities in a modified "brute-force" attack—something which would take impossibly long. A human being can correct and enlarge partial solutions. And there is no machine yet devised that can, as quickly as the living computer inside the skull, make an inspired guess on the basis of a half-forgotten news item in the *Washington Post* of a month ago and last night's television news that the formless mess of letters *i-go-e-ia* must be a garbled *Indonesia*. Finally, and above all, a human brain must decide which tests the computer should run on a sheaf of cryptograms. Cryptanalysis still has room—indeed, may have more room than ever before—for flair, intuition, experience, individual brilliance. The computers at N.S.A. are—as they are wherever computers are used—the tools of their operators, not their replacements. They are robot cryptanalysts to a very limited degree. Thus, in the last half of the twentieth century, in the flowering of the computer age, cryptanalysis often comes down to exactly the same problem that four centuries earlier faced the West's first great cryptanalyst, Giovanni Soro of Venice: Does x stand for *a* or *o*?

The quality of the systems N.S.A. attacks varies greatly from country to country. Competence in cryptology, as in other fields of endeavor, seems to vary in direct proportion to the technological knowledge and the economic wealth of a country. On this basis, the United States probably has the most secure cryptosystems and the most informative communications intelligence in the world. Of the nations whose cryptograms N.S.A. attempts to solve, unquestionably the most sophisticated must be the Soviet Union, Great Britain, and France, probably in that order.

In all probability, N.S.A. attempts to solve all cryptosystems of all countries—at least in principle. But manpower and monetary limitations afflict N.S.A. like other agencies, and these and the incessant emergencies that must require pulling a cryptanalyst off his regular task make the ideal unattainable. Thus, though N.S.A. might want to attack, for example, the middle-echelon military systems of a Near Eastern country, it might have to concentrate the cryptanalysts that would be assigned to it on a Russian system that could be expected to yield more valuable results. How long it will keep a team working upon a system probably depends upon the information it thinks it will obtain. The agency may well keep a team examining cryptograms in a given system for two or three years, even though it has had no success, in the hope that one of the cipher clerks may some day blunder and open the way to a solution. For in modern systems, properly used and with frequent key changes, a cryptographer's error is the cryptanalyst's only hope. And when nations will pay their code clerks only $60 a week, as Italy did in Washington in the 1960s, to await such errors may not be pointless.

In addition to the general cryptanalytic effort, N.S.A. may mount special attacks if one of its customers requests it. The State Department, for example, may request such a solution in advance of a high-ranking official's visit to another country or before a major diplomatic conference.

N.S.A. cryptanalysts probably solve foreign cryptosystems in degrees of completeness that range from total reading of all messages in a given system, to fairly full solutions with a few questionable patches, to partial solutions with many holes, to solutions in which, say, one or two rotors of several have been reconstructed but no plaintext has been read, to an absolute blank. Solutions probably also vary in time: the cryptanalysts may read a complicated system for a few months, then lose out again in a change of key.

The solutions must go to organizations in the U.S. government that require that information—military details to the Defense Department, diplomatic to State, and so on. These, together with the C.I.A., must be N.S.A.'s chief customers. Probably each class of messages has a distribution list. Individual messages may well be read at meetings of the National Security Council and the U.S. Intelligence Board. During the Korean War, the White House itself reportedly called for solutions, even though some were fragmentary. Currently, the President sees the N.S.A. "Black Book" every morning, brought to him by his military aide.

What does it all consist of? How successful is N.S.A., and how valuable are its results?

It is likely that N.S.A. reads only a small minority of the total volume of intercepts sent it—perhaps under 10 per cent. In peacetime, encipherers can work more slowly and more accurately than in war—yet even in the wartime conditions of the Russian front, with a great volume of messages and unquestionably many more errors, Germany's Army Group North solved less than 30 per cent of Russian military cryptograms. Moreover, the N.S.A. intercept posts probably concentrate on messages in the highest priority systems, yet these must be the best systems and must often resist solution, thus lowering N.S.A.'s average.

Nevertheless, N.S.A. does solve enough cryptograms to produce information of great value to the nation. Martin and Mitchell delineated the extent of N.S.A. success. The agency, they said, solved the codes of more than 40 nations—or just about half of all that there were when they spoke. Asked which ones, Martin replied: "Italy, Turkey, France, Yugoslavia, the United Arab Republic, Indonesia, Uruguay—that's enough to give a general picture, I guess." This range is remarkable. France is one of the world's great powers and has a long and strong cryptologic tradition. It stands as an American ally in the free world, as do the other major European country (Italy), the small Latin American country (Uruguay), and the neighbor of Russia (Turkey). Indonesia and the U.A.R. are both important neutrals in the Cold War. Yugoslavia is a renegade Communist country. The two defectors would not say whether the United States reads Soviet messages. But the Soviet predilection for the one-time pad in diplomatic messages, and its known cryptologic sophistication, make it most unlikely, except by a lucky accident.

Hamilton, the Arab, filled in some details of the Martin-Mitchell outline:

> I was listed as an expert on the Near East Sector in the office designated ALLO, which means "All other countries." This sector concerns itself with the U.A.R., Syria, Iraq, Lebanon, Jordan, Saudi Arabia, Yemen, Libya, Morocco, Tunisia, Turkey, Iran, Greece, and Ethiopia. The duties of my colleagues in ALLO included the study and breaking of military ciphers of these countries, and also the deciphering of all correspondence reaching their diplomatic representatives in any part of the world.... N.S.A. reads the ciphers of all these countries by applying cryptanalysis....
>
> I knew for a fact that the State Department and Defense Department systematically read, analyzed, and utilized in their own interests the enciphered correspondence between the U.A.R. embassies in Europe and the U.A.R. government in Cairo.
>
> For example, I had in my desk all the deciphered communications between Cairo and the U.A.R. Embassy in Moscow relating to the visit of the U.A.R. government mission to the U.S.S.R. in 1958 for the purpose of purchasing petroleum in the Soviet Union. N.S.A. sent all these communications to the State Department just as it continually sends it the deciphered instructions of the U.A.R. Ministry of Foreign Affairs to its embassy in Washington....

It is especially important to note that American authorities take advantage of the fact that the U.N. headquarters is located on American soil. Their high-handedness has reached the point where the enciphered instructions of the governments of the U.A.R., Iraq, Jordan, Lebanon, Turkey, and Greece to their missions to the U.N. General Assembly fall into the hands of the State Department before arriving at their proper address.

The intelligence that flows out of Fort Meade mingles with intelligence from many other sources to help high officials determine national policy and tactics within the framework of American goals. N.S.A. intelligence is not as voluminous as C.I.A.'s, a former top C.I.A. official has said, but it is of a higher grade. All intelligence is evaluated for credibility, and cryptanalyzed intelligence must nearly always get the highest rating (some messages may be dummies) because it comes straight from the mouths of the subjects themselves. N.S.A.'s intelligence covers the gamut of communications of modern nations, from the minutiae of legation routine to the secret instructions to ambassadors. Even at its most complete, however, it can illuminate but part of the intelligence picture. The solutions allude to persons and facts and basic policies half known or unknown to the interceptor; they presuppose a common knowledge not at his disposal; they do not include information exchanged by personal contact, letter, telephone. Most messages mean little standing alone; only context makes them comprehensible. Cryptanalysis thus complements other forms of intelligence, overt and covert, just as they complement it.

Perhaps it is the incompleteness of cryptanalytic intelligence that led to American officials' apparently disbelieving it at the time of the Suez crisis, despite its seemingly unimpeachable authenticity. Just after that crisis had passed its peak, George Wigg, a Labor Member of Parliament, told newspapermen that the United States had broken British, French, and Israeli codes and so had prior knowledge of plans for their invasion of Egypt at the end of October and beginning of November, 1956. Though he attributed the solution to the "United States Air Research and Development Command, Griffis Air Force Base, Rome, New York," Wigg's basic point seems to have been independently confirmed by C.I.A. chief Allen Dulles, who wrote several years later of the Suez invasion: "Here intelligence was well alerted as to both the possibility and later the probability of the actions taken by Israel and then by Britain and France." Why, then, did the United States take no action? Dulles does not say, but Wigg thought "that the United States State Department knew from the middle of October what the French and the Israelis were planning to do. What I think they may have doubted was that the British Government would ever be so foolish as to get caught up in an adventure which was bound to end in disaster." Secretary of State John Foster Dulles said at the time: "We had no advance information of any kind." The later contradiction by his brother Allen suggests that this may be a cover-up for failure to act. Wigg, moreover, is not an M.P. whose inside information can be taken lightly: in 1963 he exposed the John Profumo-Christine Keeler scandal that very nearly toppled England's Conservative government. Suez has been called one of America's worst intelligence disasters. It seems more likely that the fault lay, not with the producers of intelligence, but with the consumers. No human being has ever had difficulty in finding an excuse to overlook an unpleasant fact. The consumers did not want to believe the contrary evidence of the cryptanalyzed intelligence (assuming that it existed). So they simply did not believe it—and perhaps justified their disbelief on the basis of its incompleteness. Against this human predilection no form of intelligence can prevail.

Yet where personal factors are less strongly engaged, cryptanalysis must assert itself as one of the most useful of intelligence sources. Its intermingling with other sources makes it difficult to gauge its own particular value to the American government. The message that by itself leads to results as spectacular as those of a Zimmermann telegram or a Yamamoto flight schedule must be exceedingly rare. The impact of cryptanalysis must come in the way that the falling of many snowflakes, each one imperceptible to the ear, adds up to make an audible hiss in a wood.

Occasionally, however, instances occur in which the importance of cryptanalysis has been made manifest. One such case was Hamilton's referring to "the letter in which Henry Cabot Lodge, then the American ambassador to the United Nations, expressed his appreciation to members of ALLO for information about the instructions sent by the Near East governments to their U.N. missions." Another—which showed the unsung workers at N.S.A. that the highest official in the land appreciates their work—came on March 2, 1966, when career cryptanalyst Frank B. Rowlett received the National Security Medal in a White House ceremony from the hands of the President of the United States himself.

What about other countries? Many of them do have cryptanalytic bureaus, particularly the older ones. Britain of course does; her General Communication Headquarters lies within her Foreign Office. Germany's is likewise within her Foreign Office. France's appears to be within her Ministère des Armées. It seems likely that about two thirds of the Latin American countries have codebreaking agencies, but few of the new nations of Africa do. Some Arab nations must have them, perhaps started by German cryptanalysts who went to the Near East after the war (but have reportedly since returned home). In Scandinavia, Sweden's agency remains active. In the Far East, the cryptanalytic unit within Japan's Naikaku Chosashitsu ("Cabinet Investigation Board"), a general intelligence agency, solved the codes of South Korea and exploited the information in political negotiations early in the 1960s so effectively that when South Korea found out, it stopped cabling messages to its negotiators and sent instructions by diplomatic pouch instead.

But none of these can compare with N.S.A.—any more than the countries themselves can compare with the United States in any other field. It comes down, as always, to a question of economics. Though these smaller countries are usually chiefly interested in the cryptograms of their neighbors, they cannot maintain the worldwide intercept facilities that would give them different encipherments of circular messages that are often essential for modern cryptanalysis. They cannot get enough messages to make it likely that one of them will contain an encipherer's error. They cannot support the large cryptanalytic organizations that alone can build the experience and resources to solve today's machine ciphers. In many of these countries, the cryptanalysts are more gifted amateurs than professionals. Their governments are hard-pressed to build schools and irrigation systems. They do not have the money to buy electronic computers for their codebreakers. In cryptology, as elsewhere, success breeds success.

Where, then, is the science headed? Are there any trends that can be foreseen? For there are fashions in cryptology as in other things. The one-time pad, very popular after World War II, has fallen out of favor. More popular now seem to be rotor machines—with from three to eight rotors—and Hagelin machines. For airplane and front-line messages, small codes seem to be common.

Future developments may be foreshadowed by a U.S. Air Force statement that

> One of the primary Air Force communications security objectives is total security of AIRCOMNET [the basic wire and radio teletype network] at the earliest date. It is intended to accomplish this by means of link encryption. This is a system which is integral to the communications system and which automatically secures all links of the communications system by on-line synchronous devices. When total security of AIRCOMNET is achieved, two distinct advantages will occur:
>
> (1) Unclassified common-user traffic introduced into AIRCOMNET will not be vulnerable to unfriendly intercept and analysis. U.S.A.F. Security Service has repeatedly revealed, through analysis of clear text unclassified traffic now being handled over AIRCOMNET, vital information regarding the Air Force order of battle, disposition and employment of combat air power, functions of key personnel, and similar data.
>
> (2) It will be possible to introduce classified messages up to and including SECRET into AIRCOMNET, without first resorting to off-line processing.

This is part of a more basic Air Force aim of a communications complex that will "provide full protection for information flowing within Air Force communications channels, including the exclusion of unauthorized entry into the systems. This goal will be approached, first, by providing COMSEC protection to each of the individual communications networks and later by providing total end-to-end encryption throughout the complex."

The Air Force drive toward total end-to-end encipherment carries with it a tendency toward a single all-purpose cipher, for such encipherment can most easily and most safely be applied by such a cipher. A single all-purpose cipher, simple enough for the lowest echelon, secure enough for the highest, variable enough to nullify the danger of capture or compromise, would eliminate or reduce many of the problems produced by the present multiplicity of systems—the need sometimes to reencipher a message in a system the ultimate recipient holds, the difficulties of storing, distributing, and accounting for half a dozen different sets of ciphers instead of for just one.

One possible form of this ideal cipher—perhaps the most likely—is that of a system using a long, quasi-random key generated by mathematical methods and "added" to the plaintext, either numerically as with the one-time pad or electrically as with the Vernam method. A special-purpose computer might produce such a key from a few key digits, some of them common to the whole communications net and changing at fixed intervals, some chosen at random by the encipherer for each message and inserted at a prearranged place in the cryptogram.

Many generating methods are possible. The simplest is chain addition. Successive digits of the priming key are added together and the sum tacked onto the end of the keynumber, forming part of it, and the process repeated with these digits. For example, with the priming key 3 9 6 4, 3 and 9 are 12, which is listed as 2, since all addition is noncarrying and tens digits are dropped; 9 and 6 are 5, and 6 and 4 are 0. These three figures join the key at its tail: 3 9 6 4 2 5 0. The process is then continued with 4 and 2, making 6, which is put on after the 0, with 2 and 5, making a 7 which is put on after the 6, and so on: 3 9 6 4 2 5 0 6 7 5 6 3 2 1 . . . . More complex methods are possible. The computer might multiply a base keynumber for the day by a message keynumber to ten places, then multiply the product by the basic key to ten places, that product again by the basic key to ten places, and so on, each time extracting the last four digits of each product as the final key.

These systems are not unbreakable. Recovery of any portion of a chain-added key will yield the entire key, assuming the length of the priming key is known, or one of several possible keys, assuming that the priming-key length is not known. In more complicated systems, a probable word could yield a fragment of possible key which mathematical analysis could extend forward and backward for tests and possible solution.

Nevertheless, if the key generation system could be made both sufficiently flexible and sufficiently complex, such a cipher might attain sufficient security. A computer the size of a transistor radio could produce a stream of digital pulses or numbers. Plugged into an ordinary teletype or a front-line pulse-code modulation scrambler, it could provide an on-line encipherment of sufficient security. This might be the cipher of the future, and thus cryptology would return in a more sophisticated way to a universal system, from which it has been divorced since the telegraph destroyed the nomenclator.

But what about the field as a whole? The growth of political cryptology has been exponential since it began 4,000 years ago. Will new methods like lasers, which provide hard-to-intercept line-of-sight communications, reverse that trend for the first time?

Probably not. Radio's advantage in establishing out-of-sight communication is so great that its use will probably continue to increase, just as communication and literacy itself always have. In any case, the advent of such techniques as the laser would merely shift the element of secrecy from cryptography to transmission security. It would not diminish the amount of secrecy in communication. Though in the past the amount of secrecy—the amount of cryptology, in other words—has always grown as rapidly as communication itself has, the secrecy comes not from the communication but from politics, from statecraft, from the governments who apply and seek to remove that secrecy. The future of cryptology contains many questions of technology, but the waxing or waning of the field as a whole is not among them. That question is human.

Sideshows

20

THE ANATOMY OF CRYPTOLOGY

CRYPTOGRAPHY AND CRYPTANALYSIS are sometimes called twin or reciprocal sciences, and in function they indeed mirror one another. What one does the other undoes. Their natures, however, differ fundamentally. Cryptography is theoretical and abstract. Cryptanalysis is empirical and concrete.

The methods of cryptography are mathematical. "It would not be an exaggeration to state that abstract cryptography is identical with abstract mathematics," declared Dr. A. Adrian Albert. Maurits de Vries, a Dutch statistician and theoretician of cryptology, wrote of cryptography: "The transformations are generally of a simple mathematical nature. E.g. permutations in the set of primary elements (the alphabet); coordinate transformations of lattice points; addition and subtraction in finite rings; linear algebraic transformations.... A simple example of such a secrecy-transformation is: $y = ax+b$, where x represents a letter of the message; y is the resulting letter of the cryptogram; a and b denote constants which determine this particular transformation. Calculations with the letters are easily carried out after defining a suitable algebra."

Thus the operations and results of cryptography are as universally and eternally true as those of mathematics. Within the "suitable algebra" of the ordinary 26-letter Vigenère, it would be as logically impossible to deny that plaintext *b* keyed with C yields D as to deny that $1+2 = 3$. And this holds on Mars in the 25th century as equally as in France in the 16th. Different ciphers, like different geometries, yield results that are different but equally valid.

The situation is not at all the same with cryptanalysis. Its methods are those of the physical sciences. They rest, not upon the unchanging verities of mathematical logic, but upon observable facts of the real world. The cryptanalyst must obtain these data by experiment, by measurement. Unlike the cryptographer, who can deduce any enciphering equation in Vigenère from a few initial conditions without recourse to any further experience, the cryptanalyst cannot tell from any number of statements about English which is its most frequent letter. He has to count the letters. The facts may be constants, but they are not logical necessities. They depend upon circumstance, upon reality.

Philosophy offers a useful distinction between statements like those of cryptography and statements like those of cryptanalysis. The statements of cryptography, whose denial would be self-contradictory, are analytic. The statements of cryptanalysis, whose denial would not be self-contradictory, are synthetic. It might even be said that cryptography deals with noumena, cryptanalysis with phenomena.

The empirical nature of cryptanalysis appears in its operations. These consist of the four steps of what is commonly called the "scientific method," which scientists apply in attacking problems in the natural sciences. They are: analysis (such as counting the letters), hypothesis (x might be e), prediction (if x is e, then some plaintext possibilities should emerge), and verification (they do) or refutation (they don't, so x is probably not e), either case starting a new chain of reasoning. (This common ground of scientific method between cryptanalysis and other sciences validates such metaphorical statements as "He sought to decipher the history of the earth from layers of rock.")

Within this general format, cryptanalysis operates in two ways, deductive and inductive. Deductive solutions are those based on frequency analysis; they are the general solution for any cipher system. Inductive solutions are those based on probable words or on lucky occurrences, such as two cryptograms with the same plaintext; they are special solutions.

Solutions based on frequency analysis move from a knowledge of letter frequency to an application of it to the cryptogram at hand. Reasoning that flows from the general to the specific like this is deduction. A typical syllogism in the frequency analysis of an English monalphabetic substitution would have as its major premise, "The most frequent letter in the cryptogram is probably the substitute for e," as its minor premise, "x is the most frequent letter in the cryptogram," and as its conclusion, "x is probably the substitute for e." Since all languages have well-defined characteristics of letter frequency, this deductive pattern is known to apply to any cryptogram even before it is inspected. Such a solution is thus a priori in its nature. And because this kind of solution will always work, given enough text, it is the general solution.

Inductive solutions, on the other hand, will work only when certain conditions are fulfilled. Because the cryptanalyst cannot tell whether those conditions are indeed fulfilled until after he has obtained the cryptogram and knowledge of its circumstances, inductive solutions are a posteriori in nature.

If an enemy post radios a message just after it has been subjected to heavy fire followed by a tank assault, the cryptanalyst might well conclude that the cryptogram contains *bombardment* and *attack* in its plaintext. These are probable words, which he can use to jimmy open the cryptogram. (Common words such as *the, that, and,* and so on, which are probable in all texts because of their high frequency, do not constitute probable words in this sense.) The cryptanalyst's reasoning issues from the numerous specific facts surrounding the message and crystallizes into a single conclusion concerning its plaintext. Such reasoning is inductive. So is the reasoning used in lucky-break, or

The Anatomy of Cryptology

special-case, solutions. Only after Painvin had noticed the identical bits and pieces of text in two ADFGX cryptograms could he assume that they both had identical plaintext beginnings and thus commence his cryptanalysis (which in this case might better be called a "cryptosynthesis").

Because probable words and special cases enable the cryptanalyst to bring extra information to bear, such solutions display great power and fruitfulness and are often the first to be achieved in new systems. But they are limited to particular situations, and so cryptanalysts seek the deductive general solution of frequency analysis that will always apply.

The realization that cryptography was essentially mathematical, glimpsed by Babbage and de Viaris and Hill and others, and made explicit by Albert, afforded great insight into cryptography. It also paved ways to new solutions. In cryptanalysis, the principles of letter frequency gradually expanded to help solve ciphers that at first seemed outside their ambient (such as columnar transposition). When Friedman brought those principles within the broader field of statistics, cryptanalysts could train really powerful new guns upon ciphers. But even this great expansion of knowledge did not reach to the frontiers of cryptanalysis and there confront the phenomenon upon which cryptanalysis rests—the constancy of letter frequency. Shortly after World War II, however, a remarkable new theory emerged that has provided an explanation of that phenomenon and of the whole process of cryptanalysis itself. It has not had the practical effects that Friedman's work has had, but it affords, for the first time, a thorough understanding of why cryptanalysis is possible.

The astonishing stability and universality of the phenomenon of letter frequency is not often realized. Other activities besides cryptanalysis depend upon the fixity of letter frequency, and flouting it can cause economic losses. A demonstration of these matters leads through some amusing and little-known byways.

In 1939, the Wetzel Publishing Company of Los Angeles issued a 267-page novel of but moderate literary merit but so distinctive that in its way it stands unrivalled by any other work in the entire history of the English language. Here is how the author summarizes his tale in his opening pages. The excerpt fairly illustrates the book's unique feature:

> Upon this basis I am going to show you how a bunch of bright young folks did find a champion; a man with boys and girls of his own; a man of so dominating and happy individuality that Youth is drawn to him as is a fly to a sugar bowl. It is a story about a small town. It is not a gossipy yarn; nor is it a dry, monotonous account, full of such customary "fill-ins" as "romantic moonlight casting murky shadows down a long, winding country road." Nor will it say anything about twinklings lulling distant folds; robins carolling at twilight, nor any "warm glow of lamplight" from a cabin window. No. It is an account of up-and-doing activity; a vivid portrayal of Youth as it is today; and a practical discarding of that worn-out notion that "a child don't know anything."

The title divulges the novel's distinction: *Gadsby, A Story of Over 50,000 Words Without Using the Letter E*. It is an amazing tour de force. Let the skeptical reader see how long it takes to compose even a sentence without an *e*. The author of *Gadsby*, a persevering, dauntless, white-haired old gentleman named Ernest Vincent Wright, enumerated some of the problems of his self-imposed task. He had to avoid most verbs in the past tense because they end in *-ed*. He could never use *the* or the pronouns *he, she, they, we, me,* and *them. Gadsby* had to omit such seemingly indispensable verbs as *are, have, were, be* and *been* and such basic words as *there, these, those, when, then, more, after* and *very.* A purist, Wright refused to use numbers between 6 and 30, even as digits, because an *e* was implied when they were spelled out. ("When introducing young ladies into the story, this is a real barrier," Wright complained, "for what young woman wants to have it known that she is over thirty.") Similarly, he banned *Mr.* and *Mrs.* because of the *e* in their unabbreviated form. One of the most annoying problems would arise, when, near the end of a long paragraph, he could find no *e*-less word with which to complete the thought, and had to go back and rewrite the entire paragraph. So frequently did Wright find himself wanting to use a word containing an *e* that he had to tie down the *e* typebar of his typewriter to make it impossible for one to slip in.

"And many did try to do so," he says in his preface. "As I wrote along, in long-hand at first, a whole army of little *e*'s gathered around my desk, all eagerly expecting to be called upon. But gradually as they saw me writing on and on, without even noticing them, they grew uneasy; and, with excited whisperings amongst themselves, began hopping up and riding on my pen, looking down constantly for a chance to drop off into some word; for all the world like seabirds perched, watching for a passing fish! But when they saw that I had covered 138 pages of typewriter size paper, they slid off onto the floor, walking sadly away, arm in arm; but shouting back: 'You certainly must have a hodge-podge of a yarn there without *Us*! Why, man! We are in every story ever written, *hundreds of thousands of times*! This is the first time we ever were shut out!'" The story required, Wright declared, "five and a half months of concentrated endeavor, with so many erasures and retrenchments that I tremble as I think of them."

Wright's trembling dramatizes the tenacity and pervasiveness of the mere presence of a single letter in English. Others are equally tenacious, and other writers have, as literary curiosities, produced lipograms—writings in which one or more letters are deliberately omitted. A classical Greek author named Tryphiodorus reportedly composed an Odyssey whose first book excluded alpha, the second, beta, and so on through all 24 books. But despite the inflexibility of letter frequency and the wide variation among the frequencies of individual letters in all languages, it is so inconspicuous that many people never even suspect its presence.

One such was Christopher Latham Sholes, the inventor of the typewriter and, apparently, the perpetrator of its atrocious keyboard. The keyboard arrangement first appeared in a preproduction model produced in 1872. Vestiges of an alphabetical order appear in the *dfghjkl* of the second row, and it is rumored but not substantiated that the top row included the letters of the word "typewriter" so that salesmen could find them easily in demonstrations. The inefficiency of the *qwertyuiop* keyboard costs businessmen time and money. In a right-handed world, it gives the left hand 56 per cent of all strokes. Of all motions for successive letters, 48 per cent use only one hand instead of two. Thus words like *federated* and *addressed* force the left hand to leap frantically among the keys while the right languishes in unemployed torpor. Much more efficient is the even rhythm of the two-handed *thicken*. As if to emphasize the problem, touch-typing places the two most agile fingers of the right hand directly on keys for two of the least frequent letters of the alphabet, *j* and *k*.

These glaring faults have spurred design of numerous keyboards. The Minimotion keyboard, developed after an exhaustive statistical analysis by engineer Roy T. Griffith, raises the percentage of right-handed strokes to 52, of two-handed motions to 67 and of strokes in the touch-typist's home row to 71 over the *qwertyuiop* keyboard's 32. Tests in a Chicago elementary school showed that pupils learned to type twice as fast on another simplified keyboard, the Dvorak-Dealey, than on the standard. Experiments by a New York management consultant firm conclusively demonstrated the superiority of a keyboard that fits instead of fights principles of frequency. But all reform has been blocked by the inertia of typists who do not want to learn a new touch system all over again and by business firms who do not want to pay for the conversion of standard-keyboard typewriters.

Where men take advantage of the facts of letter frequency, they may reap extra profits. Samuel F. B. Morse is probably the best example. When he decided about 1838 to use an alphabetical system of signals for his newly invented electromagnetic telegraph, he counted the letters in a Philadelphia newspaper's typecase so he could assign the shorter dot-and-dash symbols to the more common letters. He found 12,000 *e*'s, 9,000 *t*'s, 8,000 each of *a*, *o*, *n*, *i*, and *s*, 6,400 *h*'s, and so on. With few exceptions, he followed this list in his original code, assigning the shortest symbol, a dot, to the most common letter, *e*, another short symbol, a dash, to *t*, and so forth. With the modern International Morse Code, slightly different from his original American Morse, transmission of an English message of 100 letters requires about 940 dot-units. (The duration of a dot equals one dot-unit, a dash equals three dot-units, space between dots and dashes of a letter equals one dot-unit, space between letters equals three dot-units.) If the symbols had been assigned at random, the same message would run about 1,160 dot-units—or about 23 per cent longer. Morse's perspicacity may have rewarded his successors financially by making it possible to handle almost one quarter more messages on a telegraph line within a rush period than if he had made up his code haphazardly.

742   THE CODEBREAKERS

Long before Morse, typefounders realized that it was to their advantage not to case as many *q*'s or *z*'s as *e*'s in a font, though they had to add extras in the rare letters to allow for occasional odd combinations, such as Hamlet's "Buzz, Buzz!" The practice is still current: the font of 12-point Bodoni Book (a standard body type) sold by American Type Founders contains 53 lower-case *e*'s and only 6 *z*'s. Similarly, Ottmar Mergenthaler decided that the letter matrices in his Linotype should be arranged in order of the demand for each

```
AAAAAAAAAAAAAAAAAAAAAABBBBBBBBCCCCCCCCCCCCDDDDDDDDDDD&&&&EEE
EEEEEEEEEEEEEEEEEEEEEEFFFFFFFFFFGGGGGGGGIIIIIIIIIIIIIIIIIHHHHHHHH
HHJJJJJJKKKKKKKLLLLLLLLLLLLLMMMMMMMMMMMNNNNNNNNNNNNNNNNNN
NNOOOOOOOOOOOOOOOOOOOOPPPPPPPPPPPQQQQRRRRRRRRRRRRRRRRRZZZ
ZSSSSSSSSSSSSSSSSSSSSTTTTTTTTTTTTTTTTTTTTUUUUUUUUUUUVVVVV------WWW
WWWWW::::XXXX;;;;YYYYYYYY!!!![[["""""""]]]""""(((""""))),""",,,,,,,,,,,,,,,,,,,,,,,,,,,.............????

aaaaaaaaaaaaaaaaaaaaaaaaaaaaaaaaaaabbbbbbbbbbbbbbbbcccccccccccccccccccc-----ddddd
dddddddddddddddddddddddffffffffffffffffeeeeeeeeeeeeeeeeeeeeeeeeeeeeeeeeeeeeeeeeee
gggggggggggggggg!!!hhhhhhhhhhhhhhhhhhhhhhhhhiiiiiiiiiiiiiiiiiiiiiiiiiiiiiiiiiiijjjjjjjjjkkkkk
kkkkklllllllllllllllllllllllmmmmmmmmmmmmmmmmmmmmm"""nnnnnnnnnnnnnnnnnnnn
nnnnnnnnnnnnnnnnnnoooooooooooooooooooooooooooooooooo""""ppppppppppppppp
pqqqqqrrrrrrrrrrrrrrrrrrrrrrrrrrrrrrrrrrrssssssssssssssssssssssssssssssssssssttttttttttttttttt
ttttttttttttttttttttttuuuuuuuuuuuuuuuuuuvvvvvvvvvwwwwwwwwwwwwxxxxxxyyyyyyy
yyyyyyyy;;;zzzzzz:::fiflfl""""ffffffffyyyyy,,,,,,,,,,,,,,,,,,,fifififfi................???""""(((())))[[[]]]ffifflffl

11111111111122222222222333333333334444444444455555555556666666666677777
7777777----88888888888,,,,,,,,,99999999999.............0000000000000000$$$$$$$$$$
```

A font of type, showing the greater quantities of high-frequency letters

letter, perhaps to speed composition by having the more frequent letters traverse a shorter distance. This put lower-case *e* at the extreme left, followed by *t*, *a*, *o*, and so on. Since the key that controls each letter must be situated under its matrices' channel, the keyboard as assembled reflects the frequency of letters in English:

```
            e     s     c     v     x
            t     h     m     b     z
            a     r     f     g     fi
            o     d     w     k     fl
            i     l     y     q     ff
            n     u     p     j     ffi
```

The Anatomy of Cryptology

This accounts for the *etaoin shrdlu* sometimes seen in newspapers: linotypists just run their fingers down the keys to fill out an incorrect line.

Even more scientifically designed is the panel of the Mergenthaler company's Linofilm system. This system passes light through pictures of letters onto a film, where the successive images form text usable in offset photo-lithography. The pictures are mounted on the panel in an arrangement that exploits not only monographic but digraphic frequencies to minimize the shifting of the panel during composition. For example, *t* and *h* lie next to one another.

These examples imply that the frequencies of letters do remain fairly constant. Actual frequency counts back this up. A number of cryptologists have counted the numbers of *e*'s in German texts of about 1,000 letters, and their percentages vary only slightly: Kasiski, 18.4; Valério, 18.3; Carmona, 18.5; Hitt, 16; Givierge, 18; Lange and Soudart, 18.8; Baudouin, 19.2; Pratt, 16.7. These may be compared with a frequency count that is as close to completeness as anyone is likely to get—a tabulation of no fewer than 59,298,274 letters, derived from a count of 20,000,000 German syllables made for linguistic purposes in 1898 by the philologist F. W. Kaeding, who was nothing if not indefatigable. Kaeding found 10,598,015 *e*'s, or 17.9 per cent. What is perhaps most striking is that the eight shorter counts average to 18.0 per cent—a difference of only one *e* per thousand letters from the Kaeding standard. Thus does language cleave to its statistical norms!

Why? The answer may be found within the theory formulated after World War II that not only explains cryptanalysis but also extends far beyond. It is called "information theory" or, sometimes, a "mathematical theory of communication." It deals in general with the mathematical laws that govern systems designed to communicate information. Originating in transmission problems of telephony and telegraphy, it has grown to embrace virtually all information-processing devices, from standard communications systems to electronic computers and servomechanisms, and even the nerve networks of animals and men. Its ideas have proved so suggestive that they have been adapted to such fields as psychology, linguistics, molecular genetics, history, statistics, and neurophysiology. Because of this fertility, and because of its potential in helping to manage the information explosion of the 20th century, information theory may eventually rank, *Fortune* magazine has speculated, among the "enduring great" theories of man. The brilliant mind that fathered it also sired its cryptologic applications.

Claude Elwood Shannon was born in Petoskey, Michigan, on April 30, 1916, and was raised in nearby Gaylord, a small town in the north-central portion of Michigan's southern peninsula. He majored in electrical engineering and mathematics at the University of Michigan and there developed an interest in communications and cryptology. At the Massachusetts Institute of Technology, where in 1940 he was awarded a Ph.D. in mathematics, he wrote a master's thesis of such originality that it had an immediate impact on the designing of telephone systems. After a year at the Institute for Advanced Study in Princeton, he joined the staff of the Bell Telephone Laboratories.

There he built a maze-solving mouse, used to study circuitry for logic machines, and worked on a chess-playing machine, which may be regarded as the first step in the construction of computers for evaluating military situations and deciding the best move. At one time, he was an expert tightrope walker and unicycle rider and could be seen riding his one-wheeler up and down the halls of the Bell Laboratories. These proficiencies resulted from his attempts to design a form of Pogo stick that would bounce around by itself; this never materialized, but he did succeed in producing a bicycle that maintained its own balance. He has been teaching at M.I.T. since 1956. A thin (135 pounds on a five-foot, ten-inch frame), shy man, he likes science fiction, jazz, chess, and mathematics and admits to changing hobbies very rapidly. He lives with his wife and co-worker, Betty, and their three children in a house full of awards and honors in Winchester, Massachusetts.

"During World War II," he has said, "Bell Labs were working on secrecy systems. I'd worked on communication systems and I was appointed to some of the committees studying cryptanalytic techniques. The work on both the mathematical theory of communications and the cryptology went forward concurrently from about 1941. I worked on both of them together and I had some of the ideas while working on the other. I wouldn't say one came before the other—they were so close together you couldn't separate them." Though the work on both was substantially complete by about 1944, he continued polishing them until their publication as separate papers in the abstruse *Bell System Technical Journal* in 1948 and 1949.

Both articles—"A Mathematical Theory of Communication" and "Communication Theory of Secrecy Systems"—present their ideas in densely mathematical form, pocked with phrases like "this inverse must exist uniquely" and expressions like "$T_i R_j (T_k R_l)^{-1} T_m R_n$." But Shannon's terse and incisive style breathes life into them. The first paper gave birth to information theory; the second dealt with cryptology in information-theory terms.

Chief among their new concepts is that of redundancy. Redundancy retains, in information theory, the essence of its lay meaning of needless excess, but it is refined and extended. Roughly, redundancy means that more symbols are transmitted in a message than are actually needed to bear the information. To take Shannon's own elementary example, the *u* of *qu* is redundant because *q* is always followed by *u* in English words. Many of the *the*'s of ordinary language are redundant: persons sending telegrams get along without them. Just how great the excess of symbols is in English words is vividly demonstrated by some of those Army or Air Force adjutant-general communications that take off into a wild blue yonder of abbreviated words and phrases like "Off pres on AD for an indef per." The initiated usually has no trouble in understanding this as what would normally be written, "Officer present on active duty for an indefinite period."

Redundancy arises from the excess of rules with which languages burden themselves. These rules are mostly prohibitions—"Thou shalt not say 'dese' or 'dose' for *'these'* or *'those'*"; "Thou shalt not spell 'separate' as 'seperate'"; "Thou shalt not say 'is' after 'I.'" All such limitations exclude perfectly usable combinations of letters. If a language permitted any permutation of, say, four letters to be a word, such as "ngwv," then 456,976 words would exist. This is approximately the number of entries in an unabridged English dictionary. Such a language could, therefore, express the same amount of information as English. But because English prohibits such combinations as "ngwv," it must go beyond the four-letter limit to express its ideas. Thus English is more wasteful, more redundant than this hypothetical four-letter language.

The rules that lead to redundancy come from grammar ("I am," not "I is"), phonetics (no word in English may begin with *ng*), idiom ("believe" alone may not be followed by an infinitive, only by a clause beginning with "that"). Others come from etymology, in which the derivation of a word has left many now-silent letters, as in "through" or "knight." Still others come from limitations on vocabulary. A teen-ager who uses "swell" to mean what an adult might designate by a dozen different terms of approbation utters speech that is much more redundant, more restricted, less variable, less flexible than the adult's. As Shannon wrote, "Two extremes of redundancy in English prose are represented by Basic English and by James Joyce's book *Finnegans Wake*. The Basic English vocabulary is limited to 850 words and the redundancy is very high. This is reflected in the expansion that occurs when a passage is translated into Basic English. Joyce on the other hand enlarges the vocabulary and is alleged to achieve a compression of semantic content."

Two other sources of redundancy are of particular importance for their role in determining the frequency table. One derives from the relationships to which human beings refer so often and which language necessarily reflects. These are the relations of one person to another ("the son of John"), of one object to another ("the book on the table"), of an object to an action ("put it down"). English expresses many of these relationships by separate words, called "function words." Pronouns, prepositions, articles, conjunctions are all function words. Some stand for purely grammatical relationships that serve as a kind of linguistic shorthand—saying "I" instead of repeating one's name all the time. Function words mean nothing standing alone. Yet they are among the most common words in English because the relationships they express are so common. In English, only ten of these words constitute more than one quarter of any text: *the, of, and, to, a, in, that, it, is,* and *I* totalled 26,677 of 100,000 words in a count made by Godfrey Dewey. Inevitably this preponderance will affect the frequency table. *H*, for example, owes most of its occurrences to *the*.

The second source of redundancy stems from the human laziness that favors sounds easier to pronounce and identify. The voiceless stops /ptk/

require less energy to articulate than the corresponding voiced stops /bdg/ and they average twice the frequency of voiced stops in sixteen widely varying languages surveyed by George K. Zipf. Similarly, short vowels are markedly more frequent than long vowels or diphthongs. In the same way, auditors of English, at least, seem to prefer sounds that are easier to identify. Tests made with nonsense syllables show that listeners seldom confuse consonants produced with the vocal organs held in the same position but used in a different manner (such as /ntrsdlz/), but usually fail to distinguish consonants produced with the vocal organs used in the same manner but held in different positions (such as /ptk/). In the first group (the alveolar consonants), the tongue stays at the upper gum ridge but molds or interrupts the breath stream in different ways. In the second group (the voiceless stops), all the consonants block the breath stream and explosively release it, but at different positions of the lips and tongue. It is interesting to note that the easy-to-identify alveolar consonants comprise seven of the eight more-frequent consonants in English, while the two stops that are not alveolar (/pk/) lie well down in the frequency table. Incidentally, this preference for easily distinguishable consonants is one of the few explanations for the arrangement of even a few of the letters in the English frequency table.*

All these prohibitions and rules and tendencies help create redundancy. English is about 75 per cent redundant.† In other words, about three quarters of English text is "unnecessary." English could theoretically express the same things with one quarter its present letters if it were wholly nonredundant. A literary curiosity demonstrates graphically how a few letters carry most of the information of a text while the others are redundant. The curiosity is entitled "Death and Life":

	cur	f	w	d	dis	and p
A	sed	iend	rought	eath	ease	ain
	bles	fr	b	br	and	ag

In this, 65 per cent of the letters are in the central row (reading it twice), and serve both contradictory meanings equally well. Thus they add nothing to the information of the passage, all of which is carried in the remaining 35 per cent.

Anyone who knows English will know the rules of spelling and grammar and pronunciation that help engender its redundancy, and he will know these rules prior to the receipt of any new text in the language. This is almost tautological: it is only the existence of such rules that makes communication possible. If a hearer interprets "to" to mean "from," he will not understand very much. If he pronounces a written *m* as /v/, a *t* as /s/, and so on, he will not get through to his listeners. These redundant elements, these rules, may be considered the invariant portion of language. They may not be changed

---

* Note 1, at end of chapter, discusses other proposed explanations.
† Methods of determining this percentage are given in Note 2 at end of chapter.

without loss of comprehension. But one may say what he wishes as long as he follows them. They are the preexistent mold into which the free-will portion of a communication is poured. Hence the enormous range of texts, from laws to poems, in the same language—which is to say, following the same rules.

If one hears the fragment "It's not hard for you to . . . ," the redundant elements say that a verb is likely to follow, although the free-will portion makes it impossible to know which one. This same prior knowledge, or, in other words, the redundant elements, detects and corrects errors that arise during the transmission of messages. This is why language tolerates so heavy a burden of redundancy. For example, if a dot is dropped in a telegraphed message in English, so that an *i* (··) becomes an *e* (·) and "individual" becomes "endividual," the recipient will know that an error was made because English lacks the sequence "endividual." But if the language used were the hypothetical four-letter language, in which all sequences of four letters were used and therefore all were potentially acceptable in the message, the same dropping of a dot would go undetected. "Xfim," meaning perhaps "come," would be changed to "xfem," maybe meaning "go" and, without redundancy, no alarm bells would ring. (There is, of course, a higher order of redundancy— that mandated by context—which might sound the alarm. If "xfem" meant "green," it would not fit the context. A perfectly nonredundant language can therefore probably not exist, since at least a few basic agreements that a few recurring experiences of the real world will be represented by the same verbal symbols appear to be essential for communication.)

Where the language has no redundancy—as with telephone numbers, where a single wrong digit can lead to a wrong connection—people put in their own redundancy. They repeat the number in giving it to someone. Or, in spelling out names, they say "B as in baby, not v as in Victor." For the greater the redundancy, the easier it becomes to detect mistakes. If a language consisted only of alternations of consonants and vowels, any deviation from that pattern would flag an error.

This detection of errors is the first step toward their correction. And in this correction redundancy again plays the central role. After the recipient of "endividual" has hunted through his memory and his dictionary and found that it does not exist in English, he brings up the sequence "individual," which does exist, from his store of prior information about English, and corrects his message. If the reader of a business letter sees the sequence "rhe company," he will recognize "rhe" as a nonword, will remember that the rules of English often call for a similar-appearing group of letters, "the," before a noun like "company," will perhaps consider that *r* is near *t* on the typewriter keyboard, and then will conclude that "rhe" should be "the."

This process is a first cousin to cryptanalysis.

For cryptanalysts bring to bear in their solutions the same prior knowledge of rules and spelling and phonetic preferences (that is, redundancy) that the ordinary reader does to correct a typographical error. What laymen do with accidental errors, cryptanalysts do with deliberate deformations. Of course a cryptogram is immensely more involved and obscure than an isolated misprint, but it has an underlying regularity that the single random error does not, and this structure assists and confirms the successive "corrections" that constitute a cryptanalysis.

But how does the cryptanalyst begin in the first place? In correcting a typographical error, all the redundant elements lie in plain view, ready for use. With a cryptogram, they are obscured. The cryptanalyst begins by breaking these elements down to their atomic form—letters. He then compares them to the redundant elements of a language that have been reduced to the same common denominator. In other words, he takes a frequency count of the letters of the cryptogram and matches it against a frequency count of the letters of the assumed plaintext language. (These counts must sometimes be modified by the conditions of the cipher. In polyalphabetics, a count must be made for each alphabet; in digraphics, the count must be of pairs. If the cryptogram is in code, the atomic forms are words, but the same principle applies.)

Having done this, how can the cryptanalyst be confident that the cryptogram's plaintext will have approximately the same frequencies as those of plaintext in general? Why won't the differences in subjects of discussion, in vocabulary, in expression, upset the frequencies? Because the redundant elements of language far outweigh the variable ones. The 75 per cent redundancy in English overwhelms the 25 per cent of "free will"—though this 25 per cent does keep frequency counts from matching one another exactly. The redundant elements in any text converge to make its frequency table. The need in any English text to use "the" frequently ensures that *h* will be a high-frequency letter. English's preference for alveolar consonants will make *n*, *t*, *r*, *s*, *d*, and *l* all high- or medium-frequency letters. The language's aversion to *p* and *k* keeps their frequencies low. These redundant elements are fixed and predetermined—necessarily so, if communication is to take place—and hence they stabilize the frequency tables that reflect them. The enormous preponderance of redundancy manifests itself in the closely equal proportions of *e* in the nine separate German frequency counts. And of course it manifests itself in the daily successes of cryptanalysts.

Shannon's insight, his great contribution to cryptology, lay in pointing out that redundancy furnishes the ground for cryptanalysis. "In . . . the majority of ciphers," he wrote, "it is only the existence of redundancy in the original messages that makes a solution possible." This is the very basis of codebreaking. Shannon has here given an explanation for the constancy of letter frequency, and hence for the phenomena that depend on it, such as cryptanalysis. He has thus made possible, for the first time, a fundamental understanding of the process of cryptogram solution.

From this insight flow several corollaries. It follows that the lower the redundancy, the more difficult it is to solve a cryptogram. Shannon's own two extremes of redundancy illustrate this. The last few words of *Finnegans Wake* are these: "End here. Us then. Finn, again! Take. Bussoftlee, mememormee! Till thousendsthee. Lps. The keys to. Given! A way a lone a last a loved a long the." This would interpose distinctly more difficulties to a cryptanalyst than a portion of the New Testament in Basic English: "And the disciples were full of wonder at his words. But Jesus said to them again, Children, how hard it is for those who put faith in wealth to come into the kingdom of God!"

Puzzle cryptograms achieve their goal of being as hard as possible to solve by using archaic and esoteric words dredged from the far corners of the dictionary and combined in almost meaningless texts. Their redundancy is relatively low. One such cryptogram gives a self-description: *Tough cryptos contain traps snaring unwary solvers: abnormal frequencies, consonantal combinations unthinkable, terminals freakish, quaint twisters like 'myrrh.'* But even here the redundant elements win out. Though a few may be suppressed, others remain, and these permit solution. The interesting question of whether the differences in redundancy among natural languages make cryptograms in some inherently more difficult to solve seems never to have been put to a test.

The problem of low redundancy arises in practice with a vengeance when the cryptanalyst is faced with enciphered code. To strip the encipherment from encicode, the cryptanalyst must solve a cryptogram whose plaintext consists of codewords and which may look like IXKDYWUKJTPLKJE.... This is of very low redundancy because of the more even use of letters, the greater freedom in combining them, the suppression of frequencies by the use of homophones, and so on. But the unavoidable repetitions of orders and reports, the pressure of the redundancy of the language pent within the vessel of the code, and the engineering of codewords so that garbles can be corrected—all these give the underlying codetext a fibrous enough texture for the cryptanalyst to grasp it for solution.

These considerations suggest that reducing the redundancy will hinder cryptanalysis. Shannon himself prescribes operating on the plaintext "with a transducer which removes all redundancies.... The fact that the vowels in a passage can be omitted without essential loss suggests a simple way of greatly improving almost any ciphering system. First delete all vowels, or as much of the message as possible without running the risk of multiple reconstructions, and then encipher the residue." Experts who have attacked cryptograms from whose plaintexts only the letter *e* has been eliminated have found that the difficulty of solution increased noticeably. Reducing redundancy is especially effective because it robs the cryptanalyst of one of his chief tools for attack instead of just bolstering the wall of secrecy. Cryptographers of the Italian Renaissance did this when they ordered cipher clerks to drop the second letter of a doublet, as the second *l* in *sigillo*.

Such techniques rely upon the cipher clerks' knowledge of their language to supply the suppressed elements of redundancy. Abbreviations likewise may have such low redundancy, may require such an extensive furnishing of information, as *bn* for *battalion*, that they may not only make plaintexts harder to solve, but may themselves function as a rough form of cryptography. Two gossips, for example, may refer to a third party by her initials. They hope that no one within hearing will have sufficient knowledge of the contextual situation to restore the eliminated portion of the name. Much of the Masonic ritual is printed in that form: "Do u declr, upn ur honr, tt u r promptd to. . . ."

Another corollary is that more text is needed to solve a low-redundancy cryptogram than one with a high-redundancy plaintext. Shannon has managed to quantify the amount of material needed to achieve a unique and unambiguous solution when the plaintext has a known degree of redundancy. He calls the number of letters the "unicity distance" (or "unicity point"), and he calculates it by means of a rather complicated formula. This formula naturally differs for different ciphers, but it always includes the redundancy as one of its terms. In his original paper, in which he considered the redundancy of English at only 50 per cent, Shannon found the unicity point for monalphabetic substitution at 27 letters, for polyalphabetics with known alphabets at twice the period length, for those with unknown alphabets at 53 times the period length, for transposition at the keylength times the logarithm of the keylength factorial.

One of the most interesting uses of the unicity-point formula is in determining the validity of an alleged solution to a cryptogram, especially one of the questionable solutions, such as those claimed to be hidden in the Shakespearean plays to prove that Francis Bacon wrote them. "In general," wrote Shannon, "we may say that if a proposed system and key solves a cryptogram for a length of material considerably greater than the unicity distance the solution is trustworthy. If the material is of the same order or shorter than the unicity distance the solution is highly suspicious." Shannon's formula was not applied to most of these "decipherments" because most were published before his work was; furthermore, the formula would ramify to unmanageable terms to account for the many subrules and exceptions in these extremely flexible "systems." It triumphed in its only known combat action—one that took place in the pages of *Life* magazine on a solution proposed by Ib Melchior, son of the opera star Lauritz Melchior.

Melchior thought that the decipherment of a cryptogram that he detected on Shakespeare's tombstone might lead him to an early text of a play. He obtained a numerical ciphertext by counting the number of successive capitals and small letters in the epitaph on Shakespeare's grave. This he solved to read: *elesennrelaledelleemnaamleetedeeasen*. But the eleven letters *ledelleemna* made no sense to Melchior, and, noting that they came from the letters between the two THE ligatures on the tombstone, he concluded that they were change symbols to signal a shift in cipher alphabets. With this change, the new "solution" read: *elesennrelaedewedgeeereamleetedeeasen*. Taking away the "obvious nulls" and modernizing the Elizabethan spelling, Melchior read: *Elsinore laid wedge first Hamlet edition.* This was supposed to mean that a first edition of *Hamlet* was buried in a wedge-shaped cell deep within the castle of Elsinore. But even granting the generously low redundancy of only 50 per cent, a crucial section of the cipher flunks the Shannon unicity test completely, while the remaining letters barely meet the minimum and do not fulfill the requirement for a "length of material considerably greater than the unicity distance." Despite this implied prediction of failure, Melchior, backed by a *Life* expedition, went to Elsinore anyway. Cryptologists were not surprised when the team brought back an excellent picture story for the magazine—but no "first Hamlet edition."

The concept of redundancy thus repeatedly demonstrates its power by bringing under a single broad generalization numerous cryptologic phenomena that had heretofore to be given individual explanations. Why are puzzle cryptograms harder to solve than ordinary messages? Previously, cryptanalysts could only say that it was because they used rarer and odder words; today they can invoke the wide-ranging principle of redundancy and point out that such cryptograms have a lower redundancy than the normal ones. Why have stereotyped expressions—"Reference your telegram of . . ."—so often helped cryptanalysts? Because they raise the redundancy to delightfully high levels. On the other hand, the use of codenames for places, operations, and so forth, within a plaintext lowers redundancy. As General Marcel Givierge wrote, "the fact that one expects to find *Paris* in a text will cause him to search for the letters and syllables in *Paris* and not that of the codename which replaces *Paris*." Similarly, bisection of a message—cutting it in half and tacking the start onto the end—buries the frequently routine start of a message in the middle and brings the middle of a phrase to the head of the message. This substantially lowers the redundancy of that vulnerable point. Shannon's information theory shows how to make cryptanalysis more difficult and tells how much ciphertext is needed to reach a valid solution. In all these ways it has contributed to a deeper understanding of cryptology.

Shannon has also viewed cryptology from a couple of other perspectives, which, while not as useful as information theory, are enlightening. The first, in fact, is a kind of corollary to the information-theory view.

"From the point of view of the cryptanalyst," Shannon wrote, "a secrecy system is almost identical with a noisy communication system." In information theory, the term "noise" has a special meaning. Noise is any unpredictable disturbance that creates transmission errors in any channel of communication. Examples are static on the radio, "snow" on a television screen, misprints, background chatter at a cocktail party, fog, a bad connection on the telephone, a foreign accent, perhaps even mental preconceptions. Shannon is suggesting that noise is analogous to encipherment. "The chief differences in the two cases," he wrote, "are: first, that the operation of the enciphering transformation is generally of a more complex nature than the perturbing noise in a channel; and, second, the key for a secrecy system is usually chosen from a finite set of possibilities while the noise in a channel is more often continually introduced, in effect chosen from an infinite set."

When Carl W. Helstrom, author of *Statistical Theory of Signal Detection*, was asked whether the techniques of isolating signals from noise had any relevance to cryptanalysis, he replied: "I suspect that the analogy between the enciphering rule of 'key' and random noise will not prove very fruitful. It seems to me more appropriate to regard the encipherment as a filtering of the original message to produce a transformed version. The 'filter' is a definite transformation rule, but the analyst doesn't know what it is. . . . The problem is then to discover the transformation rule, or the nature of the filter, when given the statistics of the input and output. It is like finding the structure of an electrical filter by passing random noise through it and measuring the statistical distributions of the input and output voltages."

Cryptology may also be regarded as a conflict in the sense employed in *The Theory of Games and Economic Behavior* by John Von Neumann and Oskar Morgenstern. As Shannon, who first made the allusion, puts it: "The situation between the cipher designer and cryptanalyst can be thought of as a 'game' of a very simple structure; a zero-sum two-person game with complete information, and just two 'moves.' [A zero-sum game is one in which one contestant's advances are made at the expense of the other.] The cipher designer chooses a system for his 'move.' Then the cryptanalyst is informed of this choice and chooses a method of analysis. The 'value' of the play is the average work required to break a cryptogram in the system by the method chosen."

Cryptology is, by definition, a social activity, and so it may be examined from a sociological point of view. It is secret communication, and communication is perhaps man's most complex and varied activity. It encompasses not just words but gestures, facial expressions, tone of voice, even silence. A glance can express a tale more sweetly than a rhyme. Basically, all forms of communication are sets of agreements that certain sounds or signs or symbols shall stand for certain things. One must be a party to these preconcerted rules if one wants to communicate.

But all forms of communication are not at all times and all places known. Those who happen to know one system that others around them do not can use it for secret communication. Irish troops sent to the Congo as part of the United Nations force in 1960 spoke Gaelic over the radio, and the U.N. commander, General Carl von Horn of Sweden, called it the best code in the Congo. This is a kind of cryptography by default, depending upon a fortuitous ignorance—a defective cryptography. Effective cryptography deliberately establishes special rules of communication that deny information to those who would otherwise understand the messages.

This withholding of information constitutes the essential element of that which is called "secrecy." All the manifestations of secrecy—hiding places, disguises, locked doors—share the basic idea of not communicating objects or information. Its extreme form is silence (which conjures up an Orwellian nightmare of the extreme form of eavesdropping—detection and interpretation of brain waves). An exhaustive investigation of the concept of secrecy would require, as Maurits de Vries has pointed out, "a complete examination of the relations between individuals and between groups in our society," because secrecy is the antithesis of communication, and communication—as that which makes man a social being—encompasses all aspects of cultural behavior. Cryptography combines these antitheses into a single operation; a wag might define it as "noncommunicating communication."

The relation between cryptography and cryptanalysis is not logically necessary; it is contingent. One can envision men communicating by secret means with others not even thinking of prying. But in the real world, the cryptanalyst—or more accurately the potential cryptanalyst—comes first. What need for cryptography if no one would eavesdrop? Why build forts if no one would attack? Thus the assumption that someone will attempt a cryptanalysis, no matter how tentatively or incompetently, engenders cryptography.

Experience of the interreaction between cryptography and cryptanalysis has precipitated out certain practical principles. They all refer to time, because all practical matters involving mortal men connect eventually with that one inexorable, irreversible, irretrievable factor.

Time, for the cryptographer, controls a variable relationship. The most general of the cryptographer's principles deals with the sliding ratio between speed and security; as the need for speed in communications increases, the need for security decreases. Early in the planning of a major operation, messages demand great security because the enemy, if he could read them, would have time to prepare countermoves. But in the heat of battle, commanders may use plain language because the enemy, though he intercepts the messages, may not have time to react effectively. This principle arranges a nation's cryptosystems in a hierarchy in which front-line systems are simple and diplomatic systems secure and more complex. "Of each such system," Friedman wrote, "the best that can be expected is that the degree of security be great enough to delay solution by the enemy for such a length of time that when the solution is finally reached the information thus obtained has lost all its 'short term,' immediate, or operational value, and much of its 'long term,' research, or historical value."

The paramount requirement for all cryptosystems is reliability. This means that cryptograms must be decipherable without ambiguity, without delay, and without error. It implies, for example, that cipher machines will be sturdy enough to withstand ordinary abuse so that they will be ready to operate properly when a message comes in. Usually the simpler the system, the more reliable. The requirement excludes from the combat zone ciphers of more than two steps. Any encipherer's errors or garbles should be correctable without having to call for a retransmission. This bans systems in which a single error garbles the message from the point of error on, as in autokey ciphers (such systems are said to have an undesirable error-propagation characteristic). Obviously, if a general cannot rely upon the validity of messages that come out of his cipher machines, the cryptosystem is worse than useless.

Secondary requirements for a cryptosystem are security and rapidity. Which one comes first depends upon the needs of the users. Further down the scale of importance stands the requirement of economy. This rules out any system that requires several men to encipher, makes the ciphertext more than twice as long as the plaintext, or is too complicated or expensive to manufacture or distribute.

In addition to these general requirements, military and diplomatic cryptosystems must meet two specific ones—both first enunciated by Kerckhoffs. The first rests upon the almost universal employment of telegraphy or radiotelegraphy for military and diplomatic communications. No system is acceptable whose cryptogram characters cannot be sent in Morse code; excluded are squares, angles, crosses, or other designs. The second rests upon a working assumption of military cryptography: that the enemy knows in general how a cipher works. Secrecy must depend upon the keys used. No method is acceptable that does not accede to this requirement, that does not provide for both a general system and specific keys.

For the cryptanalyst, time's demands remain fixed. Always at his back he hears time's winged chariot hurrying near. He seeks to get out his solutions as quickly as possible. It is probably true that a message will always have some historical value, but that is small comfort to a commander who does not get a cryptanalysis that would have warned him of an enemy attack until after the attack is under way. The factors that affect the time required to solve cryptograms—aside from external factors, like the speed of sending the intercepts back to the cryptanalyst—are the strength of the system, the soundness of the regulations for its use, how closely the cipher clerks follow those regulations, the volume of text, the size and skill of the cryptanalytic organization, and the amount and character of collateral information.

Bringing skill into the picture raises the question of whether cryptanalysis is a science or an art. It is both. On the one hand, cryptanalysis—or, more properly in this context, cryptanalytics—is an organized body of knowledge. It studies and controls phenomena. Its whole spirit is scientific, but that of an applied science, like engineering. On the other hand, cryptanalysis—here meaning the steps performed in solution—clearly depends upon personal ability. Some cryptanalysts are better than others. In this sense, cryptanalysis is an art. So, in this sense, is any human activity that demands a certain aptitude for its superior practice. Yardley said that outstanding cryptanalysts were gifted with "cipher brains," and rather glamorized the faculty, but in fact "cipher brains" are just the cryptologic manifestation of a general

The Anatomy of Cryptology

characteristic—talent in a given field. Who possesses "cipher brains" and why, however, raise complicated questions.

Human knowledge not only cannot answer them now, it does not even understand how the mind performs the basic psychological operation of cryptanalysis—pattern recognition. How the brain can supply the missing letters to a fragment of plaintext which it has never before seen resembles such problems as how one can read words in a handwriting one has never seen or recognize a piece of music as Mozart's even though one has never heard it before. These problems remain among the still unsolved ones of psychology and biochemistry, as convoluted as the cerebral cortex and molecular chains which may hold the answer.

Nor does anyone know the emotional bases of cryptology. Freud stated that the motivation for learning, for the acquisition of knowledge, derives ultimately from the child's impulse to see the hidden sexual organs of adults and other children. If curiosity is a sublimation of this, then cryptanalysis may be even more positively a manifestation of voyeurism. This view has won some qualified support. Psychoanalyst Theodor Reik, author of *Listening with the Third Ear*, *The Secret Self*, and many other books, replied to a query about it: "I am inclined to assume that there is at the bottom of the wish to break a code a continuation of the infantile desire to find out what is the secret of sexuality which the parents or the adult hide before the little boy.... I think that it is ... one of the roots of scientific inquiry," he added, suggesting the Freudian view that scientists, art critics, and anyone else whose work involves either literal or figurative looking is similarly motivated. Psychologist Erich Fromm, author of *Escape From Freedom* and *May Man Prevail?* conceded that the voyeuristic explanation "may sometimes be correct, but by no means as generally as the Freudians believe." The eminent psychiatrist Karl Menninger assented to the idea, adding that "this is not a new 'theory.'"

But this view has been challenged, and by a Freudian psychiatrist. Jeptha R. Macfarlane thought that cryptanalysis represents a power drive. "The codebreaker isn't interested in the content of the message but in the solution of the code," he said. "He does not take a sneaking interest in the cryptogram but pride in its mastery. Cryptanalysis is not peeking through a keyhole. It is breaking down a door." Supporting Macfarlane's hypothesis are remarks by or about cryptanalysts. Werner Kunze of Pers z, excusing his lack of knowledge of the results of his work, said that he did not pay much attention to what the messages said, and lost interest after the system had been solved—hardly a voyeuristic impulse! Of John Wallis it was said that he "never concerned himself in the matter, but only in ye art & ingenuity." Even the experience of the solvers of newspaper cryptograms attests to Macfarlane's power explanation: they are not curious about the answer, they only want to solve the puzzle.

Though the evidence seems to support the power hypothesis better, neither it nor the voyeuristic one has ever been put to the test. Perhaps part of the answer to the apparent contradiction lies in the theory that the voyeuristic motivation might lead a man to a general interest in cryptanalysis and that the power drive leads him to success in specific solutions.

What relation, if any, these explanations have to those for an interest in cryptography, in inventing secret codes and unbreakable ciphers, is not wholly clear. Reik thought this interest "might be a suspiciousness that others could find out about ourselves (not only about our sex-life, but our hostility, aggressiveness, and so on) and a wish to prevent them." Fromm's view was not dissimilar, though he linked cryptography and cryptanalysis: "I think the interest in deciphering, as well as in secret codes, may have a great deal to do with a person's relatedness to the world, and specifically with the sense of aloneness and isolation and the hope that he might find the related soul with whom he could communicate . . . the world is closed to him . . . and hence he has to decipher what is not meant for him." Psychologist Harold Greenwald, who was once interested in cryptology, wrote: "The patients I have seen who were interested in this subject seemed to display another motive [than voyeurism]. Predominantly they were the kind of people who attempted to establish feelings of power through either hiding their own behavior (putting things in secret code) or discerning the things that others wish to keep secret (breaking codes)." A psychological study of secrets in general states that secrets have their origin in the anal stage of psychosexual development. This implies that cryptography may come ultimately from the infantile sexual pleasure that Freud says children obtain from the muscle tension of retaining the feces.

There appear to be as many theories as there are writers. Ernest Jones, the distinguished psychoanalyst and biographer of Freud, put his finger on what may be a significant point. Many youngsters become interested in cryptology when they are 12 or 13, and Jones told in his autobiography how "When I was nearly twelve, the secretiveness that so often heralds the approach of puberty combined with an always strong curiosity to impel me towards a passionate interest in ciphers, about which I still know a good deal. I devised one myself which I was satisfied would baffle any opponent; I must admit, however, that it would not have been a convenient code for purposes of rapid communication, since it involved the interplay of so many subciphers that it took the best part of a day to transcribe a sentence into it. The complex, thus allayed, was able to transmute itself into a more useful form . . . ," which was shorthand. Unfortunately, Jones never said why he thought secretiveness was related to puberty.

Novelist Aldous Huxley seemed to have glimpsed the voyeuristic idea for cryptanalysis and inverted it into antivoyeurism as an explanation for cryptography. In *Those Barren Leaves*, he wrote:

> Did she love me? At any rate she often said so, even in writing. I have all her letters still—a score of scribbled notes sent up by messenger from one wing of the Hotel Cecil to the other and a few longer letters written when she was on her

holiday or week-ending somewhere apart from me. Here, I spread out the sheets. It is a competent, well-educated writing; the pen rarely leaves the paper, running on from letter to letter, from word to word. A rapid writing, flowing, clear and legible. Only here and there, generally towards the ends of her brief notes, is the clarity troubled; there are scrawled words made up of formless letters. I pore over them in an attempt to interpret their meaning. "I adore you, my beloved... kiss you a thousand times... long for it to be night... love you madly." These are the fragmentary meanings I contrive to disengage from the scribbles. We write such things illegibly for the same reason as we clothe our bodies. Modesty does not permit us to walk naked, and the expression of our most intimate thoughts, our most urgent desires and secret memories, must not—even when we have so far done violence to ourselves as to commit the words to paper—be too easily read and understood. Pepys, when he recorded the most scabrous details of his loves, is not content with writing in cipher; he breaks into bad French as well. And I remember, now that I mention Pepys, having done the same sort of thing in my own letters to Barbara; winding up with a "Bellissima, ti voglio un bene enorme," or a "Je t'embrasse en peu partout."

This is illuminating, though no more conclusive than the other theories. But if the psychological roots of cryptology remain obscure, the biological roots are clear. Those roots reach back through the eons to the first protozoa struggling for life in the warm seas of the primordial earth. For cryptography and cryptanalysis, though they are highly sophisticated technologies, retain at their inmost cores, like chromosomes that determine their heredity, the most primitive of functions.

Cryptography is protection. It is to that extension of modern man—communications—what the carapace is to the turtle, ink to the squid, camouflage to the chameleon. Cryptanalysis corresponds to the senses. Like the ear of the bat, the chemical sensitivity of an amoeba, the eye of an eagle, it collects information about the outside world.

The objective is self-preservation. This is the first law of life, as imperative for a body politic as for an individual organism. And if biological evolution demonstrates anything, it is that intelligence best secures that goal. Knowledge is power. In an atmosphere of competition, it may exist in two modes: mine and mine enemy's. All organisms attempt to maximize the former and minimize the latter. Cryptography and cryptanalysis exemplify the two modes. Cryptography seeks to conserve in exclusivity a nation's store of knowledge, cryptanalysis to increase that store.

But knowledge alone is not power. To have any effect it must be linked to physical force. Cryptology, like the services of supply and transportation and administration, aids the fighting troops that constitute a main element of national power. Nations use that power to advance their political and social goals. Cryptography and cryptanalysis are means to those ends. And that is their position in the ultimate scheme of things.

Even when the ends that they serve are purely defensive in regard to other nations, there exists a difference in morality between the means of cryptanalysis and such means as armies and navies. The latter are honest and above-board, open deterrents to aggression; they are like strong men armed. Cryptanalysis is itself an aggression—often a preventive one, to be sure—but still an aggression, a trespass. Moreover, it is surreptitious, snooping, sneaking; it makes its government hypocritical. It is the very opposite of all that is best in mankind. It shatters the highest ethical precept: to do unto others as we would have others do unto us.

Is it, then, ever morally justified? It is. A single act can be both moral and immoral, depending on circumstances. Killing is permissible in self-defense. So is cryptanalysis. In war, of course, cryptanalysis can look like a positive good, especially when it saves lives. Even in peace, cryptanalysis may be a form of self-defense. It can warn of hostile intent and enable the government to preserve life and liberty, without which there is no doing to others of any kind. But when a nation is not threatened, it is wrong for it to violate another's dignity by clandestine pryings into its messages, just as it is wrong to indiscriminately tap telephone lines or invade the privacy of a man's castle. That is why it is indefensible for the United States to read the messages of friendly nations like Norway, Britain, or Peru.

Even when justified, cryptanalysis remains an evil, and it goes against the American grain. Ever since July 4, 1776, the United States has stood for morality and integrity, in international affairs as in domestic, in the Fourteen Points as in the Emancipation Proclamation. It is this stand that, in large measure, makes America great. Cryptanalysis therefore poses a much greater problem for the United States than for other nations. It perhaps reflects this concern that the United States places her national cryptanalytic agency within the Defense Department, where it belongs in ethical terms, while Great Britain puts hers in the Foreign Office, where it belongs in a practical way.

Only once has cryptanalysis been treated as the sin against morality that it is: in 1929, before Hitler and the Japanese militarists, with no nations potentially dangerous to the United States and self-preservation not at issue, Henry L. Stimson closed Yardley's Black Chamber. Even though it was done at a time when the United States could afford it, the decision was a profoundly moral one, and it marched in the center rank of American belief. Was it softheaded, unrealistic? No. Idealism is the ultimate realism. Ideas of truth and justice always eventually triumph. Mankind can learn. America's whole history shows this, as does humanity's ascent from barbarism. The growth of wisdom and morality—urged on in these present times by the very real danger of total annihilation—may some day lead mankind to beat its swords into plowshares. When it does, it will no longer need cryptanalysis, and will dismantle organizations like N.S.A. and the Spets-Otdel. Their nonexistence then will testify to a true peace on earth. And may such be their glorious destiny!

Note 1: Variations in Letter Frequency

The problems of why certain letters should be more frequent than others within a language, and why one language should prefer sounds that another abhors, remain unsolved. Why should *e* be the most frequent letter in English? (This question is admittedly complicated in English by the discontinuity between speech and spelling, but even languages whose orthography fits their phonetics have high- and low-frequency letters.) Why should *o* be the most common in Russian, *a* in Serbo-Croatian, and *e* again in German, French, and Spanish?

Various hypotheses have been proposed; none is entirely satisfactory. The theory that the most common sounds are those learned earliest in babyhood has been proven false. The suggestion that people inhabiting a cold, damp area might select a set of sounds requiring minimal lip-opening is not supported by the facts. Nor is the opposing one that a community of fishermen will evolve a language rich in vowels to better communicate over great distances and the noises of the sea. The tendency toward economy of effort explains many phenomena, such as the greater frequency of voiceless stops compared with voiced stops, but founders on other facts, such as the development in some languages of sounds harder to pronounce than those they are replacing. An entire book has discussed the correlation between the geographic distribution of the o-factor in blood and the development of the /th/ sounds in Europe to demonstrate that hereditary factors predispose populations to certain speech sounds. But, as a reviewer has pointed out, the two correspond "only because both reflect the distribution, movement and mixing of historic people and not for any causal relation" between genetics and phonetics. Theories that languages tend to fill holes in their linguistic patterns, that sounds are selected on the basis of auditory or articulatory distinctiveness, that unusual sounds gain in popularity because they are more expressive than ordinary ones, that the culture of a community (such as agricultural versus nomadic) affects its sound complement—each of these may contain a grain of truth and explain certain isolated phenomena. But no one thesis provides a single explanation of why one language evolves one set of sounds and another a different set, nor explains why each language favors certain sounds over others.

Note 2: Calculation of Redundancy

Determining the percentage of redundancy begins with the calculation of a quantity called "entropy." Shannon borrowed this term from physics because the form of the equation that he developed for the amount of information in a set of utterances is identical with that used in physics to represent entropy. In both fields, entropy measures disorder, randomness, lack of structure. The greater the entropy, the greater the chaos. It marks a negative, dispersive tendency. Entropy is of great importance in physics because it figures in the second law of thermodynamics, perhaps the sovereign physical principle. This states that "entropy always increases" —that energy, in other words, always passes from the more organized state to the less organized, as, for example, a star dissipates its energy in radiation. This one-way flow has given entropy the epithet of "time's arrow," because an increase in entropy invariably means an increase in the age of an (isolated) physical system. If this process were to continue to its end within the universe, Sir James Jeans wrote, "there would be neither sunlight nor starlight, but only a cool glow of radiation uniformly diffused through space." This state of ultimate maximum entropy has been called the "heat-death of the universe."

Since an increase in entropy means an increase in anarchy, the language with the most entropy is the language with the greatest freedom. This is obviously a language with no rules at all to limit it. Such a language would naturally have no statistics to govern which letters would be used most often, which letters would be likely to follow a given letter, and so on. A text can be written in such a language by putting the 26 letters and the space (eliminating, for simplicity's sake, signs of punctuation, capital letters, etc.) into an urn, drawing one item out, recording it, replacing it, stirring the elements, and redrawing. Chance alone controls, and the text would be purely random. It would look like the sample Shannon composed by just such a process:

XFOML RXKHRJFFJUJ ZLPWCFWKCYJ
FFJEYVKCQSGXYD QPAAMKBZAACIBZLHJQD

The Argentine author Jorge Luis Borges has written a haunting short story about an imaginary and infinite Library of Babel whose volumes were written in just such a random fashion. It therefore contains every possible combination of letters, and, consequently, "all that it is given to express in all languages. Everything: the minutely detailed history of the future, the archangels' autobiographies, the faithful catalogue of the Library, thousands and thousands of false catalogues, the demonstration of the fallacy of those catalogues, the demonstration of the fallacy of the true catalogues . . . the true story of your death, the translation of every book in all languages. . . . I cannot combine some characters—dhcmrlchtdj—which the divine Library has not foreseen." When the people of the library realized that it was total, they rejoiced because they knew it contained the answers to the mysteries of the world. Their elation was followed by extreme depression: they could not find the answers. Thus the entropy of the library as a whole was great as it could be. The coherent texts were as much the result of chance as a line of poetry accidentally tapped out by those typewriting monkeys of Émile Borel.

But natural languages are not random affairs. Their many rules impart a highly organized structure and so lower their entropy. In theory, to compute the entropy, one must 1) count each letter in the universe of discourse, figure its probability of occurrence by dividing into the total number of letters, multiply this probability by its logarithm and then add up all these products, changing the minus signs to plus; 2) count each letter-pair, figure its probability of occurrence, multiply the probability by its logarithm, total the products, change the signs, then divide by two (since entropy is specified on a per-letter basis); 3) count each trigram, figure its probability, total the products of their probabilities and the logarithms of these probabilities, change signs, and divide by three; 4) tally all the four-letter groups, figure the probability of each, multiply their probabilities by the logarithms of their probabilities, sum the products, change signs, and divide by four; 5) repeat this process with ever-increasing sizes of letter-groups up to the largest utterances that can give a valid probability of occurrence. Each step gives a closer approximation to the entropy of the language as a whole.

The Anatomy of Cryptology

Shannon has actually carried out the first three steps on a sufficiently large sample. Using a 27-item alphabet (including the word-space) and English frequency tables, he found that the entropy for single letters is 4.03 bits* per letter. For digraphs, it falls to 3.32 bits per letter, and for trigrams to 3.1 bits per letter. The decrease stems from the fact that each letter influences what follows it: a *t* is more likely to drag an *h* behind it than an *l*. This probability constitutes an increase in order and a decrease in entropy.

This direct technique cannot be extended very far in practice, because the frequency counts rapidly become unwieldy. By the time 12-letter groups are reached, more than a billion billion frequency pigeonholes would be needed. Consequently, Shannon resorted to indirect methods, which draw upon the fact that "anyone speaking a language possesses, implicitly, an enormous knowledge of the statistics of the language." Mathematics can extract the entropy from these results. In one experiment, Shannon counted how many guesses a subject needed to determine the right letter in an unknown text. The number beneath the letter gives the number of guesses one subject made:

```
T H E R E   I S   N O   R E V E R S E   O N   A   M O T O R C Y C L E
1 1 1 5 1  1 2  1 1 2 1  1 15 1 17 1 1 1 2 1 3 2 1 2 2 7 1 1 1 1 4 1 1 1 1
A   F R I E N D   O F   M I N E   F O U N D   T H I S   O U T
3 1 8 6 1 3 1 1 1 1 1 1 1 1 1 1 1 6 2 1 1 1 1 1 1 2 1 1 1 1 1 1
R A T H E R   D R A M A T I C A L L Y   T H E   O T H E R   D A Y
4 1 1 1 1 1 1 1 11 5 1 1 1 1 1 1 1 1 1 1 1 1 6 1 1 1 1 1 1 1 1 1 1 1 1
```

Of the 102 symbols, the subject guessed right on the first try 79 times and required three or more guesses only 15 times. Most of these occur where the line of thought has more possibilities of branching out.

In another experiment, subjects tried to complete a phrase from which the spaces and the vowels had been deleted, yielding a text half as long as the original:

```
F C T S S T R N G R T H N F C T N
```

Six subjects restored an average of 93 per cent of the deletions, and several reconstructed the full text: *Fact is stranger than fiction*.

On the basis of tests like this, Shannon estimated that the entropy of English in 100-letter groups stands at about 1 bit per letter. It is this low because the cumulative effect of the long preceding passage quite substantially constrains the last letter.

---

* "Bits" is a blend-word for "binary digits." Binary digits are the two figures in a system of numerical notation that uses only two different numbers to express quantities; the two digits are commonly 0 and 1. Ordinary notation uses decimal digits in its ten-number system. To count in bits, one goes through the same procedure with two numbers that one goes through in decimal digits with ten. Thus the quantities which in decimal notation are 0, 1, 2, 3, 4, 5, 6, 7, 8, 9, 10, 11, are in binary notation 0, 1, 10, 11, 100, 101, 110, 111, 1000, 1001, 1010, 1011. Binary digits express results in terms of a choice of one of two exclusive possibilities, in terms of this or that, on or off, all or nothing, 1 or 0. Thus 4.03 bits per letter simply means that 4.03 yes-no choices must be made to determine the right letter. This form has a variety of conceptual advantages in information theory over the 10 alternatives presented by decimal digits. The binary is just another form of numerical notation, like the octal system used in computers and the duodecimal system sometimes urged for daily life because 12 has more divisors than 10. The binary system requires the use of logarithms to the base 2 instead of to the base 10 in calculations.

Actually, other tests indicate that entropy ceases to decline after about 32 letters are taken as a group. In other words, 32 letters exert virtually the same influence over those that follow them as 100 do.

Naturally, no such cohesion exists in the "urn language," or that of the Library of Babel, where letters were generated independently. Nor are there any frequency variations, because chance will select all equally often. This "urn language," whose entropy is strictly a function of the number of elements in its alphabet, becomes the standard against which natural languages are measured. The result of the comparison is redundancy. Technically speaking, redundancy is the ratio of the entropy of a language to the maximum value entropy can have with the same number of elements, subtracted from 1. It is expressed as a percentage. The maximum entropy of an alphabet of 27 items is the logarithm of 27, or 4.76 bits per letter, of 26 items, 4.70. With English's entropy of 1 bit per letter, this gives a redundancy for English of $1 - 1/4.7$, or 79 per cent, which is usually reduced to the simpler and more conservative 75 per cent.

21
HETEROGENEOUS IMPULSES

FEW FALSE IDEAS have more firmly gripped the minds of so many intelligent men than the one that, if they just tried, they could invent a cipher that no one could break. Many have tried and, although only a fraction of their ciphers have been published or patented, the quantity and variety of even this small sample is astounding.

Emile Myzskowski, a retired French colonel, devised a kind of repeated-key transposition and published it in his *Cryptographie indéchiffrable*. Collon, a Belgian Army officer, proposed a number of fractionating systems. One Rozier marched his plaintext letters through the interior of a Vigenère tableau in a dizzily twisting path in an attempt to lose the cryptanalyst. The so-called Phillips cipher enciphers five letters monalphabetically in a 5 × 5 square, then shifts the lines of the square and repeats the process. The Amsco transposition cipher accepts both single letters and pairs as its plaintext elements. A. de Grandpré filled a 10 × 10 square with ten 10-letter words whose first letters form a mnemonic acrostic, then ranged coordinates on the outside and used these to encipher; the use of plaintext words inside provides homophones in approximately the proportion required to disguise the frequencies of normal plaintext. A French major, Louis-Marie-Jules Schneider, concocted an enormously complex polyalphabetic whose alphabets were generated one from the other; this was one of the systems William F. Friedman broke in evolving the principle of the index of coincidence. A mathematician named Arthur Porges devised a system based upon a continuing fraction. The Nicodemus cipher sets out a plaintext beneath a keyword, enciphers it in Vigenère according to that keyword, and then transposes it vertically by keynumbers derived from the keyword. The Count de Mirabeau, an 18th-century French revolutionist, enciphered in a Polybius square whose sets of coordinates both ran from 1 to 5; he wrote each two-digit equivalent vertically and then transcribed all of the first digits and then all of the second, inserting numbers from 6 to 0 at will as nulls. Some amateurs just propose enciphering a message in Vigenère and superenciphering the text in Playfair. There have been autokey transpositions and a cipher invented by W. B. Homan that produces a cryptogram in which every letter of the alphabet occurs as often as every other.

Beyond these pencil-and-paper systems, the files of the patent offices bulge with quantities of cipher disks—probably the most popular single kind of cipher invention—and with gear arrangements, grilles, cylinders, mechanized tableaux, strip systems, and so on. (Most of these mechanisms produce substitution ciphers because of a very basic difference between substitution and transposition. A transposition cipher resembles what industrial engineers call a "batch" manufacturing process, in which quantities of material are cooked at a time, the product issuing in batches. This is because a transposition requires a whole group of letters that will all be mixed together, and it is hard for a mechanical device to store letters. A substitution cipher, on the other hand, is like a "continuous" process. Here the raw materials—letters in one case, ingredients in the other—flow continually, are not stored, and may be cut off at any point.)

Probably most ciphers get invented as a bit of recreation, as a part of the spell of interest in cryptology that so many people seem to go through. Sooner or later it occurs to every cryptologist that an acquaintance will say, "It can't be too hard to make a cipher that can't be solved." The friend then offers his theories, which often involve some crude sort of polyalphabeticity or a book code. Frequently he dredges up some system from his adolescence and, taking half an hour to put a ten-word message into that cipher, challenges the cryptologist to break it on the spot. William Jerdan, a 19th-century British journalist, told in his autobiography a very typical story of the birth of a cipher, reporting with a refreshing touch of humor on the dreams of glory that often accompany the nativity.

One evening, while Jerdan and his young friends were talking, the subject of ciphers came up. Jerdan boasted that "I myself could frame a system which nobody on earth could decypher and read" and bet a dinner on it. Then somebody pulled down an encyclopedia to show him the many systems that had been invented, and, said Jerdan, "when I retired to rest [I] was on no very pleasant terms with myself, for I had looked very like what I had no chance of inventing—a Cypher." But in the morning he awoke "with a secret cypher concocted in my brain," which he discussed with his friends, among them Thomas Wilde, a future Lord Chancellor. They agreed that "It ought to be laid before the government, and I cannot tell how immense a reward I was to reap for my wonderful discovery. No castle in the air was ever more stupendous and gorgeous than mine. . . . Wilde and I were now all agog for an audience of the Prime Minister, to put him in possession of the good fortune which had befallen his government, and ourselves in the way of wealth and promotion." They did manage to describe the cipher to a government secretary, and many years later, Jerdan, visiting a high Foreign Office official, saw a cipher being used based on his principle. He naturally thought that it was his, but it may have been invented independently by someone else.

Nearly every inventor of a cipher system has been convinced of the unsolvability of his brainchild. (The tendency to claim this in patents has, however, been receding with the rise of cryptologic sophistication.) In 1744, Leonhard Euler, the great Swiss mathematician, sent to a friend a monalphabetic substitution cryptogram that had a few homophones, expressing his belief that it could not be deciphered. He was only slightly more naïve than most inventors. A representative of the humanities, Walter W. Skeat, a distinguished English philologist and editor of Chaucer, proposed a cipher in 1896 that amounted to a Vigenère with key ABCDE; when hordes of amateur cryptanalysts knocked it off, he had the grace to bow and retire. Nearly all the cryptographic fossils entombed in dusty books or in old files of patent offices deserve their oblivion. They are too prone to error or too easy to solve or too cumbersome. Many an inventor delights in intricacy. Poorly endowed with empathy, he never considers the possibility that cipher clerks will not dote as lovingly upon the complex calculations of his cipher as he does; he fails to realize that to the clerks ciphering is not a pleasant after-hours recreation but a day-long, dull, boring job, about as exciting as adding up columns of figures, and that they would rather be out on a date with a girl friend.

Charles Babbage asserted that no man's cipher was worth looking at unless the inventor had himself solved a very difficult cipher. This rule holds true in the great majority of cases and if observed would have saved cryptologists a great deal of time. But it would be like having required Thomas Edison to pass a stiff examination in acoustical theory before deigning to look at his phonograph. The Babbage rule would have deprived cryptologists of some of the most important features of modern cryptography, such as the Vernam mechanism, the rotor, the Hagelin machine. Cryptologists must process a lot of ore to get something valuable—but so must diamond miners.

In evaluating their ciphers, many inventors err by thinking that the cryptanalyst must retrace the decipherment steps in his solution and that, since some of these steps are recoverable only with the key, the cipher must remain inviolate. For example, a simple cipher decomposes the plaintext into the coordinates of a checkerboard, regroups these by uniting the second coordinate of each letter with the first coordinate of the next letter (combining the leftover coordinates of the first and last letters), and recomposes them as letters:

	1	2	3	4	5
1	L	B	S	A	C
2	T	R	D	V	O
3	F	W	M	H	X
4	I	K	Y	G	N
5	Z	U	P	E	Q

plaintext   a   t   t   a   c   k   n   o   w
decomposition 1 4 2 1 2 1 1 4 1 5 4 2 4 5 2 5 3 2
recomposition   K   B   L   I   E   V   U   P   T
 to ciphertext

To the inventor, it appears that because the cryptanalyst does not know the coordinates of the letters, which are necessary to reconstruct the intermediate numerical text—which in turn seems essential to the recovery of the plaintext—he cannot make an entry into the cryptogram. A smooth unbroken surface, upon which the cryptanalyst can find no purchase, apparently protects the cipher. But the cryptanalyst does not think like that. Analyzing the structure and not the operation of the cipher, he observes that the second, or column, coordinate of the ciphertext letter K is the first, or row, coordinate of the unknown plaintext letter, and that the first, or row, coordinate of the next ciphertext letter, B, forms the second, or column, coordinate of that same plaintext letter. This observation circumvents any need to find the actual numerical coordinates, and from there the cryptanalyst can proceed with his solution.

Many inventors also invoke the vast number of combinations of keys afforded by their system as proof of its invulnerability. To exhaust the possible solutions would take eons, they contend, unwittingly using the same argument to defend their systems as Cardano used to defend a monalphabetic—and with the same lack of validity. For, as Shannon has shown, the cryptanalyst does not go after these possibilities one by one. He eliminates millions at a time. Moreover, the trials progress from the more probable to the less probable hypotheses, increasing the cryptanalyst's chance of striking the right one early. "Whereas complete trial and error requires trials to the order of the number of keys," Shannon wrote, "this subdividing trial and error requires only trials to the order of the key size in bits," a very much smaller number.

Such observations seldom have much effect upon a determined inventor. If a cryptologist points out a chink in the cryptologic armor, the inventor patches it with an extra complication. The less the inventor knows about cryptology, the more stubbornly will he cling to his conviction of unbreakability; and the more intelligent he is, the more ingeniously will he palter with the cryptologist. If the cryptologist objects that the cipher will not stand up to heavy traffic or will engender too many bad errors, the inventor replies that the cipher must be used properly for it to remain unbreakable. By "properly" he means the conditions that obtain only in cryptography's Utopia—no enciphering or transmission errors, no traffic volume exceeding the prescribed bounds for a particular key.

But this at once reduces his cipher to triviality as a practical method of cryptography. For with such a definition of "properly" any cipher may be regarded as unbreakable. Even a monalphabetic substitution would be used properly, in this sense, if only a single, very short cryptogram were sent in it. The inventor, concentrating on those rare occasions on which his cipher would be used properly, refuses to see the vast domain in which it will not serve. But the ratio of the area in which a cipher will serve to the area in which it will not counts as much in evaluating it as its intrinsic merits. The cryptologist of course sees this, but when he attempts to direct the inventor's gaze to this outside world the inventor tells him, "I am not talking about that." The cryptologist and the inventor are indeed talking about two different things, and each in his way is right. The inventor is right when he says that the cipher is impregnable within its tiny duchy. But the cryptologist is even more right when he says that it is insignificant.

Classic in the annals of cryptographic invention is the case history of J. F. Byrne, who stuck with his cipher through repeated rebuffs for more than 35 years. Byrne was an intimate of James Joyce; they were students together at Dublin, and Joyce modeled Cranly in his *Portrait of the Artist as a Young Man* upon Byrne, and made Byrne's residence, 7 Eccles Street, Dublin, the home of Leopold and Mollie Bloom, the two protagonists of his great *Ulysses*.*
It was in 1918 that Byrne hit upon the principle of his "Chaocipher," which he never disclosed publicly but was an autokey. It required nothing more than a cigar box and a few bits of string and odds and ends for its operation. When he showed it to his cousin, she exclaimed that it would bring him a Nobel Prize—not for science, apparently, but for ushering in an age of universal peace by conferring the gift of perfect security upon the communications of all nations and all men. Wrote Byrne:

> When I first set out to discover a system for concocting an indecipherable cipher, I had it clearly in mind that such a system would and should be universally available. I envisioned, for instance, the utilization of my method and machine by business men for business communications, and by brotherhoods and social and religious institutions. I believe that my method and machine would be an invaluable asset to big religious institutions, as for example the Catholic Church with its world-wide ramifications. I had, and still have in mind

---

* It may not be coincidence that in *Ulysses* an inventory of Mr. Leopold Bloom's locked private drawer at 7 Eccles Street included, among other things, "3 typewritten letters, addressee, Henry Flower, c/o P.O. Westland Row, addresser, Martha Clifford, c/o P.O. Dolphin's Barn: the transliterated name and address of the addresser of the 3 letters in reversed alphabetic boustrephodontic punctuated quadrilinear cryptogram (vowels suppressed) N.IGS./WI.UU.OX/W.OKS.MH/Y.IM: . . . ." "Quadrilinear" meant to set the cipher in four lines; "reversed alphabetic" indicated the key of $a = z$, $b = y$, etc.; "boustrephodontic," an adjective concocted from the adjective "boustrephodon," a technical term in paleography referring to writing that runs left and right in alternate lines, indicating that the lines of the cryptogram were to be read in that way. Unfortunately, Joyce or Bloom forgot about this in the fourth line, which incorrectly reads left to right. The cryptogram and its solution thus are:

```
N . I G S .
m a r t h a

W I . U U . O X
d r o f f i l c

W . O K S . M H
d o l p h i n s

Y . I M
b a r n
```

the universal use of my machine and method by husband, wife, or lover. My machine would be on hire, as typewriter machines now are, in hotels, steamships, and, maybe even on trains and airliners, available for anyone anywhere and at any time. And I believe, too, that the time will come—and come soon—when my system will be used in the publication of pamphlets and books written in cipher which will be unreadable except by those who are specially initiated.

Byrne corresponded with Colonel Parker Hitt, and in 1922 demonstrated his machine before Friedman and Colonel Frank Moorman, former head of G.2 A.6, then handling cryptography for the Signal Corps. They did not want it. He offered it to the State Department, which replied with a form letter stating that its "ciphers are adequate to its needs"—a statement that Byrne rightly damned as "a paragon of smugness." He submitted it to the Navy in 1937–38, negotiating apparently with Commander Joseph N. Wenger, and to A. T. & T.'s Ralzemond D. Parker, chief of company development and research and Vernam's boss when he invented the on-line mechanism. Nobody took it.

Byrne's faith remained undaunted. He had a little brochure printed in which he enciphered known texts in his Chaocipher and defied the world to break it. Toward the close of his life, he wrote a book of reminiscences. It told much about his days with Joyce, but his real reason for writing it was not to shed light on early Joyce but to get his Chaocipher before a larger audience. The 21st and last chapter of *Silent Years: An Autobiography with Memoirs of James Joyce and Our Ireland*, comprising fully one eighth of the book, recapitulated the story of his Chaocipher. Byrne concluded by betting $5,000 or the total royalties of the first three months after publication of his book that no one would be able to solve the message in Chaocipher that he printed in extenso in the final pages. He flung the challenge also at the amateurs of the American Cryptogram Association and the New York Cipher Society and at Norbert Wiener, father of cybernetics, and to other believers in the capabilities of the electronic calculating machines.

Nobody ever claimed the money, and Byrne died a few years later. One may presume that the reason both for the failure of the public to read his cipher and the failure of the government to adopt it was that while the cipher probably had many merits, its many demerits outweighed them for practical use. Byrne, like many inventors, both won and lost. His cipher was never broken. But his dream never came true.

Codemaking appears to be such a popular sport because it is literally fancy-free. If cryptography is a form of abstract algebra, then inventing a new cipher system is nothing more than building abstract castles in the air with material and design of one's own choosing. To make the system work is little more than to avoid self-contradiction, yet when the answer comes out right it always satisfies the inventor. Codemaking is much more popular than codebreaking because it is easier and more esthetic; it flings together shining theories however it pleases, whereas cryptanalysis forces the mind to concentrate upon the data, upon the coarse rubble of reality. But cryptanalysis is much more rewarding. For it subdues these hard and unyielding facts; it represents a victory of the mind over something, whereas codemaking represents a triumph over nothing. This mental mastery is the keen pleasure-pang of solution; it is what men of the intellectual caliber of Babbage and Wheatstone see in cryptanalysis, and it explains the most extraordinary testimonial ever given to cryptanalysis. The testimonial's phraseology is undistinguished and the cryptogram was elementary; what gives it its weight is that it was uttered by Harry Houdini. "I managed, after some worry, to solve the message, and very few things in after life gave me as much pleasure as did the unraveling of that code," wrote the man who, one would think, would say that about his ability to untangle the physical puzzles of knotted ropes and straitjackets and of locks on trunks thrown into the water to which he daily owed his life.

Consequently it is not surprising to learn that those addicted to this mental enjoyment have banded together to assure themselves of it. The American Cryptogram Association was founded in 1932 by members of the National Puzzlers League who wanted to concentrate more on cryptology, taking as their motto "The cryptogram is the aristocrat of puzzles." Today the A.C.A. numbers about 500 members, including some from Japan, Australia, New Zealand, India, Israel, Algeria, England, Netherlands, Spain, Northern Ireland, Germany, Sweden, Argentina, Venezuela, and Canada. Their professions are varied; included are lawyers, editors, physicians, professors, civil servants, teachers, housewives, widows, engineers, mathematicians, computer programmers, a puzzle maker, and retired people. Most of the members affect a nom de plume, or sort of sprightly codename, like B. NATURAL, AB STRUSE, FRINKUS, DR. CRYPTOGRAM; this is a carry-over from the National Puzzlers League and is alleged to increase informality among the membership. Every other month, the association publishes *The Cryptogram*, a magazine usually of 24 pages with articles on cryptanalysis, new ciphers, and cryptologic history. It offers the members several kinds of cryptograms for solution—monalphabetics with word divisions ranging from the simplest to the kind with the most twisted syntax and vocabulary (these are called "Aristocrats" in recognition of the association's motto), monalphabetics without word divisions ("Patristocrats"), cryptograms in all the varieties of cipher that can be solved within the compass of a 150-letter message, sometimes with tips, and cryptograms in foreign languages, including occasionally Esperanto, Latin, and Hungarian. Solvers' noms and scores are listed. The association holds an annual convention at which members hear talks on cryptology, engage in a cipher contest, are interviewed by slightly befuddled newspapermen, and banquet. In the larger cities, members have banded together to form local groups, such as the New York Cipher Society, which usually meet monthly to talk, exchange ideas, and socialize. The association appears to be the only one of its kind in the world, though France has an Amicale des Réservistes du Chiffre, a quasi-official organization of Army, Navy, and Air reservists and active officers in cryptology.

Tens of thousands of people not in the A.C.A. get the thrill of cryptanalysis by solving the monalphabetic substitutions printed in daily newspapers as puzzles much like the crossword puzzle. Some of these are relatively simple, using ordinary words in a quotation from a famous author, while other newspapers print short, rather tough cryptograms made of rare and almost nonsensical words. Most of these cryptograms are syndicated. In addition, crossword puzzle magazines usually include a few monalphabetics. One magazine, which paid a dollar apiece for the cryptograms, got most of its supply from an inmate of an Ohio prison.

While many people make and break ciphers in sport, others do it in earnest. The variety and quantity of nonpolitical cryptography can only equal the number of motives that impel people to secrecy, and these motives, like their ciphers, are most heterogeneous.

In the graveyard of New York's Trinity Church, on Broadway at the foot of Wall Street in the very heart of the financial district, stands a tombstone with an epitaph partly in cipher. Under it lies James Leeson, who died September 28, 1794, aged 38. The cipher inscription is in the ancient pigpen cipher, whose use goes back hundreds of years, and it reads *Remember Death*. Why Leeson had it carved there no one, perhaps, will ever know, but his motive may well have been that of the ancient Egyptians who first used cryptography in their sepulchral inscriptions: to stay passersby and bring the dead to life in their memory.

More obscure are the motives that led several people to encipher entries in church registers, though the conjectures can be tantalizing. At Cleator, Cumberland, England, someone used the very simple cipher

a	e	i	o	u	l	m	n	r
1	2	3	4	5	6	7	8	9

with the rest of the plaintext letters left unenciphered to record in Latin the baptism on January 1, 1645, of Janet Barne, daughter of William Barne, curate of the parish. The mother's name is not given. Could the encipherer have been Barne himself? And if so, was he perhaps hiding an illegitimate birth? The same system was used in the fee-book for the parish of Iver near Uxbridge, England, to note on January 17, 1767, the marriage of 188 b58y48. Why Ann Bunyon's name should be veiled while her husband's was left in clear remains unknown.

In two spirals on a minute of a letter of September 14, 1750, Gabriel Cramer, a teacher of mathematics at the Calvin Academy in Geneva, who corresponded with the most learned men of his time, inscribed two cipher messages. Simple columnar transpositions, they counseled: "The oracle tells thee to fear nothing; thou art permitted to hope for everything; dare boldly; banish fear; thou canst surely give thyself over to joy." Cramer almost certainly composed the messages only for his own pleasure or encouragement, perhaps choosing the spiral because it symbolized unrolling time and so a future to which he may have looked forward.

The location of a hidden treasure remains concealed beneath a cryptogram that has resisted the digging of cryptanalytic treasure hunters for more than a century. The story begins in 1817, when one Thomas Jefferson Beale and his company of 30 men were following an immense herd of buffalo about 250 miles north of Santa Fe. They camped for the night in a small ravine, and in the firelight something sparkled in the rocks: gold! For 18 months, Beale and the others mined quantities of both gold and silver. He and ten companions returned to Virginia in November, 1819, to hide half a ton of gold and almost two tons of silver in an excavation six feet deep "in the county of Bedford about four miles from Bufords." Two years later he deposited almost a ton of gold, half a ton of silver, and $13,000 worth of jewels. Beale then left again for the West. He never returned. But he had left a locked box with Robert Morris, a tavern keeper for whose integrity he had great respect, asking Morris to wait ten years and then, if Beale had not returned, to open it.

Morris waited more than twenty years before breaking the lock. Inside he found several sheets of paper covered with numbers and two letters addressed to him. They told the story of the discovery of the gold and directed him to divide the treasure into 31 equal parts—one part for himself and one to be given to the next of kin of each of the 30 men. The cryptograms gave the names of the next of kin and the location of the treasure. The letters promised that their key would be sent to Morris, but none had ever arrived.

Morris set about trying to solve the cryptograms. He got nowhere. After a number of years of failure, he shared the secret with James B. Ward, of Campbell County, Virginia, who also strove to read the messages. Ward eventually succeeded in breaking the cipher of the paper marked No. 2, which specified the amount of the treasure and how and when Beale had buried it. But it did not say where. The message ended: *Paper Number One describes the exact locality of the vault, so that no difficulty will be had in finding it.*

The key to Paper No. 2 lay in the Declaration of Independence. Beale had numbered each word from 1 to 1322 and had used the word's number as the cipher equivalent for the first letter of the word. But the Declaration of Independence did not unlock the desperately sought cryptogram of Paper No. 1. This is a numerical message of 496 groups ranging from 1 to 2906, with a moderate quantity of repeats. Cryptanalysts—or more accurately, would-be cryptanalysts—have attacked it repeatedly, trying the Constitution, books of the Bible, plays of Shakespeare. Nothing has worked. A copy was sent to Fabyan's Riverbank Laboratories, but no solution came back. In

1964, Dr. Carl Hammer, of Washington, D.C., ran elaborate statistical tests on an electronic computer, the Univac 1107, to determine the cryptogram's properties. "Among others," he wrote, "I have analyzed the distribution of the numbers themselves, their residues modulo 26, their cross sums, and even their autoregressive patterns ranging from frames 2 to 100." These have confirmed to his satisfaction that Paper No. 1 is indeed enciphered in the same general system as Paper No. 2. But he has not solved the cryptogram. To the man who does will go one of the richest rewards in cryptanalysis.

Cryptography has protected not only material secrets, but spiritual ones as well. Secret societies have long used ciphers. The Free and Accepted Masons monopolized the antique pigpen cipher to such an extent that it is often called the Freemasons' cipher. Its most common modern form is this:

Thus *Scottish rite* would be enciphered **VLE≫ΓVΠ FΓ>◻** . These symbols stand out here and there in the printed manuals of Masonry; they comprise part of the mixture of cryptography, abbreviation, and rebus with which the Masons disguise their secret rituals. In the postbellum South, the Knights of the Golden Circle, a kind of Ku Klux Klan, used essentially the same cipher for their occasional correspondences.

In its early days, Phi Beta Kappa had strong strains of secrecy, and a charter sent to Harvard in 1780 from the parent body at Williamsburg required that "all correspondencies shall be through the President of each Society by means of the Table herewith transmitted." It consisted of 13 reciprocal substitutions, and the Harvard chapter used it in a letter of March 23, 1782, to the Yale chapter, beginning IZ BUGZ BPWX ZUNDWZXB FHHFN-BARWBG . . . (*We take this earliest opportunity* . . .), to inform them of the establishment of the Harvard chapter and to invite them "to the advantages of a literary correspondence." The members took their cryptography rather seriously, for the president of the Yale chapter wrote Harvard on October 10: "I must observe that I have now written many things which ought to have been written by the T[abl]e but as I forgot to obtain it before I left N. Haven it is not in my power to avail myself of it."

The Carbonari, an antimonarchical, liberal, secret political society that flourished in Italy, and later in France, early in the 19th century, may have used a cipher based on a keyphrase. This phrase was written beneath the plaintext alphabet, thereby becoming the ciphertext alphabet. Superscribed numerals differentiated repeated letters in the keyphrase. Paul Féval, a prolific author of popular adventure novels, employed such a system in *Les*

Compagnons du Silence, a novel published in 1857 and involving a Carbonari-like secret society. The keyphrase was the fictional society's motto, meaning "Happy friends, let us go to suffering," but Féval erroneously used ALLIEGRE for ALLEGRI, throwing most of the phrase out of phase:

a b c d e f g h i j k l m n o p q r s t u v w x y z
A M I C I^2 A^2 L L^2 I^3 E G R E^2 A^3 N D I^4 A^4 M^2 O A^5 L^3 L^4 A^6 P [E N A]

In this, *carbonari* would become IAA^{4}MNA^{3}AA^{4}I^3. In 1834 a cryptogram with a similar aspect was seized upon a member of the French Carbonari.

Though the whole aim of science is to bring things to light, scientists have sometimes had to conceal their results for fear of persecution. Porta's Accademia dei Lincei corresponded in cipher with Johann Eck. When Galileo Galilei discovered with his new telescope that Venus went through phases like the moon, thereby powerfully supporting the Copernican theory, he risked getting into serious trouble with the Catholic Church, which was soon to declare that theory heretical. Consequently he recorded his discovery as an anagram in a letter to Johannes Kepler: HAEC IMMATURA A ME JAM FRUSTRA LEGUNTUR O.Y. ("These unripe things are now read by me in vain"), with the O.Y. two letters that he could not fit in. The plaintext further hid the names of the celestial bodies under mythological allusions, referring to Venus' character as the goddess of love, and Cynthia's as the goddess of the moon: *Cynthiae figuras aemulatur mater amorum* ("The mother of love imitates the phases of Cynthia"). In the same way, Christiaan Huygens established his priority in the discovery that Saturn had rings. Instead of anagramming his plaintext into another sensible text, however, he simply alphabetized it in a letter to a friend: 7 A's, 5 C's, 1 D, 5 E's, 1 G, 1 H, 7 I's, 4 L's, 2 M's, 9 N's, 4 O's, 2 P's, 1 Q, 2 R's, 1 S, 5 T's, and 5 U's. This stood for *Annulo cingitur tenui plano, nusquam cohaerente, ad eclipticam inclinato* ("It is girdled by a thin flat ring, nowhere touching, inclined to the ecliptic"). In 1711, the great English architect Sir Christopher Wren, stimulated by the promise of a reward offered by Parliament to the inventor of a means of determining the longitude of a ship at sea, transmitted three short cipher messages to the Royal Society describing three instruments for this: (1) OZVCVAYINIXDNCVOCWEDCNMALNABECIRTEWNGRAMHHCCAW, (2) ZEIYEINOIEBIVTXESCIOCPSDEDMNANHSEFPRPIWHDRAEHHXCIF, (3) EZKAVEBIMOXRFCSLCEEDHWMGNNIVEOMREWWERRCSHEPCIP. Each was to be read backwards, omitting every third letter. There are a few errors. Why Wren enciphered something that he should have been making plain as day remains unknown, but in any event he did not win the reward.

More recently, Alfred C. Kinsey and his associates encoded the replies of interviewees about their sexual habits for *Sexual Behavior in the Human Female*. Only four persons on the staff of the Institute for Sex Research could read the code, which recorded the answers in the forms of x's and a few checks, dashes, and incomprehensible abbreviations in columns. Kinsey explained that "Recording the data in code in the presence of the subject has done a good deal to convince him or her of the confidence of the record. Even though anonymity is ordinarily guaranteed by the statement which caps most questionnaires, many persons still fear that there may be some means by which they can be identified if they write out answers to printed questions. They fear, and not without some justification in the history of such studies, that a record made in plain English may be read by other persons who obtain access to the file. It is not to be forgotten that our sex laws and public opinion are so far out of accord with common and everyday patterns of social behavior that many persons might become involved in social or legal difficulties if their sexual histories became publicly known."

Lovers could sometimes find themselves in the same difficulties if their liaisons became known. Consequently Ovid, in his *Art of Love*, offered counsel on how to correspond clandestinely, mentioning some primitive forms of secret ink:

> Tuta quoque est fallitque oculus e lacte recenti
> Littera: carbonis pulvere tange, leges.
> Fallet et umiduli quae fiet acumine lini,
> Et feret occultas pura tabella notas.

Or: "A letter is also safe and escapes the eye when written in new milk; touch it with coal dust and you will read. That too will deceive which is written with a stalk of moistened flax, and a pure sheet will bear hidden marks." He also advised using pronouns of the opposite sex, such as HIM for *her*.

Secret correspondence among lovers ranges from simple notes clandestinely passed in schoolrooms to the far more elaborate systems of the rich, the royal, and the famous. In 1631, John Winthrop the younger, a future governor of Connecticut, then in his twenties, fell in love with his cousin, Martha Fones, an orphan and ward of his father, John, first governor of the Massachusetts Bay Colony. Somehow they managed to get married, when he was 24, and, since the mails were irregular and letters were sealed only with wax, they embowered their rather lyrical correspondence the next year within a monalphabetic symbol substitution, he from London, she from Groton. But she died with her first-born and he later remarried. In the 1890s, Seaman L. Wetherell, who had been convicted in Vermont of having had sexual intercourse with a girl under 14, mailed her from prison a copy of *The Black Cat* magazine, in which he had marked and dotted certain words and letters, spelling out what the court ponderously called "a communication in epistolatory form, expressive of love, and containing a request to write, and an injunction to remember her promise." Jonathan Swift, whose pen could be sharper and more satiric than any man's, melted into almost cloying sweetness in the "little language," which was not much more than a kind of baby talk, of his *Journal to Stella*, who was really 12-year-old Esther Johnson. He also used a null cipher, in which only the alternate letters counted, as in AL BSADNUK LBOINLPL DFAONR UFAINFBTOY DPIONUFNAD for *a bank bill for fifty pound*.

Heterogeneous Impulses

Marie Antoinette maintained a most elaborate cryptographic ménage for amatory correspondence, which with her often had political overtones. Though she lived in the age of the nomenclator, she employed a Porta-like cipher for correspondence in Italian, and another based on the novel *Paul et Virginie* for her Paris correspondence, mostly with Bertrand de Moleville. She enciphered her love letters to Count Axel Fersen, the tall, grave, handsome young Swede who was apparently her lover from the middle of 1783, after his return from helping America in the Revolutionary War. "I can tell you that I love you and indeed that is all I have time for," one letter began. It ended, "Farewell, most loved and loving of men. I kiss you with all my heart." Fersen also handled the voluminous correspondence of the Queen and the King in the two months before their famous attempt to escape the Revolution. He used a polyalphabetic system to encipher and decipher the letters to and from the co-conspirators:

A	ab	cd	ef	gh	ik	lm	no	pq	rs	tu	xy	z&
B	bk	du	ei	fl	gn	ho	my	ps	qx	rt	ac	&z
C	lr	ad	bg	cz	s&	ek	fm	th	ix	np	oq	uy
.	..	..	..	..	..	..	..	..	..	..	..	..

The letters of the keyword were found in the column of capitals and the plaintext letter sought in the lowercase pairs, the cipher letter being the other letter of the pair. Thus with key B, *d* = U and *u* = D. Fersen used as keys not words like ROI or LOUIS or ROYALE, which might be easily guessed, but simple words like DEPUIS, VOTRE, BATTRE, SEROIT, and so on, which he changed frequently. In addition, he represented important persons by a single letter in a little code list: B = *Empress of Russia*, F = *King of Spain*, N = *the King*, R = *Count Fersen*, and so on. The messages held their secret well, including the one of May 26, 1791, enciphered with the keyword VERTU, which stated that "the King approves the route." It was not cryptography's fault that the escape a few days later of Louis and Marie, disguised as servants and riding in a berlin, was discovered. At Varennes, a cart full of furniture barred the way across a little bridge, and just 24 hours after Marie had pretended to go to bed at the Tuileries, there were cries of "Stop!" and the King and Queen of France and their family were again prisoners of the Revolution—and, eventually, its victims.

Among the strange means of secret communication to which lovers in the 1800s resorted was perhaps the most public of all channels—the personal advertisements in newspapers, sometimes called the "agony columns." Apparently unable to contact one another directly through the mails because of parental or other restrictions, the lovers could easily bring a newspaper into the house and thus receive their messages. For secrecy, these were enciphered, but usually in so elementary a system that anyone who applied himself could read their intimacies. In February of 1853, *The Times* of London carried a Caesar substitution, in which *a* = V, addressed to Cenerentola:

Until my heart is sick have I tried to frame an explanation for you, but cannot. Silence is safest, if the true cause is not suspected. If it is, all stories will be sifted to the bottom. Do you remember our cousin's first proposition? Think of it. A few months later, on August 19, the same paper carried a cryptogram in an ordinary reversed alphabet—$a = $ z, $z = $ A—with numbers representing a few words like *the* and *that*. The message began *My darling, need I say how delighted I was to receive your letter of dear remembrance on my birthday? I beg you not to think I wrote under any irritation. I fear my letters being read by others.* . . . Wheatstone and Babbage often amused themselves by solving these simple missives. Babbage easily read a Caesar substitution of May 13, 1859, addressed to Robert: *Why do you not come or write for me? Such grief and anxiety!— Oh! Love Love!* His most difficult was a numerical cryptogram of December 21, 1853, addressed to Flo and beginning 1821 82734 29 30 84541. After, apparently, months of trying it as a polyalphabetic and as a homophonic substitution, he finally discovered that it was a polyphonic substitution, in which each cipher number stood for from one to four plaintext letters. It began (with two enciphering errors): *Thou image of my heart!*

Sometimes people inserted cryptograms just to see if anyone would make them out. A piece of advice about education, enciphered in a Caesar substitution, dated Kensington, was followed a week later by a cleartext advertisement addressed to Kensington, saying, *Your cipher is made out; but such good maxims should be written in plain English, that all might benefit.* On February 10, 1852, *The Times* was used to circulate calumny against itself—in cryptographic form, of course: TIG TJOHW IT TIG JFHIIWOLA OG TIG PSGVW. It stood for *The Times is the Jefferies of the press*, enciphered in a progressive Vigenère with key ABCD . . . beginning anew with each word. The reference to George Jeffreys, a 17th-century English judge, meant that *The Times* was a pusillanimous tool of the government and mercilessly severe to its opponents. When the editor of *The Times* heard about the cryptogram, he, like his queen, was not amused. The family of the explorer Richard Collinson communicated with him privately during his explorations even though they did not know where he was by inserting coded personal notices in *The Times*. Use of the enciphered personal advertisement seems to have died out, however, perhaps owing to the censorship restrictions of two world wars, perhaps because of the telephone or relaxed parental restrictions.

Still cryptography serves lovers. Early in the 1930s, Thelma, Lady Furness, was being courted by the Prince of Wales, later to become Edward VIII. They cabled each other in code. "I used to resent the time it took me to decode them," she gushed later. "When one is in love, one wants to know everything all at once, and as the messages were usually long, it seemed to take forever to find out what they said. But the wait was always worth while because in code one need not leave unsaid all the things dear to a woman's heart." Unfortunately, she made the mistake, on the eve of a visit to the United States, of asking a friend to look after the prince for her while she was away, and the friend promised that she would. Her name was Wallis Warfield Simpson.

The privacy sought in such communications is sometimes sought even in missives to oneself—in diaries or private notebooks. Well known are the notebooks of Leonardo da Vinci, which he wrote partly in his left-handed mirror writing, partially concealing many of the ideas that were so advanced for their time, such as armored military vehicles and flying machines. Perhaps the earliest diary to be kept cryptographically was that of the Swedish government official Erik Brahe, who kept one in secret characters—a line a day—from 1592 to 1601. Others followed. In colonial America, William Byrd of Virginia, an ancestor of the late Senator Harry F. Byrd of the same state, kept a diary irregularly for a total of about seven years between 1709 and 1741. He wrote in shorthand, using a system identified late in the 1930s by Edward J. Vogel, a Chicago court stenographer who had worked in Yardley's MI-8, as William Mason's "La Plume Volante," or the flying pen. Mrs. Marion Tinling transcribed it, finding some difficulty because Byrd often omitted the vowels in that shorthand. Parts of the diary are still unpublished, presumably because of its exceedingly racy character.

General Henri-Gatien Bertrand, Napoleon's companion during his years of exile on Saint Helena, kept a diary in such highly abbreviated French that it was virtually a code. The entry for January 20, 1821, reads: "N. so. le mat. en cal: il. déj. bi. se. trv. un peu fat; le so. il est f.g." The interpreter, Paul Fleuriot de Langle, who called his work "translating from French into French—the singular sport and strange pastime," rendered this passage as *Napoléon sort le matin en calèche. Il déjeune bien, se trouve un peu fatigué; le soir, il est fort gai* ("Napoleon goes out in the morning in a carriage. He lunches well, finds himself a little tired; in the evening, he is very gay").

Most famous of secret diaries—and deservedly so—is, of course, Samuel Pepys'. This English civil servant kept his tart, frank diary, probably the most continuously fascinating ever written, from January 1, 1660, to May 31, 1669, when failing eyesight forced him to discontinue it. It fills more than 3,000 closely written pages, all in a shorthand of Thomas Shelton's called "tachygraphy." Eleven of its shorthand letters were little removed from the outlines of the ordinary longhand forms, and it had five places for the vowel-dots, but a vowel in the middle of a word was expressed by placing the following consonant in the position that the vowel-dot would have assumed. Shelton suggested a list of contracted words—books of the Bible, frequent sermon phrases—and gave arbitrary characters to 265 common words. Among these were 2 for *to*, a larger 2 for *two*, 3 for *grace*, 4 for *heart*, 5 for *because*, 6 for *us*, and so on.

Pepys probably learned it at Magdalene College, Cambridge, where it was in favor; he seems to have based his diary upon the edition of 1641, apparently the sixth since Shelton's first publication in 1620. But though this apparently widespread knowledge would seem to have made it impossible for

Pepys to have used shorthand for secrecy, that appears in fact to have been one of his motives for using it. In the first place, he once remarked to a friend about how undesirable it would be to have it generally known that he kept a diary. In the second place, shorthand was uncommon enough in 17th-century England for many people to believe it could be used as a secret cipher.

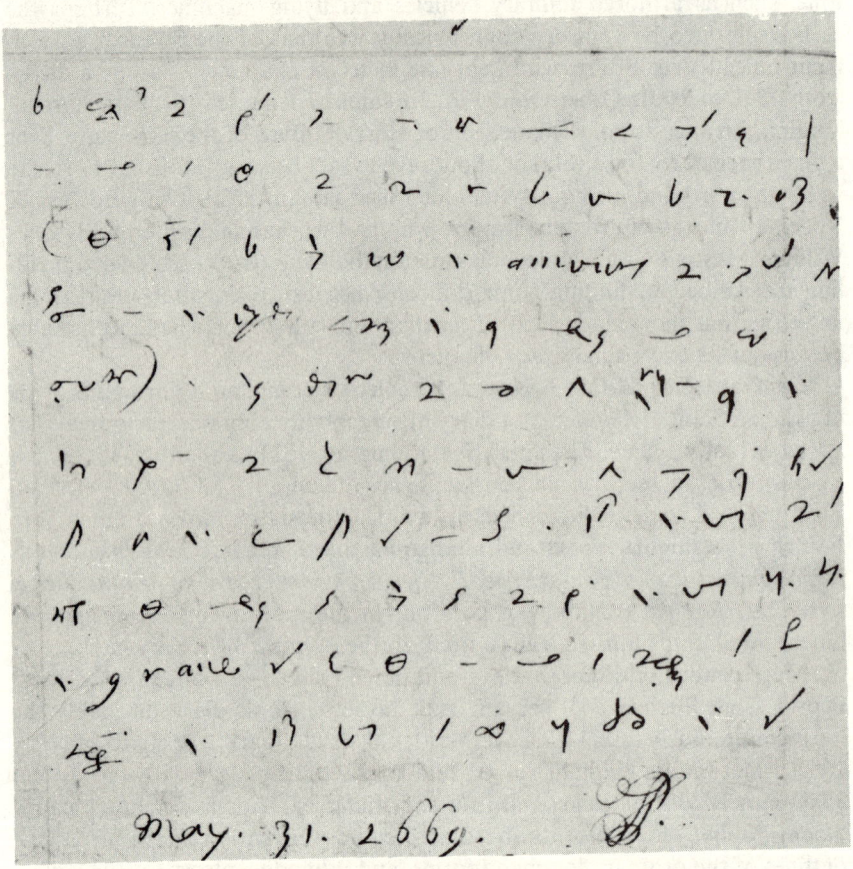

A page of Samuel Pepys' original shorthand diary

Some Protestants, fearing that the Catholics would entirely suppress the Bible if they had the opportunity, copied it out in shorthand to preserve it. Pepys increased the secrecy by writing the more salacious passages usually in French, sometimes in Latin, Greek, or Spanish, and by interpolating null symbols of his own invention. In addition to the secrecy of shorthand, Pepys undoubtedly liked its convenience, and much of the charm of his diary may derive from the mentally uncensored way in which shorthand's speed permitted him to write it.

The six small octavo volumes of the diary reposed in the Pepysian collection at Magdalene College for three or four generations after Pepys' death, unread beneath its semisecret script. Shelton's tachygraphy had joined the multitude of all-but-forgotten outdated shorthand systems; the volumes contained no key; and although the collection included Pepys' longhand transcript of his shorthand account of the adventures of Charles II, the librarians did not know about it. Upon the publication of the diary of John Evelyn, Pepys' contemporary, the master of Magdalene thought that Pepys' diary might also shed light on that exciting period in English history, since Pepys had held some high posts in the Admiralty. He showed the diary apparently to Thomas Grenville, a statesman and book collector. According to oral tradition at the college, Grenville took the diary up to bed with him one evening and reappeared at breakfast the following morning with several pages deciphered. He gave this key to John Smith, an undergraduate in St. John's College and a shorthand reporter, who took from 1819 to 1822, working usually 12 or 14 hours a day, to transcribe the diary. He did it with skill and accuracy—in general, only half a dozen minor errors will be found in 20 pages.

When he finished, he had disclosed, not just some titillating personal recollections, but a document unparalleled for the way it reveals a man. The diary was published in 1825 and has probably never been out of print since. Smith afterwards spent an uneventful life, dying in 1870 after 38 untroubled years as rector at Baldock, Hertfordshire. The diary has become a classic of literature, and literature must owe this ornamant in part to the cryptographic secrecy of the shorthand, in which Pepys felt safe in setting down his most intimate, his most human thoughts.

Cryptology has enriched literature in other ways. Many of the authors of antiquity—among them Homer and Herodotus—mention secret writing. But they allude to events believed to be historical. Not until the Renaissance, when cryptology became more widely used and hence known to many literate men, could it serve as a topic in literature. The author who first employed it did not merely brush the subject, he seized it with both hands, danced it around, and exuberantly roared out a stream of mirth poking fun at the whole business. He was, naturally, François Rabelais:

> When Pantagruel had read the superscription [in a missive from a lady, saying "To the most loved by the fair and the least loyal of the brave"], he was much amazed, and therefore demanded of the said messenger the name of her that had sent it: then opened he the letter, and found nothing written in it, nor otherwayes inclosed, but only a gold ring, with a square table-diamond. Wondering at this, he called Panurge to him, and shewed him the case; whereupon Panurge told him, that the leafe of paper was written upon, but with such cunning and artifice, that no man could see the writing at the first sight, therefore to finde it out he set it by the fire, to see if it was made with Sal Ammoniack soaked in

water; then put he it into the water, to see if the letter was written with the juice of Tithymalle: after that he held it up against the candle, to see if it was written with the juice of white onions.

Then he rubbed one part of it with oile of nuts, to see if it were not written with the lee of a fig-tree: and another part of it with the milk of a woman giving suck to her eldest daughter, to see if it was written with the blood of red toads, or green earth-frogs: Afterwards he rubbed one corner with the ashes of a Swallowes nest, to see if it were not written with the dew that is found within the herb Alcakengie, called the winter-cherry. He rubbed after that one end with eare-wax, to see if it were not written with the gall of a Raven: then did he dip it into vinegar, to try if it was not written with the juice of the garden Spurge: After that he greased it with the fat of a bat or flitter-mouse, to see if it was not written with the sperm of a whale, which some call ambergris: Then put it very fairly into a basin full of fresh water, and forthwith took it out, to see whether it were written with stone-allum: But after all experiments, when he perceived that he could finde out nothing, he called the messenger, and asked him, Good fellow, the lady that sent thee hither, did she not give thee a staffe to bring with thee? thinking that it had been according to the conceit whereof Aulus Gellius maketh mention, and the messenger answered him, No, Sir. Then Panurge would have caused his head to be shaven, to see whether the Lady had written upon his bald pate, with the hard lie whereof sope is made, that which she meant; but perceiving that his hair was very long, he forbore, considering that it could not have grown to so great a length in so short a time.

Then he said to Pantagruel, Master, by the vertue of G— I cannot tell what to do nor say in it; for to know whether there be any thing written upon this or no, I have made use of a good part of that which Master Francisco di Nianto the Tuscan sets down, who hath written the manner of reading letters that do not appear; that which Zoroastes published, *Peri grammaton acriton*; and Calphurnius Bassus, *de literis illegibilibus*: but I can see nothing, nor do I beleeve that there is any thing else in it then the Ring: let us, therefore, look upon it.

And inside the ring, of course, is the message of reprobation from the lady. Half of this lusty episode—was ever a discussion of invisible inks rendered with more glee?—turns on real things, and illustrates Rabelais' vast erudition, while the half that makes it an outrageous burlesque is purely Rabelais' invention. The inks made with ammonium chloride, onions, alum, and tithymallus will all work, while the red toads, the ear wax, and the bat fat lampoon the exotic formulas and the unnecessary mystery with which the would-be magicians of the day, rather like Trithemius and, in a different way, like Porta, loved to surround themselves. The staff, of course, is a skytale, which the Roman writer Aulus Gellius describes in his *Attic Nights*. The head-shaving story kids Herodotus' tale of Histaeius and his tattooing of a secret message on a slave's head. The three books are purely imaginary. And the climax of the episode—with the message just where they should have looked to begin with—satirizes the whole business of unearthing secret messages. Here, in the volcanic writings of a titan, cryptology explodes into incandescent literary life.

The greatest writer of all, William Shakespeare, never mentioned cryptology as such, but did touch upon its older brother, interception. In *Henry V*, Henry's brother, the Duke of Bedford, is discussing with two other peers a conspiracy that three other lords were hatching against the king. "The King hath note of all that they intend,/By interception which they dream not of," Bedford says. Not long thereafter Henry presents the three traitors with proofs of their guilt—probably the intercepted letters themselves. The effect is dramatic: "Why, how now, Gentlemen?/What see you in those papers that you lose/So much complexion?" Henry exclaims. "Look ye, how they change! /Their cheeks are paper. Why, what read you there/That hath so cowarded and chas'd your blood/Out of appearance?" They immediately confess, and, in the play, are promptly executed.

Though this was a historical play, Shakespeare's sources—the chronicles of Raphael Holinshed and of Edward Hall—do not mention interception. This aspect must therefore have sprung from Shakespeare's imagination, which may have drawn its inspiration from the knowledge, probably fairly common then, that letters were intercepted and opened by the authorities to obtain information.

It perhaps testifies to Shakespeare's scope that discussions of cryptology in works of the imagination in the 200 years that succeeded his appear nonexistent, or at least were so rare and tangential to the main theme of a work that they left no traces in the critical literature. Then, in 1829, literary cryptology took a step sideways when Honoré de Balzac published *The Physiology of Marriage*, one of the works that make up his immense *Human Comedy*. It is a long, amusing, sardonic dissertation on marriage, and in a section on "Religion and confession, considered in their relation with marriage," Balzac wrote: "La Bruyère has said very spiritually: 'It is too much against a husband [to require both] devotion and gallantry: a wife must choose.' The author thinks that La Bruyère is mistaken. In reality,"—and there followed four pages of the most confused typographical mishmash, with letters upside down, letters sideways, type standing on its head and printing on its feet, none of it making the least bit of sense, but with a final "en effet" slyly inserted near the end. In the errata, which serve "to caution you against the errors you have made in reading this work," Balzac cited the four pages and observed: "To really understand the sense of these pages, a reader who is honest with himself ought to reread its principal passages several times; for the author has placed all his thought there."

Could it be a real cryptogram? Commandant Bazeries wondered, and, taking a later edition, analyzed the cryptic text, found the cryptogram to be neither a transposition nor a substitution, and concluded that it was no cipher at all. He could have determined this more easily simply by comparing his edition with the first, or with any one of the successive editions—some of which appeared during Balzac's lifetime. He would have seen that Balzac, evidently not wishing to reveal his feelings on religion and confession, had

La Bruyère a dit très-spirituellement : —
C'est trop contre un mari que la dévotion et
la galanterie : une femme devrait opter.

L'auteur pense que La Bruyère s'est trompé.
En effet, [cryptogram text]

DES RELIGIONS ET DE LA CONFESSION, CONSIDÉRÉES DANS
LEURS RAPPORTS AVEC LE MARIAGE.

La Bruyère a dit très-spirituellement : « C'est trop contre
un mari que la dévotion et la galanterie : une femme devrait
opter. »

L'auteur pense que La Bruyère s'est trompé. En effet :
[cryptogram text]

DES RELIGIONS ET DE LA CONFESSION, CONSIDÉRÉES DANS
LEURS RAPPORTS AVEC LE MARIAGE.

La Bruyère a dit très-spirituellement : — " C'est trop
contre un mari que la dévotion et la galanterie : une femme
devrait opter."

L'auteur pense que La Bruyère s'est trompé. En effet :
[cryptogram text]

266   THE PHYSIOLOGY OF MARRIAGE

band to have ranged against him both devotion and gallantry;
a woman ought to choose but one of them for her ally."

The author thinks that La Bruyere is mistaken. For
instance : anresfs mirhcaraf.: farmhcsdalhd laiadttfhmsl, aidl
annersnsffiNfidgdc.: "pqtpvgvtmfto. dt-aipo; todfda:dhoiOo
tdasadecssmcirersqvt" odht.tditoadgdaodtgd scmwywgbm wp
ctoliygfb chuykgbvTOIj qwfmhi nihecmlunfbmcthan numfkw
arolfmecml uwfmbraod rfhmsewyuniuwan csn cwyuniahmrl
shrluf bmhraoinpywffgbmhrjNIDFMB nlwgbmharod inudr
ehfgkqjp ylidrmbv csthaoildmbyun drARMT,..; dfarhlnldr
eccmrodwlunldrfmh bmh fdwyluULDFMBH,. ylwfmhranlf
cmb fwdilyqkgbmhtarlmeshrdwkflffffnjpul dra h nurmrafpu
and in similar vein to the end of the paragraph.

Balzac's fake cryptogram in The Physiology of Marriage, *showing differences in different editions, beginning with the first edition in 1840 (upper left), a "new" 1840 edition (upper right), an 1847 edition (lower left), and an English 1901 edition (lower right)* ordered his printer to set pi, for the "cryptogram" changed from one edition to the next!

A few years later, literary cryptology took its greatest step forward with the work of Edgar Allan Poe, whose story "The Gold-Bug" remains unequalled as a work of fiction turning upon a secret message.

That the early American writer should have become interested in cryptology seems almost inevitable. He urged exactness in thinking, talked about "ratiocination," and wrote stories, like "The Purloined Letter," that demanded a methodical logic. But he also wrote poems of an unearthly beauty and the macabre *Tales of the Grotesque and Arabesque*, and he looked into such irrational subjects as mesmerism and phrenology. Cryptology, more than other subjects, is split the same way. It beams the hard bright searchlight of reason upon the phenomena it investigates. At the same time it glimmers with the pale, eerie, indistinct moonshine of mysticism and spooky powers. This double aspect of cryptology played upon Poe's dual nature—its science upon his intellect, its occultism upon his emotions—and aroused thereby a whole-souled response.

Evidence of Poe's interests in writing and mystery appeared in *The Narrative of Arthur Gordon Pym*, when outlines on maps and flakings of cavern walls inexplicably spelled out words in Ethiopian and Arabic. His first known mention of cryptology itself occurred, however, in an article entitled "Enigmatical and Conundrum-ical" that appeared in the December 18, 1839, issue of *Alexander's Weekly Messenger*, a Philadelphia newspaper. After printing a riddle that had baffled one of the paper's subscribers, Poe wrote:

> We sympathize with our correspondent's perplexity, and hasten to remove it—especially as we have a *penchant* for riddles ourselves. In spite of the anathemas of the over-wise, we regard a good enigma as a good thing. Their solution affords one of the best possible exercises of the analytical faculties, besides calling into play many other powers. We know of no truer test of general capacity than is to be found in the guessing of such puzzles. In explanation of this idea a most capital Magazine article might be written. It would be by no means a labor lost to show how great a degree of rigid *method* enters into enigma-guessing. So much is this the case, that a set of rules might absolutely be given by which almost any (good) enigma in the world could be solved instantaneously. This may sound oddly; but is not more strange than the well known fact that rules really exist, by means of which it is easy to decipher any species of hieroglyphical writing—that is to say writing where, in place of alphabetical letters, any kind of marks are made use of at random.*

And the footnote to this read:

> * For example—in place of A put † or any other arbitrary character—in place of B, a *, &c. &c. Let an entire alphabet be made in this manner, and then let this alphabet be used in any piece of writing. This writing can be read by

means of a proper method. Let this be put to the test. Let any one address us a letter in this way, and we pledge ourselves to read it forthwith—however unusual or arbitrary may be the characters employed.

Replies poured in on Poe. At first they came just from Philadelphia and environs, but later they arrived from Alabama, Massachusetts, New York, Ohio, Indiana, and Iowa—the correspondent from Iowa being 17-year-old Schuyler Colfax, later to be Vice President in Grant's first term. The cipherers used wild combinations of asterisks, question marks, numbers, paragraph marks, and once "the ugliest and drollest hieroglyphics imaginable (we having no type in our office which would come within a mile of them)." The volume increased so that he asked his readers: "Do people really think that we have nothing in the world to do but to read hieroglyphics? or that we are going to stop our ordinary business and set up for conjurers? Will any body tell us how to get out of this dilemma? If we don't solve all the puzzles forwarded, their concocters will think it is because we cannot—when we can. If we *do* solve them we shall soon have to enlarge our sheet to ten times the size of the Brother Jonathan" (a "mammoth" New York newspaper about two feet by three). Things never got that bad, but the great number of messages afforded Poe a lucky opportunity to explain why he limited his challenge to ciphers that were—for him—so easy to solve: "Were we to engage in the solution of *every kind of puzzle* sent us, we should have our hands full. We said that we could and would solve every cipher, of a stipulated character, which we should receive, and we have kept our pledge more than ten times over."

In the 15 numbers of *Alexander's Weekly Messenger* in which he had articles on cipher, Poe published the ciphertexts and solutions of 11 cryptograms and the solutions only of 16; he merely stated that he had solved three others. Six he had not solved: one he had lost, one he had had no time to examine, one was written in pencil and defaced, two were "impositions" (false cryptograms), and one had 51 different cipher characters and hence lay outside the limits of strict monalphabeticity with no homophones that he had laid down in his original challenge.

During all these months, he never once revealed how he solved the cryptograms, though his readers begged, "Just let us into the secret, as we are fond of the marvelous." Teased Poe: "Well, what will he give us for the secret?— it is a wonderful one and well worth paying for. Let him send us on a list of forty subscribers, with the money, and we will give him a full explanation of our whole method of proceeding." After solving an alliterative message that used, apparently, a different alphabet for each line, he promised to reveal his method of solution. But he evidently realized that the mystery heightened interest, for in the next issue he recanted: "Upon second thought, we must decline giving our *mode of solution* for the present."

The closest he ever came to doing so was when he demonstrated how he deduced that a challenge sent him by G. W. Kulp, of Lewiston, Pennsylvania, was a false cryptogram. He picked out three words in the cryptogram—MW, LAAM, and MLW. Since "all English words of but two letters consist of a vowel and a consonant," he wrote, MW must be one of 30 words, which he listed. He then inserted every letter of the alphabet in the middle of all 30 words in an exhaustive trial process to see which letters would make a sensible word out of MLW. Here he found 18, including *ash* and *tho'*. Turning to LAAM, he observed, that "if MLW be *ash*, then LAAM will be a word of this form, *s . . a*, in which the dots represent two unknown letters of the same kind." He ran through his 18 words in this way, and found that the only one that gave a possible meaning for LAAM was *h . . t*, or *hoot*. "LAAM is then *hoot* or nothing. But the hypothesis of the word *hoot* is founded upon that of the word *tho'*. . . . We now arrive at a definite conclusion. Either Mr. Kulp's puzzle is not genuine, or MW stands for *to*, MLW for *tho'*, and LAAM for *hoot*. But it is evident that this latter cannot be—for in that case both W and A represent the letter *o*. What follows?—why that Mr. Kulp's puzzle is no puzzle at all. This demonstration is as absolutely conclusive as any mathematical one could be. The process of reasoning here employed is that employed also in the solution of the cyphers."

All his *Alexander's* cryptograms were simple monalphabetics with word divisions (except one which appears to have been some kind of Cardano grille, whose solution only he gives). None of Poe's correspondents tried to stump him with puzzle-type cryptograms that use bizarre words and twisted syntax, which would have been perfectly within the limits of his rules. In fact, they often made it especially easy for him by using well-known pieces for their plaintext, such as the Lord's Prayer or the opening lines of *Twelfth Night*. Identification of a word or two of these would give away the entire message, and indeed "a single glance" enabled Poe to read the Lord's Prayer cryptogram. Most employed symbol alphabets constructed without any key, though one correspondent actually used an $a = 1$, $b = 2$, $\ldots$, $z = 26$ substitution. Poe solved them quickly: "Our correspondent will know by the date of his communication, that we could only have received it on the morning when we go to press (Tuesday)—consequently we must have read his puzzle *instanter*," he wrote in giving his first solution in *Alexander's*. He also solved some sloppily, giving solutions with errors or omissions. This rather suggests that he attacked his cryptograms inductively, guessing at words by trying combinations of letters, as in the Kulp demonstration, rather than carefully analyzing ciphertext frequencies and characteristics. This intuitive approach, which offers a bolder and easier solution, would accord well with his habits of thought and work.

Poe's solutions for *Alexander's* became the narrow foundation upon which he erected an exaggerated reputation as a cryptanalyst. He enlarged the foundation slightly in 1841 when he solved cryptograms in a polyphonic substitution, a little more difficult than ordinary monalphabetic substitution, submitted by readers of another magazine. It was his publicitywise skill at magnifying these rather ordinary deeds, however, plus the testimony of others, that created the legend of his almost supernatural cryptanalytical prowess. An article on "Quick Perception" in the *Philadelphia Saturday Museum* in 1843 reported how Poe was shown a cryptogram and "immediately" gave the answer. He supplied material for a biography of himself in the same issue which cited the most difficult cryptogram that he had ever solved as the easiest: "This cryptograph, however," the article observed falsely, "was simplicity itself in comparison with others resolved by the subject of our memoir." A friend reported in a letter how Poe solved a cryptogram "in a much shorter time" than it took to encipher it—and Poe promptly published the letter. The legend appeared in full flower less than a year after Poe's death. A Massachusetts clergyman, telling how Poe read a cryptogram "in one-fifth of the time it took . . . to write it," concluded that "The most profound and skilful cryptographer who ever lived was undoubtedly Edgar A. Poe."

The myth has shrunk since then. But vestiges linger. Poe student W. K. Wimsatt, Jr., has contended that Poe's cryptanalytic powers were "far beyond the ordinary." Beyond the ordinary individual, of course, and even beyond the person who may have a curiosity about ciphers. But not beyond the ordinary amateur. Most amateurs that do any solving at all solve monalphabetics with quite the same facility as Poe. Just a modicum of experience endows a solver with an apparently miraculous facility to recognize words and word-patterns at a glance—KVBK stands out as *that*, KVILI as *there*, AVTOV as *which*. The solution of such ciphers is not only simple but also becomes, upon the slightest practice, mechanical. On the available evidence, then, it is wrong to say that Poe's cryptanalytic skill exceeded the ordinary. But what about his latent capacity, what Wimsatt called his "native power"? Other amateur cryptologists of the day—Babbage, Wheatstone, Kasiski—sometimes solved ciphers much more difficult than monalphabetic substitution. Would Poe have been able to do so too? The question is unanswerable. Poe limited himself to the simplest kind of cipher. To decide on the basis of no evidence whether he did so because he feared to tackle the more complicated systems, or because, as he said, he did not have time, would be arbitrary and useless.

Nevertheless, Poe's reputed cryptanalytic superiority has colored the whole picture of the man. "Doubtless nothing contributed to a greater extent than did Poe's connection with cryptography to the growth of the legend which pictures him as a man at once below and above ordinary human nature," wrote Joseph Wood Krutch. For by associating himself with cryptology, Poe clothed himself in the spectral aura that has always shimmered about it.

Poe quit *Alexander's* in May of 1840. A year later, when he had become editor of *Graham's Magazine* in Philadelphia, he found an opportunity to exploit the same sure vein of journalistic interest that he had struck in *Alexander's*. Reviewing *Sketches of Conspicuous Living Characters of France* in the issue of April, 1841, he offered, in almost the same words he had used in *Alexander's*, to read cryptograms that readers might send him:

> In the notice of [the lawyer Antoine] Berryer it is said that, a letter being addressed by the Duchess of Berry to the legitimists of Paris, to inform them of her arrival, it was accompanied by a long note in cypher, the key of which she had forgotten to give. "The penetrating mind of Berryer," says our biographer, "soon discovered it. It was this phrase substituted for the twenty-four letters of the alphabet—*Le gouvernement provisoire!*"
>
> All this is very well as an anecdote; but we cannot understand the extraordinary penetration required in the matter.... anyone who will take the trouble may address us a note, in the same manner as here proposed, and the keyphrase may be in either French, Italian, Spanish, German, Latin, or Greek (or in any of the dialects of these languages), and we pledge ourselves for the solution of the riddle. The experiment may afford our readers some amusement —let them try it.

The keyphrase cipher, which apparently has never been used in practical cryptography before or after the Duchess of Berry,* uses the keyphrase as a substitution alphabet:

```
a b c d e f g h i j l m n o p q r s t u v x y z
L E G O U V E R N E M E N T P R O V I S O I R E
```

The French plaintext *vraiment* ("truly"), which has no repeated letters, would become OOLNEUNI. Thus, O represents both *v* and *r*, and N both *i* and *n*. The keyphrase produces a polyphonic substitution—one in which a given ciphertext letter may stand for two or more different plaintext letters, and which consequently may create some decipherment ambiguities. Its ciphertext may exhibit such dismaying peculiarities as three or four identical ciphertext letters in a row. But any difficulties that this may occasion the cryptanalyst are counterbalanced by the coherence of the keyphrase, which he reconstructs along with the ciphertext.

While waiting for responses to his challenge, Poe wrote "A Few Words on Secret Writing," the longest of his writings on cryptology, for the July *Graham's*. It comprised a medley of cryptographic information, presented with pace and vigor but giving little new. It did include a dictum that he had promulgated in *Alexander's* but that here assumed the form in which it became classic in cryptology—long considered a truism but now known to be

---

* And perhaps not even by her. The system described is virtually the same as that apparently used by the Carbonari at the same period except that the superscribed differentiating numbers are omitted. It may well have been Berryer's biographer who omitted them, either because someone did not give him all the details of the system or because he misunderstood. It is true that the Duchess of Berry was a royalist and the Carbonari were antimonarchical, but both were opposed to the line then occupying the throne upon the Duchess' return to France in 1832. They might have shared the Carbonari system, or, more probably, it might have just been in the air at that time and therefore widely used. Thus the keyphrase cipher may owe its existence to Poe's creating it as a result of a mistake!

false: "It may be roundly asserted that human ingenuity cannot concoct a cipher which human ingenuity cannot resolve." Most of the article's "scraps of erudition," as critic Wimsatt well put it, came straight from the *Encyclopaedia Britannica*, and perhaps also from the *Encyclopaedia Americana*. Poe faithfully reproduced the *Britannica*'s error in abbreviating Giovanni Battista Porta's name as "Cap. Porta." Poe here gave cryptology its first discussion of skytale cryptanalysis: wrap the strip of parchment around a cone and slide it up and down until sense appears; the diameter of the cone at that point is the diameter of the skytale. But he still did not say anything about how to solve the monalphabetic substitutions; he still did not disclose the secret for which his readers had clamored. Indeed, he deepened the mystery. He concluded the article by stating (incorrectly) that one could find in writings on cryptology no rules for solving ciphers that one did not "in his own intellect possess."

On July 1, a friend in Washington, F. W. Thomas, a novelist who held a position in the Treasury Department and who was helping Poe in his efforts to get a government job, forwarded two keyphrase cryptograms from a friend of his who had accepted Poe's challenge in the April *Graham's*. Poe solved one of them at once; the other had the same keyphrase: BUT FIND THIS OUT AND I GIVE IT UP. It was the most difficult he had ever solved, owing to its plaintext, part of which read: *Without dubiety incipient pretension is apt to terminate in final vulgarity, as parturient mountains have been fabulated to produce muscupular abortions.* Elatedly, he sent the solution to Thomas "by return of post" on July 4, asking for testimonials. These he used in the August issue of *Graham's*, in which he published the text of the cryptogram and offered a year's subscription to *Graham's* and *The Saturday Evening Post* to the first solver. A few days after sending this number to press, he received another cipher from Thomas, this one from the son of the Secretary of the Treasury, to whom Thomas had been speaking of Poe. "Decypher Mr. P. Ewing's cryptograph in your August number if you can—Let me have it by return of mail," Thomas wrote. But it did not yield to Poe's analyses, and Poe, who up to this point had apparently depended solely upon rules that he already possessed in his own intellect, and who might have been helped in getting a job he wanted if he solved the Ewing cipher, sought new sources of information.

Several times before, he had had good results with *The Cyclopaedia* of Abraham Rees, finding materials for articles on Palestine and Stonehenge. Now he turned to it again and this time discovered the superb article on "Cipher" by William Blair, an English surgeon. It ran 30 pages and about 35,000 words—the length of a small book—and for almost a century, or until Parker Hitt wrote his *Manual for the Solution of Military Ciphers* in 1916, it remained the finest treatise in English on cryptology. Blair had done considerable original research among manuscripts for historical material; he described thoroughly the major systems of cryptography and gave the bases of cryptanalysis and a number of examples—including attempts taken (with credit) from Falconer, to solve polyalphabetics. On the back of the envelope of Thomas' letter, Poe copied a variety of linguistic observations—"*y* seldom in middle of word"—plus what appears to have been his first and only frequency count, though from his work with printers he must have already been aware that letters differ in their frequency of use.

In giving the frequencies, Blair had divided vowels from consonants and had ranked the frequencies of the consonants in four groups, in each of which he listed the individual consonants alphabetically: "To find out one consonant from another, you must observe the frequency of *d, h, n, r, s, t*; and next to those, *c, f, g, l, m, w*; in a third rank may be placed *b, k, p*, and lastly, *q, x, z*." As for the vowels, "you will generally find *e* occur the oftenest; next, *o*, then *a*, and *i*; but *u*, and *y*, are not so often used as some of the consonants, especially *s* and *t*." In compressing Blair's information, Poe ignored Blair's distinctions, erroneously transposed *a* and *o*, and listed as the "order of frequency e a o i d h n r s t u y c f g l m w b k p q x z." Both Blair and Poe omitted *j* and *v*.

This help, however, did not enable Poe to solve the Ewing cipher, which was very short. Nor did he use this frequency count for notes on cryptology in the October and December issues of *Graham's*, though he did make use of much of Blair's information—without ever giving credit to the source. In fact he made it appear as if the knowledge were his. For example, on the basis of the Blair-Falconer discussion of polyalphabetic solution, he wrote in December regarding the Vigenère tableau: "Out of a thousand individuals nine hundred and ninety-nine would at once pronounce this mode inscrutable. It is yet susceptible, under peculiar circumstances, of prompt and certain solution." Poe's readers no doubt drew the conclusion that he wanted them to draw about just who could effect that solution.

Cryptology had made the biggest hit of any of his journalistic writings. A story based upon the sure-fire topic of a secret message seemed a natural, and a story explaining the technique of cryptanalysis—the mystery with which he had teased his readers for two years—seemed a certain success. Half a dozen years before, he had reviewed Robert M. Bird's *Sheppard Lee*, whose hero frantically searched for the legendary treasure of the pirate Captain William Kidd. Poe remembered a comical Negro servant from the novel, and this brought back his Army days in the South in 1828, when he served at Fort Moultrie on Sullivan's Island, outside Charleston, South Carolina. Sullivan's Island became the locale of the story and, recalling some natural history studies with an acquaintance there, Poe combined the click beetle, *Alaus oculatus*, with its death's-head spots, and the gold beetle, the gleaming *Callichroma splendidum*, into the gold-bug that gave its name to the story he wrote.

In spite of the story's length, George Rex Graham, the publisher of *Graham's Magazine*, snapped it up. He paid only a minimum price, however, and when Poe heard that the *Dollar Newspaper* was offering a $100 prize for the best story, he got "The Gold-Bug" back from Graham and entered it in the competition. (Unable to return Graham's money, he had to make it up with a series of reviews.) "The Gold-Bug" won the prize and was published in two installments in the *Dollar Newspaper* on June 21 and 28, 1843. It made an instant hit. So great was the demand that it was reprinted in the *Saturday Courier*, and then reprinted again in the *Dollar Newspaper*. Playwright Silas S. Steele adapted it, and on August 8 it was given as a curtain raiser at the Walnut Street Theatre in Philadelphia. The tale was—and is—by far the most popular of any of Poe's stories. In 1845, it was published in book form for the first time, in *Tales*. Poe revised the plaintext slightly—changing a *forty* to a *twenty*—and corrected the ciphertext to agree; but, human as he was, he forgot to make the appropriate changes in his frequency count. The *Tales* count also omits one character, the (representing *r*. Most editors have reproduced these slightly erroneous figures. In November of 1845, a French translation by Alphonse Borghers appeared in *La revue britannique*, and in 1856 the great French symbolist poet whom Poe had so influenced and who in turn influenced so much of French poetry, Charles Baudelaire, published his translation as "Le Scarabée d'or." "The Gold-Bug" was both the climax and the conclusion of Poe's cryptologic writings; he published nothing more on the subject, although he solved cryptograms sent him by correspondents during the next two years. He eventually stopped this, complaining in a letter to a friend that "I have lost, in time, which to me is money, more than a thousand dollars, in solving ciphers."

"The Gold-Bug" opens with the hero, William Legrand, living a secluded life on Sullivan's Island with an old Negro servant, Jupiter. A sort of amateur naturalist, Legrand has found a new specimen, a gold-colored bug; he sketches it for his friend, the first-person narrator of the story, upon a scrap of parchment that he has picked up on the beach. The narrator accidentally holds the parchment near a fire. When he looks at it, he sees only a reddish death's-head. Legrand becomes abstracted upon seeing this. During the next month or so his behavior becomes increasingly strange. Jupiter fetches the narrator, and upon Legrand's request they set off into the woods, carrying shovels. Halting at a large tree, Legrand makes Jupiter climb it, find a skull at the end of a branch, and drop the gold-bug (which Legrand has gotten back from the friend to whom he lent it) through one eye. Following a line determined by the bug and the tree, they dig—and exhume a fabulous treasure of glittering gold coins and jewels, buried there by Kidd. The mystery of how Legrand knew how to find it is resolved when he explains how, using heat, he developed a cryptogram in invisible ink on the parchment, and then (using the frequency count that Poe had copied out of the Blair article) how he solved the cryptogram.

The story is full of absurdities and errors. The parchment was found near "the remnants of the hull of what appeared to have been a ship's long boat," which "seemed to have been there for a very great while; for the resemblance to boat timbers could scarcely be traced." This was the boat in which Kidd had brought ashore his treasure. Would the parchment have remained in the same place for generations? If it did, would it not have suffered from the elements, as the timbers did? The invisible ink, Poe specifies, is "regulus of cobalt, dissolved in spirit of nitre." Unfortunately, this gives cobalt nitrate, which is readily soluble in water. Would any trace of ink have remained on the parchment after decades on the beach? Even if any had, it would have been obliterated when Legrand washed the parchment in warm water to remove dirt. Legrand spotted the skull from a hillside seat through a rift in the trees; as soon as he moved from the seat, the skull disappeared. Poe implies that for that very reason the pirates chose that seat, that tree, and that branch. Would that narrow rift have remained unchanged through 150 years of arboreal growth? The first traces of the ink were accidentally brought out when the narrator's hand, holding the parchment, dropped close to a fire; but heat strong enough to bring out the ink would probably have scorched the narrator's hand. The frequency table was of course absurd, though Poe paid no attention whatever to it after using it to identify *e*. Finally, one may wonder whether Kidd would have employed so ridiculously melodramatic a manner of recording the treasure location, and have been so careless as to lose the note.

All of these criticisms are valid. They show that Poe was less concerned with accuracy than with the appearance of accuracy, that he affected a learning which he did not have and to this extent was not intellectually honest. Beyond that, and to the reader, none of them matters. For no one thinks of these problems when caught up in the powerful narrative current of the story. The tale perhaps owes some of its force to Poe's using it to vent some of his frustrated desires. "I cannot keep from thinking with sadness how the unfortunate E. Poe must have dreamed more than once about how to discover such treasures," wrote Baudelaire. The plot, with its finding of buried treasure, may seem trite to readers of today. But that is for the same reason that *Hamlet* seems loaded with clichés: its virtues have made its lines so well known. Something of how it struck contemporaries, however, may be felt in what Baudelaire wrote: "How beautiful is the description of the treasure, and how good a feeling of warmth and dazzlement one gets from it! For they find the treasure! *it is not a dream*, as generally happens in all these novels, where the author awakens us brutally after having excited our minds with appetizing hopes; this time, it is a *real* treasure, and the decipherer has really won it." The construction of the story, which ends, not with the finding of the treasure, as lesser writers might have done, but with the resolution of the cryptogram, is exactly right. Moreover, the exposition of that crucial part of the story, on which all turns, is a masterpiece of lucidity. "As we follow the steps of the argument," wrote critic Wimsatt, "we have the impression of intricacy and precision, of Legrand's shrewdness and patience—each detail receives attention—and yet we are never lost, the main outlines remain clear, the reasoning turns where it should, the momentum, or rhythm of the whole is sustained. The writing of this kind of prose was, as I see it, one of Poe's most impressive gifts."

The story's excellence wells up from deeper springs, however. The reader watches fascinatedly as a chain of logic appears link by link and ends in the disclosure of the answer to the central problem. "The Gold-Bug" and one or two of Poe's other stories are the first to employ this intellectual operation as their theme, and so they are called the first detective stories. But "The Gold-Bug" has something that other detective stories do not. All mystery stories give the reader, who identifies with the hero, the mental satisfaction of resolving a puzzle. Beyond that, the reader gets nothing out of it, for in most cases the conclusion reaches out to a third party—it merely punishes the murderer. "The Gold-Bug," however, rewards the hero-reader. Unlike other detective fiction, "The Gold-Bug" purges, in an Aristotelian sense, man's craving for wealth and power. The story satisfies the emotions. It adds that extra dimension to the intellectual one. In that may lie the story's special merit, its perennially engaging quality, while the breadth of its appeal may lie in the universality of the desire it brings to catharsis.

At the same time, the cryptological element in "The Gold-Bug" exists on the same two levels: the levels of reason and desire that summoned up so intense a response in Poe. On the surface, the story deals only with the scientific aspect of cryptology: the text handles it strictly as a subject for "ratiocination," for logical investigation. But the structure of the story utilizes cryptology as a form of divination. The mysterious symbols of the message contain the secrets of great wealth, and the man who reads them compels the earth to yield up these hidden treasures. These are precisely the operations of divination and magic, which seek to fulfill human desires by foretelling and so controlling nature, and these are the operations that the plot executes and so confirms. On this deeper, almost subliminal level, then, Poe set up anew a sympathetic vibration between cryptology and magic. Poe, in other words, glamorized cryptology.

The effect was to popularize it. He was the first to do so. The immense success of his story gave far wider currency to valid information about cryptology than any mere textbook could have given. "Popular interest in this country in the subject of cryptography received its first stimulus from Edgar Allan Poe," wrote Friedman. Interest extended to England, where the mathematician Charles Lutwidge Dodgson, better known as the writer Lewis Carroll, copied Poe's table of letter frequencies into a notebook, along with a few other cryptologic odds and ends. "The Gold-Bug" was the first widely available and easily palatable lesson on the subject, and it continues as such. People still read it, learn from it—and are inspired by it. The contributions of those thereby attracted to cryptology probably cannot be measured, but whether they be few or many, cryptology owes them to Poe.

It also owes him much of its literature. Since Poe showed the way, other writers have used secret writing in their stories. And not a few of their tales would be more honestly entitled "Return of the Gold-Bug" or "Son of Gold-Bug," since they utilize the same hidden-treasure motif. (It is in reading many of these stories and then rereading "The Gold-Bug" that Poe's genius becomes apparent.) Their cryptologic episodes are often well done, however, and the quality of the writer often shows itself in the way he handles the cryptology. The ciphers may be more plausible, the exposition of their solution clearer, their connection with the plot—where they are not merely a flourish—more intimate. Nearly always the ciphers are simple ones, for to explain or solve a complicated one slows the narrative pace too drastically and involves more explanation than the reader of fiction will put up with. Sometimes, of course, the author himself does not know enough to write effectively about the subject.

The number of well-known authors who have touched upon cryptology in their works is surprising. William Makepeace Thackeray, the six-foot four-inch author of *Vanity Fair*, employed a Cardano grille in 1852 in *The History of Henry Esmond*, the novel that has been called his most artistic and for which he did months of research in the British Museum. The cipher was used in the book's account of the plot to put the would-be James III on England's throne—the same plot in which Bishop Atterbury was convicted, largely on cryptanalyzed evidence. No cryptanalysis was involved here, though, simply the transmission of a message.

Jules Verne heightened the excitement of three of his novels with the mystery of secret writing. In general, he handled cryptology as well as he did other technical matters. But he marred his two solutions with a physical or a psychological improbability. These hurt the credibility of his cryptanalyses more than the technological improbabilities injured the credibility of his science-fiction fantasies, because they violated immutable laws of nature whereas the fantasies merely exceeded man's then-current technical capabilities. On the other hand, just as he foresaw submarines, projectiles from the earth to the moon, and speedy trips around the world, so Verne anticipated a technique of cryptanalysis.

He began the book that was his second great success and that clinched his reputation, *Voyage to the Center of the Earth*, with a three-step cryptogram. On a slip of parchment, it flutters out of an old runic manuscript that Professor Otto Lidenbrock has just bought. It too is in runic—21 groups of six characters each. Lidenbrock converts it into roman letters; it makes no sense, so he rearranges the letters in the form of a columnar transposition, then transcribes them. Still no luck. Later, his young nephew, Axel, "mechanically" fanning himself with the paper bearing the transcription, sees the writing through its back and discovers that it is simply a Latin text written in reverse. Here the plausibility slips a little on several counts: Can one read through paper so easily? Would Axel have been able to grasp the significance of the letters, which would appear backward? Probably not. But all is forgotten in the excitement of reading the plaintext: "Descend the crater of the volcano of Sneffels when the shadow of [Mount] Scartaris comes to caress it before the calends of July, audacious voyager, and you will reach the center of the earth. I have done it. Arne Saknussemm." And Lidenbrock and Axel, following the cryptanalyzed instructions, do it too.

In *La Jangada*, Judge Jarriquez, after failing to solve a cryptogram as an ordinary monalphabetic, concludes that it is a Gronsfeld (a Vigenère with numerical key) because it contains a group of three repeated letters. This induction is poorly founded—many ciphers produce three of the same letters in a row—and is the flaw in the solution. A Gronsfeld it is, however, and Jarriquez solves it by trying, on the basis of outside information, the name *Ortega* as the probable word that ends the message as a signature. He sees at once that the six final letters, SUVJHD, all stand farther back in the alphabet than the letters of *Ortega*, which supports his hypothesis. Jarriquez uses the probable word to recover the key 432513 and then tests it at the beginning of the cryptogram. He gets a lucky break when the one chance in six that the key begins with the 4 works out, and he reads the plaintext right off. Though this rather obvious technique may well have been used before, Verne's exposition of it here in 1881 is the first to appear in print, and it may even be regarded as the forerunner of the identical method of using a probable word to recover a polyalphabetic key that Bazeries published twenty years later with the boastful cry that it was "a new procedure of decipherment which neither Kasiski, nor Kerckhoffs, nor Josse, nor Viaris, nor Valério have described!"

Verne's final fictionalization of cryptology, in *Mathias Sandorff*, involved no solution, since Sarcany finds the grille that enciphered the message. In this book, published in 1885, Verne cited Eduard Fleissner von Wostrowitz's *Handbuch der Kryptographie*, published four years earlier, which eulogizes grilles. Verne probably also read Kerckhoffs' *La Cryptographie militaire*, published two years before *Mathias Sandorff*, since Verne's language in discussing the requirements of good ciphers is strongly reminiscent of Kerckhoffs'. He did not absorb all Kerckhoffs' information, however, since he proclaimed the grille and enciphered code as unbreakable.

The most famous of fictional detectives, Sherlock Holmes, encountered ciphers not once but three times in his distinguished career (excluding a simple signaling system of light flashes and a word puzzle). In "The 'Gloria Scott,'" the great detective soon discovers that a secret message is hidden within an open-code text as every third word. In "The Valley of Fear," given a numerical code message from an accomplice of his arch rival, Professor Moriarty, he reasons his way brilliantly not only to the conclusion that it is a book code, but to the very volume used. The book must be both readily available and standardized as to format. This excludes the Bible, which meets the requirement of availability to perfection but that of standardization of pages not at all—and also because "I could hardly name any volume which would be less likely to lie at the elbow of one of Moriarty's associates." The only volume which fits both requirements is *Whitaker's Almanac*. The current edition yields the senseless *Mahratta government pig's bristles,* but last year's gives perfect sense. Thus Holmes solves the cryptogram purely by use of his famed deductive powers and without really needing to know cryptanalysis.

But his thorough knowledge of that subject, as of all others needed in his chosen profession, becomes manifest in his "Adventure of the Dancing Men." The dancing men—little stick figures with their arms and legs in various positions—constitute the cipher symbols. An American gangster, Abe Slaney, "the most dangerous crook in Chicago," writes threatening notes in them to a former childhood sweetheart, Elsie, who has married an English squire. The squire copies the messages, which are chalked on window sills and tool houses, and brings them to Holmes. Holmes solves them, but the squire is killed by Slaney in an exchange of shots before Holmes can prevent the tragedy. Slaney escapes. Holmes, who knows where he is from the solved

A message in the Dancing Men cipher, solved by Sherlock Holmes

cryptograms, carefully composes a message out of cipher symbols that he has recovered and sends him a note urging him to *Come here at once.* (Holmes perhaps borrowed this scheme from Thomas Phelippes, who, Holmes knew, had in 1587 forged a cipher postscript to a letter of Mary, Queen of Scots, to learn the names of the intended murderers in the Babington plot against Elizabeth.) Slaney, naïvely believing that only Elsie and others of his Chicago gang at the Joint could read the cipher and that the note must therefore have come from her, returns to the squire's home. He is at once arrested and, naturally, confesses.

Holmes is, as he himself says, "fairly familiar with all forms of secret writings, and am myself the author of a trifling monograph upon the subject, in which I analyse one hundred and sixty separate ciphers, but I confess that this is entirely new to me." He referred, of course, to the use of the dancers "to give the idea that they are the mere random sketches of children," and not to their nature as a monalphabetic substitution. That he promptly recognized that they belonged to this class of ciphers is proved by his embarking at once upon a solution without any false starts. His task was considerably more difficult than that of any other fictional cryptanalyst, because his text was exceedingly short, disconnected, and elliptical and loaded with proper names. It eventually consisted of five messages in telegraphic English: (1) *Am here Abe Slaney*, (2) *At Elriges*, (3) *Come Elsie*, (4) *Never*, (5) *Elsie prepare to meet thy God.* But to begin with Holmes had only the first message, on which he made his start, and he broke the cipher only with that message plus the next three. They total only 38 letters, eight of them occurring but once; out of the nine words, four are proper names, and of the other five none is among the ten most frequent words in English, which normally make up a quarter of English text.

The difficulty of such a solution demonstrates the power and flexibility of the great detective's mind. Holmes would quite evidently have preferred to solve the cryptogram with his usual rigorous deductions, which means by frequency analysis. He began that way. The first message contained 15 dancing men, of which four are in an ecstatic spread-eagle position and three have their left leg bent. Holmes at once marked down the four spread-eagle dancers as *e*. Now, neither letter frequencies nor any other statistical phenomena are reliable in small samples; it was quite possible that the three bent-left-leg dancers represented *e*, or that one of the single dancers did, or even that no *e* at all occurred in the first message. It is inconceivable that Holmes did not know this. Nevertheless, he fixed the symbol for *e* "with some confidence." He was right, of course, but why? No doubt Holmes, having recognized that the figures holding flags marked the ends of words, noticed that two of the four spread-eagle dancers carried flags, and instantly connected this with the well-known fact that *e* is the most frequent terminal letter in English. His swift mind may also have observed the variety of the *e* dancers' contacts. But all this flashed through his great brain just below the threshold of his consciousness—this perhaps helps explain the characteristic rapidity of his deductions—and consequently he did not articulate it in his explanation to Watson. Or perhaps he did not want to burden Watson with all those details.

He did realize, however, that neither frequency analysis nor anything else could go further in the first message, and so he awaited more text. Upon the arrival of the next three messages, he saw that frequency analysis would not serve with so short a text. Unable to progress with his beloved deductions, he deftly switched to induction. He performed brilliantly, guessing first that a five-letter word with *e* as the second and fourth letters and comprising a message in itself must be *never*, and then conjecturing that the name *Elsie* might occur in the messages and finding it. With these values he was fairly on his way, and with further arduous labor completed the solution.

Some cryptologists have affected to sneer at Holmes's taking two hours to solve these cryptograms, covering "sheet after sheet of paper with figures and letters" as he did so. With so short and difficult a text, however, the time is not only understandable, but admirable. Moreover, the dancers caper in no recognizable pattern when placed in alphabetical order, and when they pose in a graduated order of choreography, no regularity appears in the letters. In other words, the cipher of the dancing man is purely arbitrary. Some members of the Sherlock Holmes fan club, the Baker Street Irregulars, which included

Alexander Woollcott, Christopher Morley, and Franklin D. Roosevelt, have kept their gaslights burning late in attempts to discover a regular basis of construction. It is wasted energy. The fact that Holmes limited himself to already recovered letters in his "Come here at once" message to Slaney suggests that he did not discover any regularity which would have permitted him slightly more latitude in composing that message. And surely had there been such a key pattern, Holmes would have discovered it. The inventor of the cipher, Elsie's father, Patrick, "the boss of the Joint," may have gotten the idea for the dancing men from a cipher based on human figures in the semi-official *Manual of Signals* by Albert Myers, the founder of the U.S. Army Signal Corps, or from the same unknown place as the inventor of a slightly later United States patent that uses manikins for cipher symbols, or from the ubiquitous Carbonari, whose call-sign is made by extending the arms horizontally in the form of a cross and the reply by pressing two fists one above the other on the breast. Holmes may well have known of these possible sources. But even if Patrick did borrow the idea from one of them, he has altered the arrangement so thoroughly that cryptanalysis is left as the only way of resolving the problem.

A final point remains to be cleared up in the case of the dancing men: the source of the cryptographic errors that appear in all printed accounts. In the very first publication of "The Adventure of the Dancing Men," the cryptograms use the same dancer for the v in *Never* and the p's in *prepare*, and use an identical dancer for the b in *Abe* and for the r in *Never*. The Baker Street Irregulars have expended a great deal of energy on this problem. It is in their attempts to find the "correct" version that they have falsely assumed a regularity in the cipher alphabet, constructing tables of arm and leg positions and extrapolating the ciphertext symbols for the eight letters (f, j, k, q, u, w, x, z) that do not occur in the messages. They have also sought to determine the cause of the errors. Their efforts, however, have served only to show why they are the disciples and Holmes the master. All of them engage in armchair thinking without investigating the facts. There has been a suggestion that the errors "are in the messages of the villain of the story and may be laid, if one so wishes, to the poor devil's confusion and despair," but no one has raised the equally likely possibility that the squire may have made the mistakes while copying the messages to bring them to Holmes. In fact, however, the errors are neither Slaney's nor the squire's, for the errors were not present when Holmes solved the cryptograms. If the same symbol had been used for v and p in the originals, Holmes would have produced the partial plaintext *vrevare* in the fifth message after guessing *Never* instead of the *?re ?are* that he shows, with the two p's as unknowns. Similarly, if the r and b had been confounded in the original, he would have shown a partial solution *?re* (for the correct *Abe*) after guessing *Never*, but in fact he shows a partial solution *? ?e* with the b still unknown. Holmes' own account thus proves that the errors did not exist in the original messages—and it is fortunate that they did not, for they occur at junctures crucial to the analysis and, coupled with the other difficulties, might have rendered the cryptograms almost impossible to read, even for Holmes. The errors must therefore have been made by Dr. Watson in transmitting the canon to the world. Later publications have compounded Watson's original errors, but these have passed through the hands of literary and journalistic types, notoriously frivolous and unreliable as to facts, and need not be considered.

After Holmes' feat, all other solutions look pale. Westrell Keen, the Tracer of Lost Persons, an elderly, distinguished-looking, unfailingly courteous man, conceived by Robert W. Chambers, is given a cipher consisting of rectangles with crossing diagonals, some of the lines of which are crossed by ticks. Like every fictional cryptanalyst, Keen must set forth superexcellent credentials and then marvel at the surprising uniqueness of the present system. Keen's statement is classic:

> "It's the strangest cipher I ever encountered," said Mr. Keen—"the strangest I ever heard of. I have seen hundreds of ciphers—hundreds—secret codes of the State Department, secret military codes, elaborate Oriental ciphers, symbols used in commercial transactions, symbols used by criminals and every species of malefactor. And every one of them can be solved with time and patience and a little knowledge of the subject. But this"—he sat looking at it with eyes half closed—"this is *too* simple."

Notwithstanding, he solves it in short order, finding that the ticks mark the lines that in each rectangle form a crude drawing of a number. These numbers serve as the cipher message in a system where $1 = a$, $2 = b$, and so on. The message, directed at handsome Captain Kenneth Harren of the Philippine Scouts, reads, *I never saw you but once. I love you. Edith Inwood.* Keen discovers from his voluminous files that Miss Inwood, 24, a 1902 graduate of Barnard, is an assistant to Professor Boggs of the American Museum of Inscriptions and an authority on Arabian cryptograms. Keen unites the lovers.

H. Rider Haggard, author of *She* and *King Solomon's Mines*, had the eponymous hero of his *Colonel Quaritch, Q.V.*, poor, plain, and middle-aged, solve a cipher that enabled him to find a buried treasure and marry the young woman who loved him. This saved her "from a fate sore as death," namely, marrying a young, rich, and handsome man whom—alas!—she did not love. The solution of the cipher, a null system, must rank among the strangest in fiction: "Now, as the match burnt up, connected probably with the darkness and the sudden striking of light upon his eyeballs, it came to pass that Harold [Quaritch], happening to glance thereon, was only able to read four letters of this first line of writing of the cryptogram. All the rest seemed to him but as a blur connecting those four letters. They were: D....e....a....d, being respectively the initial letters of the first, the sixth, the eleventh, and the sixteenth words of the line given above." It is a cryptanalysis by optical illusion. Interestingly, a niece and a nephew of Haggard later served in England's Room 40. Perhaps if Haggard had written the book after their experience there, his solution might have been a little less farfetched.

Lloyd C. Douglas inserted a journal kept in a railfence cipher in *Magnificent Obsession*. It began:

```
R   A   E   I   O   S   D   R   O   M   F   I   N
  E   D   R   C   N   I   E   Y   U   Y   R   E   D
```

O. Henry penned a sardonically amusing story about "Calloway's Code." Calloway, a newspaper correspondent, gets a scoop past the censor's eye by using the first half of a newspaper cliché as the codeword for the second half, which forms the plaintext. Thus, FOREGONE meant *conclusion*; DARK, *horse*; BRUTE, *force*; BEGGARS, *description*. And—sad to say—the journalists in New York understand it. Robert Graves gave the ancient Romans two ciphers, an ordinary (the Caesar) and a special (a polyalphabetic), in *I, Claudius*. India's great Rabindranath Tagore recorded the directions to a secret treasure in gūḍhalekhya, a classical Indian system of cryptography, in his story "Gupta-dhana" ("The Hidden Treasure").

But most cryptograms appear in mystery stories. Bram Stoker, the author of *Dracula*, based *The Mystery of the Sea* upon an enormously complicated concealment system; the book, like Byrne's *Silent Years*, may have been written partly to show off the method. The solution leads to a fabulous treasure. Agatha Christie, one of the most artistic of mystery writers, employed an open code using flower names in "The Four Suspects," solved, of course, by her prim Aunt Jane Marple. E. C. Bentley, author of *Trent's Last Case*, has his Philip Trent likewise tangle with an open-code flower system in "The Ministering Angel." Lillian de la Torre has her Dr. Samuel Johnson solve a skytale cipher that used a peg leg as the skytale in "The Stolen Christmas Box." In Montague Rhodes James' ghost story "The Treasure of Abbot Thomas," a solution leads to a treasure. And there have been scores of others—sometimes in short stories, sometimes as decoration for the major plot in books. Even Fu Manchu thrust *The Hand of Fu Manchu* into cryptology. The cryptograms have been of all kinds, based on everything from the Dewey Decimal classification system used in libraries to the roulette wheel.

They have grown more complicated as readers have grown more sophisticated. In 1932, Dorothy Sayers' urbane Lord Peter Wimsey solved a Playfair in *Have His Carcase*—and quite an elegant solution it is, too. Undoubtedly the most complex cryptogram ever to appear in novel form is the mixed-alphabet polyalphabetic in Helen McCloy's *Panic*, published in 1944, when interest in cryptology was high. The author displays a fair knowledge of cryptology and its literature, listing some of the standard works in describing the contents of her cryptologist victim's bookshelves. The cryptologist's niece solves the cipher somewhat intuitively, though with a fair amount of analysis, and the solution leads to the killer. In 1957, Ian Fleming gave his hero, James Bond, the task of capturing the cipher machine Spektor, whose workings were, unfortunately, not described; the book, *From Russia, With Love*, was one of the favorites of President John Kennedy.

Cryptology has insinuated itself into motion pictures as well. In *Dishonored*, Marlene Dietrich rolled out a few magnificent chords in which was supposed to be concealed some secret message with the notes representing letters. During the 1930s, when Saturday afternoon movie serials were so popular, Paul Kelly starred in a 15-part thriller entitled *The Secret Code*, which had very little to do with cryptology but displayed an awful lot of cliff-hanging action. *Rendezvous*, the film based on Yardley's *The Blonde Countess*, of course had a touch of cryptology, as did the film version of *From Russia, With Love*, which flashed the Spektor—which resembled no cipher machine in existence—upon the screen for the briefest moment. The wartime documentary *The House on 92nd Street* had a brief scene showing German spies being instructed in cryptography at a Hamburg spy school, complete with a Vigenère-like tableau.

Cryptology played a big role during daytime radio serials in the late 1930s and early 1940s, before television. Such favorites as Captain Midnight and Little Orphan Annie would send their faithful young listeners cipher disks or secret codes to decipher secret messages about tomorrow's adventure. The numbers or letters were read by an announcer with a portentous voice.

Even music has a touch of cryptology. About 1898, composer Sir Edward Elgar, best known for his *Pomp and Circumstance* march, wrote *Variations on an Original Theme*, in which he musically depicted in each variation a member of his circle of friends, his wife, and, to end the piece, himself. Elgar labeled the basic theme in G minor, on which the individual portraits were the variations, "Enigma," and said that it was itself a variation on another piece of music—which he never disclosed. "The Enigma I shall not explain—its 'dark saying' must be left unguessed," he wrote, adding, "... the principal theme never appears." Many persons have tried to guess what the Enigma theme might be: a phrase from *Parsifal*, one from *Pagliacci*, or the theme of *Auld Lang Syne*. None has won acceptance. But it is possible that a clue to the Enigma lies hidden in a cryptogram that Elgar sent to one of the "variationees" in 1897—Miss Dora Penny, the Dorabella of Variation X. As a girl in her twenties she spent much time with Elgar, and when she asked him about the Enigma, protesting that she simply could not figure it out, she was told by the composer, "I thought you, of all people, would guess it." He would say no more. The cryptogram consists of 87 characters consisting of one, two, or three curves in various positions and looking as a whole rather like a flock of sheep. Nobody has solved it, and so nobody knows whether it will shed any light on the Enigma. But if it does, it may help resolve one of the oddest mysteries in the musical domain.

Finally, there is the case of the painting with its title in code. This might perhaps be more understandable if the painting were abstract, but in fact it is a powerful representational image of two conspirators, one whispering into the ear of the other. Part of a series of 12 × 16-inch tempera panels depicting the birth of the United States and its struggle for freedom, the picture, by Jacob Lawrence, bears part of Benedict Arnold's dictionary-code message to John André in its title: "120.9.14. 286.9.33.ton 290.9.27. be at 153.9.28 110.8.19. 255.9.29. evening 178.9.8 . . . —An Informer's Coded Message."

22

RUMRUNNERS, BUSINESSMEN, AND MAKERS OF NONSECRET CODES

THE STAR PROSECUTION WITNESS in the New Orleans Federal Court on May 2, 1933, was a new kind of detective. Instead of tailing suspects through the mazes of the underworld, she tracked down letters through the tortuous labyrinths of code and cipher. Instead of dusting surfaces for fingerprints, she applied sensitive analytical tests that developed traces of plaintext. Yet her evidence could be fully as incriminating as the gumshoe methods of ordinary police work. Mrs. Elizebeth Smith Friedman, a cryptanalyst for the Coast Guard, was about to testify to her solutions of coded messages of the Consolidated Exporters Company, Prohibition's largest and most powerful bootlegging ring—messages that at last connected the ringleaders to the actual operations of the rumrunning vessels.

It was not the first time Mrs. Friedman had done this. As the national thirst grew during year after year of Prohibition, as speakeasies sprang up and disregard for the law became rampant, geniuses of crime battened on the illegal demand. Small-time hoodlums like Al Capone burst forth as big businessmen. Whole syndicates, rivaling in intricacy and geographic dispersion the industrial giants of America, came into being just for smuggling. Crime became organized—and the foundations laid in those days support the Mafia and the Cosa Nostra of today.

The lessons of organization learned by the bootleggers on land were taught to the rumrunners at sea, who brought in from foreign countries the flow of liquor without which the whole criminal operation would dry up. While the hoodlums ashore had to contend with Prohibition agents of the Department of Justice, those afloat had to contend with the United States Coast Guard—charged, during Prohibition no less than before or after, with preventing smuggling into the United States. As the rumrunners became more numerous and better organized, they turned increasingly to radio to control their offshore fleets. Messages between ship and shore stations warned of Coast Guard countermeasures, told ocean-going ships where to meet the small fast craft that would run the liquor in to some secluded cove, ordered decoy tactics by one ship to let another slip past a picketing Coast Guard patrol, reported that a Coast Guard ship was tailing a rumrunner and advised that no speedboats be sent out, and in general coordinated rumrunning activities in a highly efficient and effective manner.

Naturally their messages were coded. But although Coast Guard radiomen had long been intercepting them and forwarding them to headquarters, no law-enforcement agency could break them down. By April of 1927, hundreds of intercepts had accumulated in the Coast Guard intelligence office files.

Then Commander Charles S. Root conferred with the Bureau of Prohibition, and Prohibition employed Mrs. Friedman and established her in the Coast Guard office in Washington. At the same time, Prohibition furnished the personnel and the Coast Guard the equipment for two intercept stations, one in San Francisco, one in Florida, to assure a continuing flow of material. Within two months Mrs. Friedman had solved the bulk of the messages; she then began concentrating on intercepts from Coast Guard stations on the West Coast that dealt with current activities. Most of it emanated from two rival rum fleets—the giant Consolidated Exporters Corporation, whose messages she was to confront again and again in her work, and the so-called Hobbs interests, both operating out of Vancouver. She solved the messages in Washington and forwarded the results to the Pacific, by telegraph if they were of immediate value, by airmail otherwise. To save time and make intercepts immediately available in plain language at the point where they were needed, Mrs. Friedman went to the West Coast in June of 1928 to teach C. A. Housel, of the office of the Coordinator of the Pacific Coast Details, how to decrypt rumrunners' messages in systems that Mrs. Friedman had already solved. Housel proved himself apt and industrious, and in the next 21 months he handled 3,300 messages between four or five shore stations and two dozen vessels.

As a result of the information obtained from cryptanalysis and from direction-finding, the Coast Guard put increasing pressure on the smugglers' activities. Evidently the bootleggers discovered the weakness of their wireless operation, particularly their codes and ciphers, for in two years their radio and cryptographic organizations ramified at an enormous rate. Whereas in 1927–28 only two general systems were in use, changed only every six months, in mid-1930 practically every rum boat on the Pacific Coast had its own code or cipher. In May of 1930, for example, the Consolidated Exporters Corporation, with three shore stations, employed a different cryptosystem from its headquarters to each of its "blacks," or rumrunning craft, while the mother ship corresponded with these blacks in an entirely different system. In the fall of 1929, this giant, which had gobbled up most of its competition in the Pacific, established a branch in Belize, British Honduras. Traffic in this Gulf Coast branch rapidly climbed to several hundred cryptograms a month. On the Atlantic side of Florida, 25 cryptograms a day were intercepted, while in the New York region, in only five days in February of 1930, a radio inspector heard no fewer than 45 unlicensed stations from within ten miles of New York. They were involved in operations from Nova Scotia to the Bahamas. It was reported that one syndicate paid its radio expert $10,000 a year—this during the Depression! A retired lieutenant commander of the Royal Navy devised the systems for Consolidated Exporters' Pacific operation, though its Gulf and Atlantic groups made up their own as needed.

His name was unknown, but his cryptologic expertise was apparent. The smugglers' systems grew increasingly more complicated. "Some of these are of a complexity never even attempted by any government for its most secret communications," wrote Mrs. Friedman in a report in mid-1930. "At no time during the World War, when secret methods of communication reached their highest development, were there used such involved ramifications as are to be found in some of the correspondence of West Coast rum running vessels." One such system, employing two different commercial codes, passed through five steps: The clerk (1) encoded the plaintext in the commercial *ABC Code*, 6th edition, (2) added 1000 to the numerical codegroup, (3) looked up this codenumber in another commercial code, the *Acme*, (4) transcribed the codeword opposite that codenumber, and (5) enciphered that codeword in a monalphabetic substitution. Much of this complexity, however, was vitiated by the clerk's habit of only partially encoding messages and enciphering the rest in a monalphabetic substitution that appears to have been the same as for the code. Mrs. Friedman illustrated the process with an actual message (which may have some slight errors in it):

plaintext	Anchored	in harbor.	Where	and	when	are you sending	fuel?
in ABC Code	07033	52725				24536	
+1000	08033	53725				25536	
Acme Code *word*	BARHY	OIJYS				WINUM	
substitution	MJFAK	ZYWKH	QATYT	JSL	QATS	QSYGX	OGTB

Mrs. Friedman solved the system. "In this case," she wrote, "an inspection determined that the system employed came under the general classification of Enciphered Code. Then began what seemed endless experimentation to determine the particular type of enciphered code. There are hundreds of public codes any one of which might have been used, and in order to discover which, it was necessary to solve the cipher applied. With enormous difficulty the cipher alphabet was built up, by which the groups actually appearing in the messages were resolved into code groups of the *Acme Code*. But as this resulted in no intelligible meaning, it was obvious that further steps were necessary in order to reach clear language. The processes of experiment continued, the search among hundreds of code books was again prosecuted, and finally the whole laborious process was revealed."

In her office—first in a building near the Bureau of Printing and Engraving, then in a building on Pennsylvania Avenue opposite the Willard Hotel—Mrs.

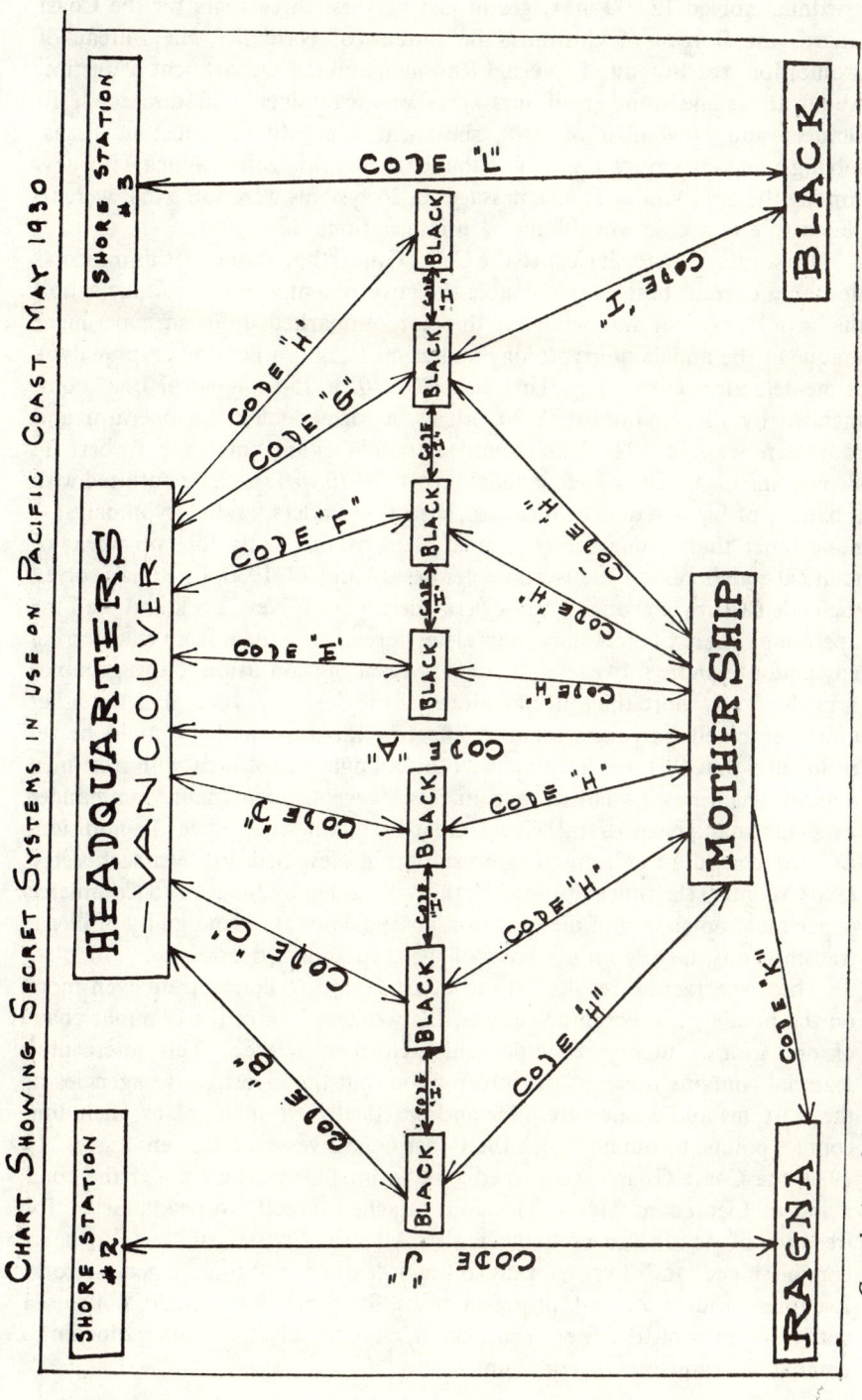

Complexity of the code organization of a bootlegging syndicate during Prohibition. "Black" means a rumrunning ship

Friedman solved 12,000 messages in just her first three years for the Coast Guard, the Bureau of Customs, the Bureau of Narcotics, the Bureau of Prohibition, the Bureau of Internal Revenue, and the Department of Justice. About the same number of messages were examined and discarded. In October and November of 1929, she spent a month in Houston, Texas, solving a mass of smuggling traffic subpoenaed by the United States Attorney. Among the approximately 650 messages in 24 systems were some that were to play a role in a case world-famous in international law.

Her solutions made it clear to the Coast Guard that obtaining this information on a current basis would enable the government agencies to take action that would prevent smuggling. It therefore embarked upon an experiment unique in the annals of cryptology and criminology: a floating cryptanalytic crime-detection laboratory. This was *CG-210*, a 75-foot patrol boat commanded by Lieutenant Frank M. Meals, a former telegraph operator and radioman who in 1924 had compiled, with civilian employee Robert T. Brown, the Coast Guard's first codebook. *CG-210* was specially outfitted with a battery of high-frequency receivers, direction-finders, and a cryptanalyst— none other than William F. Friedman, lent by the Army for two weeks of nautical codebreaking. Between September 14 and 27, 1930, Friedman solved the code used by a group of smugglers operating off New York and read the operating orders to their ships, completely preventing them from transferring any liquor to shore for several days. "The resulting confusion to this group of rum ships was more than all the efforts of the destroyer force and the other units combined have been able to effect in months—and it should be remembered that this was accomplished by a single patrol boat with nine men aboard which never went near 'rum row,'" wrote Lieutenant Commander F. J. Gorman, head of the Coast Guard's intelligence office. In addition, *CG-210* located an unlicensed radio station in New Bedford, Massachusetts, used to control the rum ship *Nova V*; this was raided by Justice and Commerce department officials, and the operator, Joseph Travers, found guilty of illegal transmissions, largely on the basis of the cryptanalyzed evidence.

These spectacular results led the Coast Guard to concentrate even more on the bootleggers' communications, the weakest link in the criminal chain of operations. Intelligence office chief Gorman wrote: "This intercepted material contains much of the information that the investigative agencies of the Customs and Justice are after and practically all of the plans, including contact points, to obtain which the Coast Guard vessels cruise endlessly." In 1930, the Coast Guard established a radio-intelligence unit under the command of Lieutenant Meals. The unit, attached directly to headquarters for freedom of action, covered the entire Atlantic Coast. At New York six commissioned and five warrant officers learned radio-intelligence work. Eventually four more 75-foot patrol boats, fitted out like *CG-210*, put to sea with a commissioned officer in command, a cryptanalyst, and six radiomen to combat the rumrunners' communications.

The cryptanalysts who went to sea did not, however, have either the experience or the material with which to undertake the long and difficult solution of some of the systems employed by the rumrunners. Their work was primarily current, involving perhaps the stripping of a superencipherment from a rumrunner code. Unfortunately, the headquarters cryptanalytic unit—on which the whole radio-intelligence operation depended—consisted of only Mrs. Friedman and a clerk. She explained in a memorandum how this situation cramped Prohibition law enforcement:

> For the past several years intercept activities maintained both by the Coast Guard and by other agencies concerned with the enforcement of the law regarding smuggling have yielded a very large volume of communications passing between shore stations and ships engaged in smuggling. With the extremely limited personnel available for work in connection with the solution of this intercepted traffic little has been accomplished compared with what might have been and still might be accomplished were an adequate and trained force available for solution activities. For the most part the smugglers use extensive code books which they usually compile or have compiled for them by code firms. From a technical point of view the solution of code messages is much more difficult and requires much greater time and effort than does the solution of ciphers. Moreover, in the case of code the mere breaking down of the basic system is only the beginning of the work, because, unlike cipher systems, the solution of one message discloses very little about the remaining messages. The solution of code is a *long-drawn-out* process, which must be continued through the life of the code, if all messages are to be read. It may be stated that every system employed by the smuggling interests has been solved but in no case has it been possible to read all of the messages in view of the large amount of labor involved and the lamentable lack of personnel to accomplish the work.

As an example, Mrs. Friedman gave a series of intercepts sent between a shore station and the rumrunner *Bear Cat* that were solved only much later. A 125-foot Coast Guard cutter was trailing *Bear Cat*, which, upon reporting this, was instructed to head for the open sea as if she were starting across the Atlantic. On September 22, 1930, *Bear Cat* wirelessed: *Am now 120 miles south east Fire Island Light and still going. Advise.* Replied the shore station: *Keep on going. Cutter not likely to stay much longer.* And indeed the next day the cutter, apparently convinced of *Bear Cat*'s legitimacy, now that she was 200 miles out, dropped the chase—whereupon *Bear Cat* promptly returned to her original rendezvous and made contact. "If the contents of the foregoing messages had been made known to the base to which the 125-footer belonged," Mrs. Friedman wrote, "the latter would certainly have been ordered to stay with the Black indefinitely."

Mrs. Friedman consequently urged the establishment of a seven-man cryptanalytic section at headquarters, consisting of a cryptanalyst in charge at $4,000 a year, an assistant cryptanalyst in charge at $2,000, a senior cryptographic clerk at $2,000, a cryptographic clerk at $1,800, and three assistant cryptographic clerks at $1,620 each, for a total of $14,660. "Fuel maintenance alone of one destroyer amounts annually to a sum thousands of dollars in excess of the total cost of operating this central unit," she wrote in her memorandum. "At the present time each Coast Guard vessel travels thousands and thousands of miles annually in a blind search over a given area. In the future, under such a plan as outlined, all such aimless activity could be eliminated and the mileage reduced to a very marked degree because the course and contact positions of any given rum-runner would be known." These arguments convinced. The Coast Guard included money for this cryptanalytic section in its budget, Congress approved it, and on July 1, 1931, it came into being. The personnel were mostly Coast Guard radiomen.

On April 7 and 8, 1932, it did just as Mrs. Friedman had foreseen. Radio-intelligence units solved messages from an offshore rumrunner saying that she was then alongside a collier and loading her with liquor. Since the name of the collier and its destination were unknown, the Coast Guard advised all units to search all colliers arriving in Atlantic ports within the next few days. On April 8, *Maurice Tracy* and *Eastern Temple* arrived in New York and were searched. Nothing was found on *Eastern Temple*, but after the cargo of coal was discharged from *Maurice Tracy*, inspectors found a large quantity of liquor concealed in a special compartment. Again, early in November, 1932, *CG-214* intercepted and read messages from the Canadian rumrunner *Amacita* indicating that she would land liquor in Buzzards Bay, Massachusetts. The Coast Guard vessels coolly waited until *Amacita* steamed into the bay, then pounced and seized her with a full load of liquor. The penalty assessed was $107,661.

More often, however, the radio-intelligence organization did not realize its optimistic expectations of being able to read current messages quickly enough to have them acted upon—perhaps because the Depression reduced bootlegging activity. Nevertheless, the cryptanalytic section at headquarters and the floating radio-intelligence units under Lieutenant Meals did furnish information that helped capture and convict one "rummy" after another. For example, the organization solved messages of the rumrunner *John Manning* long after they were of current value. A typical message was that sent at 5 p.m. on September 28, 1930, giving 4AR, a shore station, the location of CEE, the *John Manning*: CEE YIBOG NW WFYLO WFYJE WYDHO WYBEC WYBUG WYBFO ZABYS, meaning, *John Manning's position now 42 miles south by east Fire Island Lightvessel*. A few months later, a message on February 24, 1931, told *John Manning* to *Go to 25 miles east by south from Winter Quarter Lightvessel to meet a Bull Line ship at 11 p.m. there*.... Though the message was solved too late to catch the two ships in the act of transferring liquor, the mention of the Bull Line caused the Coast Guard to undertake an investigation, and eventually to seize the Bull Line freighter *Arlyn* in New York. The cryptanalyzed evidence helped to convict its master and three others and to sentence them to a year and a day in jail for conspiracy to smuggle liquor into the United States, while *Arlyn*'s owners paid $10,000 to release the vessel.

In addition, the five floating radio-intelligence cutters, plus some shore-bound interceptors, helped furnish information that led to one raid after another on shore stations, often leading to captures of the smugglers' codebooks. On December 15, 1930, for example, Coast Guard radiomen began picking up traffic from an unlicensed station. At 2:59 p.m. January 2, 1931, Radioman 1/c E. D. Bump in Brooklyn copied this message to 1FJ, one of the station's call-signs, from 3JP, a rum ship: 1FJ DE 3JP R HW MSG CK25 AHOHR AFAZQ ACXED STOP AGATA AETCU AHGHM AFHCD AGYSE AHMMS AIALN AFMZC AGEBC STOP ABYTM WILL QRS AGATA AHIPY ACYJF TMW AM STOP AFXKY LATER AR AR. Triangulation soon located the station at 5671 Hudson Boulevard, North Bergen, New Jersey. Law-enforcement officers raided it on January 23, 1931, arresting Frank H. Brown and finding a codebook that ran from 00001 ABACT = *again* to 03108 AJLHI = *bank*, together with "two sheets of cipher alphabet." With this aid the message of January 2 was read as: *R HW* [meaning unknown] *Message check 25* [groups]. [*We will*] *try lose cutter Stop Position is 12 miles southwest Fire Island Lightvessel 9 p.m. Stop Boat will wait position there daylight tomorrow morning Stop Password later.* The doubled AR at the end may have been a signature. This and other messages were collected for use as evidence for a rumrunning prosecution.

In another case, after almost two months of intercepting such messages as Z 5 GR 8 Q844 Q997 Q823 Q985 Q833 L394 T269 Q797 T239 AR AS, lawmen swooped down on 448 Highland Avenue, Newark, New Jersey. As the New York *Journal* put it in the supercharged style of the day: "Federal agents struck with a vicious hand today at the very vitals of a gigantic rum ring, raiding its $100,000 radio broadcasting station at Newark and silencing the unseen voice that guides its carriers of contraband into sheltered coves at night." The entire top floor of a 14-room house was given over to a 500-watt radio station controlling a fleet of eight fast 125-foot rum ships that carried 4,000 to 6,000 cases of liquor on each trip from Canadian ports. In addition, three codebooks were found, one of them an extract for ready reference of the larger basic code, a third using obscene language and apparently for the personal messages of the crew. They enabled Boatswain John M. Gray of the radio-intelligence unit to decode the Z 5 message to *Do you believe we can load tonight around midnight*. These messages too served as evidence.

Mrs. Friedman, meanwhile, was solving not only rumrunners' messages but those of other highly organized smuggling gangs that had adopted their methods. She went to Vancouver to testify in a trial of Gordon Lim and several other Chinese that their secret messages, cast in a complicated system involving Chinese, dealt with opium-smuggling. They were convicted and sentenced to seven years' imprisonment. In San Francisco, the solution of such messages as *Our shipment goes today. It consists of 520 tins of smoking opium and 20 tins sample, 70 ounces cocaine, 70 ounces morphine, 40 ounces heroin* ... induced dope-runners Israel and Juda Ezra to plead guilty. They were sentenced to twelve years in jail—"twelve years," a Pacific Coast columnist wrote, "in which to try to devise a code that a woman couldn't break."

The climax of her criminal work came, however, at the celebrated Consolidated Exporters Corporation trial in New Orleans. After taking over in the Pacific and establishing its large operation at Belize, British Honduras, this syndicate of crime spun a network of activities completely surrounding the United States. Its agents were not only in Mexico and Belize, they also infiltrated New Orleans, Miami, Havana, Nassau, and Montreal. Consolidated virtually monopolized rumrunning in the Pacific and the Gulf of Mexico. It became one of the largest liquor-smuggling outfits in the country.

During all this time, the Coast Guard intelligence office in Mobile was intercepting hundreds of the outfit's messages, and when law-enforcement agents swooped down on 2831 North Rampart Street, New Orleans, on April 11, 1932, they seized many more. In the same raid they found a large consignment of liquor and arrested many of the bootleggers. The messages were sent to Coast Guard headquarters in Washington where the cryptanalytic unit, headed by Mrs. Friedman, broke them down. The messages directed the rumrunners *Ouiatchouan*, *Rosita*, *Albert*, and *Concord* to the vicinity of locations to which they had earlier been tracked by the Coast Guard, thus affording a positive link between the ringleaders and the actual operations of the smuggling vessels.

After Mrs. Friedman related this vital evidence, the grand jury in November indicted 35 rumrunners for conspiracy to violate the National Prohibition Act. Part of the indictment charged

> (11) That a secret code or codes would be and were framed and constructed for use in sending and receiving messages over said radio apparatus from and to the premises and places aforesaid, and from and to the ships at sea, hereinbefore referred to as "rum-runners," and more particularly, the ships hereinbefore described, and to a radio station located in Belize, British Honduras;
>
> (12) That said messages, transmitted, broadcasted and received, unlawfully as aforesaid, would have to do with the location and time of arrival of said "rum-runners," and the smuggling and landing of large quantities of intoxicating liquors from said "rum-runners" into the United States by the means, the manner and methods aforesaid; that said radio messages in said secret code would be sent and received over said radio apparatus from the State of Louisiana to the stations and ships aforesaid, concerning the smuggling of intoxicating liquors into the United States.

The trial began May 1, 1933, in the United States District Court for the Eastern District of Louisiana, before Judge Charles B. Kennamer. The case was so important that the Justice Department sent Colonel Amos W. W. Woodcock, former Director of Prohibition, to prosecute it in person. He said in his opening statement that Albert M. Morrison, Nathan Goldberg,

Merchant D. O'Neal, and the latter's brother, Joseph O'Neal, were the "brains of the ring which purchased millions of dollars of contraband whisky from Canada and other foreign countries and smuggled it into points along the Gulf coast, from which it was distributed inland." Mrs. Friedman took the stand after wireless technician Roy E. Kelly identified 32 messages intercepted from March 24 to April 10, 1931, between the rum ships and stations in New Orleans and in Belize. One, sent at 7:06 a.m. March 25, read:

GD (HX) GM GA HX (GD) R GM OB BT HR CK 25 BT BERGS SUB SMOKE CAN CLUB BETEL BGIRA CLEY CORA STOP MORAL SIBYL SEDGE SASH (?) CONCOR WITTY FLECK SLING SMART SMOKE FLEET SMALL SMACK SLOPE SLOPE BT SA BACK TO THE WORD SLDGE its SEDGE INSTEAD OF SLEDGE HW

Two days later, a message was picked up at 6:22 p.m.:

HX (GD) HR CK 16 BT QUIDS SEEMS ROSE FLAKE GAUDY WHICH FRAIL SNEAK SNOWY SHEER SNIPE FRAME SNOUT SNORE SNEAK SNIPE AR HW

After Mrs. Friedman had been sworn in, Woodcock qualified her as an expert in cryptanalysis by having her state that she had been doing that work since 1916, mostly with the United States government, and that she had been employed by the War, Navy, State, and Treasury departments. After a mild objection by the defense, Judge Kennamer ruled that "The witness is qualified." Then, without describing her method of analysis or the system, Mrs. Friedman testified to her solutions of the Consolidated Exporters Corporation messages. The rummies had used a rather complex method. They had compiled their own vocabulary and assigned to its terms the five-letter English words that the *Western Union Travelers' Code Book*, a 68-page pocket code given out free by that telegraph company, employed as codewords to represent such phrases as *Detained here in Quarantine*. But the rumrunners shifted these equivalents according to indicators. Thus, in a message beginning with the indicator BERGS, the plaintext number *nine* would be represented by the codeword SMART, whereas in a message beginning with indicator CABER, *nine* would be SMASH and SMART would now represent plaintext *eight*. There were nine of these indicators, including QUIDS, and hence nine sets of equivalents in the messages, making it a kind of code polyalphabetic system. The messages of 7:06 and 6:22 read (after eliminating the call-signs and abbreviations): *Substitute 50 Canadian Club balance Blue Grass for Corozal Stop Repeat Tuesday wire Concord go to latitude 29.50 longitude 87.44* and *When Rosita is loaded proceed latitude 29.35 longitude 87.25*.

The defense objected to each of the solutions on the ground that the witness's testimony "elicits a conclusion and it is opinion." Mrs. Friedman made a statement that "This is not a matter of opinion. There are very few people in the United States, not many it is true, who understand the principle of this science. Any other experts in the United States would find, after proper study, the exact readings I have given these. It is not a matter of personal opinion—" at which point Woodcock cut in and said, "Well, never mind that." Defense attorney Walter Gex, Sr., asked that "all that be excluded. I think it is very improper." The judge ruled it out of the jury's consideration.

Gex cross-examined Mrs. Friedman, putting to her the usual questions that oversimplify the problem of cryptanalysis in an attempt to undermine the credibility of the solution. He evidently was unaware of the shifting nature of the code symbols; otherwise he would surely have capitalized on that difficulty—for each additional link in the complicated chain of cryptanalytical reasoning makes it less certain and therefore less incriminatory.

- Q How shall I address you, Madam or Miss?
- A I am Mrs. Friedman.
- Q Mrs. Friedman, I understand the symbols sent you, you know nothing at all about them, but you received a copy of the symbols, which they asked you to analyze and translate?
- A Yes.
- Q Before you could properly translate those symbols, somebody had to tell you it was symbols in reference to the liquor transportation?
- A Oh, no. I might receive symbols pertaining to murder or narcotics.
- Q Could the same symbols be used in a conspiracy in the Mann Act of bringing girls here from another country?
- A They could have, but it would be my business—
- Q Well—

Mr. Woodcock: Let her answer.

Mr. Gex: I thought she was through. Go ahead.

- A (*witness continuing*)——Such symbols could be used for such purposes, but it would not be possible for me to say they referred to liquor when they actually referred to the Mann Act.
- Q Well, what symbols refer to liquor as a symbol itself?
- A This is a code. You cannot say that—I cannot tell you which symbol refers to liquor without going through the entire thing.
- Q It is not a standard code; a code these gentlemen may have made up themselves?
- A Yes.
- Q Then you had to take all the words and the whole correspondence to fit them in?
- A Yes. That is my business to analyze.
- Q You mean to tell this jury the same words could not have been used in a conspiracy to violate the Mann Act?
- A Not with the meaning that was given them here.
- Q I know; you gave them the meaning?
- A No, I did not give them the meaning. The meanings were not created by me and put alongside the code words. I obtained these meanings by scientific analysis. I did not obtain them by any guess work.
- Q Suppose I used the word CORA to mean *whiskey* and the Colonel here used the word AIM to mean *whiskey*, how would you analyze it?

OBJECTION: *Mr. Woodcock.*
That is not a fair question. I object.
Mr. Gex: She is under cross-examination.
The Court: Just explain.
A If I did not receive anything except those two words, it would be impossible for me to state that one meant one thing and the other meant another thing, or that both meant the same thing. My business is to analyze material of which I have a sufficient amount to demonstrate with the scientific analysis applied. I do not state that I can solve anything. It depends upon the amount of material I have on the type of system used.
Q You would not tell this jury that the same symbols these gentlemen used to mean what you say, *whiskey, beer, position*, could not have been made up by people in code for transportation of women from Europe?
A Those symbols could have been used for that purpose, yes.
BY THE COURT:
Q But you say that they were not used for that purpose in this case?
A Yes.
Q And you determined that from study of all symbols you used in their relation one to the other?
A Certainly.

After a five-day trial, Morrison, the two O'Neals, and two other smugglers were convicted, Goldberg and the others acquitted. Morrison, the ringleader, was sentenced to two years in the Federal Penitentiary at Atlanta and was fined $5,000 after his conviction was upheld by the United States Circuit Court of Appeals. And on June 28, 1933, Woodcock wrote the Secretary of the Treasury: "I am taking the liberty to bring to your attention the unusual service rendered by Mrs. Elizebeth Smith Friedman in the trial of the largest smuggling case which the Bureau of Prohibition made during the last two years.... Mrs. Friedman was summoned as an expert witness to testify as to the meaning of certain intercepted radio code messages.... Without their translations, I do not believe that this very important case could have been won."

Neither before nor since have criminals ever used such extensive and complicated systems of secret writing, and neither before nor since has so strong an effort been mounted against them. Mrs. Friedman fought in this arena as the champion of the law, at first singlehandedly and then, late in the game, as the leader of a small band. Appropriately enough, she crowned this work with solutions of messages that helped destroy one of the largest smuggling rings in the United States. While she had the satisfaction of a job well done, Woodcock's letter must have come as a very welcome appreciation. It was probably not lost upon her that he had prosecuted in the name of the United States of America.

In 1934, some of Mrs. Friedman's earlier solutions helped to extricate the United States from an embarrassing diplomatic tangle and to establish a point of international law. Among the intercepts that she had solved during her trip to Houston in 1929 were 23 that had no connection with any case then under investigation by the United States Attorney there. Between October 2, 1928, and March 15, 1929, they had been exchanged between the cable address CARMELHA, which belonged to the well-known liquor import-export firm of C. A. Melhado in Belize, and the New York cable addresses HARFORAN and MOCANA, both of which were unregistered. The American authorities had intercepted them as they passed over the radio circuits of the Tropical Radio Company at New Orleans. A typical message was this:

> HBA69 6 Wireless—NS Belize BH 29 427P
> MOCANA
> NEW YORK
> YOJVY RYKIP PAHNY KOWAG JAJHA FYNIG IKUMV

Mrs. Friedman had little difficulty in discovering that they had been encoded in *Bentley's Complete Phrase Code* and that the placode group had been replaced by the codegroup five places forward in the codebook. This message's plaintext then read: *Arrived. Some repairs necessary. Will leave 2d February. Telegraph instructions.* None of the messages carried any signature.

On her way back to Washington, she stopped off at New Orleans and gave her solutions to Edson J. Shamhart, supervising customs agent there. Shamhart practically leaped out of his chair with a whoop. He had been trying to help the State Department resolve the difficult case of the schooner *I'm Alone*. This handsome two-master had been built in Nova Scotia in 1924 for the liquor trade, which she had plied vigorously and profitably. In 1928 she was sold to new owners, but her mission remained the same. On March 20, 1929, when the Coast Guard cutter *Wolcott*, suspecting her of running liquor, ordered her to heave to, she refused. The ships' positions then were given by the boatswain in command of *Wolcott* as 10.8 miles from shore, well within the 12-mile territorial limit, and by the captain of *I'm Alone* as 15 miles from shore. A chase began. *Wolcott* fired a warning shot, then turned her guns on the schooner itself, damaging her sails and slightly wounding the captain. Shoal water caused *Wolcott* to fall back, however, and it was not until March 23 that she and another cutter, *Dexter*, again caught up with *I'm Alone*. This time, at a point 220 miles from shore and well out of American jurisdiction, *Dexter* poured shells into *I'm Alone* and sank her with her Canadian flag waving.

Relations between the United States and Canada were already somewhat strained over the liquor question, since the exporting of liquor was entirely legal in Canada, and the *I'm Alone* sinking exacerbated feelings. A member of the Canadian Parliament even claimed that the attack was an act of war if it had been carried out under official instructions. Canada demanded $386,000 for loss of the vessel and its cargo. This claim was based on the presumption that the vessel was Canadian-owned. American officials contended that the ship had been challenged in territorial waters, that hot and continuous pursuit had ensued, and that international admiralty custom sanctioned her sinking. In addition, they strongly suspected that the schooner belonged to Americans, in which case the affront of sinking a Canadian flag could be adjusted between friendly powers by a formal apology and a token cash indemnity.

Unfortunately, they had little success in tracing the owners—until Mrs. Friedman walked into Shamhart's office with her translations of messages to and from New York. For the dates of arrival and orders to sail and quantities of alcohol listed in the messages agreed perfectly with the sailing dates of *I'm Alone* from Belize and with the quantities of Scotch, rye, and malt in her manifests. Some detective work discovered that the cable addresses MOCANA and HARFORAN belonged to one Dan Hogan, a New York bootlegger and half-owner of *I'm Alone*, who was arrested and convicted. In the winter of 1934-35, a Canadian and an American justice of the two countries' Supreme Courts sat as a court of arbitration in the *I'm Alone* case. They agreed that the doctrine of hot pursuit—the rule that lets a policeman who begins chasing a speeder in his own state arrest him in another—held in international law, settling this moot point for the first time. They granted Canada $50,666 for the flag insult (the United States also formally apologized), but ruled against the Canadian claim for restitution to the owners of *I'm Alone*. At the time they decided, among the items of evidence before them were the 23 solutions of Elizebeth Smith Friedman.

The great Teapot Dome oil scandal of the 1920s revealed corruption and rottenness in the dealings of some of the highest ranking and wealthiest men in America. The list began with the Secretary of the Interior, Albert B. Fall, who had leased out for development the rich Teapot Dome naval oil reserve in Wyoming to Harry F. Sinclair and the Elk Hills reserve to Edward C. Doheny of the Pan American Petroleum Company. This he did in secret on the ground of national security.

When this came to light early in 1924, the Senate Public Lands Committee began an investigation. It soon obtained an admission from Edward B. McLean, editor-president of the *Washington Post*, that he had lent Fall $100,000 for which he had neither canceled checks nor stubs nor any kind of receipt. McLean denied knowing Sinclair or anything at all about the oil reserves matter. But then the committee dug up a number of messages in code, mostly to and from McLean, one to Doheny. It turned them over to the Army for an attempt at solution. On March 4, 1924, the committee heard sworn testimony concerning their readings from the chief of the code section in the Signal Corps, William F. Friedman. His task had not been too difficult, because he had access to all three of the codes used. The Doheny message used a private code of the Pan American Petroleum Company; the company furnished a decode of the message to the committee, who gave it to Friedman, who merely checked it. The McLean messages were encoded either in

Bentley's Complete Phrase Code, used straight, or, surprisingly, in a code of the Department of Justice's Bureau of Investigation (forerunner of the F.B.I.). It gave rise to such messages as the one to McLean on January 9, 1924, whose odd-sounding language tickled the fancy of many newspaper readers:

> ZEV HOCUSING IMAGERY COMMENSAL ABAD OPAQUE HOSIER LECTIONARY STOP CLOT PRATTLER LAMB JAGUAR ROVED TIMEPIECE NUDITY STOP HOCUSING LECTIONARY CHINCHILLA PETERNET BEDAGGLED RIP RALE OVERSHADE QUAKE STOP . . . .

The Justice Department code partook of the characteristics of both a one-part and a two-part code. Like the German diplomatic code 13040, which figured in the Zimmermann telegram, it was a hybrid. Thus, in the encoding section, while the plaintext ran alphabetically from *a* to *z*, the initial letters of the codewords ran from R to W, from N to Q, and from A to M. The breaks occurred in the middle of the plaintext *e*'s and *i*'s. Thus *eight* was WIPPEN and *end* was NAUTCH, *interrogation* was QUAKE (appropriately enough) and *is* was ACERBATE. The January 9 message thus read: *Zevely thinks trend of investigation favorable to you. Not impressed with Walsh as cross-examiner. Thinks you need have little apprehension about forthcoming interrogation.* . . .

Friedman read the McLean messages by "means of a code book which I obtained at the Department of Justice from Mr. [William J.] Burns," director of the Bureau of Investigation. (The codeword for *burns* in that code was SNIVELING—how that must have given the punsters a field day!) And how had McLean gotten this official code? Soon after Warren G. Harding was elected President, McLean explained, he himself was made a special agent of the Department of Justice and was given a little card, a badge, and the Justice Department code. The sender of the January 9 message, William O. Duckstein, McLean's private secretary, was a former Justice agent who seems simply to have kept the book. Burns later took the stand to explain to the committee that when he came into the Justice Department he found that the old code was so widely held that he had a new one made up, only two copies of which were given to each branch. He instructed the agents in charge "that whenever an agent went out on a more important case, where it would require the use of an absolutely secret code in order to communicate with either me or the local office, they were to use this new secret code. The other code is used by the agents in the field when they get into a little town and do not care to write out a telegram that the operator could spread. Mr. McLean had a code book. Every agent that asked for one could have one; but not so with the new code."

Friedman's decodings of the McLean messages showed McLean exhibiting an intense interest in a matter about which he had said he knew nothing. The plaintext readings tended to suggest that McLean's $100,000 loan to Fall was in fact involved in the oil reserves matter and was not just some pleasant isolated transaction. It was soon discovered that the money had really come from Doheny. Fall was later convicted of accepting a $100,000 bribe and served a year and a day in jail. Doheny and Sinclair were acquitted of trying to bribe a public official, but their leases on the reserves were canceled.

Cryptology did not supply an essential link to these events. Its contribution seems peripheral. Friedman's testimony spiced the proceedings with the mystery of code and cipher and helped revitalize flagging public interest in the exposé—and public interest is, in the long run, the only force for honesty in government.

Criminals, like anyone else, will bother with codes and ciphers only when they have to, and the only time they really need them is in international smuggling, when illegal movements have to be coordinated in secrecy over great distances. In 1934, Swedish police gave cryptologist Yves Gyldén some cipher messages sent by smugglers, a typical one of which read: 16 48 59 74 29 53 99 32 86 28 60 0 St-a 55 67 29 07 28 67 55 44 46 63 80 90 02 99 06 03 15 05 74 59 69 00. He quickly determined that it was a rather simple homophonic substitution and that the plaintext read: *Överlämna 28600 St-a allt klart henom* [error for *genom*] *spärren*, with the 00 meaning *period*. As a result of these solutions, completed August 19, the police lay in wait for the fast, low *Kismet*, whose crew discovered that things were not "allt klart" when they were nabbed on September 26 with 5,000 liters of illegal liquor.

The greatest era of international smuggling—Prohibition—created the greatest era of criminal cryptology. Complicated criminal systems of code and cipher are now rare. They survive only in the drug traffic—the only major international smuggling racket still in existence. For example, two heroin smugglers, John D. Voyatzis and Elias Eliopoulos, encoded their messages in the *Universal Trade Code*, then moved the center digit to the front, and replaced the new digit with the equivalent five-letter codeword in that book. Thus the plaintext *sold* was encoded to 58853; this became 85853, which was turned into XIQWD. Much simpler systems exist side by side with the better ones. In 1955 some dope traffickers that used the aircraft of the British Overseas Airway Corporation as their transport wired some accomplices in Bahrein, ORDERING 19 COULD MANAGE MORE IF AVAILABLE, which meant *Arrive Bahrein 19th. Could carry more opium than last time.*

Today, most criminal cryptology springs from the efforts of bookmakers to conceal or nullify evidence of their illegal activity. The systems are highly specialized and suitable only for bookmaking. Usually they combine encipherment of numbers with abbreviations for recording bets and payoffs; they do not have sufficient scope to encipher ordinary plaintext. Their solution demands as great a knowledge of the various illegal forms of gambling as the bookie's own, for the "plaintext" will be only a series of numbers!

One highly popular game is policy, or the numbers racket. The bettor puts his money—which may be as little as a dime—on a three-digit number. If the number turns up, he wins 666 times his wager. These odds considerably favor the house. Many variations and combinations exist beyond this basic bet. He can play any permutation of the three-digit number, winning correspondingly less if one of the six permutations shows up. (Usually the three-digit number is determined by a syndicate from the last digits of the total amount wagered on three successive horse races at a nearby track.)

Perhaps the world's expert in solving policy codes was Abraham P. Chess, who, before his transfer to another bureau of the New York City government, frequently broke them for the New York City Police Department as a sideline to his normal work as an attorney in the department's legal bureau. He had become interested in cryptology when he read Poe's "The Gold-Bug" at 18, but got into criminal cryptanalysis quite by accident.

In 1940, a New York City detective spent the greater part of a day watching a policy collector take bets and, it appeared, note them down. But when the detective made his arrest, he found to his surprise that the notes constituted not the usual bet record, but several sheets of music, neatly staffed and scored, complete with treble clefs, slurs, and hold and crescendo marks. Without evidence that the collector was actually engaged in bet-taking rather than some odd but wholly legal activity, the arrest would not stick. The detective felt sure that the music constituted some kind of code, but the New York City Police Department laboratories had no cryptanalysts. Then another detective remembered that a young lawyer in the legal bureau was interested in cryptology, and the "music" was sent to 30-year-old Abe Chess.

When he tried it on a piano it proved to be virtually unplayable and absolutely unmusical. He soon observed that only ten different notes were used and that the measures were highly irregular. In seven hours he discovered that each note represented a number, the number being determined by the note's position on the staff. The bottom line, normally E in music, stood for *1*, the bottom space, normally F, for *2*, the second line from the bottom, normally G, for *3*, and so on to the first space over the scale, normally G, for *0*. Each measure, set off by a bar, recorded a separate wager, and the repeat sign of two dots at the end of a measure indicated a combination play. Altogether, the score held 10,000 bets. Chess's testimony in court brought about a conviction that, without his evidence of bet-taking, would have been impossible.

From that first solution, Chess went on until by 1951 he attacked 56 such systems, or more than one a week. Their variety was astonishing. To represent numbers, the gamblers used Greek letters or Hebrew letters or even ancient Phoenician letters; or they invented characters or used the system that equates the numbers with a 10-letter word that has no repeated letters. If this keyword were CUMBERLAND, a policy bet of 25 cents on the number 137 would be written CMLUE—the number is ordinarily given first with the bet following, usually without a space between them. One system appeared at first to be shorthand notes in which some of the characters were identical with others except for their shading, some being dark and some light, just as in Pitman shorthand. Chess soon discovered that a light diagonal slanting from the upper left was *1*, that the same diagonal written heavily was *2*, and that the other numbers were coded similarly. Another policy collector's notebook contained long, bizarre words like SINKKATYUNDEYO. Chess puzzled over this for almost three hours until he suddenly recalled that the suspect came from French West Africa. The "code" was nothing more than French numerals written phonetically as they are pronounced in the suspect's dialect, except that zero was represented simply by the letter O. SINKKATYUNDEYO meant *cinq quatre un deux zéro*, or, on number 541, a 20-cent bet. Chess compiled frequency tables for policy games, which the New York City Police Department still uses in its solutions. Chess eventually left the Police Department, but the work he started proved so valuable to law enforcement that today the department has a number of individuals to solve all the gamblers' codes it gets. The Chief Inspector's Investigations Unit, the Police Academy, the Police Laboratory, and the Police Commissioner's Confidential Unit all have cryptanalysts.

Police departments not fortunate enough to have an Abe Chess—and this means nearly all of them—often call upon the F.B.I. for the solution of encoded bookmaking records. The F.B.I. does this work in its Cryptanalytical and Translation Section, whose existence it seeks, for some reason, to conceal; it has even lied about its location. In fact the section operates in a plain cream-colored concrete building with no markings except its street number—215 Pennsylvania Avenue, South East, in Washington, D.C. A marquee testifies to its former use as Frank Small's auto agency, but the show window has been bricked up and even the owner of the liquor store next door knows only that it houses some hush-hush activity. Though the building stands almost within the shadow of the Capitol dome, it is so situated that no one can look into its windows. On the ground floor is a classroom and a green blackboard, sometimes covered with exercises in symmetry of position; on the upper floors are the offices. Entrance is through a courtyard in the rear.

But if the F.B.I. hides the place where it effects its solutions of bookmaking codes for law-enforcement agencies, it does not hide its light under a bushel when it comes to telling of its successes.

> Cryptosystems involving bookmaking usually fall into one of two general categories. The most common system involves digital encryption, that is, reduction of most of the betting data to numbers and then enciphering these numbers. Tracks are assigned arbitrary number or letter equivalents, horses are identified by post position or racing sheet numbers, amounts and types of wagers are indicated by numbers significant by their position in the entries as well as their identity. Super-encipherment is frequently the substitution of letters or symbols, or combinations of these, for the code numbers. The second general class of "bookie" cryptosystems involves phonetic and related types of abbreviations, including use of foreign or corrupted language text.

Cryptanalytic techniques employed by the F.B.I. Laboratory to break these "bookie" ciphers are conventional in the sense that they rely heavily upon letter and digital frequency characteristics of the various types of bookmaking entries, and trial and error testing of probable betting data. F.B.I. experts have examined and broken literally thousands of encrypted betting entries during the past dozen years [1950 to 1961] and have developed a highly skilled acuity for penetrating this type of material. This skill is a combination of pure cryptanalytics and a very comprehensive knowledge of betting procedures and operations.

Indeed. To understand the plaintext, much less the cryptanalysis, would require an extended course of tuition at Churchill Downs, Pimlico, and Saratoga, with perhaps a week at Las Vegas for postgraduate work. The entries are highly abbreviated, so that a few code symbols can represent what would take a few dozen words to spell out. The bookmakers also rely heavily on their memory for many details, including especially the names of bettors, which are almost never entered. Nevertheless, the F.B.I. cryptanalysts nearly always master the systems. In one case, Hebrew script served to encipher the numbers, Yiddish phonetics the names of the horses, and the arrangements of numbers combined with symbols like parentheses the types of bets. After an F.B.I. cryptanalyst took the stand at the bookie's trial in Lancaster, Pennsylvania, the bookie changed his plea from innocent to guilty. He was fined and sent to jail.

When Boston police raided a betting parlor, they confiscated racing forms, racing magazines, sports editions of newspapers, and a pocket notebook containing handwritten symbols like Greek letters. When questioned about this, the suspect told police that he was a student of the classics; he conceded that he was trying also to work out a system for beating the horses, but denied that he was a bookie. Privately, however, he boasted to friends that the cops would never break his code and that until they did he was going to continue to book horses. Boston police sent the notebook to the F.B.I., who soon established, for example, that $\alpha = 1$, $\phi = 2$, $\sigma = 9$, $\beta = 11$, $\delta = 12$, both H and O = 50,) = *parlay*, and so on. The entries proved so highly abbreviated that even after the plaintext meanings were established considerable interpretation was necessary. With the testimony of an F.B.I. agent, the Boston prosecutor was able to prove that the defendant had maintained "apparatus for the registering of bets on the result of a contest of speed or endurance of a certain beast, to wit, a horse," and to win a conviction.

Another Boston case depended wholly upon the solution of 200 pages of coded information found in three notebooks in a raided clothing store suspected of being a bookmaking front. The F.B.I. solved it relatively quickly, and found that the basic encipherment involved transforming letters into numbers with the key

1	2	3	4	5	6	7	8	9	0
B	E	G	I	N	T	O	D	A	Y/Z

Other cipher symbols included BRD for *$1 on a daily double*, ERD for *$2 on a daily double*, NYD for *50¢ on a daily double*, BLT for *$1 across the board*, NLT for *$5 across the board*, a check to indicate a payoff, and so on. Thus the cipher $\sqrt{}$IG BZBZ GB meant a bet on the No. 4 horse in the third race of $10 to win and $10 to place; the horse paid $6.20 on a $2 bet to place for a return of $31 on the $10. After a three-hour trial, during which an F.B.I. cryptanalyst testified to the solution, the clothing store operator was convicted of bookmaking.

Less common than bookie and policy systems are the occasional ciphers used to plan jail breaks, to note proposed robberies or burglaries, to record illicit activities. Nearly always these are of an extremely simple nature, usually a monoalphabetic substitution using symbols. When New York City police broke up a ring in 1959 that produced and sold pornographic films, they found enciphered records that listed the names and addresses of 300 actresses and what they would perform for the cameras. Police easily broke the cipher, a rather simple one consisting largely of abbreviations and symbol substitutions, and began making arrests wholesale. Prisoners use the ubiquitous knock cipher, based on the checkerboard, to transmit information from one cell to another. Thus one knock followed by two means *b*, two knocks followed by one indicates *f*. The system serves in jails all over the world. Less specifically criminal but still outside the law was the "code" used by New York City employment agencies to designate the race or color preferences of employers. One agency used NO NFU'S—the latter originally standing for "Not for us"—to mean *No Negroes*. Another wrote RECOMMENDED BY REDBOOK to mean that Negroes are not wanted and MUST PLAY SAXOPHONE to mean that Jews should not bother to apply. Such designations are prohibited by the New York State law on fair employment practices, and in 1962 at least one employment agency signed a consent order in which it promised not to use them again. In 1960, the United States accused five big electrical concerns—including General Electric Company and Westinghouse Electric Corporation—of violating the antitrust laws. The firms' executives replaced the names of the firms with numbers as a simple code to help conceal their agreeing to fix prices and to rig bids so that profits would be assured. Thus 1 stood for *General Electric*, 2 for *Westinghouse*, 3 for *Allis-Chalmers Manufacturing Company*, and so on. The system was transparent, however, and the executives got 30 days in jail.

Card sharks mark their cards, which constitutes a kind of cryptography, and they communicate clandestinely with one another by various body or voice signals. Particular ways of holding a cigarette or scratching an itch can indicate various suits or cards. In one common hand-signal, a gambler quickly, almost casually, places his hand against his chest, thumb spread, to mean *I'm going to take this game. Anybody want to partner with me?* A right hand, palm down, on the table, means *yes*; a fist on the chest or table means, *No, I'm working single, and I discovered these guys first, so scram.* In one of the English whist clubs of Victorian days, a player would tell his partner which suit to lead by a casual comment, the first letter of which was the same as the first letter of the suit. Thus "HAVE YOU SEEN OLD JONES IN THE PAST FORTNIGHT?" would mean that hearts was to be led. Such systems are limited only to the ingenuity of the gamblers. The position of cards on the table can represent ace, king, queen, or jack. Knees can be touched under the table. Accusations of cheating by such means at the world bridge championships in Buenos Aires in May, 1965, were hurled at the British team of Boris Shapiro and Terence Reese. But the subtlety of the signals—a way of puffing a cigar, of scratching an ear, of breathing, of anything that people might ordinarily do—made it extremely difficult to prove the accusation true or false.

Jargon, because of its allusive nature and easy comprehension, seems to be widely used in illegal activities that involve considerable contact with the public, such as vice. In 1961, police in Graz, Austria, noticed that curio dealer Alexander Kotzbeck got more customers than a nearby milk store. Checking, they discovered that he was telephoning his customers to report that the BAROQUE ANGEL had arrived, or that the ROCOCO STATUE could be picked up immediately. The "angels" and the "statues" turned out to be living dolls—call girls aged between 18 and 24. The police, having broken the code, broke up the vice ring.

Spoken jargon of this kind borders upon argot, the language of thieves. Argot is just one of many specialized vocabularies used in various social groups, from children to sailors to printers. Because such social factors as exclusiveness, mutual experiences, the need to discuss common technical operations, and delight in word games engender such specialized "languages," they arise all over the globe. Tinkers in Ireland use one called Shelta. Cockneys speak rhyming slang (STORM AND STRIFE for *wife*). Medical students at London University occasionally used Medical Greek, a transformation of pairs of English words, so that *smoke a pipe* would become POKE A SMIPE. Primitive tribes like the Langos and the Todas have secret languages. The Chinese use them. Children are prolific in inventing them; each natural language seems to have at least one particular children's cipher. Well known in English is Pig Latin: the speaker beheads the initial consonant sound of the word, attaches this sound to the end of the word, and adds the syllable AY. Thus *third* becomes IRDTHAY. For words beginning with a vowel, the speaker simply adds WAY to the end—*and* becomes ANDWAY. Tut Latin, or the King Tut language, interpolates a TUT between syllables.

Argot differs from these languages in being, perhaps, more developed, more extended; in addition, while, like the others, it includes many necessary technical terms and serves as a sign that the speaker belongs to an in-group, it incorporates a much darker strain of secrecy. Argot is not an international thieves' language, though some terms may be international. It varies from country to country because it is essentially a modification of the national language. When speakers of argot desire secrecy, they can transmute either the meaning of a word or its form. Metaphor plays a large role in the former.

A *lawyer* is a MOUTHPIECE; *money* is BREAD or DOUGH (this metaphor occurs in French as well); the *electric chair* is the HOT SEAT; *solitary confinement* is the COOLER. Substitutions of form include abbreviation (ALKY for *alcohol*, CON MAN for *confidence man*), and systems like Pig Latin. These are not widely used in English argot but are relatively common in French. One French system is largonji, so-called from its deforming the word *jargon* according to its own system: moving the initial consonant to the back of the word, adding an I, and putting an L on the front of the word. French argot devised many ingenious systems, most of them short-lived; several replaced a word's normal ending with a peculiar-sounding one. Thieves in Peshawar, India, insert a syllable with a *z* in it into words, so that *piu* ("father") becomes PIZEO and *usko bula* ("call him") becomes UZUSKUZO BUZULEZA.

In the Occident, argot apparently began in France in the 1100s, in the warren of thieves' dens and culs-de-sac on the site of the present Place Maubert in Paris that was the most famous Court of Miracles, inhabited by highly stratified and closed bands. In England it originated in the 16th century, in America in the 18th. Argot was for hundreds of years a secret language, as much owing to the isolation of its speakers as to any inherent cryptography. Some poems written in argot by the 15th-century poet-thief François Villon remain partly incomprehensible even today. Argot lost most of its secret character when, in the early 19th century, the demolition of the old quarters, the creation of municipal police, the breakdown of social barriers, destroyed the old criminal bands. They melted into the population at large and their language filtered into the common speech. Most terms disappeared; some of the more colorful became slang. Though today criminals still use argot, its secret character has faded—the police understand nearly all of it; scholars write about it—and it consists mainly of technical and professional terms. Crime, like everything else, has become a business.

And business, too, uses secret languages. The need to conceal financial information from the unscrupulous led the early church to encipher some of its financial transactions by using Greek letters to represent numbers. The Knights Templars, the semimilitary, semireligious order of the Middle Ages, enciphered letters of credit that Templars carried instead of cash from one of their 9,000 commanderies in Europe to another. The cipher alphabet, like their chapels, was based on the Maltese cross. In the 19th century, the Ottoman Turks in Egypt used qirmeh, an abbreviated sort of writing, to record their tax and financial transactions.

Free enterprise entails secrecy almost inevitably. Entrepreneurs must keep secrets not only from competitors, but often from consumers. Thus, cloth merchants in Peshawar insert MIRI as a kind of null into words to create their secret languages, much as Pig Latin adds -AY at the end of words. Goldsmiths in Kashmir drastically alter the form of words. Where the normal forms of "one," "two," "three" and "Will you sell?" in their Zergari dialect are *akara, sanni, trewai,* and *choande* the goldsmiths convert them into BIN, HANDISH, YANDIR, and PHETZU WAHNO. Other trades in India have their own dialects—probably reinforced by the caste barriers. Butchers in Hanoi move the initial consonant of a word to the end, replace it with a CH sound, and add an -IM onto the end of the word. Fish dealers at the Fulton Fish Market in New York use impromptu codes to conceal their prices. Professional magicians use codes with their assistants in "mind-reading acts"; the assistant, passing among the spectators, keeps up a patter that tells the magician what objects the spectators hold, or the serial number of a dollar bill, or their names. Among written secret languages within various trades, perhaps the oldest, most widespread, and best known is that of the hoboes, who chalked various marks on the walls or doorposts of houses to inform one another that the owner is a soft touch, or has a vicious dog, or calls the police upon being approached, or makes one work for the handout. But Social Security is gradually eroding this particular cryptography.

Often, retail merchants will encipher wholesale prices on price tags so that they will know how much discount they can afford to give while keeping the customer ignorant of the original price. Generally they will replace the numbers with letters according to a keyword, rather like the bookmakers. Dealers in antiques and other flexibly priced items probably use these systems more than anyone else, though in the 1890s the impresario George Broadhurst, then manager of a theater in Minneapolis, encoded the night's receipts by means of the word REPUBLICAN before telegraphing them to the Baltimore headquarters of the theater chain. Such systems have been solved—sometimes with valuable commercial results. In one case Macy's, the giant New York department store, was bound to observe manufacturers' minimum prices until it could prove that others did not. It cracked the price-tag code of Masters, Inc., a large New York discount house, and used the information for business tactics that improved its own competitive position.

From these simple beginnings commercial secrecy evolves into levels of much greater complexity. The Swedish match king, Ivar Kreuger, employed cryptography to mask the hollowness of the enormous financial empire he built up. For his own use, he carried about with him a tableau of 26 mixed alphabets graven on a small ivory plaque. In his office he used cipher machines, which he employed often enough to have a sign printed "Ciphering in progress here" to deny access to that office. Rumor said that the giant J. P. Morgan Company banking house had tried to break his messages. Perhaps because of this, Kreuger hired Yves Gyldén to teach two of his employees cryptography. The course of instruction ended suddenly when Kreuger committed suicide and his business honeycomb collapsed.

Business espionage, which in some respects is almost as elaborate as governmental espionage, with undercover agents, long-range cameras, hidden microphones, and bribes to get the contents of firms' wastebaskets, has rarely gone as far as cryptanalysis, however. In addition to the Macy's and alleged

Morgan cases, the only other case known is that of a firm in Hong Kong that obtained the messages of a rival firm from an employee of a cable office. These had been encoded with a commercial code that was sold publicly, and the intercepting firm had no trouble reading the messages—and then submitting bids of its own that were half a cent lower than those of its rival, thus stealing considerable business. When the other firm learned about this, it began enciphering its code messages. Evidently this proved too much for the intercepting firm, for it no longer won bid after bid.

Nevertheless, to prevent this sort of thing from even getting started, many firms encipher their messages or—more frequently—encode them with their own private code. Usually they are not superenciphered, secrecy being obtained by small printings, restricted distribution, and careful supervision of the codebooks. Though these would not guarantee protection against the attacks of government cryptanalysis, they adequately guard the firm's message from the casual inspection of cable clerks or from cryptanalysis by their rivals. Firms in such highly competitive businesses as oil and mining, where information about a possible rich field can be worth hundreds of millions of dollars, are the greatest users of such private codes.

In the 1920s, with the sudden expansion of international trade following World War I, a number of individuals saw opportunities in what they thought was the need for secrecy in the booming capitalistic economy. Inventors directed promotional efforts for the first time more at business than at armies or diplomats. The understandable desire to get rich motivated the efforts of such men as Damm, Hebern, and Scherbius, the inventors of the rotor; the A. T. & T. Company promoted Vernam's machine in the hope of profit. The inventions of these men enriched cryptology if not themselves, but the efforts of many others contributed nothing either to cryptology or to their own pockets. The best known was Alexander von Kryha, a handsome engineer of Ukrainian extraction who energetically promoted his machine. It consisted of a simple cipher disk, attractively housed, with gears controlling the number of spaces it turned and a spring mechanism driving it. The encipherer found the plaintext letter in an outer alphabet and took the letter inside it as its ciphertext; he then depressed a button, allowing the disk to turn an irregular distance and stop, presenting a new set of cipher equivalents. Von Kryha got a German professor of mathematics, Georg Hamel, to calculate the number of different permutations of alphabets that were possible with the movable letters of the cipher alphabet, multiplying this immense figure by the number of possible gear combinations, and then by all the other variables to "prove" that only immortals could break the cipher. Unfortunately, the mechanism came down to a simple polyalphabetic cipher with a single cipher alphabet and a period of a few hundred letters—solvable within hours, not millennia. But the company probably failed less because of its product's technical weaknesses than because of the same lack of interest that firms like Damm's and Scherbius' encountered in the business world at large.

The effort to sell secrecy to the business world runs like an irregular thread through the fabric of cryptologic history. A number of firms manufacture cipher machines today and offer them to the commercial world. Ottica Meccanica Italiana, a Roman company, produces a rotor machine. Standard Elektrik Lorenz of Stuttgart makes the Mi-544, a heavy, solid, one-time tape machine. Hagelin sells his machines. Gretag, Limited, of Regensdorf-Zurich, Switzerland, produces two machines. The KFF-58 is an electro-mechanical device using sprocket wheels as the keying mechanism. The TC-534 is a solid-state digital device that generates a pseudo-random key for use in a Vernam-like device. And other companies manufacture cipher machines upon occasion. But the sales effort never really succeeds because the commercial market is too small. Mining and oil companies may buy a few, but almost no one else. At the time of the coronation of England's Queen Elizabeth II, when the National Broadcasting Company and the Columbia Broadcasting System were competing hotly to get their films on television first, N.B.C. encoded its transatlantic messages to keep its plans away from C.B.S. But even here, with millions of dollars at stake, N.B.C. probably did not use machines. The commercial cipher machine market is minuscule.

Even in financial dealings, banks seem to prefer to rely upon codes and ordinary precautions. The system works well enough, if the experience of 26-year-old David Hermoni is any guide. Hermoni, one of three employees of the Hollandsche Bank Unie in Haifa who knew the bank's private code, opened two accounts in a Zurich bank on September 1, 1958, on his way back from a vacation. The accounts bore only numbers, not his name. He then cabled three New York banks (the Irving Trust Company, the Manufacturers Trust Company, and First National City Bank) in the private code, instructing them to transfer $229,988 to his two accounts. After calling in sick at his job, he flew to Zurich, identified himself to the Swiss Bank Corporation as the owner of an account, and withdrew $150,000. He then went to Crédit Suisse and drew out $50,000 from his other account. But when he returned to the Swiss Bank to get another $25,000, he was arrested; a confirmation cable to Haifa from one of the New York banks had tripped him up. Since things like this could happen as well with cipher systems, banks find it unnecessary to invest in them. The International Monetary Fund, on the other hand, employed Mrs. Friedman soon after it was created to set up an elaborate cryptographic system, based upon the one-time tape; the fund built a big safe to hold all its tapes. But its situation differs from those where banks deal with private transactions; the fund's activities may have international repercussions, and interested governments may seek to discover its plans so that they may take self-advantageous economic action.

Commercial secrecy has had a moderate success in one field: telephonic communication. The convenience and universal use of the telephone and the prevalent fear—if not the actual prevalence—of wiretapping or switchboard eavesdropping has led some businessmen to buy scramblers. Excluding the installations constructed by the large communications companies to protect their radiotelephone traffic, at least three companies in the United States make scramblers. Delcon Corporation of Palo Alto, California, produces several kinds, from a simple, portable telephonelike device that fits, hand-held, over an ordinary telephone to scramble the outgoing words and descramble the incoming, to more elaborate radio-scrambler attachments. They are inverters and the company describes the effect as an "unintelligible jargon which can be vaguely identified as the sound of an incomprehensible foreign language, similar to the effect of a phonograph record player in reverse." Delcon provides different ciphony arrangements for different customers—presumably different inversion points. Among those customers, oil companies and mining firms again lead the pack. Prospecting teams will carry a scrambler with them so that they can report back from the field without fear that a wiretap will reveal their information. The Shell Oil Company used them, for example, for talks with drillers and lease buyers. The helicopters that scout for fish report the locations of large schools via Delcon's radio scramblers so that rivals will not learn where the good fishing is. The ships themselves scramble their price discussions with canneries so competitors will not underbid them. During their multimillion-dollar proxy battle with Allan P. Kirby for control of the $6 billion Alleghany Corporation in 1961, brothers John and Clint Murchison of Texas telephoned one another using portable scramblers. Police use the radio scramblers on stake-outs so that criminals with police radios will not know that they are being watched. The prices range from about $150 for the portable hand-scrambler to $450 for the radio scrambler.

The Westrex Company, a New York City division of Litton Systems, Incorporated, makes two inverters which differ only in some minor technical details. Both accept a speech band of from 250 to 2,750 cycles per second and invert it about the midpoint of 1,500 cycles. El Al Israel Airlines used the Westrex system to provide privacy for radiotelephone calls from its airplanes high over the Atlantic. Most elaborate—and most expensive—of the commercial scramblers are those of Lynch Communication Systems, Incorporated, of San Francisco. Its E-7 is a 319-pound band-splitter offering 233 combinations; several of these have reportedly been sold to some Latin American countries and to some communications firms. Lynch also makes a 71-pound inverter, the B-69, which appears to preserve the quality and intelligibility of the speech much better than the other inverters.

The most primitive form of human graphic communication—pictures—resisted subjugation to the methods of secrecy much longer than its younger brother, writing. Images had to await the invention of technical means of reproduction before they could be distorted or scrambled for secrecy. Cryptographic literature records a few rare cases where spies clandestinely transmitted plans of fortifications by disguising them as parts of a drawing of a butterfly or a landscape. But this belongs to steganography.

Cryptoeidography (from the Greek "eidos," "form") encompasses two basic ways of making pictures secret. One is based upon optics; it takes the image directly and distorts it. The other way is based upon electricity; it distorts, not the image, but an electrical current that represents it. Whether the former is akin to code or not, the latter resembles cipher and, in respect of its clear analogy to ciphony, is called "cifax" (from "cipher" +a shortening of "facsimile").

It might seem at first that the optical systems would be the older. But though lenses for distorting have been available since at least the time of Anton van Leeuwenhoek, there was for a long time no way of recording the distorted image. And when Louis Daguerre devised such a method, it soon became clear that no amount of viewing an out-of-focus photograph through correcting lenses would reproduce the original external object with clarity. Since this would mean that an encoded picture could never be decoded, no systems based on this method were devised. (Microphotography served in communications, but that is a method of steganography.)

Perhaps the first cryptoeidographic system to employ classical optical principles was a stereoscopic one. A stereoscopic photograph actually consists of two pictures taken simultaneously by two cameras a small distance apart; when the two images are viewed in a special holder together, the eyes combine them to give a three-dimensional appearance to what they see. The two films differ only in very slight displacements of the images of the objects shown—displacements ranging from only a fraction of a millimeter to about three millimeters. "Because the significant stereo differences are those of lateral displacement, it is easy to imitate them in hand work," wrote Herbert C. McKay, director of the Stereo Guild. A plaintext is scattered through a cover-text—which may be intelligible, but need not be—consisting of many nonsignificants. The encipherer typewrites this cover-text on a sheet of paper. He types it a second time on another sheet, omitting the letters of the plaintext, then shifts the paper in his typewriter ever so slightly and fills in the significant letters of the plaintext. He sends the two sheets by different routes to the recipient, who inserts them in his stereoscope. The plaintext optically leaps up off the page at him in relief. "Because similar irregularities will not affect stereo relief," explained McKay, "it is possible to introduce random irregularities which will not change the stereo appearance but will positively prevent any attempt to read the message by measurement of spacing." Though the system labors under some practical disadvantages—both messages must reach the recipient; the interceptor needs only a stereoscope to solve them—it has an intrinsic theoretical interest. A later system based on classical optical principles employs many tiny lenses to separate the plaintext image into small portions and then to rotate these portions out of alignment with one another. This system was first devised in 1960 at Bausch & Lomb, perhaps because it could not work efficiently until plastics technology developed a method of molding in a single piece the scores of lenticles needed.

A more sophisticated form of optical cryptoeidography emerged with the evolution of what came to be called "fiber optics." It had long been known that light would travel in a curved path by repeatedly reflecting itself from the inner surface of a thin, curved conductor, which could be water or glass or other substances. But until the 1950s it had never been possible to transmit a picture along such a path. Then Dr. Narinder Singh Kapany, then in his late 20s and at the University of Rochester, bunched many glass fibers, each about a thousandth of an inch thick, into a bundle. Each of these hair-thin "light pipes" picked up a point of light from an illuminated image and transmitted it faithfully to the opposite end of the bundle. Here the fibers, which occupied the same relative position at both ends, reproduced the image in the form of hundreds of thousands of microscopic points of light and dark. Kapany realized that if the two ends of the bundle were not alike, if the fibers occupying, say, the edges of the input face occupied the center of the output face, then the emerging image would be scrambled. To decode, the image need only be sent backward through the same or an identical bundle. He tested the idea, and it worked. A picture of numbers and lines emerged from a bundle of about a quarter of a million fibers as an absolutely random and shapeless grouping of black and white dots. Its decode appeared grainy—as do all such images—with some "holes" in parts of the numbers and lines, but fully intelligible.

In this form, however, the fiber-optic coder labored under several practical difficulties. To make one, the fibers of a bundle are scrambled in the middle of the bundle, which is cut at that point. The two halves then serve as the encoder-decoder pair. It is, however, extremely difficult to reproduce a particular scramble; moreover, the loss of fiber material during the cut decreases the accuracy of the decode. To eliminate these problems, Robert J. Meltzer of Bausch & Lomb, Incorporated, dissected the plaintext image not with individual fibers but with many small bundles of fibers about a tenth of an inch thick. They pick up the light of the image at the input face, offset it through a scramble of the bundles, and emit it in jumbled form at the output face.

For once there appeared to be a fair potential in business for a coding device. If someone finds a bank passbook or an identification card with the owner's signature on it, the finder can forge the signature to withdraw money or gain improper access somewhere. Personal credit companies reportedly have sustained considerable financial losses in this way. But if the signature were encoded, the finder would be virtually unable to reconstruct it. Three companies have offered signature-encoding systems to industry: the LeFebure Corporation of Cedar Rapids, Iowa, a subsidiary of Craig Systems, Incorporated, with an Autho-Visor system, R.C.A., with its Signa-Guard systems, and Bausch & Lomb. In general, they convert the signatures into broken wavy lines, rather like a highly magnified fingerprint. But despite the apparently bright prospects, sales of the systems—which cost several thousand dollars—have not mounted very high.

Cifax systems have never succeeded commercially, either. Probably the most primitive are those for enciphering the telautograph, which reproduces handwriting at a distance. Gilbert S. Vernam used a gear mechanism on the telautograph to add a circular rotation to the original motion of the hand-guided pen, producing a scrawl. The decipherer followed the scrawl, and his mechanism, subtracting the rotation, traced out the original writing. Vernam also invented a mechanism that analyzed a picture into shades of white, light gray, dark gray, and black, converted them into holes on punched tape, and enciphered them with a keytape according to the Vernam principle.

Cifax took a major step forward with the invention of wirephoto and radiophoto. A photograph is mounted on a rotating drum. A photoelectric cell scans the entire surface of the picture and converts the gradations of gray into a fluctuating electric current for long-distance transmission. The brighter

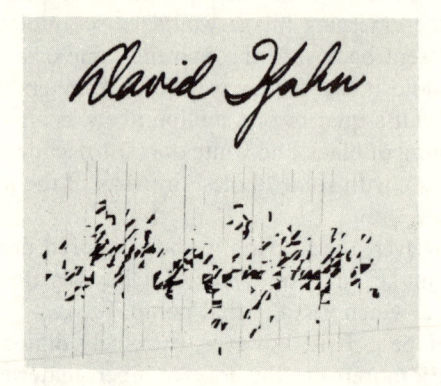

The author's signature scrambled by fiber optics

the spot of the photograph being scrutinized by the electric eye, the more current it will send out. At the receiving instrument, light-sensitive paper on a similar drum turns beneath a light source that shines brighter or dimmer in ratio to the electric current; gradually the entire sheet is exposed. Normally, the two drums rotate at the same constant speed; if they are out of synchronization, distorted images result. The French engineer who invented this system, Edouard Belin, seized upon this weakness and made it a cryptoeidographic strength. He rotated the drums at irregular intervals according to a prearranged key. As long as the sender and receiver ran according to the same pattern, the deciphered images appeared normal. But an interceptor would get only a blur of smudges, streaks and white spots.

Belin's was the best-known system for enciphering still pictures, but many others were invented, for the electric current of wirephoto could be deformed in just as many ways as the electric current of a telephone. Engineers could invert it. They could divide it into frequency bands—representing here levels of brightness instead of levels of voice—and substitute one for another. They could subject it to a time-division scramble, or bury it in noise and extract it at the receiver. But few of these methods were ever used: no one needed them.

Then came television, and in the 1950s in the United States a great battle over subscription television, also called "pay-TV," "toll-TV," or simply "fee-vee." In pay-TV viewers pay a nominal sum to see first-run movies, Broadway plays, sports events, opera, ballet, and other attractions not normally on television—and to see them uninterrupted by commercials. Apart from the struggle within the industry as to whether the Federal Communications Commission should license any kind of pay-TV at all, the fee-vee partisans disputed among themselves as to the best kind of subscription. Some favored broadcasting the subscription programs scrambled so that only subscribers with a decoder attached to their television sets could get a comprehensible picture. The subscribers would pay an installation and monthly rental fee for the decoder and an additional fee for each program they watch. Other subscription TV firms proposed bringing the programs into the subscribing homes by wire. In urging wired TV before the F.C.C., the Jerrold Electronic Corporation of Philadelphia showed how easy it would be for a pay-TV bootlegger to solve any broadcast scramble and to sell information or equipment to unscramble it to the public. Jerrold's two reports, by Donald Kirk, Jr., its vice president and director of research, comprised perhaps the first discussion in cryptology of TV cryptanalysis.

Television cifax operates upon certain characteristics of the television signal, and it is no more possible to understand it without knowing how television works than it is to understand codes and ciphers without knowing what letters and words are. The TV camera converts the light and dark parts of the image focused by its lens upon a photosensitive surface into proportional fluctuations of electric current, which is transmitted as a radio wave. The brighter the spot, the greater the amplitude of this wave. The television receiver transforms the fluctuations of this wave into equivalent fluctuations of a beam of electrons directed at the phosphorescent face of the picture tube. The greater the amplitude of the incoming wave, the heavier the beam of electrons pumped out by the receiver—and consequently the brighter that spot on the picture tube. The camera scans the photosensitive surface 30 times a second, the close succession of pictures giving the impression of motion. Naturally, the electron beam in the receiver must sweep in exact synchronization with the camera, and to assure this the transmitter sends out at the proper times a pulse that tells the receiver, "Now start again at the lefthand edge of the picture and begin sweeping toward the right at the predetermined rate." American television divides the picture into 525 horizontal lines. The horizontal position pulse is transmitted for each of these lines, or about 1,500 times a second. To further assure the synchronization, the transmitter also sends out a vertical position pulse that tells the receiver, "Now start again at the top of the picture."

This system makes several variables available to cifax. The most obvious is the basic video signal—the one determining the amount of light, or brightness, of the parts of the picture. This signal is analogous to the one that carries the frequency of a voice, and cifax may deform it just as scramblers distort the frequency signal. Simplest of all is inversion. The blacks become whites and vice versa, and gray tones invert around a midpoint. A video band-splitting would divide TV brightness into five groups, ranging from dark to light, and replace, say, group 1 with group 4, group 2 with group 3, and so on. If these assignments remained unchanged, Kirk observed, the result would constitute a kind of cifax monalphabetic substitution. But he noted that a one-time system, affording perfect security, was theoretically possible. As the transmitter scans across a line of the image, it discerns about 300 individual spots of light. Filters would discriminate each of these into one of television's approximately 25 levels of brightness. Then a one-time key would control the substitution of one level for another. Between the extremes of monalphabeticity and one-time keys lay many possibilities, Kirk wrote. "In a conventional LP [long-playing] record of the 33 1/3 r.p.m. type if one considers that the frequency response is out to 5,000 cycles and that this record plays for some 30 minutes, then one might conceivably get 10,000,000 pieces of coding information on the record. Now if this record were to last for one month and during that month there were to be 250 hours of television programming (this is about one million seconds of television programming), then one can see that this information stored on an LP record might be used to shift the coding signal some ten times each second. . . . Of course, it is unlikely that one could record as much information as has been listed here on an LP record and expect it to stay synchronized [with the LP record used at the transmitter to encipher the signal] for 250 hours of television programming."

Noise might be added to the TV signal. Synchronization problems would again require this to be of a fairly simple type. Black or white bars might stripe the picture. A problem here is that using the ends of the video spectrum for enciphering reduces the amount of spectrum available for the picture, resulting in less contrast and a washed-out image. The transmitter might scan the successive horizontal lines at varying rates instead of the standard uniform speed. "This would pose a great problem in all TV receiver designs," Kirk wrote, "because much attention has gone into cutting as much of the cost out of the sweep circuits of the receiver as possible. This has resulted in a sweep circuit of fixed design. To either speed up or slow down this sweep circuit by an appreciable amount would require major modifications, and, therefore, costly additions to the average TV receiver."

TV normally fixes the horizontal and vertical position of the picture on the screen by sending the horizontal position pulses and the vertical position pulses at regular intervals. If a transmitter electronically manipulated these, the image would become displaced on the screen. Varying the manipulations would shred the picture, so that parts normally appearing in juxtaposition would become separated. A nose might appear to the right of an eye, an ear below a mouth. Other manipulations would "jitter" the image like a movie film that has jumped its sprockets. These arrangements, Kirk wrote, would "require only inexpensive changes in the position-circuits of the receiver."

Various pay-TV companies proposed different forms of the keys that they would sell to subscribers to enable them to unscramble the program. Skiatron Electronics and Television Corporation would send out each month an I.B.M. card on which electric circuits would be imprinted. The subscriber would insert this into his decoder, which could then reverse that month's enciphering key to reverse the two basic video enciphering processes that Skiatron would use—shifting the horizontal lines to one of three different positions and inverting the video signal. It would also decipher the audio scramble, a band-shift. Zenith Radio Corporation's decoder had five key knobs, each of which had seven positions. To unscramble a particular program, a customer would have to set his decoder knobs to one of the 16,000 possible positions. And to prevent one person from buying numbers and furnishing them to his neighbors, Zenith would wire its decoders differently so that different decoders would require different numbers for the same program. Zenith would encipher its video in essentially the same way as Skiatron. A third system, that of the International Telemeter Corporation, employed a decoding card within a coin-operated device. Holes in this card, which was to be changed monthly at the same time coins were collected from the decoder, permitted electrical contacts to make circuits that unscramble the programs. More recently, Blonder-Tongue Laboratories and Teleglobe Pay-Television System have proposed other methods.

Kirk demonstrated how fee-vee bootleggers could steal the keys of the three systems. In each case, the bootlegger would have to subscribe legitimately to the system to get the unscrambling information, which he would then use to break the system and peddle the results to nonsubscribers at a rate lower than subscribers would be paying. For Skiatron, he could sell a card that would fit into the decoder and would contact all of the circuits; switches attached to it would permit shutting the circuits on or off. Then he would simply translate his knowledge of the current key into settings for the switches and sell the settings. For Zenith, all the decoders would have to be able to unscramble the same signal, even though the knob settings would be different; the bootlegger could quickly correlate the setting for a knob on one decoder with the setting for a knob on another decoder and obtain equivalences between the two decoders. To sell to a particular subscriber, the bootlegger would merely have to compare a few of that man's keys with his own keys for the same period. Telemeter's system would require breaking into the decoder to copy the card.

But how would he break the system in the first place? Kirk observed that "for successful operation of a scrambled television system, long-term security

—in fact, indefinite security—is mandatory." Yet, "even if one used a very complex coding arrangement and delivered the coding devices only into hands of those people who made adequate payment for them, this would represent only short-term security. With decoders located in living rooms and thousands of technicians (not sworn to secrecy as in the military case) receiving training, it is unlikely that a bootlegger could long be prevented from obtaining a decoder or an instruction book containing circuit information. In fact, these technicians, trained at the expense of the television scramblers, might well become the first bootleggers." Since any such system would be used extensively, it would have to be relatively simple, and once installed on millions of TV sets it naturally could not be changed very easily. Moreover, television transmits at a very high rate, providing an enormous volume of traffic for solution. TV's approximately 500 lines per picture and 300 spots per line make about 150,000 spots of light per picture; Kirk equated the 25 levels of brightness with the 26 letters of the alphabet, and noted that 30 pictures are sent per second. "This corresponds to sending $4\frac{1}{2}$ million letters per second, or in terms with which we are more familiar, some 900,000 words per second. This is the equivalent of five or ten books per second in terms of information transferred by letters." Finally, the TV signals are very highly redundant. The image does not radically change every one-thirtieth of a second; usually it stays essentially the same. The only television picture that would have low redundancy would be one that shows grains of sand of various shades of black and white blowing across the screen: that picture would change from image to image.

Kirk contemptuously dismissed inversion as "not . . . a coding procedure because a simple inverter and two-position switch is all that is needed" to reinvert it. He ignored the problem of finding the inversion point, but that is a minor problem. Bars across the picture can be removed by examining the voltage of the video wave to find features—such as spurts of amplitude—"which can be eliminated to bring order to the picture." Kirk did not discuss solving the video equivalent of band-splitting, presumably because no pay-TV firm proposed such a system, and he also did not discuss a one-time system, because synchronization problems render such encipherments practicable in home TV sets only with a wired link from transmitter to receiver to bring in the key pulses. To solve shiftings of horizontal lines involves merely electronically comparing the frequencies of the horizontal sweep signals with the frequencies of the video signals; these will be out of phase by a fixed number corresponding to the shift. "Thus," Kirk wrote, "it may well be possible for a bootlegger to build a decoding device . . . which . . . simply utilizes the fact that the encoding process at the transmitter end will insert in the signal a stop phase shift which can be detected by a phase detector at the receiver end."

The most general question involved the displaced or jiggled image. Kirk's technique resembles the speech-scrambler solution technique of recording the scrambled sounds on a spectrogram and then matching the lines as in a jigsaw puzzle until a smooth flow is established.

> Assume for the moment that the television signal is received, and instead of being displayed on a picture, the lines of the picture are simply recorded on a tape. This means that one will have available on tape the series of lines which contain variations in intensity from black to all shades up to white. These lines will be received in the order that they are supposed to come in the picture. The only thing that is out of order is that the edges of the lines don't match up. If one matches the ends of these lines, then the picture doesn't match up.
>
> If these were given to an individual with the requirement that he sort them out to make a picture, he could certainly do this in very short order. He would simply look for the like looking blobs of black and white on the adjacent lines and then match these up by shoving one first a little to the right and the other a little to the left as necessary. Very shortly he would have the completed picture....
>
> If now one makes an electronic circuit which can control the horizontal position of the picture and feeds this circuit from a computer which computes which alignment of picture elements will keep things on adjacent lines most nearly the same, the result will be a circuit which is capable of electronically decoding the television signal.

Kirk's exposition made a very strong technical case against the security of fee-vee. Toll-TV proponents in effect conceded this. But they replied on the much broader and, in the case of profit-seeking firms, the controlling ground of economics.

They denied, first, Kirk's premise that "long-term security ... is mandatory." "Pay-television systems do not have to have a cryptographic security comparable to the security of military systems," wrote William C. Rubinstein, vice president of Telemeter. "After all, what is at stake is merely a sports event or a movie." He then argued that the relatively low security of pay-TV's own scrambles sufficed.

> The world is full of systems which function satisfactorily in the business world but which have no more security than the most rudimentary secret television system.... Chewing gum and peanuts stand in glass bowls on every street corner exposed to the theft of any little boy with a brick....
>
> Obviously, a criminal organization can be established to manufacture decoders and to periodically forge code cards. Is the threat of such criminal activity serious? It sounds to me much easier to bootleg liquor instead of paying the high federal tax or engaging in a large variety of other less technically complicated criminal activities....
>
> What about the genius who uses correlation techniques, builds a device in his garage, etc.? We figure that no substantial percentage of the population can or will do this. This genius probably doesn't want to watch the programs anyhow. He is probably too busy tinkering in his garage.

Finally, the pay-TV proponent said, experience backed up these arguments. "In Hartford, Connecticut, a cryptographic pay-television system has now operated successfully for four years. The RKO General Corporation is now expanding the system. The provisions for security are now being minimized because it has become obvious that there is no security problem in pay-television.... I notice that the Jerrold organization, although it has had four years in which it could have gotten rich by building bootleg decoders in Hartford, has done nothing along these lines. Instead it has proceeded along making a fortune minding its own business."

Nevertheless, the F.C.C. has not yet approved either televised fee-vee or Jerrold's wired version. The real reason lies in an economic argument that is even more broadly based than the economic argument against insecure scrambles. This is that the American public prefers free-vee.

Despite heady flirtations with the dark attractions of secrecy, business chose the dependably beneficial quality of economy for its long-term association with codes. In that association lies the saga of the nonsecret code—a saga that is now all but ended.

The roots of the nonsecret code reach back to the prearrangements of signals required for the most primitive means of rapid long-distance communication. Tom-toms, smoke signals, beacons of fire at night work only when the recipient knows what the signal-pattern means. These prearrangements constitute a code in the sense that a language is a code; their purpose is the very opposite of secrecy: it is to make communication possible, not impossible. Though the Romans had more than 3,000 towers for fire signals throughout their empire, rapid long-distance communication did not become available for business until 1794, when Claude Chappe installed an "aerial telegraph" from Paris to Lille. This consisted essentially of a semaphore system, with hilltop towers supporting the signal apparatus. A signal was repeated from tower to tower, and in good visibility would cover the 16 stations in the 140 miles from Paris to Lille in two minutes and the 116 stations from Paris to Toulon on the Mediterranean in 20 minutes. This was so much faster than messengers that Chappe's system spread rapidly, not only in France, where it eventually created a network of 534 stations that served 29 towns, but in other countries of Europe.

To speed up transmission, Chappe's cousin, Leon Delaunay, made up a code representing 10,000 expressions by one to four figures. After using this for a while, Chappe devised a more efficient code in which 92 of the semaphore's 196 positions were set aside as code positions. Three vocabularies, each of 92 pages with 92 expressions on each page, provided a lexicon of more than 25,000 elements. When similar lines were set up in other countries, similar codes sprang up and, by 1825, had become common. In 1830, Chappe expanded his code by assigning 184 semaphore positions to code use, giving a code of almost 34,000 elements. A Russian-language code appeared in St. Petersburg in 1839 for the Chappe network between that capital and Kronstadt and Warsaw that helped bridge the immense distances of the Russian

Rumrunners, Businessmen, and Makers of Nonsecret Codes

empire. In 1845 a rather extensive *Telegraphic Vocabulary for the Line of Semaphoric Telegraphs between Liverpool and Holyhead* was published in London.

At about the same time, England was improving maritime signals. During the American Revolution, Admiral Richard Kempenfeldt issued the first scientific naval signal book, which, after a struggle, finally established itself in the Royal Navy. In 1817, Captain Frederick Marryat published the first international code of signals, in which colored flags represented the numbers

Part of a page of one of the vocabularies for Claude Chappe's "aerial telegraph," showing the three-armed semaphore's two-position signals assigned to ships' names

of words listed in a 9,000-item signal book. In 1857, the British Board of Trade published a draft code of more than 70,000 signals, which was adopted by many seafaring nations. Hoists of colored flags, of which there were 18, standing for all consonants but x and z, represented codewords in the book, which contained words and expressions used by sailors.

In 1843, the first public electric telegraph line had been laid in England, and in 1844 Morse established the first public telegraph line in the United States. The electric telegraph, much faster than the Chappe semaphore, and usable in night and rain and fog, quickly supplanted the older system and spread very quickly through Europe and America. In 1845, former Maine

Congressman Francis O. J. Smith, then 39, whom Morse had taken into partnership in the hope of finding in Smith the business acumen that artist Morse himself so lacked, published his *The Secret Corresponding Vocabulary: Adapted for Use to Morse's Electro-Magnetic Telegraph*, the first code intended for the electric telegraph. Smith, a rather unscrupulous lawyer, may have gotten the idea for his code from one that Morse himself had compiled but discarded. The 1835 model of Morse's telegraph transmitted ten symbols corresponding to the ten digits, and to convey words by means of them, Morse spent considerable time numbering words to form a special vocabulary for use with his apparatus. He used it in his first public demonstration of his telegraph, in 1837. But the invention of what is now the Morse code, which permitted the direct transmission of words by dots and dashes without the extra step of encoding, supervened and Morse jettisoned his vocabulary.

Smith's *Vocabulary* and one compiled at about the same time by Henry Rogers, entitled *The Telegraph Dictionary and Seaman's Signal Book, Adapted to Signals by Flags or Other Semaphores; and Arranged for Secret Correspondence, Through Morse's Electro-magnetic Telegraph*, both emphasized secrecy. But although businessmen desire secrecy in communication, they demand speed, accuracy, and economy before it. These motives soon became paramount in the public telegraph codes that followed Smith's and Rogers', such as John Wills' *Telegraphic Congressional Reporter* of 1847, and in the private codes that American firms began to improvise as early as 1848. Their lexicons expanded and grew richer in phrases. And since groups of figures were more expensive to send than words and much more liable to error—the change of a single digit, which in the Morse code could result from the simple dropping of a dot, could mean an entirely different word—the codes shifted to the use of regular words as codewords. Thus CAT might mean *sell* and DOG, *buy*. By 1854, one eighth of the telegrams between New York and New Orleans passed in code.

In 1866, the laying of the Atlantic cable gave an immense impetus to commercial codes, as these nonsecret codes came to be called. Cable messages cost so much that the reduction in length made possible by code afforded enormous economies. Within eight years there appeared the first edition of the first public code destined to have a wide sale and a long life, *The ABC Code*, compiled by William Clausen-Thue, 40 years old, a shipping manager later elected a Fellow of the Royal Geographical Society. *The ABC Code*, which went through many editions, probably owed its success to its enormous vocabulary, which represented many business expressions of several words by a single dictionary codeword. The cable companies charged for codewords as if they were plain language, limiting both plain and codewords to a maximum of seven syllables.

Codes could save so much money for telegraph and cable users that, it seemed, everyone who ever sent a telegram had one. In 1874, the Hebrew Orphan Asylum Printing Establishment issued *M. Abenheim's Telegraph-*

Code for Exclusive Use With His Correspondents. Detwiller & Street, a fireworks firm, had its own 20-page *Telegraphic Chart*, with some appropriate codewords (*mammoth torpedoes, 3 case* = FESTIVAL). India's Department of Revenue and Agriculture had its 325-page *Weather and Famine Telegraphic Word-Code*, a two-part code (ENVELOPPE = *Great swarms of locusts have appeared and ravaged the crops*). The mackerel industry had a 5-page cable code of its own (ABDIC = *extra quality, very fat and white*), and so did the sausage industry. There were codes for tourists and the press. The big companies naturally had their own codes, the Erie Railroad Company's running to 214 pages, Swift & Company's to 554 pages (not counting the 364 pages of the separate code for its provision department), Lehman Brothers' to two volumes. Wells, Fargo & Company prudently did not supply printed a codeword for the plaintext *robbed*, evidently preferring to fill this in by hand to afford some secrecy.

Among the great code compilers of this era were John Charles Hartfield, who published *The Merchants Code* of 15,000 dictionary words in 1877, and followed it with eleven others before 1890, when he was joined by his son, John W. Hartfield, in the business; Henry Harvey, who published 21 codes or lists of codewords between 1878 and 1899; and Benjamin Franklin Lieber, compiler of eight codes, one of them becoming widely used and being translated into French and German. In France there was F. J. Sittler, whose four-digit code sold widely; Bazeries and de Viaris published codes as well. Italy had its Baravelli. These Continental codes, mostly numerical, which lent themselves easily to superencipherment, seemed to aim quite as much at secrecy as at economy, in contradistinction to the American public codes, which emphasized dictionary words as affording greater savings than code-numbers.

But the use of dictionary words, chosen at random, of varying length and irregular construction as regards placement of vowels and consonants, and often closely resembling one another, entrained difficulties. The words were subject to phonetic, orthographic, and telegraphic errors which, unlike errors in plain language, could not be corrected from context. For example, in codetexts spoken aloud, as they were in the days when the mirror galvanometer served in cable telegraphy and one operator watched its movements and called out the signals to an operator who wrote them down, codewords like ACCEPT and EXCEPT or SERIAL and CEREAL would be confused. In handwritten codetexts, JEERING might be confused with PEERING, or MORNING with MOANING. The most prolific source of errors came from the telegraphic transmissions themselves. A telegraph company's records showed that fully half its errors stemmed from the loss of a dot in transmission, and another quarter by the insidious false spacing of signals. These errors often turned one word into another. For example, dropping the single dot that represents E would convert the French verb CITERONS ("[we] shall point out") to the French word for "lemons," CITRONS. AMENDING might become ATTENDING if the two dashes of its M sounded, not as a single letter, but as two separate dashes to make two T's (–). With two spacing errors in a single word, the result might bear almost no similarity to the original, as BANEFUL (–··· ·– –· · ··–· ··– ·–··) might become DUTIFUL (–·· ··– – ·· ··–· ··– ·–··).

These errors sometimes transmuted a codeword into one whose decode made sense, or, because telegrams were often only partially encoded, into what the recipient took for a plain-language word. When the recipients acted upon the basis of this erroneous information, financial losses sometimes ensued. The senders of the messages then sued the telegraph companies to recover these losses, on the ground that the faulty transmission had caused the loss. The classic case went to the Supreme Court of the United States.

In June of 1887, Frank J. Primrose, a Philadelphia wool dealer, sent William B. Toland as his agent out to Kansas and Colorado with instructions to buy 50,000 pounds of wool and then await further instructions. Toland did just this, exchanging many messages with Primrose in their telegraphic code during the course of his buying. On June 16, Primrose encoded the following message to Toland: *Yours of the 15th received; am exceedingly busy; I have bought all kinds, 500,000 pounds; perhaps we have sold half of it; wire when you do anything; send samples immediately, promptly of purchases.* He wrote out the codetext in his own hand: DESPOT AM EXCEEDINGLY BUSY BAY ALL KINDS QUO PERHAPS BRACKEN HALF OF IT MINCE MOMENT PROMPTLY OF PURCHASES. He gave it to Western Union, which transmitted it correctly to the relay station at Brookville, Kansas, but added a dot between Brookville and Ellis, Kansas. The extra dot changed the A (·–) of BAY into a U (··–), and so when the message reached Toland at Waukeney, instead of reading the *I have bought* that BAY represented, he interpreted BUY as another plain-language word. He consequently bought 300,000 pounds of wool. Primrose, in settling with the sellers, lost more than $20,000 because of that one dot. He sued the Western Union Telegraph Company for this amount, on the ground that they had been negligent in performing their contract with him to transmit the message correctly. But the Supreme Court, in a 33-page decision, ruled that Primrose could not recover more than the cost of the message, as the terms printed on the back of the message blank stipulated, because he had not requested that the message be repeated back to him, which could have made Western Union liable. The telegram had cost $1.15.

Even before this landmark decision, however, code compilers had begun to recognize the danger of promiscuously using any dictionary words as codewords. They employed experienced telegraphers to eliminate words telegraphically too similar. They deleted words that might make sense in the business in which the code was used. Most important, they included only words that differed from one another in spelling by at least two letters. Thus, if MORNING were admitted to the code, MOANING, which differed from it by only one letter, would not be, but LOANING, which differed from MORNING by two letters, would be. This principle became known as that of the "two-letter differential." Finally, although eight languages were allowed in cable traffic, some American codemakers deemed foreign words too hard for Americans to spell and to telegraph and struck them out as well. All these restrictions so limited the number of usable words that code compilers made up codewords by tacking English suffixes onto English words, even though the suffixes made no sense. For example, to the word NIGH, one code added 49 suffixes, resulting in such strange neologisms as NIGHANT, NIGHBAKE, NIGH-CAST, and so on. The compilers justified these on the very practical ground that both code clerks and telegraphers found them easier to handle than many legitimate foreign words, such as AARDMIJTEN, and this was undoubtedly true.

These were among the first artificial codewords. Others were created by hooking code syllables, each with a particular meaning, onto dictionary words to modify them. In one such code, for example, the syllable FI meant *you* or *yours*, TI meant *it*, MI meant *me, I,* or *mine*, ZI meant *they, them, theirs*, and so on. The codeword ACCESA meant *What do—advise—to do?* and the addition of the syllables FI and ZI, making the codeword ACCESAFIZI, filled in the blanks to make the completed plaintext *What do you advise them to do?* Some codes provided syllables that the user could combine into an entire artificial codeword that included several ideas. Usually each syllable stood for a variation of a particular idea, as the FI, TI, MI . . . series of pronouns. But the syllable systems did not conform to the principle of the two-letter differential and, the dangers of transmission error rendering such systems too risky, code compilers moved to the root-and-terminal system. Instead of just using two- or three-letter syllables, they provided groups of four or five letters to indicate different ideas. The code clerk would combine two of these into a single artificial codeword. For example, in one root-and-terminal system, the root APARL meant *We order 1500 at 28 shillings*, the terminal ANFRO meant *140 jute sacks Duluth Imperial, net c.i.f. London*, and the codeword for the entire order was APARLANFRO. The terminal ANERE changed the destination to Liverpool.

Still another, and perhaps the most voluminous, source of artificial codewords was the code condenser. A condenser converts figure codegroups into letter groups, usually resembling artificial words. Because there are more letters than numbers, it is possible to reduce a seven-figure group to a five-letter group (26^5, or 11,881,376, being greater than 10^7, or 10,000,000), but most condensers reduce only six figures to five letters because they want to retain a certain alternation of vowels and consonants to keep its letter groups pronounceable. Condensers are essentially tables of letter-number equivalents. In one condenser, the code clerk would convert the group 484704 into ILIKE by finding that 04 is E on the first page of the condenser, and, using the tables on that page, substituting IL for 48 and IK for 47. To reverse the process, he determines the vowel-consonant pattern of the first two syllables. Since it is vowel-consonant, vowel-consonant, or UCUC, he goes to the first page and reads off the equivalents. If the combination were UCCU, the codeword would have been taken from the second page and accordingly those tables would have been used, if CUUC, the third page, and if CUCU, the fourth. Condensers offered several advantages. Words usually cost less to cable than figures. They are less subject to error. Condensers further compress messages—twelve 5-digit codegroups could be reduced to ten 5-letter codewords. Moreover, each 5-digit codegroup usually has counted as a single cable word, while for codewords a 10-letter group usually constituted the unit of charge. This would cut the toll in half. A final advantage sacrificed economy for accuracy. To ensure correct reception, code clerks would add up the five digits of a codegroup and tack on the units digit of the result as a "check digit." If the codegroup was 18250, the check digit would become 6, and the clerk would then pass 182506 through his condenser. If the codeword was mutilated in transmission, the failure of the check digit to confirm the total would alert the recipient to the error, and he could request a retransmission.

The code compilers strove constantly to find new ways of reducing cable tolls for users—this was, after all, their raison d'être. Consequently, many of their innovations can be best understood as efforts to circumvent the tariff regulations of the International Telegraph Union, to which most of the nations of Europe belonged. In 1875, the Union's conference in St. Petersburg reduced the maximum length of a word in extra-European traffic from seven syllables—a regulation that had given rise to considerable abuses, such as CHINESISKSLUTNINGSDON, which had 21 letters but only six syllables—to ten letters. Four years later, the London conference promulgated two regulations that occasioned innumerable disputes, which, in turn, eventually led to the creation of the modern commercial code. Article 8 of the convention stated, in part: "In the extra-European regime code-language telegrams can contain only words belonging to the German, English, Spanish, French, Italian, Dutch, Portuguese, or Latin languages. Every telegram can contain words taken from all of the aforementioned languages." Article 9 stated that "The following are considered as telegrams in cipher language: (a) those which contain a text in figures or in secret letters; (b) those which include either series or groups of figures or letters, the significance of which is not known to the office of origin; or of words or names, or of groups of letters not complying with the conditions for plain language or code language." This article threw into the high-priced category of cipher language all the systems employing artificial and invented words, and the code-using public at once began violating it.

But though the counter clerks of the government-owned communication monopolies of European states contested these evasions, the privately owned cable companies did not fight them too hard—for if they did, the user would simply take his business to a more complaisant company. This tendency was aggravated by the fact that domestic telegraph companies in the United States—which did not adhere to the International Telegraph Union—counted any pronounceable group or any dictionary word as a single word. American codes had come to use these artificial groups, and American users saw no reason why they should not use them outside the United States just as they did within. Moreover, the telegraph personnel themselves often found the artificial words, composed as they were of fairly regular alternations of vowels and consonants, simpler to handle than the clusters of consonants sometimes found in English or German.

To end the increasing number of abuses, the Union's Paris conference of 1890 provided for an official code-language vocabulary. Within Europe, all code-language words would have to come from this vocabulary, but it would be optional on the Europe-America cables. This did not make much sense, since nearly all the abuses occurred in the transatlantic traffic. Nevertheless, the International Telegraph Bureau, the secretariat of the Union, compiled the vocabulary, consisting of 256,740 words of from five to ten letters in the eight authorized languages, and published it in an edition of 15,000 copies in 1894. It met with a clamor of opposition, primarily because it would eventually outlaw many existing codes at great financial loss. So the Budapest conferenec in 1896 authorized the Bureau to approve or disapprove the words in existing codes. Submitted were 218 codes, containing more than 5,750,000 codewords. The Bureau actually completed its herculean task and published four gigantic volumes in 1900 and 1901 with 1,174,864 words, plus a small appendix, bringing the total of approved words to 1,190,000. But all that immense labor went for nought. The London conference of 1903 dropped the entire idea of an official vocabulary, and, bowing to the pressures of business and to common sense, authorized the use of artificial words. These were to be "formed of syllables capable of being pronounced" in one of the eight standard languages and were to be no more than ten letters long. The Union had in mind words of from five to ten letters that, by alternations of vowels and consonants, would resemble real words. It was in for a shock.

In February of 1904, four months before the new regulations were to go into effect, there appeared in England *Whitelaw's Telegraph Cyphers: 400 Millions of Pronounceable Words*. The volume consisted of 20,000 codewords, or "cyphers," all of five letters each—FREAN, LUFFA, FORAB, LOZOJ—without phrases attached to them. Whence the 400,000,000? Since the maximum permissible length of codewords was ten letters, and since each of Whitelaw's five-letter words was pronounceable, any one could be combined with any other one in a single ten-letter word, making 20,000 × 20,000, or the 400,000,000. Through this loophole, unforeseen by the Union, the combining of two codewords into one made it possible to halve cable tolls. Whitelaw's gimmick was immediately adapted by many private firms. In 1905 Ernest Lungley Bentley, 45, who had revised the private code of a shipping agency where he was private secretary to a partner, founded a code company, which the following year published the compact, well-constructed, moderately priced *Bentley's Complete Phrase Code*, first of the modern five-letter codes. It has sold well—

about 100,000 copies—and remains today perhaps the best known and most widely used of commercial codes. Bentley, a plump, jovial man of medium height, who had a good baritone and always sang in the choir of the church he attended, including St. Paul's Cathedral's honorary evening choir, saw this success, living until 1939. The cut in cable costs that the five-letter codes made possible led to an upsurge in cable traffic and inspired the publication of many new codes. Within half a decade, the new five-letter codes had swept the dictionary-word type from the field.

Eventually, codes were compiled for virtually every industry that was not strictly local. A list of even some of them suggests the incredible diversity of modern commerce. There were codes for automobile dealers, bankers, brokers, canned goods, clothing, coal, coffee, commission merchants, cotton, cottonseed, dry goods, electric supplies, flour, fruit, fur, grain, groceries, hay, insurance, iron and steel, leather, liquor, livestock, lumber, meat packing, mining, oil, papermaking, phonographs, potatoes, produce, railroads, rice, rubber goods, the sash-door-and-blinds trade, seeds, ship brokers, shipping, sugar, tailors, textiles, theaters, ticket brokers, tobacco, transportation, travelers, vegetables, wastes, wool. In addition, private firms published their own codes in the fields of butter and cheese, boots and shoes, cordage, dentists' supplies, drugs, elevators, fire insurance, flaxseed, harness, hides, hops, lead, lime, machinery, millinery, peanuts, printing ink, smelting and refining, soap, spices, steam and gas fittings, steam engines, steamboats, suretyship and guaranty, tanning, tea, wagons, and yarn.

To open these books is to feel the life pulse of the business. The *Waste Merchant's Standard Code* offers a consignment of *cast iron scrap, excessively rusty* with IQUA. Using *Tilton's Income Tax Code*, the taxpayer declares firmly MIRASOL for *I (we) will not pay*—and the tax advisor retorts promptly NASA (*The penalty is ...*). An airline pilot regretfully wires VAOIK (*Forced landing account engine trouble*) using the *Avico Aviation Code*, and a lawyer sternly advises IYGWG (*habeas corpus*) in the *Legal Telegraphic Code*, which is even bound to resemble a law book. A U.S. immigration agent, using the *Telegraphic Code* of the Immigration and Naturalization Service, embarrassedly telegraphs his chief GAXEW (... *Escaped after being placed on shipboard for deportation*). A missionary seeks out HAUCD in the 724-page *The Missions Code* to sadly report to his home church that (*Mission*) *property* (*at——*) *has been destroyed*, and then adds a hopeful SWAMK (*Join us in prayer for funds*). Sometimes the codebooks reveal not just the life of an organization or industry, but also its very soul. Thus the *Cinema-code* of 1923 has under the heading *Picture*: *is a charming love story* = EPWCY, *is a classic production* = EPWMI, *is a country life drama* = EPWOK, *is a detective story* = EPWSO, ... *is a marvelous, vivid drama* = EPXOX, *is a spectacular production* = EPXUD. But even the Hollywood fairyland met with brutal reality at times, and the compiler, Richard Poillon, felt compelled to include EPXIR (*is a great disappointment*).

Rumrunners, Businessmen, and Makers of Nonsecret Codes   845

In the 1920s, the explosion of international commerce that had been bottled up by the World War created the golden age of the commercial code. More codes were produced in the five or six years after the war than in the 20 years before it. Many of the great commercial codes date from this era—the *ABC* 6th edition, the *Acme*, the *Boe*, *Farquhar's*, the *Lombard*, the *Rudolf Mosse*, *Peterson's*, the *United Telegraph*, the *Western Union*. They were large tomes of hundreds or even a thousand pages, comparing favorably in poundage with a Webster's Unabridged, and costing in the neighborhood of $25. Many of the codes of this period were produced by the world's handful of code compilers, nearly all Americans, representing the second generation of workers in this recondite field: John C. Hartfield, son of John W. Hartfield, C. Bensinger, Ernest F. Peterson, Thomas C. Wilwerth, Cyrus F. Tibbals, Cosmo Farquhar, and William J. Mitchel. At least two made fortunes—Peterson and Tibbals.

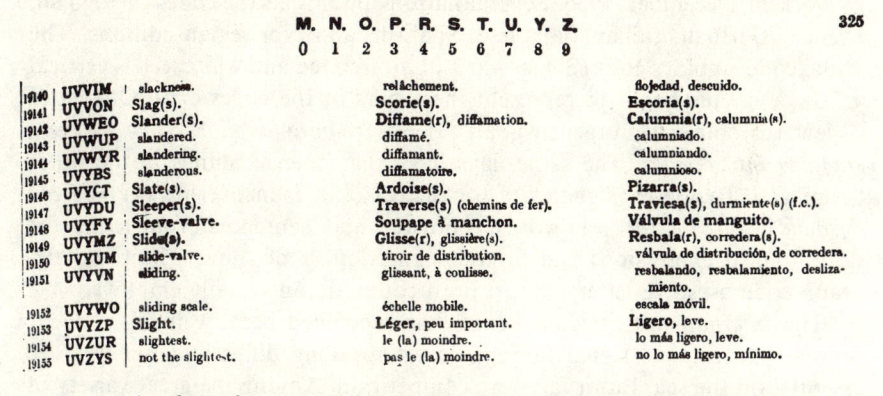

		M. N. O. P. R. S. T. U. Y. Z.			325
		0 1 2 3 4 5 6 7 8 9			
19140	UVVIM	slackness.	relâchement.		flojedad, descuido.
19141	UVVON	Slag(s).	Scorie(s).		Escoria(s).
19142	UVWEO	Slander(s).	Diffame(r), diffamation.		Calumnia(r), calumnia(s).
19143	UVWUP	slandered.	diffamé.		calumniado.
19144	UVWYR	slandering.	diffamant.		calumniando.
19145	UVYBS	slanderous.	diffamatoire.		calumnioso.
19146	UVYCT	Slate(s).	Ardoise(s).		Pizarra(s).
19147	UVYDU	Sleeper(s).	Traverse(s) (chemins de fer).		Traviesa(s), durmiente(s) (f.c.).
19148	UVYFY	Sleeve-valve.	Soupape à manchon.		Válvula de manguito.
19149	UVYMZ	Slide(s).	Glisse(r), glissière(s).		Resbala(r), corredera(s).
19150	UVYUM	slide-valve.	tiroir de distribution.		válvula de distribución, de corredera.
19151	UVYVN	sliding.	glissant, à coulisse.		resbalando, resbalamiento, deslizamiento.
19152	UVYWO	sliding scale.	échelle mobile.		escala móvil.
19153	UVYZP	Slight.	Léger, peu important.		Ligero, leve.
19154	UVZUR	slightest.	le (la) moindre.		lo más ligero, leve.
19155	UVZYS	not the slightest.	pas le (la) moindre.		no lo más ligero, mínimo.

A trilingual commercial code: The Marconi International Code

New York was the world center of commercial code activity because commercial codes served mainly in cables between Europe and America. English was the language of most codes, not only because it has always been the language of commerce but because most messages went to America. To cross language barriers, some codes, such as Bentley's and Lieber's, were translated into other languages; some were bilingual. Marconi's Wireless Telegraph Company Limited made a supreme effort in this field: its code, compiled by James C. H. Macbeth, a quiet, blue-eyed Scot in his early thirties who had become interested in codes while in business in Malaya, encompassed nine languages—English, Dutch, French, German, Italian, Japanese, Portuguese, Russian, and Spanish. Each of its four massive volumes contained three languages, one of which was always English. The eight other languages had indices referring to the place in the code, which was arranged according to the English word-sequence, where a particular expression would be found. It was to serve as a kind of automatic translator. An American would encode the word *a* or *an* as ABABA, and a Frenchman, receiving that codeword, would decode it as *un* or *une*. This sort of thing can be done with code because code operates upon linguistic entities. The idea stands in the line of great efforts to create a universal language, and in 1663, in fact, Athanasius Kircher compiled a Marconi-like code of 1,048 words from each of five languages, the coded version to serve as an international language.

The only one of these proposals that seems ever to have worked is the *International Code of Signals*. The 1857 British Board of Trade code was improved by a conference in Washington in 1889 and distributed to maritime powers in 1897, enabling a ship of one nation to hoist flags which would be read by a ship of another nation in its own language by virtue of a codebook in that language. The International Radiotelegraph Conference of Washington in 1927 agreed that two codes, one visual, one radio, should be compiled. The editorial committee assembled in London in October, 1928, and completed its work in December, 1930. Several nations published the codes in English, French, German, Italian, Japanese, Spanish, and Norwegian editions. The visual code employs colored flags—U is quartered red and white, G has vertical yellow and blue bars—to represent the letters of the codewords. One-letter codewords stand for urgent signals: G = *I require a pilot*; U = *You are standing into danger*. The same flags have the same meanings in the other languages. Two-letter signals are for distress and maneuvering (AP = *I am aground*), three-letter for words, phrases, and sentences, four-letter for geographical expressions and for the signal letters of ships. The radiotelegraph code uses five-letter groups. Both codes are universally employed.

The *International Code of Signals* has succeeded because it fills a need: mutually intelligible signals among crews speaking different languages are essential on the sea. But it faced no competition. Among the great variety of commercial codes, any of which could have filled the need for cutting cable tolls, why do some succeed and some fail? There appear to be two reasons, one intrinsic, the other extrinsic.

The extrinsic factor is the salesmanship of the compiler, and this often outweighs all else. The *Acme Code* succeeded commercially because its compiler, William J. Mitchel, was a convincing salesman, whereas the *Universal Trade Code* of Yardley and Mendelsohn, intrinsically about as good a code, never sold well because its compilers, busy with other matters, never pushed it. The intrinsic factor, or the quality of the code, refers primarily to its condensing power: how many plain-language words are represented by a single five-letter codeword. The later codes average a condensing power of between 5:1 and 10:1, which means that they reduce messages to one fifth or one tenth of their plain-language length. The ratio depends, of course, upon the vocabulary. How, then, is a vocabulary constructed?

"By reading telegrams," said Mitchel, who has compiled not only the public *Acme Code* but also many private ones. The code compiler must read thousands of business telegrams to get the most-used phrases, which he writes

Combat cryptography: an American soldier, rifle slung on back, enciphers with an M-209 *during the Korean War*

National Security Agency headquarters

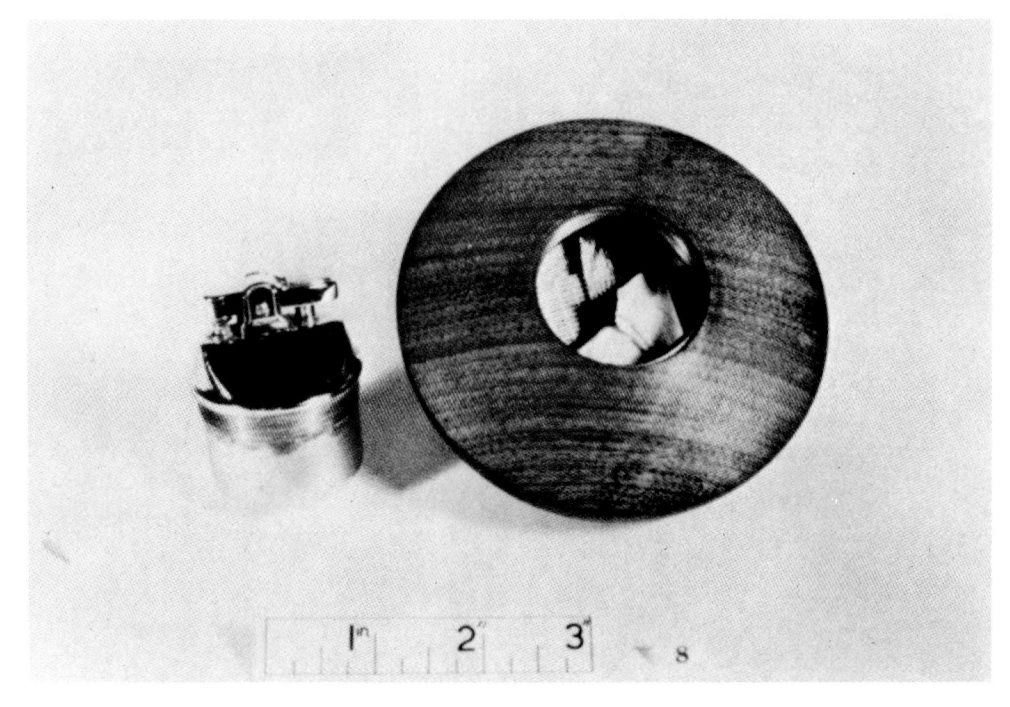

Soviet spies Helen and Peter Kroger hid their one-time pads in this table cigarette lighter in their suburban cottage in 1951

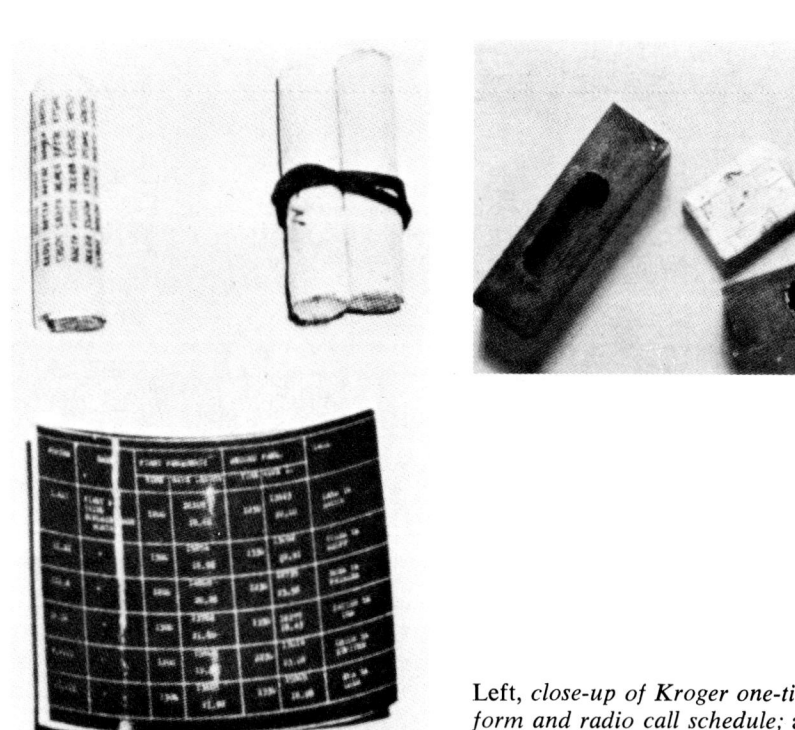

Left, *close-up of Kroger one-time pads in scroll form and radio call schedule;* above, *Soviet spy Rudolf Abel's wrapped-up one-time pad, which he hid in the hollowed-out wood blocks*

Electronic countermeasures: radar scope jammed by noise from three locations and filled with blips produced by false-target generator

Frank Byron Rowlett, Special Assistant to the Director of the National Security Agency, receiving the National Security Medal from President Johnson. Rowlett was cited as a "leading force for more than three decades in the nation's cryptologic efforts."

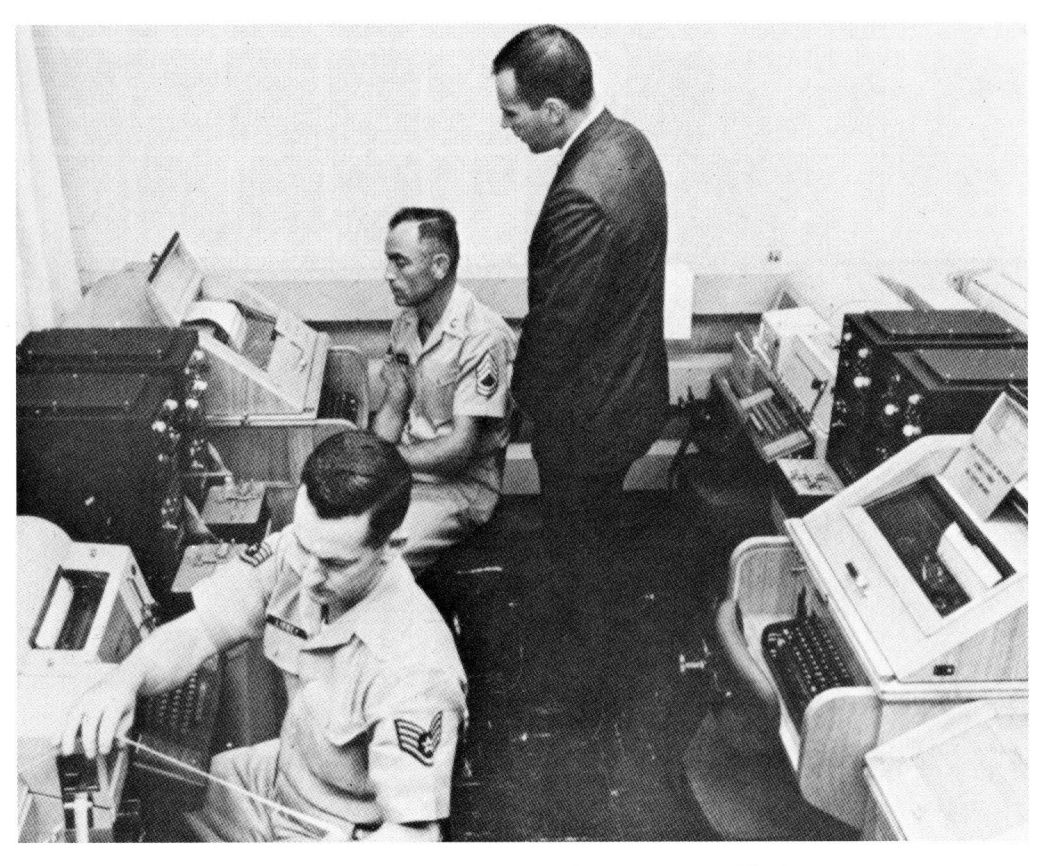

American end of the Moscow-Washington "hot line," with black one-time tape cipher machines standing between the teleprinters

Above, *O.M.I. rotor cipher machine;* left, *Hagelin hand cipher machine*

The original Sherlock Holmes coolly appraises a message in the Dancing Men cipher

Claude E. Shannon, who explained cryptanalysis

Radio scrambler sold by Delcon

E. L. Bentley, compiler of commercial codes

Scrambled television. Above, the clear image; below, the picture encoded by the Zenith Radio Corporation for its subscription-television operation in Hartford, Connecticut. Light tones appear dark, and darks, light, and portions of the picture appear cut in bands and shifted. This is how the picture would appear on a television set not equipped with the subscription-TV decoder.

Francis Bacon, enigmatologists' victim

A page of the still unsolved Voynich manuscript

Ignatius Donnelly, the first enigmatologist

The 85-foot radio telescope at Green Bank, West Virginia, tilts to listen for messages from other worlds

out on slips of paper. These not only give him specific entries for his code, but also suggest others, in the manner described in the 1930s by John W. Hartfield:

> I had a great mass of material accumulated from years past, different codes, and gleanings of suggestions made by different people and so forth. I took these and made notes of them on sheets of paper, writing phrases on sheets of paper. As I wrote phrases, other phrases suggested themselves and I interpolated those. I read the phrases and as I read them, other phrases suggested themselves and I wrote those. Then I rewrote them into alphabetical sequence, and as I rewrote them into alphabetical sequence other phrases suggested themselves, and those I interpolated. Then I went through this different data I had and made further additions, kept on enlarging various subjects. Some people suggested to me that the subjects in my 1905 book were not adequate and should be improved upon. These subjects I enlarged, amplified.

And so the books grew.

Larger codes usually have a greater condensing power than small ones because they can include many long phrases, some with 20 or 30 words. But more important than size is how well a code's phraseology accords with business usage. Thus Cyrus Tibbals' *Western Union Code*, whose 300,000 equivalents make it probably the largest commercial code ever compiled, did not afford as much economy as the 100,000-codeword *Acme Code* because its vocabulary was not as good. Business firms compared codes by using them in their cables to see which saved more money before investing several hundreds or thousands of dollars in buying scores of copies of a code for their offices around the world. Many companies had private codes compiled in which their products are listed in great detail. Though this may cost a large firm up to $50,000 (including printing), they soon recover that amount in their cable toll savings; they also get a dividend of secrecy, which is sometimes important.

Up to the mid-1920s, the codewords of a code did not affect its quality very much, since all included the two-letter differential. Then Mitchel introduced a new safeguard in his *Acme Code*: no codeword was included if it could be formed from an already existing codeword by the transposition of two adjacent letters. Thus, if the code included LABED, excluded would be ALBED, LBAED, LAEBD, and LABDE. Since such transpositions are not at all rare in communication, both code and plain, resulting usually from psychological rather than telegraphic slips, Mitchel's idea spread rapidly.

To generate the enormous quantities of codewords needed, compilers used construction tables. For five-letter codes, these consisted of a square of single letters with two squares of letter-pairs adjoining it, one at the top and one at the side. The letter pairs were so chosen and arranged that all in a given column or row in a square differed by two letters from one another. To keep the codeword stock free of transpositions of adjacent letters, the squares must have an odd number of cells on each side. Since the normal alphabet has

26 letters, this can be done either by dropping one letter or by adding an extra character and then eliminating from the code stock all words formed with it; the latter procedure, which saves the 26th letter, naturally produces more codewords. A miniature codeword construction table, based on the six-letter alphabet, A, B, C, D, E, and F, with † as the extra character, can demonstrate the procedure:

AA	AB	AC	AD	AE	AF	A†
BB	BC	BD	BE	BF	B†	BA
CC	CD	CE	CF	C†	CA	CB
DD	DE	DF	D†	DA	DB	DC
EE	EF	E†	EA	EB	EC	ED
FF	F†	FA	FB	FC	FD	FE
††	†A	†B	†C	†D	†E	†F

A	B	C	D	E	F	†	AA	BB	CC	DD	EE	FF	††
B	C	D	E	F	†	A	BA	CB	DC	ED	FE	†F	A†
C	D	E	F	†	A	B	CA	DB	EC	FD	†E	AF	B†
D	E	F	†	A	B	C	DA	EB	FC	†D	AE	BF	C†
E	F	†	A	B	C	D	EA	FB	†C	AD	BE	CF	D†
F	†	A	B	C	D	E	FA	†B	AC	BD	CE	DF	E†
†	A	B	C	D	E	F	†A	AB	BC	CD	DE	EF	F†

To construct codewords, the compiler takes two elements from the same column and two elements from the same row, with the single letter at the pivot of the column and row. Thus, the codeword series would run AAAAA, AAABB, AAACC, ... AAA††, AABBA, AABCB ... , AA†F†, ABBAA, ABBBB ... , ABB††, ABCBA ... , A†FF†, BBBBA, BBBCB, BBBDC .... These words all show a 2-letter difference and exclude alternate-letter transpositions. The number of 5-letter codewords using a 26-letter alphabet showing a simple 2-letter differential is 26^4, or 456,976. The alternate-letter restriction lowers this to 440,051 codewords constructed with a 27-character alphabet, or 390,625 if constructed with a 25-letter alphabet. These are theoretical maximums, however, and although some cryptologists, notably Friedman, Mendelsohn, and Schauffler, have used mathematics to examine the best ways of constructing stocks of codewords, "most codemakers," Schauffler has written, "are pure empiricists" and "many an inelegant solution" robs them of usable codewords. But what deprived the code compilers of the greatest number of codewords was the International Telegraph Union rule that the words be pronounceable. This slashed the number available from about 400,000 to about 100,000.

The pronounceability rule consequently became increasingly unpopular during the code-boom period of the early 1920s. It restricted the size of codes when they were bursting at the seams. It caused innumerable arguments at the telegraph counters. It engendered disputes between the cable companies and the governmental telegraph administrations. So the 1925 Paris conference of the International Telegraph Union sent the entire codeword question to a special 15-delegate committee, which met for a month in 1926 at the resort town of Cortina d'Ampezzo, Italy. It scrutinized the answers to questionnaires it had sent out, read the comments submitted to it by operators and users and code compilers, discussed the problem, and decided (all but the British delegation) to recommend to the next conference that "Code words must be formed of a maximum of five letters, chosen at the will of the sender, without any condition." But the 1928 Brussels conference ignored this recommendation. It sought instead to quantify pronounceability by requiring that all codewords of ten letters have at least three vowels. The rule ran into strong opposition, and finally, at Madrid in 1932, what had become the International Telecommunications Union at long last abandoned any effort to legislate the nature of codewords and acceded, in effect, to the Cortina proposal. Much of the rationale for pronounceability was dissolving with the introduction of teletypewriters into the cable circuits. The sound of the codewords may have mattered to the Morse-code operators who listened to the signals of the Morse sounder; it did not matter to touch typists. What did matter was that the codewords became five letters long instead of ten. The teletypist could now take in and remember a word at a single glance, which he could not do with the artificial ten-letter words, even if they were pronounceable, without a fair proportion of errors. The new regulations thus speeded transmission and reduced errors.

Simultaneously, the number of permissible codewords bounded upward. This did not mean much in most public codes, where codes of 50,000 to 100,000 elements are the largest practicable, since beyond that size no code clerk takes the time to search out the most precise and economical phrase. But in private codes the many new codewords were very advantageously employed. When Ernest F. Peterson revised a cash register company's 100,000-word code, he found that 1,000 words in the old code, from KAJAN to KUTAZ, conveyed shipping instructions. Thus, KUBOR meant *We are shipping to you, in care of your agent at Shanghai.* The description of the machine had to go into the next codeword. Taking advantage of the new wealth of codewords, Peterson combined each of the 10,000 shipping instructions with each of the firm's 200 models of cash registers, and assigned each a codeword. This used 200,000 words, or twice as many as the old code had had altogether. But it saved a cable word, and when Peterson finished making similar changes elsewhere, the code could express common transactions that had formerly required four five-letter codewords in just two, greatly lowering the firm's cable bill. Similarly, he expanded a bank's code from 100,000 to 400,000 words.

Such savings were important in the Depression, and commercial codes were widely used—though the code compilers suffered as much from the economic slump as the rest of the business world. World War II, whose numerous national censorships frowned on codes and limited the number of permitted ones, dealt the code business a severe blow. And after the war, the rising cost of labor dealt it a mortal one. It often cost more to have a clerk code a message than the coding would save in cable tolls. At the same time, the greater ease of international communications militated against the use of codes. Sending a cable message once involved a mystique of writing it out on a blank in telegraphic English and having a messenger take it down to the cable office, a dramatic place where men could touch a key and make something go "click" in Europe, a week away by boat. Codes and coding were part of this mystique. But when business firms installed teletypewriters that could be linked directly to the cablehead, or even to a firm's European branch, it became simpler just to sit down at the keyboard and type out the message without bothering with the whole rigamarole of coding. Transatlantic telephone calls and letters by jet, which leave London one day and arrive in New York the next, stole business from the cables and reduced the need for codes.

At the same time, the march of progress was making codes less and less useful. For a code once compiled does not retain its value forever. A code reflects the world at a particular instant, and as the world moves on it outmodes the code. New products, new ways of doing things, new political or economic facts begin to make its vocabulary old-fashioned. No codes compiled in the 1920s or 1930s had any phrases referring to transatlantic air travel, yet cable traffic today is replete with such references. Ironically, the better a code is at the moment of its compilation, the more closely its vocabulary fits the business requirements of its time, the more rapidly will it obsolesce. Of course many phrases will remain viable, but the lack of many badly needed phrases renders the code as a whole almost useless. Why bother to encode at all if half the message has to be sent in plain anyway?

Thus the use of code fell off drastically after World War II. Many companies resorted to code only when they needed a modicum of secrecy—a return, at the moment of the commercial code's death, to the motive advanced as its main reason for being at the moment of its birth. Today only commodity exchanges use commercial codes extensively (for economy, not secrecy). Old codes are still reprinted and sold, but the printings have dropped in size. Only a handful of commercial codes—probably all private—were compiled in the 1950s, and it is almost certain that since 1960 not one has been. There is today not a single practicing code compiler in the United States, and probably not one in the world.

Even an injection of the wonder drug of modern business—the electronic computer—failed to stem the decline. Robert W. Bemer of I.B.M. proposed placing a business vocabulary in a computer memory and assigning digital "codewords" to its words and phrases on the basis of frequency—shorter groups of digits for the common phrases, longer groups for the less used ones. The computer would automatically encode the message. Bemer called the idea "digital shorthand" and found that it would compress a message to one third its normal length, thereby in effect tripling the capacity of a communications link. But though the method was technically feasible, economically it never got off the ground, and the code business remained moribund.

The rise and fall of an industry is not a new story in the history of the world. As a business, the making of nonsecret codes is as dead as armor making or buggy-whip making. Did it have any aftereffect on civilization, after fulfilling its function of helping that civilization advance? Did it leave anything beyond hundreds of dusty tomes filled with outmoded references to ships being coaled and defunct names like St. Petersburg, and some lessons in codeword construction? There is one thing that may be distilled from any human experience because it represents the universal, and that is art. Commercial codemaking stimulated the best humor in cryptology—a small contribution to the world's store of art, but one that gives lasting pleasure nonetheless. The author, Jack Littlefield, offered some "Melancholy Notes on a Cablegram Code Book" to the readers of the July 28, 1934, issue of *The New Yorker**—the code in question being the *Acme*.

> Every time I receive a cablegram in code, I have the same feeling of pleasureable excitement. There is the familiar envelope lying on my desk, marked "Cablegram: Urgent." I rip it open and discover inside the single mysterious word BIINC. The message is from our Venezuela office. Visions at once loom of secret documents, beautiful women, and dark Latin-American intrigue. Then I turn to my code book and find BIINC: *What appliances have you for lifting heavy machinery?* This sort of thing can be very debilitating.
>
> It is not the fault of the code book, either. That handy volume is full of interesting messages that my correspondents never seem to get around to sending. For years I have been on the watch for wires like NARVO (*Do not part with the documents*), OBNYX (*Escape at once*), ARPUK (*The person is an adventurer, have nothing to do with him*), or BUKSI (*Avoid arrest if possible*), but they never seem to arrive. And yet, if the code book is to be believed, they are fair samples of the kind of thing with which our telegraph wires are humming daily.
>
> Not all the code-book suggestions, of course, are on this high level of adventure. Our telegraph-users, it would seem, have a wide range of concerns. At this very moment a perplexed customer in some distant part of the globe is inquiring URPXO (*For what use was the mixing machine intended?*); in the next town, perhaps a ship's captain is reporting diffidently ELJAZ (*Will have to get bottom examined before proceeding*); while somewhere a new parent is voicing his elation in the form of AROJD (*Please advertise the birth of twins*).
>
> The dominating note of the code book, however, is one of resigned melancholy. Its pages are replete with such gloomy sentiments as ZULAR (*Unfortunately too true*) and CULKE (*Bad as possibly can be*), expressions that seem only too justified when we consider the extraordinary series of disasters that has been stored up for users of the code. Every possible variety of mishap has been foreseen and embalmed in a group of doleful entries ranging from the comparatively trivial AIBUK, which describes the bursting of a donkey boiler, to the truly cataclysmic PYTUO (*Collided with an iceberg*). Even the usually trustworthy mail and

---

* Reprinted by permission, copyright © 1934, 1962 The New Yorker Magazine, Inc.

express services share in the general debacle. Our very letters, it is predicted, will be *unreadable, the writing having been obliterated by water* (SKAAE); and shipments will inevitably arrive *in clammy condition* (HEHST). It is all very sad.

Nor is the code book a volume to be recommended for shipboard reading. Never frolicsome, it is at its gloomy best when describing sea accidents. This it does not only with gusto but with an unpleasantly convincing eye for detail. Listings like LYADI, for example (*Arrived here with decks swept, boats and funnel carried away, cargo shifted, having encountered a hurricane*), are just circumstantial enough to be a trifle discommoding to the ocean-traveller. And when, a few pages farther on, he encounters the still more ominous UZSHY (*Body now lies in the mortuary*), he cannot help feeling an awful assurance as to the identity of the corpse in question.

Then, too, there is the matter of the ship's captain, that dignitary whom we are accustomed to think of as a strong, silent man—alert, commanding, and always on the job. The code-book picture of him is different and more than a little disconcerting. By the time we have finished reading messages like *Captain lost overboard, Captain not to be found, Captain drunk, Captain refuses to leave vessel*, and *Captain insane*, it is with considerable relief that we light upon the entry *Arrest the Captain*. It would seem to have come not a moment too soon.

But even if the captain avoids these pitfalls, and the ship itself escapes the ravages of the storm, the code has still other hazards in store for the unhappy voyager. At any moment the ship may be *captured by pirates* (ENIMP) or *plundered by natives* (YBDIG). There is always the chance that the captain will receive cabled instructions to *arrest all passengers* (ZEIBI). Even less consoling to the prospective traveller are such glimpses of world hygiene as IDDOG (*Ship in port, all hands down with scurvy*) and OAVUG (*An epidemic of foot-and-mouth disease has broken out here*). The only ray of light is provided by EWIXI (*Very few cases of cholera are now reported*), and even that statement is not without its depressing implications.

There is no denying, however, that the code book is full of helpful information. Should you ever, for example, feel the need of *lard, in bladders*, the word is CHOOG. Flannel shirts are GOLPO. Cod-liver oil is called GAHGU—and a very good word for it, too, as is FOOLP for ship's biscuit. A niblick is, of course, a GAZEB, but the word for foot-warmer is FREIZ. No matter what commodity it is you desire, you will find it covered in the code, which includes a list of nearly a thousand necessities of life, ranging all the way from arsenic to ostrich feathers, from blasting charges to porch umbrellas. Even the commodities, however, are blighted by the same spirit of melancholy that pervades the entire code, and the result is such decadent listings as ZOKIX (*unhealthy trees*) and GNUEK (*rubber, slightly moldy*).

But it is in its cross-references that the code book reaches the logical limits of pessimism. For gratuitous gloom, it would be difficult to equal such groupings as "Ankles: see Accidents" or "Chief topic on the Stock Exchange: see Failure." In other cases, however, the effect is merely rococo, as in "Marriage: see Hotel Accommodations" or "Noses: see also Fittings, Machinery, and Spare Parts."

Valuable as it is from both the literary and the practical standpoint, it is plain that the code book was intended for people who get around more than I do. Such well-meant suggestions as DEOBI (*A great battle is now raging here*), PUMZI (*Can you combine horses and grain?*), and EZUCZ (*Calling at Elephant Point for orders*) can hold for me at best only an academic interest. But any of these messages is a monument of utility beside the picturesque YBTUA, which deals with the transportation to Mecca of *pilgrims—at the prevailing price per head*! And however much I may regret my inability to send a message like WUMND (*Have every reason to believe oil will be struck*), at least I feel certain that I shall never rise, Phoenix-like, from my own ashes to cable that most fantastic of all code words, AHXNO: *Met with a fatal accident.*

23

CIPHERS IN THE PAST TENSE

ALL CRYPTANALYSTS have not borne arms for Mars. Some of the most prolific have served Clio, the muse of history. Many of these unsung heroes—the only cryptologists whose contributions enlightened all mankind—worked in the 19th century. The immense influence of Leopold von Ranke's objective school of history, which demanded a study of the original documents, sent droves of historians to mine state papers and diplomatic correspondence in the archives, whose doors had been unlocked for the first time by the nationalism and democracy of the 1800s.

The researchers found many of the documents in cipher, or partly so. Invariably, it seemed, the crux of a dispatch was enciphered. In the mid-1500s, a Venetian ambassador wrote home about his talk with Henry II of France concerning English affairs. "His Majesty suddenly turned to me, taking a troubled aspect and shrugging his shoulders, added to me these very words . . . ." and the rest is in cipher! Historians realized that the most important parts were the most likely to be put into cipher. Some, unfamiliar with cryptanalysis, apparently regarded the resultant cryptogram as an act of God, an insuperable obstacle which they would have to live with as with a hole in the document. "Were we able to decipher the letters written on congressional politics by Richard Henry Lee and his correspondents . . . no doubt much of the cloud which hangs over the congressional intrigues of that critical period would be removed," mourned Francis Wharton in 1889 in *The Revolutionary Diplomatic Correspondence of the United States.*

But other scholars looked upon the cryptograms as a challenge. One of the first of these was a transplanted German whose services to English historiography were of high importance.

Gustave Adolph Bergenroth was born February 26, 1813, at Marggrabowa, which his biographer called "an insignificant town in the remotest and dreariest corner of East Prussia." He attended the University of Königsberg, where he was very popular with his fellow students and where he sustained a severe injury to his right wrist in duelling. After working in Cologne and Berlin as an assessor, with time out for a trip to Italy necessitated by his liberal views, he quit his job and sailed in 1850 for California as a pioneer. The racy style of his first composition in English, "The First Vigilance Committee," drew favorable attention, and he determined to write. After some literary work, he began a history of Tudor England. Finding the available materials insufficient, he set out, late in his forties, for that great repository of documents for those years when Spain bestrode the world, the Archivio General at Simancas in northwest Spain. His letters home soon won him a stipend from England's Master of the Rolls to find, list, and summarize the state papers at Simancas that related to English history and to prepare a volume for the Spanish series of the endless Calendars of State Papers. He forgot his Tudor history.

He arrived at Simancas in September, 1860, and established himself in a kind of hotel, the Parador della Luna, where he would do much of his cryptanalysis. An Englishman who visited him painted the scene: "Simancas is a collection of wretched hovels, half buried in dust and sand. There is not a good house in the place. The one in which Mr. Bergenroth lives belongs to a farm bailiff, consists of two storeys, all the rooms of plaster, and the floors of brick. No fireplace in any of the rooms, and, as the winter is very intense here from November to February, and the walls full of holes, nothing but the strongest desire to do service to history could reconcile any man to so much hardship." Bergenroth had, moreover, to overcome some of the oddest phenomena ever to interfere with cryptanalysis. The plaza beneath his room was crowded with shouting donkey-drivers and visited frequently by a dulciana, whose "shrill notes, continually playing an air from Traviata and one Spanish melody, and nothing else, drive me almost mad." His landlady liked to strum on her guitar, and "none but drivers of bullock-carts could, for a single night, stand the music of the Lady della Luna." The kitchen girl "hangs my linen and that of the whole family over my balcony for drying, and then, with laudable resolution, sets to ironing it on my writing-table."

More troubles faced him at the Archivio General. It consists of an old castle, with crenellated walls pierced by loopholes, surrounded by deep moats and drawbridges. Its 46 rooms contain more than 100,000 bundles, or legajos, in each of which are filed from 10 to 100 documents, making a total of several million. From this staggering accumulation Bergenroth had to select the pertinent items. It was hard for him even to get at them. When Spain's archives administration finally granted him entrée, the crabbed Renaissance semiuncials made long and dogged practice necessary before he could read the handwriting. Indeed, the archivist himself had often been defeated by it, and in his jealousy at Bergenroth's success he deliberately hampered the historian's work by refusing access to such cipher keys as were in his possession. Bergenroth had to recover them by himself, as well as those keys that had been lost.

The story of his cryptanalytic endeavors can be pieced together from several of his writings.

> I did not go to Spain quite unprepared for my work. I had carefully studied the *Paléographie* of Christoval Rodriguez; I had also spent much time in

deciphering such old Spanish documents as were to be found in the libraries of London and Paris. . . .

[At Simancas.] The first thing I considered it necessary to do was to study most carefully, not only the Spanish orthography of the period, but that of each statesman in particular who could be supposed to have written any of these letters. Even this was not sufficient. I had to study the turns of thought, and the favourite words and expressions of each statesman. Long and curious lists, covering many sheets of paper, lay during many months on my writing-table, and were stuck up against the wall of my room.

I did not discover any of the keys to the ciphers in a methodical manner. Whilst engaged in copying I was constantly on the watch for a weak point, convinced that no man can for any length of time succeed so completely disguising his thoughts but that he will occasionally betray himself to a close observer. Wherever I thought that that was the case, I tried to guess the meaning of the signs. A hundred times I may have done so in vain, but at last I triumphed. . . .

When copying an instruction to the Duke [de Estrada], I discovered little dots, like full stops, behind two signs of cipher. As interpunction is never used in cipher of this kind, the dots could only be signs of abbreviation. But even abbreviations (a skilful writer would never have made use of them) offer so many difficulties that they can be employed only on the most common occasions, as, for instance, V. A. for Vuestra Alteza, or n.f. for nuestra fija, or nuestro fijo. From obvious reasons [in this case], I decided in favor of "nuestra fija," and inferred further that the preceding signs must correspond to "princesa de Gales." The breach was opened, and before three o'clock in the next morning I was in possession of eighty-three signs, representing the letters of the alphabet, and of thirty-three monosyllables, signifying words. The key is far from being complete, but there remain no longer unconquerable difficulties. . . . [This cipher] of the Duke de Estrada is the most difficult, and at the same time the most important of all, as a greater number of undeciphered despatches are written in it than in any other kind of cipher. . . .

The question may be asked, whether my decipherings are trustworthy? I answer with full confidence in the affirmative. I have more reason than one for doing so. After I had deciphered the despatches, I found, in some instances, that they were only ciphered copies of drafts in plain writing. Thus I had an opportunity of comparing my interpretations with the originals, and found that in all essential points they were identical. The key of De Puebla and the fragments of the two other keys, which were given to me after my return from Madrid, provided me with an additional test. The keys which I had already formed before seeing them coincided perfectly with them. . . . But the general and most decisive proof consists in the meaning of the despatches, concealed behind the cipher.

In ten months, Bergenroth surpassed the feats of many professional cryptanalysts by reconstructing 19 nomenclators—an average of about one every two weeks, some with 2,000 or 3,000 elements. This was in addition to his own copying, his supervising of a copyist, his searching for documents, his battles with the bureaucracy, and his frequent letters home. He did not like the cryptanalysis: "Nothing but sheer necessity would have forced me to attempt such a task, which, I think, is one of the most laborious that any man

Ciphers in the Past Tense

could undertake." Yet by July 23, 1861, ten months after his arrival, he could report, "The despatches in cipher are all copied and deciphered, with the exception of two small letters (the one of them from John Stile to Henry VII.), which I intend to decipher in Barcelona or in London. I am now too fatigued for a work which requires so much concentration of thought as the discovery of keys to unknown cipher does." He did solve the Stile letter, but not the other, a short one from King Ferdinand and Queen Isabella dated at Segovia on August 20, 1503, the only one in that key. This key was the only one of those used by Spain during the reign of England's Henry VII (1485–1509) that he failed to read.

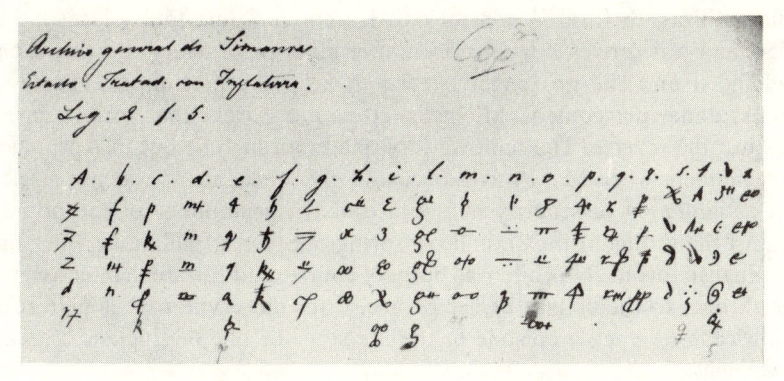

Gustave Bergenroth's reconstruction of a Spanish cipher

One long dispatch, whose solution took a week, typifies the treasures he unearthed. It is a letter of July 25, 1498, from Don Pedro de Ayala in London to Ferdinand and Isabella, reporting on England's fitting out of an expedition to some islands in the New World which, Ayala thinks, had already been discovered by Columbus and were owned by Spain. He apparently referred to the second voyage of John Cabot, on whose discoveries the English claims to North America rested. Though some of the nomenclators that Bergenroth recovered were later found in the archives, many others never were, and only his cryptanalyses brought the documents to light. Bergenroth died in 1869 of a fever contracted at Simancas, but the results of his labors shine today in the close-printed pages of his *Calendars of Letters, Despatches, and State Papers Relating to the Negotiations Between England and Spain*. To their résumés of hundreds of documents, the historians return time and again, with gratitude.

Bergenroth had been assisted in his cryptologic work at Simancas by Paul Friedmann, who appears to have been some kind of itinerant archivist. For France's Bibliothèque Nationale he compiled a collection of ciphers employed by various French political correspondents of the 16th century. In

1868 he became interested in the cipher messages of Giovanni Michiel, Venetian ambassador to the court of England's Queen Mary, sister and predecessor of Elizabeth I. No one in the archives of Venice could read the dispatches, and, though photographs of them were sent to England for attempts at solution there, they continued to baffle everyone. In Venice, Friedmann examined the Michiel correspondence and "soon arrived at the conviction that the cipher was not one of extraordinary difficulty, that it was not always used with sufficient care, and that with a little labor the sense might be discovered." It used about 200 signs, and within a few months he had solved it. Thus d^{11} was *bo*, d^{12} was *g*, t^{25} *Sua Maesta*, and so forth.

"Michiel's correspondence is of a considerable value," Friedmann wrote. "It will redress many errors, and fill many a gap in the narratives . . . ." For example, historians had generally considered that the transfer of the future Queen Elizabeth from Woodstock to Hampton Court took place in June, 1554, and was a release from prison after all hope of Mary's having a child had faded and she no longer needed to keep the presumptive Protestant heiress under her control. Michiel's letters make clear that what happened was just the reverse. The removal took place not in June but in April, at the very moment when Mary was expected to give birth, and it was not a release but a tightening of security in the face of the grumblings of the populace against the thought of a Catholic offspring of Spain's Philip and Mary upon the English throne. No child was born, of course, and Elizabeth later ascended the throne, to the delight of her people. Thus did cryptanalysis help rectify knowledge of a tense episode in the life story of one of England's greatest sovereigns.

Friedmann bitterly complained that an Italian archivist, Luigi Pasini, attempted to claim credit for the Michiel solution when, in fact, he merely augmented it. This was true, but Pasini did achieve some notable cryptanalyses. He had begun work in the Archivio di Stato of Venice in 1855, when he was 20. Ten years later, he became interested in the Venetian ciphers and began collecting keys and documents concerning them.

His enlargement of the Michiel nomenclator won him the commendation of the Master of the Rolls, and when a French scholar, Armand Baschet, heard of it, he encouraged Pasini to attack the enciphered dispatches of the Venetian ambassadors to the court of France for the last four years of the reign of Henry II, the three-year reign of Francis II, and the first five years of Charles IX, for all of which no decipherments or keys could be found. Pasini, an intelligent and likable young man, succeeded in solving about 5,000 lines, and Baschet, who had at first considered not publishing the dispatches for those years because the most valuable information was concealed under the cipher, could declare: "Thanks to his [Pasini's] extraordinary aptitude, the dispatches of six Venetian ambassadors for a period of twelve years, written in the impress of great events such as the last struggles of the King of France with the [Holy Roman] Emperor and the Spaniards, and the first religious wars, have recovered their extreme interest." Pasini also assisted Baschet cryptologically in a study of the letters of Aldus Manutius, the great printer. He continued to collect material on the history of Venetian ciphers until his death in 1885.

Another Italian archivist, Domenico Pietro Gabbrielli, an abbot, was positively awesome in his cryptanalytic industry. He was appointed an apprentice archivist in the diplomatic section of the Archivio di Stato of Florence early in 1854, when he was 30. Ten years later he began a nine-year marathon of historical cryptanalysis, becoming probably the most expert solver of nomenclators who ever lived. He solved 400 in his first seven years, a rate of better than one nomenclator solution per week. He owed this apparently incredible facility to his progression from the simple ciphers of the 1400s to the full nomenclators of the 1700s, which familiarized him with the quirks and trends and phraseology of Florentine cryptography, to the probable similarity of many of the nomenclators, to the great volume of material at hand, and to his own ability. In addition to his solutions, he reconstructed twice as many nomenclators from existing plain and cipher versions of dispatches.

Gabbrielli solved or reconstructed 1,755 nomenclators, dating from 1414 to 1742. They fill 16 volumes arranged either administratively (as Volume III, 130 keys to the correspondence of Cosimo I de Medici, ruler of Florence from 1536 to 1574) or geographically (as Volume XVI, 142 keys to the correspondence from France from 1542 to 1735). Death halted his work on November 26, 1873, while he was in the midst of compiling a 17th volume on ciphers for Spain. An unfinished, unbound file containing attempts, excerpts, and various keys testifies mutely to his persistence.

In the United States, Edmund C. Burnett solved many of the letters that Wharton did not in editing the great collection of *Letters of Members of the Continental Congress*. In Germany, more recently, Bernard Bischoff has reconstructed the ciphers used in scores of medieval manuscripts, often from just a sentence or two. Guillermo Lohmann Villena, a Peruvian diplomat, solved a number of ciphers during his exhaustive researches into the systems used by Spain during her colonization of the New World.

These mass-production artists are followed by many one-shot historical cryptanalysts who have encountered a cipher or two during their researches and have cracked it. In the late 1930s, Howard Peckham of the William L. Clements Library at the University of Michigan solved parts of the André dictionary-code correspondence that was involved in the Benedict Arnold treason. "The reason I was able to decode [letter] No. 31 was because No. 30 exists here in both coded and decoded form, and also Washington's proclamation, which [Carl] Van Doren mentioned [in his *Secret History of the American Revolution*] but did not print, is there in code and could be decoded by reference to a plain copy. These two items gave me quite a vocabulary to work with, without the dictionary." Derek J. Price, professor of the history of science at

Yale, tackled a monalphabetic substitution in an astronomical manuscript by Geoffrey Chaucer and solved it, bringing to light a cipher message by one of the greatest names in English literature.

The enormous volume of Spanish letters in the early years of modern history makes their solution a subspecies in themselves. The Belgian J. P. Devos, who published a large collection of Spanish nomenclators in 1950, found it necessary to solve an enciphered dispatch to reconstitute one of them. About the same time, Miguel Gómez del Campillo solved messages of Tomás Perrenot, señor de Chantonnay, sent to Philip II and the Duke of Alba. In 1926, a young Mexican historian, Don Francisco Monterde García-Icazbalta, won a prize of 200 gold pesos established by a merchant for the first solution of an enciphered letter by Cortéz, which is the oldest extant example of New World cryptography. Shortly before his death in 1934, the German Robert Fuchs solved a 15-page letter of Charles V that gave instructions in 1546 to a cardinal on his way to Rome. And early in the 1900s, Henry Biaudet, who forgot his copy of the key of Don Juan de Zúñiga y Requesens when he went to Geneva to study that Renaissance diplomat's correspondence, "was able to reconstruct it on the spot without the least difficulty."

More recently, Raoul Brunon solved several 16th-century nomenclators for the sumptuous volume, with many facsimiles of the actual cipher letters, that he and his brother Jean published in 1952, *Les Français en Italie sous Henri II*. In 1947, Dr. Rebeca Rosell Planas reconstructed the keys used by José Martí of Cuba in his correspondence before the Cuban revolution against Spain and read some of the never-before-solved portions of his letters. A century before, Dietrich C. von Rommel published the key to the nomenclator that Henry IV of France had used with Maurice the Wise. The Babbage and Wheatstone solutions of royal letters of the 1600s fall into this category. And there must be dozens more who have similarly succeeded in a bit of cryptanalysis like this.

The thought of tearing away the veil that has enshrouded a message for perhaps hundreds of years exerts a potent lure upon all minds. Not even the professional cryptologist, who daily solves cryptograms of immediate importance, remains immune. Étienne Bazeries succumbed often. He solved nomenclators of Francis I, Francis II, Henry IV, Mirabeau, Napoleon. But his greatest historical effort led to what he thought was the solution of one of the most tantalizing of mysteries—the identity of the Man in the Iron Mask.

In 1891, Commandant Gendron of the French General Staff found himself stymied in his study of the campaigns of Marshal Nicolas de Catinat, one of Louis XIV's generals, by five ciphered dispatches to Catinat from Louis himself and by two from Louvois, the minister of war. Gendron appealed for help to Bazeries, who, after examining them, boldly declared that he would solve them—to the astonishment of Gendron, who had submitted the messages in vain to other cryptologists. Bazeries felt so confident because he had observed that the cipher numbers ran from 1 to the high 500's and that repetitions were rife. This convinced him that the cipher numbers mostly represented plaintext syllables—a method rare since the telegraph had killed the nomenclator, and probably the reason for the failure of the other cryptologists.

Bazeries first made a frequency count of the 12,125 groups of the dispatches, finding that the most frequent group was 22, appearing 187 times. Then followed 124, with 185 occurrences, 42 with 184, 311 with 145, 125 with 127, and so forth. With no tables of syllable frequencies available, Bazeries had to guess. He supposed the order to be *le, la, les, de, des, du, au, il, et, vous, que,* and so on. Then, surmising that the phrase *les ennemis* would crop up frequently in military dispatches, he split it into syllables and matched it with five figures that appeared together several times with only slight variations. These variations, he conjectured, represented homophones. To discover them is the first step in the solution of nomenclators. Thus, he assumed that

	124	22	146	46	469
	124	22	125	46	574
	124	22	125	46	120
	124	22	125	46	584
	124	22	125	46	345
all stood for	*les*	*en*	*ne*	*mi*	*s*

He inserted these values throughout the cryptograms, giving him the meaning of approximately one group in every eleven. At one point, he read,

52	124	22	88	374	46	284
	les	*en*			*mi*	

Obviously, this was a case in which the second syllable of *les ennemis* had been broken up into letters; the 284 was still another equivalent for the plural ending, and 52 stood for *que* ("that"). Proceeding like this, Bazeries gradually pulverized the two-part nomenclator, possibly composed by Bonaventure Rossignol himself. He found it to consist of 587 equivalents for letters, syllables, words, and nulls, which also served as punctuation marks. One sign had the interesting function of erasing the previous sign.

After solving the dispatch of July 8, 1691, Bazeries read how displeased the king was that one of Catinat's commanders, Vivien Labbé, Seigneur du Bulonde, had disobeyed Catinat's orders and raised the siege of the northern Italian town of Coni. The action defeated the French Army, ended its campaign in Piedmont, and rudely jolted the pride of the haughty Sun King. The dispatch ordered Catinat to arrest Bulonde and "conduct him to the fortress of Pignerol, where His Majesty desires that he be guarded locked in a cell of that fortress at night and having the liberty during the day of walking on the battlements with a 330 309." These two figures appeared nowhere else in the dispatches, and Bazeries, who knew that the mysterious masked prisoner of the

Bastille had come there from Pignerol and was treated as a person of considerable importance, concluded that 330 represented the infrequent word *masque* and 309 a period or stop and published to the world his finding that Bulonde had been the Man in the Iron Mask.

The determination has been attacked on psychologic, linguistic, and cryptologic grounds. Bulonde, runs one counterargument, was a relatively minor soldier who did not warrant the deference that later gave rise to the speculation that the masked prisoner was an illegitimate son of Louis. Moreover, the text as cryptanalyzed would have meant "with a masked person" to Louvois, who would have said "en masque" instead of "avec un masque." The word *masque* does not belong in a military repertory, and, indeed, an exhaustive examination of the much larger nomenclators of succeeding rulers of France shows not one that includes it.

But what most impedes a wider acceptance of the theory is that in 1708, five years after the death of the mysterious masked prisoner of Pignerol and the Bastille, Bulonde was still alive.

Solutions more valid than Bazeries' wild leap at *masque* can, on the other hand, revolutionize some long-accepted views of events in history. One such provides unexpected support to the lingering but unsubstantiated theory that the murder of Abraham Lincoln was engineered by his own Secretary of War, the ambitious and highhanded Edwin Stanton, as part of a plot to seize control of the government and impose a hard and bitter peace upon the South.

In a bound volume of *Colburn's United Service Magazine* for the second half of 1864 that he had bought for 50 cents, New Jersey chemist and Civil War buff Ray A. Neff noticed one day in 1962 what appeared to be cipher messages written in pencil in the inner margins of a few pages. The one on page 183, for example, began: J O 5 O F X 2 S P N F 6 U I F S F 8 X B M L F E.... Neff enlisted the aid of Leonard Fouché, a self-styled professional cryptographer of Collingswood, New Jersey. It could not have taken Fouché long to find that the cipher was the simplest possible, each plaintext letter being replaced by the one following it in the normal alphabet, with the numbers indicating word separations. The cryptogram on page 183 solved out as a long allegorical poem, beginning: *In new Rome there walked three men, a Judas, a Brutus, and a spy. Each planned that he should be the kink* [king] *when Abraham should die....* Neff also found a series of much longer messages spelled out by placing dots under letters on the volume's printed pages, reading from right to left and from bottom to top. Page 106 began the narrative: *It was on the tenth of April, Sisty-five when I first knew that the plan was in action* (evidently no *x* appeared on that page, so the cipherer used an *s* instead in *sisty*). Page 107 continued: *Ecert had made all the contacts, the deed to be done of the forteenth* [the date of Lincoln's assassination]. *I did not know the identity of the assassin but I knew most all else when I approached E. S. about it.* Page 120 reported that *there were at least eleven members of*

Ciphers in the Past Tense

Congress involved in the plot. After a long gap, there appeared on page 245 an ominous *I fear for my life. LCB.*

Who was L.C.B.? Neff developed on an outer margin an invisible-ink signature of Lafayette C. Baker, chief of the secret National Detective Police. Neff feels that the "E.S." in the dot message and the "Judas" in the substitution refer to Stanton. The Judas metaphor rests upon Stanton's hypocrisies vis-à-vis Lincoln, such as in secretly opposing many of the President's policies in Congress. Brutus connects with John Wilkes Booth, the actual assassin and a noted Shakespearean actor. As for the spy who walked in new Rome, the cryptogram concludes: *But lest one is left to wonder what has happened to the spy, I can safely tell you this, it was I. Lafayette C. Baker. 2-5-68.* Neff further believes that "Ecert" was really Thomas T. Eckert, general superintendent of military telegraphs, whose name Baker intentionally misspelled because no *k* appears on page 107 until near the top and Baker did not want to leave so long a gap in his dot message. Lincoln had wanted the tall and strong Eckert as his bodyguard at Ford's Theatre; the major declined, saying he had work to do; but in fact he did not work that night and was home when notified of the shooting.

It is possible that Baker, a notorious charlatan, scoundrel, and liar, could have left the message simply to embarrass Stanton and Eckert. But Neff adduces circumstantial evidence tending to show that the secret service chief was poisoned by arsenic in a vain attempt to silence him. Furthermore, Baker pricked out a notice that *The names of these known conspirators is presented without comment or notation in Vol. one of this series.* Perhaps this cryptogram will force a reappraisal of one of the cruelest moments in the whole of American history—if only somebody could find the first half of the 1864 *Colburn's United Service Magazine.*

The longest, the best known, the most tantalizing, the most heavily attacked, the most resistant, and the most expensive of historical cryptograms remains unsolved. It fills an anonymous, untitled volume that has been called "the most mysterious manuscript in the world." In 1962, rare book dealer Hans P. Kraus of New York attracted worldwide attention when he asked $160,000 for this book that no one can read.

The volume itself is unprepossessing. A large octavo of about 6 × 9 inches, it has 204 pages; 28 others are lost. Its covers, of vellum like the leaves, are off. Dozens of tiny female nudes, astrological diagrams, and about 400 drawings of fanciful plants illuminate the book in blue, dark red, light yellow, brown, and an especially vivid green. Running among these decorations is the text itself. The manuscript somewhat resembles an herbal—a book, common in the Middle Ages, listing plants with medicinal properties and often giving recipes for extracting drugs from them.

At first glance, the text that is the heart of the mystery appears to be no problem at all. It does not look cryptic. It looks like ordinary late-medieval handwriting. The symbols preserve the general form of letters of that time, which they are not; they are like old friends whose names are on the tip of one's tongue. The writing flows smoothly, as if a scribe were copying an intelligible text; the symbols do not seem to have been printed one by one. In the most cursory examination of a single page, the eye recognizes the same letters again and again, and then it sees repeated groups and even repeated words, sometimes with slightly different endings.

All this sounds as if the text, if not in a known language disguised to the modern eye by the unfamiliar handwriting, should be in some easily ascertainable tongue. Yet scholars in the most recondite languages have stated that they could not understand it. Palaeographers have declared that the script was not known to them. And cryptanalysts, whose frequency counts of the approximately 29 symbols (some blend into others and are hard to define) looked like those of an ordinary monalphabetic substitution, and who laughed to themselves when they spotted all those repetitions that this would be simpler than the puzzle cryptograms in newspapers, turned away in chagrin when their attempt to resolve the text into church Latin, or Middle English, or langue d'oc, or some other appropriate tongue, failed utterly.

This is not to say that no one has ever claimed to have solved it. Indeed, one solution that was announced temporarily transformed the manuscript into perhaps the most important document in the history of science. Unfortunately, it, as well as the others, has been disproved.

Mystery has beclouded the manuscript since its recorded history began. That was on August 19, 1666, when Joannes Marcus Marci, the highly respected rector of the University of Prague, sent the book to his former teacher, Athanasius Kircher, the most famous Jesuit scholar of his time. Kircher had, three years earlier, published a book on cryptology and a universal language, and had boasted of having solved the riddle of hieroglyphics. In a letter accompanying the book, Marci recalled that the former owner of the book had sent Kircher a portion of the text for possible solution. To that work the owner "devoted unflagging toil ... and he relinquished hope only with his life. But his toil was in vain, for such Sphinxes as these obey no one but their master, Kircher. Accept now this token, such as it is and long overdue though it be, of my affection for you, and burst through its bars, if any there be, with your wonted success." Bars there were, but Kircher, who never shrank from bragging of what he thought were his successes, did not burst through them, for his silence on this point is eloquent.

Marci wrote that the manuscript had been bought for 600 ducats by the Holy Roman Emperor Rudolf II. More of a scholar than a ruler, Rudolf founded observatories for Tycho Brahe and Johannes Kepler, established a botanical garden, and set up an alchemical laboratory to which he invited numberless scientists. The presence of the manuscript at his court in Prague was later proved by the discovery in a margin of the autograph of Johannes de Tepenecz, a Bohemian scientist who was a favorite of Rudolf.

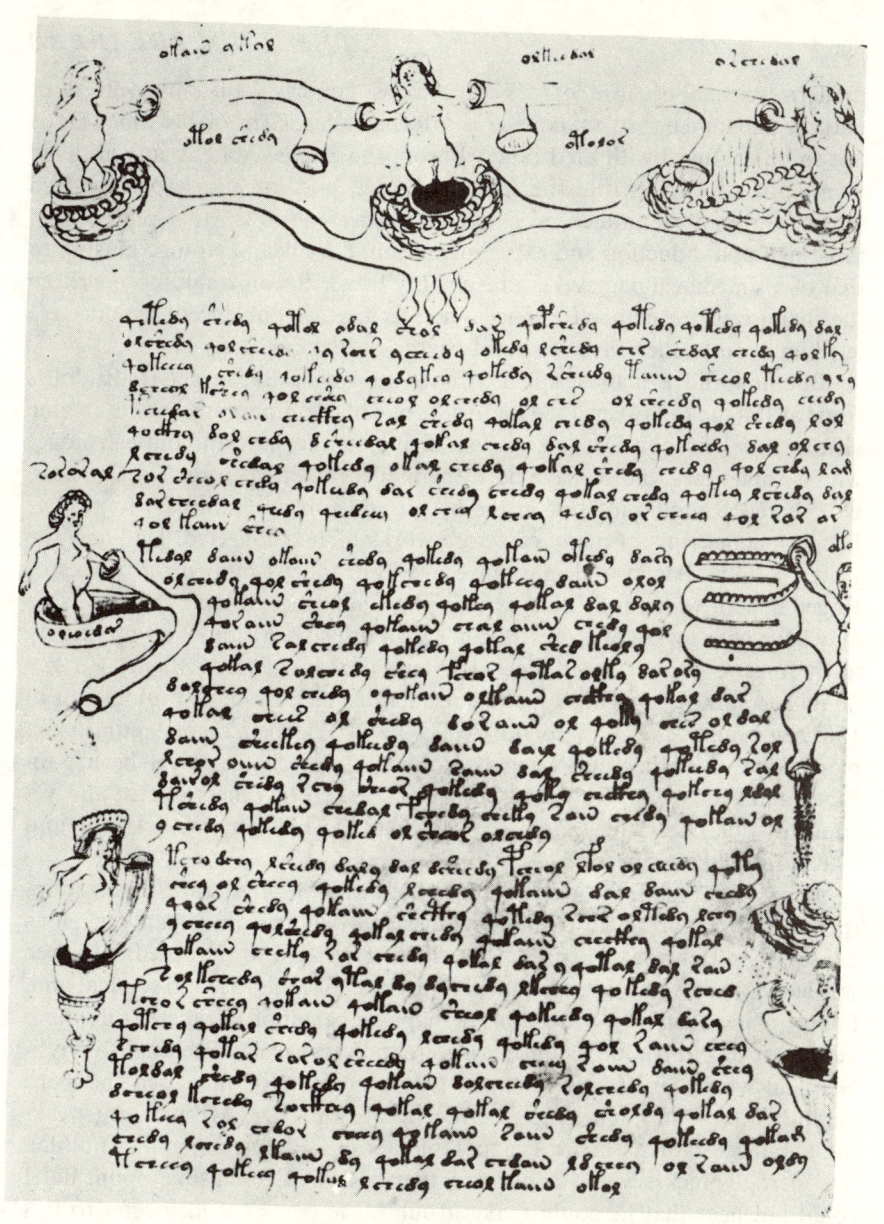

A page of the Voynich manuscript

Marci also reported the belief that the author of the manuscript was Roger Bacon, the English Franciscan friar who lived from about 1214 to 1294. Bacon had speculated, centuries before they became reality, on the possibility of microscopes and telescopes, motorboats, horseless carriages, and flying machines. Popular legend credited him with great magical abilities, a reputation probably enhanced by his extensive writing on alchemy. He interests modern science because of his precocious emphasis on observation of natural phenomena, so unlike the a priori scholasticism of his time. He is not to be confused with Sir Francis Bacon, the English statesman who lived from 1561 to 1626, wrote the famous *Essays*, and largely shaped modern science through the influence of his philosophy—although that philosophy, insisting upon induction and experimentation, does bear a strange kinship to that of his medieval namesake. Presumably Roger Bacon would have written the manuscript in cipher to conceal secrets that, if publicized, would have left him open to the grave medieval charge of black magic.

But how did a manuscript attributed to Roger Bacon get to Rudolf's court at Prague? Between 1584 and 1588, one of the Emperor's most welcome visitors was Dr. John Dee, an English divine, mathematician, and astrologer who is sometimes said to have been the model for Prospero in *The Tempest*. Dee shared Rudolf's interest in the occult and was an enthusiast for Roger Bacon, manuscripts of many of whose works he had collected. He knew the young Francis Bacon and may have even introduced him to the works of Roger Bacon, which may help explain the similarities in their thought. Dee may have been aware of Roger Bacon's own brief discussion of cryptography in the *Epistle on the Secret Works of Art and the Nullity of Magic*. He certainly had some knowledge of, and considerable interest in, cryptology, for in 1562, he bought for Sir William Cecil, Queen Elizabeth's great minister, a manuscript of Trithemius' "Steganographia," which had not yet been published and "for wch a Thousand Crownes have ben by others offred, and yet could not be obteyned." Dee spent ten days "with contynuall Labor and watch" in making himself a copy.

It may be that Dee had somehow obtained the mysterious manuscript (possibly from the Duke of Northumberland, who pillaged many religious houses when Henry VIII broke up the monasteries, and with whose family Dee was associated), was told or assumed that it was Bacon's, tried to solve it, and, failing, made a gift of it to Rudolf, perhaps on behalf of Elizabeth, for whom he was serving at Rudolf's court as a secret political agent. The English physician and writer Sir Thomas Browne (who, incidentally, first used the word "cryptography" in English) related that Dee's son, "Dr. Arthur Dee (speaking about his father's life in Prague) told about . . . book containing nothing but hieroglyphicks, which book his father bestowed much time upon, but I could not hear that he could make it out." The comment may refer to this very manuscript.

This is conjectural, however. What is certain is that Kircher deposited the manuscript in the Jesuit Collegium Romanum, and that in 1912 an American rare book dealer named Wilfred Voynich purchased it for an undisclosed sum from the Jesuit school of Mondragone in Frascati, Italy.

Eager to read the manuscript, Voynich generously supplied photostats to anyone who seemed likely to solve it. Many tried. Botanists thought they could read it by identifying the plants and assuming their names as probable words; one difficulty here was that most of the flora were imaginary. Astronomers recognized stars such as Aldebaran and the Hyades but could not force a solution. Philologists tried the methods used for reading lost languages and failed. Cryptanalysts observed characteristics in common with ordinary ciphers and found that it resisted their well-tried techniques. Voynich heard from many specialists who were interested in the problem: palaeographer H. Omont of Paris' Bibliothèque Nationale, who had written a learned article about a 15th-century cryptographic manuscript on alchemy; Professor A. G. Little, a foremost authority on Bacon; a Harvard professor of anatomy; George Fabyan of the Riverbank Laboratories; the vice president of the Royal Astronomical Society in London; even Dom Aidan, Cardinal Gasquet, prefect of the Vatican Archives, who offered to help get any documents from those archives that might throw light on the problem. Almost certainly many of these and others tried to solve the cryptogram. Among the others in 1917 was Captain John M. Manly, then second in command of Yardley's MI-8. He had cracked the Lother Witke cipher that had baffled all his colleagues but, like the others, with the Voynich manuscript he failed. And so did Yardley.

In 1919, some of Voynich's reproductions found their way to William Romaine Newbold, a professor of philosophy and former dean of the Graduate School at the University of Pennsylvania. Newbold, 54, a brilliant man who had stood first in his class of 1887 at Pennsylvania, had wide-ranging interests, many of which had in common an element of the occult—spiritism, the Gnostics, the Great Chalice of Antioch, supposed by some to be the actual chalice of the Last Supper, which is known in legend as the Holy Grail. He knew many languages and later became proficient in cryptanalysis: in 1922, Theodore Roosevelt, Jr., then Assistant Secretary of the Navy, thanked him for his "time and trouble in deciphering espionage correspondence that had baffled the Departments here in Washington."

Newbold saw microscopic shorthand symbols in the macroscopic characters of the manuscript text and began his decipherment by transliterating them into Roman letters. A secondary text of 17 different letters resulted. He doubled all but the first and last letters of each section: the secondary text *oritur* would become the tertiary text *or-ri-it-tu-ur*. Any of these groups that contained any of the letters of the word *conmuta*, plus *q*, underwent a special substitution. The resultant quaternary text was then "translated": Newbold replaced the pairs of letters with a single letter, presumably according to a key, which, however, he never made clear. Newbold regarded some letters of this reduced quinary text as equivalent to one another because of phonetic similarity. When required, therefore, he interchanged *d* and *t*, for example, *b*, *f*, and *p*, *o* and *u*, and so on. Finally, Newbold anagrammed the letters of this senary text to produce the alleged plaintext in Latin.

In April, 1921, Newbold announced the preliminary results of his solution according to this method before brilliant and learned audiences. These results stamped Roger Bacon as the greatest scientific discoverer of all time. According to Newbold, Bacon had recognized the Great Nebula in Andromeda as a spiral galaxy, identified biological cells and their nuclei, and come close to seeing the union of the sperm with the ovum. He had therefore to have not merely speculated about but to have actually constructed a microscope and a telescope and used them to make discoveries that anticipated the 20th century. Newbold's cryptanalysis of a caption on a sketch that somewhat resembles a pinwheel and that he took to represent the Andromeda nebula reads in part: "In a concave mirror I saw a star in the form of a snail ... between the navel of Pegasus, the girdle of Andromeda, and the head of Cassiopeia." Newbold asserted that his solution could not be subjective because "I did not know at the time [of solution] that any nebula would be found within the region thus defined."

Newbold's solution created a sensation in the world of scholarship. Many scientists, though declining to pass upon the validity of the cryptanalysis, which they did not think themselves competent to do, accepted the results with alacrity. One eminent physiologist went so far as to specify that some of the drawings probably represented the columnar epithelial cells with their cilia, drawn to a magnification of 75. The public at large was fascinated. Sunday supplements had a field day. One poor woman came hundreds of miles to beseech Newbold to use Bacon's formulas to cast out the demons that possessed her. The cipher itself drew mixed reviews. Manly, back at the University of Chicago, half accepted, half rejected it. "Professor Newbold's theory and system now seem much more reasonable than they did a year ago when he first explained them to me," he wrote in *Harper's Magazine*. But a writer in *Scientific American Monthly*, J. Malcolm Bird, observed acutely, in relation to the tertiary text of interlocking pairs, as *or-ri-it-tu-ur*, that "Professor Newbold has not in any of his public utterances explained satisfactorily how, in the original encipherment, it is possible to ... get letter-pairs that interlock as in the above example." In other words, although the system might work in deciphering it did not seem to work in enciphering. Many one-way ciphers have been devised: it is possible to put messages into cipher, but not to get them back out. Newbold's seemed to be the only example extant of the reverse situation. For this and other reasons, Bird rejected the solution.

The excitement simmered down. Newbold went back to continue his solutions; other scholars weighed his conclusions. In 1926, Newbold died. But his working notes, his solutions, and the chapters for the book that he had projected were faithfully edited by his friend and colleague Roland Grubb Kent. In 1928, they were published as *The Cipher of Roger Bacon*. An important French philosopher, Étienne Gilson, later one of the 40 "immortals" of the Académie Française, though bewildered by the method, accepted the results; a French specialist in Bacon, Raoul Carton, enthusiastically endorsed both method and results. American and British historians of medieval science were cooler.

In 1931, Manly, who had studied the Newbold method in detail, concluded that it "is open to objections of so grave a character as to make it impossible to accept the results." Warning that these results "threaten to falsify, to no unimportant degree, the history of human thought," he demolished them in a 47-page article. He pointed out that the cipher postulated by Newbold permitted many different "solutions." The encipherer could never be certain that his message would get through correctly; the decipherer would never know whether he was reading the intended message. The chief cause of this flexibility lay in the anagramming process—the one that finally produced the Latin plaintext. Anagramming rearranges letters of one text into another; it is a kind of unkeyed transposition. Often many anagrams are possible: *live*, *veil*, *evil*, *vile*, and *Levi* are all anagrams of the "ciphertext" EILV, each as valid as the next. As the number of letters involved rises, the possible anagrams increase in geometric proportion. The 31 letters of the angelic salutation, "Ave Maria, gratia plena, Dominus tecum," have afforded thousands of different anagrams, all perfect in spelling, diction, and syntax. One zealot turned out 1,500 pentameters and 1,500 hexameters; another 3,100 anagrams in prose and an acrostic poem; another composed a "Life of the Virgin" in 27 anagrams—all these of the salutation. Newbold tended to anagram Bacon's message in blocks of 55 or 110 letters. How certain could he then be that his anagram was the right one? The answer is that he could not be certain at all.

Manly also showed that the alleged shorthand signs were nothing more than the breaking up of the thick ink on the rough surface of the vellum into shreds and filaments that Newbold had imagined were individual signs. Newbold himself conceded that "I frequently, for example, find it impossible to read the same text twice in exactly the same way." Manly pointed to different solutions from the same text. Finally, he criticized the texts of the solutions themselves on the ground that they "contain assumptions and statements which could not have emanated from Bacon or any other thirteenth century scholar."

How, then, to explain Newbold's cryptanalyzing information that he said he never knew, such as the position of the spiral nebula? The answer is that he must have known it, though subconsciously. Newbold, a scholar of immense erudition who casually learned the Catalan language and read a thousand pages in it in pursuit of a minor point of the solution, must have swept up that detail in his extensive studies and slipped it into the depths of his brain, where it lay hidden from his active mind until the solution drew it forth. No one ever questioned Newbold's integrity; he was a victim, Manly said, "of his own intense enthusiasm and his learned and ingenious subconscious."

The spectacular collapse of the Newbold theory has not deterred other scholars from attacking the manuscript, though it has made them a bit more cautious in publishing their "solutions." In 1943, however, a Rochester,

New York, lawyer, James Martin Feely, recklessly exposed to the world—and to its ridicule—a solution that makes little sense in Latin and not much more in English: "The feminated, having been feminated, press on the forebound; those pressing on are moistened; they are vein-laden; they will be broken up; they are lessened."

Two years later, Dr. Leonell C. Strong, a highly respected cancer research specialist, concluded that the Voynich manuscript was the work of one Anthony Ascham, an English scholar of the 1500s and author of an herbal. Strong cryptanalyzed out of the manuscript several texts in alleged medieval English, including a contraceptive formula, by means of a "double reverse system of arithmetic progressions of a multiple alphabet," by which he apparently meant some form of polyalphabeticity. The contraceptive works, and anyone who wishes to prove it may do so, since Strong published it; but he has not seen fit to do the same with his method of cryptanalysis, and it therefore remains unproved and unaccepted. His published texts have been severely attacked on linguistic grounds, and the formula has been explained on the same basis of subconscious knowledge as Newbold's spiral-nebula solution.

There have been many more attempts that did not result in publication because the would-be solvers honestly admitted defeat. Scores of persons have worked at home on the illustrations in the Newbold volume without success. In 1944, from among specialists in languages, documents, mathematics, botany, and astronomy then doing war work in Washington, William F. Friedman organized a group to work on the problem. Unfortunately, by the time they had, working after hours, completed the task of transcribing the text into symbols that tabulating machines could process, the war was over and the group disbanded.

Their preliminary results had the effect of deepening the mystery. For they found that words and groups of words repeat *more* often in the manuscript than in ordinary language. This fact alone differentiates the manuscript from all other cryptograms, for all known cipher systems seek to suppress repetitions, not to intensify them.

What causes this difference? Friedman thinks that the manuscript represents a text in an artificial language that has divided all existence into categories, assigned each a basic symbol, and indicated subclasses by additional symbols tacked onto the first. The first artificial language, that of the Scot George Dalgarno, was of this kind. He distributed knowledge into 17 main classes and labeled each with a consonant: for example, *K* stood for political matters, *N* for natural objects. He subdivided these into subclasses and assigned a vowel to each. Thus *Ke* was "judicial affairs," *Ku* "war." Finer divisions were represented by alternating consonants and vowels. Many other artificial languages of this type have been invented, one by Bishop John Wilkins, who wrote the first book on cryptology in English. Obviously a text in such a language would repeat its "roots" over and over while its suffixes would vary—and this phenomenon is very common in the Voynich manuscript. Friedman planned to test this hypothesis (in which the English cryptologist Brigadier John H. Tiltman concurs) on an R.C.A. 301 computer, but the work did not progress very far.

Another explanation for the great redundancy is that it reflects the many repetitions of pharmaceutical formulas that are likely to occur in an herbal or any medical tract. This is the view of the late Father Theodore C. Petersen, Ph.D., of St. Paul's College in Washington, D.C., an expert in ancient documents who made a 40-year study of the Voynich manuscript. He thought that minute variations in the shape of the characters and in their hooks and other appendages might represent the syllables of a medieval shorthand. He never did collect the statistical evidence he needed to confirm or refute this hypothesis.

Yet men have solved mysteries far more abstruse. Why hasn't anyone unriddled this? The reason, Manly said, is that "the attack has proceeded on false assumptions. We do not, in fact, know when the manuscript was written, or where, or what language lies at the basis of the encipherment. When the correct hypotheses are applied, the cipher will perhaps reveal itself as simple and easy...."

Is it, then, just a gigantic hoax, like the Cardiff giant or the Piltdown man or the fossils of Professor Beringer? Nobody involved with it seems to think so—and this includes those who have been rebuffed by it. The work is too well organized, too extensive, too homogeneous. Nothing repeats larger than a group of five words, whereas in actual hoaxes, such as the fake hieroglyphic papyri sometimes sold to tourists in Egypt, much longer phrases are repeated. Moreover, the words in the text recur, but in different combinations, just as in ordinary writing. Even if it were a hoax, there seems to be no point to having made it so long. Most critically, the medieval quasi-science that was seeking the philosopher's stone and the elixir of life while the manuscript was being written was too credulous to entertain the concept of a hoax.

Voynich died in 1930. His wife, Ethel, kept the manuscript in a safe-deposit box at the Guaranty Trust Company in New York for 30 years, until her death in 1960, aged 96.* Her estate sold it to Kraus. He priced it at $160,000 because he believes that the manuscript contains information that could provide new insights into the record of man. "The moment someone can read it," he says, "this book is worth a million dollars." Others do not think so. They contest the attribution to Bacon, observing that the manuscript

---

* Mrs. Voynich deserves a footnote. Her novel, *The Gadfly*, has sold more than 2,500,000 copies in translation in the Soviet Union, where critics revere her as one of the all-time greats in English fiction. The patriotic romance, a best-seller when it was published in England in 1897, is read by most Russian schoolchildren, forms the subject of Soviet doctoral theses, and has been made into a movie and an opera. The Russians think so highly of it that they paid Mrs. Voynich one of the very few royalty fees they ever gave to an American.

looks much more like a 16th- than a 13th-century work. They feel, as did an American foundation that turned down Friedman's application for funds to attack it, that it contains nothing new, that it may be, after all, only some kind of fanciful herbal.

But no one yet knows, and the book lies quietly inside its slipcase in the blackness of Kraus' vault, possibly a time bomb in the history of science, awaiting the man who can interpret what is still the most mysterious manuscript in the world.

24

THE PATHOLOGY OF CRYPTOLOGY

SICKNESS APPEARS IN CRYPTOLOGY as cryptanalytic hyperactivity. Its victims overcryptanalyze documents, and they bring forth invalid solutions. A case in point is William R. Newbold's "solution" of the Voynich manuscript. It is not necessary, however, that the cryptic text be patent, that it be, in other words, a cryptogram. The text subjected to the excessive cryptanalysis may be a steganogram, which conceals the presence of the real, the secret message beneath an innocent cover-text. Steganography opens a much wider field of search for those seeking documents on which to vent their excessive cryptologic energies, for they may postulate that any text contains a hidden communication beneath a dissembling surface. The literary excellence of the outer text will then only attest to the superiority of the steganography; the less suspicious the outer text by virtue of its literary qualities, the better the steganogram. And, indeed, those who suffer from the most virulent form of this mania attack what on this basis would be the greatest steganogram of all time—the plays of William Shakespeare, seeking to draw forth solutions demonstrating that the real author was Francis Bacon.

They are not entirely without cryptologic warrant. Just as systems of cryptography have transmitted valid messages despite abuses like Newbold's, so systems of steganography have preserved legitimate messages beneath an innocent camouflage. Among these are steganograms of authorship. In 1897, the eminent philologist Walter W. Skeat was editing *The Testament of Love*, which had been attributed to Chaucer in its only known copy, a printing of 1532, when he noticed that the initial letters of the various chapters were intended to form an acrostic. With some emendation, they spelled out *Margarete of Vitrw, have merci on thin*[e]—*Usk*—indicating as some other scholars had suggested, that the real author was not Chaucer but Thomas Usk. Other cases are known, probably the earliest of which is in cuneiform— the only case in which a cuneiform author gives his name. The most famous authorship steganogram involves the famous *Hypnerotomachia Poliphili*, published by Aldus Manutius at Venice in 1499 with no author listed. It is regarded as one of the most beautiful books ever printed, and its typeface has inspired many of the ones used today. The title is made up of five Greek roots and has been translated as "The Strife of Love in a Dream." As early as 1512, however, readers discovered that the first letters of the 38 chapters spelled out *Poliam frater Franciscus Columna peramavit* ("Brother Francesco Colonna passionately loves Polia"). Colonna was a Dominican monk, still alive when the book was published, and the reason for the secrecy was clear. Polia is still unknown.

It was thus perfectly possible for Francis Bacon to have used steganography to simultaneously conceal and reveal his authorship of the Shakespeare works. The question is, Did he?

The first to assert that he did was one of America's most colorful political figures, a round-faced man of great wit, ability as a public speaker, and personal popularity. Ignatius Donnelly became lieutenant governor of Minnesota at 28, and, four years later, in 1863, began the first of three terms in the House of Representatives. A political quarrel there blocked a fourth nomination. He quit the Republican party and, his radical reforming proclivities coming to the fore, became a Granger and a Greenbacker and won repeated election to the State Senate. But in 1878, following his rejection by the voters in a contest for Congress, he espoused two theories of pseudo science—the existence of Atlantis and the devastating prehistoric collision of the earth with a comet. At the same time, having chanced across a description of a steganographic system by Francis Bacon in a book belonging to one of his children, *Every Boy's Book*, and apparently having heard of the new theory that attributed Shakespeare's plays to Bacon, he determined that in the winter of 1878–79 "I will reread the Shakespeare plays, not, as heretofore, for the delight which they would give me, but with my eyes directed to discover whether there is or is not in them any indication of a cipher.... The things to be on the lookout for in my reading were the words *Francis, Bacon, Nicholas* [father of Francis], and such combinations of *Shake* and *Speare* or *Shakes* and *peer* as would make the word *Shakespeare*."

This search served as a recreation during Donnelly's more serious work of supporting his family by his pen. In 1882 there appeared *Atlantis: The Antedeluvian World*. With enormous and wide-ranging but undisciplined erudition, Donnelly gave Plato's legend of the lost continent coherent form for the first time. He regarded it as the actual Garden of Eden. As evidence for its existence, he marshalled similarities in flood myths, pyramid-building, knowledge of embalming, and a 365-day calendar between the civilizations of ancient Egypt and of the Aztecs and Mayans in the New World. The book was an immense success. Within eight years, it had gone through 23 editions in the United States and 27 in England (and in the 1960s a paperback publisher issued it anew). It brought Donnelly his first secure and comfortable income, and made him probably the most discussed literary figure outside of professional and intellectual circles. The following year he offered *Ragnarök: The Age of Fire and Gravel*. This volume, a predecessor of Immanuel Velikovsky's controversial *Worlds in Collision* of 1950, argued that earth had collided with a mighty comet in its infancy. The stories of Sodom and Gomorrah and Joshua's commanding the sun to stand to still, together with race-memories of similar events in other cultures, testified to this catastrophe, Donnelly said. *Ragnarök* (whose title was taken from an Old Norse term for "doom of the gods") also sold well.

Even while writing it, however, Donnelly was quoting in his diary for September 23, 1882: "I have been working ... at what I think is a great discovery I have made, to wit: a cypher in Shakespeare's Plays ... asserting Francis Bacon's authorship of the plays ... I am certain there is a cypher there, and I think I have the key; all this cannot be accident." A year later the solution of this cipher had become his consuming passion: "I think about it all day and dream about it all night; it is hideously complicated and perplexing." By May, 1884, its calculations had wearied him, and he turned with relief to the composition of the book that was to be his magnum opus, *The Great Cryptogram*.

In September of that year, when he was running again for Congress, an acquaintance broke the news that Donnelly had found a cipher in Shakespeare. It stirred up some interest, but it did not win the election for him. Nevertheless, he continued his political activities side by side with his cryptologic. In 1887, the year that he won election to the State Legislature on the Farmers' Alliance ticket, Joseph Pulitzer's New York *World* sent a professor of mathematics to Donnelly's home in Nininger City, Minnesota, to examine the cipher system, which involved a great deal of arithmetic. On August 28 the newspaper splashed the professor's favorable appraisal on its front page. During the winter, Donnelly worked from 10 a.m. to 11 p.m. to complete the book, called it "a terrible task," and finished the last page with "an infinite sense of relief."

What had he discovered? He found, as he had expected he would, a narrative revealing that *Skaks't spur never writ a word of them* and *It is even thought here that your cousin of St. Albans* [Bacon was Viscount of St. Albans] *writes them*. "Them" referred, of course, to the plays. Some of the decipherment was in the third person; why, Donnelly never explained. How had he discovered all this?

He had begun by misapprehending Bacon's cipher. Based upon this, he had sought an interrelationship of numbers that would locate the words of the hidden message in the open message of the plays by their serial position on the page or in an act. In its simplest form, the system would, for example, find that the 17th, 18th, 19th, and 20th words on pages 17, 18, 19, and 20 spelled out "I, Bacon, wrote this." After beginning with a fruitless search in a modern edition of the plays—as if Bacon, in addition to his other talents, foresaw the exact pagination to be used 200 years after his death—Donnelly woke up and turned to a facsimile of the famous First Folio of Shakespeare's plays, published in 1623, three years before Bacon died.

At last he began to get results. They were not simple. Nor were they as straightforward as the fictitious example above. By some reasoning that he never set forth, Donnelly settled upon 505, 506, 513, 516, and 523 as "root-numbers." From these he subtracted "modifiers," or sometimes "multipliers"; from the differences he deducted the number of italic words on a page, sometimes counting stage directions, sometimes not; these results were altered by the addition or subtraction of the number of hyphenated and bracketed words—although he confesses that "we sometimes counted in the bracketed and additional hyphenated words ... and sometimes we did not." The final figure showed the position of the plaintext word on the page—then the page itself varied, and sometimes the first column was selected, sometimes the second, and occasionally counting began at the beginning of a scene instead of the page, and occasionally at the bottom of the page. Donnelly neglected to say why he chose one alternative over another, though he did set out his computations in impressive detail:

computations	word number	page and column	plaintext
$516-167 = 349-22b$ & $h = 327-30 =$ $297-254 = 43-15b$ & $h = 28$	28	75:2	Shak'st
$516-167 = 349-22b$ & $h = 327-248 = 79.$ $193-79 = 114+1 = 115+b$ & $h = (121)$	(121)	75:1	spur
$516-167-349-22b$ & $h = 327-254 = 73-$ $15b$ & $h = 58.$ $498-58 = 440+1 = 441$	441	76:1	never

The "b & h" means that he is counting bracketed and hyphenated words. Donnelly does not explain the mid-course changes after the periods in the computations for "spur" and "never," nor the sudden backwards counting of "(121)." The First Folio pages the Comedies, Histories, and Tragedies separately, and Donnelly's figures refer to the pages of the Histories in the Staunton reproduction.

Donnelly's book, *The Great Cryptogram*, consisted of "deciphered" passages accompanied by their derivations and interspersed with polemics defending the method and setting the hidden story in perspective. The publisher, R. S. Peale and Company of Chicago, brought in a special printer to set up crucial portions of the book without seeing the rest. But Peale had a premonition of what was in store when he encountered an unexpected resistance to the anti-Shakespeare idea as he sought prepublication subscriptions in England. He set the first edition at 12,000 copies. But despite the reputation of the author, the book flopped. Hostile reviews battered it. Readers found the demonstration of the cipher confusing, and the book as a whole lacked flow. Worst, the cipher itself suffered crippling blows.

At one point, after deciphering the names Cecil (as *seas-ill*), Marlowe (as *More-low*), and Shakespeare (as *Shak'st-spur*), Donnelly had asked: "Are there four other columns, on three other consecutive pages, in the world, where six such significant words can be discovered? And, if there are, is it possible to combine them as in the foregoing instances, not only by the same root-number, but by the same modification of the same root-number? If

The Pathology of Cryptology

you can indeed do this in a text where no cipher has been placed, then the age of miracles is not yet past."

Another Minnesotan, Joseph Gilpin Pyle, promptly demonstrated that it was not. He parodied both the title and the method of *The Great Cryptogram* in his own *The Little Cryptogram*, in which he extracted by a similar method the following message from *Hamlet*: *Don nill he* [Donnelly], *the author, politician, and mountebanke, will worke out the secret of this play. The Sage* [of Nininger, Donnelly's sobriquet] *is a daysie.* In some respects his calculations were much simpler than his subject's: *Don* was simply 523 minus 273, making the 250th word on page 273, column 2. Pyle was seconded in a

Some of Ignatius Donnelly's calculations

devastating work by the Reverend A. Nicholson, who in a cruel coincidence happened to be the incumbent clergyman at Bacon's own home of St. Albans. In a brilliant refutation, Nicholson used Donnelly's own root of 516 on the very pages in which Donnelly first glimpsed his solution to produce a "decipherment" diametrically opposed to Donnelly's: *Master Will I am Shak'st spurre writ the play and was engaged at the Curtain.* One computation ran: $516 - 167 = 349 - 22b$ & $h = 327 - 163 = 164 - 50 = 114 - 1h = 113$, pointing to the 113th word on page 76, column 2, which was "*Will.*" Nicholson clinched his demonstration by producing the same text four times from Donnelly's four other root-numbers. It became evident to all but Donnelly that Pyle and Nicholson had merely done consciously what Donnelly had done subconsciously: selected the words of the hidden message, then found the figures and arithmetic that supported them.

Donnelly, unbowed, went to Europe to lecture on his decipherment. At the University Union at Oxford, where he debated a Shakespearean, a poll of the audience routed him, 167 to 27. Criticism grew increasingly harsh, and when he returned after five months, Peale told him that the book was dead. Donnelly refused to believe it, kept the controversy alive in letters to editors, and had the Pinkerton Agency check on Peale's records. Eventually the publisher sued him for $4,000 in advance royalties that had not been earned. To settle, Donnelly traded the publisher lots in St. Paul for the plates for the book. "I will . . . put them in my garden, and build a little house to cover them," he wrote pathetically in his diary on December 22, 1892. "The little building will be my monument of colossal failure. Every time I look at it, I shall think of wrecked hopes and ruined ambitions."

He was unusually depressed because he had just lost an election for governor on the Populist ticket, for which he had, that summer, written a ringing platform that became the creed of this third party and foreshadowed many modern reforms. Nevertheless, he soon rebounded and continued his fight for the underdog. He had, interestingly, depicted Bacon in his decipherment somewhat as he visualized himself—a courageous, honest, struggling politician victimized by greedy, corrupt officeseekers. Donnelly never lost his own faith in his Baconian revelations, and he continued to labor at the cipher. In 1899 he privately published *The Cipher in the Plays and on the Tombstone*. It passed directly into limbo. His political fortunes followed it the next year, when the Populists, who had nominated him for Vice President, smothered in the McKinley victory. On January 1, 1901, the first day of the twentieth century, Donnelly died.

Of Donnelly's "system" it may be remarked that nothing like it has appeared in cryptology before or since. And with good reason, for the system is no system at all; there is neither rhyme nor reason to the choice of numbers that lead to the result. It may also be remarked that, in an open-code system, the hidden message controls the cover-text, which is merely a function of the hidden plaintext. Donnelly, though he worked only on a few pages of the two parts of *Henry IV*, therefore presupposed that the magnificent language of the plays all resulted merely from the inner workings of a cipher. Did Falstaff, marvelous Falstaff, exist so exuberantly only to make sure that Bacon would have the right words for an open code? The thought is hard to bear.

Donnelly's murder of logic, like the slaying of Banquo, started a line of phantoms that threatens to stretch out to the crack of doom. Among the Baconians, these apparitions are "ciphers" that are not really ciphers. Likewise, the technique of descrying them is not really cryptanalysis, and the results are not solutions or decipherments. They are the deliriums, the hallucinations of a sick cryptology. The suggestion to call this whole area "enigmatology" comes from a Baconian; and it is a good one, for it will prevent using the terms of cryptology for noncryptology, will prevent calling a "cipher" that which is not a cipher. On this basis, then, a Baconian "cipher system" would be an "enigmaplan," the verb for its obscuration would be "enigmalyze," and the result would be an "enigmaduction"—a term every bit as graceful, as purebred, and as well constructed as that which it denotes.

The more important of these enigmaplans have come under the cool scrutiny of the Friedmans in *The Shakespearean Ciphers Examined* (a nice anapestic trimeter of a publisher's title which they dislike because it implies that ciphers exist in Shakespeare). In its uncondensed form, this book won the Folger Shakespeare Library Literature Prize of $1,000 in 1955. The Friedmans pointed out that, unlike, say, a professor of English, they had "no professional or emotional stake in any particular claim to the authorship of Shakespeare's plays" and that the anti-Shakespearean "claims based on cryptography can be scientifically examined, and proved or disproved." They say that they will accept as valid any cipher that fulfills two conditions: that its plaintext make sense, and that this plaintext be unique and unambiguous—that, in other words, it not be one of several possible results. So saying, they set out to see if anyone had discovered valid cryptologic proof that Non-Shakespeare wrote Shakespeare.

They find no such proof. But they have a fascinating trip. They pass through a surrealist landscape where logic and the events of history both resemble and do not resemble the real things, like the oozing watch of Salvador Dali, where supermen of literature outperform the most harried of hacks in volume and the most thoughtful of philosophers in profundity—and then sit up nights enciphering secret messages to tell about it, where enigmatologists frantically nail together wild tottering structures upon the quicksands of conjecture. Though sometimes reviled by the natives, the Friedmans never lose their composure. As guides, they are wise, courteous, and quite entertaining.

They introduce their readers to Orville Ward Owen, a Detroit physician. His basic tool was a "cipher wheel," which consisted of 1,000 pages of Elizabethan writing glued onto 1,000 feet of canvas wound on two giant spools. With its help, he enigmalyzed from those pages an autobiography in which Francis Bacon revealed that he was the natural son of Queen Elizabeth and Robert Dudley, Earl of Leicester, and had written not only the works of Shakespeare but those of Christopher Marlowe, Edmund Spenser, Robert Burton (*Anatomy of Melancholy* only), George Peele, and Robert Greene. Indeed, he had done so primarily to conceal the story that Owen laid bare. Owen's enigmaplan depended upon four key words, FORTUNE, HONOR, NATURE, and REPUTATION. The Friedmans summarized its rules as: "first find one of your key words (or one of its various derivatives); then look for a suitable text somewhere near the place where it occurs; and if you find one which fits into the story as you want it to be, there you are—another triumph of decipherment." That Owen drew one enigmaduction from a translation prepared 22 years after Bacon's death only confirmed the immortality of the Lord Chancellor's genius. Owen learned that Bacon left the original manuscripts of the plays in a set of iron boxes on the grounds of Chepstow Castle in England. He went there and excavated, shifting his spot several times as the enigmaplan issued varying instructions. No manuscripts were found.

Some Baconians claim to have discovered "cipher signatures" of their hero in the Shakespeare plays. Walter Conrad Arensberg, a wealthy Philadelphian, showed that for hundreds of years millions of readers had been blind to Bacon's authorship when he found such a signature in Polonius' famous advice to Laertes (*Hamlet* I. iii. 70-73):

> Costly thy habit as thy purse can buy;
> But not exprest in fancie; rich, not gawdie:
> For the Apparell oft proclaimes the man.
> And they in France of the best ranck and station, . . .

"Consider in these lines," wrote Arensberg, "the following acrostic letters:

> Co
> B
> F
> An

Read: F. Bacon."

The Friedmans refuted this sort of nonsense by painstakingly counting the initial letters of 20,000 lines of the First Folio. They calculated that chance would assemble the letters b, a, c, o, and n in that order only 0.0244 times in the approximately 100,000 lines of the First Folio. Significantly, Arensberg did not find any such straight acrostic. Instead, he had to widen his field to include second letters, such variants as "Baco" and "F. Baco," and anagrammed forms of these. This promptly brought the pure-chance probabilities well within the range of the First Folio—and it is these that Arensberg "discovered." If a die turns up a deuce 1,000 times out of 6,000 throws, can this prove more than that what will probably happen has indeed happened?

In their discussion of William Stone Booth's "string cipher" (which, incidentally, bears no relation to the string cipher for which it was named), the Friedmans pointed out time and again how the enigmatologists stretch, ignore, or break their own rules when these stand in the way of a needed enigmaduction. They cast a skeptical eye upon the many anagrams of the longest word in Shakespeare, found in the Clown's remark (*Love's Labour's Lost* V. i), "I marvell thy M[aster]. hath not eaten thee for a word, for thou art not so long by the head as honorificabilitudinitatibus: Thou art easier swallowed then a flapdragon." Sir Edwin Durning-Lawrence enigmalyzed it to the Latin *Hi lu-di F Ba-co-nis na-ti tui-ti or-bi* ("These plays, F. Bacon's offspring, are preserved for the world"). The Friedmans proved these offspring to be illegitimate by citing a quantity of other, equally valid anagrams of this word, one of which, by its very presence, hints that Dante, who died two hundred years before Shakespeare was born, may have rather literally ghost-written the Bard's plays: *Ubi Italicus ibi Danti honor fit* ("Where there is an Italian, there honor is paid to Dante").

Some of the gayest moments in cryptology come when the Friedmans disprove some enigmaplans by showing that they are so loosely constructed that they can render multiple enigmaductions. In the poem "To the Reader" underneath the famous Droeshout portrait of Shakespeare in the First Folio, one Edward D. Johnson saw a symmetrical diagram of 22 letters that when rearranged spelled, for him, the 25-letter ejaculation *Fr Bacon author author author*. The triple repetition must have bolstered his confidence, for he issued a challenge: "If after checking the signatures ... the reader is still of the opinion that they are all accidental, the writer would ask him to try a small experiment. Let him take from any book, ancient or modern, 20 consecutive lines of prose or poetry, place the letters in a Table, and then try to see if he can make up any word out of the letters the same distance apart in the text in the form of a chain."

The Friedmans found it "hard to resist this courteous request. We decided to use the text of one of Johnson's own examples; and the poem 'To the Reader' divulged the message 'No kidding, Francis Bacon: *I* wrote these plaies!—Shakespeare.' ... Our message is nearly twice the length of Johnson's; it is a complete sentence; and it uses each letter of the diagram once and only once. But the disadvantage of this 'method' comes out very clearly here. Since our chosen letters do not have to 'appear' in their correct 'order' (i.e., we can arrange them any way we please), there may be several alternative 'messages' to choose from: amongst them, one (giving a very different sense to the pattern) runs: 'No kidding! I, Francis Bacon, wrote these Shakespeare plaies.' This alone is enough to show that Johnson's method is worthless as a piece of cryptography."

Indeed it is. Virtually all the Baconian enigmaplans suffer from the grave weakness of multiple answers, as the Friedmans amply demonstrate. This fault instantly vitiates any alleged method of secret communication. For such a method, though intended to be secret, is first and foremost a method of communication. Of what value is it if the encipherer can never be sure that the message he puts in will be the one the decipherer will get out? If Walter Raleigh inserted into *Julius Caesar* a message beginning *Dear Reader: The Asse Will Shakespeare brought William Hatton down to his grave* to prove Bacon's authorship, as the economist Wallace McC. Cunningham asserted he did, and the Friedmans, attempting to extract it by the rather vague rules that Cunningham said Raleigh used, read instead *Dear Reader: Theodore Roosevelt is the true author of this play ... Friedman can prove that this is so by this cock-eyed cypher*, what good did all of Raleigh's work do?

Practical considerations such as that rarely trouble the Baconians. Nor do they often deign to answer these criticisms. When they do, their defense usually resembles a remark that Arensberg made. The Friedmans had just used his enigmaplan to enigmalyze *The author was William F. Friedman* from one of Arensberg's own books to show him the invalidity of it all. Replied he with equanimity: "What you have done does not disprove the presence of the sentence *The author was Francis Bacon* which I found in *The Tempest*." But the sentence is not present in *The Tempest*. Arensberg imposed it upon the thousands of letters that make up the play. It is like looking up at the hundreds of stars in the night sky and projecting upon a few neighboring ones the image of some mythic hero or animal. Orion and Pegasus exist only in the mind of the beholder, as does Arensberg's sentence. The proof is that other minds, like the Friedmans', may organize other patterns.

Enigmatology resembles nothing so much as the Rorschach tests given by psychologists, in which a subject tells what he sees in an ink blot. The blot is formless, of course, and so anything that the subject reports can come only from within himself. The test thus discloses a great deal to the psychologist. To the enigmatologists, the Shakespearean plays may serve as a kind of literary Rorschach—and the snobbery and the fantasies of incest and adultery that appear in many enigmaductions may themselves be revelatory. This may partly explain the great emotional involvement of Baconians in their theories. Certain it is that to think that these mental pictures, whether inspired by ink blots or stars or letters, exist in external reality is to be out of touch with that particular area of reality.

One system of steganography, and one alone, of all those applied by the Baconians to the First Folio, is valid. It has a special attraction, for it was invented by Francis Bacon himself "in our youth, when we were at *Paris*," or some time between the ages of 15 and 18 during his service under the English ambassador from 1576 to 1579.

He alluded to it in 1605 in his *Of the proficience and advancement of Learning, divine and humane*. In discussing "cyphars," he wrote, in a statement that has become classic in cryptology, that "the vertues of them, whereby they are to be preferred, are three; that they be not laborious to write and read; that they bee impossible to discypher; and in some cases, that they bee without suspition. The highest Degree whereof, is to write OMNIA PER OMNIA [anything by anything]; which is undoubtedly possible, with a proportion Quintuple at most, of the writing infoulding, to the writing infoulded, and no other restrainte whatsoever." He did not expand this ellipsis until the publication, in 1623, of *De Augmentis Scientarum*, an enlarged Latin version of the *Advancement*. This influential volume, whose classification of the sciences shaped man's view of human knowledge for nearly two centuries, subsumed "ciphers" under writing, which he considered a branch of grammar, which in turn formed "the organ" of the "traditive doctrine, which takes in all the arts relating to words and discourse." From here Bacon ascended the epistemo-

The Pathology of Cryptology 883

logical ladder via rungs of logic, faculties of the soul, human philosophy, knowledge of man, and philosophy to encompass at last all learning. At 62, he felt his own system "a thing that yet seemeth to us not worthy to be lost" and so gave it place in this grand design.

He began by replacing the 24 letters of his alphabet (Bacon naturally used both *i* and *j* and *u* and *v* interchangeably) by permutations of two symbols, A and B, taken five at a time:

a AAAAA	e AABAA	i ABAAA	n ABBAA	r BAAAA	w BABAA
b AAAAB	f AABAB	k ABAAB	o ABBAB	s BAAAB	x BABAB
c AAABA	g AABBA	l ABABA	p ABBBA	t BAABA	y BABBA
d AAABB	h AABBB	m ABABB	q ABBBB	v BAABB	z BABBB

Thus *but* becomes AAAAB BAABB BAABA. He needed five places because two things taken five at a time produce 2^5 or 32 permutations, whereas taken four at a time they yield 2^4 or only 16, too few for all the letters. Modern terminology would call this a quinquiliteral binary alphabet, and modern notation would replace the A's and B's by 0's and 1's, so that *d* would be 00011, but Bacon called it "bi-literal," and the name has stuck. He went on: "Neither is it a small matter these *Cypher-Characters* have, and may performe: For by this *Art* a way is opened, whereby a man may expresse and signifie the intentions of his minde, at any distance of place, by objects which may be presented to the eye, and accommodated to the eare: provided those objects be capable of a twofold difference onely; as by Bells, by Trumpets, by Lights and Torches, by the report of Muskets, and any instruments of like nature." The raising of a torch could signify A, its lowering B. The teletypewriter utilizes Bacon's binary principle by sending five marks or spaces within a given time to represent a letter (though its equivalents differ from his).

The conversion of a message to biliteral form is only the first step in Bacon's scheme to write "without suspition." This scheme requires a cover-text. Now, among the objects "capable of two differences" are faces of printing type. These come not just in two but in scores of different styles, usually named for their designers, as Caslon, Baskerville, Bodoni, Garamond, each with its roman and its italic. Bacon's system can be most clearly illustrated however, by using the roman and the italic forms of the present typeface as if they were different faces. The A's of the hidden message become roman letters in the cover-text, and the B's of the hidden message become italic letters in the cover-text. Thus, the cover-text "Do not go till I come" would represent the hidden message *fly*, which is AABAB ABABA BABBA, by setting the D and the O in roman, the N in italic, the O in roman again, the T in italic, and so on, like this:

A A   BAB   AB   ABAB   A   BB A -
Do   *not*   go   t*il*l   I   *come*

The cover-text says exactly the opposite of the hidden message; it is, of course, entirely independent of it, and this is what Bacon means when he refers to writing "omnia per omnia," or anything by anything.

This example is not very subtle because of the obvious difference between the roman and italic type styles. Bacon's original suggestion was, however, not to use two strongly contrasting forms of the same typeface, but to use two separate typefaces with only slight differences between them, one face for the A's, the other for the B's. If these two resemble one another as closely as do, for example, Caslon and Baskerville, the ordinary reader might never even suspect the presence of the two. The decipherer, of course, would have to observe some very fine differences in the shading and curvature and dimensions of, say, the lowercase *r*'s in the two faces so that he will be able to distinguish the A *r* from the B *r*.

One of Francis Bacon's own examples of his biliteral cipher, in which plaintext Fuge *("Flee") is concealed under covertext* MANERE TE VOLO DONEC VENERO *("Stay till I come to you"). Note the difference between the A-form and the B-form e's in Manere.*

Yet the procedure is valid. If the encipherer prevails upon a friendly, patient printer to set type following copy suitably marked, the message that he inserts will be the one that the decipherer extracts. There will be no ambiguities, no looseness, no multiplicity of decipherments. What is commonly called the "Bacon biliteral cipher" is therefore in no way an enigma-plan, but a true system of steganography, and an exceedingly clever and useful one at that. Technically, a message in it would fall into the category of the semagram, for its substitutes are not really the letters of the cover-text but the forms or shapes of those letters.

It was only natural that Baconians should turn to their hero's own system in an attempt to prove their case. The first enigmaduction based on it to see print applied it, not, however, to the First Folio but to an "uncouth mixture of large and small letters" that uncertain tradition records as the inscription of the original Shakespeare tombstone at Stratford. The carving of the epitaph seemed made to order for the Baconian biliteral:

> Good Frend for Iesus SAKE forbeare
>
> To diGG TE Dust Enclo-Ased HE.RE.
>
> Blese be TE Man Ƹ spares TEs Stones
>
> And curst be He Ƹ moves my Bones.

In 1887, Hugh Black took the lowercase letters as A-forms and the uppercase as B-forms. Regarding the G's of diGG as lowercase and the TY as a single capital, he produced *saehrbayeeprftaxarawar*. "To an ordinary person," commented the Friedmans, "the resultant message would be enough to prove that there is no cipher being used. The difference between the ordinary person and the Baconian is, shall we say, one of degrees of persistence and ingenuity." Black arranged his text in a special formation, drew a line to divide it into two parts, anagrammed one part into *Shaxpeare* and the other into *Fra Ba wrt ear ay*, and confidently interpreted the latter to mean "Francis Bacon wrote Shakespeare's plays."

Black's work was emended and expanded by one Edgar Gordon Clark. He enigmalyzed *Fra Ba wryt ear. AA! Shaxpere* and *Fra Ba wrt ear. HzQ AyA! Shaxpere* out of the tombstone. These, to him, meant "Francis Bacon wrote here. Aye Aye! Shakespeare" and "Francis Bacon wrote here. His cue. Aye Aye! Shakespeare." Among the many other tombstone enigmatologists was Ignatius Donnelly, who had so thoroughly misconstrued the biliteral early in his Baconian career that he turned it into his number cipher, but later learned enough so that he could mismanage it. Taking advantage of a "double-back-action quality" that Bacon, the inventor of the system, had neglected to mention, repeating some groups and omitting others, and anagramming, he cheated his way to a superb proof of Baconian authorship. And there have been others, equally valid.

In 1899, the same year that Donnelly's effort appeared, there was published the first report of a Baconian cipher message hidden in the way that Bacon himself had suggested—in printed books. This was *The Bi-literal Cypher of Sir Francis Bacon Discovered in his Works and Deciphered by Mrs. Elizabeth Wells Gallup*. A Michigan high school principal, then 51, Mrs. Gallup was an honest, gentle, religious woman who had studied at the Sorbonne and at the University of Marburg. Bacon interested her and Dr. Owen's "word cipher" attracted her and she worked with him on it. She evidently accepted his results, for her own paralleled them, but rejected his method, for she began her own search for a message based on the biliteral cipher.

Struck by the variations of type used to set the First Folio, she studied the printing with a magnifying glass to see if these differences represented Bacon's use of the biliteral cipher. Since the differences are sharpest in the italic letters, she tried first to decipher the Prologue to *Troilus and Cressida*, which is almost entirely in italic in the First Folio. Slowly and painstakingly, she drew from that page and from others bits and pieces of a sensational life story of Bacon quite similar to the biography enigmalyzed by Owen, and soon found that it was continued, also in biliteral form, in the books of Marlowe, Jonson, Spenser, Burton, Peele, and Greene, all of whom served, as in Owen's work, as masks for Bacon. The tale skipped about from place to place; a sentence broken off in one book resumed in another; and the substance repeated over and over again, as if Bacon were making sure that at least one message would be found.

Mrs. Gallup found the nub of the story in the "Catalogue," or table of contents, of the First Folio:

> Queene Elizabeth is my true mother, and I am the lawfull heire to the throne. Finde the Cypher storie my bookes contain; it tells great secrets, every one of which, if imparted openly, would forfeit my life.   F. Bacon.

Bacon's father was Robert Dudley, the Earl of Leicester, Mrs. Gallup discovered, and she drew forth a hair-raising tale of how Elizabeth, "unwilling in th' seventh month to proclaim herself a woman wedded and pregnante," gave birth to the unwanted child whom she later entrusted to Nicholas Bacon for upbringing: ". . . she who bore me, even in the hour of my unwelcom'd coming, outraging every instinct of a naturall woman, in the pangs and perills of her travail cherisht one infernal purpose. 'Kill, kill,' cried this madden'd woman, 'kill.' "

The publication of the book stirred great interest, as do nearly all reports of new "proofs" of Baconian authorship of Shakespeare. A second edition appeared in 1900 and a third in 1902. Mrs. Gallup was berated; she replied mildly. The most sensible statement in the uproar was that the Baconian controversy had been shifted to new ground. In 1907 she sailed for England to look for manuscripts that her readings told her were in Canonbury Tower in London, where Bacon once lived, or in his country home at Gorhambury. But the first was reconstructed, the second in ruins and, no more than Dr. Owen, who was digging at the same time, did she find any manuscripts.

After her return to the United States a few years later, she was hired by George Fabyan to work at his Riverbank Laboratories in Geneva, Illinois, and "decipher" the manuscripts there, with the assistance of a staff and photographic equipment for enlarging the letters of the First Folio. The wealthy Fabyan hoped to be revered as a literary pioneer after the expected Baconian victory; he had financed Owen's excavations and had been introduced to Mrs. Gallup by a mutual friend. In his campaign to "sell" her work to the academic world, he invited prominent scholars to Riverbank at his expense, fed, housed, and entertained them at his villa, treated them on their first day to a well-organized lantern-slide lecture on the biliteral cipher, urged them to observe the staff at work and to talk with Mrs. Gallup, and reiterated the need to keep an open mind. Mrs. Gallup remained at Riverbank until a few years before her death in 1934 at 87; during all those years she never produced another "decipherment."

The Laboratories' staff members were told, however, that she was working on Bacon's *New Atlantis*. Among her assistants was William F. Friedman. Though head of the Riverbank Department of Genetics, he helped make the photographic enlargements. Instead of clarifying the slight differences between the A and B forms of the letters, however, the enlargements obscured them, because many proved to be the result of damaged type, imperfections in the paper, poor presswork, or ink-spread around the actual printed letter.

Nevertheless, the work went on. Elizebeth Smith, the future Mrs. Friedman, collated the A and B assignments of the other workers on the basis of a tally and attempted to read the secret message. When, as invariably happened, she failed to get more than a word or two, she brought the text to Mrs. Gallup, who produced extensive readings with little apparent effort. When Miss Smith would say, "But you must have changed some of the assignments," Mrs. Gallup would point out that the group had missed the position of the dot over an *i* or some similar minutia. Miss Smith, who at first admired Mrs. Gallup's acute facility in extracting intelligence from what she herself could see only as gibberish, found her admiration turning to "uneasy questioning, and then to agonizing doubt, and then to downright disbelief. I can state categorically that neither I nor any other one of the industrious research workers at Riverbank ever succeeded in extracting a single long sentence of a hidden message; nor did one of us so much as reproduce, independently, a single complete sentence which Mrs. Gallup had already deciphered and published."

This tells heavily against the Gallup results. If the biliteral cipher were present, all decipherers should be able to obtain the same message. That her results were at least partially subjective she conceded in her admission that "I sometimes think inspiration" is "absolutely essential." Critics leveled objections at the use of words in her texts in senses they did not have in Bacon's time, and at such barbarous abbreviations as *adoptio*' and *ciphe*' that no one but she ever used. Her "decipherments" in general have a vague pointlessness: "Seeke the keyes untill all bee found. Turne Time into an ever present, faithfull companion, friend, guide, light, and way. For he who seeks an entrance here, must be furnished in that manner aforesaid." Was this the secret message, the primary text to which the plays, with all their soaring eloquence and profundity, were but secondary? Would Bacon have spent so much of his time enciphering this drivel, and expended so much of his cash to have a printer set it in the painstaking manner required? Would one of the most acute thinkers and most pithy of English writers (who on the Baconian theory also composed the poetry of Shakespeare) have considered such maunderings his greatest secret? No open-minded man will believe so.

Even the slight possibility that this is so is eliminated by the technical criticisms that utterly demolish the Gallup "decipherment." Dr. Fred M. Miller, a document expert of the F.B.I. whom the Friedmans had interested in the problem, pointed out that Mrs. Gallup was notoriously inconsistent in her letter assignments. For example, some of her A-form *t*'s resembled B-form *t*'s more than they do other A-form *t*'s. The Friedmans, checking up, caught her frequently adding or dropping letters of the cover-text. And finally, they found that she did not consistently "decipher" the same pieces of type the same way. Printers pick up the type of the page headings from one form and use it for other signatures; the identical type should result in identical decipherments. With bibliographical help, the Friedmans identified the lifted headings and found that more often than not (in the first 21 pages of the First Folio) Mrs. Gallup's "decipherments" of them varied.

This devastating analysis consigned her "solution" to the dustbin of enigmaduction, but it did not deny the possible existence of a biliteral cipher in the First Folio; Mrs. Gallup may simply have misread it. The Friedmans, however, assembled expert evidence to show that none does.

Experts in printing showed that the printers of the time changed authors' spellings in order to justify lines more easily; this practice would break up the even flow of the biliteral. Poor inking made letters printed from the same piece of type look as if they had been printed from different ones. Paper was dampened before printing; it often dried unevenly and shrank identical letters to different sizes. Frequently, closed letters like *a, e, o* filled with ink, obscuring differences. And Dr. Charlton Hinman, who has collated dozens of First Folios letter by letter and traced hundreds of distinctive pieces of type through their pages for his massive typographical study, *The Printing and Proofreading of the First Folio of Shakespeare*, has found that any given copy contains "large numbers of variant readings" as a result of the customary printing practice of the time. Consequently, no biliteral message would have been transmitted with absolute fidelity. His studies "have certainly revealed nothing to encourage the idea—to put it in very moderate terms—that the book contains biliteral cipher." All these points militate against any probability of its use in the First Folio.

Conclusive proof that it was in fact not used came from two experts. One was Frederick W. Goudy, one of America's most distinguished typographers. Fabyan had commissioned him in 1920 to look into the possibility of a biliteral cipher in the First Folio—and then had suppressed the report. For Goudy, himself a designer of typefaces, had measured, sketched, analyzed, and compared the letters of the First Folio, and had concluded that a multiplicity of typefaces had been used, not just the two that the biliteral required. (This finding, incidentally, accorded with the then current practices of English printing, which had fallen to a low estate.) Independently, the F.B.I.'s Dr. Miller concurred: "No characteristics were found which support the classification into two fonts, such as A-font and B-font."

It may put the Baconians into perspective to recognize that they are not the only enigmatologists. Gabriele Rossetti, the 19th-century Italian nationalist who was the father of the English poets Dante Gabriele Rossetti and Christina Rossetti, found in Dante's *Divine Comedy* a secret language in which a secret society, opposing political and ecclesiastical tyranny from the earliest times, expressed its aims and informed its members of its affairs. Professor David S. Margoliouth, who had served in England's M.I. 1(b) in World War I and should have known better, rearranged the colophons of the *Iliad* and the *Odyssey* and found two incantations to the muse which neither appear to make much sense nor add anything to the epics. Anti-Baconian Ib

Melchior fell victim to his opponents' obsession and enigmalyzed from Shakespeare's tombstone a message in alleged Elizabethan English that supposedly meant, "Elsinore laid wedge first Hamlet edition"; his enigmaduction enjoys the dubious prestige of being the first to have been laid low by Claude Shannon's unicity-point formula. Baconian Pierre Henrion has extended his enigmaplan to Jonathan Swift; by anagramming the nonsensical names in *Gulliver's Travels*, substituting letters, and then anagramming again, he "proves" that LEMUEL GULLIVER really means *Jonathan Svvift* and that LILLIPUT is *Novvhere*. A British artillery colonel, H. W. L. Hime, has "deciphered" a text proving that Roger Bacon invented gunpowder; unfortunately, while the most important letters of this text appear in printed versions through some errors, they do not exist in the original manuscript.

Other enigmaductions have been elicited from the Bible, Chaucer, Aristotle. Lesser minds have enigmalyzed less exalted texts. Hans Omenitsch, an anti-Semite who lived in Jackson Heights, New York, found that the Dick Tracy comic strip of April 18, 1936, concealed the plaintext *Nero mob in fog rob Leroy apt rat in it are a goy*. He had equal success with the Harold Teen comic strip and ordinary news stories in various New York dailies. He explained to a Congressman: "A criminal system of codes is operated daily in the press by the real masters of the country, who not only control the press and the politicians in power but who also control and direct the so-called red movement (international) as a sham to hide their real operations." His enigmaplan was unclear, and as for his enigmaduction, the Congressman said that "it does not mean anything to anyone."

Just as the Baconians are not the only enigmatologists, so the enigmatologists are not the only expositors of false historical and scientific theories. Science and history have their sicknesses, too. Various groups of oddballs maintain their belief in a flat earth, in a hollow earth, in dowsing rods, in the prophecies incorporated in the measurements of the Great Pyramid of Cheops, in the existence of Atlantis (it is no coincidence that Donnelly fell for both this and the Baconian theory), in flying saucers, in such medical cults as iridiagnosis, which diagnoses illnesses from the appearance of the iris. The enigmatologists form but the literary sector of this lunatic fringe. Both they and the other pseudo scientists seize upon the possible as if it were the probable, fantasize behind a mask of rationality, multiply entities beyond necessity, and refuse to test their hypotheses.

The techniques for eliciting universal truths from the Great Pyramid resemble the Baconian enigmaplans so strikingly because of these shared attitudes. For example, one Pyramid theory holds that its internal measurements embrace practically all of man's historical and scientific knowledge. Various multiplications of measurements of height, side, the length of the Grand Gallery, and so on, produce the dates for past and future events in world history. The Creation (4,004 B.C.), the Flood, Christ's birth, the Great

Tribulation before his Second Coming, all are indicated. Other combinations yield scientific truths—the distance from the earth to the sun, the earth's mean density, the mean temperature of its surface, and so on. With so many lengths possible in so complex a structure, and no strict rules to go by, it is obviously possible to juggle them to produce figures which coincide with important dates or scientific facts. Such manipulations parallel the undisciplined combining of letters in the First Folio to produce Baconian authorship proofs.

Both the Baconian and the Pyramid assertions claim to be legitimate scientific theories, but their behavior in the face of criticism or embarrassing fact strips them of such pretensions. Their proponents do not reconsider, request new tests, submit to verification. Rather, they vilify their critics, dodge, equivocate, explain away. Never do they concede that they might be wrong. When Mrs. Gallup, in a tight corner, had to read a B-form as an A-form to make sense, she summoned up a phony explanation that she never had to use in any of her previous determinations: the wrong form was deliberately inserted to confuse because "ciphers are made to hide things, not discover them." When the Friedmans knocked enigmaplans wholesale into a cocked hat, the Baconians suddenly came up with something that not one had ever mentioned: "while an Elizabethan cipher may be considered invalid by modern standards of rigid cryptography, it may well have provided its institutors with a fairly safe method of recording historical facts, or personal opinions, which they could not express without grave risk. An Elizabethan cryptogram may be suggestive rather than conclusive, and these suggestions may ultimately, by their very frequency, command assent." Not an iota of evidence exists for this, outside of the Baconian claims themselves, and it is safe to say that for every Baconian "suggestion" drawn forth, someone could, if he wanted to, extract an equivalent Shakespearean one. But it would be as idle to do so as to talk back to a phonograph. For the Baconians do not seek knowledge—they have the faith; they are not scholars, but advocates.

The situation which the enigmatologists and the other pseudo scientists exemplify almost ideally is not at all uncommon, and philosophers have examined it often. A. J. Ayer of Oxford is especially clear: "A man can always sustain his convictions in the face of apparently hostile evidence if he is prepared to make the necessary ad hoc assumptions. But although any particular instance in which a cherished hypothesis appears to be refuted can always be explained away, there must still remain the possibility that the hypothesis will ultimately be abandoned. Otherwise it is not a genuine hypothesis. For a proposition whose validity we are resolved to maintain in the face of any experience is not a hypothesis at all, but a definition."

The Baconians so maintain their view. They insist that their theory is true, but if it may be true it may also be false, and this they will not concede. For upon what evidence would they abandon their assertions? The finding of a holograph of *Hamlet*? If experience is any guide, they would say that Shakespeare copied it out at Bacon's orders. The discovery of a note by Bacon that he hated Shakespeare's plays and would have nothing to do with such claptrap? Obviously a clever trick to throw contemporaries off the trail. The Baconians cannot lose. But then they cannot claim to have won, either.

People ask, "Does it matter who wrote the Shakespeare plays? After all, it is the plays themselves that count, not who wrote them." It matters because truth matters. The Baconian error has implications far beyond the Bacon-Shakespeare question. "If one can argue that the evidence in Shakespeare's case does not mean what it says," a scholar has written, "that it has been falsified to sustain a gigantic hoax that has remained undetected for centuries, then one can just as surely argue that other evidence is not to be trusted and that, as Henry Ford said, 'history is bunk.' "

It is as pointless to try to convince the Baconians of this on rational grounds as it would be to demonstrate to an inmate of a mental hospital, with pictures of Napoleon's funeral and tomb and attested documents of Napoleon's death, that he is not Napoleon. For neither he nor the Baconians hold their views rationally. They hold them emotionally. The problem of enigmatology is, at heart, not logical but psychological. This is not to say that Baconians are psychotics—on the contrary, in non-Baconian spheres they function adequately, perhaps even outstandingly. But as Baconians they live in a fantasy world. Enigmaductions are classic instances of wishful thinking, of unconscious projection, of figments of the imagination. These results of an overactive cryptanalytic gland, these bloated growths of a chaotic imagination are like cancers on the corpus of normal codemaking and -breaking. They constitute the pathology of cryptology.

Paracryptology

25
ANCESTRAL VOICES

IN THE FALL OF THE YEAR, the staid *Journal of Hellenic Studies* issues its annual volume. Its articles examine in exhaustive detail some lesser points of Greek philology or literature—the individual bricks of scholarship that raise mankind's house of knowledge. Their prose is flat and unemotional, their titles restrained.

The volume for 1953 contained an article that in all outward forms resembled the others. Its text was a thicket of Greek verb endings and grammatical forms, its title as carefully circumscribed as the others: "Evidence for Greek Dialect in the Mycenaean Archives." Yet for many readers it evoked the ringing plains of windy Troy, the coruscating helmets and dancing horsehair plumes of Homeric heroes crowding beneath the walls and topless towers of Ilium, and ancient Crete, with its bull-dancer frescoes, its sinister labyrinth, its Minotaur, Theseus, and the House of the Double Ax.

For the article reported the decipherment of a lost writing, a script called Linear B scratched on clay tablets when Achilles and Agamemnon, Helen and Menelaus walked the earth. It was the most recent in the long series of decipherments that have given tongue to mute stones, brought to life Pharaoh and Nineveh and the panoply of ancient civilizations, allowed ancestral voices silenced for millennia to whisper across gulfs of time and space to the men of today. Some of these decipherments must rank among the noblest achievements of the human mind. For how to read the unknown writing of those long dead? How to speak the words of those whose voices murmur only in the sighing of the wind?

The solution of the problem shares some techniques with cryptanalysis. In one way the linguistic problem is easier, for there has been no deliberate attempt to conceal, but in another way it is harder, for sometimes an entire language must be reconstructed. In general, the linguistic problem involves two factors—the writing and the language. Either may be known or unknown. Four cases therefore arise.

In Case 0, both script and language are known. No problem exists: an Englishman can read English in its customary alphabet. In Case I, the language is known but not the writing. This is the simplest problem, equivalent to that of a substitution cipher. If the writing is alphabetic, the solution resembles that of a monalphabetic substitution; if syllabic, like kata kana, that of a nomenclator; if logographic, like Chinese, that of a code. In Case II, the script is known but not the language. An American who does not know Italian may be able to read aloud a newspaper article in an approximation of that language—but he will not understand what he is saying. The problem that faces the decipherer in Case II parallels the one that would face an American who wanted to teach himself Italian without any grammars or dictionaries, helped only by any pictures that might accompany the texts, by an English translation, or by a knowledge of related languages, such as French, Spanish, and Latin. Without any of these external elements, solution is probably not possible. In Case III, neither writing nor language is known. If this occurs in cultural isolation, so that neither can ever be known, no solution can ever be reached. But it has happened that although neither is known at the beginning of a study, outside information—usually a proper name known from another culture—determines the sound-values of the writing system and this, with the help of a translation or cognate languages, leads to the reconstruction of the language as well. The problem resolves into a succession of Cases I and II.

Case I solutions sometimes read like textbook explanations of elementary cryptanalysis.

In the summer of 1946, Édouard Dhorme, an eminent Orientalist who was a dean at the Sorbonne's School of Advanced Studies, undertook the study of some inscriptions dug up in Syria at Byblos, the town that gave its name to the Bible. The writing resembled hieroglyphics, but it made no sense read that way. From the location of the inscriptions and from their approximate age, Dhorme felt confident that the language underlying the approximately 100 sign-images was Phoenician. The number of signs suggested a syllabary, in which each sign would represent a syllable, like /ta/. But the usual Phoenician writing followed the Semitic trait of writing only the consonantal skeleton—"mister," "master," "muster," "mystery," and "mastery" would all be written *mstr* in the Semitic convention. Since no one knew how the words sounded, Dhorme could not hope to recover the vowels of his syllabary. But since the Phoenicians who wrote the inscriptions knew the vowels, and presumably used different signs for, say, *ta*, *ti*, and *tu*, Dhorme had to expect to find several signs for what he would know only as *t*.

These difficulties did not daunt the 65-year-old scholar, who had been made an officer of the Légion d'Honneur for cryptanalytical work in World War I and who had been one of three independent decipherers of another script in 1929. He boldly attacked the Byblos pseudo-hieroglyphics, beginning with the assumption that seven vertical marks in the lower left corner of a tablet represented a regnal date.

> I did not hesitate to give to the four signs preceding the number the value *b'šnt*, "in the years, in the year." This hypothesis had the advantage of permitting

me to ignore the appearance of the sign in determining its [sound-]value. All my work consisted of carrying forward these four letters wherever the corresponding signs were found and of filling the empty spaces with cross-checkings suggested

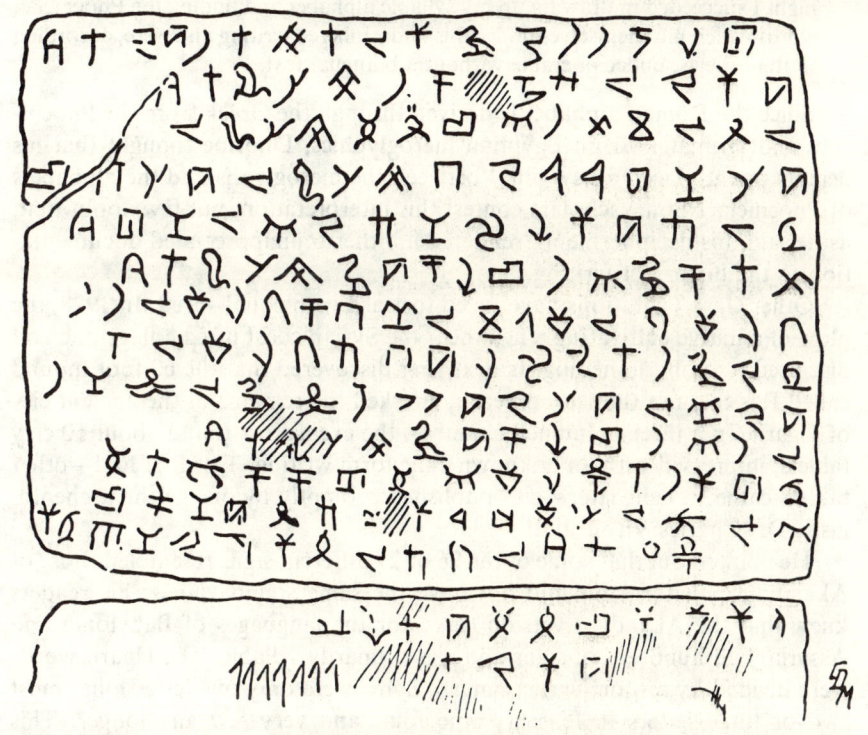

The tablet from Byblos that Édouard Dhorme used to start his solution of the pseudo-hieroglyphics

by Phoenician. In the first line of Tablet C, I found the group *n-ḥ* and, since a copper tablet was involved, I reconstituted the word *nḥš*, "copper, bronze." The *ḥ*, thus identified with the sign of the bird, gave me in lines 6 and 10 the final of a group, --*bḥ*, where I recognized the word *mzbḥ*, "altar." The *m* thus obtained, carried forward as penultimate of line 14, gave me *b'tm-*, which could only be the designation of the month "in Tammuz." I thus had a second *z* which I marked z_1. The month must have been preceded by the mention of the day. Since there was no number at all in line 14, I recognized in the group *š-š* the name of a number and I thought first of *šlš*, "three." After some fruitless trials of the consonant *l* wherever it appeared, I finally perceived that the number was not *šlš*, "three," but actually *šdš*, "six" in its primitive form. The *d* was thus added to the identified signs. The group following *šdš* could only be the word "days," in the plural like "years" in line 15, and I read this group *ymm* (*yâmîm*), which furnished me with *y* and two other *m*'s. Thus the filling in of correct solutions not only in Tablet C but also in Tablet D permitted me to obtain new values, always ignoring the form of the signs and resorting only to the suggestion of the contexts. All those who have practiced this kind of cryptography, where the pencil and the eraser are unremittingly in action, where one successively carries forward the hypothetical values to replace them with others which end by yielding place to the definitive values—these will understand by what obsessive work of day and night I succeeded in drawing up my syllabic alphabet and finding the Phoenician words which hid themselves under this undeciphered writing and were, according to the experts, undecipherable without a bilingual text.

Since the Roman alphabet is derived through the Greek from the Phoenician and ultimately from Egyptian hieroglyphics, Dhorme thought that his decipherment placed a new link "between the hieroglyphs and the alphabets of Phoenicia." Some scholars contest this interpretation, but few doubt that, as he said, his decipherment "rendered a hitherto unappreciated documentation to the history of writing."

Other Case I solutions have raced forward with equal speed. In 1928, the plow of a native cultivating a field near the Syrian coast lifted a flagstone and disclosed a tomb; archeologists next year discovered that the 60-foot mound called Ras Shamra that stood nearby marked the remains of the ancient city of Ugarit. In a three-columned chamber, the excavators found about 50 clay tablets, impressed with an unknown cuneiform writing. This first find—other tablets came to light later—was published promptly by one of the archeologists, Dr. Charles Virolleaud.

He pointed out that some of the 26 or 27 different signs resembled those of Akkadian cuneiform but did not have the same sound values; his readers knew that the Akkadian version (used for the languages of Babylonia and Assyria) had hundreds of signs and was primarily syllabic. The Ugarit words were divided by a short vertical mark. Some were only one letter long, most two or three letters in length, some four, and very few any longer. This indicated a consonantal script to Virolleaud. He did not have to add that the tablets came from a locale where Semitic languages had long predominated.

He commented that the shortest text, a six-sign inscription on four bronze ax handles, might represent the name of the owner. A fifth ax handle had the same six signs preceded by a word of four letters, which he said probably stood for "ax" or "hatchet" or "pick." He saw that a sign of three vertical wedges that preceded the probable names also appeared in the first line of one of the tablets, and he suggested in his paper that this might stand for the Semitic letter *l*, which means "to."

Virolleaud's publication came to the hands of Dr. Hans Bauer of the University of Halle on April 22, 1930. A big, heavy man and a brilliant philologist, then 52, who knew not only the Western and Near Eastern languages but those of the Far East as well, he set to work at once to try to solve them. Like Dhorme, he had had some cryptanalytic experience in World War I. His technique, in fact, depended primarily upon statistics, as do the general solutions of cryptanalysis, and only secondarily upon guessing at words for the actual reconstruction of the text—one of the few decipherments in archeological history to sustain that order of importance. It began with a study of the letters in the West Semitic languages that could appear as initials, terminals, or as one-letter words. Among other things, this showed that *m*, *k*, and *w* could appear in all three places. He correlated the list he compiled with a similar list that he made for the signs of the Ras Shamra tablets.

Based on this, he decided that two signs could represent either *w* or *m* and that two others could stand for either *n* or *t*. Then, picking up Virolleaud's possible *l*, he looked for the probable word *mlk*, "king."* He found it, and extended his decipherment by filling in other possibilities. Within five days he had recovered 20 letters. When he tested these against the four-letter word on the ax handle that Virolleaud had thought might mean "ax," he produced *grzn*, a Semitic word meaning "ax." On April 28 he reported his recoveries to the French archeologists. On June 4, he published a preliminary report in the *Vossische Zeitung* which gave the values of *t*, *r*, *n*, and *alef*, a guttural sound, and the deciphered names of the gods Ba'al, Astarte, Ashera, and El.

At the same time, Dhorme, who was then in Jerusalem, had been working on the texts independently. He, too, began with Virolleaud's suggestion for *l*. "This consonant furnished me with the word *b'l* ('Ba'al'), which repeats in all the lines of [Tablet] No. 14," he wrote on August 15, 1930. "Unhappily, in striking out from the consonant *b*, I read *bn*, 'son,' where it was necessary to read *bt* (*bath*, 'daughter,' or *bayt*, 'house'), and vice versa. This derailment on two letters as frequent as *n* and *t* had rendered my subsequent efforts vain so that I was only put back on the track by an article which Professor [W. F.] Albright procured for me in the middle of June.... M. Hans Bauer, professor at the University of Halle, announced in it that he had discovered the key of the Ras Shamra texts.... I did not have Bauer's alphabet before me, but the elements contained in the above-mentioned article permitted me to believe that it corresponds, outside of a sign or two perhaps, to that which I composed according to the information from that article and my personal researches."

Virolleaud, meanwhile, had solved the tablets on his own. He had looked for a three-letter word with his *l* in the middle as a possible *mlk*. He found it, then *Ba'al*, then an itemized list that gave him the spelled-out forms of numbers, which virtually completed the alphabet. He was about to publish his decipherment when Bauer beat him to it. Like Dhorme, Virolleaud did not agree with all of Bauer's values. Bauer was corresponding with Dhorme and, on comparing his work with the Frenchman's, he soon found that a scribe's dropping of a word separator had led him astray. His primary findings of *k* and *m*, as well as *p*, *q*, *s*, and *š*, had been wrong. He freely admitted this "with a perfect scientific loyalty" in a letter of October 3 to Dhorme. His other identifications had been sufficiently right to give them the clues they needed to decipher the texts, however. The three men thus solved, partly indepen-

---

* This word, which plays a central role in the decipherment of Semitic languages, will be familiar to Jews from the blessings for bread and wine. It appears in the phrase "elohenu melech ho'olam" ("Our God, King of the Universe").

dently, partly together, the alphabet for what has been called "the most important corpus of ancient literature discovered so far in the twentieth century."

For dozens, even scores, of parallels have been observed between Ugaritic literature and the Bible. One Ugaritic tablet declares: "Ah, thy enemies, O Ba'al; ah, thy enemies, you will strike them down; Thus you will slaughter your adversaries." Psalm 92 proclaims: "For, lo, Thine enemies, O Lord, For, lo, Thine enemies shall perish; All the workers of iniquity shall be scattered." Another tablet refers to "The dew of heaven, the fat of the earth," which is almost word for word Genesis 27:28's "The dew of heaven, the fatness of the earth." A third says, "Thy kingdom is everlasting, thy power (endureth) to all generations," which is not unlike Psalm 145: "Thy kingdom is an everlasting kingdom, and thy dominion endureth throughout all generations." Even Job's moving expression of faith, "But as for me, I know that my Redeemer liveth" (19:25), which Handel set to music in his *Messiah*, may echo a Ugaritic tablet: "I know that Alein-Ba'al is living."

The parallels can illuminate many obscure or unique words in the Bible. They can help explain strange practices. The reason for the prohibition of Exodus 23:19, "Thou shalt not seethe a kid in its mother's milk," the basis of the kosher law that forbids mixing meat and dairy foods, had never been clear. A Ugarit tablet reading in part "Cook a lamb in milk, a lamb in curdled milk" suggests that the Hebrews reacted against a Canaanite practice and thereby set themselves apart. The name El, which Bauer found applied to a Ugarit god in his very first solution, is the very name given to the Hebrew God Yahweh in Genesis (often in the plural of majesty, Elohim). Indeed, a possible god *Yw* appears in the Ugarit tablets, and Ba'al himself, as a son of god, is put to death and rises again. It well may be that the literature made available by the three-man decipherment of Ugaritic will illuminate much of the Holy Scriptures of the Judaeo-Christian ethos.

Case II solutions—in which the script is known but the language is not—are really not decipherments. They are linguistic reconstructions. Many have been made, particularly during the explosive growth of linguistic science during the nineteenth century.

Gothic, the oldest known form of the Germanic languages (of which English is a member), had become extinct by about the 900s; it survived only in such Latin alphabet manuscripts as the magnificent Codex Argentius, a translation of the four Gospels. A host of German scholars determined its grammar, the meaning of its words, how they sounded—and in doing so shed light on the development of modern languages. Ancient Persian, the 2,000-year-old language of the Zend-Avesta, was reconstructed by the successive efforts of Anquetil du Perron, Rasmus Rask, Eugene Bournouf, Niels Ludvig Westergaard, and A. V. Williams Jackson. The original form of Slavic, called Old Slavic, necessary for a knowledge of the interrelationships of such modern tongues as Russian, Bulgarian, Polish, Czech, Serbian, and Slovakian, was found only in scattered church manuscripts. Philologists such as Joseph Dobrovský, Franz von Miklošić, and August Leskien painstakingly assembled a picture of the dead language from these bits and pieces.

Perhaps the most interesting Case II involved Tokharian. Expeditions sent out by scholarly societies in the 1890s discovered in the ruined towns of Eastern Turkestan—the westernmost part of China—bundles of manuscripts almost perfectly preserved by the bone-dry climate and the overlying sands. One group proved to be written in the Brahmī script, used in ancient India and the script from which all later Indic scripts are descended. The language, however, was unknown. Careful analysis of the manuscripts by F. W. K. Müller showed that they were written in what turned out to be two new members of the great Indo-European family of languages. He named them Tokharian A and B. Surprisingly, though they were two of the most easterly members of that family, they resembled the western branch more. This threw new light on the prehistoric migrations of Central Asia.

In such reconstructions, philologists make use of translations (usually in the form of bilingual inscriptions), of glosses (marginal notes in manuscripts explaining the meaning of some obscure or foreign word), of remarks in other literatures about the meaning of alien terms. Philologists have also learned enough about how languages develop internally to identify several normal types of linguistic change. The pair "man, men" is an example of one such regular variation, known as umlaut. This alters one vowel to another under the influence of a succeeding sound. In the Primitive Germanic, the plural of man was "manni"; speakers, anticipating the front-of-the-mouth /ee/ sound of the plural, shifted the /a/ forward in the mouth to become the /eh/ sound, and this remained when the final syllable fell away. Other types of change, such as assimilation, dissimilation, diphthongization, and articulative intrusion, enable the philologist to trace sounds back like a movie run in reverse and so to arrive at an earlier point in the development of the language. These principles also assist in determining differences between languages descended from a common ancestor, so that the vocabulary and syntax of a known tongue can be applied on a basis of analogy to help determine those of the unknown one.

These processes commingle with those of Case I in Case III decipherments. Incomparably the most romantic instance is that of the Egyptian hieroglyphs.

Probably the most beautiful system of writing ever created, hieroglyphics burst suddenly into being just before the unification of Upper and Lower Egypt into one kingdom about 3200 B.C. They appeared first in rudimentary form on small seals and decorative palettes and developed rapidly. By the Fourth Dynasty, artists were painting columns of hieroglyphs on the chamber walls of the immense pyramids, all around the reddish men with the strange eyes and contorted bodies who march and hunt and sail eternally—comrades for the departed kings. Pharaohs with names like Amenhotep and Thutmose and Ramses carved monumental inscriptions in it on the massive temples of Karnak and Luxor. The writing itself comprises lovely drawings of birds, snakes, squares, feathers, shepherd's crooks, whorls, stools, hands, banners, and hundreds of other images.

Egypt held many mysteries for the foreigner. No one knew the source of the Nile, nor why it annually spread its gift of fertile soil upon the land. The Greeks puzzled over this old civilization, indisputably developed independently of their own, so at variance with their opinion of barbaric foreigners, so wounding to their own confident superiority. The abyss between the Oriental and Occidental world-views—the one mystical, the other rational—prevented total comprehension, and the Greeks sensed that something was not coming through in their intercourse with the Egyptians. They thought that a mysterious knowledge lurked behind this impenetrable veil. They came to regard Egypt as the fount of an ineffable wisdom of the East. Their admiration for what Pythagoras called "the symbolic and occult teachings" of Egypt distorted their preconceptions of the hieroglyphics.

For the Greeks never really learned the complex writing system. The meanings of a few hieroglyphs were explained to them, but they never grasped the relation between the sound and the image. Rather they misinterpreted this relation as an allegorical one. Thus, one writer knew that the Egyptians used the picture of a goose to represent the Egyptian word for "son," but he thought that they did so because this animal supposedly loved its offspring more than any other. This false view of hieroglyphics perfectly fitted the Platonic theory of forms, in which the concrete objects of the real express the abstract notions of the ideal. Plato's congeniality to Christianity fixed this impression strongly in men's minds and long prevented proper understanding. A neoplatonist philosopher, Plotinus, himself born in Egypt, gave the idea of hieroglyphics the formulation that became universally accepted: the Egyptians, in their superior wisdom, had imbued these pictures—which transcended ordinary writing—with symbolic qualities that intuitively revealed to the initiated a vision of the very essence of things. Plotinus drew part of this conception from the Egyptians themselves, who regarded writing as possessing magical powers. His view endowed the hieroglyphics with the fascinating aura of esoterism and hidden knowledge and eternal truth that surrounds them to this day.

In ancient Egypt, hieroglyphics transmitted the solemn proclamations of the divine king and his priestly viziers to the gods and to his subjects; the word "hieroglyph" itself means "sacred carvings." But the domination of foreigners, beginning with the Persian conquest of 525 B.C. and continuing with the Greeks under Alexander, cut the script off from its political roots. The writing became a professional secret of the priests. The people began to write their language in the Greek alphabet of the rulers. The hieroglyphic vocabulary contracted. Inscriptions grew increasingly stereotyped. With the advent of Christianity and the collapse of the pagan religion, the hieroglyphic tradition flickered out here and there over Egypt. It resisted longest on the Island of Philae near the First Cataract of the Nile, where a fanatic Nubian clergy defended the cult of Isis in dilapidated temples amid memories of past glories. Here the last hieroglyphic inscription was recorded in 394 A.D. The last man to know the ancient writing as a living tradition must have gone to his grave soon thereafter. So the gods departed from Egypt. Isis and Osiris, Ra and Thoth fell silent for more than a thousand years.

But their memory lingered. The Pyramids stood. The Sphinx brooded. The shadowy notion of Egypt's omniscience haunted Europe, and the currents that stirred the Renaissance quickened the never-quite-forgotten curiosity about the hieroglyphs. Leon Battista Alberti attempted to reconstruct them from written descriptions, and urged their use as imperishable inscriptions on monuments. The great *Hypnerotomachia Poliphili*, printed by Aldus Manutius in Venice in 1499, scattered hieroglyphic emblems throughout its exquisite woodcuts. Much of this activity stemmed from the discovery in 1419 of the only manuscript on the subject preserved from antiquity, the *Hieroglyphics* of a fourth-century author known only as Horapollo, which was immediately accepted as the accurate authority on the subject and which fixed the course of investigation for centuries. Circulating at first in manuscript, it was published by Aldus Manutius in 1505. Horapollo knew what some of the signs meant, probably because Egyptians had told him. But his derivations of sense from symbol are totally wrong, and so he could not interpret the inscriptions. His ideas in general followed those of Plotinus, who had written in the third century. He therefore assumed that the hieroglyph of a bird stood for that particular bird or for some idea associated with it, as speed or flight. He supposed that the vulture was used for "mother" (as it was) because no male vultures exist!

This allegorical interpretation of Horapollo contaminated the many other attempts to comprehend the meaning of hieroglyphics that followed his. One such became the first "modern" authority on the subject. Its author was Pierius Valerianus, a famous scholar whose secular name was Giovan Pietro della Fosse and who tutored the future Pope Leo X and later became his private secretary. Hieroglyphic problems fascinated him, and at various times during his life he wrote the 58 books of what was published in 1556 as his *Hieroglyphica*, a remarkably unified and elegant work. Each book deals with the symbolic significance of one or more hieroglyphs in explanations drawn from Horapollo and other classics dealing with the subject. The elephant symbolizes purity because it bathes in rivers at full moon. Alone, the lion stands for "nobleness of mind," yoked with a wild boar, for "strength of mind and body," roaring, for "bestial ferocity," and with a cock, for "pious timidity" because of its supposed awe of the fowl. The work was reprinted at least eleven times and translated thrice.

Through the history of those years runs the continuous thread of interest in the problem, visible in comments in books widely scattered in time and space. While many authors attempted to draw out of the hieroglyphs the profound wisdom that they supposedly enclosed, none seriously attempted a new decipherment until the 17th century. By then the first extensive collection of authentic hieroglyphic inscriptions, J. F. Herwath von Hohenburg's *Thesaurus Hieroglyphicorum*, had been published.

The most ambitious attack on the meaning of the Egyptian writings was mounted by the Jesuit Athanasius Kircher, who later in his life was to fail to read the mysterious manuscript attributed to Roger Bacon. Kircher was the most famous and prolific scholar of his time, author of a book on cryptology and universal language, and for several years a professor of mathematics. If Leibnitz was the last man to know everything, Kircher may have been the next to last. His lifework sought to combine the totality of knowledge into a universal cosmology, in which divine truth moved the universe. Christianity manifested this truth perfectly, but Kircher found its highest pre-Christian form in the Egyptian philosophical and magical treatises attributed to Hermes Trismegistus. Kircher believed that Hermes Trismegistus was a real Egyptian priest who had lived in remotest antiquity, but the treatises had actually been written by early Christians and so, despite their pagan and gnostic elements, were theologically consistent with Christianity. Kircher was certain that he knew in general what the hieroglyphic texts contained: the esoteric knowledge of ultimate reality said by Plotinus to have been possessed by the Egyptians. His hope of confirming this by reading the texts and thereby proving the truth of his cosmology motivated his prodigious efforts to decipher them.

In 1636 appeared his *Prodromus coptus sive ægypticus*, which put forth the original view that Coptic—the language of Egypt that Arabic had displaced but that was still used, written in Greek characters, in the liturgy of the Coptic, or Egyptian Christian, church—"was formerly the Pharaonic language." In other words, Coptic was the latest form of the same Egyptian language that had been written in hieroglyphs. In this, and in his further statement that a knowledge of Coptic would be needed for a solution of hieroglyphics, Kircher was absolutely correct. His *Lingua ægyptiaca restituta* of 1644 laid the foundation for Coptic studies. But then his great work on the interpretation of hieroglyphs ignored his own advice. The *Œdipus ægyptiacus* of 1652–1655 identified each hieroglyph with a philosophical concept in the old allegorical way and so was able to make them reflect Kircher's cosmology. Kircher read a group that stood for nothing more than the name of the pharaoh Apries as "The benefits of the divine Osiris are to be procured by means of sacred ceremonies and of the chain of the Genii, in order that the benefits of the Nile may be obtained." Another of his hieroglyphic works, the *Sphinx mystagogica*, interpreted the simple phrase "Osiris says" as "The life of things, after the defeat of Tryphon, the moisture of Nature, through the vigilance of Anubis." Kircher made a few lucky guesses, such as that three wavy lines stood for both "water" and the sound /m/ because the Coptic word for water was "mu." But these few grains of truth were submerged in a sea of nonsense. This quickly became evident to other scholars, particularly in the critical Age of Reason that followed.

The collapse of Kircher's ambitious attempt quelled any further major trials at solution for a century and a half. Interest nevertheless remained high, fed in part by the inscriptions that continually came to light. The Great Seal of the United States, designed in 1790, depicts an Egyptian pyramid capped by an eye, the supposed hieroglyphic symbol of divine justice; this can be seen on the back of every U.S. dollar bill. Mozart set *The Magic Flute* in and around the Temple of Isis and Osiris and peopled it with the high priest and an Egyptian prince. The opera was produced in 1791, when the West had gotten no further in the reading of hieroglyphics than it had a thousand years before. Indeed, in 1797, Georg Zoëga, in his enormous 700-page resumé of Egyptological matter, declared the problem insoluble. Two years later, an Egyptian laborer named Dhautpoul was building a fort for the French conquerors of his native land near a town in the Nile Delta whose native name was Rashid. His eye was caught by an irregular slab of fine-grained black basalt, either lying on the ground, as some accounts say, or built into an old wall which he was demolishing. It was covered with three bands of writing—hieroglyphs, something thought to be Syriac, and Greek. Pierre-François Bouchard, an alert French officer of engineers in charge of the gang, thought that they were probably three versions of the same text and that the Greek might serve as a key to solving the mystery of hieroglyphics. He knew of the large group of scientists that Napoleon had taken with him on his Egyptian expedition to study the antiquities, and he sent the stone to his commander, reporting that it had been found near a town known to Europeans as Rosetta.

The stone's importance was instantly recognized. In Cairo, copies were made of it. When the French surrendered to the British in Egypt in the spring of 1801, Article XVI of the Treaty of Capitulation gave the Rosetta Stone to the British. It eventually reached the British Museum, where it reposes today at the south end of the Egyptian Sculpture Gallery, probably the most famous single archeological discovery in history. It measures 3 feet 9 inches high, 2 feet 4 inches wide, and 11 inches thick. Both upper corners and the lower right corner are broken off. The Greek text consists of 54 lines; of the hieroglyphic there remain only 14, corresponding to the last 28 of the Greek, all but two of which are missing part of the ends. The central band proved to be in a writing called demotic, "the language of the people," a simplified form of script used in business. Demotic had evolved out of hieratic, itself a simplified form of hieroglyphics that had developed for writing on papyrus. At times in Egyptian history all three existed side by side, employing essentially the same principle of expressing sound in script, though the forms differed greatly.

Several translations were made of the Greek text. It was dated on the fourth day of the Greek month Xandikos (April) of the ninth year of the reign of Ptolemy V Epiphanes, which would be 196 B.C. A convocation of

Egyptian priests set forth the benefits which this pharaoh had conferred upon them and upon Egypt—gifts of money and corn to the temples, remission of taxes, conquest of the town of Shekan, and so forth. In return, they honored him by making his birthday a festival day forever, erecting golden statues of him in every temple of Egypt, and cutting Egyptian and Greek copies of this decree upon slabs of basalt in the three writings and placing them in the temples next to the statues. This last point confirmed the probability that the three texts were three versions of the same text and permitted scholars to compare them with assurance.

Yet the mere existence of the Rosetta Stone did not make solution automatic. The most eminent Orientalist of the day, Sylvestre de Sacy, professor of Arabic in Paris, very sensibly tried to locate the proper names of the Greek text in the demotic, beginning with this because he felt it to be alphabetic. The hieroglyphic script frightened people off because many still regarded it as a secret symbolology and because it was so badly damaged. He found the approximate groups for "Ptolemy" and "Alexander," but the 15 letter-values that he obtained would not yield Coptic-like words elsewhere in the text. He frankly admitted his failure and handed over his material to the Swedish diplomat and scholar, Johan David Åkerblad. A talented linguist and student of Coptic, Åkerblad managed to solve in two months many of the problems that had baffled de Sacy. Using the same general approach, he established a demotic alphabet of 29 letters, half of which were correct, and educed words that were more or less identical to the Coptic, thus proving that the language of the ancient Egyptians was indeed related to Coptic. But his insistence that demotic was entirely alphabetic blocked further progress.

He did not touch the hieroglyphs. The few who did treated them as allegorically as had Kircher, with results about as valuable. One case, in fact, was more extreme than anything that had gone before. Another Swedish diplomat, Count N. G. Palin, thought that the Psalms of David were Hebrew translations of Egyptian texts. If, he suggested, the Hebrew were to be translated into Chinese, the Chinese would provide a key to the decipherment of the hieroglyphs!

In 1814, the Rosetta Stone came to the attention of Thomas Young. A British physician, then 41, whose hobby was science, he revived the wave theory of light on the basis of his discovery of the principle of interference, advanced the theory that the eye sees color by fibers that respond to red, green, and violet light, described the visual defect of astigmatism, contributed to the theory of tides, defined a coefficient of elasticity (Young's modulus), and investigated epicycloidal curves, spiders, the atmosphere of the moon, capillarity, and diseases of the chest. He knew modern languages, including Arabic, Ethiopic, and Turkish, and some ancient ones, such as Hebrew, Persian, and Coptic. With their help, he made some progress with the demotic inscription and then turned to the hieroglyphic.

He first assumed that the hieroglyphs enclosed in ovals with a straight line at one end, called cartouches, represented the names of royalty. His comparisons of the demotic, hieratic, and hieroglyphic scripts convinced him that the first had been derived from the second, and that hieratic had come from hieroglyphic. The signs of the demotic seemed to be letters that stood for sounds; could the signs of the older script be just more elaborate versions of those letters? If this were so, scribes in a conquered country like Egypt might well resort to them to spell out the names of foreigners, which might not be otherwise reproducible in the native script. He might test this hypothesis by seeing if the writing in the cartouches yielded the name that he knew from the Greek version, "Ptolemy."

The five cartouches contained only two sets of hieroglyphics. The eight signs of the shorter appeared as the first eight signs of the longer, which had 16 signs. Young had seen that in the Greek text the longer form of Ptolemy included titles. He concentrated on the simpler short version, and equated its eight signs with the ten letters of the Greek form "Ptolemaios" by agglomerating the Greek letters into six rather arbitrary syllables (p, t, ole, ma, i, os), by counting a doubled sign (two feathers side by side) as a single letter, and by regarding another sign (a loop) as a kind of silent letter. This gave him the Egyptian equivalents for the six sounds. He inserted these equivalents into a similar cartouche from the ceiling of a temple at Karnak, and, by filling in known sound-values and guessing at new ones, identified the name of the pharaoh Ptolemy I Soter. He did the same for that of the queen, Berenice.

Here he stopped. Though he had managed to read six signs correctly out of the 13 that he had identified and three partly correctly, he declared that he had been unable to find any cases in which the alphabetical signs were used for native words or names and that it was therefore idle to try reading the pure hieroglyphic with them. Actually, his correct identifications had produced such names as "Ptah," which occurred in his own vocabulary. But he evidently did not recognize them and he quit the field, having made the crucial breakthrough of recognizing the presence of alphabetic elements in a script formerly thought to be purely logographic and symbolic.

The attack was pressed by a young man of sallow complexion and burning genius, a prodigy whose lifelong passion had been to disclose the mystery of the hieroglyphs. Jean-François Champollion was born in Lot, France, on December 23, 1790; five years later he achieved his first decipherment by teaching himself to read. The seeds of his destiny were sown when he was 10 and the mathematician Jean-Baptiste Fourier, then at Grenoble where Jean-François was studying, showed the boy his collection of Egyptian antiquities. The youngster announced that when he was big he would read the writing on them. His life from then consisted of one long preparation for his accomplishment. At 17, he read a paper on "Egypt Under the Pharaohs" to the staff of the Grenoble high school; they were so impressed they elected the youth to the faculty on the spot. Continuing his studies in Paris, he learned Sanskrit,

Arabic, Persian, Hebrew, and, above all, Coptic. He had determined not to tackle the difficult problem until he had thoroughly prepared himself.

He made intensive comparisons of the three kinds of writing, though at first he thought that the more recent demotic was the older. He clung to the conventional symbolistic view of the hieroglyphs. But he was able to confirm an ingenious observation of Åkerblad, based on the Coptic, that a horned viper represented /f/, which meant "he" at the end of certain words. Champollion extended this to some other end-letters that stood for other personal pronouns. About 1819, however, personal and political troubles so depressed him that he began to doubt even his best results. He reverted to such fantasies as thinking that the lion crouched in the middle of Ptolemy's cartouche represented his name as a symbol of war, which in Greek was "polemos," the word from which came Ptolemy's name (which means "mighty in war").

To discipline himself, he undertook a meticulous comparison of the signs of all known Egyptian texts. This corrected his chronology of the three scripts and enabled him to trace a sign from hieroglyphic through hieratic to demotic. In December, 1821, his counts showed that the hieroglyphic text of the Rosetta Stone contained 1,419 signs whereas the Greek text consisted of only 486 words. This made untenable the old theory that each sign represented a whole word; he therefore decided to test once and for all the theory that at least some of these hieroglyphs represented sounds. He transcribed the name "Ptolemy," which on linguistic grounds he now spelled *Ptolemis*, from the demotic version (known from the Rosetta Stone, and thought to be alphabetic) to hieratic to hieroglyphic. He arrived at a spelling that was virtually identical with the hieroglyphs of the Rosetta Stone. This proved that the hieroglyphs represented sounds, and buried the theory that each hieroglyph was purely the symbolic expression of an idea.

A month later, a friend sent him a new lithograph of a bilingual inscription from a granite obelisk found at Philae in 1815. The Greek text showed it to be a priestly appeal to—interestingly enough—the children of the Ptolemy eulogized in the Rosetta Stone; their names were Ptolemy and Cleopatra. Champollion recognized the cartouche of this Ptolemy from the cartouche for the same name on the Rosetta Stone. And he observed that several of its hieroglyphs reappeared in the Cleopatra cartouche in positions that showed that the signs corresponded to sounds that the two names had in common. Thus, the first sign of *Ptolemis*, a square, was the fifth of *Cleopatra*, proving it to be /p/. The third sign of *Ptolemis*, a noose, was the fourth of *Cleopatra*, proving it to be /o/. A lion was the fourth sign of *Ptolemis* and the second of *Cleopatra*, proving it to be /l/. And the vulture that stood in the sixth position of *Cleopatra* also stood in the ninth, proving it to be /a/. The only irregularity was that the two words used different signs for their /t/'s; he regarded this as a case of homophony. Like Young, he considered the double feather in *Ptolemis* to be a single letter, the /i/.

It was January, 1822. Within a few feverish months, the 31-year-old

Ancestral Voices 909

decipherer turned out an almost complete translation of the hieroglyphic names of rulers of Egypt from Alexander to Antoninus Pius. He derived the sound-values of the other phonetic hieroglyphs by the cryptanalytic method—substituting known values, guessing at the names, and testing the presumed

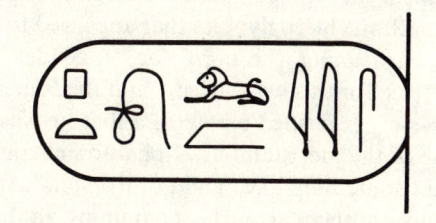

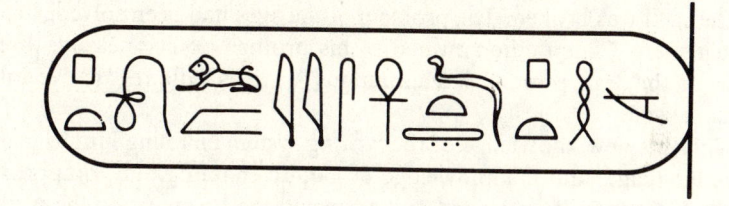

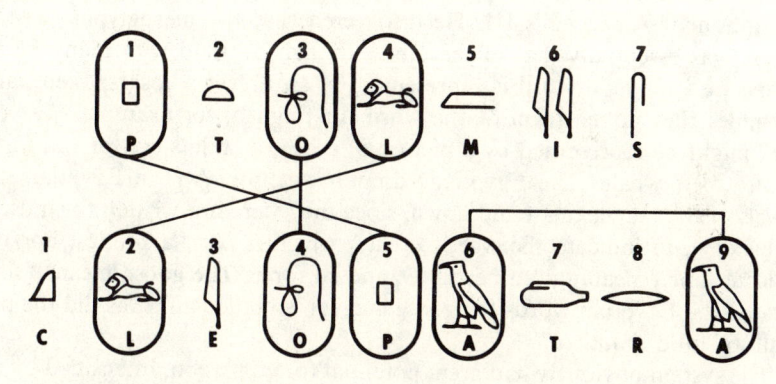

Champollion's cross-checking of hieroglyphic sound-values in royal names

values elsewhere. But this solution, while undoubtedly correct, might have proved of only secondary importance had these alphabetic signs served only for foreign names and played no part in spelling out the native Egyptian tongue. Had he come this far only to face the same difficulty that Young had?

On September 14, 1822, he received some inscriptions from the colossal rock-hewn temple of Abu Simbel on the Nile. Unquestionably it antedated

Graeco-Roman times. One inscription contained a cartouche with four signs: a circle with a dot in it, which represented the sun, a three-pronged sign whose meaning was unknown to him, and two occurrences of a sign like a shepherd's crook that he knew from *Ptolemis* stood for /s/. Coptic had taught him that the sun was called "ra" or "rē," and the three-pronged sign occurred in a part of the Rosetta Stone hieroglyphics that appeared to represent the complex of Greek words meaning "be born" or "engender" that added up to "birthday." The Coptic for this was "mīse," and the four symbols could thus stand for "Ra-mise-s-s." It flashed before him that he was reading the hieroglyphic form of one of the most famous of pharaonic names, "Ramses," and that the name meant something like "child of the sun." At the same moment his eye was caught by another cartouche, containing an ibis, known as a bird of the god Thoth, the three-pronged sign, and another shepherd's crook /s/, and he realized in a dazzling instant that *this* was "Thutmose," another well-known pharaonic name, which obviously meant "child of Thoth."

The spell was broken. The problem of the ages had been solved. In a fever of excitement Champollion rushed to his brother's office nearby, threw his papers on the desk, pronounced his famous "Je tiens l'affaire!" ("I've got it!"), and collapsed.

With this new knowledge of the writing system enabling him to penetrate to the language, and his knowledge of Coptic enabling him to approximate Egyptian, Champollion refined and corrected the language by the script and the script by the language. Within three years he had arrived at an understanding of both accurate enough to enable him to translate an Early Egyptian inscription of Amenophis III. He discovered that the hieroglyphic writing system was essentially that of the rebus, though overlaid with many refinements. In a rebus, a word is represented by an object whose spoken name resembles the spoken form of the word. In English, for example, the verb "be" might be represented by a picture of a bee; a child's cry, or wail, by a picture of a whale. The Egyptians drew a swallow, /wr/ in Egyptian (the vowels of the language are unknown, since they were not written for most of its history), to indicate the word "great," which is /wr/, a beetle (/hpr/) to indicate /hpr/, meaning "to become," and so forth. The goose meant "son" because the Egyptian words for goose and son sounded alike, as did the pair "vulture" and "mother."

The system obviously had great potential for confusion, intensified by the lack of vowels; to preclude as much of it as possible the Egyptians tacked onto their words mute explanatory signs called determinatives. Thus, a picture of a seated man always followed names or designations of men, a pelt with a tail followed mentions of mammals, a jug was used for citations of liquids, a pair of legs for movement, a circle with an open cross inside (representing a walled city with intersecting streets) for towns, a papyrus roll for spiritual matters.

Champollion distinguished these from the true logograms that Egyptians also used. Thus, a picture of an eye meant "eye," of a bow meant "bow"; a stylized representation of a loaf meant "bread," of an angle meant "corner." The Egyptians further used logograms to stand for verbs and adverbs by extending their images to associated concepts. A man with a stick in his hand meant "to beat"; a leg and foot, "to walk"; a stooped man leaning on a staff, "old age"; a lily, the flower characteristic of Upper Egypt, to mean "south." There were hundreds of these in common use. They had in part inspired the old allegorical view of hieroglyphs, and they gave it the only validity it had had.

Someone reading hieroglyphics aloud would therefore have to know whether a given sign represented a single sound that formed part of a word, a concept whose spoken form would not have anything to do with the picture (as the sound of "lily" in Egyptian has nothing to do with that of "south"), or a determinative that was not to be uttered at all. Nor did that end the complexity of hieroglyphics. Not content with determinatives, the Egyptians often added extra phonetic signs to words, to make absolutely sure the sense would come through. Though the swallow adequately represented /wr/, the Egyptians liked to draw a mouth, standing for /r/, after the swallow. Though "to hear" was effectively expressed by the picture of an ear, they would append an owl, standing for /m/, the last sound of /sdm/ ("to hear") just after the ear. Often it seemed as if they could not pile up enough of these pleonastic symbols —to the decipherer, however, each one acted as a kind of null.

The final complication of Egyptian writing were the homophones— different signs standing for the same sound. In Champollion's original decipherment, a semicircle stood for the /t/ in *Ptolemis* and a hand for the /t/ in *Cleopatra*. Champollion found many homophones: so many, in fact, that they retarded general acceptance of his decipherment. Eventually the German scientist Richard Lepsius showed that many of these phonetic signs stood for two- or three-letter consonantal groups. The three-pronged sign that had appeared in "Ramses" and "Thutmose" stood, not just for /m/, as Champollion had thought, but for /ms/—with the extra /s/'s that Champollion had found in those words just pleonasm. Lepsius' decipherment of the lengthy bilingual Decree of Canopus, discovered in 1866, cleared up many of the details that Champollion had not been able to resolve.

For he had died in 1832, aged 41, less than ten years after his solution. Yet he had had the satisfaction of having resolved the riddle which the silent Sphinx had guarded since time immemorial. Like the rising sun warming the colossus of Memnon, Champollion's brilliance struck sound from statues and inscriptions dumb through a long darkness. He animated a whole vast civilization once known only through its relics. The decaying temples, the rock-hewn tombs, the Pyramids, became the setting for a shimmering pageant of barges on the Nile, of slaves and nobles, of an expedition to Punt returning with cinnamon-wood and apes and ivory, of strange religious beliefs and incestuous royalty and a brave doomed fight for monotheism, of the young warrior-pharaoh, Ramses II, recording upon the walls of Luxor and Thebes the very thoughts he thought when he beat back an enemy army that almost overpowered him at faraway Kadesh—a drama of human joys and sorrows reaching back into unsuspected depths of antiquity. Champollion let man see more of his past than perhaps any other human being. It is an enviable accomplishment.

It is not only the dead men of Egypt who have told their tales. Decipherers have also conjured forth the annals of ancient Babylonia. Their decipherment of cuneiform is a more astonishing feat in a way than that of hieroglyphics because it was achieved without the aid of a bilingual. Only after a simple cuneiform used for a known language had been read could progress be made on the complicated form and its unknown tongue—the tongue of Nineveh and Babylon.

The solution was begun by a 27-year-old schoolteacher of Göttingen, Georg Friedrich Grotefend, who had written a book on a universal language and who enjoyed solving ciphers and word puzzles. He equated a common and repetitive series of signs in the cuneiform inscriptions with the frequent and repetitious formula "king of kings" and "son of the king X" that was known from the Greek versions of later Persian inscriptions. He shrewdly compared the formulas in two inscriptions and discerned a succession of father, son, and grandson in which the son and grandson were kings but the father was not. Historical evidence had fixed the approximate period of the dynasty, and the kings of Persia were well known from Greek historians. Grotefend found that only Hystapes, Darius, and Xerxes fitted the pattern. He obtained the modern Persian forms of the names from the Zend-Avesta, substituted these sound-values back into the cuneiform, and obtained 13 correct values and four incorrect ones for the alphabet of 42 signs. This was the breakthrough, but much of the subsequent work in recovering the Old Persian language was done by the Danish philologist Rasmus Rask.

Independently, an Englishman, Henry C. Rawlinson, clinging like a fly to the sheer face of the high cliff of Behistun to copy the trilingual inscription carved thereon like a giant billboard from antiquity, also solved the Old Persian cuneiform. He too found a series of signs that he recognized as kings' names, identified them, and broke into the script. He recovered rather more of the alphabet than did Grotefend, and this provided the key for the next and far more important step: solution of the syllabic cuneiform used to write Akkadian, the language of Babylonia and Assyria.

In terms of numbers of signs, this script was the most complicated of the three found at Behistun and on other trilingual inscriptions. Rawlinson and other scholars located the repeated schemata that included the names of the kings. Comparisons of these with their sounds and meanings—now known from the Old Persian solution—showed that the Akkadian script was partly syllabic, partly logographic. For example, it represented the word "king" by a single sign whereas it spelled out the names of the kings with several signs. The number of signs used in these names equalled the number of consonants in them. This led the Swede Isidor Löwenstern to conclude that the language was Semitic, a family whose later scripts, at least, write only the consonants as letters, representing the vowels by points and lines. However, he discovered an abnormal number of signs representing a single consonant. An Irish clergyman, Edward Hincks, showed that these actually stood for syllables based on that consonant, such as /ra/, /ri/, /ru/, /ar/, /er/, /ir/, /ur/. He also recognized that a single sign could serve as a word-sign, a syllable-sign, or a determinative much like the hieroglyphic determinatives.

Rawlinson, meanwhile, continued to substitute new-found phonetic values back into the cuneiform texts. At times the suggested values appeared jarringly out of place, and after many occurrences in which a single sign appeared to be wrong in a word that context compelled to be right, a regularity in these apparent errors impressed itself upon him. He finally concluded that a single sign could possess several different sound values, much as the English *c* can sound like either an /s/ or a /k/. Thus, in the Akkadian, Rawlinson discovered, the sign that usually represents /ud/ can also stand for /tam/, /par/, /lah/, and /his/. The 246 polyphonous symbols that he established by 1851 proved in the long run to be almost entirely correct. They were confirmed by finding, among the 20,000 clay tablets of the library of Ashurbanipal, about 100 on which students learning the complicated language had correlated the various signs, syllabic polyphones, and logograms. Only then was it possible to understand why the name *Nabu-kudurrī-uṣur* ("Nebuchadnezzar"), meaning "O Nabu, protect my boundary mark," came out as AN-AG-ŠA-DU-ŠIŠ. It turned out that AN-AG was a logographic symbol for the god Na-bi-um, ŠA-DU represented the word *kudurru* ("boundary mark"), and šiš stood for *naṣāru* ("to protect"), the imperative form of which was *uṣur*.

In view of complexities like this, it was hardly surprising that many scholars jeered at the results as pure imagination. To settle the question of reliability, the Royal Asiatic Society in 1857 sent a newly discovered cuneiform inscription to four experts, Rawlinson, Hincks, William Henry Fox Talbert, and Jules Oppert, with the request that they work on it independently. The sealed envelopes containing the four solutions were opened at a formal meeting. In all essential points their translations agreed.

Within fifteen years, a world that still largely believed in the revelatory uniqueness of Holy Scripture was reading in shocked surprise the Epic of Gilgamesh, in which a story of an ancient flood parallels the Biblical narrative down to the details of the release of a bird to see whether the waters had subsided. Then, at the turn of the century, a broken black diorite stele covered with 3,600 lines of cuneiform was found to be the law code of Hammurabi—with crimes and punishments and even phrases that the later Mosaic Law had evidently copied. The decipherment of cuneiform showed that what the West had regarded for centuries as God-given truths had come merely from the human minds of a pagan civilization and, by undermining the divine authority of the moral law, helped pave the way for the ethical and philosophical revolution of today. It revealed so much about the ziggurat lands of Assyria and Babylonia, with their winged bulls, their bearded kings, their royal lion hunts, their astronomy, and their deities like Marduk and Ishtar, that modern man knows far more about them than the most learned traveler of ancient Greece, who was 2,000 years closer to them in time.

Scholars have elucidated many other lost languages—indeed, every tongue that has become extinct and has been recovered falls into the category. Many involve obscure dialects of half-forgotten peoples, and so have not had the impact on history that the solution of the hieroglyphic and cuneiform writing of two great civilizations has had. Surprisingly often, the basic solution is the work of a single scholar, though almost invariably his work is extended and checked, usually in the infinitely detailed field of philology, by others.

Of these other solutions, perhaps the most important is Bedřich Hrozný's 1916 reading of the Hittite cuneiform. The Czech scholar, a lively, generous man, then 37, read the Hittite cuneiform texts using the sound-values and occasional logograms of Akkadian cuneiform, but the language seemed to make no sense. Eventually he found a sentence that included the logogram for bread, and he transliterated the rest of it as: *Nu-BREAD-an ezzateni, wadar-ma ekuteni*. It seemed to echo a familiar phrase, and suddenly he saw that it referred to eating bread and water, *wadar* resembling Germanic *watar* and, of course, the English *water*, and *ezzateni* being cognate with German *essen* and English *eat*. The language thus turned out to be Indo-European, flying in the face of nearly all philologists, who had assumed it to be almost anything but. This placed the language on the proper footing for its reconstruction, and within 20 years a satisfactory understanding of it had been gained. This helped clear up some of the mystifying details about the history of this people, who are mentioned in the Bible and in the chronicles of other ancient peoples. (The Hittites also wrote in their own hieroglyphics; several scholars, each adding a detail or a hypothesis to the corpus of the decipherment, are still laboriously working out the solution.)

Most of the other solutions have come from Mediterranean lands, the seedbed of civilization. Meroitic, the language of the "Ethiopian" kingdom of Meroë, which flourished south of Egypt from about 100 B.C. to 300 A.D., proved to be an offshoot of Egyptian when Francis Llewellyn Griffith solved it in the 1920s. Lycian, spoken in southwestern Asia Minor, was in large measure deciphered with the help of epitaphs whose rigid formula was ascertained from others nearby, written in Greek. Lydian, the language of King Croesus, was read with the aid of both Aramaic and Greek bilinguals. Sidetic, spoken in the city of Side on the southern coast of Asia Minor, could not be read at first because the Greek bilinguals were too short; but a longer one discovered in 1949 enabled Helmuth T. Bossert to make considerable headway. In 1843, F. C. de Saulcy read Libyan, also called Numidian, the language spoken in northwestern Africa at the time of Carthage and written in what appears to be a specially invented script; he had the aid of bilinguals in Latin and in Punic, the language of Carthage, and of philological insights from Numidian's modern descendant, the language of the Berber tribesmen. The Iberian script, used in about 150 inscriptions found in Spain, the longest only 342 letters, was deciphered in the mid-1920s by Professor Manuel Gómez Moreno; some points are still in question. Writings of South Arabia, such as the graceful Sabaean alphabet, have been deciphered; they provide knowledge of the earliest dialects of Arabia. The North Arabian Safaitic inscriptions, which were mainly incised on volcanic rocks near es-Safa southeast of Damascus in the first two centuries A.D., were largely read by the German E. Littmann.

James Prinsep, professor of Sanskrit at Oxford, who died in 1840 at age 41, solved not one but two important ancient scripts and has been called "one of the most talented and useful men that England has given to India." He first unraveled the Pahlavi script after finding bilingual coins in it and in Greek from the Bactrian empire of Persia that flourished after Alexander the Great. Greek proper names on them suggested the sound values of letters in Pahlavi, which proved to be Persian written in a Semitic alphabet. Then he turned his attention to the inscriptions of the Buddhist king Asoka, who in the third century B.C. ruled the greatest empire that ever existed in India. They were written using the then-unknown Brahmī alphabet in the common language of the people, Prakrit (as distinguished from the literary tongue, Sanskrit). In 1837, Prinsep saw a number of brief inscriptions on objects found in a temple near Bhopal in Central India and concluded that they meant somebody's "gift" to the temple. Equating the known sounds of the Prakrit word for "gift" and of the Prakrit proper names with the letters, Prinsep worked out the oldest known writing of India. The solution filled in much of early Indian history and some of the development of Indian language and writing, with consequences important for the knowledge of other Indo-European languages. It also paved the way for Müller's reconstruction of Tokharian, which was written in the Brahmī script.

Müller also played a major role in the decipherment of Sogdian. This was the lingua franca of Central Asia during the first millennium A.D. when that melting pot—today a sparsely populated sandy waste—was a rich land of smiling cities like Samarkand, criss-crossed by caravans bearing spices and emeralds to Europe. Like Pahlavi, the language was an eastern dialect of Middle Persian, the alphabet also a descendant of the Aramaic.

Other abandoned scripts from the oddest corners of the Orient have yielded to the analyses of linguists. Mon, a script employed in Burma about the eleventh century A.D., fell before the attack of C. O. Blagden, whose principal weapon was a quadriliteral of Mon, Pyu, Pali, and Burmese. Some inscriptions in Khmer, a fifth-century language of Cambodia, were solved in the 1920s by G. Coedès. A group of scholars collaborated in reading, with the help of

Sanskrit bilinguals, an Indian tongue written in a script called Central Asian Slanting Gupta.

The decipherment that is sometimes cited as the most typical of armchair decipherments involved another writing from Central Asia. In 1889, explorers discovered two large inscribed stones near the Orkhon River about 40 miles north of Karakorum. A short Chinese text on one declared that it had been erected in memory of a Turkish prince in a year that corresponded to 732 A.D. A second and longer inscription on that stone was graven in an angular script that resembled Germanic runes. Both inscriptions were published in 1892. The next year a Danish scholar, Vilhelm Thomsen, after failing to match the Chinese rendering of the prince's name ("K'we-te-kin") to the rune-like characters that represented it, discovered that the Turkish form of the prince's name was *Kül-tigin* and matched the characters to that. Then he found the Turkish word *tängri* ("heaven") in a group that occurred where the Khan's appellation of "Celestial" might appear. These two words together contained all the characters necessary for reading a word that occurred very frequently—*türk*, the name of Kül-tigin's people. The language proved to be the oldest and purest Turkish dialect known, before it was affected by the Moslem conquest; the script, now called Kök-Turki runes, was shown by other discoveries to be a national script that the Turks later forsook. Thus, on November 25, 1893, with the aid of a Chinese bilingual, Thomsen deciphered the writing, and so completely and accurately had he done it that since then there has been almost nothing to add or correct.

It must not be thought that every script has surrendered. Many remain books sealed with seven seals. Etruscan, written in Latin letters and contemporaneous with the early Latin culture, is one of the most tantalizing. It is a Case II problem which has been partly solved. A few words have been identified with a fair degree of probability, but the 8,000 texts are too stereotyped (many are funerary inscriptions) and too brief (many are mere fragments) to allow much progress to be made in reconstructing the language. The few bilinguals that exist (with Latin) are epitaphs. The state of the question can be dramatized by pointing out that disagreement is rife concerning even the numbers, which have been found in written form on dice.

The hieroglyphics of the Indus Valley civilization, which flourished in the northwest corner of India more than 4,000 years ago, remain unread. During World War II, Hrozný, then in his dotage, mounted an attack upon all the undeciphered scripts of the world and announced a decipherment of the approximately 250 signs of the Indus Valley script, but other scholars have discredited it. Some investigators see a resemblance between this script and that of the "talking boards" of Easter Island. A number of the signs do look surprisingly alike, but their enormous separation in time and space makes it most unlikely that they have any connection. Easter Island natives call the writing rongo-rongo, and their tradition holds that bards merely used the little figures of what appear to be men and plants as cues for a whole line in a story. None of the native informants could actually explain the 500 symbols when they were discovered in 1870, but Thomas S. Barthel has recently claimed to have deciphered the talking-board writing.

Many would-be decipherers have exercised their ingenuity upon the Phaistos Disk, a circular tablet six inches in diameter, found at Phaistos in Crete in 1902. Its 241 signs were printed into the fine-grained clay with stamps; the writing uncoils from the center in five spirals on both sides. Forty-five highly pictorial representations of humans, animals, tools, and body parts form the signary. This has led to statistical calculations that the original signary had between 50 and 60 pictograms. The disk apparently dates from about 1700 B.C. Many solutions have been announced. None has been generally accepted.

A Case III problem which has caused many a sleepless night is that of the Maya hieroglyphics. It remains unconquered, despite a recent onslaught by that all-conquering of modern weapons, the digital computer. Three young Soviet mathematicians from the Novosibirsk Institute of Mathematics of the Soviet Academy of Sciences, E. V. Yevreinov, Y. G. Kosarev, and V. A. Ustinov, became the first to apply a computer to a decipherment problem. They assumed that the most frequent Mayan glyphs would represent the written form of the most frequent sounds of the Mayan language. The language, and its sounds, were known primarily from Mayan texts written by their priests in the alphabet of the conquistadores, secondarily from two Maya-Spanish dictionaries compiled at the same time, thirdly from the degenerate form of Mayan still spoken in Yucatán. The mathematicians codified the 60,000 words of these texts on the punched cards and magnetic drums that served as the computer's memory. They found that 70 letter-pairs in the texts accounted for half the word-beginnings, and that 73 glyphs similarly accounted for half the word-beginnings. On this basis they predicated an identity between the two groups, and, by correlating other relationships between endings and medial groups in a lightning 40-hour electronic "decipherment," concluded that they had solved the Mayan writing. Sample solutions: "The young maize god fires pottery from white clay"; "The woman's burden is the god of war." But criticism both as to their general method and as to details of result has razed this elaborate structure.

Of all the decipherments of history, the most elegant, the most coolly rational, the most satisfying, and withal the most surprising occurred in 1952. The story begins, as all stories of the Aegean must, with Troy.

In the 1870s, a wealthy German businessman who refused to accede to the general opinion that the *Iliad* and the *Odyssey* were pure myth proved his dogged belief that they enclosed a germ of truth. Heinrich Schliemann discovered the site of the historical Troy at the 85-foot mound of Hissarlik in Turkey three miles from the sea. He unearthed the thick circuit walls around which Achilles dragged Hector's body and which only the trickery of the wooden horse had breached. He found golden cups in what he thought was Priam's treasure. The site was right but his dating was wrong by a thousand years. He thought that the second level of the oft-rebuilt city was Homer's Troy; an American expedition in the 1930s under Dr. Carl W. Blegen of the University of Cincinnati showed that the much later seventh level of Troy was the Ilium that Homer had immortalized.

Homer had also sung of "Mycenae rich in gold," and Schliemann, again trusting the poet, promptly dug up at Mycenae on the mainland of Greece a circle of royal graves in which the interred kings wore crowns and death masks of gold. He thought that these were the tombs of Agamemnon, "king of men," ruler of Mycenae, overlord of all the Greeks in the Trojan War, and of his Trojan captive Cassandra, both murdered soon after his return by his wife Clytemnestra and her lover Aegisthus. As with Troy, Schliemann was hundreds of years too early. But his instincts were magnificently right.

A young British archeologist named Arthur Evans became curious about the writing that he felt must have been used by the wealthy and cultured inhabitants of this era. He found some engraved gems in Greece that had some appearance of script, traced them to Crete, and began to dig at Knossos. He discovered writing, as he had hoped, but the stupendous nature of his other discoveries soon drove this modest original goal out of his mind.

For Evans had excavated the spectacular ruins of an advanced ancient civilization. He had found the vast palace of the legendary King Minos, so rambling and so confused in plan that it might well have given rise to the myth that Minos built a labyrinth in which to pen the Minotaur, the monstrous offspring of his own queen and a bull. Evans saw wall frescoes of youths grasping the horns of a bull and being tossed onto its back—the bull-dancers that intimated that some elements of the story of the Minotaur, filtered through the dark lenses of legend, were the race-memory of actual events. Scattered through the palace were representations of the royal symbol, the two-headed ax, in such profusion that Evans called the palace the House of the Double Ax. The civilization he named Minoan, after its legendary founder.

Evans had begun his excavations in March of 1900. On the 31st of the month he unearthed the first clay tablet with the writing he had originally sought; on the 6th of April he found a whole hoard of inscribed tablets. Some were embedded in charred wood, presumably the remains of the wooden box in which they were originally stored. The dull gray tablets came in two shapes, a long and narrow "palm-leaf" type and a 5 × 10-inch "page" type. The Cretans did not bake the tablets but merely dried them; a leak in one of Evans' roofs once reduced a boxful to a pulpy mass. The clay still held the fingerprints of the scribes who had patted them flat. Most tablets were broken, but often the fragments could be joined together.

Ancestral Voices

Evans found four kinds of writing. The oldest appeared as three-dimensional carvings on gems like those that had started his quest and on seals an inch across. It was markedly pictographic, and Evans called it the Hieroglyphic Script of Class A, though it bore no relation to the hieroglyphs of Egypt. He found a stylized form of this written on clay which he called the Hieroglyphic Script of Class B, and he traced further simplifications of this into two forms of cursive writing, much more linear than the hieroglyphs, on the tablets. Evans called one the Linear Script of Class A, and the other, the most recent of the four scripts, the Linear Script of Class B. Linear A was found at locations all over Crete, while Linear B was found only at Knossos. They had not coexisted; Linear B replaced Linear A. The relationship among the four was not entirely clear. Some forms progressively simplified from Hieroglyphic A to B to Linear A to B. But Linear B has some signs that do not exist in Linear A, and some Linear B forms are more complex than their apparent Linear A counterparts. The linear scripts run from left to right.

The individual signs of Linear B are rather fanciful and resemble a whole variety of objects—a Gothic arch enclosing a vertical line, a ladder, a heart with a stem running through it, a bent trident with a barb, a three-legged dinosaur looking behind him, an A with an extra horizontal bar through it, a backward S, a tall beer glass, half full, with a bow tied on its rim; dozens look like nothing at all in this world. Evans counted 70 in common use (there were about 90 altogether), and presumed from this and from the average number of signs included between the upright lines that often divided the words that "it is probable that the signs have a syllabic value."

The Linear B tablets appeared to be primarily inventories, lists, business documents. In addition to the signs, they bore pictograms of horses, chariots, wheels, men, women, swords, cereals, and so forth, accompanied by strokes that evidently indicated the number of the depicted item in a decimal system. Several tablets were found with a totaling entry on the bottom line. Some tablets were indexed on their edges so that the bookkeeper would not have to pull out a whole batch to get the one he needed.

Evans classified the tablets into groups suggested by their pictograms—olive culture, saffron culture, cereals, flocks and herds, chariots, and so on. He divided the signs themselves into four groups based on phonetic, ideographic, numerical, or agricultural associations. He listed what appeared to be male and female names, counted sign-occurrences in the male group, and suggested that regular changes in names in the female group constituted "good evidences of declension." He identified what he claimed were determinatives for royal and religious words. He remarked that one sign looked much like a Semitic letter, wisely stopping short of making the unsubstantiated suggestion that they both represented the same sound.

He did not read the script. The basis for the decipherment—the language underlying the writing—remained unknown. Historical considerations pointed strongly in a certain direction, however.

Evans believed that the Minoan civilization that he had uncovered had dominated the mainland Greeks from its inception to its fall. As evidence, he cited early features that were original at Knossos and derivative in the contemporaneous Mycenaean civilization discovered by Schliemann—primarily similar architecture and the so-called Palace style of pottery. Given this "Knossocentric" premise, there followed inexorably the corollary that the language of Linear B was related to Semitic or Etruscan or Hittite or to the language of whatever racial stock, probably non-Indo-European, that had first ruled in Crete. Had the language of Linear B been the Greek that the Mycenaeans presumably spoke—which seemed improbable in the first place, because the script presumably would have been a relatively easy Case I solution—Evans' thesis would have been untenable. But an apparent demonstration that the language was not Greek seemed to prove the Minoan hegemony.

Linear B strikingly resembled the writing used centuries later on the nearby Mediterranean island of Cyprus. The general configurations of the characters agreed, and some signs matched perfectly. Scholars could read the Cypriote script, in use from 700 to 100 B.C., because the English Assyriologist George Smith had deciphered it in the 1870s. The number of its characters—55—had convinced him that they represented syllables. In a bilingual inscription of Phoenician and Cypriote, Smith picked out the two Cypriote words corresponding to the two Phoenician occurrences of "king." The next-to-last signs in the Cypriote differed from one word to the other. From their positions in the text, Smith decided that the differences resulted from declension—one form being the nominative case, "king," the other the genitive case, "of the king." He then looked for a neighboring language in which the next-to-last syllables of the word "king" varied from the nominative to genitive. He found the Greek *basileús*, nominative, and *basiléōs*, genitive. With this and the help of proper names, "I thus obtained, with more or less certainty, the phonetic values of eighteen of the Cypriote characters, and I tried by means of this help to decipher the remainder of the inscription. Unfortunately, the parts of the Cypriote inscription which contained the rest of the proper names were mutilated...." On the evidence of *basileús* and other similarities with Greek, he thought that "the language was allied to, although not the same as, the Greek." At this point Smith quit the problem, partly because he could not go any further, partly because he was about to set out on the expedition that was to find the Babylonian tablets of the Flood and the Gilgamesh Epic.

His work was continued by others, particularly Samuel Birch, Johannes Brandis, and Moriz Schmidt. Eventually it became clear that the language was Greek, but written in a script so utterly unlike the familiar alphabetic system of Greek that it seemed mangled almost beyond recognition. The signs of this script could represent only pure vowels or syllables in the form of consonant-vowel; single consonants, vowel-consonant groups, and consonant-vowel-consonant groups were excluded. Among other peculiarities, the script did not distinguish the sounds of /ta, da, tha/, but used a single sign for all of them. It ignored nasals before a consonant: "panta" ("all") was written *pa-ta*. It wrote consonants at the end of a word with an unpronounced auxiliary vowel: "theoīs" ("to the gods") becomes *te-o-i-se*. A syllable beginning with two consonants had to be written as if with two syllables. All this imparted a barbarous awkwardness to the written language of the Greeks of Cyprus, which was contemporary and similar to that spoken by the mainland Greeks during their Golden Age. The Greek "anthropos" ("man") appeared in Cypriote as *a-to-ro-po-se*.

Evans pointed out the similarity of this script to the Cretan ones and may even have tried to decipher Linear A and B with the Cypriote values. If so, he failed, as others who did try it later failed. A singular fact seemed to ratify this failure. The most common final consonant in Greek is *s*, which the Cypriote script rendered as *se*. Now, the Cypriote sign for *se* is identical to one of the Linear B signs. But in Linear B this sign rarely ends words. This phenomenon repelled the hypothesis that Greek underlay Linear B. The failures, plus this linguistic evidence, reinforced Evans' archeological evidence for his Knossocentric thesis of Crete's dominance over Greece. His own magisterial prestige soon elevated it to orthodoxy.

Yet a few brave heretics challenged it. Brave they had to be: one, Alan J. B. Wace, paid for his impudence with an unwanted retirement from the British School in Athens in 1923 and with exclusion from work in the Minoan field for several years. The heretics differed with Evans only for the period from 1450 B.C. to the end of the Bronze Age in 1125 B.C. These years encompassed the heroic age of Greece and the Trojan War (about 1240 B.C.) and are consequently of supreme importance; the Linear B tablets were written during this time. Both schools of thought agreed that, earlier in the Bronze Age, before 1450, Crete prevailed in the Aegean. The legend of Athens' subjugation to Minos and its annual tribute of seven youths and seven maidens to the Minotaur, eventually slain by the Athenian hero Theseus, may mount from this time as a kind of literary artifact. This period, in which Linear A was used, ended with the destruction, by earthquake and fire, of the original Palace of Minos.

Wace and the others felt that Evans had ignored important evidence for the questioned years. Archeological evidence, such as size of palaces, increasingly showed that the mainland was rising in power and influence during and just prior to these years and that Crete was declining. This, Wace thought, made a mainland domination of Crete more likely than the reverse.

A 1939 discovery gave this theory an enormous boost. After finishing his work at Troy, Carl Blegen excavated at Pylos in Greece. He unearthed the palace of Nestor, the oldest of the Greek chieftains at Troy, wise and garrulous, one of the Argonauts who sailed with Jason in quest of the Golden Fleece. Blegen's very first trench ran through the archives room, where he found 600 fragments of clay tablets inscribed in Linear B. If Linear B represented the language of Minoan culture, why should it be found only at Knossos and nowhere else on its native Crete, and yet be in use by a Greek king for keeping his accounts on the mainland far from its home? Wace theorized that Pylos was a home of Linear B and that conquering Greeks brought it to Knossos. Unfortunately, this virtually required Linear B to be Greek, and the probabilities appeared to stand strongly against this. Evans' words boomed out in victorious affirmation of this thesis: "... there is no palace either at Mycenae or at Thebes for Greek-speaking dynasts ... the culture, like the language, was still Minoan to the core."

Despite Evans' confidence, only the solution of the language could definitely confirm or deny his statement. And this looked far off. Evans had, in 1909, published the hieroglyphic inscriptions then known and a couple of the Linear A tablets from Knossos in his folio-sized *Scripta Minoa I*, but only 14 of the approximately 1,600 Linear B tablets that he had unearthed. In 1935, he presented 120 more during a richly suggestive 160-page discussion of them in the second part of the fourth and final volume of his magnum opus, *The Palace of Minos*. But he never carried out his intention of publishing the main corpus of the tablets in successive volumes of the *Scripta Minoa* series, and at his death in 1941, aged 90, it was still closed to scholars. Custom in archeology gives the discoverer the privilege of publishing his finds first, but it imposes in return the duty of publishing them promptly. Evans has therefore been taxed with depriving two generations of scholars of the opportunity of working on Linear B. The only other Linear B texts that were generally known were 38 of the Knossian tablets, published by the Finnish professor Johannes Sundwall, who incurred Evans' displeasure for even that small breach of archeological etiquette. World War II forced Blegen to cache his trove in the vaults of the Bank of Athens and prevented him from publishing it.

Despite the insufficiency of material, many would-be decipherers had attacked the puzzle. In 1931, for example, F. G. Gordon went *Through Basque to Minoan* and came out in a never-never land in which the Knossos inventories read like elegiac poems. Miss Florence Melian Stawell dared to counter Evans by seeing Greek in the Minoan scripts. She arbitrarily assigned a syllabic or alphabetic value to each hieroglyphic or Linear A sign based on the Greek name of the object shown on the tablets, permitting herself a good many terms "which had died out before Homer." Difficulties with Linear B compelled her to read each sign as a whole word, with the absurd result that the words, which were divided by vertical lines, became in her view whole sentences.

The error of her ways was demonstrated in a 1940 article in the *American Journal of Archaeology* by one M. G. F. Ventris, who, whoever he was, was evidently not a professional archeologist, since, where most contributors listed their university affiliations, he gave only "London." Yet his article was good enough to be published. Ventris cleared the field of opposition views—

"The theory that Minoan could be Greek is based of course on a deliberate disregard for historical plausibility, and the wonder is that the Greek readings have been got into publishable form at all"—before presenting his own case for a similarity with Etruscan. He based it upon the lack in both Etruscan and the Cypriote syllabary of the voiced stops /b/, /g/, /d/ and the apparent derivation of Cypriote from Minoan. He deciphered some Linear B names with the help of the syllabary and obtained some "name-radicals," which did not add much except confusion. Concluded Ventris bravely: "It [the decipherment] can be done."

Meanwhile, Bedřich Hrozný, who had disposed of the Indus Valley hieroglyphics to his satisfaction, knifed through Linear B with a facility that made everyone who had been stymied by its difficulties look like fools. He assigned the phonetic value /ha/ to a Linear B sign, for example, on the basis of resemblances that he saw between it and a Hittite sign for *hà*, an Egyptian sign for *he*, a Sabaean for *ḥ*, a Carian and Etruscan for *kh*, and a Phrygian for *χ*. He related another sign to a value deduced from his Indus Valley decipherment. The solution consisted of a hodgepodge of words from a mixture of different actual and derived languages. Critics condemned it on methodological, philological, and evidentiary grounds. "When the decipherer is as thoroughly acquainted with as many languages as Hrozný certainly is," one critic observed gently, "the range of possible satisfactory combinations of sound and sense is very large, and few inscriptions will seem entirely without sense." Most importantly, Hrozný's readings did not correspond to what the tablets appeared to be talking about.

At about the same time, Vladimir Georgiev of the University of Sofia offered an 81-page decipherment. He wrote that his study of Aegean placenames and Greek vocabulary had established that the Linear B language was an unknown Indo-European tongue which he named Pelasgian or Eteocretan. His readings seemed arbitrary, however, and did not secure conviction.

Essays more modest appeared from time to time. In 1950, the German scholar Ernst Sittig, who had served in the German Foreign Office cryptologic section from 1919 to 1924, assumed that the language underlying some non-Greek inscriptions written in the Cypriote syllabary was related to Minoan. He then matched these signs to Linear B on the basis of resemblances in form and in frequency, and announced the identification of 14 signs. With these as a start, he began work to recover the Minoan language.

The most valuable of the limited studies was a series of articles by Dr. Alice B. Kober, assistant professor of classical studies at Brooklyn College. In 1944 she presented a close textual analysis of tablets with an adze ideogram, and in 1945 pointed out that the final signs in words on ten "chariot" tablets varied. As Evans had suggested ten years earlier, she concluded that "it is highly probable that the language of the Linear Class B documents was inflected."

In an inflected language, changes in the form of words—usually endings—

924   THE CODEBREAKERS

indicate differences in tense, gender, number, person, case, and so on. Only a few such changes, or inflections, survive in English. An -*s* on nouns marks a plural. An -*ed* on verbs indicates past tense. Inflections are much more common in older languages, as anyone who has grappled with Latin grammar knows. Thus, where English would use the simple form *earth* in all cases, Latin declines it from *terra* to *terrae, terrae, terram,* and so on, depending on whether it is a singular noun in the nominative case, the genitive case, the dative case, or some other case. The part of the word that does not change—*terr*—is the stem.

"If a language has inflection," Miss Kober wrote, "certain signs are bound to appear over and over again in certain positions of the written words." She detected such repetition, though she conceded that "the types of inflection used, and their significance are still unknown."

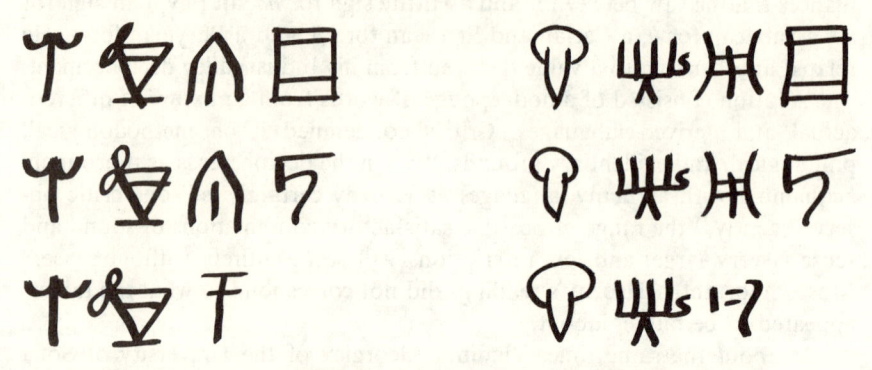

The Linear B nouns that Alice Kober used in her original analyses

The next year she identified the signs that constituted the inflections. She began by assuming that the words in a tablet headed with the ideogram for "woman" were all nouns (probably names) and all in the same case. Then she postulated that "if a certain sign or group of signs occurs regularly or with fair frequency as a word ending in a given inscription . . . this ending is usual for . . . the particular case." In Latin, the -*ae* of the genitive singular will recur in *terrae, fossae, barbae,* and so on. She found a sign that recurred thus frequently as a word ending. It looked like a ladder and was referred to for typographical convenience as "7." She labeled it the ending for Case I. She could not tell, of course, whether the case was nominative, accusative, or what. Next she looked in other tables for the same words with a different common ending. She could recognize the "same" words by the invariant stem. She found another ending, which looked somewhat like a 5, referred to as "40," and labeled it the Case II ending.

When she had done this for all the common endings, she found several nouns that were declined in three cases. For her analysis, she in effect picked out a pair that exhibited some puzzling characteristics and concentrated on them, hoping that explaining the characteristics would help solve Linear B. The two nouns thus chosen may be tagged by letting J K represent the signs of the stem of one and L M the signs of the stem of the other. She set them out in two paradigms, each listing all forms of one word:

Case I	J	K	2	7		L	M	36 7
Case II	J	K	2	40		L	M	36 40
Case III	J	K	59			L	M	20

Miss Kober then dared a conjecture that might explain these variations. Suppose, she said, that the signs of the Linear B syllabary could represent only either pure vowels or syllables of consonant-vowel formation. She based this assumption upon the resemblance of the Linear B to the Cypriote syllabary, which could express sounds only in that very way—syllables like *a* and *da* permitted, syllables like *ad* and *dap* and lone consonants like *d* excluded.

Suppose further, she said, that both the JK and LM stems ended in consonants. This assumption was justified; most stems in most languages seem to end in consonants—*hom* for Latin *homo*, for example. The end of the stem would be followed by the beginning of the inflection, and in a Cypriote-like syllabary, the consonant would have to be followed by a vowel. Thus the syllabary would link together in a single sign the consonant of the stem ending and the vowel of the inflection's beginning—the *m* and the *o* of *homo* into *mo*, if Latin had been written in that syllabary. Such a sign would straddle or bridge the natural division between stem and inflection. It would stand with one foot in the stem and the other in the inflection, the first foot being a consonant, the second a vowel. It may be called a "bridge sign."

Now in a paradigm, the first vowel of the case ending often varies as part of the variation that differentiates one case from another. Thus, in the Latin paradigm *dominus, domini, domino*, the first vowel of the inflection is successively *u, i,* and *o*. Hence, in a Cypriote-like syllabary, the bridge signs that would incorporate these varying vowels would themselves vary, because *nu, ni, no* would necessarily have different signs. Miss Kober observed this phenomenon in the variation between signs 2 and 59 in the JK noun and between signs 36 and 20 in the LM noun. She therefore regarded them as bridge signs. But—concentrating on JK—signs 2 and 59 each stand with one foot on the unchanging final consonant of the stem. Thus both these signs begin with the same consonant. For generality, Miss Kober illustrated this principle with an Akkadian noun, *sadanu*, whose stem is *sad-* and whose case endings are *-anu, -ani,* and *-u:*

Case I	J	K	2	7
		sa	da	nu
Case II	J	K	2	40
		sa	da	ni
Case III	J	K	59	
		sa	du	

Miss Kober did not suggest that these were the actual meanings of the Linear B signs. She simply wanted to demonstrate how signs 2 and 59 shared the fixed consonant of the stem. By the same reasoning, signs 36 and 20 of the LM noun began with a consonant in common. In neither noun did she know what the consonant might be. (She could not draw any conclusions about signs 7 and 40, for though in Akkadian they happened to have the same consonant, in Linear B they might not. Case II might be something like *sadalo*.)

The Brooklyn College scholar thus ascertained that some signs shared a common consonant. She thereby drove the thin edge of a wedge into the theretofore unbreached façade of Linear B. In her next move, Miss Kober widened this crack into a substantial fissure.

She cross-compared the JK and LM nouns. She recalled her original search and conclusions: JK and LM had the same signs at their tails and so had the same case endings. She focused on Case I. Since both words had the same case endings, both contributed the same vowel to their respective bridge signs—2 in JK, 36 in LM. But if the vowels were the same, why were the bridge signs different? Because, she answered herself, JK was a different word from LM, the different words had different stems, and the different stems furnished different final consonants to the bridge signs. Therefore they differed. But the vowel did not change. It remained the same in both bridge signs. And so Miss Kober ascertained two signs that had a vowel in common.

The situation can be depicted with the made-up word *petanu*, of the same declension as *sadanu*, and consequently with the same endings *-anu*, *-ani*, and *-u*.

Case I	J	K	2	7	L	M	36	7
		sa	da	nu		pe	ta	nu
Case II	J	K	2	40	L	M	36	40
		sa	da	ni		pe	ta	ni
Case III	J	K	59		L	M	20	
		sa	du			pe	tu	

Even though signs 2 and 36 differ because they have different stem consonants, they have the vowel of the case ending in common. Likewise 59 and 20 have a vowel in common.

Miss Kober had thus discovered some Linear B signs that had vowels in common and some that had consonants in common. Some signs belonged to both groups, and when this occurred she could arrange them in a two-dimensional pattern, with the signs sharing the same vowel in a single row and those sharing the same consonant in a single column:

	C_1	C_2
V_1	2	36
V_2	59	20

Her method was ingenious, rigorous, and powerful in the extreme. It precluded wild guesses as to the meaning of a sign, for any phonetic assumption would have to validate itself with the consonants of its column in the pattern and the vowels of its row. In other words, if *du* looked good for 59, *d* would have to make sense as a consonant wherever 2 appeared, and *u* as a vowel wherever 20 appeared. At the same time, it would suggest new values. If *du* was 59, then the insertion of *d?* wherever 2 appeared, as in *??-d?-nu,* might suggest that 2 was *da,* giving a new vowel value. Then 36 would have to be *?a,* and this in turn might suggest *ta* to make *??-ta-nu.*

Miss Kober purposely refrained from the critical step of assigning phonetic values to the signs because she felt it unwarranted with the paucity of material then available. But she wrung a few more details from the tablets, such as the demonstration that the two forms of a two-sign word at the foot of several lists represented masculine and feminine forms of "total." Most important, by 1948 she had extended her consonant and vowel equivalents from four signs to ten, which she arranged in a "tentative phonetic pattern" two vowels deep and five consonants wide. Two years later, aged 43, she was dead of cancer.

A few months before her death in May, 1950, she had received a questionnaire on the Linear B problem from Michael Ventris, who had propounded the Etruscan theory in the *American Journal of Archaeology* in 1940. The ten-year hiatus in his work was the result of interruptions by World War II, in which he served as a navigator in a Royal Air Force bomber, and by his studies at the Architectural Association School in London, from which he was graduated with honors in 1948. For Ventris was an architect, not a professional scholar, and he was not yet 30. He had written his 1940 paper when he was only 18, a fact that he had carefully concealed from the editor and that makes the article's acceptance all the more impressive.

He was born on July 12, 1922. His father was a British Army officer in India, his mother a beautiful woman who brought Michael up in an artistic atmosphere. He himself was uncommonly handsome. He went to school in Switzerland and then won a scholarship to Stowe School in England. His aptitude for languages was marked: he taught himself some Polish (his mother was half Polish) when he was 6, and as a young man learned enough Swedish in a few weeks to get a temporary job in Sweden. He had been taught in French and German in Switzerland, and had studied Greek at Stowe. He combined a remarkable visual memory with a good ear. As an architect, he worked for a while designing schools for the Ministry of Education, and in 1956 won the first research fellowship awarded by the *Architects' Journal.* His wife, also an architect, designed a modern home for them and their two children. By all accounts he was charming and modest, serious yet with an occasional flash of gaiety, affable, able to explain things simply, and brilliant.

Ventris' interest in the Linear B problem had been roused when, at 14, he heard Sir Arthur Evans himself lecture on fabulous Crete and its mysterious writing. At that impressionable age, when so many lifetime enthusiasms are formed, he took up the challenge of the undeciphered script, reading the literature and, later, corresponding with the experts. The publication of seven newly discovered tablets in 1950 encouraged him to resume his analyses, beginning by determining the "state of the art." The questionnaire that he sent Miss Kober in 1950 also went to eleven other scholars who he knew were working on Linear B. Ten of the twelve answered. Hrozný, then past 70, did not, nor did Miss Kober, who believed—with some justification—that discussion of unproved theories is a waste of time. Ventris circulated the replies, which summarized what was known about Linear B 50 years after Evans' discovery of the first tablets and which has come to be called the "Mid-Century Report." The consensus was that the underlying language was probably related to Hittite; a minority, including Ventris, held that it was more closely related to Etruscan.

In 1951, 556 of the Linear B tablets that Carl Blegen had found at Pylos in 1939 were published, thus at one stroke quadrupling the quantity of text available for study—the Evans tablets still not having been released. The publication of Blegen's find was supervised by one of Blegen's students, Emmett L. Bennett, Jr. Bennett, who had worked as a cryptanalyst during World War II, had written his doctoral thesis on "The Minoan Linear Script from Pylos." Like Miss Kober, he proceeded with caution; progress was slower than if he had attacked the problem wholesale with sign substitutions and the like, but it was substantially surer. In a 1950 article, he clarified the numerical and mensural systems of both Linear A and B. But his greatest contribution was the establishment of the signary by recognizing variant forms. This first step, which can be quite difficult in an unknown script—and sometimes is not easy with just an unfamiliar handwriting—supports all the rest; it is therefore essential, but no one before Bennett had really done it. Bennett also classified the signs according to their form and established an order which others numbered to make it easier to cite the signs in print.

By then Ventris was circulating Work Notes averaging eight pages each that he duplicated and mailed at his own expense to two dozen interested scholars. These notes reported his theories, comparisons, wild surmises. He was, in a sense, working in public, allowing each of his steps to be seen and criticized by his colleagues, and—what is frequently important among scholars, who are rewarded in fame and honor and not in cash—risking that his suggestions might touch off a train of thought in a colleague's mind, letting him achieve the final solution. The first Work Note, mailed out in January, 1951, reviewed the evidence for inflection and for Miss Kober's phonetic pattern. Ventris adopted it—though he placed the vowels at the top, the consonants at the side—and called it a "grid." He drove nails into a board and hung tags on them marked with the Linear B signs.

The second Work Note suggested that a button-like sign represented an enclitic "and"—a conjunction like the Latin suffix "-que," which was tacked onto the end of words, as in "Senatus Populusque Romanus," the full form of SPQR, "the Senate and the people of Rome." Several succeeding Work Notes tested possible parallels with a postulated Aegean language or with Etruscan, which Ventris still regarded as the probable answer. And all this time he was slowly filling in the grid by repeating Miss Kober's technique of comparing words to determine signs sharing the same vowels and consonants. He moved the tags from one nail to another as he tested assumptions, noting whether a sign hung in a certain column seemed to have the same vowel as the signs already there.

Work Note 8 tabulated the frequencies of each sign as initial, final, or medial. The enormous frequency of three signs at the beginning of words—one looking like a double ax, the second a throne, the third like an A with an extra bar—suggested that they might be pure vowels. In languages written syllabically, statistics showed, the pure vowels have the highest initial frequencies. Ventris thought, as others had privately, that the double ax represented *a* and the throne *i*. The assignments of pure vowels were independent of the grid; they did not affect it nor it them.

The next Work Note set forth evidence that certain signs represented similar sounds. Ventris observed that certain words exhibited slight differences in spelling and, because these words occurred in identical sentences, he concluded that the differences represented, not inflection, but slight variations in pronunciation. One scribe might write "father," another—from the Knossos equivalent of Brooklyn—might set down "fadder." No dictionaries existed to standardize spelling; the scribes wrote what they heard. Ventris, coming across such variations in identical contexts, assumed that /th/ and /dd/ represented similar sounds. He could then place them in either the same column or the same row of the grid, depending on whether the consonant or the vowel varied, information that came from other sources. These spelling variations greatly expanded the grid.

Work Note 10 resumed the discussion of the enclitic "and." Work Note 11 showed that two alternating phrases represented male and female genders of "servant." Work Note 12 classified the sign-groups into what Ventris thought were personal names, names of institutions or places, names of trades and titles applied to men and women, and a general vocabulary. Work Notes 13 and 14 showed that men's names were declined in at least six different declensions. The lack of a regular sign for a nominative ending in -*s* militated against Greek or any related Indo-European language. Work Notes 15 and 17 expanded the grid and proposed a few tentative phonetic assignments. By September 28, 1951, Ventris, in Athens, drafted a grid in his beautiful hand that inserted 50 signs in its 85 cells.

During the winter of 1951–52 Ventris made advances in elucidating a variety of minor points. In February, 1952, appeared *Scripta Minoa II*, edited by the elderly Sir John Myres, Evans' old colleague, and presenting at last the tablets that Evans had found half a century before. Work Note 19 of

March 20 gave considerable space to possible parallels in Etruscan for the inflectional activity of a particular sign.

Ventris then took up a puzzling spelling variation that had grown more evident with the publication of *Scripta Minoa II*. To improve the symmetry of a corner of the grid in the light of this feature, he returned to the value *jo* for a sign for which he had, in Work Note 9, summarily rejected that value. This would make the many men's names end (in the genitive) in -*jo* or -*jojo* (the *j* is a semiconsonant, like *y*). Ventris found precedents for this in derivative Greek, Etruscan, and Lycian names. The grid automatically compelled every sign in that column to share the vowel -*o*. Ventris thought that the throne sign was *i* and—even though the grid did not require him to do so— gave the same vowel to the signs that he had placed in that column. This was bolstered by the near identity of the sign for Cypriote *ti* and a sign in the throne column. He stuck with *a* for the double ax and the signs of that column, and with the help of this made his third consonant assumption, *n*, because of the similarity of the Cypriote *na* and a sign in the -*a* column.

With these in mind, he looked again at some of the very words that Miss Kober had used in her original analysis. He thought that certain of these might be names of places. Their longer forms had added on the symbols for *jo* and *ja* to form masculine and feminine adjectives, just as "France" expands to "français" and "française." In the words' short forms, all their vowels were known. In the first word, for example, the grid showed that all three vowels were the same; the *jo* assumption made them *o*. The consonants were not known, but here again the grid showed that, in the first name and the second, the last consonants were the same. Moreover, the second consonant of the first word was the same as the third consonant of the second— even though they were mated to different vowels. The partial decipherments, in which the unknown consonants are represented by the numbers of the row of the grid in which the Minoan sign stood, were:

6*o*-8*o*-13*o*   *a*-7*i*-8*i*-13*o*

Among the place-names likely to occur in tablets found at Knossos would be that of its harbor town, Amnisos, which would have to be spelled with an extra vowel between the *m* and the *n* to conform to the consonant-vowel nature of the script. As Ventris later wrote, "It did not require very great imagination to realize" that the second of the two could be *A-mi-ni-so*. If so, the imperatives of the grid demanded that the first name become 6*o-no-so*, which, again on the basis of an inserted vowel, could be *Ko-no-so*, or *Knossos* itself. This looked good. Perhaps the scribes dropped the final -*s*. This might explain the puzzling failure of the sign that so resembled the Cypriote *se* to appear at the end of words as often as it would have in Greek. Though the inserted vowels differed in the two cases, they both followed the rule of anticipation: they were the same as the vowel of the following syllable.

By a chain reaction, the grid now determined part of the sounds of dozens of other signs and the entire phonetic value of several others, just as it had indicated the consonant of *no* in *Ko-no-so*. For example, the sign like a tall beer glass stood at the intersection of the row for *k* and the column for *i*. It had to be *ki*. That was the beauty of the grid system. It forced its decipherment out of itself.

Ventris looked at the two-sign word that Miss Kober had determined stood for "total." The first sign stood in the same row as *ti* and in the *o* column; it had to be *to*. The second sign in the masculine form was *so*, and the second sign in the feminine form stood in the same row but in the *a* column: *sa*. Thus the two words were *to-so* and *to-sa*. They strongly resembled archaic forms of the Greek *tossos* and *tossa*, "so much," or *tossoi* and *tossai*, "so many." Greek? Everybody, including Ventris, thought that the Linear B language had to resemble some Aegean tongue that reflected the cultural domination of the Cretans, whose ethnic origin was widely regarded as non-Greek. The occurrence of an isolated word in a different language would not shake this view. It would not mean that Linear B was Greek any more than the presence of "habeas corpus" in a Supreme Court decision would mean that it was written in Latin.

Borrowed words usually indicate a need in the borrowing language. Words for common, everyday things, on the other hand, are usually filled from the native stock. Consequently Ventris may have been a bit surprised when the first syllable of the word that, in masculine and feminine forms, had been identified by ideograms as "boys" and "girls" deciphered as *ko*, the beginning of the classical Greek "kouros" ("boy") and "korē" ("girl"). Even this would not be conclusive: the English words for such homely concepts as "uncle" and "sky" have been imposed by invaders and do not come from Anglo-Saxon.

Then Ventris recalled that philologists had reconstructed the primitive Greek forms of "koros" and "kore" as "korwos" and "korwa." He thought that these primitive forms might be rendered in Linear B as *ko-wo* and *ko-wa*, and he drew from the back of his mind the suspicion that the barred A sign represented the pure vowel *e*. This would make *-e-wo* part of a common declension, and he remembered another reconstruction: *-ewos*, the primitive Greek genitive of the many words ending in *-eus*, such as the names "Odysseus," "Peleus," "Idomeneus." He made further assumptions—perhaps just in the spirit of seeing where they would lead. These produced a whole phrase of what appeared to be mutilated archaic Greek from a table with a chariot ideogram; it translated as "fitted with reins."

Greek had now thrust itself upon him in vocabulary, syntax, and meaning. Always the assumptions, rigidly controlled by the grid, mutually interlocked. Could it be that the Linear B tablets were—contrary to every tenet of orthodox Bronze Age archeology—written in Greek?

Ventris was not convinced. In Work Note 20 of June 1, 1952, which set out these results, he wrote: "If pursued, I suspect that this line of decipherment would sooner or later come to an impasse, or dissipate itself in absurdities." He scrupulously pointed out that the button sign would not fit the archaic Greek word that scholars had reconstructed for an enclitic "and," which was *te*. He called the Work Note "a frivolous digression," and regarded the appearance of the Hellenic language as "the Greek chimera."

But while the Work Note still was in the mail, Ventris discovered that the chimera was astonishingly real. He had pursued the line of decipherment and found that the Greek solution could not be denied. His logic had conquered his preconceptions. He had recovered archaic forms of four well-known Greek words (for "shepherd," "potter," "goldsmith," and "bronzesmith") and translated eight phrases. On a B.B.C. broadcast over which he had previously been invited to give a talk on the general problem of the scripts, he

Michael Ventris' grid of Linear B signs

said, "Once I made this assumption [that the tablets were written in Greek], most of the peculiarities of the language and spelling which had puzzled me seemed to find a logical explanation." In June of 1952, Ventris felt that he had deciphered Linear B. Work Note 20 was the last.

One of the most interested listeners to the broadcast was a young Cambridge philologist specializing in Greek, John Chadwick. At the time, the Ventris theory was just the latest in a long line of supposed "solutions," every one of which had failed. But Chadwick, who had himself failed to read the tablets on the assumption that they were Greek, was interested. He obtained Ventris' Work Notes from Sir John Myres and went home to test the solution for himself. Within four days he was convinced. He had deciphered 23

Ancestral Voices 933

plausible Greek words, some of which had not then been read by Ventris. On July 9, Chadwick wrote to the architect, congratulating him on the solution. They formed a close association and together wrote a report of the decipherment under a title which they had carefully chosen to avoid extravagant claims: "Evidence for Greek Dialect in the Mycenaean Archives."

It gave a decidedly confusing explanation of the decipherment. And it did not gather up all the loose ends. Some signs remained unknown; some translation difficulties arose. Yet its conclusions were cogent. In the first place, the deciphered words made sense. The language was Greek, truncated and primitive as compared to the polished classical tongue, but Greek. Its roughness could be attributed to the fact that the language of the tablets was a thousand years older than that of Plato, "a difference in date," they noted, "as great as between Beowulf and Shakespeare." Besides, many of the archaic forms agreed with predicted ones. In the second place, the deciphered texts reflected what

The "tripod" tablet that clinched the decipherment of Linear B

the tablets appeared to be talking about. Where the grid produced the word for "sword," a pictogram of a sword stood nearby. The two young authors submitted their article to the editors of the *Journal of Hellenic Studies*, who, recognizing its importance, made room for it in the 1953 volume despite the backlog of World War II articles that was still crowding their pages.

While waiting for it to appear, Ventris heard favorably from many experts who knew of his work. Professor Sittig, for example, who had been working on his own method of decipherment, now abandoned it and wrote to Ventris on May 22, 1953: "Your demonstrations are cryptologically the most interesting I have yet heard of, and are really fascinating." Of course, not everybody climbed on the bandwagon. But in that same month Ventris received a letter from Blegen that settled the matter:

> Since my return to Greece I have spent much of my time working on the tablets from Pylos, getting them properly ready to be photographed. I have tried your experimental syllabary on some of them.
>
> Enclosed for your information is a copy of P641, which you may find interesting. It evidently deals with pots, some on three legs, some with four handles, some with three, and others without handles. The first word by your system seems to be *ti-ri-po-de* and it recurs twice as *ti-ri-po* (singular?). The four-handled pot is preceded by *qe-to-ro-we*, the three-handled by *ti-ri-o-we* or *ti-ri-jo-we*, the handleless pot by *a-no-we*. All this seems too good to be true. Is coincidence excluded?

It was. The obvious relation of *ti-ri-* to *tri-*, of *a-* to the prefix meaning "nothing" or "without," of *-po-de* to Greek root *-pod-* meaning "foot," and of *-o-we* to the Greek *-oues* for "ear" or "handle" could not be denied. The language of Linear B was indubitably Greek. The tripod tablet results brought immediate agreement in principle by the vast majority of scholars competent in the field—including many who had themselves been defeated by the solution, such as Georgiev, Sundwall, and Bennett.

But some disagreed. The same journal that published "Evidence" provided space for a rebuttal by A. J. Beattie, professor of Greek at the University of Edinburgh. He did not understand the grid—a misapprehension that was due not to any obtuseness of his but to the obscurity of the Ventris-Chadwick account. "Let us suppose that he [Ventris] used *all* the texts available to him," Beattie wrote, "and that he counted every single sign in initial, medial and final positions, and so obtained three figures and an overall total for each sign, as well as an assortment of information about alternatives or concomitants. Are we then to suppose that these figures fell naturally into groups, so that the signs to which they referred could be disposed lengthwise and crosswise in such a way that they would ultimately be found to correspond to series of the type, *i, pi, ti, ki*, etc. and *pa, pe, pi*, etc.? This is evidently what Mr. Ventris means us to believe." This same lack of understanding misinformed Beattie's more valid linguistic criticisms: "What Mr. Ventris has given us by his transcription is not in fact the Greek language but a language of his own making. It is a strange language, which looks like Greek because he has been careful to provide it with a selection of Greek suffixes.... And by devising spelling-conventions of primitive simplicity, he has ensured that the syllables preceding the suffix of each word may occasionally be intelligible as Greek word-stems." Even Beattie admitted that the tripod tablet yielded some Greek, however, and in the end was reduced to impugning, not the results, but the data itself: "We should in any case suspect the validity of a list that has no one-handled or two-handled pots but knows only those with three or four handles or none at all."

Unlike the attacks upon the Hrozný and Georgiev "solutions" of Linear B, the critics' objections failed to convince. The solution rapidly won acceptance, and classical circles began to use its results. The most important result was, of course, the very fact that the language was Greek. Greek was spoken at the seat of former Minoan power in Knossos because Greeks ruled there. This vindicated Wace's rebel view that the mainland dominated Crete during the questioned years of 1400 to 1125 B.C. and thereby revised the Late Bronze Age history of the Aegean.

But what did the tablets say?

Sample texts read like this: "Koldos the shepherd holds a lease from the village: 48 litres of wheat." "At Pylos: five sons of the Ti-nwa-sian weavers (sons of rowers at A-pu-ne-we), two boys." "Four (or more) slaves of Koradollos in charge of seed-corn." "One pair of wheels bound with bronze, unfit for service." The tripod tablet, with pictograms in italic capitals: "Two tripods: Aigeus the Cretan brings them: 2 *TRIPODS*. One tripod: it is not sound as regards one foot: 1 *TRIPOD*. One tripod: the Cretan brings it; charred around the legs. . . . 1 *TRIPOD*. Wine-jars: 3 *JARS*. One larger cup with 4 handles: 1 *CUP*. Two larger cups with 3 handles: 2 *CUPS*. One smaller cup with 4 handles: 1 *CUP*. One smaller cup with 3 handles: 1 *CUP*. One smaller cup with no handle: 1 *CUP*." A votive tablet reporting, "To all the gods, one amphora of honey: 1 *AMPHORA*. To the Mistress of the Labyrinth, one amphora of honey: 1 *AMPHORA*," reads in the syllabic script *pa-si-te-o-i me-ri AMPHORA* 1/*da-pu-ri-to-jo po-ti-ni-ja me-ri AMPHORA* 1."

None of the tablets contains any literary work, nor any diplomatic instructions, personal letters, religious texts, historical writings, nor anything, in fact, beside these minutely detailed bureaucratic records of petty commercial transactions. Professor Denys Page describes the impression they make as a whole:

> These palace archives are the records of a comprehensive and pervasive bureaucracy, administering for hundreds of years a most elaborately organized society. . . . It is as if everything done by everybody was open to official inquiry and subject to official orders. We possess a part only of the archives for a single year at Pylos: they record thousands of transactions in hundreds of places. . . . But even more astonishing and significant is the omniscience, the insatiable thirst for intimate detail. Sheep may be counted up to a glittering total of twenty-five thousand; but there is still a purpose to be served by recording the fact that *one* animal was contributed by Komawens and another by *E-te-wa-no*. Restless officialdom notes the presence in *Pe-se-ro*'s house of one woman and two children; the employment of two nurses, one girl, and one boy, in a Cretan village; the fattening of an insignificant number of hogs in nine places; the existence somewhere of a single pair of brassbound chariot wheels and labelled "useless". . . . One would suppose that not a seed could be sown, not a gram of bronze worked, not a cloth woven, not a goat reared or a hog fattened, without the filling of a form in the Royal Palace; such is the impression made by only part of the files for a single year.

But was this all? Was this piddling minutiae to be the only result of a brilliant achievement? Was there to be no Epic of Gilgamesh, no Code of Hammurabi, no pharaonic boasts of kings conquered and cities sacked— only the Bronze Age equivalent of some incomplete county clerk records, some transactions of a farm cooperative, and some small donations to a parish church? Only that. But although no poetry has been discovered, the information contained in the tablets has, by inference, illuminated some of the greatest of Western man's poetry—the *Iliad* and the *Odyssey*.

The tablets do so because they are 400 years older than the time of Homer and contemporary with the events of which he sings. Linear B represents the written form of the language spoken by the almost legendary figures of the Trojan War. The clay tablets found at Mycenae and Pylos were written at almost the very moment that Agamemnon and Nestor, the kings of those cities, were waging war on the Trojan plain. Soon thereafter, waves of impoverished and barbaric Dorians from the north, brandishing their iron weapons, overran the Bronze Age civilization of heroic Greece. They extinguished the light of learning and the love of art, and for four centuries Greece dwelled in the illiterate darkness of its early Iron Age. In the eighth century B.C. the Hellenes began to emerge from this eclipse. They started to write with the Phoenician alphabet—the precursor of the present Latin alphabet. At the same time, a blind genius molded the stories of gods and men that had been transmitted orally from the past into a great unified theme and won undying fame for his name—Homer. The names and noble deeds and language of his epics in turn helped fix the ideals of the classical Greek civilization that flowered a few centuries later, and so helped mold the West.

By preserving many circumstantial details of the heroic world, the Linear B tablets assist in showing to what extent the *Iliad* is historical, to what extent poetic imagination has transmuted factual dross to fictional gold. Basically, the tablets confirm what archeology—beginning with Schliemann—had already shown, but they do provide additional details. For example, the tablets have two high titles in common with the epics: "wanax" and "basileus." In the tablets, "wanax" referred to the supreme king in the palace, and "basileus" to one of the many district governors. The epics often confer the title "basileus" on men who were clearly "wanaktes," showing a generalization of the term. But subconsciously the poet knows that the inferior title of "basileus" may never be applied to a god, though he may with perfect propriety be called "wanax." "The existence of the title 'wanax' in the *Iliad* is a plain proof of the continuity of the Greek epic from the Mycenaean period onwards," wrote Denys Page. Another proof of the historicity of the *Iliad* lies in the many names in *-eus* that occur in both the tablets and the epics—but not in later Greece. Dorian names were different, and, since the Mycenaean names survived only because the stories did, they testify to the fact that the Siege of Troy was already the subject of oral poetry within a generation of the destruction of the historical city, Troy VII.

Before Ventris deciphered Linear B, the oldest known specimen of Greek (and hence of European) writing existed on a vase dating from about 750 B.C.; it reads, "The dancer who performs most gracefully of all shall receive this." Ventris pushed back the frontiers of the language by some 700 years. He disinterred the earliest form of a language that still lives, 32 centuries later, and one of the earliest known forms of the western branch of the Indo-European languages. This has filled in some details of linguistic and semantic change.

Similarly, the Linear B tablets help depict life in Bronze Age Greece, and so throw additional light upon these obscure origins of Greek history. As Professor T. B. L. Webster declared, "By seeing the Greeks against this background we can measure more clearly than ever before the achievement of the

Greeks in leaping out of this context to become the founders of modern civilization."

Yet these results are, in the broadest sense, limited. They provide some minor details for literary appreciation; they permit a slightly greater understanding of a brilliant cultural achievement; they rectify an upside-down picture of the relation between two neighboring areas during a brief and distant moment of time, without much altering the view of the inner life of those areas. It is true that no decipherment can ever have the impact upon man that a new scientific discovery can, although the one may equal the other as a mental accomplishment. But even on its own ground of historical importance, the decipherment of Linear B cannot match that of hieroglyphic or that of cuneiform. They painted whole civilizations in rich detail on large and colorful canvases. Linear B slightly embellished one already known. William H. McNeill, in his recent one-volume world history, relegated the results to a footnote.

The greatness of the decipherment lies not in its substance but in its method. It shines with a clean Euclidean beauty. In it, man thinks more purely rationally, depending less upon external information and more upon logical manipulation of the data to derive new conclusions, than perhaps anywhere else in the humanities. The foundations of the decipherment utilized almost exclusively the observable interrelationships of the script symbols. The decipherers subjected these relationships to a minute scrutiny and, on the basis of only a few simple hypotheses from philology, extracted a pattern of vowels and consonants and then rewove them into a meaningful whole. The decipherment was sufficient unto itself. Everything discovered in the analysis found its place in the synthesis. From this economy and simplicity the decipherment gains its elegance and its great sense of satisfaction. And when, in the phonetic breakthrough, the decipherer necessarily departed from the givens of the script, he borrowed the very minimum of information from the outside world. He needed no bilingual Rosetta Stone, no dusty chronicles of Persian kings—only the single inescapable fact of where the tablets had been found.

The decipherment's pattern, more valuable than the information it produced, gives the work its great vitality—a vitality that has overcome the human mortality of its decipherers. For Ventris, like Alice Kober, had died young. Aged 34, he collided with a truck near Hatfield, England, while driving home late one night. But though all men die, to few is it given even in the full span of human existence to produce some useful work that endures beyond their years and makes them immortal. Michael Ventris and Alice Kober, despite their premature deaths, won that victory. They created the model decipherment.

26

MESSAGES FROM OUTER SPACE

OF ALL THE PROBLEMS CHALLENGING MAN in the modern realms of space and communication, perhaps the most intriguing is the one that lies at their juncture: how to solve messages from other worlds. The detection of a communication from another planet in another solar system would be one of the greatest events in human history. The discovery that other beings inhabit the same corner of eternity as man, that "they" are out there and "we" are down here, that life is not only an earthly state of being, that man must now surrender his last claim to uniqueness in the universe, would profoundly affect human thought. At the same time, it would open unimaginable vistas of technological growth that might help men solve the problems of war, disease, hunger. This would require an exchange of information, something beyond the mere hearing of a signal from outer space.

Yet, paradoxically, the very dissimilarities that would make the transfer of knowledge so fruitful might impede it. Could man understand a message from beings whose very modes of consciousness might differ from his? Could he extract information sent by creatures whose experience might seem at first glance to be utterly remote from his, who might not even respond to the same sense stimuli as humans, whose ways of thought might be as different from man's as man's are from the ant's? No doubt men would try, as Ulysses tried,

>To follow knowledge, like a sinking star,
>Beyond the utmost bound of human thought.

But could they do it?

The problem is not merely academic. Before dawn on the clear, cold morning of April 8, 1960, a young radio astronomer, Dr. Frank D. Drake, and a handful of technicians arrived in the electronics-packed control room nestling beneath the 85-foot radio telescope that stands in a grassy meadow at tiny Green Bank, West Virginia. They aimed its parabolic dish at Tau Ceti, an average-sized nearby star in the constellation of the Whale that was then rising over the eastern rim of the mountainous horizon. They set clockwork to track the star as it moved across the vault of the sky. Drake turned on the loudspeaker that would bring into the control room the radio emanations that the radio telescope—which is basically a giant directional radio antenna—

would pick up. He started the recording device whose pen would trace the emanations on a moving strip of paper. At about 6 a.m., he reached the last switch in his long series—the one for the mechanism that would automatically tune the receiver to listen in to one radio frequency after another. With a certain sense of destiny, he flicked it.

Mankind had begun the first major search that could lead to perhaps the most important discovery in its history—messages from outer space.

Two years later, in the dimly lit caucus room of the House of Representatives, Emilio Q. Daddario, a Congressman from Connecticut who, like most of his colleagues, is usually concerned with much more down-to-earth problems, put a question that might have seemed to belong, not to the august halls of Congress, but to science fiction, cereal boxes, comic strips, or teenage speculations. "I wonder," he asked the distinguished British astronomer Dr. Bernard Lovell, "taking into consideration the status of all of the possibilities of planets including those which might have life of one kind or another, what are the possibilities of receiving signals from other planets, and what kind of program should we have if any, and what would it involve?" Ten years earlier, such a question would have made Daddario the butt of laughter and might even have cost him some votes back home. On March 21, 1962, nobody laughed, and the question got a serious answer: "Well, sir, I think that now one has to be sympathetic about an idea which only a few years ago would have seemed rather farfetched." And then the Congressmen and the scientists went on to discuss that idea.

Just a few months earlier, the National Academy of Sciences had sponsored a conference at Green Bank, at which 11 scientists explored in some depth the questions of extraterrestrial life and its detection. And by 1965, some scientists had grown so trigger-happy over the possibility of hearing messages from outer space that three Russian astronomers announced that they had heard radio waves on a 100-day cycle from quasar CTA-102 indicating a supercivilization—only to retract it, after an almost unanimous chorus of skepticism, the very next day.

Men have long wondered whether other beings exist elsewhere in the universe. Lucretius thought it "in the highest degree unlikely that this earth and sky is the only one to have been created." A Chinese philosopher, Teng Mu, thought along the same lines, and Plutarch wondered about the habitability of the moon. But for centuries Ptolemaic astronomy, with its earth at the center of its universe, precluded any such thoughts from being any more than idle speculation. Then the Copernican revolution broke through the Ptolemaic spheres, and the Newtonian discovery of the laws of gravitation, which tie together the earth and the most distant stars, proposed to men's minds the new thought that nature might behave in the same way throughout the universe, that celestial phenomena might follow the same laws as terrestrial.

Soon thereafter a number of scientists and philosophers expressed the idea that there might be a plurality of worlds. Christiaan Huygens, discoverer of the rings of Saturn, looked up at the starry heavens and wondered, "Why may not every one of these stars or suns have as great a retinue as our sun, of planets, with their moons to wait upon them?" Bishop John Wilkins, author of the first book on cryptology in English, published *The Discovery of a World in the Moone, or a Discourse tending to prove that 'tis probable there may be another Habitable World in the Planet.* Poets found these ideas a fertile ground for fancy. Milton wondered in *Paradise Lost* whether the moon might not have clouds and rain and also fruits and creatures to eat them. He contended that it was disputable whether the entire universe existed only to convey shards of starlight to the earth, but ended by urging Adam and Eve to "Dream not of other worlds, what creatures there / Live, in what state, condition or degree," but to be happy in Eden. Alexander Pope thought that any knowledge of "what other planets circle other suns" might help man to know himself better. A number of writers of early science fiction discussed the question of life on other planets.

But for centuries such speculations were sanctioned only by imagination. Mankind's anthropocentric philosophy and religion even frowned upon them. Science turned up no evidence for the possible existence of other solar systems, and the more it learned about this one, the less hospitable other planets appeared as cradles of life. Mercury was too hot, Jupiter and Saturn and the other outer planets too cold. Venus and Mars, on the other hand, emerged as possibilities. Then, in 1877, the Italian astronomer Giovanni Schiaparelli "discovered" the so-called canals of Mars. Their ruled-line precision seemed best explainable as the work of intelligent beings. Other astronomers, equally respectable, confirmed the canals and reinforced the implication that the red planet could support life by their observation of the darkening of certain areas during Martian springs, as if vegetation were growing. These ideas caught the public fancy, and from these few threads of evidence Sunday supplement writers wove entire tapestries of Martian biology and sociology.

Interest in the problem periodically rose to a peak whenever Mars approached Earth closely in their orbits, which occurred every 15 to 17 years. Men animatedly discussed whether the Martians might be trying to contact Earth, and a few attempts were actually made to detect any signals. But nothing was heard, and the progress of scientific research soon made it highly improbable that any kind of intelligent life could exist on Mars. It was too cold, and there was too little water. Continued astronomical observations reduced the "canals" to a few faint lines on the Martian surface. As for Venus, its cloud-covered surface seemed to preclude gaining any visual evidence of life there.

At the same time, science seemed to have decided that life, if it existed at all elsewhere in the universe, was extremely rare. The birth of the solar system apparently required a freak occurrence. In the immeasurable depths of the void—where, if the sun were an apple placed at New York, the nearest star would be another apple at Moscow—two stars approached one another and swung past, each drawing out of the other long filaments of gas that condensed into planets. Anyone who has ever tried to get a golf ball into a stationary hole a few hundred yards away will appreciate the difficulty of intionally getting the two "apples," both in motion, to hit each other, and much more the chance of their accidentally grazing one another while on random courses. So infrequently would this event have occurred that in the whole history of the universe only the sparsest sprinkling of planetary systems would have come into being. The probability of other life in the universe would consequently be so low as to be negligible.

Theories were propounded that the solar system might have formed out of a great whirling mass of gas, floating in the universe, that condensed under gravitational attraction into the sun and its satellites. This ran into the problem that the sun's gravitation would apparently prevent the formation of planets. Though this difficulty still plagues cosmologists, the collision theory began to encounter even greater inconsistencies, such as the presence of an iron core in the earth when the sun, from which the earth was putatively born in the cosmic accident, has so little of that element. As a result, the condensation theory came to be accepted more and more by astrophysicists. Moreover, external evidence tends to support it, such as observations of what appear to be stars forming by condensation elsewhere in the universe.

The great implication of the condensation theory is that planetary systems must come into existence almost routinely as a by-product of the gaseous contraction and swirling that produce stars, and that a fair proportion of stars must have them. Evidence exists that this is so. Stars with planetary systems rotate much more slowly than those without, because the planets carry much of the system's spin, or angular momentum. Observation of many stars shows a sharp difference in their rotation speeds—some spinning on their axis in a matter of hours, others, like the sun, taking 25 days for a single revolution. Furthermore, all stars above a certain temperature and mass spin rapidly, while all those below spin slowly. Astronomers know how many stars exist of each of type, and this tells them that the Earth's galaxy alone, the Milky Way, contains millions of slowly spinning stars. Almost certainly these stars have planets. The pendulum of scientific opinion had begun its swing away from the theory of a scarcity of life in the universe toward one of its prevalence.

More direct evidence that planets exist elsewhere—though none have yet been seen—has been accumulating since World War II. If sufficiently heavy, a planet orbiting a star will tug sufficiently at its parent star to make it wiggle in its motion across the celestial sphere. This wiggle has been observed in two stars, 61 Cygni and Barnard's star. Calculations indicate that the satellite of 61 Cygni is about eight times the mass of Jupiter and that it circles its parent body every 4.8 years. That of Barnard's star revolves in a 24-year orbit and is half again as big as Jupiter.

It thus began to appear that planetary systems are not unusual but common in the universe. Of course, only those fulfilling certain conditions would be suitable as abodes of life. The main conditions appear to be a parent star long-lived and stable enough to permit the emergence of life, a planet large enough to retain an oxygen atmosphere, and an orbit that stays within a "habitable zone," defined basically as a zone in which water remains liquid. But even when, from the number of stars that probably have planets, those that are not suitable for one reason or another to support life are successively eliminated, the quantity of stars in just the Milky Way galaxy is so immense that there still remain hundreds of thousands of potential life-bearing worlds.

While astronomers were coming to these conclusions, biologists were experimenting to show that the chance of life's arising on these planets was good. Their work actually began in 1828 when Friedrich Wöhler synthesized an organic compound, urea, found in living creatures, from inorganic elements. The biggest step was Darwin's, of course, in advancing the theory of evolution that showed a continuous development of life forms, from the simplest to the most complex. There remained the problem of how it all started. Darwin himself thought that a few stray molecules containing the critical elements of hydrogen, oxygen, carbon, nitrogen, and phosphorus, cooked in the warm seas of the primordial earth, jolted by discharges of electricity, might have prepared a compound "ready to undergo still more complex changes." Serious testing of this hypothesis did not come until the late 1950s and early 1960s. In perhaps the most famous experiment, Dr. Stanley L. Miller subjected a mixture of water vapor, methane, ammonia, and hydrogen —thought to be, on the basis of spectrographic analysis of the atmospheres of Jupiter and Saturn, main constituents of the Earth's early atmosphere— to a 60,000-volt spark. He circulated the mixture in a sealed system of flasks and tubes for a week. By the end of the first day it had turned pink, and by the end of the week a deep red. Upon analysis, the mixture proved to have converted its simple compounds into glycine, alanine, lactic acid, acetic acid (vinegar), urea, and formic acid. All are organic compounds of importance in life, particularly glycine and alanine, which, as amino acids, constitute proteins, perhaps the most important biological materials.

At the same time, other scientists were working out the so-called "code of life" of the nucleic acids, DNA (deoxyribonucleic acid) and RNA (ribonucleic acid). These giant molecules are composed of a few simple chemical compounds, including amino acids like those synthesized by Miller, only repeated hundreds of thousands of times in a complicated pattern. Their structure resembles a twisted ladder whose sidepieces form a double spiral; the molecule unzips down the rungs to form two separate semimolecules, each of which attaches to itself compounds floating in the environment—thereby twice re-creating the ladder and reproducing the original molecule. The pattern with which the compounds of these nucleic acids fit together—a pattern that differs from one animal species to another—carries the instructions of heredity. Thus DNA and RNA are responsible for the essential characteristic of life: its ability to persist, its continuity. They themselves lie at the border between the animate and the inanimate. These biological experiments tended to show that life could arise spontaneously from ordinary, nonliving chemical compounds present on the primitive Earth. And if it could happen on that typical planet, Earth, it could happen on others.

Thus astronomy and biology converged upon the likelihood that life exists elsewhere in the universe. Man is just now reaching that conclusion. But the galactic time-scale reduces to the blink of a gnat's eye man's existence on Earth. Consequently, it is unlikely that other forms of life elsewhere have evolved to precisely the same point of cosmic consciousness. Chance alone would predict that on half the other planets life might be still in the unicellular state or in their equivalent of Neanderthal man. But on the other half civilization might have soared far beyond Earth's still primitive efforts.

In 1959, as all these avenues of investigation were reaching the crossroads that meant life exists elsewhere, a question asserted itself to several minds at almost the same time. Might these superior civilizations be trying to contact us? Frank Drake was beginning the thinking that culminated in Project Ozma. And two physicists from Cornell, who had long been interested in the general question of life in outer space, finally spent a few days to see whether communication was feasible between different solar systems. Their calculations showed that it was, and they sent the report of their investigations to *Nature*, the prestigious British scientific weekly. Its publication of their paper on September 19, 1961, made discussion of this science-fiction question "respectable," brought it out into the open, and stimulated a vigorous colloquy among scientists that is still continuing.

The article, by Philip Morrison and Giuseppe Cocconi, was entitled "Searching for Interstellar Communications." After briefly recapitulating the likelihood that long-lived civilizations might arise in other solar systems, they said:

> It follows, then, that near some star rather like the Sun there are civilizations with scientific interests and with technical possibilities much greater than those now available to us.
>
> To the beings of such a society, our Sun must appear as a likely site for the evolution of a new society. It is highly probable that for a long time they will have been expecting the development of science near the Sun. We shall assume that long ago they established a channel of communication that would one day become known to us, and that they look forward patiently to the answering signals from the Sun which would make known to them that a new society has entered the community of intelligence. What sort of channel would it be?

Communication may be effected in two ways: in person, which is to say by direct face-to-face contact, and not in person, which is by writing, radio, telegraph, telephone, flashing lights, or other similar long-distance means.

Communication in person is far easier than not in person, for it has access to many more resources.

Probably the first problem of a spaceman on another planet would be to decide whether the three-headed monster that meets him is trying to signal "Welcome, earthling" or "Scram, one-head!" If this question is settled amicably, both sides could proceed to the setting up of a more extended communication. As a preliminary step, the spaceman would obviously have to determine which of his five senses could be used to "talk" to a creature that may have only some of them.

Smell seems useless. Roy Bedichek, in *The Sense of Smell*, tells why:

> It may be worth a pause here to consider the problem of producing a language—that is, a give and take of important information—by means of odors alone. There is first the chemical difficulty of creating a countless number of distinctive odors. Only perfumers, perhaps, can appreciate the unreasonableness of this demand. Solve it, however, and you have made hardly a beginning. Each species must have a broadcasting equipment competent on the instant to generate the odor molecules carrying the particular message the animal at the moment wishes to communicate. After this seemingly impossible task has been accomplished, there remains the technology of devising a receiving set of high selectivity to receive the broadcast, decodify it and pass it on to the power with authority to prescribe and enforce appropriate action.

The other chemical sense, taste, suffers from these defects and more: taste organs can respond only to substances that they contact and that are dissolved in water.

Touch, however, has served humans as a relatively useful means of expression. Perhaps the most dramatic example is Helen Keller. Blind and deaf since the age of nineteen months, she learned by matching the vibrations of her teacher's vocal cords to objects she felt with her hands. Eventually she managed to comprehend, speak, and write. Though this system depends upon the peculiar accessibility of the human larynx, its remarkable success in the face of severe obstacles suggests that the basic method may be adapted to conversations with Martians—meaning here the inhabitants of any other planet. Perhaps the spaceman could give an object to the Martian and let him first feel it with his antennae, then run those antennae over the Braille word for the object. Or, while the Martian is handling the object, the spaceman might send him the signal for the object in "vibratese," an experimental system of tactile communication by buzzes of different intensity and length applied to various parts of the body. But touch itself is hampered by its relative grossness and its need to physically contact the communicator. These serious limitations will probably relegate it to a subordinate role in man-to-Martian communication, just as on Earth.

Sight and hearing, then, are left as the most workable senses for conversations involving humans. With these two, communication would probably begin with a simple show-and-tell process, like that used in many schools to teach reading. The spaceman could pick up a rock and say "rock," could run a short distance and say "run," and so forth. Eventually communication might be established. But if the Martians—or any life forms on nearby planets, if such exist—are a subhuman species, communication, in the sense of a two-way exchange with men, would probably not be possible. These lower forms would not have the intelligence for it. Men might, however, observe their communications among themselves. This usually amounts to an instinctual behavior highly restricted in the information that it conveys. Such, for example, is the "language" of the bees. The German zoologist Dr. Karl von Frisch found that when a bee arrived at her hive laden with nectar, she would perform a sort of "dance" with great vigor. Suddenly one of the other bees would fly out of the hive. Others would follow. Within minutes some of these bees would appear at the source of the nectar, which was often some distance away and not visible from the hive. Through repeated experiments, von Frisch found that the rate at which the bee turned during her dance indicated the distance of the food source from the hive. When the food was only 100 yards away, the bee turned between nine and ten times in 15 seconds. At 200 yards, she turned seven times, and at about a mile, only twice. Her dance then pinpointed the food source by giving its direction from the hive. When she danced at an angle of, say, fifty degrees to the left of vertical on the hive wall, the food source was located fifty degrees to the left of a line between the hive and the sun. So precise is the apian system of communication, von Frisch found, that it steers bees directly even to food hidden behind the ridge of a mountain. But this study, while valuable in learning about the creatures that man might find on other planets, has little relevance to communicating with them.

In any event, communication by direct contact occupies but a small part of the problem of messages from outer space. It is highly questionable whether intelligent life even exists on Venus or Mars, and the frozen black voids of interstellar space are so inconceivably vast that many scientists feel that man will never attempt to cross them in spaceships. Relativity limits any vehicle to the speed of light, and in a galaxy 60,000 light-years across it would take eons even at that speed—which no human conveyance shows any sign of even approaching—to penetrate even part way into the more populous neighborhoods of the galaxy.

Some scientists think, nevertheless, that some sort of tangible object might be sent on such a flight by one advanced civilization seeking to contact another. Leslie C. Edie wondered whether one might not fill a maintenance-free package with a great deal of information and set it adrift in the gravitational currents of space, rather like a message in a bottle intended for a distant shore. Perhaps the messages might be graven microscopically on ultrathin metal plates, or perhaps even organized into the structure of the molecules to convey information—surely as compact a message as is possible. Edie suggested looking again at meteorites to see whether anything like this has already been done with the carbonaceous material sometimes found therein.

A rather similar technique was envisioned in 1962 by Dr. Ronald N. Bracewell, a leading radio astronomer. Bracewell has suggested that the traveling package might consist of a radio with tape-recorded messages, or perhaps directed by a microminiaturized computer with the size and memory-capacity of a human brain. The advanced society would aim this to swing silently among the planets of the target star, scanning all radio frequencies. When it heard a signal, it would mimic back that signal on the same frequency. If the planet then repeated this message once again, indicating that it was ready to accept the information, the probe would automatically pour out its information. Presumably it would carry an encyclopedic store of knowledge. "Such a probe may be here now, in our solar system, trying to make its presence known," Bracewell wrote. As evidence, he offered several unexplained radio "echoes" heard in 1927, 1928, and 1934 by several careful scientists. These "echoes," Bracewell thought, were in reality the probe's repeating back to Earth the signals that it had heard to alert Earth to its presence. His idea has been criticized on several grounds, among them that while it might not cost too much for a civilization to spray such probes into the surrounding space, it seems exceedingly difficult to armor them against the erosion of space for hundreds of millions of years. In any event, the theory has not received widespread acceptance.

Perhaps the object to be sent might consist of the lightest "things" in the universe—electrons. An electron gun could shoot beams of these charged particles through space. They would be received by a scintillation detector, which gives off flashes of light whenever an electron hits it. The system can carry a great deal of information with high efficiency, but its range seems limited to about 100,000 miles—far under the trillions needed for interstellar communication. The same general idea has been proposed for another subatomic particle, the neutrino. It would be ideal for long-distance communication, since it weighs nothing and carries no electric charge, and hence would not be distracted from its course by the magnetic fields of space. There is a little problem in that scientists on Earth are hard put to detect their presence at all—neutrinos pass all the way through Earth without leaving any evidence of their passage—and observing a modulated beam of them seems definitely beyond present terrestrial capacities. Other civilizations, however, may have solved these problems.

The fastest and cheapest means of interstellar communication appears to be, not by object, but by electromagnetic waves. These are the waves of radio, heat, light, ultraviolet, X rays, and gamma radiation. All, of course, travel at the speed of light. And it is clearly easier to push a radio signal out into space than to launch a probe. "Interstellar communication across the galactic plasma without dispersion in direction and flight time is practical, so far as we know, only with electromagnetic waves," wrote Cocconi and Morrison.

The question at once arises, Which waves? Natural considerations quickly limit the possibilities. Signals by X rays cannot be focused. Gamma rays are given off by radioactive materials; perhaps these unwanted by-products of a nuclear reactor might find useful employment in space communication. Unfortunately, they do not carry beyond 100,000 miles, and, so, like electrons, have insufficient range.

Morrison has made the imaginative suggestion that a civilization fling an opaque screen, perhaps consisting of many individual morsels of matter, into space on a line between the parent sun and the target star. The civilization would move the screen, perhaps by magnetism, into and out of that line, thereby causing the whole parent sun to appear to blink. The pattern of the blinks would, of course, form the signal. An effort of this magnitude might not be too difficult for an advanced society. A subtle refinement of this, suggested by Drake, uses a cloud of material that would absorb, not all the light, but only certain wavelengths of it. These missing wavelengths, which would leave a black line in a spectrogram of the star's light, would indicate the existence of an artificial element and consequently of a civilization. Though Drake seemed to propose this more as an indicator than as a signal device, it might be possible to shift this cloud, or renew it in the face of its dispersion by the outflow of gas from the star, and so transmit messages. Another possible light-wave system uses the natural absorption by elements in a star's atmosphere of certain wavelengths of the light emitted by its incandescent body. This absorption likewise leaves a black line in the otherwise bright and rainbowlike spectrogram of its light. Dr. Charles Townes, who won a Nobel Prize for fathering the maser and its optical cousin, the laser, suggested, with a colleague, Robert N. Schwartz, that laser light, which can be very finely tuned, might be focused into the narrow slot of the black absorption line, like fitting a key into a keyhole, and turned on and off to send messages. Astronomers on distant planets, seeing the fine inner line of light where nature would not have it, would recognize it as artificial.

While all these methods may be feasible despite their great technical difficulties, the most practical method of all appears to be radio. Man today has a sophisticated understanding of radio's superiority. But in an almost instinctive fashion, man recognized radio as a natural choice for interplanetary communication soon after it was invented. Nikola Tesla, who was a pioneer in the field and who, though an eccentric, made solid contributions, observed at his radio laboratory in Colorado in 1899 periodic "electrical actions" with "a clear suggestion of number and order that were not traceable to any cause then known to me." "The feeling is constantly growing on me," he wrote, "that I had been the first to hear the greeting of one planet to another." Twenty-one years later, the inventor of radio, Guglielmo Marconi, was reported as saying that some inexplicable radio signals heard by his company on both sides of the Atlantic might be signals from another planet. They are now thought to be the phenomenon known as "whistlers," caused by lightning, heard by Marconi years before others had noticed them.

With the close approach of Mars to Earth in 1924, the question of Mars–Earth communication erupted into excited discussion. Lieutenant Commander Fitzhugh Green asked, "Could We Decode Messages From Mars?" in *Popular Science Monthly*, and went on to note that "Twenty-one different methods have been suggested to communicate with Mars this summer"—none of them particularly acute. David Todd, former head of the astronomy department at Amherst College, sought to have all radio stations on Earth shut down during the passage and listen for signals from Mars. The Army and Navy actually ordered their stations to avoid unnecessary transmissions and to listen for unusual signals. The executive officer of the Signal Corps announced that the chief of its code section, one William F. Friedman, was standing by to decipher any messages received. At Camp Alfred Vail, the Army's major Signal Corps center, now Fort Monmouth, three radio stations did listen. Others may have searched the radio bands too. This was, despite its haphazard, transient, and superficial nature, man's first known attempt to listen for messages from other worlds. On the night of August 24 recorded dashes followed by a voice pronouncing words were heard. Nothing was done about it, as it seemed to be just a human radio test. In addition, a Washington man named Jenkins, an early television pioneer, heard some mysterious signals that he recorded on moving photographic strips from 1 p.m. August 22 to 5 p.m. August 23, 1924. Accepting the Signal Corps' implied invitation, he brought the strips to Friedman's office. Recalled Friedman: "I thought him a sort of visionary and didn't try to do anything with his record. I was probably wrong!"

Since that time, the development of radio astronomy and general advances in radio technique have made it possible to eliminate large portions of the radio spectrum as likely channels for any messages from outer space. For a number of technical reasons—attenuation in space, power required, facility of reception—"The wide radio band from, say 1 Mc [megacycle] to 10^4 Mc, remains as the rational choice," Cocconi and Morrison wrote. But where precisely in this still enormous range should man listen? The question is that which faces the driver of a car who is in a part of the country where he does not know the radio stations but wants to pick up the broadcast of a particular major-league ball game. He has to tune his radio across the entire dial, listening at each station, until he finds what he wants. With interstellar broadcasts, not only is the dial immensely broader, but also the signal would be far weaker and far less recognizable than the voice of a familiar announcer.

Fortunately, "just in the most favored radio region," Cocconi and Morrison pointed out, "there lies a unique, objective standard of frequency, which must be known to every observer in the universe." This is the so-called radio emission line of neutral hydrogen, only discovered by man in 1951. For physical reasons, the axis of the spinning of the hydrogen electron around its nucleus wobbles, or precesses, at the rate of 1,420,405,752 times a second. Out in space, individual hydrogen atoms occasionally collide with one another. This gives them a bit of extra energy, which they later cast off in the form of an electromagnetic wave vibrating at the same rate as the precession of the spin axis. This is a radio wave of 1,420,405,752 cycles per second, or roughly 1,420 megacycles. Since all electromagnetic waves travel at the same speed, this frequency corresponds to a wavelength of 21 centimeters, or $8\frac{1}{2}$ inches. Vast clouds of hydrogen float in the galaxy, and all the individual atomic emissions combine into a steady hum of radio noise at that frequency, or "station," on the celestial dial. In a sense, this produces a homing beacon, a standard landmark in the radio range of the electromagnetic spectrum. "Therefore we think it most promising to search in the neighborhood of 1420 Mc/sec," the two physicists wrote. Not directly on the hydrogen emission line, for anyone foolish enough to send his signals right at that frequency would have them jammed by the hydrogen noise, but at frequencies nearby, or perhaps at double or half that frequency. The listening frequencies should be relatively free of cosmic radio noise, or static, which stars and nebula generate just as they generate light and heat in other parts of the electromagnetic spectrum.

The next question to be faced in the process of narrowing down the potential channels is: Where are the broadcasts likely to come from? It is not practicable simply to tune a receiver to 1,420 megacycles and start listening for a signal from anywhere in the sky. Cosmic noise from all over space would drown it out. Rather, any searchers would have to direct their antennae at a possible sender to better pick up any signals—just as a portable radio plays louder when its antenna is pointed at the transmitter. The question of "where" really amounted to a consideration of the stars that were likely to have planets that may have evolved life. This meant long-lived, slow-turning stars rather like the sun. Naturally, the nearer stars would be considered first. Many of the 45 that lie within 16 light-years of the solar system must be excluded because they do not meet the conditions. The nearest star, Alpha Centauri, is actually a triple star—three stars revolving around one another—for which an orbit with a habitable life-zone seems most unlikely. In the neighborhood of the solar system, then, only a dozen or so stars met the requirements. Some of them, however, lay directly against a background of stars that produced a great deal of cosmic noise, which meant that it would be extra hard to detect any signals from them. Ruling these out left two nearby stars as the most likely contenders: Tau Ceti, in the constellation of the Whale, and Epsilon Eridani, in the constellation of the River Eridanus. Both are rather smaller than the sun, with one third its luminosity, but both, like the sun, are long-lived and slow-turning. These conclusions were reached independently by a number of theoreticians, including Drake, Cocconi and Morrison, and Su-Shu Huang, who first formulated the concept of habitable zones.

Consequently, it was at Tau Ceti that Drake first aimed his 85-foot radio telescope on the morning of April 8, 1960. Because of the probable difficulty of isolating the possible intelligible signals from the constant background crackle of cosmic static, he had worked out several ingenious techniques to make any signal stand out more clearly. They resemble somewhat the electronic warfare techniques of electronic counter-countermeasures—and it may be significant that Drake spent three years of military service as electronics officer aboard the heavy cruiser U.S.S. *Albany*. They may also owe something to techniques developed to detect radar echoes from Venus that were extremely faint—one hundredth of a billionth of a billionth of a watt.

In one of Drake's techniques, the radio telescope looked alternately at the star and at a patch of sky near the star. The latter delivered to the telescope only general cosmic noise, without any emissions from the star, while the former delivered noise plus any emissions. Drake's equipment compared the two and took note only of any emission from the star whose strength rose above the general noise level. This would be the signal. The other technique depended upon the fact that one potato more does not make much difference to a carload but does to a grocer weighing out a pound. Electronic equipment balanced two unequal incoming emissions: a very broad band of noise and a narrow band within it. The radio telescope listened on successive narrow bands within the broad one. If a signal were present in the broad band but not in the narrow one being listened to, its strength would be negligible compared with all the noise and so the emissions would remain balanced. But if the narrow band picked up the signal, the signal would concentrate all its weight in that band and would throw the two emissions out of balance. The difference between them would constitute the artificial signal.

Drake called his effort "Project Ozma," after the name of the queen of the imaginary land of Oz—"a place very far away, difficult to reach, and populated by exotic beings." His equipment tuned automatically across 400,000 cycles of the radio spectrum, centered on the hydrogen frequency. The switch that automatically tuned the receiver from one 100-cycle band to the next after a minute's observation was the last one he snapped on the historic morning of April 8, 1960, as man began his first major attempt to find life in other solar systems.

Throughout the day the giant saucer of his radio telescope swiveled slowly as it followed Tau Ceti, its light invisible in the glare of the sun, across the sky. Only the hisses and buzzes of cosmic noise had come in on the loudspeaker, only the formless wiggles of its graphic representation on paper had been recorded. As Tau Ceti began setting in the west, Drake, who had been in and out of the control room during the day, decided to swing to Epsilon Eridani, his other possibility. No sooner had he done so than the pen, Drake said, "went bang off scale"—knocked there by some very powerful signal. With the volume turned down, the pen smoothly wrote a uniform series of pulses, eight to the second. They could only have been produced artificially, by some intelligence. There was, Drake said, "a moderate amount of pandemonium" in the control room. Checks of the equipment showed no flaws. And before the telescope could be moved to see if the signal remained strong from other directions of the sky, which would indicate a non-Epsilon Eridani source, it abruptly stopped.

Drake strongly doubted that he had actually trapped an interstellar signal on his first try. The chances were much too remote. He said nothing about it, and two weeks later, when he heard the marching pulses again, he tested their origin by steering the antenna off the star. As he had suspected, the pulses continued, proving that they came from somewhere on Earth, probably as a result of some radar countermeasures work.

Project Ozma continued for a total of about 150 hours of listening through July of 1960, without any evidence of interstellar signals. Then it was suspended, mainly because the telescope was needed in other projects, but also partly out of flagging interest in the face of no results. Drake had hoped to resume listening with a new 600-foot radio telescope that the Navy was then constructing, but this project was abandoned, and Ozma left in abeyance.

Occasionally, during the public discussion of Ozma, a voice would be heard protesting against it. Perhaps, to the advanced creatures of another civilization, men might be nothing more than a tasty-looking herd of beef cattle. Why tempt fate? There were a number of answers to this. One was the immense distances to be covered and the unlikelihood that anyone would travel so far just for a steak. Another was the length of the voyage: by the time they arrived, Earth might well be able to protect itself. Another was that a civilization advanced enough to be able to contact Earth would probably have figured out its food supply problem for itself. All may be summarized in a single point of view: that the only thing worth traveling for (over great distances) is information. It would not be worthwhile to mine diamonds or iron on Mars; synthetics made on Earth would be much cheaper. Nobel Prize winner Edward Purcell, discoverer of the hydrogen radio emission line, felt certain that "No one can threaten anyone else with objects," and that interstellar conversation would be, "in the deepest sense, utterly benign."

What, some people asked, if everybody is listening and no one is sending? For example, Dr. Harrison S. Brown told Congressman Daddario during the hearings of the Committee on Science and Astronautics: "I would say that the success of Project Ozma will depend almost entirely upon how Congressmen in these other systems have behaved. Have they allocated the funds, the very substantial funds necessary to build the fantastically powerful transmitting systems which could be necessary? And here I am perhaps gloomy. I try to think how you gentlemen would react to a proposal to build at great expense a transmitter which would send signals which the inhabitants of another star may or may not hear in a few million years, and I believe that such a bill probably would receive somewhat less than enthusiastic attention." Brown was probably politically right but technologically wrong. It seems possible that advanced civilizations could detect emerging ones by stray radio signals that leak out into the cosmos as part of the planet's ordinary activities—radio broadcasting, high-powered military communications, satellite relay transmissions, and especially long-range radar. In the case of Earth, some wags, thinking of soap operas and disk jockeys, have remarked that this might deter more than invite.

One of the most curious facts about any interstellar conversation will be the long delays it would involve. Since it takes radio waves traveling at the speed of light 20 years to reach a planet 20 light-years away, conversation would have to proceed at a leisurely pace. Obviously, men would not transmit a message, then do nothing for 40 years until a reply came back. Both sides would exchange continual streams of information. The answers would, in a sense, be a legacy for the inquirers' children. And perhaps, Walter Sullivan suggests in his *We Are Not Alone*, just as children are a form of physical immortality for men, so knowledge might constitute a form of intellectual immortality for whole worlds. "Bertrand Russell has pointed out that 'all the labours of the ages, all the devotion, all the inspiration, all the noonday brightness of human genius, are destined to extinction in the vast death of the solar system.' Yet it seems that life, in a sense, may be eternal. Perhaps true wisdom is a torch—one that we have not yet received, but that can be handed to us by a civilization late in its life and passed on by our own world as its time of extinction draws near."

But how would we actually communicate? What would the language of the transmission be? No simple show-and-tell process will be possible.

Many scientists think that other civilizations will hail us with a special calling signal. "We expect that the signal will be pulse-modulated with a speed not very fast or very slow compared to a second, on grounds of bandwidth and of rotations," wrote Cocconi and Morrison. "For indisputable identification as an artificial signal, one signal might contain, for example, a sequence of small prime numbers of pulses, or simple arithmetical sums." Nikola Tesla envisioned the same thing when he imagined that terrestrial astronomers would announce the first cosmic contact with the words: "Brethren! We have a message from another world, unknown and remote. It reads: one . . . two . . . three . . . "

As for the language of the text, no one on Earth can make a useful guess. Probably the one overriding principle of the outer-spacelings will have been to make their message as clear as possible. It will be coded, but in a code designed for clarity and not for obscurity—a kind of cryptography in reverse, as Edward Purcell has said, an anticryptography. Will the skills of the cryptologist be required to help read it? His specialized knowledge of letter frequencies and Kerckhoffs superimpositions will naturally be useless and unnecessary on a plaintext in an unknown language. But his talent for seeing patterns in unfamiliar texts may well prove of vital assistance. Perhaps the cryptologist will attend the translation conference with the logician, the mathematician, the linguist, the biologist, the astronomer, the radio engineer. If so, it would mark the fitting summit of a career whose long road began more than 4,000 years earlier; for cryptology, it would be the ultimate solution.

While it is impossible to predict what the language of the outer-spacelings' message is likely to be, Russian linguist N. D. Andreyev of the Leningrad Academy of Sciences has recently proposed a method that he believes will enable men to decipher any language. Using what he calls "statistical-combinatory" analysis, he measures six different parameters in a text, such as the distance of one word from another in a sentence, to arrive at a semantic relationship between words. Testing this on human languages, he has ascertained the meaning of verbal symbols. "The data are uneven," he wrote. "For several words their exact meanings are obtained; other words group themselves into clearly delimited and semantically homogeneous sets with a definite meaning in common (but without specifying individual notions belonging to single members of a set); some words reveal only their broad semantic class and do not permit any delimitative grouping." His work on the problem has just begun, but it seems to show promise.

But how will man reply? Here the thinking has been primarily that of logicians, mathematicians, and astronomers. Their proposals may be said to fall into two categories. One group bases its language primarily on mathematical logic. The other depends basically upon pictures.

It is evident that no one is going to try to beam a message in Esperanto to the creatures of another world. That artificial language rests too directly upon those of Earth; it belongs to the type of artificial language called a posteriori because it is based upon existing tongues. But the logico-mathematical proposals for an interstellar language have in their background the other kind of artificial language, the kind called a priori, in which all experience is categorized logically and the language molded upon these categories. The first artificial languages were of these kind; it is the kind that Friedman thinks may lie under the mystery of the Voynich manuscript. Many different systems have been proposed. They arose early in the 1600s, as Latin, which had been the international language, fell into disuse in scholarship and governmental institutions. In a letter in 1629, Descartes urged the creation of a philosophical language in which simple ideas would be so denominated that they could be combined into more complex ones as are letters into words. Leibnitz likewise dreamed of such a language, which he hoped would avoid many philosophical problems based solely on linguistic confusions. Such languages were even worked out, the first by George Dalgarno. Bishop Wilkins followed with another, using signs and attached wiggles to indicate ideas and their relations. Some were almost bizarre, using numbers to build up a scheme of existence, as Timerio, in which "I love you" became 1-80-17, or using musical notes, like Solresol, in which "Domisol" signifies "God" and "Solmido" means "Satan." Its inventor, Jean-François Sudre, noted that it could be sung or, if the seven notes were replaced by seven colors, painted.

Near the end of the 19th century, the Italian mathematician Giuseppe Peano sought to reduce as much as possible of the language used in mathematics and logic to formulas. He tried to formalize not the subject of mathematical thought—the equations in the books—since this had been done long before, but mathematical thought itself, the running text that surrounds the equations. For this he created symbols for "and," "or," "not," "implies," "every," and other logical terms that previously had to be expressed verbally. He hoped this would facilitate scientific thought in nonmathematical areas, just as mathematics did in quantitative areas. (Peano also invented a simplified Latin for ordinary discourse, which he described in a speech in Turin in 1903. He began in almost classic Latin, and as he explained his various simplifications he introduced them into his talk, ending up with his almost grammarless "Latino sine flexione.") Peano's ideas of a mathematical language were picked up by Alfred North Whitehead and Bertrand Russell, whose revolutionary *Principia Mathematica* exposed the foundations of mathematics and showed those of logic to be identical. Today, mathematical logic, the outgrowth of their work, boasts a large vocabulary of syntactical terms with which to express relations between ideas.

This syntax serves as the skeleton of the interstellar language based on logic. The flesh of the language is formed by its vocabulary, and this is the work of Dr. Hans Freudenthal, professor of mathematics at the University of Utrecht in the Netherlands. Freudenthal designed it more as an exercise in logical language than as a serious proposal for interstellar communication, though he believes that it could fulfill that function. He called his language "Lincos," from "lingua cosmica." Its sounds consist of radio signals of various lengths and frequencies; its word-divisions and punctuation consist of pauses of varying duration. Freudenthal did not specify what the actual radio signal will be for a given word, as this does not really matter; it can be left up to the technicians. In print, he often represented his words by abbreviations of Latin words meaning the same thing. Thus "Inq," evidently deriving from the Latin "inquirere," stands for whatever signal is used for "ask."

Lincos would have to be taught to the creatures of outer space before it could be used as a medium of communication, and Freudenthal proposed to do this by transmitting the statements of Lincos, which he hoped would be relatively self-evident, over and over again until the recipients catch on to their meaning.

He began his program by sending a series of messages to teach the terms "plus" and "equals." His first message might be *beep beep beep beep bloop beep beep tweet beep beep beep beep beep beep*. Next he might send *beep beep bloop beep tweet beep beep beep*. After sending enough of these for the outerspacelings to catch on to the idea that *bloop* is "plus" and *tweet* is "equals," he might transmit a message with a new signal, like *beep beep beep blip beep tweet beep beep*. Soon the spacelings would realize that *blip* means "minus." Similarly, Freudenthal would build up an entire mathematical vocabulary.

He would then introduce the notion of time by sending, say, a seven-second dash, then a Lincos word meaning "second," then seven pulses. By repeating this pattern with dashes of different lengths, the listeners would eventually notice that the duration of the dash is proportional to the number following, and would thus ascertain the length of Earth's time-unit.

3 01 3.   * Ha Inq $Hb \cdot ? x . 100 x = 1010$:
   Hb Inq $Ha . 1010/100$:
   Ha Inq Hb Mal :
   Hb Inq $Ha . 1/10$:
   Ha Inq Hb Mal :
   Hb Inq $Ha . 101/10$:
   Ha Inq Hb Ben *

   * Ha Inq $Hb \cdot ? x . x = 10 + 10$:
   Hb Inq $Ha . 10 + 10$:
   Ha Inq Hb Mal :
   Hb Inq Ha 100 :
   Ha Inq Hb Ben *

   * Ha Inq $Hb \cdot ? x . x^{10} = 11001$:
   Hb Inq $Ha . 101 \times 101 = 11001$:
   Ha Inq Hb Mal :
   Hb Inq $Ha \cdot 101 \times 101 = 11001 . \in$ Ver :
   Ha Inq $Hb \cdot$ Ver Tan Mal : $\neg \cdot x^{10} = 11001 . \rightarrow . x = 101$:
   Hb Inq $Ha . 101 \backsim - 101$:
   Ha Inq Hb Ben *

   * Ha Inq $Hb \cdot ? ˇx . x^{10} = 11001$:
   Hb Inq Ha 101 :
   Ha Inq Hb Ben *

   * Ha Inq $Hb \cdot ? ˇx . x^{10} = 11001 \cdot$
   Hb Inq $Ha : ˇx . x^{10} = 11001 \cdot \in \cdot ↑x . x^{10} = 11001 \cdot$
   Ha Inq Hb Mal *

A page of the cosmic language "Lincos" in the notation of mathematical logic which its inventor uses as its script, showing a discussion between **Human a** *and* **Human b**

Human behavior would be demonstrated through a kind of Lincos radio-play. A new signal would be followed by an incomplete Lincos statement, such as "six plus four equals . . . " A second new signal would be followed by the Lincos word for "ten." These two new signals would continue querying one another on mathematical problems—the only topic available for discussion to beginning speakers of Lincos. During these colloquies they would use—and therefore teach—the Lincos terms "says," "good," "bad," "who," "allows," and so forth. The outer-space listeners would also divine, Freudenthal expected, that the signals are actually the Lincos names for sapient beings. Eventually, Freudenthal would have two beings perceive the same event at different times—and therefore in different places. This new notion, location, would lead into definitions of distance, motion, and mass, and hence into the whole field of mechanics. Universal constants, such as the speed of light or the hydrogen atom's radio wavelength, would (with the known Earth time-unit) establish Earth's units of length. This important step would permit description of the earth, the solar system, human beings, and so forth. From here, Freudenthal planned to strike out into geography, anatomy, and physiology, and, on a more profound level, into human behavior.

The plan is well founded and elaborately prepared, with hundreds of proposed messages fully worked out in Freudenthal's book, *Lincos: Design of a Language for Cosmic Intercourse*. But some interesting criticisms have been made. One mathematician wondered how Freudenthal can be so certain that the outer-spacelings would think as he does? Perhaps their mathematics is different. Perhaps they would try to seek a pattern in the meaningless variation of the numbers of beeps used as illustration in teaching the elementary concept of "plus" instead of concentrating on the invariant "plus" signal. To these Freudenthal has replied: "I suppose that the receivers are mentally humanlike. Otherwise I would not know how to communicate with them." He went on to explain that he referred primarily to mutual possession of the mathematics known to humans, the only kind that humans can imagine. As for the variations, "The words 'plus' and 'equal' are so different from the regularly fluctuating signals that you cannot be mistaken. I am absolutely sure that any Chinese peasant who has never understood the English words 'plus' and 'equal' will understand what you have said."

Lancelot Hogben, a Fellow of the Royal Society, editor of the best-selling *The Loom of Language*, and himself inventor of an interstellar language, agreed with Freudenthal up to the establishment of temporal signals. But he thought—and, many believe, rightly—that the step after that would be to set up a common factual framework based on mutual experience, which would have to be celestial phenomena. "The last topic about which we could hope to achieve understanding would be the actions of persons in general and the concept of the ego in particular," he wrote. Hogben also saw no advantage in converting the messages into the Lincos logistical form. The only necessity for cosmic speech is that "terms and constructions conform to the requirements of rigorous semantic rectitude," he said. But he seems to have missed the point that the very purpose of Lincos is to secure that rectitude.

Hogben's own proposal, called "Astraglossa," shared many of the basic principles of Lincos, but it does not give the impression of solid logical structure, and hence of communicative power, that Lincos does. He devised it at the invitation of the British Interplanetary Society early in the 1950s, before thoughts of other worlds had ripened. He envisioned it in the form of a communication by light flashes with Mars, but explained that it could be generalized to any planet, using radio waves.

Hogben began, like Freudenthal, by teaching elementary signals for "plus" and "equals." He suggested teaching time in conjunction with astronomy. By selecting a reference point on Mars and a celestial event visible there, Earth would send n dashes at n time-intervals before the event would be seen at the Martian point, then $n-1$ dashes at $n-1$ time-intervals, and so on. For example, 9 dashes might be sent 9 minutes before Martian eyes would see Earth occult its moon, then 8 dashes 8 minutes before, and so on. The danger that they would think this simply a lesson in astronomy could be averted by sending the numbers as triangular factors: $1+2$ instead of 3, $1+2+3$ instead of 6, $1+2+3+4$ instead of 10. Hogben suggested moving from simple flashes for integers to numeration, which is more efficient, proposing base 2 or base 12, preferably the latter because it is more compact. The Martians—who, if they are picking up the communication, can detect electromagnetic energy—may have also discovered the absorption lines in spectrograms of the portion of the electromagnetic spectrum that is visible to humans. "This opens the possibility of associating the concept of number and duration with the concept of matter in its several elementary forms," Hogben hypothesized.

To establish negation, Hogben would set up a new flash and insert an erroneous term in the series in juxtaposition to a foregoing correct message. By repeating the lesson, the Martians would infer that the new flash indicates negation. He would explain interrogation by substituting, for the affirmative declaratory annunciatory flash that normally precedes a message, a new dual flash meaning "what" is the "xth" term in a number series. Next, Hogben would set up assent and denial. Eventually a question-and-answer technique, combined with ability to detect signals from different transmitting stations, would make possible the differentiation of "we" and "they." Hogben would then be in a position to ascend to new levels of communication.

The earliest system proposed for cosmic talk partakes of some features of both the mathematical and the pictorial approaches, but its feet stand firmly in the former. It was devised in 1896, after a near approach of Mars to the Earth, by Sir Francis Galton, the founder of eugenics and an early proponent of the use of fingerprints to identify criminals. It being before the days of radio, Galton imagined that the Martians were communicating with Earth by flashing an immense assemblage of large heliographs, all worked simultaneously, to reflect sunlight back toward Earth. The Martians used three signals—a dot of $1\frac{1}{4}$ seconds, a dash of $2\frac{1}{2}$ seconds, and a line of 5 seconds. With these three they built up a system of numeration to the base 8, either because, Galton speculated, they were using only three different signals ($8 = 2^3$), or because they are highly developed ants who count to eight on six limbs and two antennae. After instruction in addition, subtraction, and the other arithmetical processes, the Martians transmitted figures giving, for each of the five major planets, its mean distance from the sun, radius, and time of rotation, with Earth's measurements given as 100.

Next, the Martians industriously sent over signals defining π, and with the help of this drew a polygon of 24 sides. They named each side, and, by transmitting one name after another, used the polygon to draw pictures. The first was of half of Saturn—the other half not being needed because the planet is symmetrical. This took 105 "stitches." Next came a picture of the North American continent, which required 88 stitches, 16 of them fractional because of the indentation of its shores, while South America, which followed, required only 52. Night after night the scintillations came down, progressing to domestic and sociological drawings. Galton implied that communication ceased only when the two planets drew too far apart along their orbits.

Galton sugared his discussion with some humor, and he deserves credit as the pioneer in a new field of communication. Both his program and Hogben's, however, suffer a serious loss of generality in assuming communication with a planet so close that external phenomena are visible—eclipses or occultations in Hogben's Astraglossa, terrestrial geography in what might be called Galton's Martiansprache. This gives them an easy way out of what is the hardest step for the mathematically based languages—the leap from the conceptual to the physical, from ideas to things. In Lincos, which is much more rigorously logical than either of the others, this transfer is the weakest point.

Concreteness is, on the other hand, the strength of the pictorial approach. The astute space expert and writer Arthur C. Clarke first mentioned this idea, which television apparently suggested to him. Like the logico-mathematical approach, the pictorial has roots in precosmic human activity.

Writing itself, of course, began as a series of pictures. In China, a script that consists of formalized pictures is read and understood to mean identical things by Chinese whose speech is mutually unintelligible. The principle is that of a skull and crossbones on a medicine bottle, which means danger or poison to an American, a Frenchman, a German. Many other symbols serve to communicate between persons whose languages differ: road signs, chemical formulas, notes of music, Arabic numerals.

The first attempts to signal man's presence on Earth to the creatures of another planet—Mars—employed diagrams. The German mathematician Karl Friedrich Gauss, whose name lives in English today in the verb "degauss," meaning to neutralize the magnetic field of a ship, suggested planting broad lanes of forest in Siberia in the form of a gigantic right-angled triangle, filling the inside with wheat to make it stand out more clearly. This geometric shape would clearly be an artificial creation. Man could drive the point home by erecting squares on each side of the triangle to illustrate the Pythagorean theorem. Not long thereafter, the Viennese astronomer Josef Johann von Littrow proposed digging canals in the Sahara to form geometric figures with twenty-mile sides. At night kerosene would be poured upon the water and set ablaze. Charles Cros in France conceived the idea of a huge mirror to reflect sunlight, like a giant heliograph, toward Mars.

These devices could not convey much more than that intelligence exists on Earth. Moreover, they depend upon a visual contact, which is not possible in interstellar communication. To express any real information, man would have to radio a plurality of pictures or detailed diagrams to the other world. Two ways of doing so have been proposed. Both expect that the recipients would arrange the message, which arrives in a long one-dimensional string of pulses, in a two-dimensional array. One method depends upon spatial relationships to clue the recipients to this rearrangement, the other upon temporal relationships.

Shortly after the Green Bank conference on extraterrestrial life in 1961, Frank Drake sent to the participants, and later to other scientists as well, a message based on the spatial form. It consisted of 551 binary digits—zeros and ones, which might have been transmitted as pulses and blanks or as two kinds of pulses. The solution of the problem resembled the cryptanalysis of a columnar transposition cipher. The fact that 551 is the product of two primes, 19 and 29, suggested arranging the digits in a rectangle of those dimensions. With 29 digits across the top, no pattern emerged, but when the digits were laid out in lines of 19 characters, several groupings of the units—which might be envisioned as dots or marks lying amid the white space of the zeros—appeared. Drake's message was highly concentrated, depicting a two-legged creature rather like a man, evidently the sender of the message; schematic drawings of the carbon and oxygen atoms, implying that the creature's chemistry was, like man's, based on them; the sun and five planets of the creature's solar system, with modified binary numbers for 1 to 5 opposite them and a series of longer binary numbers that probably represent the populations of the planets (No. 4, with 7 billion, apparently being the home planet and two others, with 3,000 and 11, apparently being colonized or explored by astronauts); and, finally, the creature's height, given as 31, probably 31 times the wavelength on which the message was sent. Of course, a great deal of this information is read into the message on the basis of human experience, and it is doubtful whether so compact a message would be transmitted at first. But Drake remarked:

> The content of the message was designed to contain the data we would first like to know about another civilization, at least in the opinion of many scientists who have thought about this problem.
>
> In preparing the message, an attempt was made to place it at a level of difficulty such that a group of high quality terrestrial scientists of many disciplines could interpret the message in a time less than a day. Any easier message would mean that we are not sending as much information as possible over the transmission facilities, and any harder might result in a failure to communicate. In trying this puzzle on scientists, it has been true so far that scientists have understood the parts of the message connected with their own discipline, but have

usually not understood the rest. This is consistent with the philosophy behind the message.

The use of two dimensions has made possible the transmission of a great deal of information with few bits. This is because it is possible to arrange the symbols of the message in positions relative to one another such that even the arrangement carries information, when we employ logic and our existing knowledge of what may possibly occur in another planetary system. Thus the 551 bits are equivalent to approximately 25 English words, but the information content of the message appears much greater than that. This is because much of the message tells us, by the placement of a single symbol, which of several complicated possibilities is the one that has occurred in the other planetary system, without using bits to spell out precisely the possibility that has occurred.

Even though Drake's message was too compressed, the principle certainly works. It could even be extended to produce a three-dimensional model. The

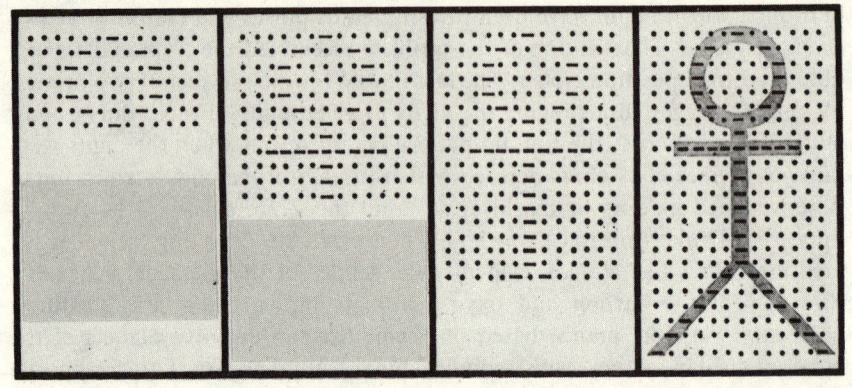

Interstellar communication by picture: the position of the dashes among the dots inside the picture frame builds up the image of a human form

use of a number of pulses that is the product of three primes might hint at this, just as a number resulting from two primes suggested the two-dimensional array. So far, it seems not to have been tested.

The temporally based method of transmitting images has been urged by Philip Morrison. To mark off each line of the picture, he would send two synchronizing pulses. These would be distinctive and each pair would be separated in time by the same interval as every other pair. They would frame the picture. Between the beginning and ending pulses of each line, Morrison would transmit the information-carrying signals. The outer-spacelings would have to align these one under the other to form the picture, hopefully being guided to do so by the frame of the synchronizing pulses, and perhaps helped by the near-similarity and slight divergencies of successive lines.

Morrison would send as his first picture a circle—a kind of test pattern. The message would consist of a number of units, all equal in time, all marked off at the beginning and end by identical pulses. The first segment would consist of these two synchronizing pulses with a single distinctive message pulse sent midway between them. The second segment would have two message pulses, one sent slightly before and the other slightly after the middle of the segment. The third segment would likewise have two message-pulses, both likewise symmetrically spaced in time about the midpoint but farther from it. Successive lines would continue to widen the interval between the two pulses until a maximum was reached, then would begin to narrow it again, until the final segment would again comprise a single message pulse in the middle of the time interval. When these are lined up one under the other—voilà! A circle.

"Of course," said Morrison, imagining the use of this method by the outer-spacelings in sending messages to Earth, "they may not scan linearly. Maybe they scan in logarithmic spiral. It makes no difference to the method. As long as they supply us with a simple geometric pattern and some algebraic clue to it, we cannot take very long to make out the nature of their scanning raster." The method, is, of course, adaptable to sending more complex images, like Drake's, though it is perhaps not as suitable for three-dimensional structures.

The temporal scanning principle is, of course, that used in television. Actual television as known here on Earth would not be used for interstellar communication, even if it were taught to the outer-spacelings, because it requires too much power for long distances and is not efficient in transmitting information. But two of its characteristics—moving pictures and tones of gray (instead of just black or white, as in Drake's diagram)—might eventually help convey additional information. For motion, the simple principle of movie cartoons would serve. A series of images, each differing slightly from its predecessor, would be sent. When viewed in rapid succession they would appear to move—at least to humanlike eyes. For tint gradations, Drake would convert the brightness of each spot in an image into a number proportional to the brightness. White spots might be coded as 10, medium-gray as 5, very dark gray as 2, black as 1. These numbers would be transmitted instead of the binary digits of his basic scheme. In a test of just such a system for commercial purposes (because it uses less bandwidth than television), Bell Telephone Laboratory engineer R. L. Carbrey found that pictures of a pretty girl with only three levels of brightness were perfectly recognizable. By using a special transmission code, he used seven pulses per spot to obtain 128 levels of brightness ($2^7 = 128$). But this might be rather sophisticated early in the interstellar game.

The great advantage of the pictorial approach lies in its grasp of the real. A picture can indeed be worth a thousand words. But pictures without captions, objects without concepts to relate them to one another and to the higher realms of generalization, would afford the creatures of outer space but a grotesque parody of life on Earth, and would in fact exclude the more important things of that life. Needed are both the abstract and the concrete, and needed in interstellar communication, therefore, are both the logico-mathematical and the pictorial approaches. It seems most probable that the messages to outer space would combine some form of Lincos-like instruction with Drake's pictures. Morrison envisaged such a combination in his television picture of a circle; he preceded it with a brief lesson in arithmetic followed by a numerical series that converged on π. It would only be after the television raster was taught and enough test patterns sent to make the principle sink in that man would flash pictures of his world—still or moving—upon the screen of the extraterrestrial TV set.

Man's next step might well be to use pictures to create a dictionary for a second-level, verbal language. He would send a picture of a triangle and whatever radio signal will be used for it, a picture of the carbon atom and then its radio signal, a picture of a man and its radio signal. What might be the composition of these radio signals? Morse code might be used, and sending *dadah didah dadit* (= *man*) would be faster than sending the picture of a man. But the great redundancy of English and all natural languages makes this inefficient. Much more economical would be the commercial code principle: as the radio signal for "man" or "carbon" or "triangle," use a group of numbers or a combination of radio frequencies. The redundancy would be minimal—only that required to detect and correct errors. The numbers need not be limited to base 10 any more than only ten different radio frequencies need be used.

Still more economy would be obtained by varying the lengths of the radio signals, giving those with the fewest elements to the more frequent concepts. For example, the idea "hydrogen line emission" would probably be used much more frequently than the term "blue," and so it would get a much shorter signal. This is, of course, the principle of economy used by Morse in devising his telegraph code. Algorithms are known to communications engineers that optimally assign digital groups of varying lengths to messages of varying frequencies; these could be used to construct the most efficient language. At first the communication engineers would have to guess at the probable frequency of the words in this language. Later, a corrected version, based on experience, might be constructed. The arrangement of words and ideas in this verbal interstellar language would then depend solely upon their frequency. This represents a new kind of artificial language. It is based on efficiency and differs from both the "rational" categorization of the a priori type and the natural-language imitations of the a posteriori type.

Sometimes it may be necessary to send words as pictures, as in the case of captions labeling objects shown in a picture being sent on the interstellar television. The letters and numbers of existing Earth alphabets are wasteful in design, of course, and special symbols would probably be invented. The combination of symbols for a given word should naturally correspond exactly to the combination of radio frequencies in that word's radio signal, thereby saving both men and outer-spacelings innumerable headaches in spelling.

All this, of course, is to think and act like humans in communicating with nonhumans. Some scientists are trying to gain some knowledge about this very problem of interspecies communication by working with the bottle-nose dolphin, or porpoise. This mammal may have an intelligence approaching or equaling man's, and its marine environment may make it a more alien race than any man may encounter in space. In comparison with man's brain, its brain is slightly larger, appears as dense in nerve fibers as man's (which is not true of elephant and whale brains, which are much larger than man's), and is even richer in cortical folds, usually taken as a rough index of intelligence. Moreover, it has a complex and efficient vocal language for talking to other dolphins. This consists mostly of sharp, high-pitched whistles, but it has imitated human voices that it has heard in the laboratory. Dolphins have helped other dolphins, and even humans, in distress. They have learned in a single try to push a switch giving them a pleasurable electrical sensation, whereas monkeys usually need 300 or more attempts.

Dr. John C. Lilly, who is working on man-dolphin communication at his Communications Research Institute, stated with conviction:

> If we are ever to communicate with a non-human species of this planet, the dolphin is probably our best present gamble. In a sense, it is a joke when I fantasy that it may be best to hurry and finish our work on their brains before one of them learns to speak our language—else he will demand equal rights with men for their brains and lives under our ethical and legal codes!
>
> Before our man-in-space program becomes too successful, it may be wise to spend some time, talent, and money on research with the dolphins; not only are they a large-brained species living their lives in a situation with attenuated effects of gravity, but they may be a group with whom we can learn basic techniques of communication with really alien intelligent life forms.

So far, however, Lilly has made little fundamental progress—and this in itself may be significant.

Man's situation in regard to the creatures of outer space and their messages may resemble that of the human beings in Plato's parable of the cave. Trapped in an underground den, they thought that their shadows, thrown on the wall before them by a fire, were their substances. A whole school of linguists thinks that men are trapped, intellectually, by their languages. Following Benjamin Lee Whorf, they point out that the way each language dissects reality imposes a world-view upon its speakers. Whorf thought, for example, that Western civilization emphasizes history, clocks, calendars, exactness in sequences of events, wages on the basis of time, and business records because Indo-European languages analyze time and all aspects of the world in spatial terms. Thus even nonspatial entities are envisioned by Western minds as "something like a ribbon or scroll marked off into equal blank spaces, suggesting that each be filled with an entry." The Hopi language does not emphasize chronology so much, Whorf said, because it structures life differently. Many of its verbs are conjugated on the basis of whether the speaker saw the action directly or had it reported to him. On this view, men cannot project their minds further than their linguistic preconceptions will allow. It is like trying to see a rainbow in all its colors while wearing red glasses. The implication is that interstellar communication may be fraught with obstacles and misconceptions of which man will be wholly unaware.

Moreover, men cannot even read the primitive Mayan hieroglyphs or the Voynich manuscript, and the simple process of translation from one common language to another still plagues the cause of peace. If this be so between individuals of the same species inhabiting the same planet, how difficult would it be to communicate with an utterly different species having nothing in common with man and living on a planet invisible to him!

Nothing seems more certain than that integers, the basic system of counting, will be known to both sides. Yet perhaps the outer-spacelings think in terms of continua, of curves, of Fourier analyses; perhaps their thinking begins with aleph-null, the first number past infinity, and works down to integers, which would then be the last thing they would introduce. Perhaps, as cosmologist Fred Hoyle has suggested, the values man observes for such dimensionless numbers as the fine-structure constant might "be connected with the particular oscillating and finite region [of the universe] in which we happen to live." Perhaps the outer-spacelings amplify the minute electrical fluctuations that constitute their brain waves and transmit them directly from mind to mind. Perhaps they communicate through some kind of music, having refined it into a much more intimate and emotional communication than men now dream of.

So much is unknown! Who knows what the beings of outer space are like, or how they think or sense? The simple idea of communication by picture presupposes that they see. Yet nothing about them can be assured in advance —the wildest imaginings are probably but feeble simulacrums of the truth. Fact has always been stranger than fiction. Of course they will try to make their messages as clear as possible, but what is clear to them may not be clear to humans. How, then, does man dare hope that he can read any messages from outer space?

Nothing can guarantee that he will. Perhaps he will not, if the communicators differ too radically. It may be, as Ulysses found, that the horizon of "that untravell'd world" "fades/ For ever and for ever when I move," that man in trying to read such messages will never arrive at an answer. Yet to succeed he must begin somewhere. And he has no choice but to start from within his own mental cage: "That which we are, we are." He must seek in order to find, he must start in order to end, he must strive in order to succeed.

Man's hope lies in his intelligence. With it, he has riddled out the secrets of stars and atoms. He has traced the thin thread of causality back from a tremor in an adult's hand to a long-forgotten trauma in childhood. He has mastered the complexities of transfinite algebra and deciphered the histories of unknown men from speechless stones. He has freed himself from the grip of Earth and swims at the shores of the universe. These achievements of the human intellect father the hope that man will solve whatever message may come from the stars. Perhaps some day Earth will be enriched by the profound knowledge of glittering civilizations, and Man, in turn, will endow them with the magnificent creations of his Shakespeares and the noble philosophies of his Christs.

The New Cryptology

27

CRYPTOLOGY GOES PUBLIC

The great struggle in cryptology during the final quarter century of the millennium came over openness. A field that had for centuries been a secret government monopoly exploded into public consciousness under the impact of technology, economics, politics, and history. This development engendered conflict between the people engaged in open cryptologic activities in these new fields and the governmental agencies charged with making and breaking codes for their countries, which require secrecy for success. The individuals and the businesses sought not only the advancement of individual and corporate freedom but also personal and professional profit. The agencies fought not only for national security but also for jobs and bureaucratic power. The expansion of communications, a constant in history now exponential in its growth, has vastly increased the stakes in this fight.

This expansion meant that, by the last half of the twentieth century, communication security and communication intelligence operated in many more places than ever and, more than ever, risked exposure by events. And indeed, a number of episodes brought electronic intelligence to the attention of many.

Several embarrassing airborne episodes, such as when Francis Gary Powers was shot down in his U-2, led the United States to supplement its Cold War intelligence collection with ships. These were seen as platforms that could carry bigger intelligence teams and larger, more sensitive instruments than planes, work an area longer, and navigate more precisely to stay out of dangerous areas. So, in 1963, the Navy began putting such vessels—converted from surplus World War II freighters—into service. The larger of them were called AGTRs, for auxiliary general technical research vessels; the smaller, AGERs, for auxiliary general environmental research vessels.

The Navy's official description of one such vessel probably typified them all: she supported "U.S. Navy electronic research projects which include electromagnetic propagation studies and advanced communications systems." While not, strictly speaking, inaccurate, the statement obfuscated her mission. Communications technicians aboard her intercepted, recorded, took bearings on, and analyzed radar emissions and radio transmissions. This activity probably obtained locations and operating characteristics of radars, order-of-battle information on armed forces, and noted foreign military and civilian activities. The intelligence was forwarded to the National Security Agency at Fort Meade, Maryland, for further refinement and transmission to higher military and civilian authorities. The information was certainly useful, for the intelligence community kept putting more AGTRs and AGERs into service. But the theory that ships would be safer than planes did not always prove to be true.

In the spring of 1967, the smoldering hostility between the Arab nations and Israel intensified. The situation was fraught with global danger, because the Soviet Union supported the Arab countries and the United States, Israel. The possibility of renewed hostilities grew. Now, it is well known to cryptologists that the start of fighting, with its corrections to misdirected messages and improperly used cryptosystems, yields a bumper crop of radio intelligence. To harvest this, in case war did break out, and to gather any information on possible Soviet forces in the Arab countries, the United States dispatched into the eastern Mediterranean an AGTR outfitted to collect such intelligence.

She was the U.S.S. *Liberty*, AGTR-5, a 22-year-old, 7,600-ton, former cargo ship commissioned on December 30, 1964. The three huts of her SOD, or special operations detachment, housed dozens of communications technicians. She arrived at her station off Port Saïd just about the time the soon-to-be-called Six-Day War erupted on June 4, 1967, between Israeli and Arab forces. Among *Liberty's* primary targets were the Tupelov TU-95s currently in Egypt: policymakers in Washington wanted to know whether these airplanes were controlled by the Egyptians or their Soviet "advisors." In the fast-moving fighting, the Israelis drove the Egyptians back and the Jordanians out of the Old City of Jerusalem. Four days later, as Israeli forces reached the Suez Canal and the tip of Sinai to control the whole peninsula, Israeli airplanes reconnoitered the *Liberty*, which was flying a large American flag, more than half a dozen times. At 2:00 p.m., Israeli jets swooped down and fired machine guns and rockets at the *Liberty*. Within half an hour, the air attack was supplemented by machine-gun fire and torpedoes from three Israeli torpedo boats. One torpedo passed only 75 feet astern of the *Liberty*. In the SOD hut, the eavesdroppers continued their work. Marine Staff Sergeant Bryce F. Lockwood ran up to Lieutenant James M. Ennes, Jr., and cried exultantly that "We've got the Bears"—the TU-95s—"They're Russian!" A moment later, a torpedo slammed into the *Liberty*, killing 25 and putting the ship all but out of commission. After an hour and a quarter, the Israeli forces retired, and the *Liberty* staggered into Malta.

The United States protested, and Israel immediately apologized for what it called a "tragic accident." At least two suggestions have been offered as to the possible reason for the attack on the ship of a friendly nation. The Israelis, who the day after the *Liberty* incident launched a surprise attack on Syria, driving her forces out of the Golan Heights, and who did not know what the *Liberty* was listening for, may have wanted to prevent the spy ship from overhearing their plans for the assault. Or perhaps Israel feared that the intercepts would show that she had started the war against the Arab states. But no proposed motive has been satisfactory.

Though the incident showed that spy ships were almost as vulnerable as spy planes, it did not stop the N.S.A. from dispatching them. One was the U.S.S. *Banner,* covernamed the AGER-1. She fished the airwaves above the frigid waters of the Siberian Sea, netting a good enough catch for the United States to send the AGER-2 to cruise off North Korea. A cockleshell of a ship, a converted cargo carrier like the *Liberty* though, at 900 tons, only an eighth her size and with a third the intelligence crew, she was named the *Pueblo.* Her operational orders called for her primarily to "(1) determine nature and extent of naval activity vicinity of North Korean (Korcom) ports . . . , (2) sample electronic environment of east coast North Korea, with emphasis on intercept/fixing of coastal radars, (3) intercept and conduct surveillance of Soviet naval units operating Tsushima Straits in effort to determine purpose of Soviet presence in that area since Feb 1966." She was to do this 15 to 20 nautical miles off the coast of North Korea from about January 10 to January 27, 1968; then she was to work off the Tsushima Straits until she had to leave to arrive at her base at Sasebo, Japan, on February 4.

With Commander Lloyd M. Bucher as her skipper, the *Pueblo* rolled and pitched through heavy storms to reach her station. Though her latitude, about 39 degrees north, was that of Kansas City or Washington, ice soon coated her decks and superstructure and had to be chipped off. Meanwhile, the technicians developed information about the number, type, and position of coastal radars, and Bucher and the head of the intelligence unit, Lieutenant Stephen R. Harris, prepared reports. But then, on January 23, 1968, while Bucher was lunching, a North Korean SO-1 submarine chaser raced out from port and began circling the ship. Soon, three torpedo boats joined her. They too surrounded the *Pueblo* at a distance of 50 yards, aiming their machine guns at the *Pueblo*'s bridge. The SO-1 signaled, "Heave to or I will fire." When Bucher signaled back, "Am in international waters," the SO-1, which by now had been joined by two other North Korean vessels, fired a long burst from her 57-millimeter cannon. The shells struck the radar mast and other parts of the ship. Splinters wounded several, including Bucher. He ordered destruction of classified material, but it was not so easy to do. Some of the gear had heavy metal covers, and 8-pound sledgehammers bounced off them. Though some documents were burned and some torn up and thrown overboard, the volume was too great: all of it could not be destroyed. The North Korean boats drew closer, but Bucher, under instructions not to act provocatively, did not fire his own machine guns. Suddenly, eight or ten North Koreans armed with automatic weapons climbed over the *Pueblo*'s fantail, and she became the first American warship captured without a fight since 1807, when the U.S.S. *Chesapeake* surrendered to Britain's H.M.S. *Leopard* off the Virginia capes. She was taken into Wonsan; the crew went into captivity.

The Navy, even while saying that each ship's cryptosystem was unique and that the *Pueblo* loss would not disclose the Navy's communications secrets, changed some elements of some of its cryptosystems as a general precaution. Exactly what material fell into North Korea's hands was never revealed, but some intelligence equipment, technical manuals, and results probably had. Presumably this gave Communist powers information on how to counter American techniques and made it harder for the United States to gain intelligence.

The crew was imprisoned for almost a year. In December, after the United States signed a confession of spying inside North Korean waters that it branded false, the 82 surviving crewmembers were released.

By then, a third episode had further highlighted the vulnerability of spy ships. In February 1968, the engines of the U.S.S. *Joseph P. Muller* failed as she was on station off Cuba. She began drifting toward the hostile island. Navy vessels sought to tow her to safety, but line after line snapped. Finally, shortly before she crossed into Cuba's territorial waters, one held and she was pulled away. This incident was the last straw. The United States took its spy ships out of service. The loss, however, was not total, for satellites had, in part, replaced them.

Shortly after the *Pueblo* incident, in the early 1970s, the world was electrified by public disclosure of the greatest codebreaking operation of the Second World War: Ultra.

The origins of what has been called the longest sustained intelligence success in history had deep roots. Though the success took place in World War II, it originated during World War I. In August 1914, a German cruiser, the *Magdeburg*, grounded in shallows at the mouth of the Gulf of Finland. Fearing capture by the enemy Russians, its captain burned or jettisoned three of its four copies of the main German naval codebook, the *Signalbuch der Kaiserlichen Marine*. But in the turmoil he forgot the one in his cabin, and it fell into the hands of the Russians. Perhaps after making a copy for themselves, they gave the original to their allies, the British. This large, fat, blue-bound tome enabled the chief naval power to read German naval messages and to parry Germany's repeated attempts to sortie into and control the North Sea. In part because of this intelligence, the island nation, which needed to dominate the seas if she were not to lose the war, ruled the waves during the Great War.

In 1923, when the Allied victory was history, Winston Churchill, who, as the political head of the Royal Navy, had received the original codebook, revealed the story of the *Magdeburg* capture in his inimitable dramatic style. The Germans suddenly saw why their naval moves had been frustrated. They needed, they felt, a cryptosystem that would not have the fatal flaw of a codebook: that the capture of any one copy compromises the entire edition. The Kriegsmarine had, in fact, declined one in 1918 that fulfilled this condition. A machine based on revolving wired codewheels, or rotors, called the Enigma, it had so many keys that even an enemy in possession of a copy would not be able to run through them in time to be of use. Its inventor, engineer Dr. Arthur Scherbius, calculated that if 1,000 cryptanalysts, each with a captured Enigma, tested four keys a minute all day every day, it would take the team 1.8 billion years to try them all. And other methods of solution, such as superimposition, would be excluded by proper encipherment. After the government declined to buy his machine, Scherbius offered it on the commercial market. It thus became known to foreign cryptologic agencies.

Now the German Navy saw that the Enigma fulfilled its needs. It was, moreover, the best practical cipher system then available in the world. After changing some elements of the commercial machine, the Kriegsmarine ordered a quantity of three-rotor Enigmas. From about February 1926, the Enigma served as the German Navy's main cipher system. It proved good enough for the Army to adopt it on July 15, 1928. Thus the Enigma became the main high-level cryptosystem of both German armed services (they retained hand systems for lower-level communications) and, later, of other agencies such as the railroads (though never the Foreign Office).

Germany was, in the 1920s, enraged at the post–World War I re-creation of Poland. Lands that had been Germany's since the partitions of the 1790s now constituted the western provinces of Poland, and Germany wanted them back. She thundered out ceaseless propaganda about this and pressed incessantly for a "rectification" of borders. Poland, concerned, sought as much information about her belligerent neighbor as possible.

Now it had happened that in 1920, when Russia's new Communist government had invaded westward in the hope of turning all Europe Red, Poland had created a cryptanalytic section in its Army General Staff. As hoped, the unit gained information that helped Poland block the Russians before Warsaw. Once the Russian threat had receded, the unit, the Biuro Szyfrów, or Cipher Bureau, added Germany as a target. It seems to have solved the German Army double transposition hand cipher, but when in 1928 messages with quite different letter frequencies appeared, it failed. Through analysis or spies, it learned that the new system was the Enigma machine. And here the head of the Biuro Szyfrów proved himself more farsighted than any country's cryptanalytic chief in the 1920s. Franciszek Pokorny recognized that the increased volume of communications, foreshadowed by World War I, was mechanizing cryptology, that these cipher machines operated not on linguistic entities, such as words, as did the codes that were then popular, but on individual letters that would, for example, separate the t from an h in *the,* and that consequently, what was needed to solve them were not classical scholars and philologists but mathematicians. They might reconstruct a cryptosystem without ever reading a word of plaintext, not unlike the way William Friedman worked when he devised the index of coincidence. Pokorny recruited young mathematicians through classes in cryptology attended by about 20 at the university in Poznán. Most of the students soon dropped out, but three young men proved outstanding: Marian Rejewski, Henryk Zygalski, and Jerzy Różycki. After they had completed their studies—or, in the case of Rejewski, the oldest, after he had completed a postgraduate year at Göttingen—they accepted jobs at the Biuro Szyfrów in Warsaw. When they had passed their apprenticeship by solving a German naval code, they were turned loose on Enigma.

At about this time, a 44-year-old employee of the German Army cipher bureau named Hans-Thilo Schmidt, who was discontented with his life and wanted money, offered the French the operational manuals for Enigma. The French bought them, but because the manuals did not provide the keying information needed, the cryptanalysts got nowhere. The French then passed copies of the manuals to the Poles, with whom they had signed a treaty of mutual military assistance—primarily directed against Germany—in 1921. The brochures told the young mathematicians a useful fact about the enciphering procedure of the German Army Enigma: For each message, the enciphering clerk chose, at his whim, the three rotors' starting positions, which were indicated by letters. To help correct any garbles, he repeated the three letters: PDQPDQ. He enciphered them under the common, army-wide key for that day. The six enciphered letters, say, MKFXRC, called the indicator, were transmitted at the head of each message to the recipient. He used that day's army-wide key to decipher the indicator, determine the three original letters, and set up his Enigma to read the incoming messages.

But the repetition of the three letters, which was a plus in reliability, proved a minus in security. The three Polish cryptanalysts saw that, as a consequence of the repetition, which made the first and fourth, second and fifth, and third and sixth letters of the preencipherment indicator the same, all the indicators in a single day's message that had, say, M as its first letter had, say, X as its fourth. The same thing held true for the second and fifth and the third and sixth letters. Now, another enciphering clerk might have chosen PLM as his key setting instead of PDQ. The encipherment of that indicator might be MRAXTT. It might happen that on a single day two indicators were MRAXTT and XYULKO. Rejewski, the best of the three, strung together MX and XL into MXL, the first links in a chain. Other indicators provided other links. Eventually, the chain would close upon itself, but if Rejewski had about 60 indicators, he sometimes could link all 26 letters, though never in one chain but always in several. When he assigned numbers to the letters, these chains, or cycles, enabled Rejewski to set up six long equations that, if solved, would disclose the wiring of the rightmost, or fast, rotor. But they had too many unknowns for him to solve.

Meanwhile, the French continued to receive information from Schmidt. At one rendezvous, he gave them the Enigma keys for August and September 1932. This converted some of the unknowns in Rejewski's equations to knowns. After struggling with these, he had a flash of inspiration. Perhaps the wiring from the keyboard to the rotor input plate did not run from Q (the first letter on the keyboard) to A (the first contact on the plate) but from Q to Q and likewise for the other letters. He adjusted his equations. "The very first trial yielded a positive result," he wrote. "From my pencil, as if by magic, began to issue numbers designating the wiring in rotor N [the rightmost]."

The 27-year-old cryptanalyst had uncovered part of the secret heart of the Enigma. Similar work enabled him to reconstruct the wiring in the other two rotors and in the reflecting rotor. Around Christmas 1932, he handed in his first solutions. It was a remarkable feat of cryptanalysis—one of the finest in the history of the art—but Rejewski recognized what was often to become a necessity in the cryptanalysis of modern systems: that it succeeded only with help from stolen or otherwise compromised material. ". . . the intelligence material furnished to us should be regarded as having been decisive in the solution of the machine," he wrote.

Great as Rejewski's achievement was, it marked not the end of his work but only the end of its beginning. For while Poland now had, in effect, a copy of the

Wehrmacht's Enigma, its cryptanalysts stood only at the point that was the main reason for Germany's adoption of the machine: even if an enemy had an Enigma, he would not be able to read messages in it because so many keys existed that he would not be able to find the right one in any useful time. The Poles were thus faced with the problem of discovering the daily keys.

They exploited the repetition of the indicators, devised a technique for determining the rotor locations by matching pairs of letters, and ascertained the rotors' starting position sometimes by guessing that the messages began with *AnX* (German for *to* plus *X* as a word divider), sometimes simply by trying all 17,576 possible starting positions by hand. When they had enough of the right kind of messages, the three young Poles could reconstruct the daily keys and read all the messages enciphered that day on that network. Their work would frequently take a full day. But this was much less than the eons the Germans thought would be needed. It was one of the great achievements of cryptology.

But the Poles could not rest on their laurels. As Germany rearmed, the volume of messages rose. Signal officers stepped up the pace of their key changes. Rotor locations, originally changed every three months, began to be changed monthly and then daily. The Poles fought back with mechanical devices they called "bombes"—the roots of protocomputers. But when, late in 1938, the Germans added two rotors to the three available for insertion into the machine, the work required outstripped the Poles' resources. By then, Germany's threats against Poland had become all but deafening. After Hitler, who had said at Munich that he wanted no more territory after the Sudetenland, seized all of Czechoslovakia, Britain and France promised that, if Hitler attacked Poland, they would come to her aid. With this guarantee, Poland decided to offer her allies her Enigma results in return for the material help that would enable her to continue her solving. At a conference near Warsaw beginning Monday, July 24, 1939, the Poles revealed their reconstructed Enigmas, their electromechanical codebreaking aids—their "bombes"—and other technical information needed to read the system to the astonished Allied cryptanalysts.

The French and the British were at first incredulous, then overjoyed. They sent the items home under diplomatic seal and began work there.

Five weeks later, Germany flung her panzers and her stukas against Poland. Their might overwhelmed any information the codebreakers supplied—and incidentally provided a fundamental lesson in intelligence: no matter how good intelligence may be, it is all but useless without sufficient force. The same thing, yielding the same lesson, occurred in France in 1940.

Britain now stood alone. But she had an advantage that the other countries did not. The British codebreaking establishment, the so-called Government Code and Cypher School, or G.C. & C.S., had recruited, as war threatened, a number of linguists and mathematicians. Among the latter was an authentic genius. Alan Turing had become a fellow of King's College, Cambridge, at the almost unprecedented age of 22 when the dons recognized his ability. Tallish, powerfully built, with deep-set blue eyes, he wore unpressed clothes, sidled through doors, stammered, fell into long silences. He had, four years earlier, proved a fundamental theorem in mathematics: that it was not possible to ascertain whether certain problems could be solved. To prove it, he envisioned a mechanism that could move to the left or to the right an infinitely long tape marked into squares, and could read and change or read and leave unchanged the blank or the mark—the 0 or the 1—in each square. He demonstrated that this machine could compute anything that could be calculated. Then he showed that even this machine could not tell whether the unknown problems could be solved. This machine, later called the "universal Turing machine," has come to be recognized as the idealization of general-purpose computers and Turing, therefore, as the intellectual father of the computer.

This genius turned his mind to the problem of solving Enigma messages. He took the Poles' bombe and advanced it by a quantum leap. He conceived a device that would take a cryptogram's presumed plaintext—as the Poles had done with *AnX,* only longer—and run it through all possible rotor combinations until it found one that would yield the known ciphertext from the presumed plaintext. This combination would constitute that day's key on that cipher net and would allow the British to read all that net's messages for that day. The presumed plaintexts, or cribs, would come from radiomen's chatter, service messages, solutions of messages sent in hand systems, plaintext intercepts, captured documents, prisoner interrogations, guesses based on events.

The system offered far greater cryptanalytic potential than the Poles' system. G.C. & C.S. had a machine to implement it built by the British Tabulating Machine Company. It was about four feet wide, as tall as a man, and with six stacks of two horizontal rectangles, each holding three wired codewheels, the analogues of the rotors, on its front. This, the first British bombe, was installed March 18, 1940, in one of the long, peak-roofed, wooden huts that had been built as a non-London headquarters for the cryptanalysts on an estate, Bletchley Park, or B.P., in the railroad junction town of Bletchley, 50 miles northwest of the capital. It began work at once seeking to determine Enigma keys.

The British concentrated at first on Luftwaffe messages. The Luftwaffe signalmen were not as well trained as the more veteran signalmen of the German Army and Navy; they were less disciplined in their cryptographic work, engaging in such forbidden practices as using a girlfriend's name for a key setting or beginning a second message with the same setting as that left at the ending of the first. This sloppiness, together with a greater knowledge of probable plaintexts, enabled B.P. to begin reading the Luftwaffe's general key, which B.P. called RED, with regularity on May 22, 1940. RED provided the British with some insights into the Luftwaffe's plans during the Battle of Britain, though most of the information that helped Britain win that crucial victory came from radar and plain language intercepts. The British continued to read RED to the end of the war. It provided valuable information about land operations as well, primarily through the intercepts of reports from and instructions to the *Flivos,* or *Fliegerverbindungsoffiziere,* the air liaison officers who knew what the ground forces to which they were attached were doing.

Prerequisite to the ground victories, however, was victory in the war at sea. And enormously helpful—one cannot say essential—to that victory was the winning of the code battle. This was more difficult than the land or air solutions because the Kriegsmarine employed an entirely different Enigma keying system. It lacked the weakness of the repeated key indicators or the use of girlfriends' names, for example, because it utilized a book of random indicators, which were themselves enciphered. This all but precluded a purely cryptanalytic attack on the Navy system. It became evident that only obtaining the indicator lists and their enciphering tables, through seizure or betrayal, would lead to solution.

One intelligence officer who saw this was a man with an inventive turn of mind: Ian Fleming, the future author of the James Bond books. But his idea for seizing the documents—by crashing a captured German bomber in the North Sea and then boarding the boat that came to rescue the "airmen"—failed when suitable circumstances did not materialize. The thought of seizure took root in the mind of another young B.P. worker, a longish-haired, corduroy-trousered Cambridge undergraduate: F. Harry Hinsley. Hinsley knew, from his studies of intercepted German naval traffic, that the Kriegsmarine had stationed converted fishing vessels northeast of Iceland to collect and report the meteorological data that the high command needed to forecast the weather for its bombing raids and its blitzkriegs. He knew, too, that these ships enciphered their messages in Enigma and that they patrolled alone. Hinsley proposed that a task force be sent to seize their key lists, thereby enabling B.P. to read Enigma messages during the month or two that the key lists remained valid.

The Admiralty accepted the proposal. A flotilla of a cruiser and four destroyers were dispatched to the German Navy's grid square AE39, some 54 miles on a side, about 300 miles northeast of Iceland. At a little past 5:00 p.m. on May 7, 1941, the task force surprised the *München.* Her crew threw her Enigma overboard, but the British boarders got the Enigma keys for June. These found their way to B.P.—as did complementary documents taken from the *U-110,* a German submarine that a British destroyer had boarded after an action in the North Atlantic. The cryptanalytic results were dramatic. Toward the end of May, when B.P. was attacking Enigma messages analytically, it was taking from 38 hours to 11 days to read them—when they could be read at all. When the June keys came into effect, the first message intercepted in them, picked up at 12:18 a.m. June 1, was forwarded from the intercept post to B.P., deciphered and translated there, and teleprinted to the Admiralty in just 4 hours 40 minutes. And for the rest of the month, intercept-to-teleprint time averaged six hours.

But after the June keys expired, Hinsley foresaw, the problems of slow solutions would recur. He concluded that the job would have to be done again, and he so persuaded the Admiralty. On Saturday, June 28, 1941, another task force of a cruiser and three destroyers seized the *Lauenburg,* an immaculate, three-year-old trawler—and with her the July Enigma keys. They reached B.P. on July 2, and the solution time fell from about 40 hours, to which it had risen when the June keys expired, to under three.

Yet it cannot be said that this speedier intelligence immediately affected the Battle of the Atlantic. As many ships were sunk in the slow-solution months of May and August as in the fast-solution months of June and July. Intelligence was outweighed by too many other factors. Yet gradually it gained in importance. It did so as the new knowledge of German naval terms, reports, forms of orders, stereotypical phraseology, and the like gave B.P. cribs that the growing number of bombes could masticate to spit out the daily U-boat keys. These keys let B.P. read U-boat messages, telling the Admiralty where the U-boats were patrolling and where they had been ordered to go. The Admiralty could then detour its convoys around the wolfpacks.

Convoy HX155 typified the technique. Its 54 ships sailed from Halifax, Nova Scotia, on October 16, 1941, carrying grain, sugar, fuel oil, aviation gasoline, steel, copper, and tobacco, among other goods. But its original route, decided a week before it sailed, would have run it close to a couple of U-boat concentrations whose presence had only since then become known. As a consequence, the Admiralty ordered it to swing more to the west and then, as more information about U-boat positions became known, still farther to the west. When it had steamed far enough north to avoid the concentrations, the Admiralty ordered HX155 to turn eastward again. And with these directions, the convoy sailed safely past the U-boats. As the Admiralty later said: "All ships now arrived." The supplies so badly needed for Britain to continue her fight against the Axis had reached the island kingdom, thanks in part to the backroom boys of B.P.

The struggle against the Enigma continued throughout the war, as the Germans improved the device—not because they thought it had been compromised but because they feared that the growth in communications might produce a leak. A long blackout throughout most of 1942, due in part to the addition of a fourth rotor to the mechanism and in part to the change of a weather cipher that had permitted useful cribs, ended when a capture restored the cribs. From then on, naval Enigma was read with relative regularity. It permitted not only the defensive diversion of convoys but an offensive against the U-boats by aircraft from small escort carriers. These seriously disrupted the submarine dispositions and greatly blunted their attacks. Thus, B.P. helped win the Battle of the Atlantic. It did not win it alone. The merchant mariners, the shipwrights who built more vessels than U-boats could ever sink, the airplanes that gave convoys cover and forced U-boats to submerge to ineffectualness, the sailors on the warships escorting convoys—all were the chief winners of the war at sea. But codebreaking substantially shortened the struggle. And by doing so, it saved lives. And what contribution could be greater than that?

The great story of the solution of the Enigma machine and its effects on World War II remained a tightly held secret for almost 30 years. Only a few tiny shards of light about it escaped, and they revealed nothing about the vast scope of the work and its vast influence on the war. The tens of thousands of people involved in the work remained utterly silent about it for decades—probably the best example of general security in history. The British government insisted upon this silence because it had given the thousands of Enigma machines that it had gathered up after the end of the war to its former colonies as they gained independence and needed secure systems of communication. (Their officials were not stupid: probably they surmised that, if the mother country was giving them these cipher machines, she could read them. But they were concerned less with Britain than with their neighbors—India with Pakistan, for example—and they were almost certainly right in that those neighbors could not break the Enigma.)

Then, by the early 1970s, the last Enigmas in service wore out, physically. There was no longer any need to keep the story secret. There was, on the other hand, the possibility of showing the world Britain's remarkable feat with communications and protocomputers. Among them was an electronic codebreaking device, called Colossus, for a non-Enigma cipher machine, that could be seen as a precursor of the information age. A Royal Air Force officer who had played a role in the distribution of the codebreaking results during the war, Group Captain F. W. Winterbotham, had been pestering Her Majesty's Government for permission to tell the entire Enigma story, which he subsequently received. *The Ultra Secret* appeared in 1974 in Britain, at first excerpted in newspaper series, and in 1975 in the United States, where a review in *The New York Times Book Review* beginning "This book reveals the greatest secret of World War II after the atom bomb" helped set it on the road to best-sellerdom. Since then, dozens of books, sustained by an outpouring of documents into the American and British archives, have amplified the story. Together, they awakened a wide public to the existence of codebreaking. More important, they taught that public, which previously thought only of spies and cameras as kinds of intelligence, that codebreaking was the most important source of all.

Coincident with this growing public sensitivity to cryptology, though not driven by it, but spurred instead by the growth in computers and communications, the U.S. government moved to put into service a publicly available cryptosystem that would protect such items as bank messages or health information in data banks while allowing broad intercommunication among its users. It would do this by utilizing a cryptosystem that would be known to all but would have users establish private keys between themselves to keep their messages secret. In 1973 and 1974, the National Bureau of Standards, as the National Institute of Standards and Technology was then named, solicited candidate cryptosystems in the *Federal Register.* A handful of proposals was sent in. One of these was based on a system devised by Horst Feistel of the International Business Machines Corporation. Feistel, who had immigrated from Germany in 1932, had worked on I.F.F., or identification-friend-or-foe, systems during and just after World War II. This interested him in the problem of authentication and coded texts and, when he joined I.B.M. in 1967, he began trying to see how the monoalphabetic substitution, the most general substitution of all, could be used in a good system. He was accustomed to working with computer technology and in binary digital form.

Computer memory enabled him to incorporate transposition into his system, something that had not been practicable with devices using letters. Binary operations facilitated his changing numerical bases from 2 to 8 (though always expressed in binary form) to devise a critical contraction that made it hard for a would-be cryptanalyst to track back through the cipher system. Computer technology thus let him devise this cipher, which, because of its complexity, could never be implemented by hand. Feistel wanted to name it "Dataseal," but I.B.M. just shortened the term "demonstration cipher" to "Demon." Later, the name was changed to "Lucifer," which, in addition to maintaining what Feistel called "the evil atmosphere" of "Demon," contained the word "cipher."

The system was not an elegant one. It operated on blocks of 64 plaintext bits, which it transposed, divided, replaced, and combined in complicated ways, repeating some of the steps 16 times. Because the individual operations were simple, the system could run fast enough to keep up with the demands of computer communications.

Before I.B.M. submitted it as a candidate for the proposed Data Encryption Standard, it conferred with the National Security Agency to strengthen it. The meetings resulted in an improvement of a key component called the S (for substitution) boxes and in a reduction of the length of the key that Feistel had designed, down to 56 bits (plus eight extra as parity, or checking, bits). This was the modified version of Lucifer that I.B.M. submitted to the bureau.

Of all the candidate cryptosystems, it proved to be the only one the bureau believed met even the minimal demands of computer security and communications requirements. The bureau published it in the *Federal Register* of August 1, 1975, as a proposed federal information processing standard—the data encryption standard, or D.E.S.

Very quickly a storm blew up. The growing community of nongovernmental cryptologists, who worked in academe and for businesses such as banks, international oil conglomerates, communication equipment manufacturers, and communications companies, suspected something fishy. The involvement of N.S.A. led them to believe either that a "trap door" had been built into the data encryption standard that enabled N.S.A. to solve it easily, or that N.S.A. had deliberately weakened the system by reducing the length of its key to where the system was just strong enough to keep business firms from solving competitors' messages but just weak enough to let the government read messages in it. Articles appeared in the technical, trade, and general press about it; panels argued over the issue at professional conferences; the standards bureau called meetings to discuss the matter and, it hoped, to convert attendees to its point of view. In the end, most people seemed to stick with the positions they had had at the beginning of the controversy—and the standards bureau issued the standard as it had originally proposed it, with the 56-bit key, on January 15, 1977, as the 18-page Federal Information Processing Standards Publication 46. The publication stated that the D.E.S. was to be used by federal departments and agencies for any of their nonnational-security data that an authorized official decided needs "cryptographic protection."

Perhaps more important, the publication said that the D.E.S.'s use by "commercial and private organizations" was to be "encouraged."

With a market thus assured, manufacturers such as Motorola began producing D.E.S. chips for incorporation into computers. Rival firms selling cipher machines the world over warned that the D.E.S.'s approval by the U.S. government meant that that government could read D.E.S.-encrypted messages. But D.E.S. manufacturers maintained instead that the U.S. government had in effect certified the system as solid and that, if a firm feared that the N.S.A. could read D.E.S., it could doubly or triply encrypt its messages, thus assuring secrecy. Businesses either accepted this point or didn't care about government spying, for more and more began encrypting messages using D.E.S. It has become the de facto standard for much of business around the world. And despite occasional rumors that this researcher or that has solved the D.E.S., despite successful attacks on parts of the system or on it up to its 15th round, despite the growth in computer power since the D.E.S. was promulgated, there is no authenticated case of anyone's breaking it. Can the N.S.A. do so? No one outside the agency knows, but one standards institute official has said that, from the standpoint of national security, the D.E.S. was the worst mistake the N.S.A. ever made.

The controversy over the D.E.S. brought the government into conflict with at least parts of the broad new cryptologic public. This conflict expanded into other areas with some ham-handed attempts to control that public. Several persons who had been invited to speak at a conference at Cornell University were warned in a letter from an individual, later determined to be an N.S.A. employee, that discussing cryptology would violate the federal International Traffic in Arms Regulations. These forbid the export of cryptologic equipment or information on cryptology without government approval, and speaking before an audience that included non-U.S. citizens constitutes an export. The speakers, fearful of violating U.S. law, refrained from talking. At about the same time, the government slapped secrecy orders on a few applications for patents for cryptosystems. This raised protests. Then a new director of the N.S.A., Vice Admiral Bobby R. Inman, a tall, slender Texan, brought the agency out of the dark, and into the non-national-security world. He spoke to the media! He visited the offices of *Science* magazine and explained N.S.A.'s point of view. One upshot was the establishment of a committee under the American Council on Education to look into the problem of publishing material on cryptology that might harm the national security. The committee, consisting mainly of professors of mathematics who worked in cryptology, proposed a system of voluntary censorship. Authors of works on cryptology would be asked to submit their material to N.S.A., which, without any enforcement power, would urge the writers to delete or blur sensitive matter. The system was put into operation and has been working satisfactorily.

Meanwhile, revelations in the press about excesses of the intelligence community led the U.S. Senate and the House of Representatives to investigate it. Included was the N.S.A. The agency, the investigations showed, had monitored the domestic conversations of Americans without the proper court warrants. It was chastised and forbidden to overhear such communications, and Congress established a special court to grant national-security wiretaps.

Public interest in cryptology was further—and greatly—stimulated by the invention of a new form of cryptography that prompted more work in the field than anything else in its history. This was public-key cryptography. For the first time, a form of secret communication used different keys for encryption and decryption. The idea was first proposed by Dr. Martin Hellman of the Stanford University Department of Electrical Engineering and Whitfield Diffie, a graduate student. It was a dramatic breakthrough, for it had not occurred to anyone else in the long history of cryptology that the deciphering key could be anything other than the inverse of the enciphering key. The asymmetry permitted, for the first time in cryptology, the possibility of authenticating a message sent electrically. The two discussed the possibility in a pathbreaking article entitled "New Directions in Cryptography." In it, however, they offered only partial implementations of their idea.

The theory put forth in the article came to the attention of three mathematicians at the Massachusetts Institute of Technology. Ronald Rivest, Len Adleman, and Adi Shamir were intrigued with the possibility and sought to realize it. After some failed attempts, they devised a system based upon the mathematical phenomenon that it is easy to determine whether a number is a prime but, if it is not, hard to determine its factors. Under the system, anyone may send a secret message to a particular person but only that person can read it. The system works like this: the person wishing to receive secret messages selects two large prime numbers, p and q, which must be kept secret, and another large number, e, which is public. He or she multiplies the primes together to produce n, which is also public. The numbers e and n, which must be prime to one another, constitute the public key. They are published, as a telephone number is in a phone directory. The person then calculates another number, d, by finding the greatest common denominator of $p-1$ and $q-1$, multiplying this number by the product of $p-1$ times $q-1$, adding 1, dividing this total by e, and taking the remainder. He keeps d secret. Someone wanting to send a message first converts it into numerical form (as $a = 10$, $b = 11$, etc.), multiplies it by itself e times, divides the result by n, discards the quotient and takes the remainder as the cryptogram. When the recipient gets this, he multiplies it by itself d times, divides it by n, and takes the remainder as the numerical plaintext. The system resists to the degree that n is hard to factor into p and q.

It offers a number of fascinating possibilities. If a person encrypts a message with her decrypting key, she cannot deny that the message came from her, because no one else knows her key. By the same token, the recipient knows it came from her: the message is thus authenticated. She can secure her message by encrypting it with the recipient's public key. Now no one can read it except the legitimate recipient, who can decrypt the message with his secret key and then encrypt the result with the sender's public key to obtain the plaintext.

When Martin Gardner mentioned the system in his column on Mathematical Games in *Scientific American,* explaining how it could both authenticate messages (assure the recipient that they came from whom they said they came) and make them undeniable by the sender, an avalanche of 5,000 requests for their article poured in to M.I.T. The interest stemmed from the apparent impossibility of doing what it claimed it would do: the event was counterintuitive. But the system did do what it said it would do, and it did it in so elegant a mathematical fashion that it attracted hundreds of researchers to the field. The system came to be known as the RSA, from the initials of its inventors.

Dozens of applications of public-key cryptography presented themselves, such as digital cash. But the system runs much more slowly than, say, the D.E.S. because it requires heavy computation. So it has come mainly to encrypt keys between correspondents in cryptographic networks in which there are so many correspondents that it is difficult to exchange keys before secret communication needs to take place.

Public-key cryptology, the D.E.S., cryptosystems using shift registers, cryptosystems based on elliptic curves and other mathematical techniques—all are implemented today not on the alphabet of 26 letters, as the Enigma machine and the hand cipher systems of yesteryear were, but on the binary digital alphabet of 0s and 1s. The reason is that this is the international alphabet of computers and communications, and therefore of the Internet.

The openness of the Internet makes it easy for unauthorized persons to approach the gates of computers and computer networks and, if those gates are not properly guarded, to hack through them and gain entry to those computers. Inside, they can read personal and business files out of a morbid curiosity, or, if they are more vicious, to change or even destroy them. When film or TV viewers see young hackers tapping away at their computers, they are watching the characters attempting to gain entry to a system by trying likely passwords. Once inside, they are writing instructions in a computer language, such as C or Intel assembly language, to open up files or to alter them.

Cryptology plays a role in this because it is the only technology that, if good enough, can block access to files in storage or in transit. Passwords can be encrypted so that they cannot be read even if the file in which they are stored is accessed. Files can be encrypted so that their contents can remain secret. The need to protect the ever-growing number of files as communications expands at its present lightning rate in e-mail, the World Wide Web and other functions of the Internet, internal business networks, and cellular telephones explains why more than a thousand firms now offer cryptologic systems for data, voice, and fax, why manufacturers are now building them into the software packages they sell. And this growth of cryptographic systems explains the justified anxiety of law-enforcement agencies about such systems getting into the hands of drug dealers, terrorists, kidnappers, and other criminals. These agencies have proposed cryptographic systems that would let trusted organizations hold the keys, to be delivered to the law-enforcement agencies upon a court order; they could then read messages encrypted with these keys. But the plan, called key escrow, faces practical difficulties and philosophical opposition, and has not yet been put into practice.

The anxiety of these agencies, and of N.S.A., is justified because cryptosystems today can be made unbreakable. This means that it is computationally infeasible to reconstruct the system and the key in use to read the message it is protecting. In many systems, this infeasibility holds true even if the cryptanalyst himself chooses the plaintext to try to trace back to it from the ciphertext. People ask, Can't computers break these systems? The answer is no. While computers helped make them, the systems are so complex that they defeat attempts at reconstruction. A rule of thumb in cryptology holds that every time the cryptographer doubles the number of combinations in a system, the cryptanalyst must square the number of trials he must make: one goes from 5 to 10, the other from 5 to 25. This means that, although errors will occur that will occasionally enable the cryptanalyst to solve systems analytically, when systems are good enough and are properly used, they cannot be broken. The war of cryptographer against cryptanalyst has been won by the cryptographers. The only way properly encrypted messages can be read nowadays is by theft or betrayal—that is, noncryptologic means. It had already begun with the German naval Enigma.

Does this mean that the story of secret writing has ended? In the long term, yes. Of course, cipher clerks will always make mistakes, apparently good cryptosystems will have unsuspected weaknesses, and people will invent and use foolish cryptosystems, so cryptanalysis will always have its niche. But massive solutions, as of Enigma, are becoming a thing of the past.

Near the end of his ever-fascinating book *The American Black Chamber,* published in 1931, Herbert O. Yardley, speaking about the Vernam one-time tape system, the oldest practically and theoretically unbreakable system, wrote, "Sooner or later all governments, all wireless companies, will adopt some such system. And when they do, cryptography [meaning cryptology], as a profession, will die."

His prediction is coming true.

BIBLIOGRAPHY

This is not a full listing of all works used in the writing of this book. Most of the sources are not required beyond the period covered by a single chapter, and full references are given in the notes to each chapter, or sometimes in those for the preceding chapter or two. If references are widely separated they are repeated in full. The notes therefore comprise a kind of classified bibliography of the subject, and to repeat the works in a general listing would serve no useful purpose.

Rather this is a listing of some of the more important sources that are used throughout the book, together with the abbreviations by which they are cited. The cryptological books mostly serve to give information on cryptanalysis for cipher systems mentioned herein, and they may be consulted with confidence because they are good solid works. Except for Gaines and Sacco (in French), they are all out of print, but they may often be found in large libraries.

ABBREVIATION	REFERENCE
Add. Ms.	British Museum, Additional Manuscript. Followed by number of the manuscript in the Add. Ms. series.
AMS	*American Men of Science*, 10th edition.
DAB	*Dictionary of American Biography*.
DGFP	United States, Department of State. *Documents on German Foreign Policy*, Series D (1937–1945). Washington, D.C.: U.S. Government Printing Office, 1949–. Followed by volume number.
DNB	*Dictionary of National Biography*.
DSDF	National Archives, Record Group 59, Department of State Decimal File. Followed by number of item.
NA, RG	National Archives, Record Group. Followed by number of record group.
PHA	United States, Congress, Joint Committee on the Investigation of the Pearl Harbor Attack. *Pearl Harbor Attack*. Hearings. 79th Congress: 1st and 2nd Sessions. Washington, D.C.: U.S. Government Printing Office, 1946. Followed by part number and pages: "12:154–157, 281" means part 12, pages 154 to 157 and page 281.
Articles	United States, War Department, Office of the Chief Signal Officer. *Articles on Cryptography and Cryptanalysis Reprinted from The Signal Corps Bulletin*. Washington, D.C.: U.S. Government Printing Office, 1942. Followed in parentheses by date article first appeared in *The Signal Corps Bulletin*.
Bazeries	Bazeries, Étienne. *Les chiffres secrets dévoilés*. Paris: Librairie Charpentier et Fasquelle, 1901.

ABBREVIATION	REFERENCE
Eyraud	Eyraud, Charles. *Précis de cryptographie moderne.* Paris: Éditions Raoul Tari, 1953.
Friedman	Friedman, William F. *Military Cryptanalysis.* War Department, Office of the Chief Signal Officer. Washington, D.C.: U.S. Government Printing Office. I: *Monoalphabetic Substitution Systems* (1942, 3rd edition). II: *Simpler Varieties of Polyalphabetic Substitution Systems* (1943, 3rd edition). III: *Simpler Varieties of Aperiodic Substitution Systems* (1939). IV: *Transposition and Fractionating Systems* (1941). Dates given are those of volumes, herein cited to section instead of page to facilitate reference in other printings.
Gaines	Gaines, Helen F. *Elementary Cryptanalysis.* Boston: American Photographic Publishing Co., 1939. Reprinted as *Cryptanalysis*, New York: Dover Publications, Inc., 1956.
Galland	Galland, Joseph S. *An Historical and Analytical Bibliography of the Literature of Cryptology.* (Northwestern University Studies in the Humanities, No. 10.) Evanston, Ill.: Northwestern University, 1945.
Givierge	Givierge, M[arcel]. *Cours de cryptographie.* Paris: Berger-Levrault, 1925.
Gyldén	Gyldén, Yves. *The Contribution of the Cryptographic Bureaus in the World War.* A translation by the Military Intelligence Division of the War Department General Staff of *Chifferbyråernas insatser i världskriget till lands* [Stockholm: Militärlitteratur-föreningens förlag, 1931]. Washington, D.C.: U.S. Government Printing Office, 1935. References are to this volume and not to original publication of the translation in *The Signal Corps Bulletin*, No. 75 (November–December, 1933) to No. 81 (November–December, 1934).
Harris	Thompson, George Raynor, and Harris, Dixie R. *The Signal Corps: The Outcome (Mid-1943 through 1945).* (United States Army in World War II: The Technical Services.) Department of the Army, Office of the Chief of Military History. Washington, D.C.: U.S. Government Printing Office, 1966.
Kerckhoffs	Kerckhoffs, Auguste. *La Cryptographie militaire.* Paris: Librairie militaire de L. Baudoin & Cie., 1883.
Sacco	Sacco, Luigi. *Manuale di crittografia.* 3rd edition. Rome: Istituto Poligrafico dello Stato, 1947. Translated by J. Brès as *Manuel de cryptographie*, Paris: Payot, 1951. Cited to section instead of page to facilitate reference in both languages.
Terrett	Terrett, Dulany. *The Signal Corps: The Emergency (To December 1941).* (United States Army in World War II: The Technical Services.) Department of the Army, Office of the Chief of Military History. Washington, D.C.: U.S. Government Printing Office, 1956.
Thompson	Thompson, George Raynor, Harris, Dixie R., Oakes, Pauline M., and Terrett, Dulany. *The Signal Corps: The Test (December 1941 to July 1943).* (United States Army in World War II: The Technical

Bibliography

ABBREVIATION	REFERENCE
	Services.) Department of the Army, Office of the Chief of Military History. Washington, D.C.: U.S. Government Printing Office, 1957.
Wolfe	Wolfe, J[ack]. M. *A First Course in Cryptanalysis*. Revised. In 3 volumes. Brooklyn: Brooklyn College Press, 1943.
Yardley	Yardley, Herbert O. *The American Black Chamber*. Indianapolis, Ind.: The Bobbs-Merrill Company, 1931.

Citations of these authors by name only always refers to these books. Their other works are cited with full or short title following their names.

In citations to Congressional committee hearings and reports, I have eliminated the "United States, Congress" that should precede. They thus begin with "Senate" or "House of Representatives." I have abbreviated the "Washington, D.C.: U.S. Government Printing Office" to "GPO" in these cases. The full citation "74th Congress, 1st Session" becomes "74:1." The term "Hearings" after the title distinguishes the published transcript of the hearings from the committee's report, which often bears the same title. "Senate, Subcommittee on Internal Security" refers to Senate, Committee on the Judiciary, Subcommittee to Investigate the Administration of the Internal Security Act.

"Hardie" means Bradford Hardie, M.D. In manuscript and old book references, "f." means "folio," "r" means "recto," and "v" means "verso." I have copied quotations errors and all without using that supercilious "[sic]."

NOTES TO TEXT

A FEW WORDS

The best definitions of cryptologic terms in English today are to be found in *Webster's Third New International Dictionary of the English Language Unabridged* (Springfield, Massachusetts: G. & C. Merriam Co., 1961). The definer was Martin Joos, Ph.D., professor of German and linguistics at the University of Wisconsin, a World War II cryptologist and an experienced lexicographer. The definitions are based on actual usage. For a discussion and a list of the cryptologic terms in the dictionary, see my *Plaintext in the New Unabridged: An Examination of the Definitions on Cryptology In Webster's Third New International Dictionary* (New York: Crypto Press, 1963).

I have in general followed these definitions, in their technical senses. In a few places I have tried to fix meanings more specifically, and here and there I have invented a word where one seemed needed or given an old word a new meaning. Among the new words are "cryptoeidography," meaning the encoding of pictures or images, and "semagram," meaning a steganographic message transmitted by anything other than letters or numbers, as by the order of cards in a deck. The chief old word that has been given a new meaning is "steganography" (ultimately from the Greek steganos "covered" + graphein "to write"). This was the original term for cryptography (a word which comes ultimately from the Greek kryptos "covered" + graphein); it had fallen into desuetude. Following the suggestion of George E. McCracken in "Athanasius Kircher's Universal Polygraphy," *Isis*, XXXIX (November, 1948), 215–228, at footnote 7, I revived it and assigned it as the term so badly needed for methods that conceal the very presence of a secret message.

Naturally all books on cryptology will give explicit or implicit definitions of terms; the best of these is Friedman; more compact and more accessible is his article "Cryptology" in the *Encyclopaedia Britannica*. Most complete of the technical glossaries is the United States Army Security Agency's; more recent is David Shulman's *Glossary of Cryptography* (New York: Crypto Press, 1961). The official definitions of a number of cryptologic terms are given in United States, Department of Defense, Joint Chiefs of Staff, *Dictionary of United States Military Terms for Joint Usage* (Washington, D.C.: U.S. Government Printing Office, 1964), and United States, Department of the Army, *Dictionary of United States Army Terms* (Army Regulations 320–5. Washington: 1958). (These official definitions persist in making physical and personnel security part of signal security. But while physical and personnel security are undoubtedly essential to signal security, they are not essential to it alone. They extend throughout the military sphere. It thus is wrong to define signal security in terms of them. They are accompanying characteristics, not defining ones. The official definitions fail to see this distinction. Interestingly, however, they do not make the complementary activities of theft and betrayal part of signal intelligence.) For other places where cryptologic definitions may be found, see Appendix II of *Plaintext in the New Unabridged.*

Chapter 1 ONE DAY OF MAGIC

Since the question of responsibility for the Pearl Harbor disaster is steeped in such bitter controversy, I feel that I should make known my views. I believe that the theory is false that Roosevelt and his cabal teased the Japanese into attacking to trick a reluctant United States into the war, and that they assured the Japanese success at Pearl Harbor by withholding vital information from the Hawaiian commanders. These are the views expressed by John T. Flynn, Rear Admiral Robert A. Theobald, George Morgenstern, and Charles A. Beard, among others, in their books and pamphlets. I hold that Pearl Harbor resulted from Japanese duplicity, audacity, and security; from the difficulty of predicting what others will do; from a concatenation of dozens of minor mistakes, omissions, false assumptions, and failures, none intentional; from a poor administrative setup (most evident in the defense of Hawaii and in the evaluation of intelligence); and from the unwillingness of the American public to believe war likely and to pay for military preparedness. The causes of Pearl Harbor were not one but many, not simple but complex—as are the causes of most great events.

This is essentially the view of the majority of the Congressional committee. Samuel E. Morison gives a short but devastating rebuttal of Theobald and the other revisionists in his *Two-Ocean War* (Boston: Little, Brown & Co., 1963), 69-76. He observes that a Japanese defeat at Pearl Harbor would have better served a warmongering policy by preserving the forces of war. The most thorough analysis of the problem is Roberta Wohlstetter's *Pearl Harbor: Warning and Decision* (Stanford, Calif.: Stanford University Press, 1962), which shows the difficulties of detecting the true signals of future events amid the roar of the false. After the fact, of course, the true portents stand out in high relief, whereas the others, unneeded and therefore forgotten, recede into the background. The revisionists, looking back with the 20-20 vision of hindsight, select the true indications and disregard all others, thus making it appear as if even a deaf and blind idiot could have seen Pearl Harbor coming. But it was not like that for those who were there.

A problem that occupied much of the committee's time was that of the winds code execute. Safford maintained that it had been received on December 4 and suggested that all records of it had been destroyed by Marshall and King to cover up their failure to warn Pearl Harbor (*PHA*, 8:3579, 3652, 3655-6, 3686-7). The revisionists, accepting this at face value, argue that had notification of the winds execute been sent to the Hawaiian commanders, it would have alerted them sufficiently to prevent the debacle. Though Safford very manfully stuck to his guns under harrowing cross-examinations, I cannot believe his story. Too many other witnesses who would have seen such an execute had it been received testified that they never did. Consequently I have eliminated from my account all references to

Notes 991

this nonexistent "true" execute. Furthermore, I believe, as the committee majority did, that, even if it had been received, it would not have added any important information to what was already known. For a detailed discussion of the matter, see Appendix E of the committee's report.

I have relied almost exclusively upon *PHA*. Its 39 parts, or volumes, include the hearings, exhibits, and reports of the seven previous Pearl Harbor investigations. The joint Congressional investigating committee's own Report is entitled *Investigation of the Pearl Harbor Attack*, Senate Document No. 244, 79:2 (GPO, 1946), which includes the minority report. Citations in the form 33:765 always refer to *PHA*.

I regret that space prohibits my identifying the witnesses to whose testimony the numbered citations refer. The multiple references result sometimes from the scattering through the record of the separate items that go to make up a complete statement, sometimes from my supporting the detailed statement of a less-than-authoritative witness with a (briefer) statement by the best witness. In general, I have documented only the individual cryptologic data, and not the details of the Pearl Harbor strike mission, which come mostly from Walter Lord, *Day of Infamy* (New York: Henry Holt & Co., 1957); Mitsuo Fuchida, "I Led the Air Attack on Pearl Harbor," *United States Naval Institute Proceedings*, LXXVII (September, 1952), 939–952; and Samuel E. Morison, *The Rising Sun in the Pacific, 1931–April, 1942*, History of United States Naval Operations in World War II, vol. III (Boston: Little, Brown & Co., 1950).

In the notes, "Report" means the committee's report. IMTFE refers to the proceedings of the International Military Tribunal for the Far East; a set of the mimeographed documents of these "Tokyo Nuremberg Trials" is available at the National Archives. "Navy biography" or "Army biography" means the official biographies issued by the respective public information offices.

Japanese names are given in the American style, with family name last, and not in the Japanese form, with family name first, in which they are found in many of the sources. Times are always local date and time, and I have tried to indicate this in the text.

I want to thank Mrs. Wohlstetter for reading the draft of this chapter and offering some corrections.

PAGE

1   1:28, 1:37: IMTFE, Exhibit 2964, affidavit of Kazuji Kameyama, Foreign Office cable chief, gives 28 minutes past the hour as the time of transmission. *PHA*, 14:1416, from American intercept records, gives 18 minutes past for the start of transmission and 37 past for the end. In view of the brevity of the message and the fact that the equally short 14th part took only five minutes to transmit (14:1415), I think that 9 minutes is a more likely time for transmission than 19. Accordingly, I have used the Japanese figure. These two references serve for all times of transmission and interception in this chapter.

1   teletype: 33:765, 8:3559.
1   page-printer: 8:3579.
1   carbon, yellow and pink: 8:3806, 9:4123.
1   apparatus: 3:1130, 9:4001.

PAGE
- 2 key: 8:3778.
- 2 orientation: 8:3897.
- 2 sticker, hand-carried: 33:765, 844.
- 2 after 5 a.m.: my estimate. Decryption on the PURPLE machine would take "a very few minutes ... less than fifteen" (9:4001). Brotherhood does not remember whether an Army translator was on duty by 4 a.m., which suggests that, since he was thinking about translation, he had decrypted the message by then, but does remember that by 7 a.m., he had made one or two trips to the Army office (33:844). Thus, the intercept went to the Army some time between 4 and 7 a.m.
- 2 "Will the Ambassador": 12:248.
- 2 14th part: 12:245.
- 2 Pering: 33:765.
- 2 Kramer arrives: 9:4006.
- 2 Bryant: 8:3611.
- 2 14 copies: 33:848.
- 3 Anderson names MAGIC: Wohlstetter, 75; Anderson, telephone interview, January 8, 1965.
- 3 McCollum, traffic and other deliveries: 9:4006, 4038, 4043-7.
- 3 Kramer sees one o'clock message: 8:3908.
- 3 unusual hour: 2:930.
- 3 time circle: 8:3910.
- 4 folders and briefcases: 29:2451, 34:95, 3:1324, 4:1927.
- 4 inserts dispatches, deliveries: 8:3908-9, 3393-4.
- 4 on the double: 9:4109.
- 4 "merits": Report, 232.
- 5 Zacharias: his *Secret Missions* (New York: G. P. Putnam's Sons, 1946), 83-84, 88-90, 97-108.
- 5 Rooms 2646 and 1649: Zacharias, 83; Claus Bogel, letter, May 8, 1925, in Manly Papers, University of Chicago Library.
- 5 to Corregidor: 26:387.
- 5 other units: 36:61.
- 5 Army: Yardley, 37, 240, 370, 250-317; *The Origin and Development of the Army Security Agency*, anonymous, undated, mimeographed document, but apparently based on official sources, at 2-4; Harris, 330-333.
- 6 1934: Lindsay Parrott, International News Service story of May 24, 1934; interview, Juichi Yoshida, September 12, 1962; Senate, Committee on Armed Services, *Enhancing Further the Security of the United States*, Report No. 1433, 80th Congress, 2nd Session, May 28, 1948 (GPO, 1948), 4.
- 6 Enigma: [United States, Department of the Army.] Headquarters, Army Forces Far East, Military History Section, *Operational History of Naval Communications: December 1941–August 1945*, Japanese Monograph No. 118 (Department of the Army: Office of the Chief of Military History, 1953), 67. Other information that came to my attention too late to include in my text is in Ladislas Farago, *The Broken Seal* (New York: Random House, 1967), 59-60, 74-75. Farago's material must, however, be used with great caution, as it has many errors.

Notes

PAGE

6 HATO: *Ibid.*, 94; *PHA*, 35:463.
6 1936 to 1940: 9:4584, 34:10–11.
6 Mauborgne: 2:951, 3:1546, 34:83; his *An Advanced Problem in Cryptography and its Solution* (Fort Leavenworth, Kansas: Press of the Army Service Schools, 1914); Terrett, 13; Mauborgne, "One Method of Solution of the Schooling 'Absolutely Undecipherable' Cryptogram," *Articles*, 227–240 (April–June, 1939); *The Origin and Development of the Army Security Agency*, 9–12; Army biography; "Secrecy for Sale" chapter and notes.
7 "If we have war . . . ": Lord, 12.
7 Rochefort: Navy biography; 10:4672–3, 8:3395, 3403–4, 26:217.
7 Combat Intelligence Unit: 32:358, 10:4673–4, 4697–8.
7 Japanese naval codes: 18:3335, 10:4673.
7 unit's personnel: 10:4673.
8 net: 28:863, 23:675.
8 KUNA 1: 37:744.
8 reliance on radio intelligence: 36:14–15, 8:3383.
8 three stages: 28:870, 10:4834–5.
9 blank condition, low power: 10:4903–4, 23:659.
9 covering force, July, February: 10:4839, 4833.
9 S.I.S. size and organization: *The Origin and Development of the Army Security Agency*, 14; *PHA*, 3:1146.
9 Doud: 35:105; Army biography.
9 no Japanese military solutions: 35:106, 37:1061.
9 Rowlett, Svensson: 35:34.
9 OP-20-G: 8:3611, 29:2362, 33:769.
10 Safford: 8:3555–6; Navy biography; "Secrecy for Sale" and "Two Americans" chapters.
10 functions: 9:3962.
10 GI, GL: 36:91, 327.
10 division of cryptanalyses: 8:3560, 26:388, 10:4698.
10 Corregidor unit: 3:1559, 36:45, 61, 5:2425; Navy biography of Fabian.
10 Navy personnel: 4:1794, 8:3560, 26:388 for "young, enthusiastic, and capable."
11 subsections and duties: 8:3572, 3611, 3895–6, 3936, 3574, 3576, 36:313.
11 Kramer: 8:3611, 3411, 3893–4, 9:4075, 36:72; Navy biography; George Morgenstern, *Pearl Harbor: The Story of the Secret War* (New York: Devin-Adair, 1947), 400.
11 Craig, Marshall attitudes: 3:1100–1, 1146.
12 cable companies' refusal: 10:4676, 35:836.
12 95 per cent radio: 36:64, 312, 328, 37:1081.
12 Navy stations, Bainbridge duties: 8:3559, 3581, 3802.
12 kana, typewriter: 10:4705, 8:3579, 3394.
12 Army stations: 35:35, 37:1082–3; see also Harris, 333–335.
12 airmail: 8:3896, 35:82, 10:4720, 37:1082–3.
12 teletypewriter: 8:3559, 3805, for Navy, 35:106–108 for Army.
12 radio for PURPLE, RED, J19: 8:3896, 36:47, 227, 311.
13 all but four: 6:2916. Less clear-cut figures at 10:5137, 11:5352, 37:1081–2.

PAGE

13 Yoshikawa: Takeo Yoshikawa with Norman Stanford, "Top Secret Assignment," *United States Naval Institute Proceedings*, LXXXVI (December, 1960), 27–39; Naval Intelligence and F.B.I. reports on Honolulu consulate espionage, *PHA*, 35:352–392, at 363, 431; 12:260.
13 telephone taps: 35:84, 36:222, 37:889.
13 Sarnoff, December 1: 33:856, 26:336, 36:163, 23:646, 653.
14 odd-even: 8:3923, 3900.
14 hierarchy: 33:1133–4 for an American formula.
14 variety of codes: 12:208, 35:403–409, 433, 439, 462–463, 676, 684.
14 priority schedule: 8:3395, 34:83, 36:311, 313.
14 LA: Code reconstructed by the author by comparing coded messages given in part 38 with solutions and translations in part 37. The year-end bonus message, for example, is 38:153 in code form, 37:983 in Japanese and English. My reconstruction is corroborated by an independent and much more complete one by Hardie, who has generously made it available to me. 36:68 for 1925.
15 PA-K2: Code reconstructed by the author in the same way, and corroborated by independent reconstructions by Hardie and by Howard T. Oakley. Hardie's is especially complete. Yoshikawa message at 37:997, 38:172, 226. Cryptanalysts' worksheets at 38:124, 237. Japanese keying instructions at 35:458–460. American names and times of solution at 4:1860–1, 10:4675, 35:103, 106, 36:67.
16 J series: Transposition method reconstructed by Hardie from key given at 37:1066 for message at 38:210–211, translations at 12:215 and 35:472, 679. Introduction and solution dates, 37:663, 12:310, 5:2082–3, 36:64, 67, 85.
18 J19 vs. PURPLE percentages: 36:314.
18 PURPLE machine: reports of interviews in Japan by Bernard Krisher of Shiroji Yuki, Takeshi Kajiwara, Masana Horiuchi, and Hiroshi Hori, former code clerks, June 1963; report of interview by Shin Kawai of Kazuji Kameyama, May 1962; my Yoshida interview. *PHA*, 33:833 for general type; 12:209, 35:673 for YU GO; 12:299 for plugboard; 12:1, 3, 137 for superencipherments; 8:3898 corrected 11:5309 for three-letter codewords; 34:84, 33:833, 12:7, 314 for RED. Interviews, Drs. Werner Kunze, May 4, and Rudolf Schauffler, May 6, 1962, German cryptanalysts who solved the RED machine. See also Farago, 78–81 for RED, 90–92 for PURPLE.
20 first essays: my suppositions.
20 codeword PURPLE: 1:258, 14:1401, 15:1423 for ORANGE; 35:47 for Holtwick.
21 "Most of the time": Rosario Candela, *The Military Cipher of Commandant Bazeries* (New York: Cardanus Press, 1938), 25–26.
21 "When the PURPLE": 34:84–85.
21 Friedman: "Two Americans" chapter.
22 techniques of solution: my suppositions based on PURPLE's cipher. See also Farago, 95–100.
22 mechanism: 3:1130, 9:4001.
22 first solution: 36:312, 34:84.

Notes

995

PAGE

22 "Naturally": 34:85.
22 captain of the team: 36:70.
23 breakdown: my suppositions; 34:34, 82, 36:312.
23 other PURPLE machines: 8:3561, 36:347, 34:85, 3:1197, 10:4773. See also Farago, 102, 253–254.
23 key prediction: 8:3778, 9:4005.
23 PURPLE+CA+K9: 12:8; IMTFE, Exhibit 808, for "highest type."
24 balancing: 2:793.
24 "I see no use": 7:3363. This was Vice Admiral William Ward Smith, who had had some experience in cryptology himself; see "Two Americans" chapter.
24 reasons for secrecy: 2:792, 907.
24 January 23 agreement: 2:788, 4:1734.
24 extra recipients: 5:2173, 2:464, 789, 790, 9:4033, 4529, 3:1196, 1151, 35:90, 16:2015, 34:93.
24 field commands excluded: Report, 181; 2:791–792, 3:1176–7, 6:2540.
25 July 8: 3:1212, 14:1326.
25 Philippines: 36:73, 61, 47, 4:1741–2, 10:4722, 4715.
25 COPEK cipher: 33:855, 863–864, 10:4717, 4831, 36:46. A photostat of the message of December 4 at 37:1065, marked "COPEK," appears in Portfolio 5, Box 52, Records of the Joint Congressional Committee on the Pearl Harbor Attack, NA, RG 128.
25 McCollum letter: 10:4845–7.
26 serial numbers, July 19, December 3: 14:1398–9, 1408.
26 Memo 9, Watson, F.B.I.: 11:5475, 8:3725, 3:1147.
26 Thomsen: *DGFP*, XII, 661. See also Farago, 191–199.
26 messages of May 3, 5, 20, Nomura, June 23, November 25: 4:1861–3, 12:314, 35:671.
27 J12, Code s: 9:3984 corrected 11:3510, 4:1863, 5:2070.
27 distribution procedures: 10:4723, 3:1100, 34:11, 8:3558–9, 3681, 3902, 9:4509, 4561.
28 "I intervened": 3:1196.
28 pouches: 3:1324, 1575, 34:95, 8:3681.
28 surrenders key: 34:94.
28 Kramer explains, messenger stands by: 9:4109, 2:789, 3:1038, 4:1735.
28 departures from ideal: 3:1559, 8:3902, 29:2451.
28 advance telephoning: 8:3899–900.
28 "leave his office": 34:45.
28 Hull, Knox, conferences: 9:4035, 4235, 8:3903, 5:2468.
28 copies returned, filed, burned: 2:447, 789, 3:1038, 9:3938, 4529, 29:2451, 8:3902, 36:345, 34:25.
28 bottleneck, increase, "most highly skilled": 10:4275, 8:3896, 3400, 2:808, 4:1733.
29 year's experience: 36:318.
29 telegraphic Japanese, "the so-called translator": 2:808, 8:3400.
29 Mrs. Edgers, "not a reliable": 36:303, 8:3446.
29 partial or no translation: 9:3947.

PAGE

29 speed: 10:4723, 9:4600, 33:852.
29 volume: 35:25, 33:915, 848, 851, 37:1082, 1084–5.
30 winnowing: 29:2450, 10:4750–1, 34:11–13, 35:25, 8:3926, 3941, 9:3933, 4195, 4584.
30 Marshall complaints: 33:824, 3:1211, 1515.
30 pencil, clips: 4:1735, 1927, 5:2173, 9:4582.
30 twice a day, to homes: 8:3904, 11:5373, 8:3627, 10:4623.
30 exchange of messages, competition: 10:4927, 34:83, 8:3580, though denied 10:4740. Cooperation on a lower level was mandatory (37:1137).
30 hell, no hell: 29:2455, 3:1325.
30 White House distribution: 11:5475.
31 "witness," "intensely interested": 2:447, 11:5373.
31 most reliable: 2:792.
31 15 per cent: 4:1977.
31 USAFFE command: 29:2452.
31 speedily: 3:1147, 1196.
31 "priceless asset": 3:1362.
31 "too much of it": 33:824.
31 "This time": Shigenori Togo, *The Cause of Japan*, translated by Fumihiko Togo and Ben Bruce Blakeney (New York: Simon and Schuster, 1956), 61.
32 Proposal B, "final," "because": 12:96–7, 99, 100.
32 dummy traffic: Lord, 17; *PHA*, 11:5356, 1:185, 238.
32 Circular 2353: 12:154.
33 "There are reasons," "Tokyo time": 12:165, 173.
33 Kochi: Lord, 21.
33 telephone open code: 12:178 (more clearly at 35:652), 188–91.
37 INGO DENPO: 12:186–8, 35:669.
37 translation of HATTORI equivalent: 36:308, 341–2, 35:678, 33:862.
38 solved November 28: Translation dates are given at foot of each intercept.
38 winds intercept efforts: 10:4700, 4706–7, 18:3304–6, 26:393, 35:83, 8:3915.
38 swamping: 8:3924, 9:4145 corrected 11:5312, 26:393.
38 "Should Japan," "Say very secretly": 12:202, 204.
39 F.D.R.: 9:4072.
39 call-sign change: 17:2601, 2636, 10:4680.
39 November 1 change: 37:754, 23:664, 10:4903, 6:2522, 26:866. The October 31 date is Hawaii time; it was November 1 in Japan.
39 like July and February: 10:4833, 4839.
39 "Admiral Kimmel said": 36:128.
40 O.N.I. report, "dotting i's": 15:1896, 10:4892.
40 new security measures, Rochefort spots: 10:4893, 36:37, 128, 17:2635–6, 37:745, 756.
40 December 2 and 3 summaries: 17:2638–9. Layton's testimony before the Congressional committee, especially at 10:4829–42, 4892–4, and 4903–4, and Kimmel's remarks at 6:2523, are very enlightening about the limitations of traffic analysis. Ironically, Rochefort's unit had detected on November 3 the creation of the 1st Air Fleet (37:755)—the Pearl Harbor strike force—but was unable to follow it further.

Notes

PAGE

40 code-destruction messages: 12:137, 208–209.
41 "Climb Mount Niitaka": 13:713, 426, 1:185, 216; Robert J. C. Butow, *Tojo and the Coming of the War* (Princeton, N.J.: Princeton University Press, 1961), 370.
41 F.B.I. taps: 35:48, 36:222, 336.
41 "At 4 p.m.": 35:205–206.
41 Circular 2445: my composite of 12:215, 35:472, 679.
42 sends HARUNA: 38:250.
42 Tsukikawa: 35:363.
42 Kühn: 35:320–322; Ronald Seth, *Secret Servants: A History of Japanese Espionage* (New York: Farrar, Straus & Cudahy, 1957), 9–10.
42 signal system: 12:267–268, 35:221–322, 38:158, 161.
42 Street gives Mayfield: 36:243, 331–332.
43 "burn all": 12:215.
43 "chances had diminished": 2:503.
43 F.D.R.: 11:5284 corrected 5513.
43 embassy, Robert, paper codes, destruction: Yoshida, Kajiwara, Hori; *PHA*, 9:4576.
44 Iguchi and code clerks: IMTFE, Exhibit 2967, affidavit of Shiroji Yuki.
44 HARUNA messages: 5:2077.
44 "If you rupture": 9:4226.
45 "Highly reliable," "Circular 2444": 14:1407–8.
45 meaning of "PURPLE": 10:4842, 36:136.
45 "Memorize," "Destroy this system": 14:1408–9.
45 false winds execute: 33:839–840, 8:3386–7, 18:3305, 3320. This is the execute which Safford thought to be true.
46 Liaison Conference: Togo, 199; Butow, 372–374.
46 "that the high command": Togo, 208–209.
47 Yoshikawa messages and errors: 12:266, 268; 35:388–389.
47 Kase, Koshi: 13:427–428; Lord, 25.
47 redrafted, special frequency: comparison of messages; my supposition.
47 10 per cent, "not . . . vital," December 4, 8: 18:3335–6; 26:220, 10:4674.
47 "Five numeral": 37:1065.
47 flag officers' system unsolved: 18:3335–6.
48 Mayfield gets second batch: 23:673, 36:224, 263, 331.
48 hard to say No: Dyer, interview, December 12, 1963.
48 Woodward, Dyer, Wright: 36:262, 319, 323; Navy biographies.
48 Radio Intelligence Publications: 36:38, 10:4677.
48 1:30, 12-hour days, "nothing but junk": 36:319–20, 322, 37:983.
48 Mori: 23:360, 30:2979–81; Lord, 5–6.
49 pilot message: 12:238–239, 9:4510–13.
49 S.I.S. closed, reopens: 35:107, 36:315, 8:3558, 9:4001, 10:4927.
50 Navy handles: 8:3558.
50 "At first glance": 36:303, 345.
50 parts 1 and 2, Cave: 8:3576, 36:314–315, 37:1084.
50 3 p.m., part 8: 8:3898, 11:5509.
50 Linn clears garbles: 8:3562.

PAGE

50   6 p.m., parts 9 and 10: 8:3906; 14:1414–15 shows only these parts decoded by Army.
51   7:30: 8:3899.
51   garbles left: 12:240–245. Correct plaintexts from original document as handed to Hull, NA, RG 59.
51   Terasaki party: Yuki affidavit and interview; Butow, 379; Wohlstetter, 207.
51   9 p.m., 10 hours: Joseph C. Grew, *Ten Years in Japan* (New York: Simon and Schuster, 1944), 497.
51   Mori tap and transcript: 23:640, 26:360, 27:737–739, 29:1666, 36:223.
52   "very suspicious": 28:1542.
52   Yomiuri feature: Lord, 211.
52   6:01 p.m. message: 12:270, 35:453, 390, 38:149, 233.
52   Kramer prepares folders, begins rounds: 8:3899–901.
53   Schulz, F.D.R.: 10:4659–65.
54   Knox: 8:3902–3, 9:3991, 4514; Report, 432–433.
54   Wilkinson's home: 9:3903, 10:3993, 2:925.
54   back to Navy Department: 9:3904.
54   "cage," Martin: 35:107–108; 12:270 shows message marked "2-TT" indicating teletype from Post 2.
55   looking for 14th part: 10:4642, 4932; 8:3575.
55   Serial Nos. 380, 381: 33:765.
55   an hour to break: 33:845.
56   barrage balloons, final messages: 12:269; Lord, 25–26.
56   Ono, bits of paper: Lord, 25, 35.
56   Kramer arrives, smooths copy, delivers: 9:4006, 4043, 8:3907, 3393.
56   Beardall, F.D.R.: 11:5282–3, 5273–4.
57   14th part at State: 9:4046–7, 4545, 16:2015.
57   9 a.m., "stunned me": 9:4517. An unsolved question is why this message remained in S.I.S. at least two and probably four hours, when it would have required only five to ten minutes to translate (8:3785). Brotherhood brought the message to S.I.S. for translation probably a little after 5 a.m., but no later than 7 a.m. (33:844). Yet it had not come back to GZ by 9:30, when Kramer left to deliver the 14 parts, nor to Bratton by 8 a.m., when he had arrived at his office (9:4516). The earliest reference to it after Brotherhood's is Bratton's seeing it at 9 a.m. I have been unable to discover any reason for the delay. Would speed have averted Pearl Harbor? Possibly, but I doubt it. A translation on Bratton's desk by 8 a.m. might have enabled him to catch Marshall before his Sunday morning horseback ride and perhaps get a warning out much earlier. But then there is no reason to believe that R.C.A. in Honolulu would have delivered it any sooner than it did. Stark had not wanted to send another warning on the basis of this intercept, and his seeing it at 8 a.m. instead of at 9:30 probably would not have changed his thinking. Surprisingly, neither the Congressional committee nor its staff nor any writers on the attack ever noticed this hiatus.
57   "Please go out," Miles, Marshall call back: 9:4524–5.
57   Kramer orders folders, S.I.S. decrypts: 8:3908–9, 9:4017, 37:1084.

Notes

PAGE

57 INGO DENPO: 36:83, 9:3970–1.
58 Kramer at White House: 11:5481.
58 Kramer perspires, corrects INGO DENPO: 9:4109, 9:3971, 36:343, 349.
58 Safford estimates, GY log: 33:779, 37:1084.
59 delay: Grew, 497; Butow, 391.
59 Grew sees Togo: Grew, 486–487; Togo, 219–220.
60 Marshall sees 1 p.m. message: 3:1108–9, 33:822, 9:4546–7, 15:1633.
60 Stark: 5:2184.
60 Marshall message: 15:1640.
60 scrambler: 3:1173, 1289, 1212–3, 29:2313, 2:934. See "Censors, Scramblers, and Spies" chapter for German solutions.
60 transmission of warning message: 14:1409–10, 3:1523, 23:1102–3, 27:109, 29:2311, 34:33, 22:237–238; Thompson, 9–10.
61 "I passed solemnly": Togo, 223.
62 "To," "Tora": Fuchida, 947–948.
62 "The Japanese envoys": Cordell Hull, *The Memoirs of Cordell Hull* (New York: The Macmillan Company, 1948), II, 1095–7.
62 Togo exonerates, talking point: Togo, 210–213; Butow, 383.
63 IMFTE charge: IMTFE, *Judgment of the International Military Tribunal for the Far East* (November, 1948), Appendix A-6. Violation of the Third Hague Convention was made a part of many of the counts, including the chief ones accusing the Japanese leaders of waging wars of aggression.
64 Fuchikama delivery: Lord, 174–175; *PHA*, 7:3163–4, 11:5297.
65 destruction of U.S. codes: 16:1950–5; Letter of Grew to William D. Mitchell, Box 5, Records of the Joint Congressional Committee on the Investigation of the Pearl Harbor Attack, NA, RG 128.
66 Honolulu burning: 22:192, 23:873, 28:1545, 10:5109, 5114.
66 "Nothing coming": 37:983, 996. The message in question (37:1001–2) seems, however, to be properly encoded. Worksheets at 38:181, 257; ciphertext at 38:237; plaintext at 12:269.
66 solves others: 37:996.
66 Kramer breaks out charts, Marshall comment: 36:345, 3:1138.
66 Kühn system not used, he imprisoned: 35:320, 331, 13:639; Don Whitehead, *The FBI Story* (New York: Random House, 1956), 344.
67 winds execute: 18:3327.
67 F.D.R. speech: Report, 443.
67 "contributed enormously": Report, 232.

Chapter 2 THE FIRST 3,000 YEARS

71 Egyptian cryptography: three articles by Etienne Drioton, "La cryptographie égyptienne," *Revue Lorraine d'Anthropologie*, VI (1933–1934), 5–28; "Essai sur la cryptographie privée de la fin de la XVIIIe dynastie," *Revue d'Égyptologie*, I (1933), 1–50, at 1 for Khnumhotep's tomb, and 49–50 for reasons for the use of cryptography; "Procédé acrophonique ou principe

consonantale," *Annales du Service des Antiquités de l'Égypte*, XLIII (1943), 319–349. Price E. Newberry, *Beni Hasan*, I, Archeological Survey of Egypt, ed. F. L. Griffith (London: Kegan Paul, Trench, Trübner & Co., 1893), 2, 56, for description of Khnumhotep's tomb and inscription; the author refers to the scribe's many "blunders." H. W. Fairman, in two articles ("Notes on the Alphabetic Signs Employed in the Hieroglyphic Inscriptions of the Temple of Edfu," *Annales du Service des Antiquités de l'Égypte*, XLIII (1943), 193–310, and "An Introduction to the Study of Ptolemaic Signs and Their Values," *Bulletin de l'Institut Français d'Archéologie Orientale*, XLIII (1945), 51–138, esp. at 52–54) vigorously attacks the whole idea of hieroglyphic cryptography. I have tried to take into account those of his criticisms which seem valid. But too many other Egyptologists consider the inscriptions in question cryptographic for the cryptography to be, as Fairman says, "a figment of the imagination" of Drioton. See the many references in Drioton's articles; see also Gustave Lefebre, *Grammaire de l'Égyptien Classique*, 2nd ed. (Cairo: Imprimerie de l'Institut Français d'Archéologie Orientale, 1955), 38–39; Eric Iversen, *The Myth of Egypt and Its Hieroglyphs in European Tradition* (Copenhagen: Gad, 1962). I am grateful to Eric Young of the Department of Egyptian Art of the Metropolitan Museum of Art in New York for calling my attention to Fairman's works and for clarifying some hieroglyphic obscurities for me.

73   Chinese cryptography: letters, Kwang-chih Chang of the Department of Anthropology, Yale University, June 25 and July 7, 1963, for "la wan"; Lien-sheng Yang, professor of Chinese history, Harvard University, July 20, 1963, for military code; Y. R. Chao of the Department of Oriental Languages, University of California, October 14, 1964, for impracticality of deformation of ideographs; Owen Lattimore, Department of Chinese Studies, University of Leeds, March 13, 1964. Chao-ying Fang, interview at his office in Columbia University, November 18, 1963. None knew of any actual use of cryptography in pre-Western China. The Library of Congress reported, May 18, 1962, that the only evidence it could find for pre-Western Chinese or Japanese secret communications involved the recognition signs of secret societies, such as the Black Dragon Society; these are made with teacups or chopsticks; I have not included them. Chao-ying Fang, "Yin-t'ang," in *Eminent Chinese of the Ch'ing Period*, ed. Arthur W. Hummel, The Library of Congress (Washington, D.C.: U.S. Government Printing Office, 1944), II, 927–929. The full citation for "Essentials from Military Classics" is *Wu-ching tsung-yao, ch'ien-chi* 15.12a–13b, in *Ssu-k'u ch'uan-shu chen-pen, ch'u-chi*. For oral secrecy, Y. R. Chao, "Eight Varieties of Secret Language Based on the Principle of Fanchieh," *Bulletin of the Institute of History and Philology*, Academia Sinica, II (1931), 312–354, in Chinese; I have not read it.

74   Indian cryptography: T. C. H. Raper, assistant keeper, India Office Library, letters, March 2, April 1, May 21, June 17, 1964; these gave me all my references and include some translations of hitherto untranslated items.

Notes

PAGE

Kauṭilya's Arthaśāstra, trans. Dr. R. Shamasastry, 4th ed. (Mysore: Sri Raghuveer Printing Press, 1951), Book I, chs. 12 and 16 (at pp. 21 and 31). *Lalita-Vistara, or Memoirs of the Early Life of Sakya Sinha*, trans. Rajendralala Mitra, Bibliotheca Indica (Calcutta: Asiatic Society of Bengal, 1882–1886), ch. 10 (at 182–184). *Ibid.*, notes at 186–187, and Raper, March 2, 1964, for *Kāma-sūtra* and Yaśodhara; Raper observes that Sir Richard F. Burton's translation (reprinted New York: E. P. Dutton & Co., 1962), incorrectly uses the word "cypher" in connection with the preceding (44th) yoga. Anil Baran Ganguly, *Sixty-Four Arts in Ancient India* (New Delhi: The English Book Store, 1962), 168–174, for specific forms of secret communications. A. L. Basham, *The Wonder That Was India* (1954, reprinted New York: Grove Press, 1959), 121, 183, mentions cryptography in its social context.

75 cuneiform cryptography: C. J. Gadd and R. Campbell Thompson, "A Middle-Babylonian Chemical Text," *Iraq*, III (1936), 87–96, and letters, Dr. Benno Landsberger, January 27, 1964, and Dr. A. Leo Oppenheim, February 21, 1964, both of the Oriental Institute of the University of Chicago, for glaze text. O[tto]. Neugebauer, ed., *Astronomical Cuneiform Texts* (Princeton, N.J.: Institute for Advanced Study, by Lund Humphries: London, 1955), I, 11, 161–163, for lunar-eclipse tablet. Erle Leichty, "The Colophon," in *Studies Presented to A. Leo Oppenheim* (Chicago: Oriental Institute, 1964), 147–154 at 152–153; Musée du Louvre, Département des antiquités orientales, *Tablettes d'Uruk*, ed. F. Thureau-Dangin, Textes cunéiformes, VI (Paris: Librairie Orientaliste Paul Geuthner, 1922), No. 51, and F. Thureau-Dangin, "L'exaltation d'Istar," *Revue d'assyriologie*, XI (1914), 141–158, for Ishtar tablet. France, Ministère de l'Éducation Nationale et des Beaux-Arts, *Textes Scolaires de Suse*, ed. P. E. v. d. Meer, Mémoires de la Mission Archéologique de Perse, XXVII (Paris: Librairie Ernest Leroux, 1935), Nos. 233 and 234, for possible code lists. The references cited by v. d. Meer do not throw any light on this problem. I am greatly indebted to Dr. William W. Hallo, curator, Babylonian Collection, Yale University Library, who furnished me with these references and helped me with a number of details in letters of November 22, 1963, and September 8 and October 12, 1964, and at an interview, spring, 1964. E. Weidner, "Geheimschrift," *Reallexikon der Assyriologie*, eds. Erich Ebeling and Bruno Meissner (Berlin: Walter de Gruyter & Co., 1964), III, 185–188, and R. Borger, "Geheimwissen," *Ibid.*, 188–191, cover the subject thoroughly but came to my attention too late for use.

77 Sheshach: almost any edition of the Bible will cite SHESHACH as a cipher for *Babel* or *Babylon*. The earliest traditional reference I could find was *Midrash Rabbah*, Numbers, 18:21, trans. Judah H. Slotki, eds. Rabbi H. Freedman and Maurice Simon (London: Soncino Press, 1939), 739. The commentaries on Scripture are endless, but among the best on SHESHACH that I have found are "Sheshach" in *Encyclopedia Biblica*, eds. T. K. Cheyne and J. Sutherland Black (New York: The Macmillan Company, 1903), which proposes "editorial manipulation" as a probable answer;

A. S. Peake, ed., *Jeremiah and Lamentations*, II, The New-Century Bible (New York: Henry Frowde, Oxford University Press, 1912), 20–21. Both have extensive references. Later studies do not add anything. Dr. John Paterson, Drew University, letter, February 16, 1964, suggests that SHESHACH may be "a tour de force on the part of a late scribe." "Jeux des Moines," *Intermédiaire des Chercheurs et Curieux* (May, 1958), cols. 389–391, for monks' word games.

77　Leb Kamai: The earliest traditional reference that I could find is *Targum Jonathan*, Jeremiah 51:1; I am indebted to Harry Sherman for a translation of the latter. "Leb-Kamai" in *Encyclopedia Biblica* suggests that the encipherment could be "the trifling of a scribe in athbash," but could also be a corruption of other words.

77　atbash: The system seems never to be explained in the traditional literature, only used. It is used in: Babylonian Talmud, *Seder Mo'ed*, Shabbath, 104a, trans. Rabbi H. Freedman, ed. Rabbi Isidore Epstein (London: Soncino Press, 1938), 501–502; Babylonian Talmud, *Seder Mo'ed*, Megillah, 6a, trans. Maurice Simon, ed. Rabbi H. Freedman (London: Soncino Press, 1938), 29, note 11 to Rashi's interpretation; Palestinian Talmud, *Ta'anith*, III, 67a; *Pesikta Rabbati*, 43:181b, for the translation of both of which I am indebted to Harry Sherman. I am grateful to Dr. Abraham J. Heschel, professor of Jewish ethics and mysticism, Jewish Theological Seminary of America, for these references. For discussions, see "Cryptography," *Universal Jewish Encyclopedia*, and Solomon Gandz, "Hebrew Numerals," *Proceedings of the American Academy for Jewish Research*, IV (1932–1933), 53–112 at 89, 94.

78　albam: notes to the *Midrash Rabbah*, Soncino edition, at 739, explain albam.

78　TABEEL: Despite the *Midrash Rabbah*, neither "Tabeel," *Encyclopedia Biblica*, nor George B. Gray and Arthur S. Peake, *A Critical and Exegetical Commentary on the Book of Isaiah*, International Critical Commentary (New York: Charles Scribner's Sons), 118, even mention a cipher, regarding it as a corruption or a contemptuous epithet.

79　Shadrach, Meshach, Abednego: James A. Montgomery, *A Critical and Exegetical Commentary of the Book of Daniel*, International Critical Commentary (New York: Charles Scribner's Sons, 1927), 112–123, 128–130.

79　atbah: Babylonian Talmud, *Seder Mo'ed*, Sukkah, 52b, ed. Rabbi I. Epstein (London: Soncino Press, 1938), 249. Notes give a clear explanation.

79　handwriting on the wall: *Daniel* 5. Montgomery, 262–264, is the clearest explanation; Gordon, interview, spring, 1963. Babylonian Talmud, *Seder Nizikin*, Sanhedrin, 22a, ed. Rabbi I. Epstein (London: Soncino Press, 1935), 121–122, suggests that the writing was in atbash or a transposition as a possible explanation for the difficulty of solution; no evidence exists to support either hypothesis. See also John D. Prince, *Mene Mene Tekel Upharsin* (Baltimore, 1893), and E. G. Kraeling, "The Handwriting on the Wall," *Journal of Biblical Literature*, LXIII (1944), 11–18.

80　Homer: *Iliad* vi.168ff. Trans. E. V. Rieu (Harmondsworth: Penguin Classics, 1950), 120. "Deciphered" is not to be taken literally, of course. I have recently learned that Chr. Johnen, *Geschichte der Stenographie* (Berlin,

Notes

PAGE

1911), says, 106–111, that the oldest Greek cryptographic text is that of the Acropolis stone, fourth century B.C.

81 Herodotus: i.123–124; v.35; vii.239. Trans. Aubrey de Sélincourt (Harmondsworth: Penguin Classics, 1954), 498 for Demaratus story.

82 skytale: Thucydides i.131; Plutarch *Parallel Lives: Lysander* xix.4–7; Xenophon *Hell.* iii.3(8). The seventh-century-B.C. poet Archilochus uses the term "skytale" to designate an apparently nonsecret communication in No. 224 of his *Fragments*, trans. André Bonnard (Paris: Société d'Édition "Les Belles Lettres," 1958); see also Introduction at lxxi. For other uses of the term, see "skytale" in Liddell & Scott, *Greek Lexicon*.

82 Aeneas: xxxi. For commentary, Hermann Diels, *Antike Technik* (Leipzig: Teubner, 1920), ch. 4.

83 Polybius: *Histories* x.43–47.

83 Caesar: *Gallic Wars* v.48.

84 Suetonius: *The Twelve Caesars: Julius* 56, *Augustus* 88.

84 Caesar's more complicated ciphers and Probus' treatise: Aulus Gellius *Attic Nights* xvii.9.

84 cryptography not uncommon: C. Iul. Victor *Ars rhet.* 17 *de epist.*, ed. C. Halm *Rhet. lat. min.* (Leipzig, 1863), 448. For other references to cryptology in classic literature, see Viktor Gardthausen, *Griechische Palaeographie*, (1879, reprinted Leipzig: Verleg von Veit, 1911), vol. II, part III, ch. 4, "Kryptographie"; W. Süss, "Über antike Geheimschreibemethoden und ihr Nachleben," *Philologus*, LXXVIII (June, 1922), 142–175; Edgar C. Reinke, "Classical Cryptography," *The Classical Journal*, LVIII (December, 1962), 113–121.

84 Cicero: *Letters: ad Att.* ii.14, 16, 17, 20, 23.

84 Yezidis, Tibetans, Nsibidi: David Diringer, *The Alphabet: A Key to the History of Mankind*, 2nd ed. (New York: Philosophical Library [1949?]), 296–299, 355, 148–149.

85 Thailand: O. Frankfurter, "Secret Writing in Siamese," *The Journal of the Siam Society*, III (1902), 62–72.

85 Maldive Islands: Diringer, 393.

85 Malaya: R. A. Kern, "A Malay Cipher Alphabet," *The Journal of the Royal Anthropological Institute of Great Britain and Ireland*, XXXVIII (1908), 207–211 and plate xvii.

85 Armenia: Prof. Werner Winter, "Armenian Cryptography: Notes on Some Samples in the Collection of H. Kurdian, Wichita, Kansas," *The Armenian Review*, VIII (Autumn, 1955), 53–56.

86 Persia: Ibn al-Nadīm, *Kitab al-Fihrist*, ed. Gustav Flügel (Leipzig, 1871–1872), 14, for shah-dabiriya and raz-sahriya. I am grateful to Miss J. R. Watson, India Office Library, letter, November 4, 1964, for this reference and a translation. Abū Bakr Muḥammad b. Yaḥyā aṣ-Ṣulī, *Adab al-kuttāb*, ed. Muḥ. Bahjat al-Atharī (Cairo, 1341/1922-3), 186–187 for birds and lunar mansions.

86 St. Jeremias graffiti: J. E. Quibell, *Excavations at Saqqara* (1907–1908) (Cairo: Service des Antiquités de l'Égypte, 1909), 67, 13, 58, 10. On Coptic cryptography in general, Jean Doresse, "Cryptographie Copte et

Cryptographie Grecque," *Bulletin de l'Institut d'Égypte*, XXXIII (1950–1951), 215–228.

86 oldest surviving cipher key: The Metropolitan Museum of Art, *Egyptian Expedition: The Monastery of Epiphanius at Thebes* (New York: Metropolitan Museum of Art, 1926), II, item 616. Henry C. Fischer of the Department of Egyptian Art kindly made the ostracon itself—Accession No. 14.1.219—available for my inspection.

86 runes: R. Derolez, *Runica Manuscripta: The English Tradition* (Bruges: De Tempel, 1954), lx, 89, 133–146; Ralph W. V. Elliott, *Runes: An Introduction* (Manchester: University Press, 1959), 1–2, 43–44, 85, 107; George Stephens, *The Old-Northern Runic Monuments of Scandinavia and England* (Edinburgh: Williams and Norgate, 1884), III, 42–47.

88 ogham: R. A. Stewart Macalister, *The Secret Languages of Ireland* (Cambridge: University Press, 1937), 18–19, 28, 38–59; *Auraicept na n-eces: The Scholar's Primer*, ed. George Calder (Edinburgh: John Grant, 1917), 272–299, 300–319; *The Book of Ballymote* [a facsimile], ed. Robert Atkinson (Dublin: Royal Irish Academy House, 1887), 311–314.

89 medieval cryptography: Bernhard Bischoff, "Übersicht über die Nichtdiplomatischen Geheimschriften des Mittelalters," *Mitteilungen des Instituts für Österreichische Geschichtforschung*, LXII (1954), 27 pages listing nearly all known occurrences; Gardthausen. "Jeux des Moines" for a broader picture of scribes' word and letter games.

89 St. Boniface: Wilhelm Levison, *England and the Continent in the Eighth Century* (Oxford: Clarendon Press, 1946), 138–139 and Appendix VIII, "St. Boniface and Cryptography," 290–294.

89 Sylvester II: Julien Havet, "L'écriture secret de Gerbert," Académie des Inscriptions et Belles-Lettres: *Comptes-Rendus*, 4th series, XV (1887), 94–112 at 97, 98. For quasi-cryptographic stenography, see his "La tachygraphie italienne du Xe siecle," *Ibid.*, 351–374, and Emile Chatelain, "La tachygraphie latine," *Revue des Bibliothèques* (January–March, 1902), 40 pages.

89 Hildegard von Bingen: Bischoff, §60.

89 Dubthach: James F. Kenney, *The Sources of the Early History of Ireland* (New York: Columbia University Press, 1929), I, 556; R. Derolez, "Dubthach's Cryptogram," *L'Antiquité Classique*, XXI (1952), 359–375.

90 Bacon: *Roger Bacon's Letter Concerning the Marvelous Power of Art and of Nature and Concerning the Nullity of Magic*, trans. Tenney L. Davis (Easton: Chemical Publishing Co., 1923), 39–41; William R. Newbold, *The Cipher of Roger Bacon* (Philadelphia: University of Pennsylvania Press, 1928), 25–26. On the work in general, Lynn Thorndike, *A History of Magic and Experimental Science* (New York: Columbia University Press, 1926–1958), II, 659–661.

90 Chaucer: *The Equatorie of the Planetis*, ed. Derek J. Price (Cambridge: University Press, 1955), Appendix I, "Cipher Passages in the Manuscript," 182–187; 75, 77, 78, 79, 85, 87.

91 "perforce commune": William F. Friedman, "Edgar Allan Poe, Cryptographer," *American Literature*, VIII (November, 1936), 266–280 at 267.

Notes

- 91 "sundry very ancient": *Parallel Lives: Lysander* xxvi.2.
- 91 Leiden papyrus: F. L. Griffith and Herbert Thompson, *The Demotic Magical Papyrus of London and Leiden* (London: H. Grever & Co., 1904, 1909), I, 97; III, 105–112. I am grateful to Father Theodore C. Petersen for this and many other references to medieval magical cryptology, in an interview, December 16, 1963, and a letter, December 26, 1963.
- 91 Arnaldus de Bruxella: W. J. Wilson, "An Alchemical Manuscript by Arnaldus de Bruxella," *Osiris*, II (1936), 220–405 at 345. Wilson's "Catalogue of Latin and Vernacular Alchemical Manuscripts in the United States and Canada," *Osiris*, VI (1939), 1–836, notes passages in cipher at 312, 316, 317, 433, 545.
- 91 kabbalah: Gershom G. Scholem, *Major Trends in Jewish Mysticism*, 3rd ed. (New York: Schocken Books, 1961), esp. p. 17.
- 92 "truth stands more firmly": Babylonian Talmud, *Seder Mo'ed*, Shabbath, 104a, ed. Rabbi Isidore Epstein (London: Soncino Press, 1938), 501 and note 11.
- 92 gematria: Scholem, 100, 127, 135; Gandz, 86, 93; "Gematria," *Jewish Encyclopedia*; "Gematria," *Universal Jewish Encyclopedia*.
- 92 later writers: Johannes Trithemius (the abbot), Jacques Gohorry, Jacques Gaffarel, Claude Menestrier, Gabriel Naudé, and others. See Thorndike. Andrew D. White, *A History of the Warfare of Science with Theology in Christendom* (New York: Appleton, 1910), 382–383, for church proscription of magic. The discovery of the arcane writings attributed to Hermes Trismegistus probably intensified the association. I think that Madeleine V.-David makes too sharp a division between cryptology and symbolism in her *Le Débat sur les Écritures et l'Hiéroglyphe aux XVIIe et XVIIIe siècles*, Bibliothèque Générale de l'École Pratique des Hautes Études, VIe Section (Paris: S.E.V.P.E.N., 1965), 17–42, 66. See my section on Trithemius.
- 93 ben-Waḥshiyya: his book has been translated by Joseph Hammer as *Ancient Alphabets and Hieroglyphic Characters Explained* (London: W. Bulmer & Co., 1806).
- 93 treatise on magic: [Paul] Casanova, "Alphabets Magiques Arabes," *Journal Asiatique*, 11th series, XVIII (July–September, 1921), 37–55.
- 93 spy letter and misirli alphabet: M. J. A. Decourdemanche, "Note sur quatre systèmes turcs de notation numérique secrète," *Journal Asiatique*, 9th series, XIV (September–October, 1899), 258–271 at 267–269.
- 93 manuscript on war: Wüstenfeld, "Eine arabische Geheimschrift entziffert," *Nachrichten der Gesellschaft der Wiss. zu Göttingen* (1879), 349–355.
- 94 Persian model, Ghaznavids: Miss J. R. Watson, letter, November 4, 1964, citing Baihaqi, *Tarikh i Mas'udi*, ed. Ghani and Faiyad (Tehran, 1324/ 1945–6), 654–655, 688; C. E. Bosworth, *The Ghaznavids* (Edinburgh: University Press, 1963), 95.
- 94 "he was eloquent": Evariste Lévi-Provençal, ed., *Documents inédites d'Histoire Almohade* (Paris: Librairie Orientaliste Paul Geuthner, 1928), 59.

PAGE

94   Ibn Khaldūn: *The Muqaddimah: An Introduction to History*, trans. Franz Rosenthal, Bollingen Series XLIII (New York: Pantheon Books, 1958), II, 391–392. Toynbee, *A Study of History*, 2nd ed. (London, 1935), III, 322.

94   qirmeh: Ibrahim el Mouelhy, "Le Qirmeh en Égypte," *Bulletin de l'Institut de l'Égypte*, XXIX (1946–1947), 51–82. H. Kazem-Zadeh, "Les chiffres siyak et la comptabilité persane," *Revue du Monde Musulman*, XXX (1915), 1–51, for ciphered forms of numerals in Persian financial accounts.

94   Qalqashandi: C. E. Bosworth, "The Section on Codes and Their Decipherment in Qalqashandi's *Ṣubḥ al-a'shā*," *Journal of Semitic Studies*, VIII (Spring, 1963), 17–33, giving large portions in translation preceded by a commentary on Arabic cryptology. This is perhaps the most important single article on the history of cryptology, and I am grateful to Bosworth, of the University of St. Andrews, for sending it to me, and for further information and discussion in letters of November 28, 1963, and January 8, July 24, and August 23, 1964. A colleague, John R. Walsh of the William Muir Institute in Edinburgh, argues strongly in letters of January 26 and February 18, 1964, that there "never was" a science of cryptology among the Arabs. He regards it as significant that Qalqashandi, though an official of the chancellery, had no first hand knowledge of the subject and "was compelled to turn for information to what was probably a merely theoretical treatise by a certain Ibn Duraihim." Moreover, "Amongst the millions of documents preserved in the Ottoman archives, I have yet to hear of one being written in code." These are strong arguments, but I feel that the tone of the Qalqashandi-Ibn ad-Duraihim work could have come only from experience with cryptology and that Qalqashandi's casual reference to "thorough probes into all letters" is too weighty to be denied. Consequently, though moderating Bosworth's probably extravagant view, at 19, that "the use of codes for administrative and diplomatic purposes became widespread," I have regarded both cryptography and cryptanalysis as fairly well known in the Moslem world. My text reflects this.

96   probable beginnings of Arabic cryptanalysis: Bosworth, letter, July 24, 1964; *Cambridge Mediaeval History*, IV, 290–291, for Arabic grammar.

97   al-Khalīl: John A. Haywood, *Arabic Lexicography: Its History, and Its Place in the General History of Lexicography* (Leiden: E. J. Brill, 1960), 20–21, 28, 31.

97   "Occasionally, skillful secretaries": *The Muqaddimah*, II, 391. Parentheses in Rosenthal's translation have been changed to brackets here; they mean an editorial interpolation of needed sense. I have changed his "decoding" to "cryptanalysis" and his "deciphering" to "solving."

98   cipher of abd al-Wahid: Georges S. Colin, "Note sur le système cryptographique du Sultan Aḥmad al-Mansūr," *Hésperis*, VII (1927), 221–228.

99   cryptanalysis of monalphabetic substitution: Any book on cryptology in any language will explain how to solve such ciphers in that language. The better expositions are those in the books listed in the Bibliography.

Notes 1007

Chapter 3 THE RISE OF THE WEST

Citations to Meister, *Diplomatischen* and Meister, *Päpstlichen* refer respectively to the two indispensable books by Dr. Aloys Meister, professor of history at the University of Münster: *Die Anfänge der Modernen Diplomatischen Geheimschrift* (Paderborn: Ferdinand Schoningh, 1902), 65 pages, and *Die Geheimschrift im Dienste der Päpstlichen Kurie* (Paderborn: Ferdinand Schoningh, 1906), 450 pages. Citations in the form *Calendar, Foreign, January–July 1589* refer to a volume in the endless and equally indispensable *Calendars of State Papers* published by Great Britain's Public Record Office. Following *Calendar* comes the name of the series in short title, as *Foreign* or *Venice*, and then the dates covered by the particular volume in the series, as *January–July 1589*. Since this will identify the volume, I have thought it unnecessary to burden these notes with full dates and places of publication and editors.

PAGE

106 slow growth: Meister, *Päpstlichen*, 2–3.
106 origins of code: Meister, *Päpstlichen*, 3–12.
106 origins of cipher: Meister, *Päpstlichen*, 12–19.
107 Lavinde's manual: Meister, *Päpstlichen*, 21–22, and 171–176 for the keys. The Lavinde document has sometimes been called the first book on cryptology, but since it is nothing more than a collection of cipher alphabets, it does not deserve that title. Perhaps the oldest modern Western discussion of cryptography, as distinct from its mere use, is the "Occulte Scribendi Modus"—apparently a monalphabetic—in British Museum, Sloane Mss. No. 416, f. 155r, dated April 19, 1455. It is almost certainly the oldest such discussion in English (despite its Latin title).
107 Mantuan alphabet with Simeone de Crema: Meister, *Diplomatischen*, 41.
108 nondiffusion of cryptanalysis: This is the opinion of an expert in Arabic influences on Europe. The probable indigenous origin is my supposition.
108 use of cipher in secular principalities: Meister, *Diplomatischen*, 15; Sacco, §133.
108 homophones for consonants, small code lists: Meister, *Päpstlichen*, 46–49.
108 stimulus for cryptology: Meister, *Diplomatischen*, 1; Garrett Mattingly, *Renaissance Diplomacy* (London: Jonathan Cape, 1955), 11–12.
109 Venetian cryptologic organization: Meister, *Diplomatischen*, 16–25; Armand Baschet, *Les Archives de Venise: Histoire de la Chancellerie Secrète* (Paris: Plon, 1870), 576–579; *Calendar, Venice, 1509–1519*, Appendix II, Rawdon Brown, "History of Italian Cipher," lxix–lxxii at lxxi–lxxii.
109 Soro: Meister, *Diplomatischen*, 21–23; Meister, *Päpstlichen*, 30–31; Brown, xix, lxxi; *Calendar, Venice, 1509–1519*, 293, *1520–1526*, 607.
110 Marco Rafael: *Calendar, Venice, 1527–1533*, 277. The same document cites a paper on cipher presented to the Council of Ten by Alvise Borgi in 1548, which is not mentioned by Meister.
110 Florentine cryptology: Meister, *Diplomatischen*, 42–50.
110 "is due first place": Matteo Argenti, in Meister, *Päpstlichen*, 161.

PAGE

110 Machiavelli: Book vi, trans. by a Gentleman of the State of New York (Albany: Henry C. Southwick, 1815), 264–265.

110 Milan: Meister, *Diplomatischen*, 25–33, 35 for Modena cipher.

110 Simonetta: P.-M. Perret, "Les règles de Cicco Simonetta pour le déchiffrement des écritures secrètes," *Bibliothèque de l'École des Chartes*, LI (1890), 516–525; Bibliothèque Nationale, Ms. italien 1595, ff. 441–442.

111 Babou, "ofttimes decipher": *Dictionnaire de Biographie Française*; Blaise de Vigenère, *Traicté des Chiffres* (Paris: Abel l'Angelier, 1586), 34v–35r.

112 Antonio Elio: Meister, *Päpstlichen*, 50.

112 "decipher with much facility": Matteo Argenti in Meister, *Päpstlichen*, 161.

112 Bencio: Meister, *Päpstlichen*, 50; his successors, 51–54.

112 solution of Philip II cipher: Meister, *Päpstlichen*, 216, reproduces a "Cifra del Card. di Burgos con il re Philippo, decifrata alli x di febraro 1557 in Bologna."

112 Great Vicar of St. Peter: Vigenère, 35r.

112 Argentis: Meister, *Päpstlichen*, 54–65, 123–124. Their ciphers and rules are described *passim* in their manuals, extracts of which are given at 65–113, 148–162, 176–221, 283–445. A good résumé of their work is Yves Gyldén, "Cryptologues italiens aux XVe et XVIe siecles," *Revue Internationale de Criminalistique*, IV (1932), 195–205; another good review, with some new material, is Pierre Speziali, "Aspects de la cryptographie au XVIe siecle," *Bibliothèque d'Humanisme et Renaissance*, XVII (May, 1955), 188–206. I have examined Matteo's manual in the Chigi Library, Rome.

114 early Spanish ciphers: *Calendar, Spain, 1485–1509*, xi–xii, and Gustave A. Bergenroth, "Remarks on the Ciphered Dispatches in the Archives at Simancas," *Ibid.*, cxxxvii–cxlvi.

114 Columbus cipher: Pietro Martire d'Anghiera, *De Orbe Novo* (1530), Decade I, ch. 7, trans. by Francis Augustus MacNutt as *The Eight Decades of Peter Martyr d'Anghera* (New York: G. P. Putnam's Sons, 1912), I, 149.

114 Philip changes ciphers: J. P. Devos, *Les chiffres de Philippe II et du Despacho Universale Durant le XVIIe Siècle* (Bruxelles: Académie Royale de Belgique, 1950), 61–62.

115 pattern of Spanish cryptography: survey of the ciphers reproduced in Devos and in Mariano Alcocer's two articles entitled "Criptografía espanola" in *Revista de Archivos, Bibliotecas y Museos*, 3rd época, XXV (October–December, 1921), 628–640, and in *Boletín de la Academia de la Historia*, CV (July–December, 1934), 337–460, and in Miguel Gomez de Campillo, "De cifras," *Boletín de la Real Academia de la Historia*, CXXIX (October–December, 1951), 279–307, and of photocopies obtained from Spanish archives. Joaquín Carmona, *Tratado de Criptografía* (Madrid: Sucesores de Rivadeneyra, 1894), lists, 181–192, official keys preserved at the Archivio General de Simancas.

115 nomenclators for Spanish America: Guillermo Lohmann Villena, two articles entitled "Cifras y claves indianas," *Anuario de Estudias Americanas*, XI (1954), 285–380, and XIV (1957), 351–359.

115 Cortés: "Carta de Hernán Cortés, Marqués de Valle, a su pariente y procurador ad litem el Licenciado Francisco Núnez, México, 25 de Junio de

Notes

1009

1532," *Anales del Museo Nacional de Arquelogia, Historia y Etnografia,* 4th época, III (1925), 123–130, for letter in cipher; "La carta cifrada de Don Hernán Cortés," *Ibid.,* 436–443 for solution.

116 Despacho Universal: Devos, 20, 72.

116 suppression of decipherments, errors: Bergenroth, cxlv.

116 no Spanish cryptanalysis: Neither actual solutions nor reports of them from this time appear in the literature on Spanish cryptology, though two very short treatises on elementary cryptanalysis, dating from the 15th and 16th centuries, are reprinted in Carmona, 200–202.

116 Viète's life: *Encyclopaedia Britannica; Biographie Universelle;* Tallement des Réaux, *Les Historiettes,* chapter entitled "Viète," Bibliothèque de la Pléiade (Paris: Librairie Gallimard, 1960), I, 191–192, notes at 872–873; Jacque-Auguste de Thou, *Histoire Universelle,* trans. from 1604 Latin original (London: 1734), XIV, 164–166; Frédéric Ritter, *François Viète: inventeur de l'algèbre moderne. 1540–1603. Notice sur sa vie et son œuvre* (Paris: Revue Occidentale, 1895), 21–23, who mentions that in February, 1603, Viète addressed to Sully a memoir on cryptanalysis; I cannot find it in Sully's papers.

116 Farnese solution: Devos, 59.

117 Moreo plaintext: quoted in Bazeries, 222–232, with citation to original printed document in Bibliothèque Nationale, Les 500 de Colbert, No. 33.

117 Moreo nomenclator: Devos, 328–334.

117 bits and pieces: in Viète's letter to Henri, quoted in Bazeries, 220–222.

117 Ivry: Auguste Poirson, *Histoire du Règne de Henri IV* (Paris: Didier, 1862), I, 171–172. Neither Viète nor his solution are mentioned.

117 "And do not get anxious": in Bazeries, 220–222.

117 "He had just told me": Baschet, 576–579. Mocenigo's report was the one of June 5, 1595.

117 della Caselle cipher: André Lange and E.-A. Soudart, *Traité de cryptographie* (Paris: Librairie Félix Alcan, 1925), suggest, at 34, that this is a Cardano grille. If so, Viète's comment that "For that, you have to skip a lot" might be taken as an indication that he knew the cipher and perhaps could solve it. Mocenigo's remark that "he only knew portions of it" does not necessarily militate against this view. Meister does not mention any grille ciphers having been used by Venice, though they were used elsewhere.

118 Spanish complaint at Rome and its boomerang: de Thou, XIV, 166: "Mais tout l'avantage qu'ils retirèrent de cette calomnie, fut qu'ils s'attirèrent le mépris & l'indignation de toutes les personnes raisonnables." I think this is the original source for this famous story, since de Thou was a contemporary of Viète.

118 Marnix: *Biographie Universelle; Biographie Nationale* of the Académie Royale de Belgique.

118 "noble, wise, gracious": description by Paolo Rinaldi, treasurer of the Duke of Parma, quoted in Leon van der Essen, "Contribution à la biographie de Phillipe Marnix de Sainte-Aldegonde," *Analectes pour servir à l'histoire ecclésiasticale de la Belgique,* XXXIII (1911), 53–66 at 56.

PAGE

118 Marnix's solution of Moreo letter: van der Essen, 53–66. *Calendar, Foreign, January–July 1589*, 278, 284, 287, mentions Marnix's solution of a letter of Parma's secretary indicating that the Duke intends to try to surprise Ostend or, failing that, to besiege it; the Public Record Office does not have the solution itself.

119 Don Juan, de La Noue's interception, Marnix: Conyers Read, *Mr. Secretary Walsingham and the Policy of Queen Elizabeth* (Cambridge: Harvard University Press, 1925), II, 355–358; A. J. Butler, "Some Elizabethan Cipher-Books," *Transactions of the Bibliographical Society*, VI (October, 1900–March, 1902), 127–135 at 130.

119 Don Juan's cipher: Butler, 131; Carmona, 195–196. The solution is in Great Britain, Public Record Office, State Papers 106/1, no. 58; the original is in the Archivio General de Simanca, Estado 826, f. 168. They match perfectly.

119 Rogers' report: *Calendar, Foreign, 1577–1578*, 24.

120 increased watchfulness at time of Armada: The report in Spencer Walpole, *The Life of the Rt. Hon. Spencer Perceval* (London: Hurst & Blackett, 1874), I, 4, that his ancestor, Richard Perceval, alerted England to the Armada by his solution of Spanish dispatches is not supported by any of the *Calendars* nor by the standard histories of the Armada.

120 end of Don Juan's plot: Read, II, 358–359.

121 Walsingham–Davison letters: *Calendar, Foreign, 1577–1578*, 552 for March 20, 597 for April 5, 474–476 for Giraldez' letter.

121 Walsingham sends Phelippes cryptograms in Paris: *Calendar, Foreign, 1578–1579*, 37.

121 Phelippes: *Mary Queen of Scots and the Babington Plot*, ed. John Hungerford Pollen (Edinburgh: Printed at the University Press for the Scottish History Society, 1922), liii–lv, cxlii.

122 beer keg: Read, III, 10.

122 Mary's security: Pollen, 141–146; numerous cipher letters of Mary catalogued in *Calendar, Scotland*, II, at 906, 907, 933, 947, 948, 984, 999, 1001, and in many other places. Three of Mary's cipher keys are depicted in John Holt Schooling, "Secrets in Cipher," *Pall Mall Magazine*, VIII (1896), "I: From Ancient Times to Late-Elizabethan Days" (January), 119–129, at Nos. 8, 9, 12.

122 delivered to Walsingham: Read, III, 11–13.

122 decrypted by Phelippes: *Calendar, Scotland*, II, 946, 947, 948, 984, 997, 998, 999 for July 18 and 22, 1000, 1001, 1002. *DNB* states, at "Peter Bales," that Bales, an English calligrapher, served as a cryptanalyst and forger in the Babington plot.

122 Babington letter: *Calendar, Scotland*, II, 995.

123 Mary's reply: Pollen, 26; *Calendar, Scotland*, II, 998.

123 forged postscript: Read, III, 43; Pollen, 45; original in Public Record Office, State Papers, 53/18, no. 55.

123 Babington's cipher alphabets: *Calendar, Domestic, 1581–1590*, 355. Reproduction using modern sorts in Alan Gordon-Smith, *The Babington Plot* (London: The Macmillan Company, 1936), 251.

PAGE

123 Mary's trial and death: Agnes Strickland, *Life of Mary Queen of Scots* (London: George Bell & Sons, 1907), II, 422–423, 456.

Chapter 4 ON THE ORIGIN OF A SPECIES

This chapter depends heavily upon Dr. Charles J. Mendelsohn's important article, "Blaise de Vigenère and the 'Chiffre Carré,' " *Proceedings of the American Philosophical Society*, LXXXII (March 22, 1940), 103–129, which traces the evolution of polyalphabeticity through the various authors, and upon Luigi Sacco's *Un Primato Italiano: La Crittografia nei Secoli XV e XVI* (Roma: Istituto Storico e di Cultura dell'Arma del Genio, 1958), which, though the author sometimes goes overboard in trying to prove that everything was an Italian first, is generally accurate and includes much valuable source material. The first is cited simply as "Mendelsohn," the second as "Sacco, *Primato*."

125 "Dato and I": My translation from the two Italian translations of Alberti's manual, in his *Opuscoli Morali*, trans. Cosimo Bartoli (Venice: Francesco Franceschi, 1568), 200–219, and in Sacco, *Primato*, 37–50.

126 Alberti: *Enciclopedia Italiana; Biographie Universelle*; Giorgio Vasari, *Lives of the Most Eminent Painters, Sculptors and Architects*, trans. Gaston du C. de Vere (London: Medici Society, 1912–1915), III, 43–48; Lauro Martines, *The Social World of the Florentine Humanists, 1390–1460* (Princeton, N.J.: Princeton University Press, 1963); Meister, *Päpstlichen*, 25–26.

126 Burckhardt: (1860), Part II, ch. 2, trans. S. G. C. Middlemore (1929, reprinted New York: Harper Torchbooks, 1958), 148–150.

126 Symonds: *Renaissance in Italy: The Revival of Learning* (1877, reprinted London: John Murray, 1929), 246–249; and *Renaissance in Italy: Italian Literature* (1881, reprinted London: John Murray, 1927), 159–189, at 188 for "He presents."

126 "You've always been": very free translation from the Italian translations.

127 1466 or 1467: Girolamo Mancini, *Vita de Leon Battista Alberti* (Firenze: G. C. Sansoni, 1882), 459.

127 Alberti's treatise: Latin original reprinted in Meister, *Päpstlichen*, 125–141; Charles J. Mendelsohn, "Bibliographical Note on the 'De Cifris' of Leone Battista Alberti," *Isis*, XXXVIII (February, 1948), 48–51; translations by Mendelsohn, the part dealing with cryptanalysis in manuscript in Mendelsohn Collection, Rare Book Room, University of Pennsylvania Library, Philadelphia, and the part dealing with cipher disk in William F. Friedman, "Edgar Allan Poe: Cryptographer—Addendum," *Articles*. In this article Friedman observed that Alberti "suggests a two-part arrangement of the contents of the code, thus deserving the credit for being first to describe (if not to invent) this important feature." It is true that Alberti describes the two-part arrangement when he says: "It may be advisable for me to have two tables and for you likewise to have two;

in one set the numerals will be arranged in order at the beginnings of the lines conveniently for the reader; in the other set the phrases will be alphabetically arranged under the headings of the letters so that they will not have to be looked up in various headings in the table and may be readily at hand for the writer." But the purpose of a two-part arrangement is increased secrecy, and I do not think that Alberti was thinking of this. He did not specifically say that the numbers must stand in mixed order against the plaintext as he did for the ciphertext letters on his disk, while he specifically did refer to the convenience of the arrangement. It is difficult to assign motives at a range of half a millennium, and on principle I would prefer to rest upon purely objective evidence; but since the secrecy that is an essential element of cryptography is a human desire, motives must be weighed. As Friedman said, Alberti has described *a* two-part code (though not in thoroughly mixed order), but on the ground that he did not intend secrecy in making two code lists, I deny that he invented *the* two-part code, in the full sense of the term. The invention belongs to Antoine Rossignol.

130 "This man": Symonds, *Literature*, 159.

130 Trithemius: Paul Chacornac, *Grandeur et Adversité de Jean Trithème* (Paris: Éditions Traditionelles, 1963); R. W. Seton-Watson, "The Abbot Trithemius," in *Tudor Studies*, ed. R. W. Seton-Watson (London: Longmans, Green, 1924), 75–89; Thorndike, V, 438–439, 441, 606.

131 "first bibliographically minded scholar": Theodore Besterman, *The Beginnings of Systematic Bibliography* (London: Oxford University Press, 1935), 6–9.

131 occult background for Trithemius: Frances A. Yates, *Giordano Bruno and the Hermetic Tradition* (London: Routledge and Kegan Paul, 1964), 6, 18, 84–85, 102.

131 ciphers of "Steganographia": Chacornac, 137–139, 151–156.

131 third book of "Steganographia": D. P. Walker, *Spiritual and Demonic Magic from Ficino to Campanella*, Studies of the Warburg Institute, No. 22, ed. G. Bing (London: Warburg Institute of the University of London, 1958), 86–90; Yates, 145–146, 270. Chacornac, 156–157, says that Book III does not appear to be authentic Trithemius because it oversteps the bounds set for the work in the Preface and because its style differs from that of the other two books. However, he is a great apologist for Trithemius, and without further proof, in the form of early manuscripts that do not contain Book III, or statements by Trithemius or other commentators, or a detailed explication of the text, I do not accept his assertion. No one else seems to have made it.

132 "Steganographia" on Index: Chacornac, 139.

133 dates of writing *Polygraphiae*: from dates given in the book itself.

133 publication of *Polygraphiae*: Chacornac, 168. Woodcut borrowed from Trithemius' *Liber octo questionum* (Oppenheim, 1511). Chacornac says, 73, that it is the work of Hans Scheiffelein, a favorite student of Albrecht Dürer. Campbell Dodgson, *Catalogue of Early German and Flemish Woodcuts Preserved in the Department of Prints of the British Museum*

Notes

PAGE

(London: British Museum, 1903), 376, 405–406, gives an elaborate explanation of the woodcut without ever realizing that it was used in an earlier work (with the single slight change of a lamp into a crozier). This throws into doubt his attribution of the woodcut to Hans Springinklee, another student of Dürer's, and his statement that the book was actually printed in Basle by Adam Petri for Haselberg. He gives no sources or reasons for these statements.

133 540 pages: my examination of a copy in the Bibliothèque Sainte-Geneviève, Paris, from which no signatures are missing or repeated. The collation in Library of Congress Catalog Card No. 32-17914 is correct, except for its omission of the separately printed "Clavis Polygraphiae," but then it inexplicably gives "300 leaves" for the total. One must beware of the confusion between the *Polygraphiae* and the *Steganographia* that exists in many bibliographies: Library of Congress Catalog Card No. 17-17876 states for the latter that "The first edition appeared Oppenheim, 1518, under title: Polygraphiae libri sex."

133 Collange: *Polygraphie et Vniverselle escriture Cabalistique de M. I. Trithème Abbé* (Paris: Jacques Kerver, 1561). Collange omits Book II and hence his book numbers do not coincide with Trithemius' after Book I. He calls the Clavis Polygraphiae Book VI.

133 numbers of alphabets: my examination of the Bibliothèque Sainte-Geneviève copy.

135 contents of books: Chacornac, 163–167, correcting the numbers of his Books because he has, without saying so, depended upon Collange.

136 tabula recta: *Polygraphiae*, f. sig. o$_{ij}$ r.

136 HXPF GFMNCZ . . . : *Polygraphiae*, f. sig. B$_{vi}$ r. For some reason, Mendelsohn, 118, gives a later and more complicated encipherment as an example of Trithemius' first polyalphabetic system.

136 first letter-by-letter encipherment: Mendelsohn.

136 progressive key: Gaines, ch. 20.

137 putative Father of Cryptology: Gyldén suggests that the German tradition of emphasizing cryptography to the neglect of cryptanalysis poisoned the wells of German cryptology in World War I and left their ciphers at the mercy of the Allies; he traces German cryptology to Selenus, who does little more than comment on Trithemius. I think, however, that the reasons for the German emphasis on cryptography are to be found elsewhere than in Latin books which the later authors probably never read; likewise the reasons for the Allied successes.

137 Belaso: Meister, *Päpstlichen*, 36; Vigenère, 36r.

137 Belaso booklet: (Venice, 1553). Second edition, 1557. Third edition entitled *Il Vero Modo di Scrivere in Cifra* (Brassa: Iacobo Britanico, 1564). Sacco, *Primato*, §7; F. Wagner, "Studien zu einer Lehre von der Geheimschrift (Chifferkunste)," *Archivalische Zeitschrift*, XI (1886), 156–189, XII (1887), 1–29, XIII (1888), 8–44, at XII, 11–13.

137 first literal key: Mendelsohn, 119–120, 126; Sacco, §22b.

137 Porta: Derek J. Price, "Giambattista della Porta and his *Natural Magic*," in *John Baptista Porta's Natural Magick* (facsimile of first English edition,

1568), The Collector's Series in Science (New York: Basic Books, 1957), v–ix; *Biographie Universelle; Enciclopedia Italiana*; Meister, *Päpstlichen*, 44; Yates, 380; Walker, 76, 158; George Sarton, *Six Wings: Men of Science in the Renaissance* (Bloomington: Indiana University Press, 1957), 84–88, 94. Though Porta's name is now given everywhere with the "della," none of his books has it in his name, and he signed it without a "della."

138 Lynxes: Among the accusations was one that they were writing in cipher; this was true, for examples of their ciphered correspondence with Johann Eck appear in Vatican ms. lat. 9684, ff. 23–26. 131–133, 140, 144–146. The ciphertext consists of symbols and the system appears to be monalphabetic.

138 *De Furtivis*: (Naples: Apud Ioan. Mariam Scotum, 1563), trans. Keith Preston (1916), in manuscript in Fabyan Collection of The Library of Congress, from which the English quotations are taken. Sacco, §144; Wagner, XII, 14–19. An extensive résumé of the 1602 edition is given in D*** (Pierre François Duchesne), *Notice Historique sur la vie et les ouvrages de J.-B. Porta, gentilhomme napolitain* (Paris: Poignée, An IX [1801]), 174–209.

138 quotations from *De Furtivis*: given by book (roman numerals) and chapter (Arabic numerals) to facilitate reference in the various editions: Rosicrucian, ii.14; digraphic, ii.13; threefold classification, ii.1; synonyms and misspellings, ii.6; conversion, ii.11; "deflowered," ii.20; undivided monalphabetic, iii.9, 10, 11; probable word, iii.2; work techniques, iii.1; practical experience, iii.2; polyalphabetic system, ii.16.

142 polyalphabetic solution: The disk solution is outlined in iii.16 and illustrated with an example in iii.17, with suggestions for solving systems without word divisions or with nulls at iii.18–20. The 1602 edition solution is in its ii.16. Charles J. Mendelsohn, "The Earliest Solution of a Multiple Alphabet Cipher Written with the Use of a Key," *Articles*.

142 pirated edition: A. W. Pollard and G. R. Redgrave, *A Short-Title Catalog of Books Printed in England, Scotland, and Ireland, and of English Books Printed Abroad 1475–1640* (London: Bibliographical Society, 1926), No. 20118a.

143 "He was, in my opinion": Mendelsohn, 113.

143 Cardano: Oystein Ore, *Cardano, the Gambling Scholar* (Princeton: Princeton University Press, 1953), ch. 1. *De subtilitate libri xxi* (Norimbergae: apud J. Petreium, 1550); *De rerum varietate libri xvii* (Basilae: per H. Petri, 1557).

144 Cardano's cryptology: Charles J. Mendelsohn, "Cardano on Cryptography," *Scripta Mathematica*, VI (October, 1939), 157–168.

145 Vigenère: Denyse Métral, *Blaise de Vigenère: Archéologue et Critique d'Art* (Paris: Librairie E. Droz, 1939), 6–31, 57–69; Mendelsohn, 103–107.

146 2,000 ecus: Vigenère, 210r.

146 *Traicté des Comètes*: White, *Warfare of Science with Theology*, 197.

146 *Traicté des Chiffres*: Sacco, §145; Sacco, *Primato*, 28–32; Wagner, 23–28.

146 "un inestimable": 12r.

146 Japanese ideograms: Galland, 193.

Notes

PAGE

146 "All the things in the world": 53v- 54r. Pascal quoted in E. Littré, *Dictionnaire de la Langue Française* (1863), at "chiffre."
146 Pancatuccio: 197r–199r, translation at Mendelsohn, 104–105.
147 field of stars: plate following 258v.
147 key methods and autokey: 48v–50r; Mendelsohn, 127–129.
148 standard system: Mendelsohn, 107–109; Gaines, Wolfe, Givierge, etc.
148 "impossible of translation": "A New Cipher Code," *Scientific American Supplement*, LXXXIII (January 27, 1917), 61, taken from the *Proceedings of the Engineers' Club of Philadelphia*.
148 Argenti solution: Meister, *Päpstlichen*, 294–295; Mendelsohn, "Earliest Solution."
150 Callières: in chapter on ciphers.
150 anonymous Brussels "Traitté": H. Seligmann, "Un Traité de Déchiffrement du XVIIe Siecle," *Revue des Bibliothèques et Archives de Belgique*, VI (1908), 1–19, at 12, 15–18.
151 Jesuit polyalphabetic: Lohmann Villena, "Cifras y claves indianas."
151 Caetano's cipher: Meister, *Päpstlichen*. It is my assumption that the cipher was the one broken by Chorrin.
151 Chorrin: Eugene Vaillé, *Le Cabinet Noir* (Paris: Presses Universitaires de France, 1950), 47, quoting Agrippa d'Aubigné.
151 Elizabethan ciphers: Great Britain, Public Record Office, State Papers 106/1–3 at 106/1 ref. 2 for Asheley; at 106/1 ref. 27, 106/2 ref. 106, 106/3 refs. 160 and 186 for Porta-like tableaux; at 106/3 ref. 187 for sliding card cipher. Photographs of the latter two in Schooling (January) at No. 5 and (February) at No. 19.
152 Cospi: quoted in Kerckhoffs.
152 Brussels writer flounders: Seligmann, 12–15.
152 allegiance to Spain: Of the author of the treatise: Seligmann, 6; Devos, 72. Of Martin: During the years (1652–1658) when Retz was using the cipher and Condé (Louis II of Bourbon) was employing Martin, Condé was in the Low Countries fighting as a general in the armies of Spain against his own monarch, Louis XIV. Thus, in serving Condé at this time, Martin was serving Spain, not France. The *Biographie Nationale* of the Académie Royale de Belgique does not list any cryptologic feats among its contemporary Martins, Martens, Martinis, etc.
152 Retz: *Mémoires* in *Oeuvres*, eds. A. Feillet and J. Gourdault (Paris: Librairie Hachette & Cie., 1876), IV, 515–518.
152 in Brussels, at Utrecht: Retz, note 1, p. 518, cites Joly as saying in his *Mémoires* that when Retz went to visit Condé in Brussels in 1658, Retz was living in Holland, mostly at Utrecht. Joly's *Mémoires* do not seem to refer to the solution.
153 used cipher six years: Retz, 334, refers to his use of the indecipherable cipher with La Palatine in September, 1652.
153 Casanova: Jacques Casanova de Seingalt, Vénitien, *Histoire de Ma Vie* (Wiesbaden and Paris: F. A. Brockhaus and Plon, 1960), III, 107, 115–116; William F. Friedman, "Jacques Casanova de Seingalt, Cryptologist," *Casanova Gleanings*, IV (1961), 1–12.

PAGE

153 solutions in early 1800s: by Charles Babbage, for example. See Babbage in text.
154 lesser writings: Sacco, §147.
154 Silvestri: Meister, *Päpstlichen*, 31–32; Sacco, §142; Sacco, *Primato*, 6; Wagner, XII, 1–9.
154 *Cryptomenytices*: (Luneberg: Sternen bibliopolarum).
154 Augustus' ancestry: Lewis Melville, *The First George in Hanover and England* (London: Sir Isaac Pitman & Sons, 1908), genealogical table in vol. I. For his life, *Biographie Universelle; Allgemeine Deutsche Biographie*.
154 book: a translation by Dr. John W. H. Walden is in the Fabyan Collection of The Library of Congress. Quotation and "sportive poem" from preface. See also Wagner, XI, 174–178, Chacornac, 141–142, and Charles P. Bowditch, *The Connection of Francis Bacon with the First Folio of Shakespeare's Plays and with the Books on Cipher of his Time* (Cambridge: The University Press, 1910), 13–15, for letters of Augustus suggesting that his likeness and that of Trithemius be in title-page engraving.
154 Kircher: *Catholic Encyclopaedia*; Galland, 102–103; George E. McCracken, "Athanasius Kircher's Universal Polygraphy," *Isis*, XXXIX (November, 1948), 215–228; Wagner, XI, 178–181.
154 Schott: *Catholic Encyclopaedia*; Galland, 163–164; Thorndike, VII, 591, 598; Wagner, XI, 181–184.
155 *Mercury*: (London: I. Norton). Wagner, XIII, 9–12.
155 Wilkins: *DNB*; "lustie, . . ." from John Aubrey, *Brief Lives*.
155 words: Wilkins, 14; Oxford *New English Dictionary*.
155 geometrical ciphers: Wilkins, 93–94.
155 *Cryptomenytices Patefacta*: (London: D. Brown).
155 Falconer's life: Untitled genealogical book in New York Public Library, catalogued as by Thomas Falconer, marked on spine as "Falconer's Writings" (London, 1866), 3–5. This seems to be source for *Biographie Universelle* reference cited by Galland, 62. Falconer is not listed in the Index of F. M. G. Higham's *King James II*, or *The Memoirs of James II: His Campaigns as Duke of York, 1652–1660*, trans. A. Lytton Sells (Bloomington, Ind.: Indiana University Press, 1962), or in standard histories and encyclopedias. The British Museum *General Catalog of Printed Books* lists the author of *Cryptomenytices Patefacta* separately from an approximately contemporaneous John Falconer, a Jesuit biographed in *DNB*.
155 polyalphabetic: 20–24.
155 keyed columnar: 62.

Chapter 5 THE ERA OF THE BLACK CHAMBERS

157 Réalmont siege: Ch. Pradel, ed., "Mémoires de Jean Olès sur la dernière guerre du duc de Rohan, 1627–1628," *Revue Historique, Scientifique et Littéraire du Département du Tarn*, XXIV (1907), 1–25, 138–162, at 155–157.

Notes

PAGE

157 Rossignol's role: [Charles] Perrault, *Les hommes illustres qui ont paru en France pendant ce siècle* (Paris: Antoine Dezallier, 1696), 57–58 at 57.

157 La Rochelle: Perrault, 57; Tallement des Réaux, *Les Historiettes*, Bibliothèque de la Pléiade (Paris: Librairie Gallimard, 1960), in chapter on Richelieu, I, 256–258 at 256; Bois-Robert, *Épistres en Vers*, Maurice Cauchie, ed., Société des Textes Français Modernes (Paris: Librairie Hachette, 1921), I, note at 82, which cites Archives des Affaires Étrangères, Mém. et doc.: France, 806, f. 218v, for his appointment. For surrender: *Cambridge Modern History*, IV, 133.

158 Juvisy: Hubert Arvengas, "Antoine Rossignol et le grand Chiffre de Louis XIV," *Bulletin de la Société des Sciences, Arts et Belles-Lettres du Tarn*, XVI (new series) (January–December, 1955), 511–516, at 514–515; personal visit, June 1966, to the chateau, now the city hall of Juvisy-sur-Orge.

158 Hesdin, reticence, no solutions: Tallement, I, 256–258. Bazeries, at 45, thinks that Tallement is wrong in his charge of no solution, but concedes, at 47, that he could find none of Rossignol's cryptanalyses in the archives. However, he seems not to have investigated the archives of the Ministère des Affaires Étrangères, in which—to take one volume of many—*Correspondance Politique, Angleterre*, 47, contains much correspondence of 1638–1639 between Charles I and Britain's ambassadors in England. This was almost certainly intercepted and cryptanalyzed, probably by Rossignol, although the documents bear no annotations specifying their provenance.

158 Richelieu: *Lettres, Instructions Diplomatiques et Papiers d'État du Cardinal Richelieu*, ed. Denis L. M. Avenel, Collection de documents inédits sur l'histoire de France, 1ère série: Histoire Politique (Paris: Ministère de l'Instruction Publique: Imprimerie Impériale, 1853–1877), at IV, 569, for "It is necessary" and VII, 56, for "I saw." Other references to Rossignol at I, xxiii–xxiv, VI, 401, 695, 710, 774, VII, 57, 70.

158 deathbed recommendation: Perrault, 57.

158 master of Chamber of Accounts: H. Constant d'Yanville, *Chambre des Comptes de Paris* (Paris: J.-B. Dumoulin, 1866–1875), 541, showing coat of arms, 984.

158 Mazarin forwards letter: *Lettres de Cardinal Mazarin pendant son ministère*, ed. Adolphe Chéruel, Collection de documents inédits sur l'histoire de France, 1ère série: Histoire Politique (Paris: Ministère de l'Instruction Publique: Imprimerie Nationale, 1872–1906), VII, 517. Other references to Rossignol at II, 202–203, VI, 47, VII, 636, VIII, 595, 611.

158 room near king's study: Arvengas, 512.

158 marriage: Bois-Robert, note at 83.

158 Boisrobert: Tallement, 589; Emile Magne, *Le plaisant Abbé de Boisrobert* (Paris: Mercure de France, 1909), at 151–153, 302–305. Poem to Madame Rossignol is Épistre XXXII, at Bois-Robert, 212–214. Poems of unhappiness and thanks, both addressed to Rossignol, are Épistres IX and X, at Bois-Robert, 81–88, 89–94. Épistre XXIX is at 200–202. Bois-Robert also refers to Rossignol in Épistres XXVIII, XXX, and XXXVI.

PAGE

159 Épistre 29: English verse translation by Jenny Hauck.
159 Saint-Simon: Duc de Saint-Simon, *Mémoires*, ed. A. de Boislisle, Les Grands Écrivains de la France (Paris: Librairie Hachette, 1897), XIII, 149–150.
160 Mazarin regrets, "for the insult": Mazarin, VIII, 727, 768.
160 largesse: Tallement, I, 257; Saint-Simon, note at 150.
160 "in a fashion so marvelous": Fletcher Pratt, *Secret and Urgent* (Indianapolis: Bobbs-Merrill, 1939), 128–129, from Bazeries, 45.
160 "rossignol" in 1406: Pierre Guirard, *L'Argot*, Que sais-je, No. 700 (Paris: Presses Universitaires de France, 1956), at 11.
160 Albi neighbors: Tallement, 257.
161 two-part nomenclators: based upon examination of several nomenclators of the time. Bazeries, 45, credits him with this invention.
161 Louis XIV visit: Perrault, 58; Arvengas, 515, describing a painting of the event.
161 death: Saint-Simon, note at 149. Rossignol was buried in a chapel he built at the Palais episcopale in his native Albi.
162 tutored his son: Saint-Simon, 150, and note at 149.
162 "intriguer, very ugly:" Père Léonard de Saint-Catherine in his manuscript "Familles de Paris" (Archives nationales, MM 827, at f. 109), cited in Saint-Simon, XIII, Appendix V, at 525.
162 Sévigné and Dangeau: Eugène Vaillé, *Le Cabinet Noir* (Paris: Presses Universitaires de France, 1950), 77. Information on cryptology is scattered throughout the 408 pages of this scholarly work.
162 *Mercure Galant*: (October, 1705), 232–237 at 235 for "The King himself . . ."
162 "he became adept": Saint-Simon, 150.
162 Bonaventure's sons: Saint-Catherine; Yanville, 984.
162 Vimbois and La Tixeraudière: Bazeries, 48.
162 Nancre: Vaillé, 72–3.
162 Luillier: Saint-Simon, note at 150.
162 frequent changes, Louvois in 1676 and 1690: Vaillé, 72–74.
163 Louis in 1711: unpublished letter of Voysin, dated at Marly, May 6, 1711, in Archives Nationales, Dépôt général de la Guerre, A 1-2335, at 299, kindly communicated by Lieutenant Colonel R. Léger, formerly chief of the French Army cipher service.
163 Louis XV nomenclators: unpublished study by Léger, of the nomenclators dating from 1709 to 1760 in the archives of the Ministère de la Guerre, A 4 101.
163 Georgel: Duc de Broglie, *Le secret du roi: Correspondance secrète de Louis XV avec ses agents diplomatiques 1752–1774*, 3rd ed. (Paris: Calmann Lévy, 1879), at II, 514–519. The pertinent portion of Georgel's *Mémoires* is reprinted in *Correspondance secrète inédite de Louis XV sur la politique étrangère*, ed. M. E. Boutaric (Paris: Henri Plon, 1866), at II, 378–382.
163 Vienna best: James W. Thompson and Saul K. Padover, *Secret Diplomacy: A Record of Espionage and Double-Dealing, 1500–1815* (London: Jarrolds, Ltd., 1937), at 117.
163 Austrian cipher bureau: F. Stix, "Zur Geschichte und Organisation der

Notes

PAGE

Wiener Geheimen Ziffernkanzlei (von ihren Anfangen bis zum Jahre 1848)," *Mitteilungen des Österreichischen Instituts für Geschichtsforschung*, LI (1937), 132–160. I am indebted to Maurits de Vries for an impromptu oral translation of this important article.

164 British ambassador complains: Padover, 117.

164 "our ciphers of 1200": dispatch of Prince de Rohan, July 4, 1774, in Boutaric, at II, 384–385.

165 Koch letters: *Correspondance Secrète entre le Comte A[nton]. W[enzel]. Kaunitz-Rietberg, ambassadeur impérial à Paris, et le Baron Ignaz de Koch, secrétaire de l'Impératrice Marie-Thérèse, 1750–1752*, ed. Hans Schlitter (Paris: E. Plon, Nourrit et Cie., 1899), at 117, 125. Other references to cryptanalyzed correspondence at 196, 137, 144, 264.

165 bases of strategy: Rohan in Boutaric, II, 385.

166 Wallis biography: *DNB*; *Encyclopaedia Britannica*.

166 "adding withall," other early solutions: John Wallis, "A Collection of Letters and other Papers, which were at severall times intercepted, written in Cipher," 1653, Oxford University, Bodleian Library, Ms. e Mus. 203, in preface. This preface has been reprinted in John Davys, *An Essay on the Art of Decyphering* (London: Gulliver & Clarke, 1737), at 9–23 as "A Discourse of Dr. Wallis." References to this hereafter will be as "Discourse." It might be noted that in 1961 and 1962 the Bodleian acquired two more Wallis manuscripts: Ms. Eng. misc. c. 475, essentially a copy by Wallis of his "Collection," and Ms. Eng. misc. c. 382, a volume, 323 ff., of Wallis' own copies of his solutions of political intercepts, nearly all French, from June 14, 1689, to August 29, 1703. I regret I saw this extremely valuable volume too late for use in my text.

166 "made known to me": C. H. Firth, "Thomas Scot's Account of his Actions as Intelligencer during the Commonwealth," *English Historical Review*, XLV (January, 1897), 116–126 at 121.

167 self-taught: "Discourse," 13–14.

167 calculating feats: W. W. Rouse Ball, *Mathematical Recreations & Essays*, revised by H. S. M. Coxeter, 11th ed. (London: Macmillan, 1942), at 351.

167 Aubrey: *Brief Lives*, ed. Oliver L. Dick (Ann Arbor: University of Michigan Press, 1957), lxxxix.

167 Nottingham in 1689: David Eugene Smith, "John Wallis as a Cryptographer," *Bulletin of the American Mathematical Society*, XXIV (1917), 83–96 at 87. This reprints some of Wallis' important letters from his "Letter-Book," Add. Ms. 32,499, which also includes many solutions.

168 "seven weeks": reprinted Wallis letter, *Monthly Magazine* (October 1, 1802), 252–253 at 252.

168 waiting messenger: reprinted Nottingham and Wallis letters, *Monthly Magazine* (June 1, 1802), 446–447. The issue of July 1, 1802, publishes, at 560–561, another Wallis letter.

168 effects of his solutions: Smith, 87, 90–91.

168 no publicity: Smith, 87.

168 prowess: *DNB* for gold chain, which is shown in portrait by Sir Godfrey

PAGE

　　　　Kneller, the court painter; Smith, 91; and "Letter-Book," ff. 301–305, 307–314, for medal.

169　Leibnitz: Davys, 30; Smith, 82. The correspondence is reprinted in Wallis, *Opera mathematica* (Oxoniae, 1699), III, 674, 687, 688, 693, 695. This gives, at III, 659–672, two solutions of nomenclators, but no cryptanalytic details. For Leibnitz' interest in cryptology, see references in Louis Davillé, *Leibniz Historien: Essai sur l'activité et la méthode historiques de Leibniz* (Paris: Félix Alcan, 1909), 500, 502, 607.

169　grandson: Smith, 83–84; Great Britain, Public Record Office, *Calendar of Treasury Papers for 1697–1701/2*, ed. Joseph Redington (London: Longman & Co., 1871), 465.

169　Blencowe: *DNB*; Kenneth Ellis, *The Post Office in the Eighteenth Century: A Study in Administrative History*, University of Durham Publications (London: Oxford University Press, 1958), 128. The footnotes in this 176-page book are a rich source of leads to further study of British cryptanalysis in the 1700s.

169　Keill: *DNB*; Ellis, 128.

170　Willes: Ellis, 128–130; Stephen Hyde Cassan, *Lives of the Bishops of Bath and Wells* (London: C. & J. Rivington, 1829), 166–170; Great Britain, Public Record Office, *Calendar of Treasury Papers preserved in Her Majesty's Public Record Office, 1714–1719*, ed. Joseph Redington (London: Longmans & Co., 1883), 206.

170　Swedish plot: Ellis, 128; Basil Williams, *Stanhope: A Study in Eighteenth-Century War and Diplomacy* (Oxford: Clarendon Press, 1932), 246.

170　Atterbury: *DNB* under Atterbury and James Francis Edward Stuart (the would-be James III); Great Britain, Parliament, *Journals of the House of Lords*, XXII (1722–1726), 150–188 at 152 for deposition and 183 for May 7; other testimony at 162, 170, 172, 173, 184, 186, 188.

171　Willes family: Ellis, 129–130. The graves of Bishop Willes and his sons Edward and Francis form part of the flooring of Westminster Abbey's north ambulatory just east of its intersection with the nave. Add. Mss. 45, 518–545, 523, the Willes papers, throw additional light on their cryptologic activities.

171　other cryptanalysts: Ellis, 129–130, 133.

171　Secret Office: Ellis, 65, 69.

171　Bode: Ellis, 66, 81, 95, 105, 76.

171　legality: Ellis, 62–63; Great Britain, Parliament, *Report of the Committee of Privy Councillors appointed to inquire into the interception of communications*, October 1957 (London: Her Majesty's Stationery Office, 1957), esp. Part I, "The authority of the Secretary of State to intercept communications," 7–15.

172　Decyphering Branch: Ellis, 126 for location; 67 for funds; 75, 152 for security; 74 for Nienburg; 71 for imported cryptanalysts and royal interest; 70 for cribs; 73 for output.

172　public awareness of interception: Thomas E. May, *The Constitutional History of England* (London: Longmans, Green & Co., 1912), at II, 153–156.

172　volume of solutions: Ellis, 73; Add. Mss. 32,258 to 32,303, which are the

PAGE

solutions, keys, and worksheets of the cryptanalysts; Ellis, letter, July 11, 1962, on delays in solutions.

172 read by king: Ellis, 70; Add. Ms. 24,321, ff. 88–105.
172 uses of cryptanalyzed documents: Ellis, 70–74.
173 Seven Years' War: H. W. V. Temperley, "Pitt's Retirement from Office, 5 Oct. 1761," *English Historical Review*, LXXXI (April 1906), 327–330 at 329; Philip Yorke, *The Life and Correspondence of Philip Yorke, Earl of Hardwicke, Lord High Chancellor of Great Britain* (Cambridge: University Press, 1913), at III, 274–279; Thomas Babington Macaulay, "The Earl of Chatham," *Critical and Historical Essays*, I, Everyman's Library, No. 225 (New York: E. P. Dutton & Co., Inc., 1961), 404–478 at 423, 425.
173 "owe the Esteem": Callières, 195. A number of diplomatic manuals of this period discuss the importance of ciphers. See, for example, Juan Antonio de Vera y Zúñiga, Conde de la Roca, *El Embaxador* (Sevilla, 1620), trans. by Lancelot as *Le Parfait Ambassadeur* (Paris, 1642), Book III, 467–474.
173 effect of economics: K. L. Ellis, "British Communications and Diplomacy in the Eighteenth Century," *Bulletin of the Institute of Historical Research* [London University], XXXI (November, 1958), 159–167 at 163–164. The extensive footnotes here are, like those in Ellis' book, a very rich source of leads to the effects of cryptology.
174 diplomats' cryptographic errors: *Ibid.*, 165–167.
174 "a bishop charged": Vaillé, 185–186.
174 Voltaire: article "Poste" in his *Dictionnaire Philosophique*.
174 Church incident: Douglas Southall Freeman, *George Washington* (New York: Charles Scribner's Sons), III (1951), 544–552, with pictures of cryptogram following 541; John Bakeless, *Turncoats, Traitors and Heroes* (Philadelphia: J. B. Lippincott Company, 1959), at 9–23. The original cryptogram is in The Library of Congress, Papers of George Washington, XVIII, 119, solution at 120.
174 biographical data: *DAB* and Freeman, III, 474–475, for Church. *DAB* for West. *DAB* for Gerry. Sylvester Judd, *History of Hadley* (Northampton, Mass.: Metcalf & Co., 1863), 556, and Harvard University, *Quinquennial Catalogue*, for Porter.
176 Benedict Arnold: Carl Van Doren, *Secret History of the American Revolution* (New York: Viking Press, 1941), 196–198 for Odell and Stansbury; 200, 440, 442 for Blackstone; 441, 449 for Bailey's Dictionary; 459–460 for unidentified small dictionary. Van Doren gives the decoded correspondence; the original coded documents are in the University of Michigan, William L. Clements Library, Sir Henry Clinton Papers.
177 superencipherment by adding 7: Howard H. Peckham, "British Secret Writing in the Revolution," *Quarterly Review of the Michigan Alumnus*, XLIV (Winter, 1938), 126–131, at 130.
177 Woodhull and Townsend nomenclator: Morton Pennypacker, *General Washington's Spies on Long Island and in New York* (Brooklyn: Long Island Historical Society, 1939), 209, 252, 218; photograph of part of code opposite 218.

PAGE

177 invisible ink: Pennypacker, 51–52, for Jay and Washington letters, 61 for cover-text and blank sheets, 17 for Washington's appreciation; Sanborn C. Brown and Elbridge W. Stein, "Benjamin Thompson and the First Secret-Ink Letter of the American Revolution," *Journal of Criminal Law and Criminology*, XL (January–February, 1950), 627–636. Victor Hugo Paltsits, "The Uses of Invisible Ink for Secret Writing during the American Revolution" [The New York Public Library] *Bulletin*, XXXIX (May, 1935), 361–364, has some additional information.

178 British systems: Peckham; Bakeless, 148–150, 269–270. Originals, including Clinton grille, in Clinton Papers.

180 Lovell: *DAB*; Peckham, 128; Bakeless, 88; *Letters of Members of the Continental Congress*, ed. Edmund C. Burnett (Carnegie Institution of Washington: Washington, 1921–1936), note at VI, 328. Referred to hereafter as *Letters*.

181 Lovell endorses Lee proposal: Edmund C. Burnett, "Ciphers of the Revolutionary Period," *The American Historical Review*, XXII (January, 1917), 329–334, at 330.

181 Gates and Adams systems: Burnett, 331; *Letters*, IV, 84, 155.

181 Randolph-Madison: Irving Brant, *James Madison* (Indianapolis: Bobbs-Merrill Company, 1941–1961), at II, 440; Burnett, 332, 331; *Letters*, VI, 332, 383, 452.

182 Greene intercepts: *Letters*, VI, 224 and note. I reconstructed the alphabet and system from the intercepts in NA, Papers of the Continental Congress, 1774–1789, Item 51, "Intercepted Letters, 1775–1781," I, ff. 705–739. The Papers have been issued by NA as Microcopy No. 247; these documents are on Roll 65.

182 "It is not improbable": *Letters*, VI, 223–224.

182 "My secretary has taken": *Letters*, VI, 224.

183 recovery of Clinton letters: *Journal* of Elias Boudinot, quoted in *Letters*, VI, 239–240; letters of McKean to Washington, *Letters*, VI, 237–240, for "by means of a little address" and "the beach is so extensive."

183 "I found . . . Entick's:" *Letters*, VI, 241.

183 same alphabets: a copy of Clinton to Cornwallis, September 24, 1781, in enciphered form, is in the Clinton Papers. Test shows it to be written in the same alphabet, at $a = 7$.

184 Clinton letter: Earl Cornwallis, *An Answer to that Part of the Narrative of Lieutenant-General Sir Henry Clinton which relates to the Conduct of Earl Cornwallis during the Campaign in North America in the Year 1781* (London: J. Debrett, 1783), at 202–203.

184 "Since I wrote": *Letters*, VI, 241.

184 "My intelligence was true": *Letters*, VI, 239.

184 "The British General": McKean to deGrasse, October 14, 1781, The Historical Society of Pennsylvania, McKean Papers.

184 Washington loses "not an instant": Papers of George Washington, CLXXXVI, 16, 17.

184 Livingston forms: Burnett, 332.

184 Madison-Jefferson cipher-code: Burnett, 333.

Notes

1023

PAGE

185 Madison stares: Brant, III, 379.
185 Mr. Monroe's cypher: Burnett, 333–334.
185 Franklin cipher: Burnett, 330–331; American Philosophical Society, Franklin Papers, L (i), 24; Edward Koch, *Cryptography or Cipher Writing* (Belleville, Ill.: Buechler Publishing Co., 1936; revised 1942), at 58–61.
185 Carmichael: *The Papers of Thomas Jefferson*, ed. Julian P. Boyd (Princeton, N.J.: Princeton University Press, 1950–), at VIII, 251.
186 French-English lexicon: *The Papers of Thomas Jefferson*, VI, xi, 226.
186 Lee brothers: Burnett, 330; *Letters*, III, 231.
186 Burr: Walter Falvius McCaleb, *The Aaron Burr Conspiracy* (New York: Dodd, Mead & Co., 1903), at 73–75; Thomas Perkins Abernethy, *The Burr Conspiracy* (New York: Oxford University Press, 1954), at 59–62, 148, 176, 228, 239, 248; Nathan Schachner, *Aaron Burr: A Biography* (New York: Frederick A. Stokes Company, 1937), at 322–323, with reproduction of first page of the letter; *The Trial of Col. Aaron Burr*, T. Carpenter, reporter (Washington City, 1808), at III, Appendix L; Parke-Bernet Galleries, Catalog 1878, Item 29, for cipher disk and letters of 1800 and 1804, which were solved in 1959 by Miss Barbara Harris of the New York Cipher Society.
187 solutions of American correspondence: Add. Ms. 24,321, at ff. 24–28 for white ink, ff. 32–35 for businessman's letter, ff. 62–70 for Lafayette letter, ff. 86v, 106 for overboard, ff. 88–105 for seen by king; Add. Ms. 32,303, ff. 8–45, solution of three-part correspondence, ff. 46–52 for Spanish.
187 shrinkage of Decyphering Branch: Ellis, 130–131.
187 France not idle: Brant, VI, 64, with photostat of solution in Library of Congress, France, Ministère des Affaires Étrangères, Correspondance Politique, États-Unis, LXVIII, f. 344. For Napoleon's use of the black chamber, see Gen. [Charles-Tristan] Montholon, *Recits de la Captivité de l'Empereur Napoléon à Sainte-Hélène* (Paris: Paulin, 1847), entry for January 18, 1816.
188 outcry over opening of mail: Howard Robinson, *The British Post Office: A History* (Princeton, N.J.: Princeton University Press, 1948), ch. 24; Ellis, 138–142.
188 Austria shutters black chamber in 1848: Stix.
188 end of Cabinet Noir: Vaillé, 384–391.

Chapter 6 THE CONTRIBUTION OF THE DILETTANTES

189 "secrecy in correspondence": (Portland: Thurston, Ilsley & Co.), in unpaged "To the Reader."
189 "means should be taken": anonymous, untitled review of eight articles on telegraphy in *Quarterly Review*, XCV (June, 1854), 118–164 at 148.
189 telegraph kindled interest: A secondary source of interest was Edgar Allan Poe's "The Gold-Bug" (see "Heterogeneous Impulses" chapter).

PAGE

190 telegraph's importance in war: Cyril Falls, *A Hundred Years of War* (London: Gerald Duckworth & Co., 1953), 12; letter, Major General J. F. C. Fuller, January 6, 1964.

190 one-part government codes: for example, Mexico, *Diccionario Telegrafico* (Mexico: Imprenta Imperial, 1866).

192 *A Dictionary*: (Hartford: for the Proprietor, 1805), but printed at London. A copy is in the New York Public Library.

192 Jefferson: For dating of the wheel cypher, I am indebted to Dr. Julian P. Boyd, editor of *The Papers of Thomas Jefferson*, who, in the absence of documentary information, discussed the question in long letters of June 23 and 26, July 8, and August 13, 1964.

193 "Turn a cylinder": Jefferson Papers, Library of Congress, f. 22138. (This bears the penciled notation "1802," but on what authority I do not know.) I have used this fair copy instead of the rough draft, f. 41575, from which it differs only slightly. Boyd thinks that a note on f. 22138 erroneously calculating 36 factorial as "4648 &c . . . to 42 places!!" is in Patterson's hand.

194 Lewis and Clark cipher: Jefferson Papers, f. 22608. Depicted in Library of Congress, *Catalogue of the Library of Thomas Jefferson*, ed. E. Millicent Sowerby (Washington, D.C.: U.S. Government Printing Office, 1952), opposite IV, 333.

194 Patterson's cipher: Jefferson Papers, ff. 20446-9.

194 "I have thoroughly": Jefferson Papers, ff. 20947-8.

195 "We are introducing": Jefferson Papers, f. 21071. Other letters from Patterson on the cipher at ff. 21119-20 and 27086-8; Jefferson's own description of it at ff. 22130-2 and 41578-80.

195 Wadsworth: *List of Officers of the Army of the United States from 1779 to 1900*, comp. William H. Powell (New York: L. R. Hamersly & Co., 1900), 649; letter of September 20, 1962, from Major General H. F. Bigelow, assistant deputy chief of staff for logistics; Constance McL. Green, *Eli Whitney and the Birth of American Technology*, ed. Oscar Handlin (Boston: Little, Brown & Co., 1956), 116-117, 126, 156, 162, 291.

195 Wadsworth device: Owned by the Hamden Historical Society, Inc., it is held in the museum of the New Haven Colony Historical Society, New Haven, Connecticut. I am indebted to Miss Ella Wood, secretary of the Hamden society, for making the device available for my inspection.

195 built by Whitney: opinion of late civil engineer Charles Rufus Harte. The device was also found in the home of a Whitney heir. Information from statements by members of the Hamden Historical Society contained in letter of Miss Wood, October 15, 1962.

196 Wheatstone: *DNB*; *Columbia Encyclopedia*.

197 Charles I: Physical Society of London, *The Scientific Papers of Sir Charles Wheatstone* (London: Taylor and Francis, 1879), 321-341.

197 Exposition Universelle: Kerckhoffs, 61.

197 instructions: *Scientific Papers*, 344-345.

198 Laussedat: Kerckhoffs, 62-63.

Notes

PAGE

198 "C.P.B.": "Ciphers and Cipher-writing," *Macmillan's Magazine*, XXIII (1871), 328–338. C.P.B. may be Charles Babbage, though elsewhere he never used a middle initial. For a solution of the Wheatstone, see [William F. Friedman], *Several Machine Ciphers and Methods for their Solution*, Riverbank Publication No. 20 (Geneva, Ill.: Riverbank Laboratories, 1918), 6–36.

198 cipher invented for telegraph by Wheatstone: article in *Quarterly Review*, 148.

198 Playfair: *DNB*.

198 friend of Wheatstone: Wemyss Reid, *Memoirs and Correspondence of Lyon Playfair* (London: Cassell and Co., 1899), 74, 154–155.

198 Granville dinner: Reid, 158–159.

200 rectangle: Babbage Papers, Add. Ms. 37,205, f. 80. This manuscript is referred to henceforth as Babbage Papers.

201 Foreign Office: Reid, 159.

202 Britain keeps Playfair secret: Great Britain, War Office, General Staff, *Manual of Cryptography* (1911), mentions the Playfair at 37–39, but this manual was not made public.

202 Beaufort: *Columbia Encyclopedia*.

202 card: *Cryptography. A System of Secret Writing by the late Admiral Sir Francis Beaufort, K.C.B., adapted for telegrams and postcards.* (London: Edward Stanford). No date on the copy in the Mendelsohn Collection of the University of Pennsylvania Library, but Galland cites 1857.

202 Sestri: *Metodo Brevissimo & assoluto per scrivere occulto in tutto le lingue...* (Roma: Bernabò, 1710). Unpaged.

203 Chase: *DAB*.

203 Chase ciphers: "Mathematical Holocryptic Cyphers," *The Mathematical Monthly*, I (March, 1859), 194–196.

204 Babbage: *DNB*; *Charles Babbage and his Calculating Engines*, eds. Philip Morrison and Emily Morrison (New York: Dover Publications, 1961), xi–xxxii. Quotations from Babbage are cited to this volume, which reprints his *Passages*.

205 "Deciphering is": Morrison, 103.

205 solved personal advertisements: Babbage Papers have numerous clippings of such ciphers and Babbage's worksheets and solutions of them, as at ff. 12, 35 et seq., 42, etc.

205 "The bigger boys": Morrison, 103.

205 Henrietta Maria: Babbage Papers, opposite f. 220.

205 recommends Wheatstone: Babbage Papers, f. 211.

205 Flamsteed: Francis Baily, *An Account of the Revd John Flamsteed, the First Astronomer-Royal* (London: Lords Commissioners of the Admiralty, 1835), 346–347, 391.

206 Kinglake: Babbage Papers, f. 81 et seq.

205 Henry's cipher: Babbage Papers, f. 35 et seq.

206 double Vigenère: C[harles Babbage]., "Mr. Thwaites's Cypher," *Journal of the Society of Arts*, II (September 1, 1854), 707–708, and (October 5, 1854), 776–777. These in reply to articles by John H. B. Thwaites in

PAGE

same *Journal*, "Secret or Cypher Writing" (August 11, 1854), 663–664; "Secret or Cypher Writing" (September 15, 1854), 732–733, and "Mr. Thwaites's Cypher" (October 13, 1854), 791.

206 "singular characteristics" and autokey: Morrison, 103–105.

207 algebra: Babbage Papers at f. 13 et seq. for Gilbert cipher and at ff. 135, 184, and others.

207 Kasiski: *Geschichte des Fusilier-Regiments Graf Roon (ostpreussisches) Nr. 33*, in annex 9; information kindly communicated in a letter of June 15, 1962, by Herbert Flesch, Osnabrück, West Germany; M. W. Bowers [pseud. Zembie], "Major F. W. Kasiski—Cryptologist," *The Cryptogram*, XXXI (January–February, 1964), 53, 58–59; Kasiski's scholarly articles in *Schriften der Naturforschenden Gesellschaft in Danzig*, 1872, 1873, 1875, 1876, 1878; *Zeitschrift für Ethnologie*, 1875, 1877; *Baltische Studien*, 1876, 1877; *Encyclopaedia Britannica* citation in 11th edition, XIX, 441, in article on "Neustettin." These articles were discovered by David Shulman. The Deutsches Zentralarchiv, Potsdam, reports that Kasiski's personnel records fell within the competence of the former Heeresarchivs, Potsdam, and that these archives were destroyed in an air raid in 1945 (letter, December 7, 1964).

208 Kasiski examination: Gaines, ch. 14; Wolfe, lesson 5.

209 Kasiski examination and solution: Kasiski ("calculate the distance" at § 78); Gaines, chs. 14 and 15; Wolfe, lessons 5, 6, and 7; Friedman, II, §§ iii and iv.

213 mixed-alphabet polyalphabetic solutions: Gaines, ch. 18; Givierge, ch. 7; Sacco, §§ 91 and 92; Eyraud, chs. 9 and 10; Friedman, II, §§ iv–x.

Chapter 7 CRISES OF THE UNION

I am grateful to Watt P. Marchman of the Rutherford B. Hayes Library for reading the draft of the section of this chapter dealing with the 1876 telegrams.

214 Stager: *DAB*.

214 early history of route cipher: William R. Plum, *The Military Telegraph during the Civil War in the United States* (Chicago: Jansen, McClurg & Co., 1882), I, 44.

214 nulls: See, for example, NA, RG 109, message of June 1, 1863, to Sheldon from Thos. T. Eckert, and accompanying deciphering chart.

215 diagonals: Plum, II, 372.

215 Beckwith: Plum, I, 55.

215 12 and 36 pages: Plum, I, 56; David Homer Bates, *Lincoln in the Telegraph Office* (New York: Century Co., 1907), 53.

215 series of 12: Plum, I, 47–56.

215 department ciphers: Plum, I, 59.

215 polyalphabetics and Hawley: Albert J. Myer, *A Manual of Signals*, new ed. (New York: D. Van Nostrand, 1868), 307–311, plate XXVII. Brigadier

General Myer founded the Signal Corps, which competed with the U.S. Military Telegraph. One of his patents, No. 50,946, is a kind of cipher disk.
215 sample encipherment: NA, RG 109. Cipher No. 9 is reproduced in full in Plum, II, 370–377.
215 Eckert: *DAB*.
215 telegraph office: Bates, 38, 144, 147.
216 "Outside the members": Bates, 9, 3, 7.
216 raisins: Bates, 41; Albert Chandler, "Lincoln and the Telegrapher," *American Heritage*, XII (April, 1961), 32–33, reprinted from an uncited issue of the *Sunday Magazine*.
216 fast: Bates, 199.
216 over shoulders: Bates, 40.
216 Jeffy D: Bates, 205.
216 Beauregard: William E. Beard, "YIYKAEJR GZQSYWX," *U.S. Naval Institute Proceedings*, XLIV (August, 1918), 1829–1836 at 1831. This article cites the Official Records of the Union and Confederate Armies and Navies for the systems described.
216 Davis: Dunbar Rowland, ed., *Jefferson Davis, Constitutionalist* (Jackson: Mississippi Department of Archives and History, 1923), V, 225. Ciphers also mentioned on 396, 452, 475, 476, 532, 539.
217 Maffitt, Semmes: Beard, 1830, 1831.
217 Vigenère: For example, NA, RG 109, War Department Collection of Confederate Records, Office of the Secretary of War, Telegrams Received, 1865, Nos. 3900–4210, has all enciphered messages apparently in Vigenère. Vigenère messages also occur in many other places in the Confederate archives. "A Civil War Secret Service Code," ed. John G. Westover, *The Journal of Southern History*, VII (November, 1942), 556–557, depicts a Vigenère held, not by a secret agent, but by a general in the Missouri State Guards. Cipher disk in NA, RG 109, Records of the Office of the Chief Signal Officer, folder D10, OSO, 1865.
217 Cunningham: Plum, I, 40.
217 "It would sometimes": U. S. Grant, *Personal Memoirs* (New York: Charles L. Webster & Co., 1886), II, 207–208.
218 Johnston message and solution: Beard, 1834; Bates, 68–71.
218 Devoe: Beard, 1832.
218 Keith cryptogram: Bates, 71–76; Bates, "A Rebel Cipher Despatch," *Harper's New Monthly Magazine*, No. 577 (June, 1898), 105–109; Plum, I, 41.
220 6,500,000: W. G. Fuller, "The Corps of Telegraphers under General Anson Stager during the War of the Rebellion," in *Sketches of War History, 1861–1865*, Papers Read Before the Ohio Commandery of the Military Order of the Loyal Legion of the United States, 1886–1888 (Cincinnati: Robert Clarke & Co., 1888), II, 392–404 at 398.
220 tapped: Beard, 1829.
220 newspapers: Plum, I, 60.
220 captures and new lists: Plum, I, 47, 49, 52, 55.

PAGE

220 Booth: Theodore Roscoe, *The Web of Conspiracy* (Englewood Cliffs, N.J.: Prentice-Hall, Inc., 1959), 186 and photographs following 274.
220 cipher reel: Roscoe, 277–279 and photographs; Benn Pitman, *The Assassination of President Lincoln and the Trial of the Conspirators*, facsimile ed. (New York: Funk and Wagnalls, 1954), 41. Myer, plate XXVII, depicts one.
221 Deuel: Roscoe, 455; Pitman, 42.
221 last message: Philip Van Doren Stern, *Secret Missions of the Civil War* (Chicago; Rand McNally & Co., 1959), 320.
221 641: Edward S. Holden, "The Cipher Dispatches," *The International Review*, VI (1879), 405–424 at 408–410.
222 leak, editorials: Harry W. Baehr, Jr., *The New York Tribune Since the Civil War* (New York: Dodd, Mead & Co., 1936), 170.
222 more dispatches: Baehr, 171.
222 subscriber suggestions: Royal Cortissoz, *The Life of Whitelaw Reid* (New York: Charles Scribner's Sons, 1921), I, 411.
222 Saratoga: Cortissoz, 410.
222 Patrick message: Holden, 411; Baehr, 168; House of Representatives, Select Committee on Alleged Frauds in the Presidential Election Investigation, *Presidential Election Investigation*, 45:3, Miscellaneous Document 31, Part IV, "Testimony Relating to Cipher Telegrams" (GPO, 1879), 111–112. Referred to hereafter in this chapter as "Testimony."
223 September 4: Cortissoz, 412.
223 Hassard: *DAB*; Baehr, 27, 128; James J. Walsh, "John R. G. Hassard," *The Catholic World*, XCVII (June, 1913), 349–359; Blanche Mary Kelly, "John Rose Greene Hassard," United States Catholic Historical Society: *Historical Records and Studies*, XV (March, 1921), 19–34.
223 Grosvenor interested: *The Cipher Dispatches* (*New York Tribune*: Extra No. 44: New York, 1879), ii. This publication, which reprinted the *Tribune* stories with a foreword by Reid, is referred to hereafter as *Tribune Extra No. 44*.
223 Grosvenor: *DAB*; Baehr, 134.
224 Reid quotation: Cortissoz, 413.
225 Holden: *DAB*.
225 Holden quotation: "Testimony," 326.
225 Hassard-Grosvenor priority: "Testimony,"112, by Reid.
225 transposition system: *New York Tribune*, October 7, 1878; Holden, 420–423; John R. G. Hassard, "Cryptography in Politics," *North American Review*, CXXVIII (March, 1879), 315–325 at 322–325; Paul L. Haworth, *The Hayes-Tilden Election* (1906, reprinted Indianapolis: Bobbs-Merrill Co., 1927), 318.
226 Holden description: "Testimony," 326.
226 multiple anagramming: Gaines, 56–59; Sacco, § 76.
227 *geodesy:* Holden, 412; Hassard, 322; *Tribune Extra No. 44*, iii.
227 other ciphers: Hassard, 319–321; Holden, 413.
227 all but three: *Tribune Extra No. 44*, iii.
229 results of publication: Haworth, 320–321; Baehr, 173; Cortissoz, 423.

PAGE

229 Tilden: Haworth, 323–326; Alexander C. Flick, *Samuel Jones Tilden: A Study in Political Sagacity* (New York: Dodd, Mead & Co., 1939), 435.
229 *Sun*: quoted in Baehr, 173.
229 "As a result": Flick, 437.
229 "It had pilloried": Cortissoz, 424.

Chapter 8 THE PROFESSOR, THE SOLDIER, AND THE MAN ON DEVIL'S ISLAND

230 Kerckhoffs biography: France, Archives Nationales, F^{17} 22927 and F^{17} 40236. These are Kerckhoffs' dossiers as a high school teacher and as a member of the Académie de Paris. Previous works are listed opposite title page of *La cryptographie militaire*, his memberships and posts on title page. He is buried in Paris' Cimetière de Montparnasse.
231 Volapük: L. Couturat and L. Leau, *Histoire de la Langue Universelle* (Paris: Librairie Hachette, 1903), xxx, 142–151; Albert Léon Guérard, *A Short History of the International Language Movement* (London: T. Fisher Unwin, 1922), 97, 103, 135–136.
233 Kerckhoffs: "La Cryptographie Militaire," *Journal des Sciences militaires*, 9th series, IX (January, 1883), 5–38; (February, 1883), 161–191. Future page references will be to the book, published under the same title in 1883 by Librairie Militaire de L. Baudoin & Cie., Paris. An English translation was made in 1964 by Warren T. McCready of the University of Toronto; it circulates in manuscript.
233 features in book: "Austrian writer," 24; wire service dispatch, 41; German practice and French ciphers, 4–6; Wheatstone, 62.
233 "I have therefore thought": Kerckhoffs, v.
234 field ciphers in 1600s: Kerckhoffs, 3–4.
234 "It is necessary": Kerckhoffs, 8.
234 "I am stupefied": Kerckhoffs, 6–7.
235 six requirements: Kerckhoffs, 8.
235 "the secret matter": Kerckhoffs, 9.
235 "the material part of the system": Kerckhoffs, 10.
235 "not require secrecy": Kerckhoffs, 8.
235 "a process that": Kerckhoffs, 10.
235 "it is not necessary": Kerckhoffs, 10.
236 superimposition: Kerckhoffs, 48–52.
236 Krohn: *Buchstaben- und Zahlen-systeme für die Chiffrierung von Telegrammen, Briefen und Postkarten* (Theobald Grieben); Kerckhoffs, 37.
237 symmetry of position: Kerckhoffs, 46–48.
238 latent symmetry of position: Gaines, 175–184; Friedman, II, 52–77, 119–129; Sacco, §§91(d), 96; articles in *The Cryptogram* for April–May, 1943, February–March and April–May, 1948, February–March, 1949, July–August, 1958, and, probably the best, October–November, 1950.
238 St.-Cyr slides: Kerckhoffs, 27–29.

PAGE

240 second-rate writers: See Galland; [Yves Gyldén], "Bibliographie cryptologique," in Edmond Locard, *Traité de criminalistique* (Lyon: Joannès Desvigne, 1935), VI, 904–931; and André Lange and E.-A. Soudart, *Traité de Cryptographie* (Paris: Librairie Félix Alcan, 1925), bibliography at iii–xii.

240 Josse: "La cryptographie et ses applications à l'art militaire," *Revue Maritime et Coloniale*, LXXXIV (February, 1885), 391–432; (March, 1885), 640–699. This was published as a book in 1885 by Librairie Militaire de L. Baudoin & Cie., Paris. "Pencil and paper," 695. "M. Kerckhoffs, whose name," 668.

240 de Viaris biography: Service Historique, Ministère des Armées (Marine), letter, October 25, 1962; Musée Nationale de la Légion d'Honneur, dossier of de Viaris.

240 de Viaris cipher machine: H. Léauté, "Sur les Mécanismes Cryptographiques de M. de Viaris," *Le Génie Civil*, XIII (September 1, 1888), 278–281.

240 Vinay and Gaussin: mentioned in Th. du Moncel, *Exposé des applications de l'électricité* (Paris: Librairie Scientifique, Industrielle, et Agricole, 1874), III, 529–538. Kerckhoffs, 61, says that the device, though portable, is still too big for wartime use and that cryptographically it has no value whatsoever. It was never patented (Institut Nationale de la Propriété Industrielle, letter, July 1, 1964), and I have not been able to find a description. First names from their joint French patent, No. 80,186.

240 de Viaris in *Génie Civil*: XIII (1888) (May 12), 24–27; (May 19), 38–39; (May 26), 55–56; (June 2), 72–75; (June 9), 84–88; (June 16), 104–107. The book is *Cryptographie* (Paris: Publications du Journal Le Génie Civil, 1888).

242 second de Viaris book: *L'art de chiffrer et déchiffrer les dépêches secrètes* (Paris: Gauthier-Villars, 1893).

242 Valério: "De la cryptographie," *Journal des Sciences militaires*, 9th series. XLVIII (December, 1892), 385–402; IL (January, 1893), 37–49; (February, 1893), 244–260; L (April, 1893), 75–97; LI (July, 1893), 102–116; LII (November, 1893), 248–276; LIII (March, 1894), 443–468; LVII (January, 1895), 124–152; LVIII (April, 1895), 127–142; (May, 1895), 285–300. Valério also served as a handwriting "expert"—who made a false identification—in the Dreyfus affair; for an analysis of this work, see Edmond Locard, *Les Faux en Ecriture et leur Expertise* (Paris: Payot, 1959), 131–134.

242 Delastelle biography: William Maxwell Bowers, "F. Delastelle—Cryptologist," *The Cryptogram*, XXX (March–April, 1963), 79–82, 85; (May–June, 1963), 101, 106–109. This is based on documents in the Mairie of Saint-Malo and on recollections of Delastelle's niece. His first book was *Cryptographie nouvelle* . . . (Paris: P. Dubreuil, 1893).

242 "only catalogues": Delastelle, 2.

243 Playfair invention: Delastelle, 72–82.

243 bifid: Delastelle, 86–93. For methods of solution, see Friedman, IV, ch. x; Sacco, §103A; William Maxwell Bowers, *The Bifid Cipher*, Practical Cryptanalysis, II (American Cryptogram Association, 1960).

PAGE

243   trifid: Delastelle, 101–106. For methods of solution, see Sacco, §103B; William Maxwell Bowers, *The Trifid Cipher*, Practical Cryptanalysis, III (American Cryptogram Association, 1961).

243   slide dispositions: Delastelle, 52–63; Sacco, §31; Friedman, II, ch. ii and appendix 1.

244   Bazeries biography: *Dictionnaire de Biographie Française*; Musée National de la Légion d'Honneur, dossier of Bazeries; Pierre Sourbès, "Le Commandant Bazeries: l'Homme Qui 'Cassait' les Codes," *Le Miroir de l'Histoire*, No. 153 (September, 1962) 282–289. The Sourbès article is based on an interview with Mme. Jean Yon, Bazeries' daughter, but is dangerously unreliable in relating Bazeries' cryptologic career. As just one instance of many, Sourbès gives 1876 as the date of an incident that Bazeries himself says occurred in 1890. In addition, the conclusion—that Bazeries solved cryptograms enabling the French to place their forces to halt the Germans at the Battle of the Marne—is false. These cryptograms were not solved until after the battle, according to the chief of the cryptologic bureau at G.H.Q., Givierge, vi. Some additional personal and professional details come from my interviews with Mme. Yon, then 98, at Perpignan, July 15 and 19, 1966.

244   Nantes solution: Bazeries, 34–35.

245   Bord: Bazeries, 121–127.

245   ciphers solved: Bazeries, 200, 128–139, 151–184. Étienne Bazeries, *Les 'Chiffres' de Napoléon Ier Pendant la Campagne de 1813* (Fontainebleau. Maurice Bourges, 1896); Étienne Bazeries et Emile Burgaud, *Le Masque de Fer* (Paris: Firmin-Didot, 1893), 257–272.

245   anarchists: Bazeries, 111–114.

245   Gronsfeld: Gaspar Schott, *Magia universalis* . . . (Nuremberg, 1659), IV, 33.

246   Orléans: Bazeries, 114–119. False repetitions, 243–247. "Merde," 248–249. Joseph Reinach, *Histoire de l'Affaire Dreyfus* (Paris: Charpentier et Fasquelle, 1905), V, 6, translated in Rosario Candela, *The Military Cipher of Commandant Bazeries* (New York: Cardanus Press, 1938), 3.

247   train-ride solution: Bazeries, 201.

247   two proposed systems: Bazeries, 203–207.

247   "knocking his brains out": Bazeries, 207.

247   cylindrical cryptograph: Bazeries, 207–212, 250–261; M. le Capitaine Bazeries, "Cryptograph à 20 rondelles-alphabets (25 lettres par alphabet)," *Compte rendu de la 20e session de l'Association Française pour l'Avancement des Sciences* (Paris: Au secrétariat de l'Association, 1892), 160–165.

247   de Viaris solution: *L'art de chiffrer* . . . , 100–109. For an exposition in English, see [William F. Friedman], *Several Machine Ciphers and Methods for Their Solution*, Riverbank Publication No. 20 (Geneva, Illinois: Riverbank Laboratories, 1918), 37–58.

249   U.S. Army adopts: United States [War Department], Chief Signal Officer, *Instructions for Using the Cipher Device Type M-94*, February, 1922 (Washington, D.C.: U.S. Government Printing Office, 1922); Harris, 335.

PAGE

249 pencil and paper cipher: Bazeries, 262–274. See Candela for solution.
250 comments in Bazeries' book: "revelation," 2–3; "willful blindness," 3; "retreated," 34; "routine," 214; "public danger," 33; survey of current literature, 56–80; "to abandon," 34.
250 Spanish Army cipher: Carmona (Madrid: Est. Tip. Sucesores de Rivadeneyra), 99–117.
251 Martí: *Las Claves de Martí y el Plan de Alzamiento para Cuba*, deciphered by Dr. Rebeca Rosell Planas, Publicaciones del Archivo Nacional de Cuba, XVI (La Habana, 1948), frontispiece, 3, 65–71.
251 Ethiopia: L. Zehnder, "Geheimaltung drahtloser Telegramme," *Prometheus: Illustrierte Wochenschrift über die Fortschritte in Gewerbe, Industrie und Wissenschaft*, XXIII (May 18, 1912), 524. I am indebted to Maurits de Vries for this reference.
251 codes for diplomats: for example, Mexico, *Diccionario Telegrafia* (México: Imprenta Imperial, 1866); Portugal, Ministerio da Marinha e ultramar, *Diccionario cryptographico* (Lisbon: Typ. do Instituto Geográphico Portuguez, 1890).
251 superencipherment of codenumbers into letters: [W. Clausen-Thue], *The ABC Fifth Edition Universal Commercial Electric Telegraphic Code* [London, 1901], vii–ix.
251 Sittler transposition: F.-J. Sittler, *Dictionnaire Abréviatif Chiffré*, 4th ed. (Paris: Imprimerie Lefebre, 1879), section "Correspondance Secrète" at back of volume.
252 additive superencipherment: one of nine methods proposed in [United States, War Department] *Telegraphic Code to Insure Secrecy in the Transmission of Telegrams*, J. F. Gregory, compiler (Washington, D.C.: U.S. Government Printing Office, 1886).
252 Navy cryptographic responsibility: Captain L. S. Howeth, U.S.N. (Ret.), *History of Communications-Electronics in the United States Navy* (Washington, D.C.: U.S. Government Printing Office, 1963), 7, 8, 9, 233.
252 David Porter message: Letters to Officers, Ships of War, VIII, 486, 510, NA, RG 45.
252 1877 Vigenère: message of March 12, 1877, from Commander T.V. McNair, commanding *Kearsarge* at Nagasaki, to Rear Admiral William Reynold, commanding U.S. Naval Force on Asiatic Station, NA, RG 45.
254 Dewey message: "Reception of the Report," *New York Tribune* (May 8, 1898), 1, 2; Dewey to Long, May 1, 1898, Naval Records Collection of the Office of Naval Records and Library, Area 10 File, 1798–1910, January 1898 to May 10, 1898, NA, RG 45, for codetext. Conclusion about apparent superencipherment stems from the lack of a fixed relationship between the codewords in this and other code messages in that file and their plaintexts as given in NA, RG 45, Ciphers Sent, October 27, 1888, to May 31, 1898.
254 Dreyfus: Background information on the case comes largely from Guy Chapman, *The Dreyfus Case: A Reassessment* (New York: Reynal & Co., 1955), which has a useful bibliography. Material on the Panizzardi telegram comes from Reinach, I, 244–251, and Henri Guillemin, "L'Affaire

Notes

PAGE

Dreyfus: Le Télégramme du 2 Novembre," *Mercure de France*, CCCXXXIX (August, 1960), 596–616. Because the primary sources in the Dreyfus affair are a chaos of transcripts, depositions, First Revisions, and Second Revisions that terrify all but the professional Dreyfus-case experts, and because the Reinach and Guillemin analyses are keyed almost sentence by sentence back to these original materials, thus permitting any hardy—or foolhardy—soul who wants to spelunk among them to do so, I have thought it better not to burden these notes with point-by-point references to the primary sources. I have checked the primary sources to make certain of the accuracy of all statements in the two articles bearing on the solution of the Panizzardi telegram. Only items not included in either of them are given notes here. To begin with, there is the telegram code-text itself. It is in France, Archives Nationales, BB^{19} 75, dossier 1.

255 cipher bureau members: France, Ministère des Affaires Étrangères, *Annuaire Diplomatique et Consulaire de la République Française pour 1894*, new series, XVI (Paris: Berger-Levrault, 1894), 1, 2, 170, 283, 214, 184, 147, 151, 216. Bazeries: Ministère des Affaires Étrangères, Direction des Archives Diplomatiques, letter, December 15, 1962, says that the archives of the cryptanalytic service were destroyed in 1940.

256 Baravelli: Published by Ermanno Loescher; reprinted 1896.

257 Duchess Grazioli: Maurice Paléologue, *An Intimate Journal of the Dreyfus Case*, trans. by Eric Mosbacher (New York: Criterion Books, 1957), entry for November 10, 1894, 29–32.

258 Baravelli elements: The fragmentation of *Dreyfus* and the subsequent one of *Schlissenfurt*, the reconstruction of the cryptanalysts' worksteps, and the determination of the superencipherment result from my comparison of the telegram's encicode with its plaintext and with the codebook.

260 Matton incident and quotations: La révision du Procès de Rennes, *Enquête de la Chambre Criminelle de la Cour de Cassation* (Paris: Ligue Française pour la Défence des Droits de l'Homme et du Citoyen, 1908), 240–241. Called the Second Revision in the Dreyfus literature. Page numbers used in my citations are those of the Imprimerie Nationale edition, which are given in the margin of the Ligue republication.

261 date of Schlissenfurt telegram: Second Revision, 249.

261 Foreign Office does not know that Army had plaintext: Only Delaroche-Vernet says that the Army had given the Schlissenfurt plaintext to the Foreign Office to help it achieve an accurate solution of the November 2 message, which he says was not fully solved. Paléologue, Matton, and the unnamed chief of the cryptanalytic service all agree that the phony message served only to check the completed solution of the November 2 message. Reinach, I, 249, with all citations. Indices to Reinach indicate that none of the cryptanalysts ever testified.

261 Munier: Conseil de Guerre de Rennes, *Le procès Dreyfus*, Compte rendu sténographique in extenso (Paris: P. V. Stock, 1900), II, 228. Munier said that the ciphertext consisted of 20 groups of four-digit numbers, which is not true in the first place. He then said either that the 10th and 17th groups are identical, which is false, or that two 10's and two 17's

1034 THE CODEBREAKERS

appear in the message, which is also false. On the basis of whatever he meant he alleged that "All the groups No. 10 and No. 17 correspond to interchangeable expressions; now, this condition is realized in Version No. 2. Thus Version No. 1 can apply to the authentic ciphered text." The episode shows to what lengths the enemies of Dreyfus would go to shore up their false case against him. Munier died before he could be questioned about his conclusions.

262 French solution of Italian code: Paléologue, entries of November 29, 1897, 93, and August 26, 1899, 267–268.
262 French solution of German code: Raymond Poincaré, *Memoirs*, trans. by Sir George Arthur (New York: Doubleday & Co., 1928), III, 251; Gyldén, 17–18.
262 Commission on Military Cryptography: Gyldén, 10–11; [François Cartier], "Souvenirs du Général Cartier," *Revue des Transmissions*, No. 85 (July–August, 1959), 23–39, for part I, No. 87 (November–December, 1959), 13–51, for part II, at I, 23–24, 34, 35.
263 German cryptology: Gyldén, 14–19.
263 prewar England and Italy: Gyldén, 19–20, 23; Sacco, §§157–158.
263 Austria: Gyldén, 21–22; Maximilian Ronge, *Kriegs- und Industri-espionage* (Zurich: Amalthea–Verlag, 1930), trans. by Adrien F. Vochelle and published in a slightly abbreviated edition as *Espionage* (Paris: Payot, 1932), 29–30. All my citations refer to French edition unless otherwise specified.
263 blank code, Serbian code, Italian code: A former Austrian code officer, "Ciphers and Cipher Keys," *The Living Age*, CCCXXXIII (September 15, 1927), 491–495.
264 English–French codebook: Cartier, "Souvenirs," II, 30. See also Barbara Tuchman, *The Guns of August* (New York: The Macmillan Company, 1963), 55.

Chapter 9   ROOM 40

Because of the importance of the Zimmermann telegram, a note on major printed sources might not be inappropriate. Admiral Sir William James, *The Eyes of the Navy: A Biographical Study of Admiral Sir William Hall* (London: Methuen, 1956), also published in New York the same year by St. Martin's Press as *The Code Breakers of Room 40*, based his Zimmermann telegram chapter upon Hall's own story of it in his uncompleted autobiography and Hall's papers; James was himself administrative head of Room 40 later in the war. Burton W. Hendrick, *The Life and Letters of Walter H. Page* (Garden City: Doubleday, Page & Co., 1925), III, ch. 12, "The Zimmermann Telegram," 331–364, gives much material unobtainable elsewhere, but does not cite any sources and seems in error in a few places. Barbara W. Tuchman, *The Zimmermann Telegram* (New York: Viking Press, 1958), is a masterly study of the political circumstances surrounding the telegram and its publication. Unfortunately, it was written before the declassification on January 20, 1965, of William F. Friedman and Dr. Charles J. Mendelsohn,

Notes 1035

The Zimmermann Telegram of January 16, 1917 and its Cryptographic Background, War Department, Office of the Chief Signal Officer (Washington, D.C.: U.S. Government Printing Office, 1938), a very thorough study, detailing the role of Code 0075, based upon examination of the then extant messages in the State Department archives and upon Mendelsohn's studies of German diplomatic codes; Mendelsohn, a professor at the College of the City of New York, served as a cryptanalyst in Yardley's M.I. 8 and his American Black Chamber. All citations to "James" refer to the American edition of his work, to "Tuchman" to the above cited book; their other works are cited in full or short title. Among the major nonprinted sources are DSDF; a letter of the German Foreign Office, March 30, 1965, translated by Hardie, in response to my query of November 20, 1964, cited simply as "GFO"; and James's letters of September 12, October 8, and November 7, 1962, and—after reading a draft of the chapter—of February 1, 4, and 17, 1964, for which I am deeply grateful.

PAGE

266 *Telconia:* Tuchman, 10–11; Hugh Cleland Hoy, *40 O.B., or How the War Was Won* (London: Hutchinson & Co., 1932, republished 1935, to which references are cited), 21–22.

266 Oliver mentions intercepts: "War Work at the Admiralty," *The* [London] *Times* (December 14, 1927), 16, a report of Ewing's disclosures of his work in Room 40 at a lecture in Edinburgh; Admiral Sir William James, "Room 40," *Edinburgh University Journal*, XXII (Spring, 1965), 50–54, at 50.

266 "futile" mechanism: A. W. Ewing, *The Man of Room 40: The Life of Sir Alfred Ewing* ([London:] Hutchinson & Co., [1939]), 174.

266 Ewing's appearance: Ewing, 178.

267 life and work: Ewing; *Who Was Who, 1929–1940; Columbia Encyclopedia.*

267 Lloyd's, four friends: Ewing, 174–175; James, letter, February 1, 1964.

267 *Göben* message and incident: James, 60; Tuchman, *The Guns of August*, ch. 10.

267 "thick of office work": Ewing, 176.

268 German codebooks, intercept stations: James, 28–29.

268 "Ewing Admiralty": Ewing, 174.

268 no previous knowledge, exhilarated, October 25: Ewing, 175–177.

268 *Magdeburg:* Winston S. Churchill, *The World Crisis* (New York: Charles Scribner's Sons, 1923), at I, 503. All Churchill references in this chapter are to this work.

268 October 13, copied, Rotter: James, 29, 56.

268 German naval code: James, letter of September 12, 1962; French Strother, "German Codes and Ciphers," *The World's Work* (June, 1918), 143–153 at 152–153. Sacco, §110, gives methods of solving superencipherments with known codes. The "German High Fleet code" depicted in Yardley, opposite p. 218, was probably used in the latter part of the war.

269 three weeks: Churchill, I, 503–504.

269 crowding, Room 40, I.D. 25: James, 56; James, letters, September 12, 1962, and February 1, 1964; Ewing, 178–179; Francis Toye, letter, March 9, 1963.

PAGE

269 trawler: James, 56–57. This code may have been VB 718 (Tuchman, 79).
269 staff expansion: James, 57, 70, 90; Francis Toye, *For What We Have Received: An Autobiography* (New York: A. A. Knopf, 1948), at 166, 186–187.
270 direction-finding: "War Work at the Admiralty"; Churchill, I, 504; James, 68.
270 Hartlepool raid: Churchill, I, 505–513; James, 58; Filson Young, *With the Battle Cruisers* (London: Cassell & Co., 1921), 97–99.
271 Dogger Bank: Churchill, II, 124–137 for intercepts and action; James, 128, Ewing, 187, for aftermath.
271 50 stations: James, letter, September 12, 1962.
271 new superencipherment: James, 67–68; alphabet reconstructed from Odenwald messages in Strother, 152–153.
272 key changes and solutions: James, 25, 29, 67–68; "War Work at the Admiralty"; Admiral Sir William James, *The Sky Was Always Blue* (London: Methuen, 1951), 104.
272 Jutland: Churchill, III, 114 for preliminary intelligence; Churchill, III, 116, James, 117, and Sir Julian S. Corbett, *History of the Great War based on Official Documents: Naval Operations* (London: Longmans, Green & Co., 1920–1931), III, 326, for call-sign transfer; Churchill, III, 157, and James, 119, for Regensburg error; Churchill, III, 156, and Corbett, III, 402, for Scheer's messages and their solution; James, 119, for omission of 9:06 message; Churchill, III, 157, for Jellicoe rejection. Jellicoe does not mention the Admiralty message to him in his *The Grand Fleet 1914–1916* (London: Cassell, 1919).
273 gamma epsilon and gamma u: James, letters, October 8, 1962, February 4, 1964.
273 German suspicion: Churchill, III, 113.
273 change of code: James, 115.
273 L-32: James, 116.
273 Miller: "A War Secret," *The Saturday Evening Post*, CCII (October 23, 1926), 44, 46, 74.
274 pneumatic tube: James, 129; Ewing, 182; James, letter, September 12, 1962.
274 15,000: W. R. Hall, affidavit of March 28, 1932, Mixed Claims Commission, *U.S.A. on behalf of Lehigh Valley Rr. et al. against Germany*, Docket 8103, Exhibit 920. Reprinted in Friedman and Mendelsohn, 30–32. Cited henceforth as "Hall affidavit." Ewing, in "War Work at the Admiralty," stated that sometimes 2,000 intercepted messages were dealt with in 24 hours. He does not specify that they were solved, however, as Hall does. Many of the 2,000 might have simply served for direction-finding fixes.
274 round the clock: James, letter, September 12, 1962.
274 Zeppelin raids: Hoy, 190; James, letter, February 1, 1964. By reading German messages, Room 40 could warn British defenses of imminent Zeppelin raids—a warning of particular importance because the Zeppelins flew so high that without it the slow-climbing pursuit planes of the day could not attack the airships. Early in the war, Room 40 learned of the raids through Zeppelin messages reporting "Only HVB on board." HVB, or Handelsschiffsverkehrsbuch, was the German mercantile code, a

nonconfidential one which was the only one carried over enemy territory. Beginning March 31, 1916, Room 40 was able to solve messages (probably meteorological) indicating raids and to alert defense commands. On August 24, this procedure resulted in the downing of the L-13. See Hoy, chs. 14 and 15; Kenneth Poolman, *Zeppelins Against London* (New York: John Day, 1961), at 51; François Cartier, "Le service d'écoute pendant la guerre," *Radio-Electricité*, IV (November 1, 1923), 453–460, (November 15, 1923), 491–498, at 460.

274 staff increased: James, 129.
274 staff: James, *Sky Was Always Blue*, 104, 106; Toye, 188; James, letters, February 1 and 4, 1964; *Who's Who, 1962*, for Adcock, Toye, Beazley, Savory, Waterhouse, Fraser, Willoughby; *Who Was Who, 1929–1940*, for Clarke, Monkbretton; *1941–1950*, for Dilwyn Knox; *1951–1960*, for Ronald Knox, McCarthy, Tiarks, Young; also for Young, James, 90, and George Young and Joseph M. Kenworthy, *Freedom of the Seas* (New York: Liveright, 1929), at 80–81. Great Britain, Admiralty, *The Navy List*, gives, in its quarterly issues, under Director of Naval Education (until transfer of the cryptanalysts to Hall), a list of many names of persons presumably assisting in the work; but James states in his letters that the lists—or at least that for July, 1916, which is typical—include several who did not make much of a contribution or were only occasional helpers, and omitted several who did much more and much better work than those so listed. I have therefore followed his recommendations. On Father Ronald Knox, though Evelyn Waugh states in *Monsignor Ronald Knox* (Boston: Little, Brown & Co., 1959), at 156, that Knox (who did not convert until September, 1917) worked in the War Office and does not mention his Room 40 service, James says that "It is understandable that Evelyn Waugh did not know that he came to us for the last few months of the war."
275 50 cryptanalysts: "War Work at the Admiralty."
275 social types, typists: Toye, 188; James, xviii, 32–33.
275 Lady Hambro: W. Lionel Fraser, *All to the Good* (London: Heinemann, 1963), 62. His ch. 5, 52–62, gives some interesting sidelights on Room 40.
275 Ewing retirement: Ewing, 195–208; "War Work at the Admiralty" for "pedestrian wits."
276 Hall: James, xxiv, 2, 6, 13; Tuchman, 8; Hendricks, 361; Toye, 188–189.
277 French naval solutions: Marcel Givierge, "Questions de chiffre," *Revue Militaire Française*, LXXXXIV (new series) (June 1, 1924), 398–417, (July 1, 1924), 59–78, translated as "Problems of code," *Articles*, 4–31, at 19, 23, 27; [Georges J. Painvin], "Conférence de M. Georges Jean Painvin," *Bulletin de l'A.R.C.* [Amicale des Réservistes du Chiffre], VIII (new series) (May, 1961), 5–47, at 8. There is a discrepancy with James's statements: Givierge says that the three-letter code was for U-boats and was monalphabetically enciphered. Painvin's article—essential for the study of World War I cryptology—is based upon his original working papers.
277 Nauen solutions: Cartier, "Souvenirs," II, 49–50.

PAGE

277 minimal reciprocation, cruiser, Berlin-Madrid: Cartier, "Souvenirs," II, 34–36, 32, 33; Painvin, 10. Room 40 also read Berlin-Madrid messages through a captured code (James, 69; Ewing, 199–200; Hoy, 155–157).

278 Mata Hari: Painvin, 10; Sam Waagenaar, *Mata Hari*, adaptation by Jacques Haubert (Paris: Fayard, 1965), at 198–203, 215, for texts of intercepts, 206–207, 223 for discussion.

278 Austro-Hungarian codes: Cartier, "Souvenirs," II, 33; Painvin, 9–10; James, xx, 159. The cryptanalyst was Painvin, whom the Italians awarded the Cross of the Chevalier of the Crown of Italy for his solutions.

278 Neumünster: Churchill, III, 113; Corbett, III, 395; James, 120.

279 Cypher SA: Great Britain, Admiralty, *C.B. 0565A: Memorandum No. 7 regarding Ship Cypher* ([London], 1918). "The Navy's War Code," *The New York Times Magazine* (September 11, 1932), 19:3, for Davidson.

280 "cryptographers' department": Churchill, III, 112. He adds that Room 40 spared Britain the ordeal of German naval bombardment of her coastal towns because the fleet could not have stayed continuously at sea to prevent it.

281 Persia: Young and Kenworthy, 80; James, 92; Ewing, 199.

281 Trebitsch Lincoln: Hoy, 108–114; James, 36–37; Trebitsch Lincoln's own memoirs.

281 Casement: Strother, 145, for reproductions of Devoy's messages; Hoy, 116–123 for OATS and code; James, 112–114 for diary; Ewing, 192–194.

281 bird, code expert: Hoy, 92, 89–90.

282 half-past ten: James, 136.

282 1,000 groups: Robert Lansing, *War Memoirs* (Indianapolis: Bobbs-Merrill, 1935), 226.

282 code 0075 used for message: GFO. Friedman and Mendelsohn guessed this (15, 17) and remarked that 0075 was "apparently reserved for messages of the highest importance" (19).

282 cryptanalysts working for six months: Hayden Church, "A Sherlock Holmes of Secret War Codes," *The New York Times Magazine* (November 8, 1931), 17. This is an interview with Ewing, in which Church states that "The deciphering of the code used by Bernstorff, the German Ambassador to the United States, took nearly six months and involved the piecing together of thousands of scraps of paper resembling an immense jigsaw puzzle." He adds that "In this code the name given to the German Foreign Office was 'Arthur Foxwell.'" This must be a Room 40 play on Zimmermann's first name and his attempts at deception. German diplomats were not using jargon codes, and if they were Room 40 would not have taken six months to solve one.

282 other codes in 0075 series: Friedman and Mendelsohn, 15. Another German diplomatic code is given in skeleton form in NA, RG 76, Mixed Claims Commission, Exhibit 86.

282 distribution places and date of 0075: GFO. This verifies the "six months" statement of Church.

282 0075 to Bernstorff by *Deutschland:* GFO; guessed by Friedman and Mendelsohn, 18, on the basis of Bernstorff's statement that he received new

Notes

	codes and ciphers on each trip of the U-boat (in *Official German Documents Relating to the World War* [New York: Carnegie Endowment for International Peace, 1923], I, 313–315).
283	partial text: The two sources, James, 136, and Hendrick, 336–337, appear to be different copies from the original partial solution. I have collated them with each other and with the final German text. Unsolved portions are indicated by ellipses between parentheses, questionable readings by parentheses, extremely questionable readings by question marks within the parentheses. The single question mark is given, with ellipses, by both James and Hendrick, but what it indicates is not clear, since in the German text only the words "to keep Stop" appear, and these are given in the English partial solution. The bracketed "of Mexico" is my insertion.
283	copies burned, no word to Foreign Office: James, 136, 138.
283	political situation: Tuchman, 4, 114, 107–108, 142–144.
284	Eckardt: German Foreign Office, letter, January 10, 1964.
284	routes of message: Hendrick, 335–342; Tuchman, 101–104, 128–136; James, 132–133; Friedman and Mendelsohn, 6–14. Britain's 1915 positive knowledge of German superencipherment: Friedman and Mendelsohn, 9–10. Hendrick, Tuchman, and James list a third route, by radio from Nauen to Sayville, but Friedman and Mendelsohn, 7–8, give strong evidence against the likelihood of this channel's being used for the Zimmermann telegram, and I have therefore omitted it. Finally, GFO gives only the American route for the message, which may mean that the Zimmermann telegram did not go by the Swedish roundabout. Opposing this is the fact that important messages between Washington and Berlin were frequently transmitted by several routes to ensure their reception. The archivist, Royal Ministry of Foreign Affairs, Sweden, says, in letter of June 1, 1966, that German telegrams "were in fact brought to the Ministry from the German Embassy in Stockholm for further delivery to the Royal Telegraphic Service, where they later were burnt." Nor were copies kept either by the Ministry or the Swedish mission in Argentina. No copies of the codetext in 0075 thus seem extant, except those in the Room 40 archives.
285	"highly entertained": Ewing, 205.
285	de Grey: *Who Was Who, 1951–1960*; *Burke's Peerage, 1963*, at 2499–2500; John de Grey, letters, June 3, 1963, and undated, several weeks later.
285	Montgomery: R. D. Whitehorn, letter, February 4, 1958, to Mrs. Tuchman (who kindly lent it to me) and enclosed record from St. John's College, Cambridge, and undated newspaper clippings; Church, 17, for postcard—I assume the clergyman he mentions is Montgomery, the only one listed in *The Navy List*.
286	methods for solution of code: Yves Gyldén, interviews, May 28–31, 1962; Valério; Sacco, §§104–108; Givierge, ch. 15.
287	additional traffic: James, 139, 140. These implications that the code was only partially solved at this time are reinforced by a statement of Page's in a telegram of September 10, 1917, that the Zimmermann telegram "went in a code which the British had at that time only partly succeeded

in deciphering" (DSDF, 862.20235/537). This incompleteness of the solution explains why the section concerning dismemberment of the U.S. was not present in the first partial solution that Montgomery showed Hall.

287 reasons against disclosing telegram: my assumptions, based in part upon those in Friedman and Mendelsohn, 26–27.

289 February 5: James, 140.

289 agent T: James, 140–141, 133–135.

289 Code 13040: GFO for distribution; David Kahn [pseud. Ishcabibel], "A Partial Reconstruction of a German Diplomatic Code," *The Cryptogram*, XXVIII (September-October, 1960), 1, 4–7, for construction of code; also Friedman and Mendelsohn, 15–16. Hall's affidavit states that "The German cipher book covering this system of ciphering [Code 13040] is in our possession, it having been captured by the British authorities in the luggage of a German consul named Wasmuss who was stationed at Shiraz while Wasmuss was engaged in an endeavor to cut a British oil pipe line." This story is elaborated by James, 69, and Tuchman, 19–21. But it must be some lapse of memory on Hall's part. As Friedman and Mendelsohn remark, at 17, "It seems unlikely that a German consul engaged in an expedition to cut a pipe line should carry a diplomatic code book in his baggage." They suggest that the British found parallel plain and code messages in Wassmuss' baggage. According to GFO, 13040 was never distributed to Wassmuss nor to any German missions in Persia. However, other codes were, and the British discovered "two 'dictionary' cyphers" wrapped in several pairs of long woolen underwear in the German consulate at Bushire, Persia, on March 9, 1915 (C. J. Edmonds, "The Persian Gulf Prelude to the Zimmermann Telegram," *Journal of the Royal Central Asian Society*, XLVII, January, 1960, 58–67 at 65), and perhaps Hall confused that code with 13040. It is not known what code Wassmuss did have. Hall did not make his statement to cover up British cryptanalysis because earlier in his affidavit he stated that sometimes "our cipher experts were able to decipher the German ciphers." Whatever the reason for Hall's statement about a capture, it seems certain that Room 40 solved and did not capture 13040. Friedman and Mendelsohn, 17, point out that the copy of 13040 given by Britain to the United States after America entered the war gives every evidence of being a reconstruction, comprising about half the vocabulary with words and phrases from all sections and with some identifications marked as doubtful, and GFO reports that German archives show no reports of loss or compromise of that code. My text reflects my belief that 13040 was cryptanalyzed. Consequently, I have excluded the romantic stories of Wilhelm Wassmuss and of Alexander Czek, who is supposed to have stolen a German diplomatic code, which in any case may not have been 13040 or 0075 but any of the others; Hall in any event denied any knowledge of Czek (Robert Boucard, *Les Dessous des Archives Secrètes* [Paris: Les Éditions de France, 1929], 69–83).

291 variations between the two texts: comparison of them. Printed versions at

Notes

PAGE

Official German Documents, II, 1337, for Berlin to Washington; Hendrick, 345–346, and Tuchman, 201–202, for Washington to Mexico.

291 Britain deliberately holds the message for release: No evidence exists for this crucial statement. That many historians agree in it (views summarized in Samuel R. Spencer, *Decision for War, 1917* [Rindge, New Hampshire: Richard R. Smith, 1953], at 62–64) means little, since they were unaware of the underlying cryptologic and espionage problems. Friedman and Mendelsohn, 26–28, believe that the desire to protect the espionage secrets motivated the delay, and both they and Mrs. Tuchman, who has made the closest study of the political circumstances, think that the timing of giving the note to the Americans was based on political factors. I concur in these conclusions. No evidence exists for any different reason for the release, either.

291 "The danger is": Hendrick, 324–325.

291 "much that of a soda-water bottle": the military attaché, Spring-Rice, quoted in Walter Millis, *Road to War: America 1914–1917* (New York, 1935), 403.

291 Bell: James, 142.

292 text of message: James, 141; Hendrick, 333, and 345–346 and Tuchman, 201–202 for German.

292 conference and Balfour: Tuchman, 163–164, 166.

292 Page telegrams: Hendrick, 332–334. Original is DSDF, 862.20212/69.

293 Polk, "Much indignation": Tuchman, 168.

293 Lansing and Wilson: Lansing, 226–228.

293 Hood, news stories: Tuchman, 175. For some reason the text was given out in a different and weaker translation than that furnished by Page to the State Department.

293 "Please endeavor": DSDF, 862.20212/69, Lansing to Page, February 28, 1917.

293 "never used straight": Hendrick, 344.

294 Carlton: Tuchman, 171.

294 "Some members": DSDF, 862.20212/82A. The original Bernstorff-to-Eckardt Western Union telegram follows this and bears the same file number.

294 "Bell took": Hendricks, 345. Bell's original decode is DSDF, 862.20212/81½. But only the first page and a few lines of the second are in his handwriting; most of page 2 and pages 3–8 are in handwriting identified by John de Grey in an undated letter of 1963 as that of his father, Nigel. James erroneously states, at 143, that the message was decoded by Bell in the American embassy so that Wilson could say it was decoded by Americans on American soil.

294 statement to Senate: Tuchman, 180.

294 pet theories: Hendrick, 356.

294 Hall instigates: "Admiral Hall on the Zimmermann Telegram," *The World's Work*, LI (April, 1926), 578–579.

294 Berlin-Eckardt messages: Hendrick, 357–360. Though at first sublimely confident that their code had not been broken (Tuchman, 189, 194),

the Germans later resorted to a dictionary code to try to bribe Mexico to remain neutral (Yardley, ch. 6).
296 hilarity: Hendrick, 356; "Admiral Hall on the Zimmermann Telegram."
297 Zimmermann admits: Tuchman, 183.
297 American reaction: Tuchman, 184–187.

Chapter 10 A WAR OF INTERCEPTS: I

298 radio: see also Major R. B. Moran, "Powers and Limitations of Radio Communication Within a Modern Field Army," *Articles*, 89–113 and 114–134, at 95–96 (July–August and September–October, 1936); William F. Friedman, *American Army Field Codes in the American Expeditionary Forces During the First World War*, War Department (Washington, D.C.: U.S. Government Printing Office, 1942), 3; "Signal Communications," *Encyclopaedia Britannica*.
299 first days: Givierge, "Problems," 5.
299 French intercept service: Cartier, "Service d'écoute." This includes numerous photographs of intercept posts and one of Cartier.
299 direct wire: Cartier, "Souvenirs," I, 33.
300 traffic analysis: Cartier, "Service d'écoute," summarized at Gyldén, 31.
300 language separation: Givierge, "Problems," 25.
300 Circourt: Gyldén, 35–36.
301 ÜBCHI: Painvin, 11–12.
302 solution of single-columnar transposition: Gaines, ch. 4; Sacco, §§78–79; Wolfe, ch. 9; Friedman, IV, §§i–iv; Wayne G. Barker, *Cryptanalysis of the Single Columnar Transposition Cipher* (Rutland, Vt.: Charles E. Tuttle Co., 1961). Frequencies from Wolfe. Adding up the logarithms of these frequencies instead of the frequencies themselves will give a more accurate result.
302 solution of double-columnar transposition: Sacco, §84; Friedman, IV, §28g.
303 key in force: Painvin, 12.
303 cryptanalysts' difficulties: Carter, "Souvenirs," I, 25, II, 17; Givierge, "Problems," 7.
303 key reconstruction: Givierge, 200–204; Friedman, IV, §27.
304 October 1: Givierge, "Problems," 7. All first names of officers come from 1914 and 1919 editions of France, Ministère de la Guerre, *Annuaire officiel de l'armée française* (Paris: Berger-Levrault).
304 gossip and subsequent solutions: Givierge, "Problems," 8–9.
304 Thielt: Painvin, 12.
304 new system: Givierge, "Problems," 8, for November 18; 12, for illusory complication; 9, for December 10; Painvin, 12, for operation; Givierge, 218–223, for methods of solution. Painvin gives December as the date for the introduction of the system, but he was not officially in cryptanalysis then and Givierge was.

Notes 1043

PAGE

304 Painvin note, first solutions, goes to Bureau: Painvin, 11, 13.
304 Painvin: *Who's Who in France, 1961–62*; J. Rives Childs, letter, August 27, 1962; Yardley, 224; General Desfemmes, "Réflexions sur la guerre éléctronique," *L'Armée*, No. 24 (December, 1962), 21–33 at 28.
305 echelons: Givierge, "Problems," 16; Marcel Guitard, "Conférence de Marcel Guitard," *Bulletin de l'A.R.C.*, VIII (new series) (May, 1961), 47–52 at 48; Gyldén, 30, 40.
306 1915: Painvin, 14.
306 other problems: Cartier, "Souvenirs," I, 26; Gyldén, 42.
306 retrospective solutions: Givierge, vi, and "Problems," 9–10; Gyldén, 38.
306 French solutions: Givierge, "Problems," 14, 7, 18–24, 25, for "terrible regularity"; Gyldén, 38 for faked attacks, 36 for guessed keys; Guitard, 49, for proverbs.
307 ABCD: Painvin, 14. A confusing explanation of the cryptanalysis, translated from the French, appears in J. Rives Childs, Cipher Papers, I, §2, a paper mistitled "On the Italian & S.E. Front." These Childs Cipher Papers, deposited at the library of Childs' alma mater, Randolph-Macon College, Ashland, Virginia, comprise five volumes of cryptologic documents—intercepted cryptograms, solutions, reports, memoranda—from Childs' service as an American cryptanalyst in World War I.
307 substitution ciphers: Painvin, 14–15; Childs Cipher Papers, I, §2, "System in Use by the Germans Between Berlin and Constantinople."
308 grilles: Painvin, 15; "Instructions for Grill Cipher," Translation of a Captured German Document in J. Rives Childs, *German Military Ciphers from February to November, 1918*, War Department, Office of the Chief Signal Officer (Washington, D.C.: U.S. Government Printing Office, 1935), at 48–50, for codenames. Gaines, ch. 5; Wolfe, ch. 10 at 8–11, 22–26; Friedman, IV, ch. vii; Sacco, §§13, 81–82, for methods of grille construction and solution.
309 British setup: inferred from Childs, *German Military Ciphers*, 22, 24.
309 Hay: *Who's Who*, 1963; *Burke's Peerage, 1963*, at 2448–9; obituary in *The Scotsman*, December 28, 1962; introduction by Thomas Sugrue to Hay's *The Foot of Pride* (London: Beacon Press, 1950), at xi–xix; Mrs. Hay, letters June 4, 18, and 25, 1963. I am most indebted to Mrs. Hay for her help.
309 personnel: Names in memorandum dictated by Hay in 1956; *Who's Who, 1963*, for Sansom and Jopson; *Who Was Who, 1951–1960*, for Leeds, Minns, Strachey; *1941–1950*, for Tyndale, Brooke; *1929–1940*, for Margoliouth, Hunt.
310 5 Cork Street: Sir George Sansom, letter August 27, 1963; [J. Rives Childs], *Before the Curtain Falls* (Indianapolis: Bobbs-Merrill, 1932), at 122. This work of disguised nonfiction, published anonymously, contains considerable cryptologic color. Names are slightly altered: Hay appears as Day, Brooke-Hunt as Brooke, Hitchings as Herbert, Painvin as Pinson, and so on.
310 French help: James, 28; Cartier, "Souvenirs," II, 33.
310 skilled cryptanalysts: Childs, *German Military Ciphers*, 24, for Turkish

and Brooke-Hunt; Great Britain, War Office, letter, 22 May 1963, and *Before the Curtain Falls*, 123, for Brooke-Hunt.

310 Für GOD: Childs, *German Military Ciphers*, 1–4; J. Rives Childs, "History and Principles of German Military Ciphers" (unpublished typescript, April 5, 1919, deposited with Childs Cipher Papers as Vol. V), ch. 4; *Before the Curtain Falls*, 123–124; Hay memorandum for his close relations with Hall; Hoy, 157–159, for Abd el Malek. Hoy states that the Malek messages were solved by Room 40, but a study of the political situation, plus the fact that Malek is mentioned in at least two Für GOD messages (October 2, 1917, and January 10, 1918), leads me to believe that it was a Für GOD solution that sank the submarine. Für GOD plaintexts in Childs Cipher Papers, I, §9.

311 Hay and duties: Sansom letter for "very good chief"; photographs of the book of remembrances from Mrs. Hay; Hay memorandum for duties.

311 Hitchings: his widow, Mrs. Jean B. Hitchings, letters, November 11 and December 2, 1963; Childs, letters, September 11 and 16, 1963.

311 Intelligence E(c), 2nd echelon: Friedman, *Field Codes*, 15.

311 Le Touquet: *Before the Curtain Falls*, 135, 136.

311 Macgregor: Hay memorandum; Childs, letters, September 11 and November 6, 1963.

311 army cryptanalysts and POW: Childs, *German Military Ciphers*, 24; Childs, letter, September 16, 1963.

312 Playfair: Gyldén, 44; Colonel Andreas Figl, *Systeme des Chiffrierens* (Graz: Ulr. Mosers Buchhandlung, 1926), at §47; William F. Friedman, "The Use of Codes and Ciphers in the World War and the Lessons to be Learned Therefrom," *Articles*, 192–205 at 198 (July–September, 1938).

312 Lawrence of Arabia: Sir Ronald Storrs, *Memoirs* (New York: Putnam, 1937), 186.

312 code chiffré: Friedman, *Field Codes*, 51–71 for facsimiles of the Series 65 code; Givierge, "Problems," 13 for changes; Colonel Givierge, *Le chiffre*, Conférence faite le 6 février 1927, École de Perfectionnement des Officiers de Réserve de Penthièvre (Paris: Imprimerie F. Essertier, n.d.), 13; Givierge, 256, and André Lange and E.-A. Soudart, *Traité de cryptographie* (Paris: Librairie Félix Alcan, 1925), 87–88, for dangers of partial encoding. The Mendelsohn Collection at the University of Pennsylvania Library has a 28-page *Code Chiffré*, Série 64 (Ministère de la Guerre, Cabinet du Ministre, Section du Chiffre, no date or place of publication), a three-digit superenciphered code whose users are enjoined specifically to encode *only* the important words in a message; I do not know where, when, or why this code was used.

312 French mixed-alphabet polyalphabetic: Gyldén, 44.

312 French interrupted columnar: Givierge, "Problems," 13; Gyldén, 44, 43 for no solution, and footnotes by William F. Friedman on 41 and 44; Figl, §20. For French errors in handling—by officers, no less—see Givierge, "Problems," 12.

312 no cryptanalysts: Friedman, note in Gyldén, 41; "Lessons," 197.

312 no German military cryptanalysis: Gyldén, 15, states that only the German

Notes

Foreign Office engaged in cryptanalysis, and that to a very limited extent.

313 side effect: Givierge; "Problems," 14; Gyldén, 54.
313 on French territory: Gyldén, 34.
313 Abhorchdienst: Gyldén, 45. This pertains only to the Western Front. In the East, the Germans intercepted much Russian plaintext and solved a few of the poorly enciphered cryptograms soon after the war started; for details, see chapter on Russian cryptology. I believe that this activity did not spread to the West because no cryptanalytic organization existed to disseminate methods and results, because the fronts were widely separated and theater commanders almost independent, and because solutions occurred even in the East only rarely and haphazardly, and at great distances from one another.
313 Neumünster and Playfairs: Commandant X, "Les grandes heures de la T.S.F.," *QST Français et Radio-électricité réunis*, IX (April, 1928), 24–26 at 24.
313 mathematicians: W. Nicolai, *The German Secret Service* (London: Stanley Paul, 1924; a translation of *Geheime Machte*), 211. See also Gyldén, 19.
314 Spa: Gyldén, 55.
314 Germans never caught up: Gyldén, 43–44.
314 telephone eavesdropping: Givierge, "Problems," 15; untitled captured German document in Lange & Soudart, 88–91; "Eavesdropping in the War," *Infantry Journal*, XVII (October, 1920), 350–352; Frank Moorman, "Code and Cipher in France," *Infantry Journal*, XVI (June, 1920), 1039–1044 at 1043, for crawling across no man's land; R. E. Priestley, *The Signal Service in the European War of 1914 to 1918 (France)* ([London?]: Institution of Royal Engineers, 1921), 105–106, for Ovillers-la-Boiselle; "Signal Communication," *Encyclopaedia Britannica*, for overall picture; Henri Morin, *Service Secret: A l'Écoute devant Verdun*, ed. Pierre Andrieu (Paris: G. Durassie & Cie., 1959).
314 Dubail: Givierge, *Le chiffre*, 15.
314 carnets de chiffre: Givierge, "Problems," 15.
314 carnet réduit: Friedman, *Field Codes*, 7, and 37–50 for facsimiles of pages from OLIVE and URBAIN.
315 Befehlstafel: Givierge, "Problems," 15; Painvin, 15.
315 Satzbuch: Givierge, "Problems," 17; Friedman, *Field Codes*, 91–113, for facsimiles of pages from Satzbuch 140; Yardley, 189, for reprint of Satzbuch page; note by Friedman in Gyldén, 53; Painvin, 15–16.
315 KRU solutions: Painvin, 16; Givierge, "Problems," 17 for 30 codes, 16 for December 5 to 15.
315 British prediction and French discussion: Childs Cipher Papers, I, §1, Second Lieutenant J. Rives Childs, "Report on Investigations of Codes and Ciphers...," March 22, 1918, at 3. The visitor was, of course, Childs.
315 Schlüsselheft and Geheimklappe: note by Friedman in Gyldén, 53; Friedman, *Field Codes*, 9, 75–90, for facsimiles of pages; Childs Cipher Papers, II, has an Allied reconstruction of a Schlüsselheft dated July 31, 1918, plus a reconstruction of a Geheimklappe encipherment dated March 23, 1918.

PAGE

316 Austrian solutions from June to October: Ronge, 108–109, 134. These references are still to the French edition unless otherwise specified. Gyldén cites the original German. All first names and ranks are taken from the index to the German edition, however.
317 "paying for itself": Ronge, 109.
317 cifrario tascabile: Figl, §44; Sacco, §§23–24.
317 Chaurand: Gyldén, 23; Sacco, §158.
317 Mengarini: Gyldén, 79; General Odoardo Marchetti, *Il Servizio informazione dell'esercito Italiano nella grande guerra* (Roma: Tipografia Regionale, 1937), 182.
317 May 20, June 1 and 8, Isonzo: Gyldén, 80; Ronge, 158–159.
317 Austrian cryptanalytic organization: Ronge (German ed.), 403. In 1918, the Rumanian group was taken over by Johann Baleanu and the Russian by Rudolf Lippmann. The Austro-Hungarians also employed cryptanalysts and secret-ink experts for its counterespionage work. For some interesting details see Arthur Scheutz [pseud. Tristan Busch], *Entlarvter Geheimdienst* (Zurich: Pegasus Verlag, 1946), trans. Anthony V. Ireland as *Secret Service Unmasked* (London: Hutchinson, n.d.), chs. 9–17.
318 Rumanian: Gyldén, 74–75; Ronge, 170, 205.
318 Sacco and Italian cryptanalysis: Sacco, interview, May 10, 1962; Sacco, §157; Marchetti, 87–88, 132.
319 Austrian systems: Childs Cipher Papers, I, §3, "Notes on radio-telegraphy and cryptography of the Austrian Army," translation of report of May 6, 1918, by Section R, Intelligence Service, General Headquarters, Rome, and accompanying papers.
319 solution of June 20: Sacco, §108.
319 Italian solutions: Sacco, §§157, 111 for diplomatic code, 157 and interview of May 10, 1962, for naval.
319 Italian cryptographic improvements: Marchetti, 161 for January attempt, 173 for cifrario rosso débacle and replacement of cifrario tascabile; Sacco interview, for change to enciphered code after Caporetto; Cartier, "Souvenirs," II, 37–38 for his visit; Ronge, 247, and James, 159, for Allied mission. The group from Room 40 apparently included de Grey, according to his *Who Was Who* biography. Sacco, §158, denies that the Allies reorganized the Italian cipher organization.
320 Austrian preponderance: Gyldén, 81–82.
320 tribute: Ronge, 249. The sentence is also quoted in Marchetti, 181, who passionately denies that the Austrians could have gotten very much information from Italian interceptions. He is not, however, entirely convincing.

Chapter 11 A WAR OF INTERCEPTS: II

All citations from the previous chapter carry over to this one.

321 first steps: Details of technical conferences, Muirhead's paper and students' responses, in a notebook entitled "Military Cryptography" in the Fabyan

Notes

PAGE

Collection, The Library of Congress. The puerility of American cryptography at this time is illustrated in War Department, Office of the Chief Signal Officer, *Visual Signaling*, Manual No. 6 (Washington, D.C.: U.S. Government Printing Office, 1910), ch. 6, "Codes and Ciphers," 84–97.

321 Mauborgne pamphlet: *An Advanced Problem in Cryptography and Its Solution* (Fort Leavenworth: Press of the Army Service Schools, 1914).

321 Hitt: War Department, Adjutant General's Office, *Official Army Register*, January 1, 1934; Hitt, memorandum, November 26, 1962; Hitt, letters, February 22 and August 4, 1963; Hitt, interview, December 8, 1963.

322 "very much interested": Hitt to Reber, January 9, 1915, in Hitt Papers. Hitt very kindly turned over his cryptologic documents to me, and they are referred to henceforth as Hitt Papers.

322 solutions: all the kinds cited are preserved in Hitt Papers.

323 "I have a mass of material": Hitt Papers.

323 35 cents: Hitt to O'Bleness, January 25, 1917, Hitt Papers.

323 *Manual:* 2–3 for cryptanalytic offices, 16–19 for intercept procedures, 95–101 for error correction, 2 for "luck," v for "excludes the use of codes."

324 served as textbook: Frank Moorman, "Wireless Intelligence," Lecture delivered to the officers of the Military Intelligence Division, General Staff, February 13, 1920, printed in Friedman, *Field Codes*, 265–270, at 266; *Before the Curtain Falls*, 102; Harris, 329; Yardley, 21.

324 cipher disk: Friedman, *Field Codes*, 1, 31; *Visual Signaling*, 89–93; Harris, 335.

324 Larrabee: Hitt, 53–54.

324 Hitt urges Playfair: Hitt Papers.

325 "This device is based": Hitt Papers; for other details, correspondence with Friedman, 1930 and 1944, and photograph of original device, Hitt Papers.

325 Mauborgne contribution: William F. Friedman, "Edgar Allan Poe—Cryptographer: Addendum," *Articles*, 183 (October–December, 1937); Harris, 335.

326 "1. The enclosed": Hitt Papers. Many other similar requests in Hitt Papers.

326 General Orders: United States, Department of the Army, Historical Division, *Bulletins and General Orders, G.H.Q., A.E.F.*, United States Army in the World War, 1917–1919 (Washington, D.C.: U.S. Government Printing Office, 1948). No. 8 is dated July 5, 1917. Other general orders bearing on cryptology are No. 3 of June 28, 1917, of which section 21 specifies permissible commercial codes and section 25 mandates use of War Department Telegraph Code for messages on troop movements, casualties, supplies, etc.; No. 103 of June 26, 1918, setting forth the different uses of the War Department Telegraph Code (between A.E.F. G.H.Q. and War Department), Staff Code (between G.H.Q. and divisions), Trench Code (within divisions), Playfair (for emergency) and special codes; No. 148 of September 3, 1918, on codes between French and American units; No. 152 of September 10, 1918, establishing the Army Radio Corps for interception and direction-finding; No. 172 of October 7, 1918, regulating the distribution of trench codes; No. 190 of October 29,

PAGE

1918, giving detailed instructions on sending code messages, prohibiting mixed code and cleartext, and permitting messages in clear only "on the written order of an officer."

326 December of 1917: Friedman, *Field Codes*, 9.

326 Barnes: United States, Department of State, *Register*, December 15, 1916 (Washington, D.C.: U.S. Government Printing Office, 1917), 72, 23; Friedman, *Field Codes*, 14.

326 Barnes' staff: Howard R. Barnes, "Report of the Code Compiling Section," in Friedman, *Field Codes*, 9. Since large portions of this report are cited in *Field Codes*, future citations to Barnes will refer directly to pages in that work.

326 three authorized means: Friedman, *Field Codes*, 17, 27.

327 Trench Code, Front-Line Code: Barnes, 9–10.

327 "To him more than to any other": Barnes, 27.

327 Childs: Friedman, *Field Codes*, 10–14; 117–130 for a facsimile of Childs' report, and 131–142, 223–229 for facsimiles of the two codes and their enciphering alphabets.

327 "I concur": Hitt Papers.

327 security burden: Barnes, 13, 17.

327 June 24: Friedman, *Field Codes*, 17.

327 River and Lake series: Barnes, 17–18, and United States, War Department, Office of the Chief Signal Officer, *Report of the Chief Signal Officer to the Secretary of War, 1919* (Washington, D.C.: U.S. Government Printing Office, 1919), ch. 33, "Code Compilation Service," 536–538, for publication and issuance of codes; Friedman, *Field Codes*, 151–197, for facsimiles of sample pages from each. The Mendelsohn Collection at the University of Pennsylvania Library has several of these codes bound in a single volume under U.S. Army, A.E.F. 1917–1920, Collection of Secret Codes.

329 printing secrecy and distribution: Barnes, 21, 30 for British officer; General Orders No. 172 for seals.

329 cryptanalytic tests: Friedman, *Field Codes*, 14–17 for Hay, Hitchings, and Hitt letters; 143–149 for Hay and Hitchings supporting reports.

329 supplementary and unauthorized codes: Barnes, 19–20; Friedman, *Field Codes*, 209–220, 230–246, 253–256, for facsimiles.

331 general orders nonuse of code: Barnes, 22.

331 "there certainly never": Moorman, "Code and Cipher in France, " !040.

331 security service: Barnes, 22–25; *Report of the Chief Signal Officer*, 323, 326, 331; Moorman, "Wireless Intelligence," 265, 269, for "hang . . . the offenders"; Moorman, "Code and Cipher in France," 1043–1044; Friedman, *Field Codes*, 261–263, for letters of reprimand, and 23–24, for extract on "Security Service" from an unspecified report of Moorman, whence "only a few" quotation is taken.

332 improvements in code: Barnes, 17, 18, 26–27, 19; see also Instructions to Staff Code, Friedman, *Field Codes*, 217.

332 Turner: "The Significance of the Frontier in American History" (1893), last paragraph.

Notes

PAGE

333   DAM: covers of codes reproduced in Friedman, *Field Codes*.

333   Moorman: United States, War Department, Adjutant General's Office, *Official Army Register*, January 1, 1934; Mrs. Naomi Moorman, his widow, letters, September 20 and October 22, 1963; Hitt, *Manual*, 78; Childs, letter, September 16, 1963.

333   "Glass House": William E. Moore, "The Jerry Who Spoiled the War," *The American Legion Weekly*, IV (September 1, 1922), 7–8, 26–28, at 7.

333   personnel: Moore, 8; Childs, letter, August 27, 1963; Childs Cipher Papers, I, §1, an assignment sheet giving staff list as of April 1, 1918; Moorman, "Wireless Intelligence," 265–266.

333   G.2 A.6 work: Moorman, "Wireless Intelligence," 265.

333   traffic analysis, fake messages, aircraft: Moorman, "Wireless Intelligence," 267–268; "Code and Cipher in France," 1040–1041.

334   Woellner: Childs Cipher Papers, I, §12.

334   St.-Mihiel: Moorman, "Code and Cipher in France," 1043.

334   training in ciphers, "we were reading," first real victory: Moorman, "Wireless Intelligence," 266.

334   Radio Section: *Report of the Chief Signal Officer*, 321–335, at 327 for figures on intercepts and bearings, 321 for working conditions; Moorman, "Wireless Intelligence," 266 for appreciation; Moore, 27 for accuracy on March 11; Childs Cipher Papers, I, §12, untitled report by Lieutenant Lee West Sellers on value of Signal Corps interceptions, at 6 for only Americans picked up.

335   Berthold's solution: Moore, 8, 26–27; William F. Friedman, *Elements of Cryptanalysis*, Training Pamphlet No. 3, Office of the Chief Signal Officer, May, 1923 (Washington, D.C.: U.S. Government Printing Office, 1924), at §103, for correlation of plaintexts and ciphertexts; Childs Cipher Papers, II, "Three Number Code," March 11, 1918, for intercepts as distributed in G.2 A.6; Moorman, "Wireless Intelligence," 266; "Code and Cipher in France," 1044, for "cost the lives," where the date is erroneously given as February, 1917; *Before the Curtain Falls*, 118, 145, for description of Berthold.

336   9:05 message: *Report of the Chief Signal Officer*, 332.

336   "unnecessary work": Moorman, "Wireless Intelligence," 267.

336   Jaeger: Moore, 8; Moorman, "Code and Cipher in France," 1040.

336   "Woe to him": Childs Cipher Papers, I, §11, undated "Special Code Section Report," message of 6:40 p.m., April 1 [1918].

337   Childs: *Who's Who in America, 1963*; Childs Cipher Papers, I, §1, travel orders and "Report of Investigations of Codes and Ciphers"; Childs, *German Military Ciphers*, 19, 22, 24; *Before the Curtain Falls*, 116–117, 122, 125; excerpts from Childs' as-yet-unpublished manuscript tentatively entitled "Between Two Worlds."

337   Für GOD keys: Childs, *German Military Ciphers*, 1–4.

337   von Kressenstein message: Childs Cipher Papers, I, §6, for ciphertext, solution, and G-2 survey; I, §5, untitled page, message of 21:10 hours August 8 for "use forbidden"; John Buchan, *A History of the Great War* (Boston: Houghton Mifflin Co., 1922), IV, 299, for importance of Baku.

PAGE

339 ALACHI solution: Childs, *German Military Ciphers*, 9–12; Moorman, "Wireless Intelligence," 267.

339 Constantinople and Mackensen messages: Childs, *German Military Ciphers*, 35–41, 14; *Before the Curtain Falls*, 143–146, for "By reason of its length," translation of Mackensen message, and excitement at G.H.Q.; R. W. Seton-Watson, *A History of the Roumanians* (Cambridge: at the University Press, 1934), 535, for situation in Rumania. Original ciphertext in Childs Cipher Papers, III, " 'Richi' ADFGVX Cipher," November 3, 1918, message of 7:06 p.m. November 4. German plaintext in Childs Cipher Papers, I, §5, "Special Code Section Report," November 5, 1918.

339 ADFGVX: Painvin, 16–45, for detailed exposition of cryptanalyses; Eyraud, 215–219, for abbreviated exposition. Military details have been largely drawn from the excellent articles on "World War I," "St. Quentin, Battle of," and "Chemin-des-Dames, Battle of" by Captain B. H. Liddell Hart in the *Encyclopaedia Britannica*.

340 conference of German specialists: Desfemmes, 30.

340 perplexity: *Before the Curtain Falls*, 125.

341 "Poor Painvin": Painvin, 17.

341 "best informed man": Guitard, 49.

344 no general solution: Painvin, 39. For such a solution, Sacco, §102; Friedman, IV, §§41–43.

344 keys solved: Childs, *German Military Ciphers*, 13. Daily volume ranged from 25 messages a day at the inception of the system to 148 in the last days of May. During July, the system, formerly confined to the Western Front, began to be used by Berlin to communicate with its troops on the Eastern Front. These messages bore the indicator RICHI in the preamble, in contrast to those on the Western Front, which were prefaced by CHI (the RI from "orient"?). Both prefaces were followed by the number of letters in the message. The Eastern Front keys had a life of two days and later of three, in comparison with one day in the West. G.2 A.6 read 17 RICHI keys covering 44 days from July to November. No keys for constructing the checkerboard or the numerical transposition sequence were ever recovered for any ADFGVX solution.

344 other solutions: Painvin, 39. Childs Cipher Papers, I, §10, includes some of the original mimeographed notifications of the keys.

344 "in short": Painvin, 39.

345 times of solution: Painvin, 40.

346 Ludendorff troubles: Erich Ludendorff, *Ludendorff's Own Story* (New York: Harper & Brothers, 1919), II, 271. "St Quentin, Battle of" for typical use of night cover.

346 French intelligence, Guitard enters: Desfemmes, 26.

346 telegram text: Painvin, 44, corrected by a letter of August 12, 1962, from Painvin.

347 French preparations and the attack: [Ferdinand Foch], *The Memoirs of Marshal Foch*, trans. by T. Bentley Mott (Garden City, N.Y.: Doubleday, Doran & Co., 1931), 323, for aerial reconnaissance; Raymond Recouly,

Notes 1051

PAGE

La Bataille de Foch (Paris: Librairie Hachette, 1920), 77–78, for deserters and Mangin counterattack; General Bartholemew Palat, *La Grande Guerre sur le Front Occidental*, XIII (*Offensives Suprêmes de l'Allemagne*) (Paris: Berger-Levrault, 1929), 365–366, for "offensive is imminent"; Colonel Ripert d'Alauzier, "La bataille de Courcelles-Méry," *Revue militaire française*, 95th year (new series) (August 1, 1925), 234–252, (September 1, 1925), 372–392, (October 1, 1925), 68–83, at 383 for bombardment, and *passim* for details of the entire battle. Foch says that the French knew German intentions by May 30, which would be before the Painvin solution. But Recouly, who wrote much more closely to the event, and Palat, who is the official French military historian, specifically credit the munitions cryptogram with alerting the French to the attack. I believe that Foch was simply a few days off in the question of warning. The message—which has recently been given the name of "le radiogramme de la victoire" in French cryptologic literature—is also mentioned in Givierge, "Problems," 17, where it appears to be a Schlüsselheft solution; in Gyldén, 48, who credits the Mangin attack with turning the tide of the war; and in Cartier, "Souvenirs," II, 19–20.

347 "thorough preparation": Ludendorff, II, 271.
347 no surprise: all parties agree on this—Liddell Hart in "World War I"; Buchan, IV, 259; even Ludendorff, II, 271.
347 importance of the battle: Recouly, 78; Buchan, IV, 260; Hanotaux and Lavisse, quoted in Desfemmes, 27.
347 Painvin: Eyraud, 219; *Who's Who in France, 1961–1962*; Painvin, letter, August 12, 1962, for satisfaction and "indelible mark."
348 chamber analysis dead: Gyldén, 3.
348 cryptologic executive: Gyldén, 39–40.
349 Bacon: *The Tvvoo Bookes of Francis Bacon of the Proficience and Advancement of Learning* (London), at 61r.
349 "encode well": Givierge, "Problems," 31.

Chapter 12 TWO AMERICANS

351 Yardley biography: *Who Was Who in America, 1951–1960;* United States, Department of State, *Register*, December 15, 1916 (Washington, D.C.: U.S. Government Printing Office, 1917), 24, 144; Yardley, 17–21; Herbert O. Yardley, *The Education of a Poker Player* (New York: Simon and Schuster, 1957), v, 5, 65. Ladislas Fargo, *The Broken Seal* (New York: Random House, 1967), 9–31, 56–58, 67–72, which came to my attention too late for use in my text, gives additional material on Yardley, but his interpretations must be viewed with extreme caution.
351 House message: Yardley, 21–22.
351 Wilson systems: Permanent exhibit on second floor of The Library of Congress shows a superencipherment; George Sylvester Viereck, *The Strangest Friendship in History* (New York: Liveright Publishing Corporation,

PAGE

1932), 353 for jargon code, 358–359 for another superencipherment edition.

351 memorandum, Yardley symptom: Yardley, 26–30.

352 MI-8 organized: Yardley, 31–36.

352 Manly: Yardley, 38–39; *DAB*, supplement 2; *Who Was Who in America, 1897–1942*.

352 others: David Stevens, letters of May 3 and 11, 1963; *Who's Who in America, 1938–1939* for Stevens; *Who Was Who in America, 1897–1942*, for Luquiens; *1943–1950* for Knott, Beeson.

352 subsections: United States, War Department, *Annual Reports, 1919: Report of the Chief of Staff* (Washington, D.C.: U.S. Government Printing Office, 1920), 329. Yardley, 47, names a code and cipher solution subsection instead of the code instruction subsection cited in the official report. Childs, "History and Principles of German Military Ciphers," at 1, for teaching at Army War College; Manly Papers, University of Chicago Library, for Problem 20.

352 locations: Frederick Livesey, "Memoirs" (1959), typescript in possession of his widow, Vera, to whom I am indebted for making it available to me. For Livesey, *Who's Who in America, 1956–1957*.

352 shorthand: Yardley, 54.

353 secret inks: Yardley, 60–85; ch. 5, for Victoria; Scheutz, 95. Charles E. O'Hara and James W. Osterburg, *An Introduction to Criminalistics* (New York: The Macmillan Company, 1952), 500, 504, and Edmond Locard, *Manuel de Technique Policière*, 4th ed. (Payot: Paris, 1948), 241–242, for general reagent. *Report of the Chief of Staff*, 329, for 2,000 and 50 letters.

353 diplomatic solutions, mostly Spanish: Yardley, 206; Livesey. I cannot bring myself to believe the figure of 10,000 telegrams solved that Yardley gives.

353 "it rather worried me": Yardley, 198.

354 Waberski: Yardley, ch. 7, who, regrettably, does not give Manly credit for the solution; Henry Landau, *The Enemy Within: The Inside Story of German Sabotage in America* (New York: G. P. Putnam's Sons, 1937), 120–127; Stevens, letter of May 3, 1963. Stevens, incidentally, solved the PQR cipher (Yardley, 150–152). Yardley, ch. 6. for Eckardt's dictionary code.

354 Yardley in Europe: Yardley, chs. 9–12; *Before the Curtain Falls*, 157–158; Livesey.

355 origin of the American Black Chamber: DSDF 894.727/10, Secretary of War to Secretary of State, September 1, 1931.

355 American Black Chamber: Yardley, 240, 250, 265; Livesey, 75–76; Mrs. Edna Yardley, interview, November 3, 1961, for personnel. "Yardley Surprised at Denials," *New York Sun*, June 8, 1931, 3:2–3, and Manly, letter, January 24, 1921, addressed to Yardley at 141 East 37th Street, Manly Papers, for addresses. *Who Was Who in America, 1897–1942*, for Mendelsohn. Of the three locations, 3 East 38th Street has been replaced by a five-and-dime store, 141 East 37th Street is now a woman's residence, and 52 Vanderbilt Avenue still stands as an office building.

Notes

PAGE

356 Japanese solutions: Yardley, chs. 14–16, at 268–269 for "By now"; Livesey, 77–79. It should be recorded that in 1932 the then Captain W. A. van der Beck, a Dutch officer stationed in Batavia and assigned to solve Japanese codes, singlehandedly solved an early edition of the Japanese LA code. He made his initial break by correctly guessing that certain repeated codegroups in circular telegrams represented addresses. The solutions helped the Dutch fend off tough Japanese demands in a trade conference (van der Beck, letters, March 25, April 23, June 16, 1962).

357 Kowalefsky: Yardley, 279; Shiro Takagi, "Nippon Kaigun No Kimitsushitsu" ("The Black Chamber of the Japanese Navy"), *Shukan Asahi* (Showa 36, Junigatsu 8 [December 8, 1961]), 24–26 at 24.

358 Jp: Yardley, 289–290. He states that this code employed three-letter codewords to disrupt the regularity of the two-letter groups, and that this gimmick delayed solution forty days. But a photograph of a Jp code message with its partial decryptment (opposite 312) shows no three-letter groups.

358 "sees all": Yardley, 305.

358 most important telegram: Yardley, 312–313.

358 "nothing to do": Yardley, 317.

359 Hughes letter of commendation: mentioned DSDF 894.727/10.

359 nervous breakdowns: Yardley, 318–321. However, Livesey, who was probably the "most valuable assistant" that Yardley mentions, states that "this page about me is purely imaginative." He says that Yardley had to let him go because of cutbacks, but got him severance pay and a job in the State Department, which Livesey made his career.

359 security: Yardley, 323–331; Mrs. Edna Yardley, interview, for taking papers home and size of staff. Manly, letter to Yardley, December 5, 1924, Manly Papers, for appropriation cut.

359 45,000: Yardley, 332.

359 code telegrams from telegraph companies: DSDF 894.727/25, copy of Yardley letter to Bobbs-Merrill Company, March 18, 1931.

359 end of the Black Chamber: Yardley, "The American Black Chamber," original typescript in possession of Mrs. Edna Yardley, ch. 20, p. 2, which differs in significant detail from the printed version; Yardley, ch. 20. Henry L. Stimson and McGeorge Bundy, *On Active Service in Peace and War* (New York: Harper & Brothers, 1947), 188, for "Gentlemen" and "In 1929"; Elting E. Morrison, *Turmoil and Tradition: A Study of the Life and Times of Henry L. Stimson* (Boston: Houghton Mifflin Company, 1960), 639. Neither the National Archives nor the State Department seem to have any records of the Black Chamber or its dissolution.

360 $6,666: *The Origin and Development of the Army Security Agency*, anonymous, undated mimeographed document, but evidently based on official sources, at 4.

360 $98,808.49 and $230,404: DSDF 894.727/10. Letter from Victor Weiskopf to Manly, September 16, 1929, Manly Papers, mentions that the rent was prepaid to September.

PAGE
- 360 "less than nothing," loan, "I hadn't done": Letters of Yardley to Manly, August 29, 1930, and undated from Worthington; letter of Manly to Yardley, January 30, 1931, all Manly Papers.
- 361 *The Saturday Evening Post*: "Secret Inks," CCIII (April 4, 1931), 3–5, 140–142, 145; "Codes," (April 18, 1931), 16–17, 141–142; "Ciphers," (May 9, 1931), 35, 144–146, 148–149. Demand was so great that he wrote another, more general article, "Cryptograms and Their Solution," for the November 21 issue, at 21, 63–65.
- 361 critics: *Book Review Digest*, XXVII (March, 1931–February, 1932), for Roberts and others. The best-selling mystery-book author, Erle Stanley Gardner, calls *The American Black Chamber* "one of the most interesting books I have ever read" and commends it to "any ambitious writer" as an example of "the possibilities of the human mind when its self-imposed brakes are removed" in ch. 7, *The Writer's Handbook*, ed. A. S. Burack (Boston: The Writer, 1963), 30–31.
- 361 official statements: "Deny Our Statesmen Read Envoys' Ciphers," *The New York Times* (June 2, 1931), 18:3. Also "State and War Officials Silent on Yardley Book," *New York Herald Tribune* (June 9, 1931).
- 361 St.-Mihiel Story: Yardley, 42–45; Friedman, *Field Codes*, 10–13, 25–26. Manly wrote to Friedman, July 24, 1931, that he had the same impression of the episode as Yardley (Manly Papers).
- 362 Friedman circularizes, Hitt, Moorman reply: Letter from Friedman and enclosed photostats, Manly Papers; Childs Cipher Papers, I, §12. Friedman, *Field Codes*, 10, refers to *The American Black Chamber* as "a book which, in most libraries, is undoubtedly catalogued under the class of non-fiction."
- 362 "you might incur," "I approve": letters of January 30 and April 24, 1931, Manly Papers.
- 362 Friedman criticism: Letters of August 24, 1931, for breach of ethics, and of November 22, 1931, for "great harm," Manly reply of August 28, [1931], Manly Papers.
- 362 extra work: Solomon Kullback, interview, December 7, 1962.
- 362 "dramatise": undated letter and letter of April 30, 1931, Manly Papers.
- 362 letter to the editor: *New York Evening Post* (June 23, 1931).
- 363 *Liberty* article: VIII (December 19, 1931), 8–14.
- 363 sales: memorandum of November 28, 1962, from William J. Finneran, sales manager, trade division, Bobbs-Merrill Company.
- 363 furor: DSDF 894.727/9, report of counselor of embassy in Tokyo, enclosing newspaper clippings and translations; DSDF 894.727/11, Forbes report of November 5.
- 364 language students: *PHA*, 10:4909.
- 364 Togo: Togo, 61.
- 364 Hornbeck memorandum: DSDF 894.727/20.
- 364 seizure: "Code Expert's Ms. On Japan is Seized," *The New York Times* (February 21, 1933), 3:4.
- 364 Yardley bill and debate: 73rd Congress, House of Representatives Reports 18 and 206, Senate Report 21; *Congressional Record*, LXXVII, 2698,

Notes 1055

PAGE

2699, for passed and reconsidered; 3125–3139, for debate and Senate passage; 5218, 5333–5334, for House acceptance and passage; 6198, for President signs; 3129, for Yardley justifications.

367 Bobbs-Merrill petition: DSDF 894.727/25½.

368 Yardley novels: both published 1934 by Longmans, Green & Company of New York.

368 *Rendezvous:* Undated publicity material—which, incidentally, states falsely that the film is based on *The American Black Chamber*; André Sennwald, "William Powell as the Star of 'Rendezvous,' a Spy Melodrama Now at the Capitol Theatre," *The New York Times* (October 26, 1935), 12:2–3. J. Rives Childs, letter, June 27, 1964.

368 China: Yardley, *Education of a Poker Player*, 65–66; Theodore H. White, *Fire in the Ashes* (New York: William Sloan Associates, 1953), 357–358. Herbert O. Yardley and Carl Grabo, *Crows Are Black Everywhere* (New York: G. P. Putnam's Sons, 1945), 78–80, for ciphers. J. Rives Childs, letter, June 27, 1964, for salary and Queens.

369 personality: Mrs. Yardley interview for golf and duck-hunting. *Education of a Poker Player*, v, for poker, 67, for whorehouses. Letter from Theodore H. White, May 10, 1963, for virtual orgy. Emily Hahn, *China to Me* (Garden City, N.Y.: Doubleday & Company, 1944), 167–168. Childs, "Between Two Worlds," for cynicism.

369 restaurateur, Canadian bureau, forced out: John O'Donnell, "Capital Stuff," New York *Daily News* (February 27, 1945), 4:4–5.

369 "father of American cryptography": Associated Press.

369 inspired amateurs: as for example, Rosario Candela, who pays tribute to Yardley in his *The Military Cipher of Commandant Bazeries* (New York: Cardanus Press, 1938), xiv.

369 Friedman traits: my observations.

370 Friedman biography: *Who's Who in America, 1962–63*; interview, December 11, 1962, for all information up to 1921, except as otherwise noted.

370 Fabyan: *Who Was Who in America, 1897–1942;* William F. and Elizabeth S. Friedman, *The Shakespearean Ciphers Examined* (Cambridge: University Press, 1957), at 205; Harris, 329.

371 Elizabeth Smith Friedman: *Who's Who of American Women, 1963–1964*; interview, December 11, 1962.

371 Hindu ciphers: W. F. Friedman, "The Hindu Cipher," *Information Bulletin* of the Office of the Chief Signal Officer, No. 11 (December 1, 1921), 23–27; Strother, 151; Thomas M. Johnson, "Secrets of the Master Spies," *Popular Mechanics Magazine*, LVIII (September, 1932), 409–413; for checkerboard system. This, incidentally, is essentially the same as the so-called Nihilist substitution (Schooling, IV, 616–617; Gaines, 164–167; Wolfe, II, ch. 8). Inspector Thomas J. Tunney, *Throttled! The Detection of the German and Anarchist Bomb Plotters* (Boston: Small, Maynard & Co., 1919), 80–81 and pictures opposite 80 and 90, for book cipher; Friedman, I, 102, for solution methods.

372 Pletts solution: Friedman, "The Use of Codes and Ciphers in the World War and Lessons to be Learned Therefrom," *Articles*, 42–43; Friedman,

PAGE

        interview, 1961; Yardley, 358, for illustration of the device, which appears not to have been patented.

374 Riverbank Publications: No. 15 published in 1917; Nos. 16 to 21 in 1918; No. 22 in 1922.

376 Lohr: letter, January 15, 1948.

376 Cartier false-dating: Friedman.

376 treating frequency distribution as a statistical curve: In the Introductory to No. 22, Friedman farsightedly remarked that "when such a treatment is possible, it is one of the most useful and trustworthy methods in cryptography."

376 theory (of monographic coincidence): Friedman, II, Appendix 2; 114 for 1925 solution.

377 κ_r, κ_p: Sacco has computed a constant called "presences" that differs from language to language and that figures in his formula for "mean quadratic frequency," or "mfq," to distinguish mono- from polyalphabetic texts. See his Appendix II and Table 28; also his "Dérivation de la formule des présences," *Revue Internationale de Criminologie et de Police Technique*, No. 4 (October–December, 1957), 300–302.

378 kappa, phi, and chi tests: Friedman, III, §§11, 12, 14.

384 greatest single creation: Friedman, interview, April 16, 1963.

384 bewildering variety: see, for instance, Figl.

384 "cryptanalysis": letter quoted in David Kahn, *Plaintext in the New Unabridged* (New York: Crypto Press, 1963), 33–34.

384 *Elements of Cryptanalysis*: (Washington, D.C.: U.S. Government Printing Office, 1924). Kerckhoffs and, to a lesser extent, Delastelle had classified ciphers, but their efforts, in addition to being outdated in 1923, did not strike through to fundamentals as Friedman's did.

385 ex-prizefighter: "William F. Friedman's Remarks at His Retirement Ceremony," *The NSA Newsletter*, No. 25 (November, 1955), 7–8, 10, at 8.

385 first two patents: 1,522,775 and 1,516,180.

385 Teapot Dome: Senate, Committee on Public Lands and Surveys, *Leases upon Oil Reserves*, Hearings, 68:1 (GPO, 1924), 2483–7, 2515–21, 2548–51.

385 Mars: "Radio Hears Things as Mars Nears Us," *The New York Times* (August 23, 1924).

386 Signal Corps: *The Origin and Development of the Army Security Agency* for all administrative details of Army cryptology; also Harris, 330–331.

386 Navy: Smith, letter of October 30, 1963; Safford's official Navy biography; *PHA*, 8:3556. Farago, 36–53, 76–77 has good material on this period. Smith's "Solution of the Playfair Cipher" in André Langie, *Cryptography*, trans. J. C. H. Macbeth (London: Constable & Co., 1922), 170–188. Smith felt compelled to emend Macbeth's sample text by changing *fornication* to *intoxication*, cutting off its *i* to make it fit.

387 Zacharias: *Secret Missions: The Story of an Intelligence Officer* (New York: G. P. Putnam's Sons, 1946), 83–91 at 89 and 101.

388 solution of Hitt machine: DSDF 119.25/782½.

388 Friedman interests: see listing in Galland.

Notes 1057

PAGE

389 Walter Reed Hospital: Friedman's official Army biography.
390 picture: cover of *The NSA Newsletter*, No. 25 (November, 1955).
390 "avalanche": David Kahn, "Decoding the Bard," *The New York Times Book Review* (October 6, 1957), 3, 41.
390 $100,000: 84th Congress, 2nd session, H.R. 2068 (Private Law 625, May 10, 1956), and accompanying House Report 260 and Senate Report 1815; transcript of hearing (not printed) held by the Committee on the Judiciary. Previous bills were H.R. 5278, 82nd Congress, and H.R. 1152, 83rd Congress.
391 three Friedman patents: 2,395,863, 2,552,548, 2,877,565.
392 Safford and Rowlett bills: 85th Congress, 2nd Session, S. 1524 (Private Law 494, July 22, 1958); 88th Congress, 2nd Session, H.R. 7348 (Private Law 358, October 13, 1964).

Chapter 13 SECRECY FOR SALE

I am grateful to Boris Hagelin for reading portions of the manuscript and offering suggestions, to R. D. Parker for his several letters and interview, and to the American Telephone and Telegraph Company for making patent files available.

394 telegraph section, 17th floor: Ralzemond D. Parker, interview, December 4, 1962; Ralph E. Pierce, interview, May 9, 1963.
394 Vernam: *Encyclopedia of American Biography*, XXXI (new series) (New York: American Historical Company, 1961), 217–218; Vernam's daughter, Mrs. Per W. Nielssen, and his brother, Harold, interview, October 22, 1962; *The Aftermath of the Class of 1914 of the Worcester Polytechnic Institute* (Worcester, 1914), 132; Parker interview; R. B. Shanck, interview, August 9, 1963, for "What can I invent now?"
394 summer: G. S. Vernam, "Secret Telegraph Systems—Western Electric Patent Applications," Memorandum of August 1, 1918, in A. T. & T. File of Correspondence, Memoranda, and Notes Removed from Issued Application Folders for U.S. Patent 1,310,719, at 6.
394 multiplexing: *Report of the Chief Signal Officer, 1919*, at 139.
395 altering connections: Vernam memorandum of August 1.
395 enciphering technique and arrangement: Vernam's U.S. Patent 1,310,719; G. S. Vernam, "Cipher Printing Telegraph Systems for Secret Wire and Radio Telegraphic Communications," *Journal of the American Institute of Electrical Engineers*, XLV (February, 1926), 109–115.
397 sketch of December 17: Vernam memorandum of August 1, in which he states that "this sketch is the first record which we have of this suggestion."
397 meetings of February 18 and March 27 and tests: Vernam memorandum of August 1.
397 Morehouse keytape modification: U.S. Patent 1,356,546.
398 8,000 feet: G[ilbert] S V[ernam], "Secret Telegraphy—Double Key System," Memorandum of June 10, 1918, in A. T. & T. File of Correspondence,

Memoranda, and Notes Removed from Issued Application Folders for U.S. Patent 1,356,546.

398 invention of the one-time system: Though Vernam invented the pulse adding device, no clear-cut contemporary record states who invented the cryptographic method that accompanied it—the one-time system. Following is the evidence on which I base the conclusions that my text embodies.

Vernam seems to have evolved the randomness of the key. Parker and Vernam's co-worker, Ralph E. Pierce, both credit him with it, and though no other evidence supports them, none contests them either. Because Vernam had had no prior interest in cryptology, I think it likely that he created the random key in an unthinking way—"let's punch out some characters for the key"—rather than first making up a coherent key and then realizing its cryptographic weaknesses and deciding to nullify them with a random key. This requirement of randomness, which is not stated either in Vernam's or Morehouse's patents or in the A. T. & T. files on either, is first mentioned in Vernam's *Journal of the A.I.E.E.* article, p. 113.

The first mention of nonrepetition of polyalphabetic keys that I have found anywhere in cryptology occurs in a Parker Hitt "Memorandum for Chief of Staff" dated May 19, 1914: "No message is safe in the Larrabee cipher unless the key phrase is comparable in length with the message itself" (Hitt Papers). This was written about six months after Mauborgne had left the Army Signal School for the Philippines, but the statement, which stands without argumentative support, seems so positive and unquestioned as to imply a fairly long period of acceptance. Consequently, I think it probable that it was formulated with Mauborgne present, quite probably with his assistance, and that he adapted the principle to the Vernam machine keys.

Before I discovered this mention in the Hitt Papers, I had asked both Mauborgne and Parker who invented the nonrepetition feature. Mauborgne replied (letter, March 5, 1963) that "yes, I did it." (While he was referring to the work with Vernam, this may support the probability of his participation in the formulation of the principle at the Army Signal School.) Parker (letter, March 4, 1963) and Pierce (interview) both denied Mauborgne's claim, asserting that Vernam invented the feature. However, while the A. T. & T. files not only contain no reference supporting Vernam, they do include documents corroborating several statements that Mauborgne made in his letter. Moreover, without going into details, I believe that the line of development implied by the Mauborgne claim is more likely than that urged by Parker and Pierce, and some evidence that the implied Mauborgne line of development actually happened comes from engineer Donald B. Perry (letter, July 1, 1963). Admittedly, Perry did not join A. T. & T. until June, 1920, and so his testimony is at second hand, but he was a colleague of Vernam's on the cipher machine from those early days. Pierce's memory, incidentally, seems influenced by a Parker memoir on the subject; his is not an entirely independent recollection. But in any case I think that the Hitt statement

Notes

fairly well settles the matter in favor of Mauborgne, though the proof is not absolute.

All this seems to call for the conclusion that Mauborgne welded the two elements together, and I have consequently used it, even though no documentary evidence exists for it. Other Vernam co-workers threw no light on the question of invention (David E. Branson, letter, June 26, 1963; Roy B. Shanck, interview, August 9, 1963). The National Archives could not find any documents filed by Mauborgne at the time of his work with the Vernam machine, nor any report filed by Lieutenant Griffiths.

398 unbreakable: William F. Friedman states in his article, "Cryptology," in the *Encyclopaedia Britannica* that "a letter-for-letter cipher system which employs, once and only once, a keying sequence composed of characters or elements in a random and entirely unpredictable sequence may be considered holocryptic, that is, messages in such a system cannot be read by indirect processes involving cryptanalysis, but only by direct processes involving possession of the key or keys, obtained either legitimately, by virtue of being among the intended communicators, or by stealth."

400 reasons for only partial use: Friedman, III, 71–72; Hans Rohrbach, "Mathematische und maschinelle Methoden beim chiffrieren und dechiffrieren," *FIAT Review of German Science, 1939–1946: Applied Mathematics* (Wiesbaden: Office of Military Government for Germany: Field Information Agencies, Technical, 1948), I, 233–257, at 242.

401 Mauborgne and tri-city circuit: *Report of the Chief Signal Officer, 1919*, at 140–141.

401 Gherardi-Fabyan correspondence: photocopies in Pierce's possession; originals in A. T. & T. Confidential File 3710.

401 demonstrations: *Demonstrations for the Delegates to the Preliminary International Communications Conference* ([New York:] American Telephone and Telegraph Company [1920]), 7–8; Vernam, "Cipher Printing Telegraph Systems," 115; Vernam's Diary, entry for February 9, 1926.

402 German activities: interviews with Adolf Paschke, May 3; Werner Kunze, May 4; Rudolf Schauffler, May 6, all 1962.

403 publicity on Vernam's system: "A Secret-Code Message Machine," *The Literary Digest*, LXXXIX (April 17, 1926), 22; "Automatic Code Messages," *Science*, LXIII (new series) (February 19, 1926), unnumbered page in "Science News" section; Yardley, 363–365; Yardley, "Are We Giving Away Our State Secrets?" *Liberty*, VIII (December 19, 1931), 8–13.

403 Vernam cryptographic inventions: U.S. Patents 1,416,765 for stunts, 1,584,749 for handwriting, 1,613,686 for pictures.

403 to I.T.T.: Vernam's Diary, July 1, 1929.

403 SIGTOT: Harris, 586–588.

403 Vernam's death: *The New York Times* (February 10, 1960).

404 Gioppi: *La crittografia diplomatica, militare e commerciale* (Milano: Ulrico Hoepli, 1897), at 45–46. Friedman's Riverbank Publication No. 18 contains a section on "Digraphic and Trigraphic Substitution" at 5–9.

PAGE

404 Levine trigraphic substitution: Levine, letter, October 10, 1964. Another of his is in *The Cryptogram,* XXVIII (January–February, 1961), 54–56.

404 "Cryptography in an Algebraic Alphabet": *American Mathematical Monthly,* XXXVI (June–July, 1929), 306–312.

404 Hill: obituaries in *The New York Times* and *New York Herald Tribune* (January 10, 1961); Mrs. Hill.

404 *Telegraph and Telephone Age:* "The Role of Prime Numbers in the Checking of Telegraphic Communications," No. 7 (April 1, 1927), 151–154, and No. 14 (July 16, 1927), 323–324; "A Novel Checking Method for Telegraphic Sequences," No. 19 (October 1, 1926), 456–460.

404 patent: Hill Papers, in my possession.

405 "Linear Transformation Apparatus": *American Mathematical Monthly,* XXXVIII (March, 1931), 135–154.

405 previous proposals: Buck cited in bibliography by Maurits de Vries; Levine mentioned in M. E. Ohaver, "Solving Cipher Secrets," *Flynn's Weekly* (November 13, 1926), 794–800 at 799–800.

405 methods of encipherment: A good elementary introduction to the Hill system is given in Lyman C. Peck, *Secret Codes, Remainder Arithmetic, and Matrices* (Washington, D.C.: National Council of Teachers of Mathematics, 1961), and a clear explanation in Wolfe, III, Lesson 14.

407 comparison of matrix and linear systems: J. M. Wolfe with Salvatore Bonafide, *On Algebraic or Polygraphic Ciphers,* annotated translation of Sacco's Appendix I-D, "Sulla Cifratura Algebraica e Poligrammica" (mimeographed, no date or publisher), notes 13 and 18.

408 cryptanalysis: I am grateful to Dr. Jack Levine for his comments on the cryptanalytic defenses of the Hill system, and especially for his checking out of my suggestion concerning the possible weakness of two encipherments of a single message. For details, see his "Some Elementary Cryptanalysis of Algebraic Cryptography," *The American Mathematical Monthly,* LXVIII (May, 1961), 411–418; "Some Applications of High-Speed Computers to the Case $n = 2$ of Algebraic Cryptography," *Mathematics of Computation,* XV (July, 1961), 254–260; "Analysis of the Case $n = 3$ in Algebraic Cryptography with Involutory Key-Matrix and Known Alphabet," *Journal für die reine und angewandte Mathematik,* CCXIII (1963), 1–30; and, with Joel V. Brawley, Jr., "Involutory Commutants with some Applications to Algebraic Cryptography" *Journal für die reine und angewandte Mathematik,* CCXXIV (1966), 20–43.

408 Hill patent: 1,845,947 (with Louis Weisner).

408 Hill's later papers: Hill Papers.

408 Bruton: *New York Herald Tribune* obituary.

410 Albert: *Who's Who in America, 1962–63.* His paper, "Some Mathematical Aspects of Cryptography," seems never to have been published. It circulates in manuscript. Wolfe discusses pedagogical value of mathematics in cryptology at I, ii.

411 rotors: Givierge, 281–285; Sacco, §83c; Eyraud, §§108–109; patents; study of a Hebern machine.

Notes

PAGE

413 rotor solution: Rohrbach, 253; Sacco, appendix I-B; Ottico Meccanica Italiana, *Cryptograph C.R.: A Modern Patented Coding Machine* (Roma: Ottico Meccanica Italiana, n.d.), at 13–17; Arne Beurling, interview, November 9, 1963; my own investigations. NA, Microcopy T-311, Roll 83, Frame 7108489, cites a rotor solution.

415 Hebern: Mrs. Ellie Hebern, his widow, telephone interview, January 16, 1963, and letter, January 21, 1963. The name is pronounced HEE-burn.

415 early patents: 1,084,010 and 1,096,168 for checks; 1,086,823 and 1,123,738 for keyboards; 1,136,875 for blocks; 1,141,055 for typewriter. The two-typewriter arrangement is mentioned in U.S. Patent Office, Interference 77,716, *Edward H. Hebern vs. Austin R. Noll*, November 13, 1939, at 14–15 of hearings testimony.

415 1917: Interference 77,716, Hebern brief. This date is crucial because it awards the priority of the rotor invention to Hebern even though his application for a rotor patent was not filed until after two other inventors had filed theirs. The 1918 date of construction is corroborated by the statement printed in 1922 that the first machine was "completed about four years ago." (H. H. Dunn, "Electrical Machine Can Make Eleven Million Codes," *Popular Mechanics Magazine*, XXXVIII [December, 1922], 849–850; it has photographs of Hebern, a rotor, and the machine.)

415 Navy in 1921: Admiral Milo F. Draemel, letter, November 23, 1963.

415 "something radically better": United States Court of Claims, Case 213–53, *Ellie L. Hebern, executrix of the estate of Edward H. Hebern, deceased, and Hebern Code Inc., a corporation, vs. United States of America*, May 19, 1953, "Memorandum of Conference on 8 September [1956] in the office of the Judge Advocate General re Hebern Code Inc. infringement, etc.," at 5–6, quotation of Rear Admiral S. C. Hooper, U.S.N., Retired.

417 Hebern corporate history: This is assembled from stockholders' reports of March 1 and October 1, 1922; August 1 and November 1, 1923; August 28, 1924, and November 20, 1925; from news stories in the Oakland *Tribune* on January 28 and December 9, 1923; April 28 and 30, May 2, June 18 and 27, August 6, September 23 and 30, and December 12, 1924; March 15 and 18, April 9 and 30, May 2 and 14, June 18, July 7 and 8, August 27 and 28, and September 12, 1925; January 19, February 1, March 1, 2, 3, 4, and 8, May 14, June 16, 23, and 28, 1926; July 29, 1927; September 10, 1947; and from the proceedings of Interference 77,716 and the Court of Claims case. Hebern's rotor patents include 1,510,441, 1,683,072, 1,861,857 (the biggest U.S. patent on cryptography), 2,269,341, and 2,373,890.

419 Friedman solution: Friedman, II, 114.

419 top naval cryptosystem: Safford in Court of Claims case testimony, at 8–9.

419 IBM: This is Interference 77,716; Noll was an employee of IBM. Interferences 77,445 and 77,446 were combined with 77,716. Interferences 78,370 and 79,267, also brought on by Hebern against IBM employees, were dissolved.

PAGE

420 Koch: information from his son, H. E. Koch of The Hague, obtained by Maurits de Vries, March, 1963. Octrooiraad, letter, March 7, 1963, for patent assignment. The corresponding U.S. patent is 1,533,252.
420 Scherbius: biographical information from German patents 318,911, 331,419, and 331,683.
420 Scherbius patents: in the United States, 1,556,964 for codewords; 1,584,660 for numerical rotors; 1,657,411 for standard rotors.
421 Enigma models: Dr. Siegfried Türkel, *Chiffrieren mit Geräten und Maschinen* (Graz: Verlag von Ulr. Mosers Buchhandlung, 1927), 71–94, plates M-P.
421 Gewerkschaft Securitas: assignee of first Scherbius patent.
421 Chiffriermaschinen Aktiengesellschaft: *Handbuch der Deutschen Aktien-Gesellschaften* (Berlin: Verlag für Börsen- und Finanzliteratur), 1925, II, 2888, for founding; 1930, III, 3988; 1935, V, 6610, for no dividends and dissolution. Hardie translations.
421 Postal Union: Türkel, 77–78.
421 *Radio News:* Dr. Alfred Gradenwitz, "Secrecy in Radio," V (January, 1924), 878, 997–998.
421 flyers and pamphlets: *Die Schreibende Enigma-Chiffriermaschine*, undated one-page broadside; *Ciphering Typewriter Enigma*, undated 16-page pamphlet, with "natural inquisitiveness" at 5.
422 dimensions: NA, Microcopy T-78, Roll 153, Frame 6085796.
422 top Army and Air Force system, signal officers' views: Colonel Herbert Flesch, retired signal officer of the Luftwaffe, letter, March 22, 1964.
422 patent 52,279: The operation of this patent can be best understood from General Cartier, "Le Secret en Radiotélégraphie," *Radio Electricité*, VII (January 10, 1926), 6–10. It is also described in H. Stålhane, *Hemlig Skrift: Coder och Chiffrermaskiner* (Stockholm: Lindfors Bökforlag, 1934), at 217–220. The corresponding U.S. patent is 1,502,376.
422 Damm biography: Yves Gyldén, interviews, April 28, 29, 30, 1962; C. A. Lindmark, untitled manuscript of recollections of his work as an engineer with Damm, March 12 and 15, 1959. I am grateful to Bertil R. Gustring for his oral translation.
424 Craig: assignment of his patent rights, June 8, 1915, filed at the patent office, Stockholm (information supplied by Dr. Käärik).
424 founding of firm: Gyldén interviews; Lindmark; Bertil R. Gustring, "Ciphers and Ciphering Machines," *The Bulletin of the American Society of Swedish Engineers*, XXXVI (October, 1941), 6–9, at 8; Boris C. W. Hagelin, interviews, May 8 and 9, 1962.
424 machines: Lindmark; Stålhane, 217–229 (with illustrations); *Aktiebolaget Cryptograph* [an illustrated advertising pamphlet] (Stockholm, 1922). U.S. Patent 1,502,376 incorporates the influence letter; 1,484,477 for codewords; 1,644,239 for links; others are 1,233,035, 1,540,107, and 1,663,624.
425 business difficulties: Lindmark.
425 Hagelin enters: Hagelin interviews; Gustring, 8.
425 Swedish Army: Hagelin interviews.

Notes

PAGE

425 B-21 and B-211: Stålhane, 242–246 (with photographs); U.S. Patent 1,846,105; *The Hagelin Cryptographers: Ciphering Machines, type B-211 and C-36* (Stockholm: A. B. Cryptoteknik, 1936), at 4–5; Eyraud, 200–201.

425 purchase of firm: Gyldén interviews.

426 most compact, French request: Gustring, 8.

426 adding machine: Hagelin interviews.

426 C-36: *The Hagelin Cryptographers*, at 6–7.

426 5,000: Philip Lorraine, "Miljonar pa Chiffer," *Allt*, No. 6 (1956), 48–50 at 49.

426 turning point, time not ripe: Gustring, 8; Hagelin interviews.

426 Gyldén analyses: Yves Gyldén, *Analysis, from the Point of View of Cryptanalysis, of "Cryptographer Type C-36," Provided with 6 Key Wheels, 27 Slide Bars, the Latter Having Movable Projections, Single or Multiple* (Stockholm, May 9, 1938), and Yves Gyldén, *Analysis of the "Model C-36" Cryptograph* [5 keywheels, 25 slidebars] *from the Viewpoint of Cryptanalysis* (Stockholm, February 26, 1936). Both are typewritten documents marked "Translated from the French" and annotated by Friedman.

427 American negotiations, "a normal visa": Hagelin interviews; Philip L. Lorraine, "The Cipher No Spy Can Crack," *Industria*, LI, No. 11E, (1955), 62–63 at 63; Harris, 335.

427 M-209, division to battalions: United States, War Department, *Converter M-209, M-209-A, M-209-B (cipher)*, Technical Manual 11-380, March 17, 1944 (Washington, D.C.: U.S. Government Printing Office, 1944), at 1; Harris, 335–336.

427 400 a day, 140,000, Italian Navy: Hagelin interviews.

427 royalties: 84th Congress, Senate, Committee on the Judiciary, Hearings on H.R. 2068 (Friedman bill), testimony of Stuart Hedden, Hagelin's lawyer, at 17.

427 operation: machine itself.

431 M-209 solution: Howard T. Oakley, *The Hagelin Cryptographer (Model C-38)—Converter M-209: Reconstruction of the Key Elements* (mimeographed, May 12, 1950); Gyldén analyses. NA, Microcopy T-501, Roll 322, Frame 108, reports a German M-209 solution; so does Harris, 90–91.

432 "with my earnings": Lorraine, 63, corrected by Hagelin.

432 move to Zug: Hagelin interviews.

432 factory: visits during Hagelin interviews.

433 machines: pamphlets issued by Crypto AG: II 3011-a, *Cryptographer Type C-52* (January, 1958); II 3096, *Pocket Cryptographer Type CD-55* (August, 1959); II 3076c, *Auxiliary Devices for Teleciphering (Telecrypto) Series T-55* (October, 1959); 3052b, *Keyboard Attachment Unit Type B-52* (December, 1958). Prices and total costs from Boris Hagelin, Jr., interview, November 3, 1961.

433 customers: Hagelin interviews.

434 "tremendous number," "not good business practice": Crypto AG pamphlet V. 7002e, *Usage of Hagelin Cryptographer C-52* (October, 1962), at 1, 3.

Chapter 14 DUEL IN THE ETHER: THE AXIS

In this and succeeding chapters, citations in the form "T-175:477:7334380–411" refer to captured German World War II records published on microfilm by the National Archives. T-175 is the microcopy number, which varies for different groups of records; 477 is the microfilm roll number; 7334380–411 means microfilm frame numbers 7334380 to 7334411. A citation to "*Guide 39*" will refer to No. 39 of the *Guides to German Records Microfilmed at Alexandria, Va.* (Washington, D.C.: National Archives, 1958–), an indispensable series of mimeographed finding aides. "Churchill, IV, 200" will mean page 200 of volume IV (*The Hinge of Fate*) of his *The Second World War* (Boston: Houghton Mifflin Company, 1948–1953).

I want to thank Miss Katherina (Bucha) Frowein for her researches on my behalf amongst the interminable spools of German microfilm.

PAGE

435 prewar Polish solution: Wilhelm F. Flicke, *War Secrets in the Ether*, trans. Ray W. Pettengill (Washington, D.C.: National Security Agency, 1953), 128.

435 message of August 31: Birger Dahlerus, *The Last Attempt* (London: Hutchinson & Co., [1948]), 106; William L. Shirer, *The Rise and Fall of the Third Reich* (New York: Simon and Schuster, 1960), 587–589; Mario Toscano, "Probleme particolari della storia della seconda guerra mondiale," *Rivista di Studi Politici Internazionali*, XVII (July–September, 1950), 388–398 at 397. Dahlerus says that the message was received at 12:45, but I cannot credit that it was cryptanalyzed, translated, and delivered in less than an hour.

436 Selchow: Flicke, 81; *Trials of War Criminals before the Nuernberg Military Tribunal under Control Council Law No. 10, Case 11: United States of America vs. Ernst von Weizsaecker, et al.*, Nuernberg, October, 1946–April, 1949, testimony of Kurt Selchow, September 8, 1948, 20458–20484 at 20460. This transcript is mimeographed. Referred to henceforth as Selchow.

436 Referat I Z, Pers Z: German Foreign Office organizational charts at T-120: 247:183913, T-120:1029:406770, T-120:1780:406640, T-120:236:170704.

436 Ribbentrop takes Chifferbüro: Selchow, 20464.

436 two groups of cryptanalysts: Hans Rohrbach, interviews, May 2 and 3, 1962.

436 Kunze: interview, May 4, 1962.

437 Paschke: interview, May 3, 1962.

437 Schauffler: interview, May 6, 1962. Schauffler received his doctorate in mathematics with a dissertation involving cryptanalytics—*Eine Anwendung zyklischer Permutationen und Ihre Theorie* (Marburg: mimeographed, 1948); it has been translated by Hardie.

437 Schauffler's studies for Pers z: See bibliography in Hans Rohrbach, "Mathematische und maschinelle Methoden beim chiffrieren und dechiffrieren," *FIAT Review of German Science, 1939–1946: Applied Mathematics*, Part I (Wiesbaden: Office of Military Government for Germany: Field Information Agencies, Technical, 1948), 233–257. This article is of

Notes 1065

PAGE

primary importance for a knowledge of modern cryptology. Bradford Hardie has made an excellent translation. Several other translations exist, including a French one; to facilitate reference I cite the paper by section instead of by page, and as Rohrbach *FIAT* to distinguish it from his interviews. As for the papers listed in the bibliography: Pers z hid them under the eaves of Burgscheidungen Castle when the Americans captured Pers z. But when Schauffler and Rohrbach sent one of Rohrbach's students to bring the box back from the castle, which was in the Soviet zone of occupation, the caretaker of the castle tipped off the Russians. They confiscated the box as the student was waiting with it at the railroad station.

438 Langlotz, Hoffman, Scherschmidt: T-120:247:183913.
438 recruiting: Miss Asta Friedrichs, interview, August 15, 1963.
438 Rohrbach: interview; *Wer Ist Wer*, XIV.
438 Köthe: interview, May 21, 1964; *Wer Ist Wer*, XIV.
438 Deubner: Friedrichs.
438 locations: Rohrbach interview, Friedrichs, Köthe.
439 von der Schulenberg: Not Count Friedrich Werner von der Schulenberg, German ambassador to Russia at the time of the Hitler attack, nor Count Fritz von der Schulenberg, both of whom were executed in connection with the July 20 attack on Hitler, on November 10 and August 10, 1944, respectively (Shirer, 1072).
439 security measures: Friedrichs.
439 Selchow a Nazi: Selchow, 20460-1.
439 statistics, information group, language bonuses: Friedrichs.
440 machines: Rohrbach *FIAT*, §F.
440 Krug: Rohrbach interview, Friedrichs.
440 difference method: Rohrbach *FIAT*, §G3; Rohrbach interview; Eyraud, 240-245. My example is adapted from one provided by Bradford Hardie, to whom I am indebted for it. A rudimentary but precocious form appears in Kerckhoffs, 57.
443 translucent paper: Rohrbach *FIAT*, §F2.
444 Italian, French, English 40,000-additive codes: Kunze, Köthe.
444 Japanese code: Rohrbach interview.
445 von Papen message: T-120:1768:028378.
445 Woermann memo: T-120:598:001669-70; Rohrbach interview. Ribbentrop took into account British knowledge of Italian cryptograms in a memorandum of April 21, 1941 (*DGFP*, XII, 593).
445 "This is good to know": Count Galeazzo Ciano, *The Ciano Diaries, 1939–1943*, ed. Hugh Gibson (Garden City, N.Y.: Doubleday & Company, 1946), entry for May 25, 1941.
445 small countries' codes: Friedrichs.
445 Selchow distribution: Selchow, 20472.
445 green F, "Kann nicht": Friedrichs.
446 Brown as Bundy: Rohrbach interview, Köthe.
446 nations whose codes Pers z solved: affidavits of Paschke and Selchow (they are identical, Selchow's being based on Paschke's), respectively Exhibits

55 and 54 in Trials of War Criminals . . . , Case 11. Originals in NA, RG 238. I have substituted "Dominican Republic" for their "Santo Domingo."
446 Forschungsamt: Flicke, 103–109; Walter Schellenberg, *The Labyrinth: Memoirs of Walter Schellenberg*, trans. Louis Hagen (New York: Harper & Brothers, 1956), 254–255.
447 Prince Christoph of Hesse: *Almanach de Gotha*, 1941.
447 Braune Blätter: *Guide 17*, 45; T-77:661:1863503. These were evidently so called because the solutions were distributed on sheets of light brown paper.
447 27 recorded conversations: [United States], Office of the United States Chief of Counsel for Prosecution of Axis Criminality, *Nazi Conspiracy and Aggression* (Washington, D.C.: U.S. Government Printing Office, 1946), V, 628–654.
447 milk-marked ballots: Shirer, 273–274.
449 diplomatic telegrams, telephone conversations: *Guide 32*, 128; *Guide 33*, 6.
449 RSHA: invaluable outline of its administrative history by Robert Wolfe in preface to *Guide 39*. Amt I was personnel; Amt II, organization, administration, and law.
449 Austrian cryptanalytic documents: Schellenberg, 31.
449 Höttl and Figl: Wilhelm Hoettl, *Hitler's Paper Weapon*, trans. Basil Creighton (London: Rupert Hart-Davis, 1955), 132. Höttl's chronology is telescoped but may be straightened out by the dates that Jost headed Amt VI (1938 to early 1942).
449 plaintext telegram: *Guide 33*, 4.
450 Spanish code: Himmler File, Box 402, Folder 65, German Papers, Manuscript Division, Library of Congress. I am indebted to Maxwell W. Bowers of Clarksburg, West Virginia, for a tentative reconstruction of the code, which varies in some particulars from mine.
450 Ominata: Robert Boucard, *Les Dessous de l'Espionnage, 1939–1945* (Paris: Éditions Descamps, 1958), 130.
450 Schellenberg and Heydrich requests: Schellenberg, 237, 235.
450 Schellenberg sees Göring: Schellenberg, 254–255.
450 Amt VI secret communications department: Schellenberg, 364. Dr. Otto-Ernst Schüddekopf of the Anglo-American branch of Amt VI prepared an elementary treatise on cryptology which is preserved in the RSHA archives, T-175:458:2974805-25.
450 digraphic cipher: T-175:477:7334380-411.
450 RSHA cipher machines: receipts at T-175:60:2576855-70.
450 "Every three weeks": Schellenberg, 361–362. He names Fellgiebel and Thiele.
450 Göring raid on Pers z: Selchow, 20464.
451 Operation Cicero: L. C. Moyzisch, *Operation Cicero*, trans. Constantine Fitzgibbon and Heinrich Fraenkel (New York: Coward-McCann, Inc., 1950), esp. 50, 52, 111; Eleysa Bazna, *I Was Cicero* (New York: Harper & Row, 1962); Schellenberg, 337, 340; Kunze, Paschke.
452 Höttl and Hungarians: Hoettl, *Hitler's Paper Weapon*, 132–138. The mid-1944 date is fixed by the dates of Sztojay's premiership (March 22 to August 24, 1944).

Notes

PAGE

453 Abwehr: Paul Leverkuehn, *German Military Intelligence* (London: Weidenfeld & Nicolson, 1954), 1, 28–31, 41; T-175:470:2991464; Shirer, 1026.
454 Buschenhagen cryptanalytic service: Flicke, 81.
454 "In order to cultivate": T-79:65:211. Hardie translation.
454 German military communication intelligence in the 1920s and 1930s: Flicke, 85–99, 115–117.
455 Fellgiebel: personnel file in NA, World War II Records Division. These records are cited henceforth as NA, WW2.
455 Amtsgruppe WNV: "Auszug aus den Dienstanweisungen und Arbeitsplänen von Chef WNV, Ag WNV und den unterstellten Abteilungen," September 28, 1944, in NA, WW2.
455 Thiele: personnel file in NA, WW2.
456 Kempf and Kettler: personnel files in NA, WW2; Flicke, 293, 151.
456 Chiffrierabteilung and officials: "Arbeitsplan der Abteilung Chi der Ag WNV" [1944], in NA, WW2. 1945 organization deduced from OKW telephone directory listing for Chi, T-78:43:6005283. Schellenberg, 113, for description of Madrid intercept post.
457 Fenner, Novopaschenny: Flicke, 291–293.
458 Stein: telephone interview, August 25, 1964.
458 superencipherment-stripping device: Rohrbach *FIAT*, §F2.
458 locations of Chi: Gisbert Hasenjaeger, a mathematician who was on the staff, interviews, September 24 and November 21, 1964; T-78:43:6005283.
458 Fellgiebel and Thiele removals: personnel files; Shirer, 1057, 1072.
458 Praun: personnel file in NA, WW2.
458 German Army ciphers: Hagelin interviews; T-78:158:6085796; T-311:134: 7108488–9, 7179071, 7179122, 7179138–9 (latter for "Tarntafeln..."). Sacco, §46c; U.S. Patent 1,912,983; Hans Rohrbach, "Chiffrierverfahren der neuesten Zeit," *Archiv der elektrischen Übertragung*, II (December, 1948), 362–369, at §13 (translation by Howard Oakley), for Siemens machine.
459 Fernmeldeaufklärung 7: Colonel Karl-Albert Mügge, "Die Deutsche Heeres-Fernmeldeaufklärung in Mittelmeerraum," *Fernmelde-Impulse*, VII (May, 1964), 9–17, translated by Hardie.
460 Yugoslav solutions: Flicke, 140–141; Wilhelm Hoettl, *The Secret Front*, trans. R. H. Stevens (New York: Frederick A. Praeger, Inc., 1954), 165.
460 German solution of M-209: T-501:322:108; Dr. K. A. Hirsch, letter, September 1, 1962, conveying information from Dr. Rudolf Kochendorfer; Harris, 90–91.
460 52nd Anti-Aircraft brigade, grid square 43835, no firing: T-501:321:575, 329; T-501:322:219.
461 wadi bombing: Mügge, 16.
461 Carrocetto factory: quoted in Peter Tompkins, *A Spy in Rome* (New York: Simon and Schuster, 1962), 119–120.
461 "Yet the actual attack": Major General F. W. von Mellenthin, *Panzer Battles*, trans. H. Betzler (Norman, Okla.: University of Oklahoma Press, 1956), 325.

PAGE

461 Nachrichten-Verbindungswesen: organizational chart of Luftfahrtministerium, 1944, T-177:1: frame unknown; organizational chart of O.K.L., T-321:75: frame unknown.

461 Luftwaffe cryptosystems: Flesch; T-321:R70:4820996–1001; T-321:75: frame unknown.

461 Funkaufklärungsdienst: Notebook Concerning the Organization and Equipment of the Funkaufklärungsdienst of the Luftwaffe, Miscellaneous German Air Force Collection, Box 501, German Papers, Library of Congress Manuscript Division; T-321:75: frame unknown.

463 Syko: Howard K. Morgan, *Codes and Ciphers: Prepared for aircraft flight and ground crews* (Washington, D.C.: The Infantry Journal, 1944), 58–59, for early Syko; Eyraud, 192–194; Sacco, §29; Charles Eyraud, interview, May 14, 1962; Tompkins, 119; Alexander d'Agapeyeff, *Codes and Ciphers* (London: Oxford University Press, 1949; rev. ed., third impression, 1960), 117–119.

464 Ploesti: James Dugan and Carroll Stewart, *Ploesti: The Great Ground-Air Battle of 1 August 1943* (New York: Random House, 1962), 86–87.

465 B-Dienst early successes: Captain S. W. Roskill, *The War at Sea, 1939–1945* (London: Her Majesty's Stationery Office, 1954—), I, 19, 267; Duncan Grinnell-Milne, *The Silent Victory: September 1940* (London: Bodley Head, 1958), 133.

465 Norway invasion: Grand Admiral Erich Raeder, *My Life*, trans. Harry W. Drexel (Annapolis, Md.: U.S. Naval Institute, 1960), 307; Grinnell-Milne, 134.

465 "completely outwitted": Churchill, I, 600.

465 *Atlantis:* Wolfgang Frank and Captain Bernhard Rogge, *The German Raider Atlantis*, trans. R. O. B. Long (New York: [Pocket Books, Inc.] Ballantine Books, 1956), 68, 40–42, 49, 68, 86; Roskill, I, 281, 283.

466 BAMS code: Great Britain, Admiralty, Signal Department, *Merchant Ships' Signal Book*, I: *Visual Signalling Code and Instructions*; II: *Merchant Ships' Code*; III: *Wireless Signalling Instructions* (various dates).

466 value of merchant solutions: Harald Busch, *U-Boats at War*, trans. L. P. R. Wilson (New York: [Pocket Books, Inc.] Ballantine Books, 1955), 40.

466 "The Battle of the Atlantic": Churchill, V, 6.

466 Western approaches messages: Roskill, I, 468.

468 "These situation reports": Admiral Karl Doenitz, *Memoirs: Ten Years and Twenty Days*, trans. R. H. Stevens (Cleveland, Ohio: World Publishing Co., 1959), 325, 242; Roskill, II, 364.

468 March convoys: Doenitz, 326–328; Roskill, II, 365–366.

468 "It was the greatest": Doenitz, 328.

468 darkest hour of the war, "The Germans never": Donald Macintyre, *The Battle of the Atlantic* (New York: The Macmillan Company, 1961), 181.

468 Italian naval cryptanalysts: Franco Maugeri, *From the Ashes of Disgrace*, ed. Victor Rosen (New York: Reynal & Hitchcock, 1948), 31. Maugeri was director of the Servizio Informazione Segreto.

Notes

PAGE

468 scout plane message solution: Maugeri, 23.
469 solution of order to Cunningham and results: Marc' Antonio Bragadin, *The Italian Navy in World War II*, trans. Gale Hoffman (Annapolis, Md.: U.S. Naval Institute, 1957), 91; Roskill, I, 427.
469 S.I.M. Sezione 5: *Il Processo Roatta* (Roma: Donatello de Luigi, 1945), 29–30, 194; General Cesare Amè, *Guerra Segreta in Italia 1940–1943* (Rome: Gherardo Casini, 1954), 5–6, 8, 47–50; Amè, interview, May 11, 1962. Amè was director of the S.I.M.
469 Gamba: Amè interview; Amè, *Guerra Segreta*, 48; Agencia Nazionale Stampa Associata (ANSA), "Morto Asso Controspionaggio Italiano" (January 23, 1965); "Crittografia," *Enciclopedia Italiana*, XI, 986–988 (1931).
469 Mancini: Amè interview.
469 Italian codes: Eyraud interview.
469 Yugoslavia: Amè, *Guerra Segreta*, 74–76.
469 "naked rear": Churchill, III, 172.
470 3,500 solutions, Bulletin I: Amè, *Guerra Segreta*, 51, 50.
471 Italy's Rumanian and Turkish solutions: *The Ciano Diaries*, March 10, 1942, October 18, 1940, July 20, 1941, August 16 and 31, 1942, January 4, 1943.
471 Italy's British solutions: *The Ciano Diaries*, September 9, December 24 and 30, 1942, January 16, 1943.
472 Loris Gherardi and theft in Rome: Colonel Norman E. Fiske, letters, May 4 and 24, June 16 and 30, 1964, April 27, 1965; Wickersham (Fiske's civilian aide), letters, May 16 and June 20, 1964, April 24, 1965; Department of State, letter, June 21, 1964; Amè, letter, September 27, 1964. Paul Carell, *The Foxes of the Desert*, trans. Mervyn Savill (London: Macdonald & Co., 1960), 213, 227, says that Bianca Bergami, the daughter of a high-ranking Fascist militia officer, "borrowed" the code. My efforts to trace her in Rome have borne no fruit, and Amè says in his letter that he thinks that the tale of Bianca and the implication of seduction are "fantasy." The United States Army has not yet declassified its counterintelligence report on the case.
473 Fellers: service biography. In letters of July 18 and August 8, 1963, Fellers said that the British did not habitually advise him of future operations and that he only once reported an advance operation on the basis of British information; his other predictions were based on personal estimates and guesses.
473 Fellers messages: Amè, *Guerra Segreta*, 96–98; Flicke, 193–196; Carell, 227; Leonard Mosley, *The Cat and the Mice* (New York: Harper & Brothers, 1958), 91–92.
474 message No. 11119: declassified from U.S. Army files. This message agrees perfectly with Amè's, at 104.
474 Malta message and operation: Amè, 104–105; Flicke, 195; Roskill, II, 69–72.
475 "The approach": Churchill, IV, 302.
475 Seeböhm unit: Mellenthin, 52, 135; Churchill, IV, 415, for El Adem; Carell, 227; Mosley, 89–90.

PAGE

476 "a very important factor": Mellenthin, 110–111.
476 Rommel independent reading of Fellers: Mosley, 90–91.
476 Seebőhm death: Mellenthin, 135; NA, WW2, letter, January 19, 1965.
476 two officers check Fellers: Fellers, letter, August 8, 1963.
476 prisoner of war: Mosley, 90–91.
476 British pick up messages: Fellers letter; Mosley, 92.
476 "long, detailed": Mosley, 92.
476 British tell Americans: This is the most likely, in view of their picking up the messages, as opposed to the incredible tales given in Flicke, 196, and Mosley, 93.
476 Fellers citation: service biography.
476 no M-138 solution: Flicke, 197
477 profit from Fernmeldeaufklärung capture: Major General R. F. H. Nalder, *The History of British Army Signals in the Second World War* (London: Royal Signals Institution, 1953), 257–260.
477 Alamein build-up and camouflage: Lieutenant General Fritz Bayerlein, "El Alamein," in *The Fatal Decisions*, eds. Seymour Friedin and William Richardson (New York: William Sloane Associates, 1956), at 107–109.
477 "Before Alamein": Churchill, IV, 603.

Chapter 15 DUEL IN THE ETHER: NEUTRALS AND ALLIES

All citations and abbreviations from the previous chapter carry over in this. There is one addition. Citations consisting of a virgule followed by a number, as "/310," refer to the item numbers in DSDF 119.25, "Cipher and Telegraph Codes.". In full the citation would be DSDF 119.25/310. Other DSDF items are cited in full. DSDF 811.727 ("Telegraph Codes—United States") is without interest.

478 50 in villa: Eyraud interview; Eyraud, letter, March 15, 1962.
478 Mandel cipher failure: "Vichy's Experts Stumped by Code Mandel Used," *The New York Times* (April 26, 1941).
478 Swedish cryptanalytic bureau: Unless otherwise noted, all details are from Yves Gyldén, interviews, April 28, 29, 30, 1962, with notes corrected by Dr. Käljo Käärik, an amateur cryptologist and acquaintance of Gyldén's in Sweden; Dr. Carl-Otto Segerdahl, interview, May 1, 1962; Dr. Arne Beurling, interviews, September 17 and November 9, 1963, November 21, 1964.
478 Torpadie solution: "Några ord om chifferskrift," *Historisk Tidskrift*, VII (1888), 376–383.
479 *Chifferbyråernas* ... : *Revue Militaire Française* (1931), 211–231.
479 Warburg: Gyldén. Warburg wrote "Chiffer," *Nordisk Familjebok*, 3rd ed. (1923–1937), XXI, columns 830–835.
479 talks to coeds: *Stockholm Tidningen* (March 3, 1939).

Notes

479 Feilitzen: *Vem Är Det: Svensk Biografisk Handbok, 1963*. Feilitzen denied in a telephone interview that he was a wartime cryptanalyst, but I think that was pro forma and is not to be believed.
479 Beurling: *Who's Who in America, 1962–63*; AMS.
480 Nazi fish-price code: Segerdahl; system is also mentioned by Schellenberg, 100.
481 Sandler: *Vem Är Det: Svensk Biografisk Handbok, 1963*; Joachim Joesten, *Stalwart Sweden* (Garden City, N.Y.: Doubleday, Doran & Co., 1943), 18–29. Sandler's book is *Chiffer: En Bok om Litterära och Historiska Hemligskrifter* (Stockholm: Walhström & Widstrand, 1943).
481 Achilles: Segerdahl; German Foreign Office, letter, January 10, 1964.
483 Bohemann tells Cripps: "Telegram fran Churchill banade vag till Roosevelt" and "Tyskarnas hemliga kod forcerades av srenskar," both *Svenska Dagbladet* (October 30, 1964), 5; "Churchill stor beundrare av Karl XII: Chifferbragd i UD," *Dagens Nyheter* (October 30, 1964), 29; "Han dechiffrerade tyska krigskoden pa fjorton dagar," *Dagens Nyheter* (November 1, 1964), 1.
483 Germans use Swedish wires: See demand in *DGFP*, XII, 1041.
483 $60,000 a year: /630, a letter from the American chargé d'affaires at San Salvador, December 7, 1925, reporting a conversation with the British chargé there a few years earlier.
484 Department of Communications: Sara Turing, *Alan M. Turing* (Cambridge: W. Heffer & Sons, 1959), 67.
484 Bletchley Park: D. C. Low, *The History of Bletchley Park and Mansion* (mimeographed, no publisher, 1963).
484 MI 8: Nalder, 118. Administrative problems of the British military cryptographic organization at 252–256, 162.
484 August 20 change: Captain Ellis M. Zacharias, *Secret Missions: The Story of an Intelligence Officer* (New York: G. P. Putnam's Sons, 1946), 86–88.
485 "a great setback": quoted, Roskill, I, 264.
485 30,000: *PHA*, 3:1147, 29:2408.
485 solutions 097975 and 098846: *PHA*, 35:669, 690.
485 distribution: *PHA*, 35:674 and other messages.
486 "in their original form": Churchill, II, 654.
486 Joint Intelligence Committee: James R. M. Butler, *Grand Strategy*, United Kingdom Military Series (London: Her Majesty's Stationery Office, 1953), 585.
486 Britain had more cryptanalyzed intercepts: *PHA*, 3:1197.
486 PURPLE keys radioed to London: *PHA*, 36:68.
486 U.S.-British-Canadian-Australian cooperation: *PHA*, 2:947, 8:3594, 34:85, 36:64.
486 Cynthia: H. Montgomery Hyde, *Room 3603: The Story of the British Intelligence Center in New York during World War II* (New York: Farrar, Straus & Co., 1962), 105–108 for Lais, 108–120 for French codes, 215–216 for Spanish. Churchill, III, 218 and 220 for "Towards the end of March" and "disposed of all." Hyde implies, at 115, that the request

to get the French ciphers resulted from plans to invade North Africa. But this operation was not definitely decided upon until July, 1942, several months after the request was made, and I think it much more likely that Madagascar was the stimulant for the request, particularly in view of Churchill's request for "extreme vigilance about any [French] convoys" (VI, 227). An illustration of the French superencipherment tables appears opposite 116. The matter of the timing is corrected, Cynthia's real identity disclosed, and further details given on the Italian and French code thefts, in Hyde's later book, *Cynthia: The Spy Who Changed the Course of the War* (London: Hamish Hamilton, 1966). In a suit by Lais' heirs against Hyde in Milan, Paolo Comel, described as the head of the Italian Navy code communication department during the war, said the code used by the warships in the Cape Matapan battle was issued four months earlier, when Lais was already in the U.S., and that it was used only between the ships and naval headquarters in Rome and was issued to no one else (Associated Press story, "Quiet Canadian," November 23, 1966).

489 binding color designates codes: /332.
489 RED and BLUE codes have five-figure groups: /359.
489 "better and less expensive": /73.
489 "open book": /468.
489 Larrabee: Hitt, 53–54; /87, /317, /318 for PEKIN and POKES. DSDF 119.25 contains many other references to losses of Larrabee cards, changes of keywords, etc. DSDF 763.7211H68/73 assigns keyword LIBERTY to consuls at Batavia and Penang.
489 "In reference to": /117.
489 no funds: /118.
489 Mexicans obtain RED code: /174, reply to DSDF 812.00/16037.
490 minister to Rumania: Allen W. Dulles, *The Craft of Intelligence* (New York: Harper & Row, 1963), 73–74.
490 "special cipher": /698.
490 GREEN code: My reconstruction, based on codetext given in DSDF/862.-20212/82A, message 4494 of March 1, 1917, from State Department to American Embassy, London, outgoing plaintext of which is marked into sections for encoding, incoming plaintext of which has codetext attached.
490 foreign employees had run of embassies: Yardley, 211; Robert Murphy, *Diplomat Among Warriors* (Garden City, N.Y.: Doubleday & Company, 1964), 6.
490 clerk to Pearl Harbor commandant: House of Representatives, Committee on Naval Affairs, *Sundry Legislation Affecting the Naval Establishment, 1935*, Hearings, 74:1 (GPO, 1935), 793.
490 Leipzig: Murphy, 7.
490 rumors of British solution of U.S. Codes: "U.S. Secret Code Known in England," *St. Paul Dispatch* (May 8, 1916); /217.
490 monthly key change, "I never realized": /364.
490 *Universal Pocket Code:* /411, /421, /424.
491 GRAY used for confidential messages: /410.

Notes

PAGE

491 Thurber: "Exhibit X," *The New Yorker*, XXIV (March 6, 1948), 26–28 at 26.
491 State-Navy cipher: /468, /631.
491 farewell speech in GRAY: Charles W. Thayer, *Diplomat* (New York: Harper & Brothers, 1959), 150.
491 San Salvador chargé suggestion: /630.
492 16th-century codes: Yardley, 362.
492 "The Department is in receipt": /779. So little thought did the Department give to these communications that it used "25th instant" in a letter written on the 2nd of the month!
492 "There is only one," "Nothing less": Yardley, 365, 366.
492 "Suggest telegrams": /722.
492 Hornbeck minute: DSDF 793.94/2149.
493 broken wax seals: /828.
493 "I could not help": /823, DSDF 793.94/4727.
493 Guggenheim: interview, November 3, 1964.
493 Roosevelt prodding, BROWN code stolen: Thayer, 144–145.
493 C-1, D-1 superencipherment: DSDF 124.946/147; Thayer, 145.
493 Munich crisis: Thayer, 149.
493 M-138: DSDF 124.946/147 dates some M-138 sets in 1939; Rohrbach, interview.
493 triple priority message: *PHA*, 15:1717 shows this message divided into groups of 30 letters for encipherment.
493 Roosevelt uses naval codes: "Letters to *The Times:* Position of Mr. Bullitt" (February 19, 1948), 22:6–7; "Admiral Standley Reports Leaks in State Department Code in War" (September 19, 1948), 1:6–7; "Code's Weakness Held Known in '41" (December 10, 1948), 4:3–6, all *The New York Times;* Murphy, 232. "State Department Now Nation's Nerve Center," *The New York Times* (April 16, 1939), IV, 6:1–2 for feature on code room.
494 Madrid embassy: Ambassador Carton J. H. Hayes, *Wartime Mission to Spain*, quoted in Henry J. Taylor, *Men and Power* (New York: Dodd, Mead & Co., 1946), 49–50.
494 Thomsen messages: *DGFP*, IX, 73, and XI, 227.
494 German ambassador in Spain: *DGFP*, XI, 975.
494 German ambassador in Italy: *DGFP*, IX, 417.
494 Tyler Kent, "The removal": United States, *Department of State Bulletin* (September 3, 1944), 243–245 at 244.
495 "Because of his treachery": quoted in Bernard Newman, *Epics of Espionage* (New York: Philosophical Library, 1951), 150.
495 Ango Kenkyu Han and its successes: International Military Tribunal for the Far East, Exhibit 2964, affidavit of Kazuji Kameyama; *Ibid.*, Transcript, 10570, 26204–26206; Herbert Feis, *The Road to Pearl Harbor* (Princeton, N.J.: Princeton University Press, 1950), 173.
495 "One of the high": *PHA*, 2:582.
495 "Prince Konoye knows": Joseph C. Grew, *Ten Years in Japan* (New York: Simon and Schuster, 1944), 415.

PAGE
495 "Dear Cordell": DSDF 740.0011 Pacific War /856.
495 Grew misapprehension: *PHA*, 2:692.
496 deliberate delay: Robert J. C. Butow, *Tojo and the Coming of the War* (Princeton, N.J.: Princeton University Press, 1961), 391.
496 Pers z solution of American codes: Rohrbach *FIAT*, §G3, identified as American by Rohrbach interview; dates of 1925 and 1940 ascertained by dates of monographs on solving the system.
497 Müller, Friedrichs help solve 72,000-group code: Friedrichs.
497 Murphy's activities help: Friedrichs.
497 Murphy insists on State codes: Murphy, 291–292, 156. "Nazis Got U.S. Secrets, Diplomatic Book Hints," (Washington) *Evening Star* (May 11, 1959), for Murphy's confidence (even after the war) that Germans had not solved State Department codes.
497 "For Murphy," "From Murphy": Friedrichs. Corroborated by examination of messages in United States, Department of State, *Foreign Relations of the United States, Diplomatic Papers, 1942, II: Europe* (Washington, D.C.: U.S. Government Printing Office, 1962), at, for example, 443, 444, 449, 459, etc.
497 "We knew," "I wanted": Friedrichs.
498 solved messages of July 21 and August 2: T-120, frames FI/0568–0574. Originals in the above-cited *Foreign Relations* . . . 396–398, 406–407.
498 "documentary proof": *Ibid.*, 466.
498 "Fortunately, it was not," "I was never able," "only for messages," "the Germans never": Allen W. Dulles, *Germany's Underground* (New York: The Macmillan Company, 1947), 130–131.
499 Bibo's Dulles solutions: Hoettl, *The Secret Front*, 285.
499 naval systems: Original of the message of January 3, 1943, in the Franklin D. Roosevelt Library at Hyde Park, is on a naval communications form.
499 "Former Naval Person," "I sent my cables": Churchill, II, Book I, ch. 1.
499 attack on M-138: Rohrbach *FIAT*, §G3; Rohrbach interview.
501 State gets cipher machines: "Department of State Communications," in Senate, Committee on Government Operations, Subcommittee on National Security Staffing and Operations, *Administration of National Security*, Hearings, 88:2 (April 8, 1964), 505–509 at 505.
501 Parke to State: United States, Department of State, *Biographic Register, 1963*.
501 Division of Cryptography: United States, Office of the Federal Register, *United States Government Organization Manual, 1949* (Washington, D.C.: U.S. Government Printing Office, 1949), 97.
501 codewords: Bill Hines, "Operation Codename," *Infantry Journal*, LX (March, 1947), 42–43; Ray S. Cline, *Washington Command Post*, United States Army in World War II: The War Department (Department of the Army: Office of the Chief of Military History) (Washington, D.C.: U.S. Government Printing Office, 1951), 131.
502 crossword puzzles: Cornelius Ryan, *The Longest Day: June 6, 1944* (New York: Simon and Schuster, 1959), 46–48, 168–169. Perhaps as a result,

Notes

PAGE

"French Bar Crossword Puzzles [in newspapers]," *The New York Times* (September 22, 1944).

502 "I have crossed out": Churchill, V, 662.

503 "The name 'Round-up'," "boastful, ill-chosen," "hastened to rechristen": Churchill, IV, 436–437, 447.

503 Churchill coins OVERLORD: Omar Bradley, *A Soldier's Story* (New York: Henry Holt & Company, 1951), 172.

503 "The signals from": quoted in Ladislas Farago, *The Tenth Fleet* (New York: Ivan Obolensky, Inc., 1962), 223.

503 "the most gabby": Farago, 224.

503 Safford: Navy biography.

504 direction-finder net and operation: Farago, 224–227.

504 *U-158*: Samuel E. Morison, *The Battle of the Atlantic, September 1939–May 1943, History of United States Naval Operations in World War II*, I (Boston: Little, Brown & Co., 1947), 226–228.

504 *U-66*: Farago, 208–210, 225, for rapid horizon scanning.

504 intercept net: Farago, 225, 227.

504 *U-505* capture: Rear Admiral Daniel V. Gallery, *We Captured a U-Boat* (London: Sidgwick & Jackson, 1957), 200–201, 232–233, 243–244. The Radio Log Books of *U-505* (plaintext only) are in Box 374, German Papers, Manuscript Division, Library of Congress.

506 "climactic single episode": Farago, 270.

506 "In the latter half": Harald Busch, *U-Boats at War*, trans. L. P. R. Wilson (New York: [Pocket Books, Inc.] Ballantine Books, 1955), 138, 144. See also Farago, 161, 183, 221.

507 "Battles might be won": Churchill, III, 111–112.

507 "Reduced to the simplest": Farago, 221.

507 radio intelligence companies: Thompson, 386; Harris, 65 for "outstanding," 348 for "of material value" and "most constantly," 49, 118, 179.

507 German strategy from Japanese sources: Marshall at *PHA*, 3:1132.

508 loss of military attaché code: *PHA*, 3:1133.

508 Oshima Westwall message: I have heard this story from a number of sources, so that I believe it is true, but I have not been able to confirm it. Japanese archives report that Oshima's dispatches were destroyed in air raids (Mrs. Michi Freeman, letters, March 9 and July 15, 1964); Oshima himself burned all his papers and does not recall any such report (letter, June 5, 1964). In addition, General Sir John F. M. Whitely, intelligence chief for Eisenhower, does not recall the intercept (letter, August 16, 1964). However, entries in the OKW Kriegstagebuch for October 23 and November 4, 1943, refer to Oshima's tour.

508 FORTITUDE cover plan: Major L. F. Ellis, *Victory in the West, I: The Battle of Normandy*, United Kingdom Military Series (London: Her Majesty's Stationery Office, 1962), 103, 127; Bernard Fergusson, *The Watery Maze: The Story of Combined Operations* (New York: Holt, Rinehart, and Winston, 1961), 333–334.

509 "The final result": Churchill, V, 596.

509 "the enemy will probably": quoted in L. F. Ellis, 323.

PAGE

509 "to meet a very": Bradley, letter, January 7, 1965. General Lucius D. Clay, letter, January 18, 1965, could not recall any cases in which solutions played a critical role and said that cryptanalytic results "were not too important."
509 849th: Dr. Joseph S. Schick, letter, March 4, 1965.
509 pre-Bulge solutions: Edgar C. Reinke, letter, February 2, 1964.
509 failure to heed intelligence: Milton Shulman, *Defeat in the West* (London: Secker and Warburg, 1947), 223.
509 "young, trigger-smart": Colonel Robert S. Allen, *Lucky Forward* (New York: Vanguard Press, 1947), 56.
510 TYPEX: Eyraud interview; Kunze interview.
510 SIGABA never solved: Harris, 90, 344–345, 582.
510 loss of the SIGABA: Thomas M. Johnson, "Search for the Stolen Sigaba," *Army*, XII (February, 1962), 50–55; Frederick Ayer, Jr., *Yankee G-Man* (Chicago: Henry Regnery Co., 1957), 146–150; Col. David G. Erskine, letter, November 18, 1963.

Chapter 16 CENSORS, SCRAMBLERS, AND SPIES

I am grateful to Colonel Shaw and Walter Koenig for reading the parts of the manuscript dealing with their work and for suggesting corrections.

513 World War I censorship: Childs Cipher Papers, IV, and "Liverpool Codes," NA, RG 98, contain photocopies of cryptic messages intercepted by British censors in World War I.
513 Joe K: Hyde, 79–83; Alan Hynd, *Passport to Treason: The Inside Story of Spies in America* (New York: Robert M. McBride & Co., 1943), 148, 181; Michael Sayers and Albert E. Kahn, *Sabotage! The Secret War Against America* (New York: Harper & Brothers, 1942), 32–40, for reproductions of the secret-ink letters; Don Whitehead, *The FBI Story* (New York: Random House), 193–194, 344.
513 Luning: Theodore F. Koop, *Weapon of Silence* (Chicago: University of Chicago Press, 1946), 6–15.
515 14,462: Koop, 10.
515 90 buildings, 1,000,000 letters: Mary Knight, "The Secret War of Censors vs. Spies," *The Reader's Digest*, XLVIII (March, 1946), 79–83 at 79, 80.
515 banned items: Koop, 61–63, 70.
515 Madame Defarge: Charles Dickens, *A Tale of Two Cities* (1859, New York: Houghton Mifflin Co., 1931), Book II, chs. 15, 16; Book III, ch. 8, at 169, 170, 173, 177, 299–300. This has been called a purl of a system.
515 cable regulations, flowers: Koop, 64–65.
516 "dead...deceased": Fletcher Pratt, *Secret and Urgent* (Indianapolis: Bobbs-Merrill Company, 1939), 58.
516 codes: "British Lift Ban on Codes for Commercial Cables," *The New York Times* (December 29, 1939); "Modify Code Restrictions," *The New York Times* (April 6, 1940). *Restrictions of Service Imposed by Foreign*

Notes

PAGE

Governments on International Telegrams and Revised U.S. Censorship Regulations Now in Effect, issue of December 15, 1943 (New York: R.C.A. Communications, Inc.), for code regulations. "Argentina Limits Messages of Axis" (December 4, 1942), "Axis Envoys Protest Curb in Argentina" (December 18, 1942), "Argentina Ends Code Leaks; Moves to Curb Axis Agents" (May 29, 1943), "Holy See First to Suffer by Argentine Code Ban" (June 15, 1943), all *The New York Times*.

516 want ads, radio precautions: Koop, 62, 179–180.

516 Max Baer: Alfred Toombs, "Washington Communication: Cryptographic Broadcasts," *Radio News*, XXV (January, 1941), 15.

517 T.O.D. and Shaw: Harold R. Shaw, untitled 27-page manuscript dealing with his work in censorship (spring, 1964), at 3–7, 14–15. I am deeply indebted to Colonel Shaw for preparing this for me.

518 O.S.R.D. group: Shaw, 24. *Who Was Who in America, 1951–1960* for Lamb; *Who's Who in America, 1964–1965* for Chadwell, Brown; *AMS* for Eaton, Evans, Lothrop, Pierce.

518 hobbies catalogued, swimmer: Koop, 34.

518 economic clues, rare languages: Knight, 80.

519 security assistant: Shaw, 15.

519 New York field office: Melville F. Abrams, interview, May 18, 1964. Abrams was chief of its code and cipher section from September 1942 to July 1943. See also "2,000 Here Censor All Foreign Mail," *The New York Times* (May 15, 1942).

519 early jargon codes: Meister, *Päpstlichen*, 5–6, for papal; Bazeries, 10–13, for French.

519 stilted language: Koop, 60; Knight, 81.

519 cigars: Hoy, 102–104.

520 Dickinson: "Woman Accused of Using Letters on Dolls to Convey Military Data" (January 22, 1944), " 'Doll Woman' Enters Guilty Plea in Censor Case, Faces 10 Years" (July 29, 1944), " 'Doll Woman' Sentenced to Prison for 10 Years and Fined $10,000" (August 15, 1944), all *The New York Times*. Also Shaw, 19–20; Whitehead, 194–195.

521 "Pershing sails . . . ": Church, 17. The German ambassador to the United States in World War I, Count Johann von Bernstorff, says in his *My Three Years in America* (New York: Charles Scribner's Sons, 1920), 154, that he used null ciphers in press cables to pass messages to his Foreign Office through British Censorship.

521 "beating the censor," servicemen: Koop, 59–60, 45–46; Shaw, 11.

521 Nutsi: "A.E.F. Full of Steganographists but Censors Detect Their Codes," *The New York Times* (July 24, 1943).

521 family codes: "Navy Warns on 'Family Codes,'" *The New York Times* (May 29, 1943).

521 Trevanion: C. C. Bombaugh, *Oddities and Curiosities*, ed. Martin Gardner (reprinted New York: Dover Publications, Inc., 1957).

521 U-boat officers: Shaw, 16–17; Koop, 109.

522 semagraphic drawings: For some good examples, together with some null ciphers, see Melville Davisson Post, "German War Ciphers," *Everybody's*

Magazine, XXXVIII (June, 1918), 28–34. For semagrams, see Edmond Locard, *Traité de criminalistique*, VI (Lyon: Joannès Desvignes, 1937), "Les Correspondances secrètes," 831–931 at "Cryptographie à l'aide des objets," 901–903.

522 frustrating experience: Abrams.

522 technological steganography: For elementary forms see Allan Fea, *Secret Chambers and Hiding-Places* (London: S. H. Bousfield, 1901).

522 Pliny the Elder: *Natural History* xxvi.62, trans. W. H. S. Jones, Loeb Classical Library (Cambridge, Mass.: Harvard University Press, 1956), VIII, 311.

522 Ovid: iii.627ff. For other secret inks in antiquity, see Süss and Thorndike, I, 467.

522 Philo of Byzantium: Ch. Graux, "Notes Paléographiques: 2, L'encre à base métallique dans l'antiquité," *Revue de Philologie, de Littérature, et d'Histoire Anciennes*, nouvelle série, IV (1880), 82–85, at 83, quoting Philo's *Veteres Mathematici*, 102.

522 Qalqashandi: quoted in Bosworth, 23. Siegfried Türkel, "Eine orientalische sympathetische Tinte im Mittelalter," *Archiv für Kriminologie*, LXXVIII (1926), 166, for another Arabic secret ink.

522 secret inks in the Renaissance: Devos, 76; Meister, *Päpstlichen*, 18–19; Great Britain, Public Record Office, *Calendar of State Papers, Foreign Series*, XX (September, 1585–May, 1586) (London: His Majesty's Stationery Office, 1921), 705–708.

522 book with secret ink: Giovanni Battista Verini, *Secreti: e modi bellissimi nouamente inuestigati*, no date or place of publication, cited in Prince d'Essling, *Les livres à figures vénitiens* (Florence & Paris: Olschiki & Leclerc, 1909), No. 2572, and Max Sander, *Le livre à figures italiens* (New York: Stechert, 1941), No. 7552, who gives 1530 date.

522 Rautter: Knight, 83; Shaw, 18.

522 sympathetic inks in general: Dr. Edmond Locard, *Manuel de Technique Policière* (Paris: Payot, 1948), 238–242; Georges Écard, "Les encres invisibles," *Revue internationale de criminalistique*, X (1938), 225–256.

523 Dasch: Eugene Rachlis, *They Came to Kill: The Story of Eight Nazi Saboteurs in America* (New York: Random House, 1961), 64, 72–73, 162, 203.

523 striping: Dr. Sanborn C. Brown, interview, April 20, 1963.

524 4,600, 400: Knight, 81, 82.

524 Collins: Shaw, 14; Yardley, 60–76.

524 splitting, transfer: Brown.

525 Wurlitzer organ: Shaw, 25–26; Brown.

525 microdots: J. Edgar Hoover, "The Enemy's Masterpiece of Espionage," *The Reader's Digest*, XLVIII (April, 1946), 1–6; Shaw, 20–21; Brown. Both Herbert C. McKay, "Notes from a Laboratory," *American Photography*, XL (November, 1946), 38–49, 50, and A. Cuelenaere, "A Short History of Microphotography (High-Reduction Photography)," *Journal of Forensic Sciences*, IV (January, 1959), 83–90, with many photographs, provide historical background. Some of the original 1870 microphotographs may be seen in France's Musée Postal, Paris. See also G. W. W.

Notes

PAGE

Stevens, *Microphotography: Photography at Extreme Resolution* (New York: John Wiley & Sons, 1957). For concealing messages photographically, see A. Cuelenaere, "Cryptophotography," *International Criminal Police Review*, No. 102 (November, 1956), 284–290; Gilbert Renault (pseud. Rémy). *Comment devenir agent secret* (Paris: Éditions Albin Michel, 1963), 119–121.

526 R.I.D.: George E. Sterling, "The U.S. Hunt for Axis Agent Radios," *Intelligence Articles*, n.d., 35–54; George E. Sterling, "The R.I.D. Story," *Spark-Gap Times*, No. 16 (August 1, 1963), 13–23; No. 17 (October 1, 1963), 25–39; No. 18 (December 1, 1963), 7–27; No. 19 (February, 1964), 6–7. I am most grateful to Commissioner Sterling for sending me the *Spark-Gap Times* articles and for other help.

526 "In the routine": *Intelligence Articles*, 38.

527 McIntosh and Checkoway: George E. Sterling, letter, November 8, 1963.

528 Latin America: Sterling articles; Whitehead, 215–224. *Intelligence Articles*, 46–48, for cipher; Whitehead, 223, for "cardinal mistake."

530 CQ DX v W2 and its cipher: *Spark-Gap Times*, No. 17, at 36; Whitehead, 168–169; Sayers and Kahn, 24–32. The cipher of the two German agents in Newark, Axel Wheeler-Hill and Felix G. A. Jaahnke, is described in "F.B.I. Tells of Work of Spy Ring Here," *The New York Times* (December 1, 1943), 10:6. Though the news story speaks of providing "substitutions for the alphabet," the description of taking the first nine different letters on the first line of a page of a book and then taking letters of the "left hand marginal line" of the page to form a key accords so closely with the LIR system that it must be the same. The Newark key book was *Half Way to Horror*.

531 ND98: Whitehead, 196–198.

531 greatest radio deception: Flicke, 172.

531 "The word implies": Ladislas Farago, *Burn After Reading: The Espionage History of World War II* (New York: Walker & Company, 1961), 56.

531 Operation North Pole: Unless otherwise specified, all information comes from H. J. Giskes, *London Calling North Pole* (London: William Kimber, 1953), with an Epilogue by H. M. G. Lauwers. The R.S.H.A. head in the operation, Joseph Schreieder, has written *Het Englandspiel* (Amsterdam: Van Holkema & Warendorf, n.d.), which I have not been able to read because it is in Dutch; however, its appendix, 305–336, describes various ciphers used—double transposition, Playfair, bifid, null, and a Vigenère type. The Kingdom of the Netherlands investigated the debacle exhaustively and published the hearings and results in three huge volumes: Enquêtecommissie Regeringsbeleid 1940–1945, *Verslag Houdendē de Uitkomsten van het Onderzoek*. Deel 4: *De Nederlandse Geheime Deinsten te London de Verbindingen met het Bezette Gebeid* ('s Gravenhage: Staatsdrukkerij-en Uitgeverijbedrijf, 1950). Deel 4B, "Bijlagen," contains Bijlage 26, a report on the cryptographic-security check problems by H. Koot, J. A. Verkuyl, and A. N. Baron de Vos van Steenwijk, at 88–94, and Bijlage 40, the statement of the British Foreign Office, at 122. Another primary source is Pieter Dourlein, *Inside North Pole:*

	A Secret Agent's Story, trans. F. G. Renier and Anne Cliff (London: William Kimber, 1953).
534	Lauwers security check, "he wanted": Lauwers in Giskes, 181–185.
536	poor abilities, 5 to 15 per cent, "identity check omitted"; Bijlage 26, §§A7, B17.
536	"inconclusive": Bijlage 40, §9. The Foreign Office then makes an understatement of a proportion remarkable even for the British: "It was later realised that the decision to continue the operation was mistaken."
536	Hitler sees messages: T-175:124:2599027–30, marked "Hat dem Führer vorgelegen."
537	Lauwers attempts: Lauwers in Giskes, 189–194, 196–198.
538	items in German hands: Bijlage 16, at 30.
538	worst Allied defeat: Giskes, 202; Farago, 241.
539	Maquis: Jacques Bergier, *Secret Weapons—Secret Agents*, trans. Edward Fitzgerald (London: Hurst & Blackett, 1956), 57 for *tobacco*; pictures opposite 156 and 112 for plaintext and ciphertext of a message. Gilbert Renault (pseud. Rémy), *Mémoires d'un Agent Secret de la France Libre* (Paris: Éditions France-Empire, 1960), II, 127–129; Renault, *Comment devenir agent secret*, 94–101 for double transposition, 103–105 for code and one-time pad.
539	O.S.S.: Abrams, who served in the specialist group in its cryptographic headquarters for more than two years.
539	Tompkins: Peter Tompkins, letters, April 14, 1962, and undated, with enclosures.
539	double transposition solved: Charles Eyraud, interview, May 14, 1962.
540	Vanek: Case 5–1942, Rädhusrätten, Stockholm, obtained by Dr. Käljo Käärik; Per Meurling, *Spionage och Sabotage i Sverige* (Stockholm: Lindfors Bokforlag, 1952), 125–138. Beurling, interview, September 17, 1963, for his solution; Flicke, 215, for German solution and effects.
541	"Thus, on the night": Peter Tompkins, *A Spy in Rome* (New York: Simon and Schuster, 1962), 131.
541	MARCO POLO: Bergier, 45, 48, 90.
542	Red and Green Plan codewords and impact: Cornelius Ryan, *The Longest Day: June 6, 1944* (New York: Simon and Schuster, 1959), 85; Gordon A. Harrison, *Cross-Channel Attack*, United States Army in World War II: The European Theater of Operations (Department of the Army: Office of the Chief of Military History) (Washington, D.C.: U.S. Government Printing Office, 1951), 205–206; David Howarth, *D Day: The Sixth of June, 1944* (New York: McGraw-Hill, 1959), for "The arrow pierces steel."
542	Verlaine message: Ryan, 30–34, 84–85, 96–97; Harrison, 275–276; Philippe de Vomécourt, *An Army of Amateurs* (Garden City, N.Y.: Doubleday & Company, 1961), 229–230; Lieutenant General Bodo Zimmerman, "France, 1944," in *The Fatal Decisions*, eds. Seymour Frieden and William Richardson (New York: William Sloane Associates, 1956), 197–245 at 212–213.
544	O.K.H. teletype of June 2: T–78:451:6426880–1.

Notes 1081

PAGE

545 Manhattan District secrecy: Unless otherwise specified, all information from Fletcher Knebel and Charles W. Bailey II, *No High Ground* (New York: Harper & Brothers, 1960), primarily at 59–62, 64, 115–116, 119, 207. Groves quotations and checkerboard, Groves: letter, August 16, 1961. Hiroshima striking code: Thomas F. Farrell, letter, September 8, 1961.

549 Axis wiretaps: Shirer, ix, 338, 585–586; *Ciano Diaries*, entries for May 10, June 9, June 24, 1940, October 13, 1941, January 25, 1942; Churchill, IV, 602.

549 Choctaws: "The Sun's Rays: Choctaw Stopped War Wire Tappers," *The* (New York) *Sun* (February 2, 1938), 30:1–2. A. Lincoln Lavine, article in *New York American* (November 13, 1921), says they were in Company E, 142d Infantry.

550 Indians in World War II: "Comanches Again Called for Army Code Service" (December 13, 1940), "Indians' 'Code' Upsets Foes" (August 31, 1941), "Navajo Code Talk Kept Foes Guessing" (September 19, 1945), all *The New York Times*; Harris, 218.

550 Navaho language: Clyde Kluckhohn and Dorothea Leighton, *The Navaho* (Cambridge, Mass.: Harvard University Press, 1946), 186–187, 191, 198, 196.

551 Rogers: *DAB*; U.S. Patent 251,292.

551 sound: For a clear explanation of speech acoustics, with spectrograms, see George A. Miller, *Language and Communication*, McGraw-Hill Series in Psychology (New York: McGraw-Hill, 1951), 26–41.

552 scrambler types: List adapted from W. Koenig, "Final Report on Project C-43; Continuation of Decoding Speech Codes," Bell Telephone Laboratories for Office of Scientific Research and Development, National Defense Research Committee, Communications Division (Division 13, Section 3), Part I: "Speech Privacy Systems—Interception, Diagnosis, Decoding, Evaluation," October 12, 1944, at ch. III. Part II is "Appendix Including All Preliminary Reports," November 30, 1944. This is a superb report on the state of the art at the time—clear and comprehensive. The Library of Congress has published it, together with all other O.S.R.D. scrambler reports, on microfilm Reels 184, 185, and 186 of O.S.R.D. Technical Reports. My list omits vocoders and multiplexing systems because they are not primarily scramblers. U.S. patents on scramblers, mostly in Class 179 Subclass 1.5, offer valuable information. Among the earliest is one (1,123,119) by Lee De Forest that does for radio what Rogers did for telephony—send messages on two different wavelengths.

554 hams listen to Catalina: Lloyd Espenschied, interview, August 27, 1963. Espenschied, one of the A. T. & T. pioneers in radiotelephone and scramblers, worked on the Catalina installation.

554 East Coast, Roberts: Ed G. Raser, letter, June 19, 1964, and enclosed circuit diagrams for Roberts De-Scramblers.

554 A-3: L. Schott, "Final Report on Project C-66: Frequency Time Division Speech Privacy System," May 29, 1943, Bell Telephone Laboratories for O.S.R.D., at 6–8.

1082 THE CODEBREAKERS

PAGE
554 Japanese query: *PHA*, 35:82–83, 22:243–245.
554 Roosevelt, control room: Hal Borland, "Diplomacy in Scrambled Words," *The New York Times Magazine* (September 22, 1940), 5, 15; "Roosevelt Protected in Talks to Envoys by Radio 'Scrambling' to Foil Spies Abroad," *The New York Times* (October 8, 1939), 47:2–3.
555 Deutschen Reichspost: T–175:129:2654865–9, with sample conversation at –70–74. T–175:122:2647449–51 for Churchill-Butcher, –60–62 for Clark, and –52–59 for conversation between British Embassy in Washington and a Mr. Cunningham in London. Hardie translations. Flicke, 233, for Hitler and system changed.
556 F.D.R.–Churchill 1943 conversation: Germany, Oberkommando der Wehrmacht, *Kriegstagebuch des Oberkommando der Wehrmacht*, eds. Helmuth Griner and Percy Ernst Schramm (Frankfurt am Main: Bernard & Graefe Verlag für Wehrwesen, 1963), III, part 2, 854; F. W. Deakin, *The Brutal Friendship* (London: Weidenfeld & Nicolson, 1962), 501–502.
556 F.D.R.–Churchill 1944 conversation: Schellenberg, 366.
558 early U.S. activities: Koenig, 1.
558 lab, Koenig: Walter Koenig, interview, April 19, 1962; *AMS*.
558 "Beginners": Koenig, 33.
558 47 and 76 per cent: Schott, 17.
558 speech safety factor: Miller, 63–65, 69.
559 "The fact that": Koenig, 33.
559 spectrograph solutions: Koenig.
560 Camp Coles, Japanese scramblers: Koenig, Part II, Preliminary Reports 24, 23, 2; Koenig, letter, June 18, 1965.
560 British 2-D solution: A. D. Fowler and E. C. Thompson, "Project 13–106, Report No. 2: Analysis of Recording of Speech Scrambled by British 2-Dimensional Privacy System," Bell Telephone Laboratories for O.S.R.D.
560 improvement of privacy: "Project C-32, Final Report: Speech Privacy Decoding," January 31, 1942, Bell Telephone Laboratories for O.S.R.D.
560 "privacy" not "secrecy": Marshall in *PHA*, 3:1213.
560 teletype: Murray Teigh Bloom, "Teletype: The Amazing Mechanical Messenger," *The Reader's Digest*, XXV (December, 1956), 188–194, at 192.
560 Marshall: *PHA*, 29:2313.

Chapter 17 THE SCRUTABLE ORIENTALS

Notes to this chapter will be considered as an extension of those to "One Day of MAGIC." All forms, abbreviations, authors' names, carry over, with these additions: Documents in the Navy Department, Naval History Division, Classified Operational Archives, bear "COA" at the end of the citation. "USSBS (201), 3, 5" means "United States Strategic Bombing Survey, Interrogation Number 201,

Notes 1083

pages 3 and 5"; copies are in NA, RG 43. Space prohibits my naming the subject and position of the person interrogated. These mimeographed interrogations are not to be confused with the printed report, United States Strategic Bombing Survey (Pacific), *Japanese Military and Naval Intelligence Division*, April, 1946 (Washington, D.C.: U.S. Government Printing Office, 1946), cited as *Japanese Intelligence*. The *Operational History of Naval Communications* is cited here as just *Operational History*.

I am grateful to Ikuhiko Hata for reading this chapter and offering some valuable suggestions.

PAGE

561 Japan's Midway strategy: Mitsuo Fuchida and Masatake Okumiya, *Midway, The Battle that Doomed Japan: The Japanese Navy's Story* (Annapolis, Md.: U.S. Naval Institute, 1955); Thaddeus Tuleja, *Climax at Midway* (New York: W. W. Norton & Company, 1960); Samuel E. Morison, *The Two-Ocean War* (Boston: Little, Brown & Co., 1963), 147–151. All references to Morison without roman numeral volume numbers will be to this book unless otherwise specified.

562 details of Combat Intelligence Unit and cryptanalytic work: Unless otherwise specified, all from Dyer and Wright, separate interviews, December 12, 1963; letters from them correcting notes to those interviews, December 27 and 19, 1963, respectively; Wright, telephone interview, May 14, 1964.

562 three days after Pearl Harbor: 18:3336; also Wright letter.

563 Dyer, Wright: Navy biographies; 36:247, 261.

564 Japanese attempts to change code: Dyer.

564 Navy Code Book D, administrative confusion: *Operational History*, 76, 91, 78.

565 April 17: Morison, 141. General foreknowledge of Coral Sea: 3:1132; Louis Morton, *Strategy and Command: The First Two Years*, United States Army in World War II: The War in the Pacific (Department of the Army: Office of the Chief of Military History) (Washington, D.C.: U.S. Government Printing Office, 1962), 275.

565 code pad error: Morison, 143; Chester W. Nimitz and E. B. Potter, eds., *The Great Sea War: The Story of Naval Action in World War II* (Englewood Cliffs, N.J.: Prentice-Hall, Inc., 1960), 216.

566 Holtwick: Navy biography; 35:46, 36:262 (transcribed incorrectly as "Hopewick").

566 monitoring: 23:677–678.

566 Holmes: Navy biography.

566 Holmes to Draemel to Nimitz: Admiral Milo F. Draemel, U.S.N., Ret., letters of November 29 and December 4, 1963.

567 200 ships in operation, more fuel: Fuchida, 79, 68.

567 Nimitz scents offensives: Samuel E. Morison, *Coral Sea, Midway, and Submarine Actions, May 1942–August 1942*, Vol. IV, *History of United States Naval Operations in World War II* (Boston: Little, Brown & Co., 1949), 80, 165–166; Morton, 280.

567 Nimitz, King views: Tuleja, 58.

PAGE
568 naval forces: Tuleja, 51–52, 62.
568 May 20 order: Fuchida, 108, 80–84.
569 CHI-HE system: *Operational History*, 245–246.
569 coordinate AF, fresh water: J. Bryan, III, "Never a Battle Like Midway," *The Saturday Evening Post*, CCXXI (March 26, 1949), 24–25, 50, 52–75 *passim*, at 50; independent recollection by Wright.
570 Finnegan: 36:251.
570 "The enemy is expected": United States Navy, Commander in Chief Pacific Fleet, Operation Plan 29–42, May 27, 1942, p. 2, COA. Nimitz' estimate of enemy forces in this plan omitted the entire main body of battleships and heavy cruisers that Yamamoto planned for the coup de grâce. Why this should have happened, in view of the apparently complete cryptanalytic intelligence available to him, has never been explained. Perhaps the error was corrected after his plan was promulgated. Morison, IV, 84, notes but does not explain this.
571 Theobald suspects: Nimitz, 227.
571 Nimitz never mentioned cryptanalysis: Vice Admiral William Ward Smith, U.S.N., Ret., letter, November 17, 1963.
571 mail for Midway: Admiral Toshiyuki Yokoi, *Teikoku Kaigun Kimitsushitsu* ("*The Black Chamber of the Imperial Japanese Navy*") (Tokyo: Shinseikatsu Publishing Co., Showa 28 [1953]), ch. 9, "The Midway Naval Battle," at §3, trans. Flo Morikami; 3:1158 for "bit too thick."
571 "Japanese are adept": Operation Plan 29–42, 19.
571 Midway battle details and assessment: Morison; Fuchida; Tuleja; Nimitz
573 "I must also tell you": Tuleja, 30.
573 "Midway was essentially": Nimitz, 245.
573 "We were able": 3:1132.
573 Goggins: Navy biography.
573 Melbourne unit: Fabian Navy biography; 35:87.
573 OP-20-G split-up: 9:3962, 8:3776–7; Senate, Committee on the Judiciary, *Laurance F. Safford*, Report No. 1473 to accompany S. 1524, 85:2 (April 28, 1958), 11–12 for Safford inventions.
574 Navy cedes diplomatic: 37:1083.
574 Nebraska Avenue: 29:2371.
574 Navy crypto growth: 4:1794, 3:1147.
574 Army cryptologic growth and organization: Harris, ch. 11, "Signal Security and Intelligence," 327–350; *The Origin and Development of the Army Security Agency*, 14–17. Marshall gives very slightly different figures at 3:1146–7.
574 Vint Hill Farms: Thompson, 444, 445; Fred Paulmann, interview, April 19, 1962. Paulmann served at Vint Hill.
575 mechanization: Harris, 442, 443, 584, 592.
575 traffic volume: Harris, 49, 65, 90, 259, 585.
577 C.B.: Harris, 241–242, 340.
577 Sinkov: Army biography; Wilson Yulson, interview, May 18, 1963. Yulson served with the 138th Signal Company (Radio Intelligence), which trained briefly at C.B.

PAGE

577 101st: Thompson, 298. He also lists the 117th, 121st, 122nd, 123rd, 128th, 849th, and 955th Signal Companies (Radio Intelligence) and the 860th Signal Company (Radio Intelligence, Aviation).
578 138th: Yulson. Nimitz, 344, for Hollandia; Harris, 258, for value of signal intelligence.
579 1925, Naval Ministry building: Naotsune Watanabe, untitled manuscript dealing with his experiences as a wartime Japanese naval cryptanalyst of American systems (spring, 1962), trans. Flo Morikami, at 13. All references are to pages of Japanese text. I am deeply grateful to Dr. Watanabe for preparing this memoir for me.
579 "Tokumu Han": *Japanese Intelligence*, 29.
579 Morikawa, Kamisugi, and all early details: Shiro Takagi, "Nippon No Black Chamber" ("The Black Chamber of Japan"), *All Yomimono* (Showa 27, Juichigatsu [November, 1952]), 157–175, at §§1–5, and Shiro Takagi, "Nippon Kaigun No Kimitsushitsu" ("The Black Chamber of the Japanese Navy"), *Shukan Asahi* (Showa 36, Junigatsu 8 [December 8, 1961]), 24–26.
580 Owada built: *Operational History*, 5; Takagi, "Nippon No Black Chamber," §5.
580 10 full time, 10 part time, 60 recruits: Watanabe, 15.
580 Tokumu Han expansion and training: Watanabe, 16, 8, 7, 3–4; USSBS (433), 1, (437), 3.
580 fleet units: USSBS (219), 2, (437), 3, (309), 3.
580 Owada equipment: *Operational History*, 57.
580 20 prisoners of war: Watanabe, 18.
580 several thousand: Watanabe, 17.
580 nisei girls: Watanabe, 66: Takagi, "Nippon Kaigun No Kimitsushitsu."
580 1943 move: Watanabe, 17; USSBS (431), 5.
580 2nd Branch, its sections: *Japanese Intelligence*, 30; Watanabe, 9.
581 3rd Branch, Morikawa: USSBS (208), 2, (431), 2; Watanabe, 10, 13.
582 Tokumu Han command: *Japanese Intelligence*, 29.
582 Kakimoto: Watanabe, 12.
582 Nomura: USSBS (208), 2.
582 failed on solving U.S. messages: Yokoi, ch. 9, §1.
582 no medium- or high-echelon: Takagi, "Nippon No Black Chamber," §7.
582 AN 103: Watanabe, 23–25; Takagi, "Nippon No Black Chamber," §6.
582 BAMS: USSBS (208), 4, (201), 7, (238), 8.
582 worked most on strip cipher: My supposition, based on emphasis in sources.
582 CSP 642: Senate, *Laurance F. Safford*, Report No. 1473, at 12. Methods of use deduced from Japanese cryptanalytic techniques.
582 strips captured at Wake and Kiska: USSBS (208), 4; Shiro Takagi, untitled manuscript dealing with his experiences as a wartime naval cryptanalyst of American systems (spring, 1962), trans. Flo Morikami, at 1. Referred to henceforth simply as "Takagi" to distinguish it from his published articles. References are to pages of Japanese text. I am grateful to Mr. Takagi for preparing this memoir for me. Rear Admiral W. Scott Cunningham, who surrendered Wake to the Japanese, says

PAGE

in his *Wake Island Command* (Boston: Little, Brown & Co., 1961), that the Japanese read the coded dispatch ordering Cunningham to put War Plan 46 into effect after Pearl Harbor. Cunningham says that he destroyed all codes and ciphers before surrender and that the Japanese boasted that they had broken a code. I think it more likely that they found one that had not been destroyed.

582   I.B.M. tabulators: Takagi, 33–34
582   BIMEC, FEMYH: Watanabe, 36.
583   Shimizu, Oda, methods of solution: Takagi, 21–36.
583   solvers of strip ciphers: Takagi, 19.
583   Tokumu Han gives up on strips: Watanabe, 59; Yokoi, ch. 9, §1.
583   "Our whole analysis": USSBS (431), 5. *Operational History*, 320–326, illustrates the poverty of fleet communications intelligence as well.
583   graphing: Watanabe, 35, 53; USSBS (431), 2–3.
583   bulge: USSBS (369), 7, (431), 3–4.
583   Philippines, Marshalls: USSBS (437), 4, (208), 3.
584   Arisue: USSBS (238), 10.
584   Army communications intelligence: *Japanese Intelligence*, 31. I cannot locate any of these places in the *Lippincott Columbia Gazetteer*.
584   Yofuen, Machida: Takagi, 41–42.
584   Army field units, wiretapping: USSBS (451), 5, (450), 5.
584   "We did not break": USSBS (450), 3.
584   14th Army cryptanalysts: United States, Navy, South West Pacific Command Headquarters, Allied Translator and Interpreter Section, *Japanese Ten Day Period Reports on Monitoring of Allied Wireless Communications in the Philippines . . . Issued 11 January 1943 to 28 December 1943 by Watari Group (Shudan) (14th Army) Staff Section Counter-Intelligence Squad*, Limited Distribution Translations, No. 31, March 29, 1945, COA.
585   U.S. cipher disk: George E. Sterling, *Intelligence Articles*, 36; Harris, 272, says this was the M-94.
585   M-94s captured: Yokoi, ch. 9, §1.
585   "If you know": John Keats, *They Fought Alone* (Philadelphia: J. B. Lippincott Co., 1963), 181–182.
585   seven-page cipher: Colonel Allison Ind, *Allied Intelligence Bureau: Our Secret Weapon in the War Against Japan* (New York: David McKay Co., Inc., 1958), 122, 139.
585   Cebu number cipher: *Japanese Ten Day Period Reports*, 18.
585   "a special code": *Ibid.*, 27.
585   Peralta system solution: *Ibid.*, 36.
585   double transpositions: *Ibid.*, 46 (called "double substitution," the use of which seems highly improbable here).
585   "on the general organization": *Ibid.*, 55.
585   "standstill": *Ibid.*, 61.
585   214 messages: *Ibid.*, 65.
585   back files solved: *Ibid.*, 75.
585   captured American yields keywords: *Ibid.*, 77.

PAGE
- 585 direction-finding units: *Ibid.*, 58.
- 585 raids: *Ibid.*, 75–76, 73.
- 585 "Although enemy wireless": *Ibid.*, 84.
- 585 "a fatal blow," "as always": *Ibid.*, 99.
- 586 Heindorf House, Ferguson, impressive proportions: Ind, 193, 209.
- 586 outline of Japanese naval cryptography: Adapted from *Operational History*, 91–94. That D and RO are JN25 and that KO is the flag officers' system are my suppositions.
- 587 *Taiho* code: *Operational History*, 326.
- 587 Japanese Army codes: 37:1061; IMTFE, Exhibits 833, 3729; United States, Navy, Pacific Fleet, South Pacific Force, Combat Intelligence Center, Item 964, "Excerpt from Notebook of Unknown Owner," captured near Bougainville, November 27–29, 1943, COA.
- 588 code revision and code areas: *Operational History*, 77, 91, 81–84; Dyer for JN25's dozen editions: "By the end of the war, they had gone through half the alphabet in new editions."
- 588 administration and distribution: *Operational History*, 77–81, 63–64.
- 589 security lapses: *Operational History*, 86–89.
- 590 *I-1*: *Operational History*, 85–86; Halsey, 148–149.
- 590 water-soluble ink: *Operational History*, 64–66.
- 591 Army code exhortation: United States, Navy, Pacific Fleet, South Pacific Force, Combat Intelligence Center, Item 2a, "Translation of Captured Japanese Documents: 'Revision of Codes, December 1, 1942,' " 34–39, at 35, 36, 39, COA.
- 591 Kiska "proof": *Operational History*, 90–91.
- 591 2,000,000 copies: *Operational History*, 89.
- 591 *PT-109:* All noncryptologic details from Robert J. Donovan, *PT-109: John F. Kennedy in World War II* (New York: McGraw-Hill, 1961). Cryptologic details from my reconstruction of the cipher system and key squares from plain and cipher messages in log of Arthur Evans, photographs of which he kindly supplied.
- 593 direction-finding system not solved, 75 solutions: Dyer.
- 594 direct line, noon positions, complaints: Lockwood, letters, May 22 and November 25, 1964; Lockwood, *Sink' Em All: Submarine Warfare in the Pacific* (New York: E. P. Dutton & Co., 1951), 110; 29:2403.
- 594 importance of submarines, Tojo statement: Nimitz, 422–423; Morison, 493.
- 594 primary contribution: Dyer.
- 594 40,000 soldiers: *Congressional Record*, XCI (October 25, 1945), 10053.
- 594 *Yamato:* Dyer; Nimitz, 223, 537–539.
- 595 Yamamoto presence in the Solomons: Nimitz, 285.
- 595 additive changed April 1: Lieutenant Commander Tatsuo Sagara, *Taihei Yo Senso* ("*The Pacific War*") (Tokyo: Chuokoron Publishing Co.), III. Citation supplied by Ikuhiko Hata.
- 595 date and text of itinerary message: War History Office, National Defense College, Japan Defense Agency, Tokyo. The present translation was very kindly supplied by Fred C. Woodrough, Jr., of Silver Spring, Maryland, a wartime translator of Japanese for the Navy. Sagara says message was

1088 THE CODEBREAKERS

PAGE

        sent in the most secret code; this, together with the use of the additive, virtually confirms that the code was JN25. I do not think that the conclusion of a Japanese Navy court of inquiry after the war that an Army code was at fault need be taken seriously.

595 cryptanalytic details: Wright and Dyer; confirmed Lasswell, telephone interview.

595 Lasswell: Marine Corps biography.

598 pros and cons: Rear Admiral Edwin T. Layton, letter, October 26, 1964.

598 Yamamoto personal details: Fuchida, 73–76; Zacharias, 92–93; James A. Field, Jr., "Admiral Yamamoto," *U.S. Naval Institute Proceedings*, LXXV (October, 1949), 1105–1113; Halsey, 155.

599 Nimitz authorization: Layton, who states that the decision to shoot down Yamamoto was Nimitz' alone, with no approval required of higher authority in Washington.

599 Wilkinson query: 4:1737.

599 cover story: Layton.

599 cryptologic dangers: My suppositions, confirmed by Dyer.

599 reply to Wilkinson: 4:1737; Layton.

599 Mitchell-Lanphier mission: Lanphier's own story in *The New York Times* (September 12, 1945), 1:6, (September 13, 1945), 5:1, (September 14, 1945), 7:1–3, from which all quotes are taken; *The Army Air Forces in World War II*, eds. Wesley F. Craven and James Lea Cate, Vol. IV, *The Pacific: Guadalcanal to Saipan, August 1942 to July 1944* (Chicago: University of Chicago Press, 1950), 213–214.

601 burial, "There was only one": Field, 1111; Andrieu d'Albas, *Death of a Navy: Japanese Naval Action in World War II*, trans. Anthony Rippon (New York: Devin-Adair, 1957), 254.

601 major victory: All sources agree on this evaluation: Nimitz, 285; Morison, 274; Morton, 415; Masanaro Ito with Roger Pineau, *The End of the Imperial Japanese Navy* (New York: W. W. Norton & Co., Inc., 1962), 92.

601 "particularly high plane": United States, Navy, Commander South Pacific Area and South Pacific Force, C. W. Nimitz, first endorsement to Serial 00740, April 26, 1943, forwarding Combat Report of Air Command Solomon Islands, April 21, 1943 [the Mitchell-Lanphier mission], COA; Halsey, 157.

601 Americans learn from Japanese newscast: Field, 1112; *The New York Times Index* (1943, 1944, 1945).

601 citizen telephones Marshall, his attempts to suppress talk: 3:1157, 1208–9.

602 not to field commands: 2:800.

602 "We have told them": 29:2404.

602 "No action," convoys, coastwatchers: 29:2403.

603 *Chicago Tribune* case: *The New York Times*, 1942, (August 8), 4:4, (August 9), 26:1, (August 11), 17:1, (August 12), 22:1, (August 14), 7:1, (August 18), 18:7, (August 19), 7:7, (August 20), 28:5–6.

603 switch to JN25d: Safford says, 8:3738, that this switch was due to the Johnston story. But the insistence in *Operational History*, 90–91, on the

inpregnability of their codes, the absence of any reference to the matter in their discussion of routine post-Midway code change at 76–77, and the absence of any reference to the Johnston story in any Japanese postwar discussions of American cryptanalysis, militate against this view.

604 Holland: *Congressional Record*, LXXXVIII (August 31, 1942), 7011–2; "McCormick's Paper Accused of Tip to Japan," *New York Herald Tribune* (September 1, 1942).

604 Dewey and Pearl Harbor charges: John Chamberlain, "Pearl Harbor," *Life*, IX (September 24, 1945), 110–114, 116, 119–120.

604 charges in politics: *The New York Times Index* (1944).

604 Harness: *Congressional Record*, XC (September 11, 1944), 7649.

604 Bissell, Marshall, Clarke: 3:1129–37. Letter at 3:1132–3.

607 not same code, Bell, two days: Letter of Dewey, November 1, 1945, to William D. Mitchell, Box 5, Records of the Joint Congressional Committee on the Investigation of the Pearl Harbor Attack, NA, RG 128; "Dewey Is Silent on Japanese Code," *The New York Times* (September 22, 1945), 4:1.

608 "no further reference": 3:1136. My examination of *The New York Times Index* (1944) confirms this: there was continued interest in the Army and Navy board investigations into Pearl Harbor, but no further Republican charges about suppression of the truth or demands for inquiries, as earlier in the year.

608 Task Force 34 incident: Nimitz, 389–390; Halsey, 220–221; Morison, 466–468.

609 *Indianapolis:* Richard F. Newcomb, *Abandon Ship: Death of the U.S.S. Indianapolis* (New York: Henry Holt & Co., 1958), 19, 271, 178–179.

610 Togo-Sato intercepts: *The [James] Forrestal Diaries*, ed. Walter Millis (New York: Viking Press, 1951), 74–77, 82–83, 84.

610 President sees: Herbert Feis, *Japan Subdued: The Atomic Bomb and the End of The War in the Pacific* (Princeton, N.J.: Princeton University Press, 1961), 57–58, 98.

610 "Probably as a result": My supposition, concurred in by Robert J. C. Butow, letter, July 2, 1964. His statement in *Japan's Decision to Surrender* (Stanford, Calif.: Stanford University Press, 1954), 130, that this intelligence was not turned to good account, is based on other considerations. He emphasizes the limitation of unconditional surrender to the armed forces at 133.

610 B-29s: Takagi, "Nippon No Black Chamber," §7; USSBS (284), 3; Fletcher and Knebel, *No High Ground*, 15–16.

610 "swallowing our tears": Watanabe, 56.

611 occupation: 3:1137, 1157–8.

611 400: a rough total from 72 in G.2 A.6 (Moore, 8), 200 in MI-8 (Yardley, 204), my estimate of half a dozen in the Code Compiling Section, a dozen in the Navy, and 100 intercept operators in the Signal Corps Radio Section, divided into *World Almanac* figure of 4,355,000 as peak U.S. armed forces strength in World War I for one in 10,000.

PAGE

611 16,000: 3:1147; divided into *World Almanac* figure of 12,300,000 as peak U.S. armed forces strength in World War II, for one in 800.
611 M-209 keys and machine: Martin Joos, interview, summer 1964.
613 shortened war by a year: "Germans Tapped Atlantic Phones," *The New York Times* (December 9, 1945), 32:5. The official is not named, but the reporter was the late Anthony Leviero, who won a Pulitzer Prize in 1952. I tried but failed to get estimates of the value of cryptology to the Allies in the prosecution of the war from Churchill, Eisenhower, and MacArthur.
613 Amè: interview.
613 "It won the war": Anderson, telephone interview, January 8, 1965.
613 "I believe": *Congressional Record*, XCI (October 25, 1945), 10053.

Chapter 18 РУССКАЯ КРИПТОЛОГИЯ

Some of the full references for these notes will be found in the notes to earlier chapters dealing with the periods to which the notes refer. Thus a citation on a World War I episode will be found in full in the notes to one of the World War I chapters.

614 monks' ciphers: M. N. Speransky, "Taynopis' v Yugo-Slavyanskikh i Russikh Pamyatnikakh Pis'ma," *Entsiklopediya Slavanskoy Philologii* (Leningrad: Izdatel'stvo Akademiya Nauk SSSR), IV, part 3 (1929), 56–161; "Kryptographiya," *Bolshaya Sovietskaya Entsiklopediya* (1953), XXIII, 401, trans. Madeleine Albright; Boris Unbegaun, "Russkaya Taynopis' XVII Vyeka," *Obshchestva Druzey Russkoi Knigi*, IV (1938), 81–86; Akademiya Nauk SSSR Biblioteka, *Istoricheskiy Ocherk I Obzor Fondov Rukopisnogo Otdela Biblioteka Akademiya Nauk* (Moskva: Izdatel'stvo Akademiya Nauk SSSR, 1956), II, 103, 120; David Diringer, *The Alphabet*, 2nd ed. (New York: Philosophical Library, [1949?]), 485.
614 first Russian solution: Add. Ms. 32,288, f. 1.
614 Swedish code of 1700: Chifferklaver XI:3, Riksarkiv, Stockholm. Henning Stålhane, *En Misslyckad Kungamiddag* (Stockholm: Hugo Gebers Förlag, 1937), gives additional details of 17th- and 18th-century Swedish diplomatic codes at 91–136, 273.
614 Russian ciphers and codes: Add. Ms. 32, 292, passim.
615 "many nulls," superencipherment: Add. Ms. 32,292, ff. 45, 50.
616 January 22: Count Nikita Petroviya Panin, *Material' dlya Zhizneoisaniya*, ed. A. Briknera (St. Petersburg: Typographiya Imperatorskoi Akademii Nauk), V (1891), 245–246.
616 Madrid discontinued: Add. Ms. 32,292, f. 82.
616 "Your confidential reports," "Not having at hand": Panin, 484, 362.
617 black chambers and Chétardie: Thompson and Padover, 142–144.
617 "we possess": Panin, 284.
617 Napoleon: Bazeries, 152–184, 275–277; [Jacques Etienne J. A. Macdonald], *Souvenirs du Maréchal Macdonald* (Paris: Librairie Plon, 1892), 308–309. The great fire in Moscow burned many of Napoleon's ciphers and he had

to issue orders organizing his retreat in clear, many of which were seized by the Russians; "perhaps the fate of France and the face of Europe depended upon the desuetude of steganography," says General Étienne A. Bardin, *Dictionnaire de l'Armée de Terre* (Paris: Corréard, 1851), "Chiffre stéganographique," I, 1281–3, citing *Spectateur militaire*, IX (June, 1830), 302, 389.

618 black chambers: A. T. Vassilyev, *The Okhrana: The Russian Secret Police*, ed. René Fülöp-Miller (London: George G. Harrap & Co., 1930), 90–95; Richard W. Rowan, *Spy and Counter-Spy* (London: John Hamilton Ltd., [1929]), 188–193; S. Maiskii, "Chernyi Kabinet," *Byloe* (January, 1918), 185–197; P. Zavarzine, *Souvenirs d'un Chef de l'Okhrana (1900–1917)*, trans. J. Jeanson (Paris: Payot, 1930), 43–44.

618 Zybine: Zavarzine, 45–48; Vassilyev, 93–94.

619 fraction system as standard: The cipher is also described in V. Bakharev, *O Shifrah* ("On Ciphers") (Geneva: Tipografiya Soyuza, 1902), 3–5. This 24-page booklet, dated at Tyurvma in 1902, and Pavel I. Rosental: (pseud. A. Bundevets), *Shifrovannoe Pis'mo: Kritika upotreblyaemykh u nas sistem shifra* ("Cipher Writing: A Critique of the Cipher Systems Used by Us") (Geneva: Imprimerie israelite, 1904), 113 pages, are the only Russian works on cryptology known to me. Both simply discuss different types of ciphers and do not discuss cryptanalysis. Both appeared in Switzerland while Lenin was there; this may be significant, but neither author is listed even in the first (pre-purge) edition of the *Bolshaya Sovietskaya Entsiklopediya*, nor in biographies of Lenin, nor in the New York Public Library Card Catalog. Columbia University catalog gives "Bundovets' " real name but no other information.

620 checkerboard: George Kennan, "Russian Provincial Prisons," *The Century Illustrated Monthly Magazine*, XXXV (January, 1888), 397–406 at 403–405; and "A Russian Political Prison: The Fortress of Petropavlosk," *Ibid*. (February, 1888), 521–530 at 528; Bakharev, 19.

620 handwritten concealment: Kennan, 406.

620 Nihilist substitution: Kennan, 404–405; Schooling, IV, 614–618. For methods of solution: Gaines, 164–167; Wolfe, II, ch. 8; Mauborgne and Friedman, *Articles*, 227–240, 245–249, on their separate solutions of Schooling's 20-letter challenge cryptogram. The Nihilists also used a transposition cipher: Kerckhoffs, 12–14; Gaines, 17–25 for solution.

621 Foreign Ministry: Vladimir de Korostovetz, "The Black Cabinet," *The Contemporary Review*, No. 951 (March, 1945), 162–165; Gyldén. Savinsky, in his *Recollections of a Russian Diplomat* (London: Hutchinson & Co., 1927), says only (p. 5): "I was guardian of the most secret Ministerial archives."

621 Cartier: "Souvenirs," II, 23–29.

622 Andreiev's fear: Arthur Scheutz [pseud. Tristan Busch], *Secret Service Unmasked*, trans. Anthony V. Ireland (London: Hutchinson & Co., [1948]), 58.

622 Tannenberg: general military details from Barbara Tuchman, *The Guns of August* (New York: The Macmillan Company, 1962), 290–309.

PAGE

622 wire and radios: Lieutenant General Nicholas N. Golovine, *The Russian Campaign of 1914*, trans. by Captain A. G. S. Muntz (Fort Leavenworth, Kans.: Command and General Staff Press, 1933), 171–172; Major H. C. Ingles, "Tannenberg–A Study in Faulty Signal Communication," *Articles*, 41–54 at 50 (July–August, 1929).

622 no key for XIII Corps, messages in clear: Golovine, 172; Germany, Reichsarchiv, *Der Weltkrieg: 1914 bis 1918* (Berlin: Mittler & Sohn), II (1925), 351.

623 Hoffman proposal: Major General Max Hoffman, *War Diaries and Other Papers*, trans. Eric Sutton (London: Martin Secker, 1929), II, 249, 330.

623 motorcyclist, initiative, intercept texts, Königsberg: Wilhelm F. Flicke, *War Secrets in the Ether*, trans. Ray Pettengill (Washington, D.C.: National Security Agency, 1953), 12, 9, 5; Hoffman, II, 332.

623 messages compared with directive: Golovine, 209–211.

626 "Rennenkampf's formidable host": Erich Ludendorff, *Ludendorff's Own Story* (New York: Harper & Brothers, 1919), I, 57–58.

626 intercept at headquarters on 25th: *Der Weltkrieg*, II, 136; Hoffman, II, 265.

626 text of Rennenkampf radiogram: Flicke, 6.

626 intercept at Montovo, cars: Hoffman, II, 267.

626 text of Samsonov radiogram: Flicke, 7; *Der Weltkrieg*, II, 136–137.

627 "one of the great victories": quoted in Tuchman, 306.

627 importance of Tannenberg: Tuchman, 306–309; John Buchan, *A History of the Great War* (Boston: Houghton Mifflin Co., 1922), I, 188.

627 "We had an ally," "The Russians sent": Hoffman, I, 41, 18.

628 September 14: Ronge, 67. All references are to French edition unless specified otherwise.

628 Russian Army cipher: Colonel Andreas Figl, *Systeme des Chiffrierens* (Graz: Verlag von Ulr. Mosers Buchhandlung, 1926), 84–85 and Appendix 19; Henning Stålhane, *Hemlig Skrift* (Stockholm: Lindfors Bokforlag, 1934), 65–69; W[illiam]. F. F[riedman]., "Note on the Russian Cipher System," in Gyldén.

628 September 19: Ronge (German ed.), 116.

628 solutions of Novikov and Engalitschev: Ronge, 68–70.

629 first key change and solution: Ronge, 72.

629 Deubner: Gyldén, 60, 62; *Der Weltkrieg*, V (1929), 422.

629 "quite geniuses": General [Max] von Hoffmann, *The War of Lost Opportunities* (London: Kegan Paul, Trench, Trubner & Co., 1924), 28. Subsequent Hoffmann references are to this book.

629 Ludendorff: Flicke, 18–19; General Dupont, "Le Haut Commandement Allemand en 1914," *Revue Militaire Française*, XCI (new series) (July 1, 1921), 9–38, at 14–15.

629 telegraph connections: Flicke, 18.

629 good harvest: Ronge, 74.

630 not much different from Stavka: Ronge (German ed.), 127; *Der Weltkrieg*, VI (1929), 46.

630 military details of November 11–25: Buchan, I, 395–399.

Notes

PAGE

630 message of 2:10 p.m. and Mackensen order: *Der Weltkrieg*, VI, 71–72;
630   Ronge, 75; Gyldén, 67.
November 15 messages: *Der Weltkrieg*, VI, 83.
630 Russian retreat order and countermand: Hoffman, 72; Ludendorff, I, 126.
631 Russians suspect German solution, change alphabets: Ronge, 76; Gyldén, 69.
631 Zemanek, von Marchesetti: Gyldén, 81; Ronge (German ed.), index, for first names.
631 Pokorny solves: Ronge, 76.
631 December 14 cipher change, solution, and abandonment: Gyldén, 71; Ronge, 77.
631 Caesar cipher: Gyldén, 57–58; Figl, 85.
631 RSK: Flicke, 18.
632 "most brilliant period": Ronge, 94.
632 Russian mystification: Colonel A. M. Nikolaieff, "Secret Causes of German Successes on the Eastern Front," *Coast Artillery Journal* (September–October, 1935), 373–377, reprinted *Articles*, 78–89, at 84, 85–86.
632 spy mania: Ronge, 95.
632 cipher change of May: Ronge, 100.
632 December 20: Ronge, 127.
632 300-group code: Ronge, 127. Figl, 187–190 and Appendix 38, gives a small code of 120 groups with Russian plaintext, but no date or place of usage, nor even any mention of Russian origin.
632 French tell Russians: Cartier, "Souvenirs," II, 29.
632 Russian direction-finding, school: Ronge, 153.
632 old system continued, 8th Army, 70 dispatches: Ronge, 161.
633 German decryptments: Gyldén, 60.
633 Boldeskul, von Marchesetti, Lippmann: Ronge, 171 and (German ed.) 403.
633 cipher changes of November and December, 1916: Ronge, 172. Figl, 183–187 and Appendix 37, gives a Russian system in which three-digit groups replace digraphs. He cites no date or place of usage.
633 333 radiograms: Ronge (German ed.), 298.
633 "We were always," "Only once": Hoffmann, 132.
634 1919 transposition: Yardley, 242–247; Dr. Käljo Käärik [pseud. CLIFF], "The 'Soviet Spies' Cipher," *The Cryptogram*, XXX (November–December, 1962), 32–34; W. M. Bowers [pseud. ZEMBIE], "The 'Soviet Spies' Cipher," *Ibid.* (January–February, 1963), 58–61.
634 Morrow: Theodore Draper, *The Roots of American Communism* (New York: Viking Press, 1957), 366–367. Open codes at 339–340.
635 dubok, old practices used anew: David Dallin, *Soviet Espionage* (New Haven, Conn., Yale University Press, 1955), 1.
635 Amtorg, "the cipher used": House of Representatives, Special Committee to Investigate Communist Activities in the United States, *Investigation of Communist Propaganda*, Report No. 2290, 71:3 (January 17, 1931), 35.

PAGE

635 "Not one expert": *Congressional Record,* LXXVII (April 3, 1933), 1152. Yardley, 325, refers to this failure; he also depicts, opposite p. 237, a Russian codebook, though he does not specify its provenance.

635 Copenhagen: Gyldén interviews, April–May, 1962.

635 Argentis: Meister, *Päpstlichen,* 156.

636 Meurling system: Per Meurling, *Spionage och Sabotage i Sverige* (Stockholm: Lindfors Bokförlag AB, 1952), 425, is merely illustrative. The actual key M DEL VAYO comes from minutes of his trial for espionage in Sweden examined by Dr. Kaljo Käärik of Enskede, Sweden; the multiplication feature comes from Meurling himself by a telephone call from Käärik (Käärik, letters of August 20, 1962, and October 10, 1964). General Walter G. Krivitsky, *In Stalin's Secret Service: An Exposé of Russia's Secret Policies by the Former Chief of the Soviet Intelligence in Western Europe* (New York: Harper & Brothers, 1939), states at 99–100 that Russian agents in Spain radioed vital information daily.

637 AFNO: "Red Pair Arrested for Theft of Codes," *The New York Times* (November 25, 1926), 28:7-8.

637 Persian spies, Dachnaks: George Agabekov, *OGPU: The Russian Secret Terror,* trans. Henry W. Bunn (New York: Brentano's, 1941), 103, 109, 99.

637 Rumanian: "Says Moscow Got Code," *The New York Times* (May 28, 1930), 11:3.

637 Shanghai: Vladimir Orloff, *The Secret Dossier: My Memoirs of Russia's Political Underworld,* trans. Mona Heath (London: George G. Harrap & Co., 1932), 241.

637 Prague: "Stolen Soviet Codes Found," *New York Herald Tribune* (November 29, 1935).

637 Japanese correspondence: Krivitsky, 15–20.

637 Russian-Spanish code: "Soviet Code Reported Stolen from Valencia," *New York Herald Tribune* (August 4, 1937), 7:2.

637 Lyushov: Chalmers Johnson, *An Instance of Treason: Ozaki Hotsumi and the Sorge Spy Ring* (Stanford, Calif.: Stanford University Press, 1964), 148.

637 King: Isaac Don Levine, "Execution of Stalin's Spy in the Tower of London: Inside Soviet Underworld, III," *Plain Talk,* III (November, 1948), 21–25; Senate, Subcommittee on Internal Security, *Internal Security Annual Report for 1956,* Report No. 131, 85:1 (March 4, 1957) (GPO, 1957), 30; "British Tell of '39 Spy," *The New York Times* (June 8, 1956).

637 Azarov: United States District Court for the Eastern District of Pennsylvania, Civil Division Case 614, *Maria Azarov and Vladimir Azarov vs. Cunard White Star Limited,* October 24, 1939, "Complaint." The court papers do not record the amount of the settlement; plaintiff's lawyers cannot find the file; defendants' lawyers decline to reveal amount.

638 "pumpkin papers," "decidedly yes": House of Representatives, Committee on Un-American Activities, *Hearings Regarding Communist Espionage in the United States Government,* 80:2 (GPO, 1948), II, 1387–8.

Notes

PAGE

638 Communists read American codes: *Ibid.*, II, 1405.
638 Currie: *Ibid.*, I, 519, 553, 853; Senate, Subcommittee on Internal Security, *Hearings on the Institute of Pacific Relations*, 82:1 (GPO, 1951), II, 423.
639 *Amerasia:* Senate, Subcommittee on Internal Security, *Interlocking Subversion in Government Departments*, 83:1 (July 30, 1953) (GPO, 1953), 16.
639 secret police, military intelligence: Dallin, 2–5.
639 Cheka resumes: Vassilyev, 294.
639 2nd Special Directorate: Edward Spiro [pseud. E. H. Cookridge], *The Net that Covers the World* (New York: Henry Holt & Co., 1955), 67; *The Soviet Secret Police*, eds. Simon Wolin and Robert M. Slusser, Studies of the Research Program of the U.S.S.R., No. 14 (New York: Frederick A. Praeger Inc., 1957), 108. A 2nd Special Division is said to have existed in the K.G.B. at an unspecified time doing the same kind of black-chamber work as the M.V.D.'s 2nd Special Directorate (Wolin and Slusser, 169).
640 Information Administration: Wolin and Slusser, 199. The agency which received suspicious coded letters from this administration is here called the "Special Administration (SPEKO)"; SPEKO is the acronym for the Spets-Otdel (Agabekov, 263); "administration" may be an almost synonymous translation of *otdel* ("department").
640 Spets-Otdel: Commonwealth of Australia, Royal Commission on Espionage, *Official Transcript of Proceedings* (various places and printers, 1954–1955), 68. Henceforth cited as *Transcript*.
640 quasi-independent, responsible to central committee: Agabekov, 257.
640 attached to foreign directorate: Vladimir and Ekdovia Petrov, *Empire of Fear* (London: Andre Deutsch Ltd., 1956), 55. The Petrovs declined to answer some questions about their cryptologic experience that I wanted to put to them (Australian Embassy, letter, 1964).
640 as 5th Directorate: Petrov, 80. I cannot find any description of an N.K.V.D. 5th Directorate to confirm this.
640 Boki: Petrov, 129–130; *Transcript*, 68–69, 99; Agabekov, 264; Orloff, 173; *Bolshaya Sovietskaya Entsiklopediya* (first ed.), VI (1927), cols. 686–687, trans. Mrs. Albright. He is not listed in the second edition.
640 buildings: Petrov, 86, 126–127, 129; *Transcript*, 68.
641 cryptographic sections: *Transcript*, 69–70; Petrov, 101.
641 section 6, Koslov, Petrov: *Transcript*, 68–69; Petrov, 153.
641 Ilyin, Degtjarov, Shevelev: Petrov, 60, 80, 84.
641 Section 6 growth: Petrov, 56; *Transcript*, 69.
641 Petrov's job: Petrov, 56; *Transcript*, 69.
641 Bokov: Petrov, 80–82.
641 linguistic subsections: Petrov, 134, 142.
641 Kharkevich section: *Transcript*, 151; Petrov, 127.
641 Gusev: *Transcript*, 151; Petrov, 129; *Bolshaya Sovietskaya Entsiklopediya* (first ed.), XX (1930), cols. 27–28, trans. Mrs. Albright. He is not listed in the second edition.

PAGE

641 Japanese section: Petrov, 128–129.
642 aristocrats, Krivoshes: Petrov, 127, 134, 140.
642 security: Petrov, 127, 129.
642 précis: Agabekov, 263.
642 Madame Moritz: Petrov, 149.
642 "carries on the work": "OGPU—Reminiscences of the Chekist, G. Agabekoff," trans. from *Novoye Russkoye Slove* of New York (October 13, 1930), in House of Representatives, Special Committee to Investigate Communist Activities in the United States, *Investigation of Communist Propaganda*, Hearings, 71:3 (December, 1930), Part I, Vol. 5 (GPO, 1931), 147–154 at 149.
642 "first-class lot": Agabekov, 263.
642 section 8: testimony of Ismail Ege in Senate, Subcommittee on Internal Security, *Hearings on Interlocking Subversion in Government Departments*, 83:1 (GPO, 1953), XV, 1012–14.
643 Soviet military intelligence: Igor Gouzenko, *The Iron Curtain* (New York: E. P. Dutton & Co., 1948), 120, 67–68.
643 O.R.D.: Dallin, 14. *Transcript*, 76, mentions a Colonel Vorobiev as head of a similar Otdel Radyosluzhby of the Komitet Informatsyi, a merger of the secret police and military intelligence (or at least of some of their foreign political intelligence functions) under the Foreign Ministry from 1946 to 1951.
643 Kravchenko: Gouzenko, 68–69, 168.
643 "I well remember": Gouzenko, 65.
643 cipher-clerk training: Gouzenko, 59–61, 120, 150–151; Petrov, 49–55; *Transcript*, 67.
644 Leningrad signal school, Sokolniti institute: Ege testimony, 1002–3.
644 "We are being fired on": General Gunther Blumentritt in *The Fatal Decisions*, eds. Seymour Friedin and William Richardson (New York: William Sloane Associates, 1956), 56.
644 enciphered code: Arne Beurling, interviews, September 17 and November 9, 1963; Paschke, May 3, 1962; NA Microcopy T-311, Rolls 83 and 84, Frames 7109028, 7110093–4. Henceforth this series of monthly reports of cryptanalytic activity of the German Army Group North on the Russian front from May 1943 to May 1944, trans. Hardie, is cited only by frame number. I think it likely that the O.K.W.'s translucent light device for solving enciphered codes, at first two-digit codes, was probably devised for this Russian system.
644 replacement: Many of the monthly reports refer to new systems solved, as 7109555 and 7109719.
644 reappearance: 7109555, 7109880.
644 shared and separate systems: Beurling interviews; 7110323.
644 Beurling solutions: Beurling interviews.
645 Swedish cryptanalytic help at Suomussalmi and Salla: Gyldén interviews.
645 44th Division advance, "the enemy's casualties": [Field Marshal Baron Carl Mannerheim], *The Memoirs of Marshal Mannerheim*, trans. Count Eric Lewenhaupt (New York: E. P. Dutton & Co., 1954), 340. Manner-

Notes

PAGE

heim says only that the "news" of this advance reached Finnish headquarters.
645 Red Air Force solutions: Segerdahl interview.
645 Finnish-German intercept exchange: 7109555.
646 no 5-digit solutions: 7109028, 7109123, 7109213.
646 no radio-intelligence service: Colonel-General Franz Halder, quoted in Heilbrunn, 147.
646 good order-of-battle information, Air Force betrayal: Flicke, 146.
646 "The best and most reliable," "In those days," "The Russians were," "The Red Army": Major General F. W. von Mellenthin, *Panzer Battles: A Study of the Employment of Armor in the Second World War*, trans. by H. Betzler (Norman, Okla.: University of Oklahoma Press, 1956), 246, 260, 261, 260.
647 November, December, January new systems: 7109555, 7109719, 7109880.
648 table of solutions: Compiled by me from 7109028, 7109123, 7109213, 7109313, 7109446, 7109555, 7109719, 7109880, 7110093, 7110236, 7110321, 7110432.
649 February 1944 report: 7110094.
649 German cryptanalytic failure, cryptanalyst's judgment: Flicke, 146–152, 166, 206, 209.
649 Enigma solved, "it is forbidden": 7108488–9.
650 no Russian Foreign Office messages read: Paschke, Friedrich, and Beurling interviews; Selchow testimony, 20479 (and, by implication, omission of the Soviet Union from his affidavit listing those countries whose messages Pers z solved); United States Strategic Bombing Survey, *Japanese Intelligence*, 31. Paschke for 1930 start of one-time pad. Beurling cited some technical details of how he failed to solve the messages but recovered some serial numbers that indicated a one-time pad to him. These independent, widespread, repeated, and highly circumstantial admissions make the failure to solve Russian diplomatic messages perhaps the best attested fact of World War II cryptology. Yet during 1941 at least, the German consul at Harbin, Manchuria, repeatedly forwarded to Berlin "intercepted" Soviet diplomatic messages from Moscow (*DGFP*, XII, 250–251, 793; some telegrams from Harbin are at T-120:105:113116–7, T-120:107:113431–2, which I have examined). Harbin was usually forwarding German translations of the Russian messages three days after they were sent from Moscow. Though none of my sources indicated that the Russians used ciphers of a lower grade than the one-time pad for diplomatic purposes, I think that this is the most likely explanation, particularly in view of the fact that all the Harbin intercepts appear to be circulars to all missions.
650 standard Soviet spy cipher: Clausen described his system in detail and deciphered the message of March 3, 1940, for his Japanese captors; an abstract is given in the official Japanese transcript of the Sorge ring interrogation, *Gendai-shi shiryō* (*Materials on Modern History*) (Tokyo: Misuzu Shobō, 1962), I, 93–98, kindly communicated by Chalmers Johnson. In addition, complete descriptions of the cipher are given in

Alexander Foote, *Handbook for Spies* (Garden City, N.Y.: Doubleday & Company, 1949), 250–256, and in the Eriksson case, Case 13–1941, Rådhusrätten of Scheelegatan, Stockholm, with appeal in Nedre Justitie Revisionen. Dr. Käärik examined the court papers and very kindly made his notes and his analyses of the cipher available to me. Dr. Käärik also independently recovered the SUBWAY keyword from a photograph of a Clausen encipherment in Major General Charles A. Willoughby, *Shanghai Conspiracy: The Sorge Spy Ring* (New York: E. P. Dutton & Co., 1952), 97.

651 keys: Willoughby, 98, for Clausen. Foote, 253; Dallin, 216, for Swiss. Eriksson case papers.
654 Sorge ring: general information from Willoughby and Johnson.
655 Clausen radio abilities: Johnson, 164–166; Willoughby, 39–44, 96.
655 "My heart jumped": Willoughby, 235.
655 transmission details: Willoughby, 63, 98, 236.
655 Sorge teaches cipher: Johnson, 101.
655 "I always encoded": Willoughby, 235.
656 Sorge discovered date of Nazi attack: Willoughby, 105; Johnson, 155–156.
656 groups sent: Johnson, 167; Sorge, 121.
656 Japanese interception, no solution: Willoughby, 96, 98; Johnson, 165; Schellenberg, 164; F. W. Deakin and G. R. Storry, *The Case of Richard Sorge* (London: Chatto and Windus, 1966), 208–209, 212.
656 "There will be no attack": Johnson, 158.
656 importance of Sorge information: John Erickson, *The Soviet High Command: A Military-Political History, 1918–1941* (London: Macmillan & Company, 1962), 631; "Soviet Admits Sorge Was Its Spy in Wartime Japan," *The New York Times* (September 5, 1964), 3:1–4; Deakin and Storry, 233.
657 Rote Kapelle: Dallin, 141–143, 152–155, 243–253; Flicke, 174–184; Erickson, 638.
657 Schulze-Boysen in Forschungsamt: Shirer, 1043.
657 June 26: Flicke, 174.
657 six direction-finders: Heilbrunn, 24–25.
657 "proctor": Schellenberg, 280–281; Flicke, 176; Dallin, 153.
658 Teramond: W. F. Flicke, *Spionagegruppe Rote Kapelle* (Kreuzlingen: Neptun Verlag, 1949), a fictionalized account of the spy ring, refers at 147 to "proctor" and at 131 to *Le miracle du Professeur Teramond* by Guy de Lecerf. No such book or author seems to exist, and it seems to be a juggling of the author and title of the Teramond opus, which has a zoologist Lecerf as a character and a geometer Dartifol, which is the name of the landlady in Flicke's story. The book was published at Paris: Édition du Monde Illustré, 1910. I skimmed its 286 pages but did not find "proctor," though its subject matter makes its presence likely.
658 120 messages: Dallin, 252–253.
659 Swiss network: Foote; Dallin, 182–233; Pierre Accoce and Pierre Quet, *La Guerre a Été Gagnée en Suisse* (Paris: Librairie Académique Perrin, 1966.)
659 sources: Accoce and Quet, 80–81, 176.

Notes

PAGE

659 March 12: Foote, 60.
660 "Having returned": Foote, 125–126.
660 six a day: estimate from Dallin, 198.
660 100 words: examination of "250 Intercepted Messages to and from Moscow," a selection of the Swiss ring messages, in Dallin D Papers.
660 radio procedure: Foote, 76–77.
660 "My transmission time": Foote, 126.
660 "On October 19": Foote, 126–127.
660 "Moscow very largely": Foote, 95. Erickson, 638, quotes this approvingly.
661 "splintering crash": Foote, 165.
661 keys in Canada: Gouzenko, 190; Dominion of Canada, Royal Commission to Investigate the Facts Relating to and the Circumstances Surrounding the Communication, by Public Officials and Other Persons in Positions of Trust, of Secret and Confidential Information to Agents of a Foreign Power, *Report*, June 27, 1946 (Ottawa: Edmond Cloutier, 1946), 12. Henceforth cited as Canada, *Report*.
661 security in Australia: *Transcript*, 97, 100–101, 130, 157; Commonwealth of Australia, Royal Commission on Espionage, *Report*, August 22, 1955 (Sydney: A. H. Pettifer, 1955), 85. Henceforth cited as Australia, *Report*.
661 Ottawa fire: "Russians Scored on Embassy Ruin," *The New York Times* (January 3, 1956).
662 photographed documents, burning, P.M.V.: *Transcript*, 21, 49, 121–123, 126.
662 acid: Pawel Monat with John Dille, *Spy in the U.S.* (New York: Harper & Row, 1961), 55–56.
662 new cipher keys: *Transcript*, 9–92.
662 one-time pads in embassy: Australia, *Report*, 86.
662 different branches, different ciphers: Canada, *Report*, 13; *Transcript*, 117–118.
662 semisecret jargon: Australia, *Report*, 53; *Transcript*, 111–112.
662 codenames: Australia, *Report*, 53, 116; *Transcript*, 20; Canada, *Report*, 731–733, and 685 for "we have been unable."
662 sensitive terms removed and separately enciphered: *Transcript*, 27, 122, 162, 208; Australia, *Report*, 86. This system was used during World War II by the French Resistance (Renault, *Comment devenir agent secret*, 117–118.)
662 letter of November 25, 1952: Australia, *Report*, 41–55, with photographs.
663 one-time pad types: Postage stamp is Abel's, size given on F.B.I. photograph; scrolls are Krogers', size given in Wide World Photos photographs; 1954 pad is that of Gregory Liolios, and 1958 is that of Eleftherious Voutsas, both Greek Communists, information from Greece's General Security Police via Apostle G. Millis of Amarousion in letters of September 27, 1962, and January 8, 1963, for which I am greatly indebted; 1957 pad is Abel's; 1961 pad belonged to a group of North Korean Communist spies captured November 20, 1961, by Japanese police, who sent me a photograph of it; booklet pad is Abel's, with details from James B. Donovan, *Strangers on a Bridge: The Case of Colonel Abel* (New York: Atheneum, 1964), 47, 84, and United States

PAGE

District Court for the Eastern District of New York, Criminal Case 45094, *United States of America vs. Rudolf Ivanovich Abel*, transcript of trial, 424–426.

664 typists: study of a page of the Voutsas one-time pad by Dr. Käärik, December 31, 1963, corroborated by Howard T. Oakley.

664 wastebasket: Donovan, 47.

664 Krogers' pads: "An Innocent Looking Suburban House was the Hub and Bank of Spy Ring, Prosecution Allege," *The* [London] *Times* (March 14, 1961), 4:1–7.

664 Martelli: "Britain Says Nuclear Scientist Had Spy Equipment in Office," *The New York Times* (May 16, 1963), 4:4–5.

664 spy for East Germany: "Briefkasten an der Weser-Fähre," *Der Spiegel*, XVIII (February 26, 1964), 24, 26; trans. Hardie.

665 Abel radio details: Donovan, 150, 211, 55–56.

665 Kroger radio details: *London Daily Telegraph* (February 10, 1961), 24; *The* [London] *Times* (March 16, 1961), 7; (March 17, 1961), 7; (February 8, 1961), 5, for "Mrs. Kroger showed."

666 microdots: Donovan, 164–165,

666 Swedish Communist ciphers: Night Lead "Spies," United Press dispatch UP41 (March 15, 1955).

666 Iran: "170 More Seized in Iran in Drive on Red Spy Net," *New York Herald Tribune* (September 8, 1954); "Red Spy Network Smashed by Iran," *The New York Times* (September 11, 1954); "Iran Forms Court for Spying Trials," *Ibid.* (September 17, 1954); Isaac Don Levine, "The Anatomy of a Red Spy Ring," *Life*, XXXIX (November 21, 1955), 172–174, 177–178, 181–182, 187–188, 191. Mr. Levine kindly sent me photographs of messages in the trigonometric code; these were analyzed by Howard Oakley.

668 drops, soft microfilm: Sanche de Gramont, *The Secret War: The Story of International Espionage Since World War II* (New York: G. P. Putnam's Sons, 1962), 227, 227–228.

669 Hayhanen cipher: David Kahn, *Two Soviet Spy Ciphers* (Great Neck, N.Y.: privately printed, 1960), 4–12; reprinted in slightly altered form with some additional details as "Number One From Moscow," *Intelligence Articles* of the Central Intelligence Agency, V (winter, 1961), A15–A28; diagrammed in David Kahn, "Modern Cryptology," *Scientific American*, CCXV (July, 1966), 38–46 at 45.

670 "riddle": Winston Churchill.

671 Russians solve American cipher: Senate, Subcommittee on Internal Security, *The Wennerstroem Spy Case: A Translation Prepared for the Subcommittee*, 88:2 (GPO, 1964), 151.

Chapter 19 N.S.A.

To save space in the following notes, I use the following abbreviations: "*GOM*" for Office of the Federal Register, *United States Government Organization Manual*,

Notes 1101

1964–1965 (GPO, 1964), with years being indicated only for other annual volumes; "AR" for Army Regulation and "AFR" for Air Force Regulation; "Martin-Mitchell" for "Text of Statements Read in Moscow by Former U.S. Security Agency Workers [William H. Martin and Bernon F. Mitchell]," *The New York Times* (September 7, 1960), 10. (As printed there, typographical errors wrongly cite Harry Howe Ransom's *Central Intelligence and National Security* (Cambridge, Mass.: Harvard University Press, 1958) as the source of a great deal of information. In fact the Ransom quote is two paragraphs long and ends with "world-wide scale.")

I have relied extensively upon the following Department of the Air Force Manuals dealing with Air Force Communications–Electronics Doctrine (CED): *Basic Concepts, Missions, and Functions with Communications-Electronics Applications*, Air Force Manual 100–11; *C-E Publications and Training*, Air Force Manual 100–12; *Communications-Electronics Policy*, Air Force Manual 100–13; *Utilization of USAF Communications Services*, Air Force Manual 100–16; and *USAF Communications Complex (AIRCOM)*, Air Force Manual 100–32, published at times ranging from 1959 to 1962. They categorize their topics according to a CED number, such as CED 1105.4b. The first two digits are the same as the number of the manual in the 100 series; CED 1105.4b is thus in Air Force Manual 100–11. The other digits refer to sections, paragraphs, and subparagraphs. I use CED numbers in all my citations because of their brevity and because they are more likely to remain unchanged through various editions and corrections than page numbers.

All government agencies issuing the documents cited are understood to be those of the United States, except in the case of a few British agencies, indicated as such.

At several points in this chapter, I have used the word "probably" or the verb "may" to indicate that the statement is my own supposition.

PAGE

672   Defense Communications System: wall display at headquarters of Defense Communications Agency, Arlington, Virginia; *GOM*, 201; CED 1107.5h.

672   *Annapolis:* " 'Network' Casts Off for Atlantic Fleet," *The New York Times* (March 8, 1964), 84:4; "Seagoing Pentagon Is Ready," *New York Sunday News* (July 16, 1961), 10, for a similar vessel.

672   helmet radios: Department of Defense, *Getting the Word . . . Military Communications*, Pamphlet 1–8 (GPO, 1957), 6.

673   Air Force networks: CED 3201–3219.

674   N.S.A. origin: *PHA*, 35:87 for Willoughby, 9:4499 for Clausen, 10:4909 for Layton.

674   Dulles memorandum: quoted in Ransom, 218, 223.

674   "liaison with": AR 10–125, "Organization and Functions: Army Security Agency" (February 23, 1949), §3e.

675   1949: dates in Navy biographies of assignment to AFSA of Safford (January, 1949), Dyer (June, 1949), Wenger, and Stone (both July 15, 1949). I think the Safford date might have been a misreading of "Jun" for "Jan."

675   November 4, 1952: footnote to CED 1206.5a reads: "Prior to 4 November 1952, the National Security Agency was known as the Armed Forces Security Agency." Canine Army biography confirms the month.

PAGE

675 NSA description: *GOM 1967-1968*, 208. General Canine illuminated the peculiar administrative status of NSA when he testified that it is "within but not a part of the Defense Department," in Senate, Committee on the Post Office and Civil Service, "Transcript of Proceedings" (July 6, 1956), on H.R. 11040, 84:2 (not printed), 17, in NA, RG 46; referred to henceforth as "Canine testimony." I have been unable to find any official references to NSA's intelligence role, but among the official statements describing its security mission are those in CED 1206.5 ("The National Security Agency has the authority and responsibility for the preparation and production of all cryptographic material"), in Department of Defense Instruction 3135.1 (June 4, 1963) ("The Director, National Security Agency, shall establish guidelines and provide technical guidance and support for cryptographic equipment technical training conducted by Department of Defense agencies. . . ."), in AFR 5-38 (February 26, 1963), and references to "mandatory security modifications" of State Department cipher machines "prescribed by the cognizant national authority" and to "standards set by the U.S. communication security authority" in House of Representatives, Committee on Appropriations, Hearings on Department of State Appropriations for fiscal 1965, 400, 402. (For full reference, see below.)

676 first address: *GOM, 1957–1958*, 137.

676 NSA building: "Security Agency at Fort Meade to Cost $30 million," *Washington Evening Star* (May 3, 1953); "Washington Firm Will Install Ft. Meade Security Utilities," (January 7, 1954); "Army Awards Contract for NSA Building," (July 10, 1954); "Work To Start Soon on NSA Building," (July 13, 1954); "NSA to Pinch Buffer County," (June 16, 1957); "New NSA Home Is Efficient, Secure," (June 19, 1957), all *Washington Post*.

676 Annex: Department of the Army, Corps of Engineers, Baltimore Engineer District, *Advance Notice to Bidders*, ENG-18-020-63-38 (March 25, 1963), and C. F. Pfrommer, chief, engineering division, Baltimore Engineer District, letter, October 8, 1964.

677 Agency growth: Canine testimony, 14, for 9,000; Martin-Mitchell; David Wise and Thomas B. Ross, *The Invisible Government* (New York: Random House, 1964), 222, for C.I.A. size and space-utilization figures. Stewart Alsop, "The Battle for Secret Power," *The Saturday Evening Post*, CCXXXVI (July 27, 1963), 17–21, at 18 for NSA "employs more people than CIA;" "C.I.A.: Maker of Policy, or Tool," *The New York Times* (April 25, 1966), 1:2–4, 20:1–8 at 20:4 for budget twice as large as C.I.A.'s.

677 Scientific Advisory Board: General G. B. Erskine, USMC, Ret., letter, February 4, 1955.

677 IDA: "DD Gives Analyses Institute Research Pact in Cryptology," *Electronic News* (March 30, 1959); IDA 3rd, 4th, and 5th annual reports. *AMS* for Albert, Rosser, Liebler; *Who's Who in America, 1962–63*, for Albert.

678 NATO: CED 1105.4e, Figure 11–12.

Notes

PAGE

678 Army Security Agency: *GOM*, 159; *The Origin and Development of the Army Security Agency*, 18; For administrative arrangement and current personnel, see current edition of Department of Defense, *Telephone Directory*, in classified section.

679 A.S.A. customers: *GOM*, 154, 156.

679 Signal Communications Security Agency: AR 10-128, "Organization and Functions: United States Army Signal Communications Security Agency" (December 19, 1957), and AR 380-41, "Military Security: Control of Cryptomaterial" (July 27, 1961).

680 Naval Security Group: *GOM*, 167. For current personnel, see current edition of Department of Defense, *Telephone Directory*, in classified section.

680 10,701: House of Representatives, Committee on Appropriations, Subcommittee on Department of Defense Appropriations, *Department of Defense Appropriations for 1965, Part 1: Military Personnel*, Hearings, 88:2 (GPO, 1964), 201.

680 USAFSS: press kit; *GOM*, 199; AFR 5-38, "Specialized USAF Communications Security Publications" (February 26, 1963).

681 ASA reserve: AR 140-192, "Army Reserve: Military Intelligence and Army Security Units: Organization, Training, Assignment and Retention Criteria" (March 1, 1963), § VII. " 'Why Us?' Reserves At Fort Devens Ask" and "Reservist Who Sent Complaint to Paper Punished by Army," both *The New York Times* (December 4, 1961), 1:7 and 19:4.

681 J-6: CED 1108.2 and Figure 11-27; *GOM*, 130.

681 Military Communications–Electronics Board: CED 1108.3 and Figure 11-28; "Should Communications Have Single Management?" *Armed Forces Management*, VI (January, 1960), 15-18 at 17.

681 NSA reports to Deputy Director: John P. Grigrich, executive assistant, special intelligence staff, Deputy Director of Defense Research and Engineering, letter, September 28, 1964. This arrangement abolished an older one (see *GOM, 1959-1960*, 143-4). The "special committee of the National Security Council" to whose direction and control NSA was ultimately subject in the late 1950s (*GOM, 1957-1958*, 137, *1958-1959*, 193) no longer exists (Bromley Smith, executive secretary, National Security Council, letter, September 14, 1964).

681 Director of Telecommunications Management: *GOM*, 61; CED 1107.4b.

684 United States Intelligence Board: "Intelligence Unit Listed by Dulles," *The New York Times* (February 18, 1960); Wise and Ross, 197-198.

684 President's Foreign Intelligence Review Board: *GOM*, 546. It replaced the President's Board of Consultants on Foreign Intelligence Activities, established in 1956. NSA supervision: J. Patrick Coyne, PFIAB executive secretary, letter, September, 1964.

684 $380,000,000, $100,000,000: Martin-Mitchell. "C.I.A.: Maker of Policy, or Tool," 20:4, says that in the mid-1960s the N.S.A. budget was twice as large as C.I.A.'s $500,000,000.

685 Woikin: Canada, *Report*, 496.

685 Rhodes: "G.I. Tells of Sale of Data to Soviet," *The New York Times* (October 22, 1957), 1:1.

PAGE

685 Clarence: "Briton Sentenced to 5 Years as Spy," *The New York Times* (December 23, 1954), 6:3; "U.S. 'Mystery Man' Will Testify in Russian Spy Trial in Britain," *New York Post* (December 14, 1954), 16.

685 Ceylon: Senate, Committee on the Judiciary, *Exposé of Soviet Espionage, May 1960*, Prepared by the Federal Bureau of Investigation, 86:2, Document No. 114 (GPO, 1960), 35–36; "Ceylon Changes Codes," *The New York Times* (July 16, 1957); Ceylon, Parliament, *Parliamentary Debate (Hansard)*, House of Representatives, Official Report, XXVIII (July 15, 1957), columns 651–654.

685 Kirilyuk: *Exposé of Soviet Espionage, May 1960*, 38. "Soviet Spy Tried to Win American," *The New York Times* (May 24, 1960). Henry Cabot Lodge, U.S. Ambassador to the United Nations, included the Kirilyuk episode in an exposé of Soviet spy activities in the United States that he gave to UN Secretary General Dag Hammarskjöld in 1960 ("U.S. Gives Details of Soviet Spy System in This Country to the U.N.," *The New York Times* [May 25, 1960]).

685 Ollier: Australia, *Report*, 171, for letter; 173, for "If, then"; *Transcript*, page F, for Anglo-American bloc ciphers.

686 success in Paris: "Reds Had French Code, Obtained Dien Secrets," *New York Mirror* (October 5, 1954); "Inside Story of Spy Ring Told by Paris Code Expert," New York *Journal-American* (October 13, 1954), 1.

686 Scarbeck: "The Gal Who Gave Her All Says Doc Gave the Reds Just Trifles," *New York Daily News* (October 6, 1961), 5.

686 Formosa: Night Lead "Formosa," United Press dispatch UP52, (May 27, 1957); "State Department Record of Dulles' News Conference," *The New York Times* (May 30, 1957), 2:3–8.

686 "United States Government," "success in at least": Martin-Mitchell.

686 "NSA also obtains": Victor Norris Hamilton, "Ya Vybral Svobodya" ("I Chose Freedom"), letter to the editor, *Izvestia* (July 23, 1963), 6. I am deeply grateful to Marjorie and Howard Oakley for translating this.

687 Georgiev: "Bulgarian Says He Spied for U.S.," *The New York Times* (December 27, 1963), 1:1.

687 Khrushchev: "U.S. Agents Sell Info to Reds: K," *New York Daily News* (October 3, 1959); Wise and Ross, 208.

687 separate cryptographic storage: AFR 100–40 (April 17, 1964), prescribes establishing communications-security accounts.

687 AR 380–5: (June 6, 1952), §IV.

687 Executive Order 10964: "Amendment of Executive Order No. 10501, Entitled 'Safeguarding Official Information in the Interests of the Defense of the United States,'" (September 20, 1961), §§1 and 5.

687 Public Law 513: Approved by Truman May 13, 1950. For background, see Senate, Committee on Armed Services, *Enhancing Further the Security of the United States by Preventing Disclosures of Information Concerning the Cryptographic Systems and the Communication Intelligence Activities of the United States*, 81:1, Report No. 111 (March 11, 1950), and House of Representatives, Committee on the Judiciary, *Enhancing Further . . .*, 81:2, Report No. 1895 (April 6, 1950). The only discussion of the bill

Notes

on the floor of Congress was a brief explanation at the request of Senator Robert A. Taft (*Congressional Record*, VC [March 18, 1949], 2774–5). Votes were not recorded. An identical bill in the 80th Congress, 2nd Session (S. 2680) never got passed. A bill in the 79th Congress (S. 805) that was essentially similar but would have penalized disclosure of any material that had been enciphered, such as diplomatic telegrams, was vigorously denounced in the House (*Congressional Record*, XCI [October 25, 1945], 10046–52) as gagging Congress and the press; it died in the House. A bill identical to S. 805 in the 80th Congress, 1st Session (S. 1019) was never passed. Hearings on S. 805 and S. 277 appear to have been held in executive session.

688 NSA security: my observations; Dick Schapp, "The Strange Case of the Psycho Traitors," *True*, XLII (June, 1961), 44–47, 89–93 at 44; United States District Court for the Eastern District of Virginia, Alexandria Division, Criminal Case 3049, *United States of America vs. Joseph Sidney Petersen, Jr.*, transcript of hearing before sentence, January 4, 1955, testimony of Dr. Lawrence W. Shinn, 37–39. Henceforth referred to as "Petersen transcript."

689 U.S. Mission to U.N. code room: my observations.

689 NSA funds: United States, *The Budget of the United States Government for the fiscal year ending June 30, 1965, Appendix* (GPO, 1964), shows no NSA, Army Security Agency, Naval Security Group, Air Force Security Service, or cryptology in its index. Nor is NSA listed in the detailed breakdowns of individual agency personnel. (The Army has two cryptologic advisors budgeted for a total of $35,527.) GAO confirmed its audit of NSA funds in telephone interview, October 30, 1963.

689 employee security standards: Department of Defense, press release of Statement by Vincent J. Burke, Jr., general counsel of the Department, before the Special Subcommittee for Investigation of Intelligence Matters of the House Armed Services Committee (September 15, 1960), at 4–11. Henceforth cited as Burke statement.

689 sex questions: House of Representatives, Committee on Government Operations, *Use of Polygraphs as "Lie Detectors" by the Federal Government*, 89:1, House Report 198 (GPO, 1965), 43.

690 NSAers never tell wives: testimony of Frank W. Lewis, Petersen transcript, 32. Walter Millis comments in *Individual Freedom and the Common Defense* (New York: The Fund for the Republic, 1957), at 72: "Probably few who have not engaged in top secret work can appreciate the personal and social and educational consequences of a situation in which a husband cannot even mention to his wife or children the matters which engage his whole working time and energy."

690 "Our job," "But to St. Peter": *The NSA Newsletter*, No. 25 (November, 1955), 9, 2.

690 Petersen: Petersen transcript and the case's indictment (October 20, 1954) and the bill of particulars (November 9, 1954); J. A. Verkuyl, interview, May 19, 1962; "Code Expert Heard on Petersen," *New York Herald Tribune* (October 19, 1954); "Netherlands Got Petersen Secret Data,"

PAGE

Washington Post (October 20, 1954); Bureau of Prisons, letter, September 10, 1964.

692 Martin-Mitchell: Burke statement; "The Defectors," *Newsweek* LVI (September 19, 1960), 33–37; news stories in *The New York Times* (for full listing, see its *Index* for 1960) and in the *Washington Post* on September 8, 15, 16, and 20, 1960; Jack Anderson for Drew Pearson, "The Washington Merry-Go-Round," *Washington Post* (September 4, 1960); Arthur Watson, "The Red Subway—Mexico to Moscow," *New York Sunday News* (August 21, 1960), 70–71; House of Representatives, Committee on Un-American Activities, *Security Practices in the National Security Agency*, Report, August 13, 1962 (GPO, 1962); Sanche de Gramont, *The Secret War* (New York: G. P. Putnam's Sons, 1962), 390–404; J. Bernard Hutton, *School for Spies* (London: Neville Spearman, 1961), 204–206. The defection stirred up enormous interest—it was the lead story of *The New York Times* for the day and ran under a two-column headline—and there was a continuing fallout of news stories from the investigations into the defection. In my article, "Lgcn Otuu Wllwqh Wl Etfown," *The New York Times Magazine* (November 13, 1960), 71, 83–84, 86, 88, 90, I stated that, after the Martin-Mitchell disclosures, "virtually every nation in the world must have taken the elementary precaution of changing their codes and ciphers" and that as a probable result of this "the United States has been plunged into a communications-intelligence blackout unparalleled in the cold war." I have since learned that these statements are incorrect.

696 Klein and Reynolds: *Security Practices in the National Security Agency*, 10–12; "Security Agency Aide Bungles His Own File," *Washington Post* (August 2, 1961); "Favor-Taking Cited, 2nd NSA Man Quits," *Newsday* (November 22, 1961), 7.

696 Hamilton: "Ousted N.S.A. Aide Defects to Soviet; Accuses Code Unit," *The New York Times* (July 23, 1963), 4:3; "Russia Claims Yank Defects," *Newsday* (July 23, 1963).

696 Dunlap: Don Oberdorfer, "The Playboy Sergeant Who Spied for Russia," *The Saturday Evening Post*, CCXXXVII (March 7, 1964), 40, 44–45; "Suicide Bares Red Spy in U.S. Code HQ," *New York Daily News* (October 11, 1963), 1; "G.I. Suicide Sold Secrets to Russia," *The New York Times* (October 11, 1963), 1:7.

697 road signs: my observations.

698 "It identifies it": Petersen transcript, 40.

698 "result in serious": Executive Order 10501.

698 "Past efforts," "In 1960," "The results," tightened employment practices: *Security Practices in the National Security Agency*, 12–13, 16, 17, 18–19.

698 "proved most beneficial," "The committee is confident": *Ibid.*, 17, 2.

699 "NSA, as the Agency": Educational Testing Service, *National Security Agency: Professional Qualification Test*, bulletin for 1964–65 (Princeton, N.J.: Educational Testing Service, 1964), 3.

699 no Dunlap investigation: Senate, Committee on the Judiciary, Subcommittee on Internal Security, letter, October 28, 1963; House of Representatives,

Notes

PAGE

Committee on Un-American Activities, letter, October 29, 1963; Senate, Committee on Armed Services, letter, October 31, 1963.

699 "If a similar": Oberdorfer, 45.

699 "The NSA particularly": Stewart Alsop, "Affairs of State: Hogwash about the CIA," *The Saturday Evening Post*, CCXXXVII (February 15, 1964), 15.

699 "The sensitive nature": *Security Practices in the National Security Agency*, 4.

700 "The committee was so": *Congressional Record*, CII (June 20, 1956), 10695.

700 Public Law 36: Approved by President Eisenhower, May 29, 1959. This was H.R. 4599, 86:1. Committee Report numbers were Senate, 284, House, 231. Hearings were apparently in executive session and there was no debate on the bill on the floor of either house.

700 summary-discharge power bill: Public Law 290, 88th Congress. Approved by President Johnson March 26, 1964. This was H.R. 950. Committee Report numbers were Senate, 926, House, 108. House debate and passage: *Congressional Record*, CIX (May 9, 1963), 8127–8156. No Senate debate. The identical bill in the 87th Congress was H.R. 12082. "This [bill] is": *Congressional Record*, CVIII (September 17, 1962), 19623.

700 "After an exhaustive," "The members": *Congressional Record*, CVIII (September 17, 1962), 19633.

701 "The Agency is faced": House of Representatives, Committee on Un-American Activities, *Amending the Internal Security Act of 1950 to Provide for Maximum Personnel Security in the National Security Agency*, 87:2, Report No. 2120 (August 2, 1962), 5.

702 "whatever power": quoted in Wise and Ross, 356.

702 NSA directors: service biographies. "The Eavesdropper," *Newsweek* (May 31, 1965), 21–22 for "I've had some beauts."

704 NSA deputy directors: Wenger, Navy biography; Ream, *Who's Who in America, 1964–65*; Engstrom, *AMS* and Sperry Rand biography; Tordella, *AMS*.

705 Agency divisions: Martin-Mitchell say that "NSA headquarters is subdivided into four main offices": Production, Research and Development, Communications Security, and Security. This is not quite correct. The Office of Security, by which they mean the Office of Security Services, is only one of several administrative support units.

705 size of agency divisions: Prorated roughly into 12,000 persons on the basis of the following quotas for a Community Chest fund drive: Research and Development, $1,994; Communications Security, $1,606; Production, $8,257; agency total, $14,710 (from *The NSA Newsletter*, No. 25 [November, 1955], 12).

706 recruitment: Canine testimony; Burke statement; Educational Testing Service bulletin; National Security Agency, *Opportunities Unlimited* (GPO, 1956); National Security Agency, *A Challenging Future* (undated).

707 modern management: *The NSA Newsletter*, 5, 9, 11.

707 Campaigne, Jacobs: *AMS*.

707 R/D's three divisions: Martin-Mitchell. I have elaborated on their functions by applying likely duties given in *Opportunities Unlimited* and *A Challenging Future*.

PAGE
708 new transmission techniques: Ken Gilmore, "The Secret Keepers," *Popular Electronics*, XVII (August, 1962), 41–44, 102, 104.
709 dictionaries and grammars: in Library of Congress.
709 "All cryptographic material": CED 1206.5a (2).
709 AFKAG-2: AFR 5-38, §4b.
709 courses of instruction, regulations: Department of Defense, Instruction 3135.1 (June 4, 1963).
709 COMSEC functions: I have elaborated these by applying likely duties given in *Opportunities Unlimited* and *A Challenging Future*.
709 amateur cryptologists: Solomon Kullback, interview, December 7, 1962.
710 Agency will not promise not to use ideas: my experience.
711 PCM: J. R. Pierce, *Symbols, Signals and Noise: The Nature and Process of Communication* (New York: Harper & Brothers, 1961), 132, 138, 276.
711 PCM scrambler: U.S. Patents 2,777,897, 3,071,649, for examples.
711 KY-9: House of Representatives, Committee on Appropriations, Subcommittee on Deficiencies, *Supplemental Appropriation Bill, 1962*, Hearings, 87:1 (August 17, 1961) (GPO, 1961), 539–540. Subsequent references to hearings on supplemental appropriation bills will carry only the title of the hearings, Congress session, date, and page. "Voice scramble," *Army Navy Air Force Journal*, XCIII (December 10, 1955), 8; Joseph Albright, "U.S. Unit Plans for All—Including MIG Attacks," *Newsday* (February 22, 1963).
712 speech compression and scramblers: Martin Weinstock, "The Army and Speech Compression," in *Proceedings of Seminar on Speech Compression and Processing*, L. G. Hanscom Field, Bedford, Massachusetts, September 28–30, 1959 (Department of Commerce, Office of Technical Services). Good bibliography on speech compression and related problems in Paul G. Edwards and John Clapper, Jr., "Better Vocoders Are Coming," *IEEE Spectrum*, I (September, 1964), 119–129.
712 State Department: "Department of State Communications," in Senate, Committee on Government Operations, Subcommittee on National Security Staffing and Operations, *Administration of National Security*, Hearings, 88:2 (April 8, 1964), 505–509, for growth of departmental communications, surplus cipher machines,
712 15 times as much by machine: Department of the Army, [William F. Friedman], *Basic Cryptography*, Technical Manual 32-220, April, 1950 (GPO, 1950), §79b(5).
712 "responsible for providing": *GOM, 1949*, 97.
712 Cryptography Staff: *GOM, 1962–63*, 83, 67; House of Representatives, Committee on Appropriations, Subcommittee on Departments of State and Justice, the Judiciary, and Related Agencies Appropriations, *Departments of State and Justice, The Judiciary, and Related Agencies Appropriations for 1962: Department of State*, Hearings, 87:1 (March 14, 1961) (GPO, 1961), 505. Subsequent references to hearings in this series will carry only the subtitle (*Department of State*), Congress session, date, and page. Department of State, *Biographic Register*, 1959, for Parke.

Notes

PAGE

712   traffic volume: "Department of State Communications," 505; *Supplemental Appropriation Bill, 1962*, 87:1 (August 17, 1961), 546.

713   Cuban crisis: "Link to Moscow Delights Capital," *The New York Times* (April 4, 1963), 1:7.

713   "prepares and executes": *Department of State*, 88:2 (February 5, 1964), 380.

713   growth of Communications Security Division: *Ibid.*, 377, 402. *Department of State*, 89:1 (February 22, 1965), 398–399; *Department of State*, 89:2 (February 16, 1966), 284.

713   cryptanalyst qualifications: Civil Service Commission, *Qualification Standards*, Cryptanalyst Series, GS-1541.

713   Goodman: Department of State, *Biographical Register*, 1963.

714   program completed in 1965: *Department of State*, 89:1 (February 16, 1965), 3; *Department of State*, 89:2 (February 15, 1966), 4.

714   HW-28: *Department of State*, 88:2 (February 5, 1964), 383–384, 407.

714   KW-7: *Ibid.*, 389, 396.

714   KW-1: *Department of State*, 87:2 (March 5, 1962), 549, 565–566.

714   "for the purchase": *Department of State*, 87:1 (March 14, 1961), 515.

714   leased wires, dummy filler: "Electronic Coder Keeps U.S. Secrets" (May 6, 1954), 10:3–4; "Soviet Approves U.S. Message Link" (November 28, 1964), 9:2–3, both *The New York Times*.

715   green operators: House of Representatives, Committee on Un-American Activities, *Investigation of Communist Penetration of Communications Facilities—Part I*, Hearings, 85:1 (July 18, 1957) (GPO, 1957), 1447, 1452, 1462.

715   16,200,000 words—about three out of every five messages being in code: *Department of State*, 89:1 (February 16, 1965), 11, (February 22, 1965), 421.

715   KY-3, KG-13, KY-8: *Department of State*, 88:2 (February 5, 1964), 386, 396, 400, 407.

715   hot line agreement: Department of State, *United States Treaties and Other International Agreements*, XVI, Part 1, 1963 (GPO, 1964), 825–835.

715   "In our negotiations": Sampson, letter, April 13, 1964.

716   ETCRRM II: Visible in U.S. Army Photographs SC 605685 and –6 of the American terminal; Standard Telefon og Kabelfabrik A/S, *Cryptographic Equipment ETCRRM II and II-S* (Oslo, no date); Joseph Tusso of I.T.T., interview, April 19, 1962, for $1,000.

716   test messages: "Gromyko One-Ups U.S. Over 'Hot Line' Testing," *The New York Times* (December 8, 1964), 23:5; " 'Hot Line' Tested Every Hour," *New York Herald Tribune*, European Edition (January 21, 1966).

716   "to help reduce": "U.S. and Soviet Sign 'Hot Line' Accord in Geneva," *The New York Times* (June 21, 1963), 1:3–5.

716   President's communications: *GOM*, 201; "President's Trip Big Logistics Job" (October 9, 1961), 19, "Where Kennedy Goes, There Goes White House" (June 28, 1963), 3:5–7, both *The New York Times*; "The President Gets a New Car," *Popular Science Monthly* (September, 1961), 90–91; "The Flying White House," *Look*, XXVIII (June 2, 1964), 86–96 at 95;

"Adenauer's Phone Tapped, He Tells Bonn Parliament," *The New York Times* (November 10, 1962), 1:6.

717 warrant officers: Fletcher Knebel, "Face of Crisis," *Look*, XXVI (January 2, 1962), 36–38; "Johnson Took Trip Without His Doctor or Code on Plane," *The New York Times* (September 9, 1964), 31:3.

717 "my most solemn": "Text of McNamara's Statement to Platform Group," *The New York Times* (August 18, 1964), 18:2–6.

717 reliability of strike message: CED 1301.10; "Radio to Cut Cost in Firing Missile" (December 14, 1960), "SAC Is Improving Link to Its Bases" (July 12, 1964), 40:3, both *The New York Times;* "Earth Wave Signals Now in the Works," *New York Daily News* (October 10, 1960), 26.

718 strike-order and fail-safe codes: Peter Wyden, "The Chances of Accidental War," *The Saturday Evening Post*, CCXXXIV (June 3, 1961), 17–19, 60–63 at 61; Richard B. Stolley, "How It Feels to Hold the Nuclear Trigger," *Life*, LVII (November 6, 1964), 34–41; "Code Guards Against War-by-Goof," *New York Mirror* (March 1, 1960); "Pentagon Backs 'Fail-Safe' Setup" (October 21, 1962), 69:1–8, "SAC's Flying HQ in the Air 4 Years" (February 4, 1965), 11:4, both *The New York Times*.

718 Johnson asserts overall control: "Johnson Pledges Full Safeguards on Nuclear Arms," *The New York Times* (September 17, 1964), 1:8.

718 missile monitoring: "2 Soviet Rockets Failed, U.S. Says," *The New York Times* (February 11, 1960), 5:1.

718 PROD's eight sections: Martin-Mitchell stated that PROD had only five: ADVA, GENS, ACOM, ALLO, MPRO. They were wrong.

719 listening net: Martin-Mitchell; "U.S. Listening Net Checks on Soviet" (February 8, 1959), 1:1, "U.S. Network Aided Rusk" (October 1, 1964), 2:4-6, both *The New York Times;* "Intelligence," United Press International dispatch NX107, (February 9, 1959).

719 electronic reconnaissance: Martin Mann, "Our Secret Radar War with Russia," *Popular Science Monthly* (January, 1961), 66–69, 225–227; James H. Winchester, "The Soviets' Little-Known 'Wet War,'" *Reader's Digest*, LXXX (April, 1962), 182–191; William L. White, *The Little Toy Dog* (New York: E. P. Dutton & Co., 1962), 5–12, 131; Robert J. Schlesinger, *Principles of Electronic Warfare* (Englewood Cliffs, N.J.: Prentice-Hall, Inc., 1961), ch. 4, 51–80; Harris, 327–350; John M. Carroll, *Secrets of Electronic Espionage* (New York: E. P. Dutton & Co., 1966).

720 satellite reconnaissance: "Big Picture," *Newsweek* (December 31, 1962), 36; Wise and Ross, 303–306; "Soviet Asserts U.S. Spies from Space" (June 10, 1964), 12:6–8, "Satellite Spying by Soviet Hinted" (September 14, 1963), 2:7, both *The New York Times*; Carroll, 187–196.

721 "The Wizard War": Winston S. Churchill, *Their Finest Hour*, Book II, Ch. 4.

722 ECM and ECCM: *Countermeasures*, reprint from *Aviation Week* (November 18 and 25, 1957); *Aerospace Electronics*, reprinted from *Space/Aeronautics* (April, 1960), with bibliography; *The Navigator*, VII (January, 1961); Schlesinger, especially chs. 1, 2, 7; Carroll, *passim*.

Notes 1111

PAGE

724   voice interception: for a sample recording, released by the United States to prove Soviet downing of a U.S.A.F. C-130 that had "strayed" into Soviet Armenia, see "Documents on U.S. Plane's Disappearance over Soviet Union," *The New York Times* (February 6, 1959), 2:2-6. Officials refused to say how the recording had been made. Martin-Mitchell said that the plane was doing electronic reconnaissance.

726   computers: NSA has been reported to have the Whirlwind computer; this is not so.

727   "Black Book": Stewart Alsop, "The Battle for Secret Power," 17.

728   forty nations: Martin-Mitchell.

728   "Italy, Turkey ...": "Two Code Clerks Defect to Soviet; Score U.S. 'Spying,'" *The New York Times* (September 6, 1960), 1:7-8.

729   Suez: "Briton Says U.S. Solved Secret Codes of Allies," *The New York Times* (November 23, 1956); George Wigg, letter, January 2, 1957; Allen Dulles, *The Craft of Intelligence* (New York: Harper & Row, 1963), 168; Wise and Ross, 118, for John Foster Dulles quote; *Proceedings of the House of Commons* (Hansard's) (November 29, 1956), column 576.

730   Rowlett award: The White House, Press Release, March 2, 1966; "Johnson Salutes (Sh!) Code Expert," *The New York Times* (March 3, 1966), 35.

730   Britain: Great Britain, *The British Imperial Calendar and Civil Service List, 1964* (London: H.M.'s Stationery Office, 1964), columns 322, 326; *Who's Who*, 1964 for Sir Eric Jones, Sir Clive Lochnis, Leonard J. Hooper, Brig. John H. Tiltman.

731   "One of the primary," "provide full protection": CED 1301.10d, CED 3204.8a. Other goals at CED 1301.6, −.7, −.8.

Chapter 20   THE ANATOMY OF CRYPTOLOGY

I am grateful to Claude Shannon and to David Slepian for reading an early draft of the parts of this chapter on information theory and making helpful suggestions.

737   "It would not be": A. Adrian Albert, "Some Mathematical Aspects of Cryptography," unpublished paper delivered before the American Mathematical Association, November 22, 1941.

737   "The transformations are": Maurits de Vries, "Concealment of Information," *Synthèse*, IX (1953), 326–336 at 330.

739   stability of letter frequency: for an explanation of this—based on de Saussure's axiom of the independence of sound and meaning—see G. Herdan, *Quantitative Linguistics* (London: Butterworths, 1964), 5–11.

740   Gadsby: Ernest Vincent Wright, *Gadsby, A Story of Over 50,000 Words Without Using the Letter E* (Los Angeles: Wetzel Publishing Co., 1939), 5, 19.

740   lipograms: J. R. Pierce, *Symbols, Signals and Noise* (New York: Harper & Brothers, 1961), 48; C. C. Bombaugh, *Oddities and Curiosities of Words*

and Literature, ed. Martin Gardner (New York: Dover Publications, 1961), 25–26. For language oddities in general, see Dmitri A. Borgmann, *Language on Vacation* (New York: Charles Scribner's Sons, 1965).

740 typewriter: Bruce Bliven, Jr., *The Wonderful Writing Machine* (New York: Random House, 1954), 145–148; Bruce Bliven, Jr., "The Wonderful Writing Machine," *Collier's*, CXXXIII (May 14, 1954), 102–105; "Faster Typewriter," *Time*, XXXIII (March 20, 1939), 39; Roy T. Griffith, "The Minimotion Typewriter Keyboard," *Journal of the Franklin Institute*, CCXLVIII (November, 1949), 399–436.

741 Morse: Edward L. Morse, "The Dot-and-Dash Alphabet," *The Century Illustrated Monthly Magazine*, LXXXIII (March, 1912), 695–706; Wolfe, I, ch. 1, 3–6; Frank G. Halstead, "The Genesis and Speed of the Telegraph Codes," *Proceedings of the American Philosophical Society*, XCIII (November 30, 1959), 448–458.

743 Kaeding: *Haufigkeitswörterbuch der deutschen Sprach* (Berlin: Mittler & Sohn, 1898), 643.

743 Shannon: *Who's Who in America, 1964–1965*; press release, M.I.T., February 4, 1957; Shannon, telephone interview, November 27, 1961; David Slepian, interview, October 28, 1962.

744 Shannon's papers: "A Mathematical Theory of Communication"; *Bell System Technical Journal*, XXVII (July, 1948), 479–523, (October, 1948), 623–656, reprinted in Bell Telephone System Technical Publications as Monograph B-1598; "Communication Theory of Secrecy Systems," *Bell System Technical Journal*, XXVIII (October, 1949), 656–715, reprinted in Bell Telephone System Technical Publications as Monograph 1727.

744 information theory in general: Pierce; Francis Bello, "The Information Theory," *Fortune* (December, 1953), 136–158; Claude E. Shannon, "Information Theory," *Encyclopaedia Britannica;* David Slepian, "Information Theory," *Collier's Encyclopedia*. An example of the theory's use in history is Roberta Wohlstetter's *Pearl Harbor*, which fruitfully uses the concepts "signal" and "noise" to help explain the catastrophe.

744 redundancy: "A Mathematical Theory of Communication," Colin Cherry, *On Human Communication* (New York: John Wiley & Sons, 1957), 115–120, 180–187; George A. Miller, *Language and Communication* (New York: McGraw-Hill, 1951), chs. 4 and 5. The latter are extremely valuable books.

745 four-letter language: adapted from G. T. Guilbaud, *What Is Cybernetics?*, trans. by Valerie MacKay (New York: Grove Press (Evergreen), 1960), 102.

745 "Two extremes of redundancy": "A Mathematical Theory of Communication," §7.

745 Dewey's count: *Relative Frequency of English Speech Sounds* (Cambridge, Mass.: Harvard University Press, 1923), 17–19.

746 voiced stops: George K. Zipf, *Human Behavior and the Principle of Least Effort* (Cambridge, Mass.: Addison-Wesley Press, 1949), 99–107; Miller, 86–88.

746 English 75 per cent redundant: Claude E. Shannon, "Prediction and En-

Notes

tropy of Printed English," *Bell System Technical Journal*, XXX (January, 1951), 50–64, reprinted in Bell Telephone System Technical Publications as Monograph 1819, at 50.

747 nonredundant language: John Locke discusses the impossibility of something approaching this in *Essay on Human Understanding*, Book III, ch. i, §3 and ch. iii, §§2–4; Jonathan Swift, in *Voyage to Laputa*, ch. iii, describes a word-frame in the Grand Academy of Lagado that produces something like it.

748 matching of cryptogram and plaintext frequency counts: for a mathematical demonstration of the validity of the process, see Gustav Herdan, *The Advanced Theory of Language as Choice and Chance* (Berlin: Springer-Verlag, 1966), 182–185.

748 "in . . . the majority of ciphers": Shannon, "Secrecy Systems," §12.

749 puzzle cryptogram: Prosper Buranelli and others, *The Cryptogram Book* (New York: Simon and Schuster, 1928), No. 168.

749 "with a transducer": Shannon, "Secrecy Systems," §17.

749 "The fact that the vowels": *Ibid.*, §19.

750 Masons: *King Solomon and His Followers* (Brooklyn: Allen Publishing Co., 1908), 20.

750 unicity distance: "Communication Theory of Secrecy Systems," §§14–16. Shannon was examining when a solution is valid; interestingly, René Descartes used the cryptanalyst's feeling of certainty when he reaches a solution to help prove a point of his philosophy in his *Principles*, IV, §205 (1644), in *Œuvres et Lettres*, ed. André Bridoux, Bibliothèque de la Pléiade (Paris: Gallimard, 1949), 530–531.

750 Melchior: Ib Melchior, "A Hamlet Enigma at Elsinore," *Life*, XXXVII (August 9, 1954), 81–92; "Hamlet Enigma Again," *Life*, XXXVII (August 30, 1954), 4. John Sack devastatingly parodies the Melchior "solution" in "My Solution of the Grant's Tomb Cipher," *The New Yorker*, XXX (September 18, 1954), 35–36.

750 codeword for *Paris*: Givierge, "Problems of Code," in *Articles*, 24.

751 "From the point of view": Shannon, "Secrecy Systems," §11.

752 Helstrom: letter, March 24, 1961.

752 game theory: Shannon, "Secrecy Systems," §21.

752 best code in Congo: Cathal Og O'Shannon, "Grievances of the Irish in Congo," *The* [Dublin] *Irish Times* (September 6, 1960).

753 "complete examination": de Vries, 329.

753 "Of each such system": [William F. Friedman], *Basic Cryptography*, Department of the Army Technical Manual 32–220 (Washington, D.C.: U.S. Government Printing Office, 1950), §17.

753 practical requirements: *Ibid.*, §18.

754 factors affecting cryptanalysis time: *Ibid.*, §16.

754 "cipher brains": Yardley, 39. He was referring to Manly.

755 pattern recognition: Cherry, ch. 7; Oliver D. Selfridge, "Pattern Recognition and Learning" in *Information Theory: Papers Read at a Symposium on "Information Theory*," ed. Colin Cherry (London: Butterworths, 1956), 345–353.

1114 THE CODEBREAKERS

PAGE

755 Freud: "Three Contributions to the Theory of Sex" in *The Basic Writings of Sigmund Freud*, ed. A. A. Brill, Modern Library Giant 39 (New York: Random House, 1938), 594–595; see also *Psychological Abstracts*, XXIV (1950), No. 6119. I am grateful to Dr. Hanna Marlens for general guidance in this field and to Dr. Pierre A. Bensoussan for reading this section.

755 Reik: letter, March 22, 1961.

755 Fromm: letter, April 14, 1961.

755 Menninger: letter, December 20, 1961.

755 Macfarlane: interview, October 3, 1964.

756 psychological study of secrets: *Psychological Abstracts*, X (1936), No. 4450, English translation at XXV (1951), No. 7298. See also *Ibid.*, XXIX (1955), No. 495, and Raoul de la Grasserie, *De l'Instinct Cryptologique et de l'Instinct Phanérique* (Paris: Librairie Félix Alcan, 1911).

756 Jones: *Free Associations: Memoirs of a Psychoanalyst* (New York: Basic Books, 1959), 43.

756 Huxley: ch. 5.

758 hypocrisy: The basic hypocrisy is, of course, doing the communication intelligence and pretending or claiming that one is not doing it. A more subtle example appears in the *Radio Regulations* of the International Telecommunications Union, drawn up at the International Radiocommunication Conference at Atlantic City in 1947. The signatory nations here appear to be safeguarding the privacy of international radio communications, but, in fact, by a weaseling insertion of the term "authorize," give themselves a license to invade that privacy. Ch. IX, Art. 21, "Secrecy," reads: "[§485] The administrations bind themselves to take the necessary measures to prohibit and prevent: [§486] a) the unauthorized interception of radiocommunications not intended for the general use of the public; [§487] b) the divulgence of the contents, simple disclosure of the existence, publication or any use whatsoever, without authorization, of information of any nature whatever obtained by the interception of the radiocommunications mentioned in 486." The signatories include the major powers of the earth, including the U.S. and the U.S.S.R. Signing for Italy was radio expert and cryptologist Luigi Sacco.

759 varying frequencies of letters: L. F. Brosnahan, *The Sounds of Language* (Cambridge: W. Heffer and Sons, Ltd., 1961), chs. 1–3; review by Morris Swadesh, "Pro and Contra Darlington," *Science*, CXXXIV (September 1, 1961), 609.

759 entropy: William Cecil Dampier, *A Shorter History of Science* (1944, reprinted New York: Meridian Books, 1957), 97–99, 168–169.

760 Borges: "The Library of Babel," in *Labyrinths* (New York: New Directions, 1962), 51–58.

760 calculation of redundancy: Shannon, "A Mathematical Theory of Communication" and "Prediction and Entropy of Printed English"; George A. Miller and Elizabeth A. Friedman, "The Reconstruction of Mutilated English Texts," *Information and Control*, I (September, 1957), 38–55; David Slepian, interview, October 28, 1962.

Chapter 21 HETEROGENEOUS IMPULSES

A citation in the form *N&Q*, 4:5:254, 285, means *Notes & Queries*, Series 4, Volume 5, pages 254 and 285. References to common works of literature are given by chapter instead of by the page of a particular edition.

PAGE

763   Myzskowski: *Cryptographie indéchiffrable* (Paris: Société Française d'imprimerie et de librairie, 1902), at 44–46.
763   Collon: articles in *Revue de l'Armée Belge* (1899); Sacco, §37.
763   Rozier: Rosario Candela, *The Military Cipher of Commandant Bazeries* (New York: Cardanus Press, 1938), 76.
763   Phillips: Gaines, 185–190.
763   Amsco: Gaines, 51.
763   Grandpré: *Cryptographie pratique* (Paris: Boyveau & Chevillet, 1905).
763   Schneider: *Description d'un système cryptographique à l'usage de l'armée* (Paris: L. Fournier, 1912); W. F. Friedman, *The Index of Coincidence and Its Application in Cryptography*, Riverbank Publication 22 (Geneva, Ill.: Riverbank Laboratories, 1922).
763   Porges: "A Continuing Fraction Cipher," *The American Mathematical Monthly*, LIX (April, 1952), 236.
763   Nicodemus: Gaines, 216.
763   Mirabeau: Gaines, 209.
763   Homan: Communication to the author, 1948. This "equifrequency" cipher was broken by Howard T. Oakley; see also his "An Equi-Frequency System," *The Cryptogram* (July–August, 1955), 60–62.
764   cipher mechanisms: In the U.S. Patent Office, inventions dealing with cryptology are classed in the following classes and subclasses—what the Patent Office calls the "field of search for cryptography." Not every patent in these classes deals with cryptography. Class 35, "Education," Subclasses 2–4, for cryptography generally; Class 197, "Typewriting Mechanisms," Subclass 4, for cryptographic typewriters; Class 283, "Printed Matter," Subclasses 11 and 17, for cryptographic printed matter; Class 178, "Telegraphy," Subclass 5.1 for secret facsimile and secret television, Subclass 22, for secret telegraphy; Class 179, "Telephony," Subclass 1.5, for secret telephony; Class 325, "Modulated Carrier Wave Communication Systems," Subclasses 32–35 and 122, for modulated carrier wave systems involving secrecy; Class 116, "Signals and Indicators," Subclasses 18–20, for code signaling generally; Class 340, "Communications, Electrical," Subclasses 345–365, for electrical communications involving code converters and transmitters; Class 234, "Selective Cutting," Subclasses 69–70, 94–108, for cutting or punching involving coding. A list of the patents in each of these subclasses, as well as the patents themselves, may be purchased from the Patent Office. (U.S. Patent Office, letters, November 21, 1962, and November 17, 1965.) About 1950, Howard T. Oakley compiled a mimeographed *List of U.S. Patents Dealing with Cryptography* that gives a one-line

description of the mechanism of many of the patents. Among the patentees, incidentally, is motion-picture star Hedy Lamarr, who, under her married name of H. K. Markey, patented, with a few others, a "Secret Communication System" to guide torpedoes to their targets by secret radio remote control; this is No. 2,292,287.

764 transposition cipher machine: described at Gaines, 13; this appears to be that of Nicoletti, U.S. Patent No. 1,311,457.

764 Jerdan: William Jerdan, *Autobiography* (London, 1852), I, 40–44.

765 Euler: P[ierre]. Speziali, "Le logogriphe d'Euler," *Stultifera navis: Bulletin de la Société suisse de bibliophiles*, X (April, 1953), 6–9.

765 Skeat: *N&Q*, 8:9:6–7, 33, 58–59.

765 fractionating cipher: This is described in Givierge with no inventor named. It turned out to be a bad choice to illustrate the ignorance of inventors, because I have since found that in the earliest exposition I know of this system ("Systèmes de Cryptographie," *Revue Scientifique* [March 24, 1888]), the author, one Pomey, thoroughly analyzed the structure of the system mathematically. This did not lead him, however, to the solution.

766 "Whereas complete trial": Shannon, "Communication Theory of Secrecy Systems."

767 Byrne: J. F. Byrne, *Silent Years: An Autobiography with Memoirs of James Joyce and Our Ireland* (New York: Farrar, Straus, and Young, 1953), 264–307; *Book Review Digest*, 1953; Lynn Caine, publicity director of Farrar, Straus and Cudahy, telephone interview, May 28, 1962.

767 Bloom's cipher: James Joyce, *Ulysses* (Paris: Shakespeare and Company, 1922), 673. G. Smith, Jr., "The Cryptogram in Joyce's Ulysses: a Misprint," *PMLA*, LXXIII (September, 1958), 446–447, discusses errors in later editions.

769 Houdini: *Houdini on Magic*, eds. Walter Gibson and Morris N. Young (1930, 1932; New York: Dover Publications, 1953), 244.

769 American Cryptogram Association: membership from 1965 Directory.

770 newspaper cryptograms: The two types are represented by the "Daily Cryptoquote" in *Newsday* and by the daily cryptogram in the regretted *New York Herald Tribune*.

770 Trinity Church epitaph: Meyer Berger, "About New York," *The New York Times* (January 2, 1957); Charles L. Wallis, *Stories on Stone: A Book of American Epitaphs* (New York: Oxford University Press, 1954), 202–203.

770 church register cryptograms: *N&Q*, 14:157:134, 214.

770 Cramer cryptogram: Pierre Speziali, "Une curiosité parmi tant d'autres," *Les Musées de Genève*, VI (March, 1949), 1.

771 Beale treasure: P. B. Innis, "The Beale Fortune," *Argosy*, CCCLIX (August, 1964), 70–71, 82–84; photostats of Beale Paper cryptograms, Roanoke Public Library, Roanoke, Virginia; Carl Hammer, letter, November 25, 1964, and print-outs from computer, for which I am most grateful.

772 Masons: *King Solomon and his Followers* (Brooklyn: Allen Publishing Co., 1908).

772 Knights of the Golden Circle: NA.

PAGE

772 Phi Beta Kappa: "U Butdz ofn Hpw Tzbu Quhhu, Or, A Table for Phi Beta Kappa," *The Key Reporter*, XXIV (July, 1959), 1.

772 Carbonari: *Intermédiaire des Chercheurs et Curieux* (March, 1954), col. 98, for 1834 cryptogram; Paul Féval, *Les Compagnons du Silence* (1857; Paris: Michel Levy Frères, 1861), Part 2, ch. 7, for key; Prologue, chs. 5, 8, 9, Part 2, ch. 8, Part 5, chs. 1, 5, 13, for enciphered messages. André Lange et E.-A. Soudart, *Traité de cryptographie* (Paris: Félix Alcan, 1925), discuss Féval cipher in Annexe X, 322–326. E. T. Bourg [pseud. M. Saint-Edmé], *Constitution et Organization des Carbonari* (Paris: Corby, 1821), does not give anything about Carbonari cryptology per se, though he does cite letters used as mystic signs (181–182).

773 Lincei-Eck correspondence: Vatican Library, Ms. Vat. lat. 9684, ff. 23–26, 131–3, 140, 144–146.

773 Galileo and Huygens anagrams: William F. and Elizabeth S. Friedman, *The Shakespearean Ciphers Examined* (Cambridge: University Press, 1957), 17. John Wallis duped Huygens with a number of anagrams; see Christiaan Huygens, *Œuvres Complètes* (La Haye: Martinus Nijhoff, 1888), I, 338, 396, 402; II, 306.

773 Wren: Sir David Brewster, *Memoirs of the Life, Writings, and Discoveries of Sir Isaac Newton* (Edinburgh: Thomas Constable & Co., 1855), II, 263; *N&Q*, 5:12:316.

773 Kinsey: Alfred C. Kinsey et al., *Sexual Behavior in the Human Female*, Institute for Sex Research (Philadelphia: W. B. Saunders Co., 1953), 59.

774 Ovid: *Artis Amatoriae* iii.627–630; i.489 for HIM instead of *her;* i.137; also *Amorum* i.4.16ff., ii.5.18.

774 Winthrop: Harry Andrew Wright, "Those Human Puritans," *Proceedings of the American Antiquarian Society*, L (new series) (April 17, 1940), 80–90.

774 Wetherell: 40 *Atlantic Reporter* 728, also at 70 *Vermont* 274; Windham County Clerk, letter, July 25, 1963.

774 Jonathan Swift: *Journal to Stella*, ed. Harold Williams (Oxford: Clarendon Press, 1948), I, lv–lix for discussion of the "little language"; 208 for null cipher (in letter of February 24, 1710/11).

775 Marie Antoinette ciphers: Yves Gyldén, "Le chiffre particulier de Louis XVI et de Marie-Antoinette lors de la fuite de Varennes," *Revue Internationale de Criminalistique*, III (1931), 248–256; this ciphered correspondence was reportedly published by Alma Soderhjelm in 1930 and 1934. Princess de Lamballe, *Secret Memoirs of the Royal Family of France during the Revolution* (Philadelphia: H. C. Carey & I. Lea, 1826), frontispiece, 366, 367.

775 newspaper advertisements: "Secrets Exposed," *Littell's Living Age*, No. 494 (November 5, 1853), 342–344 (taken from *Chambers' Journal*); Babbage Papers, Add. Ms. 37205, ff. 221 for Robert, 68–76 for Flo, 65, 79, 207, 222–224, 227 for others; Wemyss Reid, *Memoirs and Correspondence of Lord Lyon Playfair* (London: Cassell and Co., 1899), 154–155, for *The Times*' editor; Richard J. Cyriax, "The Collinson Cryptograms in 'The Times,' " *N&Q*, CXCII (July 20, 1947), 322–323.

PAGE

776 "I used to resent": Thelma, Lady Furness, "The Prince and I," *The American Weekly* (June 20, 1954), 9.

777 Erik Brahe: Sven Tunberg, "Riksrådet Erik Brahes chifferkalendarium," *Personhistorisk tidskrift*, XX (1918–1919), 37–65; XXIII (1922), 31–38.

777 William Byrd: *The Secret Diary of William Byrd of Westover, 1709–1712*, eds. Louis B. Wright and Marion Tinling (Richmond, Va.: Dietz Press, 1941), vii; *Another Secret Diary of William Byrd of Westover, 1739–1741*, ed. Maude H. Woodfin, trans. Marion Tinling (Richmond, Va.: Dietz Press, 1942), iv.

777 Bertrand: General H. G. Bertrand, *Journal: Cahiers de Sainte-Hélène*, ed. Paul Fleuriot de Langle (Paris: Éditions Gulliver, 1949), I, 16.

777 Pepys: John Eglington Bailey, "On the Cipher of Pepys's 'Diary,'" *Papers of the Manchester Literary Club*, II (1876), 130–137; W. Matthews, "Samuel Pepys, Tachygraphist," *Modern Language Review*, XXIX (October, 1934), 397–404; W. Matthews, "Pepys's Transcribers," *Journal of English and Germanic Philology*, XXXIV (April, 1935), 213–224; *Encyclopaedia Britannica; DNB*. Thomas Grenville as first solver of the diary is theory of D. Pepys Whitely, Pepys Librarian at Magdalene College, Cambridge (letter, November 19, 1965). His second choice is Grenville's older brother, William Wyndham Grenville, Baron Grenville. Both were uncles to Richard Griffin Neville, 3rd Baron Braybrooke, first editor of the diary and, as holder of the barony of Braybrooke, hereditary visitor of Magdalene College. None of their *DNB* biographies shed any light on the question.

779 Rabelais: *Pantagruel* (1532), ch. 24, trans. Sir Thomas Urquhart (1653; Philadelphia: J. B. Lippincott Co., 1912), I, 270–271. Rabelais' *Third Book*, ch. 20, has an episode involving symbolism. Notes by ed. Jean Plattard in the edition Les Textes Français (Paris: Éditions Fernand Roches, 1929) say that Zoroaster never wrote anything on letters hard to understand and that if Bossus, a grammarian contemporary with Domitian, ever wrote the book cited, it is unknown. Notes by eds. Jacques Boulenger and Lucien Scheler in the edition of the Bibliothèque de la Pléiade (Paris: Gallimard, 1955), say that Zoroaster is a grammarian of the time of Domitian and that Bossus and his alleged book are unknown. I can find nothing about ciphers of Zoroaster's and nothing at all about Bossus. *N&Q*, 9:3:128, refers to a "Cyphral Dispatch" at end of one of translator Urquhart's tracts.

781 Shakespeare: *The Life of King Henry the Fifth*, II.ii.6–7, 71. William F. Friedman, "Shakespeare, Secret Intelligence, and Statecraft," *Proceedings of the American Philosophical Society*, CVI (October, 1962), 401–411, demonstrates, in my opinion, that the proofs of guilt that Henry shows the traitors are indeed the intercepted letters. But I think Friedman has fallen victim to an unnecessary interpretation when he argues that the letters had been enciphered and that Henry's agents had cryptanalyzed them. His arguments are purely hypothetical and without basis in the play. One might as well suppose that the letters were also in invisible ink. The original documents had no effect on Shakespeare's play, of course, but M. McGuinness of the Public Record Office wrote on May 9,

Notes

PAGE

1963: "A number of documents (other than those printed in *Rymer's Foedera* IX, p. 300 et seq., and in *Rotuli Parliamentorum* IV, pp. 64–67) relating to the conspiracy against Henry V were found in Miscellanea of the Exchequer (E.163/7/7) and are printed in the Forty Third Report of the Deputy Keeper of the Public Records, 1882, p. 582 et seq. The original documents are written *en clair* and I have not found any evidence to suggest that they were originally enciphered. Documents produced for and at the trial of the conspirators at Southampton would normally have been filed among Ancient Indictments (KB 9) but I have been unable to trace any at the appropriate date; nor any entry on the Plea Roll for Michaelmas 1415 (KB 27/618)."

781 Balzac: *La Physiologie du Mariage* (Paris, 1829), Meditation XXV, §1, at II, 207–210 and 347 for erratum. In the Notes to the edition of the Bibliothèque de la Pléiade (Paris: Gallimard, 1960), which was based on the last text reviewed by Balzac himself, editor Marcel Bouteron says, at 895, that "One need not seek any sense in the text, designedly indecipherable, on page 835. Balzac wanted to hide his opinion on religion and confession from us; he managed it by a typographic jest in the fashion of his favorite author, the English humorist [Laurence] Sterne, in having printed letters assembled by chance." Bazeries, 90–98; Lange & Soudart, Annexe VI, 305–307; *N&Q*, 10:3:368.

783 Poe's interest in cryptology: For other theories on its origin, see *DAB* and Clarence S. Brigham, *Edgar Allan Poe's Contributions to Alexander's Weekly Messenger* (Worcester, Mass.: American Antiquarian Society, 1943), 11, which reprints Poe's articles in that paper. This brochure is reprinted from the Society's *Proceedings*, LII (April, 1942), 45–125. Reference to Poe's articles will be made by date to *AWM* (for *Alexander's Weekly Messenger*). I am grateful to W. K. Wimsatt, Jr., for reading my section on Poe and commenting upon it.

783 *The Narrative of Arthur Gordon Pym*: ch. 23.

784 Schuyler Colfax: *AWM* (April 29, 1840), 2:4.

784 "ugliest and drollest": *AWM* (January 22, 1840), 2:5

784 "Do people really": *AWM* (February 12, 1840), 2:5.

784 "Were we to engage": *AWM* (March 25, 1840), 2:6.

784 statistics on number of cryptograms solved: W. K. Wimsatt, Jr., "What Poe Knew About Cryptography," *PMLA*, LVIII (September, 1943), 754–779 at 755.

784 "Just let us into," "Well, what will": *AWM* (January 22, 1840), 2:5.

784 seven alphabets, promise to reveal method: *AWM* (February 19, 1840), 2:2–3. William F. Friedman, "Edgar Allan Poe, Cryptographer," *American Literature*, VIII (November, 1936), 266–280, at 270–272, raises the question whether this seven-alphabet message might have been a keyword polyalphabetic. Wimsatt, 762, dismisses this possibility, and I agree: Had Poe actually solved one such, he would have crowed about it.

784 "Upon second thought": *AWM* (February 26, 1840), 2:4; Wimsatt, 779.

784 Kulp false cryptogram: *AWM* (February 26, 1840), 4:3–5.

785 Cardano grille: *AWM* (February 26, 1840), 4:3–5.

PAGE

785 Lord's Prayer, "Twelfth Night": *AWM* (February 26, 1840), 2:4, (March 11, 1840), 2:3.
785 "single glance": *AWM* (February 26, 1840), 2:4.
785 unkeyed symbol alphabets: My tabulation, based on cryptograms as printed in *AWM. a* = 1 alphabet, *AWM* (April 22, 1840), 2:3.
785 "Our correspondent will": *AWM* (January 15, 1840), 2:4.
785 errors and omissions: *AWM* (April 22, 1840), 2:3, for example; Wimsatt, 765.
785 Poe's reputation: Brigham, 11; Wimsatt, 765 for "immediately," 777 for "This cryptograph," 765 for "much shorter time," 760 for "in one-fifth," 778 for "The most profound."
786 "far beyond the ordinary," "native power": Wimsatt, 778. Wimsatt's article is the definitive study of Poe's cryptology and stands up extremely well under scrutiny; most of its judgments are valid, and I am indebted to it for the framework of my own study, but I think that here Wimsatt's lack of familiarity with the practice of cryptanalysis has led him astray. This charge cannot be leveled against William F. Friedman, who concludes his "Poe" article with the judgment that "Had he [Poe] an opportunity to make cryptography a vocation, there is no doubt that he would have gone far in the profession." But this is a pure guess, not even based on the evidence of the Alexander's articles, which had not then been discovered, and its force seems to be negated by a nearby sentence (280): "Against his will he [the serious student of cryptography] is driven to the conclusion that Poe was only a dabbler in cryptography." Even Poe never claimed to be anything else. Moreover, the article is unfair to Poe, evaluating him from a modern and not a contemporary point of view. It belittles what the achievement of a polyalphabetic solution would have been in those pre-Kasiski days and taxes Poe with not knowing some things (about Renaissance cryptology) that no one else in his time knew. The article was, nevertheless, the first study of Poe's cryptography. In sum, I think that the Wimsatt and Friedman judgments of an exceptional cryptanalytic ability for Poe are unwarranted.
786 "Doubtless nothing": quoted Friedman, "Poe," 266.
787 "In the notice": quoted Friedman, "Poe," 268.
787 keyphrase cipher: Friedman, "Poe," 268–270; Gaines, 103.
787 "A Few Words on Secret Writing": printed in *The Complete Works of Edgar Allan Poe*, ed. J. A. Harrison (New York, 1902), XIV.
788 "It may be roundly": quoted Wimsatt, 776. *AWM* (March 25, 1840), 2:6, (April 22, 1840), 2:3.
788 "scraps of erudition," sources: Wimsatt, 767–771.
788 "in his own intellect": quoted Wimsatt, 769.
788 Thomas episode: Friedman, "Poe," 272–276; Wimsatt, 756–759, 764–765, with facsimile.
788 Blair article: William Blair, "Cipher," in Abraham Rees, *The Cyclopaedia* (London: Longman, Hurst, Rees, Orme & Brown, 1819), VIII, unpaged. *DNB* for Blair.
789 Poe's borrowings from Blair: Wimsatt, 771–775, with facsimile.

Notes

PAGE

789 "Out of a thousand": quoted Friedman, "Poe," 277.
789 sources for "The Gold-Bug": William Bittner, *Poe: A Biography* (Boston: Little, Brown & Co., 1962), 184–185; Hervey Allen, *Israfel: The Life and Times of Edgar Allan Poe* (New York: George H. Doran Co., 1927), I, 209–220.
789 publication history of "The Gold-Bug": Bittner, 185–186; *Famous Stories of Code and Cipher*, ed. Raymond T. Bond (New York, 1947), introduction to "The Gold-Bug"; Edgar Allan Poe, *Oeuvres en Prose*, trans. Charles Baudelaire, ed. Y.-G. LeDantec, Bibliothèque de la Pléiade (Paris: Gallimard, 1951), 1081.
790 last cryptographic publication: Wimsatt, 759.
790 correspondence, "I have lost": Wimsatt, 759–760.
790 absurdities and errors: J. Woodrow Hassell, Jr., "The Problem of Realism in 'The Gold Bug,' " *American Literature*, XXV (May, 1953), 179–192; Bittner, 185; Edward Wagenknecht, *Edgar Allan Poe: The Man Behind the Legend* (New York: Oxford University Press, 1963), 102–104, bibliography, 241.
791 narrative drive of "The Gold-Bug": Allen, II, 566; Hassell, 192; Wagenknecht, 104.
791 "I cannot keep," "How beautiful": Poe, Bibliothèque de la Pléiade, 1032.
791 "As we follow": Wimsatt, 779.
792 Poe glamorized cryptology: Wimsatt, 778.
792 success of "The Gold-Bug": Allen, II, 565–566.
792 Lewis Carroll: frequency list under "Alphabet Cipher" in Modern Library edition of his complete works.
792 "Popular interest": Friedman, "Poe," 266.
793 Thackeray: *The History of Henry Esmond*, Book III, ch. 8.
793 Jules Verne: William F. Friedman, "Jules Verne as Cryptographer," *Articles;* Lange & Soudart, Annexe IX, 311–322; Charles W. R. Hooker, "The Jules Verne Cipher," *The Police Journal*, IV (January, 1931), 107–109; *Voyage au Centre de la Terre* (1864), chs. 2–5; *La Jangada* (1881); *Mathias Sandorff* (1885), Part I, chs. 1, 3, 4.
794 Sherlock Holmes: in A. Conan Doyle, *The Complete Sherlock Holmes* (Garden City, N.Y.: Garden City Publishing Co., 1938), the cryptogram and solution in "The Valley of Fear," Part I, ch. 1, appears at 904–907, in "The 'Gloria Scott,' " at 429 and 436–437. The light flashes are in "The Adventure of the Red Circle," 1066 and 1073, and the word puzzle in "The Musgrave Ritual."
796 cryptologists sneer: Fletcher Pratt, "The Secret Message of the Dancing Men," in *Profile by Gaslight: An Irregular Reader about the Private Life of Sherlock Holmes*, ed. Edgar W. Smith (New York: Simon and Schuster, 1944), 274–282 at 275; Bond's introduction to the story in his anthology, *Famous Stories of Code and Cipher*.
796 dancing-men sources: Albert J. Myer, *A Manual of Signals*, new ed. (New York: D. Van Nostrand, 1868), 281; U.S. Patent No. 1,267,640; E. T. Bourg, 181–182. Pratt theorizes that Watson eliminated the real cipher from the story he told and inserted in its place the dancing men, whose

1,568 arm and leg positions form the cipher symbols of a small code in which Holmes recorded a secret account of Moriarty's gang. He bases this upon the equivalence between the 1,568 possible positions and the statement that Bazeries, after solving a nomenclator of Antoine Rossignol (which Pratt calls Rossignol's "Great Cipher," which it was not), "reported that the possible total of characters was exactly 1,568." This statement is false: Bazeries never said any such thing. (Émile Burgaud and Commandant Bazeries, *Le Masque de Fer* [Paris: Firmin-Didot, 1893], 257–289.) Nor, in point of fact, is the possible total 1,568. End of theory.

797 errors: original publication is A. Conan Doyle, "The Return of Sherlock Holmes. III: The Adventure of the Dancing Men," *The Strand Magazine*, XXVI (December, 1903), 602–617. [Edgar W. Smith], "Addendum," *The Baker Street Journal*, V (new series) (April, 1955), 90–91; Bond's introduction.

797 tables of arm and leg positions: three articles in *The Baker Street Journal* (new series): Remsen TenEyck Schenck, "Holmes, Cryptanalysis and the Dancing Men," V (April, 1955), 80–90; Robert H. Pattrick, "A Study in Crypto-Choreography," V (October, 1955), 205–209; Howard R. Schorin, "Cryptography in the Canon," XIII (December, 1963), 214–216. Other studies of Holmes's cryptology are David Shulman, "Sherlock Holmes: Cryptanalyst," *The Baker Street Journal*, III (1948), 233–237; Lord Donegall, "Baker Street and Beyond," *The New Strand*, I (August, 1962), 1048-1050, II (February, 1963), 1717–1720.

798 Westrell Keen: Robert W. Chambers, *The Tracer of Lost Persons* (New York: D. Appleton & Co., 1906), chs. 9 and 10.

798 *Colonel Quaritch, Q.V.:* (London: Longmans, Green & Co., 1911), chs. 4 and 39. W. Lionel Fraser, *All to the Good* (London: Heinemann, 1963), 59, for Haggard's niece and nephew in Room 40.

799 *Magnificent Obsession:* (1929), chs. 5 and 6.

799 O. Henry: in Bond.

799 Tagore: Cited in Anil Baran Ganguly, *Sixty-Four Arts in Ancient India* (New Delhi: English Book Store, 1962), 173.

799 *The Mystery of the Sea:* (New York: Doubleday, Page & Co., 1902), frontispiece, ch. 12, Appendices A-D.

799 Christie, Bentley, de la Torre, James: all in Bond.

799 *Have His Carcase:* (1932), ch. 26.

799 *Panic:* (New York: William Morrow & Co., 1944).

800 *From Russia, With Love:* (New York: The Macmillan Company, 1957).

800 *Dishonored:* Pratt, *Secret & Urgent;* cited also (under film's other title, *X-27*) by M. Berry, "De la Cryptographie Musicale," *Revue Internationale de Criminalistique*, X (1938), 212–224.

800 *The Secret Code:* advertising material for the series, in my possession.

800 Elgar's Enigma: Irving Kolodin, "What is the Enigma?" *Saturday Review*, XXXVI (February 28, 1953), 53, 55, 71.

801 Jacob Lawrence coded title: "Birth of a Nation," *Time*, LXIX (January 14, 1957), 82.

Notes 1123

Chapter 22 RUMRUNNERS, BUSINESSMEN, AND MAKERS OF NONSECRET CODES

PAGE

802 rumrunners' use of radio and codes: Malcolm F. Willoughby, *Rum War at Sea* (Washington, D.C.: U.S. Government Printing Office, 1964), 105–106; an Assistant Secretary of the Treasury, letter of December 17, 1931, to Secretary of State, in folder "Radio Stations, Illicit," Box 20, Records of U.S. Coast Guard Intelligence Division, NA, RG 26. This folder is henceforth cited simply as " 'Radio Stations, Illicit.' "

803 hundreds of messages accumulate: Elizebeth Smith (Mrs. William F.) Friedman, "History of Work in Cryptanalysis, April, 1927–June, 1930," NA, RG 26, at 1. Cited henceforth as "E. S. Friedman."

803 Prohibition hires Mrs. Friedman, intercept stations: Lieutenant Commander F. J. Gorman, "Memorandum for the Commandant," October 10, 1930, NA, RG 26, at 2. Cited henceforth as "Gorman."

803 Mrs. Friedman solves, Housel: E. S. Friedman, 1–3.

803 growth of rumrunners' cryptography: E. S. Friedman, 3–5.

804 $10,000 a year: Gorman, 4.

804 retired lieutenant commander, Gulf and Atlantic groups make up own codes: Mrs. Friedman, interview, December 2, 1962.

804 "Some of these," "At no time": E. S. Friedman, 3.

804 "anchored in harbor" system and message: E. S. Friedman, 6–8.

804 "In this case": E. S. Friedman, 7.

804 Mrs. Friedman's offices: Mrs. Friedman, interview, December 2, 1962.

806 12,000 messages solved, customers: E. S. Friedman, 5–6.

806 month in Houston: E. S. Friedman, 4.

806 Meals: Willoughby, 108, 110.

806 *CG-210*: Willoughby, 109–112; Gorman 2–3. Dates of Friedman's service from his Army biography.

806 "This intercepted material": Gorman, 1.

806 radio-intelligence unit: Willoughby, 112–113; Gorman, 5–6 for recommendation.

807 headquarters cryptanalytic unit: "Memorandum Upon a Proposed Central Organization at Coast Guard Headquarters for Performing Cryptanalytic Work" and "Memorandum for Commander Gorman Upon the Personnel for a Proposed Central Organization at Coast Guard Headquarters for Performing Cryptographic and Cryptanalytic Work," NA, RG 26. Both memoranda are undated and unsigned, but their content, style, purpose, and addressee make it highly likely that Mrs. Friedman wrote them, and I have incorporated this assumption in my text. "For the past several years," "Fuel maintenance alone," in "Memorandum upon a Proposed Central Organization" at 2, 7.

808 cryptanalytic unit comes into being: undated remarks by Lieutenant Commander Gorman following Admiral Billard's speech in "Radio Stations, Illicit."

808 Coast Guard radiomen: Willoughby, 113.

PAGE

808 *Maurice Tracy:* Willoughby, 114–115.
808 *John Manning:* "Memorandum Upon a Proposed Central Organization," 4, 5; Willoughby, 114.
809 1FJ case: Lieutenant Frank M. Meals, letter, February 27, 1931, re special investigation No. S233, in "Radio Stations, Illicit."
809 Highland Avenue case: Lieutenant Frank M. Meals, letters of January 24 and February 16, 1931, re special investigation No. S232, in "Radio Stations, Illicit"; New York *Journal* (January 20, 1931). The same folder contains a number of records of other cases involving codes, and Thomas M. Johnson, "Secrets of Bootleggers' Grapevine," *Popular Mechanics*, LVIII (November, 1932), 744–747, gives a picture of a rumrunner's codebook.
809 Mrs. Friedman's other solutions: Leah Stock Helmick, "Key Woman of the T-Men," *The Reader's Digest* (September, 1937), 51–55; Royal Canadian Mounted Police, letter, February 21, 1963.
810 Coast Guard intercepts Consolidated messages, others seized: Lieutenant Commander F. J. Gorman, "Memorandum" to Commandant, July 8, 1933, NA, RG 26.
810 raid of April 11, 1932: "Wireless Station Operator Called in Rum Ring Trial," New Orleans *Times-Picayune* (May 2, 1933), 1, 12. I am grateful to Donald E. Newhouse for helping make newspaper clippings of the case available to me.
810 "That a secret code or codes": District Court of the United States of America for the Eastern District of Louisiana, *United States vs. Albert M. Morrison et al.*, Criminal Case No. 7255, indictment, 9.
811 "brains of the ring": "Wireless Station Operator Called in Rum Ring Trial."
811 Kelly messages: Criminal Case 7255, Exhibits X1 to X32. The two cited are X6 and X7.
811 Mrs. Friedman's testimony: Criminal Case 7255, Transcript, 141–174, at 141–143 for qualification. Cited henceforth as "Transcript."
811 code system used: This was reconstructed from the intercepts and plaintext by W. M. Bowers of Clarksburg, West Virginia, to whom I am most grateful. For the rumrunners compiling their own vocabulary, Mrs. Friedman, interview, December 2, 1962.
811 solution of messages: Transcript, 150, 154.
811 "elicits a conclusion": Transcript, 145.
811 "This is not": Transcript, 147.
812 Gex cross-examination: Transcript, 163–166.
813 Morrison sentence: United States Court of Appeals, Fifth Circuit, *United States vs. Albert Morrison et al.*, Case 16,981, Warrant on Sentence.
813 "I am taking the liberty": copy attached to Lieutenant Commander F. J. Gorman, "Memorandum" to Commandant, July 8, 1933, NA, RG 26.
814 *I'm Alone* case: United States, Department of State, *"I'm Alone" Case: Joint Interim Report of the Commissioners and Statements of the Agents of Canada and the United States Pursuant Thereto with Supporting Affidavits*, Publications of the Department of State: Arbitration Series

Notes

PAGE

No. 2 (6) (Washington, D.C.: U.S. Government Printing Office, 1935), at 183–196, Document 12, "Affidavit of Elizabeth Smith Friedman, of November 30, 1934, Describing the Decoding of the 'Carmelha,' 'Mocana,' and 'Harforan' Telegrams"; Katherine A. Kellock, "She Breaks Up Smugglers' Plots by Decoding Their Notes for Uncle Sam," Washington (D.C.) *Star* (July 22, 1934); Helmick, 54–55; Willoughby, 128–130.

815 Teapot Dome: Senate, Committee on Public Lands and Surveys, *Leases Upon Naval Oil Reserves*, Hearings, 68:1 (GPO, 1924), with Friedman testimony at Part 10, 2483–7, 2515–21, 2548–51. Pertinent McLean testimony at 2680, 2692–5, 2688–9, 2709.

816 Justice Department code: my reconstruction.

816 "means of a codebook": *Leases Upon Naval Oil Reserves*, Hearings, 2486.

816 "that whenever an agent": *Ibid.*, 2503.

817 code testimony revitalized interest: Burl Noggle, *Teapot Dome: Oil and Politics in the 1920s* (Baton Rouge, La.: Louisiana State University Press, 1962), 131–132.

817 Gyldén solution, results: Gyldén papers in my possession; "Skottsaker smugglarbåt," *Stockholm Aftonbladet* (September 27, 1934), 1.

817 complicated criminal codes rare: M. Girerd of Interpol, interview, August, 1965, said that he could recall no case in which smuggling rings had used cryptograms. In this connection I might note here that almost none of the articles on cryptology in criminological journals discuss any actual cipher systems used by criminals. They simply review the basic elements of cryptology, giving perhaps a single example—which in most cases might even be fictitious—of a monoalphabetic substitution, or some hobo's signs. Better than most, however, are Don L. Kooken, "Cryptography in Criminal Investigations," *The Journal of Criminal Law and Criminology*, XXVI (March, 1936), 903–919, XXVII (May–June, 1936), 75–96; Edmond Locard, *Les Faux en Écriture et leur Expertise* (Paris: Payot, 1959), ch. 7, "Écritures Secrètes," 369–389; Francisco García de Parada, "Criptografia," *Investigación*, XXVIII (December, 1960), 38–40, XXIX (February, 1961), 57–59, (March, 1961), 57–59, (June, 1961), 51–53. Edmond Locard, *Traité de criminalistique*, VI, *L'Expertise des Documents Écrits* (*Seconde Partie*) (Lyon: Joannès Desvigne & Cie., 1937), "Les Correspondances secrètes," 831–931; he offers some juicy real-life cryptograms at 866–871.

817 Voyatzis system: Robert Rice, *The Business of Crime* (New York: Farrar, Straus & Cudahy, 1956), 116–117.

817 ORDERING 19: Donald Fish, *The Lawless Skies: The Fight Against International Air Crime* (New York: G. P. Putnam's Sons, 1962), 174, picture opposite 65.

818 Abraham P. Chess solutions: Dan Paonessa, "Code Detective," *Coronet*, XXXVI (August, 1954), 35–37; "Codes Are Fragile," *Spring 3100*, XXXIII (April, 1952), 10–12, with many illustrations of the policy codes.

819 post-Chess N.Y.P.D. cryptanalysts: Joseph G. Martin, deputy commissioner, letter, November 29, 1965.

PAGE

819   F.B.I. Cryptanalytical and Translation Section: personal visit, April 16, 1963. Not to be confused with the F.B.I. Coding Unit in Room 4642 of the Justice Department building.

819   "Cryptosystems involving bookmaking": untitled memorandum prepared for me by the F.B.I., January 8, 1962, and later condensed as "FBI Cryptanalysts Decipher 'Bookie' Codes and Ciphers," *FBI Law Enforcement Bulletin*, XXXI (July, 1962), 15–17, (August, 1962), 15–17, (September, 1962), 28–29.

820   bookie cryptosystems: *Ibid.*

821   pornographic film code: "Identify 300 Sin Film Girls; Cops Break Code, Start Hunt," *New York Daily News* (March 24, 1959), 1, 3; telephone call to prosecutor.

821   knock cipher: used even in Estonia—William Tomingas, *Vaikiv Ajastu Eestis* (New York: Eesti Ajaloo Instituut, 1961), 327–328.

821   employment codes: "Coded Bias Notes Barred by State," *The New York Times* (September 11, 1962); Benjamin R. Epstein and Arnold Forster, *Some of My Best Friends...* (New York: Farrar, Straus & Cudahy, 1962).

821   electrical price-rigging codes: "5 Big Electrical Concerns Charged with Bid Rigging," *The New York Times* (February 17, 1960), 1:2–3; "Price-Rigging Electric Execs Get Shock: Jail," *New York Daily News* (February 7, 1961), 2:1–2; William L. Maher, Chief, Middle Atlantic Division, Antitrust Division, Department of Justice, letter, March 13, 1961, quoting District Court of the United States of America for the Eastern District of Pennsylvania, *United States vs. General Electric Co. et al.*, Criminal Case 20235, indictment, §11h, and transcript, 245.

821   card sharks: Frank Garcia, *Marked Cards and Loaded Dice* (Englewood Cliffs, N.J.: Prentice-Hall, 1962), 79–83.

822   cheating at world bridge tournament: *The New York Times;* "Un bridgeur fume un cigare: 'Je suis en train de tricher, prouvez-le,' "*France-Soir* (August 10, 1965).

822   Kotzbeck jargon code: "Ye Olde Curiosity Shop Deals in Ye Olde Vice," *New York Sunday News* (February 19, 1961).

822   specialized languages: Macalister, *Secret Languages of Ireland*, 136, for Shelta; "Language Codes," *Fraternal Order of Police Journal* (November, 1933), 12, 18–19, for Medical Greek; "Secret Languages," *Encyclopaedia Britannica*, for Langos and Todas; personal experience for Pig Latin; Jenny Hauck for King Tut language; Iona and Peter Opie, *The Lore and Language of Children* (Oxford: at the Clarendon Press, 1959), "Secret Languages," 320–322. Other works on secret languages, which I have not seen, are G.-S. Colin, *Le parler enfantin de Rabat et de Tangier*; R. Iversen, *Secret Languages in Norway* (1944–1950).

822   argot: Pierre Guiraud, *L'Argot*, Que sais-je, No. 700 (Paris: Presses Universitaires de France, 1963), with bibliography.

823   English argot: Eric Partridge, *A Dictionary of the Underworld* (London: Routledge & Kegan Paul Ltd., 1950).

823   thieves in Peshawar: Gottlieb William Leitner, *Section I of linguistic fragments discovered in 1870, 1872 and 1879 ... relating to the dialect of*

Notes

the Maggadds and other wandering tribes, the argots of thieves, the secret trade-dialects and systems of native cryptography in Kabul, Kashmir and Punjab ... (Lahore: Punjab Government Civil Secretarial Press, 1882), xiv.

823 early church financial encipherments: Clara Fabricius, "Die Litterae Formatae im Fruhmittelalter," *Archiv für Urkundenforschung*, IX (1925), 39–86, 168–194.

823 Knights Templars: J.-H. Probst-Biraben and A. Maitrot de la Motte-Capron, "Les Templiers et leur Alphabet Secret," *Mercure de France*, CCXCIII (August 1, 1939), 513–532 at 522, 530.

823 merchants in Peshawar, goldsmiths in Kashmir: Leitner, xv, xvi.

824 butchers in Hanoi: Guiraud, 66–61.

824 magicians' mind-reading codes: John Nanovic [pseud. Henry Lysing], *Secret Writing: An Introduction to Cryptograms, Ciphers and Codes* (New York: David Kemp & Co., 1936), 80–88.

824 antique dealer code: for the solution of one of these codes, see André Langie, *Cryptography*, trans. J. C. H. Macbeth (London: Constable, 1922), 116–121.

824 Broadhurst: George Broadhurst, "Some Others and Myself," *The Saturday Evening Post*, CIC (October 23, 1926), at 42.

824 Macy's solves Masters code: Richard Austin Smith, "Business Espionage," *Fortune*, LIII (May, 1956), 118–126, 190, 192, 194, at 119.

824 Kreuger: 26 × 26 ivory plaque in possession of Boris Hagelin, who kindly showed it to me; "Ciphering in progress here" sign in possession of W. F. Friedman; Gyldén instruction reported by Gyldén, interview, May, 1962. I have not been able to confirm or refute the J. P. Morgan cryptanalysis rumor.

824 no business cryptanalysis: Ulmont O. Cumming, who has done considerable business espionage, says in a letter, October 30, 1963, that he has never heard of any cryptanalysis for business espionage.

825 Hong Kong solutions: William J. Mitchel, interview.

825 Kryha: U.S. Patent 1,744,347; various advertising pamphlets; Hamel's *Die Chiffriermaschine Systeme Kryha* (1927); Sacco, §45 for description, §114 for solution.

826 Ottica Meccanica Italiana: advertising pamphlet for its Cryptograph; Italian Patents 452,848 and 490,996.

826 Mi-544: Gerhard Grimsen, "Cryptographic Telegraph Equipment Mi-544," *Electrical Engineering*, XXV (1958), 209–214.

826 Gretag: *The Concept of Ciphering, Gretag Teleprinter and Ciphering Device Type KFF*, and *Transmission Control and Ciphering System TC-534* (all three Regensdorf-Zurich: Gretag, n.d.); R. Winter, letter, September 23, 1966.

826 NBC encodes messages: "Long Live the Queen!" *Time*, LXI (May 25, 1953), 67.

826 Hermoni: "Robs Banks Via Cable; Caught by Own Line," *New York Sunday News* (September 14, 1958).

826 commercial scramblers: David Kahn, "The Sound of Secrecy," *Newsday* (December 1, 1961), 1c. Delcon Corporation, *Telephone Security* (Palo

1128 THE CODEBREAKERS

PAGE

Alto, Calif.: Delcon Corporation, 1960), and *Product Bulletins 101, 102, 103* (n.d.); U.S. Patent 3,114,800; "The Murchisons and Allan Kirby," *Life* (April 28, 1961), 79, for picture of Clint Murchison using Delcon scrambler. Westrex Company, *Type 58 Privacy* (New York: Westrex Corporation, 1961), and *Type 59 Privacy* (New York: Westrex Corporation, 1960); "Airline to Offer Telephone Calls," *The New York Times* (January 27, 1960); Philip J. Klass, "El Al to Use In-Flight Phone Service," *Aviation Week* (July 6, 1959). Lynch Communication Systems, *E-7 and B-69 Speech Privacy Equipment* (San Francisco: Lynch Communication Systems, 1960).

826 fortification plans concealed: Robert S. S. Baden-Powell describes this in relating his experiences in the Boer War.

828 stereoscopic cryptography: Herbert C. McKay, "Notes from a Laboratory," *American Photography*, XL (November, 1946), 38–39, 50; Herbert C. McKay, "Stereo Photography," *U.S. Camera*, XIII (October, 1950), 16, with example.

828 plastic lenticle system: U.S. Patent 3,178,993.

829 fiber optic cryptography: Narinder S. Kapany, "Fiber Optics," *Scientific American* (November, 1960), 72–81, with diagrams of fiber optic coder and photographs of encode and decode at 77; "Picture Tube," *Time* (December 3, 1956), 69–70. I have not seen Brouwer et al., "Two Dimensional Coding of Optical Images," *Optica Acta*, II (April, 1955).

829 difficulties of fiber-optics coders: R. J. Meltzer, letter, August 23, 1965.

829 Bausch & Lomb fiber-optic encoders: U.S. Patents 3,145,247 and 3,178,993.

829 LeFebure Corporation: *Instant Verification* (no place or date of publication); "Signature Scrambler Foils Forgery," *Management and Business Automation* (September, 1960), 53.

829 R.C.A.: *Signature Verification* (Camden, N.J.: R.C.A., n.d.); R.C.A. press release, "RCA Develops New Signature Scrambling Device to Block Bank Passbook Forgery," October 11, 1960.

830 Vernam cifax: U.S. Patents 1,613,686 and 1,657,366.

830 Belin mechanism: U.S. Patent 1,657,366; Sacco, §46.

831 pay-TV: Federal Communications Commission, *Subscription TV and the FCC*, INF Bulletin No. 20-G (September, 1964). Pay-TV is the F.C.C.'s Docket 11279.

831 Jerrold's reports: Don Kirk, "Engineering Report on Encoding Television Signals," in *Wired TV is the Best Way to Bring Toll TV to the American Public* (Philadelphia: Jerrold Electronics Corporation, 1955); "Technical Description of Proposed Television Codes and Methods of Decoding Zenith, Skiatron and Telemeter Scrambled Broadcasts," Appendix to Jerrold Electronics Corporation, *Reply to Comments in Response to Notice of Proposed Rule Promulgated by the Commission on February 10, 1955*; Before the Federal Communications Commission, Docket No. 11279 (Philadelphia, Pa.: Jerrold Electronics Corporation, September 8, 1955). I would like to thank Mr. Kirk for his kindness in reading the draft of this section.

832 systems of encipherment: abstracted from above reports.

Notes 1129

PAGE

832 monalphabetic substitution, one-time system: "Engineering Report," §B.
832 "In a conventional LP": "Engineering Report," §C2a.
832 "This would pose": "Engineering Report," §C2b.
833 "require only inexpensive": "Engineering Report," §C2b.
833 Skiatron, Zenith, and Telemeter systems: "Technical Description."
833 "for successful operation," "even if one": "Technical Description," 32, 31.
834 "This corresponds to": "Engineering Report," §A.
834 "not . . . a coding procedure": "Technical Description," 32.
834 "which can be eliminated": "Engineering Report," §D2.
834 "Thus, it may well be": "Technical Description," 38.
835 "Assume for the moment": "Engineering Report," §D2.
835 "Pay-television systems do not": William C. Rubinstein, letter, January 10, 1966.
835 "The world is full": *Ibid.*
835 Hartford test: "Fee-Vee," *Time* (July 5, 1962), 39. Perhaps the only other place in the country that broadcasts scrambled television is New York City's Channel 31, which televises pictures of criminal line-ups to half a dozen police precinct houses, saving detectives and witnesses from having to go down to headquarters to view suspects; the pictures are scrambled to protect the rights of suspects ("20 Police Stations Get Television Sets in Test of U.H.F.," *The New York Times* [March 22, 1962]; Ira Kamen, "Scrambled Line-Up," *Popular Electronics*, XVII [August, 1962], 57; Walter Arm, deputy commissioner, New York City Police Department, letter, April 17, 1963). New York City enacted Local Law No. 271 on March 18, 1963, making it a misdemeanor for unauthorized individuals to unscramble the telecasts; this became §434a-38.0 of the Administrative Code of the City of New York.
836 Chappe: "Chappe, Claude" and "Télégraphe" in *La Grande Encyclopédie*; Jean Laffay, *Les télécommunications*, Que sais-je? No. 335 (Paris: Presses Universitaires de France, 1961), 10–14.
836 Chappe's codes: Col. Pamart, "Abraham Chappe, fut-il le premier transmetteur militaire?" *Revue des Transmissions*, No. 47 (November, 1952), 5–6, 9–12, 15–20, 23–27, at 5. France's Archives Nationales has a copy of the *Grand Vocabulaire* in four large handwritten volumes; this is F^{90} 11690. What seem to be official codes based on the Chappe system are F^{90} 11660-3; the Archives catalog says they were used in the July Monarchy and the Restoration (1830–1848). The Musée Postal at Paris has a number of handwritten sheets on which words and syllables are represented by two or three positions of the Chappe semaphore. The U.S. Library of Congress has an anonymous *Telegraphic Dictionary* (Brooklyn, T. Kirk, printer: 1812), whose 382 pages list words in columns with no numbers or codewords next to them. There is no explanation for its use and I do not know for what it was intended.
837 1845 *Telegraphic Vocabulary:* William F. Friedman, *Report on the History of the Use of Codes and Code Language, the International Telegraph Regulations Pertaining Thereto, and the Bearing of This History on the Cortina*

Report, International Radiotelegraph Conference of Washington: 1927, Delegation of the United States of America (Washington, D.C.: U.S. Government Printing Office, 1928), 6. Friedman was technical adviser to the American delegation. I have depended heavily upon this superb report in my discussion. It is cited henceforth as "Friedman, *Report*."

837 British maritime signals: "Signalling," *Chambers's Encyclopaedia*.

838 Smith: *Biographical Dictionary of the American Congress*; Robert Luther Thompson, *Wiring a Continent* (Princeton, N.J.: Princeton University Press, 1947), 13.

838 Morse's special vocabulary: Friedman, *Report*, 7.

838 Rogers: in the Library of Congress. All commercial codes henceforth mentioned in the text may be found in the Library of Congress; I have therefore deemed it unnecessary to give bibliographical information for them unless the text calls for it.

838 shift from figures to dictionary words: Friedman, *Report*, 7–8.

838 one eighth in code: cited to Alexander Jones, *Historical Sketch of the Electric Telegraph* (New York, 1854).

838 Clausen-Thue: Royal Geographical Society, letter, April 16, 1963.

838 codewords charged as if plain language: Friedman, *Report*, 11.

838 M. Abenheim and other codes: all the Library of Congress.

839 dangers of dictionary words: Friedman, *Report*, 15–20; *Guide to the Correction of Errors in Code (and Other) Telegrams*, 4th ed. (London: ["The Electrician" Printing and Publishing Co., Ltd.], 1890), for proportions of errors.

840 Primrose: *Frank J. Primrose vs. The Western Union Telegraph Co.*, 154 *U.S.* 1. The case was heard in the October term, 1893, and decided May 26, 1894. The opinion of the court was delivered by Justice Horace Gray, with only Justice John Marshall Harlan (grandfather of the Justice of the same name appointed by President Eisenhower) dissenting—as was his wont. The decision cites, at pages 32 and 33, other cases involving errors in cipher messages. Two later cases are 128 *Southeastern Reporter* 500, involving a change from BLUFFNESS to BLUFFING in a 1923 message and causing a loss of $663, in which the North Carolina Supreme Court ruled for the telegraph company, and 35 *Southern Reporter* 190, in which ALIKE was received as ALIVE in 1892, causing a loss of $304.89, and in which the Mississippi Supreme Court held that the customer was entitled to recover that amount—the only court to do so. The other cases involving telegraphic error—31 *Southern Reporter* 222 and 18 *Southern Reporter* 425—became tangled in jurisdictional problems and were not settled on the basic question. References to other legal problems of cipher-message transmission may be found in *American Jurisprudence* under "Cipher" and "Telegraphs and telephones—cipher messages," *Corpus Juris Secundum* under "cipher," "cipher messages," and "code book," *Words and Phrases* under "cipher, cipher dispatch or message," and *Abbott New York Digest* under "Cipher messages" and "Telegraphs and Telephones—cipher messages." Many of these other cases involve the failure to deliver a message, such as 245 *New York Reports* 284, or the

Notes
1131

PAGE

failure to stop one, such as 139 *New York Supplement* 289. In reading these cases, one sometimes comes across famous names. 245 *N.Y.R.* 284 was argued for the appellant by Vincent R. Impellitteri, later mayor of New York, and was decided by Judge Benjamin R. Cardozo, later a great U.S. Supreme Court justice. 139 *N.Y.S.* 289 was decided by Justice Samuel Seabury, later to gain fame as the man who cleaned up Jimmy Walker's New York.

840 compilers eliminate dangerous words: Friedman, *Report*, 21.
841 artificial codewords: Friedman, *Report*, 21–25.
841 code condenser: example taken from *The Standard 12 Figure Converter Code*.
842 I.T.U. tariff regulations: Friedman, *Report*, 11–15, 25, 31–32; George A. Codding, Jr., *The International Telecommunications Union*, Université de Genève: Institut Universitaire de Hautes Études Internationales (Leiden: E. J. Brill, 1952), 67–75, 153–154.
843 I.T.U. official vocabulary: Friedman, *Report*, 29–30, 32–33.
843 artificial codewords admitted: Friedman, *Report*, 35–39.
843 *Whitelaw's*: Friedman, *Report*, 39.
843 Bentley's and five-letter codes: Friedman, *Report*, 40–43.
844 Bentley: H. B. Bentley, memorandum, May 2, 1963, and letter, May 11, 1963.
844 codes for all industries: from Library of Congress Card Catalog under subject entry "Cipher and Telegraph Codes.'
845 more codes after war: Friedman, *Report*, 59.
845 American code-compilers: William J. Mitchel, interview, June 10, 1965.
845 Macbeth: R. W. Bell, historian, Marconi's Wireless Telegraph Co., letter, May 3, 1963.
846 Kircher: George E. McCracken, "Athanasius Kircher's Universal Polygraphy," *Isis*, XLIX (November, 1948), 215–228. For other written forms of international languages, see M. Monnerot-Dumaine, *Précis d'Interlinguistique* (Paris: Librairie Maloine, 1960), 11–16.
846 *International Code of Signals:* "Signalling," *Chambers's Encyclopaedia*.
846 salesmanship: Mitchel interview.
846 "By reading telegrams," methods of code-compiling: Mitchel interview.
847 "I had a great mass": 91 *Federal Reporter Second* 998. Hartfield had sued Peterson for copying his code; U.S. Circuit Court Judges Martin T. Manton, Learned Hand, and Augustus N. Hand upheld the award of $5,000 damages to Hartfield.
847 business firms compare codes: Mitchel interview.
847 no transposition of letters: Mitchel interview; Paul D. Green, "Lost Your Money? Wire KUBIT," *The Saturday Evening Post* (November 6, 1948).
848 code construction chart: William F. Friedman and Charles J. Mendelsohn, "Notes on Code Words," *The American Mathematical Monthly*, XXXIX (August–September, 1932), 394–409 at 408.
848 "most codemakers": Rudolf Schauffler, "Über die Bildung von Codewörtern," *Archiv der Elektrischen Übertragung*, X (1956), 303–314 at 312. Hardie translation.

1132   *THE CODEBREAKERS*

PAGE

848   unpopularity of pronounceability: Friedman, *Report*, 50–58.
849   Cortina proposals: Friedman, *Report*, 59–70.
849   three vowels per codeword: Friedman and Mendelsohn, "Notes on Code Words," 394.
849   effect of teletypewriters: Friedman, *Report*, 62.
849   effect of 1932 regulations: Jesse F. Gelders, "The Strange Language of the Cables," *Popular Science Monthly*, CXXVIII (March, 1936), 22–23, 86.
850   not a single practicing code compiler today: Mitchel interview.
850   "digital shorthand": Robert W. Bemer, "Do It By the Numbers—Digital Shorthand," *Communications of the Association for Computing Machinery*, III (1960), 530–536; mimeographed I.B.M. press release, " 'Digital Shorthand' Can Triple Data Link Capacity," July 5, 1960.

Chapter 23   CIPHERS IN THE PAST TENSE

For the problem in general, see F. Stix, "Geheimschriftkunde als historische Hilfswissenschaft," *Mitteilungen des Österreichischen Instituts für Geschichtsforschung*, XIV, 453–459, and C. Trasselli, "La crittografia, scienza ausiliaria della storia," *Nuova Critica*, Nos. 3, 4 (1945).

854   "His Majesty suddenly": Armand Baschet, *Les Archives de Venise: Histoire de la Chancellerie Secrète* (Paris: Plon, 1870), 312.
854   "Were we able": Wharton, I, 281, quoted in Edmund C. Burnett, *Letters of Members of the Continental Congress* (Washington, D.C.: Carnegie Institution of Washington, 1921–1936), III, xxxiii.
854   Bergenroth: *DNB*; W. P. Cartwright, *Gustave Bergenroth: A Memorial Sketch* (Edinburgh: Edmonston and Douglas, 1870), 3–11.
855   "Simancas is a collection": Cartwright, 89–90.
855   "Shrill notes," "none but drivers," kitchen girl: Bergenroth letters quoted in Cartwright, 67–68, 54, 56.
855   castle, administrative difficulties: Cartwright, 58–64, 93, 95–97.
856   cryptanalytic endeavors: These are pieced together from Bergenroth's letters to the Master of the Rolls in 1860 and 1861, printed in Cartwright, and from his "Remarks on the Ciphered Despatches in the Archives at Simancas," originally published in Great Britain, Public Record Office, *Calendar of Letters, Despatches and State Papers Relating to the Negotiations between England and Spain* (London: Longman, Green, Longman & Roberts, 1862), I (*Henry VII: 1485–1509*), ed. Gustave Bergenroth, at cxxxvii–cxlvi, and reprinted in Cartwright, to which reference is made in this note. "I did not," Cartwright, 205; "The first thing," 209; "When copying," 91; "The question," 213.
856   "Nothing but," "The despatches": Cartwright, 206, 98.
857   only key not read: Cartwright, 207.
857   Ayala: Cartwright, 76.
857   Friedmann assists: Cartwright, 53, 163. Friedmann is not listed in *DNB*, no biographical notices are given in the catalogue of the New York

PAGE

Public Library, and the Public Record Office has no biographical information on him (letter, January 8, 1965).

857 Bibliothèque Nationale: Manuscrits français, nouvelle acquisition 4206, a small notebook with 19 cipher keys marked "Don de M. Paul Friedmann, . . . 8 février 1880."

858 Michiel: *Les dépêches de Giovanni Michiel*, ed. Paul Friedmann (Venice: Imprimerie du Commerce, 1869), v–xvi; Paul Friedmann, "Some New Facts in the History of Queen Mary," *Macmillan's Magazine*, XIX (November, 1868), 1–12, at 1–3.

859 Pasini: *Les dépêches de Giovanni Michiel*, xiv; Baschet, 82, 111–112, 309–312; Galland, 16; Archivio di Stato, Venice, letter, October 19, 1964.

859 Gabbrielli: Archivio di Stato, Florence, letter, March 12, 1964; G. E. S[antini]., "Dispacci in cifre del R. Archivio di Stato di Firenze," *Archivio Storico Italiano*, III series, XIV (1871), 473–476 at 476 for 400 solutions; Meister, *Diplomatischen*, 42–47.

859 Burnett: III, xxxiii: "The present editor has deciphered all such letters as have been found."

859 Bischoff: "Übersicht über die nichtdiplomatischen Geheimschriften des Mittelalters," *Mitteilungen des Instituts für Österreichische Geschichtsforschung*," LXII (1954).

859 Lohmann: "Cifras y claves indianas," *Anuario de Estudios Americanos*, XI (1954), 285–380, XIV (1957), 351–359.

859 "The reason": Peckham, letter, August 15, 1962.

859 Price: *The Equatorie of the Planetis*, ed. Derek J. Price (Cambridge: University Press, 1955), 182–187.

860 Devos: *Les chiffres de Philippe II et du Despacho Universal durant le XVIIe Siècle* (Brussels: Académie Royale de Belgique, 1950), 418.

860 Gomez del Campillo: "De Cifras," *Boletín de la Real Academia de la Historia*, CXXIX (October–December, 1951), 279–307.

860 Monterde: "La carta cifrada de Don Hernán Cortés," *Anales del Museo Nacional de Arqueología, Historia y Etnografía*, 4th época, III (1925), 436–443.

860 Fuchs: Robert Fuchs and Gottfried Buschbell, "Die Instruktion Karls V. für den Kardinal von Trent, Cristoph Madruzzo, nach Rom (von 11. June 1546)," *Archiv für Urkundenforschung*, XIV (1935), 188–210.

860 Biaudet: "La correspondance diplomatique de Don Juan de Zúñiga y Requesens," *Suomalaisen Tiedeakatemian Toimituksia*, series B, VIII (1912), 31–41 at 35.

860 Brunon: Jean Brunon and Jean Barruol, *Les Français en Italie sous Henri II* (Marseilles: Collection Raoul et Jean Brunon, 1952), 44–45, 48, 76–78.

860 Rosell Planas: *Las claves de Martí y el plan de alzamiento para Cuba*, Publicaciones del Archivo Nacional de Cuba, XVI (Havana: Talleres del Archivo Nacional de Cuba, 1948).

860 Rommell: "La clef des chiffres dans la correspondance inédite de Henri IV avec Maurice le Savant," *Allgemeine Zeitschrift für Geschichte*, V (1846), 402–404.

PAGE

860 Bazeries: 201.
860 Man in the Iron Mask: Émile Burgaud et Commandant Bazeries, *Le Masque de Fer* (Paris: Firmin-Didot, 1893), 257–272 for solution, 1–3 for message of July 8; Lieutenant Colonel Léger, "Le masque de fer," *Le Monde Militaire*, No. 70 (October 21, 1949), 7, 10, for refutation.
862 Neff: Robert H. Fowler, "Was Stanton Behind Lincoln's Murder?" *Civil War Times*, III (August, 1961), 4–23.
863 description and history of Voynich manuscript: William R. Newbold, *The Cipher of Roger Bacon*, ed. Roland G. Kent (Philadelphia: University of Pennsylvania Press, 1928), 1–51; *Thirty-Five Manuscripts*, Catalogue 100 (New York: H. P. Kraus, 1962), 42–46.
866 Dee: *DNB*; John E. Bailey, "Dee and Trithemius's 'Steganography,'" *N&Q*, 5:9:401-402, 422–423.
866 "Dr. Arthur Dee": Charlotte Fell-Smith, *John Dee*, at 311–312, quoted Newbold, 40.
866 attempts at solution: John M. Manly, "The Most Mysterious Manuscript in the World," *Harper's Magazine*, CXLIII (July, 1921), 186–197 at 190.
867 specialists: correspondence relating to the manuscript, in Kraus's possession; letters, Yardley to Manly, February 18, 1921, and January 13, 1922, Manly Papers.
867 Newbold: Kent foreword in Newbold, xi–xiv.
867 Newbold cipher: most clearly at Newbold, 106–107.
867 results and excitement: Manly, 186–187; John M. Manly, "Roger Bacon and the Voynich Ms.," *Speculum*, VI (July, 1931), 345–391; "Roger Bacon's Cipher Manuscript," *The American Review of Reviews* (July, 1921), 105–106.
868 "In a concave mirror," "I did not know": Newbold, 124, 123.
868 cilia, "Professor Newbold's theory": Manly, 193, 195.
868 J. Malcolm Bird: "The Roger Bacon Manuscript," *Scientific American Monthly*, III (June, 1921), 492–496, at 495 for "Professor Newbold has not."
868 Carton, Gilson: Manly, 347.
868 American and British: Lynn Thorndike, review in *American Historical Review*, XXXIV (January, 1929), 317–319; Robert Steele, "Science in Medieval Cipher," *Nature*, CXXII (October 13, 1928), 563–566.
869 "is open to objections," "threaten to falsify": Manly, 347.
869 "I frequently": Newbold, 103.
869 different solutions of the same text: Manly, 358–360.
869 "contain assumptions": Manly, 348.
869 1,000 pages in Catalan: Newbold, xxvi.
869 "of his own intense": Manly, 390.
870 Feely: *Roger Bacon's Cipher: The Right Key Found* (Rochester, N.Y.: privately printed, 1943), at 41. This is the translation for line 28 of the manuscript's folio 78r (Newbold, plate V).
870 Strong: "Anthony Ascham, the Author of the Voynich Manuscript," *Science*, new series, CI (June 15, 1945), 608–609; L. C. Strong and E. L.

Notes 1135

PAGE

McCawley, "A Verification of a Hitherto Unknown Prescription of the 16th Century," *Bulletin of the History of Medicine*, XXI (November–December, 1947), 898–904. Criticism from W. F. Friedman in interviews.

870 1944 Friedman attempt: Friedman, letters to Mrs. Voynich's secretary, Miss Anne M. Nill, May 25, June 29, August 5, 1944; Elizebeth Smith Friedman, " 'The Most Mysterious MS' Still an Enigma," *The Washington Post* (August 5, 1962), E1, E5.

870 Dalgarno and others: Frederick Bodmer, *The Loom of Language*, ed. Lancelot Hogben (New York: W. W. Norton & Co., 1944), 448–460; Mario Pei, *One Language for the World* (New York: Devin-Adair, 1958), 88–90, 143–150; M. Monnerot-Dumaine, *Précis d'Interlinguistique* (Paris: Librairie Maloine, 1960), 72–81, 11–16.

871 Petersen: interviews, July 3, 1962 (by telephone), December 15, 1963.

871 "the attack has": Manly, 391.

871 no hoax: Petersen interviews; Friedman, telephone interview, June 19, 1962.

871 Ethel Voynich: "A Best Seller in Russia," *Look*, XXII (July 8, 1958), 68–70; "Ethel L. Voynich, Novelist, Was 96," *The New York Times* (July 29, 1960).

871 "The moment someone": H. P. Kraus, interview, June 19, 1962.

872 16th-century work, foundation: E. S. Friedman, " 'The Most Mysterious MS' Still an Enigma."

872 probably an herbal: Petersen.

Chapter 24   THE PATHOLOGY OF CRYPTOLOGY

873 Thomas Usk: *The Complete Works of Geoffrey Chaucer*, VII: *Supplement: Chaucerian and Other Pieces*, ed. Walter W. Skeat (Oxford: Clarendon Press, 1897), xix–xx.

873 cuneiform acrostic: W. G. Lambert, "Ancestors, Authors, and Canonicity," *Journal of Cuneiform Studies*, XI (1957), 1–14 at 1, citing *Zeitschrift für Assyriologie*, XLIII, 34.

873 *Hypnerotomachia Poliphili:* J. A. Symonds, *Renaissance in Italy*, IV; [New York Public Library] *Bulletin*, XXXVI (July, 1932), 475–486, LVIII (September, 1954), 419–428.

874 Donnelly: *DAB*; Martin Ridge, *Ignatius Donnelly: The Portrait of a Politician* (Chicago, Ill.: University of Chicago Press, 1962), especially ch. 14, "The Great Cryptogram," 227–244.

874 "I will reread": Ridge, 227.

874 *Atlantis* and *Ragnorök*: Martin Gardner, *Fads and Fallacies in the Name of Science* (New York: Dover Publications, 1957), 164–166, 35–37; Ridge, 202.

875 "I have been working": Ridge, 228.

875 "I think about it": Ridge, 229.

PAGE
875 New York *World*: Ridge, 231. The mathematician was Thomas Davidson.
875 "terrible task," "infinite sense": Ridge, 233–234.
875 workings of cipher: Mostly from William F. Friedman and Elizebeth S. Friedman, *The Shakespearean Ciphers Examined: An Analysis of Cryptographic Systems Used as Evidence That Some Author Other Than William Shakespeare Wrote the Plays Commonly Attributed to Him* (Cambridge: University Press, 1957), ch. 3, "Ignatius Donnelly and The Great Cryptogram," 27–50; some from Ignatius Donnelly, *The Great Cryptogram: Francis Bacon's Cipher in the So-Called Shakespeare Plays* (Chicago, Ill.: R. S. Peale & Co., 1888).
876 root-numbers: Donnelly, 583.
876 "Shaks't spur": Donnelly, 719.
876 special printer: Ridge, 232.
876 book's failure: Ridge, 233–237.
876 criticism: Friedman and Friedman, 35–45, 49–50.
878 European tour, "I will put": Ridge, 237–243.
878 *The Cipher in the Plays and on the Tombstone:* (Minneapolis, Minn.: Verulam Publishing Company, 1899); Ridge, 244.
878 "enigmatology": Pierre Henrion, *Jonathan Swift Confesses, I: Gulliver's Secret* (Versailles: privately printed, 1962), 49. This appears to be a renaming of the "generalised cryptology" which he opposes to modern, scientific, rigid cryptography in *Baconiana*, No. 160, at 43, 46, 47, and No. 161, at 111.
879 Owen, Arensberg, Booth, Durning-Lawrence, Johnson, Cunningham: Friedman and Friedman, chs. 5, 10, and 9, and pp. 106–107 and 83–85, and plates iv and v.
882 "in our youth": Francis Bacon, *Of the Advancement and Proficience of Learning*, trans, Gilbert Wats (Oxford: Leon Richfield for the University, 1640), 265. This is the first English translation of *De Augmentis Scientarum*. The cipher section is in Book VI, ch. 1.
882 *Of the proficience and advancement of Learning, divine and humane* (London: Henrie Tomes, 1605), 60v–61r.
883 "a thing that yet": *Of the Advancement and Proficience of Learning*, 265.
883 "Neither is it": *Ibid.*, 266. For a cipher that contains many elements of Bacon's, including the variation of typefaces but not the clever use of an independent covertext, see Blaise de Vigenère, *Traicté des Chiffres* (Paris: Abel l'Angelier, 1586) 200r, 241r–243r. This was printed after Bacon assertedly invented his but before he published it. Perhaps the idea was current in Paris at the time.
884 tombstone cipher: Friedman and Friedman, ch. 4.
885 biliteral cipher in the plays, Mrs. Gallup: *Ibid.*, chs. 13–18.
885 Gallup: (Detroit, Mich.: Howard Publishing Co.). Second edition 1900, third 1901, Part III, *Deciphered Secret Story, 1622 to 1671* (1910).
886 "Queen Elizabeth is": Gallup, 2nd ed., 166.
886 "unwilling," "she who bore me": Gallup, Part III, 11, 13.
887 "But you must have," "uneasy questioning": Friedman and Friedman, 210, 211.

Notes

PAGE

887 "I sometimes think": quoted Friedman and Friedman, 198.

887 "Seeke the keyes": Gallup, 2nd ed., 168. The maundering quality of many of the Baconian enigmaductions may result from their being, at heart, Markoff chains based on word-sequence probabilities, rather like discourse put together according to frequency tables, as in Jonathan Swift, *Voyage to Laputa*, ch. iii. See Colin Cherry, *On Human Communication* (New York: John Wiley & Sons, 1957), 181–182; George A. Miller, *Language and Communication* (New York: McGraw-Hill, 1951), 190.

887 inconsistent assignments: Friedman and Friedman, 223–224, plate x.

887 lifted headings: Friedman and Friedman, 243.

888 Hinman: (Oxford: Clarendon Press, 1963).

888 "large numbers of variant": quoted Friedman and Friedman, 228.

888 "have certainly revealed": Hinman, letter, January 28, 1965.

888 Goudy: Friedman and Friedman, 217–221.

888 "No characteristics": quoted Friedman and Friedman, 223.

888 Rossetti: E. R. Vincent, *Gabriele Rossetti in England*, Oxford Studies in Modern Languages and Literature (Oxford: Clarendon Press, 1936), ch. 4, "Critic," 73–109. Vincent, 109, says he will not attempt "the futile and impossible task of proving or disproving the existence of a medieval sect with a secret code for which no evidence appears to exist apart from works arbitrarily understood according to that code."

888 Margoliouth: *The Colophons of the Iliad & Odyssey* (Oxford: Basil Blackwell, 1925).

889 Henrion: *Jonathan Swift Confesses*.

889 Hime: "Roger Bacon and Gunpowder" in *Roger Bacon Essays*, ed. A. G. Little (Oxford: Clarendon Press, 1914), ch. 12, 321–336. For refutations, Lynn Thorndike, "Roger Bacon and Gunpowder," *Science*, XLII (1915), 799–800; Robert Steele, "Luru Vopo Vir Can Utriet," *Nature*, CXXI (February 11, 1928), 208–209. For another solution from these nonexistent letters, see *Nature*, CXVIII (September 4, 1926), 352.

889 Bible: Margoliouth in *Saturday Review* (September, 1924); Raymond Abellio, *La Bible: Document Chiffré*, in two vols. (Paris: Gallimard, 1950). A poignant instance of imagined ciphers in the Bible is the demand of DeWitt T. Kennard, an inmate of Peoria State Hospital, that George Fabyan take up the interest in ciphers described in an article about Fabyan in the *American Magazine*, XCIX (January, 1925), 36–39, 60, 62, and solve the ciphers in the Bible that prove that Kennard is the Messiah (*The New Embodiment: Letters of the Lord God to Colonel George Fabyan* [December 24, 1925], Fabyan Collection No. 417, Rare Book Room, The Library of Congress).

889 Chaucer: Ethel Seaton, "The Parlement of Foules and Lionel of Clarence," *Medium Ævum*, XXV (1957), 168–174; Katherine T. Emerson, "A Reply," *Ibid.*, XXVI (1957), 107–111; William F. Friedman and Elizebeth S. Friedman, "Acrostics, Anagrams, and Chaucer," *Philological Quarterly*, XXXVIII (January, 1959), 1–20.

889 Aristotle: David S. Margoliouth, *The Homer of Aristotle* (Oxford: B. Blackwell, 1923).

PAGE
- 889 Omenitsch: *Congressional Record,* LXXX (April 22, 1936), 6121–6122; worksheets of Omenitsch apparently sent to Donald D. Millikin, 1936, in my possession.
- 889 oddballs: Gardner, ch. 15, for Pyramidologists.
- 890 "ciphers are made": quoted Friedman and Friedman, 242.
- 890 "while an Elizabethan": *Baconiana,* No. 160, at 3.
- 890 Ayer: *Language, Truth and Logic* (1936, reprinted New York: Dover Publications), 95. For errors the Baconians commit, John Hospers, *An Introduction to Philosophical Analysis* (Englewood Cliffs, N.J.: Prentice-Hall, 1950); for what they should be doing, Henry Margenau, *The Nature of Physical Reality* (New York: McGraw-Hill, 1950), chs. 5 and 6.
- 891 "If one can argue": Frank W. Wadsworth, *The Poacher from Stratford* (Berkeley, Calif.: University of California Press, 1958), 164. Another general study of the problem is H. N. Gibson, *The Shakespeare Claimants* (London: Methuen, 1962).
- 891 psychological problem: See Harry Trosman, "Freud and the Controversy over Shakespearean Authorship," *Journal of the American Psychoanalytic Association,* XIII (July, 1965), 475–498. I am grateful to Dr. Trosman for reading portions of the manuscript and making a number of valuable suggestions. An analysis of the same problem in history in general has been made by Richard Hofstadter, *The Paranoid Style in American Politics* (New York: Alfred A. Knopf, 1965).

Chapter 25 ANCESTRAL VOICES

Since the material on which this chapter is based is widely known and easily available, I have not thought it necessary to give notes as detailed as those for the other chapters. I want to thank Dr. Emmett L. Bennett, Jr., for reading the Linear B section of this chapter, and Dr. I. J. Gelb for reading the other sections. Both offered many valuable suggestions and corrections, most of which I have adopted, and for which I am deeply grateful.

- 895 general problem of decipherment: Pentti Aalto, "Notes on Methods of Decipherment of Unknown Writings and Languages," *Studia Orientalia,* XI, No. 4 (1945), 1–26; P. E. Cleator, *Lost Languages* (New York: John Day, 1961), 23–24; Henry Sweet, *The Practical Study of Languages* (1898, reprinted London: Oxford University Press, 1964), 254–261.
- 896 Dhorme: *Who's Who in France, 1963–1964;* telephone interview with I. J. Gelb, November 17, 1964; Ernst Doblhofer, *Voices in Stone,* trans. Merven Savill (New York: Viking Press, 1961), 213, and Leo Deuel, *Testaments of Time: The Search for Lost Manuscripts and Records* (New York: Alfred A. Knopf, 1965), 236, for cryptanalytic experience.
- 897 "I did not hesitate": E. Dhorme, "Déchiffrement des inscriptions pseudo-hiéroglyphiques de Byblos," *Syria,* XXV (1946–1948), 1–35 at 2–3.
- 898 "rendered a hitherto": *Ibid.,* 4; David Diringer, *The Alphabet* (New York: Philosophical Library, 2nd ed., n.d.), 161–165; I. J. Gelb, *A Study of*

Notes

PAGE

Writing, rev. ed. (Chicago: University of Chicago Press, 1963), 157–158.

898 Ugaritic: Charles Virolleaud, "Les inscriptions cunéiformes de Ras Shamra," *Syria*, X (1929), 304–310, plus 20 plates; Hans Bauer, "Die Entzifferung des Keilschriftalphabets von Ras Schamra," *Forschungen und Fortschritte*, VI (August 20, 1930), 306–307.

899 "This consonant": Dhorme, "Un Nouvel Alphabet Sémitique," *Revue Biblique*, XXXIX (October, 1930), 571–577.

899 Virolleaud solution: "Le déchiffrement des tablettes alphabétiques de Ras Shamra," *Syria*, XII (1931), 15–23.

899 "perfect scientific loyalty": Dhorme, "Première Traduction des Textes Phéniciens de Ras Shamra," *Revue Biblique*, XL (January, 1931), 32–56 at 32.

900 "the most important": Cyrus H. Gordon, *Ugaritic Literature* (Rome: Pontificium Institutum Biblicum, 1949), 1.

900 Biblical parallels: J. W. Jack, *The Ras Shamra Tablets: Their Bearing on the Old Testament*, Old Testament Studies, No. 1, Society for Old Testament Study (Edinburgh: T. T. Clark, 1935), 48–49; Robert de Langhe, *Les Textes de Ras Shamra-Ugarit et leurs Rapports avec le Milieu Biblique de l'Ancien Testament*, Universitas Catholic Loaveniensis, Dissertationes..., Series II, Vol. 35 (Gembloux: J. Duculot, 1945), I, 370–375.

900 linguistic reconstructions: Holger Pedersen, *The Discovery of Language: Linguistic Science in the Nineteenth Century*, trans. John Webster Spargo (1931, reprinted Bloomington, Ind.: Indiana University Press, 1962), for Gothic, Persian, Slavic, Tokharian. E. H. Sturtevant, *Linguistic Change* (1917, republished Chicago: University of Chicago Press, 1961), for principles of internal change.

901 hieroglyphs: Erik Iversen, *The Myth of Egypt and Its Hieroglyphs in European Tradition* (Copenhagen: G. E. C. Gad, 1961), is my source for nearly all the information on the Greek impressions of hieroglyphics, their decline, their impact on European thought, the false solutions, and Young's and Champollion's correct solutions. This is a fascinating book. See also Madeleine V.-David, *Le débat sur les écritures et l'hiéroglyphe aux XVIIe et XVIIIe siècles et l'application de la notion de déchiffrement aux écritures mortes*, Bibliothèque générale de l'École Pratique des Hautes Études, VIe Section (Paris: S.E.V.P.E.N., 1965).

904 Hermes Trismegistus: Frances A. Yates, *Giordano Bruno and the Hermetic Tradition* (Chicago: University of Chicago Press, 1964).

904 Pharaoh Apries misinterpretation: Sir Alan Gardiner, *Egyptian Grammar*, 3rd ed., rev. (London: Oxford University Press, 1957), 12.

904 Rosetta Stone: E. A. Wallis Budge, *The Rosetta Stone* (London: British Museum, 1922; revised 1950).

904 Dhautpoul: Karl Marek [pseud. C. W. Ceram], *Gods, Graves, and Scholars*, trans. E. B. Garside (New York: Alfred A. Knopf, 1951), 90.

907 Champollion's solution: Iversen, 124–149; Johannes Friedrich, *Extinct Languages*, trans. Frank Gaynor (New York: Philosophical Library, 1957), 5–25; Cleator, 29–64; Doblhofer, 38–84; Marek, 85–116;

PAGE

        Champollion, *Lettre à M. Dacier* . . . (Paris: Firmin Didot Père et fils, 1822), 2, 3–4.

912 cuneiform: Friedrich, 29–67; Cleator, 64–112; Pedersen, 154–160; Aalto, 4–5.

914 Hittite cuneiform: Friedrich, 69–79; Cleator, 118–119.

914 Meroitic, Lycian, Lydian, Libyan, Iberian, Sabaean, Safaitic, Pahlavī, Brahmī, Sogdian, Mon, Khmer, Gupta: Friedrich, Pedersen, Diringer, Gelb.

916 Kök-Turki: Pedersen, 196–199; Doblhofer, 271–293.

916 Etruscan: Friedrich, 137–143; M. Pallottino, *The Etruscans*, trans. by J. Cremona (Harmondsworth: Penguin Books, 1955), 229–280.

916 Indus Valley, Easter Island: Friedrich, 169–173; Gelb, 90–91; Doblhofer, 301–311; Thomas S. Barthel, "The 'Talking Boards' of Easter Island," *Scientific American*, CXCVIII (June, 1958), 61–68.

917 Phaistos Disk: Diringer, 78; Gelb, 155–157; Aalto, 6. A very full bibliography in E. Grumach, *Bibliographie der kretisch-mykenischen Epigraphik* (Munich and Berlin, 1963).

917 Maya: E. V. Yevreinov, Yu. G. Kosarev, and V. A. Ustinov, three 1961 articles from different Russian sources translated and published as *Foreign Developments in Machine Translation and Information Processing*, No. 40, by the United States, Department of Commerce, Office of Technical Services, Joint Publications Research Service, No. 10508; and criticism by Yu. V. Knorozov, *Ibid.*, No. 102, same publisher, No. 14318; Felix Shirokov, "Computer Deciphers Maya Hieroglyphics," *The UNESCO Courier*, XV (March, 1962), 26–32.

917 Linear B: Unless otherwise specified, all decipherment details are from John Chadwick, *The Decipherment of Linear B* (Cambridge: University Press, 1958), and Michael Ventris and John Chadwick, *Documents in Mycenaean Greek* (Cambridge: University Press, 1956), 11–25. Archeological details mostly from Marek, 29–67, and Paul MacKendrick, *The Greek Stones Speak* (New York: St. Martin's Press, 1962), 3–117.

918 March 31: Correction by Bennett of Leonard R. Palmer, *Mycenaeans and Minoans* (New York: Alfred A. Knopf, 1962), 48.

919 four types of writing: Gelb, 91–95.

919 "it is probable": Evans in *Annual of British School at Athens*, VI, 59, quoted Chadwick, 17.

919 Evans classification: Arthur Evans, *The Palace of Minos*, IV, part 2 (London: Macmillan & Co., Ltd., 1935), 716–725 for cultures, 681 for associations, 714 for male and female, 715 for "good evidence of declension," 713 for Semitic letter.

920 Cypriote: Friedrich, 124–131; Doblhofer, 227–237; Pedersen, 168–171; Gelb, 153–155, for interrelationships of Cretan and Cypriote.

921 pro- and anti-Evans views: "Editorial Notes," *Antiquity*, XXVII (March, 1954), 1–2.

922 "there is no palace": Evans, 755.

922 160-page discussion: Evans, 666–825.

922 Gordon, Stawell: Chadwick, 28–30.

Notes

PAGE

923 "The theory that": M. G. F. Ventris, "Introducing the Minoan Languge," *American Journal of Archaeology*, XLIV (October-December, 1940), 494–520 at 494.

923 "It can be done": *Ibid.*, 520.

923 Hrozný: Bedřich Hrozný, *Les Inscriptions Crétoises, Essai de Déchiffrement*, trans. Madeleine David, Monografie Archivu Orientalního, XII (Prague: Orientální Ústav, 1949), at 10 for *ha*.

923 "When the decipherer": review by Emmett L. Bennett, Jr., *American Journal of Archaeology*, LIV (January, 1950), 81–82. Friedrich, 165.

923 Georgiev: "Le déchiffrement des inscriptions minoennes," *Annuaire de l'Université de Sofia, Faculté Historico-Philologique*, XLV (1948/1949), Livre 4, No. 2, 1–81, at 13.

923 Sittig: *Who's Who in Germany, 1960*; Chadwick 32; Friedrich, 165–166.

923 Kober: obituary in *The New York Times* (May 17, 1950).

923 adze and chariot: "The 'Adze' Tablets from Knossos," *American Journal of Archaeology*, XLVIII (January–March, 1944), 64–75; "Evidence of Inflection in the 'Chariot' Tablets from Knossos," *Ibid.*, XLIX (April–June, 1945), 143–151, at 151 for "it is highly probable," and 143 for "if a language." Near the end of both these articles Miss Kober wrote the identical and—fortunately—totally misleading remark, "Further conjecture is useless."

926 identical vowels and identical consonants: "Inflection in Linear Class B: 1—Declension," *Ibid.*, L (April–June, 1946), 268–276. No other article of what Miss Kober evidently intended to be a series ever appeared.

927 "total": "'Total' in Minoan (Linear Class B)," *Archiv Orientální*, XVII (1949), 386–398.

927 "tentative phonetic pattern": "The Minoan Scripts: Fact and Fancy," *American Journal of Archaeology*, LII (January–March, 1948), 82–103, at 98.

927 Ventris: Chadwick, 1–4; Leonard Cottrell, *Realms of Gold* (Greenwich, Connecticut: New York Graphic Society Publishers, 1963), 7.

928 Bennett: *Directory of American Scholars*, 1957.

933 "Evidence": *The Journal of Hellenic Studies*, LXXIII (1953), 84–103.

933 "Since my return": Chadwick, 81.

934 Beattie: "Mr. Ventris' Decipherment of the Minoan Linear B Script," *The Journal of Hellenic Studies*, LXXVI (1956), 1–17, at 2, 8, 14.

934 sample texts: *Documents;* Chadwick.

935 "These palace archives": Denys Page, *History and the Homeric Iliad*, Sather Classical Lectures, XXXI (Berkeley, Calif: University of California Press, 1959), 180–181.

936 wanax, basileus: Page, 188.

936 names in -eus: Page, 197.

936 "By seeing the Greeks": *From Mycenae to Homer* (London: Methuen, 1958), 3.

937 McNeill: *The Rise of the West* (Chicago: University of Chicago Press, 1963), 97. Another result might be the solution of Linear A, which takes off from the solution of Linear B, claimed by Dr. Cyrus H. Gordon of

Brandeis University ("Link Greek Culture to Hebrew," *New York Herald Tribune* [April 4, 1958], 1, 8; Cyrus H. Gordon, *Before the Bible* (New York: Harper & Row, 1962), 206–217; Cyrus H. Gordon, "The Decipherment of Minoan," *Natural History*, LXXII (November, 1963), 22–31; Rolland Emerson Wolfe, "Not from the Head of Zeus," *The Unitarian Register and The Universalist Leader* (mid-summer, 1962), 14–16. However, not only has Dr. Gordon failed to convince me of the soundness of his method, whatever its linguistic merits or demerits, but also the criticisms directed against his thesis suggest that acceptance of it should, for the present, be withheld (Maurice Pope, "The Linear A Question," *Antiquity*, XXXII [June, 1958], 97–99; M. I. Finley, "Hellas and Israel," *New Statesman*, LXV (January 11, 1963), 47–48). Consequently I have not included his results.

Chapter 26 MESSAGES FROM OUTER SPACE

In these notes, *IC* refers to *Interstellar Communication*, ed. A. G. W. Cameron (New York: W. A. Benjamin, 1963), a valuable collection of reprints and original contributions by several authors on the problem, but unfortunately rather repetitious and badly arranged. I have cited authors and titles in it only where necessary. "Sullivan" refers to Walter Sullivan, *We Are Not Alone: The Search for Intelligent Life on Other Worlds* (New York: McGraw-Hill, 1964), a very thorough and workmanlike discussion on which I have leaned heavily. All references in the text to Cocconi and Morrison refer to Giuseppe Cocconi and Philip Morrison, "Searching for Interstellar Communications," *Nature*, CLXXXIV (September 19, 1959), 844–846, reprinted, *IC*, 160–164. I am grateful to Frank Drake, William F. Friedman, and Mario Pei for reading a very early draft of what was to become this chapter, and, in the case of Drake and Friedman, offering some valuable suggestions.

938   "To follow knowledge": Alfred, Lord Tennyson, "Ulysses."
938   April 8, 1960: Drake, telephone interview, February 9, 1962.
939   "I wonder": House of Representatives, Committee on Science and Astronautics, *Panel on Science and Technology: Fourth Meeting*, Hearings, 87:2 (March 21 and 22, 1962) (GPO, 1962), 73.
939   Green Bank conference: *IC*, 287–293; Sullivan, 245–265.
939   Russian report: "Russians Say a Cosmic Emission May Come From Rational Beings" (April 13, 1965), 1:6–7; "Russians Temper Space Wave View" (April 14, 1965), 3:1–4; "Radio Emissions From Space Spur Disagreement Between American and Soviet Astronomers" (April 18, 1965), 1–8, all *The New York Times*.
939   development of idea of extraterrestrial life: Sullivan.
940   Milton: *Paradise Lost*, viii.
940   Pope: *An Essay on Man*, Epistle I, 1. 26.
943   Cocconi and Morrison spend a few days: Morrison, telephone interview, February 9, 1962.

Notes 1143

PAGE

944 "It may be worth": Roy Bedichek, *The Sense of Smell* (Garden City, N.Y.: Doubleday & Company, 1960), 133.

945 bees: Frisch's books and articles.

945 Edie: "Messages from Other Worlds," letter to the editor, *Science*, CXXXV (April 13, 1962), 184.

946 Bracewell interstellar probe: *IC*, 239–241; Sullivan, 207–209; for criticism, *IC*, 263–264.

947 opaque screen: *IC*, 270; Sullivan, 221–222.

947 laser light: *IC*, 223–231; Sullivan, 209–217.

947 Tesla, Marconi, Todd: Sullivan, 177–179.

948 Green: CV (August, 1924), 27–28. Other discussions were those of H. Winfield Secor, "Hello Mars!" *Electrical Experimentor*, VII (April, 1920), 1248–50, 1302, 1304, 1306–9; Clement Fezandie, "My Message to Mars," *Ibid.*, VIII (July, 1920), 267, 318–322.

948 Camp Alfred Vail listens: Captain John P. Ferriter, letter to William F. Friedman, September 5, 1924, quoted in Friedman, letter, November 13, 1960. Friedman thinks that the Ediphone cylinder recordings may still be at Fort Monmouth.

948 Jenkins: Friedman, letter, November 13, 1960. Friedman has photographic copies of the strips.

948 narrowing down of radio search and of star search: Sullivan.

950 Drake's signal-isolation techniques: *IC*, 172, 174; Sullivan, 202.

950 "a place very far away": *IC*, 172.

950 false signals: Drake, telephone interview; Sullivan, 204–205.

951 information the only thing worth traveling for: Morrison in *IC*, 262.

951 "No one can threaten": *IC*, 142.

951 "I would say": *Panel on Science and Technology: Fourth Meeting*, 74–75.

951 stray signals: J. A. Webb in *IC*, 178–191.

952 legacy for the children: *IC*, 142.

952 intellectual immortality: Sullivan, 290–291.

952 special calling signal: Sebastian von Hoerner in *IC*, 272–286.

952 Tesla: Sullivan, 177.

952 message as clear as possible: Frank Drake, letter, November 17, 1960.

952 cryptography in reverse: *IC*, 140.

953 "The data are uneven": N. D. Andreyev, letter, October 6, 1965. Dr. Andreyev's forthcoming book, "Statistical-Combinatory Methods in Theoretical and Applied Linguistics" will include a chapter named "Language Universals and Investigation of Unknown Languages," extraterrestrial ones being meant. The principles of his statistical-combinatory method, as applied to human languages, may be found in his paper "Algorithms for the Statistical-Combinatory Modeling of Syntax, Word-Formation and Semantics," published in *Materialy po matematicheskoy lingvistika i mashinnomu perevodu*, II (Leningrad University, 1963), which has been translated as *Foreign Developments in Machine Translation and Information Processing*, No. 161, United States, Department of Commerce, Office of Technical Services, Joint Publications

Research Service, No. 26209. Dr. Andreyev has proposed an intermediary computer language for intercommunication on earth, and an intermediary language of the second order for communication with extraterrestrial beings, in his "Linguistic Aspects of Translation," *Proceedings of the Ninth International Congress of Linguists*, Cambridge, Massachusetts, August 27-31, 1962, ed. Horace G. Lunt (The Hague: Mouton & Co., 1964), 625-637 at 634.

953 artificial languages: The best recent discussion is M. Monnerot-Dumaine, *Précis d'Interlinguistique* (Paris: Librairie Maloine, 1960).

954 Lincos: Hans Freudenthal, "Towards a Cosmic Language," *Delta* [Netherlands Institute for International Cultural Relations] (Summer, 1958), 37-48; Hans Freudenthal, *Lincos: Design of a Language for Cosmic Intercourse* (Amsterdam: North-Holland Publishing Co., 1960). George A. W. Boehm, "Are We Being Hailed from Interstellar Space?" *Fortune*, LXIII (March, 1961), 144-149, 193-194, has illustration at 148 of what such a message might look like recorded by a pen.

956 Lincos criticisms and replies: Maurits de Vries, letter, December 2, 1960; Lancelot Hogben, "Cosmical Language," *Nature, Supplement*, CXCII (December 2, 1961), 826-827; Freudenthal, letters, February 19, 1960, and February 17, 1961.

956 Astraglossa: Lancelot Hogben, "Astraglossa, or First Steps in Celestial Syntax," *Journal of the British Interplanetary Society*, XI (November, 1952), 258-274.

957 Galton's proposal: "Intelligible Signals Between Neighboring Stars," *Fortnightly Review* (November, 1896), 657-664.

958 Gauss, Littrow, Cros: Sullivan, 175.

959 Drake 551-digit message: forwarded by him. A less condensed form appears in Sullivan, 267-269.

959 "The content": Drake's notes to solution of 551-digit message.

960 Morrison television: *IC*, 268-269.

961 R. L. Carbrey: "Video Transmission over Telephone Cable Pairs by Pulse Code Modulation," *IRE Proceedings*, XLVIII (September, 1960), 1546-1561.

962 dictionary, artificial language based upon efficiency: Kahn.

963 dolphins: John C. Lilly, *Man and Dolphin* (New York: Doubleday & Company, 1961); John C. Lilly, "Some considerations regarding basic mechanisms of positive and negative types of motivations," *American Journal of Psychiatry*, CXV (December, 1958), 498-504, for "If we are ever."

963 Whorf: See the collection of his writings, *Language, Thought and Reality* (New York: John Wiley & Sons, 1956). To test his thesis, a logical language was synthesized; see James Cooke Brown, "Loglan," *Scientific American*, CCII (June, 1960), 53-63.

964 outer-spacelings may think in terms of continua, aleph-null: Maurits de Vries, letter, December 2, 1960.

964 "be connected with": Prof. F. Hoyle, "Recent Developments in Cosmology," *Nature*, CCVIII (October 9, 1965), 111-114 at 114.

ACKNOWLEDGMENTS FOR ILLUSTRATIONS

I am grateful to the following institutions for their kindness in granting permission for the reproduction as illustrations in this book of the following items, which belong to them:

Trustees of the British Museum, London. Medal by Matteo de' Pasti of Leo Battista Alberti; Add. Mss. 32288, f. 102; 32292, f. 4; 32303, f. 30; 32307, folio unknown; 32499, f. 344; 37205, ff. 80, 249.

France, Ministère de l'Éducation Nationale, Bibliothèque Nationale. Gravure de Blaise de Vigenère sculpté par Thomas de Leu.

Great Britain, Public Record Office. Crown copyright acknowledged for S.P. 106/1, f. 58; S.P. 53/18, no. 55; P.R.O. 31/11/11.

London, The National Gallery. Painting by Rembrandt van Rijn of "Belshazzar's Feast," Accession No. 6350. Reproduced by courtesy of the Trustees, The National Gallery, London.

Magdalene College, Cambridge. Page of Diary of Samuel Pepys.

Metropolitan Museum of Art, New York. 17.3.756.1423, Jacob de Gheyn: Portrait of Philip van Marnix, The Metropolitan Museum of Art, Dick Fund, 1917.

The Master and Fellows of Peterhouse, Cambridge. Ms. 75.1, f. 30v.

University of Cincinnati, Cincinnati, Ohio. Ta 641.

William L. Clements Library, University of Michigan, Ann Arbor, Michigan. Benedict Arnold code letter to Major John André of 15 July 1780.

NOTES TO ILLUSTRATIONS

The full citations will be found in the notes to the text for each chapter.

Chapter 1

One o'clock message: NA, RG 319.
Japanese code page: DSDF, 894.727/3-8.
HARUNA *message*: (*PHA*, 38:250): Department of the Navy.
Yoshikawa final message: (*PHA*, 38:233): Department of the Navy.
14th part: NA, RG 319.
Japanese note: DSDF, 711.94/2594-7/8.

Chapter 2

Hieroglyphs: E. Drioton, "Essai sur la cryptographie privée de la fin de la XVIIIe dynastie," 24, showing equivalents established by Drioton from stele V 93 of Leyden.
Cuneiform: *Tablettes d'Uruk*, Textes cunéiformes, VI, No. 51r.
Siamese cryptography: Frankfurter, 4.
Rök stone: George Stephens, *The Old-Northern Runic Monuments of Scandinavia and England* (Edinburgh: Williams & Norgate, 1884), III, 46.
Ogham cryptography: Royal Irish Academy, "Book of Ballymote," 313.
Chaucer: "The Equatorie of the Planetis," Cambridge University, Peterhouse, Ms. 75.1, f. 30v.
Davidian alphabet: Ahmed bin Abubekr Bin Washih, *Ancient Alphabets and Hieroglyphic Characters Explained*, trans. Joseph Hammer (London, 1806), 39.

Chapter 3

Simeone de Crema: Mantua, Archivio di Stato, Busta E.I. 2a, No. 32.
Medici nomenclator: Florence, Archivio di Stato, Cifrari della Repubblica e medicei, No. 457.
Cortés letter: Spain, Archivio General de Indias, Papeles de Justicia de India, Autos entre partes vistos en el Consejo de Indias, Audencia de Mexico, Estante 51, Cajón 6, Legajo 6.23.
Marnix solution: Great Britain, Public Record Office, State Papers 106/1, f. 58.
Forged postscript: Great Britain, Public Record Office, State Papers 53/18, no. 55.

Notes to Illustrations 1147

Chapter 4

Alberti cipher disk: Meister, *Päpstlichen*, 28.
Trithemius title page: 1518 edition. Caption description by Dodgson, 405–406, corrected by Chacornac, 73–74.
Ave Maria: 1518 edition of *Polygraphiae*.
Digraphic system: Porta, 90.
Porta cipher disk: Porta, 73.

Chapter 5

Wallis solution: Add. Ms. 32499, f. 344.
Decyphering Branch solution: Add. Ms. 32307.
Church cipher message: The Library of Congress, Papers of George Washington, XVIII, 119.
Benedict Arnold message: University of Michigan, William L. Clements Library, Sir Henry Clinton Papers.
Lovell's Cornwallis solution: NA, Papers of the Continental Congress, Item 51, I, f. 722.
Jefferson's 1785 nomenclator: The Library of Congress, Jefferson Papers, 5th series, XI, f. 35.
Solution of letter to John Quincy Adams: Add. Ms. 32303, f. 20.

Chapter 6

M-94: U.S. Army, *Signal Communications* (field manual).
Wheatstone cipher device: Kerckhoffs, 62.
Wheatstone description of Playfair cipher: Add. Ms. 37205, f. 80.
Babbage uses mathematics: Add. Ms. 37205, f. 249.

Chapter 7

Confederate cipher telegram: NA, RG 109, War Department Collection of Confederate Records, Telegrams, 4161.
Confederate agents' message: Plum, 41 (slightly different copy in Bates, 73).
Electoral telegram: Photolithic Copies of Dispatches, To Accompany the Presidential Election Investigation, in Edward L. Parris Papers, Rutherford B. Hayes Library, Fremont, Ohio.
Nast cartoon: Harper's Weekly (November 2, 1878), 869.

Chapter 8

De Viaris cipher device: Léauté, 279.
Bazeries cylinder: Bazeries, 252.
Long to Dewey: NA, RG 45, Naval Records Collection of the Office of Naval Records Library, Area 10 File, 1798–1910, February 26, 1898; translation in "Ciphers Sent," October 27, 1888, to May 31, 1898, at 524.
Baravelli code: Dizionario per corrispondenze in cifra (1895), 75.
Panizzardi telegram: France, Archives Nationales, BB[19]75, dossier 1.

Chapter 9

Zimmermann telegram: DSDF 862.20212/82A.
de Grey's transcription: DSDF 862.20212/81½.
Kirby cartoon: The [New York] *World* (March 3, 1917), 8:4–8.

Chapter 11

Hudson Code and Emergency Code List: Collection of Secret Codes of U.S. Army, University of Pennsylvania Library, Rare Book Room.
G.2 A.6 solutions: Childs Cipher Papers, I, §11.

Chapter 12

Hindu book cipher: Tunney, opposite p. 90.

Chapter 13

Hagelin machine: Eyraud, 195.

Chapter 14

"Brown Sheet": Wi VI/149, Records of Headquarters, O.K.W., Bundesarchiv, Koblenz.
R.S.H.A. encipherment table: T–175:477:7334402.
Luftwaffe code: T-321, Roll 75, frame unknown.
Syko card: Morgan, 59.

Chapter 15

Cartoons: Great Britain, Admiralty, *Merchant Ships Signal Book*, III, 27, 28.
"Dear Cordell" note: DSDF 740.0011 Pacific War/856.
Pers-Z solution: Microcopy T-120, Frame F1/568.
Churchill message: Franklin D. Roosevelt Library, Hyde Park, New York.

Chapter 16

San Antonio River drawing: Colonel Shaw. The drawing, produced by the San Antonio postal censorship station, uses short blades of grass along riverbank for dots and long blades for dashes to spell out, in Morse code, *Compliments of CPSA MA to our chief Col Harold R. Shaw on his visit to San Antonio May 11th 1945.*
Invasion open code: Germany, Militärgeschichtliches Forschungsamt, Kriegestagebuch des Armeeoberkommandos 15/Ic vom 5.6.1944.
Scrambler diagrams: Brown-Boveri Review (December, 1941), 399, 402.
Churchill transcript: T-175:122:2647449.

Chapter 17

Tokumu Han organization and Japanese Navy intelligence: United States Strategic Bombing Survey (Pacific), Japanese Military and Naval Intelligence Division, *Japanese Intelligence* (April, 1946), 30.

Notes to Illustrations

Japanese Navy code: supplied by Ikuhiko Hata from Japan, Defense Ministry Archives.
Evans' decipherment: Supplied by Evans.

Chapter 18

Russian monalphabetic key: Add. Ms. 32292, f. 4.
Solution of nomenclator: Add. Ms. 32288, f. 102.
Russian military message: T-314, Roll 212, frame unknown.
Erickson cipher worksheets: Sweden, Nedre Justitie Revisionen, Case 13-1941 of Radhusrattan, photographed by Dr. Käärik.
One-time pad: Japanese police.
"Trigonometric" cipher: Supplied by Isaac Don Levine.

Chapter 21

Balzac's fake cryptogram: in first edition, 207-210; "new" 1840 edition, Charpentier, 265; 1847 edition, Charpentier, 299; English 1901 edition, Dana Estes & Co., 266.
Dancing Men: The Strand Magazine, XXVI (December, 1903), 604.
Pepys: Magdalene College Library, Cambridge.

Chapter 22

Bootlegging code chart: NA, RG 26.
Fiber optic scramble: provided by R. J. Meltzner, Bausch & Lomb, Inc., Rochester, New York.

Chapter 23

Bergenroth: Great Britain, Public Record Office, P.R.O. 31/11/11.
Voynich manuscript: kindly supplied by Hans Kraus.

Chapter 24

Donnelly calculations: Minnesota Historical Society.
Bacon's biliteral: Of the Advancement of Learning, trans. Gilbert Wats (Oxford: Leon Lichfield for the University, 1640), 268.

Chapter 25

Pseudo-hieroglyphic tablet: Syria (1929), 6.
Grid: Ventris and Chadwick, "Evidence," 86.
Tripod tablet: Archeology (Spring, 1954), 18.

Chapter 26

Lincos: Freudenthal, 93.
Dot-and-dash picture: Warren Weilbacher, *Newsday* (April 20, 1962).

Photographic Inserts

Rembrandt painting: London, The National Gallery, Accession No. 6350.

Alberti medal: copyright, British Museum; George Francis Hill, *A Corpus of Italian Medals of the Renaissance Before Cellini* (London: British Museum, 1930), No. 161, says the medal, by Matteo de' Pasti, dates from 1446–1450 while Alberti was in his middle forties in Rimini.

Porta: frontispiece from his *Magiae Naturalis libri XX* (Naples, 1589).

Cardano: frontispiece from his *De Rerum Varietate* (1557).

Vigenère: engraving by Thomas de Leu, Bibliothèque Nationale, Paris.

Trithemius: sculpture in Neumünster church in Wurzburg by Tilman Riemenschneider, one of Germany's greatest Renaissance sculptors.

Viète: *Galérie Française, ou Collection des Portraits*... (Didot, 1821), I, plate 24.

Marnix: engraving by Jacob de Gheyn, 1599; The Metropolitan Museum of Art, New York, Dick Fund, 1917.

Rossignol: anonymous engraving from Charles Perrault, *Les Hommes Illustres Qui Ont Paru en France Pendant ce Siècle* (Paris, 1696), opposite p. 57.

Willes: portrait by Thomas Hudson in Wells Palace, Wells, England.

Wallis: engraving by W. Faithorne, New York Public Library, Prints Division.

Gerry: engraving by J. B. Longacre from a drawing by Vanderlyn, New York Public Library, Manuscript Division, Emmet 2134.

M-94: author's collection.

Jefferson: United States Bureau of Engraving and Printing.

Wheatstone, Playfair, Babbage: all *The Illustrated London News* (November 6, 1875), 461; (December 6, 1873), 528; (November 4, 1871), 424, respectively.

Cipher disk: NA, RG 92.

Holden: *Harper's Weekly*, XXXVIII (1894), 1144.

Kerckhoffs: Eugen Drezen, *Historio de la Mondo Lingvo* (Leipzig, 1931), 102.

Bazeries: photo supplied by Mme. Jean Yon, his daughter.

de Grey: wearing uniform of Royal Naval Volunteer Reserve, 1914 or 1915; photo supplied by his son.

Hay: wearing uniform of Gordon Highlanders, 1915; photo supplied by his widow.

Hitchings: during World War I; photo supplied by his widow.

Hitt: NA, photo 111-SC-23349.

Sacco: photo supplied by Sacco.

Painvin: photo supplied by Painvin.

Friedman: U.S. Army Photograph, P-2229 (this photograph is dated October, 1933, but Friedman's clothes are identical with two photographs dated 1928; I therefore think that one or the other is in error and have struck the average for my date of 1930).

Childs and Yardley: NA, photo 111-SC-51371.

Yardley: Wide World Photos.

Powell: publicity still from "Rendezvous," supplied by Metro-Goldwyn-Mayer.

Sinkov, Rowlett, Kullback: U.S. Army Photographs P-3599, P-4303, P-3946, respectively.

Notes to Illustrations

Friedmans: Cambridge University Press.
Vernam: picture taken for graduation with Class of 1914 of Worcester Polytechnic Institute, supplied by his daughter.
Mauborgne: NA, photo 111-SC-101413.
Hebern: photo (mid-1920s) supplied by his widow.
Hebern cipher machine: photo supplied by Mrs. Ellie Hebern.
Hagelin: Wide World Photos.
Paschke: photo supplied by Paschke.
Kunze and Gylden: author's photographs.
Kramer-Safford, Rochefort: both Wide World Photos.
Dyer: photo supplied by Dyer.
Shaw: photo supplied by Shaw.
Koenig: Bell Telephone Laboratories photo, July, 1964.
Japanese cruiser: NA, 80-G-414422.
Spectrograms of speech: Bell Telephone Laboratories photos.
Traffic analysts: U.S. Army Photograph SC 223683.
U-505: NA, photo 80-G-49172.

Combat cryptography: U.S. Army Photograph SC 370625, showing message center of the 3rd Division, U.S. Infantry, Hyopchong, Korea, October 1, 1951.
NSA headquarters: U.S. Army Photograph SC 574898.
Kroger one-time pads: both Wide World Photos.
Abel pad: Federal Bureau of Investigation.
Electronic countermeasures: Sperry Gyroscope Company, Lake Success, New York.
Johnson and Rowlett: United Press International photo.
hot line: U.S. Army photograph SC 605685.
Hagelin hand machine: author's collection.
O.M.I. machine: Ottico Meccanica Italiana, Rome.
Holmes: drawing from the first publication of Arthur Conan Doyle, "The Adventure of the Dancing Men," *The Strand Magazine*, XXVI (December, 1903), at 604.
Shannon: Bell Telephone Laboratories.
Radio scrambler: photo of Model 106 from Delcon, Inc., Palo Alto, California.
Bentley: photo at about age 60, supplied by his son.
scrambled television: Zenith Radio Corporation, Chicago, Illinois.
Bacon: engraving by W. Hollar, New York Public Library, Prints Division.
Ignatius Donnelly: Minnesota Historical Society.
Voynich manuscript: Hans Kraus.
Radio telescope: National Science Foundation.

INDEX

THE INDEX covers only the cryptological aspects of this book. Thus, although there is a passage describing Japan's war strategy, the index does not cite it because cryptology played no essential role in it. On the other hand, there is a reference to the Battle of Midway because cryptology was crucial to it. Subjects that are discussed in relation to cryptology are listed under their names; thus, music in cryptology is listed under "music" and not under "cryptology, music in." The major subject headings, such as "cryptography," deal only with that subject when it is considered as a whole in its various aspects. In general, they are cross-referenced to entries of coordinate value.

There are few chronological references because the book's structure is largely chronological, but there are geographical and national entries.

To cite every occurrence, or even just major occurrences, of a common general system, such as polyalphabetic substitution, would make an entry so long as to be useless. But rarer systems, as polygraphic substitution, or specific named systems, as PA-K2, are listed in all essential occurrences. In such headings the term "code" or "cipher" is omitted.

0075 code, 282–97 *passim*
13040 code, 289, 290

A-1 (U.S. Navy), 387
A-1 (U.S. State Department), 491–92
A-3, 554, 555, 557
Abbasi, A., 666–67
ABC, 304–05, 306, 307
ABC Code, 516, 838, 845
ABCD, 307
Abel, R., 664, 665, 668
Abhorchdienst, 313–14
Abwehr, 453–55, 531, 533, 534, 535, 537
Academy of Lynxes, 138, 773
Accademia Secretorum Naturae, 138
Accidental repetitions, 208, 213
Acme Code, 516, 845, 846, 847, 851
Adams, J. Q., 187
Additive, 252, 440, 444
Adleman, L., 982

ADFGVX, 339, 340, 344–45, 388
ADFGX, 338, 340–43
Advertisements, personal, in newspapers, 775
A.E.F. *See* American Expeditionary Force
Aeneas the Tactician, 82, 83
Aerial telegraph, 836–37
African nations, 730
A.F.S.A. *See* Armed Forces Security Agency
Afu, 532
AGERs, 969–70
Agony columns, 775
AGTRs, 969–70
AIRCOM, 672
AIRCOMNET, 673
AIROPNET, 673
AK, 319
Åkerblad, J. D., 906
Akkadian, 898, 912, 913, 914, 925

1153

Aktiebolaget Cryptograph, 424
Aktiebolaget Cryptoteknik, 432
ALACHI, 338
Albam, 78, 79
Albert, A. A., 410, 677, 737, 739
Alberti, L. B., 125–30, 903
Algebraic cryptography 405–08
   see also mathematics
Al-Khalil, 97
Allison, H., 388
Alphabet
   cipher, 103, 107
   definition, xiii
   normal profile, 210–11
   primary, reconstruction from secondary alphabets, 374
   symmetry of position, 237–38
Alphabetical Typewriter (cipher machine), 18, 19
Amadi, A., 109–10
Amateurs, 767–70
   see also inventors
AMCOMNET, 673
Amè, C., 470, 613
American Black Chamber. See Black Chamber
American Black Chamber, The, 361–64, 367–68, 984
American Council on Education, 981
American Cryptogram Association, 769
American Expeditionary Force, 326–39
American Indian languages, 549–50
American Revolution, 174–85
American Telephone and Telegraph Company, 394–403, 554, 555, 558, 768, 825
American Trench Code, 327
Amjadi, M., 666
Amtorg Trading Corporation, 635
AN-103, 582
Anagramming, 103
   multiple, 226, 303, 309
Anderson, W. S., 3, 613
André, J., 176
Andreyev, N. D., 953
Anglo-French code book, 264
Ango Kenku Han, 495
Annapolis, 672

Antoinette, M., 775
Arabs, 93–99
Arensberg, W. C., 880, 882
Argenti, G. B., 112–14, 130, 148–49, 151
Argenti, M., 112–14, 130, 151
Argot, 822, 823
Arisue, S., 584
Armed Forces Security Agency, 675
Armenia, 85
Army Security Agency, 13, 576, 577, 678–79, 681, 699
Arnold, B., 176–77, 178, 252, 859
Artha-śāstra, 74, 75
A.S.A. *See* Army Security Agency
ASSCOMS, 386
Assyria, 75–76, 912
Astraglossa, 956–58
Atbah, definition, 79
Atbash, 92
   definition, 77–78, 79
Atlantic, Battle of, 468, 978
Atlantis, 465–66
Atlantis: The Antedeluvian World, 874
Atlas computer, 726
Atomic bomb project, 545–49
A. T. & T. *See* American Telephone and Telegraph Company
Atterbury, F., 170–71
Augustus Caesar, 84
Augustus II, 154
Aulus Gellius, 780
Australia, 486
Austria
   black chamber, 163–65
   cryptanalytic organization in World War I, 316–18
   cryptographic systems, 278, 319
Austria-Hungary
   Dechiffrierdienst, 316–18, 320
   Kriegschiffriergruppe, 318
   pre-World War I, 263–64
   World War I systems, 319
Authenticators, 571
Autokeys, 143, 144, 147, 206, 754
"Automatic cryptography," 397
Ave Maria cipher, 135
Ayer, A. J., 890
Azarov, A. and M., 637–38

Index

B-1, 491–92
B-21, 425
B-211, 426, 691
B-69, 827
Babbage, C., 204–07, 240, 765, 776, 860
Babington, A., 122–23
Babou, P., 111
Babylonia, 75–76, 912
Bacon, Sir Francis, 349, 866
Bacon, R., 90, 865, 866, 868
Baker, L. C., 863
Balzac, H. de, 781
BAMS, 466, 467, 582
Band-splitters, 554
Banks, 826
Banner, 971
Baravelli code, 256, 257, 839
Barber, R. T., 600
Barne, J., 770
Barne, W., 770
Barnes, H. R., 326, 327, 332
Bates, D. H., 216, 218
Baudot code, 395, 482
Baudot, J. M. E., 395
Bauer, H., 898–900
Bausch & Lomb, 829
Bazeries cylinder, 247
   solution of, 247–49
   see also multiplex system
Bazeries, E., 240, 244–50, 839, 860
Bazna, E., 451
B-Dienst. *See* Beobachtung-Dienst
Beale, T. J., 771
Beattie, A. J., 934
Beatty, Sir David, 271
Beaufort cipher, 202–03, 242, 324
Beaufort, F., 202
Bedicheck, R., 944
Befehlstafel, 315
Behistun, 912
Belaso, G. B., 137, 143, 144, 146
Belin, E., 830
Bell Telephone Laboratories, 558–60, 744
Bemer, R. W., 850
Bennett, E. L., Jr., 928
Bensinger, C., 845
Bentley, E. L., 799, 843–44
Bentley's Complete Phrase Code, 516, 843

Beobachtung-Dienst, 465–68, 484
Bergenroth, G. A., 854–57
Bernstorff, J. H. A., von, 282–97 *passim*
"Berthas," 540
Berthold, H. A., 333, 335
Bestuzhev-Ryumin, A., 617
Beurling, A., 482, 541, 644, 645
Biaudet, H., 860
Bible, 76–80, 896, 900
Bibo, Major, 452, 499
Bicknell, G. W., 51
Bien Bien Phu, 686
Bifid, 243
Bigram, definition, xiv
Bingen, H. von, 89
Bipartite substitution, 243
Bird, J. M., 868
Bischoff, B., 859
Bissell, C. L., 604, 605, 608
Biuro Szyfrów, 973
BLACK, 472–74
Black chambers, 162, 163–65, 171–72, 187–88, 617, 618
   American, 5, 31, 355–60, 361–64, 367, 368, 758
Black, F. F., 321
Black, H., 884–85
Blackstone's *Commentaries,* 177
Blair, W., 788–89
Blake, G. A., 702, 703
Blegen, C., 921, 928, 933
Blencowe, W., 169
Bletchley Park, 976
Blonder-Tongue Laboratories, 833
BLUE, 489
Bohlen, L. von, 530
Boki, G. I., 640
"Book of Ballymote," 88, 89
Bookmaking, 817–21
Booth, J. W., 220, 863
Bozart, J., 669
Bracewell, R. N., 946
Brahmi, 901, 915
Bratton, R. S., 27
Braune Blätter, 447, 448
Britain, Battle of, 976
British Broadcasting Corporation, 541–45
British Security Coordination, 486

British Tabulating Machine Company, 976
Brooke-Hunt, G. L., 310, 354
Brotherhood, F. M., 1, 2, 11
Brousse, C., 487, 488
BROWN, 493, 579
Brown, F. H., 809
Brown, R. T., 806
Browne, Sir Thomas, 866
Brunon, R., 860
Bruxella, A. de, 91
Bryant, H. L., 2, 3, 4, 50
Bucher, L. M., 971
Buck, F. J., 405
Bulge, Battle of the, **509**
Bullitt, W. C., 493
Bupo, 661
Bureau du Chiffre
    Army, 305–06
    Foreign Ministry, 255–56, 259
Burke, J. P., 718
Burnett, E. C., 859
Burns, W. J., 816
Burr, A., 186
Busch, H., 506
Bush, V., 559
Business, 823–27
Byblos inscriptions, **896**
Byrne, J. F., 767–**68**

C-1, 493
C-36, 426
C-48, 433
C-52, 433
Cabinet Noir, 162, 188
"Cablegram Code Book, Melancholy Notes on," 851
Cablegrams. *See* commercial codes
Cables, German transatlantic, cutting of, 266
Caesar alphabet, 84, 619
Caesar, J., 83
Caesar substitution, 83, 136, 619, 631, 775
Callières, F. de, 173, 174
Campillo, M. G. del, 860
Canada, 486
Canaris, W., 453, 542
Canine, R. J., 390, 702
Caporetto, Battle of, 319

Carbonari, 772, 787
Card playing, 821–22
Cardano, G., 143–45
Cardano grille, 144, 519, 521
Carmona, J. G., 251
Carnet de chiffre, 314
Carnet réduit, 314
Carnia, 319
Carr, D., 13, 51
Carter, M. S., 702, 703
Cartier, F., 262, 277, 299, 300, 303–06
    passim, 315, 319, 348, 376, 621
Casanova, J., 153
Casement, Sir Roger, 281
Cave, R., 49
Cavendish-Bentinck, V. F. W., 486
CD-55, 433
Censorship, U.S., 513–26
Central Intelligence Agency, 674, 681, 688, 699, 729
Ceylon, 685
CG-210, 806
Chadwick, J., 932–33
Chaff, 721, 722, 723
Chamber analysis, 348, 479
Chambers, R. W., 798
Chambers, W., 638
Champollion, J.-F., 907–11
Chandler, A. B., 216, 218
Chaocipher, 767, 768
Chappe, C., 836–37
Chase, P. E., 203–04
Chaucer, G., 90, 354, 873
Checkerboard, 83, 86, 203, 546, 620, 650, 651
Checkoway, A., 527
Chesapeake, 971
Chess, A. P., 818–19
Chétardie, Marquis de la, 617
Chi test, 380–82, 388
Chiffres Secrets Dévoilés, Les, 250
Chiffrierabteilung, 456–57
Chiffriermaschinen Aktiengesellschaft, 421
CHI-HE, 569, 587
Childs, J. R., 327, 333, 337–39, 355
China, 73–74
Chorrin, 151

Index

Christie, A., 799
Christoph, Prince of Hesse, 448
Church, B., 175
Churchill, W. L. S., 268, 502–03, 556, 721, 972
C.I.A. *See* Central Intelligence Agency
Ciano, G., 445, 471–72, 498
Cicero, operation, 451–52
Cifax, 828, 831–33
Cifra general, 115
Cifra particular, 115
Cifrario rosso, 316, 319
Cifrario servizio, 316
Cifrario tascabile, 317, 319
Cipher
  definition, xv
  first modern Western political ciphers, 106
  first Western military ciphers, 82
  oldest surviving key, 86
  oldest Western keys, 107
  telegraph fosters, 191
  unbreakable, 398–400
  see also code; field cipher
Cipher alphabet. *See* alphabet
Cipher device
  Byrne, 767–68
  cipher reel, 220
  Hawley, 215
  see also cipher disk; cipher machine; grille; multiplex system; skytale
Cipher disk, 239
  Alberti, 127–29
  Befehlstafel, 315
  Burr, 186
  Confederate, 217
  Danish Communist, 635
  Mexican Army, 322
  most popular invention, 764
  Porter, 139
  U.S. Army, 324, 326, 584
  see also cipher device; cipher machine
Cipher machine
  de Viaris, 240
  Friedman, 385, 391
  Gretag, 826
  Hitt, 388
  Kryha, 825
  mathematical models of, 708
  Mi-544, 826
  Ottica Meccanica Italiana, 826
  Pletts, 372–74
  presently popular, 731
  RSHA, 450
  Safford, 388
  Siemens and Halske, 459, 482
  State Department, 712
  typewriter caps, 321, 415
  U-boat, 506
  U.S. Army, 575
  Vinay and Gaussin, 240
  Wanderer Werke, 459
  see also Damm; Enigma; Geheimschrijf machine; Hagelin; Hebern; Hill; M-134-C; M-228; M-325; ORANGE; PURPLE; RED; SIGABA; SIGTOT; Vernam; Wheatstone
Cipher Machines Corporation, 421
Cipher Secretary, papal, 112
Cipher telegrams, New York *Tribune* publication of, 221
Cipher wheel, Owen's, 879
Ciphertext, definition, xv
Ciphony, 551–60
Civil War, 214–21
Clarence, J., 685
Clark, E. G., 885
Clark, H. L., 21
Clarke, A. C., 958
Clarke, C. W., 604–05
Clarke, R., 268
Clausen, H., 674
Clausen, M. G. F., 650, 651, 654, 655, 656
Clausen-Thue, W., 838
Cleartext, definition, xvi
Clinton, Sir Henry, 180, 182–84
Clopfruna, 88
Cocconi, G., 943, 946, 948, 952
Code
  book, 177
  commercial. *See* commercial code
  definition, xiv
  dictionary, 177, 181, 183, 186, 216–17, 222–23
  enciphered. *See* enciphered code
  field, 314–16, 326–33

Code (*cont.*)
  first printed, 192
  hybrid, 289, 816
  nomenclators engender today's, 190
  oldest existing, 76
  origin of Western, 106
  solution of, 242, 286–87, 289, 335
  trench, 314–16, 324
  see also cipher; commercial code; enciphered code; open code
Code Compilation Section, 326–33, 611, 678
Code Compiling Company, 359
Codebreaking, definition, xv
Codegroups, definition, xiv
Codemaking, interest in, 768–70
Codenames, 501–03, 751
  see also under individual codenames
Codenumbers
  compared to codewords, 251
  condensers for, 841–42
  definition, xiv
Codetext, definition, xv
Codewords
  compared to codenumbers, 251
  construction of, 847–48
  definition, xiv
  in commercial codes, 838–44, 847–49
Colfax, S., 222, 783
Coincidence, theory of, 376–80
Cold War, 969
Collins, S. W., 524
Colophons, 75, 76, 888
COLORADO, 332
Colossus codebreaking device, 979
Columnar transposition, 155, 195
  double, 301, 302, 539
  interrupted, 312–13, 669
  irregular, 303, 634
  regular, 303
  single, 302, 529
  solution of, 16, 302–03, 440, 539
Combat Intelligence Unit, 7, 8, 10, 13, 39, 562–70, 573
COMLOGNET, 673
Commercial code, definition, xv, 189–90, 836–53

Communications intelligence, 718
  definition, xvi
Communications Intelligence Summary, 40
Communications security, definition, xvi
"Communication Theory of Secrecy Systems," 744
Compton, A., 547
Computers and tabulators, 440, 443–44, 458, 562, 563–64, 566, 568, 576, 582, 585, 595, 707–08, 725–26, 732, 917, 975, 976, 983–84
COMSEC, 709–18
  D.E.S. development, 979–81
  Condenser, commercial code, 841–42
  Confederate States of America, 216–21, 324
  Congress, U.S., 981–82
  Consolidated Exporters Corporation, 802, 803, 810–13
  Contact chart, 100–01
  Convoy HX155, 978
COPEK, 25, 31, 47, 564, 570
Coptic, 86, 904, 908, 910
Coral Sea, Battle of, 565
Corbiere, A., 170
Corderman, W. P., 388, 517, 575
Corner reflector, 722
Cornwallis, Lord, 182–84
Cory, Mr., 38
COSMOS, satellites, 720
Council of Ten, 109
Countermeasures
  definition, 722
  see also electronic countermeasures
Craig, M., 11
Cramer, G., 770–71
Criminals, 802–13, 815–22
Crisis Center, 711
Cryptanalysis,
  as a physical science, 737–38
  becomes a major element of intelligence, 348
  becomes most important element of intelligence, 612–13
  becomes specialized, 348–49
  coining of term, 384
  contrasted with cryptography, 298, 737–39, 768–69

Index

definition, xv
first, 80
general and special methods, 140, 738–39
independently invented in West, 108
linguistic basis of, 744–48
linked to statistics, 384
machines for. *See* robot cryptanalysts; computers and tabulators
mathematization of, 612
outgrows chamber analysis, 348
relation to cryptography, 753
science of, invented by Arabs, 93, 96–98
science or art, 754–55
scientific method in, 738
time element in, 754
see also cryptanalytics; enigmatology
Cryptanalytic bureaus of smaller countries, 730
Cryptanalytics, 754
Cryptanalyze, definition, xv
Crypto Aktiengesellschaft, 432, 433
Cryptoeidography, 827–36
definition, 828
Cryptogram, definition, xv
Cryptogram, The, 769
Cryptograph, Inc., 424
Cryptographia, 155
Cryptographie militaire, La, 230–39, 794
Cryptography
as mathematics, 410, 737, 739
as noise in a communications channel, 751–52
binary digital alphabet, 983
contrasted with cryptanalysis, 298, 737–39, 768–69
defective and effective, 752
definition, xiii
first recorded instance of, 71
hierarchy of systems, 14, 192, 587
in Middle Ages, 89
Internet, 983
machines for. *See* cipher machines
mechanization of, 575, 612
practical principles, 233–36, 753–54
public interest in, 980–83
public key, 982–83
relation to cryptanalysis, 753
spontaneous cultural generation of, 84
time element in, 753
see also cryptoeidography; cryptophony; steganography
Cryptologia, 155
Cryptology
administrative organization, 305, 611–12
as a black art, 91–93, 783, 792
biological roots of, 757
definition, xvi
effect of permanent embassies, 108
effect of radio, 298–90
effect of telegraph, 189–92, 298–99
effect of World War I, 348–50
effect of World War II, 611–13
first appears as cryptography plus cryptanalysis, 93
future of, 731–33
in ancient or primitive civilizations, 72–73
in theory of games, 752
linked to mathematics, 383–84, 408–10
logic of, 738–39
morality of, 758
psychological bases of, 755–57
recorded history opens, 71
sociology of, 752–53, 757
terminology, xiii-xvi, 384
U.S. takes world lead in, 385
West takes lead over East in, 127
Cryptomeneses, 155
Cryptomenytices et Cryptographiae, 154
Cryptomenytices Patefacta, 155
Cryptophony, definition, 551
Cryptotyper, 424
CSP-642, 582
see also multiplex system
Cuba, 251, 972
missile crisis, 713, 715
CULPER JR., 179
CULPER SR., 179
Cuneiform
cryptography, 75–76
decipherment of, 912–14
signs, 898, 912
Currie, L., 638

CW, 319
Cylinder, Bazeries, 247–49
    see also multiplex system
CYNTHIA, 486, 487, 488
Cypher SA, 279–80
Cypher W, 279
Cypriote, 920, 921, 925, 930
Czechoslovakia, 540–41, 975

D-1, 493
Dachnaks, 637
Daddario, E. Q., 939
Dahlerus, B., 435
Dalgarno, G., 870
Damm, A. G., 422–25, 478, 612, 825
Dancing Men cipher, 795–98
Daniel, 79–80
Darwin, C., 942
Data Encryption Standard, 979–81, 983
Dato, L., 126
Davidian alphabet, 93
Davidson, J. C. F., 279
Dawes, C. G., 492
D-Day, 542–45
Deceptions and dummy traffic, 40, 508–09, 714–15
Dechiffrierdienst, 318
Decipher, definition, xv
Decode, definition, xv
Decoys, 722, 724
Decypherers, British, 169–74, 187
Decyphering Branch, 171–74, 187–88, 704
Dee, J., 866
De-fa tana, 85
Defense Communications System, 672
De Furtivis Literarum Notis, 138
De Grey, N., 282, 285, 287, 294, 485
De la cryptographie, 242
Delafield, J. W., 540
Delastelle, F. M., 240, 242–44
Delaunay, L., 836
Demotic, 905
Delcon Corporation, 827
Denniston, A. G., 274
De-Scrambler, 552
Despacho Universal, 115
De Subtilitate, 143

Deubner, L., 438, 629, 631, 633
Deubner, O., 438
Deutschen Reichspost, 555
Devers, J. L., 511
Devos, J. P., 860
Devoy, J., 281
De Vries, Marquis, 737, 753
DEW Line, 720
Dewey, George, 254
Dewey, Godfrey, 743
Dewey, T. E., 364, 604–08
Dhorme, E., 896–99
Diaries, 777–79
Dickinson, V., 520
Difference method, 440–43
Diffie, W., 982
Digital shorthand, 850
Digraph, definition, xiv
Digraphic substitution, 198–202, 404, 450
    first, 139
Direction-finding, xvi, 7–8, 270, 334, 503–04, 708
Disk, cipher. *See* cipher disk
Distant Early Warning Line, 720
Division of Cryptography, 712
DNA, 942–43
Dogger Bank, Battle of, 271
Doheny, E. C., 815–17
Dolphins, 963
Dönitz, K., 465
Donnelly, I., 874, 885
Double-key cipher, 151
Double transposition. *See* columnar transposition, double
Doud, H. S., 9
Douglas, L. C., 799
Draemel, M. F., 415, 491, 566
Drake, F. D., 938, 947, 949–51, 959–61
Dreyfus, A., 254–62, 469
Driscoll, A. M., 417, 418
Drugs, smuggling of, 817
Dubthach, 89
Dulles, A. W., 390, 498–99, 674
Dulles, J. F., 729
Dumbell cipher, 180
Dunlap, J. E., 696–97
Dunning, M. J., 49
Durbodha, 74

Index

D'Urfe, Madame, 153
Dusenbury, C. C., 28
Dvorak-Dealey keyboard, 741
Dyer, T. H., 48, 562–64, 593, 595

E-7, 827
Eastern Island script, 916
E.C.C.M. *See* electronic counter-counter-measures
Eckhardt, H. von, 289, 294, 354
Eckert, T. T., 215, 863
E.C.M. *See* electronic countermeasures
Edgers, D., 29, 50
Edie, L. C., 945
Edward, Prince of Wales, 776
Egypt, 970
Eisenhower, D., 325
Electric Code Machine, 416
Electric Coding Machine, 25
Electro-Crypto Model B 1, 424
Electronic counter-countermeasures, xvi, 721, 723
Electronic countermeasures, xvi, 721
  active, 722–23
  passive, 722
Electronic fingerprinting, 539
Electronic intelligence, xvi, 720–21
  outline of, xvi
Electronic reconnaissance, xvi, 719–20
Electronic security, xvi, 721
  outline of, xvi
Electronic warfare, 719–24
Elements of Cryptanalysis, 384
Elgar, Sir Edward, 800
Eliopoulos, E., 817
Emanuel, T., 13
Emergency Code List, 329
Emission security, xvi, 721, 723
Encicode, definition, xv
Encipher, definition, xv
Enciphered code, 129, 251–52, 402, 644
  Austrian, 278, 319
  criminal, 222–23
  definition, xv
  first, 129–30
  French, 312, 402
  German, 268–69, 271–2, 273, 315–16
  Italian, 256–59, 469

Japanese, 7, 15–16, 23–24, 563, 588
  Russian, 616, 644–45
  solution of, 258–59, 268–69, 440–44, 496–97, 564, 749
  U.S., 252, 491–92, 493, 496–97
Encode, definition, xv
ENGLANDSPIEL, 533
Engstrom, H. T., 705
Enigma, 6, 18, 421, 422, 423, 425, 459, 461, 510, 649, 972–77, 984
  public discourse of, 978–79
"Enigma" *Variations,* 800
Enigmaduction, definition, 879
Enigmaplan, definition, 879
Enigmatology, 878–91
  definition, 878
Ennes, J. M., Jr., 970
Eno, A. L., 394
Entick's *Dictionary,* 177, 183, 186
Entropy, 759–62
Epsilon Eridani, 950–51
Eriksson, B. E. G., 652
"Erring Siamese," 85
Error detection and correction, 747
Erskine, D. G., 511–12
ETCRRM II, 716
Ethiopia, 251
Etruscan, 916
Euler, L., 765
Evans, A., 918–23
Evans, A. R., 591
Ewing, Sir Alfred, 266, 275, 276
Eyraud, C., 478
Ezra, I., 810
Ezra, J., 810

F and P inks, 353
Fabian, R. J., 10, 25, 40, 563, 564, 568, 573
Fabyan, G., 370, 401, 867, 886, 888
Falconer, J., 155
Fall, A. B., 815–17
Family codes, 521
Farquhar, C., 845
Federal Bureau of Investigation, 26, 41, 524, 528, 530, 531
  Cryptanalytical and Translation Section, 819–21

Federal Communication Commission, Radio Intelligence Division of, 526–29
Federal Information Processing Standards Publication 46, 980–81
Federal Register, 979, 980
Feely, J. M., 870
Feistel, H., 979–80
Fellers, B. F., 473–76 *passim*
Fellgiebel, E., 455, 458
Fenner, W., 457
Fernmeldeaufklärung, 459, 475, 476
Ferrett airplanes, 719
Ferret satellites, 720
Fersen, A., 775
Féval, P., 772–73
Fiber optics, 829
Field cipher, 202, 234–36
    in World War II, 459
    invention of, 191
    most famous, 339
    requirements for, 235
Fielder, K. J., 52
Figl, A., 316, 449–53 *passim*
Filter, noise, 752
Fingerprinting, electronic, 539
Fingerprinting apparatus, radio, 708
Finland, 644–45
Fish, H., Jr., 635
"Fists" of radiotelegraphers, 32, 527, 536, 539
Five-letter commercial codes, 843, 844, 847
Five-numeral system. *See* JN-25
Five-Power Treaty, 358, 364
Fleet Radio Unit, Pacific Fleet. *See* FRUPAC
Fleming, I., 800, 977
Fletcher, F. J., 565
Flint, C., 509
Flivos, 976
Florence, 110, 114
Foote, A., 650–51, 659–60
Forschungsamt, 446–48, 450
Forschungsanstalt, 555–57
FORTITUDE, 508–09
Fosse, G. P., della, 903
Fourier, J.-B., 907
Fouché, L., 862

Fractionating ciphers, 203–04, 243
France
    Bureau de Chiffre (Army), 305–06; (Foreign Ministry) 255–56, 259
    Commission on Military Cryptography, 261, 262, 299, 304
    diplomatic codes, 402, 481–82
    Foreign Ministry, 255–61, 303
    interrupted columnar transposition, 312–13
    military codes, 312, 314
    nomenclators, 162–63
    pre-World War I, 239–40, 262, 264
    Service du Chiffre, 305
    Vichy, 478, 487
    War Ministry, 299–301, 303–09
    see also Babou, Cabinet Noir, Rossignol, Viete
Franklin, B., 185
Franz, W., 458
Freemasons' cipher, 772
Frequency of letters, analysis of, 99, 100, 107, 127, 201, 210, 738
Frequency counts
    comparison of, 380–83
    digraphic, 202
    in solution, 97–99, 99–102, 209, 210–11, 748
    stability of, 739–43, 748
Freud, S., 755
Freudenthal, H., 954–47
Friedman, E. S.
    Baconian studies, 885, 879–82, 887–88
    children, 389
    early life, 371
    I'm Alone case, 814–15
    International Monetary Fund, 826
    rumrunning solutions, 802–14
Friedman, W. F.,
    and Yardley, 361–62, 369
    as teacher, 384, 517
    at Riverbank Laboratories, 371–74, 384
    Baconian studies, 390, 879–82, 885, 886–88
    characteristics, 21, 369–70, 389
    children, 389

Index

codeword construction, 848
Congressional compensation, 390–92
contributions to cryptology, 21, 392–93, 612
decorations, 390
early life, 370–71
first writing on cryptology, 374
greatest single creation, 384
Hindu solutions, 371–72
in G.2 A.6, 333, 374
in N.S.A., 390
in Signal Corps Code & Cipher Compilation Section, 5, 360, 384–86
in S.I.S., 5, 386, 388–90
Index of Coincidence, 376–80, 382–84, 973
interest in cryptology, 371
inventions, 385, 389, 391, 510
makes U.S. world leader in cryptology, 385
Mars messages, 385, 948
nervous breakdown, 23, 389
Pletts machine solution, 372, 374
PURPLE solution, 1, 9, 21–22, 389, 508
retirement, 390
Riverbank Publications, 374–84
rotor solution, 385
rumrunning solutions, 806
Teapot Dome, 385, 815–17
Vernam-device solutions, 401
Voynich manuscript, 870, 953
word coinages, 384
writings, 374–84, 385, 388, 390, 699, 706
Friedmann, P., 857–58
Friedrichs, A., 438, 439, 446, 497–98
Frisch, K. von, 945
Fromm, E., 755
Front-Line Code, 327
Frost, L. H., 702, 703
FRUPAC, 573, 594, 595
Fuchs, K., 661
Fuchs, R., 860
Funkabwehr, 661
Funkaufklärungsdienst, 461
Funkspiel, 531–38 *passim*
Für GOD, 310, 464
Furness, Lady Thelma, 776

G.2 A.6, 326, 329, 331, 333–39, 678
Gabbrielli, D. P., 859
Gabuli tana, 85
Gadsby, 740
Gallery, D. V., 504, 506
Gallup, E. W., 371, 885–88
Galton, Sir Francis, 957–58
Gamba, V., 469
Gambling, 817–19, 821
Gamma epsilon, 273
Gamma u, 273
Gangga malayu, 85
García-Icazbalta, D. F. M., 860
Gardner, M., 982–83
Gauss, K. F., 958
Gaussin, J., 240, 397
Geheime Kabinets-Kanzlei, 163–65
Geheimklappe, 315, 336
Geheimschrijfmachine, 420
Gematria, 92
General system, xv, 235
Generator, multiple-target, 723
Generatrix, definition, 248
Geometrical systems, 155, 519, 521
Geometrical transposition ciphers, formulae solution of, 376
Georgiev, V., 923
Germany, 730
  Abhorchdienst, 313–14
  Abwehr, 453–54, 531, 533, 534, 535, 537
  Army, 454–60
  Beobachtung-Dienst, 465–68, 484
  Chiffrierabteilung, 456–58
  Fernmeldeaufklärung units, 459–60, 461, 475–76, 477
  Forschungsamt, 446–48, 450
  Forschungsanstalt, 450, 555–57
  Funkaufklärungsdienst, 461–64
  Geheimschreiber, 482
  Heeresnachrichtenwesens, 458–61
  Kriegsmarine, 972–73, 977
  Luftwaffe, 454, 461–64, 976
  Nachrichten-Verbindungswesen, 461
  Navy, 465–68
  Pers z, 436–40, 443–46, 450, 452, 596–98
  pre-World War I, 239–40, 263

Germany (*cont.*)
  Reichsicherheitschauptamt, 449–53
  Sicherheitsdienst, 448–49
  standard Nazi spy cipher, 530
  Volunteer Evaluation Office, 454
  Wehrmachtnachrichtenverbindungen, 455, 456, 458
  World War I miscellaneous systems, 307–09
  see also 0075; 13040; ADFGVX; ADFGX; Befehstafel; Enigma; Für GOD; Geheimklappe; Satzbuch; Schlusselheft; UBCHI
Gerry, E., 176
Gestapo, 449
Gex, W., Sr., 812
Gherardi, B., 401
Gherardi, L., 472
Gifford, G., 122
Gilgamesh, Epic of, 913
Gillmore, R., 333
Gisevius, H. B., 498–99
Giskes, H. J., 531–38 *passim*
Givierge, M., 299, 348, 349
Glavnoye, Razvedyvatelnoye Upravlenie, 639, 642, 643, 650
Goggins, W. B., 573
"Gold-Bug, The," 790–92, 783, 818
Goldberg, N., 810, 813
Goodman, W. H., 713
Gorgo, 82
Göring, H., 446–47, 450
Gorman, F. J., 806
Gothic language, 900
Goudy, F. W., 888
Gouzenko, I., 643
Government Code and Cypher School, 975–76
Graham, J., 333
Grant, U. S., 217
Graves, R., 799
GRAY, 490–91, 495, 579, 638
Gray, H., 324
Great Britain
  Admiralty, 484, 977–78
  codebreaking establishment, 975–76
  diplomatic codes, 452
  Foreign Office, 483–84, 485–86
  in Singapore, 10, 563, 564
  Intelligence E(c), 2nd echelon, 311–12
  M.I. 1(b), 309–11
  naval codes, 279–80
  nomenclators, 173–74
  Playfair, 202, 312
  pre-World War I, 263, 264
  War Office, 309, 484
  see also Decyphering Branch; Phelippes; Room 40; Wallis; Willes
Great Cryptogram, The, 875, 876
Greece, ancient, 80–83
Greek language, 920–21, 931–36
GREEN, 490
Green Bank, radio telescope, 938
Greenwald, H., 756
Grew, J. C., 495
Griffiths, R. T., 741
Grilles, 180
  Cardano, 144–45, 519, 521
  turning, 308–09
Gronsfeld, Count of, 245
Grosvenor, W. M., 223–29
Grotefend, G. F., 912
Groves, L. R., 545–48 *passim*
G.R.U. *See* Glavnoye Razvedyvatelnoye Upravlenie
Gūdhalekhya, 75, 799
Gusev, 641
Gyldén, O., 424, 478
Gyldén, Y., 426, 428, 478, 479, 480, 817, 824

HA, 588
Hagelin, B. C. W., 425–34 *passim,* 612
Hagelin machines, 469, 691
  see also B-21; B-211; C-36; M-209
Haggard, H. Rider, 798
Hague Convention articles of war, 46
Hahalruna, 88
Hall, W. R., 276, 280
Halsey, W. F., 608, 609
Hamel, G., 825
Hames, M. R., 799
Hamilton, V. N., 696, 728
Hammer, C., 772
Hancock, C. B., 613
Harha tana, 85
Harnack, A., 657, 659

Index

Harness, F. A., 604
Hartfield, J. C., 839, 845
Hartfield, J. W., 839, 847
HARUNA, 42, 43, 44, 67
Harvey, H., 839
Hassard, J. R. G., 223–29
Harris, Stephen R., 971
HATO, 6
Hawley, E. H., 215
Hay of Seaton, M. V., 309–11 *passim,* 329
Hayes, R. B., 221
Hayhanen, R., 668, 669, 670
Hebern, E. H., 385, 388, 392, 415–20, 612, 825
Hebern Electric Code Inc., 417–19
Hebrew ciphers, 77–79
Heeresnachrichtenwesens, 458, 459
Heilman, G., 511–12
Hellman, M., 982
Helstrom, C. W., 752
Henry, O., 799
"Hermit metamorphosing letters," 85
Hermoni, D., 826
Herodotus, 81–82, 780
Hieroglyphic cryptography, 71–72
Hieroglyphics, solution of, 901–12
Hill, L. S., 404–10, 612, 739
Hime, H. W. L., 889
Himmler, H., 447, 449, 450
Hincks, E., 913
Hindenburg, P. von, 623, 626, 630
Hindus, 371–72
Hinman, C., 888
Hinsley, F. H., 977
Hippisley, B., 268
Hira gana, 570
Hiroshima, 549, 610
Hiss, A., 639
Histaieus, 81–82, 780
Historians, 854–72
Hitchings, O. J., 311, 329, 563
Hitler, A., 445–46, 447, 451, 460, 498, 555, 975
Hitt, P., 321–25, 329, 362, 388, 392, 403, 492, 493, 768
Hittite cuneiform, 914
H.N.W. *See* Heeresnachrichtenwesens
Hoboes, 824

Hoffmann, E., 438
Hogan, D., 815
Hogben, L., 956–57
Hohenburg, J. F., Herwath von, 904
Holden, E. S., 224
Holland. *See* Netherlands
Holland, E. J., 604
Hollerith tabulating machines, 576
Holmes, W. J., 566, 594
Holmes, S., 794–98
Holtwick, J. S., Jr., 20, 566
Homer, 80–81, 917, 918, 935–36
Homophonic substitution
    contrasted with polyalphabetic substitution, 125, 129
    definition, xiv
    expansion of, 108
    first, 96
    first Western, 107
    solution of, 113
    see also polyphonic substitution
Hoover, H., 359
Hope, H. W. W., 274
Horapollo, 903
Hornbeck, S. K., 24, 364, 492
Horner, E. W., 550
Hot line, 715–16
Höttl, W., 449–53, 613 *passim*
Houdini, H., 769
House of Representatives, U.S., 981
Housel, C. A., 803
Hoy, H. C., 274
Hrozný, B., 914, 916, 923, 928
HUDSON, 328, 332
Huffduff, 504
Hull, C., 3, 33, 49, 494
Hungary, army intelligence, 452
    see also Austria-Hungary
Hüttenhain, E., 458
Huxley, A., 756
Huygens, C., 773
HW-28, 714
Hydrogen emission line, 949, 962
Hypnerotomachia Poliphili, 873, 903

I-1, 590
I.B.M. *See* International Business Machines Corporation

Ibn ad-Duraihim, 95–98
Ibn Khaldūn, 96
I.D. 25, 270
Identification-friend-or-foe system, 718, 979
I.F.F., 718, 979
Iliad, 80–81, 917, 935–36
Illusory complication, 304
I'm Alone, 814–15
Index of Coincidence and Its Applications in Cryptography, 376–85, 973
India, 74, 979
Indianapolis, 609
Indians, American, 549–50
Indus Valley script, 916
Influence letter, 424
Information theory, 743–44
INGO DENPO, 37, 57
Inman, B. R., 981
Institute for Defense Analyses, 709, 711
Integration (anti-jamming), 723
Intelligence Bulletins, MAGIC, 30
Intelligence E(c), 311
Interception, xvi, 11–13, 298–99, 677, 724
  see also mail opening; traffic volume; wiretapping
International Business Machines Corporation
  Data Encryption Standard, 979–81
  Hebern patent interference, 419
  7090 computer, 726
  Stretch, 726
  tabulators, 562, 563, 566, 568, 576, 582, 584, 595, 726
International code of signals, 837
International Code of Signals, 846
International Code Machine Company, 419
International Communication Laboratories, 403
International Radiotelegraph Conference, 846
International Telemeter Corporation, 833, 835
International Telephone and Telegraph Corporation, 388, 403, 716
International Telegraph Union, 842, 848, 849

International Telemeter Corporation, 833
International Traffic in Arms Regulations, 981
Internet, 983
Interplanetary communication, 938–65
Interstellar language, 953–56
Inventors, 191, 709–10, 763–68, 825–26
Inversion, 552
Inverter, 554
Invisible inks, 95, 127, 138, 179–80, 187, 448, 513–14, 515, 522–25, 576, 616
Involutory transformations, 406
Isomorphic cryptograms, 20
Israel, 970
Isruna, 88
Italy
  cifrario rosso, 316, 319
  cifrario servizio, 316
  cifrario tascabile, 317, 319
  military attaché, 259, 264
  naval codes, theft of, 486–87
  Reparto crittografia, 318–19
  Servizio Informazione Militare, 469–72
  Servizio Informazione Segreto, 468–69
Ito, S., 46

J series of Japanese diplomatic codes, 16, 42, 444
J12, 27
J19, 42
Ja, 357
JABBERWOCK, 45
James, W., 274
Jamming, 722–23
Janssen, H. P. M., 519
Japan, 561–613, 730
  Anego Kenkyu Han, 495
  Army, 425, 584–88, 591
  Foreign Office, 14–19, 23–24, 32, 33–37, 42, 43, 44, 45
  INGO DENPO, 37–38, 57–58
  J12, 27
  J17-K6, 16
  J18-K8, 16
  J19-K9, 16, 32, 38, 41, 42
  LA, 14–15, 43
  maru code, 593–94

Index

Navy, 10, 47, 562–63, 564–65, 567, 586–88
97-shiki O-bun In-ji-ki, 18–19, 22, 49
Oite, 15–16
PA-K2, 15–16, 42, 43, 47, 48, 49, 55, 66
s code, 27, 593–94
Tokumu Han, 579–84, 610
TSU, 16–18, 42
see also MAGIC; PURPLE; winds code
"Japanese Diplomatic Secrets," 364
Jargon, 281, 519, 520, 541–45, 822
Jay, Sir James, 179
Jefferson, T., 184, 192–93, 194–95
  wheel cypher, 192–95
  see also multiplex system; strip cipher
Jellicoe, Sir John, 272
Jerdan, W., 764
Jerrold Electronic Corporation, 831, 836
JN25, 562, 587
JN25b, 7, 10, 564, 565, 567
JN25c, 564, 571
JN25d, 603
Johnson, H. W., 365
Johnson, L. B., 687, 730
Jones, E., 756
Joseph P. Muller, 972
Joyce, James, 745, 767
JP, 358
Jutland, Battle of, 272–73

Kabbalah, 91–92
Kaeding, F. W., 743
Kakimoto, G., 582
Kāma-sūtra, 74
Kameyama, K., 31, 49
Kapany, N. S., 829
Kappa sub p, 378
Kappa sub r, 378
Kappa test, 378, 380, 385, 413
Kasiski examination, 209, 398, 399
Kasiski, F. W., 207–08
Kasiski solution, 207–13
Kata kana, 14, 356, 570
Kautilya, 74, 75
Kautiliyam, 74
Keill, J., 169
Keitel, W., 455
Keller, H., 944

Kempenfeldt, R., 837
Kempf, S., 456
Kennamer, C. B., 810
Kennedy, J. F., 592
Kennedy, J. P., 494, 495
Kent, T., 494, 495
Kerckhoffs, A., 230–39, 240, 754
Kerckhoffs superimposition, 236–37, 378, 380, 399, 413
Kesselring, A., 459, 461
Kettler, H., 456
Key
  definition, xv
  distinguished from general system, xv, 235
  endless and random, 397–98, 402
  first mnemonic, 113
  generation of, 732
  literal in polyalphabetic substitution, 137
  progressive, 136
  recovery of in monalphabetic substitution, 103–04
  recovery of primary alphabet, 374–75, 376
  to mix cipher alphabets, 113
  see also autokeys; progressive keys; running keys
Key escrow, 983
Keynumber, definition, xv
Keyphrase, definition, xv
Keyphrase cipher, 787
Keyword, definition, xv
  length in polyalphabetic solution, 208
KFF-58, 826
KG-13, 715
Kharkevich, 641
Khnumhotep II, 71
Khrushchev, N. S., 687
King, E. J., 567
Kinkaid, T. C., 609
Kinsey, A. C., 773
Kircher, A., 154, 846, 864, 904–05
Kirilyuk, V. A., 685
Kirk, D., Jr., 831–35 *passim*
Kita, N., 13
Kitāb al-mu'ammā, 97
Kiwi, 590

Klein, M. H., 696
Knatchbull-Hugessen, Sir Hughe, 451
KNICKBEIN, 721
Knights of the Golden Circle, 772
Knights Templars, 823
Knock cipher, 821
Knossos tablets, solution of texts, 934–35
Knox, F., 3
Kober, A. B., 923–27, 937
Koch, H. A., 420
Koenig, W., Jr., 558–59
Kök-Turki runes, 916
Köthe, G., 438
Kowalefsky, J., 357, 579
Kramer, A. D., 2, 3, 4, 11, 27, 50, 56
    see also OP-20-G
Kraus, H. P., 863, 871, 872
Kreuger, I., 824
Kripo, 449
Krivosh, R., 642
Krivosh, V., 642
Kroger, H. and P., 664, 665, 666
Krohn, C. H. C., 236
KRU, 315
KRUSA, 315
Kryha, A. von, 825
Kühn, B. J. O., 42, 50, 66
Kullback, S., 386, 390, 576, 612, 707
Kunze, W., 402, 436–37, 439, 446, 563, 612, 755
KW-1, 714
KW-7, 714
KY-3, 715
KY-8, 715
KY-9, 711, 715

LA, 14–15, 43
Lagoruna, 88
Lais, A., 486, 487
Lake series, 328
Lalita-Vistara, 74
Langlotz, E., 402, 438
Languages
    decipherment of lost, 895–932
    interstellar, 953–56
    pictorial, 958–62
    reconstruction of, 900–01
    secret, 822–24

Lanphier, T. G., Jr., 599, 600, 601
Largonji, 823
LARRABEE, 324, 489
Laser, 708, 732–33
Lasswell, A. B., 48, 595, 598
Lauenburg, 977
Lauwers, H. M. G., 533, 534, 536, 537
Lavinde, G. di, 107
La wan, 73
Lawrence, J., 801
Lawrence of Arabia, 312
Laws and judicial decisions, 364–67, 390–92, 687, 691, 700
Layton, E. T., 39, 40, 596, 597
LEB KAMAI, 77
LeFebure Corporation, 829
Leichty, E., 76
Lenticles, 828
Leopard, 971
Lesson, J., 770
Letter opening device, 618
Letters of the alphabet, characteristics of, 96–97, 99–102, 127
Levine, J., 404, 405
Lexicography, Arabic, 96
Lexington, 565
Liberty, 970
Lieber, B. F., 839
Lilly, J. C., 963
Lim, G., 809
Lincoln, A., 215–16, 220, 862–63
Lincos, 954–57
Linofilm, 743
Linotype, 742
Lipograms, 740
Literacy, 74, 84, 732
Literature of cryptology
    American, 323–34, 374, 384, 388
    Arabic, 94, 95, 97
    fiction, 767, 779–800
    first biography, 159
    first printed book, 133
    first text, 82
    French and German pre-World War I, 239
    great books, 230
    in Middle Ages, 90
    most famous book, 360–61

Index

  most important publication, 376
  on World War I, 379
  poems, 95, 159
  16th and 17th centuries, 154–56
  Venetian, 109
  West's oldest text on cryptanalysis, 127
  see also Lost Books
Littlefield, J., 851
Livesey, F., 355, 357
Livingston, R. A., 184
Lockwood, B. F., 970
LOGAIRNET, 673
LOGBALNET, 673
Logograms, 910–11
Lohr, L. R., 376
Lonsdale, G. A., 664, 665, 666
Lost Books, 84, 95, 97, 109
Lovell, J., 181–86
Lovers, 774–77
Löwenstern, I., 913
Lucifer, 980
Ludendorff, E., 344, 346, 623, 626, 630, 631
Ludwig, K. F., 514
Luftnachrichten, 461
Luneberg lens, 722
Luning, H. A., 515
Lynch Communication Systems, Inc., 827
Lynn, G. W., 11

M-94, 325, 385, 584
  see also multiplex system
M-134, 575
M-134-C, 391, 510
M-138, 325, 476, 493, 495, 499–501
  see also multiplex system
  M-138-A, 325
M-209, 427, 428–32, 460, 540
M-228, 391
M-325, 391
MacArthur, D., 31
Macbeth, J. C. H., 845
McCloy, H., 799
McCollum, A. H., 3, 4
Macfarlane, J. R., 755
Macgregor, D. C., 311
Machida, Major, 584

McIntosh, A., 527
McKay, H. C., 828
Mackay Radio & Telegraph Company, 55
Mackensen, A. von, 339, 629–31
McLean, E. B., 815–17
Madison, J., 181, 184, 186, 188
Magdeburg, 268, 972
MAGIC, 1–67 *passim,* 93, 360, 674
  distribution, 24–26, 27–28, 30–31
  14-part message, 2, 3, 49–63 *passim*
  naming of, 3
  one o'clock message, 1–2, 3–4, 55, 57, 58, 60
  post-war, 610
  production of, 14–24, 28–30
  role of, 31
  security threats to, 26–27, 601–08
Magic, 91–93, 117, 131–33, 783, 792
Magnus, A. von, 295
Mail opening, 163–64, 171–72, 188, 448, 618, 639–40
Makarov, M., 657
Malaya, 85
Maldive Islands, 85
Man in the Iron Mask, 860–62
Mancini, G., 469
MANHATTAN ENGINEERING DISTRICT, 545
Manly, J. M., 352, 354, 360, 362, 867, 869, 871
Mannerheim, C., 645
Manual for the Solution of Military Ciphers, 323–24
Manutius, A., 873, 903
Maquis, French, 539
Marble, M., 222
Marci, J. M., 309, 864
Marconi, G., 947
Margoliouth, D. S., 888
Marnix, P. van, 118–21
Marryat, F., 837
Mars, 940–59 *passim*
Marshall, G. C., 11, 24, 28, 30, 31, 45, 57, 59–61, 601–08
Martin, W. H., 692–95, 719, 728
Maru code, 594
Mary, Queen of Scots, 122–24
Maser, 722

Massachusetts Institute of Technology, 982, 983
Mata Hari, 278
"Mathematical Theory of Communication, A," 744
Mathematics, 207, 240–42, 384, 405, 408–10, 612, 737
Mauborgne, J. O., 321, 401, 563
  as Chief Signal Officer, 6, 21, 389
  cryptologic highlights, 6
  invents unbreakable cipher, 397–98
Maximilian I, 134
May, A. N., 661
Maya hieroglyphics, 917
Mayfield, I. S., 13, 42, 51
Meals, F. M., 806
Mecano-Cryptographer Model A 1, 424
Medical Greek, 822
"Melancholy Notes on a Cablegram Code Book," 851
Melchior, Ib, 750
Mellenthin, F. W. von, 646, 647
Meltzer, R. J., 829
Mendelsohn, C. J., 357, 846, 848
MENE MENE TEKEL UPHARSIN, 79–80
Menet Khufu, 71
Mengarini commercial code, 317
Menninger, K. A., 755
Mergenthaler, O., 742
Mesopotamia, 75
Mexican Army Cipher Disk, 322
Mexican microdot ring, 526
Meyer, A., 415, 417
  see also Driscoll, A. M.
Meyer, H., 542–44
M.I. 1(b), 309, 484
M.I. 8 (Great Britain), 484
MI-8 (U.S.), 352–53
Mi-544, 826
Michiel, G., 858
MICHIGAN, 328
Microdot, 525–26, 666
Mid-Pacific Strategic Direction-Finder Net, 8, 10
Midway, Battle of, 561, 566–73, 603, 606
Milan, 110–11
Military Cryptanalysis, 388, 706
Miller, E. C., 273
Miller, F. M., 887, 888
Miller, S. L., 942
Minckler, R. W., 9
Mind-reading acts, 824
Ming commercial code, 690, 698
Minimotion keyboard, 741
Ministerstvo Vnutrennykh Del, 639
Minoan civilization, 918–37
Misirli, 93
Mitchel, W. J., 845
Mitchell, B. F., 692–95, 719, 728
Mitchell, J. W., 599
Mlecchita-vikalpa, 74
Mobasheri, J., 667–68
Monalphabetic substitution, 979
  definition, xiv
  solution of, 97–98, 99–105
  see also polyalphabetic substitution
Monks, use of ciphers, 106
Monoalphabetic substitution, 977
Monographic substitution, 404
Monroe, J., 185
Montdidier, Battle of, 346–47
Montgomery, B., 477
Montgomery, W., 282, 285–86, 483
Moore, W. H., 28
Moorman, F., 327, 331, 333, 336, 337, 361, 362, 768
Morehouse, L. F., 397
Moreo, J. de, 116–17
Morgenstern, O., 752
Mori, M., 48, 52, 60
Morikawa, H., 579, 581
Morimura, T. *See* Yoshikawa, T.
Morris, R., 771
Morrison, A. M., 810, 813
Morrison, P., 943, 946, 947, 948, 952, 960, 961
Morse code, 741, 754, 838
Morse, S. F. B., 189, 741
Motion pictures, 800
Motorola, 981
Mourão, J., 74
Moyzisch, L. C., 451
Mügge, K.-A., 462
Muirhead, M., 321
Muladevïya, 74
Müller, F. W. K., 901, 915

Index

Müller, H.-K., 497
Multiple anagramming, 226, 303, 305, 309
Multiple-target generators, 723
Multiplex systems, 376
   see also Bazeries cylinder; CSP-642; Jefferson wheel cypher; M-94; M-138; NCB; strip cipher
Multiplexing, 376, 394, 712
München, 977
Murphy, R., 497–98
Murray, A. A., 11
Musefili, P., 110
Music, 563, 800, 818
Mussolini, B., 471
Mycenaean civilization, 918, 920
Myres, Sir John, 929

Nachrichten-Verbindungswesen, 461
Nagasaki, 610
Napoleon, 617
Narcotics smuggling, 817
Nathan, J. P., 333
National Bureau of Standards, 979
National Communications System, 713
National Defense Research Committee, 558
National Puzzlers League, 769
National Security Agency, 672–733, 984
   amateur inventors, 709–10
   Communications Security, Office of, 705, 709–18
   computers, 726
   Congressional relations, 698–702
   cryptanalysis, 724–30
   Data Encryption Standard, 980–82
   deputy directors, 704–05
   directors, 702–04
   employees, 677, 689–90, 706–07
   expenditures, 684, 700
   functions, 675
   intelligence results, 728–29
   library, 705
   offices, 676–77, 700
   organization of, 705
   origin of, 674–75
   Personnel Services, Office of, 705, 706–07
   position in government, 675
   Production, Office of, 705, 718–19, 724–30
   relations with other organizations, 677–84
   Research and Development, Office of, 705, 707–09
   security of, 684, 688–90, 697–99
   security breaches, 690–97
   spy ships, 970–71
   supplies cryptographic equipment, 711, 714–18
   Training Services, Office of, 705, 706
National Security Council, 681
nautical signaling, 837
Navahos, 550
Naval Communications System, 672
Naval disarmament, conference for, 358
Navy Code Box, 387
NCB, 387
   see also multiplex system
Neff, R. A., 862–63
Netherlands, 532–38, 691
   see also Marnix
Neugebauer, O., 76
Neumann, J. von, 752
Neutrino, 946
"New Directions in Cryptography," 982
New York Cipher Society, 769
New York *Tribune,* 221–29
Newbold, W. R., 867–69, 873
Newspapers, personal advertisements in, 775
NIAGARA, 328
Nicholson, A., 877
Nihilist substitution, 620, 650
Nimitz, C. W., 565, 566, 569, 573, 598, 599, 601, 608, 609
97-shiki O-bun In-ji-ki, 18, 49
   see also PURPLE
Nirābhāsa, 75
N.K.V.D., 641, 650
Noise (in information theory), 751–52
Nomenclators
   definition, xv
   development of, 107
   earliest, 107
   economics of, 173–74
   evolve into codes, 190

Nomenclators (*cont.*)
  extinction of, 192
  one-part and two-part, 160–61
  preferred to polyalphabetics, 150–51
  Spanish, 115, 117, 119
Nomura, T., 582
Nonsecret code. *See* commercial code
NORDPOL, 533–38, 691
Normal profile, 210–11
Normandy, Invasion of, 509, 542–45
Norris, G. W., 366–67
North Africa campaign, 460, 474–77, 488
North Atlantic Treaty Organization, 678
North Korea, 971–72
Norway, 465, 479, 480, 481, 484
Notarikon, 92
N.S.A. *See* National Security Agency
Nsibidi script, 84
Null, definition, xiv
Null cipher, 519, 520, 521

Oberkommando der Kriegsmarine, 454, 465, 484–85
Oberkommando der Luftwaffe, 454, 461
Oberkommando der Wehrmacht, 453, 455, 475, 544
Oberkommando des Heeres, 454, 458
Occultism, 91–93, 131–33, 783, 792
Oda, Lieutenant, 583
Odyssey, 917, 935
Office of Strategic Services, 508, 539–41
Off-line encipherment, definition, 397
Ogham, 86, 88, 89
O.G.P.U., 637, 641, 642, 644
Ohnesorge, W., 555–56
Oite. See PA-K2
O.K.H. *See* Oberkommando des Heeres
Okhrana, 608
O.K.L. *See* Oberkommando der Luftwaffe
O.K.M. *See* Oberkommando der Kriegsmarine
O.K.W. *See* Oberkommando der Wehrmacht
O'Leary, J., 546
Ollier, R.-M., 685–86
Omenitsch, H., 889
On-line encipherment, definition, 397
One-time system (tape, pads), 403, 436, 438, 444, 452, 492, 539, 540, 650, 662–64, 666, 714, 715–16, 731
  first diplomatic use, 402, 403
  insolubility of, 398–400
  invention of, 398
  objections to use of, 400
O'Neal, D., 811, 813
O'Neal, J., 811, 813
OP-16-F2, 11
OP-20-G, 1–5, 9, 11, 20, 21, 23, 25, 29, 31, 32, 45, 49–51, 55, 57, 58, 66, 388, 486, 562, 563, 573–74
OP-20-GX, 11
OP-20-GY, 1, 2, 11
OP-20-GZ, 2, 11
Open code, 32–37, 41, 516, 519–21, 541–45
ORANGE, 20, 437
OSAGE, 332
Oshima, H., 26, 38, 508
Osobyi Radio Division, 643
O.S.S. *See* Office of Strategic Services
Otiosi, 138
OTSU, 587
Ott, E., 654
Outer space, messages from, 938–65
OVERLORD, 503
Ovid, 774
Owen, O. W., 879
Ozaki, H., 583, 654, 657
Ozma Project, 950, 951

PA-K2, 15, 42
Pakistan, 979
Page, D., 935
Pahlavi script, 915
Painting, 801
Painvin, G. J., 277, 304–05, 306, 307, 315, 336, 347, 355, 563, 739
  solution of ADFGVX cipher, 344–45
  solution of ADFGX cipher, 340–43
Palin, N. G., 906
Panin, N. P., 616, 617
Pāṇini, 75
Panizzardi telegram, 255–62, 469
Papal cryptology, 106–107, 109, 112–14, 126–27, 141, 148–49, 151
Papen, F. von, 445

Parke, L. W., 11, 501, 712
Parker, R. T., 394, 397, 768
Parsons, W. S., 548–49
Paschke, A., 436–37, 439
Pasini, L., 858
Passport code, 14
Patrick, J. N. H., 222–23
"Pats." *See* microdot
Patterson, R., 193, 195
Peano, G., 954
Pearl Harbor attack, 1–67 *passim*
   cryptologic results of, 674
   debate on, 604–08
Peckham, H., 859
Penkalas, 317
Pepys, S., 777–79
Pering, A. V., 2, 11
Pers z, 436–46 *passim,* 450, 452, 496, 497, 499, 501
Persian ciphers, 96
Personal advertisements, 775
Peter the Great, 614–15
Petersen, J. S., Jr., 690–92
Petersen, T. C., 871
Peterson, E. F., 845, 849
Petrov, E., 641–42
Petrov, V. M., 641, 644, 661–63, 686
Phaistos Disk, 917
Phelippes, T., 121–23
Phi Beta Kappa, 772
Phi test, 380–82, 388
Philippines, U.S. Navy cryptanalytic unit, 10, 25, 47, 563, 564
Phillips, W., 367
Physiology of Marriage, 781
Pictures
   as interstellar language, 958–62
   secrecy in, 827–30
Pig Latin, 822
Pigpen cipher, 180, 219, 770
Placode, definition, xv
Plaintext, definition, xiii, xvi
Planas, R. R., 860
Playfair cipher, 6, 202, 312, 321, 324, 326, 404, 592
   invention of, 198–202
Playfair, L., 198, 200–02
Pletts, J. St. V., 309, 372

Plotinus, 902, 903, 904
Plutarch, 82
Poe, E. A., 783–93, 818
Pokorny, F., 973
Pokorny, H., 318, 628, 631, 633
Poland, 973–75
Polyalphabetic substitution
   as a field cipher, 191, 628
   contrasted with use of homophones and polyphones, 125, 129
   definition, xiv
   first letter-by-letter, 136
   first literal key, 136
   general solution of, 236–37
   invention of, 127
   Kasiski general solution of periodics, 207–13
   modern concept of, 141–42
   myth of unbreakability, 148
   nomenclator preferred in pre-telegraph era, 150–51
   pre-Kasiski solutions of, 142, 148–54, 155, 205–06, 218
   see also monalphabetic substitution
Polybius, 83, 86, 203
Polygrams, definition, xiv
Polygraphia libri sex, 133–36
Polygraphic substitution, 405–08
Polyphonic substitution
   contrast with polyalphabetic substitution, 125, 129
   definition, 113–14
   in cypher SA, 279–80
   see also homophonic substitution
Porta, G. B., 137–43, 180, 230, 404, 788
Porter, E., 176
Postal Telegraph Cable Company, 403
POTOMAC, 327, 332
Potsdam Declaration, 610
Potter, R. K., 559
Powers, F. G., 720, 969
"Practical cryptanalysis," 636–38, 685–87
Prakrit, 915
Praun, A., 458
Price, B., 515, 517
Price, D. J., 859
Price tags, 824
Prick holes, 83

Primary Alert System, 717
Primary alphabet, reconstruction, 374
Primrose, F. J., 840
Prinsep, J., 915
Prisoners, 821
Private Office, 171
Probable word techniques, 140, 739
Probus, 84
PROD, 718–21
Progressive key, 136
Prohibition, 802–13, 817
Protocryptography, 76
Public-key cryptography, 982–83
Pueblo, 971–72
Pulse code modulation, 711
Pumpkin papers, 638
Purcell, E., 951, 952
PURPLE, 1, 11, 25, 49, 385, 437, 486, 508, 574, 718
    destruction of, 43, 44
    distribution of machines, 23
    Japanese title, 18
    most secret Japanese system, 18
    operation, 18–19
    origin of codename, 20
    solution of, 18, 19–23
Puzzle cryptograms, 749, 769
Pyle, J. G., 877
Pyramid theories, 889–90

Qalqashandi, 95, 96, 97
Qirmeh, 95
Quadratic Code, 546
Queen Mary, 528–30

Rabelais, F., 779–80
Racial discrimination, 821
Radar, 718–24
Radar-invisible materials, 722
Radio, 298–99, 348, 611
Radio Corporation of America, 13, 42, 55, 61, 64, 554, 829, 871
Radio fingerprinting apparatus, 708
Radio intelligence, 8
    see also communications intelligence
Radio intelligence companies, 577–79
Radio Intelligence Division, 526–30
Radio Intelligence Publications, 48

Radio telescope, 938, 949–51
Radiophoto, 830
Radiotelephone. *See* telephone
Rado, A., 659
Ras Shamra tablets, 899
Raven, F. A., 23, 718, 719
Rawlinson, H. C., 912–13
Rāzsahrīya script, 86
RB-47 aircraft, 720
R.C.A. *See* Radio Corporation of America
Ream, J. H., 705
RED (German), 976
RED (Japanese), 12, 20, 437
RED (U.S.), 489
Redl, A., 621–22
Redman, J., 573
Redundancy, 744–51, 759–62
Reichling, W., 543–44
Reichssicherheitshauptamt, 449–53
Reid, W., 222–29 *passim*
Reik, T., 755
Rejeweski, M., 973, 974
Renault, G., 539
Rendezvous, 368
Rennenkampf, P., 622–28 *passim*
Reparto crittografico, 318
Retail ciphers, 824
Reynolds, S. W., 696
Rhodes, R. A., 685
Rhyming slang, 822
Ribbentrop, J. von, 436, 451
Rickert, E., 354
R.I.D. *See* Radio Intelligence Division
Ridderhof, G., 532
Rihani, 93
Rin-spuns, 84
RIO GRANDE, 328
River series, 327
Riverbank Laboratories, 370, 371, 372, 384, 401, 886
Riverbank Publications, 374–84
Rivest, R., 982
RKO General Corporation, 836
RO, 588
Robot cryptanalysts, 440, 443–44, 458
Rochefort, J. J., 7, 40, 48, 562, 563, 564, 573
    see also Combat Intelligence Unit

Index 1175

Roehm, E., 447
Rogers, H., 838
Rogers, J. H., 551
Rohrbach, H., 438, 499
Rök stone, 87, 88
Rommel, D. C. von, 473, 474, 860
Ronge, M., 316, 317, 318, 319, 320
Room 40, 226–97, 309, 354, 465, 490, 799
  acquires German naval codes, 268, 273–74
  directors, 266–67, 275–76
  effects of cryptanalyses, 280, 297
  German naval solutions, 268–69, 270, 271–73
  German political solutions, 280–81, 282–97
  naming of, 269
  origin of, 266–67
  radio intelligence, 270
  relations with Allies, 277–78
  staff, 267, 269–70, 274–75
Room 100, 478
Room 2646, 387
Roos, W. R., 519
Roosevelt, F. D., 24, 30, 51, 53–54, 56–57, 59, 62, 67, 367, 495, 499, 554–55, 556
Root-and-terminal systems, 841
Rorschach tests, 882
Rosetta Stone, 905–06, 908, 910
Rossetti, G., 888
Rossignol, A., 157–61, 162
Rossignol, B., 162
Rössler, R., 659, 660
Rote Kapelle, 652, 657–58
Rotors, 411–15, 420, 510
solution of, 385
Rotscheidt, W., 458
Rowlett, F. B., 9, 386, 392, 730
Rozycki, J., 973
RSA system, 982–83
R.S.H.A. *See* Reichssicherheitshauptamt
RSK, 631
Rubinstein, W. C., 835
Rumrunners, 802–13
Runes, 86, 87
Running keys, 375

Russia, 614–71, 973
  code thefts and losses, 636–39, 685–87, 696–97
  Communist agents, 634–36, 654–61, 663–70
  cryptology appears in, 614
  Czarist diplomatic cryptology, 614–17, 621
  Czarist military cryptology, 617, 621–22, 623, 628, 629, 631–33
  effect of cryptology on, 627, 633, 649
  electronic warfare, 719–20
  enemy solutions, 628–629, 631–33, 644–49
  Lodz, battles around, 629–31
  Nihilists and revolutionaries, 619, 620–21
  quality of cryptology, 670–71
  secondary spy systems, 666–70
  secret police, 618–21, 639–40
  Six-Day War, 970
  Soviet diplomatic cryptology, 650, 661–63
  Soviet military cryptology, 642–49
  Spets-Otdel, 640–42
  standard post-war Soviet spy cipher, 663–64
  standard World War II Soviet spy cipher, 650–54
  Tannenburg, Battle of, 622–27
  U.S. defectors to, 692–96

S boxes, 980
s code, 593
Sabhasa, 75
Sacco, L., 318, 319
Sacy, S. de, 906
Safford, L. F., 10, 387, 392, 503, 573
St. Boniface, 89
St.-Cyr slides, 238–39, 243, 382
Samarasekara, D., 685
Samford, J. A., 702, 703
SAMOS satellite, 720
Sampson, G.P., 715
Samsonov, A., 623–28 *passim*
Sandler, R., 481
Sarnoff, D., 13
Satake, T., 581, 583

Satellite and Missile Observation System, 720
Sato, N., 610
Satzbuch, 315, 334
Savinsky, A. A., 621
Sayers, D., 799
Scarbeck, I. W., 686
Schauffler, R., 402, 436–37, 439, 446, 848
Schellenberg, W., 449, 450, 452
Scherbius, A., 420–22, 423, 612, 825, 972
Scherschmidt, H., 438
Schimpf, H., 447
Schindel, J. B., 28
Schleyer, J. M., 231–32
Schliemann, H., 917–18
Schlüsselheft, 315, 334, 335
Schmidt, H.-T., 973, 974
Schott, G., 155, 245
Schulze-Boysen, H., 657–59 *passim*
Schutzstaffel, 447–49
Schwartz, R. N., 947
Science, 981
Scientific Advisory Board, 677
Scientific American, 982–83
Scientists, 773–74
Scramblers, 60, 550–60, 711–12, 714, 715, 716–17, 826–27
   audio, 708
   video, 708, 831–36
Scripta Minoa I, 922
Scripta Minoa II, 929, 930
S.D. *See* Sicherheitsdienst
SEALION, operation, 484
Sebold, W. G., 530
Secret Office, 171
Secret societies, 772–73
Security check, 533, 534, 535
Seeböhm, A., 475, 476
Selchow, K., 436, 439
Selenus, Gustavus, 154
Sellers, L. W., 333
Semagram, 519–22, 884
Senate, U.S., 981
Series 65 code, 312
Service du Chiffre, 305
Servizio Informazione Militaire, 469–72 *passim*
Servizio Informazione Segreto, 468

SH, 319
Shāh-dabīrīya, 86
Shakespeare-Bacon controversy, 370–71, 750, 781, 873–91
Shakespearean Ciphers Examined, The, 390, 879
Shakespeare, W., 781, 873
Shamhart, E. J., 814
Shami, 93
Shamir, A., 982
Shannon, C. E., 743–52 *passim,* 759, 761, 766
Shaw, H. R., 517, 518, 524
Sheinwold, A., 540
Shelta, 822
Shelton, T., 777
SHESHACH, 77
Shimizu, Lieutenant, 583
Shivers, R. L., 51
Shoho, 565
Sholes, C. L., 740
Shorthand, 82, 777–79
Shungsky, 642
Sicherheitsdienst, 447–49
Siemens & Halske machine, 482
SIGABA, 510–12, 548
SIGCODE, 386
Signalbuch der Kaiserlichen Marine, 972
Signal Intelligence
   outline of, xvi
   School, 9, 388
   Service, 2–5, 6, 9, 11, 20–23, 29, 31, 42, 44, 49–50, 54–57, 386, 388, 486, 509, 575, 595
Signal Security
   outline of, xvi
   Agency, 508, 575–76, 678
   Service, 575, 611
   Battalion, 576
   Company, 9, 576
Signature-encoding systems, 829
SIGTOT, 403, 501
Silence, 753
S. I. M. *See* Servizio Informazione Militare
Simonetta, C., 110
Simpson, W. W., 777
Sinclair, H. F., 815–17
Sinkov, A., 386, 390, 577, 612, 718

Index

S.I.S. *See* Signal Intelligence Service
SITECOMNET, 673
Sittig, E., 923, 933
Sittler, F. J., 839
  commercial code, 252, 317
Six-Day War, 970
Skeat, W. W., 765, 873
Skiatron Electronics and Television Corporation, 833
Skytale, 82, 788
Slide, 152, 238–39, 243–44, 463
Smith, A. V., 489
Smith, E. *See* Friedman, E. S.
Smith, F. O. J., 189, 190, 838
Smith, G., 920
Smith, L. C., & Corona Typewriters, Inc., 427
Smith, W. W., 386
Snifter, 526
Sonderdienst Dahlem, 438
Sorge, R., 654–57
Soro, G., 109
Souchon, W., 267
Soviet Union. *See* Russia
Spain, 114–16, 250, 487, 635, 855–57
Special Operations Executive, 535–38
Spectrograph, 559–60
Speech codes, 549–51, 822–23
Speech compression, 712
Spets-Otdel, 640–42
Spurt communication systems, 712
Spy cipher, 539, 541, 634, 650–54, 663–64, 666, 669–70
Spy ships, 969–72
Square table, 135
S.S. *See* Schutzstaffel
Staff Code, 329, 332
Stager, A., 214, 215
Stain, 180
Standard Elektrik Lorenz, 826
Stanton, E., 862
STARCOM, 672
Stark, H. F., 3, 4
Starziczny, J. J. J., 528
Statistical-combinatory analysis, 953
Statistics, 376, 384–85
  see also mathematics
Stator, 238, 244

Stawell, F. M., 922
"Steganographia," 131, 132, 866
Steganography, 73, 81–83, 131, 133–34, 513, 515, 516, 519–26, 827, 873, 882
  definition, xiii
  see also cryptography
Stein, K., 458
Stereoscopy, 828
Sterling, G. E., 526
Stimson, H. L., 3, 5, 360, 547–48, 758
Stoker, B., 799
Stone, E. E., 702
Stopfruna, 88
Straddling checkerboard, 635
Strategic Air Command, 673, 718
Street, G., 42
Strip cipher, 325, 493
  Japanese solution of, 582–83
  see also multiplex system
Strong, L. C., 870
Stuyt, G., 691
Subh al-a 'sha, 95
Substitution
  basic solution of, 99–105
  compared with transposition, 250, 304, 307, 764
  definition, xiii
  distinguished from transposition, 139
  earliest recorded, 71
Suetonius, 84
Suez crisis, 729
Superimposition, 236–37, 378, 380, 399, 413, 972
Superencipherment, 251–52, 751–52
  definition, xv
  see also enciphered code
Susa, 76
Svensson, E., 9
Sweden, 87, 284, 478–83, 730
Swift, J., 889
SYKO, 463, 464
Sylvester II, 89
Symmetry of position, 237–38, 243–44
Syria, 970

T-55, 433
Tableaux, 135–36, 139, 147–48, 149, 180, 220–21, 238–39, 489

Tables à chiffrer, 161
Tables à déchiffrer, 161
Tabula recta, 136
Tabulators. *See* computers and tabulators
Tachygraphy, 777
Tadmuri, 93
Tallmadge, B., 177–79
Talmud, 79
Tannenberg, Battle of, 622–27
Tau Ceti, 949, 950
Tax officials' cryptography, 95
TC-534, 826
T.D.S. *See* time-division scramble
Teapot Dome, 815–17
Technical Operational Division, 517, 518, 524
Telautograph, 306, 830
Telconia, 266
Telecommunications Operations Division, 714
Teleglobe Pay-Television System, 833
Telegraph, 189–92, 298–99
Telegraphic Japanese, 29
Telekrypton, 560
Telephone, 550-60-712
  see also wiretapping
Teletype Corporation, 420, 714
Teletypewriter, 388, 394–97, 459, 850, 883
Television, 831–36, 961
Temurah, 92
TEN, 588
Tesla, N., 947
Thackeray, W. M., 793
Thailand, 85
Thiele, F., 455, 458
Thomas, F. W., 788
Thompson, B., 180
Thomsen, H., 26, 494
Thomsen, V., 916
Thorpe, A. E., 486
Thucydides, 82
Thurber, J., 491
Tibbals, C. F., 845, 847
Tibet, 84
Tilden, S. J., 221–29
Time-division scramble, 554, 560
Times, The, 776

Tinker, C. A., 216, 218
Tito, 460
T.O.D., *See* Technical Operations Division
Togo, S., 31, 46, 61–62, 610
Tojo, H., 31, 46
Tokharian, 901
Tokumu Han, 579–83, 610
Toland, W. B., 840
Tomographic substitution, 203
Tompkins, P., 539, 541
Tordella, L. W., 677, 705
Torre, L. de la, 799
Townes, C., 947
Townsend, R., 177
Toye, F., 269
Traicté des Chiffres, 146
Traffic analysis, xvi, 7, 8, 300, 333, 455, 566, 578, 583–84
Traffic volume, 300, 575, 712–13
Transistor, 722
Transmission errors, 839–40
Transmission security, definition, xiii
Transposition
  compared with substitution, 250, 304, 307, 764
  computer memory, 980
  difficulties of mechanizing, 764
  distinguished from substitution, 139
  first, 89
  general solution of, 226
  solution of formula, 302–03
Tratado de Criptografía, 251
Traveling wave tube, 722
Treasure, hidden, 771–72
Trench codes, 314–16, 324
Trepper, L., 657–58
Trifid cipher, 243
Trigraphic substitution, 404
Trithemius, J., 130–37, 413, 860
Troy, 917–18, 936
Truesdell, K., 321
TSU. *See* J series
Tsukikawa, S., 42
TU-16 Badgers, 720
Tupelov TU-95, 970
Türkheim, L. G. di, 404
Turing, A., 975–76
Turning grilles, 308–09

Index

Tut Latin, 822
Two-letter differential, 840–41, 847
Typewriter keyboards, 740–41
TYPEX, 510
Tyro, T., 89
Tyronian notes, 89

U-2 aircraft, 693, 720
U-110, 977
U-158, 504
U-505, 506
U-boats, 273, 466, 504–07
UBCHI, 301, 304
Ugaritic literature, 900
ULTRA, 601
Ultra Secret, The, 979
Unbreakable cipher, 398–400
Unicity distance, 750
Unicity point, 750
United States
   Air Force Security Service, 680–81
   Army, 1, 12, 398, 427, 574–75, 577
   Central Bureau, 577, 578
   Central Intelligence Agency, 681, 684
   colonial cryptology, 174–86
   Data Encryption Standard, 979–81, 983
   National Defense Research Committee, 558–60
   Navy, 5, 12, 252, 386–88, 408, 415–19 *passim,* 503–04, 680, 969, 971
   Philippines, Navy cryptanalytic unit, 10, 25, 47, 563, 564
   poor pre-World War II cryptography, 488–89
   2nd Signal Service Battalion, 576–77
   Signal Companies (Radio Intelligence), 507, 578–79
   Signal school, 321, 324, 325
   Signal Security Service, 575, 611, 678
   solution of American messages, 187, 460, 496–98, 556–57, 671
   State Department, 488–501
   superiority of current American cryptology, 730
   takes world lead, 385
   see also Army Security Agency; black chambers, American; censorship; Code Compilation Section; Combat Intelligence Unit; Federal Bureau of Investigation; Friedman; FRUPAC; G.2 A.6; Hitt; M-94; M-134; M-138; M-209; National Security Agency; Office of Strategic Services; OP-20-G; Radio Intelligence Division; Rochefort; Safford; SIGABA; Signal Intelligence Service; Signal Security Agency; SIGTOT; Stager; War Department Telegraph Code; word transposition
Univacs, 726
Universal Pocket Code, 490
Universal Trade Code, 359, 846
Universal Turing machine, 976
Uruk, 76

Valerianus, P., 903
Valério, L. P. E., 240, 242
Vanek, V., 540
Variant Beaufort, 203, 242
Vassilyev, A. T., 619
Vatican. *See* papal cryptology
Vātsyāyana, 74
Venice, 109–10, 114, 858
Ventris, M. G. F., 922–37 *passim*
Verkuyl, J. A., 691
Vernam, G. S., 394, 403, 612
   system, 395–403, 492, 501, 612, 825, 830, 984
Verne, J., 793–94
Vetterlein, Engineer, 555
Viaris, Marquis G. H. L. de, 240–42, 249, 839
Vichy France, 478, 487
Video scramblers, 708
Viète, F., 116–17
Vigenère, B. de, 145–48
   tableau and cipher, 148, 149, 194, 202–03, 217, 220, 238, 242, 317, 621
Villena, G. L., 859
Villon, F., 823
Vinay, E., 240, 397
Virolleaud, C., 898–99
Voge, R. G., 594
Voice Security Branch, 712

Volapük, 231–32
Voltaire, 174
Volunteer Evaluation Office, 454
Voris, A. C., 321
Voyatzis, J. D., 817
Voynich, E., 871
Voynich manuscript, 863–72, 873, 953
Voynich, W., 866, 871
Vries, M. de, 737, 753

Wace, A. J. B., 921
Wadsworth, D., 195–96
Wallis, J., 166–69
Walsingham, Sir Francis, 119
Wanderer Werke, 459
War Department Telegraph Code, 321, 326
Warfare, modern, development of, 190
Weather-forecast codes, Japanese, 45, 579
Webster, T. B. L., 936
Wehrmachtnachrichtenverbindungen, 455
Welker, G. W., 11
Wendland, V., 458
Wenger, J. N., 704, 845
Wenwood, G., 174
Wenzel, J., 658
Wesemann, 466
West, S. 175
Western Union Code, 847
Western Union Telegraph Company, 214, 840
Westrex Company, 827
Wheatstone, C., 196–98, 404, 776, 860
Wheatstone cryptograph, 197, 372, 376
White House Communications Agency, 716
Whitelaw's Telegraph Cyphers, 843
Whitney, Eli, 195
Wigg, G., 729
Wilkins, J., 155, 870
Wilkinson, J., 186
Willes, E., and family, 170–71, 174, 187, 188, 704
Willoughby, C. A., 674
Wills, J., 838
Willson, R., 387, 418
Wilwerth, T. C., 845
WINDOW, 721

Winds code, 32, 38, 4–46, 66–67
Winterbotham, F. W., 979
Wirephoto, 830
Wiretapping, 314, 448, 549, 717
Witzke, L., 354
"Wizard War," 721
W.N.V. *See* Wehrmachtnachrichten-
    verbindungen
Woellner, Lieutenant, 335
Woermann, E., 445
Woodcock, A. W. W., 810, 813
Woodhull, S., 177
Woodward, F. C., 48, 562
Word transpositions, 214–15, 220, 224–72
World War I, 266–350
    cryptologic preparations for, 262–65
    cryptological evolution in, 298–99, 348–50
    effect of cryptology on, 612
World War II, 435–613
    cryptological evolution in, 611–13
    effect of cryptology on, 612
World Wide Web, 983
Wren, Sir Christopher, 773
Wright, E. V., 740
Wright, W. A., 48, 562, 564, 570, 595
"Wurlitzer Organ," 525

Xenophon, 82

Yamamoto, I., 6, 562, 568, 572
    assassination, 595–601
Yamanashi, 583
Yamato, 594
Yardley, H. O.
    American Black Chamber, The, 360–64, 367–68, 984
    characteristics, 351, 369
    chief of American Black Chamber, 5, 355–60
    chief of MI-8, 324, 352–55
    contribution to cryptology, 369
    criticizes American cryptography, 363, 403, 492
    early life, 351
    fiction and films, 368
    in China, 368–69, 579
    interest in cryptology, 351–52

Index

"Japanese Diplomatic Secrets," 364
later life, 369
law aimed at, 364–67, 687
reaction to *The American Black Chamber,* 31, 361–64
solves Japanese codes, 356–59
Universal Trade Code, 359, 846
Voynich manuscript, 867
Yardley symptom, 352
Yezidis, 84
Yin-chên, 74
Yin-t'ang, 74
Yoshikawa, T., 13, 42, 47, 52
Young, T., 906–07

YU, 358
Yugoslavia, 460, 470

Zacharias, E. M., 5, 387
Zapp, Prof., 525–26
Zavarzine, P., 618–19
Zenith Radio Corporation, 833
Zievert, K., 618
Zimmermann telegram, 282–97, 388, 483, 485, 699
Zipf, G. K., 746
Zoëga, G., 905
Zybine, 618–19
Zygalski, H., 973